D1327594

THE BIBLE EXPOSITION COMMENTARY

HISTORY

THE BIBLE EXPOSITION COMMENTARY

HISTORY

WARREN W.
W I E R S B E

Run So That You May Win
ivictor.com

Victor is an imprint of
Cook Communications Ministries, Colorado Springs, Colorado 80918
Cook Communications, Paris, Ontario
Kingsway Communications, Eastbourne, England

First printing 2003
Printed in the United States of America.

1 2 3 4 5 6 7 8 9 10 Printing/Year 07 06 05 04 03

Cover Design: Peter Speach Marketing Communications

Library of Congress Cataloging-in-Publication Data

Wiersbe, Warren W.
The Bible exposition commentary / Warren W. Wiersbe.
p. cm.
Contents: 1. The Old Testament History.
ISBN 0-78143-531-5
1. Bible--Commentaries.

CONTENTS

FOREWORD

The Bible Exposition Commentary had a modest beginning in 1972 when Victor Books published my commentary on 1 John and called it *Be Real.* Nobody remembers who named the book, but for me it was the beginning of three decades of intensive Bible study as I wrote additional commentaries, all of them with Be in the title. It took twenty-three books to cover the New Testament, and they were published in two bound volumes in 1989. Then I started the Old Testament Be series, and Be Obedient, on the life of Abraham, was published in 1991. Over twenty books are now available in the Old Testament series and, the Lord willing, I hope to complete the Old Testament within a year.

This volume on the Old Testament History comprises 9 separate books covering Joshua through Esther, and we plan to issue one more volume on the rest of the Old Testament: the wisdom and poetical books (including Psalms and Song of Solomon, which will not have been published in Be books). The Bible Exposition Commentary will then be complete in six volumes, the joyful work of over thirty years. During this time I have written books for several publishers, but "doing the next Be book" was always at the top of the agenda.

Victor Books was purchased by Cook Communications Ministries in 1996, but the Be series continued to carry the Victor imprint. I owe a great debt of gratitude to the editorial staff for their encouragement and cooperation these many years, including Mark Sweeney, Jim Adair, Lloyd Cory, Greg Clouse, and Craig Bubeck. These men have been faithful to "shepherd" me through book after book, and I appreciate the friendship and ministry of each more and more. Every author should be as fortunate as I've been to work with such dedicated, skillful people who always take a personal interest in their authors. To the best of my knowledge, during these years we've ministered together, we've never had a cross word or a serious misunderstanding.

I especially want to thank the Lord for His kindness and mercy in allowing me to minister in this way through the printed page. I can think of many of my friends who could have done a far better job than I in this series, but the Lord graciously gave the privilege to me. He also gave me the wisdom and strength to get each book written on time—and sometimes ahead of time—in the midst of a very busy life as a husband and father, a pastor, a radio Bible teacher, a seminary instructor, and a conference speaker.

This leads me to say that I couldn't have done it without the loving care of my wife, Betty. She manages our household affairs so well and takes such good care of me that I've always had the time needed for studying and writing. When I started this series, our four children were all at home. Now they're all married, and my wife and I have eight wonderful grandchildren! Time flies when you're checking proofs!

The numerous readers of the Be series have been a great source of encouragement to me, even when they have written to disagree with me! I have received letters from many parts of the world, written by people in various walks of life, and they have gladdened my heart. Unless a writer hears from his readers, his writing becomes a one-way street, and he never knows if what he wrote did anybody any good. I want to thank the pastors, missionaries, Sunday school teachers, and other students of the Word who have been kind enough to write. We could compile a book of letters telling what God has done in the lives of people who have studied the Be series. To God be the glory!

As I close, there are some other people who ought to be thanked. Dr. Donald Burdick taught me New Testament at Northern Baptist Seminary and showed me how to study the Word of God. Dr. Lloyd Perry and the late Dr. Charles W. Koller both taught me how to "unlock" a Scripture passage and organize an exposition that was understandable and practical. I recommend their books on preaching to any preacher or teacher who wants to organize his or her material better.

For ten happy years, I was privileged to pastor the Calvary Baptist Church in Covington, Kentucky, just across the river from Cincinnati. One of my happy duties was writing Bible study notes for "The Whole Bible Study Course," which was developed by the late Dr. D.B. Eastep, who pastored the church for thirty-five fruitful years. No church I have ever visited or ministered to has a greater love for the Bible or a deeper hunger for spiritual truth than the dear people at Calvary Baptist. The Be series is, in many respects, a by-product of Dr. Eastep's kindness in sharing his ministry with me, and the church's love and encouragement while I was their pastor. I honor his memory and thank God for their continued friendship and prayer support.

To you who study God's Word with me, "I commend you to God, and to the word of his grace, which is able to build you up, and to give you an inheritance among all them who are sanctified" (Acts 20:32 KJV).

Warren W. Wiersbe

JOSHUA

A SUGGESTED OUTLINE OF JOSHUA

Key Theme: Claiming our victory and our inheritance in Christ
Key Verse: Joshua 1:8

I. PREPARING THE NATION—1–5
1. Encouraging the leader—1
2. Spying out the land—2
3. Crossing the river—3
4. Affirming the covenant—5

II. DEFEATING THE ENEMY—6–12
1. The Central Campaign—6–9
2. The Southern Campaign—10
3. The Northern Campaign—11
4. Summary of the victories—12

III. CLAIMING THE INHERITANCE—13–22
1. Territory assigned to the tribes—13–19
2. Cities of refuge set apart—20
3. Cities for the Levites identified—21
4. Border tribes sent home—22

IV. RENEWING THE COVENANT—23–24
1. Joshua's final message to the leaders—23
2. Joshua's final message to the nation—24

CONTENTS

CHAPTER ONE
A NEW BEGINNING
Introduction to the Book of Joshua

Why should anybody today study the Book of Joshua, an ancient book that gives a grim account of war, slaughter, and conquest? If the Book of Joshua were fiction, we might accept it as an exciting adventure story; but the book conveys real history and is a part of inspired Holy Scripture. What does it mean to us today?

"There never was a good war, or a bad peace," Benjamin Franklin wrote in 1783; but it's possible that the wise old patriot was wrong for once. After all, God called Joshua to be a general and to lead the army of Israel in holy conquest. *But there were bigger issues involved in that conquest than the invasion and possession of a land—issues that touch our lives and our faith today.*

That's why we're embarking on this study. The Book of Joshua is the book of new beginnings for the people of God, and many believers today need a new beginning. After forty years of wandering in the wilderness, Israel claimed their inheritance and enjoyed the blessings of the land that God had prepared for them, "as the days of heaven upon the earth" (Deut. 11:21). That's the kind of life God wants us to experience today. Jesus Christ, our Joshua, wants to lead us in conquest now and share with us all the treasures of His wonderful inheritance. He has "blessed us with all spiritual blessings" (Eph. 1:3), but too often we live like defeated paupers.

1. The new leader

From Exodus 3 to Deuteronomy 34, the Bible focuses attention on the ministry of Moses, God's chosen servant to lead the nation of Israel. But Moses died; and though he would not be forgotten (he's named over fifty times in the Book of Joshua), a new "servant of the Lord" (Josh. 24:29) would take his place. "God buries His workers, but His work goes on." We shall note later that this change in leadership carries with it a tremendous spiritual lesson for believers who want to experience God's best in their lives.

Joshua the slave. God spent many years preparing Joshua for his calling. He was born into slavery in Egypt and was given the name Hoshea (Num. 13:8), which means "salvation." Moses later changed it to Joshua (v. 16, NIV), "Jehovah is salvation," which is the Hebrew form of "Jesus" (Matt. 1:21; see Acts 7:45 and Heb. 4:8). When his parents gave the baby the name "salvation," they were bearing witness to their faith in God's promise of redemption for His people (Gen. 15:12-16; 50:24-26). Joshua belonged to the tribe of Ephraim and was the firstborn son of Nun (1 Chron. 7:20-27). This meant that his life was in danger the night of Passover, but he had faith in the Lord and was protected by the blood of the lamb (Ex. 11-12).

While in Egypt, Joshua saw all the signs and wonders that God performed (Ex. 7-12); and he knew that Jehovah was a God of power who would care for His people. The Lord had humiliated the gods of Egypt and demonstrated that He alone was the true God (Ex. 12:12; Num. 33:4). Joshua saw the Lord open the Red Sea and then close the waters and drown the pursuing Egyptian army (Ex. 14-15). Joshua was a man of faith who knew the Lord and trusted Him to do wonders for His people.

Joshua the soldier. The first official recorded act of Joshua in Scripture is his defeat of the Amalekites when they attacked Israel about two months after Israel's Exodus from Egypt (17:8-16). Moses was a prophet and legislator, but Joshua was a general with exceptional military skills. He was also a man of great courage, who wasn't afraid to confront the enemy and trust the Lord for victory.

Where did Joshua learn to use a sword and to command an army? Certainly he was especially gifted by the Lord, but even heavenly gifts must be discovered and developed in an earthly setting. Had Joshua in some way been involved with the Egyptian army and received his early training in its ranks? This is possible, though the Scriptures are silent and we must not be dogmatic. Just as Moses refused a high position in Pharaoh's palace but received his education there (Heb. 11:24-26; Acts 7:22), so Joshua may have turned down army promotions that he might identify with his people and serve the Lord.

According to Exodus 17:14, the writer suggests that God had chosen Joshua for a special work in the future. Unknown to Joshua, the battle with Amalek was a testing time when God was examining his faith and courage. "Make every occasion a great occasion, for you can never tell when someone may be taking your measure for a larger place" (Marsden). Joshua's conflict with Amalek was the preparation for many battles he would fight in the Promised Land.

Joshua the servant. In Exodus 24:13, Joshua is called Moses' servant ("minister"), which indicates that Joshua was now an official assistant to the leader of Israel. He accompanied Moses to the mount and went with him when he judged the people for making the golden calf (32:17). It wasn't enough that Joshua be a good warrior; he also had to know the God of Israel and the holy laws God gave His people to obey. We shall discover that the secret of Joshua's victories was not his skill with the sword but his submission to the Word of God (Josh. 1:8) and to the God of the Word (5:13-15).

During Israel's wilderness journey, Moses had a special tent set up outside the camp where he could meet with God (Ex. 33:7-11). It was Joshua's responsibility to stay at the tent and guard it. Not only was Joshua a warrior, but he was also a worshiper and knew how to live in the presence of God.

Joshua was jealous not only for the glory of God but also for the honor and authority of Moses. This is a good characteristic for a servant to have, and it showed up when God sent His Spirit upon the seventy elders Moses had chosen to assist him in his work (Num. 11:16-30). When the Spirit came upon Eldad and Medad in the camp, two men who had not assembled with the other elders at the tabernacle, Joshua protested and asked Moses to stop them from prophesying. (For a New Testament parallel, see Luke 9:49-50.) The breadth of Moses' spirit must have moved Joshua as Moses claimed no special privileges for himself. It's worth noting that when the inheritance was allotted after the conquest of the Promised Land, Joshua took his share last (Josh. 19:49–51).

Joshua the spy. When Israel arrived at Kadesh Barnea, on the border of the Promised Land, God commanded Moses to appoint twelve men to spy out the land of Canaan—Joshua among them (Num. 13). After forty days of investigating the land, the spies returned to Moses and reported that the land was indeed a good one. But ten of the spies discouraged the people by saying that Israel wasn't strong enough to overcome the enemy, while two of the spies—Caleb and Joshua—

encouraged the people to trust God and move into the land. Sadly the people listened to the faithless ten spies. It was this act of unbelief and rebellion that delayed the conquest of the land for forty years.

This crisis revealed some fine leadership qualities in Joshua. He was not blind to the realities of the situation, but he didn't allow the problems and difficulties to rob him of his faith in God. The ten spies looked at God through the difficulties, while Joshua and Caleb looked at the difficulties through what they knew about God. Their God was big enough for the battles that lay ahead!

Knowing he was right, Joshua wasn't afraid to stand up against the majority. He, Moses, and Caleb stood alone and risked their lives in so doing; *but God stood with them.* It has well been said that "one with God is a majority." It would take that kind of courage for Joshua to lead Israel into their land so they could defeat their enemies and claim their inheritance.

Think of the years of blessing in the Promised Land that Joshua forfeited because the people had no faith in God! But Joshua patiently stayed with Moses and did his job, knowing that one day he and Caleb would get their promised inheritance (Num. 14:1-9). Leaders must know not only how to win victories but also how to accept defeats. I have a suspicion that Joshua and Caleb met each other regularly and encouraged each other as the time of their inheritance drew near. Day after day, for forty years, they saw the older generation die off, but each day brought them closer to Canaan. (See Heb. 10:22-25 for a New Testament parallel.)

Joshua the successor. Throughout that wilderness journey, God was preparing Joshua for his ministry as successor to Moses. When Israel defeated Og, king of Bashan, Moses used that victory to encourage Joshua not to be afraid of his enemies (Deut. 3:21-28; Num. 21:33-35). When Moses was preparing to die, he asked God to give the people a leader; and God appointed Joshua (27:12-23; Deut. 3:23-29). In his final message to Israel, Moses told the people that God would use Joshua to defeat their enemies and help them claim their promised inheritance; and he also encouraged Joshua to trust God and not be afraid (31:1-8). Moses laid hands on Joshua, and God imparted to Joshua the spiritual power he needed for his task (34:9).

Like Moses, Joshua was human and made his share of mistakes; but he was still God's chosen and anointed leader, and the people knew this. This is why they said to Joshua, "Just as we heeded Moses in all things, so we will heed you" (Josh. 1:17, NKJV). God's people in the church today need to acknowledge God's leaders and give them the respect that they deserve as the servants of God (1 Thess. 5:12-13).

The secret of Joshua's success was his faith in the Word of God (Josh. 1:7-9), its commandments and its promises. God's Word to Joshua was "Be strong!" (vv. 6-7, 9, 18; and see Deut. 31:6-7, 23); and this is His Word to His people today.

2. The new land

The promise of the land. The word "land" is found eighty-seven times in the Book of Joshua because this book is the record of Israel's entering, conquering, and claiming the Promised Land. God promised to give the land to Abraham (Gen. 12:1-7; 13:15-17; 15:7, 18; 17:8; 24:7), and He reaffirmed the promise to Isaac (26:1-5), Jacob (28:4, 13, 15; 35:12), and their descendants (50:24). The Exodus narrative gives many reaffirmations of the promise (3:8, 17; 6:4, 8; 12:25; 13:5, 11;

16:35; 23:20-33; 33:1-3; 34:10-16), and these are repeated in Leviticus (14:34; 18:3; 19:23; 20:22-24; 23:10; 25:2, 38) and Numbers (11:12; 15:2, 18; 16:13-14; 20:12, 24; 27:12; 33:53; 34:2, 12). (See also 1 Chron. 16:14-18.)

In Moses' "farewell speech" (Deut.), he frequently mentioned the land and the nation's responsibility to possess it. The word "land" is found nearly 200 times in Deuteronomy and the word "possess" over 50 times. Israel *owned* the land because of God's gracious covenant with Abraham (Gen. 12:1-5), but their *enjoyment* of the land depended on their faithful obedience to God. (See Lev. 26 and Deut. 28-30.) As long as the Jews obeyed God's law He blessed them, and they prospered in the land. But when they turned from God to idols, God first chastened them *in the land* (the Book of Judges); and then He took them *from their land* to the land of Babylon. After they had been chastened for seventy years, Israel returned to their land; but they never fully recovered the glory and blessing that they once had known.

God called the Promised Land "a good land" (8:7-10) and contrasted it with the monotony and barrenness of Egypt (11:8-14). It was to be Israel's place of rest, her inheritance, and the dwelling place of God (12:9, 11). After enduring slavery in Egypt and misery in the wilderness, the Jews would finally find rest in their Promised Land (Josh. 1:13, 15; 11:23; 21:44; 22:4; 23:1). This concept of "rest" will show up again in Psalm 95:11 and Hebrews 4 as an illustration of the victory Christians can have if they give their all to the Lord.

The Prophet Ezekiel called the land of Israel "the glory of all lands" (Ezek. 20:6, 15), which the NIV translates "the most beautiful of all lands." Daniel calls it "the pleasant land" (8:9) and "the glorious land" (11:16 and 41). Often it is described as "a land flowing with milk and honey" (Ex. 3:8, 17; 13:5; 33:3; Lev. 20:24; Num. 13:27; Deut. 6:3; 11:9; etc.). This was a proverbial statement meaning "a land of plenty," a place of peaceful pastures and gardens where the herds could graze and the bees could gather pollen and make honey.

The importance of the land. The Prophet Ezekiel said that Jerusalem was "in the center of the nations" (5:5, NIV) and that the land of Israel was "the center of the world" (38:12, NASB). The Hebrew word translated "center" also means "navel," suggesting that Israel was the "lifeline" between God and this world; for "salvation is of the Jews" (John 4:22). *God chose the land of Israel to be the "stage" on which the great drama of redemption would be presented.*

In Genesis 3:15, God promised to send a Savior to the world; and the first step in the fulfilling of that promise was the call of Abraham. Beginning with Genesis 12, the Old Testament record focuses on the Jews and the land of Israel. Abraham left Ur of the Chaldees to go to that new land, and there Isaac and Jacob were born. God announced that the Redeemer would come from the tribe of Judah (49:10) and the family of David (2 Sam. 7). He would be born of a virgin in Bethlehem (Isa. 7:14; Micah 5:2) and one day die for the sins of the world (Isa. 53; Ps. 22). All these important events in the drama of redemption would take place in the land of Israel, the land that Joshua was called to conquer and claim.

3. The new life

It's unfortunate that some of our Christian songs have equated Israel's crossing the Jordan with the believer's dying and going to heaven, because this mistake brings confusion when you start interpreting the Book of Joshua. "Swing Low, Sweet Chariot" is a beloved spiritual, but I fear its imagery is not biblical. The hymn "On Jordan's Stormy Banks" perpetuates that same error, as does the third verse of "Guide Me, O Thou Great Jehovah":

> When I tread the verge of
> Jordan,
> Bid my anxious fears subside;
> Death of death, and hell's
> destruction,
> Land me safe on Canaan's
> side.
> (William Williams)

The events recorded in the Book of Joshua have to do with the *life* of God's people and not their *death!* The Book of Joshua records battles, defeats, sins, and failures—none of which will take place in heaven. This book illustrates how believers today can say good-bye to the old life and enter into their rich inheritance in Jesus Christ. It explains how we can meet our enemies and defeat them, and how to claim for ourselves all that we have in Jesus Christ (Eph. 1:3). What Paul's letter to the Ephesians explains doctrinally, the Book of Joshua illustrates practically. It shows us how to claim our *riches* in Christ.

But it also shows us how to claim our *rest* in Christ. This is one of the major themes of the Book of Hebrews and is explained in chapters 3 and 4 of that epistle. In those chapters, we find four different "rests," all of which are related: God's Sabbath rest after creating the worlds (Heb. 4:4; Gen. 2:2); the salvation rest we have in Christ (Heb. 4:1, 3, 8-9; Matt. 11:28-30); the believer's eternal rest in heaven (Heb. 4:11); and the rest God gave Israel after their conquest of Canaan (3:7-19).

God's promise to Moses was "My Presence will go with you, and I will give you rest" (Ex. 33:14, NKJV). The Jews certainly had no rest in Egypt or during their wilderness wanderings, but in the Promised Land, God would give them rest. In his farewell message to the people, Moses said, "For as yet you have not come to the rest and the inheritance which the Lord your God is giving you" (Deut. 12:9, NKJV; and see 3:20; 12:9-10; 25:19). *This "Canaan rest" is a picture of the rest that Christian believers experience when they yield their all to Christ and claim their inheritance by faith.*

The four geographic locations seen in the history of Israel illustrate four spiritual experiences. *Egypt* was the place of death and bondage from which Israel was delivered. They were delivered from death by the blood of the lamb and from bondage by the power of God who opened the Red Sea and took them across safely. This illustrates the salvation we have through faith in Jesus Christ, "The Lamb of God who takes away the sin of the world!" (John 1:29, NKJV) Through His death and resurrection, Jesus Christ delivers the believing sinner from bondage and judgment.

The wilderness experience of Israel depicts believers who live in unbelief and disobedience and don't enter into the rest and riches of their inheritance in Christ, either because they don't know it's there or they know and refuse to enter. Like Israel, they come to a crisis place (Kadesh Barnea), but refuse to obey the Lord and claim His will for their lives (Num. 13-14). They are delivered from Egypt, but Egypt is still in their hearts; and like the Jews, they have a desire to go back to the old life (Ex. 16:1-3; Num. 11; 14:2-4; see Isa. 30:3; 31:1). Instead of marching through life as conquerors, they meander through life as wanderers and never enjoy the fullness of what God has planned for them. It's this crowd that is especially addressed in the Epistle to the Hebrews.

Canaan represents the Christian life as it ought to be: conflict and victory, faith and obedience, spiritual riches and rest. It's a life of faith, trusting Jesus Christ, our Joshua, the Captain of our salvation (Heb. 2:10), to lead us from victory to victory (1 John 5:4-5). When Israel was in Egypt, the enemy was *around* them, making their lives miserable. When they crossed the Red Sea, Israel put the enemy *behind* them; but when the nation crossed the Jordan River, they saw new enemies *before* them, and they conquered these enemies by faith.

The victorious Christian life isn't a once-for-all triumph that ends all our problems. As pictured by Israel in the Book of Joshua, the victorious Christian life is a series of conflicts and victories as we defeat one enemy after another and claim more of our inheritance to the glory of God. The eminent Scottish preacher Alexander Whyte used to say that the victorious Christian life was "a series of new beginnings."

According to Joshua 11:23, the whole land was taken; but according to 13:1, there remained "very much land to be possessed." Is this a contradiction? No, it's the declaration of a basic spiritual truth: In Christ, we have all that we need for victorious Christian living, but we must possess our inheritance by faith, a step at a time (Josh. 1:3), a day at a time. Joshua's question to his people is a good question to ask the church today: "How long will you wait before you begin to take possession of the land that the Lord . . . has given you?" (18:3, NIV)

The fourth geographic location on Israel's "spiritual map" is *Babylon,* where the nation endured seventy years of captivity because they disobeyed God and worshiped the idols of the pagan nations around them. (See 2 Chron. 36; Jer. 39:8–10). When God's children are willfully rebellious, their loving Father must chasten them until they learn to be submissive and obedient (Heb. 12:1-11). When they confess their sins and forsake them, God will forgive and restore His children to fellowship and fruitfulness (1 John 1:9; 2 Cor. 7:1).

The leading person in the Book of Joshua is not Joshua but the Lord Jehovah, the God of Joshua and of Israel. In all that Joshua did by faith, he desired to glorify the Lord. When the Jews crossed the Jordan River, Joshua reminded them that the living God was among them and would overcome their enemies (Josh. 3:10). Through Israel's obedience, Joshua wanted all the people of the earth to know the Lord and fear Him (4:23-24). In his "farewell addresses" to the leaders (chap. 23) and to the nation (chap. 24), Joshua gave God all the glory for what Israel had accomplished under his leadership.

At least fourteen times in this book, God is called "the Lord God of Israel" (7:13, 19-20; 8:30; 9:18-19; 10:40, 42; 13:14, 33; 14:14; 22:24; 24:2, 23). *Everything that Israel did brought either glory or disgrace to the name of their God.* When Israel obeyed by faith, God kept His promises and worked on their behalf; and God was glorified. But when they disobeyed in unbelief, God abandoned them to their own ways and they were humiliated in defeat. The same spiritual principle applies to the church today.

As you look at your life and the life of the church where you fellowship, do you see yourself and your fellow believers wandering in the wilderness or conquering in the Promised Land? In the wilderness, the Jews were a complaining people;

but in Canaan, they were a conquering people. In the wilderness, Israel kept looking back, yearning for what they had in Egypt; but in the Promised Land, they looked forward to conquering the enemy and claiming their rest and their riches. The wilderness march was an experience of delay, defeat, and death; but their experience in Canaan was one of life, power, and victory.

As you look at the "spiritual map" of your Christian life, where are you living?

CHAPTER TWO
FOLLOW THE LEADER
Joshua 1

Twice during my years of ministry, I've been chosen to succeed distinguished and godly leaders and carry on their work. I can assure you that it wasn't easy to follow well-known Christians who sacrificially poured years of their lives into successful ministries. I can identify with Joshua when he stepped into Moses' sandals and discovered how big they were!

When I succeeded D.B. Eastep as pastor of Calvary Baptist Church in Covington, Kentucky, I remember how his widow and his son encouraged me and assured me of their support. I recall one of the deacons, George Evans, coming to the church office to tell me he would do anything to help me, "including washing your car and polishing your shoes." I never asked George to do either of those things, but his words expressed the encouraging attitude of all the church staff and leaders. I felt like a raw recruit taking the place of a seasoned veteran, and I needed all the help I could get!

Nearly a quarter of a century later when I succeeded Theodore Epp at Back to the Bible, I had a similar experience. The board and headquarters staff, the leaders in the overseas offices, the radio listeners, as well as many Christian leaders from all over the world, assured me of their prayer support and availability to help. When you feel like a midget taking the place of a giant, you appreciate all the encouragement God sends your way.

What a new leader needs is not advice but encouragement. "To encourage" literally means "to put heart into." General Andrew Jackson said "one man with courage makes a majority," and he was right. As God's people today face the challenges that God gives us, we would do well to learn from the threefold encouragement found in this chapter.

1. God encourages His leader (Josh. 1:1-9)

Encouragement from God's commission (vv. 1-2). Leaders don't lead forever, even godly leaders like Moses. There comes a time in every ministry when God calls for a new beginning with a new generation and new leadership. Except for Joshua and Caleb, the old generation of Jews had perished during the nation's wanderings in the wilderness; and Joshua was commissioned to lead the new generation into a new challenge: entering and conquering the Promised Land. "God buries His workmen, but His work goes on." It was God who had chosen Joshua, and everybody in Israel knew that he was their new leader.

Over the years I've seen churches and parachurch ministries flounder and almost destroy themselves in futile attempts to embalm the past and escape the future. Their theme song was, "As it was in the beginning, so shall it ever be, world without end." Often I've prayed with and for godly Christian leaders who were criticized, persecuted, and attacked simply because, like Joshua, they had a divine commission to lead a ministry into new fields of conquest; but the people would not follow. More than one pastor has been offered as a sacrificial lamb because he dared to suggest that the church make some changes.

J. Oswald Sanders writes: "A work originated by God and conducted on spiritual principles will surmount the shock of a change of leadership and indeed will probably thrive better as a result" *(Spiritual Leadership,* p. 132).

In describing the death of King Arthur, Lord Tennyson put some wise and profound words in the mouth of the king as his funeral barge moved out to sea. Sir Bedevire cried out, "For now I see the true old times are dead"; and Arthur replied:

> The old order changeth, yielding place to new, And God fulfills himself in many ways, Lest one good custom should corrupt the world.
> ["The Passing of Arthur"]

"Would that life were like the shadow cast by a wall or a tree," says the *Talmud,* "but it is like the shadow of a bird in flight." Trying to clutch the past to our hearts is as futile as trying to embrace the passing shadow of a bird in flight.

A wise leader doesn't completely abandon the past but builds on it as he or she moves toward the future. Moses is mentioned fifty-seven times in the Book of Joshua, evidence that Joshua respected Moses and what he had done for Israel. Joshua worshiped the same God that Moses had worshiped, and he obeyed the same Word that Moses had given to the nation. There was continuity from one leader to the next, but there wasn't always conformity; for each leader is different and must maintain his or her individuality. Twice in these verses Moses is called God's servant, but Joshua was also the servant of God (24:29). The important thing is not the servant but the Master.

Joshua is called "Moses' minister" (1:1), a word that described workers in the tabernacle as well as servants of a leader. (See Ex. 24:13; 33:11; Num. 11:28; Deut. 1:38.) Joshua learned how to obey as a servant before he commanded as a general; he was first a servant and then a ruler (Matt. 25:21). "He who has never learned to obey cannot be a good commander," wrote Aristotle in his *Politics.*

God commissioned Joshua to achieve three things: lead the people into the land, defeat the enemy, and claim the inheritance. God could have sent an angel to do this, but He chose to use a man and give him the power he needed to get the job done. As we have already seen, Joshua is a type of Jesus Christ, the Captain of our salvation (Heb. 2:10), who has won the victory and now shares His spiritual inheritance with us.

Encouragement from God's promises (vv. 3-6). Since Joshua had a threefold task to perform, God gave him three special promises, one for each task. God would enable Joshua to cross the river and claim the land (vv. 3-4), defeat the enemy (v. 5), and apportion the land to each tribe as its inheritance (v. 6). God didn't give Joshua explanations as to how He would accomplish these things, because God's people live on promises and not on explanations. When you trust God's promises and step out by faith (v. 3), you can be sure that the Lord will give you the directions you need when you need them.

First, God promised Joshua that **Israel**

would enter the land (vv. 3-4). Over the centuries God had reaffirmed this promise, from His first words to Abraham (Gen. 12) to His last words to Moses (Deut. 34:4). God would take them over the Jordan and into enemy territory. He then would enable them to claim for themselves the land that He had promised them. There would be no repetition of the fear and unbelief that had brought the nation into defeat at Kadesh Barnea (Num. 13).

God had already given them the land; it was their responsibility now to step out by faith and claim it (Josh 1:3; see Gen. 13:14-18). The same promise of victory that God had given to Moses (Num. 11:22-25), He reaffirmed to Joshua; and He carefully defined the borders of the land. Israel didn't reach that full potential until the reigns of David and Solomon.

The lesson for God's people today is clear: God has given us all spiritual blessings . . . in Christ" (Eph. 1:3), and we must step out by faith and claim them. He has set before His church an open door that nobody can close (Rev. 3:8), and we must walk through that door by faith and claim new territory for the Lord. *It is impossible to stand still in Christian life and service; for when you stand still, you immediately start going backward.* "Let us go on!" is God's challenge to His church (Heb. 6:1), and that means moving ahead into new territory.

God also promised Joshua **victory over the enemy (Joshua 1:5).** The Lord told Abraham that other nations were inhabiting the Promised Land (Gen. 15:18-21), and He repeated this fact to Moses (Ex. 3:17). If Israel obeyed the Lord, He promised to help them defeat these nations. But He warned His people not to compromise with the enemy in any way, for then Israel would win the war but lose the victory (23:20-33). Unfortunately, that's exactly what happened. Since the Jews began to worship the gods of their pagan neighbors and adopt their evil practices, God had to chasten Israel in their land to bring them back to Himself (Judg. 1-2).

What a promise God gave to Joshua! "As I was with Moses, so I will be with you; I will never leave you or forsake you" (Josh 1:5, NIV). God had given a similar promise to Jacob (Gen. 28:15), and Moses had repeated God's promise to Joshua (Deut. 31:1-8). God would one day give this same promise to Gideon (Judg. 6:16) and to the Jewish exiles returning from Babylon to their land (Isa. 41:10; 43:5); and David would give it to his son Solomon (1 Chron. 28:20). But best of all, *God has given this promise to His people today!* The Gospel of Matthew opens with "Emmanuel . . . God with us" (1:23) and closes with Jesus saying, "Lo, I am with you always" (28:20 NKJV). The writer of Hebrews 13:5 quotes Joshua 1:5 and applies it to Christians today: "I will never leave you nor forsake you" (NKJV).

This means that God's people can move forward in God's will and be assured of God's presence. "If God be for us, who can be against us?" (Rom. 8:31) Before Joshua began his conquest of Jericho, the Lord appeared to him and assured him of His presence (Josh. 5:13-15). That was all Joshua needed to be guaranteed of victory.

When my wife and I were in our first pastorate, God led the church to build a new sanctuary. The congregation was neither large nor wealthy, and a couple of financial experts told us it couldn't be done; but the Lord saw us through. He used 1 Chronicles 28:20 in a special way to strengthen and assure me throughout that difficult project. I can assure you from experience that the promise of God's presence really works!

God's third promise to Joshua was that **He would divide the land as an inheritance for the conquering tribes (Josh. 1:6).** This was God's assurance that the enemy would be defeated and that Israel would possess their land. God would keep His promise to Abraham that his descendants would inherit the land (Gen. 12:6-7; 13:14-15; 15:18-21).

The Book of Joshua records the fulfillment of these three promises: the first in chapters 2-5, the second in chapters 6-12, and the third in chapters 13-22. At the close of his life Joshua could remind the leaders of Israel that "not one thing has failed of all the good things which the Lord your God spoke concerning you. All have come to pass for you; not one word of them has failed" (23:14, NKJV).

Before God could fulfill His promises, however, Joshua had to exercise faith and "be strong and of good courage" (1:6). Divine sovereignty is not a substitute for human responsibility. God's sovereign Word is an encouragement to God's servants to believe God and obey His commands. As Charles Spurgeon put it, Joshua "was not to use the promise as a couch upon which his indolence might luxuriate, but as a girdle wherewith to gird up his loins for future activity" (*Metropolitan Tabernacle Pulpit,* vol. 14, p. 97). In short, God's promises are prods, not pillows.

Encouragement from God's written Word (vv. 7-8). It's one thing to say to a leader, "Be strong! Be very courageous!" and quite something else to enable him to do it. Joshua's strength and courage would come from meditating on the Word of God, believing its promises, and obeying its precepts. This was the counsel Moses had given to all the people (Deut. 11:1-9), and now God was applying it specifically to Joshua.

During the years of his leadership, Moses kept a written record of God's words and acts and committed this record to the care of the priests (Deut. 31:9). He wrote in it a reminder to Joshua to wipe out the Amalekites (Ex. 17:14). Among other things, the "Book of the Law" included "the Book of the Covenant" (24:4, 7), a record of the journeys of the people from Egypt to Canaan (Num. 33:2), special regulations dealing with inheritance (36:13), and the song that Moses taught the people (Deut. 31:19). Moses kept adding material to this record until it included everything God wanted in it (v. 24). We have reason to believe the entire five Books of Moses (Genesis through Deuteronomy) comprised "the Book of the Law," the greatest legacy Moses could leave to his successor.

But it wasn't enough for the priests to carry and guard this precious book; Joshua had to take time to read it daily and make it a part of his inner person by meditating on it (Ps. 1:2; 119:97; see Deut. 17:18-20). The Hebrew word translated "meditate" means "to mutter." It was the practice of the Jews to read Scripture aloud (Acts 8:26-40) and talk about it to themselves and to one another (Deut. 6:6-9). This explains why God warned Joshua that the Book of the Law was not to depart out of his *mouth* (Josh. 1:8). In numerous conferences, I have often told pastors and seminary students, "If you don't talk to your Bible, your Bible isn't likely to talk to you!"

In the life of the Christian believer, *prosperity* and *success* aren't to be measured by the standards of the world. These blessings are the by-products of a life devoted to God and His Word. If you set out on your own to become prosperous and successful, you may achieve your goal and *live to regret it.* "In whatever man does without God," wrote Scottish novelist George MacDonald, "he must fail miserably, or succeed more miserably." The questions God's people need to ask are: Did we obey the will of God? Were we empowered by the Spirit of God? Did we serve to the glory of God? If we can answer yes to these questions, then our ministry has been successful in God's eyes, no matter what people may think.

Encouragement from God's commandment (v. 9). God's commandments are still God's enablements for those who obey Him by faith. Gabriel's words to Mary are as true today as when he spoke them in Nazareth: "For with God nothing shall be impossible" (Luke 1:37). I especially like the translation of this verse found in the *American Standard Version* (1901): "For no word from God shall be void of power." The very word that God speaks has in it the power of fulfillment if we will but trust and obey!

In the years to come, whenever Joshua faced an enemy and was tempted to be *afraid,* he would remember that he was a man with a divine commission—and his fears would vanish. Whenever things went wrong and he was tempted to be *dismayed,* he would recall God's command—and take new courage. Like Moses before him, and Samuel and David after him, Joshua had a divine mandate to serve the Lord and do His will—and that mandate was sufficient to carry him through.

2. The leader encourages the officers (Josh. 2:10-15)

The nation of Israel was so organized that Moses could quickly communicate with the people through his officers who formed a chain of command (Deut. 1:15). Moses didn't assemble the leaders to ask for their advice but to give them God's orders. There are times when leaders must consult with their officers, but this was not one of them. God had spoken, His will was clear, and the nation had to be ready to obey.

Forty years before, at Kadesh Barnea, the nation had known the will of God but refused to obey it (Num. 13). Why? Because they believed the report of the ten spies instead of believing the commandment of God and obeying by faith. Had they listened to Caleb and Joshua—the minority report—they would have spared themselves those difficult years of wandering in the wilderness. There is a place in Christian service for godly counsel, but a committee report is no substitute for the clear commandment of God.

Instead of the command to prepare food, you would have expected Joshua to say, "Prepare boats so we can cross the Jordan River." Joshua didn't try to second-guess God and work things out for himself. He knew that the God who opened the Red Sea could also open the Jordan River. He and Caleb had been present when God delivered the nation from Egypt, and they had confidence that God would work on their behalf again.

Though he trusted God for a miracle, Joshua still had to prepare for the everyday necessities of life. In modern armies the Quartermaster Corps sees to it that the soldiers have food and other necessities of life; but Israel didn't have a Quartermaster Corps. Each family and clan had to provide its own food. The manna was still falling each morning (Ex. 16) and wouldn't stop until Israel was in their land (Josh. 5:11–12). But it was important that the people stayed strong because they were about to begin a series of battles for possession of their Promised Land.

Note that Joshua's words to his leaders were words of faith and encouragement. "You shall pass over! You shall possess the land! The Lord will give it to you!" Joshua had made a similar speech forty years before, but that generation of leaders wouldn't listen. Now that generation was dead and the new generation was ready to believe God and conquer the land.

It's unfortunate but true that sometimes the only way a ministry can move forward is by conducting a few funerals. A pastor friend of mine pleaded with his church board to build a new educational plant to house an exploding Sunday School. One of the long-time members of the board, a prominent businessman in the city, said to him, "You'll do this over my dead body!" *And they did!* A few days later, that officer had a heart attack and died; and the church moved ahead and built the much-needed educational plant.

The older we get, the more danger there is that we'll get set in our ways and become "sanctified obstructionists"; *but it doesn't have to happen.* Caleb and Joshua were the oldest men in the camp, and yet they were enthusiastic about trusting God and entering the land. It isn't a matter of *age;* it's a matter of *faith;* and faith comes from meditating on the Word of God (1:8; Rom. 10:17). How I thank God for the "senior saints" who have been a part of my ministry and have encouraged me to trust the Lord and move forward.

Joshua had a special word for the two and a half tribes that lived on the other side of Jordan and had already received their inheritance (Num. 32). He reminded them of Moses' words of instruction and warning (21:21-35; Deut. 3:12-20) and urged them to keep the promise they had made. Joshua was concerned that Israel be a *united* people in conquering the land and in worshiping the Lord. The two and a half tribes did keep their promise to help conquer the land, but they still created a problem for Joshua and Israel because they lived on the other side of the Jordan (Josh. 22).

In the nation of Israel it was the able men twenty years and older who went out to war (Num. 1:3); and the record shows that the two and a half tribes had 136,930 men available (26:7, 18, 34). But only 40,000 men actually crossed the Jordan and fought in the Promised Land (Josh. 4:13). The rest of the recruits stayed to protect the women and children in the cities the tribes had taken in the land of Jazer and the land of Gilead (32:1-5, 16-19). When the soldiers returned home, they shared the spoils of war with their brothers (Josh. 22:6–8).

It was a concession on Moses' part to allow the two and a half tribes to live outside the Promised Land. The tribes liked the land there because it was "a place for cattle" (Num. 32:1, 4, 16). Apparently their first concern was making a living, not making a life. They would rather have big flocks and herds than dwell with their brothers and sisters in the inheritance God had given them. They were far from the place of worship and had to erect a special monument to remind their children that they were citizens of Israel (Josh. 22:10ff). They represent the many "borderline believers" in the church today who get close to the inheritance but never quite claim it, no matter how successful they may seem to be. They are willing to serve the Lord and help their brethren for a time; but when their appointed job is finished, they head for home to do what they want to do.

3. The officers encourage their leader (Josh. 1:16-18)

The pronoun "they" probably refers to all the officers Joshua had addressed and not to the leaders of the two and a half tribes alone. What an encouragement they were to their new leader!

To begin with, they encouraged him **by assuring him of their complete obedience (vv. 16-17a).** "Command us and we will obey! Send us and we will go!" These officers had no hidden agendas, and they asked for no concessions. They would obey *all* his commands and go *wherever* he would send them. We could use that kind of commitment in the church today! Too many times we are like the men described in Luke 9:57-62, each of whom put something personal ahead of following the Lord.

In his novel *The Marquis of Lossie*, author George MacDonald has one of the characters say, "I find the doing of the will of God leaves me no time for disputing about His plan." That's the attitude Joshua's officers displayed. They were not so attached to Moses that they put him above Joshua. God had appointed both Moses and Joshua, and to disobey the servant was to disobey the Master. Joshua didn't have to explain or defend his orders. He simply had to give the orders, and the men would obey them.

The officers encouraged Joshua **by praying for him (v. 17).** "The Lord thy God be with thee, as he was with Moses." The best thing we can do for those who lead us is to pray for them daily and ask God to be with them. Joshua was a trained man with vast experience, but that was no guarantee of success. *No Christian worker succeeds to the glory of God apart from prayer.* "Is prayer your steering wheel or your spare tire?" asked Corrie Ten Boom, a question that especially applies to those in places of leadership. When Joshua did not pause to seek the mind of God, he failed miserably (Josh. 7 and 9); and so will we.

They encouraged Joshua by **assuring him that their obedience was a matter of life or death (1:18).** They took his leadership and their responsibilities seriously. Later, Achan didn't take Joshua's orders seriously, and he was killed (Acts 7:15). "But why do you call Me 'Lord, Lord,' and not do the things which I say?" (Luke 6:46, NKJV) If God's people today saw obedience to Christ a matter of life or death, it would make a big difference in our ministry to a lost world. We obey the Lord's orders if we feel like it, if it's convenient, and if we can get something out of it. With soldiers like that, Joshua would never have conquered the Promised Land!

Finally, they encouraged him by **reminding him of the Word of God (v. 18b).** Moses told Joshua to "be ye of good courage" when he sent him and the other men into Canaan to spy out the land (Num. 13:20). Moses repeated the words when he installed Joshua as his successor (Deut. 31:7, 23). These words were written in the Book of the Law, and Joshua was commanded to read that Book and meditate on it day and night (Josh. 1:8).

Four times in this chapter you find the words "be strong and of good courage" (vv. 6-7, 9, 18). *If we are to conquer the enemy and claim our inheritance in Christ, we must have spiritual strength and spiritual courage.* "Be strong in the Lord, and in the power of His might" (Eph. 6:10).

Soldiers of Christ, arise,
And put your armor on,
Strong in the strength which God
  supplies
Of His eternal Son.
[Charles Wesley]

The first step toward winning the battle and claiming our inheritance is to let God encourage us and then for us to encourage others. A discouraged army is never victorious.

"See, the Lord your God has given you

the land. Go up and take possession of it as the Lord, the God of your fathers, told you. Do not be afraid; do not be discouraged" (Deut. 1:21, NIV).

Be strong! The battle is the Lord's!

CHAPTER THREE
A CONVERT IN CANAAN
Joshua 2

Only two women are personally named in Hebrews 11, "The Hall of Fame of Faith": *Sarah,* the wife of Abraham (v. 11), and *Rahab,* the harlot of Jericho (v. 31).

Sarah was a godly woman, the wife of the founder of the Hebrew race; and God used her dedicated body to bring Isaac into the world. But Rahab was an ungodly Gentile who worshiped pagan gods and sold her body for money. Humanly speaking, Sarah and Rahab had nothing in common. But from the *divine* viewpoint, Sarah and Rahab shared the most important thing in life: *They both had exercised saving faith in the true and living God.*

Not only does the Bible associate Rahab with Sarah; but in James 2:21-26, it also associates her with *Abraham.* James used both Abraham and Rahab to illustrate the fact that true saving faith always proves itself by good works.

But there's more: The Bible associates Rahab with the Messiah! When you read the genealogy of the Lord Jesus Christ in Matthew 1, you find Rahab's name listed there (v. 5), along with Jacob, David, and the other famous people in the messianic line. She has certainly come a long way from being a pagan prostitute to being an ancestress of the Messiah! "But where sin abounded, grace did much more abound" (Rom. 5:20).

But keep in mind that the most important thing about Rahab was her faith. That's the most important thing about any person, for "without faith it is impossible to please Him [God]" (Heb. 11:6). Not everything that is called "faith" is really true faith, the kind of faith that is described in the Bible. What kind of faith did Rahab have?

1. Courageous faith (Josh. 2:1-7)

Both Hebrews 11:31 and James 2:25 indicate that Rahab had put her faith in Jehovah God *before* the spies ever arrived in Jericho. Like the people in Thessalonica, she had "turned to God from idols to serve the living and true God" (1 Thess. 1:9). She wasn't like the people of Samaria centuries later who "feared the Lord, and [at the same time] served their own gods" (2 Kings 17:33).

Jericho was one of many "city-states" in Canaan, each one ruled by a king (see Josh. 12:9-24). The city covered about eight or nine acres, and there is archeological evidence that double walls about fifteen feet apart protected the city. Rahab's house was on the wall (2:15).

Meanwhile, Jericho was a strategic city in Joshua's plan for conquering Canaan. After taking Jericho, Joshua could then cut straight across and divide the land; and then it would be much easier to defeat the cities in the south and then in the north.

Forty years before, Moses had sent twelve spies into Canaan; and only two of them had given an encouraging report (Num. 13). Joshua sent two men to spy out the land and especially to get information about Jericho. Joshua wanted to know how the citizens were reacting to the arrival of the people of Israel. Since

Joshua knew that God had already given him the land and the people, the sending of the spies wasn't an act of unbelief (see 1:11, 15). A good general wants to learn all he can about the enemy before he goes into battle.

How did the two spies make their way through the city without being immediately recognized as strangers? How did they meet Rahab? We certainly have to believe in the providence of God as we watch this drama taking place. Rahab was the only person in Jericho who trusted the God of Israel, and God brought the spies to her.

The Hebrew word translated "harlot" can also mean "one who keeps an inn." If all we had was the Old Testament text, we could absolve Rahab of immorality and call her the "proprietress of an inn." But there is no escape, for in James 2:25 and Hebrews 11:31, the writers use the Greek word that definitely means "a prostitute."

It's remarkable how God in His grace uses people we might think could never become His servants. "But God has chosen the foolish things of the world to put to shame the wise, and God has chosen the weak things of the world to put to shame the things which are mighty; and the base things of the world and the things which are despised God has chosen, and the things which are not, to bring to nothing the things that are, that no flesh should glory in His presence" (1 Cor. 1:27-29, NKJV). Jesus was the "friend of publicans and sinners" (Luke 7:34), and He wasn't ashamed to have a former prostitute in His family tree!

Rahab took her life in her hands when she welcomed the spies and hid them, but that in itself was evidence of her faith in the Lord. *True saving faith can't be hidden for long.* Since these two men represented God's people, she was not afraid to assist them in their cause. Had the king discovered her deception, he would have slain her as a traitor.

Since Rahab was a believer at that time, how do we defend her lies? On the one hand, she demonstrated her faith in the Lord by risking her life to protect the spies; but, on the other hand, she acted like any pagan in the city when she lied about her guests. Perhaps we're expecting too much from a new believer whose knowledge of God was adequate for salvation but certainly limited when it came to the practical things of life. If seasoned believers like Abraham and Isaac resorted to deception (Gen. 12:10-20; 20; 26:6-11), as well as David (1 Sam. 21:2), we had better not be too hard on Rahab. This is not to excuse or encourage lying, but simply to take her circumstances into consideration lest we condemn her too severely.

Lying is wrong (Prov. 12:22), and the fact that God had Rahab's lies recorded in Scripture is no proof that He approved of them. However, let's confess that most of us would hesitate to tell the truth *if it really were a matter of life or death.* It's one thing for *me* to tell the truth about myself and suffer for it; but do I have the right to cause the death of *others,* especially those who have come under my roof for protection? Many people have been honored for deceiving the enemy *during wartime* and saving innocent lives, and this was war! Suppose we looked upon Rahab as a "freedom fighter"; would that change the picture at all?

Ethical problems aside, the main lesson here is that Rahab's faith was conspicuous, and she demonstrated it by receiving the spies and risking her life to protect them. James saw her actions as proof that she was truly a believer (James 2:25). Her faith wasn't hidden; the spies could tell that she was indeed a believer.

2. Confident faith (Josh. 2:8-11)
Faith is only as good as its object. Some people have faith in faith and think that just by *believing* they can make great things happen. Others have faith in lies, which is not faith at all but superstition. I once heard a psychologist say that the people in a support group "must have some kind of faith, even if it's faith in the soft drink machine." But faith is only as good as its object. How much help can you get from a soft drink machine, especially after you've run out of money?

D. Martyn Lloyd-Jones reminds us that "faith shows itself in the whole personality." True saving faith isn't just a feat of intellectual gymnastics by which we convince ourselves that something is true that really isn't true. Nor is it merely a stirring of the emotions that gives us a false sense of confidence that God will do what we *feel* He will do. Nor is it a courageous act of the will whereby we jump off the pinnacle of the temple and expect God to rescue us (Matt. 4:5-7). True saving faith involves "the whole personality": the mind is instructed, the emotions are stirred, and the will then acts in obedience to God.

"By faith Noah, being warned of God of things not seen as yet [the intellect], moved with fear [the emotions], prepared an ark [the will] . . ." (Heb. 11:7). Rahab's experience was similar to that of Noah: *She knew* that Jehovah was the true God [the mind]; *she feared* for herself and her family when she heard about the great wonders He had performed [the emotions]; and *she received* the spies and pleaded for the salvation of her family [the will]. Unless the whole personality is involved, it is not saving faith as the Bible describes it.

Of course, this doesn't mean that the mind must be fully instructed in every aspect of Bible truth before a sinner can be saved. The woman with the hemorrhage only touched the hem of Christ's garment and she was healed, but she acted on the little knowledge that she did possess (Matt. 9:20-22). Rahab's knowledge of the true God was meager, but she acted on what she knew; and the Lord saved her.

Rahab showed more faith in the Lord than the ten spies had exhibited forty years before, when she said, "I know that the Lord has given you the land" (Josh. 2:9, NKJV). Her faith was based on facts, not just feelings; for she had heard of the miracles God had performed, starting with the opening up of the Red Sea at the Exodus. "So then faith comes by hearing, and hearing by the Word of God" (Rom. 10:17, NKJV).

Since the report of the Lord's power had traveled to the people of Canaan, they were afraid; but this is what Israel expected their great God to do. "The people shall hear, and be afraid: sorrow shall take hold on the inhabitants of Palestine. Then the dukes of Edom shall be amazed; the mighty men of Moab, trembling shall take hold upon them; all the inhabitants of Canaan shall melt away. Fear and dread shall fall upon them" (Ex. 15:14-16). God promised to do this for Israel, and He kept His promise. "This day I will begin to put the dread and fear of you upon the nations under the whole heaven, who shall hear the report of you, and shall tremble and be in anguish because of you" (Deut. 2:25, NKJV).

"The Lord your God, He is God in heaven above, and in earth beneath" (Josh. 2:11). What a confession of faith from the lips of a woman whose life had been imprisoned in pagan idolatry! She believed in *one God,* not in the multitude of gods that populated the heathen temples. She believed He was a *personal* God ("your God"), who would work on behalf of those who trusted Him. She believed He was *the*

God of Israel, who would give the land to His people. This God whom she trusted was not limited to one nation or one land, but was *the God of heaven and earth.* Rahab believed in a great and awesome God!

Our confidence that we are God's children comes from the witness of the Word of God before us and the witness of the Spirit of God within us (1 John 5:9-13). However, the assurance of salvation isn't based only on what we know from the Bible or how we feel in our hearts. It's also based on how we live; for if there hasn't been a change in our behavior, then it's doubtful that we've truly been born again (2 Cor. 5:21; James 2:14-26). It isn't enough to say "Lord, Lord!" We must obey what He tells us to do (Matt. 7:21-27). Rahab's obedience gave evidence of a changed life.

Rahab's conversion was truly an act of God's grace. Like all the citizens of Canaan, Rahab was under condemnation and destined to die. God commanded the Jews to "utterly destroy them" and show them no mercy (Deut. 7:1-3). Rahab was a Gentile, outside the covenant mercies shown to Israel (Eph. 2:11-13). She didn't deserve to be saved, but God had mercy on her. If ever a sinner experienced Ephesians 2:1-10, it was Rahab!

3. Concerned faith (Josh. 2:12-14)

Rahab, however, wasn't concerned only about her own welfare, for once she had personally experienced the grace and mercy of God, she was burdened to rescue her family. After Andrew met the Lord Jesus, he shared the good news with his brother Simon and brought him to Jesus (John 1:35-42). The cleansed leper went home and told everybody he met what Jesus had done for him (Mark 1:40-45). "The fruit of the righteous is a tree of life; and he that winneth souls is wise" (Prov. 11:30).

Rahab wanted assurance from the two spies that when the city was taken, they would guarantee her family's safety. The men gave her that guarantee in two ways: They pledged their word, and they pledged their lives that they would not break their word. In other words, they became surety for Rahab's family, the way Judah became surety for Benjamin (Gen. 43:8-9). The Book of Proverbs warns against *"suretyship"* in the business world because it involves a risk that could lead to your losing everything (Prov. 6:1ff; 11:15; 20:16; 27:13). However, in the realm of the spiritual, we are saved because Jesus Christ, who owed no debts, was willing to become surety for us (Heb. 7:22, NIV). The next time you sing "Jesus Paid It All," remember that Jesus has pledged Himself as "the guarantee of a better covenant" (Heb. 7:22, NIV). He died for us; and as long as He lives, our salvation is secure. Because of the promise of His Word and the guarantee of His eternal suretyship, we have confidence that "He is able to save completely [forever] those who come to God through Him, because He always lives to intercede for them" (v. 25, NIV).

The spies warned Rahab that she must not divulge any of this information to anybody in the city other than the members of her family. If she did, their agreement was canceled. What a contrast to the believer's relationship to Jesus Christ, for He wants *everybody* to know that He has paid the price of redemption and that they can be saved by trusting Him. If Rahab talked too much, her life was in danger; but if we don't talk enough, the lives of lost people around us are in danger.

4. Covenant faith (Josh. 2:15-24)

A covenant is simply an agreement, a contract between two or more parties, with certain conditions laid down for all parties to obey. You find a number of *divine* covenants recorded in Scripture: God's covenant with our first parents in Eden (Gen. 2:16); God's covenants with Noah (Gen. 9), Abraham (12:1-3; 15:1-20), and Israel (Ex. 19-20); the covenant concerning the land of Palestine, as explained in Deuteronomy; the messianic covenant with David (2 Sam. 7); and the New Covenant in the blood of Jesus Christ Jer. 31:31; Matt. 26:28; Heb. 12:24). You also find *human* covenants, such as the agreement between David and Jonathan (1 Sam. 18:3; 20:16) and between David and the people of Israel (2 Sam. 5:1-5).

Before the two spies left Rahab's house, they reaffirmed their covenant with her. Since the men didn't know God's plan for taking the city, they couldn't give Rahab any detailed instructions. Perhaps they assumed that the city would be besieged, the gates smashed down, and the people massacred. The men were certain that the city would fall and that ultimately the land would be taken.

Often in biblical covenants, God appointed some physical or material "token" to remind the people of what had been promised. His covenant with Abraham was "sealed" by the rite of circumcision (Gen. 17:9-14; Rom. 4:11). When God established His covenant with Israel at Sinai, both the covenant book and the covenant people were sprinkled with blood (Ex. 24:3-8; Heb. 9:16-22). God gave the rainbow as the token of the covenant with Noah (Gen. 9:12-17), and the Lord Jesus Christ used the broken bread and the cup of wine as tokens of the New Covenant (Luke 22:19-20; 1 Cor. 11:23–26).

In the case of Rahab, the spies instructed her to hang a scarlet rope out of the window of her house, which was built into the wall (Josh. 2:18). This scarlet rope would identify the "house of safety" to the army of Israel when they came to take the city. The color of the rope is significant for it reminds us of blood. Just as the blood on the door posts in Egypt marked a house that the angel of death was to pass over (Ex. 12:1-13), so the scarlet rope marked a house on the Jericho wall whose occupants the Jewish soldiers were to protect. Rahab let the men down from the window with that rope and kept it in the window from that hour. This was the "sure sign" of the covenant that she had asked for (Josh. 2:12-23).

It's important to note that Rahab and her family were saved by faith in the God of Israel and not by faith in the rope hanging out the window. The fact that she hung the rope from the window was proof that she had faith, just as the blood of the slain lamb put on the door posts in Egypt proved that the Jews believed God's Word. Faith in the living God means salvation, and faith in His covenant gives assurance; but faith in *the token of the covenant* is religious superstition and can give neither salvation nor assurance. The Jews depended on circumcision to save them, but they ignored the true spiritual meaning of that important rite (Rom. 2:25-29; Deut. 10:12-16; 30:6). Many people today depend for their salvation on their baptism or their participation in the Lord's Table (the Eucharist, Communion); but this kind of faith is vain. Rahab had faith in the Lord and in the covenant promises He had made through His servants; and she proved her faith by hanging the scarlet rope from the window. When the Jews captured Jericho, they found Rahab and her family in her house; and they rescued them from judgment (Josh. 6:21–25).

Rahab was a woman of great courage. She had to tell all her relatives about the coming judgment and the promise of salvation, and this was a dangerous thing to do. Suppose one of those relatives told the king what was going on. She also had to give a reason for the scarlet line hanging out her window. Since Jericho was "securely shut up" (v. 1, NKJV), it isn't likely that there were people outside the walls; but a stranger coming into the city for safety might have seen the scarlet cord. Or somebody visiting Rahab's house might have asked about it.

The spies left Rahab's house and hid until they were sure their pursuers had given up the chase. Then they returned to the camp of Israel and gave Joshua the good news that the fear of the Lord had brought the people of the land to a place of helplessness. Rahab not only brought hope to her family, but she also gave great encouragement to Joshua and the army of Israel.

The people of Israel, however, weren't ready yet to cross the river and conquer the enemy. They had some "unfinished business" to take care of before they could be sure of the blessing of the Lord.

CHAPTER FOUR
FORWARD BY FAITH
Joshua 3–4

We've just examined the faith of an individual, Rahab; and now the focus in the Book of Joshua moves to the faith of an entire nation. As you study, keep in mind that this book deals with much more than ancient history—what God did centuries ago for the Jews. It's about your life and the life of the church today—what God wants to do here and now for those who trust Him. The Book of Joshua is about the victory of faith and the glory that comes to God when His people trust and obey. British Prime Minister Benjamin Disraeli said, "The world was never conquered by intrigue; it was conquered by faith."

In the Christian life you're either an *overcomer* or you're *overcome*, a victor or a victim. After all, God didn't save us to make statues out of us and put us on exhibition. He saved us to make soldiers out of us and move us forward by faith to claim our rich inheritance in Jesus Christ. Moses said it perfectly: "He brought us out. . . that He might bring us in" (Deut. 6:23). Too many of God's people have the mistaken idea that salvation—being delivered from the bondage of Egypt—is all that's involved in the Christian life; but salvation is only the beginning. Both in our personal spiritual growth and in our service for the Lord, "there remains very much land yet to be possessed" (Josh. 13:1, NKJV). The theme of the Book of Joshua is the theme of the Book of Hebrews: "Let us go on" (Heb. 6:1); and the only way to go on is by faith.

Unbelief says, "Let's go back to where it's safe"; but faith says, "Let's go forward to where God is working" (see Num. 14:1-4). Forty years before, Joshua and Caleb had assured the Jews, "Let us go up at once, and possess it; for we are well able to overcome it." That's faith! But the people said, "We are not able!" That's unbelief, and it cost the nation forty years of discipline in the wilderness (see Num. 13:26-33). "And this is the victory that has overcome the world—your faith" (1 John 5:4, NKJV).

One of the joys of my Christian life has been the study of Christian biography, the lives of the men and women whom God has used—and is using—to challenge the church and change the world. The Christians I've read about were all different in their backgrounds, their training, their personalities, and their ways of serving God; but they had one thing in common: *They all believed God's promises and did what He told them to do.* They were men and women of faith, and God honored them because they believed His Word.

God hasn't changed, and the principle of faith hasn't changed. What seems to have changed is the attitude of God's people: *We no longer believe God and act by faith in His promises.* His promises never fail (Josh. 21:45; 23:14; 1 Kings 8:56), but we can fail to live by the grace of God and not enter into all that He has promised for us (Heb. 3:7-19; 12:15). God has "brought us out that He might bring us in," but too often we fail to "enter in because of unbelief" (Heb. 3:19).

In Joshua 3 and 4, God illustrates for us three essentials for moving ahead by faith and claiming all that He has for us: the Word of faith, the walk of faith, and the witness of faith.

1. The Word of faith (Josh. 3:1-13)

As the nation waited by the Jordan River, the people must have wondered what Joshua planned to do. He certainly wouldn't ask them to swim the river or ford it, because the river was at flood stage (3:15). They couldn't construct enough boats or rafts to transport more than a million people over the water to the other side. Besides, that approach would make them perfect targets for their enemies. What would their new leader do?

Like Moses before him, Joshua received his orders from the Lord, and he obeyed them by faith. "So then faith comes by hearing, and hearing by the word of God" (Rom. 10:17, NKJV). It has been well said that faith is not believing in spite of evidence but obeying in spite of consequence. When you read Hebrews 11, the great "faith chapter" of Scripture, you discover that the people mentioned there all *did something* because they believed God. Their faith wasn't a passive feeling; it was an active force. Because Abraham believed God, he left Ur and headed for Canaan. Because Moses believed God, he defied the gods of Egypt and led the Jews to freedom. Because Gideon believed God, he led a small band of Jews to defeat the huge Midianite army. *Living faith always leads to action.* "For as the body without the spirit is dead, so faith without works is dead also" (James 2:26, NKJV).

In this paragraph, you find five different messages, all of them based on the Word of God, which is the "word of faith" (Rom. 10:8). The people obeyed these messages by faith, and God took them over the river.

The officers' message to the people (vv. 1-4). Joshua was an early riser (6:12; 7:16; 8:10), who spent the first hours of the day in communion with God (1:8). In this, he was like Moses (Ex. 24:4; 34:4), David (Ps. 57:8; see 119:147), Hezekiah (2 Chron. 29:20), and our Lord Jesus Christ (Mark 1:35; see Isa. 50:4). It's impossible to live by faith and ignore the Word of God and prayer (Acts 6:4); for faith is nurtured by worship and the Word. The people God uses and blesses know how to discipline their bodies so that they can give themselves to the Lord in the early morning hours.

Joshua ordered the camp to move ten miles from The Acacia Grove (Shittim) to the Jordan; and no doubt the people in Jericho watched this march with great apprehension. It probably took Israel a day to make this journey; they rested another day; and on the third day, the officers gave them their orders: The people were to cross the river, following the Ark of the Covenant.

The Ark is mentioned sixteen times in chapters 3 and 4. It's called "the Ark of the Covenant" ten times, "the Ark of the Lord" three times, and simply "the Ark" three times. It was the "throne of God," the place where His glory rested in the tabernacle (Ex. 25:10-22) and God sat "enthroned between the cherubim" (Ps. 80:1, NIV). The Law of God was kept in the Ark, a reminder of God's covenant with Israel; and the blood of the sacrifices was sprinkled on the mercy seat on the annual Day of Atonement (Lev. 16:14-15).

The Ark going before the people was an encouragement to their faith, for it meant that their God was going before them and opening up the way. God had promised Moses, "My Presence will go with you, and I will give you rest" (Ex. 33:14, NKJV). When the nation had marched through the wilderness, the Ark had gone before them (Num. 10:33); and Moses would say, "Rise up, O Lord! May Your enemies be scattered; may Your foes flee before You" (v. 35, NIV). On that occasion, the presence of the Ark was a guarantee of the presence of the Lord.

Each of the tribes had an assigned place in the camp and an assigned order in the march when they broke up camp (Josh. 2). When the leaders of the tribes saw the priests bearing the Ark and moving toward the river, they were to prepare their people to follow. Since the people had not traveled this way before, they needed God to guide them. But they were not to get too close to the Ark, for this was a holy piece of furniture from the tabernacle; and it was not to be treated carelessly. God is our companion as we go through life, but we dare not treat Him like a "buddy."

Joshua's message to the people (v. 5). This was both an order and a promise, and the fulfillment of the promise depended on their obedience to the order. Some of God's promises are unconditional, and all we have to do is believe them; while other promises require that we meet certain conditions. In meeting these conditions, we're not earning God's blessing; we're making sure our hearts are ready for God's blessing.

If the experience of Israel at Mount Sinai was the pattern (Ex. 19:9-15), "sanctify yourselves" meant that everybody bathed and changed their clothes and that the married couples devoted themselves wholly to the Lord (1 Cor. 7:1-6). In the Near East, however, water was a luxury that wasn't used too often for personal hygiene. In our modern world we're accustomed to comfortable bathing facilities; but these were unknown to most of the people in Bible times.

In the Bible the imagery of washing one's body and changing clothes symbolized making a new beginning with the Lord. Since sin is pictured as defilement (Ps. 51:2, 7), God has to cleanse us before we can truly follow Him. When Jacob made a new beginning with the Lord and returned to Bethel, he and his family washed themselves and changed their garments (Gen. 35:1-3). After King David confessed his sin, he bathed, changed clothes, and worshiped the Lord (2 Sam. 12:20). The imagery is carried over into the New Testament in 2 Corinthians 6:14-7:1; Ephesians 4:26-27, and Colossians 3:8-14.

The promise was that the Lord would do wonders among them. As He opened the Red Sea to deliver Israel from Egypt, so also He would open the Jordan River and take them into the Promised Land. But that would be just the beginning of miracles, for the Lord would go with them into the land, defeat their enemies, and enable the tribes to claim their inheritance. "Who is so great a God as our God? You are the God who does wonders" (Ps.

77:13-14, NKJV). "How great are His signs, And how mighty His wonders!" (Dan. 4:3, NKJV)

Joshua's message to the priests (v. 6). The priests had the responsibility of bearing the Ark of the Covenant and going before the people as they marched. It was the priests who had to get their feet wet before God would open the waters. The priests would also have to stand in the middle of the riverbed until all the people had passed over. When the priests arrived on the other side, the waters would return to their original condition. It took faith and courage for these priests to do their job, but they trusted God and relied on the faithfulness of His Word.

The message of the Lord to Joshua (vv. 7-8). When Moses led the nation through the Red Sea, this miracle magnified Moses before the people; and they recognized that he was indeed the servant of the Lord (Ex. 14:31). God would do the same thing for Joshua at the Jordan; and in so doing, He would remind the people that He was with Joshua just as He had been with Moses (Josh. 4:14; see 1:5, 9). Both Moses and Joshua had received their *authority* from the Lord before these miracles occurred, but the miracles gave them *stature* before the people. It takes both authority and stature to exercise effective leadership.

Joshua's message to the people (vv. 9-13). Having instructed the priests bearing the Ark, Joshua then shared the words of the Lord with the people. He didn't magnify himself; He magnified the Lord and His gracious blessings to the nation. True spiritual leadership focuses the eyes of God's people on the Lord and His greatness. Much of what Joshua said in this brief speech was recalled from Moses' last speech to Joshua (Deut. 31:1-8), as well as the Lord's words to Joshua when he took Moses' place (Josh. 1:1-9). Joshua didn't give the people a "religious pep talk." He simply reminded them of the promises of God—the Word of faith—and encouraged them to trust and obey.

But Joshua's God was more than just the God of Israel. He was "the living God" (3:10) and "the Lord of all the earth" (vv. 11, 13). Because He is "the living God," He can defeat the dead idols of the heathen nations that then inhabited the land (Ps. 115). Because He is "the Lord of all the earth," He can go where He pleases and do what He wishes with every land and nation. "You shall be a special treasure to Me above all people," God had told them at Sinai, "for all the earth is Mine" (Ex. 19:5, NKJV). "The hills melted like wax at the presence of the Lord, at the presence of the Lord of the whole earth" (Ps. 97:5).

Joshua explained to the people that God would open the river as soon as the priests bearing the Ark put their feet into the waters of the Jordan. He also ordered each tribe to appoint a man to perform a special task that was explained later (Josh. 4:2-8). God was going before His people, and He would open the way!

As you review these five messages, you can see that the Lord gave them all the information they needed to accomplish what He wanted them to do. You find conditions that the people had to fulfill, orders they had to obey, and promises they had to believe. God always gives His "Word of faith" to His people whenever He asks them to follow Him into new areas of conflict and conquest. God's commandments are still His enablements, and God's promises do not fail. The counsel of King Jehoshaphat centuries later is still applicable today: "Believe in the Lord your God, and you shall be established; believe His prophets, and you shall prosper" (2 Chron. 20:20, NKJV). "There has not failed one word of all His good promise" (1 Kings 8:56, NKJV).

2. The walk of faith (Josh. 3:14-17)

During most of the year, the Jordan River was about a hundred feet wide; but at the spring flood season, the river overflowed its banks and became a mile wide. As soon as the priests bearing the Ark put their feet into the river, the water stopped flowing and stood like a wall about twenty miles away upstream, near a city called Adam. It was a miracle of God in response to the faith of the people.

Unless we step out by faith (1:3) and "get our feet wet," we're not likely to make much progress in living for Christ and serving Him. Each step that the priests took opened the water before them until they were standing in the midst of the river on dry ground. They stood there as the people passed by; and when the whole nation had crossed, the priests walked to the shore and the flow of the water resumed.

When God opened the Red Sea, He used a strong wind that blew the whole night before (Ex. 14:21-22). This was not an accident, for the wind was the blast of God's nostrils (15:8). When Moses lifted his rod, the wind began to blow; and when he lowered the rod, the waters flowed back and drowned the Egyptian army (14:26-28). When Israel crossed the Jordan River, it was not the obedient arm of a leader that brought the miracle but the obedient feet of the people. Unless we are willing to step out by faith and obey His Word, God can never open the way for us.

As I mentioned before, the crossing of the Jordan River is not a picture of the Christian dying and going to heaven, contrary to what is said in some songs. The crossing of the Red Sea pictures the believer being delivered from the bondage of sin, and the crossing of the Jordan River pictures the believer claiming the inheritance in Jesus Christ. Joshua is a type of Jesus Christ our Conqueror who leads us from day to day into the inheritance He has planned for us (1 Cor. 2:9–10). "He shall choose our inheritance for us" (Ps. 47:4).

What a tragedy it is when God's people fail to claim their inheritance and wander aimlessly through life as Israel did in the wilderness. The Book of Hebrews was written to challenge God's people to go on in spiritual maturity and not go backward in unbelief. In Hebrews 3-4, the writer used Israel's experience at Kadesh Barnea to warn foolish Christians not to come short of all that God had planned for them. We never stand still in the Christian life; we either move forward in faith or go backward in unbelief.

3. The witness of faith (Josh. 4:1-24)

The Lord was in control of all the activities at the Jordan River that day. He told the priests when to enter the river and when to leave and go to the other side. He told the water when to roll back and when to return. Both the water and the people obeyed Him, and everything worked out as God planned. It was a day that glorified the Lord and magnified His servant Joshua (v. 14).

Two heaps of stones were set up as memorials of Israel's crossing of the Jordan River: twelve stones at Gilgal (vv. 1-8, 10-24), and twelve stones in the midst of the river (v. 9). They were witnesses that God honors faith and works on behalf of those who trust Him.

The stones placed at Gilgal were carried over by twelve previously selected men, one from each tribe (3:12). When these men reached the midst of the river, they each picked up a large stone and carried it about eight miles to Gilgal where the nation camped for the night. Gilgal was about two miles from Jericho and excluding the Transjordan was the first territory in Canaan claimed by Israel for their inheritance. In later years Gilgal became an important center for the nation Israel crowned their first king at Gilgal (1 Sam. 11); there David was welcomed back after Absalom's rebellion was subdued (2 Sam. 19); and Samuel thought Gilgal important enough to include it in his "ministry circuit" (1 Sam. 7:16) There was a "school of the prophets" at Gilgal in the days of Elijah and Elisha (2 Kings 2:1-2; 4:38). Gilgal was important to Joshua because it became his camp and center of operations (Josh. 9:6; 10:6, 15, 43; 14:6).

This heap of twelve stones was a reminder of what God did for His people. The Jews were great believers in teaching the next generation about Jehovah and His special relationship to the people of Israel (4:6, 21; Ex. 12:26; 13:14; Deut. 6:20; see Pss. 34:11-16; 71:17-18; 78:1-7; 79:13; 89:1; 102:18). To an unbeliever, the heap of twelve stones was simply another stone pile; but to a believing Israelite, it was a constant reminder that Jehovah was his or her God, working His wonders on behalf of His people.

But also note that Joshua put an obligation on the Jews to fear the Lord and bear witness of Him to the whole world (Josh. 4:24). The God who can open the river is the God everybody ought to fear, love, and obey! Israel needed to tell the other nations about Him and invite them to trust Him too. The God of Israel cares for His people, keeps His promises, goes before them in victory, and never fails. What a witness to give to the world!

It's unfortunate that this memorial at Gilgal gradually lost its spiritual meaning and instead became a shrine where the Jews sinned against God by worshiping there. The Prophet Hosea condemned the people for worshiping at Gilgal instead of at Jerusalem (Hosea 4:15; 9:15; 12:11), and Amos echoed his warnings (Amos 4:4; 5:5). Unless we teach the next generation the truth about the Lord, they will turn away and start following the world.

Joshua set up the monument in the midst of the river (v. 9)*; and to the Jews, it must have seemed a strange thing for their leader to do. After all, who but God could see twelve stones heaped together in a riverbed? We aren't told that God commanded Joshua to set up this second monument, but it's likely that He did. At least, He didn't reproach him for doing it.

The monument at Gilgal reminded the Jews that God had opened the Jordan River and brought them safely across into the Promised Land. They had made a break with the past and were never to think of going back. The monument in the depths of the river reminded them that their old life was buried and they were now to "walk in newness of life" (Rom. 6:1-4). (When we study Josh. 5, we will see the spiritual significance for the Christian today of the establishing of this monument and the circumcising of the new generation.)

---

*The NIV text applies the verse to the monument at Gilgal, but the marginal note makes this a separate monument, which I think is the accurate interpretation. The NASB reads, "Then Joshua set up twelve stones in the middle of the Jordan at the place where the feet of the priests who carried the Ark of the Covenant were standing, and they are there to this day."

Meanwhile, whenever the Jewish children asked about the twelve stones at Gilgal, the parents would explain the miracle of the crossing of the river. Then they would add, "But there's another monument in the middle of the river where the priests stood with the Ark. You can't see it, but it's there. It reminds us that our old life has been buried, and we must live a new life in obedience to the Lord." The children would have to accept this fact by faith; and if they did, it could make a great difference in the way they related to God and to His will for their lives.

These two heaps of stones were the first of several stone monuments that the Jews put up in the land. In obedience to Moses' instructions, they also set up the two "stones of blessing and cursing" at Mt. Ebal and Mt. Gerizim (Deut. 27:1-8; Josh. 8:30-35). They raised a heap of stones over Achan and his household (7:25-26); and at the close of his life, Joshua set up a "witness stone" at Shechem (24:24-28; Judg. 9:6). The two and a half tribes that lived east of the Jordan set up a "great altar" to remind their children that they were a part of the nation of Israel, even though the river separated them from the other tribes (Josh. 22:10ff).

There is nothing wrong with memorials, provided they don't become religious idols that turn our hearts from God, and provided they don't so link us to the past that we fail to serve God in the present. Glorifying the past is a good way to petrify the present and rob the church of power. The next generations need reminders of what God has done in history, but these reminders must also strengthen their faith and draw them closer to the Lord.

God brings us out that He might bring us in (Deut. 6:23), and He brings us in that we might overcome and claim our inheritance in Jesus Christ. Because God's people are identified with Christ in His death, burial, and resurrection (Rom. 6; Gal. 2:20), they have "overcoming power," and the world (6:14), the flesh (5:24), or the devil (John 12:31) need not defeat them. In Jesus Christ, we are overcomers (1 John 5:3).

If you want to claim your spiritual inheritance in Christ, believe the Word of faith and *get your feet wet!* Step out in a walk of faith, and God will open the way for you. Surrender yourself to the Lord and die to the old life (Rom. 6), and He will bring you into the land and give you "days of heaven upon the earth" (Deut. 11:21).

The Israelites were now in the land, but they were not yet ready to confront the enemy. There was still some spiritual preparation necessary for the people and for Joshua.

CHAPTER FIVE
PREPARING FOR VICTORY
Joshua 5

The nation of Israel arrived safely on the other side of the Jordan River. Their crossing was a great miracle, and it sent a great message to the people of the land (5:1). The Canaanites were already afraid (2:9-11), and now their fears totally demoralized them.

You would have expected Joshua to mobilize the army immediately and attack Jericho. After all, the people of Israel were united in following the Lord; and the people of the land were paralyzed by fear. From the human point of view, it was the perfect time for Joshua to act.

But God's thoughts and ways are higher than ours (Isa. 55:8-9); and Joshua was getting his orders from the Lord, not from the military experts. The nation crossed the river on the tenth day of the first month (Josh. 4:19). The events described in Joshua 5 took at least ten days, and then the people marched around Jericho for six more days. God waited over two weeks before giving His people their first victory in the land.

God's people must be *prepared* before they can be trusted with victory. The triumphant conquest of the land was to be the victory of God, not the victory of Israel or of Joshua. It was neither the expertise of the Jewish army nor the emotions of the enemy that would give Israel the victory, but the presence and blessing of the Lord. There were three steps of preparation necessary before God would give His people victory over the nations in the land of Canaan.

1. Renewing the Lord's covenant (Josh. 5:1-9)

After triumphantly crossing the Jordan River, the nation had to pause at Gilgal while the men submitted to painful surgery. Why did God command this ritual at this time?

To restore their covenant relationship (Josh. 5:2-7). Israel is a covenant nation, a privilege God has given to no other nation on earth (Rom. 9:4-5). God gave His covenant to Abraham when He called him out of Ur of the Chaldees (Gen. 12:1-3), and He sealed that covenant with a sacrifice (Gen. 15). God gave circumcision as the sign of the covenant to Abraham and his descendants (17:9-14, 23-27; note especially v. 11). Other nations in that day practiced circumcision, but the ritual didn't carry with it the spiritual meaning that it did for the Jews.

Through this ritual the Jews became a "marked people" because they belonged to the true and living God. This meant that they were under obligation to obey Him. The mark of the covenant reminded them that their bodies belonged to the Lord and were not to be used for sinful purposes. Israel was surrounded by nations that worshiped idols and included in their worship rituals that were sensual and degrading. The mark of the covenant reminded the Jews that they were a special people, a separated people, a holy nation (Ex. 19:5-6), and that they were to maintain purity in their marriages, their society, and their worship of God.

The Jews had not practiced circumcision during their years of wandering in the wilderness. Thirty-eight years before, at Kadesh Barnea, they had refused to believe God and enter the land (Deut. 2:14; Num. 13-14). God disciplined the people by making them wander in the wilderness until the entire older generation had died off, except Caleb and Joshua. During that time, God had suspended His covenant relationship with Israel and didn't require the mark of the covenant on their male children. He performed wonders for them and met their every need even though they were temporarily not His covenant people.

The new generation was now in their inheritance, however, and it was important that they renew their covenant relationships with the Lord. If during their wilderness journey Israel was tempted to sin (see Num. 25), how much more they would be tempted now that they were living in the land! They would be surrounded by pagan people with immoral religious practices, and they would be tempted to compromise with their enemies. Later, this is exactly what future generations did, because they forgot the true meaning of circumcision.

This physical operation on the body was meant to be a symbol of a *spiritual operation on the heart.* "Therefore circumcise the foreskin of your heart, and be stiff-necked no longer" (Deut. 10:16, NKJV). No amount of external surgery can change the inner person. It's when we repent and turn to God for help that He can change our hearts and make us love and obey Him more. (See Rom. 2:25-29.)

But over the years, the Jews came to trust in the external *mark* of the covenant and not in the *God* of the covenant who wanted to make them a holy people. They thought that as long as they were God's covenant people, they could live just as they pleased! Moses warned them about this sin (Deut. 30:6), and so did the prophets (Jer. 4:4). When John the Baptist called them to repent, the Jewish spiritual leaders said, "We have Abraham as our father" (Matt. 3:9, NKJV). They were not unlike some people today who feel sure they're saved and are going to heaven because they're baptized, confirmed, and participate regularly in Communion. As good as these religious rites can be, they must never become substitutes for faith in Jesus Christ. (See Rom. 2:25-29.)

To test their faith (Josh. 5:8). Israel was camped in enemy territory, just a few miles from Jericho. Now they were going to *temporarily disable every male in the nation,* including every soldier in the army! What a golden opportunity for the enemy to attack and wipe them out. (See Gen. 34.) It took faith for Joshua and the people to obey the Lord, but their obedience to the Law was the secret of their success (Josh. 1:7-8). In their weakness they were made strong; and through faith and patience they inherited the promises (Heb. 6:12).

Shortly after Israel departed from Egypt, God tested them at Meribah; and they failed the test (Ex. 17:1-7; Ps. 81:7). Shortly after Israel entered the Promised Land, God tested them by commanding the men to be circumcised; and they passed the test. The people had faith to obey God, and this act gave evidence that they would obey His orders as they marched through the land.

After we've experienced an exciting victory of faith, God often permits us to be tested. Abraham arrived in the land of promise and was confronted with a famine (Gen. 12). Elijah triumphed over Baal and was threatened with death (1 Kings 18-19). After His baptism in the Jordan, the Spirit led Jesus into the wilderness to be tempted by Satan (Matt. 3:13-4:11). Since great victories can lead to great pride, God allows us to be tested in order to remind us to depend on Him. The Scottish preacher Andrew Bonar (1810-92) used to say, "Let us be as watchful after the victory as before the battle."

To remove their reproach (Josh. 5:9). The word *Gilgal* is similar to the Hebrew word *galal* which means "to roll." But what was "the reproach of Egypt"? Some suggest that this means their reproach for being slaves in Egypt, but it wasn't Israel's fault that the new pharaoh turned against them (Ex. 1:8ff). The Jews were in Egypt because God had sent them there (Gen. 46:1-4), not because they were disobedient.

It's also been suggested that "the reproach of Egypt" refers to the nation's shame because they had worshiped idols in Egypt (Ezek. 20:7-8; 23:3) and even during their wilderness wanderings (Amos 5:25-26; Acts 7:42-43). But that older generation was now dead, and the younger Israelites certainly shouldn't be blamed for the sins of their fathers. Furthermore, it's difficult for me to see the relationship between crossing the river, circumcision, and the Jews' idolatry in Egypt.

I think that "the reproach of Egypt" refers to the ridicule of the enemy when Israel failed to trust God at Kadesh Barnea and enter the Promised Land. When Aaron made the golden calf at Mount Sinai and the people broke God's law, God threatened to destroy them and make a new nation from Moses. But Moses argued that God would lose glory if He did that, because the Egyptians would only say that God delivered them in order to kill them (Ex. 32:1-12). At Kadesh Barnea Moses used the same appeal when God said He would destroy Israel (Num. 14:11-14). Moses didn't want the Egyptians to spread the word that the God of Israel couldn't finish what He had started.

Israel's sin at Kadesh Barnea was a reproach to them, but now that was all in the past. The nation was actually in the Promised Land! They had captured the territory east of the Jordan, and their people were already occupying it (Num. 32). They had crossed the Jordan River and were ready for conquest. No matter what the Egyptians and the other nations had said about Israel because of their sin at Kadesh Barnea, that reproach was now completely gone. Each man bore on his body the mark that reminded him that he belonged to God, he was a son of the covenant, and the land was his to conquer and possess.

To qualify them to eat the Passover (Ex. 12:43-44, 48). No male could participate in the annual Feast of the Passover unless he had been circumcised and was a true son of the covenant. I'll have more to say later about this great Passover celebration.

To picture some important spiritual truths. Old Testament events are often illustrations of New Testament doctrines (Rom. 15:4; 1 Cor. 10:11). Israel's Exodus from Egypt pictures the sinner's deliverance from the slavery of sin through faith in Jesus Christ (John 1:29; 1 Cor. 5:7; Gal. 1:4). Israel's crossing of the Jordan River is a picture of believers dying to self and entering by faith into their inheritance. This truth is explained in Hebrews 1-6, especially chapters 3 and 4. God doesn't want us to wander in the wilderness of unbelief. He wants us to claim our inheritance by faith, conquer our enemies, and enjoy the spiritual "rest" that He has for those who walk by faith.

Because the Holy Spirit baptizes all believers into the body of Christ (1 Cor. 12:13), all believers are identified with Christ in His death, burial, resurrection, and ascension (Rom. 6:1-10; Eph. 2:1-10). This truth is pictured in Israel's crossing of the river. We're saved from the *penalty* of sin because of *substitution:* Christ died for us (Rom. 5:8). But we're saved from the *power* of sin because of *identification:* We died with Christ (Gal. 2:20). We must believe what God says is true and reckon ourselves to be dead to sin and alive in Christ (Rom. 6:11-23). We have crossed the river!

Many New Testament scholars believe the apostolic church practiced baptism by immersion. The candidate was submerged into the water and then raised up, picturing the believer's identification with Christ in His death, burial, and resurrection. Israel pictured this truth in their crossing of the Red Sea (separated from the old life) and their crossing of the Jordan River (entering into the new inheritance).

We have also been identified with Christ in His circumcision. "In Him you were also circumcised with the circumcision made without hands, by putting off the body of the sins of the flesh, by the circumcision of Christ, buried with Him in baptism, in which you also were raised with Him through faith in the working of God, who raised Him from the dead" (Col. 2:11-12, NKJV).

The Christian's *circumcision* is in contrast to that of the Jews. They had external physical surgery, while believers have internal "spiritual surgery" on their hearts. The Jews' surgery involved only a part of the body; while for the believer, the whole "body of the sins of the flesh" (Col. 2:11) was removed. *When you accept this fact and reckon on it, you have victory over sins of the flesh that would enslave you.* Faith "in the working of God" (Col. 2:12, NKJV) can give you overcoming power.

In the early church there were false teachers who said the Gentile Christians had to be circumcised and obey the Law of Moses, or they couldn't be saved (Acts 15). They were adding human works to God's grace (Eph. 2:8-10; Gal. 5:1). Paul called these false teachers "dogs" (that's what some Jews called the Gentiles) and called circumcision "the concision" ("mutilation"), and he affirmed that Christian believers were the "true circumcision" (Phil. 3:1-3). God's children have experienced in Christ an inward "spiritual surgery" that has given them a new heart and new desires (2 Cor. 5:17; Eph. 4:24; Col. 3:10; see Ezek. 11:19; 36:26).

Just as the Jewish men at Gilgal had to submit to God's will, so believers today must yield to the Spirit and allow Him to make true in their personal experience what God says is true in His Word. We must practice "dead reckoning" (Rom. 6:11ff).

2. Remembering the Lord's goodness (Josh. 5:10-12)

"Forgetting those things which are behind" (Phil. 3:13) is wise counsel for most areas of life, but there are some things we must never forget. In his farewell address to the nation, Moses repeatedly commanded the Jews to remember that they were once slaves in Egypt and that the Lord had delivered them and made them His own people (Deut. 6:15; 15:15; 16:12; 24:18, 22). This great truth was embodied in their annual Passover feast. They were never to forget that they were a redeemed people, set free by the blood of the lamb.

Forty years before, Israel had celebrated the Passover on the night of their deliverance from Egypt (Ex. 11-14). They also celebrated Passover at Mount Sinai, before leaving for Kadesh Barnea (Num. 9:1-14); but there is no evidence that they commemorated the Passover at any time during their years of wilderness wandering. The fact that the new generation wasn't circumcised prevented them from participating, and God had temporarily suspended His covenant with His people because of their rebellion at Kadesh Barnea. That one act of unbelief had cost Israel dearly.

The death of Jesus Christ is typified in the slaying of the Passover lamb (1 Cor. 5:7), and His resurrection is typified in the "wave offering" that was presented on the day after the Sabbath that followed Passover (Lev. 23:10-14; 1 Cor. 15:23). The day after the Sabbath would be the first day of the week, the Lord's Day, the day of Christ's resurrection (Matt. 28:1). Again, we see the picture of death and resurrection, which is our only means of life and victory (Rom. 6:4).

The Passover was followed by the Feast of Unleavened Bread when for a week the Jews avoided leaven (yeast) and ate unleavened bread (Ex. 12:15, 18-20). When Israel entered Canaan, it was time for the barley harvest; thus grain was available. No doubt the inhabitants of the area had left grain behind when they fled to Jericho for safety; thus that grain was also available. The Lord prepared a table for His people in the presence of their enemies, and Israel didn't have to be afraid (Ps. 23:5).

On the day after Passover, the manna ceased; and thus ended a forty-year miracle (Ex. 16). If the Passover reminded the Jews of their redemption from Egypt, the manna reminded them of their desire to go back to Egypt! "Would to God we had died by the hand of the Lord in the land of Egypt, when we sat by the flesh pots, and when we did eat bread to the full" (Ex. 16:3). God fed His people the bread of heaven, the food of the angels (Ps. 78:23-25); and yet they still lusted for the food of Egypt (Num. 11:4-9). God easily took His people out of Egypt, but it was difficult for Him to take Egypt out of His people.

Too many professed Christians contradict their profession by exhibiting an appetite for what belongs to their past life. "If then you were raised with Christ, seek those things which are above, where Christ is, sitting at the right hand of God. Set your mind on things above, not on things on the earth" (Col. 3:1-2, NKJV). Using the imagery from Joshua, this means, "You've crossed the river and are now in your inheritance. Don't look back and desire the things of Egypt or the wilderness. Let God feed you and satisfy you with the harvest in the inheritance."

The harvest is another image of death and resurrection. The seed is buried in the ground and *dies*, but from that death comes forth beauty and fruitfulness. Jesus applied to Himself both the image of the manna (John 6:26-59) and the harvest (12:20-28), for He is the nourishment upon which we must feed.

3. Reaffirming the Lord's presence (Josh. 5:13-15)

Joshua had read in the Book of the Law what Moses had said to the Lord after Israel had made the golden calf: "If Your Presence does not go with us, do not bring us up from here" (Ex. 33:15, NKJV). The Lord had promised to be with Joshua just as He had been with Moses (Josh. 1:5), and now He reaffirmed that promise in a personal way. Like his predecessor, Joshua refused to move until he was sure the Lord's presence was with him.

This paragraph records one of the preincarnation appearances of the Lord Jesus Christ recorded in the Old Testament. To Abraham the pilgrim, the Lord came as a traveler to share in a friendly meal (Gen. 18:1-8). To Jacob the schemer, He came as a wrestler to bring him to the place of submission (32:24-32). The three Hebrew men met Him as their companion in the furnace of fire (Dan. 3:25), and Joshua met Him as the Captain of the Lord's armies. Our Lord always comes to us when we need Him and in the way we need Him.

It must have been a great encouragement to Joshua to realize that he was not alone. There is a loneliness to leadership that can be disturbing and even depressing as you realize how much your decisions affect the lives of others. "To be President of the United States is to be lonely," said Harry Truman, "very lonely at times of great decisions." Joshua must have been feeling some of that loneliness.

God had promised to be with Joshua (Josh. 1:5, 9), and the people had prayed that the Lord would be with him (vv. 16–17). The enemy knew that God was with Israel (2:8ff), and Joshua had encouraged his people with this promise (3:9ff). *Joshua was now experiencing the reality of that promise!* The Lord met him as Captain of the Lord's armies, whether in heaven or on earth. "The Lord of hosts [armies] is with us; the God of Jacob is our refuge" (Ps. 46:7, 11). Joshua would recall the song Israel had sung at the Red Sea: "The Lord is a man of war: the Lord is His name" (Ex. 15:3).

I appreciate the courage of Joshua as he confronted this stranger; for he wanted to know whose side he was on. With Joshua, there was no compromise: You were either *for* the Lord and His people or *against* them (Matt. 12:30; Luke 11:23). When Joshua discovered the visitor was the Lord, he fell at His feet in worship and waited for His orders.

In Christian ministry great public victories are won in private as leaders submit to the Lord and receive their directions from Him. It's doubtful that anybody in the camp of Israel knew about their leader's meeting with the Lord, but that meeting made the difference between success and failure on the battlefield. The Chinese Bible teacher Watchman Nee wrote, "Not until we take the place of a servant can He take His place as Lord."

Joshua was reminded that he was *second in command.* Every father and mother, pastor, and Christian leader is second in command to the Lord Jesus Christ; and when we forget this fact, we start to move toward defeat and failure. The Lord came to Joshua that day, not just to help but *to lead.* "Without Me you can do nothing" (John 15:5, NKJV). Joshua was an experienced soldier, whom Moses had trained for leadership. Yet that was no guarantee of success. He needed the presence of the Lord God.

The Lord's first order to Joshua revealed to him that he was standing on holy ground. This reminds us of God's words to Moses at the burning bush (Ex. 3:5). Joshua was standing in "heathen territory"; yet because God was with him, *he was standing on holy ground.* If we are obeying the will of God, no matter where He leads us, we are on holy ground; *and we had better behave accordingly.* There's no such thing as "secular" and "sacred," "common" and "consecrated," when you are in the Lord's service. "Therefore, whether you eat or drink, or whatever you do, do all to the glory of God" (1 Cor. 10:31, NKJV).

The sequence here is significant: first *humble worship,* then *holy walk,* then *heavenly warfare.* This parallels the "spiritual postures" found in the Epistle to the Ephesians. Joshua first bowed the knee (Eph. 3:14); then he submitted to a holy walk (4:1, 17; 5:2, 8, 15); and then he went out to battle the enemy in the power of the Lord (6:10ff). Like Joshua, we have already been given our inheritance (described in Eph. 1-2) and we must overcome the enemy in order to claim it for ourselves and enjoy it.

When Joshua met the Lord, he discovered that *the battle was the Lord's and He had already overcome the enemy.* All Joshua had to do was listen to God's Word and obey orders, and God would do the rest. God had already given Jericho to Israel (Josh. 6:2); all they had to do was step out by faith and claim the victory by obeying the Lord.

In a meeting with a small group of missionaries in China, James Hudson Taylor, founder of the China Inland Mission (now Overseas Missionary Fellowship) reminded them that there were three ways to do God's work: "One is to make the best plans we can, and carry them out to the best of our ability . . . or, having carefully laid our plans and determined to carry them through, we may ask God to help us, and to prosper us in connection with them. Yet another way of working is to begin with God; to ask His plans, and to offer ourselves to Him to carry out His purposes."[1]

Joshua followed the third plan, and that's why the Lord blessed him.

The main lesson of Joshua 5 is that we must be a spiritually prepared people if we are going to do the Lord's work successfully and glorify His name. Instead of rushing into the battle, we must "take time to be holy."

In a letter to his missionary friend Rev. Daniel Edwards, the saintly Scottish preacher Robert Murray McCheyne wrote: "Remember you are God's sword—His instrument—I trust a chosen vessel unto Him to bear His name. In great measure, according to the purity and perfections of the instrument, will be the success. It is not great talents God blesses so much as great likeness to Jesus. A holy minister is an awful weapon in the hand of God."[2]

That letter was written in 1840, but its admonition applies to God's people today. All of us are His ministers, His servants; and we want to be holy instruments that He can use successfully.

CHAPTER SIX
THE CONQUEST BEGINS!
Joshua 6

"You are but a poor soldier of Christ if you think you can overcome without fighting, and suppose you can have the crown without the conflict."

The courageous Syrian preacher and martyr John Chrysostom (347-407) said that, and he was right; for the Christian life involves challenge and conflict whether we like it or not. Our enemies are constantly waging war against us and trying to keep us from claiming our inheritance in Jesus Christ. The world, the flesh, and the devil (Eph. 2:1-3) are united against Christ and His people just as the nations in Canaan were united against Joshua and the Jewish nation.

It's unfortunate that many of the "militant songs" of the church have been removed from some hymnals, apparently because the idea of warfare disturbs people and seems to contradict the words and works of Jesus Christ. But these zealous editors with scissors seem to have forgotten that the main theme of the Bible is God's holy warfare against Satan and sin. In Genesis 3:15, God declared war on Satan, and one day He will declare the victory when Jesus comes as Conqueror to establish His kingdom (Rev. 19:11-21). *If you eliminate the militant side of the Christian faith, then you must abandon the cross; for it was on the cross that Jesus won the victory over sin and Satan* (Col. 2:13-15).

A pastor attended a court hearing to protest the building of a tavern near his church and a public school. The lawyer for the tavern owners said to him, "I'm surprised to see you here today, Reverend. As a shepherd, shouldn't you be out taking care of the sheep?"

The pastor replied, "Today I'm fighting the wolf!"

Too many Christians cultivate only a sentimental emphasis on "peace and goodwill" and ignore the spiritual battle against sin; and this means they've already lost the victory and are working for the enemy. We must never forget Paul's warning about the savage wolves that are ready to destroy the flock (Acts 20:28-29).

The Christian's warfare is not against flesh and blood, but against enemies in the spiritual realm (Eph. 6:10-18); and the weapons we use are spiritual (2 Cor. 10:3-6). Satan and his demonic armies use people to oppose and attack the church of God; and if we don't take our stand with

Christ, *we've already lost the battle.* In the army of Jesus Christ there can be no neutrality. "He that is not with Me is against Me," said Jesus; and He spoke those words in the context of spiritual warfare (Matt. 12:24-30). Since the Apostle Paul often used the military image to describe the Christian life, we dare not ignore the subject (Eph. 6:10ff; 2 Tim. 2:1-4; Rom. 13:12; 1 Thess. 5:8).

Israel's victory at Jericho illustrates three principles of spiritual conflict and victory applicable to our lives today, no matter what challenges we may be called to confront.

1. Before the challenge: remember that you fight *from* victory, not just *for* victory (Josh. 6:1-5)

The Christian soldier stands in a position of guaranteed victory because Jesus Christ has already defeated every spiritual enemy (John 12:31). Jesus defeated Satan not only in the wilderness (Matt. 4:1-11), but also during His earthly ministry (12:22-29), on the cross (Col. 2:13-15), and in His resurrection and ascension (Eph. 1:19-23). As He intercedes for His people in heaven, He helps us mature and accomplish His will (Heb. 13:20-21); and "if God be for us, who can be against us?" (Rom. 8:31)

Consider the factors involved in Joshua's victory:

The fear of the Lord (Josh. 6:1). The land of Canaan was divided up among a number of "city states," each ruled by a king (see 12:9-34). These cities were not large; Ai, which was smaller than Jericho (7:2-3), had about 12,000 people (8:25). Excavations at Jericho indicate that the city covered perhaps eight acres and was protected by two high parallel walls, which stood about fifteen feet apart and surrounded the city. It was the sight of cities like Jericho that convinced ten of the Jewish spies that Israel could never conquer the land (Num. 13:28).

But the news of Israel's Exodus from Egypt and their recent victories east of the Jordan had already spread to Canaan and put the people in panic (Josh. 2:9-11; see Deut. 2:25; 7:23; 11:25; 32:30). "I will send My fear before you," God had promised; "I will cause confusion among all the people to whom you come, and will make all your enemies turn their backs to you" (Ex. 23:27, NKJV).

It was said that Mary Queen of Scots feared John Knox's prayers more than she feared an enemy army. But is society today afraid of what God's people may do? Probably not, and it's mainly because the church hasn't done very much to display the power of God to a skeptical world. The church is no longer "terrible as an army with banners" (Song 6:4, 10). In fact, the church is so much like the world that the world takes little notice of what we do. We imitate the world's methods; we cater to the world's appetites; we solicit the world's approval; and we measure what we do according to the world's standards. Is it any wonder that we don't gain the world's respect?

But not so with Joshua and Israel! They were a conquering people who made no compromise with the enemy but trusted God to give them the victory. Theirs was a march of triumph that put the fear of God into the hearts of the enemy.

The promise of the Lord (Josh. 6:2). It's possible that the Lord spoke these words to Joshua when He confronted him at Jericho (5:13-15). The tense of the verb is important: *"I have given* Jericho into your hand" (6:2, NKJV, italics added). The victory had already been won! All Joshua and his people had to do was claim the promise and obey the Lord.

Victorious Christians are people who *know* the promises of God, because they spend time meditating on God's Word (1:8); they *believe* the promises of God because the Word of God generates faith in their hearts (Rom. 10:17); and they *reckon* on these promises and obey what God tells them to do. To "reckon" means to count as true in your life what God says about you in His Word.

"Be of good cheer," Jesus told His disciples; "I have overcome the world" (John 16:33). "And they that are Christ's have crucified the flesh with the affections and lusts" (Gal. 5:24). "Now is the judgment of this world; now shall the prince of this world be cast out" (John 12:31). Christ has conquered the world, the flesh, and the devil; *and if we reckon on this truth, we can conquer through Him.* It's possible to believe a promise and still not reckon on it and obey the Lord. Believing a promise is like accepting a check, but reckoning is like endorsing the check and cashing it.

The instructions of the Lord (Josh. 6:3-5). "Joshua did not take the city merely by a clever, human military tactic," wrote Francis A. Schaeffer. "The strategy was the Lord's."[1]

No situation is too great for the Lord to handle, and no problem is too much for Him to solve. When He saw more than 5,000 hungry people before Him, Jesus asked Philip, "Where shall we buy bread, that these may eat?" Then John adds, "But this He said to test him; for He Himself knew what He would do" (John 6:5-6, NKJV). *God always knows what He will do.* Our responsibility is to wait for Him to tell us all that we need to know and then obey it.

At the close of the last chapter, I quoted J. Hudson Taylor's words about three different ways to serve the Lord: (1) to make the best plans we can and hope they succeed; (2) to make our own plans and ask God to bless them; or (3) to ask God for His plans and then do what He tells us to do. Joshua received his orders from the Lord, and that's why Israel succeeded.

God's plan for the conquest of Jericho was seemingly foolish, but it worked. God's wisdom is far above ours (Isa. 55:8–9) and He delights in using people and plans that seem foolish to the world (1 Cor. 1:26-29). Whether it's Joshua with trumpets, Gideon with torches and pitchers (Judg. 7), or David with his sling (1 Sam. 17), God delights in using weakness and seeming foolishness to defeat His enemies and glorify His name. "For the eyes of the Lord run to and fro throughout the whole earth, to shew Himself strong in the behalf of them whose heart is perfect toward Him" (2 Chron. 16:9).

God's instructions were that the armed men march around Jericho once a day for six days, followed by seven priests each blowing a trumpet. The priests carrying the Ark of the Lord would come next, and the rear guard would complete the procession. The only noise permitted was the sound of the trumpets. On the seventh day the procession would march around the city seven times, the priests would give a long blast on the trumpets, and then the marchers would all shout. God would then cause the walls to fall down flat so that the soldiers could easily enter the city. In this plan the emphasis is on the number seven: seven priests, seven trumpets, seven days of marching, and seven circuits of the city on the seventh day. The number seven is written clearly into the life of Israel: The Sabbath celebrated on the seventh day of the week; seven weeks from Passover is Pentecost; the seventh year is the Sabbatical Year; and after forty-nine years (seven times seven) comes the Year of Jubilee. Three of Israel's feasts fall in the seventh month: the Feast of

Trumpets, the Day of Atonement (Lev. 16), and the Feast of Tabernacles. (For details about this remarkable calendar, see Lev. 23.)

In biblical numerology the number seven represents completeness or perfection. The Hebrew word translated "seven" *(shevah)* comes from a root that means "to be full, to be satisfied." When God finished His work of creation, He rested on the seventh day and sanctified it (Gen. 2:3); and this helped give the number seven its sacred significance. The Jews noted that there were seven promises in God's covenant with Abraham (12:1-3) and seven branches on the candlestick in the tabernacle (Ex. 37:17-24). Anything involving the number seven was especially sacred to them. It spoke of God's ability to finish whatever He started.

The Jews used two different kinds of trumpets, those made of silver and those made of ram's horns. The silver trumpets were used especially by the priests to signal the camp when something important was happening (Num. 10). The ram's horns were used primarily for celebrations. The common Hebrew word for "trumpet" is *shofar;* for "ram's horn," it is *jobel,* which is the root of the word *jubilee.* The "Year of Jubilee" was the fiftieth year after seven Sabbaticals, and was a special time of celebration in Israel (Lev. 25; 27:17-14). The priests blew the ram's horns to "proclaim liberty throughout all the land" (25:10).

The priests didn't use the silver trumpets in this event because Israel was not declaring war on Jericho, *for there was no war!* The Jews were announcing the arrival of the "Year of Jubilee" for Israel in their new land. God's people today can march in triumphal procession because of the victory of Jesus Christ over all the enemies of God (Rom. 8:37; 2 Cor. 2:14; Col. 2:15). We should be living like victors, not victims.

"The wall of the city shall fall down!" (Josh. 6:5) was God's promise, and His promises never fail (21:45; 23:14). God's people don't simply fight *for* victory but *from* victory, because the Lord has already won the battle. Reckon on His promises and obey what He tells you to do, and you shall have the victory.

2. During the challenge: Remember that you overcome the enemy by faith (Josh. 6:6-16, 20)

"By faith the walls of Jericho fell down, after they were compassed about seven days" (Heb. 11:30). "And this is the victory that has overcome the world—our faith" (1 John 5:4, NKJV).

Faith is not believing in spite of evidence, for the people of Israel had been given one demonstration after another proving that God's Word and God's power can be trusted. The Lord had opened the Red Sea, destroyed the Egyptian army, cared for His people in the wilderness, defeated great kings, given Israel their land, opened the Jordan River, and brought His people safely into the Promised Land. How could they do anything other than believe Him!

Joshua first shared the Lord's plan with the priests. It was important that the Ark of the Lord be in its proper place, for it represented the presence of the Lord with His people. When Israel crossed the river, the account mentions the Ark sixteen times (Josh. 3–4); and here in 6:6–15, the Ark is mentioned eight times. Israel could march and the priests blow trumpets until all of them dropped from weariness; but if the Lord wasn't with them, there would be no victory. *When we accept God's plan, we invite God's presence; and that guarantees victory.* (See Ex. 33:12-17.)

Then Joshua instructed the soldiers. He probably didn't enlist the entire army for this important event; for that would have involved far too many people. According to the military census of Numbers 26, there were over 600,000 men able to bear arms. Think of how long it would take that many men to march around the city walls! And when the walls fell down, Joshua certainly didn't need hundreds of thousands of soldiers to rush in and overcome the people. The men would have been falling over one another!

Over 2 million people were in the nation of Israel, and marching all of them around the city of Jericho would have been time-consuming and dangerous. The people no doubt watched in silence from a distance and then participated in the great shout on the seventh day. It was a victory for Israel and Israel's God, and not just for the priests and soldiers.

It's important that leaders receive their orders from the Lord and that those who follow them obey their instructions. As with the crossing of the Jordan River, so also the conquest of Jericho was a miracle of faith. Joshua and his people listened to God's orders, believed them, and obeyed; and God did the rest. When God's people rebel against spiritual leadership, as Israel often did in the wilderness, it leads to discipline and defeat.

The activities of the week were a test of the Jewish people's faith and patience. No doubt some of them were anxious to get on with the invasion so they could claim their inheritance and settle down to enjoy the rest God had promised them (Josh. 1:13). To some of them, it may have seemed a futile waste of time to devote an entire week to the taking of one city. Impatience was one of Israel's besetting sins, and God was helping them learn patient obedience; for it's through "faith and patience" that God's people inherit what He has promised (Heb. 6:12). *God is never in a hurry.* He knows what He's doing, and His timing is never off.

If the week's schedule was a test of their patience, the divine command of silence was a test of their self-control. People who can't control their tongues can't control their bodies (James 3:1-2), and what good are soldiers whose bodies are not disciplined? "Be still, and know that I am God" (Ps. 46:10). In the Christian life there's "a time to keep silence, and a time to speak" (Eccl. 3:7); and wise is the child of God who knows the difference. Our Lord is the perfect example of this (Isa. 53:7; Matt. 26:62-63; 27:14; Luke 23:9).

How did the people in the city of Jericho respond to this daily procession around the city? It's likely that the march on the first day frightened them, for they probably expected the army to raise a siege against the city. But the Jews neither built ramps against the walls nor did they try to batter down the gates. When the marchers returned to camp after making only one circuit of the walls, the citizens must have felt greatly relieved. However, as the march was repeated day after day, tension must have grown in the city as the people wondered what would happen next. They knew that the God of Israel was a "great God of wonders," whose power had defeated Egypt and the kings east of the Jordan. What would Jehovah now do to Jericho?

When the procession went around the walls seven times on the seventh day, the tension within the city must have increased to frightening proportions. Then came the blast of the trumpets and the victory shout of the people, *and the walls fell down flat!* All that the soldiers had to do was rush into the city and take over.

The Holy Spirit directed the writer of

the Epistle to the Hebrews to use this event as one of the "by faith" examples in Hebrews 11. The fall of Jericho is an encouragement to God's people to trust the Lord's promises and obey His instructions, no matter how impossible the situation may appear to be. You and I may not capture a city as Joshua did, but in our everyday lives we face enemies and high walls that challenge us. *The only way to grow in faith is to accept new challenges and trust God to give you victory.* "Do not pray for easy lives," said Phillips Brooks; "pray to be better men and women. Do not pray for tasks equal to your powers; pray for power equal to your tasks."

3. After the victory: Remember to obey God's commands and give Him the glory (Josh. 6:17–19, 21–27)

Let me quote again Andrew Bonar's wise counsel: "Let us be as watchful after the victory as before the battle." Because one soldier didn't heed this warning, Israel's next challenge in Canaan turned out to be a humiliating defeat. Joshua gave the soldiers four instructions to obey after they had taken the city.

Devote the entire city to God (Josh. 6:17–19). This meant that everything was dedicated to the Lord—the people, the houses, the animals, and all the spoils of war—and He could do with it whatever He pleased. In this first victory in Canaan, Jericho was presented to God as "the firstfruits" of the victories to come. Ordinarily the soldiers shared the spoils of war (Deut. 20:14), but not at Jericho; for everything there belonged to the Lord and was put into His treasury (Deut. 13:16; 1 Kings 7:51). It was this command that Achan disobeyed, and his disobedience later brought Israel defeat and disgrace and brought Achan and his family death.

Rescue Rahab and her family (Josh. 6:22-23, 25-26). When the walls of the city fell down, it appears that the section of the wall that held Rahab's house (2:15) *didn't fall down!* It wasn't necessary for the spies to look for a window with a red cord hanging from it (vv. 18-19), because the only house that was preserved was the house in which Rahab and her family waited. When the spies made their covenant with Rahab, they didn't know exactly how God would give them the city.

God saved and protected Rahab because of her faith (Heb. 11:31); and because she led her family to trust in Jehovah, they were also saved. These Gentile believers were rescued from a fiery judgment because they trusted the God of Israel, for "salvation is of the Jews" (John 4:22). They were "afar off" as far as the covenants were concerned (Eph. 2:11-12), but their faith brought them into the nation of Israel; for Rahab married Salmon and became an ancestress of King David *and of the Messiah!* (Matt. 1:5)

Rahab and her relatives were put "outside the camp" initially because they were unclean Gentiles, and "outside the camp" was the place designated for the unclean (Num. 5:1-4; 12:14; Deut. 23:9-14). The men in the family would have to be circumcised in order to become "sons of the covenant," and all of the family would have to submit to the Law of Moses. What grace that God spared Rahab and her loved ones, and what *abundant* grace that He chose her, an outcast Gentile, to be an ancestress of the Savior!

Like Jericho of old, our present world is under the judgment of God (John 3:18-21; Rom. 3:10-19); and His judgment will eventually fall. No matter what "walls" and "gates" this present evil world will try to hide behind, God's wrath will eventually meet them. God has given this lost world plenty of evidence so that sinners can believe and be saved (Josh. 2:8–13; Rom. 1:18ff). The tragedy is, lost sinners willingly reject the evidence and continue in their sins John 12:35-41).

Destroy the people (Josh. 6:21). It disturbs some people that God commanded every living thing in Jericho to be killed. Isn't our God a God of mercy? After all, it's one thing for the Jews to kill the enemy soldiers; but why kill women, children, and even animals?

To begin with, this commandment was not a new one. The Lord had given it to Moses years before. In the "divine law of war" found in Deuteronomy 20, the Lord made a distinction between attacking cities that were far off (vv. 10-15) and cities in the land of Canaan where Israel would dwell (vv. 16–18). Before besieging a city afar off, the Jews were to give that city an offer of peace; and if the city surrendered, the Jews would spare the people and make them subjects. But the people in the cities *in the land of Canaan* were to be destroyed completely, and their cities burned.

Why? For one thing, the civilization in Canaan was unspeakably wicked; and God didn't want His holy people contaminated by their neighbors (7:1-11). We must never forget that God put Israel in the world to be the channel for His blessing (Gen. 12:1-3), which involves, among other things, the writing of the Scriptures and the coming of the Savior. Read the Old Testament record, and you will see Satan doing everything he could to pollute the Jewish nation and thus prevent the birth of the Messiah. When the Jewish men married pagan women and began to worship pagan gods, it was a threat to the purposes God had for His chosen people (Neh. 13:23-31). God wanted a "holy seed" (Mal. 2:14-15) so that His holy Son could come to be the Savior of the world.

"God is perpetually at war with sin," said G. Campbell Morgan. "That is the whole explanation of the extermination of the Canaanites."[2] Because the Jews didn't fully obey this commandment in later years, it led to national defilement and divine chastening (Ps. 106:34-48). The Book of Judges would not be in the Bible if the nation of Israel had remained true to the Lord (Judg. 2:11-23).

There is a second consideration: The people in the land had been given plenty of opportunity to repent and turn to the Lord, just as Rahab and her family had done. God patiently endured the evil of the Canaanites from the time of Abraham (Gen. 15:16) to the time of Moses, a period of over 400 years. (See 2 Peter 3:9.) From the Exodus to the crossing of the Jordan was another forty years in Israel's history, *and the Canaanites knew what was going on!* (See Josh. 2:8-13.) Every wonder that God performed and every victory that God gave His people was a witness to the people of the land, but they preferred to go on in their sins and reject the mercy of God. Never think of the Canaanites as helpless ignorant people who knew nothing about the true God. They were willfully sinning against a flood of light.

We should also keep in mind that these historical events were written "for our learning" (Rom. 15:4) as we seek to live for Christ today. In the destruction of Jericho and its population God is telling us that *He will tolerate no compromise with sin in the lives of His people.* To quote Campbell Morgan again: "Thank God that He will not make peace with sin in my heart! I bless His name for the thunder of His authority, and for the profound conviction that He is fierce and furious in His anger against sin, wherever it manifests itself."[3]

When I was a child in Sunday School, the superintendent often chose the song

"Whiter Than Snow" for us to sing in general assembly. While we sang "Break down every idol/Cast out every foe," I confess that I didn't understand at the time what I was singing; but now I understand. *The Lord will not share my life if there are rival gods in my heart. He will not permit me to compromise with the enemy.* When you grasp this truth, you also better understand His admonition in 2 Corinthians 6:14-7:1.

Burn the city (Josh. 6:24). "Thy God is a consuming fire" was spoken by Moses in Deuteronomy 4:24 long before it was quoted by the Holy Spirit in Hebrews 12:29. Moses was warning the Jewish people against idolatry and the danger of following the religious practices of the people in Canaan. Moses added a phrase that isn't quoted in Hebrews but is still important for us to know: "even a jealous God." God is jealous over His people and will not permit them to divide their love and service between Him and the false gods of the world (Ex. 20:5; 34:14). We cannot serve two masters.

Jericho was a wicked city, *and sin is only fuel for the holy wrath of God.* Jesus compared hell to a furnace of fire (Matt. 13:42), fire that is eternal (25:41, 46); and John compared it to a lake of fire (Rev. 19:20; 20:10, 14). John the Baptist described God's judgment as "unquenchable fire" (Matt. 3:12). The burning of Jericho, like the destruction of Sodom and Gomorrah (Jude 7), is a picture of the judgment of God that will fall on all who reject the truth.

Even after he had burned the city, Joshua put a curse on Jericho. This would warn any of the Jews or Rahab's descendants who might be tempted to rebuild what God had destroyed. The curse was later fulfilled in the days of evil King Ahab (1 Kings 16:34).

As He promised, God was with Joshua (Josh. 1:5, 9); and God magnified Joshua's name in the land (v. 27; 3:7; 4:14). God's servants must never magnify themselves; and if the Lord magnifies them, they must be careful to give Him the glory. It's when we are strong that we get overconfident and forget to trust the Lord (2 Chron. 26:15).

CHAPTER SEVEN
DEFEAT IN THE LAND OF VICTORY
Joshua 7

Moses described the Promised Land as "a land of hills and valleys" (Deut. 11:11). That statement, I believe, is much more than a description of the contrast between the hilly landscape of Canaan and the flat monotonous topography of Egypt. It's also a description of the *geography* of the life of faith that is pictured by Israel's experiences in Canaan. As by faith we claim our inheritance in Christ, we experience peaks of victory and valleys of discouragement. Discouragement isn't inevitable in the Christian life, but we must remember that we can't have mountains without valleys.

The ominous word *but* that introduces Joshua 7 is a signal that things are going to change; for Joshua is about to descend from the mountaintop of victory at Jericho to the valley of defeat at Ai. Joshua was a gifted and experienced leader, but he was still human and therefore liable to error. In this experience, he teaches us what causes defeat and how we must handle the discouragements of life.

1. A disobedient soldier (Josh. 7:1, 20-21)

The sinner (Josh. 7:1). His name was Achan, or Achar, which means "trouble"; and he was from the tribe of Judah (v. 16). (See 1 Chron. 2:7; note in v. 26 that "Achor" also means "trouble.") He is known in Bible history as *the man who troubled Israel* (Josh. 7:25). Because of Achan's disobedience, Israel was defeated at Ai, and the enemy killed thirty-six Jewish soldiers. It was Israel's first and only military defeat in Canaan, a defeat that is forever associated with Achan's name.

Never underestimate the amount of damage one person can do outside the will of God. Abraham's disobedience in Egypt almost cost him his wife (Gen. 12:10-20); David's disobedience in taking an unauthorized census led to the death of 70,000 people (2 Sam. 24); and Jonah's refusal to obey God almost sank a ship (Jonah 1). The church today must look diligently "lest any root of bitterness springing up cause trouble" (Heb. 12:15, NKJV). That's why Paul admonished the Corinthian believers to discipline the disobedient man in their fellowship, because his sin was defiling the whole church (1 Cor. 5).

God made it clear that it was *Israel* that had sinned and not just Achan alone (Josh. 7:1, 11). Why would God blame the whole nation for the disobedience of only one soldier? Because Israel was *one people in the Lord* and not just an assorted collection of tribes, clans, families, and individuals. God dwelt in the midst of their camp, and this made the Jews the Lord's special people (Ex. 19:5-6). Jehovah God walked about in their camp, and therefore the camp was to be kept holy (Deut. 23:14). Anyone who disobeyed God defiled the camp, and this defilement affected their relationship to the Lord and to one another.

God's people today are one body in Christ. Consequently, we belong to each other, we need each other, and we affect each other (1 Cor. 12:12ff). Any weakness or infection in one part of the human body contributes to weakness and infection in the other parts. So it also is with the body of Christ. "If one part suffers, every part suffers with it; if one part is honored, every part rejoices with it" (1 Cor. 12:26, NIV). "One sinner destroys much good" (Eccl. 9:18, NKJV).

The sin (Josh. 7:20-21). Achan heard his commander give the order that all the spoils in Jericho were to be devoted to the Lord and were to go into His treasury (6:17-21, 24). Since Jericho was Israel's first victory in Canaan, the firstfruits of the spoils belonged to the Lord (Prov. 3:9). But Achan disobeyed and took the hazardous steps that lead to sin and death (James 1:13-15): "I saw . . . I coveted . . . [I] took" (Josh. 7:21). Eve did the same thing when she listened to *the devil* (Gen. 3:5), and so did David when he yielded to *the flesh* (2 Sam. 11:1-4). Since Achan also coveted the things of *the world,* he brought defeat to Israel and death to himself and his family.

Achan's first mistake was to look at these spoils a *second time.* He probably couldn't help seeing them the first time, but he should never have looked again and considered taking them. A man's first glance at a woman may say to him, "She's attractive!" But it's that second glance that gets the imagination working and leads to sin (Matt. 6:27-30). If we keep God's Word before our eyes, we won't start looking in the wrong direction and doing the wrong things (Prov. 4:20–25).

His second mistake was to *reclassify* those treasures and call them "the spoils" (Josh. 7:21). They were not "the spoils"; they were a part of the Lord's treasury and wholly dedicated to Him. They didn't belong to Achan, or even to Israel; they belonged to God. When God identifies something in a special way, we have no right to change it. In our world today, including the religious world, people are rewriting God's dictionary! "Woe unto them that call evil good, and good evil; that put darkness for light, and light for darkness; that put bitter for sweet, and sweet for bitter!" (Isa. 5:20, KJV)

If God says something is wrong, then it's wrong; and that's the end of the debate.

Achan's third mistake was to *covet.* "But each one is tempted when he is drawn away by his own desires and enticed" (James 1:14, NKJV). Instead of singing praises in his heart for the great victory God had given, Achan was imagining in his heart what it would be like to own all that treasure. The imagination is the "womb" in which desire is conceived and from which sin and death are eventually born.

His fourth mistake was to think that he could get away with his sin by hiding the loot. Adam and Eve tried to cover their sin and run away and hide, but the Lord discovered them (Gen. 3:7ff). "Be sure your sin will find you out" was originally said to the people of God, not to the lost (Num. 32:23); and so was "The Lord shall judge His people" (Deut. 32:36; Heb. 10:30). How foolish of Achan to think that God couldn't see what he was doing, when "all things are naked and open to the eyes of Him to whom we must give account" (Heb. 4:13, NKJV).

Achan's sin becomes even more odious when you stop to realize all that God had done for him. God had cared for him and his family in the wilderness. He had brought them safely across the Jordan and given the army victory at Jericho. The Lord had accepted Achan as a son of the covenant at Gilgal. Yet in spite of all these wonderful experiences, Achan disobeyed God just to possess some wealth that he couldn't even enjoy. Had he waited just a day or two, he could have gathered all the spoils he wanted from the victory at Ai! "But seek first the kingdom of God and His righteousness, and all these things shall be added to you" (Matt. 6:33, NKJV).

2. A defeated army (Josh. 7:2-5)

Like every good commander, Joshua surveyed the situation before he planned his strategy (Num. 21:32; Prov. 20:18; 24:6). His mistake wasn't in sending out the spies but in assuming that the Lord was pleased with His people and would give them victory over Ai. He and his officers were walking by sight and not by faith. Spiritual leaders must constantly seek the Lord's face and determine what His will is for each new challenge. Had Joshua called a prayer meeting, the Lord would have informed him that there was sin in the camp; and Joshua could have dealt with it. This would have saved the lives of thirty-six soldiers and spared Israel a humiliating defeat.

It's impossible for us to enter into Joshua's mind and fully understand his thinking. No doubt the impressive victory at Jericho had given Joshua and his army a great deal of self-confidence; and self-confidence can lead to presumption. Since Ai was a smaller city than Jericho, victory seemed inevitable from the human point of view. But instead of seeking the mind of the Lord, Joshua accepted the counsel of his spies; and this led to defeat. He would later repeat this mistake in his dealings with the Gibeonites (Josh. 9).

The spies said nothing about the Lord; their whole report focused on the army and their confidence that Israel would have victory. You don't hear these men saying, "If the Lord will" (James 4:13-17). They were sure that the whole army wasn't needed for the assault, but that wasn't God's strategy when He gave the orders for the second attack on Ai (Josh. 8:1). Since God's thoughts are not our thoughts (Isa. 55:8-9), we'd better take time to seek His direction. "Pride goes before destruction, and a haughty spirit before a fall" (Prov. 16:18, NKJV). What Israel needed was God-confidence, not self-confidence.

Ai was in the hill country, about fifteen miles from Jericho; and one went *up* to Ai because it was situated 1,700 feet above sea level. The Jewish army marched confidently up the hill but soon came down again, fleeing for their lives and leaving thirty-six dead comrades behind them.

Moses had warned Israel that they couldn't defeat their enemies unless the nation was obedient to the Lord. If they were following the Lord by faith, 1 Jewish soldier would chase 1,000, and 2 would put 10,000 to flight! (Deut. 32:30) Three Jewish soldiers could have defeated the whole city, if the nation had been pleasing to the Lord (Josh. 8:25). "But your iniquities have separated between you and your God, and your sins have hid His face from you, that He will not hear" (Isa. 59:2).

3. A discouraged leader (Josh. 7:6-15)

The leader who had been magnified (6:27) was now mortified. If some of your best plans have ever been dashed to pieces, then you can identify with Joshua and his officers.

Remorse (Josh. 7:6). The hearts of the Canaanites had melted when they had heard about the conquests of Israel (2:11). But now the tables were turned, and it was the Israelites whose hearts were melted as water! The general who had not known defeat spent the rest of the day prostrate before the Ark at Gilgal and his leaders with him. They tore their garments, put dust on their heads, lay on the ground, and cried, "Alas! Alas!" This is the way Jewish people behaved whenever they experienced great distress, such as a military defeat (1 Sam. 4:12) or personal violence and shame (2 Sam. 13:19). It was the prescribed course of action whenever the Jews turned to God in times of great danger or national sin (Neh. 9:1; Es. 4:1). Had Joshua humbled himself *before* the battle, the situation would have been different after the battle.

The Ark of the Covenant was a reminder of the presence of God with His people. The Ark had gone before Israel when they had crossed the river (Josh. 3:11ff), and the Ark had been with them when they had marched around Jericho (6:6-8). God hadn't told them to carry the Ark to Ai, but God's presence would have gone with them if there had not been sin in the camp. Without God's presence, the Ark was simply a piece of wooden furniture; and there was no guarantee of victory just because of the presence of the Ark (1 Sam. 4).

Reproach (Josh. 7:7-9). In his prayer Joshua sounded like the unbelieving Jews whenever they found themselves in a tough situation that demanded faith: "Oh, that we had stayed where we were!" They said this at the Red Sea (Ex. 14:11), when they were hungry and thirsty in the wilderness (16:3; 17:3), and when they were disciplined at Kadesh Barnea (Num. 14:1-3). The Jews had frequently wanted to go back to Egypt, but Joshua would have been willing to cross the Jordan and settle down on the other side.

"But read his prayer, and you will catch a strange note in it," wrote George H. Morrison; *"Joshua reproaches God."*[1] He seems to be blaming God for Israel's presence in Canaan and for the humiliating defeat they had just experienced.

When you walk by faith, you will claim all that God has for you; *but unbelief is always content to settle for something less than God's best.* This is why the Epistle to the Hebrews is in the Bible, to urge God's people to "go on" and enter into the fullness of their inheritance in Christ (Heb. 6:1). God sometimes permits us to experience humiliating defeats in order to test our faith and reveal to us what's really going on in our hearts. What life does *to* us depends on what life finds *in* us, and we don't always know the condition of our own hearts (Jer. 17:9).

Repentance (Josh. 7:8-9). Now Joshua gets to the heart of the matter: Israel's defeat had robbed God of glory, and for this they had to repent. If the people of the land lost their fear of Israel's God (2:8-11), this would make it difficult for Joshua to conquer the land. But the important thing was not Joshua's fame or Israel's conquests, but the glory of the God of Israel. Joshua's concern was not for his own reputation but for the "great name" of Jehovah. Joshua had learned this lesson from Moses (Ex. 32:11-13; Num. 14:13-16), and it's a lesson the church needs to learn today.

Rebuke (Josh. 7:10-15). The Lord allowed Joshua and his leaders to stay on their faces until the time for the evening sacrifice. He gave them time to come to the end of themselves so that they would obey His directions, and then He spoke to Joshua. There is a time to pray and a time to act, and the time had now come to act.

Since Israel had sinned, Israel had to deal with its sin. God told Joshua that the nation had stolen that which belonged to Him and had hidden it among their own possessions as if it were theirs. Note the repetition of the word "accursed," which is used six times in this paragraph. The nation had been sanctified in preparation for crossing the Jordan (3:5), but now they had to be sanctified to discover an enemy in the camp. They had to present themselves to God so He could expose the guilty man.

What the Lord said to Joshua helps us see Achan's sin (and Israel's sin) from the divine point of view. What they did was *sin* (7:11), a word that means "to miss the mark." God wants His people to be holy and obedient, but they missed the mark and fell short of God's standard. It was also *transgression* (v. 11), which means "to cross over." God had drawn a line and told them not to cross it, but they had violated His covenant and crossed the line.

This sin involved *stealing from God* and then *lying about it* (v. 11). Achan had taken the forbidden wealth but pretended that he had obeyed the Lord. Achan had done a foolish thing (v. 15) in thinking he could rob God and get away with it. Israel couldn't face any of her enemies until their sin had been put away. The tribes could never claim their inheritance as long as one man clung to his forbidden treasures. Everything God had done for His people up to this point was to no avail as long as they couldn't go forward in victory. What a lesson for the church today!

That evening Joshua sent word throughout the camp that the people were to sanctify themselves and prepare for an assembly to be held the next morning. You wonder whether Achan and his family got any sleep that night, or did they think they were secure?

4. A discovered sinner (Josh. 7:16-26)

The investigation (Josh. 7:16-18). "The heart is deceitful above all things, and desperately wicked: who can know it?" asked the prophet (Jer. 17:9); and he answered the question in the next verse: "I the Lord search the heart, I try the reins, even to give every man according to his ways, and according to the fruit of his doings."

Nobody can hide from God. "Can any hide himself in secret places that I shall not see him?" (23:24) Whether sinners run to the top of the mountains or dive to the bottom of the seas, God will find them and judge them (Amos 9:3). "For God shall bring every work into judgment, with every secret thing, whether it be good, or whether it be evil" (Eccl. 12:14).

God's approach was methodical. First He singled out the tribe of Judah, then the family of the Zerahites, then the household of Zabdi, and finally the culprit Achan. Perhaps the high priest used the ephod to determine God's direction (1 Sam. 23:6, 9; 30:7-8), or Joshua and the high priest may have cast lots. It must have been frightening for Achan and his immediate family to watch the accusing finger of God point closer and closer. "My eyes are on all their ways; they are not hidden from Me, nor is their sin concealed from My eyes" (Jer. 16:17, NIV). Read Psalm 10, especially verses 6, 11, 13 to see what may have been going on in Achan's mind and heart during this tense time of scrutiny.

When Joshua singled out Achan as the offender, the people watching must have asked themselves, "What evil thing did he do that the Lord was so displeased with us?" Perhaps the relatives of the thirty-six slain soldiers were angry as they looked at the man whose disobedience caused the death of their loved ones.

The confession (Josh. 7:19-23). The phrase "Give glory to God" was a form of official oath in Israel (John 9:24, NIV). Achan had not only sinned against his own people, but also he had grievously sinned against the Lord; and he had to confess his sin to Him. When he said "I have sinned," he joined the ranks of seven other men in Scripture who made the same confession, some more than once, and some without sincerity: Pharaoh (Ex. 9:27; 10:16), Balaam (Num. 22:34), King Saul (1 Sam. 15:24, 30; 26:21), David (2 Sam. 12:13; 24:10, 17; Ps. 51:4), Shimei (2 Sam. 19:20), Judas (Matt. 27:4), and the prodigal son (Luke 15:18, 21).

Before he could execute the Lord's judgment, Joshua had to present the evidence that substantiated Achan's confession. The messengers dug under Achan's tent and found "the accursed thing" that had brought defeat to Israel. The stolen goods were spread out before the Lord so He could see that all Israel was renouncing their hold on this evil treasure. The confession and the evidence were enough to convict the accused man.

The judgment (Josh. 7:24-26). Since a law in Israel prohibited innocent family members from being punished for the sins of their relatives (Deut. 24:16), Achan's family must have been guilty of assisting him in his sin. His household was judged the same way Israel would deal with a Jewish city that had turned to idols (Josh. 13:12-18). Achan and his family had turned from the true and living God and had given their hearts to that which God had said was accursed—silver, gold, and an expensive garment. It wasn't worth it!

At the beginning of a new period in Bible history, God sometimes revealed His wrath against sin in some dramatic way. After the tabernacle had been set up, Nadab and Abihu invaded its holy precincts contrary to God's law; and God killed them. This was a warning to the priests not to treat God's sanctuary carelessly (Lev. 10). When David sought to restore the Ark to its place of honor, and Uzzah touched the Ark to steady it, God killed Uzzah (2 Sam. 6:1-11); another warning from God not to treat sacred things carelessly. At the beginning of the Church Age, when Ananias and Sapphira lied to God and God's people, the Lord killed them (Acts 5:1–11).

The death of Achan and his family was certainly a dramatic warning to the nation not to take the Word of God lightly. The people and the animals were stoned, and their bodies burned along with all that the family possessed. The troubler of Israel was completely removed from the scene, the people were sanctified, and now God could march with His people and give them victory. The name *Achor* means "trouble." The Valley of Achor is mentioned in Isaiah 65:10 and Hosea 2:15 as a place where the Jews will one day have a new beginning and no longer be associated with shame and defeat. The Valley of Achor will become for them "a door of hope" when they return to their land and share in the blessings of the messianic kingdom. How wonderful the Lord is to take Achor, a place of sorrow and defeat, and make it into a place of hope and joy.

The heap of stones in the valley would be a reminder that God expects His people to obey His Word, and if they don't, He must judge them. The heap of stones at Gilgal (Josh. 4:1–8) reminded them that God keeps His Word and leads His obedient people to the place of blessing. Both memorials are needed in the walk of faith. God is love (1 John 4:8, 16) and longs to bless His people; but God is also light (1 John 1:5) and must judge His people's sins.

It had been a trying two days for Joshua and his leaders, but the situation was about to change. God would take charge of the army and lead His people to victory. When you surrender to the Lord, no defeat is permanent and no mistake is beyond remedy. Even the "Valley of Trouble" can become a "door of hope."

CHAPTER EIGHT
TURNING DEFEAT INTO VICTORY
Joshua 8

The following quotation runs contrary to what most people today think about life, including people in the church. It was said in a sermon preached on August 12, 1849, by the famous British preacher F.W. Robertson.

> Life, like war, is a series of mistakes, and he is not the best Christian nor the best general who makes the fewest false steps. Poor mediocrity may secure that; but he is the best who wins the most splendid victories by the retrieval of mistakes. Forget mistakes; organize victories out of mistakes.[1]

Henry Ford would have agreed with Robertson, because Ford defined a mistake as "an opportunity to begin again, more intelligently." Joshua would also have agreed, because he is about to "begin again, more intelligently" and organize a victory out of his mistakes.

1. A new beginning (Josh. 8:1-2)

Once the nation of Israel had judged the sin that had defiled their camp, God was free to speak to them in mercy and direct them in their conquest of the land. "The steps of a good man are ordered by the

Lord, and He delights in his way. Though he fall, he shall not be utterly cast down; for the Lord upholds him with His hand" (Ps. 37:23-24, NKJV). No matter what mistakes we may make, the worst mistake of all is not to try again; for "the victorious Christian life is a series of new beginnings" (Alexander Whyte).

You start with the Word of God. We today don't hear God's audible voice as people often did in Bible times, but we have the Word of God before us and the Spirit of God within us; and God will direct us if we wait patiently before Him.

The word of encouragement (Josh. 8:1a). Discouragement over the past and fear of the future are the two reactions that often accompany failure. We look back and remember the mistakes that we made, and then we look ahead and wonder whether there's any future for people who fail so foolishly.

The answer to our discouragement and fear is in *hearing and believing* God's Word: "Fear not, neither be thou dismayed" (v. 1). I recommend that you take your Bible concordance and study the "fear not" statements of the Bible. Note that God spoke these words to different kinds of people in various circumstances, and His Word always met the need. Be sure to check the "fear not" statements in Genesis, Isaiah 41–44, and the first eight chapters of Luke. *God never discourages His people from making progress.* As long as we obey His commandments, we have the privilege of claiming His promises. God delights "to show Himself strong in the behalf of them whose heart is perfect [wholly devoted] toward Him" (2 Chron. 16:9).

The word of instruction (Josh. 8:1b-2). God always has a plan for His people to follow, and the only way for us to have victory is to obey God's instructions. In his first attack on Ai Joshua followed the advice of his spies and used only part of the army; but God told him to take "all the people of war"(v. 1). The Lord also told Joshua to use an ambush and take advantage of Ai's self-confidence stemming from Israel's first defeat (7:1-5). Finally, God gave the soldiers the right to claim the spoils, but they were to burn the city. Had Achan waited only a few days, he could have picked up all the wealth that he wanted. *God always gives His best to those who leave the choice with Him.* When we run ahead of the Lord, we usually rob ourselves and hurt others.

The word of promise (Josh. 8:1c). "I have given" was God's promise (see 6:2) and Joshua's guarantee of victory as long as he obeyed the instructions of the Lord. "God never made a promise that was too good to be true," said evangelist D.L. Moody; but every promise must be claimed by faith. Unless the promises of God are "mixed with faith" (Heb. 4:2), they accomplish nothing. Because Israel acted presumptuously in their first attack against Ai, they failed miserably. The promises of God make the difference between faith and presumption.

You can never exaggerate the importance of the Christian soldier spending time daily in the Word of God. Unless daily we take the sword of the Spirit by faith (Eph. 6:17), we go into the battle unarmed and therefore unprepared. Spiritually minded believers are victorious because they allow the Word of God to "saturate" their minds and hearts. The Spirit using the Word controls their desires and decisions and this is the secret of victory.

No matter how badly we have failed, we can always get up and begin again; for our God is the God of new beginnings.

2. A new strategy (Josh. 8:3-13)

God is not only the God of new beginnings, but He's also the God of *infinite variety.* Remember the words of King Arthur that I quoted in chapter 2? "And God fulfills Himself in many ways/Lest one good custom should corrupt the world." God changes His leaders lest we start trusting flesh and blood instead of trusting the Lord, and He changes His methods lest we start depending on our personal experience instead of on His divine promises.

The strategy God gave Joshua for taking Ai was almost opposite the strategy He used at Jericho. The Jericho operation involved a week of marches that were carried on openly in the daylight. The attack on Ai involved a covert night operation that prepared the way for the daylight assault. The whole army was united at Jericho, but Joshua divided the army for the attack on Ai. God performed a mighty miracle at Jericho when He caused the walls to fall down flat, but there was no such miracle at Ai. Joshua and his men simply obeyed God's instructions by setting an ambush and luring the people of Ai out of their city, and the Lord gave them the victory.

It's important that we seek God's will *for each undertaking* so that we don't depend on past victories as we plan for the future. The World War II song "We did it before/And we can do it again!" doesn't always apply to the work of the Lord. How easy is it for Christian ministries to dig their way into administrative ruts that eventually become graves, simply because the leadership fails to discern whether God wants to do something new for them. The American business leader Bruce Barton (1886-1967) said, "When you're through changing, you're through."

The strategy for Ai was based on Israel's previous defeat; for God was organizing victory out of Joshua's mistakes. The people of Ai were overconfident because they had defeated Israel at the first attack, and this overconfidence would be their undoing. "We did it before, and we can do it again!"

At night Joshua and his army marched fifteen miles from Gilgal to Ai; and, using 30,000 soldiers, Joshua set up an ambush behind the city from the west (vv. 3-9). He put another 5,000 men between Ai and Bethel, which was about two miles away (v. 12). This detachment would make sure that the army from Bethel wouldn't make a surprise attack from the northwest and open another "front." The rocky terrain in the highlands around Ai made it easy for Joshua to conceal his soldiers, and the whole operation was done at night.

The plan was simple but effective. Leading the rest of the Jewish army, Joshua would make a frontal attack on Ai from the north. His men would flee as they had done the first time and by fleeing draw the self-confident people of Ai away from the protection of their city. At Joshua's signal the soldiers lying in ambush would enter the city and set it on fire. The people of Ai would be caught between two armies, and the third army would deal with any assistance that might come from Bethel.

Being a good general, Joshua lodged with his army (v. 9). He certainly encouraged them to trust the Lord and believe His promise for victory. The Captain of the host of the Lord (5:14) would go before them because they obeyed His Word and trusted His promises.

The work of the Lord requires strategy, and Christian leaders must seek the mind of the Lord in their planning. Like Joshua, we must get the facts and weigh them carefully as we seek the will of God. Too often, the work of the Lord only drifts along on the tide of time, without any rudder or compass to give direction; and the results are disappointing. Our English word *strategy* comes from two Greek words that together mean "to lead an army." Leadership demands planning, and planning is an important part of strategy.

3. A new victory (Josh. 8:14-29)

Ai emptied (Josh. 8:14-17). When morning dawned, the king of Ai saw the army of Israel positioned before the city, ready to attack. Confident of victory, he led his men out of the city and against the Jews. "They are the most in danger," said Matthew Henry, "who are least aware of it." Joshua and his men began to flee, and this gave the men of Ai even more assurance of victory.

According to verse 17, the men of Bethel were also involved in the attack; but no details are given. Whether they were already in Ai or arrived on the scene just in time, we aren't told; but their participation led to the defeat of their city (12:16) as well as Ai.

It was careless of the people of Ai to leave their city undefended, but such are the follies of self-confidence. When a small army sees a large army flee without even fighting, it gives them a feeling of superiority that can lead to defeat.

Ai captured (Josh. 8:18-20). Conscious that the battle was the Lord's (1 Sam. 17:47; 2 Chron. 20:15), Joshua waited for further instructions. God then told him to lift up his spear toward the city (Josh. 8:18). This was the signal for the other troops to enter the city and burn it, but the signal had to be given at just the right time. The men of Ai and Bethel were trapped, and it was a simple matter for the army of Israel to destroy them. Joshua held up his spear until the victory was won (v. 26), an action that reminds us of the battle Joshua fought against Amalek when Moses held up his hands to the Lord (Ex. 17:8-16).

Ai's army and people destroyed (Josh. 8:21-29). Seeing the smoke of the city, Joshua's men stopped fleeing, and they turned and attacked the army of Ai that was pursuing them. After the Jewish soldiers in Ai left the city, they joined in the battle. The enemy was then caught between two armies. "Israel cut them down, leaving them neither survivors nor fugitives" (v. 22, NIV).

Once the army was annihilated, the rest of the population of the city was destroyed, just as at Jericho (vv. 24-25; 6:21, 24). Keep in mind that this was not the "slaughter of innocent people" but the judgment of God on an evil society that had long resisted His grace and truth.

Ai's king slain (Josh. 8:23, 29). This was the final symbolic gesture of complete victory on the part of Israel. The king had no army, subjects, or city; for the Lord had destroyed them all. It was total victory on the part of Israel. Joshua killed the king with a sword and then ordered that the corpse be humiliated by hanging it on a tree until sundown (Deut. 21:22-23). The body was then buried under a heap of stones at the entrance of the gate of the ruin that had once been Ai. The previous heap of stones that Israel had raised was a memorial to Achan who had caused their defeat at Ai (Josh. 7:25-26). But this heap of stones at Ai was a memorial of Israel's victory over the enemy. By obeying the Word of the Lord, they had organized victory out of mistakes.

Ai's spoils claimed (Josh. 8:27). Since the firstfruits of the spoils of war in Canaan had already been given to God at Jericho, He permitted the army to claim the spoils at Ai. Furthermore, at Jericho, the victory was theirs because of a miracle of God;

while at Ai, because the men actually had to fight, they earned their reward. (For the laws governing the distribution of spoils, see Num. 31:19-54.) We aren't sure that these rules were strictly followed in every situation, but they give you an indication of how Israel handled the spoils of war.

When at the close of the day the men buried the king of Ai under a heap of stones, there must have been a new sense of faith and courage in Israel; for they had won another victory. The people saw that not one word of God's promise had failed. The disgrace and defeat caused by Achan had now been erased, and Israel was well on her way to conquering the Promised Land.

4. A new commitment (Josh. 8:30-35)

At some time following the victory at Ai, Joshua led the people thirty miles north to Shechem, which lies in the valley between Mt. Ebal and Mt. Gerizim. Here the nation obeyed what Moses had commanded them to do in his farewell speech (Deut. 27:1-8). Joshua interrupted the military activities to give Israel the opportunity to make a new commitment to the authority of Jehovah as expressed in His law.

Joshua built an altar (Josh. 8:30-31). Since Abraham had built an altar at Shechem (Gen. 12:6-7), and Jacob had lived there a short time (chap. 33-34), the area had strong historic ties to Israel. Joshua's altar was built on Mt. Ebal, "the mount of cursing," because only a sacrifice of blood can save sinners from the curse of the law (Gal. 3:10-14).

In building the altar, Joshua was careful to obey Exodus 20:25 and not apply any tool to the stones picked up in the field. No human work was to be associated with the sacrifice lest sinners think their own works can save them (Eph. 2:8–9). God asked for a simple stone altar, not one that was designed and decorated by human hands, "that no flesh should glory in His presence" (1 Cor. 1:29). It's not the beauty of man-made religion that gives the sinner forgiveness, but the blood on the altar (Lev. 17:11). King Ahab replaced God's altar with a pagan altar, but it didn't give him acceptance with God or make him a better man (2 Kings 16:9-16).

The priests offered burnt offerings to the Lord as a token of the nation's total commitment to Him (Lev. 1). The peace offerings, or "fellowship offerings," were an expression of gratitude to God for His goodness (3; 7:11-34). A portion of the meat was given to the priests and another portion to the offerer so that he could eat it joyfully with his family in the presence of the Lord (7:15-16, 30-34; Deut. 12:17-18). By these sacrifices, the nation of Israel was assuring God of their commitment to Him and their fellowship with Him.

Joshua wrote the Law on stones (Josh. 8:32-33). This act was in obedience to the command of Moses (Deut. 27:1-8). In the Near East of that day it was customary for kings to celebrate their greatness by writing records of their military exploits on huge stones covered with plaster. But the secret of Israel's victory was not their leader or their army; it was their obedience to God's Law (Josh. 1:7-8). In later years, whenever Israel turned away from God's Law, they got into trouble and had to be disciplined. "And what great nation is there that has such statutes and righteous judgments as are in all this Law which I set before you this day?" asked Moses (Deut. 4:8, NKJV).

Believers today have the Word of God written on their hearts by the Holy Spirit of God (Rom. 8:1-4; 2 Cor. 3). The Law written on stones was external, not internal, and could instruct the people but could never change them. Paul makes it clear in the Epistle to the Galatians that while the Law can convict sinners and bring them to Christ (Gal. 3:19-25), it can never convert sinners and make them like Christ. Only the Spirit of God can do that.

This is now the fourth public monument of stones that has been erected. The first was at Gilgal (Josh. 4:20), commemorating Israel's passage across the Jordan. The second was in the Valley of Achor, a monument to Achan's sin and God's judgment (7:26). The third was at the entrance to Ai, a reminder of God's faithfulness to help His people (8:29). These stones on Mt. Ebal reminded Israel that their success lay only in their obedience to God's Law (1:7-8).

Joshua read the Law (Josh. 8:34-35). The tribes were assigned their places in front of the two mounts, according to Moses' instructions in Deuteronomy 27:11-13. Reuben, Gad, Asher, Zebulun, Dan, and Naphtali were at Mt. Ebal, the mount of cursing; and Simeon, Levi, Judah, Issachar, Joseph (Ephraim and Manasseh), and Benjamin were at Mt. Gerizim, the mount of blessing. The tribes at Mt. Gerizim were founded by men who had either Leah or Rachel for their mother, while the tribes at Mt. Ebal were descended from either Zilpah or Bilhah, handmaids of Leah and Rachel. The only exceptions were Reuben and Zebulun, who belonged to Leah. Reuben had forfeited his status as the firstborn because he had sinned against his father (Gen. 35:22; 49:3-4).

In the valley between the two mountains stood the priests and Levites with the Ark, surrounded by the elders, officers, and judges of the nation. The people were all facing the Ark, which represented the presence of the Lord among His people. When Joshua and the Levites read the blessings of the Lord one by one (see Deut. 28:1-14), the tribes at Mt. Gerizim responded with a loud united "Amen!" which in the Hebrew means "So be it!" When they read the curses (see Deut. 27:14-26), the tribes at Mt. Ebal would respond with their "Amen" after each curse was read.

God had given the Law through Moses *at Mount Sinai* (Ex. 19-20), and the people had accepted it and promised to obey. Moses then repeated and explained the Law *on the Plains of Moab* at the border of Canaan. He applied that Law to their lives in the Promised Land and admonished them to obey it. "See, I am setting before you today a blessing and a curse—the blessing if you obey the commands of the Lord your God that I am giving you today; the curse if you disobey the commands of the Lord your God" (Deut. 11:26-28, NIV; note vv. 29-32).

Joshua now reaffirmed the Law *in the land of promise.* Since the area between Mt. Ebal and Mt. Gerizim was a natural amphitheater, everybody could hear the words of the Law clearly and respond with intelligence. By shouting "Amen" to the statements that were read, the people admitted that they understood the Law with its blessings and curses, and that they accepted the responsibility of obeying it. This included the women, children, and the "mixed multitude" (sojourners) who had joined Israel (Ex. 12:38; 22:21; 23:9; Deut. 24:17-22; 31:12). If they wanted to share in Israel's conquest, they had to submit to the Law of Israel's God.

God's people today stand in a valley between two mounts—Mt. Calvary, where Jesus died for our sins, and Mt. Olivet, where He will return in power and great glory (Zech. 14:4). The Old Testament prophets saw the Messiah's suffering and glory, but they did not see the "valley" between their era and this present age of the church (1 Peter 1:10-12). Believers today aren't living under the curse of the Law, because Jesus bore that curse "on a tree" (Gal. 3:10-14). In Christ believers are blessed with "every spiritual blessing" (Eph. 1:3, NKJV) because of the grace of God. For them life means the blessings of Gerizim and not the curses of Ebal.

However, because Christians "are not under the Law, but under grace" (Rom. 6:14; 7:1-6), it doesn't mean that we can live any way we please and ignore the Law of God or defy it. We aren't saved by keeping the Law, nor are we sanctified by trying to meet the demands of the Law; but "the righteousness of the Law" is "fulfilled in us" as we walk in the power of the Holy Spirit (Rom. 8:4). If we put ourselves under Law, we forfeit the enjoyment of the blessings of grace (Gal. 5). If we walk in the Spirit, we experience His life-changing power and live so as to please God.

Let's give thanks that Jesus bore the curse of the Law for us on the cross and that He bestows all the blessings of the heavenlies on us through the Spirit. By faith we can claim our inheritance in Christ and march forth in victory!

CHAPTER NINE
WE HAVE MET THE ENEMY AND HE IS OUR NEIGHBOR
Joshua 9:1–10:28

An anonymous wit reminds us that a dentist's mistake is pulled out, a lawyer's mistake is imprisoned, a teacher's mistake is failed, a printer's mistake is corrected, a pharmacist's mistake is buried, a postman's mistake is forwarded, and an electrician's mistake could be shocking. The novelist Joseph Conrad wrote, "It's only those who do nothing that make no mistakes."

In Joshua's case, however, doing nothing *was* his mistake; and this chapter explains what happened. It records the three stages in his second failure (after Ai) in the conquest of the Promised Land. It also tells us how Joshua turned his mistake into a victory.

1. Believing the enemy (Josh. 9:1-15)

While Israel was at Mt. Ebal and Mt. Gerizim, reaffirming their commitment to the Lord, the kings in Canaan were getting ready to attack. They had heard about the defeat of Jericho and Ai and were not about to give up without a fight. It was time for them to go on the offensive and attack these Jewish invaders. The city-states in Canaan were not always friendly with one another, but local rivals can often come together when they have a common enemy (Ps. 2:1-2; Luke 23:12).

After an experience of great blessing, God's people must be especially prepared to confront the enemy; for like Canaan, the Christian life is "a land of hills and valleys" (Deut. 11:11). But Israel's greatest danger wasn't the confederation of the armies of Canaan. It was a group of men from Gibeon who were about to enter the camp and deceive Joshua and the princes of Israel. Satan sometimes comes as a devouring lion (1 Peter 5:8) and sometimes as a deceiving serpent (2 Cor. 11:3), and we must be alert and protected by the spiritual armor God has provided for us (Eph. 6:10-18).

What the Gibeonites did (Josh. 9:3-5). Gibeon was located only twenty-five miles from the camp of Israel at Gilgal and was on Joshua's list to be destroyed. In Deuteronomy 20:10–20, God's law stated that Israel must destroy all the cities in Canaan. If after the conquest Israel was involved in other wars, they could offer peace to cities that were outside the land. (See also 7:1-11.) Somehow the Gibeonites knew about this law and decided to use it for their own protection. Since the enemy knows how to use the Word of God for their own purposes, God's people must keep alert (Matt. 4:5-7).

The Gibeonites assembled a group of men and equipped them to look like an official delegation from a foreign city. Their clothing, food, and equipment were all designed to give the impression that they had been on a long and difficult journey from a distant city. Satan is a counterfeiter and "masquerades as an angel of light" (2 Cor. 11:14, NIV). He has his "false apostles" and "deceitful workmen" (v. 13, NIV) at work in this world, blinding the lost and seeking to lead believers astray. It's much easier for us to identify the lion when he's roaring than to detect the serpent when he's slithering into our lives.

What the Gibeonites said (Josh. 9:6-13). Satan is a liar and the father of lies (John 8:44), and human nature is such that many people find it easier to tell lies than the truth. With tongue in cheek, the American political leader Adlai Stevenson said, "A lie is an abomination unto the Lord—and a very present help in trouble." The Gibeonites told several lies in their attempt to get out of trouble.

First, they said they were "from a very far country" (Josh. 9:6, 9) when they actually lived twenty-five miles away. Then they lied about their clothing and food. "This bread of ours was warm when we packed it at home on the day we left to come to you. But now see how dry and moldy it is" (v. 12, NIV). They also lied about themselves and gave the impression that they were important envoys on an official peace mission from the elders of their city. They also called themselves "your servants" (vv. 8, 9, 11), when in reality they were the enemies of Israel.

These four lies were bad enough; but when the visitors said they had come "because of the name of the Lord" (v. 9), it was blasphemous. Like the citizens of Jericho (2:10), the people in Gibeon had heard about Israel's march of conquest (9:9-10); but unlike Rahab and her family, they didn't put their faith in the Lord. These men were wise enough not to mention Israel's victories at Jericho and Ai; for that news couldn't have reached their "far country" that quickly. Satan's ambassadors can lie more convincingly than some Christians can tell the truth!

Satan knows how to use "religious lies" to give the impression that people are seeking to know the Lord. In my pastoral ministry I've met people who have introduced themselves *as seekers*; but the longer they talked, the more convinced I was that they were *sneakers*, trying to get something out of me and the church. They would make their "profession of faith" and then start telling me their sad tale of woe, hoping to break my heart and then pick my pocket. Of all liars, "religious liars" are the worst. If you need to be convinced of this, read 2 Peter 2 and the Epistle of Jude.

Why they succeeded (Josh. 9:14-15). The reason is simple: Joshua and the princes of Israel were impetuous and didn't take time to consult the Lord. They walked by sight and not by faith. After listening to the strangers' speech and examining the evidence, Joshua and his leaders concluded that the men were telling the truth. The leaders of Israel took the "scientific approach" instead of the "spiritual approach." They depended on their own senses, examined the "facts," discussed the matter, and agreed in their conclusion. It was all very logical and convincing, but it was all wrong. They had made the same mistake at Ai (chap. 7) and hadn't yet learned to wait on the Lord and seek His direction.

The will of God comes from the heart of God (Ps. 33:11), and He delights to make it known to His children *when He knows they are humble and willing to obey.* We don't seek God's will like customers who look at options but like servants who listen for orders. "If any of you really determines to do God's will, then you will certainly know" (John 7:17, TLB) is a basic principle for victorious Christian living. God sees our hearts and knows whether we are really serious about obeying Him. Certainly we ought to use the mind God has given us, but we must heed the warning of Proverbs 3:5–6 and not *lean on* our own understanding.

If this group of men had been an authentic official delegation, it would have comprised a much larger company bearing adequate supplies, including sufficient provisions for the trip home. Real ambassadors would have thrown away their "dry and moldy" bread because their servants would have baked fresh bread for them. As officials, they would have packed the proper attire so that they might make the best impression possible as they negotiated with the enemy. Had Joshua and his leaders paused to think and pray about what they saw, they would have concluded that the whole thing was a trick. "If any of you lacks wisdom, let him ask of God, who gives to all liberally and without reproach, and it will be given to him" (James 1:5, NKJV).

True faith involves exercising patience (Heb. 6:12). "Whoever believes will not act hastily" (Isa. 28:16, NKJV). Moses had told the Jews, "Be careful not to make a treaty with those who live in the land where you are going, or they will be a snare among you" (Ex. 34:12, NIV). But in their haste Joshua and the Jewish leaders broke God's Law and made a covenant with the enemy. Since their oath was sworn in the name of the Lord (Josh. 9:18), it could not be broken. Joshua and the princes of Israel had sworn to their own hurt (Ps. 15:4; Eccl. 5:1-7), and there was no way to revoke their oath or be released from their promise.

Like Joshua and the nation of Israel, God's people today are living in enemy territory and must constantly exercise caution. When you believe the enemy instead of seeking the mind of the Lord, you can expect to get into trouble.

2. Enlisting the enemy (Josh. 9:16-27)

How did the leaders of Israel discover that they had made a big mistake? Knowing that they were now out of danger, perhaps the "ambassadors" openly admitted what they had done. Or maybe the Gibeonites were overheard rejoicing in their success. Did some of Joshua's spies return to camp after reconnaissance and recognize the enemy? Perhaps the Gibeonites overheard the plans for Israel's next attack and had to inform the leaders that a solemn oath now protected those cities. However it happened, Joshua discovered that he and the princes had blundered; and no doubt they were humbled and embarrassed because of it.

We must give the leaders credit for being men of their word. To violate their oath would have been to take the holy name of Jehovah in vain, and this would have brought about divine judgment. Years later King Saul violated this oath; and God judged the nation severely (2

Sam. 21). Military leaders of lesser character than Joshua might have argued that "all's fair in love and war" and forced the Gibeonites to divulge information that would help him conquer their city. Instead, when the Jewish army arrived at Gibeon and the neighboring cities, they didn't attack them.

Why did the Jewish people grumble at what their leaders had done? Because this covenant with Gibeon would cost the soldiers dearly in plunder they would never get from the protected cities. Furthermore, the Gibeonites and their neighbors might influence the Jews with their pagan practices and lead them away from the Lord. Moses had given Israel stern warnings against compromising with the people of the land (Deut. 7), and now they had foolishly made a covenant with the enemy. However, we wonder what decisions the common people would have made had they been in the place of the leaders. It's easy to criticize after the fact!

That wasn't the end of the story. Joshua and his associates teach us an important lesson: If you make a mistake, admit it; *and then make your mistake work for you!* The leaders put the Gibeonites to work hauling water and fuel for the service of the tabernacle, where both water and wood were used in abundance. In later years the Gibeonites were called *the Nethinim* ("given ones" = given to assist the priests) and labored as servants in the temple (1 Chron. 9:2; Ezra 2:43, 58; Neh. 3:26). In Joshua 10, we shall see that God overruled Joshua's mistake and used it to give him a signal victory over five kings at one time.

Of course, the Gibeonites would rather submit to humiliating service than be destroyed as were the inhabitants of Jericho and Ai. There's no evidence in Scripture that the descendants of the Gibeonites created any problems for the Jews.

It's likely that their service in the tabernacle, and later in the temple, influenced them to abandon their idols and worship the God of Israel. The fact that over 500 Nethinim returned to Jerusalem after the Babylonian Captivity (Ezra 2:43-58; 8:20) suggests that they were devoted to the Lord and His house.

3. Defending the enemy (Josh. 10:1-28)

When you make agreements with the enemy, expect to end up paying a price and having to defend them in order to protect yourself. This is why God's people must remain separated from the world (2 Cor. 6:14-18). I wonder whether Paul had Joshua in mind when he wrote, "No one engaged in warfare entangles himself with the affairs of this life, that he may please Him who enlisted him as a soldier" (2 Tim. 2:4, NKJV).

The king's call to the armies (Josh. 10:1-5). The king of Jerusalem, whose name means "lord of righteousness," heard what the Gibeonites had done and announced that these traitors had to be punished. If a great city like Gibeon capitulated to the Jews, then one more barrier was removed against the advancement of Israel in the land. It was important for the Canaanites to recover that key city, even if they had to take it by force. Four other Canaanite kings allied with Adoni-zedek, and their combined armies encamped before Gibeon. The poor Gibeonites had made peace with the invaders and were now at war with their former allies!

As this confederation of armies and kings assembled, God in heaven must have laughed (Ps. 2:1-4), because unknown to them He was using these events to accomplish His own purposes. *Instead of having to defeat these five city-states one by one, He would help Joshua conquer them all at one time!*

Just as God used the defeat at Ai to form a battle plan for victory over Ai (Josh. 8), so also He used Joshua's mistake with the Gibeonites to protect Gibeon and accelerate the conquest of Canaan.

The mistakes we make embarrass us, especially those mistakes that are caused by our running ahead of the Lord and not seeking His will. But we need to remember that no mistake is final for the dedicated Christian. God can use even our blunders to accomplish His purposes. Somebody defined success as "the art of making your mistakes when nobody's looking"; but a better definition would be "the art of seeing victory where other people see only defeat."

The Gibeonites' call to Joshua (Josh. 10:6-7). In spite of their paganism, these Gibeonites are a good example for people to follow today. When they knew they were headed for destruction, they came to Joshua ("Jehovah is Savior") and obtained from him a promise of protection. Would that lost sinners realize their plight and turn to Jesus Christ by faith! When the Gibeonites found themselves in danger, they believed Joshua's promise and called on him for help. That's what God's people need to do when they find themselves facing the battles of life. The Gibeonites turned the whole burden over to Joshua and trusted him to keep his word, and he did.

Joshua's call to the Lord (Josh. 10:8-15). Three factors combined to give Joshua success in this attack: believing a divine promise (v. 8), using sound strategy (v. 9), and calling on the Lord in prayer (vv. 10-15).

The promise. Joshua's actions here illustrate two important verses: "Whatsoever is not of faith is sin" (Rom. 14:23) and "faith cometh by hearing, and hearing by the word of God" (10:17). Whenever we believe the promises of God and obey the commands of God, we act by faith and can expect God's help. The Jews didn't have to be afraid because God had already promised them victory. God's promises of victory had encouraged Joshua when he became leader of the nation (Josh. 1:5-9), when he anticipated attacking Jericho (6:2), and when he attacked Ai after a humiliating defeat (8:1). God's promises would be fulfilled because "there has not failed one word of all His good promise" (1 Kings 8:56, NKJV).

The strategy. But faith apart from works is dead, and Joshua proved his faith by using wise strategy. He ordered an all-night march and a surprise attack on the enemy army, strategy he had used before when attacking Ai (8:3ff). It was a long trek from Gilgal to Gibeon, and the road was uphill; but Joshua assembled his troops and made the journey as quickly as possible. No doubt the men were weary when they arrived, but the Lord was with them and gave them victory. What kept the soldiers going? They believed God's promise and knew that the victory was assured.

God assisted the weary Jewish soldiers by killing the enemy army with large hailstones. The timely occurrence of the storm was itself a miracle, but an even greater miracle was the fact that the stones *hit only the enemy soldiers*. God took His special "ammunition" out of His storehouse and used it to good advantage (Job 38:22-23). When God's people are obeying God's will, everything in the universe works for them, even "the stars in their courses" (Judg. 5:20). When we disobey God's will, everything works against us. (Read Jonah 1 for a vivid illustration of this truth.)

The prayer. But the miracle of the hailstorm was nothing compared to the miracle of extending the day so that Joshua could finish the battle and secure a complete victory over the enemy. His men were weary and the task was great; and if night came on, the enemy could escape. Joshua needed a special act from God to enable him to claim the victory the Lord had promised.

This is the last miracle recorded in Joshua and certainly the greatest. Joshua prayed for God's help, and the Lord answered in a remarkable way. This event is questioned by those who deny the reality of miracles and look only to science for truth. "How could God stop the rotation of the earth and extend the length of a day," they ask, "without creating chaos all over the planet?" They seem to forget the fact that days are *normally* of different lengths in various parts of the world without the planet experiencing chaos. At 2 o'clock in the morning, I read the newspaper *by sunlight* in Norway.

But how do you explain a miracle, *any* miracle? Of course, the simplest answer is the answer of faith: The Lord is God and nothing is too hard for Him (Jer. 32:17, 27). Day and night belong to God (Ps. 74:16), and everything He has made is His servant. If God can't perform the miracle described in Joshua 10, then He can't perform any miracle and is imprisoned in His own creation, unable to use or suspend the very laws He built into it. I have a difficult time believing in that kind of a God.

An Old Testament expert, Gleason L. Archer, points out that the phrase "hasted not to go down" in verse 13 indicates "a retardation of the movement" and not a complete cessation.[1] The sun and moon didn't stand still permanently and then suddenly go down but were held back so that the daylight was lengthened. God stopped the sun and moon and then retarded the rotation of the planet so that the sun and moon set very slowly. Such a process would not create chaos all over the globe.

A corollary to this view is that the sun and moon remained on their normal course and it only *appeared* that the day was lengthening because of the way God caused their light to be refracted. But verse 13 states twice that the sun "stood still" and once that the moon "stayed." However, these verbs need not describe a permanent situation but only the beginning of the miracle. God stopped the sun and moon in their courses and then controlled their gradual descent, all the while causing the light to be refracted for a much longer period of time.

Since verses 13b-15 are poetical in form, a quotation from the unknown Book of Jasher (see 2 Sam. 1:8), some students interpret the words symbolically. They say that God so helped Israel that the army was able to accomplish two days' work in one day. But Joshua's words sound very much like a prayer that the Lord would intervene, and the description of what occurred doesn't read like the report of an efficiency expert.

Why try to explain away a miracle? What do we prove? Certainly not that we're smarter than God! Either we believe in a God who can do anything, or we must accept a Christian faith that's non-miraculous; and that does away with the inspiration of the Bible, the Virgin Birth, and the bodily resurrection of Jesus Christ. Certainly there's room for honest questions about the *nature* of the miraculous; but for the humble Christian believer, there's never room for questioning the *reality* of the miraculous. C.S. Lewis wrote, "The mind which asks for a non-miraculous Christianity is a mind in process of relapsing from Christianity into mere 'religion.' "[2]

You find seemingly contradictory facts stated in Joshua 10:15 and 21. Why would the army go all the way back to Gilgal when the battle wasn't over? The best explanation is to see verse 15 as the completion of the quotation from the Book of Jasher, beginning at verse 13b. The temporary Jewish camp was at Makkedah, which was near Libnah; and the army didn't return to Gilgal until they had established their control over central Canaan.

Joshua's call to his army (Josh. 10:16-28). At the end of an incredible battle, Joshua performed a public ceremony that gave encouragement and strength to his soldiers. Their past victories had given them control over the central part of the land, but now they faced campaigns in both the south and the north of Palestine. "Divide and conquer" was Joshua's strategy, and it worked. Joshua wanted to remind his men that the Lord would give them victory throughout the land.

Knowing that the five kings were trapped in a cave, Joshua temporarily left them and led his men in the "mopping up" operation, which verse 20 describes as "slaying them with a very great slaughter." Only a few of the enemy soldiers escaped to the cities; but since those cities would eventually be destroyed anyway, those fugitives had no hope.

Returning to the camp, probably the next day, Joshua ordered the kings to be taken from the cave and put on the ground, their faces in the dirt. This humiliating posture announced that Joshua had won a total victory and their end had come. But there was more. He called for his officers to put their feet on the necks of the kings, symbolic not only of the past victory but also of the victories the Lord would give His people in the days ahead. The kings were slain and the five corpses hung on five trees until sundown. Then their bodies were put into the cave, with a pile of stones closing up the entrance. This pile of stones was another monument in the land speaking of the power and victory of the Lord.

In verse 25, Joshua's words must have thrilled the hearts of his brave soldiers. They echo the words God spoke to him when he began his career (1:6-9). Since Joshua is a type of Jesus Christ, we can apply this scene and these words to Christ and His people. Jesus has defeated all His enemies and will one day return and destroy them forever. No matter how they may rage and rebel (Ps. 2:1-3), our Lord's enemies are only the footstool at His feet (Ps. 110:1; 1 Cor. 15:25). Through Him, we can claim victory and put our feet on the necks of our enemies (Rom. 16:20).

As you review the whole episode of Joshua and the Gibeonites, you can't help but be both warned and encouraged. These events warn us to be alert and prayerful lest the enemy deceive us and we start walking by sight instead of by faith. Then we'll find ourselves making decisions that are wrong and getting into alliances that are dangerous. But there's also a word of encouragement: God can take even our blunders and turn them into blessings. This isn't an excuse for carelessness, but it is a great encouragement when you've failed the Lord and His people.

"And this is the victory that has overcome the world—our faith" (1 John 5:4, NKJV).

INTERLUDE
Joshua 10:29–12:24

This section of the Book of Joshua summarizes Israel's conquest of the southern (10:29-43) and northern cities (11:1-15) in Palestine, and closes with a list of the names of some of the kings whom Israel defeated (11:16-12:24). Since there is probably a map of the conquest located in the back of your Bible, consult it as you read these chapters.

Two things stand out in this record: It was the Lord who gave the victory (10:30, 32, 42; 11:6, 8); and Joshua obeyed the Lord by utterly destroying the enemy, just as Moses had commanded (11:9, 12, 15, 20). The only exception was Gibeon.

Joshua's strategy was to cut across the land and divide it, then conquer the southern cities, then the northern cities. On more than one occasion, he made a surprise attack on the enemy (10:9; 11:7); and the promises of the Lord encouraged him (v. 6; see 1:9; 8:1).

In 10:29-35, you have the record of the army fighting in the foothills; but in verse 36, the campaign moves to the mountains. The northern coalition of kings was unable to defeat Israel even though their army was much larger than that of the Jews (11:1-9).

The "long time" of verse 18 is about seven years. Israel's failure at Kadesh Barnea (Deut. 2:14), at which time Caleb was forty years old (Josh. 14:7) to their crossing of the Jordan was thirty-eight years. He was eighty-five when the conquest was over (v. 10), which means that at least seven years had been devoted to the campaign.

The Anakim mentioned in 11:21-22 were a race of giants, descendants of Anak, who were greatly feared by the ten unbelieving men who had spied out Canaan (Num. 13:22, 28, 33). The two believing spies, Joshua and Caleb, didn't fear them but had trusted the Lord for victory. Joshua's victory over the Anakim is recorded in Joshua 11:21-22 and Caleb's victory in 14:12-15.

The apparent contradiction between verses 11:23 and 13:1 can easily be explained. Joshua and his army did take control of the whole land by destroying the key cities with their kings and people. Israel didn't take every little city or slay every citizen or ruler, but they did enough to break the power of the enemy and establish control over the land. Once this was accomplished and there was rest in the land, Joshua was able to assign each tribe its inheritance; and within each inheritance, the tribes had to gain mastery over the remaining inhabitants who were still there. Even after the death of Joshua and his officers, there was additional land to be taken (Judg. 1-3).

Thirty-three kings are named in Joshua 12, beginning with Sihon and Og whose lands were east of Jordan and had been conquered under the leadership of Moses (vv. 1-8; Num. 21:21-35). The sixteen kings defeated in the southern campaign are listed in Joshua 12:9-16 and the fifteen northern kings in verses 17-24.

Now we turn to the actual assigning of the land to the tribes (chaps. 13-21) to discover the spiritual truths we need to learn and apply as we claim our own spiritual inheritance in Jesus Christ.

CHAPTER TEN
THIS LAND IS OUR LAND!
Joshua 13–21

Joshua had successfully completed the first half of his divine commission: He had conquered the enemy and was in control of the land and the cities (1:1-5). Now he had to fulfill the second part of that commission and divide the land so that each tribe could claim their inheritance and enjoy what God had given them (v. 6). (See Num. 34-35.)

The word *inheritance* is found over fifty times in these nine chapters and is a very important word. The Jews *inherited* their land. They didn't *win* their land as spoils of battle or *purchase* their land as in a business transaction. The Lord, who was the sole owner, leased the land to them. "The land must not be sold permanently," the Lord had instructed them, "because the land is Mine and you are but aliens and My tenants" (Lev. 25:23, NIV). Imagine having God for your landlord!

The "rent" God required was simply Israel's obedience to His Law. As long as the Jewish people honored the Lord with their worship and obedience, He would bless them, make their land productive, and keep their nation at peace with their neighbors. When Israel agreed to the blessings and curses at Mt. Gerizim and Mt. Ebal (Josh. 8:30-35), they accepted the conditions of what is called "The Palestinian Covenant." Their *ownership* of the land was purely the gracious act of God; but their *possession* and *enjoyment* of the land depended on their submission and obedience to the Lord. (See Lev. 26 and Deut. 27-30 for the details of the Palestinian Covenant.)

The Promised Land was a gift of God's love; and if the Israelites loved the Lord, they would want to obey Him and please Him in the way they used His land (Deut. 4:37-39). Unfortunately, they eventually defied the Lord, disobeyed the Law, and defiled the land; and God had to chasten them in the land of Babylon.

There were four main stages in the distribution of the land; and in each of these stages, you will find spiritual lessons for God's people today who want to enjoy their spiritual inheritance in Christ. As you study these chapters, I suggest you consult a map of the Holy Land that shows the boundaries of the twelve tribes and the cities that are involved.

1. The assignments made at Gilgal (Josh. 13:1-17:18)

Throughout the conquest of Canaan, Gilgal had been the center of operations for Israel. Later, Joshua moved the camp and the tabernacle to a more central location at Shiloh (18:1).

We don't know Joshua's exact age at this time in Israel's history, although he could well have been 100. Caleb was 85 (14:10), and it's likely that Joshua was the older of the two. Joshua lived to be 110 (24:19), and the events described in the last half of the book could well have taken over ten years.

The system for assigning the territories in Canaan is given in 14:1-2. Eleazer the high priest, Joshua, and one representative from each of the tribes (Num. 34:13-29) cast lots before the Lord and in this way determined His will (Prov. 16:33). When Joshua relocated the camp at Shiloh, they changed the system (Josh. 18:1-7).

The two and a half tribes east of the Jordan (Josh. 13:1-33). Reuben, Gad, and the half tribe of Manasseh had agreed to help the other tribes conquer the land before they returned to the east side of the Jordan to enjoy their inheritance (Num. 32). They had asked for this land outside the boundaries of Canaan because it was especially suited to the raising of cattle. The fact that these two and a half tribes would not be living within God's appointed land didn't seem to worry them. Moses graciously agreed to their choice and let them settle across the Jordan. When we study the twenty-second chapter of Joshua, we'll learn that while their choice may have been good for their cattle, it created serious problems for their children.

These tribes became a sort of "buffer zone" between the Jews in Canaan and the heathen nations like Moab and Ammon. Of course, their location made them extremely vulnerable both to military attack and ungodly influence; and both of these liabilities eventually brought about their downfall (1 Chron. 5:25-26). The boundaries are given for Reuben in the south (Josh. 13:15-23), and the half tribe of Manasseh in the north (vv. 29–32), with Gad sandwiched between (vv. 24–28).

> **Lesson #1.** Don't become a "borderline believer." Enter into the inheritance God appoints for you and rejoice in it. "He will choose our inheritance for us, the excellence of Jacob whom He loves" (Ps. 47:4, NKJV). The will of God is the expression of the love of God and is always the best for us.

Since the tribe of Reuben had taken its territory from Moab, it was logical for the story of Balaam to be mentioned here (Josh. 13:22-23; see Num. 22-25). When Balaam saw that God was turning his curses into blessings, he advised Balak to be friendly to the Jews and invite them to one of the Moabite religious feasts. This resulted in some of the Jewish men taking Moabite women for themselves and thus violating the Law of God. What Satan couldn't accomplish as a lion, cursing Israel, he accomplished as a serpent, beguiling Israel and leading the men into wicked compromise.

Four times in these chapters, we are reminded that the Levites were given no inheritance in the land (Josh. 13:14, 33; 14:3-4; 18:7), because the Lord was their inheritance (Deut. 18:1-8; 10:8-9; Num. 18). The priests received certain portions from the sacrifices as their due, and both the priests and Levites shared in the special tithes and offerings that the people were commanded to bring.

But other factors were probably involved in scattering the tribe of Levi. For one thing, God didn't want tribal responsibilities to distract the priests and Levites; He wanted them to devote themselves fully to serving Him. (See 2 Tim. 2:4.) Also, He wanted them to be "salt and light" in the land as they lived among the people and taught them the Law. Simeon and Levi were also scattered in fulfillment of the prophecy of Jacob (Gen. 49:5-7, see chap. 34). Simeon eventually became a part of Judah.

The two and a half tribes west of the Jordan (Josh. 14:1-17:18). The next tribes to be settled were Judah in the south (14:6-15:63), Ephraim across the middle of the land (16:1-10), and the other half of Manasseh in the north (17:1-18).

Since Caleb belonged to the tribe of Judah (Num. 13:30) and had been one of the two faithful spies, he received his inheritance first. Joshua, the other faithful spy, was the last to receive his inheritance (Josh. 19:49-51). Caleb reminded his friend Joshua of the promise Moses had made to them forty-five years before (Num. 14:24, 30; Deut. 1:34-36), that they would survive the years of wandering and receive their inheritance in the land. This promise gave Joshua and Caleb joy and courage as they endured years of wandering and waiting.

> **Lesson #2.** Be encouraged in your pilgrim journey! You have already received your inheri-

> tance in Christ and can claim "every spiritual blessing" (Eph. 1:3, NKJV). Since you have a glorious inheritance before you (1 Peter 1:3-6), keep looking up! The best is yet to come!

Caleb was eighty-five years old, but he didn't look for an easy task, suited to an "old man." He asked Joshua for mountains to climb and giants to conquer! His strength was in the Lord, and he knew that God would never fail him. The secret of Caleb's life is found in a phrase that's repeated six times in Scripture: "he wholly followed the Lord God of Israel" (Josh. 14:14; also see Num. 14:24; 32:12; Deut. 1:36; Josh. 14:8-9). Caleb was an overcomer because he had faith in the Lord (1 John 5:4).

> **Lesson #3.** We are never too old to make new conquests of faith in the power of the Lord. Like Caleb, we can capture mountains and conquer giants if we wholly follow the Lord. No matter how old we become, we must never retire from trusting and serving the Lord.

In Joshua 15:13-19, we see Caleb providing for the next generation. Some of Caleb's daring faith rubbed off on his son-in-law Othniel, who later became a judge in the land (Judg. 3:7-11). Caleb's faith also touched his daughter, for she had the faith to ask her father for a field and then for springs of water to irrigate the land. Caleb's example of faith was more valuable to his family than the property he claimed for them.

> **Lesson #4.** The older generation must provide for the next generation, not only materially but most of all spiritually. "Senior saints" must be examples of believers and encourage the younger generation to trust the Lord and wholly follow Him.

The inheritance of the rest of the tribe of Judah is described in Joshua 15:1-12 and 21-63. We're not sure why verse 32 says twenty-nine cities when thirty-six are named, but perhaps the names of some of the "villages" outside the city walls are included in the list. At that time the Jews couldn't take Jerusalem (v. 63). They held it temporarily later on (Judg. 1:8), and then David captured it permanently and made it the capital city (2 Sam. 5:6-10).

Ephraim and Manasseh were the sons of Joseph, whom Jacob "adopted" and especially blessed (Gen. 48:15-22). Since the tribe of Levi wasn't given any territory, these two tribes made up the difference so that there were still twelve tribes in Israel. The birth order was "Manasseh and Ephraim" (Josh. 16:4; 17:1), but Jacob reversed it. God rejects our first birth and gives us a second birth. He accepted Abel and rejected Cain; He rejected Ishmael and accepted Isaac, Abraham's second-born son; He rejected Esau and accepted Jacob.

In the nation of Israel the sons inherited the property but the daughters of Zelophehad saw to it that the daughters weren't discriminated against (vv. 3-6; Num. 27:1-11). Like the daughter of Caleb, these women had the faith and courage to ask for their inheritance; and they even changed the law!

> **Lesson #5.** God wants to give all His people their inheritance. "You do not have because you do not ask" (James 4:2, NKJV). In Jesus Christ, all believers are one and are heirs of God (Gal.

> 3:26-29). Nothing from your first birth should hinder you from claiming all that you have in Jesus Christ.

Joshua had a problem with the children of Joseph (Ephraim and Manasseh), who complained because the Lord didn't give them enough room! (Josh. 17:14-18) You can detect their pride as they told Joshua what a "great people" they were. After all, didn't Jacob personally adopt and especially bless them? And hadn't they multiplied in a great way? And wasn't Joshua from the tribe of Ephraim? (Num. 13:8) They were a special people who deserved special treatment.

If you compare the statistics given in 1:32-35 and 26:34 and 37, you learn that the descendants of Joseph had increased from 72,700 to 85,200, although Ephraim had 8,000 fewer people. But six other tribes had increased their number since the last census. Thus the children of Joseph weren't the only ones who were fruitful.

Joshua told his brethren that, if they were such a great people, now was their opportunity to prove it! Let them do what Caleb did and defeat the giants and claim the mountains! It's worth noting that the people of Ephraim and Manasseh seemed to be given to criticism and pride. They not only created problems for Joshua but also for Gideon (Judg. 8:1-3), Jephthah (12:1-7), and even David (2 Sam. 20:1-5). "For where envy and self-seeking exist, confusion and every evil thing are there" (James 3:16, NKIV).

> **Lesson #6.** It's not your boasting but your believing that gives you the victory and gains you new territory. Sometimes those who talk the most accomplish the least.

2. The assignments made at Shiloh (Josh. 18:1-19:51)

Five tribes now had been given their inheritance as Joshua, Eleazer, and the twelve tribal leaders cast lots at Gilgal. Then Joshua moved the camp to Shiloh, in the territory of Ephraim, where the tabernacle remained until David moved the Ark to Jerusalem (2 Sam. 6). The Lord must have directed Joshua to make this move or he would not have done it (Deut. 12:5-7). Shiloh was centrally located and was more convenient for all the tribes.

Seven tribes still had to have their inheritance marked out for them, and apparently they were slow to respond to the challenge. Unlike Caleb and the daughters of Zelophehad, these tribes didn't have faith and spiritual zeal. These tribes had helped fight battles and defeat the enemy, but now they hesitated to claim their inheritance and enjoy the land God had given them. "The lazy man does not roast what he took in hunting, but diligence is man's precious possession" (Prov. 12:27, NKJV).

At this point, Joshua and the leaders inaugurated a new system for allocating the land. After each of the seven tribes appointed three men, all twenty-one men went through the remaining territories and listed the cities and the landmarks, describing each part of the land. They brought this information back to Joshua, who then assigned the various portions to the remaining seven tribes by casting lots before the Lord.

Since Benjamin was the full brother to Joseph, his territory was assigned adjacent to Ephraim and Manasseh (Josh. 18:11–28). Simeon shared his inheritance with Judah (19:1-9; see Gen. 49:7) and eventually inhabited the cities assigned in Joshua 15:21ff. The children of Joseph wanted more territory, but weren't willing to fight for it by faith; but the people of Judah had so much land that they shared it with Simeon. What a contrast!

The area north of Manasseh was assigned to Zebulun (19:10-16), Issachar (vv. 17-23), Asher (vv. 24-31), and Naphtali (vv. 32-39). Zebulun and Naphtali later became "Galilee of the Gentiles" (Matt. 4:15-16), where our Lord ministered when He was here on earth. The "sea of Chinneroth" (see Josh. 12:3; 13:27) is the Sea of Galilee. The Hebrew word *chinnereth* means "harp," and the Sea of Galilee is shaped like a harp.

The last tribe to receive its assignment was the tribe of Dan (19:40-48), which immediately went to work and expanded its territory. Dan and Benjamin formed a "belt" across the land, connecting the Dead Sea with the Mediterranean.

Being the leader that he was, Joshua waited until the very last to claim his own inheritance; and the Lord gave him the city of Timnath-Serah (vv. 49-50). Like his friend Caleb, Joshua preferred living in the mountainous region of the land.

3. The assignment of the cities of refuge (Josh. 20:1-9)

When the nation was still on the other side of the Jordan, God told Moses to have the people set aside special cities for the Levites (Num. 35:1-5), as well as six "cities of refuge" (Ex. 21:13; Num. 35:6-34; Deut. 19:1-13). Now that the tribes had received their territories, Joshua could assign these cities.

Even before the Law of Moses was given, God had laid down the basic rule that those who shed blood should pay for their crime with their own blood (Gen. 9:5-6). This principle was enunciated repeatedly in the Law, but God made a distinction between murder and manslaughter (Ex. 21:12-14; Lev. 24:17; Num. 35:16-21; Deut. 19:11-13). "Blood defiles the land, and no atonement can be made for the land, for the blood that is shed on it, except by the blood of him who shed it. Therefore do not defile the land which you inhabit" (Num. 35:33-34, NKJV).

The six "cities of refuge" were needed because society in that day had no police force to investigate crimes. It was the responsibility of each family to see to it that murders were avenged, but how could they tell whether it was a case of premeditated murder or accidental manslaughter? In the heat of anger a relative of the dead person might kill somebody who was really innocent of a capital crime.

Joshua set apart three cities of refuge on each side of the Jordan River. On the west side, Kedesh was farthest north, in the territory of Naphtali; Shechem was in the middle of the nation in the tribe of Manasseh; and Hebron was in the south in the tribe of Judah. On the east side of the Jordan, the cities were Golan in the north in Manasseh, Ramoth in Gad, and Bezer farther south in the tribe of Reuben. Since the Holy Land is about the size of the state of Maryland, you can see that nobody was very far from a city of refuge.

The law was really quite simple. Anybody who killed another person could flee to a city of refuge and be protected from "the avenger of blood" until the elders of the city could investigate the circumstances. If they found the fugitive guilty, he or she was put to death; but if they concluded that it was a case of manslaughter, the fugitive was allowed to live in the city and be protected from the avenger. Upon the death of the high priest, the fugitive could go home again. It was a case of forfeiting freedom in order to save his or her life.

Many students have seen in the cities of refuge a picture of our salvation in

Jesus Christ, to whom we "have fled for refuge" (Heb. 6:18). The lost sinner, of course, is in danger of judgment because "the wages of sin is death" (Rom. 6:23). The avenger of blood is after him or her! God's appointed Savior is Jesus Christ (Acts 4:12), but the sinner must come to Him by faith in order to be saved (Matt. 11:28-30; John 6:37). The way to each city was kept open with roads that were cared for and marked (Deut. 19:3, NIV). God wanted it to be easy for the fugitives to find their way to safety.

Beyond this, the picture is one of *contrast.* When we come to Christ for salvation, there's no need for an investigation or a trial, because we *know* we're guilty; *and we admit it!* The only people Jesus can save are those who confess their guilt and throw themselves on His mercy.

If the fugitive prematurely left the city of refuge, he could be killed; but our salvation in Christ is not conditional. Our High Priest will *never* die, and we are forever secure. "But He, because He continues forever, has an unchangeable priesthood. Therefore He is also able to save to the uttermost those who come to God through Him, since He always lives to make intercession for them" (Heb. 7:24-25, NKJV).

The meanings of the names of the cities are interesting. Taking them in the order listed in Joshua 20:7-8, you have: Kedesh = "righteousness"; Shechem = "shoulder"; Hebron = "fellowship"; Bezer = "fortress" or "strong"; and Ramoth = "heights." Hebraists do not agree on what Golan means, but the *Gesenius Lexicon* says it means "exile."

These names then can be used to describe what sinners experience when they flee by faith to Jesus. First, He gives them His *righteousness,* and they can never be accused again. There is no condemnation! (Rom. 8:1) Like a shepherd, He carries them on His *shoulders,* and they enter into *fellowship* with Him. He is their *fortress,* and they are safe. They dwell in the *heights* even though they are *exiles,* pilgrims, and strangers in this world.

> **Lesson #7.** Unless you have fled by faith to Jesus Christ, you aren't saved! Since our sins put Jesus on the cross, all of us are guilty of His death. He is the only Savior, and apart from faith in Him, there is no salvation. Have you fled to Him?

Before leaving this theme, we should note that there is also an application to the nation of Israel. The people were guilty of killing the Lord Jesus Christ, *but it was a sin of ignorance on the part of the people* (Acts 3:12-18). When Jesus prayed on the cross, "Father, forgive them; for they know not what they do" (Luke 23:34), He was declaring them guilty of manslaughter rather than murder (1 Cor. 2:7-8). The way was open for their forgiveness, and God gave the nation nearly forty years to repent before He brought judgment. This same principle applied to the Apostle Paul (1 Tim. 1:12–14). However, no lost sinner today can plead ignorance, because God has declared *the whole world* guilty and without excuse (Rom. 3:9-19).

4. The assignment of the levitical cities (Josh. 21:1-45)

As we noted before, the tribe of Levi didn't have territory assigned to it but was scattered throughout the land. This way, they could teach the people the Law and influence each of the tribes to be faithful to the Lord. But the Levites needed places to live and pastures for their cattle. Thus God assigned forty-eight cities for them to live in, along with a specific amount of land for pasture (Num. 35:1-5). The pasture land could not be sold, but their houses could be sold; and the Levites even had special privileges for redeeming their property (Lev. 23:32-34).

The two lists of levitical cities that we have—Joshua 21 and 1 Chronicles 6:54-81—do not always agree; but names of cities and spellings change over the years, and it's possible that from time to time new cities were selected and old ones abandoned.

There were forty-eight levitical cities, six of which were also cities of refuge. Each of the tribes contributed four cities, except Judah and Simeon, who together contributed nine, and Naphtali, who contributed three. The descendants of the three sons of Aaron—Kohath, Gershon and Marari—were assigned to the various cities, although other Jews also lived in them. In Numbers 26:62, the writer states that there were 23,000 Levites before Israel entered the land, a big crowd to distribute among forty-eight cities.

It was important that Israel have qualified and authorized people to minister in the tabernacle and later in the temple, and we must never minimize the teaching ministry of the priests and Levites (2 Chron. 17:7-9). Since the common people didn't own copies of the Scriptures, it was important that the Levites identify with the people and explain the Law to them. These levitical cities were so located that nobody was too far away from a man who could help them understand and apply the Law of Moses.

This long section in the Book of Joshua closes with three wonderful affirmations:

First, God was faithful and gave Israel the land (Josh. 20:43). He kept the covenant that He made, first with Abraham (Gen. 12:7) and then with his descendants.

Second, God gave Israel victory over all their enemies and then gave them the rest from war (Josh. 20:44; see 1:13, 15; 11:23). What the ten unbelieving spies at Kadesh Barnea said could never happen *did* happen, because Joshua and the people believed God and obeyed His Word.

Third, God kept His promises (20:45). At the close of his life Joshua would remind the people of this (23:14); and Solomon reminded them of it when he dedicated the temple (1 Kings 8:56).

As the people of God, we can claim these assurances by faith. God's covenant with us is not going to fail; God's power and wisdom can give us victory over every foe; and God's promises can be trusted, no matter what the circumstances may be.

The covenant of God, the power of God, the promises of God—these are the spiritual resources we can depend on as we claim our inheritance in Jesus Christ.

CHAPTER ELEVEN
AND WHEN THE BATTLE'S OVER
Joshua 22

It was on VE-Day, May 8, 1945, when the nation heard President Truman announce over the radio: "General Eisenhower informs me that the forces of Germany have surrendered to the United Nations. The flags of freedom fly all over Europe."

I remember VJ-Day, August 14, 1945, when the downtown area of our city was jammed with people and total strangers were hugging one another and cheering. The Japanese had agreed to the Allied terms of surrender, and the war was over. My two brothers serving in the Marine Corps would be coming home!

The soldiers from the tribes of Reuben, Gad, and the half tribe of Manasseh must have been especially euphoric when the Jewish conquest of Canaan ended. For over seven years they had been away from their families on the other side of the Jordan, and now the victorious soldiers were free to go home.

But their return home was not without incident. In fact, what they did, well-meaning as it was, almost provoked another war. Let's consider the events involved and the lessons we can learn from them.

1. Their honorable discharge (Josh. 22:1-8)

"In defeat unbeatable; in victory unbearable." That's the way Sir Winston Churchill described a British army officer famous in the Second World War. The first half of the description would apply to Joshua, because he knew how to win victory out of defeat. But the last half doesn't apply at all; for as commander of the Lord's army, Joshua was magnanimous in the way he treated his troops after the victory. An Italian proverb says, "It's the blood of the soldier that makes the general great." But this general made his soldiers great! This is clearly seen in the way he discharged the tribes who lived on the east side of the Jordan.

He commended them (Josh. 22:1-3). These two and a half tribes had promised Moses that they would remain in the army until all the land was conquered, and they kept their promise (Num. 32; Deut. 3:12-20). After the death of Moses, they pledged that same loyalty to Joshua, their new leader (Josh. 1:12-18). These tribes had been loyal to Moses, to Joshua, and to their brothers from the other tribes. "For a long time now—to this very day—you have not deserted your brothers but have carried out the mission the Lord your God gave you" (22:3, NIV).

Why had they been so loyal to their leaders and fellow soldiers? Because they were first of all loyal to the Lord their God. It was *His* mission they were carrying out and *His* name they were seeking to glorify. In the service of the Lord, far above our devotion to a leader, a cause, or even a nation is our devotion to the Lord. "And whatever you do, do it heartily, as to the Lord and not to men, knowing that from the Lord you will receive the reward of the inheritance; for you serve the Lord Christ" (Col. 3:23-24, NKJV).

He discharged them (Josh. 22:4). Having fulfilled their mission and kept their promise, the tribes were now free to go home; for God had given His people rest. The concept of *rest* is important in the Book of Joshua and means much more than simply the end of the war. The word carries with it the meaning of both *victory* and *security,* and it involved Israel having their "resting place" in the land. God promised to give His people rest (Ex. 33:14; Deut. 12:9-10; 25:19; Josh. 1:13, 15), and He kept His promise (11:23; 14:15; 21:44; 22:4; 23:1).

The spiritual application of this *rest* for God's people today is made in Hebrews 3 and 4. When we trust Christ as Savior, we enter into *rest* because we're no longer at war with God (Rom. 5:1). When we yield ourselves completely to Him and claim our inheritance by faith, we enter into a deeper rest and enjoy our spiritual riches in Christ. (See Matt. 11:28-32 for our Lord's invitation.) When we *come to Him,* He gives us rest. When we *take His yoke of discipleship,* we find that deeper rest.

Imagine what it would be like for these soldiers to return home after being away for so many years! Think of the love they would experience, the joys they would find, the treasures they would share! That's just a small picture of what happens when the children of God enter into the rest God gives to those who will yield their all to Him and trust His Word.

He admonished them (Josh. 22:5). Like any good leader, Joshua was more concerned about the spiritual walk of his people than anything else. The army had experienced victory in Canaan because Joshua loved the Lord and obeyed His Word (1:7-8), and that would be the "open secret" of Israel's continued peace and prosperity. Just as they had been diligent in battle, obeying their commander, so they must be diligent in worship, obeying the Lord their God. This was the promise each of the tribes made to the Lord at Mt. Gerizim and Mt. Ebal.

The motive for their obedience had to be love for the Lord their God. If they loved Him, then they would delight in walking in all His ways and obeying all His commandments. Instead of trying to serve two masters, they would cling (cleave) to the Lord and serve Him alone, with all their heart and soul. Jesus said this was the first and greatest commandment (Matt. 22:36-38); therefore, to disobey it would mean to commit the greatest sin. "If you love Me, keep My commandments" (John 14:15, NKJV).

He blessed them (Josh. 22:6-8). It was the ministry of the high priest to bless God's people (Num. 6:22-27), but the common people could invoke God's blessing on others, especially a leader upon his people or a father upon his family (Gen. 27:4; 48:9; 2 Sam. 6:18, 20; 1 Kings 8:55). What a sight to see a great general asking God's blessing on his troops!

This blessing also involved sharing the rich spoils of battle with them and their family members back home. It was the custom in Israel that those who stayed home, or who couldn't participate in the battle for some good reason, also shared the spoils (Num. 31:25-27; 1 Sam. 30:23-25). After all, these people had protected the home cities and kept the machinery of the community going while the men had been out fighting, and it was only fair that they share in the spoils.

Indeed, for the two and a half tribes that lived east of the Jordan, it was an honorable discharge.

2. Their honest concern (Josh. 22:9-10)

As the men of Reuben, Gad, and the half tribe of Manasseh made their way east and passed landmarks that brought back memories of the great things God had done, their hearts began to disturb them. Happy as they were to be going home, it wasn't easy to say good-bye to their brothers and leave behind the nearness of the priesthood and the tabernacle. They were leaving the land that God had promised to bless. Yes, they were going home to the land that they had chosen for themselves; but somehow they began to feel isolated from the nation of Israel.

When you read and ponder Numbers 32, you discover that there is no record that Moses consulted the Lord about this decision. The thing Moses was most concerned about was that the men of Reuben, Gad, and Manasseh do their share in fighting the enemy and conquering the Promised Land; and this they agreed to do. Moses' first response was that of anger mingled with fear, lest God judge the nation as He had at Kadesh Barnea. Perhaps this first reaction was the right one.

There's no question that Canaan was God's appointed land for His people; anything short of Canaan wasn't what He wanted for them. The two and a half tribes made their decision, not on the basis of spiritual values, but on the basis of material gain; for the land east of the Jordan was ideal for raising cattle. I'm reminded of the decision Lot made when he pitched his tent toward Sodom (Gen. 13:10-11). In both instances, the people walked by sight and not by faith.

By making this decision, the people of Reuben, Gad, and Manasseh divided the nation and separated themselves from the blessings of the land of Canaan. They were farther away from the tabernacle and closer to the enemy. They became what I call "borderline believers." You'll recall that Egypt represents the world and Canaan the believer's inheritance in Christ. The wilderness wanderings represent the experience of believers who don't enter by faith into the *rest* God has for them (Heb. 3-4). The two and a half tribes portray believers who have experienced the blessings and battles of Canaan—their inheritance in Christ—but prefer to live on the border, outside God's appointed place of blessing.

"Faith can never be satisfied with anything short of the true position and portion of God's people," wrote C.H. MacIntosh in his *Notes on Numbers.* "An undecided, half-and-half Christian is more inconsistent than an open, out-and-out worldling or infidel" (pp. 457, 460).

How did they decide to solve the problem which they themselves had created? By building a large altar of stones by the Jordan River, on the Canaan side, as a reminder to everybody that the two and a half tribes also belonged to the nation of Israel. Had these tribes been living in the land of Canaan where they belonged, nobody would have questioned their nationality. But living outside the land, they gave the impression that they were not Israelites.

This is now the eighth memorial erected in Canaan (Josh. 4:9, 20-24; 7:26; 8:29-32 [three memorials]; 10:27). But it's unfortunate when believers have to resort to artificial means to let people know they're God's people. In recent years we've seen a spate of "religious" bumper stickers, jewelry, decals, and other items (including mirrors and combs with Bible verses on them), all of which are supposed to help identify the owners with Jesus Christ. While these things might occasionally open doors of opportunity for witness, how much better it would be if our Spirit-led conduct and speech made the lost sit up and take notice. When we're living as God wants us to live, we're salt and light; and the Lord uses our witness for His glory.

If the people of Reuben, Gad, and Manasseh faithfully attended the feasts in Jerusalem (Ex. 23:17), honored the Lord by obeying His Word, and talked about His Word in their homes (Deut. 6:6-9), they would be able to raise their children to know and serve the Lord. The altar on the Jordan bank, however, was no guarantee of such success.

3. Their humble submission (Josh. 22:11-29)

The alarm (Josh. 22:11-14). The word traveled quickly that the tribes east of the Jordan had erected an altar. While these Transjordanic tribes had been very sincere in what they did, their action was misunderstood; and the other tribes prepared for possible war. But wisely, they waited while an official delegation investigated what was going on. "He who answers a matter before he hears it, it is folly and shame to him" (Prov. 18:13, NKJV).

The delegation of ten princes, one from each tribe, was led by Phinehas, the son of the high priest, a man who had already proved himself courageous in defending the Law of the Lord (Num. 25; Ps. 106:30-31). It was the responsibility of the tribal leaders and the priests to investigate every situation in Israel that appeared to be a breach of the Law (Deut. 13). God had instructed the Jews to destroy the altars of the heathen nations in Canaan and not to build altars of their own. There was to be one altar of sacrifice at the one sanctuary that God had appointed (Deut. 12; Lev. 17:8-9).

The appeal (Josh. 22:15-20). It's likely that Phinehas made the speech, but note that his address represented the agreement of all the tribes. Phinehas called what they had done a *trespass* (vv. 16, 20, 22 [*transgression*, KJV], 31), which means "an act of treachery." Joshua had commended these two and a half tribes for their loyalty, and now they had proved faithless. They had *turned away* (vv. 16, 18, 23, 29), which meant they were no longer following the Lord (see v. 5). This word carries the idea of "backsliding," gradually moving away from the Lord.

The strongest word used was *rebel* (vv. 16, 18-19 [twice], 22, 29), which means deliberately resisting God's will and disobeying His Law. In building an unauthorized altar, these two and a half tribes were guilty of apostasy. "For rebellion is as the sin of witchcraft, and stubbornness is as iniquity and idolatry" (1 Sam. 15:23).

From the nation's recent history Phinehas cited two serious cases of rebellion as warning to these tribes. The first was the participation of Israel in the heathen rites of the Moabites, when the men committed harlotry with the Moabite women (Josh. 22:17; Num. 25). As a result, 24,000 people died. The second was the sin of Achan after the victory at Jericho, when he deliberately took the spoils that belonged to the Lord (Josh. 22:20; see Josh. 7). His sin led to defeat at Ai and the deaths of thirty-six Jewish soldiers. It also led to his own death and that of the members of his family.

The delegation gave a wise word of counsel: "Come over and dwell with us, because we have the Lord's tabernacle in our land" (22:19, paraphrase). No man-made altar could substitute for the presence of the Lord among His people in His tabernacle. It's too bad the two and a half tribes didn't take this advice and claim their inheritance within the land that God had promised to bless (Deut. 11:10-32).

The argument (Josh. 22:21-29). The accused tribes invoked the name of the Lord six times as they replied to the charges; and in so doing, they used the three fundamental names for the Lord: "El [the Mighty One], Elohim [God], Jehovah [the Lord]." It was a solemn oath that their intentions were pure and that the Lord knew their hearts.

Of course, the fact that the Lord knows our hearts, and that we've taken an oath, is no guarantee that our actions are right, *because we don't know our own hearts* (Jer. 17:9). All sorts of questionable activities can be shielded by, "But the Lord knows my heart!" Paul gives us the right approach in 2 Corinthians 8:21; "For we are taking pains to do what is right, not only in the eyes of the Lord but also in the eyes of men" (NIV). When a whole nation misinterprets what is supposed to be a good deed, and it brings them to the brink of war, then there must be something wrong with that deed.

The accused tribes made it clear that they weren't setting up a rival religion because the altar they built wasn't for sacrifices. Rather, they were putting up a witness that would remind the tribes west of the Jordan that Reuben, Gad, and Manasseh were a part of the Jewish nation.

It's interesting that the Transjordanic tribes pointed to the children as their concern. But it wasn't *their* children who would ask, "What have we to do with the

Lord God of Israel?" No, their children would be provoked by the children of the tribes in Canaan! Reuben, Gad, and Manasseh were not even living in the land of God's choice, *yet they feared lest the children across the river would lead their children astray!* It seems to me that the danger was just the opposite.

Not only did the Transjordanic tribes accuse their fellow Jews of having worldly children, but they even accused God of creating the problem in the first place! "For the Lord has made the Jordan a border between you and us" (Josh. 22:25, NKJV). No! *They were the ones who had made the Jordan River the dividing line!* In choosing to live east of the Jordan, the two and a half tribes separated themselves from their own people and from the land God had given to all of them. They put their cattle ahead of their children and their fellow Jews, but they blamed God and the other tribes for the problem that they created.

What kind of "witness" was this huge pile of stones? Was it a witness to the unity of the nation and to the obedience of the Transjordanic tribes? No, it was a witness to *expediency,* the wisdom of man in trying to enjoy "the best of both worlds." The two and a half tribes talked piously about their children, but it was their wealth that really motivated their decision to live east of the Jordan.

Somewhere near this "witness altar" were the twelve stones that the men had carried from the midst of the Jordan River (4:20-24). It reminded the Jews that they had crossed the river and buried their past forever. Reuben, Gad, and the half tribe of Manasseh had crossed the river *and gone back again.* Their "altar" contradicted the altar that Joshua had erected to the glory of God. "If then you were raised with Christ, seek those things which are above, where Christ is, sitting at the right hand of God" (Col. 3:1, NKJV).

4. Their happy agreement (Josh. 22:30-34)

Phinehas was pleased, the delegation was pleased, and the Children of Israel across the Jordan were pleased; *but was the Lord pleased?* The delegation rejoiced that the purpose of the altar was for witness and not sacrifice, and this seemed to settle the matter. They rejoiced that God wouldn't send judgment to the land (v. 31) and that there would be no civil war in Israel (v. 33). *But the nation was divided, in spite of the "altar of witness."* Like Abraham and Lot (Gen. 13), part of the nation had a spiritual outlook while the other part was concerned with material things.

"Peace at any price" isn't God's will for His people. This decision in Gilead was made on the basis of human wisdom and not God's truth. "But the wisdom that is from above is *first pure,* then peaceable" (James 3:17, italics mine). *The peace that God's people achieve at the price of purity and truth is only a dangerous truce that eventually explodes into painful division.* There is always a place in human relations for loving conciliation, but never for cowardly compromise. "I charge you before God and the Lord Jesus Christ and the elect angels that you observe these things without prejudice, doing nothing with partiality" (1 Tim. 5:21, NKJV).

The Transjordanic tribes named their altar "A witness between us that the Lord is God" (NIV). (The Hebrew word *edh* means "witness.") But if the Lord is God, why didn't they obey Him and live in the land He had appointed for them? The stones may have been a witness, but the people certainly were not. Surrounded by heathen nations and separated from their brothers and sisters across the river, these tribes quickly fell into idolatry and were eventually taken by Assyria (1 Chron. 5:25-26).

On September 30, 1938, British Prime Minister Sir Neville Chamberlain, just back from Germany, told a gathering at 10 Downing Street: "My good friends, this is the second time in our history that there has come back from Germany to Downing Street peace with honor. I believe it is peace for our time. We thank you from the bottom of our hearts. And now I recommend you to go home and sleep quietly in your beds."

Less than a year later, England was at war with Germany; and World War II had burst upon the world.

Church history is replete with agreements and accords that magnified unity over purity and truth, and therefore never lasted. Whether in our personal relationships in our homes and churches, or in our nation, the only peace that lasts is peace that is based on truth and purity. It's a peace that demands sacrifice and courage, and a willingness to stand up for God's Word; but the results are worth it.

The well-known Bible commentator, Matthew Henry, said it best: "Peace is such a precious jewel that I would give anything for it but truth."

CHAPTER TWELVE
THE WAY OF ALL THE EARTH
Joshua 23–24

The well-known psychoanalyst Eric Fromm wrote in *Man for Himself*, "To die is poignantly bitter, but the idea of having to die without having lived is unbearable."

Joshua the son of Nun had lived! His long life started in Egyptian bondage and ended in a worship service in the Promised Land. In between those events God had used him to lead Israel in defeating the enemy, conquering the land, and claiming the promised inheritance. With the Apostle Paul, Joshua could sincerely say, "I have fought a good fight, I have finished my course, I have kept the faith" (2 Tim. 4:7, KJV).

Joshua was about to go "the way of all the earth" (Josh. 23:14), the way you and I must go if the Lord doesn't return first. But at the end of a long and full life, Joshua's greatest concern wasn't himself. His greatest concern was his people and their relationship to the Lord. He didn't want to leave until he had challenged them once again to love the Lord and keep His commandments. His life's work would be in vain if they failed to keep the covenant and enjoy the blessings of the Promised Land.

He first called a meeting of the leaders of the nation (v. 2), either at Shiloh or at his home in Ephraim, and warned them what would happen if they deserted the Lord. Then he gathered "all the tribes of Israel to Shechem" (24:1) and gave a farewell address which reviewed the history of Israel, starting with Abraham, and challenged the people to love the Lord and serve Him alone. In these two addresses Joshua emphasized three important topics.

1. Israel's future dangers (Josh. 23:1-16)

Having assembled the leaders of the nation, Joshua presented them with two scenarios: Obey the Lord, and He will bless you and keep you in the land; disobey Him, and He will judge you and remove you from the land. These were the terms of the covenant God had made with Israel at Mount Sinai, which Moses had repeated on the Plains of Moab, and which Israel had reaffirmed at Mt. Ebal and Mt. Gerizim.

Joshua's emphasis was on possessing the land (v. 5) and enjoying its blessings (vv. 13, 15-16). While Israel had gained control of Canaan, there still remained territory to possess and pockets of resistance to overcome. (See 13:1-13; 15:63; 16:10; 17:12-13; 18:3; Judg. 1-2.) The task of the tribes wasn't finished! The great danger, of course, was that the people of Israel would gradually change their attitudes toward the pagan nations around them and start accepting their ways and imitating them.

To counteract this danger, Joshua gave the people three strong motives for remaining a separated people and serving the Lord faithfully.

What the Lord did for Israel (Josh. 23:3-4). From the day that Israel left Egypt, the Lord had fought for His people and delivered them from their enemies. He drowned the Egyptian army in the sea and then defeated the Amalekites who attacked the Jews soon after they left Egypt (Ex. 17). The Lord defeated all of Israel's enemies as the nation marched toward Canaan, and He gave His people victory over the nations in the Promised Land.

This review of history reminded Israel of two great facts: Those Gentile nations were God's enemies and therefore must be Israel's enemies; and the same God who overcame the enemy in the past could help Israel overcome them in the future. God had never failed His people; and, if they would trust Him and obey His Word, He would help them completely conquer the land. "For the Lord your God is He who has fought for you" (Josh. 23:3, NKJV).

This is a good reminder to God's people today. As we read the Bible and see what God did in the past for those who trusted Him, it encourages us to trust Him today and face all our enemies with courage and confidence. The Presbyterian missionary leader A.T. Pierson used to say that "history is His story"; and this is true. From age to age, God may change His methods; but His character never changes, and He can be trusted.

What the Lord said to Israel (Josh. 23:5-10). The secret of Joshua's success, and therefore the reason for Israel's victories, was his devotion to the Word of God (vv. 6, 14; see 1:7-9, 13-18; 8:30-35; 11:12, 15; 24:26-27). He obeyed God's commandments and believed God's promises, and God worked on his behalf. But even more, his devotion to the Word of God enabled Joshua to get to know God better, to love Him, and to want to please Him. It isn't enough to know the Word of God. We must also know the God of the Word and grow in our fellowship with Him.

God kept all His promises, and He had every right to expect Israel to keep all His commandments as well. Some of God's promises are unconditional, but some of them are conditional and depend on our obedience for their fulfillment. Israel entered and conquered the land as the fulfillment of God's promise, but their enjoyment of the land depended on their obedience to the Law of the Lord. God would enable them to claim all their inheritance if they would obey Him with all their hearts.

The most important thing was that Israel remain a separated people and not be infected by the wickedness of the Gentile nations around them (23:7-8; see Ex. 34:10-17; Deut. 7:2–4). Joshua warned them that their disobedience would be a gradual thing. First they would associate with these nations in a familiar way; then they would start discussing their religious practices; and before long Israel would be worshiping the false gods of the enemy. The Jewish men would then start marrying women from these pagan nations, and the line of separation between God's people and the world would be completely erased. Imagine the folly of *worshiping the gods of the defeated enemy!*

All of us feel the pressures of the world around us, trying to force us to conform (Rom. 12:1-21; 1 John 2:15-17); and it takes courage to defy the crowd and stay true to the Lord (Josh. 23:7). But it also takes love for the Lord and a desire to please Him (v. 8). The word translated "cleave" in verse 8 is used in Genesis 2:24 to describe a husband's relationship to his wife. Israel was "married" to Jehovah at Mount Sinai (Jer. 2:1-3; Ezek. 16) and was expected to be a faithful spouse and cleave to the Lord (Deut. 4:4; 10:20; 11:22; 13:4). How tragic that she became an unfaithful wife, a prostitute, as she turned to the gods of other nations.

The promise in Joshua 23:10 is quoted from Deuteronomy 32:30, which shows how well Joshua knew the Word of God. (See also Lev. 26:7-8.) He meditated on God's Word day and night (Josh. 1:8; Ps. 1:2) and hid it in his heart (Ps. 119:11).

What the Lord would do to Israel (Josh. 23:11-16). The Word of God is like a two-edged sword (Heb. 4:12): If we obey it, God will bless and help us; if we disobey it, God will chasten us until we submit to Him. If we love the Lord (Josh. 23:11), we'll want to obey Him and please Him; so the essential thing is that we cultivate a satisfying relationship with God.

Joshua reminded the people that God's Word never fails, whether it's the Word of promise for blessing or the Word of promise for chastening. Both are evidences of His love, for "whom the Lord loveth He chasteneth" (Prov. 3:11-12; Heb. 12:6). Charles Spurgeon said, "God will not allow His children to sin successfully."

Moses had warned Israel against compromising with the evil nations in the land (Ex. 23:20-33; 34:10-17; Deut. 7:12–26), and Joshua reaffirmed that warning (Josh. 23:13). If Israel began to mingle with these nations, two things would happen: God would remove His blessing, and Israel would be defeated; and these nations would bring distress and defeat to Israel. Joshua used vivid words like *snares, traps, scourges,* and *thorns* to impress the Jews with the suffering they would experience if they disobeyed the Lord. The final stroke of chastening would be Israel's removal from their land to a land of exile. After all, if you want to live and worship like the Gentiles, then live with the Gentiles! This happened when God permitted Babylon to conquer Judah, destroy Jerusalem, and take thousands of the Jews into exile in Babylon.

Three times in this brief address Joshua called Canaan "this good land" (vv. 13, 15-16). When God called Moses at the burning bush, He promised to take Israel into a "good land" (Ex. 3:8); and Joshua and Caleb described Canaan as "a good land" after forty days of investigation (Num. 14:7). In his farewell message Moses used the phrase "good land" at least ten times (Deut. 1:25, 35; 3:25; 4:21-22; 6:18; 8:7, 10; 9:6; 11:17). The argument is obvious: Since God has given us such a good land, the least we can do is live to please Him.

Meditating on the goodness of God is a strong motivation for obedience. James connects the goodness of God with our resisting of temptation (James 1:13-17), and Nathan took the same approach when he confronted King David with his sins (2 Sam. 12:1-15). It was not his own badness but his father's goodness that brought the prodigal son to repentance and then back home (Luke 15:17). "The goodness of God leads you to repentance" (Rom. 2:4, NKJV). The danger is that the material blessings from the Lord can so possess our hearts that we focus on the gifts and forget the Giver, and this leads to sin (Deut. 8).

Joshua's three main admonitions in this address need to be heeded by God's people today: Keep God's Word (Josh. 23:6), cleave to the Lord (v. 8), and love the Lord (v. 11). Too many Christians have not only compromised with the enemy but also have capitulated to the enemy, and the Lord is not first in their lives.

2. Israel's past blessings (Josh. 24:1-13)

In the April 15, 1978 issue of *Saturday Review,* the late author and editor Norman Cousins called history "a vast early warning system"; and philosopher George Santayana said, "Those who cannot remember the past are condemned to repeat it." A knowledge of their roots is very important to the Jews because they are God's chosen people with a destiny to fulfill in this world.

Shechem was the ideal location for this moving farewell address by Israel's great leader. It was at Shechem that God promised Abraham that his descendants would inherit the land (Gen. 12:6-7), and there Jacob built an altar (33:20). Shechem was located between Mt. Ebal and Mt. Gerizim, where the people of Israel had reaffirmed their commitment to the Lord (Josh. 8:30-35). Shechem was indeed "holy ground" to the Israelites.

If *nation* and *land* were the key words in Joshua's first address, then *the Lord* is the major focus in this second address; for Joshua refers to the Lord twenty-one times. In fact, in 24:2-13, it is the Lord who speaks as Joshua reviews the history of the nation. Another key word is *serve,* used fifteen times in this address. Jehovah gave them their land and would bless them in their land if they loved Him and served Him.

God chose Israel (Josh. 24:1-4). Abraham and his family were idolaters when God called Abraham to leave Ur of the Chaldees and go to Canaan (Gen. 11:27-12:9). "The God of glory appeared unto our father Abraham," declared Stephen in his own farewell speech (Acts 7:2), reminding the Jews that their national identity was *an act of God's grace.* Abraham didn't seek after God and discover Him; it was God who came to Abraham! There was nothing special about the Jews that God should choose them (Deut. 7:1-11; 26:1-11; 32:10); and this fact should have kept them humble and obedient.

"You did not choose Me," Jesus told His disciples, "but I chose you and appointed you" (John 15:16, NKJV). Believers were chosen in Christ "before the foundation of the world" (Eph. 1:4) and are called "God's elect" (Rom. 8:33; Titus 1:1). One of my professors in seminary used to say, "Try to explain election and you may lose your mind, but explain it away and you may lose your soul." No matter what "school" of theology we belong to, all of us must admit that *God takes the first step in our salvation.*

Abraham's firstborn son was Ishmael (Gen. 16), but God rejected him and gave His covenant to Isaac, the child of Abraham and Sarah's old age (17-18, 21). Isaac had two sons, Jacob and Esau; and God chose Jacob. Paul called these choices God's purpose "according to election"

(Rom. 9:11). Esau became the ancestor of the Edomites in Mount Seir, and Jacob became the father of the twelve tribes of Israel. Eventually, the Children of Israel went to Egypt, where God made them into a great nation.

One of the repeated titles for God in the Book of Joshua is "the Lord God of Israel," used fifteen times (7:13, 19-20; 8:30; 9:18-19; 10:40, 42; 13:14, 33; 14:14; 22:16, 24; 24:2, 23). The Jews were indeed an elect and a special people; for the Lord of heaven chose to associate His great name with them and be their God.

God delivered Israel (Josh. 24:5-7). God sent Joseph ahead to Egypt to preserve the nation during the famine (Ps. 105:16–22), and then He sent Moses and Aaron to deliver the nation from bondage (vv. 23-45). Egypt had been saved from starvation because of the Jews; but instead of being grateful, the rulers of Egypt eventually enslaved the Jews and made their lives bitter (Ex. 3:7-9). All of this was a fulfillment of what God had promised to Abraham centuries before (Gen. 15:1–17), but their suffering in Egypt only made the Israelites multiply more.

God judged the gods and rulers of Egypt by sending ten plagues to the land, climaxing with the death of the firstborn (Ex. 7-12). Only then did stubborn Pharaoh give the Jews permission to leave the land, but then he changed his mind and sent his army after them. God not only brought His people *out,* but He also led them *through* the Red Sea and drowned the Egyptian army in its waters (chaps. 14-15).

God instructed His people to observe the Passover as an annual reminder of their redemption from Egyptian bondage (chaps. 12-13). In his farewell speech Moses frequently reminded the Jews that they had once been slaves in Egypt but the Lord had set them free (5:15; 6:12; 8:14; 13:5, 10; 15:15; 16:3, 6; 20:1; 24:22). It does a believer good to remember what it was like to be in bondage to sin and then to rejoice in the redemption that was purchased so dearly for us on the cross. It's a dangerous thing to take the gift of salvation for granted.

God guided Israel (Josh. 24:8-10). God brought Israel out that He might bring them in (Deut. 6:23). His goal for them was the Promised Land, but their sin at Kadesh Barnea caused them to wander in the wilderness until the old unbelieving generation had died off As Israel marched behind the Ark of God, the Lord defeated their enemies. When Balaam tried to curse Israel, God turned the curse into a blessing (Num. 22-24; Deut. 23:5; Neh. 13:2). Whether Satan came against Israel as the lion (the army of the Amorites) or as the serpent (the curses of Balaam), the Lord defeated him.

God gave them their land (Josh. 24:11-13). The same God who took Israel through the Red Sea also took them across the Jordan River and into their inheritance. Except for a temporary defeat at Ai (Josh. 7), and a humiliating compromise with Gibeon (chap. 9), Joshua and his army defeated every enemy in the land because the Lord was with them.

The "hornet" mentioned in 24:12 (see Ex. 23:28; Deut. 7:20) may have been the insect whose sting is extremely painful, but it's possible that the word is an image of something else. Invading armies are compared to bees (Deut. 1:44; Ps. 118:12; Isa. 7:18), and some students think that's the meaning here. God sent other armies into Canaan to weaken the people and prepare them for the invasion of Israel.

But perhaps the hornets better represent the reports that came to Canaan of

Israel's conquests, reports that frightened and almost paralyzed the inhabitants of the land. The words of Rahab describe the panic of the Canaanites because of what they heard about Israel: "And as soon as we had heard these things, our hearts did melt, neither did there remain any more courage in any man, because of you" (Josh. 2:11; see 5:1 and 9:24). God had promised to do this and He kept His promise (Deut. 2:25).

In Joshua 24:13, God's words remind us of what Moses said to Israel in Deuteronomy 6:10ff. Once again, the emphasis is on the goodness of God and all that He did for Israel because He loved them. When the Jews started taking their blessings for granted, they began drifting away from sincere worship of the Lord. A grateful heart is a strong defense against the devil's temptations.

3. Israel's present responsibilities (Josh. 24:14-33)

One of the key words in this section is *serve*, used fifteen times. To serve God means to fear Him, obey Him, and worship only Him. It means to love Him and fix your heart upon Him, obeying Him because you want to and not because you have to.

Decision (Josh. 24:14-18). Joshua made it clear that the people of Israel had to make a decision to serve the Lord God of Israel. There could be no neutrality. But if they served the Lord, then they would have to get rid of the false gods that some of them secretly were worshiping. Even after the great experience of the Exodus, some of the Jews still sacrificed to the gods of Egypt (Lev. 17:7; Amos 5:25-26; Acts 7:42-43; Ezek. 20:6-8). Jacob had given this same warning to his family (Gen. 35:2), and Samuel would give the same admonition in his day (1 Sam. 7:3ff).

Joshua wasn't suggesting that the people could choose to worship the false gods of the land, and God would accept it; for there was no other option but to serve Jehovah. Being a wise and spiritual man, Joshua knew that everybody must worship something or someone, whether they realized it or not, because humanity is "incurably religious." If the Jews didn't worship the true God, they would end up worshiping the false gods of the wicked nations in Canaan. His point was that *they couldn't do both.*

The people assured Joshua that they wanted to worship and serve only the Lord God of Israel, and they gave their reasons. The Lord had delivered them from Egypt, brought them through the wilderness, and taken them into their Promised Land. (The first half of Joshua's address [Josh. 24:1-13] had made an impression on them!) Joshua had declared that he and his house would serve only the Lord (v. 15), and the people said, "Therefore will we also serve the Lord; for he is our God" (v. 18).

Devotion (Josh. 24:19-28). When the former generation had met the Lord at Mount Sinai, they had said, "All that the Lord has spoken we will do" (Ex. 19:8, NKJV). But a few weeks later, they were worshiping a golden calf! Joshua knew that it was easy for the people to *promise* obedience to the Lord, but it was quite something else for them to actually *do* it. His stern words were meant to curb their overconfidence and make them look honestly into their own hearts (Josh. 24:19).

Israel was "married" to Jehovah, and He would not tolerate any rivals in their hearts. He is a jealous God (Ex. 20:5) and a holy God, and He could never permit them to be divided in their loyalty. Just as a husband and wife are faithful to their marriage vows and jealously guard their mate's affection, so Israel and the Lord had to be faithful to each other.

Joshua warned them what would happen if they didn't get rid of their idols: They would eventually forsake the Lord, and then He would have to chasten them. They would lose all the blessings He had so graciously given them in the Promised Land. Their great need was to cleanse their hearts of allegiance to other gods and to incline their hearts only to the Lord (Josh. 24:23). If they persisted in their hidden disloyalty, God would not forgive them (Ex. 23:21) but would punish them for their sins.

Three times the people affirmed their desire to serve only the Lord (Josh. 24:16-18, 21, 24), and Joshua took them at their word. So that they wouldn't forget this solemn covenant with Jehovah, Joshua wrote it in the Book of the Law and then set up a large stone as a perpetual witness to their agreement. This is the ninth and last memorial mentioned in the Book of Joshua. The nine memorials are:

1. The stones in the midst of the Jordan (4:9).
2. The stones on the western bank of the Jordan (4:20-24).
3. The stones in the Valley of Achor (7:26).
4. The heap of stones at Ai (8:29).
5. The altar on Mt. Ebal (8:30).
6. The stones of the law on Mt. Ebal (8:32).
7. The stones at the cave at Makkedah (10:27).
8. The altar built by the Transjordanic tribes (22:10ff).
9. Joshua's stone of witness (24:26-28).

There's certainly nothing unbiblical about God's people memorializing a wonderful event or a sacred decision, so long as the memorial doesn't become the focus of idolatrous worship. It's good to remember what the Lord did and how we responded, but we must never live in the past. Religious traditions can be helpful or hurtful, depending on how we use them.

The book closes with three burials. Joshua died at the age of 110 and was buried in his own inheritance. Eleazar the high priest (Num. 20:28) died and was also buried in Ephraim, near Shiloh, where his son Phinehas had property. The bones of Joseph were buried in Shechem in the plot of ground Jacob had bought from Hamor (Gen. 33:19). Shechem became an important city for Ephraim and Manasseh, who were the two sons of Joseph. Thus it was fitting that their great ancestor be buried there. (See Gen. 50:25; Ex. 13:19; Heb. 11:22.)

Moses had named Joshua as his successor, but it's significant that God didn't tell Joshua to appoint a successor. The elders who had served with Joshua guided the nation after his death, but then the people went astray and began to disobey the Lord and worship the false gods of the Canaanites (Judg. 2:6-15). Why didn't the next generation know the Lord and what He had done for Israel? *Because the people of Joshua's generation failed to keep their promise and teach their children and grandchildren to fear and serve the Lord.*

God kept His promise and chastened His people, first by bringing other nations into the land (vv. 14-19), and then by taking the Jews out of their land, the Northern Kingdom to Assyria and the Southern Kingdom to Babylon. But one day the Lord will regather His people Israel and establish them in their land (Isa. 11-12; 51-52; Ezek. 36:24ff). Then "the earth shall be filled with the knowledge of the glory of the Lord, as the waters cover the sea" (Hab. 2:14).

CHAPTER THIRTEEN
A GREAT LIFE IN REVIEW

In his *Autobiography,* Mark Twain wrote: "Biographies are but the clothes and buttons of the man—the biography of the man himself cannot be written."

The Book of Joshua is not a biography of Joshua in the strictest sense, but it certainly tells us a great deal about this godly man. Like the rest of the Old Testament Scriptures, this book was written both to warn us (1 Cor. 10:11) and to encourage us (Rom. 15:4). Therefore, we ought to take time to review Joshua's life and ministry and learn from him lessons that will help us know the Lord better and serve Him more effectively.

1. Joshua's preparation

When God wants to accomplish something, He prepares a servant for the task and prepares the task for His servant. The Lord invested seventeen years preparing Joseph for His work in Egypt and eighty years getting Moses ready for forty years of ministry to the people of Israel. David experienced many years of trials and testings before he ascended the throne of Israel. "A prepared servant for a prepared place" is God's approach to ministry.

What were some of the "tools" God used to prepare Joshua for his ministry?

Suffering. Joshua was born into Egyptian slavery and knew what it was to suffer. In Exodus 3:7-9, the Lord's words make it clear that the Jews experienced great affliction in Egypt and cried out to God for deliverance. Nevertheless they had at least three encouragements as they suffered: God's promise to Abraham that his descendants would inherit the land (Gen. 12:7); God's prophecy concerning their deliverance from bondage (15:12-17; see Deut. 4:20); and Joseph's words concerning Israel's deliverance and possession of the Promised Land (Gen. 50:22-26).

God's pattern for life is that suffering must come before glory. This was true of our Savior (Luke 24:26; 1 Peter 1:11) and it is true of His people (1 Peter 4:13; 5:10). When we suffer in the will of God and depend on His grace, that suffering has a maturing and purifying effect on our lives. Sadly, we have too many leaders today who proudly display their medals, but they can't show you any scars. Our Lord's Calvary wounds are now glorified in heaven, eternal reminders that suffering and glory go together in the purposes of God.

Of itself, suffering doesn't make people better. Sometimes it makes them bitter. But when suffering is mixed with faith and God's grace, then it becomes a wonderful tool for building godly character (2 Cor. 12:1-10). If suffering alone gave people wisdom and character, then our world would be a far better place, because everybody suffers in one way or another. When we accept our suffering as a gift from God and use it for His glory, then it can work in us and for us to accomplish the will of God.

Submission. Joshua knew how to submit to authority. As leader of the Jewish army, he followed Moses' orders and defeated the Amalekites (Ex. 17:8-16). As Moses' "assistant" for many years (24:13), Joshua stayed with his master and served him faithfully. God's pattern for leadership is summarized in Matthew 25:21, and that pattern still stands today: when we prove ourselves faithful as servants over a few things, then God can make us rulers over many things. Joshua was able to *give* orders because he'd learned how to *take* orders.

Because he was submitted to authority, Joshua was an obedient servant. During the first half of his life, he obeyed Moses; and during the last half, he received his orders from the Lord. The key verse in Joshua's life was, "Be careful to obey all the law My servant Moses gave you; do not turn from it to the right or to the left, that you may be successful wherever you go" (Josh. 1:7, NIV). This should be balanced with 11:15, "As the Lord commanded Moses, his servant, so did Moses command Joshua, and so did Joshua; he left nothing undone of all that the Lord commanded Moses."

Delay. It's through faith and patience that we inherit what God has promised (Heb. 6:12). Had the people of Israel listened to Joshua and Caleb, they would have entered their inheritance four decades sooner and enjoyed it that much longer (Num. 13:26-14:10). Both Joshua and Caleb patiently endured the trials of the wilderness because they knew they would one day claim their inheritance in the Promised Land. In their unbelief, the Jews rejected "the work of faith" and refused to enter the land; but they couldn't rob Joshua of his "patience of hope" (1 Thess. 1:3).

Leaders must learn how to wait. Often their followers don't always see as far as they see or have the faith that they have. The vision of future victory is what motivates a true leader; but, like Israel, too often the people are looking back. I suppose every leader has at one time or another identified with Jesus when He said, "O unbelieving and perverse generation, how long shall I stay with you and put up with you?" (Luke 9:41, NIV) On more than one occasion Joshua witnessed Moses pouring out his heart to God because of the unbelief and stubbornness of the people.

2. Joshua's leadership

Are leaders born or made? Probably both. God gives them the genetic structure they need and then develops their gifts and abilities in the "school of life." Management seminars promise to teach *leadership;* but if there isn't some fuel there to ignite, the fire won't burn. Principles of leadership certainly may be taught, but what it means to be a leader can only be learned on the field of action. To think you're a leader because you attended a seminar is as dangerous as thinking you're an athlete because you watched the Olympics on television.

What were the characteristics of Joshua's leadership style?

He walked with God. Like Moses, his predecessor, Joshua was a man of God. Whoever the Holy Spirit selected to complete the Book of Joshua was led to call him "the servant of the Lord," a title not given to everybody in Scripture. We aren't told that God spoke with Joshua face to face, as He had with Moses (Deut. 34:10); but we do know that God communicated His will to Joshua and that he was obedient. Joshua meditated daily on the Law of the Lord (Josh. 1:8) and did what it said (11:15). He was a man of prayer (7:6-9), for the Word of God and prayer go together (Acts 6:4).

He had courage. At the beginning of his ministry Joshua was told four times to "be courageous" (Josh. 1:6-7, 9, 18). It takes courage to be a successful leader, courage to stand for what you believe, and courage to do what you know God wants you to do. All of us need to imitate Martin Luther when he said, "Here I stand. I can do no other."

General Omar Bradley defined bravery as "the capacity to perform properly even when scared half to death." We aren't told whether Joshua was ever afraid as he faced the enemy, but we do know that he did his job and won battle after battle. Most of us aren't called upon to lead armies, but any kind of leadership involves risks and demands moral courage. "He who loves his life will lose it, and he who hates his life in this world will keep it for eternal life" (John 12:25, NKJV). If we're timid about life and ministry, we'll never accomplish much for the Lord. It was because the servant was afraid that he hid his master's wealth and didn't take the risk of investing it (Matt. 25:24-30).

Joshua's courage involved much more than fighting the enemy, as great as that was. He also had the courage to deal with sin in the camp of Israel (Josh. 7) and to challenge the tribes to "get with it" and claim their inheritance (17:14-18). Sometimes it takes more courage to face your own people at home than it takes to face the enemy on the battlefield.

He had a plan and followed it. The conquest of Canaan wasn't a haphazard affair; it was carefully planned and skillfully executed. First, Joshua cut straight across the land and isolated the north from the south. Then he conquered the cities in the south, followed by the invasion of the north. He moved quickly to subdue the population centers and take control of the whole land. More than once, Joshua led his men on an all-night march in order to catch the enemy by surprise.

It takes planning and strategy to do the work of the Lord successfully. The leader who drifts with the tide and changes direction with every new wind isn't a leader at all. A Roman proverb says, "When the pilot doesn't know what port he's heading for, no wind is the right wind." If you know where you're going, you can adjust your sails when the storm starts to blow and still arrive at the right port.

He didn't quit. When he was defeated at Ai, Joshua admitted failure, sought the face of the Lord, went back, and won the battle. When he foolishly made a league with the Gibeonites, he admitted his mistake and put it to work for him. The successful leader isn't the one who is always right, because no such person exists. Successful leaders are people who make the best decisions they can and keep on going when they make mistakes. They learn from their mistakes and know how to snatch victory out of defeat.

The American humorist Elbert Hubbard said, "Experience is the name everyone gives his mistakes." Someone has said that experience is a tough teacher because it always gives the exam first and teaches the lesson afterward. If we turn our mistakes into mirrors, we'll see only ourselves; and this will make us miserable. But if by faith we turn our mistakes into windows, we'll see the Lord and get the strength we need to try again. To quote Elbert Hubbard again: "There is no failure except in no longer trying."

He enlisted others and commanded their respect. Except for Achan, the traitor at Jericho, and Caleb, the man of faith, we don't know the names of any of the soldiers who served with Joshua; *but he couldn't have done the job without them.* The conquest of Canaan wasn't the work of one man; it was the work of thousands of people who served faithfully in the battle and behind the lines.

True leaders don't *demand* respect; they *command* it. When you read Joshua 1:10-18 and see the way the troops responded to Joshua's orders, you can't help but conclude that he commanded their respect and loyalty. He was serving the Lord and the Lord's people, and they followed him because they knew they could trust him. His motives were pure, his life was godly, and his character was above reproach.

As Moses' successor and God's appointed leader, Joshua had *authority;* but it takes more than authority to lead others. It also takes *stature,* the kind of character and achievement that will make people look up to you and listen to you. In this day of "media magic," a public relations firm can "hype" a nobody into becoming an international celebrity; but they can't give that celebrity the kind of stature that can come only from sacrifice and service. We don't need more celebrities, but we certainly do need more servants.

Real leaders don't use people to build their authority; they use their authority to build people. Many a soldier in the Jewish army became a hero because Joshua was in command. A true leader is one who leaves behind people who have achieved far more than they would have achieved had they not followed his or her leadership.

He was concerned about the future. When King Hezekiah was told that the kingdom of Judah would eventually go into captivity in Babylon, his response was, "At least there will be peace and truth in my days" (Isa. 39:8, NKJV). I don't want to be critical of a great king, but this statement seems to reek of selfishness. Isn't a king supposed to be concerned about the generations to come?

Joshua's two farewell speeches (chaps. 23-24) give ample evidence that he was a true leader, burdened for the future of his country. He wanted to be sure that the people knew the Lord and wanted to serve Him with their whole heart. People who think only of what they can get today are only opportunists and not true leaders. Leadership means planting the right seeds that will bear fruit in years to come for the benefit of others, and Joshua did that.

He glorified God. There was a time in Joshua's life when he was jealous for the honor of his master, Moses (Num. 11:24–30); but he learned that the most important thing was the glory of the Lord. When the nation crossed the Jordan, it was God who received the glory. "By this you shall know that the living God is among you!" he told the people (Josh. 3:10, NKJV). When that miracle march was over, Joshua put up a monument so that Israel and "all the peoples of the earth may know the hand of the Lord, that it is mighty" (4:24, NKJV). A lesser man would have put up a monument glorifying himself.

As you read the book that Joshua wrote, you see that he repeatedly gave God the glory for all that happened (6:16; 8:1; 10:14; 11:6-8; 13:6; 18:3; 21:43-45). It was the Lord who conquered the enemy and gave the land to the people. It was the name of the Lord that was to be magnified in all the earth. It has been said that a leader is somebody who takes twice as much blame and half as much credit, and Joshua would qualify on both counts.

3. Joshua's message

The practical message of the Book of Joshua is that God keeps His promises and enables His servants to succeed if they will trust Him and obey His Word. The spiritual message is that God has a rich inheritance for His children *now,* and they can claim it by faith. This message is amplified in the Book of Hebrews, especially chapters 3 and 4.

We have seen that, when it comes to the things of the Lord, there are several different kinds of people in this world. Most people are still in bondage in Egypt and need to be delivered by faith in Jesus Christ. Others have trusted Christ and been delivered from bondage but are wandering in the wilderness of unbelief because they won't enter into their inheritance by faith. Still others have "sampled" the inheritance but prefer to live on the borders of the blessing. Finally, there are those who follow their Joshua (Jesus = "Jehovah is salvation") and enter the Promised Land and claim their inheritance.

Remember, crossing the Jordan and entering the land is not a picture of dying and going to heaven. It's a picture of dying to self and the old life and entering our spiritual inheritance here and now, enjoying the fullness of God's blessing as we serve the Lord and glorify Him. It's what Hebrews 4 and 5 call "entering into His rest."

The greatest need in the church today is for God's people to see how much they are missing by wandering in unbelief, or by living on the borderline of the blessing, and then to claim God's promises and enter into their spiritual inheritance. We're a deprived people because we've failed to claim our spiritual riches; and we're a defeated people because we've failed to trust our Joshua to lead us on to victory. Too many of us are like Achan, stealing from God, when we ought to be like Caleb, claiming the mountains and overcoming the giants.

4. Joshua's God

The Lord, not Joshua, is the key person in this book. As you read the Book of Joshua, you discover many wonderful truths about God.

To begin with, He is the God of His people Israel, the God of the covenant that He made with Israel through Moses. Though Moses was dead, the living God was still at work in and through His chosen people. When Joshua commanded the people, he often called God "the Lord your God." Israel belonged to Him.

But He is also "the Lord of all the earth" (Josh. 3:11). While He has a special relationship to Israel, He established that relationship in order to bring His blessing to all the nations (Gen. 12:1-3). The pagan nations in Canaan heard about what God had done for Israel, and they were frightened (Josh. 2:10-11); for none of their gods had ever done such mighty deeds.

He is the God who keeps His promises. He had promised the fathers of the Jewish nation that He would give them their land, and He kept His promise. He had promised Moses that Israel would drive out the nations in Canaan and defeat them, and He kept that promise too. At the close of his life Joshua was able to say to his people that not one thing had failed of all the good things that the Lord their God spoke concerning them (23:14).

He is a holy God who will not tolerate sin. When Achan disobeyed the ban that God had put on Jericho, God withdrew His blessing. The army of Israel was defeated at Ai, and they could not expect victory until Joshua dealt with the sin in the camp. But He is also a forgiving God who cleanses us when we confess our sins, and then gives us another opportunity for victory.

He is a God who requires obedience on the part of His people. Before Israel could enter the land, they had to submit to the requirements that God had laid down; for they were His covenant people. The Lord told Joshua that the secret of his success would be faith and obedience to the Word of God. God had a plan for the conquest of the land; all Joshua had to do was obey that plan.

He is the God who never fails! We may fail Him, but He will never fail us. "When God ordains our service," wrote J. Oswald Sanders, "He is morally obligated to see us through" (*Robust in Faith,* p. 72).

Although much more could be said, let's close on this note: He is a God who is gracious. In view of the fact that thousands of people were slain during the conquest of Canaan, it may seem strange to think about God's grace; but the grace of God was there just the same. God was gracious to delay His judgment for centuries before bringing Israel into the land (Gen. 15:16). He was gracious to send the reports about Israel into the land so that the people could fear and, like Rahab, turn to the Lord. He was gracious to wipe out the filthy religion of the Canaanites so that the Jewish boys and girls could grow up in a land where Jehovah was honored and worshiped.

When I was about to graduate from seminary, our class went on a weekend retreat; and for one of his messages, the speaker used Joshua 3:5 as his text: "Sanctify yourselves: for tomorrow the Lord will do wonders among you." I've forgotten the outline, but I remember the message: Our tomorrows can be exciting and wonderful if we are all that God wants us to be.

He is still the God of wonders, and He is still calling us to be a sanctified people who will trust and obey. The God of Joshua lives—but where are the Joshuas?

Endnotes

Chapter 5

1. Dr. and Mrs. Howard Taylor, *Biography of James Hudson Taylor* (London: China Inland Mission, 1965), p. 271.
2. Andrew A. Bonar, *Memoir and Remains of Robert Murray McCheyne* (London: Banner of Truth Trust, 1966), p. 282.

Chapter Six

1. Francis A. Schaeffer, *Joshua and the Flow of Biblical History* (Downers Grove, Ill.: InterVarsity Press, 1975), pp. 102-3.
2. G. Campbell Morgan, *Living Messages of the Books of the Bible* (Old Tappan, N.J.: Fleming H. Revell, 1912), vol. 1, p. 104.
3. Ibid., p. 114.

Chapter 7

1. George H. Morrison, *The Footsteps of the Flock* (London: Hodder and Stoughton, 1904), p. 106.

Chapter 8

1. Frederick W. Robertson, *Sermons Preached at Brighton, First Series* (London: Kegan Paul, Trench, Trubner and Co., 1898), p. 66.

Chapter 9

1. See *Encyclopedia of Bible Difficulties,* by Gleason L. Archer (Grand Rapids: Zondervan, 1982), pp. 161-62.
2. C.S. Lewis, *Miracles* (New York: Macmillan, 1960), p. 133.

JUDGES

A SUGGESTED OUTLINE OF THE BOOK OF JUDGES

Theme: Obedience brings God's blessing; disobedience brings God's discipline

Theme verse: Judges 21:25 (see also 17:6; 18:1; 19:1)

I. DISOBEDIENCE: ISRAEL TURNS FROM GOD—1-2

1. Early victories—1:1-26
2. Repeated defeats—1:27-36
3. National apostasy—2:1-15
4. Divine mercy—2:16-23

II. DISCIPLINE: THE LORD CHASTENS ISRAEL—3-16

1. Othniel, Ehud, and Shamgar—3
2. Deborah and Barak—4-5
3. Gideon—6-8
4. Abimelech—9
5. Tola and Jair—10
6. Jephthah—11:1-12:7
7. Ibzan, Elon, and Abdon—12:8-15
8. Samson—13-16

III. DISORDER: ISRAEL SINKS INTO ANARCHY—7-21

1. Religious confusion—17-18
2. Immorality—19
3. Civil war—20-21

CONTENTS

CHAPTER ONE
IT WAS THE WORST OF TIMES
Judges 1–2

FAMILY FEUD LEAVES 69 BROTHERS DEAD!

POWERFUL GOVERNMENT LEADER CAUGHT IN "LOVE NEST."

GANG RAPE LEADS TO VICTIM'S DEATH AND DISMEMBERMENT.

GIRLS AT PARTY KIDNAPPED AND FORCED TO MARRY STRANGERS.

WOMAN JUDGE SAYS TRAVELERS NO LONGER SAFE ON HIGHWAYS.

Sensational headlines like these are usually found on the front page of supermarket tabloids, but the above headlines actually describe some of the events narrated in the Book of Judges.[1] What a contrast they are to the closing chapters of the Book of Joshua, where you see a nation resting from war and enjoying the riches God had given them in the Promised Land. But the Book of Judges pictures Israel suffering from invasion, slavery, poverty, and civil war. What happened?

The nation of Israel quickly decayed after a new generation took over, a generation that knew neither Joshua nor Joshua's God. "And the people served the Lord all the days of Joshua, and all the days of the elders that outlived Joshua, who had seen all the great works of the Lord, that He did for Israel . . . and there arose another generation after them, which knew not the Lord, nor yet the works which He had done for Israel" (Judg. 2:7, 10; and see Josh. 24:31). Instead of exhibiting spiritual fervor, Israel sank into *apathy;* instead of obeying the Lord, the people moved into *apostasy;* and instead of the nation enjoying law and order, the land was filled with *anarchy.* Indeed, for Israel it was the worst of times.

One of the key verses in the Book of Judges is 21:25: "In those days there was no king in Israel; every man did that which was right in his own eyes" (see 17:6; 18:1; 19:1).[2] At Mount Sinai, the Lord had taken Israel to be His "kingdom of priests," declaring that He alone would reign over them (Ex. 19:1-8). Moses reaffirmed the kingship of Jehovah when he explained the covenant to the new generation before they entered Canaan (Deut. 29ff). After the conquest of Jericho and Ai, Joshua declared to Israel her kingdom responsibilities (Josh. 8:30-35), and he reminded the people of them again before his death (Josh. 24). Even Gideon, perhaps the greatest of the judges, refused to set up a royal dynasty. "I will not rule over you," he said, "neither shall my son rule over you: the Lord shall rule over you" (Judg. 8:23).

Deuteronomy 6 outlined the nation's basic responsibilities: love and obey Jehovah as the only true God (vv. 1-5); teach your children God's laws (vv. 6-9); be thankful for God's blessings (vv. 10-15); and separate yourself from the worship of the pagan gods in the land of Canaan (vv. 16-25). Unfortunately, the new generation failed in each of those responsibilities. The people didn't want to "seek ye first the kingdom of God, and His righteousness" (Matt. 6:33); they would rather experiment with the idolatry of the godless nations around them. As a result, Israel plunged into moral, spiritual, and political disaster.

One of two things was true: either the

older generation had failed to instruct their children and grandchildren in the ways of the Lord, or, if they had faithfully taught them, then the new generation had refused to submit to God's Law and follow God's ways. "Righteousness exalts a nation, but sin is a reproach to any people" (Prov. 14:34, NKJV). The Book of Judges is the record of that reproach, and the first two chapters describe four stages in Israel's decline and fall.

1. Fighting the enemy (Judg. 1:1-21)

The Book of Judges begins with a series of victories and defeats that took place after the death of Joshua. The boundary lines for the twelve tribes had been determined years before (Josh. 13-22), but the people had not yet fully claimed their inheritance by defeating and dislodging the entrenched inhabitants of the land. When Joshua was an old man, the Lord said to him, "You are old, advanced in years, and there remains very much land yet to be possessed" (Josh. 13:1, NKJV). The people of Israel *owned* all the land, but they didn't *possess* all of it; and therefore they couldn't *enjoy* all of it.

The victories of Judah (vv. 1-20). Initially the people of Israel wisely sought God's guidance and asked the Lord which tribe was to engage the enemy first. Perhaps God told Judah to go first because Judah was the kingly tribe (Gen. 49:8-9). Judah believed God's promise, obeyed God's counsel, and even asked the people of the tribe of Simeon to go to battle with them. Since Leah had given birth to Judah and Simeon, these tribes were blood brothers (Gen. 35:23). Incidentally, Simeon actually had its inheritance within the tribe of Judah (Josh. 19:1).

When Joshua was Israel's leader, all the tribes worked together in obeying the will of God. In the Book of Judges, however, you don't find the nation working together as a unit. When God needed someone to deliver His people, He called that person out of one of the tribes and told him or her what to do. In obedience to the Lord, Moses had appointed Joshua as his successor; but later God didn't command Joshua to name a successor. These circumstances somewhat parallel the situation of the church in the world today. Unfortunately, God's people aren't working together to defeat the enemy; but here and there, God is raising up men and women of faith who are experiencing His blessing and power and are leading His people to victory.

With God's help, the two tribes conquered the Canaanites at Bezek (Judg. 1:4-7), captured, humiliated, and incapacitated one of their kings by cutting off his thumbs and big toes. (See Judg. 16:21; 1 Sam. 11:2; and 2 Kings 25:7 for further instances about being disabled.) With those handicaps, he wouldn't be able to run easily or use a weapon successfully Thus the "lord of Bezek" was paid back for what he had done to seventy other kings, although he may have been exaggerating a bit when he made this claim.

Those seventy kings illustrate the sad plight of anybody who has given in to the enemy: they couldn't walk or run correctly; they couldn't use a sword effectively; they were in the place of humiliation instead of on the throne; and they were living on scraps and leftovers instead of feasting at the table. What a difference it makes when you live by faith and reign in life through Jesus Christ (Rom. 10:17).

Jerusalem (Judg. 1:8) was Israel's next trophy; but though the Israelites conquered the city, they didn't occupy it (v. 21). That wasn't done until the time of David (2 Sam. 5:7). Judah and Benjamin were neighboring tribes; and since the city was located on their border, both tribes were involved in attacking it (Josh. 15:63). Later, Jerusalem would become "the city of David" and the capital of Israel.

They next attacked the area south and west of Jerusalem, which included Hebron (Judg. 1:9-10, 20) This meant fighting in the hill country, the south (Negev), and the foothills. Joshua had promised Hebron to Caleb because of his faithfulness to the Lord at Kadesh-Barnea (Num. 13-14; Josh. 14:6-15; Deut. 1:34-36). Sheshai, Ahiman, and Talmai were descendants of the giant Anak whose people had frightened ten of the twelve Jewish spies who first explored the land (Num. 13:22, 28). Even though Caleb and Joshua, the other two spies, had the faith needed to overcome the enemy, the people wouldn't listen to them.

Faith must have run in Caleb's family, because the city of Debir (Judg. 1:11-16)[3] was taken by Othniel, Caleb's nephew (3:9, Josh. 15:17). For a reward, he received Caleb's daughter Acsah as his wife. Othniel later was called to serve as Israel's first judge (Judg. 3:7-11). Since water was a precious commodity, and land was almost useless without it, Acsah urged her husband to ask her father to give them the land containing the springs that they needed. Apparently Othniel was better at capturing cities than he was at asking favors from his father-in-law, so Acsah had to do it herself. Her father then gave her the upper and lower springs. Perhaps this extra gift was related in some way to her dowry.

The Kenites (1:16) were an ancient people (Gen. 15:19) who are thought to have been nomadic metal workers. (The Hebrew word *qayin* means "a metal-worker, a smith.") According to Judges 4:11, the Kenites were descended from Moses' brother-in-law Hobab,[4] and thus were allies of Israel. The city of palms was Jericho, a deserted and condemned city (Josh. 6:26), so the Kenites moved to another part of the land under the protection of the tribe of Judah.

After Judah and Simeon destroyed Hormah (Judg. 1:17), the army of Judah turned its attention to the Philistine cities of Gaza, Ashkelon, and Ekron (vv. 18-19). Because the Philistines had iron chariots, the Jews couldn't easily defeat them on level ground, but they did claim the hill country.

What is important about the military history is that "the Lord was with Judah" (v. 19), and that's what gave them victory. (See Num. 14:42-43; Josh. 1:5 and 6:27; and Judg. 6:16.) "If God be for us, who can be against us?" (Rom. 8:31)

The victory of Joseph (vv. 22-26). The tribe of Ephraim joined with the western section of the tribe of Manasseh and, with the Lord's help, they took the city of Bethel. This city was important to the Jews because of its connection with the patriarchs (Gen. 12:8; 13:3; 28:10–12; 35:1–7). Apparently it hadn't been taken during the Conquest under Joshua, or if it had been, the Jews must have lost control. The saving of the informer's family reminds us of the salvation of Rahab's family when Jericho was destroyed (Josh. 2, 6). How foolish of this rescued people not to stay with the Israelites, where they were safe and could learn about the true and living God.

2. Sparing the enemy (Judg. 1:21, 27-36)

Benjamin, Ephraim, Manasseh, Zebulun, Asher, Naphtali, and Dan all failed to overcome the enemy and had to allow these godless nations to continue living in their tribal territories. The enemy even chased the tribe of Dan out of the plains into the mountains! The Jebusites remained in Jerusalem (v. 21), and the Canaanites who remained were finally pressed "into forced labor" when the Jews became stronger (v. 28, NIV). Eventually Solomon conscripted these Canaanite peoples to build the temple (1 Kings 9:20-22; 2 Chron. 8:7-8), but this was no compensation for the problems the Canaanites caused the Jews. This series of tribal defeats was the first indication that Israel was no longer walking by faith and trusting God to give them victory.

The priests possessed a copy of the Book of Deuteronomy and were commanded to read it publicly to the nation every Sabbatical Year during the Feast of Tabernacles (Deut. 31:9–13). Had they been faithful to do their job, the spiritual leaders would have read Deuteronomy 7 and warned the Israelites not to spare their pagan neighbors. The priests also would have reminded the people of God's promises that He would help them defeat their enemies (Deut. 31:1-8). It was by receiving and obeying the Book of the Law that Joshua had grown in faith and courage (Josh. 1:1-9; Rom. 10:17), and that same Word would have enabled the new generation to overcome their enemies and claim their inheritance.

The first step the new generation took toward defeat and slavery was *neglecting the Word of God,* and generations ever since have made that same mistake. "For the time will come when they will not endure sound doctrine, but according to their own desires, because they have itching ears, they will heap up for themselves teachers; and they will turn their ears away from the truth, and be turned aside to fables" (2 Tim. 4:3-4, NKJV). I fear that too many believers today are trying to live on religious fast-food dispensed for easy consumption (no chewing necessary) by entertaining teachers who give people what they want, not what they need. Is it any wonder many churches aren't experiencing God's power at work in their ministries?

But wasn't it cruel and unjust for God to *command* Israel to exterminate the nations in Canaan? Not in the least! To begin with, He had been patient with these nations for centuries and had mercifully withheld His judgment (Gen. 15:16; 2 Peter 3:9). Their society, and especially their religion, was unspeakably wicked (Rom. 1:18ff) and should have been wiped out years before Israel appeared on the scene.

Something else is true: These nations had been warned by the judgments God had inflicted on others, especially on Egypt and the nations east of the Jordan (Josh. 2:8-13). Rahab and her family had sufficient information to be able to repent and believe, and God saved them (Josh. 2; 6:22-25). Therefore, we have every right to conclude that God would have saved anybody who had turned to Him. These nations were sinning against a flood of light in rejecting God's truth and going their own way.

God didn't want the filth of the Canaanite society and religion to contaminate His people Israel. Israel was God's special people, chosen to fulfill divine purposes in this world. Israel would give the world the knowledge of the true God, the Holy Scriptures, and the Savior. In order to accomplish God's purposes, the nation had to be separated from all other nations; for if Israel was polluted, how could the Holy Son of God come into the world? "God is perpetually at war with sin," wrote G. Campbell Morgan. "That is the whole explanation of the extermination of the Canaanites."[5]

The main deity in Canaan was Baal, god of rainfall[6] and fertility, and Ashtoreth was his spouse. If you wanted to have fruitful orchards and vineyards, flourishing crops, and increasing flocks and herds, you worshiped Baal by visiting a temple prostitute. This combination of idolatry, immorality, and agricultural success was difficult for men to resist, which explains why God told Israel to wipe out the Canaanite religion completely (Num. 33:51-56; Deut. 7:1-5).

3. Imitating the enemy (Judg. 2:1-13)

The danger. In this day of "pluralism," when society contains people of opposing beliefs and lifestyles, it's easy to get confused and start thinking that *tolerance* is the same as *approval.* It isn't. In a democracy, the law gives people the freedom to worship as they please; and I must exercise patience and tolerance with those who believe and practice things that I feel God has condemned in His Word. The church today doesn't wield the sword (Rom. 13) and therefore it has no authority to eliminate people who disagree with the Christian faith. But we do have the obligation before God to maintain a separate walk so we won't become defiled by those who disagree with us (2 Cor. 6:14-7:1). We must seek by prayer, witness, and loving persuasion to win those to Christ who as yet haven't trusted Him.

The Jews eventually became so accustomed to the sinful ways of their pagan neighbors that those ways didn't seem sinful any more. The Jews then became interested in how their neighbors worshiped, until finally Israel started to live like their enemies and imitate their ways. For believers today, the first step away from the Lord is "friendship with the world" (James 4:4, NKJV), which then leads to our being "spotted by the world" (1:27). The next step is to "love the world" (1 John 2:15) and gradually become "conformed to this world" (Rom. 12:2). This can lead to being "condemned with the world" (1 Cor. 11:32), the kind of judgment that came to Lot (Gen. 19), Samson (Judg. 16), and Saul (1 Sam. 15, 31).

The disobedience (vv. 2:1-5). In the Old Testament, the "angel of the Lord" is generally interpreted to be the Lord Himself, who occasionally came to earth (a theophany) to deliver an important message. It was probably the Lord Jesus Christ, the second person of the Godhead, in a temporary preincarnation appearance. (See Gen. 16:9; 22:11; 48:16; Ex. 3:2; Judg. 6:11 and 13:3; 2 Kings 19:35.) The fact that God Himself came to give the message shows how serious things had become in Israel.

The tabernacle was originally located at Gilgal (Josh. 4:19–20), and it was there that the men of Israel were circumcised and "rolled away" the reproach of Egypt (Josh. 5:2-9). It was also there that the Lord appeared to Joshua and assured him of victory as he began his campaign to conquer Canaan (Josh. 5:13-15). To Joshua, the angel of the Lord brought a message of encouragement; but to the new generation described in the Book of Judges, He brought a message of punishment.

The Lord had kept His covenant with Israel; not one word of His promises had failed (Josh. 23:5, 10, 15; 1 Kings 8:56). He had asked them to keep their covenant with Him by obeying His law and destroying the Canaanite religious system—their altars, temples, and idols. (In Ex. 23:20-25, note the association between the angel of the Lord and the command to destroy the false religion; and see also Ex. 34:10-17 and Deut. 7:1-11.) But Israel disobeyed the Lord and not only spared the Canaanites and their godless religious system but also began to follow the enemy's lifestyle themselves.

In His covenant, God promised to

bless Israel if the people obeyed Him and to discipline them if they disobeyed Him (see Deut. 27-28). *God is always faithful to His Word, whether in blessing us or chastening us; for in both, He displays His integrity and His love (Heb. 12:1-11).* God would prefer to bestow the positive blessings of life that bring us enjoyment, but He doesn't hesitate to remove those blessings if our suffering will motivate us to return to Him in repentance.

By their disobedience, the nation of Israel made it clear that they wanted the Canaanites to remain in the land. God let them have their way (Ps. 106:15), but He warned them of the tragic consequences. The nations in the land of Canaan would become *thorns* that would afflict Israel and *traps* that would ensnare them. Israel would look to the Canaanites for pleasures but would only experience pain; they would rejoice in their freedom only to see that freedom turn into their bondage.[7]

No wonder the people wept when they heard the message! (The Hebrew word *bochim* means "weepers.") However, their sorrow was because of the *consequences* of their sins and not because the wickedness of their sins had *convicted* them. It was a shallow and temporary sorrow that never led them to true repentance (2 Cor. 7:8-11).

4. Obeying the enemy (Judg. 2:6-23)

The sin in our lives that we fail to conquer will eventually conquer us. The people of Israel found themselves enslaved to one pagan nation after another as the Lord kept His word and chastened His people. Consider the sins of that new generation.

They forgot what the Lord had done (vv. 6-10). At that point in Israel's history, Joshua stood next to Moses as a great hero, and yet the new generation didn't recognize who he was or what he had done. In his popular novel *1984,* George Orwell wrote, "Who controls the past controls the future: who controls the present controls the past." Once they got in control of the present, both Hitler and Stalin rewrote past history so they could control future events; and for a time it worked. How important it is for each new generation to recognize and appreciate the great men and women who helped to build and protect their nation! It's disturbing when "revisionist" historians debunk the heroes and heroines of the past and almost make them criminals.

They forsook what the Lord had said (vv. 11-13). Had they remembered Joshua, they would have known his "farewell speeches" given to the leaders and the people of Israel (Josh. 23-24). Had they known those speeches, they would have known the Law of Moses; for in his final messages, Joshua emphasized the covenant God had made with Israel and the responsibility Israel had to keep it. When you forget the Word of God, you are in danger of forsaking the God of the Word, which explains why Israel turned to the vile and vicious worship of Baal.

They forfeited what the Lord had promised (vv. 14-15). When they went out to fight their enemies, Israel was defeated, because the Lord wasn't with His people. This is what Moses had said would happen (Deut. 28:25-26); but that isn't all: *Israel's enemies eventually became their masters!* God permitted one nation after another to invade the Promised Land and enslave His people, making life so miserable for them that they cried out for help. Had the Jews obeyed the Lord, their armies would have been victorious; but left to themselves they were defeated and humiliated.

They failed to learn from what the Lord did (vv. 16-23). Whenever Israel turned away from the Lord to worship idols, He chastened them severely; and when in their misery they turned back to Him, He liberated them. But just as soon as they were free and their situation was comfortable again, Israel went right back into the same old sins. "And the Children of Israel did evil in the sight of the Lord. . . . Therefore the anger of the Lord was hot against Israel, and He sold them into the hand of. . ." is the oft-repeated statement that records the sad, cyclical nature of Israel's sins (3:7-8, see also v. 12; 4:1-4; 6:1; 10:6-7; 13:1). The people wasted their suffering. They didn't learn the lessons God wanted them to learn and profit from His chastening.

God delivered His people by raising up judges, who defeated the enemy and set Israel free. The Hebrew word translated "judge" means "to save, to rescue." The judges were deliverers who won great military victories with the help of the Lord. But the judges were also leaders who helped the people settle their disputes (4:4-5). The judges came from different tribes and functioned locally rather than nationally; and in some cases, their terms of office overlapped. The word "judge" is applied to only eight of the twelve people we commonly call "judges," but all of them functioned as counselors and deliverers. The eight men are: Othniel (3:9), Tola (10:1-2), Jair (10:3-5), Jephthah (11), Ibzan (12:8-10), Elon (12:11-12), Abdon (12:13-15), and Samson (15:20; 16:31).

The cycle of disobedience, discipline, despair, and deliverance is seen today whenever God's people turn away from His Word and go their own way. *If disobedience isn't followed by divine discipline, then the person is not truly a child of God; for God chastens all of His children* (Heb. 12:3-13). God has great compassion for His people, but He is angry at their sins.

The Book of Judges is the inspired record of Israel's failures and God's faithfulness. But if we study this book only as past history, we'll miss the message completely. *This book is about God's people today.* When the psalmist reviewed the period of the Judges (Ps. 106:40-46), he concluded with a prayer that we need to pray today: "Save us, O Lord our God, and gather us from the nations, that we may give thanks to Your holy name and glory in Your praise" (Ps. 106:47, NIV).

CHAPTER TWO
THE WEAPONS OF OUR WARFARE
Judges 3

The weapons we fight with are not the weapons of the world.

That statement could have been made by a space alien in a sci-fi novel, but it wasn't. The Apostle Paul wrote those words to the believers in Corinth (2 Cor. 10:4, NIV), reminding them of a principle every Christian needs to take to heart: *When God goes to war, He usually chooses the most unlikely soldiers, hands them the most unusual weapons, and accomplishes through them the most unpredictable results.*

For example, God gave Shamgar an ox goad, and with it he killed 600 men (3:31). Jael used a hammer and tent peg to kill a captain (4:21), and Gideon routed the whole Midianite army with only pitchers and torches as weapons (7:20). Samson slaughtered 1,000 Philistines using the jawbone of an ass (15:15), and young David killed the giant Goliath with a stone hurled from a shepherd's sling (1

Sam. 17). West Point isn't likely to offer courses on how to use these weapons.

Though our world has changed dramatically since the days of the Judges, the "world system" is still the same because human nature hasn't changed (1 John 2:15-17). As long as we're in this world, God's people are involved in a spiritual battle against Satan and his armies (Eph. 6:10-19), and God is still looking for men and women who have what it takes to win: power, strategy, and courage. These three essentials for victory are illustrated in this chapter in the lives of the first three judges.

1. Othniel: the power of God (Judg. 3:1-11)

In this chapter, you will find "five lords of the Philistines" (v. 3) and the king of Moab called "lord" (v. 25); but more importantly "the Lord," meaning Jehovah God, is named fifteen times in these thirty verses. That lets us know who is really in charge. The Presbyterian missionary leader A.T. Pierson used to say that "history is His story," and he was right. As He executes His divine decrees, God never violates human responsibility, but He does rule and overrule in the affairs of individuals and nations to accomplish His great purposes on this earth.

The early church prayed, "Lord, You *are* God!" and they gladly confessed that their enemies could do only "whatever Your hand and Your purpose determined before to be done" (Acts 4:24, 28, NKJV). Poet T.S. Eliot said, "Destiny waits in the hand of God, not in the hands of statesmen."

God's mercy toward His people (vv. 1-4). The tribe of Judah was not able to hold on to the key Philistine cities they had taken (1:18; 3:3); and as we saw in chapter 1, the other tribes failed to conquer the Canaanite nations. These surviving nations adopted a "good neighbor" policy toward Israel that eventually defeated Israel from within. Sometimes Satan comes as a lion to devour, but often he comes as a serpent to deceive (1 Peter 5:8; 2 Cor. 11:3).

God could have judged Israel for sparing the wicked Canaanite nations, but in His mercy He spared them because He had purposes for them to fulfill. Israel had committed a serious blunder in not trusting God to give them victory, but God sought to use their mistake for their own good. Romans 8:28 worked even in Old Testament days.

He would use the enemy *to train Israel,* to help the new generation learn the meaning of war (Judg. 3:1-2; see Ex. 13:17). Life had been relatively easy for the Jews in the Promised Land, and they needed the challenge of ever-present danger to keep them alert and disciplined. This is not to say God always approves of war or that participating in conflict always builds character. Combat experience might do just the opposite. The point is that the Jews had to keep some kind of standing army, or their enemies could quickly unite and overpower them, especially when Israel was at such a low ebb spiritually. In the years to come, both Saul and David would need effective armies in order to overcome their many enemies and establish the kingdom.

God also used the Canaanite nations *to test Israel* and reveal whether or not His people would obey the regulations Moses had given them from the Lord (Judg. 3:4). God had made it very clear to the Jews that they were not to study "comparative religion" and get interested in the pagan practices of the Canaanites (Deut. 7:1-11). It was that kind of curiosity that had brought divine judgment on Israel in the land of Moab (see Num. 25), because curiosity is often the first step toward conformity.

Of course, Israel should have been a witness to the surviving pagan nations and sought to win them to faith in the true and living God, but they failed in that responsibility as well. What a difference it would have made in subsequent national history if the Jews had won the Canaanites to the Lord instead of the Canaanites winning the Jews to Baal!

God's anger toward His people (vv. 5-8). God had put a wall between Israel and her neighbors, not because Israel was *better* than any other nation, but because she was *different.* Instead of worshiping idols, the Jews worshiped the one true God who made the heavens and the earth. Humans did not devise the laws and covenants of Israel; God did. Israel alone had the true sanctuary where God dwelt in His glory; it was the true priesthood, ordained by God; and it had the true altar and sacrifices that God would respect (Rom 9:4-5). Only through Israel would all the nations of the earth be blessed (Gen. 12:1-3).

When Israel obeyed the Lord, He blessed them richly; *and both their conduct and God's blessing were a testimony for their unbelieving neighbors.* (See Gen. 23:6; 26:26-33; 30:27; 39:5.) The pagan people would say, "These Jews are different. The God they worship and serve is a great God!" And the Jewish people would then have had opportunities to tell their neighbors how to trust Jehovah and receive His forgiveness and blessing. (See Deut. 4:1-13.)

Alas, instead of trusting God to change their neighbors, the gods of their neighbors changed the Jews; and everything Moses warned them not to do, they did. The Jews broke down the wall of separation between themselves and their godless neighbors, and the results were tragic. Contrary to God's law, Jewish men married pagan wives, and Jewish women married pagan husbands (Gen. 24:3; 26:34-35; 27:46; Ex. 34:15-16; Deut. 7:3-4; Josh. 23:12). The idolaters gradually stole the hearts of their mates from worshiping Jehovah to worshiping false gods. King Solomon made this same mistake. After all, when you marry outside the will of God, you have to do something to keep peace in the family! (See 1 Kings 11:1-13; 2 Cor. 6:14-7:1.)

Is it any wonder that God became angry?[1] Is it any wonder He humiliated Israel by using pagan nations to discipline His own people? Since Israel was acting like the pagans, God had to treat them like pagans! "To the faithful you show yourself faithful, to the blameless you show yourself blameless, to the pure you show yourself pure, but to the crooked you show yourself shrewd" (Ps. 18:25-26, NIV).

Jehovah is the God of all the nations, "for dominion belongs to the Lord and He rules over the nations" (Ps. 22:27-28, NIV). Proud King Nebuchadnezzar had to learn the hard way "that the Most High rules in the kingdom of men, and gives it to whomever He chooses" (Dan. 4:25, NKJV).

Four times in the Book of Judges we're told that God "sold" His people to the enemy (2:14; 3:8; 4:2; 10:7; and see I Sam. 12:9; 1 Kings 21:20, 25; Ps. 44:12). The Jews acted like slaves, so God sold them like slaves. Had the Jews been faithful to the Lord, He would have sold their enemies into Israel's hands (Deut. 32:30).

The name of the king of Mesopotamia means "doubly wicked Cushan," which may have been a nickname that his enemies gave him. We aren't told where he invaded Israel, although logically the attack would have come from the north; nor are we told how much of the land he subjugated for those eight painful years. Since the deliverer God raised up was from Judah, it's possible that the invading army had penetrated that far south in

Israel when the Lord decided to intervene on behalf of His suffering people.

Charles Spurgeon said that God never allows His people to sin successfully. Their sin will either destroy them or it will invite the chastening hand of God. If the history of Israel teaches the contemporary church anything it's the obvious lesson that "righteousness exalts a nation, but sin is a disgrace to any people" (Prov. 14:34, NIV).

God's salvation for His people (vv. 9-11). There's no evidence that the people repented of their sins when they cried out to God for help, but the Lord responded to their plight and gave them a deliverer. It was the Exodus experience all over again: "And God heard their groaning, and God remembered His covenant with Abraham, with Isaac, and with Jacob.

And God looked upon the Children of Israel, and God had respect unto them" (Ex. 2:24-25). The word "knew" means much more than intellectual understanding, for God knows everything. It means that God identified with their trials and felt a concern for their welfare.

The deliverer He raised up was Othniel, the man who captured Hebron and married Caleb's daughter (1:10-13). Bible scholars don't agree as to the exact blood relationship Othniel had to Caleb. Was Othniel Caleb's nephew—that is, the son of Kenaz, Caleb's younger brother—or was he simply Caleb's younger brother? As far as the text is concerned, either interpretation is possible.

If he was Caleb's brother, then why was his father's name Kenaz instead of Jephunneh? (1 Chron. 4:13; Josh. 14:6) Perhaps Jephunneh had died, and Caleb's mother married Kenaz and gave birth to Othniel. Thus, Othniel would have been Caleb's half-brother. First Chronicles 4:13 indicates that Othniel was the *son* of Kenaz, but the word "son" is used rather broadly in Jewish genealogies and doesn't always mean a direct father/son relationship.

Fortunately, we don't have to untangle the branches in Othniel's family tree before we can benefit from the example of his life and ministry. By blood and by marriage, he belonged to a family noted for its courageous faith and its willingness to face the enemy and depend on God for the victory. When God called Othniel, he was available for the Lord, and the Spirit of the Lord came upon him and empowered him for battle (Judg. 3:10).

" 'Not by might nor by power, but by My Spirit.' says the Lord of hosts" (Zech. 4:6, NKJV). This was the secret of Othniel's strength, as it was with Gideon (Judg. 6:34), Jephthah (11:29) and Samson (14:6, 19; 15:14); and it must be the source of the believer's power today (Acts 1:8; 2:4; 4:8, 31; Eph. 5:18). One of the former directors of The Evangelical Alliance Mission, T.J. Bach, said, "The Holy Spirit longs to reveal to you the deeper things of God. He longs to love through you. He longs to work through you. Through the blessed Holy Spirit you may have: strength for every duty, wisdom for every problem, comfort in every sorrow, joy in His overflowing service."

Othniel not only rescued his nation from bondage, but also served his people as judge for forty years. This meant that he exercised authority in managing the affairs of the nation, and it was his spiritual and civil leadership that brought rest to the land. *Never underestimate the good that one person can do who is filled with the Spirit of God and obedient to the will of God.*

2. Ehud: effective strategy (Judg. 3:12-30)

Unlike Moses, who appointed Joshua to lead Israel, the judges didn't have the authority to name a successor. When God called men and women to serve as judges, they obeyed, did His work, and then passed from the scene. One would hope that their godly influence would make a lasting difference in the spiritual life of the nation, but such wasn't the case. No sooner was a judge off the scene than the people were back to worshiping Baal and forsaking the Lord.

You would think that gratitude alone would have motivated the people of Israel to obey the Lord and be faithful to His covenant, especially after enduring eight years of painful servitude. And think of all that God had done for Israel in the past! They would have been a forgotten little nation if God hadn't loved them and chosen them for Himself (Deut. 7:1-11). They would have perished in Egypt or in the wilderness if God hadn't delivered them and cared for them. They would have died on the battlefields of Canaan if the Lord hadn't given them victory over their enemies. They would have been wallowing in moral sewage if the Lord hadn't given them His Law and the priests to teach it to them. They had God's presence in the tabernacle and God's promises in the covenant, so what more could they want?

Somewhere the system broke down, and I think it was with the priests and the parents. The priests and Levites were not only to officiate at the tabernacle, but they also were to teach the Law to the people and encourage them to obey it (Lev. 10:11; Deut. 33:8-10; 17:8-9; 1 Sam. 2:12-17; Mal. 2:1-9). Jewish parents were expected to teach their children the ways of the Lord (Deut. 6:6-25; 11:18-21; and see Gen. 18:17-19 and Job 1:5) and be good examples for them to follow. During the period of the Judges, however, it appears that the older generation neglected the important ministry of instructing the new generation about the fear of the Lord (Ps. 34:11).

Eglon, the oppressor (vv. 12-14). The armies of Mesopotamia came a long distance to invade Israel; but the Moabites, Ammonites, and Amalekites were not only neighbors but also relatives of the Jews. Lot, the nephew of Abraham, was the ancestor of Moab and Ammon (Gen. 19:30-38); and Esau, the brother of Jacob, was the ancestor of Amalek (Gen. 36:12, 16; Deut. 25:17, 19).

Eglon, the King of Moab, organized the confederacy and set up his headquarters at Jericho, "the city of palm trees" (Deut. 34:3). Jericho was under a curse (Josh. 6:26), and there's no evidence that the city had been rebuilt; but the location was ideal for directing military operations, and there was an abundance of water there. For eighteen years, Eglon and his allies made life miserable for the Jews. It must have been especially galling to them to be under the heels of blood relatives who were also their longtime adversaries.

Ehud, the deliverer (vv. 15-30). Othniel, the first judge, had come from the tribe of Judah. The second judge, Ehud, a lefthanded man, came from Judah's neighbor, Benjamin—the name "Benjamin" means "son of my right hand." (The Benjamites were known for their ambidexterity. See Judg. 20:16 and 1 Chron. 12:2.) However, the text of Judges 3:15 can be translated "a man handicapped in the right hand," which suggests that he was not ambidextrous at all but able to use *only* his left hand. If that indeed is the meaning of the text, then Ehud's plan for killing Eglon was a masterpiece of strategy. It's also a great encouragement to people with physical disabilities who may have the erroneous idea that God can't use them in His service.

Ehud had several problems to solve, and he solved them successfully. At the top of the list was how to gain access to King Eglon without making anybody suspicious. He accomplished this by making himself the leader of the commission that brought the king his annual tribute. The paying of tribute not only added to the king's wealth, which he would enjoy, but it also acknowledged the king's authority over Israel; and Eglon would enjoy that as well. Of course, Eglon didn't know that Ehud was God's appointed leader to deliver Israel; otherwise, he would have had him killed on sight.

The second problem was securing a private audience with the king without exciting the distrust of his attendants and guards. Ehud did this first by leaving the king's presence together with his men after they had done homage to Eglon, and then Ehud coming back later *alone* as though he had an urgent message for the king. A solitary man with a lame right hand couldn't be much of a threat to a powerful king, and perhaps this despised Jew really did have a word from his God. Eglon may have felt proud that the God of Israel had a message for him; and since he was no doubt afraid not to listen to it, he dismissed his guards and attendants and gave Ehud a personal interview in his private chambers.

Since Ehud had to kill Eglon in a way that was quick and quiet and that would catch the king by surprise,[2] he made use of his disability. Ehud made a very sharp dagger and hid it under his clothing on his right side. Even if the guards frisked him, they would most likely examine the left side of his body where most men carried their weapons. Seeing that he was a handicapped man, they probably didn't examine him at all.

Even a king must stand to receive a message from God. When Eglon stood, Ehud may have gestured with his right hand to distract him and show him there was nothing in his hand; and then Ehud reached for his dagger and plunged it into the fat king's body. It must have been a powerful thrust because the point of the dagger came out the king's back; and Eglon was dead instantly.[3]

The next problem was how to escape from the palace without getting caught, and this he accomplished by locking the door of the private chamber and delaying the discovery of the corpse. As Ehud hastened away, the attendants concluded that the interview was over; so they went to see if their king wanted anything. The three "behold" statements in verses 24-25 indicate the three surprises that they experienced: the doors were locked, the king didn't respond to their knocks and calls, and the king was dead. All of this took time and gave Ehud opportunity to escape.

His final problem was to rally the troops and attack the enemy. The trumpet signal called the men out, and he led them to the fords of the Jordan, assuring them that the Lord had given Moab into their hands. The victory would come by trusting the Lord and not by depending on their own strength. By guarding the fords, the Israelites prevented the Moabites from escaping or from bringing in fresh troops. Since Ephraim was one of the most powerful tribes in Israel, Ehud had excellent soldiers to command. Accordingly, they killed 10,000 of the best Moabite soldiers. Not only was Moab defeated, but also the tables were turned and the Moabites became subject to Israel. We assume that Moab's defeat was the signal for their allies, Ammon and Amalek, to leave the field of battle.

If the Jews had been asked to vote on a leader, Ehud probably would have lost on the first ballot. But he was God's choice, and God used him to set the nation free. Moses was slow of speech and Paul was not imposing in his appearance, but Moses and Paul, like Ehud, were men of faith who led others to victory. Ehud turned a disability into a possibility because he depended on the Lord.

3. Shamgar: persistent courage (Judg. 3:31).

Only one verse is devoted to Shamgar and it isn't even stated that he was a judge. Judges 5:6-7 indicates that he was contemporary with Deborah and Barak. "Son of Anath" may mean that he was from the town of Beth Anath in Naphtali (1:33), which was also the tribe Barak came from (4:6; see 5:18). Since Anath was the name of a Canaanite goddess of war, perhaps "son of Anath" was a nickname that meant "son of battle"—that is, a mighty warrior.

What was significant about Shamgar was the weapon that he used. An ox goad was a strong pole about eight feet long. At one end was a sharp metal point for prodding the oxen and at the other end a spade for cleaning the dirt off the plow. It was the closest thing Shamgar could find to a spear because the enemy had confiscated the weapons of the Israelites (5:8; see 1 Sam. 13:19-22).

Here was a man who obeyed God and defeated the enemy even though his resources were limited. Instead of complaining about not possessing a sword or spear, Shamgar gave what he had to the Lord, and the Lord used it. Joseph Parker said, "What is a feeble instrument in the hands of one man is a mighty instrument in the hands of another, simply because the spirit of that other burns with holy determination to accomplish the work that has to be done."[4]

Shamgar may have killed all 600 Philistines at one time in one place (see 2 Sam. 8:8-12), but it's also possible that 600 is a cumulative total. An ox goad would be an unwieldy weapon to use if 600 soldiers had attacked Shamgar at one time. Since we don't know the details, we must not speculate. It's just encouraging to know that God enabled him to overcome the enemy though his resources were limited.

The few words that are recorded about Shamgar give me the impression that he was a man of persistent courage, which, of course was born out of his faith in the Lord. To stand his ground against the enemy, having only a farmer's tool instead of a soldier's full military equipment, marks Shamgar out as a brave man with steadfast courage.

Charles Spurgeon once gave a lecture at his Pastor's College entitled "To Workers with Slender Apparatus." Shamgar didn't hear that lecture, but I'm sure he could have given it! And I suspect he would have closed his lecture by saying, "Give whatever tools you have to the Lord, stand your ground courageously, and trust God to use what's in your hand to accomplish great things for His glory."

To paraphrase E.M. Bounds, the world is looking for better methods, but God is looking for better men and women who understand the basics: the power of the Holy Spirit, wise strategy, and steadfast courage.

Othniel, Ehud, and Shamgar have shown us the way. Will we follow?

CHAPTER THREE
"TWO ARE BETTER THAN ONE, AND

THREE ARE BETTER STILL"
Judges 4–5

The cast of characters in this drama is as follows:

Jabin: King of Hazor in Canaan; a tyrant
Deborah: a Jewish judge; a woman of faith and courage
Barak: a reluctant Jewish general
Sisera: captain of Jabin's army
Heber: a Kenite neighbor, at peace with Jabin
Jael: wife of Heber; handy with a hammer
Jehovah God: in charge of wars and weather

Now let the drama unfold.

1. Act one: a tragic situation (Judg. 4:1-3)

Jabin is the key person in act one, for God raised him up to discipline the people of Israel. For eighty years, the Jews had enjoyed rest because of the leadership of Ehud, the longest period of peace recorded in the Book of Judges.[1] But no sooner was this godly judge removed than the people lapsed back into idolatry, and God had to punish them (Judg. 2:10-19).

Israel as portrayed in the Book of Judges illustrates the difference between "religious reformation" and "spiritual revival." Reformation temporarily changes outward conduct while revival permanently alters inward character. When Ehud removed the idols and commanded the people to worship only Jehovah, they obeyed him; but when that constraint was removed, the people obeyed their own desires. The nation of Israel was like the man in Jesus' parable who got rid of one demon, cleaned house, and then ended up with seven worse demons (Matt. 12:43-45). The empty heart is prey to every form of evil.

Canaan was made up of a number of city-states, each of which was ruled by a king (see Josh. 12). "Jabin" was the official title or name of the king of Hazor (Josh. 11:1). He was also called "King of Canaan." This title probably means that he was the head of a confederacy of kings. Joshua had burned Hazor (Josh. 11:13), but the Canaanites had rebuilt it and occupied it. With his large army and his 900 chariots of iron, Jabin was securely in control of the land. As you read the narrative, however, you get the impression that Sisera, captain of Jabin's army, was the real power in the land. Jabin isn't even mentioned in Deborah's song in Judges 5!

Once again, the people of Israel cried out to God, not to forgive their sins but to relieve their suffering. (See vv. 6-8 for a hint of what life was like in those days.) Had they truly repented, God would have done much more than deliver them from physical slavery. He would have liberated them from their spiritual bondage as well. To ask God for comfort and not cleansing is only to sow seeds of selfishness that will eventually produce another bitter harvest. David's prayer is what Israel needed to pray: "Create in me a clean heart, O God; and renew a right spirit within me" (Ps. 51:10).

2. Act two: a divine revelation (Judg. 4:4-7)

God had raised up a courageous woman named Deborah ("bee") to be the judge in the land. This was an act of grace, but it was also an act of humiliation for the Jews; for they lived in a male-dominated society that wanted only mature male leadership. "As for My people, children are their oppressors, and women rule over them" (Isa. 3:12). For God to give His people a woman judge was to treat them like little children, which is exactly what they were when it came to spiritual things.[2]

Deborah was both a judge and a prophetess. Moses' sister Miriam was a prophetess (Ex. 15:20); and later biblical history introduces us to Huldah (2 Kings 22:14), Noadiah (Neh. 6:14), Anna (Luke 2:36), and the four daughters of Philip (Acts 21:9). God called Deborah a prophetess and a judge, but she saw herself as a *mother* to her people. "I, Deborah arose, that I arose a mother in Israel" (Judg. 5:7). The wayward Jews were her children, and she welcomed them and counseled them.

God revealed to Deborah that Barak ("lightning") was to assemble and lead the Israelite army and draw Sisera's troops into a trap near Mount Tabor; and there the Lord would defeat them. Mount Tabor lies at the juncture of Zebulun, Naphtali, and Issachar, not far from the Kishon River. If Barak would lead the Israelite army toward Mount Tabor, God would draw Sisera and his troops toward the Kishon River, where God would give Barak the victory.

When God wants to glorify Himself through His people, He always has a perfect plan for us to follow. God chose the leader of His army, the place for the battle, and the plan for His army to follow. God also guaranteed the victory. It was like the "good old days" of Joshua again!

3. Act three: a reluctant participant (Judg. 4:8-10)

We aren't told that Barak was a judge, which explains why he got his orders from Deborah, God's appointed leader in the land. Barak was from Naphtali, one of the tribes that would send volunteers to the battlefield (v. 6). Like Moses before him (Ex. 3-4), and Gideon (Judg. 6) and Jeremiah (Jer. 1) after him, Barak hesitated when told what God wanted him to do.

We know that "God's commandments are God's enablements" and that we should obey His will in spite of circumstances, feelings, or consequences. But we don't always do it! Was Barak's response an evidence of unbelief or a mark of humility? He didn't accuse God of making a mistake; all he did was ask Deborah to go with him to the battle. Was that because she was a prophetess and he might need a word from the Lord? Or was it to help him enlist more volunteers for the army? The fact that Deborah agreed to accompany Barak suggests that his request wasn't out of God's will, although in granting it, God took the honor from the men and gave it to the women.

Barak enlisted 10,000 men from his own tribe of Naphtali and the neighboring tribe of Zebulun (Judg. 4:6, 10; 5:14, 18). Later, volunteers from the tribes of Benjamin, Ephraim, and Manasseh west (v. 14), and Issachar (v. 15), joined these men, and the army grew to 40,000 men (v. 8). It's possible that the original 10,000 soldiers initiated the campaign that lured Sisera into the trap, and then the other 30,000 joined them for the actual battle and "mopping up" operation. The tribes that were summoned but refused to come were Reuben, Dan, Asher, and Manasseh east (vv. 15-17).

When you consider that weapons were scarce in Israel (5:8;[3] 1 Sam. 13:19-22) and that there was no effective standing army, what Deborah and Barak did was indeed an act of faith. But God had promised to give them victory, and they were depending on His promise (Rom. 10:17).

4. Act four: a victorious confrontation (Judg. 4:11-23)

The Lord is the leading actor in this scene. He not only controlled the enemy army and brought it into the trap, but He also controlled the weather and used a storm to defeat Sisera's troops.

Sisera is warned: (vv. 11-12). Verse 12 suggests that it was Heber and his family who first warned Sisera that the Jews were about to revolt and where the Israelite army was mustering. We met the Kenites in 1:16 and discovered that they were distant relatives of the Jews through Moses. It seems strange that Heber the Kenite would separate himself from his people, who worshiped Jehovah, and be friendly with idolatrous tyrants like Jabin and Sisera (4:17). Perhaps he needed the protection and business of the Canaanites as he carried on his trade as an itinerant metalworker. The Kenites seem to be attached to the tribe of Judah (1:16); but the men of Judah weren't among the volunteers in Barak's army.

It's possible, however, to view Heber from another perspective and see him as a part of God's plan to lure Sisera into the trap. Heber wasn't an ally of Jabin's; he was simply trying to maintain a neutral position in a divided society. But once the Jewish army was in place at Mount Tabor, Heber ran and gave the news to Sisera; and Sisera had no reason to question the report. Sisera began to move his army and fell right into the trap.

Sisera is defeated (vv. 13-16). The Canaanites depended on their 900 iron chariots to give them the advantage they needed as they met the Jewish army (1:19; see Josh. 17:18). What they didn't know was that the Lord would send a fierce rainstorm that would make the Kishon River overflow and turn the battlefield into a sea of mud (Judg. 5:20-22). The water and mud would severely impede the mobility of the Canaanite chariots and horses, and this situation would make it easy for the Israelite soldiers to attack and slaughter the enemy. The trap worked, and the enemy army was wiped out.

Along with the storm from the heavens and the flood from the swollen river, God sent confusion in the minds of the enemy troops. The word translated "routed" (4:15, NKJV) means "confused, thrown into panic." This is what God had done to Pharaoh's charioteers in the Red Sea (Ex. 14:24) and would later do to the Philistines in Samuel's day (1 Sam. 7:10).

One thing that helped to confuse and frighten the Canaanites was the sudden appearance of torrential rain during the traditional dry season. Since Sisera wouldn't have taken his chariots to the fields if he had suspected any kind of bad weather, we can safely assume that this battle was fought during the June-to-September dry season. When you remember that the Canaanite god Baal was the god of storms, you can see how the sudden change of weather could have affected the superstitious Canaanites. Had their own god Baal turned against them? Was the God of Israel stronger than Baal? If so, then the battle was already lost, and the wisest thing the soldiers could do was flee.

Sisera is slain (vv. 17-23). While Barak and his men were pursuing and killing the fleeing Canaanites, some of whom were in chariots and others on foot, the Canaanite captain Sisera was running for his life, probably heading toward Hazor and safety. But weariness got the best of him, and providentially he was near the tents of Heber at the oak of Zaanannim (v. 11). This famous oak was on the border of Naphtali (Josh. 19:33), about six miles east of Mount Tabor.

Since Sisera knew that Heber and his people were friendly toward Jabin, this settlement seemed a good place to stop and rest. When Heber's wife, Jael, came out to meet Sisera and invited him into her tent, the Canaanite captain was sure that he was at last safe. After all, in that culture nobody would dare enter a wife's tent except her husband. Jael gave him milk instead of water and then covered him with a blanket, and he was confident that he had found a dependable ally and could rest in peace.

But Sisera made the mistake of telling Jael to lie if anyone asked whether he was there. Being a wise woman, she concluded that Sisera was fleeing the battlefield, which meant that the Jews had won the battle and the Canaanite grip on the land was broken. If she protected Sisera, she'd be in trouble with the Jews, her own relatives. No doubt somebody was chasing Sisera, and whoever it was wouldn't be satisfied until the captain was dead.

But Sisera had no reason to suspect danger. After all, Heber's clan was friendly to the Canaanites, Jael had shown him hospitality and kindness, and no pursuing Jewish soldier was likely to force his way into a woman's tent. What Sisera didn't know was that God had promised that a woman would take his life (Judg. 4:9).

When Sisera was in a deep sleep, Jael killed him by pounding a tent peg through his head. In the Eastern nomadic tribes, it was the women who put up and took down the tents; so Jael knew how to use a hammer. When Barak arrived on the scene, he discovered that his enemy was dead and that Deborah's prediction had been fulfilled. For a captain to flee from a battle was embarrassing; for him to be killed while fleeing was humiliating; but to be killed by a woman was the most disgraceful thing of all (9:54).

Should we bless or blame Jael for what she did? She invited Sisera into her tent, treated him kindly, and told him not to be afraid; so she was deceitful. The Kenites were at peace with Jabin, so she violated a treaty. She gave Sisera the impression that she would guard the door, so she broke a promise. She killed a defenseless man who was under her protection, so she was a murderess.[4] Yet Deborah sang, "Blessed above women shall Jael the wife of Heber the Kenite be, blessed shall she be above women in the tent" (5:24)

To begin with, let's not read back into the era of the Judges the spiritual standards taught by Jesus and the apostles. Also, let's keep in mind that the Jews had been under terrible bondage because of Jabin and Sisera; and it was God's will that the nation be delivered. Both Jabin and Sisera had been guilty of mistreating the Jews for years; and if the Canaanite army had won the battle, hundreds of Jewish girls would have been captured and raped (v. 30). Jael not only helped deliver the nation of Israel from bondage, but also she helped to protect the women from the most vicious brutality. She wasn't a Semitic "Lady Macbeth" who murdered her guest for her own personal gain. There was a war on, and this courageous woman finally stopped being neutral and took her stand with the people of God.

5. Act five: a glorious celebration (Judg. 5:1-31)

When they wanted to celebrate special occasions, the Jewish people often expressed themselves in song; so the writer shifts from narrative prose to jubilant poetry. Future generations might forget what the history book said, but they were not likely to forget a festive song. (For other examples, see Ex. 15, Deut. 32, 2 Sam. 1:17-27, and Ps. 18.) The personal pronouns in Judges 5:7, 9, and 13 indicate that this was

Deborah's victory song; but just as Barak joined her in the battle, so he joined her in the victory celebration.

A poem or song isn't something you can easily outline because it's a spontaneous emotional expression that often defies analysis. Unlike classical English poetry, Hebrew poetry contains recurring themes, expressed in different ways and frequent outbursts of praise and prayer. The following outline is only a suggested approach to this magnificent song of victory.

Praise the Lord all you people! (vv. 1-12) In verses 1-9, Deborah and Barak praise the Lord for all that He did for His people. He gave unity to the leaders so that Barak could assemble an army (v. 2; and see v. 9). The same God who gave Israel victory in the past would give them victory again (vv. 4-5). Israel had entered into a covenant with the Lord at Mount Sinai, and He would fulfill His promises to His special people. Since conditions were so terrible in the land that something had to be done, God raised up Deborah to be a mother in Israel (vv. 6-9). The enemy took over because the people had turned from Jehovah to worship false gods. Deborah was concerned about the spiritual life of the people as well as their physical and political welfare. Note that this first section (vv. 2-9) begins and ends with "Praise to the Lord" and "Bless ye the Lord."

According to verses 10 and 11, Deborah and Barak summoned the wealthy nobles ("those who ride on white asses") and the common travelers to join the singers at the wells and praise the Lord for what He did to Jabin's army. Now it was safe to walk the roads, gather at the wells, and leisurely talk together. The people could leave the walled cities where they had run for protection and could return to their villages in peace. It was time for all Israel to praise God for His mercies to them.

This praise stanza closes with a call to action (v. 12). God commanded Deborah to wake up and sing and Barak to wake up and attack the enemy. Because of her faith, Deborah could sing before the battle started as well as after the battle ended.

Praise the Lord for the volunteers (vv. 13-18). Deborah was grateful that the people offered themselves willingly in the service of the Lord (vv. 2, 9) and that the nobles did their share in recruiting soldiers from the tribes (v. 13). Six tribes united in sending volunteers. Except for the people in the town of Meroz (v. 23), the men of Naphtali responded, as did the men of Zebulun, Issachar, Benjamin, Ephraim, and Manasseh west (Machir). The phrase in verse 14, "They that handle the pen of the writer" (literally, "the staff of a scribe"), may refer to the recruiting officers who wrote down the names of the soldiers. They were not "summer soldiers" but brave men who were serious about fighting the Lord's battles.

However, there were four tribes that didn't volunteer and do their share of fighting. The tribe of Reuben pondered the call to arms but finally stayed at home. They were probably considering Deuteronomy 20:1-9, Israel's law of warfare, and examining their hearts to see whether they were qualified to go to war. Since Manasseh east (Gilead) was safe on the other side of the Jordan, they also stayed home (Judg. 5:17). Dan and Asher on the coast also elected not to heed the call to battle. In contrast to these shirkers, the tribes of Zebulun and Naphtali are especially praised for risking their lives in the service of the Lord and their country (v. 18).

Keep in mind that during this period in history "every man did that which was right in his own eyes" (21:25). When Joshua was the commander of Israel's armies, *all* the tribes participated; but when Barak summoned the forces, only half of them went to war against Jabin.[5] The people of God today are not unlike the people of Israel when it comes to God's call for service: some immediately volunteer and follow the Lord; some risk their lives; some give the call serious consideration but say no; and others keep to themselves as though the call had never been given.

Praise the Lord for His victory (vv. 19-23). It's one thing to show up for duty and quite something else to go into battle. Sisera had organized an alliance of the Canaanite kings, and their united forces (with 900 chariots) met the Jewish army at Megiddo on the plain of Jezreel.[6] Since it was the dry season of the year, the charioteers expected to annihilate the army of Israel. But God had other plans. He sent a tremendous rainstorm that turned the Kishon River into a raging torrent and the battlefield into a swamp. A raindrop is a very fragile thing; but if you put enough of them together, you can defeat an army! The army of Israel trusted the Lord to give them victory because this is what He had promised (4:6-9).

Deborah and Barak didn't curse the people of Meroz; it was the angel of the Lord who did it. It must have embarrassed Barak to know that a town in his own tribe of Naphtali had refused to send volunteers to assist in this important battle. "Meroz stands for the shirker," said Philips Brooks in a famous sermon; "for him who is willing to see other people fight the battles of life, while he simply comes in and takes the spoils."[7] Note that their sin wasn't simply failing to assist *Israel;* they failed to help *the Lord!*

Praise the Lord for a courageous woman (vv. 24-31). Deborah's blessing on Jael reminds us of Gabriel's words to Mary (Luke 1:42). Because of Barak's hesitation, Deborah announced that a woman would get the credit for killing the captain of the enemy army (Judg. 4:8-9). The phrase "smote off his head" in verse 26 doesn't mean that she decapitated him with a hammer and a tent peg. The word means "crushed" or "smashed." With one stroke, she sent the tent peg through his temple, shattered his head, and killed him.[8]

The description of Sisera's death in verse 27 gives the impression that he was standing in the tent when Jael struck him and then fell dead at her feet. But he was lying down asleep when he was slain (v. 18). We may have here some Hebrew poetic license, but it's also possible that in the agony of his death Sisera raised himself up from the tent floor and then sank at her feet and expired.

The singer moves from describing Sisera's death to portraying Sisera's mother watching for her son's return (vv. 28–30). What a pathetic picture of hope where there is no hope! How many people today are looking out the window of false assumptions and expecting something to happen that will never happen. Sisera was dead; he would never come home to his mother's love again. His mother and her attendants kept telling themselves and each other that everything was fine, but it wasn't.

The closing prayer (v. 31) contrasts the enemies of the Lord—who like Sisera go out in darkness—with the people who love God, who are like the noonday sun.[9] The battle at Megiddo was more than just a conflict between opposing armies. It was a conflict between the forces of darkness and the forces of light. We either love Christ and walk in the light, or we are His enemy and perish in the darkness.

The curtain comes down on our

drama, but I predict that the cast will be making curtain calls as long as people read and study the Bible. "For whatever things were written before were written for our learning, that we through the patience and comfort of the Scriptures might have hope" (Rom. 15:4, NKJV).

CHAPTER FOUR
GOD'S MAN IN MANASSEH
Judges 6

You have a garden, and you work hard all spring and summer to make that garden produce abundantly. But every year, just about the time you're ready to gather in the harvest, your neighbors swoop down and take your produce away from you by force. This goes on year after year, and there's nothing you can do about it.

If you can imagine that scenario, then you'll have some idea of the suffering the Jews experienced every harvest when the Midianites made their annual raids. For seven years, God allowed the Midianites and their allies to ravage "the land of milk and honey," leaving the people in the deepest poverty.

About the time of the eighth Midianite invasion, God called a farmer in Manasseh named Gideon to become the deliverer of His people. Gideon started his career as somewhat of a *coward* (Judg. 6), then became a *conqueror* (7:1-8:21), and ended his career as a *compromiser* (8:22-35). But more space is devoted to Gideon in the Book of Judges (100 verses) than to any other judge;[1] and Gideon is the only judge whose personal struggles with his faith are recorded. Gideon is a great encouragement to people who have a hard time accepting themselves and believing that God can make anything out of them or do anything with them.

Before the Lord could use Gideon in His service, He had to deal with four doubts that plagued him and were obstacles to his faith. These doubts can be expressed in four questions.

1. "Does God really care about us?" (Judg. 6:1-13)

"The Lord has forsaken us!" was Gideon's response to the Lord's message (v. 13, NKJV); and yet the Lord had given Israel proof of His personal concern.

He had chastened them (vv. 1-6). "My son, do not despise the chastening of the Lord, nor detest His correction; for whom the Lord loves He corrects, just as a father the son in whom he delights" (Prov. 3:11-12, NKJV; and see Heb. 12:5-11). Charles Spurgeon said, "The Lord does not permit His children to sin successfully." God is not a "permissive parent" who allows His children to do as they please, for His ultimate purpose is that they might be "conformed to the image of His Son" (Rom. 8:29). The Father wants to be able to look at each member of His spiritual family and say, "This is My beloved child, in whom I am well pleased" (see Matt. 3:17; 12:18; 17:5).

Chastening is evidence of God's hatred for sin and His love for His people. We can't conceive of a holy God wanting anything less than His very best for His children, and the best He can give us is a holy character like that of Jesus Christ. Obedience to the Lord builds character, but sin destroys character; and God cannot sit idly by and watch His children destroy themselves.

Israel had already experienced forty-three years of suffering under the harsh rule of the neighboring nations, but they hadn't yet learned their lesson and turned away from the heathen idols. Unless our suffering leads to repentance, it accomplishes no lasting good; and unless our repentance is evidence of a holy desire to turn from sin, not just escape from pain, repentance is only remorse. Chastening assures us that we are truly God's children, that our Father loves us, and that we can't get away with rebellion.

The Midianites organized a coalition of nations to invade the land (Judg. 6:3), and all that Israel could do was flee to the hills and hide from the enemy. When the Jews returned to their homes, they found only devastation; and they had to face another year without adequate food.

He had rebuked them (vv. 7-10). Previous to this, an angel of the Lord, probably the Son of God, had come to Bochim to reprove Israel for her sins (2:1-5); and now an unnamed prophet came to repeat the message.[2] Often in the Old Testament, when the Lord denounced His people for their disobedience, He reminded them of the wonderful way He had delivered them from Egypt. He also reminded them of His generosity in giving them the land and helping them overcome their enemies. If the Jews were suffering from Gentile bondage, it wasn't God's fault! He had given them everything they needed.

When you read the New Testament epistles, you can't help but notice that the apostles took the same approach when they admonished the believers to whom they wrote. The apostles repeatedly reminded the Christians that God had saved them so that they might live obediently and serve the Lord faithfully. As God's children, they were to walk worthy of their high and heavenly calling (Eph. 4:1) and live like people who were seated with Christ in glory (Col. 3:1ff). The motive for Christian living is not that we might gain something we don't have but that we might live up to what we already have in Christ.

The purpose of chastening is to make God's children willing to listen to God's Word. Often after spanking a child, parents will reassure the child of their love and then gently admonish the child to listen to what they say *and obey it.* God speaks to His children, either through the loving voice of Scripture or the heavy hand of chastening; and if we ignore the first, we must endure the second. One way or another, the Lord is going to get our attention and deal with us.

Now He came down to help them (vv. 11-13). The people were crying out to the Lord for help (6:7), as people usually do when they're in trouble. The Israelites gave no evidence of real repentance, but their affliction moved God's loving heart. "In all their affliction He was afflicted" (Isa. 63:9). "He does not treat us as our sins deserve or repay us according to our iniquities" (Ps. 103:10, NIV). God in His mercy doesn't give us what we do deserve; and in His grace, He gives us what we don't deserve.

When you consider the kind of man Gideon was at this time, you wonder why God selected him; but God often chooses the "weak things of this world" to accomplish great things for His glory (1 Cor. 1:26-29).[3] Gideon's family worshiped Baal (Judg. 6:25-32), although we have no reason to believe that Gideon joined them. When Gideon called himself "the least in my father's house" (v. 15), he may have been suggesting that his family treated him like an outcast because he didn't worship Baal. Gideon wasn't a man of strong faith or courage, and God had to patiently work with him to prepare him for leadership. God is always ready to make us what we ought to be if we're willing to submit to His will (Eph. 2:10; Phil. 2:12-13).

Gideon's negative response to the Lord's words indicates his lack of faith and spiritual perception. Here was Almighty God telling him that He was with him and would make him a conqueror, and Gideon replied by denying everything God said! God would have to spend time with Gideon turning his question marks into exclamation points. Gideon was living by sight, not by faith, and had he remained that way he would never have been named among the heroes of faith in Hebrews 11.

2. "Does God know what He's doing?" (Judg. 6:14-24)

Gideon s first response was to question *God's concern* for His people, but then he questioned *God's wisdom* in choosing him to be the nation's deliverer. The Lord's statements recorded in verses 12 and 14 should have given Gideon all the assurance he needed, but he wouldn't believe God's Word. In this he was like Moses (Ex. 3:7-12), whose story Gideon surely knew since he was acquainted with Hebrew history (Judg. 6:13).

It has often been said that "God's commandments are God's enablements." Once God has called and commissioned us, all we have to do is obey Him by faith, and He will do the rest. God cannot lie and God never fails. Faith means obeying God in spite of what we see, how we feel, or what the consequences might be. Our modern "practical" world laughs at faith without realizing that people live by faith all day long. "If there was no faith, there would be no living in this world," wrote humorist John Billings nearly a century ago. "We couldn't even eat hash with safety."

Gideon's statement about the poverty of his family is a bit perplexing in light of the fact that he had ten servants who assisted him (v. 27). It may be that the clan of Abiezer, to which Gideon's family belonged, was not an important clan in Manasseh; or perhaps Gideon's statement was simply the standard way to respond to a compliment, as when people used to sign their letters "Your Obedient Servant." In any event, Gideon seemed to think that God could *do* nothing because he and his family *were* nothing.

Once God has revealed His will to us, we must never question His wisdom or argue with His plans. "Who has known the mind of the Lord? Or who has been His counselor?" (Rom. 11:34, NIV; see Isa. 40:13 and 1 Cor. 2:16) "Can you search out the deep things of God? Can you find out the limits of the Almighty?" (Job 11:7, NKJV) A.W. Tozer wrote, "All God's acts are done in perfect wisdom, first for His own glory, and then for the highest good of the greatest number for the longest time."[4] That being true, who are we to question Him?

When you review God's gracious promises to Gideon, you wonder why this young man wavered in his faith. God promised to be with him. God called him a "mighty man of valor" and promised that he would save Israel from the Midianites and smite them "as one man." God's Word is "the word of faith" (Rom. 10:8), and "faith comes by hearing, and hearing by the Word of God" (Rom. 10:17). But Gideon didn't receive that Word and needed assurance beyond the character of Almighty God.

Gideon asked for a sign to assure him that it was really the Lord who was speaking to him (1 Cor. 1:22), and the Lord was gracious to accommodate

Himself to Gideon's unbelief. Gideon prepared a sacrifice, which was a costly thing to do at a time when food was scarce. An ephah of flour was about a half a bushel, enough to make bread for a family for several days. It probably took him an hour to dress the meat and prepare the unleavened cakes, but God waited for him to return and then consumed the offering by bringing fire from the rock.

The sudden appearance of the fire and disappearance of the visitor convinced Gideon that indeed he had seen God and spoken to Him, and this frightened him even more. Since the Jews believed it was fatal for sinful man to look upon God, Gideon was sure he would die. The human heart is indeed deceitful: Gideon asked to see a sign, and after seeing it, he was sure that the God who gave him the sign would now kill him! There is always "joy and peace in believing" (Rom. 15:13), but unbelief brings fear and worry.

God had to give Gideon a message of peace to prepare him for fighting a war. Unless we're at peace with God, we can't face the enemy with confidence and fight the Lord's battles. It was customary for the Jews to identify special events and places by putting up monuments,[5] so Gideon built an altar and called it "The Lord is peace." The Hebrew word for "peace" *(shalom)* means much more than a cessation of hostilities but carries with it the ideas of well-being, health, and prosperity. Gideon now believed the Lord was able to use him, not because of who he was, but because of who God was.

Whenever God calls us to a task that we think is beyond us, we must be careful to look to God and not to ourselves. "Is anything too hard for the Lord?" God asked Abraham (Gen. 18:14); and the answer comes, "For with God nothing shall be impossible" (Luke 1:37). Job discovered that God could do everything (Job 42:2), and Jeremiah admitted that there was nothing too hard for God (Jer. 32:17). Jesus told His disciples, "With God all things are possible" (Matt. 19:26); and Paul testified, "I can do all things through Christ who strengthens me" (Phil. 4:13, NKJV).

3. "Will God take care of me?" (Judg. 6:25-32)

What kind of a day did Gideon have after his dramatic meeting with the Lord? Remember, he belonged to a family that worshiped Baal; and if he challenged the Midianites in the name of the Lord, it meant defying his father, his family, his neighbors, and the multitudes of people in Israel who were worshiping Baal. My guess is that Gideon had his emotional ups and downs that day, rejoicing that God was planning to deliver Israel, but trembling at the thought of being named the leader of the army.

Knowing that Gideon was still afraid, God assigned him a task right at home to show him that He would see him through. After all, if we don't practice our faith at home, how can we practice it sincerely anyplace else? Gideon had to take his stand in his own village before he dared to face the enemy on the battlefield.

Before God gives His servants great victories in public, He sometimes prepares them by giving them smaller victories at home. Before David killed the giant Goliath in the sight of two armies, he learned to trust God by killing a lion and a bear in the field where nobody saw it but God (1 Sam. 17:32-37). When we prove that we're faithful with a few things, God will trust us with greater things (Matt. 25:21).

The assignment wasn't an easy one. God told him to destroy the altar dedicated to Baal, build an altar to the Lord, and sacrifice one of his father's valuable bullocks, using the wood of the Asherah pole for fuel. Jewish altars were made of uncut stones and were simple, but Baal's altars were elaborate and next to them was a wooden pillar ("grove," Judg. 6:26; "Asherah pole," NIV) dedicated to the goddess Asherah, whose worship involved unspeakably vile practices. Since altars to Baal were built on high places, it would have been difficult to obey God's orders without attracting attention.

Gideon had every right to destroy Baal worship because this is what God had commanded in His Law (Ex. 34:12-13; Deut. 7:5). For that matter, he had the right to stone everybody who was involved in Baal worship (Deut. 13), but God didn't include that in His instructions.

Gideon decided to obey the Lord at night when the village was asleep. This showed his fear (Judg. 6:27); he wasn't sure God could or would see him through. "Why are you so fearful? How is it that you have no faith?" (Mark 4:40, NKJV) "Behold, God is my salvation, I will trust and not be afraid" (Isa. 12:2, NKJV). After all the encouragements God had given him, Gideon's faith should have been strong; but before we judge him, we'd better look at ourselves and see how much *we* trust the Lord.

It's worth noting that true believers can't build an altar to the Lord unless first they tear down the altars they've built to the false gods they worship. Our God is a jealous God (Ex. 20:5) and will not share His glory or our love with another. Gideon had privately built his own altar to the Lord (Jud 6:24), but now he had to take his public stand; and he had to do it without compromise. Before he could declare war on Midian, he had to declare war on Baal.

When ten other men are involved, it's not easy to keep your plans a secret; so it wasn't long before the whole town knew that Gideon was the one who had destroyed his father's idols. The men of the city considered this a capital offense and wanted to kill Gideon. (According to God's law, it was the idol-worshipers who should have been slain! See Deut. 13:6-9.) Gideon was no doubt wondering what would happen to him, but God proved Himself well able to handle the situation.

Joash, Gideon's father, had every reason to be angry with his son. Gideon had smashed his father's altar to Baal and replaced it with an altar to Jehovah. He had sacrificed his father's prize bull to the Lord and had used the sacred Asherah pole for fuel. (See Isa. 44:13-20.) But God so worked in Joash's heart that he defended Gideon before the town mob and even insulted Baal! "What kind of a god is Baal that he can't even defend himself?" asked Joash. (Elijah would take a similar approach years later. See 1 Kings 18:27.) "What kind of a god is Baal that he can't even plead his own cause?" Joash asked. Because of this, the men of the town gave Gideon the nickname "Jerubbaal," which means "let Baal contend" or "Baal's antagonist."[6]

Often the unbelieving world gives demeaning nicknames to faithful servants of God. D.L. Moody was known as "Crazy Moody" when he was building his famous Sunday school in Chicago, but nobody would call him that today; and Charles Spurgeon was frequently lampooned and caricatured in the British press. If we are given nicknames because we honor the name of Jesus, then let's wear them like medals and keep on glorifying Him!

Gideon learned a valuable lesson that

day: If he obeyed the Lord, even with fear in his heart, the Lord would protect him and receive the glory. Gideon needed to remember this as he mustered his army and prepared to attack the enemy.

4. "Does God keep His promises?" (Judg. 6:33-40)

The Midianites and their allies made their annual invasion about that time as more than 135,000 men (8:10; 7:12) moved into the Valley of Jezreel. It was time for Gideon to act, and the Spirit of God gave him the wisdom and power that he needed. (See Judg. 3:10; 11:29; 13:25; 14:6, 19; 15:14.) As we seek to do God's will, His Word to us is always, "Not by might, nor by power, but by My spirit" (Zech. 4:6).

When a group of British pastors was discussing the advisability of inviting evangelist D.L. Moody to their city for a crusade, one man asked, "Why must it be Moody? Does D.L. Moody have a monopoly on the Holy Spirit?" Quietly one of the other pastors replied, "No, but it's evident that the Holy Spirit has a monopoly on D.L. Moody."

Gideon blew the trumpet first in his own hometown, and the men of Abiezer rallied behind him. Gideon's reformation in the town had actually accomplished something! Then he sent messengers throughout his own tribe of Manasseh as well as the neighboring tribes of Asher, Zebulun, and Naphtali. These four tribes were near the Valley of Jezreel, and therefore the invading army affected them most. Thus at Gideon's call, 32,000 men responded.

But what chance did 32,000 men have against an army of 135,000 men plus numberless camels? (Judg. 7:12) This is the first mention in the Bible of camels being used in warfare, and certainly they would have given their riders speed and mobility on the battlefield. The Jews were outnumbered and would certainly be outmaneuvered, except for one thing: Jehovah God was on their side, and He had promised them victory.

Nevertheless, Gideon doubted God's promise. Did God really want *him* to lead the Jewish army? What did he know about warfare? After all, he was only an ordinary farmer; and there were others in the tribes who could do a much better job. So, before he led the attack, he asked God to give him two more signs.

The phrase "putting out the fleece" is a familiar one in religious circles. It means asking God to guide us in a decision by fulfilling some condition that we lay down. In my pastoral ministry, I've met all kinds of people who have gotten themselves into trouble by "putting out the fleece." If they received a phone call at a certain hour from a certain person, God was telling them to do this; or if the weather changed at a certain time, God was telling them to do something else.

"Putting out the fleece " is not a biblical method for determining the will of God. Rather, it's an approach used by people like Gideon who lack the faith to trust God to do what He said He would do. Twice Gideon reminded God of what He had said (6:36-37), and twice Gideon asked God to reaffirm His promises with a miracle. The fact that God stooped to Gideon's weakness only proves that He's a gracious God who understands how we're made (Ps. 103:14).[7] Who are we to tell God what conditions He must meet, especially when He has already spoken to us in His Word? "Putting out the fleece" is not only an evidence of our unbelief, but it's also an evidence of our pride. God has to do what I tell Him to do before I'll do what He tells me to do!

Gideon spent two days playing the fleece game with God at the threshing floor. The first night, he asked God to make the fleece wet but keep the ground dry (in this incident the Bible uses "floor" and "ground" interchangeably) and God did it. The second night, the test was much harder; for he wanted the threshing floor to be wet but the fleece dry. The ground of a threshing floor is ordinarily very hard and normally would not be greatly affected by the dew. But the next morning, Gideon found dry fleece but wet ground.

There was nothing for Gideon to do but to confront the enemy and trust God for the victory. "And this is the victory that has overcome the world—our faith" (1 John 5:4, NKJV).

CHAPTER FIVE
FAITH IS THE VICTORY
Judges 7

I don't recall too many chapel messages from my years as a seminary student, but Vance Havner gave a message that has stayed with me and often encouraged me. Speaking from Hebrews 11, he told us that because Moses was a man of faith, he was able to "see the invisible, choose the imperishable, and do the impossible." I needed that message then and I still need it today.

What was true for Moses centuries ago can be true for God's people today, but men and women of faith seem to be in short supply. Whatever our churches may be known for today, they're not especially known for glorifying God by great exploits of faith. "The church used to be known for its good deeds," said one wit, "but today it's better known for its bad mortgages."

"For whatever is born of God overcomes the world. And this is the victory that has overcome the world—our faith" (1 John 5:4, NKJV). Christians are either overcome because of their unbelief or overcomers because of their faith. And remember, faith doesn't depend on how we feel, what we see, or what may happen. The Quaker poet John Greenleaf Whittier put it this way in "My Soul and I":

> Nothing before, nothing behind;
> The steps of faith
> Fall on the seeming void, and find
> The rock beneath.

That rock is the Word of God.

The familiar and exciting account of Gideon's wonderful victory over the Midianites is really a story of faith in action, and it reveals to us three important principles about faith. If we're to be overcomers, and not be overcome, we need to understand and apply these principles.

1. God tests our faith (Judg. 7:1-8)

A faith that can't be tested can't be trusted. Too often, what people think is faith is really only a "warm fuzzy feeling" about faith or perhaps just "faith in faith." I recall being in a board meeting of an international ministry when one of the board members said enthusiastically, "We're simply going to have to step out by faith!" Quietly another board member asked, "Whose faith?" That question made all of us search our hearts.

J.G. Stipe said that faith is like a toothbrush: Everybody should have one and use it regularly, but it isn't safe to use somebody else's. We can sing loudly about the "Faith of Our Fathers," but we can't exercise the faith of our fathers. We can follow men and women of faith and share in their exploits, but we can't succeed in our own personal lives by depending on somebody else's faith.

God tests our faith for at least two reasons: first, to show us whether our faith is real or counterfeit, and second, to strengthen our faith for the tasks He's set before us. I've noticed in my own life and ministry that God has often put us through the valley of testing before allowing us to reach the mountain peak of victory. Spurgeon was right when he said that the promises of God shine brightest in the furnace of affliction, and it is in claiming those promises that we gain the victory.

The first sifting (vv. 1-3). God tested Gideon's faith by sifting his army of 32,000 volunteers until only 300 men were left. If Gideon's faith had been in the size of his army, then his faith would have been very weak by the time God was through with them! Less than 1 percent of the original 32,000 ended up following Gideon to the battlefield. The words of Winston Churchill concerning the RAF in World War II certainly applies to Gideon's 300: "Never in the field of human conflict was so much owed to so few by so many."

God told Gideon why He was decreasing the size of the army: He didn't want the soldiers to boast that they had won the victory over the Midianites. Victories won because of faith bring glory to God because nobody can explain how they happened. "If you can explain what's going on in your ministry," Dr. Bob Cook used to remind us, "then God didn't do it." When I was serving in Youth for Christ, I often heard our leaders pray, "Lord, keep Youth for Christ on a miracle basis. That meant living by faith.

Too often, we're like King Uzziah who was "marvelously helped, till he was strong. But when he was strong, his heart was lifted up to his destruction" (2 Chron. 26:15-16). People who live by faith know their own weakness more and more as they depend on God's strength. "For when I am weak, then am I strong" (2 Cor. 12:10).

In telling the fearful soldiers to return home, Gideon was simply obeying the law Moses originally gave: "What man is there who is fearful and fainthearted? Let him go and return to his house, lest the heart of his brethren faint like his heart" (Deut. 20:8, NKJV). "The fearful and trembling man God cannot use," said G. Campbell Morgan. "The trouble today is that the fearful and trembling man insists upon remaining in the army. A decrease that sifts the ranks of the church of men who fear and tremble is a great, a gracious and a glorious gain"[1]

Pride after the battle robs God of glory, and fear during the battle robs God's soldiers of courage and power. Fear has a way of spreading, and one timid soldier can do more damage than a whole company of enemy soldiers. Fear and faith can't live together very long in the same heart. Either fear will conquer faith and we'll quit, or faith will conquer fear and we'll triumph. John Wesley may have been thinking of Gideon's army when he said, "Give me a hundred men who fear nothing but sin and love nothing but God, and I will shake the gates of hell!"[2]

The second sifting (vv. 4-8). God put Gideon's surviving 10,000 men through a second test by asking them all to take a drink down at the river. *We never know when God is testing us in some ordinary experience of life.* I heard about one leading minister who always took a drive with a prospective pastoral staff member i*n the other man's car,* just to see if the car was neat and if the man drove carefully.

Whether or not neatness and careful driving habits are always a guarantee of ministerial success is debatable, but the lesson is worth considering. More than one prospective employee has ruined his or her chances for a job while having lunch with the boss, not realizing they were being evaluated. "Make every occasion a great occasion, for you can never tell when somebody may be taking your measure for a larger place." That was said by a man named Marsden; and I've had the quotation, now yellow with age, under the glass on my desk for many years. Pondering it from time to time has done me good.

What significance was there in the two different ways the men drank from the river? Since the Scriptures don't tell us, we'd be wise not to read into the text some weighty spiritual lesson that God never put there. Most expositors say the men who bowed down to drink were making themselves vulnerable to the enemy, while the 300 who lapped water from their hands stayed alert. But the enemy was four miles away (v. 1), waiting to see what the Jews would do; and Gideon wouldn't have led his men into a dangerous situation like that. One well-known preacher claims that the 300 men drank as they did so they could keep their eyes on Gideon, but the text doesn't say that either.

My assumption is that God chose this method of sifting the army because it was simple, unassuming (no soldier knew he was being tested), and easy to apply. We shouldn't think that all 10,000 drank at one time, because that would have stretched the army out along the water for a couple of miles. Since the men undoubtedly came to the water by groups, Gideon was able to watch them and identify the 300. It wasn't until after the event that the men discovered they had been tested.

"There is no restraint to the Lord to save by many or by few (1 Sam. 14:6). Some churches today are mesmerized by statistics and think they're strong because they're big and wealthy, but numbers are no guarantee of God's blessing. Moses assured the Jews that if they would obey the Lord, one soldier could chase a thousand and two would "put ten thousand to flight" (Deut. 32:30). All Gideon needed was 27 soldiers to defeat the whole Midianite army of 135,000 men (Judg. 8:10), but God gave him 300.

It is clear from 7:14 that the Midianites knew who Gideon was, and no doubt they were watching what he was doing. I've often wondered what the enemy spies thought when they saw the Jewish army seemingly fall apart. Did it make the Midianites overconfident and therefore less careful? Or did their leaders become even more alert, wondering whether Gideon was setting them up for a tricky piece of strategy?

God graciously gave Gideon one more promise of victory:

"By the 300 men that lapped will I save you" (v. 7). By claiming this promise and obeying the Lord's directions, Gideon defeated the enemy and brought peace to the land for forty years (8:28).

The soldiers who departed left some of their equipment with the 300 men thus each man could have a torch, a trumpet, and a jar—strange weapons indeed for fighting a war.

2. God encourages our faith (Judg. 7:9-15a)

The Lord wanted Gideon and his 300 men to attack the camp of Midian that night, but first He had to deal with the fear that still persisted in Gideon's heart. God had already told Gideon three times that He would give Israel victory (6:14, 16; 7:7), and He had reassured him by giving him three special signs: fire from the rock (6:19-21), the wet fleece (6:36-38), and the dry fleece (6:39-40). After all this divine help, Gideon should have been strong in his faith, but such was not the case.

How grateful we should be that God understands us and doesn't condemn us because we have doubts and fears! He keeps giving us wisdom and doesn't scold us when we keep asking (James 1:5). Our great High Priest in heaven sympathizes with our weaknesses (Heb. 4:14-16) and keeps giving us more grace (James 4:6). God remembers that we're only dust (Ps. 103:14) and flesh (78:39).

God encouraged Gideon's faith in two ways.

God gave Gideon another promise (v. 9). The Lord told Gideon for the fourth time that He had delivered the Midianite host into his hand. (Note the tense of the verb, and see Josh. 6:2.) Although the battle must be fought, Israel had already won! The 300 men could attack the enemy host confident that Israel was the victor.

Some people have the idea that confident, courageous faith is a kind of religious arrogance, but just the opposite is true.

Christians who believe God's promises and see Him do great things are humbled to know that the God of the universe cares about them and is on their side. They claim no merit in their faith or honor from their victories. All the glory goes to the Lord because He did it all! It's the unbelieving child of God who grieves the Lord and makes Him a liar (1 John 5:10).

Hope and love are important Christian virtues, but the Holy Spirit devoted an entire chapter in the New Testament—Hebrews 11—to the victories of *faith* won by ordinary people who dared to believe God and act upon His promises. It may be a cliche to some people, but the old formula is still true: "God says it—I believe it—that settles it!"

God gave Gideon another sign (vv. 10-14). It took courage for Gideon and his servant to move into enemy territory and get close enough to the Midianite camp to overhear the conversation of two soldiers. God had given one of the soldiers a dream, and that dream told Gideon that God would deliver the Midianites into his hand. The Lord had already told Gideon this fact, but now Gideon heard it from the lips of the enemy!

In the biblical record, you often find God communicating His truth through dreams. Among the believers He spoke to through dreams are Jacob (Gen. 28, 31), Joseph (Gen. 37), Solomon (1 Kings 3), Daniel (Dan. 7), and Joseph, the husband of Mary (Matt. 1:20-21; 2:13-22). But He also spoke to unbelievers this way, including Abimelech (Gen. 20), Nebuchadnezzar (Dan. 2, 4), Joseph's fellow prisoners (Gen. 40), Pharaoh (Gen. 41), and Pilate's wife (Matt. 27:19). However, we must not conclude from these examples that this is the Lord s normal method of communicating with people or that we should seek His guidance in our dreams today. Dreams can be deceptive (Jer. 23:32; Zech. 10:2), and apart from divine instruction we can't know the correct interpretation.

The best way to get God's guidance is through the Word of God, prayer, and sensitivity to the Spirit as we watch circumstances.

Since barley was a grain used primarily by poor people, the barley-cake image of Gideon and his army spoke of their weakness and humiliation. The picture is that of a stale hard cake that could roll like a wheel, not a complimentary comparison at all! The man who interpreted the dream had no idea that he was speaking God's truth and encouraging God's servant. Gideon didn't mind being compared to a loaf of stale bread, for now he knew for sure that Israel would defeat the Midianites and deliver the land from bondage.

It's significant that Gideon paused to worship the Lord before he did anything else. He was so overwhelmed by the Lord's goodness and mercy that he fell on his face in submission and gratitude. Joshua did the same thing before taking the city of Jericho (Josh. 5:13-15), and it's a good practice for us to follow today. Before we can be successful warriors, we must first become sincere worshipers.

3. God honors our faith. (Judg. 7:15b-25)

"But without faith it is impossible to please Him, for he who comes to God must believe that He is, and that He is a rewarder of those who diligently seek Him" (Heb. 11:6, NKJV). Faith means more than simply trusting God; it also means *seeking* God and wanting to *please* Him. We don't trust God just to get Him to do things for us. We trust Him because it brings joy to His heart when His children rely on Him, seek Him, and please Him.

How did God reward Gideon's faith?

God gave him wisdom to prepare the army (7:15b-18). Gideon was a new man when he and his servant returned to the Israelite camp. His fears and doubts were gone as he mobilized his small army and infused courage into their hearts by what he said and did. "The Lord has delivered the camp of Midian into your hand," he announced to the men (v. 15, NKJV). As Vance Havner said, faith sees the invisible (victory in a battle not yet fought) and does the impossible (wins the battle with few men and peculiar weapons).

Gideon's plan was simple but effective. He gave each of his men a trumpet to blow, a jar to break, and a torch to burn. They would encircle the enemy camp, the torches inside the jars and their trumpets in their hands. The trumpets were rams' horns (the *shofar)* such as Joshua used at Jericho, and perhaps this connection with that great victory helped encourage Gideon and his men as they faced the battle. At Gideon's signal, the men would blow the trumpets, break the pitchers, reveal the lights, and then shout, "The sword of the Lord and of Gideon!" God would do the rest.

Gideon was the example for them to follow. "Watch me. . . . Follow my lead. . . . Do exactly as I do" (v. 17, NIV). Gideon had come a long way since the day God had found him hiding in the winepress! No longer do we hear him asking "If—why—where?" (6:13) No longer does he seek for a sign. Instead, he confidently gave orders to his men, knowing that the Lord would give them the victory.

It has been well said that the Good News of the Gospel is we don't have to stay the way we are. Through faith in Jesus Christ, anybody can be changed. "Therefore, if anyone is in Christ, he is a new creation; old things have passed away; behold, all things have become new" (2 Cor. 5:17, NKJV).

Jesus said to Andrew's brother, "You are Simon ["a hearer"]. . . . You shall be called Cephas ["a stone"]" (John 1:42, NKJV). "You are—you shall be!" That's good news for anybody who wants a new start in life. God can take a weak piece of clay like Simon and make a rock out of him! God can take a doubter like Gideon and make a general out of him!

God gave him courage to lead the army (vv. 19-22). Gideon led his small army from the Spring of Harod ("trembling") to the Valley of Jezreel, where they all took their places around the camp. At Gideon's signal, they all blew their rams' horns, broke the jars, and shouted, "The sword of the Lord and of Gideon!" Finding themselves surrounded by sudden light and loud noises, the Midianites assumed that they were being attacked by a large army, and the result was panic. The Lord intervened and put a spirit of confusion in the camp, and the Midianites began to kill each other. Then they realized that the safest thing to do was flee. Thus they took off on the caravan route to the southeast with the Israelite army pursuing.

God gave him opportunity to enlarge the army (vv. 23-25). It was obvious that 300 men couldn't pursue thousands of enemy soldiers, so Gideon sent out a call for more volunteers. I'm sure that many of the men from the original army of 32,000 responded to Gideon's call, and even the proud tribe of Ephraim came to his aid. To them was given the honor of capturing and slaying Oreb ("raven") and Zeeb ("wolf"), the two princes of Midian. The story of Gideon began with a man hiding in a winepress (6:11), but it ended with the enemy prince being slain at a winepress.

Gideon's great victory over the Midianites became a landmark event in the history of Israel, not unlike the Battle of Waterloo for Great Britain, for it reminded the Jews of God's power to deliver them from their enemies. The day of Midian was a great day that Israel would never forget (Ps. 83:11; Isa. 9:4; 10:26).

The church today can also learn from this event and be encouraged by it. God doesn't need large numbers to accomplish His purposes, nor does He need especially gifted leaders. Gideon and his 300 men were available for God to use, and He enabled them to conquer the enemy and bring peace to the land. When the church starts to depend on "bigness"—big buildings, big crowds, big budgets—then faith becomes misplaced, and God can't give His blessing. When leaders depend on their education, skill, and experience rather than in God, then God abandons them and looks for a Gideon.

The important thing is for us to be available for God to use just as He sees fit. We may not fully understand His plans but we can fully trust His promises; and it's faith in Him that gives the victory.

CHAPTER SIX
WIN THE WAR, LOSE THE VICTORY
Judges 8

Be careful where you travel for business or vacation. You might pick a place that's dangerous.

According to an article in the June 25, 1993 issue of Pulse, there are fifty-six nations that have serious problems with land mines. Angola has 20 million mines waiting to maim or kill, Afghanistan 10 million, and Cambodia 4 1/2 million; and the expense of removing them is more than these nations can handle. The wars may be over, but the dangers haven't vanished.

The saintly Scottish Presbyterian pastor Andrew Bonar wasn't thinking particularly about land mines when he said it, but what he said is good counsel for all of us: "Let us be as watchful after the victory as before the battle." That was the counsel Gideon needed after he'd routed the Midianites, because his problems still weren't over. He discovered some "mines" that were ready to explode.

Thus far in our study of Gideon's life, we've seen his responses to the Lord's call to defeat the enemy. At first Gideon was full of questions and doubts; but then he grew in his faith, believed God's promises, and led his army to victory. In Judges 3, the account focuses on Gideon's responses to various people *after he had won the battle;* and it tells us how he handled some difficult situations.

The chronology in chapter 8 seems to be as follows: Gideon's pursuit of the two kings (vv. 4-12); his disciplining of the defiant Jews on his journey home (vv. 13-17); the protest of the Ephraimites after he arrived home (vv. 1-3); the slaying of the kings (vv. 18-21); and Gideon's "retirement" (vv. 22-35). Each of these events presented a new challenge to Gideon, and he responded differently to each one.

1. A soft answer for his critics (Judg. 8:1-3)

Why this paragraph is placed here is somewhat of a puzzle. It's not likely that the men of Ephraim would complain to Gideon while they were capturing Oreb and Zeeb (7:24-25) and while he was pursuing Zebah and Zalmunna (8:12). Fighting the enemy would have consumed all their energy and attention, and Gideon's reply in verse 3 indicates that the men of Ephraim had already captured and killed Oreb and Zeeb. Perhaps a delegation from the tribe waited on Gideon when the spoils of war were being distributed after he returned home, and that's when they complained.

Knowing that they were a large and important tribe, second only to Judah, the Ephraimites were a proud people. Gideon was from Manasseh, the "brother" tribe to Ephraim[1] and Ephraim was insulted because he didn't call them to the battle. But why would such an important tribe want to follow a farmer into battle? They had assisted Ehud (3:26-29) and Deborah and Barak (5:13-14), but that was no guarantee they would help Gideon.

When you reflect on the way the attack on Midian was handled, it was wisdom on Gideon's part that he hadn't called for volunteers from Ephraim. This proud tribe would have been incensed if Gideon had told the frightened men to go home, and their volunteers would not have tolerated his thinning out the ranks to only 300 soldiers! If Gideon had called them and then sent most of them back, they would have created a far worse problem *before* the battle than they did afterward. Ephraim was on hand to help in the "mopping up" operations, and that's what really counted.

Ephraim, however, missed out on acquiring some valuable spoils of war from over 100,000 soldiers, and this may have been what irritated them. (Usually when people criticize something you've done, there's a personal reason behind their criticism; and you may never find out what the real reason was.) Since David's unselfish law governing the dividing of the spoils of war hadn't been established yet (1 Sam. 30:21-25), those who didn't participate in the battle didn't share in the loot. When the men of Ephraim should have been thanking Gideon for delivering the nation, they were criticizing him and adding to his burdens.

As a victorious general, a national hero, and the people's first choice for king, Gideon might have used his authority and popularity to put the tribe of Ephraim in its place, but he chose to use a better approach. "A soft answer turns away wrath, but a harsh word stirs up anger" (Prov. 15:1, NKJV). Perhaps Gideon's immediate feelings weren't that cordial, but he controlled himself and treated his brothers with kindness. "He who is slow to anger is better than the mighty, and he who rules his spirit than he who takes a city" (16:32, NKJV). Gideon proved that he could control not only an army, but also his temper and tongue.

It's sad when brothers declare war on each other after they've stood together to defeat the enemy. "Behold, how good and how pleasant it is for brethren to dwell together in unity!" (Ps. 133:1) It didn't cost Gideon much to swallow his pride and compliment the men of Ephraim. He told them that their capturing Oreb and Zeeb was a greater feat than anything the men had done from his hometown of Abiezer. Peace was restored and Gideon returned to the more important tasks at hand.[2]

In *Poor Richard's Almanack* (1734), Benjamin Franklin wrote:

> Take this remark from Richard, poor and lame,
> Whate'er's begun in anger ends in shame.

And King Solomon wrote, "The beginning of strife is like releasing water; therefore stop contention before a quarrel starts" (Prov. 17:14, NKJV).

2. A stern warning for the skeptics (Judg. 8:4-17)

Gideon and his men were pursuing two of the Midianite kings, Zebah and Zalmunna, knowing that if they captured and killed them, the enemy's power would be crippled and eventually broken. The army crossed over the Jordan to Succoth in Gad, hoping to find some nourishment; but the men of Succoth wouldn't help their own brothers. The two and a half tribes that occupied the land east of the Jordan didn't feel as close to the other tribes as they should have, and Gad had sent no soldiers to help either Deborah and Barak (5:17) or Gideon. While others were risking their lives, the people of Gad were doing nothing.

The Ammonites and Moabites, relatives of the Jews through Lot, failed to help Israel with food; and God declared war on them (Deut. 23:3-6). Hospitality is one of the basic laws of the East, and custom demands that the people meet the needs of strangers as well as relatives. Hospitality was also an important ministry in the early church, for there were no hotels where guests might stay; and in times of persecution, many visitors were fleeing. (See Rom. 12:13; 1 Tim. 5:10; Heb. 13:2; 1 Peter 4:9.) Indeed, helping a hungry brother is an opportunity to help the Lord Jesus (Matt. 25:34-40).

The men of Succoth were skeptical of Gideon's ability to defeat the fleeing Midianite army and capture the two kings. If Succoth helped Gideon and Gideon failed, then the Midianites would visit Succoth and retaliate. The men of Succoth didn't think feeding a hungry brother was an opportunity to show love but was a risk they didn't want to take, and they were rather impudent in the way they spoke to Gideon. Since Gideon received the same response from the men at Peniel (Penuel), he warned both cities that he would return and discipline them.

God gave Gideon and his men victory over the fleeing Midianite hosts and enabled him to capture the two enemy kings. Triumphantly he retraced his steps and kept his promise to the men of Succoth and Peniel. Providentially, he found a young man who was able to give him the names of the seventy-seven leaders in Succoth who had refused to help him and his army. He showed them the two kings whom the elders had said Gideon would never capture, and then he chastised them, apparently by beating them with thorny branches.[3] He then went to Peniel and wrecked their tower, killing the men who had opposed him.

Why didn't Gideon show to the people of Succoth and Peniel the same kindness that he showed to the Ephraimites and simply forgive them their offenses? For one thing, their offenses were not alike. The pride of Ephraim was nothing compared to the rebellion of Succoth and Peniel. Ephraim was protecting their tribal pride, a sin but not a costly one; but Succoth and Peniel were rebelling against God's chosen leader *and assisting the enemy at the same time.* Theirs was the sin of hardness of heart toward their brethren and treason against the God of heaven. Of what good was it for Gideon and his men to risk their lives to deliver Israel if they had traitors right in their own nation?

Leaders must have discernment or they will make wrong decisions as they deal with different situations. Personal insults are one thing, but rebellion against the Lord and His people is quite something else.

3. A solemn question for his enemies (Judg. 8:18-21)

When Gideon arrived back home at Ophrah, leading Zebah and Zalmunna captive, the procession must have been as exciting as a ticker-tape parade. Gideon was a true hero. With only 300 men, he had routed the enemy camp and then pursued the fleeing soldiers across the Jordan and as far south as Karkor. He had brought his royal prisoners back, plus whatever spoils the men had gathered along the way.

Gideon had a personal matter to settle with these two kings because they had been guilty of killing his brothers at Tabor. The text doesn't tell us when this wicked act took place, but it must have occurred during one of the previous annual Midianite raids. How Gideon's brothers became involved and why they were killed isn't explained to us, but the suggestion is that the act was a unconscionable one.

According to Mosaic Law, the family was to avenge crimes like this by killing those responsible for the murder. There was no police system in the land, and each family was expected to track down and punish those who had murdered their relatives, provided the culprit was guilty (see Num. 35:9-34). In the case of Zebah and Zalmunna, the culprits were not only murderers but also enemies of Israel.

The two kings were shrewd in the way they answered Gideon, flattering him by comparing him and his brothers to princes. Someone has said that flattery is a good thing to taste but a bad thing to swallow, and Gideon didn't swallow it. How could he spare these two evil men who had taken food from the mouths of Jewish women and children and had brutally killed Jewish men?

In those days, how a soldier died was important to his reputation. Abimelech didn't want to die at the hand of a woman (9:53-54), and King Saul didn't want to fall into the hands of the Philistines (1 Sam. 31:1-6). For a child to kill a king would be the ultimate in humiliation thus Gideon told his young son Jether to execute the two criminals. By doing so, Jether would not only uphold the law of the land and humiliate the two kings, but he would also bring honor to himself. For the rest of his life, he would be known as the boy who executed Zebah and Zalmunna.

But the lad wasn't ready for either the responsibility or the honor. Even when people are guilty, enforcing justice in the land is a serious thing and must not be put into the hands of children. Because of his fear, Jether hesitated in avenging the murders of his uncles; so the two kings told Gideon to do it.

There seems to be a bit of sarcasm in their words, which may be paraphrased, "*You* kill us, Gideon. Let's see what kind of a man *you* are—or are you also just a child?" Zebah and Zalmunna didn't want the inexperienced Jether to execute them because he would have muddled the whole thing and made their deaths much more painful. The kings deliberately aroused Gideon's anger, knowing that he was a good swordsman and would dispatch them quickly, and that's exactly what he did.

4. A puzzling reply for his friends (Judg. 8:22-32)

The narrative focuses on two requests, one from the people to Gideon and the other from Gideon to the people.

The people request a king (vv. 22-23, 29-32). So popular was Gideon that the people asked him to set up a dynasty, something altogether new for the nation of Israel. This was one way they could reward Gideon for what he had done for them. But it was also somewhat of a guarantee that there would be a measure of unity among the tribes as well as the kind of leadership that would mobilize them against possible future invaders.

Their request was a confession of unbelief; for as Gideon reminded them, *God* was their king.[4] Gideon rejected their generous offer purely on theological grounds: He would not take the place of Jehovah God. Every Jew should have known that the mercy seat in the tabernacle was the throne of God from which He ruled in the midst of His people. "You who sit enthroned between the cherubim, shine forth" (Ps. 80:1, NIV). The Lord reigns, let the nations tremble; He sits enthroned between the cherubim, let the earth shake" (99:1 NIV). To set up a rival throne would be to dethrone the Lord.[5]

Moses warned that Israel would one day want a king like the other nations and forget that they were a unique nation, unlike the Gentiles (Deut. 4:5-8; 14:2; 17:14-20; Ex. 19:4-5) What other nation had the Creator, the Lord of heaven and earth, as their king?

What Gideon said was commendable, but what he did later on was very puzzling. After rejecting the throne, *he lived like a king!* Judges 8:29-32 describes the lifestyle of a monarch, not that of a judge or a retired army officer. Gideon was quite wealthy, partly from the spoils of battle and partly from the gifts of the people; and he had many wives and at least one concubine. His wives bore him seventy sons, his concubine bore him one. In fact, he named the son of the concubine Abimelech, which means "my father is a king"; and this son later tried to live up to his name and become ruler over all the land. Gideon also seems to have assumed priestly duties for he made his own ephod and probably consulted it on behalf of the people.

Nobody would deny that this courageous soldier-judge deserved honor and rewards, but his "retirement plan" seemed a bit extravagant.

Gideon requests gold (vv. 24-28). The people were only too eager to share their spoils with Gideon. After all, he had brought peace to the land (v. 28)[6] and had refused to become their king. Therefore, it was only right that he receive something for his labors. The Midianites wore gold crescents, either on the ear or the nose (Gen. 24:47), and the Israelite soldiers would have quickly taken these valuable items as they gathered the spoils. Gideon ended up with over forty pounds of gold, plus the wealth he took from Zebah and Zalmunna. No wonder he was able to live like a king!

At this point the man of faith led the people into idolatry; for Gideon made an ephod, and the people "played the harlot" with it (v. 27, NKJV). This meant that they stopped giving their true devotion to the Lord and used the ephod for an idol. In Scripture, idolatry is looked upon as prostitution (Isa. 50:1-3; 54:6-8; Jer. 2:1-3; 3:1ff; Hosea 2; James 4:4; Rev. 2:4). Gideon may have made the ephod as a representation of Jehovah, to "help the people" in their worship, but a good motive can never compensate for a bad action. He knew it was wrong to make an idol (Ex. 20:4-6).

Whether this ephod was an embellished version of the garment used by the high priest (28:6), or some kind of standing idol (see Judg. 17:5; 18:14, 17), we can't tell; but it was used in worship and became a snare to Gideon and the people (Ps. 106:36). Perhaps Gideon used it to determine the will of God and help the people with their problems. If the ephod was indeed a copy of the high priest's garment, then Gideon was definitely out of God's will in duplicating it and using it, because Gideon wasn't a priest. If it was a standing idol, Gideon was disobeying God's Law (Ex. 20:4-6) and corrupting the people as well. It was just a short step from worshiping the ephod to worshiping Baal (Judg. 8:33).

Gideon missed a great opportunity to bring reformation and perhaps revival to the land. He had torn down his father's idols, but there were many households in Israel that were still devoted to Baal, and those idols needed to be destroyed as well. The great victory over Midian gave Gideon good reason to call the nation back to the Lord and obedience to His Law. But instead of using the occasion for God's glory, he used it for his own profit; and the nation eventually lapsed into sin once again.

With his vast wealth and his great national reputation, Gideon probably thought that his children were well provided for, but just the opposite proved true. Sixty-nine of his seventy sons were killed by their half-brother who himself was slain by a woman dropping a stone on his head. *There is no security apart from the will of God.* Had Gideon practiced Matthew 6:33, subsequent events might have been radically different.

What caused Gideon's spiritual decline? I think it was pride. Before the battle against Midian, Gideon humbly depended on the Lord. During the "mopping up" operations, however, he became authoritative and even vindictive. When he refused the kingship, he sounded pious ("the Lord shall rule over you"), but I have a suspicion that he had a hidden agenda in his heart. You don't find Gideon honoring the Lord or calling the people together to make a new covenant to obey the Lord. Gideon started out as a servant, but now he was an important celebrity. The result was decline for him, his family, and his nation.

It's interesting and instructive to contrast Abraham and Gideon in the decisions they made after their respective victories (Gen. 14). Abraham took nothing for himself but made sure that others received their share of the spoils (Gen. 14:22-24). He especially refused to take anything from the heathen king of Sodom (Gen. 14:17, 21). Instead, Abraham fellowshipped with Melchizedek, King of Salem, a type of our Lord Jesus Christ

(Heb. 7-8); and in all that he said and did, Abraham gave glory to the Lord of heaven and earth.

Andrew Bonar was right: "Let us be as watchful after the victory as before the battle." After all, there may still be some land mines scattered around!

CHAPTER SEVEN
MY KINGDOM COME
Judges 9

When George Washington's army defeated the British General Charles Cornwallis at Yorktown, the end of the Revolutionary War began. Winning the war didn't automatically end the problems that the colonies faced. Things became so bad economically that one of George Washington's colonels wrote Washington a secret letter, urging him to use his army to make himself king or dictator. To the colonel, this was the only way to get the affairs of the young nation under control. Washington rejected the plan, but with his popularity and power he probably could have become king if he had so desired.

Abimelech was just the opposite. He had such a passionate desire to be king that he allowed nothing to stand in his way, not even the lives of hundreds of innocent people. This is the longest chapter in the Book of Judges and one of the most depressing.[1] The chapter records three stages in Abimelech's political career.

1. Seizing the kingdom (Judg. 9:1-21)

Abimelech was the son of Gideon by a slave woman who lived with her father's family in Shechem (8:30-31; 9:18). His name means "my father is a king." Although Gideon had certainly lived like a king, he had still refused to establish a dynasty in Israel, but Abimelech felt that his father had made a mistake. After his father's death, Abimelech decided that *he* should be king, thus he moved from Ophrah to Shechem, where he started his campaign. In what he did, Abimelech broke several of God's laws and as a result brought destruction to himself and trouble to the people.[2]

Selfish ambition (vv. 1-2). "You shall not covet" is the last of the Ten Commandments (Ex. 20:17, NKJV), but breaking it is the first step toward breaking the other nine. Of itself ambition isn't an evil thing, provided it's mixed with genuine humility and is controlled by the will of God. If it's God's wind that lifts you and you're soaring on wings that He's given you, then fly as high as He takes you. But if you manufacture both the wind and the wings, you're heading for a terrible fall.

"One can never consent to creep when one feels an impulse to soar," said Helen Keller; and her counsel is good, so long as the impulse to soar comes from the Lord. Selfish ambition destroys. "I will ascend into heaven!" turned an angel into the devil (Isa. 14:13, NKJV), and "Is not this great Babylon, that I have built" turned a king into an animal (Dan 4:28-37, NKJV). If we exalt ourselves, God has many ways of bringing us down (Matt. 23:12).

The Jews had been acquainted with the people of Shechem since the days of the patriarchs (Gen. 12:6; 33:18-20, 34:1ff). Both Jews and Canaanites lived in Shechem during Abimelech's days, which explains why he started his campaign there. His mother was a Shechemite and his father was a Jew. Therefore, if Abimelech became king, he could represent both constituencies!

Abimelech had another plank in his political platform: The Canaanites in Shechem had no indebtedness to Gideon's sons, while Abimelech was definitely one of their own. Furthermore, which of Gideon's seventy sons should be chosen king and how would he be selected? Or would all seventy try to rule the land together? With this kind of logic, Abimelech enlisted the support of both his relatives and the men of the city; and now he was ready to move into action.

Idolatry (v. 4). "You shall have no other gods before Me" and "You shall not make for yourself any carved image" are the first and second of the Ten Commandments (Ex. 20:3-4, NKJV), and Abimelech broke them both. It's obvious that he was his own god and that he had no interest in God's will for the nation. His accepting money from the Baal worshipers to finance his crusade was a public announcement that he had renounced the God of Israel and was on the side of Baal.

But Abimelech had another god beside ambition and Baal, and that was *might.* With the tainted money from the heathen temple, he hired a group of no-account mercenaries who helped him gain and keep control over the people. These vile terrorists also assisted him in his evil plot to murder his seventy half brothers and remove every rival to the throne.

The Greek philosopher Plato said, "Might is right"; and three centuries later, the Roman philosopher Seneca wrote, "Might makes right."[3] The French novelist Joseph Joubert wrote seventeen centuries later, "Might and right govern everything in the world; might till right is ready." But when *might* is in the hands of selfish dictators, *right* rarely has a chance to get ready or to take over. Might seizes control and will hold it unless a stronger power overcomes and brings freedom. The Prophet Habakkuk described these people as "guilty men, whose own strength is their god" (Hab. 1:11, NIV).

Murder (v. 5). The sixth commandment, "You shall not murder" (Ex. 20:13, NKJV), was violated scores of times by Abimelech and his mercenaries, beginning in Ophrah with their slaughter of sixty-nine of Abimelech's seventy half brothers. Why didn't somebody stop these murderers and defend Gideon's family? Because the people of Israel had forgotten both the goodness of the Lord and the kindness of Gideon (Judg. 8:33-35). They had neither the conviction to be concerned nor the courage to intervene. It doesn't take long for society to change yesterday's hero into today's scoundrel. What the Irish poet William Butler Yeats described in his famous poem "The Second Coming" was true in the nation of Israel:

> The best lack all conviction, while the worst
> Are full of passionate intensity.

"Woe to him who builds a city with bloodshed and establishes a town by crime!" (Hab. 2:12, NIV) Revelation 21:8 and 22:15 make it clear that murderers go to hell. Of course, a murderer can call on the Lord and be saved just as any other sinner can, but there's no evidence that Abimelech and his crowd ever repented of their sins. Their feet were "swift to shed blood" (Rom. 3:15; Isa. 59:7), and the blood that they shed eventually came back on their own heads.

Murder is bad enough, but when brother kills brother, the sin is even more heinous. By murdering his half brothers, Abimelech joined the ranks of other men in the Bible who committed fratricide, including Cain (Gen. 4), Absalom (2 Sam. 13:23ff), and Jehoram (2 Chron. 21:4). Not very nice company.

Dishonesty (v. 6). The third commandment says, "You shall not take the name of the Lord your God in vain" (Ex. 20:7, NKJV), and the ninth commandment forbids us bearing false witness (Ex. 20:16). Abimelech broke both commandments when he was crowned king. If he took an oath of office in the name of the Lord, it was pure blasphemy; and if he promised to protect the people and obey the law, it was further deception. (See Deut. 17:14-20.) No matter what he promised at the coronation, Abimelech had his own agenda and intended to carry it out.

The cynical journalist Ambrose Bierce defined "politics" as "a strife of interests masquerading as a contest of principles; the conduct of public affairs for private advantage." Certainly history records the names of dedicated men and women who put the good of their country ahead of the good of their party and personal gain, but in the case of Abimelech, Bierce's definition applies perfectly.

Abimelech's "coronation" was a farce, an empty ritual that was never accepted or blessed by the Lord. The new "king" not only blasphemed God by the promises he made, but he defiled a place sacred in Jewish history. The coronation took place at the "great tree at the pillar in Shechem" (Judg. 9:6, NIV). This is probably the "oak of Moreh," where the Lord appeared to Abraham and promised to give him and his descendants the land (Gen. 12:6). It was near this site that the nation of Israel heard the blessings and curses read from the Law and promised to obey the Lord (Deut. 11:26-32; Josh. 8:30-35). Jacob buried the idols here as he called his family back to God (Gen. 35:1-5), and here Joshua gave his last speech and led the people in reaffirming their obedience to the Lord (Josh. 24:25-26). All of this sacred history was degraded and dishonored by the selfish acts of one godless man.

Pride (vv. 7-21). Jotham was the only brother to escape the massacre (v. 5).[4] Perhaps the coronation celebrations were still in progress when Jotham interrupted with his parable from Mount Gerizim, which was adjacent to Shechem and the oak of Moreh. It was from Mount Gerizim that the blessings were to be read (Deut. 27:12, 28), but Jotham's story was anything but a blessing. It's worth noting that the tribe of Joseph (Ephraim and Manasseh) was to stand on the mount of blessing; but Abimelech certainly hadn't brought any blessing to Gideon's tribe of Manasseh.

This is the first parable recorded in Scripture. Many people have the idea that Jesus invented parables and that they are found only in the four Gospels, but neither is the case. Besides this "Parable of the Trees," the Old Testament also contains Nathan's "Parable of the Ewe Lamb" (2 Sam. 12:1–4), the parable by the woman of Tekoa (2 Sam. 14:5-20), the Parable of the Thistle (2 Kings 14:8-14), and the Parable of the Vineyard (Isa. 5:1-7). The prophecies of Jeremiah and Ezekiel contain both standard parables as well as "action" parables (Jer. 13, 18-19, 27-28; Ezek. 4-5, 16, 31, etc.).

Jotham pictured the trees looking for a king.[5] They approached the olive tree with its valuable oil, the fig tree with its sweet fruit, and the vine with its clusters that could be made into wine; but all of them refused to accept the honor. They would each have to sacrifice something in order to reign, and they weren't prepared to make that sacrifice.

All that remained was the bramble, a thornbush that was a useless nuisance in the land, good only for fuel for the fire. This, of course, was a symbol of Abimelech, the new king. For a thornbush to invite the other trees to trust in its shadow is a laughable proposition indeed! Often in the summer, fires would break out in the bramble bushes; and these fires would spread and threaten the safety of the trees. (See David's use of this image in 2 Sam. 23:6-7, and also Isa. 9:18-19.)

Jotham had made his point: Abimelech, the "bramble king," would be unable to protect the people, but he would cause judgment to come that would destroy those who trusted him. The men of Shechem should have been ashamed of the way they rejected the house of Gideon and honored a worthless opportunist like Abimelech. Eventually, both Abimelech and his followers would destroy one another.

Abimelech considered himself to be a stately tree of great value, but Jotham said he was nothing but a useless weed. What a blow to the new king's pride! When they chose Abimelech as their king, the men of Shechem didn't get useful olive oil, tasty figs, or cheery wine; they got only thorns— fuel for the fire.

Abimelech was actually trying to wrest the kingdom away from God (Judg. 8:23), and the Lord permitted him to have a measure of success. But God was still on the throne and would see to it that man's selfish purposes would be frustrated.

It's a dangerous thing for us to think more highly of ourselves than we ought to think (Rom. 12:3). We all need to discover the gifts God has given us and then use them in the place where He puts us. Each member in the body of Christ is important (1 Cor. 12:12-31), and we all need one another and to minister to one another. Since there's no competition in the work of the Lord (John 4:34-38; 1 Cor. 3:5-9), there's no need for us to promote ourselves. The important thing is that God receives the glory.

2. Defending the kingdom (Judg. 9:22-29)

After three years of relative success, Abimelech found himself in trouble. It's one thing to acquire a throne and quite something else to defend and retain it. The citizens of Shechem, who had helped crown him king, began to give him trouble, as well as an intruder named Gaal. All of this was from the Lord, who was about to punish both Abimelech and the men of Shechem for the slaughter of Gideon's sons. "Though the mills of God grind slowly, yet they grind exceeding small" (Longfellow, *Retribution*).

The activities of at least three days are described in this section.

Day one—the boasting of Gaal (vv. 25-33). The Lord created a breech between the king and his followers, so much so that the Shechemites started to work against the king. They began to rob the caravans that passed by the city on the nearby trade routes. Abimelech was living at Arumah (v. 41), and the activities of these bandits were robbing him of both money and reputation. The merchants would hear about the danger, take a different trade route, and not have to pay Abimelech whatever tariffs were usually levied upon them. But even more, the word would get out that the new king couldn't control his people and protect area business.

Into this volatile situation stepped a newcomer, Gaal the son of Ebed, a man who knew a good opportunity when he saw it. In a short time, he gained the confidence of the men of Shechem, who were already unhappy with their king; and when a crowd was gathered to celebrate a harvest festival, Gaal openly criticized Abimelech's administration. He reminded the people that their king had a Jewish father, while they were sons of Hamor, not sons of Jacob (Gen. 34). The plank in Abimelech's platform that he thought was the strongest (v. 9) turned out to be his thorn in the flesh.

His approach in verse 29 was effective. Gaal was living in Shechem while Abimelech was living in Arumah. The people could tell Gaal their problems, and he could give them the help they needed, but how could they go to Arubah for help? Years later, Absalom would use this same approach and steal the hearts of Israel (2 Sam. 15:1-6). Gaal closed his festival address by saying, "I would say to Abimelech, 'Call out your whole army!' " (Judg. 9:29, NIV) It was a challenge that he dared the king to take up.

Abimelech's representative in Shechem was Zebul, who wasted no time getting the information about Gaal to the king. Not only did Zebul share the contents of the speech, but he also gave the king some strategy for dealing with this boastful intruder. Zebul would be working for the king within the city, and the king would gather his troops outside the city.

Day two—the defeat of Gaal (vv. 34-41). Abimelech used some of Gideon's strategy (v. 34), although he didn't have Gideon's faith or the weapons Gideon and his men used. You get the impression that Zebul had convinced Gaal that he was his friend, for Gaal actually believed the lie Zebul told him. As the two men stood by the gate early that morning, Abimelech was setting the trap and Zebul was going to put in the bait.

When it was obvious that an army was attacking Shechem, Gaal had to act. In the decisive words of American slang, he had to "put up or shut up." If he hid in the city, he would have lost his following, been disgraced, and eventually caught and killed. If he tried to run away, Abimelech's men would have chased him and killed him. All he could do was gather his followers and go out to face Abimelech. His army was routed, and he and his cohorts were driven out of the city.

Day three—the punishment of Shechem (vv. 42-49). Abimelech had one more score to settle, and that was with the citizens of Shechem who had cursed him (v. 27) and were attacking the caravans and robbing him of both money and reputation. The next morning, when the people of Shechem went out of the city to work in the fields, Abimelech set an ambush, blocked the city gate, and slaughtered the trapped citizens. Thus the Lord avenged the blood of Gideon's sons. Indeed, the fire did "come out of the bramble, and devour the cedars of Lebanon" (v. 15). The phrase "cedars of Lebanon" represents the leading citizens of the city, who had supported Abimelech's rule (v. 20).

In order to make sure the city didn't rebel against him again, Abimelech destroyed it and sowed salt over it. The sowing of salt on a conquered city was a symbolic action that condemned the city to desolation so nobody would want to live there. "Put salt on Moab, for she will be laid waste; her towns will become desolate, with no one to live in them" (Jer. 48:9, NIV; and see Jer. 17:6).

The "tower of Shechem" may have been the same as "the house of Millo" mentioned in Judges 9:6. It was the place where the aristocracy of Shechem lived, although we don't know where it was located with reference to the main city. The people fled from Beth-Millo to the temple of El-Berith ("god of the covenant"; Baal-Berith, v. 4, and see 8:33).

Apparently they felt safer in a building devoted to one of their gods, hoping that Abimelech would respect it and leave them alone. But he turned the temple into a furnace and killed all the people in it.

3. Losing the kingdom (Judg. 9:50-57)
The shedding of innocent blood is something that God takes very seriously and eventually avenges (Deut. 19:10, 13; 21:9; 1 Kings 2:31; Prov. 6:17; Isa. 59:7; Jer. 7:6; 22:3, 17; Joel 3:19). The year 1990 was a record year for murders in the United States, with 23,438 persons being killed, an average of nearly three an hour all year long. When you add to this the thousands of innocent babies killed in their mother's wombs, it's easy to see that "the land of the free" is stained with innocent blood; and one day we will pay for it.

Abimelech paid for the murders he committed, and it happened while he was attempting to protect his throne. Since the people in the city of Thebez, about ten miles from Shechem, had apparently joined in the general rebellion against Abimelech, he went there with his army to punish them as well. Like the people from Beth-Millo, the citizens of Thebez fled to their tower; and Abimelech tried to use the same method of attack that he used so successfully at Shechem.

However, he made the mistake of getting too close to the tower, and a woman dropped an upper millstone on his head and killed him. Abimelech experienced a triple disgrace: (1) He was killed, but not really in a battle; (2) he was killed by a woman, which was a disgrace to a soldier; and (3) he was killed with a millstone, not a sword. The fact that his armorbearer finished the job with a sword didn't change anything; for centuries later, Abimelech's shameful death was remembered as being accomplished by a woman (2 Sam. 11:21).

Abimelech lost his life and lost his kingdom. The curse pronounced by his half-brother Jotham was fulfilled on both Abimelech and the people of Shechem (Judg. 9:20). "Evil will slay the wicked; the foes of the righteous will be condemned" (Ps. 34:21, NIV). "The Righteous One takes note of the house of the wicked and brings the wicked to ruin" (Prov. 21:12, NIV).

CHAPTER EIGHT
LOCAL REJECT MAKES GOOD
Judges 10–12

Life and literature are filled with the "Cinderella legend," stories about rejected people who were eventually "discovered" and elevated to places of honor and authority. Horatio Alger wrote over 100 boys' novels that focused on the "rags-to-riches" theme, and he became one of the most influential American writers of the last half of the nineteenth century. Whether it's Abraham Lincoln going "from log cabin to White House" or Joseph from the prison to the throne of Egypt, the story of the successful "underdog" is one that will always be popular. We like to see losers become winners.

The account of Jephthah, the main character in these chapters, is that kind of a story, except that it doesn't end with the hero living "happily ever after." After Jephthah's great victory over the Ammonites and Philistines, he experienced anything but happiness; and the narrative ends on a tragic note. The story can be divided into four scenes.

1. A nation in decay (Judg. 10:1-18) There were three deficiencies in Israel that gave evidence that the nation was decaying spiritually.

Israel's lack of gratitude to the Lord (vv. 1-5). For forty-five years, the people of Israel enjoyed peace and security, thanks to the leadership of Tola and Jair. We know little about these two judges, but the fact that they kept Israel's enemies away for nearly half a century would suggest that they were faithful men, who served the Lord and the nation well. Tola was from the tribe of Issachar, and Jair from the Transjordan tribes, the area known as Gilead.

If Jair had thirty sons, he must have had a plurality of wives and a great deal of wealth. In that day, only wealthy people could afford to provide their children with their own personal donkeys (5:10; 12:9, 14). In addition, each son had a city under his authority. This arrangement looks to us like nepotism, but at least it helped keep the peace.

The people of Israel, however, didn't take advantage of these years of peace to grow in their relationship to the Lord. After the death of Jair, the nation openly returned to idolatry and once again invited the chastening of the Lord. *They enjoyed forty-five years of peace and prosperity but didn't take time to thank the Lord for what He had done for them.* The essence of idolatry is enjoying God's gifts but not being grateful to the Giver, and Israel was guilty.

One of my great-uncles was a minister; and he occasionally had Sunday dinner in our home if he happened to be preaching at the church we attended. As a lad, I was impressed by him, especially the way he asked the blessing *after* the meal. Praying *before* the meal was logical and biblical, but why pray after you've finished dessert and coffee? Then I discovered Deuteronomy 8:10, "When you have eaten and are full, then you shall bless the Lord your God for the good land which He has given you" (NKJV). My Uncle Simon took this admonition seriously, and perhaps we should follow his example. If we did, it might keep us from ignoring the Lord while enjoying His blessings. Thanksgiving glorifies God (Ps. 69:30) and is a strong defense against selfishness and idolatry.

Israel's lack of submission to the Lord (vv. 6-16). If the people had only reviewed their own history and learned from it, they would never have turned from Jehovah God to worship the false gods of their neighbors. From the time of Othniel to the days of Gideon, the Jews endured over fifty painful years of oppression from the enemy. By now they should have known that God blessed them when they were obedient and chastened them when they were rebellious. (See 3:7, 12; 4:1; 6:1.) After all, weren't these the terms of the covenant that God made with Israel, a covenant the nation accepted when they entered the land? (Josh. 8:30-35)

When God chastens us in love and we're suffering because of our sins, it's easy to cry out to Him for deliverance and make all kinds of promises. But when we're comfortable and enjoying His blessings, we tend to forget God and assume that we can sin and get away with it. *Comfortable living often produces weak character.* "Happiness is not the end of life," said Henry Ward Beecher, "character is." But character is built when we make right decisions in life, and those decisions are made on the basis of the things that we value most. Since Israel didn't value the things of God, she ended up destroying her own national character.

The Lord had given Israel victory over

seven different nations (Judg. 10:11-12), but now Israel was worshiping seven different varieties of pagan gods (v. 6). No wonder God's anger "was hot against Israel" (v. 7). What foolishness to worship the gods of your defeated enemies! Israel had to be chastened again, and this time God sent the Philistines and the Ammonites to do the job. The Ammonites were distant relatives of the Jews, being descendants of Abraham's nephew Lot (Gen. 19:38). It must have given the leaders of Ammon and Philistia great joy to subdue their old enemy Israel and oppress them. Their armies invaded the area of Gilead on the east side of the Jordan and then crossed the river and attacked Judah, Ephraim, and Benjamin. It was a devastating and humiliating conquest.

History repeated itself, and the Israelites cried out to God for deliverance (Judg. 10:10; 2:11-19). But the Lord didn't send help immediately. Instead, He sent a messenger to the people who rebuked them for their lack of appreciation for all that God had done for them in the past. Then God announced that He wouldn't help them anymore. They could ask their new gods for help! (See Deut. 32:36-38.)

For the people to abandon God was one thing, but for God to abandon His people was quite something else. *The greatest judgment God can send to His people is to let them have their own way and not interfere.* "Wherefore God also gave them up. . . . God gave them up. . . . God gave them over" (Rom. 1:24, 26, 28). This was too much for the Jews, so they repented, put away their false gods, and told God He could do to Israel whatever He wanted to do (Judg. 10:15-16).

Their hope wasn't in their repenting or their praying but in the character of God. "His soul was grieved for the misery of Israel" (v. 16). "In all their affliction He was afflicted" (Isa. 63:9). "Nevertheless in Your great mercy You did not utterly consume them nor forsake them; for You are God, gracious and merciful" (Neh. 9:31, NKJV). "Yet He was merciful; He atoned for their iniquities and did not destroy them. Time after time He restrained His anger and did not stir up His full wrath" (Ps. 78:38, NIV).

Israel's lack of adequate leadership (vv. 17-18). The people were prepared to act, but from all the tribes of Israel, there was nobody to take the lead. Whether in a nation or a local church, the absence of qualified leaders is often a judgment of God and evidence of the low spiritual level of the people. When the Spirit is at work among believers, He will equip and call servants to accomplish His will and bless His people (Acts 13:1-4).

In his book *Profiles in Courage,* John F. Kennedy wrote, "We, the people, are the boss, and we will get the kind of political leadership, be it good or bad, that we demand and deserve."[1] What's true of political leadership is often true of spiritual leadership: We get what we deserve. When God's people are submitted to Him and serving Him, He sends them gifted servants to instruct and lead them; but when their appetites turn to things of the world and the flesh, He judges them by depriving them of good and godly leaders. "The righteous perish, and no one ponders it in his heart" (Isa. 57:1, NIV).

After eighteen years of suffering, the Israelites assembled to face their oppressors (Judg. 10:11). There are several places in Scripture named "Mizpeh"; this one was in Gilead (11:29; see Josh. 13:26). Israel had an army, but they didn't have a general. In order to get a volunteer to command their army, the leaders of Israel promised that their commander would be named head over all Gilead. Had the princes of Israel called a prayer meeting instead of a political caucus, they would have accomplished more.

When I was a young Christian, I heard an evangelist preach a powerful sermon on the text, "Where is the Lord God of Elijah?" (2 Kings 2:14) "We know where the Lord God of Elijah is," he said; "He's on the throne of heaven and is just as powerful today as He was in Elijah's day." Then he paused. "The question is not so much 'Where is the Lord God of Elijah?' as 'Where are the Elijahs?' "

Indeed, *where are the Elijahs?* Where are the spiritual leaders who can rally God's people and confront the forces of evil?

2. A leader in demand (Judg. 11:1-29, 32-33)

Now we are introduced to Jephthah, the man God chose to lead Israel to victory. What kind of man was he?

The unwanted brother (vv. 1-3). Jephthah wasn't to blame for his birth. His father, Gilead, had only one wife, but he consorted with a prostitute and fathered a son. At least Gilead acknowledged the boy and took him into his home, but his other sons didn't accept this "son of a strange woman." When Gilead died and the inheritance was to be divided, the legitimate sons drove Jephthah away. Little did they realize they were rejecting a future judge of Israel.

Jephthah left his father's territory and went north to the land of Tob, which was near Syria; and there he became captain of a band of "adventurers" (v. 3, NIV). The Hebrew word means "to make empty" and refers to idle people looking for something to do. (See 9:4, the "vain and light persons" who followed Abimelech. Here the word means "to be reckless.") Jephthah was already known as "a mighty man of valor" (v. 1). Thus he had no trouble forming a band of brigands.

The unopposed leader (vv. 4-11). Jephthah's brothers didn't want him, but the elders of Israel needed him and sent a deputation eighty miles to the land of Tob to ask him to take charge. Jephthah's reply sounds a good deal like what the Lord had said to the people when they turned to Him for help (10:13-14). Apparently the Jewish leaders had cooperated with Gilead's sons in expelling the unwanted brother from the land, but Jephthah listened to them and made sure their offer was valid. He was willing to lead them against the enemy if the elders would name him ruler of Gilead.

You can't help but appreciate the way Jephthah emphasized the Lord in all his negotiations with the leaders of Israel. It was the Lord who would give the victory (11:9), not Jephthah; and the agreement between him and the elders must be ratified before the Lord at Mizpah (v. 11; see 1 Sam. 11:15). Jephthah didn't see the challenge as a political opportunity for himself but as an occasion for trusting the Lord and serving Him. In addition, the writer of Hebrews makes it clear that Jephthah was a man of faith, not simply an opportunist (Heb. 11:32).

We can't help but wonder how his brothers felt when the man they renounced returned home as the captain of the army and the leader of the land! More than one "underdog" in Scripture had the same experience. Joseph was rejected by his brothers and later became their savior. It also took King David seven years to gain the full support of the twelve tribes of Israel. For that matter, the Lord Jesus Christ was rejected by His people but will be received by them when He comes again.

The unsuccessful diplomat (vv. 12-

28). Before declaring war, Jephthah tried peaceful negotiations with the Ammonites, but the negotiations failed. Nevertheless, this section does tell us two things about Jephthah: (1) He knew the Scriptures and the history of his people, and (2) he was not a hothead who was looking for a fight. Being a military man himself, Jephthah knew that a war could result in thousands of Jewish men being killed; and he wanted to avoid that if at all possible.

The King of Ammon declared that he and his men were only reclaiming land that the Jews, under the leadership of Moses, had stolen from them. If Israel would restore that land, he would call off his troops. But Jephthah presented four compelling arguments that should have convinced the Ammonites that they were wrong.

First, he presented the facts of history (vv. 14-22). Moses and his people had asked the Ammonites for safe passage through their territory, a request that the Ammonites would not grant. This led to war, and God gave the Jews the victory. Israel didn't *steal* any land; they *captured* it from the Ammonites and the Amorites (Num. 21:21-35). Furthermore, the Amorites had originally taken the land from the Moabites (Num. 21:29); so if Israel's claims to ownership by conquest weren't valid, neither were the claims of the Amorites!

His second argument was that the Lord had given Israel the land (vv. 23-24). Jephthah was always careful to give the Lord the glory for any victories Israel won (vv. 9, 21, 23-24). When the other nations captured enemy territory, they claimed that it was "the will of their god" that they take the land; and they gave their idols credit for the victory. Jephthah declared that the God of Israel was the true God and that His will had been fulfilled in allowing Israel to take the land. It was Jehovah who gave Israel the victory.

Jephthah's third argument was that Israel had lived on the land for centuries (vv. 25-26). "Three hundred years" is a round figure, but it comes close to the total number of years given in the Book of Judges for the periods of oppression and of peace. Israel had dwelt in the Transjordan area for three centuries, and that was reason enough to claim title to the land as their own. Why was the King of Ammon making his claims now? During those three centuries, the people of Ammon didn't try to reclaim their territory. In fact, back in the days of Moses, even the King of Moab hadn't tried to get his land back! If the Ammonites had a legitimate claim to the territory, they should have said something centuries ago!

Jephthah's final argument was that the Ammonites were actually fighting against the Lord (vv. 27-28). Jephthah hadn't declared war on Ammon; it was Ammon that declared war on Israel. But if God gave Israel the land, then the Ammonites were declaring war on the Lord God; and that could only mean disaster and defeat for Ammon. Jephthah had tried to reason with the King of Ammon, but he wouldn't listen.

The undefeated warrior (vv. 29-33). Empowered by the Spirit of God (see 3:10; 6:34), Jephthah called for volunteers (12:1-2) and mustered his army. In order to be certain of victory, he foolishly made a bargain with God, a subject we shall take up later. The Lord gave him victory over the Ammonites, and he captured twenty of their strongholds as he pursued the fleeing enemy army. This would guarantee freedom and safety for the Jews as they traveled in the Gilead territory.

The writer of Hebrews wrote that

Jephthah was a man of faith and his victory was a victory of faith (Heb. 11:32). *The circumstances of birth or of family are not a handicap to the person who will live by faith.* In his message to the King of Ammon, Jephthah revealed his knowledge of the Word of God; and this Word was the source of His faith. "So then faith comes by hearing, and hearing by the Word of God" (Rom. 10:17, NKJV). "And this is the victory that has overcome the world—our faith" (1 John 5:4, NKJV). Thanks to the faith and courage of Jephthah, the Ammonites didn't threaten the Israelites for another fifty years (1 Sam. 11:1ff).

3. A father in despair (Judg. 11:30-31, 34-40)

While going out to battle, Jephthah made a vow to the Lord. It was certainly acceptable to God for the Jews to make vows, provided they obeyed the laws that He had given through Moses to govern the use of vows (Lev. 27; Num. 30; Deut. 23:21-25). Vows were completely voluntary, but the Lord expected the people to fulfill them (Ecc. 5:1-6).

Jephthah's vow was really a bargain with the Lord: If God would give the Israelites victory over the Ammonites, Jephthah would sacrifice to the Lord whatever came out of his house when he arrived home in Mizpah. God did give him victory, and Jephthah kept his promise. But what was his promise and how did he keep it? What actually happened to Jephthah's daughter, his only child?

The vow. The *Authorized (King James) Version* reads: "If Thou shalt without fail deliver the children of Ammon into mine hands, then it shall be, that whatsoever cometh forth of the doors of my house to meet me, when I return in peace from the children of Ammon, shall surely be the Lord's, and I will offer it up for a burnt offering" (Judg. 11:30-31).

The *New American Standard Bible* translates this verse to say, "If Thou wilt indeed give the sons of Ammon into my hand, then it shall be that whatever comes out of the doors of my house to meet me when I return in peace from the sons of Ammon, it shall be the Lord's, and I will offer it up as a burnt offering."

The *New International Version* translates it to say, "If You give the Ammonites into my hands, whatever comes out of the door of my house to meet me when I return in triumph from the Ammonites will be the Lord's, and I will sacrifice it as a burnt offering."

The questions. The more you study Jephthah's vow, the more puzzling it becomes. He simply could have said, "Lord, if You help me defeat the enemy, when I get home, I'll offer you a generous burnt offering." But he couched his vow in ambiguous terms. How did he know who or what would come out of the door of his house? What if the first thing to greet him happened to be an unclean animal that was unacceptable to God? Then he couldn't fulfill his vow! The Hebrew word translated "whatsoever" (KJV) or "whatever" (NASB) is masculine and suggests that he expected to meet a person,[2] but what if that person turned out to be a neighbor's child or a total stranger? What right did Jephthah have to take either life and thereby offer to God a sacrifice that cost him nothing? (See 2 Sam. 24:24.)

Furthermore, surely Jephthah knew that Jehovah didn't approve of or accept human sacrifices. Jephthah gave evidence of familiarity with the Old Testament Scriptures, and he would have known about Abraham and Isaac (Gen. 22) and the commandments in the Law (Lev. 18:21 and 20:1-5; Deut. 12:31 and 18:10).

Granted, the period of the Judges was a spiritually dark era in Israel's history, and the Jews did many things that were wrong, but it's doubtful that Jephthah's friends and neighbors would have permitted him to slay his own daughter in order to fulfill a foolish vow.[3] King Saul's soldiers didn't let him kill his son Jonathan, who had violated his father's foolish vow (1 Sam. 14:24-46).

And where would Jephthah offer his daughter as a sacrifice? Surely he knew that the Lord accepted sacrifices only at the tabernacle altar (Lev. 17:1-9), and that they had to be offered by the levitical priests. He would have to travel to Shiloh to fulfill his vow (Deut. 16:2, 6, 11, 16), and it's doubtful that even the most unspiritual priest would offer a human sacrifice on God's sanctified altar, victory or no victory.[4] In fact, if people knew that Jephthah was going to Shiloh to slay his daughter, they probably would have stopped him along the way and kidnapped the girl! A national hero like Jephthah couldn't easily hide what he was doing, and surely the story would have spread quickly among the people during the two-month waiting period (Judg. 11:37-39).

Even if he made it safely to Shiloh, Jephthah could have learned from any priest that paying the proper amount of money could have redeemed his daughter (Lev. 27:1-8). As a successful soldier who had just returned from looting the enemy, Jephthah could easily have paid the redemption price.

Other pertinent questions arise. In spite of Numbers 30:1–2, would God take seriously a vow that violated both human rights and divine law? Would a Spirit-empowered man (Judg. 11:29), committed to the Lord (11:11), even make such a vow? The more I ponder these questions, the more perplexing his vow becomes and the more convinced I am that Jephthah didn't promise to offer any human sacrifice to the Lord and did not kill his own daughter.

Solutions. More than one expositor has pointed out that the little word "and?' in the phrase "and I will offer it up" (11:31) can be translated "or." (In the Hebrew, it's the letter *waw* which usually means "and." See the beginning of Ps. 119:41 for an example of what the Hebrew *waw* looks like.) If we take this approach, then the vow was twofold: Whatever met him when he returned home would be dedicated to the Lord (if a person) *or* sacrificed to the Lord (if an animal).

Since he was met by his daughter, Jephthah gave her to the Lord to serve Him at the tabernacle (Ex. 38:8; 1 Sam. 2:22). She remained a virgin, which meant that she would not know the joys of motherhood and perpetuate her father's inheritance in Israel. This would be reason enough for her and her friends to spend two months grieving, for every daughter wanted a family and every father wanted grandchildren to maintain the family inheritance.

Nowhere in the text are we told that Jephthah actually killed his daughter, nor do we find anybody bewailing the girl's death. The emphasis in Judges 11:37-40 is the fact that she remained a virgin. It's difficult to believe that "the daughters of Israel" would establish a custom to celebrate (not "lament" as in KJV) the awful sacrifice of a human being, but we can well understand that they would commemorate the devotion and obedience of Jephthah's daughter in helping her father fulfill his vow. She deserves to stand with Isaac as a faithful child, who was willing to obey both father and God, no matter what the cost.[5]

4. A ruler in defense (Judg. 12:1-15)

Accusation (v. 1). The leaders of the tribe of Ephraim expressed to Jephthah the same pride and anger they had shown to Gideon (8:1). As before, they wanted to share the glory of the victory, but they hadn't been too eager to risk their lives in the battle. The men of Ephraim were so angry that they threatened to burn Jephthah's house down. They had absolutely no respect for the new ruler of the Transjordanic tribes.

Explanation (vv. 2-3). Gideon had pacified the Ephraimites with flattery, but Jephthah took a more direct approach. To begin with, he reminded them that his first concern was to defeat the Ammonites, not to please his neighbors. Second, during the eighteen years Ammon had oppressed the people of Gilead, nobody from Ephraim had offered to come to their rescue. Third, Jephthah had issued a call for the tribes to assist him in his attack on the enemy, but Ephraim hadn't responded. Without their help, the Lord gave Jephthah and his army victory; so the proud Ephraimites (who didn't like being left out) had nothing to complain about.

Confrontation (vv. 4-7). Perhaps Jephthah should have practiced Proverbs 15:1 and 17:14 and avoided a war; but then, maybe it was time somebody called Ephraim's bluff and taught them a lesson. The men of Ephraim resorted to name-calling and taunted the Gileadites by calling them "renegades from Ephraim and Manasseh" (Judg. 12:4, NIV). Actually, the tribes east of the Jordan River—Reuben, Gad, and half of the tribe of Manasseh—had been granted their land by Moses and Joshua (Num. 32; Josh. 22). Thus the words of the Ephraimites were an insult to the Lord and His servants.

When people are wrong and refuse to accept logical reasoning and confess their faults, they often turn to violence in order to protect their reputation. This is the cause of most family disagreements, church fights, and international conflicts (James 4:1-12). But Jephthah got the best of the boastful men of Ephraim and killed 42,000 of their soldiers. The men of Ephraim themselves became "renegades," for the word "escaped" in Judges 12:5 is the same as the word "fugitives [renegades]" in verse 4. They had to eat their words and lose their lives!

The people of Ephraim had their own regional pronunciation for the word *shibboleth,* which means "stream" or "floods." They said "sibboleth," and this gave them away (Matt. 26:73). It was a simple test, but it worked. Because of this story, the word *shibboleth* has become a part of our English vocabulary and is now found in our dictionaries. It stands for any kind of test that a group gives to outsiders to see whether they really belong. Usually the *shibboleth* is an old worn-out idea or doctrine that is really unimportant. In Ephraim's case, however, it cost 42,000 people their lives.

After the defeat of Ammon and the trouncing of Ephraim, the Jews had thirty-one years of peace and security under the leadership of Jephthah and his three successors. How paradoxical that Jephthah the champion should have no family while Ibzan had thirty sons and thirty daughters and Abdon had forty sons and thirty grandsons.

Samson, however, the last judge God sent to His people, was the most paradoxical man of them all: a deliverer who couldn't deliver himself, a conqueror who couldn't conquer himself, a strong man who didn't know when he was weak.

CHAPTER NINE
THE LIGHT THAT FLICKERED
Judges 13–14

"It is a riddle wrapped up in a mystery inside an enigma." In a speech broadcast October 1, 1939 that's how Sir Winston Churchill described the actions of the Russians in his day. But what he said about Russian actions could be applied to Samson, the last of the judges, for his behavior is "a riddle wrapped up in a mystery inside an enigma."

Samson was unpredictable and undependable because he was double-minded, and "a double-minded man is unstable in all his ways" (James 1:8). It has well been said that "the greatest ability is dependability," and you could depend on Samson to be undependable.

Bold before men, Samson was weak before women and couldn't resist telling them his secrets. Empowered by the Spirit of God, he yielded his body to the appetites of the flesh. Called to declare war on the Philistines, he fraternized with the enemy and even tried to marry a Philistine woman. He fought the Lord's battles by day and disobeyed the Lord's commandments by night. Given the name Samson, which means "sunny," he ended up in the darkness, blinded by the very enemy he was supposed to conquer.

Four chapters in the Book of Judges are devoted to the history of Samson. In Judges 13-14, we're introduced to "Sunny" and his parents and we see the light flickering as Samson plays with sin. In Judges 15-16, the light goes out and Samson dies a martyr under the ruins of a heathen temple, a sad end to a promising life.[1]

Let's open Samson's family album and study three pictures of Samson taken early in his career.

1. The child with unbelievable promise (Judg. 13:1-23)

Consider the great promise that was wrapped up in this person named Samson.

He had a nation to protect (v. 1). With monotonous regularity we've read this phrase in the Book of Judges (3:7, 12; 4:1–2; 6:1; 10:6-7), and here it appears for the last time. It introduces the longest period of oppression that God sent to His people, forty years of Philistine domination.

The Philistines[2] were among the "sea people" who, in the twelfth century B.C., migrated from an area of Greece to the coastal plain of Canaan. The Jews weren't able to occupy that territory during their conquest of the land (Josh. 13:1-2). As you study your map, you'll note that their national life focused around the five key cities of Ashdod, Gaza, Ashkelon, Gath, and Ekron (1 Sam. 6:17). The land between Israel's hill country and the coastal plain was called the "Shephelah," which means "low country"; and it separated Philistia from Israel. Samson was born in Zorah, a city in Dan near the Philistine border; and he often crossed that border either to serve God or satisfy his appetites.

Samson judged Israel "in the days of the Philistines" (Judg. 15:20), which means that his twenty years in office were *during* the forty years of Philistine rule. Dr. Leon Wood dates the beginning of the Philistine oppression about 1095 B.C. and the end in 1055 B.C. with Israel's victory at Mizpeh (1 Sam. 7). About the middle of this period occurred the battle of Aphek when Israel was ignominiously defeated by the Philistines and lost the Ark and three priests (1 Sam. 4). Dr. Wood suggests that Samson's judgeship started about the time of the tragedy at Aphek and that his main job was to harass the Philistines and keep them from successfully overrunning the land and menacing the people.[3]

It's worth noting that there is no evidence given in the text that Israel cried out to God for deliverance at any time during the forty years of Philistine domination. The Philistines disarmed the Jews (1 Sam. 13:19-23) and therefore had little fear of a rebellion. Judges 15:9-13 indicates that the Jews were apparently content with their lot and didn't want Samson to "rock the boat." It's frightening how quickly we can get accustomed to bondage and learn to accept the *status quo.* Had the Philistines been more severe on the Jews, perhaps the Jews would have prayed to Jehovah for help.

Unlike most of the previous judges, Samson didn't deliver his people from foreign domination, but he began the work of deliverance that others would finish (13:5). As a powerful and unpredictable hero, Samson frightened and troubled the Philistines (16:24) and kept them from devastating Israel as the other invading nations had done. It would take the prayers of Samuel (1 Sam. 7) and the conquests of David (2 Sam. 5:17-25) to finish the job that Samson started and give Israel complete victory over the Philistines.

He had a God to serve (vv. 2-5). The tribe of Dan was originally assigned the land adjacent to Judah and Benjamin, extending to the Mediterranean Sea (Josh. 19:40-48). Since the Danites weren't able to dislodge the coastal inhabitants, however, the tribe relocated and moved north (Judg. 18-19), although some of the people remained in their original location. Zorah is about fifteen miles from Jerusalem in the foothill country near the border of Philistia.

When God wants to do something really great in His world, He doesn't send an army but an angel. The angel often visits a couple and promises to send them a baby. His great plan of salvation got underway when He called Abraham and Sarah and gave them Isaac. When He wanted to deliver Israel from Egyptian bondage, God sent baby Moses to Amram and Jochebed (Ex. 6:20); and when in later years Israel desperately needed revival, God gave baby Samuel to Hannah (1 Sam. 1). When the fullness of time arrived, God gave Baby Jesus to Mary; and that baby grew up to die on the cross for the sins of the world.

Babies are fragile, but God uses the weak things of the world to confound the mighty (1 Cor. 1:26-28). Babies must have time to grow up, but God is patient and is never late in accomplishing His will. Each baby God sends is a gift from God, a new beginning, and carries with it tremendous potential. What a tragedy that we live in a society that sees the unborn baby as a menace instead of a miracle, an intruder instead of an inheritance.

We have every reason to believe the "angel of the Lord" who visited Manoah's wife was Jesus Christ, the Son of God (see Gen. 22:1-18; 31:11-13; Ex. 3:1-6; Judg. 6:11-24). Like Sarah (Gen. 18:9-15), Hannah (1 Sam. 1), and Elizabeth (Luke 1:5-25), Manoah's wife was barren and never expected to have a child. Since it would be the mother who would have the greatest influence on the child, both before and after birth, the angel solemnly charged her what to do.

Like John the Baptist, Samson would

be a Nazirite from his mother's womb (Luke 1:13-15).[4] The word *Nazirite* comes from a Hebrew word that means "to separate, to consecrate." Nazirites were persons who, for a stated period of time, consecrated themselves to the Lord in a special way. They abstained from drinking wine and strong drink; they avoided touching dead bodies; and as a mark of their consecration, they allowed their hair to grow. The laws governing the Nazirite vow are given in Numbers 6.[5]

Manoah's wife had to be careful what she ate and drank because her diet would influence her unborn Nazirite son and could defile him. It's too bad every expectant mother doesn't exercise caution; for in recent years, the news media have informed us of the sad consequences babies suffer when their mothers use tobacco, alcohol, and narcotics during a pregnancy. Samson's Nazirite vow wasn't something he voluntarily took: God gave it to him; and his mother was a part of the vow of dedication. Not only was she to avoid anything related to the grape, but also she was to avoid foods that were unclean to the Jews (Lev. 11; Deut. 14:3-20).

Ordinarily, a Nazirite vow was for a limited period of time; but in Samson's case, the vow was to last all his life (Judg. 13:7). This was something Manoah and his wife would have to teach their son, and they would also have to explain why they didn't cut his hair. The claims of God were upon this child, and it was the obligation of the parents to train him for the work God sent him to do.

He had a home to honor (vv. 6-23). Manoah's wife immediately told her husband about the stranger's visit and message, although neither of them yet knew that the visitor was the Lord (v. 16). Manoah assumed that he was "a man of God," perhaps a visiting prophet; and he prayed that the Lord would send the man back. We can't help but be impressed with the devotion of this husband and wife to each other and to the Lord. The time of the judges was one of apostasy and anarchy, but there were still Jewish homes that were dedicated to the Lord and that believed in prayer; and God was still working through them.

God answered Manoah's prayer and gave him an opportunity to ask an important question, which the angel of the Lord never answered: "When your words are fulfilled, what is to be the rule for the boy's life and work?" (v. 12, NIV) The Old Testament Law not only gave instructions concerning Nazirites and clean and unclean foods, but also it told parents how to raise their children (Deut. 6). It wasn't necessary for the Lord to give Manoah and his wife additional instructions when the Word of God already told them what to do. The messenger simply repeated the warning he had already given to Manoah's wife.

Wanting to be a good and appreciative host, Manoah asked the guest to wait while he and his wife prepared a meal for him (6:18-19; Gen. 18:1-8). The stranger's cryptic reply was that he wouldn't eat their food but would permit them to offer a burnt offering to the Lord. After all, their promised son was a gift from God, and they owed the Lord their worship and thanks.

But Manoah thought to himself, *If I can't honor this man of God now, perhaps I can do it in the future after his words come true and the baby boy has been born.* (Note that Manoah believed the announcement and said "when" and not "if.") Manoah would have to know the man's name so he could locate him nine months later, but the man wouldn't tell his name except to say it was "wonderful." (See Gen. 32:29.)

This is the same word used to name the Messiah in Isaiah 9:6; it is translated "wondrously" in Judges 13:19 of KJV, (NIV says "an amazing thing").

Ordinarily, Jewish worshipers had to bring their offerings to the tabernacle altar at Shiloh; but since the "man of God" commanded Manoah to offer the burnt offering, it was permissible to do it there, using a rock as the altar. Suddenly, the visitor ascended to heaven in the flame! Only then did Manoah and his wife discover that their visitor was an angel from the Lord. This frightened Manoah, because the Jews believed that nobody could look upon God and live (see 6:19–23). Using common sense, Manoah's wife convinced him that they couldn't die and fulfill God's promises at the same time.

Every baby born into a godly home carries the responsibility of honoring the family name. Samson's inconsistent life brought shame to his father's house just as it brought shame to the name of the Lord. Samson's relatives had to pull his body out of the wreckage of the Philistine temple and take it home for burial (16:31). In one sense, it was a day of victory over God's enemies; but it was also a day of defeat for Samson's family.

2. The champion with undefeatable power (Judg. 13:24–25)

The baby was born and was named Samson, which means "sunny" or "brightness." Certainly he brought light and joy to Manoah and his wife, who thought they would never have a family; and he also began to bring light to Israel during the dark days of Philistine oppression. While other judges were said to be clothed with God's Spirit (3:10; 6:34; 11:29), only of Samson is it said "the Lord blessed him" (13:24; see Luke 1:80 and 2:52). The hand of God was on him in a special way.

The secret of Samson's great strength was his Nazirite vow, symbolized by his unshorn hair (Judg. 16:17); and the source of that strength was the Holy Spirit of God (13:25; 14:6, 19; 15:14). We aren't told that Samson's physique was especially different from that of other men, although he may have resembled the strong men pictured in Bible storybooks. Perhaps it was as he entered his teen years, when a Jewish boy became a "son of the law," that he began to demonstrate his amazing ability.

Only a few of Samson's great feats are recorded in the Book of Judges: killing the lion bare-handed (14:5-6); slaying thirty Philistines (v. 19); catching 300 foxes (or jackals) and tying torches to their tails (15:3-5); breaking bonds (15:14; 16:9, 12, 14); slaying 1,000 men with the jawbone of a donkey (15:15); carrying off the Gaza city gate (16:3); and destroying the Philistine building (v. 30). Judges 16:24 indicates that he had done many more feats than those listed above, feats that had aggravated the Philistine people.

As you ponder the record of Samson's life, you get the impression that he was a fun-loving fellow with a good sense of humor; and sometimes he didn't take his gifts and his work seriously. A sense of humor is a good thing to have, but it must be balanced with serious devotion to the things of the Lord. "Serve the Lord with fear, and rejoice with trembling" (Ps. 2:11). Samson's power was a weapon to fight with and a tool to build with, not a toy to play with.

Notice another thing: Samson was a loner; unlike previous judges, he never "rallied the troops" and tried to unite Israel in throwing off the Philistine yoke. For twenty years he played the champion, but he failed to act the leader. Joseph Parker said that Samson was "an elephant in strength [but] a babe in weakness." We might add that, when it came to national leadership, he was a lost sheep!

3. The man with unreliable character (Judg. 14:1-20)

According to Hebrews 11:32, Samson was a man of faith, but he certainly wasn't a faithful man. He wasn't faithful to his parents' teaching, his Nazirite vow, or the laws of the Lord. It didn't take long for Samson to lose almost everything the Lord had given him, except his great strength; and he finally lost that as well.

He lost his respect for his parents (vv. 1-4). The Lord had given Samson a godly heritage, and he had been raised to honor the Lord; but when Samson fell in love, he wouldn't listen to his parents when they warned him. Samson had wandered four miles into enemy territory where he was captivated by a Philistine woman and decided to marry her. This, of course, was contrary to God's Law (Ex. 34:12-16; Deut. 7:1-3; and see 2 Cor. 6:14-18).

Samson was living by sight and not by faith. He was controlled by "the lust of the eyes" (1 John 2:16) rather than by the Law of the Lord. The important thing to Samson was not pleasing the Lord, or even pleasing his parents, but pleasing himself (Jud, 14:3, 7, see 2 Cor. 5:14-15).[6]

When God isn't permitted to rule in our lives, He overrules and works out His will in spite of our decisions. Of course, we're the losers for rebelling against Him; but God will accomplish His purposes either with us or in spite of us (Es. 4:10-14). Samson should have been going to a war instead of to a wedding, but God used this event to give Samson occasion to attack the enemy. Because of this event, Samson killed thirty men (Judg. 14:19), burned up the enemy crops (15:1-5), slaughtered a great number of Philistines (vv. 7-8), and slew 1,000 men (v. 15). Samson hadn't planned these things, but God worked them out just the same.

He lost his Nazirite separation (vv. 5-9). When Samson and his parents went down to Timnah to make arrangements for the marriage, it appears that Samson left the main road (and his parents) and went on a detour into the vineyards; and there a lion attacked him. A vineyard was a dangerous place for a man who was not supposed to have anything to do with grapes (Num. 6:1-4). Did God send the lion as a warning to Samson that he was walking on the wrong path? The Holy Spirit gave Samson power to defeat the enemy, but Samson persisted on his path of disobedience into enemy territory and an unlawful wedding.

Some weeks later, when Samson returned to claim his bride, he once again turned aside into the vineyard, this time to look at his trophy and perhaps gloat over his victory. His sin began with "the lust of the flesh" and "the lust of the eyes," and now it included "the pride of life" (1 John 2:16). When Samson ate the honey from the lion's carcass, he was defiled by a dead body; and that part of his Nazirite dedication was destroyed. In fact, two thirds of his vow was now gone; for he had defiled himself by going into the vineyard[7] and by eating food from a dead body.

He lost control of his tongue (vv. 10-18). Since Samson hadn't brought any men with him to serve as "friends of the bridegroom" (Matt. 9:15, NKJV), the Philistines rounded up thirty men to do the job for him. These men may also have served as guards for the Philistines; for Samson's reputation had preceded him, and they were never sure what he would do next. Since the atmosphere must have been tense at the beginning of the feast, Samson sought to liven things up by posing a riddle. Sad to say, he constructed the riddle out of the experience of his sin! He didn't take seriously the fact that he had violated his Nazirite vows. It's bad enough to disobey God, but when you make a joke out of it, you've sunk to new depths of spiritual insensitivity.

It would have been an expensive thing for the thirty guests to supply Samson with sixty garments, so they were desperate to learn the answer to the riddle. Their only recourse was to enlist the help of Samson's wife. Thus they threatened to kill her and burn down her father's house if she didn't supply the answer before the week was up. Samson resolutely refused to tell her; but on the seventh day, he relented. Since the marriage was to be consummated on the seventh day, perhaps that had something to do with it. First the Philistine woman enticed him (Judg. 14:1), then she controlled him (v. 17), and then she betrayed him (v. 17), which is the way the world always treats the compromising believer. Samson could kill lions and break ropes, but he couldn't overcome the power of a woman's tears.

We wonder how his wife felt being compared to a heifer? The proverb simply means, "You couldn't have done what you did if you hadn't broken the rules," because heifers weren't used for plowing. Since the guests had played foul, technically Samson could have refused to pay the prize; but he generously agreed to keep his promise. Perhaps he found out that his wife's life had been threatened and he didn't want to put her and her family into jeopardy again.

Those who can't control their tongue can't control their bodies (James 3:2); and in Samson's case, the consequences of this lack of discipline were disastrous.

Samson lost his temper (vv. 19-20). He went twenty miles away to Ashkelon so the news of the slaughter wouldn't get back to Timnah too soon. His joke about the lion and the honey ceased to be a joke, for it led to the death of thirty men whose garments Samson confiscated. Samson was so angry that he didn't even consummate the marriage but went back to Zorah and stayed with his parents.[8] While he was away from Timnah, his wife was given to his best man. The Lord used this turn of events to motivate Samson to decide to fight the Philistines instead of entertaining them.

If Samson had won his way and married a Philistine woman, that relationship would have crippled the work God had called him to do. Believers today who enter into unholy alliances are sinning and hindering the work of the Lord too (2 Cor. 6:14-18). If Samson had sought God's leading, the Lord would have directed him. Instead, Samson went his own way, and the Lord had to overrule his selfish decisions.

"I will instruct you and teach you in the way you should go; I will guide you with My eye. Do not be like the horse or like the mule, which have no understanding, which must be harnessed with bit and bridle, else they will not come near you" (Ps. 32:8-9, NKJV). If we're looking by faith into the face of the Lord, He can guide us with His eye, the way parents guide their children. But if we turn our backs on Him, he has to treat us like animals and harness us. Samson was either impetuously rushing ahead like the horse or stubbornly holding back like the mule, and God had to deal with him.

CHAPTER TEN
THE LIGHT THAT FAILED
Judges 15–16

The life of Samson illustrates the ancient truth that a good beginning doesn't guarantee a good ending.[1] The American poet Henry Wadsworth Longfellow said, "Great is the art of beginning, but greater is the art of ending." That's why Solomon wrote, "The end of a matter is better than its beginning" (Ecc. 7:8, NIV).

At the beginning of his career, Samson served in a blaze of glory, but the light began to flicker as he yielded to his passions. In the closing scenes of his life, we watch Samson's light finally go out; and the blind champion ends up buried in the rubble of a heathen temple. Granted, he killed more in his martyrdom than he killed during his judgeship; but how different it would have been had he first conquered himself before he sought to conquer the Lord's enemies. "His whole life," said Spurgeon, "is a series of miracles and follies."

Let's look at the closing scenes in Samson's life and learn from them why he didn't end well.

1. Samson avenges himself. (Judg. 15:1-8)

The passion to get even seemed to govern Samson's life. His motto was, "As they did unto me, so have I done unto them" (15:11). I realize that as the defender of Israel, Samson's calling was to defeat the enemy; but you long to see him fighting "the battles of the Lord" and not just his own private wars. When David faced the Philistines, he saw them as the enemies of the Lord and sought to honor the name of the Lord in his victory (1 Sam. 17). Samson's attitude was different.

As Christians, we need to beware of hiding selfish motives under the cloak of religious zeal and calling it "righteous indignation." Personal vengeance and private gain rather than the glory of the Lord has motivated more than one "crusader" in the church. What some people think is godly zeal may actually be ungodly anger, fed by pride and motivated by selfishness. There is a godly anger that we should experience when we see wickedness prosper and defenseless people hurt (Eph. 4:26), but there's a very fine line between righteous indignation and a "religious temper tantrum."

He avenges his ruined marriage (vv. 1-5). Although he had never consummated the marriage, Samson thought he was legally married to the woman of Timnah. Therefore, he took a gift and went to visit her in her father's house. How shocked he was to learn that not only was he not married, but also the woman he loved was now married to his best-man![2] Samson had paid the legal "bride price" for his wife, and now he had neither the money nor the wife.

Samson was angry, and even the offer of a younger and prettier bride didn't appease him. If anybody should have been punished, it was his father-in-law. He was the real culprit. After all, he took the money and gave the bride away— to the wrong man! But Samson decided to take out his anger on the Philistines by burning up the grain in their fields.

The word translated "foxes" also means "jackals," and that's probably the animal that Samson used. Foxes are solitary creatures, but jackals prowl in large packs. Because of this, it would have been much easier for Samson to capture 300 jackals; and no doubt he enlisted the help of others. Had he tied the firebrands to individual animals, they each would have immediately run to their dens. But by putting two animals together and turning them loose, Samson could be fairly sure that their fear of the fire and their inability to maneuver easily would make them panic. Thus they would run around frantically in the fields and ignite the grain. The fire then would spread into the vineyards and olive groves. It was a costly devastation.

Why he chose to destroy the Philistine's crops in such a strange manner isn't clear to us. If others were helping him, Samson could attack several fields at the same time; and the Philistines, unable to see the animals on the ground, would be alarmed and confused, wondering what was causing the fires. The jackals would undoubtedly make a racket, especially if caught in the rushing flame or overwhelmed by the smoke. His riddle and his rhyme (15:16) indicate that Samson had a boyish sense of humor, and perhaps this approach to agricultural arson was just another fun time for him. However, we must keep in mind that God was using Samson's exploits to harass the Philistines and prepare them for the sure defeat that was coming in a few years.

He avenges his wife's death (vv. 6-8). Violence breeds violence, and the Philistines weren't about to stand around doing nothing while their food and fortune went up in flames. They figured out that Samson was behind the burning of their crops, and they knew they had to retaliate. Since they couldn't hope to overcome Samson, they did the next thing and vented their wrath on his wife and father-in-law. In the long run, her betrayal of Samson didn't save her life after all (14:15).

Samson's response? "Since you've acted like this, I won't stop until I get my revenge on you" (15:7, NIV). We don't know how many Philistines he killed or what weapons he used, but it was "a great slaughter." Following the attack, he retreated to a cave in the "rock of Etam." This is not the Etam mentioned either in 1 Chronicles 4:32 (too far away) or 2 Chronicles 11:6 (hadn't been built yet). It was some elevated place in Judah, near Lehi, from which Samson could safely and conveniently watch the enemy.

2. Samson defends himself. (Judg. 15:9-20)

If Samson could attack the Philistines, then the Philistines could retaliate and attack Israel; after all, Israel had neither weapons nor an army. The invasion of Judah didn't help Samson's popularity with his own people, who sadly were content to submit to their neighbors and make the best of a bad situation. Instead of seeing Samson as their deliverer, the men of Judah considered him a troublemaker.

It's difficult to be a leader if you have no followers, but part of the fault lay with Samson. He didn't challenge the people, organize them, and trust God to give them victory. He preferred to work alone, fighting the battles of the Lord as though they were his own private feuds. I realize that Samson's calling was to *begin* to deliver the nation (13:5), but it seems to me that he could have made a more forceful beginning. When God's people get comfortable with the status quo, and their leaders fail to arouse them to action, they are in pretty bad shape.

When the men of Judah learned that the Philistines wanted only to capture and bind Samson, they offered to help. A nation is in a sad state indeed when the citizens cooperate with the enemy and hand over their own God-appointed leader! This is the only time during Samson's judgeship that the Jews mustered an army, *and it was for the purpose of capturing one of their own men!* But Samson realized that, if he didn't give himself up to the enemy, the Philistine army would bring untold suffering to the land; so he willingly surrendered. If he defended himself, he would have had to fight his own people. If he escaped, which he could easily have done, he would have left 3,000 men of Judah easy prey for the Philistine army. There was something heroic about Samson's decision, but the men of Judah missed it.

By the power of the Holy Spirit, Samson easily broke the bonds the men of Judah had put on his arms, picked up a new jawbone of a donkey (an old one would have been too brittle) and slaughtered a thousand Philistines. We wonder what the men of Judah thought as they watched their prisoner, their own brother, kill the invaders single-handed. Did any of them feel the urge to pick up the weapons of the slain Philistines and join in the battle? Would they have known how to use them?

Samson had a way with words. At his wedding feast, he devised a clever riddle (14:14); and after this great victory, he wrote a poem. It's based on the similarity between the sounds of the Hebrew words *hamor* ("donkey") and *homer* ("heap"). James Moffatt renders it: "With the jawbone of an ass I have piled them in a mass. With the jawbone of an ass I have assailed assailants."[3]

But his victory celebration didn't last very long, for God reminded him that he was only a man and had to have water to stay alive. So often in Scripture, testing follows triumph. No sooner had the Israelites crossed the Red Sea than they became thirsty (Ex. 15:22-27) and hungry (Ex. 16). Elijah's victory on Mount Carmel was followed by his humiliating flight to Mount Horeb (1 Kings 18-19). If triumphs aren't balanced with trials, there's a danger that we'll become proud and self-confident.

If Samson had only heeded this warning and asked God not only for water but for guidance! "Lead us not into temptation" would have been the perfect prayer for that hour. How quick we are to cry out for help for the body when perhaps our greatest needs are in the inner person. It's when we're weak that we're strong (2 Cor. 12:10); and when we're totally dependent on the Lord, we're the safest.

Samson's prayer indicates that he considered himself God's servant and that he didn't want to end his life falling into the hands of the godless Philistines. Unfortunately, that's just what happened. But God was merciful and performed a miracle by opening up a spring of water in a hollow place. Samson quenched his thirst and then gave the place the name "Caller's Spring." The place where Samson slaughtered the Philistines received the name "Jawbone Hill." Some translations give the impression that the water came from the jawbone because the name of the place in Hebrew is Lehi, which means "jawbone." In the NKJV, Judges 15:19 reads, "So God split the hollow place that is in Lehi"; and the NASB and NIV are substantially the same.

3. Samson tempts himself. (Judg. 16:1-3)

Gaza was an important seaport town located about forty miles from Samson's hometown of Zorah. We aren't told why Samson went there, but it's not likely he was looking for sensual pleasure. There were plenty of prostitutes available in Israel even though the Law condemned this practice (Lev. 19:29; Deut. 22:21). It was after he arrived in Gaza that Samson saw a prostitute and decided to visit her. Once again the lust of the eyes and the lust of the flesh combined to grip Samson and make him a slave to his passions.

It seems incredible to us that a servant of God (Judg. 15:18), who did great works in the power of the Spirit, would visit a prostitute, but the record is here for all to read. The Lord certainly didn't approve of such behavior, especially on the part of a Nazirite; and the experience was for Samson one more step down into darkness and destruction. In recent years, there have been enough ministerial scandals in the United States alone to put all of us on guard. "Therefore let him who thinks he stands take heed lest he fall" (1 Cor. 10: 12, NKJV).

We can't help it when Satan and his demons tempt us; but when we tempt ourselves, we become our own enemy. God doesn't tempt us (James 1:12-15). When we pray, "Lead us not into temptation" (Matt. 6:13), we're asking that we not tempt ourselves *or put ourselves into such a position that we tempt God.* We tempt Him either by forcing Him to intervene and rescue us or by daring Him to stop us. It's possible for people's character to deteriorate so much that they don't have to be tempted in order to sin. All they need is the opportunity to sin, and they'll tempt themselves. Illicit sexual experience may begin as sweet as honey, but it ends up as bitter as wormwood (Prov. 5:1-14). Samson the man had become Samson the animal as the prostitute led him to the slaughter (Prov. 7:6-23).

Word that their enemy Samson was in town spread to the people of Gaza, and they posted a guard at the city gate to capture him and kill him in the morning. But Samson decided to leave town at midnight, while the guards were asleep. The fact that the city gates were barred didn't alarm him. He picked up the doors, posts, and bars and carried them off! Whether he carried them all the way to Hebron, a distance of about forty miles, or only to a hill that faced Hebron, depends on how you translate Judges 16:3. Both interpretations are possible.

The city gate was not only a protection for the city, but also the place where the officials met to transact business (Deut. 25:7; Ruth 4:1-2). To "possess the gate of his enemies" was a metaphor meaning "to defeat your enemies" (Gen. 22:17; 24:60). When Jesus spoke about the gates of hell (hades) not prevailing against the church (Matt. 16:18), He was picturing the victory of the church over the forces of Satan and evil. Through His death and resurrection, Jesus Christ has "stormed the gates of hell" and carried them off in victory!

4. Samson betrays himself. (Judg. 16:4-22)

The Valley of Sorek lay between Zorah and Timnah on the border of Judah and Philistia. The city of Beth-shemesh was located there. Whenever Samson went into enemy territory, he "went down" both geographically and spiritually (14:1, 5, 7, 10). This time he found a woman in the valley, not too far from home; and he fell in love with her. It's a dangerous thing to linger at the enemy's border; you might get caught.

Along with David and Bathsheba, Samson and Delilah have captured the imagination of scores of writers, artists, composers, and dramatists. Handel included Delilah in his oratorio "Samson," and Saint-Saens wrote an opera on "Samson and Delilah." (The "Bacchanale" from that work is still a popular concert piece.) When Samson consorted with Delilah in the Valley of Sorek, he never dreamed that what they did together would be made into a Hollywood movie and projected in color on huge screens.

Scholars disagree on the meaning of Delilah's name. Some think it means "devotee," suggesting that she may have been a temple prostitute. But Delilah isn't called a prostitute as is the woman in Gaza, although that's probably what she was. For that matter, Delilah isn't even identified as a Philistine. However, from her dealings with the Philistine leaders, she appears to be one. Other students believe that the basis for her name is the Hebrew word *dalal,* which means "to weaken, to impoverish." Whether or not this is the correct derivation, she certainly weakened and impoverished Samson!

Each of the Philistine leaders offered to pay Delilah a considerable sum of money if she would entice Samson and learn the source of his great strength.[4] They didn't want to kill Samson. They wanted to neutralize his power, capture him, torture him, and then use him for their own purposes. Being able to exhibit and control the great champion of Israel would give the Philistines both security and stature among the nations and would certainly satisfy their egos as they humiliated the Jews.

When Delilah began to probe for the secret of his strength, Samson should have been aware of his danger and, like Joseph (Gen. 39:12; 2 Tim. 2:22), fled as fast as possible. But passion had gripped him, sin had anesthetized him, and he was unable to act rationally. Anybody could have told him that Delilah was making a fool out of him, but Samson would have believed no one.

It's unlikely that the Philistines who hid in her chamber revealed themselves each time Samson escaped his bonds, because then he would have known that Delilah had set a trap for him. Her cry "The Philistines are upon you!" was the signal for the spies to be alert; but when they saw that Samson was free, they remained in hiding. Each of Samson's lies involved Delilah using some kind of bonds on him, but the Philistines should have known that he could not be bound (Judg. 15:13).

Delilah had to keep working on Samson or she would have lost the money and perhaps her life. After all, look at what the Philistines did to Samson's first wife! If Samson had stopped visiting Delilah, he would have kept his hair and his power,[5] but he kept going back, and each time she implored him to reveal his secret. Samson didn't know his own heart. He thought he possessed enough moral strength to say no to the temptress, but he was wrong.

Being wise in the ways of sin (Luke 16:8; Prov. 7:21), during the fourth visit, Delilah knew that he had finally told her the truth. Since the Philistine "hit squad" had quit coming after the third fiasco, Delilah summoned them quickly, and they once again hid in her chamber.

When Delilah's shout awakened Samson, he thought it was another one of her tricks and that he could handle the situation as before. But he was wrong. When he lost his long hair, the Lord left him; and he was as weak as other men. His power was from the Lord, not from his hair; but the hair was the sign of his Nazirite vow. The Spirit who had come upon him with such power had now departed from him.

Numbers 6:7 reads literally "because the consecration *(nezer)* of his God is upon his head." The basic meaning of the word *nezer* is "separation" or "consecration";

but it is also used of a royal crown (2 Sam. 1:10; Zech. 9:16; Ps. 89:39). Samson's long hair was his "royal crown" and he lost it because of his sin. "Behold, I come quickly! Hold fast what you have, that no one may take your crown" (Rev. 3:11, NKJV). Since Samson didn't discipline his body, he lost both his crown and his prize (1 Cor. 9:24-27).[6]

The Philistines easily overpowered Samson and finally had their way with him. They put out his eyes,[7] bound him, and took him to Gaza where he toiled at the grinding mill, doing work usually assigned to slaves, women, or donkeys. Someone has said that Judges 16:21 reminds us of the *blinding, binding,* and *grinding* results of sin. In his epic poem *Samson Agonistes,* John Milton has the champion say:

> O loss of sight, of thee I most complain!
> Blind among enemies, O worse than chains,
> Dungeon, or beggary, or decrepit age!

Samson is one of three men in Scripture who are especially identified with the darkness. The other two are King Saul, who went out in the darkness to get last-minute help from a witch (1 Sam. 28), and Judas, who "went immediately out: and it was night" (John 13:30). Saul lived for the world, Samson yielded to the flesh, and Judas gave himself to the devil (John 13:2, 27); and all three ended up taking their own lives.

But there was one ray of light in the darkness: Samson's hair began to grow again. His power was not in his hair but in what his hair symbolized—his dedication to God. If Samson renewed that dedication, God might restore his power. I believe Samson talked to the Lord as he turned the millstone, confessing his sins and asking God for one last opportunity to defeat the enemy and glorify His name.[8]

5. Samson destroys himself. (Judg. 16:23-31)

It was tragic that a servant of the Lord, raised in a godly home, was now the humiliated slave of the enemy. But even worse, the Philistines gave glory to their god Dagon for helping them capture their great enemy. Instead of bringing glory to the God of Israel, Samson gave the enemy opportunity to honor their false gods. Dagon was the god of grain, and certainly the Philistines remembered what Samson had done to their fields (15:1-5).

The people at the religious festival called for Samson to be brought to entertain them. They were in high spirits because their enemy was now in their control and Dagon had triumphed over Jehovah. They thought that Samson's blindness rendered him harmless. They didn't know that God had deigned to forgive him and restore his strength.

In the KJV, two different words are translated "make sport" in 16:25 ("entertain" and "perform" in the NIV). The first means to celebrate, frolic, joke, and entertain; and the second means to perform, make sport, and laugh.[9] We aren't told exactly *how* Samson entertained the huge crowd in Dagon's temple, but one thing is sure: He gave them every reason to believe he was harmless and under their control. He was even in the hands of a boy who was leading the blind man from place to place. We've seen previous indications that Samson was a clever fellow with a sense of humor. Thus no doubt he gave the audience just what it wanted.

In previous visits to Gaza, Samson had undoubtedly seen this temple and noted its construction. After all, it housed over 3,000 people, and it would be difficult for him not to notice it. During a break in the day's entertainment, Samson asked his attendant to lead him over to the pillars; and there he uttered his last prayer.[10] The fact that God answered suggests that all was right between him and his Lord (Ps. 66:18-19).

It's likely that his parents were dead by now, but his relatives on his father's side came and recovered the body and buried it. The word "brethren" in Judges 16:31 in the Hebrew carries a broad meaning of "relatives." As far as we know, Samson was an only child. The phrase "between Zorah and Eshtaol" in verse 31 reminds us of 13:25. Samson is back where he started, only now he's dead. The light has failed.

How do you assess the life and ministry of a man like Samson? I think Alexander Maclaren says it well: "Instead of trying to make a lofty hero out of him, it is far better to recognize frankly the limitations of his character and the imperfections of his religion. . . . If the merely human passion of vengeance throbbed fiercely in Samson's prayer, he had never heard 'Love your enemies'; and, for his epoch, the destruction of the enemies of God and of Israel was duty."[11]

His decline began when he disagreed with his parents about marrying a Philistine girl. Then he disdained his Nazirite vow and defiled himself. He disregarded the warnings of God, disobeyed the Word of God, and was defeated by the enemies of God. He probably thought that he had the privilege of indulging in sin since he wore the badge of a Nazirite and won so many victories for the Lord, but he was wrong.

"Whoever has no rule over his own spirit is like a city broken down, without walls" (Prov. 25:28, NKJV).

"He who is slow to anger is better than the mighty, and he who rules his spirit than he who takes a city" (Prov. 16:32, NKJV).

I wonder whether Solomon was thinking about Samson when he wrote those words.

CHAPTER ELEVEN
"THE CENTER CANNOT HOLD"
Judges 17–18

In his well-known poem "The Second Coming," the Irish poet William Butler Yeats describes the collapse of civilization in vivid and frightening imagery. Each time I read the poem, I feel chilled within; and then I give thanks that I know the One who is coming.

"Things fall apart," writes Yeats; "the center cannot hold."

The closing chapters of the Book of Judges echo that theme: "the center cannot hold." The nation that once marched triumphantly through Canaan to the glory of God now disintegrates morally and politically and brings disgrace to His name. But what else can you expect when there is "no king in Israel" and the people are flouting the laws of God?

The events described in chapters 17-21 took place earlier in the period of the Judges, probably before the forty-year rule of the Philistines. The movements of the tribe of Dan would have been difficult and the war against Benjamin impossible if the Philistines had been in charge at that time. The writer departed from historical chronology and put these events together as an "appendix" to the book to show how wicked the people had become. In three major areas of life, things were falling apart: the home, the ministry, and society.

1. Confusion in the home (Judg. 17:1-6)

God has established three institutions in society: the home, human government, and the worshiping community—Israel under the Old Covenant and the church under the New Covenant. The first of these, in both time and significance, is the home, because the home is the basis for society. When God wedded Adam to Eve in the garden, He laid the foundation for the social institutions humanity would build. When that foundation crumbles, society begins to fall apart. "If the foundations be destroyed, what can the righteous do?" (Ps. 11:3)

The name Micah means "Who is like Jehovah?" but the man certainly didn't live to honor the Lord. He had a family (Judg. 17:5), although nothing is said about his wife; and we get the impression that his mother lived with him and that she was wealthy. The "extended family" was normal in Israel.

Somebody stole 1,100 shekels of silver from Grandmother, and she pronounced a curse on the thief, not knowing that she was cursing her own son. It was the fear of the curse, not the fear of the Lord, that motivated the son to confess his crime and restore the money. Then Grandmother joyfully neutralized the curse by blessing her son. In gratitude for the return of her money, she dedicated part of the silver to the Lord and made an idol out of it. Her son added the new idol to his "god collection" in his house, a "shrine" cared for by one of his sons whom Micah had consecrated as priest.

Have you ever seen a family more spiritually and morally confused than this one? They managed to break almost all the Ten Commandments (Ex. 20:1-17) *and yet not feel the least bit guilty before the Lord!* In fact, they thought they were serving the Lord by the bizarre things they did!

The son didn't honor his mother; instead, he stole from her and then lied about it. First, he coveted the silver, and then he took it. (According to Col. 3:5, covetousness is idolatry.)

Then he lied about the whole enterprise until the curse scared him into confessing. Thus he broke the fifth, eighth, ninth, and tenth commandments; and he broke the first and second commandments by having a shrine of false gods in his home. According to Proverbs 30:8-9, when he stole the silver, he broke the third commandment and took the name of the Lord in vain. Breaking seven of the Ten Commandments without leaving your own home is quite an achievement!

The man's mother broke the first two commandments by making an idol and encouraging her son to maintain a private "shrine" in his home. According to Deuteronomy 12:1-14, there was to be but one place of worship in Israel; and the people were not permitted to have their own private shrines. Furthermore, Micah's mother didn't really deal with her son's sins; his character certainly didn't improve by the way she handled the matter. But she was a corrupt person herself, so what else could he expect?

Micah not only had a private shrine, but also he ordained his own son to serve as priest. Certainly Micah knew that the Lord had appointed the family of Aaron to be the only priests in Israel; and if anybody outside Aaron's family served as priests, they were to be killed (Num. 3:10).

Because Micah and his family didn't submit to the authority of God's Word, their home was a place of religious and moral confusion. But their home was a good deal like many homes today where money is the god the family worships, where children steal from their parents and lie about what they do, where family honor is unknown, and where the true God is unwanted. Television provides all the "images" the family will ever want to "worship," and few worry about "thus saith the Lord."

I recall hearing Vance Havner say, "We shouldn't worry because the government won't allow children to have Bibles in school. They'll get free Bibles when they go to prison."

But today our prisons are so crowded that the government doesn't know what to do. If every family would make Christ the Head of the home, we could stop some of the nation's crime right at the source. Godly homes are the foundation for a just and happy society.

2. Confusion in the ministry (Judg. 17:7-13)

Not only did God establish the home and instruct parents how to raise their children (Deut. 6), but He also instituted spiritual leadership in the worshiping community. Under the Old Covenant, the tabernacle and then the temple were the center of the community, and the Aaronic priesthood supervised both. Under the New Covenant, the church of Jesus Christ is the temple of God (Eph. 2:19-22); and the Holy Spirit calls and equips ministers to serve Him and His people (1 Cor. 12-14; Eph. 4:1-16). In His Word, God told the Old Testament priests what they were supposed to do; and in His Word today, the Holy Spirit guides His church and explains its order and its ministry.

A young Levite named Jonathan (18:30)[1] had been living in Bethlehem of Judah, which was not one of the cities assigned to the priests and Levites (Josh. 21; Num. 35). He was probably there because the people of Israel weren't supporting the tabernacle and its ministry with their tithes and offerings as God commanded them to do (Num. 18:21-32; Deut. 14:28-29; 26:12-15). Why live in one of the levitical cities if you're going to starve? When God's people grow indifferent to spiritual things, one of the first evidences of their apathy is a decline in their giving to the work of the Lord; as a result, everybody suffers.

Instead of seeking the mind of the Lord, Jonathan set out to find a place to live and work, even if it meant abandoning his calling as a servant of God. The nation was at a low ebb spiritually and he could have done something to help bring the people back to God. He was only one man, but that's all God needs to begin a great work that can make a difference in the history of a nation. Instead of being available to God, Jonathan was agreeable only to men; and he eventually found himself a comfortable home and job with Micah.

If Jonathan is typical of God's servants in that period of history, then it's no wonder the nation of Israel was confused and corrupt. He had no appreciation for his high calling as a Levite, a chosen servant of God. Not only were the Levites to assist the priests in their ministries (Num. 3:6-13; 8:17-18), but they were also to teach the Law to the people (Neh. 8:7-9; 2 Chron. 17:7-9; 35:3) and be involved in the sacred music and the praises of Israel (1 Chron. 23:28-32; Ezra 3:10). Jonathan gave up all that for comfort and security in the home of an idolater.

Jonathan's ministry, however, wasn't a spiritual ministry at all. To begin with, he was a *hireling* and not a true shepherd (Judg. 18:4; John 10:12-13). He didn't serve the true and living God; he worked for Micah and his idols. Jonathan wasn't a spokesperson for the Lord; he gave people just the message they wanted to hear (Judg. 18:6). When he was offered a place involving more money, more people, and more prestige, he took it immediately and gave thanks for it (v. 19). And then he assisted his new employers in stealing his former employer's gods!

Whenever the church has a "hireling ministry," it can't enjoy the blessing of God. The church needs true and faithful shepherds who work for the Lord, not for personal gain, and who will stay with the flock to feed them and protect them. True shepherds don't see their work as a "career" and run off to a "better job" when the opportunity comes. They stay where God puts them and don't move until He sends them.

True shepherds receive their calling and authority from God, not from people (Gal. 1:6ff); and they honor the true God, not the idols that people make. It must grieve the Lord today to see people worshiping the idols of ministerial "success:" statistics, buildings, and reputation. In today's "consumer society," self-appointed preachers and "prophets" have no problem getting a following and peddling their religious wares to a church that acts more like a Hollywood fan club than a holy people of God. And to make it worse, these hirelings will call what's happening "the blessing of God." Jonathans and Micahs will always find each other because they need each other.

The sad part of the story is that Micah now thought he had the favor of God because a genuine levitical priest was serving as his private chaplain. Micah practiced a false religion and worshiped false gods (with Jehovah thrown in for good measure), and all the while he rested on the false confidence that God was blessing him! Little did he know that the day would come when his priest and his gods would be taken from him and nothing would be left of his religion.

3. Confusion in society (Judg. 18:1-31)
God should have been the king in Israel and His Word the law that governed society, but the people preferred to "do their own thing." If the people had forsaken their idols, and if the elders of Israel had consulted God's Law and obeyed it for God's glory, Israel could have been governed successfully. Instead, "Every man did that which was right in his own eyes" (21:25), and the result was a society filled with competition and confusion.

Consider the sins of the tribe of Dan as they sought to better their situation in the nation of Israel.

Covetousness (vv. 1-2). The tribe of Dan descended from Jacob's fifth son, born of Rachel's handmaid Bilhah (Gen. 30:1-6). Though not a large tribe (Num. 1:39), it was given choice territory when the tribal boundaries were assigned (Josh. 19:40-48). The Danites, however, weren't able to defeat and dispossess the enemy (Judg. 1:34), thus they decided to go north and relocate. Most of the other tribes were able to conquer the enemy, dispossessed them, and claim their land, but the Danites coveted somebody else's land instead and took it in a violent manner.

The Lord had assigned the tribal allotments under the direction of Joshua, with the help of Eleazar the high priest and the elders from the tribes (Josh. 19:51). As He did with the nations (Acts 17:26), so He did with the tribes: God put each tribe just where He wanted it. For the tribe of Dan to reject God's assigned territory and covet another place was to oppose His divine will.

But isn't that what causes most of the trouble in our society today? Instead of submitting to God's will, people want what somebody else has; and they'll do almost anything to get it (James 4:1-3). The corruption that's in this world is fed by "evil desires" (2 Peter 1:4, NIV). Whether it's producing pornography, selling dope, or promoting gambling, money hungry people cater to human desires and end up making money and destroying lives. Thanks to the power of modern media, especially television, the advertising industry creates in people appetites for all sorts of exciting products, services, and experiences. Therefore, people go out and spend money they don't have on things they don't need to impress people who don't really care; but this is the cycle that keeps business going.[2]

The elders of Israel should have put a stop to the men of Dan as they abandoned God's assigned place and headed north to kill innocent people and steal their land. But covetousness is strong; and once people get an appetite for "something more," it's difficult to control them.

Ungodly counsel (vv. 3-6). It was Jonathan's dialect that attracted the attention of the five spies, because he didn't speak quite like a man from Ephraim. When they asked what a levitical priest was doing in a private home in Ephraim—a very good question, by the way (1 Kings 19:9, 13)—he told them the truth: He was hired to do the job! Since somebody else was paying the bill, the spies thought it was permissible to get "spiritual counsel" from Jonathan, and he told them what they wanted to hear.[3]

If the tribe of Dan had really wanted God's counsel, they could have consulted with the high priest. But they were actually rejecting God's counsel by refusing to remain in the land He had assigned to them. Therefore, it wasn't likely God would have revealed anything to them (John 7:17).

Breaking and entering, robbery and intimidation (vv. 14-26). On their way to capture Laish, the people of Dan paused at Micah's house in Ephraim. The spies told the men that Micah had a wonderful collection of gods, hinting, of course, that the collection would be valuable to them as they traveled, warred, and established their new home. While the armed men stood at the gate of the city, the five spies, who knew Jonathan, invaded the shrine and stole the gods.

When the five men, with their religious loot, arrived back at the city gate, the priest was shocked to see what they had done.[4] But the Danites silenced him by hiring him; and since he was a hireling, Jonathan was ready for a better offer. The Danites not only broke into Micah's shrine and stole his gods, but they also stole his chaplain. Not a bad day's work!

The Danites put the women and children in the front since that was the safest place, because any attacks would come from the rear. By the time the Danites had traveled some distance away, Micah discovered that his shrine was out of business, having neither gods nor priest; so he called his neighbors together, and they pursued the invaders. After all, a man must protect his gods!

It was useless. Since the Danites outnumbered him and were too strong for him, Micah and his neighbors had to turn around and go home defeated. Micah's sad question "What else do I have?" (v. 24, NIV) reveals the folly and the tragedy of religion without the true and living God. Idolaters worship gods they can carry, but Christians worship a God who carries them (Isa. 46:1-7).

Violence and murder (vv. 7-13, 27-29). The five spies had traveled 100 miles north from their encampment at Zorah to Laish ("Leshem," Josh. 19:47), a town inhabited by the Sidonians, about thirty miles east of the Mediterranean Sea. These were a peaceful people who minded their own business and had no treaties with anybody. They were "unsuspecting and secure" and "prosperous" (v. 7, NIV), an isolated people, who were a perfect target for the warlike tribe of Dan.

With 600 armed men, plus their women and children (Judg. 18:21), they marched north and captured Laish, killing all the inhabitants and burning the city. Then they rebuilt it and proudly called it Dan, after the name of the founder of their tribe. Unfortunately, what Jacob prophesied about the tribe of Dan came true (Gen. 49:17).

Someone has said that there are only three philosophies of life in today's world: (1) "What's mine is mine, I'll keep it"; (2) "What's yours is mine, I'll take it"; and (3) "What's mine is yours, I'll share it." The Danites followed the second philosophy, and so do too many other grasping people. One of the current booming industries in the United States is the installing of security systems in private homes. The number of shooting sprees in shopping malls and fast-food restaurants has frightened many people into doing their shopping by telephone. The cover story of *Time* magazine for August 23, 1993 called the United States "America the Violent."[5]

We don't know how many people lived in Laish, but the wanton murders of even a few hundred innocent people is a crime of gross proportions. I fear that we've been exposed to so much crime and violence in the media that this kind of news doesn't disturb us anymore. "We're seeing a new sort of violence," wrote Arthur Beisser in *Sports Illustrated* (March 1, 1976). "It's being used not as a means to an end, but for recreational purposes, for pleasure." We might add that violence is also a means for making money, as both the moviemakers and the television industry have proved.

Idolatry (vv. 30-31). The tribe of Dan was the first tribe in Israel to officially adopt an idolatrous system of religion. Even though there was a house of God in Shiloh, they preferred their images and idols. Years later, when the kingdom divided, Jeroboam I of Israel would set up golden calves in Dan and Beersheba and encourage the whole nation to turn away from the true and living God (1 Kings 12:25-33).[6]

The account of Micah, Jonathan, and the Danites is more than a story from ancient history. It's a revelation of the wickedness of the human heart and the hopelessness of human society without God. Our modern world has substituted idols for the true and living God and has devised its own humanistic religion, complete with "priests"—the experts who tell us that the Bible is wrong but their way is right. But neither their idols nor their priests have any power against the violence of the human heart.

When Dwight D. Eisenhower was President of the United States, he called a "White House Conference on Children and Youth," hoping to find solutions to the juvenile delinquency problem that was then plaguing the nation. I was supposed to attend that conference but couldn't go because of family obligations.

However, a friend of mine from Youth for Christ International attended and gave this report (I paraphrase): "I sat in the room for hours, listening to psychologists and educators and criminologists talk about teenagers and how to help them, and I got sick of it. Finally, I asked for the floor and told them of our experiences in Youth for Christ, how delinquents had been changed by the power of the Gospel. The room became very quiet, and then people got embarrassed and began to clear their throats and shuffle papers. The chairman thanked me for my words and immediately moved to the next item on the agenda. Then it hit me: *they didn't want to hear!"*

William Butler Yeats was right: "The center cannot hold." The home, the ministry, and society are disintegrating before our eyes, *and people don't want to hear the truth!* But whether they want it or not, the world must be told that Jesus Christ died for lost sinners, and that the power of Christ can transform hearts, homes, churches, and society if people will only trust Him.

"Christ beats His drum, but He does not press men," said English preacher and poet John Donne (d. 1631); "Christ is served with voluntaries."

Are you available?

CHAPTER TWELVE
WAR AND PEACE
Judges 19–21

After reading these three chapters, if you were to scan your daily newspaper or weekly news magazine, you'd have to admit that times haven't changed too much. For in these closing pages of Judges you find reports of wife abuse, blatant homosexuality, gang rape leading to murder, injustice, brother killing brother, and even kidnapping. It's the kind of narrative that almost makes you agree with British essayist Samuel Johnson, who said back in 1783, "I have lived to see things all as bad as they can be." What would he say today?

Of course, events like these are the daily food of people who enjoy TV violence; and researchers tell us that what happens on the screens is often duplicated on the streets. According to a study by the American Psychological Association, there are five violent acts per hour in prime-time TV programs; and on Saturday mornings when the children watch cartoons, violent acts per hour multiply five times (*USA Today* August 2, 1993). When a nation is entertained by violence, is there much hope for that nation?

When evil isn't dealt with properly, it has a tendency to grow. Sin in the city of Gibeah eventually infected the tribe of Benjamin and led to war in the land of Israel.

1. The wickedness of a city (Judg. 19:1-28)

Entertainment in Bethlehem (vv. 1-9). If you thought that the Levite Jonathan (chaps. 17-18) was a reprobate, then you'll probably conclude that this unnamed Levite was an absolute scoundrel of the basest sort. He spent most of his time partying (19:4, 6, 8, 22); he walked in darkness and jeopardized his life and the lives of those with him (vv. 9-14); he treated his concubine in the most shocking manner, while she was alive and after she was dead; and what he did to her precipitated a civil war in Israel.

A concubine was a lawful wife who was guaranteed only food, clothing, and marital privileges (Ex. 21:7-11; Deut. 21:10-14). Any children she bore would be considered legitimate; but because of her second-class status, they wouldn't necessarily share in the family inheritance (Gen. 25:1-6). If a man's wife was barren, he sometimes took a concubine so he could establish a family. Though the law controlled concubinage the Lord did not approve or encourage it; yet you will find several Old Testament men who had concubines, including Abraham, Jacob, Gideon, Saul, David, and Solomon.

This particular concubine was unfaithful to her husband and fled to her father's house in Bethlehem for protection (Lev. 20:10). The longer she was gone, the more her husband missed her; so he traveled to Bethlehem, forgave her, and was reconciled. He and his father-in-law discovered they enjoyed each other's company and spent five days eating, drinking, and making merry. Little did the Levite realize that he really had nothing to be happy about because tragedy was stalking his marriage.

To me, this Levite illustrates the careless attitude of many believers today. They are children of the day, but they act like children of the night (1 Thes. 5:1-8). Judgment is around the corner, but these people think of nothing but enjoying life. When his nation was so far from God, how could this Levite waste his time eating, drinking, and making merry? "Be afflicted, and mourn, and weep: let your laughter be turned to mourning, and your joy to heaviness" (James 4:9).

Yes, there's "a time to laugh" (Ecc. 3:4), and God wants us to enjoy His gifts (1 Tim. 6:17); but for many Christians, that time is *all the time!* In too many churches, the laughter of "religious entertainment" has replaced the holy hush of worship. The sanctuary has become a theater. When the saints get together, the most important thing is to "have fun." In order to salve our consciences, we have a "short devotional" before the fun time ends; and we piously thank God that we've had such a good time.

Nobody appreciates laughter and good humor more than I do, but I fear the church is losing its sense of awe and needs to learn how to weep. Had this laughing Levite been walking in the light, praying and seeking God's will, he would have made other plans and saved his wife from shame, abuse, pain, and death.

Hospitality in Gibeah (vv. 10-21). During the period of the Judges, it was dangerous to travel in the daytime (5:6) and even more so at night. The Levite didn't want to stay in Jerusalem because it was in the hands of the pagan Jebusites. Thus he pressed on four miles to Gibeah so he could be with his own people. *But the men of Gibeah turned out to be as wicked as the heathen around them!*

To begin with, nobody in Gibeah welcomed the visitors and opened their home to care for them. Since the Levite had plenty of provisions for his party and his animals, he wouldn't have been a burden to anybody; but nobody took them in. Hospitality is one of the sacred laws of the East, and no stranger was to be neglected; but only one man in the city showed any concern, and he was an Ephraimite. He not only took them into his home but also used his own provisions to feed them and their animals.

God's people are commanded to practice hospitality. It's one of the qualifications for a pastor (1 Tim. 3:2; Titus 1:8). "Do not forget to entertain strangers, for by so doing some people have entertained angels without knowing it" (Heb. 13:2, NIV).

Iniquity in Gibeah (vv. 22-28). Gibeah had become like Sodom, a city so wicked that God wiped it off the face of the earth (Gen. 19). The men of the city were indulging in immoral practices that were contrary to nature (Rom. 1:24-27) and the laws of God (Lev. 18:22; 20:13; see 1 Cor. 6:9-10). The word "know" in Judges 19:22 means "to have sexual experience with."

These sinners were excited because a new man was in town, and they wanted to enjoy him.

The host courageously and correctly described their desires as wickedness and folly (v. 23) and a vile thing (v. 24), and he tried to prevent them from raping his guest. Like Lot in Sodom, the host offered them his daughter, which shows the low estimate some men in that day had of women and of sexual purity. How a father could offer his own daughter as a sacrifice to the lusts of a mob is difficult to understand. Yet many parents today allow their sons' and daughters' minds and hearts to be violated by what they see and hear in movies, on television, and at rock concerts. Chastity of mind and heart is essential for chastity of the body.

Since the Levite was afraid the mob would kill him (20:5) he pacified them by giving them his concubine; and she had to endure gang rape the whole night (v. 25). Our hearts revolt at the thought of a man so insensitive to the feelings of a human being made in the image of God, so indifferent to the sanctity of sex and the responsibility of marriage, and so unconcerned about the laws of God, that he would sacrifice his wife to save his own skin. Was he punishing her for being unfaithful to him? If so, the punishment was far greater than the sin.

But it gets worse. Not only did the Levite surrender his wife to the perverted appetites of an ungodly mob, but also he was able to *lie down and go to sleep* while they were abusing her in the street! How calloused can a man become? And how naive was he to expect that she would be alive the next morning?

Finding her dead on the doorstep, but not feeling guilty about it, he put her corpse on one of the donkeys and made his way home. Then he did a despicable thing: He desecrated and mutilated her corpse by cutting it into twelve parts and sending one part to each of the twelve tribes of Israel. Of course, he wanted to mobilize the support of the tribes and punish the men of Gibeah who had killed his wife, but in fact, he was the one who had let them kill her! Surely there were other ways to call attention to Gibeah's crime.[1]

Had the Levite gone to Shiloh where the tabernacle stood (18:31), and had he consulted with the high priest, he could have dealt with the matter according to the Law of God and avoided causing a great deal of trouble. Once tempers were heated in Israel, however, it was difficult to stop the fire from spreading.

2. The stubbornness of a tribe (Judg. 20:1-48)

The assembly (vv. 1-11). The Levite's gruesome announcement produced the results that he wanted: Leaders and soldiers from the entire nation, except Benjamin (v. 3) and Jabesh-gilead (21:8-9), came together at Mizpah to determine what to do.[2] After hearing the Levite's indictment of the men of Gibeah, the people of Israel delivered a verdict and made a vow. The verdict was that the men of Gibeah were guilty and should be handed over to the authorities to be slain (Deut. 13:12-18). The vow was that none of the tribes represented would give their daughters in marriage to the men of Benjamin (Judg. 21:1-7).

The appeal (vv. 12-17). The eleven tribes had agreed "as one man" to attack Gibeah, but first they sent representatives throughout the tribe of Benjamin, calling for the people to confess their wickedness and hand over the guilty men. According to Leviticus 20:13, homosexuals were to be put to death; but that wasn't the crime the tribes were judging. Since the Levite had *willingly* given his concubine to the men of Gibeah, their sin can hardly be called adultery (Deut. 22:22). The penalty for rape was death, and gang rape would be even more serious (Deut. 22:25-26). Perhaps the tribes were citing the law concerning wicked men in a city (Deut. 13:12-18) and using that as the basis for their action.

Whatever law they were obeying, the tribes were concerned to "put away evil out of the land," a phrase that is found at least nine times in Deuteronomy. The men of Gibeah were evil men and had to be punished before the Lord could be pleased with His people and cleanse His land. But the people of Benjamin wouldn't admit that Gibeah had sinned, nor would they turn over the men who had done the wicked deed.

Some people may have interpreted the stubbornness of Benjamin as an act of patriotism: They were only trying to protect their own citizens. But their refusal to cooperate was definitely an act of rebellion against the Lord. When sin isn't exposed, confessed, and punished, it pollutes society and defiles the land. The wicked men of Gibeah were like a cancerous tumor in the body that had to be cut out. "Your glorying is not good. Do you not know that a little leaven leavens the whole lump? (1 Cor. 5:6, NKJV)

The result? The tribe of Benjamin declared war on the rest of the tribes of Israel! The eleven tribes had 400,000 men in their army (Judg. 20:2), while the Benjamites had only 26,000 swordsmen and 700 "chosen men" who were experts with slings (vv. 15-16). But in spite of the terrible odds, *it was brother fighting against brother!*

When God's people refuse to obey God's Word, the results are always tragic. The spiritual life of a church is crippled and eventually destroyed when the congregation shuts its eyes to sin and will not discipline offenders. There can never be unity among the people of God as long as some of them cover up sin and allow it to infect the body.

The attack (vv. 18-40). The representatives of the eleven tribes went to the tabernacle at Shiloh (18:31; 1 Sam. 1:9)[3] and sought the mind of the Lord, either by casting lots (Judg. 20:9) or by the priest using the Urim and Thummim (Ex. 28:30). God gave them permission to do battle, with the tribe of Judah leading the attack. That first day, God allowed the Benjamites to win and kill 22,000 Israelite soldiers.

The eleven tribes wept before the Lord and again sought His will. Note that "the children of Benjamin" in Judges 20:18 becomes "Benjamin my brother" in verse 23. Perhaps this was one reason why God permitted the Israelites to lose that first battle. It gave them an opportunity to reflect on the fact that they were fighting their own flesh and blood. But on the second day of the war, Benjamin won again, this time killing 18,000 men. The situation was very grim.

The eleven tribes again sought the face of the Lord, this time with fasting and sacrifices along with their tears. The Lord answered their prayers and not only told them to attack again but also assured them that this time they would win.

The strategy used on the third day was similar to that which Joshua used at Ai (Josh. 8). Self-confident because of two days of victories (Judg. 20:30-31, and note 16:20), the army of Benjamin met the Israelite army, killed about 30 men, but were drawn away from Gibeah and caught in an ambush. Over 25,000 Benjamites were killed on the battlefield, on the highways, or as they fled into the wilderness. Gibeah was taken, its inhabitants were slain, and the city was burned to the ground. In fact, the Israelite army wiped out several other cities in a mopping-up operation.

At the first census after the Exodus from Egypt, there were 35,400 men of war in Benjamin (Num. 1:37), and this increased to 45,600 by the time of the second census (Num. 26:41). During this three-day war, the Benjamites were left with only 600 men stranded on the rock of Rimmon, a fortresslike rock formation near Gibeah. What a price the tribe of Benjamin paid for refusing to obey the Law of the Lord!

3. The brokenness of a nation (Judg. 21:1-25)

Once their anger cooled off, the eleven tribes realized that they had just about eliminated a tribe from the nation of Israel; and this made them weep (vv. 2, 15). They offered sacrifices to the Lord, but there's no record that the people humbled themselves, confessed their sin, and sought the help of the Lord. Previously, the Lord had revealed His will to them (20:18, 23, 28); but there's no evidence that they received His Word after the battle was over.

I may be wrong, but I suspect that the Lord wasn't pleased with the people of Benjamin because they still hadn't confessed their sin and admitted they were wrong. The 600 soldiers who were stranded on the rock of Rimmon still weren't seeking God's face. They were simply fleeing from the victorious army. Had somebody suggested that they all meet the Lord at Shiloh and get the matter settled with the Lord, it might have made a difference.

Instead of getting directions from the Lord, the eleven tribes depended on their own wisdom to solve the problem (James 3:13-18). The 600 men who were left from Benjamin would need wives if they were going to reestablish their tribe, but the eleven tribes had sworn not to give them wives. Where would these wives come from?

The Israelites solved the problem by killing more of their own people! Nobody had come to the war from Jabesh-gilead, which meant two things: They hadn't participated in the oath, and the city deserved to be punished. It's possible that when the twelve parts of the concubine's body were sent throughout Israel, a warning was issued that any tribe or city that didn't respond and help fight Benjamin would be treated the same way. That's the kind of warning King Saul gave when he used a similar approach (1 Sam. 11:7).

If that's the case, then the men of Jabesh-gilead knew what was at stake when they remained at home; and the ensuing slaughter of their city was their own fault. The executioners found 400 virgins in the city, women who could become wives to two thirds of the soldiers on the rock. These men had been on the rock for four months (Judg. 20:47), but now they could take their brides and go home. What a price was paid for these wives! But such are "the wages of sin." (See Num. 31:17 and Deut. 20:13-14 for precedents.)

The elders held another meeting to discuss how they could provide wives for the remaining 200 men. Somebody remembered that many of the virgins from the tribes participated in an annual feast at Shiloh. If the remaining 200 men of Benjamin hid near the place, they could each kidnap a girl and take her home as a wife. The tribes wouldn't be violating their oath because they wouldn't be *giving* the girls as brides. The girls were being *taken*. It was a matter of semantics, but they agreed to follow the plan.

Thus, the 600 men got their brides, the eleven tribes kept their vow, the citizens of Gibeah were punished, the tribe of Benjamin was taught a lesson, and the twelve tribes of Israel were saved. The 600 men of Benjamin, with their brides, returned to their inheritance, cleaned up the debris, repaired the cities, and started life all over again.

But all of this carnage and destruction happened because one Levite didn't have the courage to stand up for what was right and treat his concubine honorably. Once again, as with Jonathan, Micah, and the Danites (Judg. 17-18), the problem started in the home. As goes the home, so goes the nation.

For the fourth time (17:6; 18:1; 19:1), the writer tells us that "there was no king in Israel"; and for the second time (17:6), he adds that "every man did that which was right in his own eyes." Today, there is no king in Israel because the nation chose Barabbas instead of Jesus (Luke 23:13-25). They said, "We will not have this man to reign over us" (Luke 19:14). Because there's no king in Israel, people are rebelling against God and doing whatever pleases them; and it will be that way until the King returns and takes His throne on earth.

But God's people today don't live in the Book of Judges; they *live in the Book of Ruth!* It's difficult to believe that the story narrated in the Book of Ruth takes place in the time of the Judges (Ruth 1:1). The story of Ruth is a *love story* about a man seeking a bride. It's a *redemption story,* about a wealthy man willingly paying the price to purchase his beloved bride and make her his very own. It's a *harvest story* about the Lord of the harvest bringing in the sheaves.

Through faith in Jesus Christ, all of God's people today share in His love. We belong wholly to Him because He redeemed us by His blood when He died for us on the cross. We are laborers together in the harvest. What a wonderful life we have in a world torn apart by sin and selfishness! And what a wonderful privilege we have to share the Good News with others!

In which book are you living—the Book of Judges or the Book of Ruth?

CHAPTER THIRTEEN
LOOKING BACK AND LOOKING AROUND

Drawing Some Lessons from the Book of Judges

As we look back at our studies and look around at our world and God's church, we can draw some conclusions about the Christian life and Christian service and make some applications for our own ministries today.

1. God is looking for servants.

He's looking for people who are available to hear His Word, receive His power, and do His will. God can use all kinds of men and women. Like Gideon, some of God's servants are weak in themselves but strong in the Lord. Like Barak, some people don't want to fight the enemy alone. All of us are different, but all of us can serve the Lord for His glory.

If God calls you to serve Him, it's not primarily because of your abilities and talents. He often calls people who seem to have no leadership qualities at all. He calls you because you are yielded to Him and available to do His will. Don't look at yourself; don't look only at the challenge; look to the Lord.

2. God rules and overrules in history. The Book of Judges makes it clear that God can work in and through all nations, Gentiles as well as Jews. God has "determined the times before appointed and the bounds of their habitation" (Acts 17:26). He's the God of both history and geography. He can use Gentile nations to chasten His own people Israel. He can put one ruler up and bring down another.

While there may not be an obvious *pattern* to history, although historians may search for it, there is definitely a *plan* to history; because God is in control. As Dr. A.T. Pierson used to say, "History is His story." Events that look to us like accidents are really appointments (Rom. 8:28). As dark as the days were in the time of the Judges, God was still on the throne, accomplishing His purposes. This ought to encourage us to trust Him and keep serving Him, no matter how grim the prospects might be in this wicked world.

3. God gives nations the leaders they deserve.

I've pointed out several times in these studies that the quality of the character of the judges deteriorated, starting with Gideon. By the time we get to Samson, we see great physical strength wedded to the weakest kind of character. Gideon, Jepthah, and Samson did the work God gave them to do, but they provided no spiritual leadership for the people.

Philosophers have debated for centuries whether or not a bad person can be a good leader. Perhaps the key question is, "What kind of leadership are you talking about?" A general who swears, bullies, lies, and ignores the Word of God, if he's an experienced soldier, can no doubt provide effective leadership for an army; but he won't provide the kind of example that builds character.

All of God's servants are flawed in some way, but that shouldn't be an excuse for us to sin or to do less than our best. We should all strive to build Christian character and to develop our skills to the glory of God. Dedication is no substitute for careless work, but success in the eyes of people is no substitute for likeness to Jesus Christ. Like David, we should serve the Lord with both integrity and skillfulness (Ps. 78:72).

4. God graciously forgives and helps us begin again.

The historical cycle in the Book of Judges assures us that God chastens when we disobey and forgives when we repent and confess our sins. It's too bad we don't learn from the failures of others and from our own past failures, but that's one of the occupational hazards of being human.

We must remember that the nation of Israel was in a special covenant relationship with God. He promised to bless them if they obeyed His Law and chasten them if they disobeyed. Nowhere in the New Testament has God promised to make His people's lives today easy and comfortable if they obey the Lord. Jesus lived a perfect life on earth, yet He suffered as no one has ever suffered; and we're called to be like Jesus. Paul was a man devoted to the Lord, yet he experienced innumerable trials.

If we obey the Lord just to get things from Him or to escape from trials, then our relationship to Him isn't very loving. It's more of a "contract" relationship: we'll obey Him if He'll give us what we want. Jesus dealt with this selfish attitude in His Parable of the Laborers (Matt. 20:1-16), which was given in answer to Peter's question, "What shall we have therefore?" (Matt. 19:27)

We should obey the Lord because we love Him. Sometimes obeying Him will lead us into trials, but He will see us through. We need to be like the three Jews who faced the fiery furnace: "Our God whom we serve is able to deliver us from the burning fiery furnace, and He will deliver us from your hand, O King. But if not, let it be known to you, O King, that we do not serve your gods, nor will we worship the golden image which you have set up" (Dan. 3:17-18, NKJV).

5. God's Word stands despite people's unfaithfulness.

The judges accomplished what they did because they believed the Word of God (Heb. 11:32-34). Sometimes their faith was weak and imperfect, but God honored their trust and glorified His name through them. But even when the leaders and the people disobeyed Him, their unbelief and disobedience didn't cancel the Word of God.

God's Word never fails. If we obey it, He is faithful to bless us, keep His promises, and accomplish His purposes. If we disobey His will, He is faithful to chasten us and bring us back to the place of submission. The Word doesn't change and God's character doesn't change.

As His children, we live on *promises* and not *explanations.* God doesn't have to explain to us what He's doing or why He's doing it that way. He will always give His servants just the promises they need to get the job done.

6. God uses human government to accomplish His will.

There was "no king in Israel," but God was still able to work. Even when there was a king in Israel, it was no guarantee that the people would obey God. Government is important, and God established government; but rulers, senates or parliaments can't limit God.

According to Romans 13, God instituted human government for our good, and it's our responsibility to respect and obey it. We may not respect the people in office, but we must respect the office. God has accomplished His purposes with His people in different kinds of political systems, including monarchies and dictatorships. We mustn't think that He needs a democracy or a constitutional monarchy in order to accomplish His will. God is sovereign!

Regardless of the form of government a nation has, Proverbs 14:34 still applies: "Righteousness exalts a nation, but sin is a reproach to any people" (NKJV).

7. When God's people are unspiritual, the nations decay.

Apostasy and anarchy go together. We're the light of the world and the salt of the earth (Matt. 5:13-16), and God wants us to exert a positive influence on society. When the church ceases to be a holy people, obedient to the Lord, the salt loses its taste and the light goes under a bushel. G. Campbell Morgan said that the church did the most for the world when the church was the least like the world. Today, many churches have the idea they must imitate the world in order to reach the world. And they are wrong!

When Israel adopted the lifestyle of the pagan nations around them, they weakened their own nation. When Israel turned to idols, God turned from blessing them. Nations don't decay and collapse because of the people who peddle pornography or narcotics, but because of Christians who are no longer salt and light. God expects sinners to act like sinners, though He disapproves of what they do; but He doesn't expect *saints* to act like sinners. Compromising Christians not only hurt themselves and their families and churches, but also contribute to the decay of the whole nation.

8. God doesn't tell the whole story all at once.

We know a good deal about Deborah, Gideon, Jepthah, and Samson, but we don't know much about Shamgar, Tola, and Jair. God hasn't seen fit to put into His Word all the works of all of His servants, yet these people played important roles in accomplishing His purposes.

The people of God may never recognize the work you do for the Lord. You may be a Tola, an Ibzan, or an Elon. Don't be discouraged! God keeps the records and will one day reward you for your faithful service. It's not important that other people see what you do and compliment you on it. It is important that we serve the Lord and seek to please Him.

There's another caution here: Don't be too quick to judge what other people are doing, and don't get the idea that you're the only one faithfully serving the Lord. During the period of the Judges, different people were serving God in different places, and not all of them knew all that was going on. So it is with the work of God today. In spite of the excellent news coverage in the Christian world, we don't always know what God is doing in and through His servants in various parts of the globe. When we feel discouraged, perhaps we'd be encouraged if we knew the whole story.

"Therefore judge nothing before the time, until the Lord come, who both will bring to light the hidden things of darkness, and will make manifest the counsels of the hearts; and then shall every man have praise of God" (1 Cor. 4:5).

9. God still blesses those who live by faith.

It has well been said that faith is not believing in spite of evidence (that's superstition) but obeying in spite of consequence. I might add that it also means obeying God no matter what we see around us or ahead of us or how we feel within us. Faith doesn't depend on our emotions (Gideon was frightened much of the time, and Samson felt he still had his old power) or our understanding of the situation. Faith takes God at His Word and does what He tells us to do.

You can't serve God without faith, because "without faith it is impossible to please Him" (Heb. 11:6). "Whatsoever is not of faith is sin" (Rom. 14:23). If we wait until we have perfect faith, we'll never do much for the Lord. He honors even weak faith and seeks to make it stronger. Exercising faith is like exercising muscles: The more you exercise, the stronger the muscles become.

10. God's story isn't finished yet.

I must confess that I occasionally felt depressed as I wrote this book. One day I said to my wife, "I'll be glad when *Be Available* is finished. There just isn't much good news in the Book of Judges!"

But the Book of Judges isn't the end of the story! In fact, the book begins with the words "now it came to pass," which is a strange way to begin a book. In the Hebrew, it reads "and it was." If I started a book with the phrase "and it was," the editors would send the manuscript back to me and tell me to brush up on my syntax.

But there are eight Old Testament

books that begin with "and it was": Joshua, Judges, Ruth, 1 and 2 Samuel, Esther, Ezekiel, and Jonah. Why? *Because they're all part of the continuing story that God is writing!* The end of the Book of Joshua doesn't end the work of God in this world, for the Book of Judges begins with "and it was." The story goes on! God is still working!

If the Book of Judges is the book of *no king,* just keep in mind that 2 Samuel is the book of *God's king;* and David takes the throne and brings order and peace to the land. When the outlook is grim, just remind yourself that *God hasn't finished the story yet.*

A friend of mine who's involved in professional basketball likes to watch videos of his team's winning games. Even during the tightest moments of the game, he can relax in front of the TV set *because he already knows how it's going to end.*

There are days when God's people look at a chaotic world, a nation given to greed and violence, and a church weak and divided, and they wonder whether it's worth it all to walk with God and do His will. When that happens, remind yourself that *God's people know how it's going to end!* The Book of Judges isn't the last installment; the Book of Revelation is! And God assures us that righteousness will triumph, evil will be judged, and faith will be rewarded.

No Christian can do everything, but every Christian can do something, and God will put all these "somethings" together to get His work done in this world.

You never can tell what God has planned for you, so *be available!*

After all, one of these days, you'll have to be accountable, and you'll want to be ready.

ENDNOTES

Chapter 1

1. The references are from Judges 9, 16, 19, 21, and 5:6 (in order).
2. Judges is the book of "no king," 1 Samuel is the book of "man's king" (Saul), and 2 Samuel is the book of "God's king" (David). The world today is living in the Book of Judges because there is no king in Israel. When presented with their rightful King, the Jews said, "We have no king but Caesar." Next on the agenda is the appearance of "man's king" (Antichrist) who will usher in world control and chaos. Then "God's King" will appear, defeat His enemies, and establish His righteous kingdom. Note that the Book of Ruth takes place during the period of the Judges (Ruth 1:1) and that it is a love story and a harvest story. God's people are living in the Book of Ruth, sharing in the harvest and waiting for the wedding.
3. The original name was Kiriath-sepher, which means "city of books." Perhaps it had a large library or it was the "county seat," where official records were deposited.
4. In the Hebrew, the words "brother-in-law" and "father-in-law" use the same letters, which helps explain the problem connected with the names Reuel, Jethro, and Hobab (Ex. 2:18; 3:1; Num. 10:29; Judg. 4:11). Some students think that Moses' father-in-law had two names, Hobab and Jethro, and that Reuel was a distant relative.
5. G. Campbell Morgan, *Living Messages of the Books of the Bible,* vol. 1 (Old Tappan, N.J.: Fleming H. Revell, 1912), 104.
6. This explains why Elijah challenged Baal to send rain (1 Kings 18).
7. God would also use these nations to test Israel (Judg. 2:22) and train the new generation for war (3:1-3). When God isn't allowed to rule, He overrules and accomplishes purposes we never imagined.

Chapter 2

1. We must never think that the wrath of God is like a child's temper tantrum. A holy God must not only hate sin but also *hate what sin does to people.* If the police arrest parents for child abuse, what should God have done when His people were sacrificing their children on pagan altars? The English poet

Thomas Traherne (c. 1636-74) said, "Love can forbear, and Love can forgive . . . but Love can never be reconciled to an unlovely object. He can never therefore be reconciled to your sin, because sin itself is incapable of being altered; but He may be reconciled to your person, because that may be restored." This explains how God can both hate sin but love the sinner; and even while He is angry at our sins, He chastens us in love "that we might be partakers of His holiness" (Heb. 12:10).

2. The fact that Ehud assassinated a ruler bothers some people, who (for some reason) aren't disturbed that Ehud and his men later slaughtered 10,000 healthy young Moabites (Judg. 3:29). If wars of liberation are justified, then how many of the enemy die is really immaterial, so long as you achieve your goal of freedom. The death rate, however, is still one apiece.
3. King Eglon's name means "little bull calf." Ehud had killed the "fatted calf."
4. Joseph Parker, *The People's Bible,* vol. 5 (London: Hazell, Watson, and Viney, Ltd., 1896), 345.

CHAPTER 3

1. You would expect Judges 4:1 to read "when Shamgar was dead" since Shamgar is the judge last named. But Shamgar's ministry was local and contemporary with that of Deborah (5:6-7). Meanwhile, Ehud exercised authority over all the land and was the architect of the eighty years of rest.
2. The selection of Deborah may also indicate that, at that time, there were no men willing and able to do the job. Even Barak was afraid to confront the enemy without Deborah's help, and he was a man of faith (Heb. 11:32). For an inspiring account of women of God who have made a difference in the church and the world, see *Daughters of the Church* by Ruth A. Tucker and Walter Liefeld (Zondervan, 1987); and *A Dictionary of Women in Church History* by Mary L. Hammack (Moody Press, 1984).
3. It's possible that this verse is speaking of deception rather than disarmament. Israel might have possessed weapons but kept them hidden from the enemy. When war was declared, the men brought them out.
4. If you were the guest of an Eastern sheik, you were under his protection; and he would not turn you over to your enemies. He would expect the people in his family and his camp to protect you as well.
5. Judah and Simeon aren't mentioned at all in Judges 4-5. Some students think these two tribes may have already been engaged in wars against the Canaanites.
6. Military leaders have called this area one of the greatest battlefields in the world. Not only did Barak defeat Sisera there, but also Gideon defeated the Midianites there (Judg. 6-7), and the "battle of Armageddon" will be fought there (Rev. 16:12-16; 17:14). King Saul died there (1 Sam. 31), and King Josiah was killed there in a battle he should never have fought (2 Kings 23:28-30).
7. "The Curse of Meroz" in *Selected Sermons of Phillips Brooks,* edited by William Scarlett (New York: E.P. Dutton, 1950), 127.
8. Sisera was killed by Jael, who had given him milk; and his army was defeated because of Deborah, whose name means "bee." Sisera discovered that "the land of milk and honey" could be a dangerous place!
9. David compared a godly leader to the rising sun and the sun shining after the rain (2 Sam. 23:3-4). When leaders obey God, as Deborah and Barak did, there is always the dawning of a new day for their people; and there will be calm and light after the storm. The armies of Israel had been through a storm, but God had given them the victory.

CHAPTER 4

1. Ninety-six verses are devoted to the last judge, Samson. The first four judges were godly people; but from the time of Gideon, the leaders began to decay until you get to Samson, the most unspiritual of them all. Because the nation wanted freedom from the enemy without being dedicated to God, they didn't deserve godly leaders. Sometimes God gives His people exactly what they deserve.
2. We usually call Samuel the first of the prophets (Acts 3:24), but there were unnamed prophets before Samuel's time.
3. The most popular image of the local church today is that of the corporation, with the pastor as the CEO. I wonder how many churches would want a CEO with the credentials of some of the people God used in the Bible? Moses was eighty years old when he began his ministry and he was

wanted for murder in Egypt. Jacob was a schemer. Elijah suffered from depression, and so did Jeremiah. Hosea couldn't keep his marriage together. Amos, a farmer, had no ministerial training. Peter tried to kill a man with his sword. John Mark was a quitter, and Paul couldn't get along with his associate Barnabas. These traits are not excuses either for leaders to sin or for churches to lower their standards, but they do remind us that God's ways aren't always our ways. The man or woman we think least qualified for God's work may turn out to be a mighty servant of God.

4. A.W. Tozer, *The Knowledge of the Holy* (New York: Harper, 1961), 66.
5. Wherever Abraham journeyed, he built an altar (Gen. 12:7-8; 13:4, 18; 22:9); and Joshua left many monuments of Israel's march of conquest through the land.
6. Joseph Parker comments: "The least one can do is to give a reformer a nickname. If we may not smite him, we may at least throw some appellation at him which we hope the enemy will take up and use as a sting or a thong" *(The People's Bible,* vol. 6, 16). But Gideon's achievements transformed a contemptible nickname into an honorable title that he was proud to wear. After all, Jehovah did prove Himself greater than Baal!
7. Joseph Parker defends Gideon when he writes, "Men cannot be courageous all at once" *(The People's Bible,* vol. 6, 14). But courage comes from faith, and faith doesn't become strong when we ask God to bless our unbelief by performing miracles. The way to grow in faith and courage is to hear God's Word, believe His promises, and obey what He tells us to do. God may stoop to our weakness once or twice, but He won't permit us to live at that juvenile level all our lives.

CHAPTER 5

1. G. Campbell Morgan, *The Westminster Pulpit,* vol. 4, 209.
2. My friend, Dr. J. Vernon McGee, used to raise the question, "Why didn't Gideon go home? After all, he was afraid!" Courage isn't necessarily the absence of fear; it's the overcoming of fear by transforming it into power. I once asked a well-known Christian collegiate star quarterback how he was able to run the ball so far down the field, and his reply was, "I was scared, just plain scared; so I kept moving!" There is a fear that paralyzes and a fear that energizes, and Gideon's fear was the latter kind.

CHAPTER 6

1. Manasseh and Ephraim were both sons of Joseph and grandsons of Jacob. Manasseh was the firstborn, but Jacob reversed their birth order when he blessed them (Gen. 41:50-52; 48:1ff). In fact, he "adopted" the two sons as replacements for Reuben and Simeon (Gen. 48:5; 49:4), and this gave Ephraim prominence in Israel.
2. Ephraim's pride later created problems for Jephthah (Judg. 12:1–6), whose response wasn't as conciliatory as Gideon's!
3. Some expositors think that Gideon made the men lie down naked on the ground, covered them with thorny branches and then drove a threshing sledge over them until they died. This seems a brutal way for him to treat his own brethren, no matter how meanly they had treated him and his men, but it's stated clearly that Gideon killed the rebels in Peniel who had treated him the same way. We must remember, however, that these were cruel times and "every man was doing that which was right in his own eyes."
4. See Pss. 47; 68:24; 74:12; 89:18; 98:6; 145:1; Isa. 6:5; 33:22; 44:6. In their song of praise after passing through the Red Sea at the Exodus, Israel acknowledged Jehovah's kingship when they sang, "The Lord shall reign forever and ever" (Ex. 15:18).
5. Remember that one of the key themes in the Book of Judges is that there was "no king in Israel" at that time (17:6; 18:1; 19:1; 21:25). The writer seems to want to emphasize the need for a king to correct the political division and spiritual decay of the nation. Later, the people asked Samuel for a king (1 Sam. 8); and God told him to grant their request. Everything Moses and Samuel warned them about their kings did to them, but fallen human nature would rather have visible human leaders instead of the invisible, immortal God of heaven and earth.
6. This is the last time you will find a period of peace mentioned in the Book of Judges. The remaining judges mainly ruled locally,

and most of them had short tenures.

CHAPTER 7

1. If the awful carnage recorded in this chapter upsets you, just be reminded that modern dictators like Idi Amin, Joseph Stalin, and Adolph Hitler have done far worse. Norman Cousins estimated that for every word in Hitler's book *Mein Kampf,* 125 people died in World War II.
2. We must not think that Abimelech reigned supremely over the entire nation. There wasn't that kind of national solidarity during the days of the judges. It was more like the post-Revolution period in American history when the colonies operated under the Articles of Confederation. Abimelech was in control of Shechem and BethMillo ("house of Millo," 9:6, KJV), Arumah (v. 41), and Thebez (v. 50), which suggests that he had direct rule over the western part of Manasseh. Judges 9:22 in the KJV implies that Abimelech actually "reigned" and that "all Israel" submitted to him for three years. But "reigned" is too strong a word; "governed" would be better. "All Israel" (at least, those who knew what had happened) had to acknowledge Abimelech as their ruler, but it's doubtful that his influence reached to all of the tribes.
3. In fairness to Plato and Seneca, it should be pointed out that they were not defending political brutality—the end justifies the means—but discussing how to bring about justice in society. "Might is right" and "might makes right" only if we sincerely want to do right.
4. Twice we're told that Abimelech killed seventy men (vv. 18, 56), but if Jotham escaped, only sixty-nine were killed. But this is no more an error than are John 20:24 and 1 Cor. 15:5, both of which call the band of disciples "the Twelve" at a time when there were only eleven apostles.
5. Ezekiel 31 and Daniel 4 both use trees to represent leaders or nations.

CHAPTER 8

1. John F. Kennedy, *Profiles in Courage* (New York: Harper and Brothers, 1955), 245.
2. *The Living Bible* reads "the first person coming out of his house."
3. Baal worship was the prevalent religion among the Canaanites, and it didn't include the sacrifice of children. The Ammonites put their children through the fire as part of their worship of Molech. Eighteen years before, the people of Israel had turned to heathen gods; and for this, the Lord had severely chastened them (10:6-9). It's unthinkable that Jephthah would adopt a heathen practice in order to get God's help when the nation had suffered so greatly for adopting heathen practices! For God to honor such a thing would make the people ask, "If heathen practices are so evil, then why did You send all that suffering?"
4. Even if a priest did offer Jephthah's daughter as a burnt offering, the sacrifice would not be acceptable because the burnt offering had to be a male (Lev. 1:3, 10).
5. If Jephthah were going to kill his daughter, he would want her home with himself and not running around on the mountains with her girlfriends. Furthermore, why would the girl lament her *virginity* if she expected to die? Of what significance is virginity if you're heading for the grave? It seems likely that she would have lamented her impending death instead. Perhaps she was lamenting the fact that she hadn't married and therefore did not leave her father any grandchildren. But if that were the case, *her father* should have been doing the grieving, because marriages were arranged by the family, not by the individuals involved.

CHAPTER 9

1. If you still have your college English literature textbook, read John Milton's epic poem "Samson Agonistes" and compare it with the biblical account. Milton presents some insights into the mind and heart of Samson that can help us better understand the impact of his life for good and for evil.
2. Our word "Palestine" comes from the word "Philistine."
3. Leon Wood, *The Distressing Days of the Judges* (Grand Rapids: Zondervan Publishing House, 1975), 302-5.
4. Other servants of God who were chosen before birth include Jeremiah (Jer. 1:4-5) and Paul (Gal. 1:15), although Psalm 139:15–16 teaches that the Lord is involved in the conception of every child.
5. "Nazirite" must not be confused with "Nazarene" (Matt. 2:23; 26:71). Since Jesus drank wine (Matt. 11:19; Mark 11:25) and

touched dead bodies (Luke 7:14; 8:54), He was obviously not a Nazirite.

6. The phrase "pleases me well" is literally "right in my eyes." It reminds us that during the period of the Judges "every man did that which was right in his own eyes" (17:6; 21:25). Instead of following the Lord, Samson was following the crowd and doing the "in" thing.
7. The week-long wedding feast (14:17) certainly involved wine, and it's probable that Samson drank it. He was the bridegroom and was expected to encourage his guests to enjoy themselves. The word translated "feast" means "a drinking party."
8. There was a form of marriage in which the wife remained with her parents and the husband visited her from time to time. But even if that were the case, the wife would expect her husband to consummate the marriage before going away. Perhaps Samson hoped to do that when he visited her at wheat harvest (15:1-3), but then he learned that she wasn't his wife!

CHAPTER 10

1. No doubt you can think of many more examples from the Scriptures. Lot had the privilege of walking with Abraham and yet ended in a cave, drunk and committing incest with his daughters. King Saul began as a humble man but ended up a suicide, destroyed by his stubborn pride. King Uzziah was a godly man until he became strong. When he tried to usurp the place of the priests, God judged him by giving him leprosy. Ahithophel was David's most trusted advisor, but he ended up hanging himself. Paul's helper Demas abandoned the ministry because he "loved this present world" (2 Tim. 4:10). May the Lord help us all to end well!
2. There are several surprised bridegrooms in the Bible. Adam went to sleep a single man and woke up to learn (happily) that he was married (Gen. 2:21-25). Jacob woke up and discovered he was married to the wrong woman (Gen. 29:21-30). Boaz woke up to find his prospective wife lying at his feet on the threshing floor (Ruth 3:1-13). Life is full of rude awakenings.
3. James Moffatt, *A New Translation of the Bible* (London: Hodder and Stoughton, 1934), 291.
4. Micah offered to pay his household priest ten pieces of silver a year, plus room and board (17:10); so Delilah was being rewarded most generously. If each of the princes of the five Philistine cities was in on the plan, as they probably were, Delilah would have received 5,500 pieces of silver. This shows how important it was to the Philistine leaders that Samson be captured.
5. Judges 16:16 suggests that Samson saw her daily ("day after day," NIV). Whether he traveled to her house every day or simply moved in with her, we aren't told. He was playing the fool, but nobody could convince him of it.
6. The Holy Spirit left King Saul because of his sins (1 Sam. 16:14), and he also lost his crown (2 Sam. 1:10). God wants us to "reign in life" (Rom. 5:17), and we will if we walk in the Spirit and yield ourselves wholly to the Lord. Sin makes slaves out of kings; grace makes kings out of sinners.
7. His eyes had gotten him into trouble (Judg. 14:1-2; 16:1), and the "lust of the eyes" had led him into sin. Had Samson walked by faith, he would have ended his career in honor, glorifying the Lord.
8. Since the Philistines knew that Samson's long hair had something to do with his great power, why did they allow it to grow again? Probably for two reasons: (1) They wanted him to be strong so they could both use his power and exhibit his feats; and (2) they were sure that his blindness prevented him from being dangerous to them anymore. However, it wasn't the length of his hair but the strength of his dedication to God that brought about the change. The Philistines had no way of knowing that God had restored Samson's strength.
9. The second word—*sahaq*—gives us the name "Isaac," which means "laughter." Both Hebrew words carry the idea of entertaining people by making them laugh. The champion is now a comedian.
10. Only two of Samson's prayers are recorded, one for water (15:18) and this one for strength to pull down the pillars. I've suggested that Samson turned his prison into a sanctuary and talked to the Lord, but his "prison prayers" aren't recorded. It's unfortunate that his final words still evidenced a spirit of revenge rather than a desire to glorify God, but let's not be too

hard on a man who was willing to give his life in one last attempt to serve the Lord.

11. Alexander Maclaren, *Expositions of Holy Scripture,* vol. 2 (Grand Rapids: Baker Book House, 1975), 256.

CHAPTER 11

1. In 18:30, Jonathan is identified as "the son of Gershom, the son of Manasseh," which is impossible since Gershom was a son of Moses and didn't belong to the tribe of Manasseh (Ex. 2:22; 1 Chron. 23:14-15). A Levite would come from the tribe of Levi. The addition of the letter *n (nun* in the Hebrew) to the name "Moses" would change it to "Manasseh." In the Hebrew original, the *nun* is found *above the line,* showing that the letter was added to the text later. Hebrew scholars believe that a scribe, zealous to protect the good name of Moses, changed the text so that there wouldn't be an idolater in Moses' family. The scribe apparently forgot about Aaron.
2. In writing this, I have no intention of indicting the entire advertising industry. Advertising performs a valuable service when it tells us where to find products and services that we really need. It's when advertisers promote unhealthy desires by creating "images" that appeal to the baser instincts of the human heart that I part company with them. Pride, covetousness, and competition for status aren't the healthiest motivations for people who want to build strong homes or a safe and just society. It's good to have the things that money can buy *if* you don't lose the things that money can't buy.
3. The fact that Jonathan's words came true doesn't absolve either him or the spies from being involved in activities outside the will of God. Jonathan's prophecy came true because the Danites were strong and the people of Laish were weak and unprotected.
4. As serious as their crimes were, I confess I can't help smiling as I envision five brave men stealing gods *that can't even protect themselves!* The Scriptures that come to mind are Isaiah 40:18-31 and 44:9-20, as well as Psalm 115.
5. However serious the present crime rate may be in the United States, let's not so idealize the past that we get things out of proportion. See *Our Violent Past* by Irving J. Sloan (New York: Random House, 1970). Violence is rooted in the human heart (Gen. 6:5, 11-12), and only the grace of God can remove it.
6. Bible students aren't agreed as to which "captivity" is meant in Judges 18:30. If it refers to the Assyrian Captivity of the Northern Kingdom in 722 B.C., then an editor had to add these words to the text at a later date. But the frequent phrase "no king in Israel" suggests that *Judges* was written during the early days of the monarchy, centuries away from the Assyrian invasion. This captivity may have been the invasion of the Philistines or perhaps some local war about which we have no information. Jonathan probably married a girl from the tribe of Dan, and his sons continued the false priesthood that he had started, but we don't know for how long. If we knew, we could determine the date of the "captivity."

CHAPTER 12

1. King Saul used a similar approach to arouse the people to fight the Ammonites, but he cut up a yoke of oxen (1 Sam. 11:1-7). The sin of Gibeah was so terrible that the Prophet Hosea referred to it centuries later as an example of great sin (Hosea 9:9 and 10:9).
2. Keep in mind that this event took place early in the period of the Judges, at a time when the nation wasn't under foreign oppression. Though they had no central government, the tribes were still united and able to muster troops and wage war together.
3. Some expositors think that they went to the city of Bethel, since "house of God" in the Hebrew is *beth-elohim* and not *bethel.* See also 20:26. The tabernacle was moved from place to place. It was first located in Shechem (Josh. 8:30-35), and then was moved to Shiloh (Josh. 18:1 and 22:12; Judg. 18:31). At one time it was at Nob (1 Sam. 21) and also Gibeon (1 Chron. 16:39; 21:29), not to be confused with Gibeah.

RUTH

A SUGGESTED OUTLINE OF RUTH

Key Theme: God providentially guides and blesses all who trust Him
Key Verse: Ruth 2:12

I. SORROW: RUTH WEEPING—CHAP. 1
1. Naomi tries to run from her problems—1:1–5
2. Naomi tries to cover up her mistakes—1:6–18
3. Naomi gets bitter against God—1:19–22

II. SERVICE: RUTH WORKING—CHAP. 2
1. A new beginning—faith—2:1–3
2. A new friend—love—2:4–16
3. A new attitude—hope—2:17–23

III. SUBMISSION: RUTH WAITING—CHAP. 3
1. Ruth presents herself to Boaz—3:17
2. Ruth is accepted by Boaz—3:8–15
3. Ruth waits for Boaz to act—3:16–18

IV. SATISFACTION: RUTH WEDDING—CHAP. 4
1. Boaz redeems Ruth—4:1–10
2. The people bless Ruth—4:11–12
3. God gives Boaz and Ruth a son—4:13–22

CONTENTS

CHAPTER ONE
YOU CAN'T RUN AWAY
Ruth 1

(In which a family makes a bad decision and exchanges one famine for three funerals)

"The efforts which we make to escape from our destiny only serve to lead us into it."

The American essayist Ralph Waldo Emerson wrote that in his book *The Conduct of Life,* and it's just as true today as when the book was published back in 1860. Because God gave us freedom of choice, we can ignore the will of God, argue with it, disobey it, even fight against it. But in the end, the will of God shall prevail; because "the counsel of the Lord stands forever" (Ps. 33:11) and "He does according to His will in the army of heaven and among the inhabitants of the earth" (Dan. 4:35, NKJV).

The patriarch Job asked, "Who has hardened himself against Him and prospered?" (Job 9:4, NKJV) Job knew the answer and so do we: *nobody.* If we obey God's will, everything in life holds together; but if we disobey, everything starts to fall apart. Nowhere in the Bible is this truth better illustrated than in the experiences of Elimelech and his wife Naomi.

We see in this chapter three mistakes that we must avoid as we deal with the problems and trials of life.

1. Unbelief: trying to run from our problems (Ruth 1:1-5)

The time. Life was not easy in those days; for during the period of the judges, "there was no king in Israel; but every man did what was right in his own eyes" (Judg. 17:6; and see 18:11; 19:1; 21:25). The Book of Judges is the story of Israel at one of its lowest points in history—it's a record of division, cruelty, apostasy, civil war, and national disgrace. Spiritually, our lives resemble elements of the Book of Judges; for there is no king in Israel, and there will not be until Jesus returns. Like Israel in the past, many of God's people today are living in unbelief and disobedience and are not enjoying the blessings of God.

It seems incredible that this beautiful love story should take place at such a calamitous period in the nation's history, but is this not true today? Today we experience national and international perplexities, moral decay, and difficulties of every kind, and yet God loves this lost world and is seeking for a bride. In spite of alarms in the headlines and dangers on the streets, we can be sure that God still loves the world and wants to save lost sinners. When you know Jesus Christ as Savior and Lord, no matter how tough the times may be, you are part of a beautiful love story.

But the Book of Ruth is a *harvest* story as well as a *love* story. During this dark time in Israel's history, God was seeking a bride and *reaping a harvest. To* be sure, Israel was reaping the harvest of their disobedience (Gal. 6:7); but God was producing the fruit of the Spirit in the lives of Ruth and Naomi. Today, the Lord is seeking a harvest and calls us to share in His labors (John 4:34-48). The harvest today is white and ready, but the laborers are still few (Luke 10:2).

The place. How strange that there should be a famine in Bethlehem, which means "house of bread"! In the Old Testament, a famine was often an evidence of God's discipline because His people had sinned against Him (Lev. 26:18-20; Deut. 28:15, 23-24). During the time of the judges, Israel repeatedly turned from God and worshiped the idols of the heathen nations around them; and God had to discipline them (Judg. 2:10-19). The godly had to suffer because of the ungodly, even in Bethlehem.

The decision. When trouble comes to our lives, we can do one of three things: endure it, escape it, or enlist it. If we only endure our trials, then trials become our master, and we have a tendency to become hard and bitter. If we try to escape our trials, then we will probably miss the purposes God wants to achieve in our lives. But if we learn to enlist our trials, they will become our servants instead of our masters and work for us; and God will work all things together for our good and His glory (Rom. 8:28).

Elimelech made the wrong decision when he decided to leave home. What made this decision so wrong?

He walked by sight and not by faith. Abraham made the same mistake when he encountered a famine in the land of promise (Gen. 12:10ff). Instead of waiting for God to tell him what to do next, he fled to Egypt and got into trouble. No matter how difficult our circumstances may be, the safest and best place is in the will of God. It's easy to say with David, "O that I had wings like a dove! I would fly away and be at rest" (Ps. 55:6). But it's wiser to claim the promise of Isaiah 40:31 and wait on the Lord for "wings like eagles" and by faith soar above the storms of life. You *can't run away from your problems.*

How do you walk by faith? By claiming the promises of God and obeying the Word of God, in spite of what you see, how you feel, or what may happen. It means committing yourself to the Lord and relying wholly on Him to meet the need. When we live by faith, it glorifies God, witnesses to a lost world, and builds Christian character into our lives. God has ordained that "the righteous will live by his faith" (Hab. 2:4; Rom. 1:17; Gal. 3:11; Heb. 10:38; 2 Cor. 5:7); and when we refuse to trust Him, we are calling God a liar and dishonoring Him.

There is a wisdom of this world that leads to folly and sorrow, and there is a wisdom from God that seems folly to the world but that leads to blessing (1 Cor. 3:18-20; James 3:13-18). "Woe unto them that are wise in their own eyes, and prudent in their own sight!" (Isa. 5:21, KJV)

He majored on the physical and not the spiritual. A husband and father certainly wants to provide for his wife and family, but he must not do it at the expense of losing the blessing of God. When Satan met Jesus in the wilderness, his first temptation was to suggest that Christ satisfy His hunger rather than please His Father (Matt. 4:1-4; see John 4:34). One of the devil's pet lies is: "You do have to live!" But it is in God that "we live and move and have our being" (Acts 17:28, NIV); and He is able to take care of us.

David's witness is worth considering: "I have been young, and now I am old; yet I have not seen the righteous forsaken, or his descendants begging bread" (Ps. 37:25, NKJV). As Paul faced a threatening future, he testified, "But none of these things move me, neither count I my life dear unto myself" (Acts 20:24, KJV). In times of difficulty, if we die to self and put God's will first (Matt. 6:33), we can be sure that He will either take us out of the trouble or bring us through.

He honored the enemy and not the Lord. By going fifty miles to the neighboring land of Moab, Elimelech and his family abandoned God's land and God's people for the land and people of the enemy. The Moabites were descendants of Lot from his incestuous union with his firstborn daughter (Gen. 19:30-38), and they were the Jews' enemies because of the way they had treated Israel during their pilgrim journey from Egypt to Canaan (Deut. 23:3-6; Num. 22-25). During the time of the judges, Moab had invaded Israel and ruled over the people for eighteen years (Judg. 3:12-14); so why should Elimelech turn to them for help? They were a proud people (Isa. 16:6) whom God disdained. "Moab is My washpot," said the Lord (Ps. 60:8, KJV), a picture of a humiliated nation washing the feet of the conquering soldiers.

The consequences. The name Elimelech means "my God is king." But the Lord was *not* king in Elimelech's life, for he left God completely out of his decisions. He made a decision out of God's will when he went to Moab, and this led to another bad decision when his two sons married women of Moab. Mahlon married Ruth (Ruth 4:10), and Chilion married Orpah. Jews were forbidden to marry Gentile women, especially those from Ammon and Moab (Deut. 7:1-11; 23:3-6; Neh. 13:1-3; Ezra 9:1-4). It was the Moabite women in Moses' day who seduced the Jewish men into immorality and idolatry; and as a result, 24,000 people died (Num. 25).

Elimelech and his family had fled Judah to escape death, but the three men met death just the same. The family had planned only to "sojourn" temporarily in Moab, but they remained for ten years (Ruth 1:4). At the end of that decade of disobedience, all that remained were three lonely widows and three Jewish graves in a heathen land. Everything else was gone (v. 21). Such is the sad consequence of unbelief.

We can't run away from our problems. We can't avoid taking with us the basic cause of most of our problems, which is an unbelieving and disobedient heart. "The majority of us begin with the bigger problems outside and forget the one inside," wrote Oswald Chambers. "A man has to learn 'the plague of his own heart' before his own problems can be solved. . ." (*The Shadow of an Agony,* p. 76).

2. Deception: trying to hide our mistakes (Ruth 1:6–18)

We need to consider the three testimonies that are in this section.

The testimony of Naomi (Ruth 1:6-15). God visited His faithful people in Bethlehem, but not His disobedient daughter in Moab. Naomi heard the report that the famine had ended; and when she heard the good news, she decided to return home. There is always "bread enough and to spare" when you are in the Father's will (Luke 15:17, KJV). How sad it is when people only *hear* about God's blessing, but never experience it, because they are not in the place where God can bless them.

Many years ago, I was in a prayer meeting with a number of Youth for Christ leaders, among them Jacob Stam, brother of John Stam who, with his wife Betty, was martyred in China in 1934. We had been asking God to bless this ministry and that project, and I suppose the word "bless" was used scores of times as we prayed. Then Jacob Stam prayed, "Lord, we've asked you to bless all these things; but, please, Lord, *make us blessable.*" Had Naomi been in that meeting, she would have had to confess, "Lord, I'm not blessable."

Whenever we have disobeyed the Lord and departed from His will, we must confess our sin and return to the place of blessing. Abraham had to leave Egypt and go back to the altar he had abandoned (Gen. 13:1-4), and Jacob had to go back to Bethel (35:1). The repeated plea of the prophets to God's people was that they *turn* from their sins and *return* to the Lord. "Let the wicked forsake his way, and the unrighteous man his thoughts, and let him return to the Lord, and He will have compassion on him; and to our God, for He will abundantly pardon" (Isa. 55:7).

Naomi's decision was right, but her motive was wrong. She was still interested primarily in food, not in fellowship with God. You don't hear her confessing her sins to God and asking Him to forgive her. She was returning to her land but not to her Lord.

But something else was wrong in the way Naomi handled this decision: *She did not want her two daughters-in-law to go with her.* If it was right for Naomi to go to Bethlehem, where the true and living God was worshiped, then it was right for Orpah and Ruth to accompany her. Naomi should have said to them what Moses said to his father-in-law, "Come thou with us, and we will do thee good; for the Lord has spoken good concerning Israel" (Num. 10:29, KJV). Instead, Naomi tried to influence the two women to go back to their families and their false gods.

Why would a believing Jewess, a daughter of Abraham, encourage two pagan women to worship false gods? I may be wrong, but I get the impression that Naomi didn't want to take Orpah and Ruth to Bethlehem *because they were living proof that she and her husband had permitted their two sons to marry women from outside the covenant nation.* In other words, Naomi was trying to cover up her disobedience. If she returned to Bethlehem alone, nobody would know that the family had broken the Law of Moses.

"He who covers his sins will not prosper, but whoever confesses and forsakes them will have mercy" (Prov. 28:13, NKJV). When we try to cover our sins, it's proof that we really haven't faced them honestly and judged them according to God's Word. True repentance involves honest confession and a brokenness within. "The sacrifices of God are a broken spirit; a broken and a contrite heart, O God, Thou wilt not despise" (Ps. 51:17). Instead of brokenness, Naomi had bitterness.

The tragedy is that Naomi did not present the God of Israel in a positive way. In Ruth 1:13, she suggests that God was to blame for the sorrow and pain the three women had experienced. "It is more bitter for me than for you, because the Lord's hand has gone out against me!" (v. 13, NIV) In other words, "I'm to blame for all our trials, so why remain with me? Who knows what the Lord may do to me next?" Had Naomi been walking with the Lord, she could have won Orpah to the faith and brought two trophies of grace home to Bethlehem.

The testimony of Orpah (Ruth 1:11-14). The two daughters-in-law started off with Naomi (v. 7), but she stopped them and urged them not to accompany her. She even prayed for them (vv. 8-9) that the Lord would be kind to them and find them new husbands and give them rest after all their sorrow. But of what value are the prayers of a backslidden believer? (Ps. 66:18) Three times Naomi told Orpah and Ruth to return (Ruth 1:8, 11-12).

When she saw them hesitating, Naomi began to reason with them. "I'm too old to have another husband and bear another family," she said. "And even if I could bear more sons, do you want to waste these next years waiting for them to grow up? You could be in your mother's house, with your family, enjoying life."

Orpah was the weaker of the two sisters-in-law. She started to Bethlehem with Naomi, kissed her, and wept with her; yet she would not stay with her. She was "not far from the kingdom" (Mark 12:34, NIV), but she made the wrong decision and turned back. Orpah kissed her mother-in-law, but we wonder whether her heart was really in it; for her decision proved that her heart was back home where she hoped to find a husband. Orpah left the scene and is never mentioned again in the Scriptures.

The testimony of Ruth (Ruth 1:15-18). Naomi was trying to cover up; Orpah had given up, but Ruth was prepared to stand up! She refused to listen to her mother-in-law's pleas or follow her sister-in-law's bad example. Why? *Because she had come to trust in the God of Israel (2:12).* She had experienced trials and disappointments, but instead of blaming God, she had trusted Him and was not ashamed to confess her faith. In spite of the bad example of her disobedient in-laws, Ruth had come to know the true and living God; and she wanted to be with His people and dwell in His land.

Ruth's conversion is evidence of the sovereign grace of God, for the only way sinners can be saved is by grace (Eph. 2:8-10). Everything within her and around her presented obstacles to her faith, and yet she trusted the God of Israel. Her background was against her, for she was from Moab where they worshiped the god Chemosh (Num. 21:29; 1 Kings 11:7, 33), who accepted human sacrifices (2 Kings 3:26-27) and encouraged immorality (Num. 25). Her circumstances were against her and could have made her bitter against the God of Israel. First, her father-in-law died, and then her husband and her brother-in-law; and she was left a widow without any support. If this is the way Jehovah God treats His people, why follow Him?

Ruth dearly loved her mother-in-law, but even Naomi was against her; for she urged Ruth to return to her family and her gods in Moab. Since Elimelech and Mahlon were now dead, Ruth was technically under the guardianship of Naomi; and she should have obeyed her mother-in-law's counsel. But God intervened and graciously saved Ruth in spite of all these obstacles. "Not by works of righteousness which we have done, but according to His mercy He saved us" (Titus 3:5, NKJV). God delights in showing mercy (Micah 7:18), and often He shows His mercy to the least likely people in the least likely places. This is the sovereign grace of the God "who will have all men to be saved, and to come unto the knowledge of the truth" (1 Tim. 2:4, KJV).

Ruth's statement in Ruth 1:16-17 is one of the most magnificent confessions found anywhere in Scripture. First, she confessed her love for Naomi and her desire to stay with her mother-in-law even unto death. Then she confessed her faith in the true and living God and her decision to worship Him alone. She was willing to forsake father and mother (2:11) in order to cleave to Naomi and the God of her people. Ruth was steadfastly "determined" to accompany Naomi (1:18) and live in Bethlehem with God's covenant people.

But there was a divine law that said, "An Ammonite or Moabite shall not enter the congregation of the Lord; even to the tenth generation none of his descendants shall enter the congregation of the Lord forever" (Deut. 23:3, NKJV). This meant permanent exclusion. How then could Ruth enter into the congregation of the Lord? By trusting God's grace and throwing herself completely on His mercy. Law excludes us from God's family, but grace includes us if we put our faith in Christ.

When you read the genealogy of Jesus Christ in Matthew 4, you find the names of five women, four of whom have very questionable credentials: Tamar committed incest with her father-in-law (Gen. 38:3); Rahab was a Gentile harlot (Josh.

2:5); Ruth was an outcast Gentile Moabitess (Ruth 1:5); and "the wife of Uriah" was an adulteress (2 Sam. 11:6). How did they ever become a part of the family of the Messiah? Through the sovereign grace and mercy of God! God is "long-suffering toward us, not willing that any should perish but that all should come to repentance" (2 Peter 3:9, NKJV). (Mary is the fifth woman in the genealogy, and she was included because of God's grace and her faith. See Luke 1:26–56.)

3. Bitterness: blaming God for our trials (Ruth 1:19-22)

The two widows probably visited the three graves of their loved ones for the last time before leaving Moab. Then they committed themselves to the Lord and set out to begin a new life. It would be interesting to know what Naomi and Ruth talked about as they journeyed from Moab to Bethlehem. Did Naomi give her daughter-in-law some basic instruction in the Law of Moses? Did Ruth ask questions about the Jewish faith, the Jewish people, and her new home in Bethlehem? We wonder what kind of answers Naomi would have given since she was a bitter woman with a faltering faith in the God of Israel.

Naomi had been away from home for ten years, and the women of the town were shocked when they saw her. (In v. 19, the pronoun of "they said" is feminine.) Their question "Is this Naomi?" suggests both surprise and bewilderment. The name Naomi means "pleasant," but she was not living up to her name. She was not the Naomi whom they had known a decade before. Her ten difficult years in Moab, and the sorrows they had brought, had taken their toll on Naomi's appearance and personality. Instead of making her better, the trials of life had made her bitter, which is the meaning of the word *mara*.

We can't control the circumstances of life, but we can control how we respond to them. That's what faith is all about, daring to believe that God is working everything for our good even when we don't feel like it or see it happening. "In everything give thanks" (1 Thes. 5:18) isn't always easy to obey, but obeying this command is the best antidote against a bitter and critical spirit. The Scottish preacher George H. Morrison said, "Nine-tenths of our unhappiness is selfishness, and is an insult cast in the face of God." Because Naomi was imprisoned by selfishness, she was bitter against God.

To begin with, she accused the Lord of dealing very bitterly with her (Ruth 1:20). She had left Bethlehem with a husband and two sons and had come home without them. She had gone to Moab possessing the necessities of life, but now she had returned home having nothing. She was a woman with empty hands, an empty home, and an empty heart. Because she didn't surrender to the Lord and accept His loving chastening, she did not experience "the peaceful fruit of righteousness" (Heb. 12:11).

Not only had the Lord dealt bitterly with her, but He had also testified against her in these afflictions (Ruth 1:21). Is this Naomi's confession of sin, her admission that she and her family had sinned in going to Moab? Is she hinting that they deserved all that they had suffered? Twice Naomi called God "the Almighty," which is the Hebrew name El Shaddai, "the All-powerful One" (vv. 20-21). It's one thing to *know* God's name and quite something else to *trust* that name and allow God to work in the difficult situations of life. "And those who know Your name will put their trust in You; for You, Lord, have not forsaken those who seek You" (Ps. 9:10, NKJV). Naomi knew the name but did not exercise the faith.

But was Naomi really that poor and empty? Or was she simply exaggerating her situation because she was weary of body and bitter of soul? Just think of the resources she had that should have encouraged her.

For one thing, she had *life;* and this in itself is a precious gift from God—a gift we too often take for granted. Naomi left three graves back in Moab, but God in His goodness had kept her alive and brought her back to Bethlehem. "Fear not that your life shall come to an end," said John Henry Newman, "but rather that it shall never have a beginning." Naomi thought that life had ended for her, but her trials were really a new beginning. Naomi's faith and hope were about to die, but God had other plans for her!

Naomi not only had life, but she also had *opportunity.* She was surrounded by friends, all of whom wanted the very best for her. At first, her sorrow and bitterness isolated her from the community, but gradually that changed. Instead of sitting looking gloomily at a wall, she finally decided to look out the window; and then she got up and opened the door! When the night is the darkest, if we look up, we can still see the stars.

One of Naomi's richest resources was *her daughter-in-law Ruth.* In fact, it is Ruth whom God used and blessed throughout the rest of this book; for Ruth was a woman who trusted God and was totally committed to Him. Naomi soon learned that God's hand of blessing was on this young woman and that He would accomplish great things through her obedience.

But most of all, Naomi still had *Jehovah, the God of Israel.* The Lord is mentioned about twenty-five times in this brief book, for He is the Chief Actor in this drama whether Naomi realized it or not. "I firmly believe in Divine Providence," said President Woodrow Wilson. "Without it, I think I should go crazy. Without God the world would be a maze without a clue." When we fear God, we need not fear anything else. On his deathbed, John Wesley said, "Best of all, God is with us!" God is not only *with* us, but He is also *for* us; and "if God be for us, who can be against us?" (Rom. 8:31, KJV)

It was barley harvest when the two widows arrived in Bethlehem, a time when the community expressed joy and praise to God for His goodness. It was spring, a time of new life and new beginning. Alexander Whyte often told his Edinburgh congregation that the victorious Christian life is "a series of new beginnings," and he was right. Naomi was about to make a new beginning; for with God, it's never too late to start over again.

Are you trusting God for *your* new beginning? After all, with God at your side, your resources are far greater than your burdens.

Stop staring at the wall and, by faith, get up and open the door to a brand-new tomorrow.

CHAPTER TWO
THE GREATEST OF THESE
Ruth 2

(In which Boaz is surprised by love, and Ruth is overwhelmed by grace)

Before God changes our circumstances, He wants to change our hearts. If our circumstances change for the better, but we remain the same, then we will become worse. God's purpose in providence is not to make us comfortable, but to make us conformable, "conformed to the image of His Son" (Rom. 8:29). Christlike character is the divine goal for each of His children.

Naomi was bitter against God, but Ruth was willing for God to have His way in her life; so God began His gracious work with Ruth. Ruth would influence Naomi, and then God would bring to pass a wonderful work that would eventually bring the Son of God into the world. Ruth and Naomi had no idea that they were part of an eternal plan that would fulfill God's promise to Abraham that his seed would bring blessing to the whole world (Gen. 12:1-3). Ruth's story begins with the death of a husband, but it will end with the birth of a baby. Her tears will be turned into triumph.

If we want God to work in our lives and circumstances and accomplish His gracious purposes, then there are certain conditions that we must meet. These conditions are illustrated in Ruth's experiences in this chapter.

1. We must live by faith in the Lord. (Ruth 2:1-3)

A Latin proverb says, "Providence assists not the idle." Since Ruth was not the kind of woman who could long remain idle, she asked Naomi's permission to glean in the fields so they would have food to eat. This was a step of faith on Ruth's part, based on God's commandment in the Law (Lev. 19:9-10; 23:22; Deut. 24:19-22). Whenever they reaped a harvest, God's people were to consider the poor and leave gleanings for them. After all, God gave the harvest; and He had every right to tell the people how to use it.

The existence of this law was proof of God's concern for the poor among His people. The nation was instructed to treat the poor with equity (Ex. 23:3, 6; Lev. 19:15; Prov. 22:22-23) and with generosity (Lev. 19:9-10). God was also concerned for the widows, many of whom were poor, and He told the people to care for them (Ex. 22:22-24; see Isa. 10:1–2). Ruth was not only a poor widow, but she was also an alien. Therefore, she had every right to look to God for His help and provision. "He defends the cause of the fatherless and the widow, and loves the alien, giving him food and clothing" (Deut. 10:18, NIV).

To live by faith means to take God at His word and then act upon it, for "faith without works is dead" (James 2:20, NKJV). Since Ruth believed that God loved her and would provide for her, she set out to find a field in which she could glean. This was completely an act of faith because, being a stranger, she didn't know who owned the various parcels of ground that made up the fields. There were boundary markers for each parcel, but no fences or family name signs as seen on our farms today. Furthermore, as a woman and an outsider, she was especially vulnerable; and she had to be careful where she went.

It is here that Boaz enters the story (Ruth 2:1, 3), a relative of Elimelech who was "a man of standing" (NIV) in the community. His name means "in him is strength." By the providence of God, Ruth gleaned in the portion of the field that belonged to Boaz. The record says Ruth "happened" to come to this portion of the field, but it was no accident. Her steps were guided by the Lord. "I being in the way, the Lord led me" (Gen. 24:27, KJV).

God's providential working in our lives is both a delight and a mystery. God is constantly working *with us* (Mark 16:20), *in us* (Phil. 2:12-13), and *for us* (Rom. 8:28) and accomplishing His gracious purposes. We pray, we seek His will, and we make decisions (and sometimes make mistakes); but it is God who orders events and guides His willing children. In a spectacular vision, the Prophet Ezekiel saw the providential workings of God depicted by a throne set on a "firmament" that was moved here and there by "wheels within wheels" (Ezek. 1). You can't explain it, but thank God you can believe it and rely on it!

2. We must live by the grace of God. (Ruth 2:4-16)

When Ruth set out that morning to glean in the fields, she was looking for someone who would show her grace (v. 2, and see vv. 10 and 13). Grace is favor bestowed on someone who doesn't deserve it and can't earn it. As a woman, a poor widow, and an alien, Ruth could have no claims on anyone. She was at the lowest rung of the social ladder.

The channel of that grace was Boaz. How good it is to know that God has good people living in bad times! If you knew only the record in the Book of Judges, you might conclude that the righteous had perished from the earth (Ps. 12:1-2; Isa. 57:1; 1 Kings 19:10; Micah 7:2). But there were still people like Boaz who knew the Lord and sought to obey His will. Boaz was concerned about his workers and wanted them to enjoy the blessing of the Lord (Ruth 2:4).

No sooner had Boaz greeted his workers than his eye caught the presence of a stranger in the field, and a lovely stranger at that. I get the impression that when he saw her, it was love at first sight; for from that point on, Boaz focuses his interest on Ruth and not on the harvest. Though an alien, Ruth was an eligible young woman whom the young men of the town would notice (3:10). Ruth 2:11 indicates that Boaz had already heard about Ruth, but now he was about to meet her personally.

Again, we marvel at the overruling providence of God. The Lord led Ruth to the field of Boaz and then led Boaz to visit his field while Ruth was there. When Boaz arrived, Ruth might have been resting in the shelter house that Boaz provided for his workers; or she might have grown weary and gone home to Naomi. When we commit our lives to the Lord, what happens to us happens by way of appointment and not by accident. Ruth was still a poor widow and an alien, but God was about to create a new relationship that would completely alter her circumstances.

Bible students have seen in Boaz a picture of our Lord Jesus Christ in His relationship to His bride, the church. Like Ruth, the lost sinner is outside the covenant family of God, bankrupt, with no claim on God's mercy. But God took the initiative and provided a way for us to enter His family through faith in Jesus Christ. (See Eph. 2:10-22.) I will have more to say about this relationship when we get to the next chapter and we consider the "kinsman redeemer."

Now let's notice the evidences of God's grace in the way Boaz related to Ruth:

(1) Boaz took the initiative (Ruth 2:8). Grace means that God makes the first move to come to our aid, not because we deserve anything, but because He loves us and wants us for Himself. "We love, because He first loved us" (1 John 4:19, NKJV). God took the initiative in salvation when we were spiritually dead (Eph. 2:1-10), without strength (Rom. 5:6), sinners (5:8), and His enemies (5:10). Salvation was not an afterthought of God but that which He planned from eternity. We have every reason to believe Boaz loved Ruth and therefore took the first steps to meet her needs.

(2) Boaz spoke to Ruth (Ruth 2:8). It

was he who first spoke to her, for she would not have dared to speak to a man, especially one who was a stranger and "the lord of the harvest." What right did a widow and an alien have to address a great man like Boaz? Yet he interrupted his conversation with his foreman to speak to a poor stranger gleaning in his field.

Several years ago, my wife, younger daughter, and I visited Great Britain and found ourselves in Lichfield, where we learned that Queen Elizabeth was coming to dedicate a new school for exceptional children. We interrupted our plans and stood on the curb, waiting patiently for the motorcade, which finally appeared. We stood perhaps ten feet from the Queen as she slowly rode by with her lady-in-waiting, waving to the crowd in her distinctive manner.

Now, suppose she had rolled down the window and called, "Hello, Warren! Hello, Betty and Judy! I'll tell my guards to take care of you!" If that had happened, everybody would have been duly impressed with our importance and perhaps asked for our autographs. Imagine, here are three American citizens to whom the Queen speaks personally!

Queen Elizabeth has never spoken to me, and probably never will; *but Almighty God has spoken to me in Jesus Christ and through His Word!* "God . . . has in these last days spoken to us by His Son" (Heb. 1:1-2, NKJV). In spite of all that a world of sinners has done to the Lord, He still speaks to us in His grace. He not only speaks the word of salvation, but He also gives us the guidance we need for everyday life. Just as Boaz instructed Ruth, so the Lord also shares His Word of wisdom to direct our daily lives. He is the "Lord of the harvest" and assigns to us our place in His field.

(3) Boaz promised to protect Ruth and provide for her needs (Ruth 2:9, 14-16). Boaz called Ruth "my daughter" because she was younger than he (see 3:10), but it was also a term of endearment. He would treat her like a member of his family. (This is what David did for Mephibosheth. See 2 Sam. 9.) Boaz instructed his young men to protect her and the young women to work with her. She was to walk with the female servants who followed immediately after the reapers. In other words, Ruth had first chance at the best of the gleanings! Boaz even instructed his workers to allow her to glean among the sheaves and told them to deliberately drop some of the harvest so she could pick it up. If she was hungry or thirsty, she could refresh herself with his workers. In fact, Boaz ate with her and personally handed her the food! (Ruth 2:14)

What a picture of the grace of God! The master became like the servants that he might show his love to a foreigner. Ruth had no idea that Boaz had commanded his workers to be generous to her, but she believed his word and found that her needs were met. Jesus Christ came to this earth as a servant (Phil. 2:1-11) that He might save us and make us a part of His family. He has shared with us the riches of His mercy and love (Eph. 2:4), the riches of His grace (v. 7), the riches of His wisdom and knowledge (Rom. 11:33), His riches in glory (Phil. 4:19), and yes, His "unsearchable riches" (Eph. 3:8, NIV). We, undeserving "foreigners," are members of the family of God and have all of His inheritance at our disposal.

(4) Boaz encouraged Ruth (Ruth 2:10-13). Ruth's response to Boaz was one of humility and gratitude. She acknowledged her own unworthiness and accepted his grace. She believed his promises and rejoiced in them. There was no need for Ruth to worry, for the wealthy lord of the harvest would care for her and Naomi. How did she *know* he would care for her? He gave her his promise, and she knew he could be trusted.

Ruth neither looked back at her tragic past nor did she look at herself and consider her sorry plight. She fell at the feet of the master and submitted herself to him. She looked away from her poverty and focused on his riches. She forgot her fears and rested on his promises. What an example for God's people today to follow!

I find that many people are miserable because they don't obey the admonition of Hebrews 12:2: "fixing our eyes on Jesus." They spend so much time looking at themselves, their circumstances, and other people that they fail to do what Ruth did, namely, center their attention on their Master. Instead of resting in His perfections, they focus on their own imperfections. Instead of seeing His spiritual riches, they complain about their bankruptcy. They go to church "to get their needs met," instead of going to church to worship the God who is greater than any need. They need to heed the counsel of the little poem a radio listener sent me years ago:

Look at self and be distressed,
Look at others and be depressed,
Look at Jesus and you'll be blessed!

(5) Boaz saw to it that she was satisfied (Ruth 2:14, 18). All of this happened to Ruth because of her faith in the God of Israel. Boaz fully knew Ruth's story, for it didn't take long for news to travel in a little town like Bethlehem. He knew that Ruth had abandoned her home and her gods and had put her faith in Jehovah. She had taken refuge "under His wings." That image sometimes refers to the hen protecting her chicks (Ps. 91:4; Matt. 23:37), but it can also refer to the wings of the cherubim in the Holy of Holies (Pss. 36:7; 61:4). Ruth was no longer a foreigner and a stranger. She was not only accepted by the God of Israel, but she was also dwelling in the very Holy of Holies with Him! (See Eph. 2:11-22.)

The word translated "answered" in Ruth 2:11 is literally "raised his voice." Boaz was getting excited! He wanted everybody to hear what he thought about Ruth, and he wasn't ashamed to be identified with her. She had trusted Jehovah, and she had proved her faith by cleaving to her mother-in-law and becoming a part of the people of Israel in Bethlehem. The phrase "spoken friendly" in verse 13 means "spoken to the heart." The Word of God comes from the heart of God (Ps. 33:11) to the hearts of His people (Matt. 23:18-23) and gives encouragement and hope (Rom. 15:4). If you listen to the voices of the world, you will be discouraged; but if you listen to the voice of God from His Word, your heart will be encouraged.

The Word of God and the Son of God can fully satisfy the heart of the believer. When we seek for satisfaction anywhere else, we will find ourselves disobedient and dissatisfied. The lost world labors for that which doesn't satisfy (Isa. 55:2), but the believer has full satisfaction because of the grace of the Lord Jesus Christ (Pss. 36:7-9; 63:5; 65:4; 103:5; 107:9). As the hymn writer put it:

Well of water ever springing,
Bread of life so rich and free,
Untold wealth that never faileth,
My Redeemer is to me.
Hallelujah! I have found Him
Whom my soul so long has craved!
Jesus satisfies my longings,
Through His blood I now am saved.
(Clara T. Williams)

We must live by faith, and we must depend on God's grace. But there is a third condition we must meet.

3. We must live in hope. (Ruth 2:17-23)

All day long, Ruth labored with a happy and hopeful heart. She didn't have to worry about the men harassing her or the other workers hindering her. She had food when she was hungry, drink when she was thirsty, and a place of rest when she became weary. The grain she gleaned amounted to about half a bushel, enough food for the two women for nearly a week. She also had some food left over from her lunch (v. 18). Ruth was not only a diligent worker, but she was also careful not to waste anything God had given her.

How will Naomi respond to Ruth's experiences? The last time we met Naomi, she was sharing her bitterness with the women of Bethlehem and blaming God for her sorrow and poverty. When Ruth had asked permission to go to the fields to glean, all Naomi said to her was "Go, my daughter" (v. 2). She gave her daughter-in-law no word of encouragement, not even the promise of her prayers.

Now we hear a new word from Naomi's lips: "Blessed!" (vv. 19-20) She not only blessed Ruth's benefactor, but she also blessed the Lord! We have moved from bitterness to blessedness. When Naomi saw the grain, she blessed the man who allowed Ruth to work in his field; and when she heard that the man was Boaz, Naomi blessed the Lord. What a change has taken place in the heart of this grieving widow! This change came about because of the new hope she had in her heart, and the one who gave her that new hope was Boaz.

Naomi had hope because of *who Boaz was*—a near kinsman who was wealthy and influential. As we shall see, a near kinsman could rescue relatives from poverty and give them a new beginning (Lev. 25:25-34). But she also had hope because of *what Boaz did:* He showed kindness to Ruth and took a personal interest in her situation. When Ruth shared with Naomi *what Boaz had said,* Naomi's hope grew even stronger because the words of Boaz revealed his love for Ruth and his desire to make her happy. That Boaz insisted on Ruth staying close to his servants and in his field was proof to Naomi that her husband's relative was making plans that included her and her daughter-in-law.

Should not we who believe in Jesus Christ rejoice in hope? When you consider who He is, what He has done for us, and what He says to us in His Word, there is no reason for us to feel hopeless. Jesus Christ is the Son of God. He has died for us, and now He intercedes for us in heaven. In His Word, He has given us "exceeding great and precious promises" (2 Peter 1:4, KJV) that can never fail. No matter how you may feel today, no matter how difficult your circumstances may be, you can rejoice in hope if you will focus your faith on Jesus Christ.

The American agnostic lecturer Robert G. Ingersoll called hope "the only universal liar who never loses his reputation for veracity." But the late Norman Cousins, former editor of *The Saturday Review,* who miraculously survived an almost incurable illness and a severe heart attack, unequivocally disagrees with Ingersoll. "The human body experiences a powerful gravitational pull in the direction of hope," Cousins wrote. "That's why the patient's hopes are the physician's secret weapon. They are the hidden ingredients in any prescription." In his work with patients at the UCLA School of Medicine,

Cousins proved the power of hope to change people's lives.

For the Christian believer, hope is not a shallow "hope-so feeling" generated by optimistic fantasies. Hope is an inner sense of joyful assurance and confidence as we trust God's promises and face the future with His help. This hope is God's gift to His children through the Holy Spirit, who reminds us of God's promises found in His Word (Rom. 15:13).

Ruth's half bushel of grain was the "firstfruits" of all that Boaz would do in the future, just as the Holy Spirit within us is the "firstfruits" of all that God has promised us (8:23). Although Ruth's supply of grain would be gone in a week, the witness of the Spirit within will remain until our hopes are all fulfilled when we see Jesus Christ.

The exciting new hope that now possessed the two widows was centered in a person, Boaz, just as our hope is centered in the Son of God. In fact, Jesus Christ is our hope (1 Tim. 1:1; 1 Thes. 1:3; Col. 1:27). Through faith in Christ, we have been born again into "a living hope" (1 Peter 1:3); and because it is a living hope, it grows stronger each day and produces fruit. The hopes that the world clings to are dead hopes, but ours is a living hope because it is rooted in the living Christ.

Naomi then explained to Ruth the law of "the kinsman redeemer" (Lev. 25:47-55). It was not just the kindness and love of Boaz for Ruth that gave Naomi confidence, for those wonderful feelings could change overnight. It was the principle of redemption that God had written in His Word that gave Naomi the assurance that Boaz would rescue them. As a near relative, Boaz could redeem the family property that Elimelech had mortgaged when he took his family to Moab. Naomi wasn't wealthy enough to redeem it, but Boaz could buy it back and keep it in the family.

However, something else was involved: The wife of the deceased went with the property. Therefore, the kinsman redeemer had to marry her and bring up children bearing the name of the deceased. They would then inherit the property, and the family name and family possessions would continue to be theirs. This is known as "levirate marriage" (see Deut. 25:5-10). The word *levir* is Latin for "a husband's brother." The author of the Book of Ruth doesn't explain how Ruth's husband Mahlon (4:10) was connected with his father's property so that Ruth had to be included in the purchase. When and why the Jewish people connected the law of the kinsman redeemer with the law of levirate marriage is not made clear to us, but that was the custom in Ruth's time.

Naomi cautioned Ruth to obey the commands of Boaz and stay close to his servants as she gleaned in the field. The barley harvest occurred during March and April, and the wheat harvest during June and July. Meanwhile, Ruth kept busy and gathered food sufficient for herself and her mother-in-law. But now she was laboring motivated by a wonderful hope: She was joyfully anticipating the day of redemption! (See Rom. 8:23 and Eph. 4:30.)

It is encouraging to see the changes that have taken place in Naomi because of what Ruth did. God used Ruth to turn Naomi's bitterness into gratitude, her unbelief into faith, and her despair into hope. One person, trusting the Lord and obeying His will, can change a situation from defeat to victory.

Ruth's faith in God's Word led her to the field of Boaz. The love of Boaz for Ruth compelled him to pour out his grace upon her and meet her every need.

(Grace is love that pays the price to help the undeserving one.) Ruth's experience of grace gave her new hope as she anticipated what her kinsman redeemer would do.

"And now abide faith, hope, love" (1 Cor. 13:13), and they still abide with us as we abide in Jesus Christ and trust in Him.

CHAPTER THREE
THE MIDNIGHT MEETING
Ruth 3

(In which a simple act of faith brings the dawning of a new day)

Ever since Boaz came into Ruth's life, Naomi has been a different person. Her concern is no longer for herself and her grief but for Ruth and her future. *It's when we serve others that we ourselves receive the greatest joy and satisfaction.* The martyred German minister Dietrich Bonhoeffer called Jesus Christ "the man for others," and the title is appropriate. "Be humble, thinking of others as better than yourself. Don't just think about your own affairs, but be interested in others, too, and in what they are doing" (Phil. 2:3-4, TLB).

When the two widows came to Bethlehem, their plan was that Ruth take care of Naomi and both of them eke out an existence the best they could. But now Naomi has a new plan: Ruth is to marry Boaz, and then all of them can live happily ever after. Naomi could tell from Ruth's report that Boaz would be in favor of the plan, so she began to set things in motion. In that day, it was the parents who arranged marriages; so Naomi was not out of place in what she did.

Keep in mind that the Book of Ruth is much more than the record of the marriage of a rejected alien to a respected Jew. It's also the picture of Christ's relationship to those who trust Him and belong to Him. In the steps that Ruth takes, recorded in this chapter, we see the steps God's people must take if they want to enter into a deeper relationship with the Lord. Like Ruth, we must not be satisfied merely with living on leftovers (2:2), or even receiving gifts (2:14, 16). *We must want Him alone;* for *when we have Him, we also have all that He owns.* It's not the gifts that we seek, but the Giver.

1. Ruth prepared to meet Boaz. (Ruth 3:1-5)

There were other men who would gladly have married Ruth (v. 10), but they could not have redeemed her. Only a kinsman could do that, and Boaz was that kinsman. Since Naomi knew that Boaz would be using the threshing floor that night and staying there to guard his grain, she instructed Ruth to prepare herself to meet him. Ruth made a fivefold preparation before she presented herself to Boaz.

First, **she washed herself (v. 3a).** Every day in the United States, 450 billion gallons of water are used for homes, factories, and farms, enough water to cover Manhattan to a depth of ninety-six feet. In the East, the heat and the dust made frequent washing a necessity; but water was not always plentiful. With regard to the Jews, the Law of Moses required ceremonial washings, and taking a bath and changing clothes usually preceded a special event (Gen. 35:1-3). Actually, Naomi was telling Ruth to act like a bride preparing for her wedding (Ezek. 16:9-12).

If we want to enter into a deeper relationship with our Lord, we must "cleanse ourselves from all filthiness of the flesh and spirit, perfecting holiness in the fear of God" (2 Cor. 7:1, NKJV). Whenever we sin, we must pray, "Wash me" (Ps. 51:2, 7); but sometimes God says to us, "Wash yourselves, make yourselves clean" (Isa. 1:16, NKJV). When we seek forgiveness, God washes the record clean (1 John 1:9); but God will not do for us what we must do for ourselves. Only we can put out of our lives those things that defile us, *and we know what they are.* It might mean cleaning out our library (Acts 19:18-20), our cassette and CD collection, the magazine rack, or perhaps the TV viewing schedule. We must separate ourselves from whatever defiles us and grieves the Father (2 Cor. 6:14-7:1; James 4:7-8).

If the Old Testament priests came into God's presence defiled, they were in danger of death (Ex. 30:17-21). The Jewish people were conscious of the need for holiness as they came to worship God (Pss. 15; 24:1-6); yet Christians today rush into God's presence without cleansing themselves of the sins that rob them of God's blessing. Is it any wonder that our worship is often an empty routine and that the power of God doesn't come to our meetings?

The next thing Ruth did to prepare was to **anoint herself (Ruth 3:3b).** Eastern peoples used fragrant oils to protect and heal their bodies and to make themselves pleasant to others. A bride would especially take care to wear fragrant perfume that would make her "nice to be near" (see Song 1:3, 12-14; 4:11-16).

Anointing oil speaks of the presence and the working of the Holy Spirit in our lives. All believers have received the anointing of the Spirit (1 John 2:20, 27), and therefore we ought to be "a fragrance of Christ" to the Heavenly Father (2 Cor. 2:15). The more we are like Jesus Christ in character and conduct, the more we please our Father; and the more we please Him, the more He can bless and use us for His glory.

I once heard Dr. A.W. Tozer say, "If God were to take the Holy Spirit out of this world, much of what the church is doing would go right on; and nobody would know the difference." We have so much in human resources available to the church today that we manage to "serve the Lord" without the unction of the Holy Spirit working in our lives. But is that what God wants?

While here on earth, Jesus lived His life and did His work through the anointing of the Holy Spirit (Luke 4:16-19). If the spotless Son of God needed the Spirit's power, how much more do we! Do we dare pray in the energy of the flesh when the Spirit is present to assist us? (Rom. 8:26; Eph. 2:18) Do we try to witness for Christ without asking the Spirit to help us? (Acts 1:8) Can we fellowship with our Lord in His Word apart from the ministry of the Spirit of God? (Eph. 1:15-23 and 3:14-21)

Ruth's third act of preparation was to **change clothes (Ruth 3:3c).** She was to put off the garments of a sorrowing widow and dress for a wedding (see Isa. 61:1-3). Ruth probably didn't have a large wardrobe, but she would have one special garment for festive occasions. Naomi had the faith to believe that Ruth would soon be going to a wedding!

In Scripture, clothing carries a spiritual meaning. After they had sinned against God, our first parents tried to cover themselves; but only the Lord could forgive them and clothe them acceptably, and He had to shed blood to do it (Gen. 3:1–8, 21). The Jewish priests wore special garments that nobody else was permitted to wear (Ex. 28). Salvation is pictured as a change of clothes (Luke 15:22; Isa. 61:10), and Christian living means taking off the "graveclothes" of the old life and putting on the "grace clothes" of the new life (Col. 3:1-17; see John 11:44).

We can't come into God's presence in our own righteousness, for "all our righteousnesses are as filthy rags" (Isa. 64:6, KJV). We can only come in the righteousness of Jesus Christ (2 Cor. 5:21), for we are "accepted in the beloved" (Eph. 1:6, KJV). If we are obedient to His will and seek to please Him, then our garments will be white (Rev. 19:8); but if we've sinned, we must confess our sins and seek His cleansing (Zech. 3). If you want to enter into a deeper fellowship with your Lord, then "let your garments always be white, and let your head lack no oil" (Ecc. 9:8, KJV).

Ruth prepared herself to meet Boaz by **learning how to present herself to him (Ruth 3:3-4).** There was nothing improper about this procedure, for it was the only way Ruth could offer herself to her kinsman redeemer. She had to put herself at the feet of the lord of the harvest, and he would do the rest.

Suppose that on her way to the threshing floor, Ruth decided to take a different approach. Why lie at the feet of the man you want to marry? Why uncover his feet and then ask him to put a corner of his mantle over you? Certainly there ought to be a better way! Had she used another approach, Boaz would have been confused; and the entire enterprise would have failed.

The Old Testament priests knew how to approach God because He gave them their instructions in the law. New Testament Christians know how to approach God because in the Word He has told us what is required. Whether in our private communion with the Lord or in public worship, we have no right to alter the principles of approach that God has laid down.

While ministering one week near Springfield, Illinois, my wife and I decided to visit the Abraham Lincoln house. In order to get in, we each had to have a ticket that could be procured at only one place. We had to follow the guide and not deviate from the route of the tour. Last but not least, we had to deposit our chewing gum in a container outside the house! If we wanted to see Mr. Lincoln's house, we had to conform to the rules.

Like the Prodigal Son (Luke 15:11-24), lost sinners can come to the Lord just as they are; and He will receive them and change them. But God's own children must "conform to the rules" if they want to fellowship with their Father (Heb. 10:19-25). When the people of God assemble for worship, we must be careful to worship Him "in spirit and in truth" (John 4:24), following the principles given in the Scriptures. When it comes to worshiping God, too often people do that which is right in their own eyes and substitute human inventions for divine instructions.

Finally, **Ruth promised to obey (Ruth 3:5).** "All that you say to me I will do" (NKJV). She was not only a hearer of the Word, but she was a doer. A willingness to obey the Lord is the secret of knowing what He wants us to do and being blessed when we do it. "If anyone is willing to do God's will, he shall know concerning the teaching" (John 7:17, literal translation). The will of God is not a cafeteria where we can pick and choose what we want. God expects us to accept all that He plans for us and to obey Him completely. Coming to God with a hidden agenda and with reservations in our hearts will only lead to grieving the Spirit and missing God's best.

2. Ruth submitted to Boaz. (Ruth 3:6-9)

The harvest season was an especially joyful time for the Jews (Isa. 9:3; 16:10), which is the way God wanted it. "The Lord thy God shall bless thee in all thine increase, and in all the works of thine hands, therefore thou shalt surely rejoice" (Deut. 16:15, KJV). Most people today live separated from the sources of their daily bread and don't realize all that's involved in producing food. Perhaps our table prayers would be more joyful and more grateful if we realized all that a farmer goes through to help keep us alive.

Harvesting and threshing were cooperative enterprises. The men of a village would take turns using the threshing floor, which was usually a raised platform outside the village and often on a hill where it could catch the evening breeze. The men would deposit the sheaves on the floor and then separate the grain from the stalks by having oxen walk on it (Deut. 25:4) or by beating the stalks (see Ruth 2:17). Once the grain was separated, the workers would throw the grain into the air; and the breeze would carry the chaff away while the grain fell to the floor. The grain would then be heaped up to be carried away for marketing or storage. The men often worked in the evening when the breeze was up, and they slept at the threshing floor to protect the harvest.

Four times in this chapter there is mention of feet (3:4, 7–8, 14). Ruth had fallen at the feet of Boaz in response to his gracious words (2:10), but now she was coming to his feet to propose marriage. She was asking him to obey the law of the kinsman redeemer and take her as his wife.

We may ask, "Why didn't Ruth wait for Boaz to propose to her?" His statement in 3:10 suggests the first reason: He fully expected that she would marry one of the younger bachelors in Bethlehem. Boaz was an older man, and Ruth was a young woman (4:12). Evidently he concluded that he was out of the running. But the most important reason is given in verse 12: There was a nearer kinsman in town who had first option on Ruth and the property, and Boaz was waiting for him to act. Ruth had forced the issue, and now Boaz could approach this kinsman and get him to decide.

"Life is full of rude awakenings!" a famous cartoon canine likes to say, and more than one biblical character would agree. Adam went to sleep and woke up to discover he'd been through surgery and was now a married man. Jacob woke up to discover he was married to the wrong woman! Boaz woke up at midnight to find a woman lying at his feet.

When he asked who she was, Ruth replied that she was Ruth; but she did not call herself "the Moabitess." Now she was the "handmaid" of Boaz. She was making a new beginning. You find Ruth named twelve times in this little book, and in five of these references she is identified with Moab (1:22; 2:2, 21; 4:5, 10).

To spread one's mantle over a person meant to claim that person for yourself (Ezek. 16:8; 1 Kings 19:19), particularly in marriage. The word translated "skirt" also means "wing." Ruth had come under the wings of Jehovah God (Ruth 2:12); and now she would be under the wings of Boaz, her beloved husband. What a beautiful picture of marriage!

3. Ruth listened to Boaz. (Ruth 3:10-14)

In the responses of Boaz to Ruth, we see how the Lord responds to us when we seek to have a deeper fellowship with Him. Just as Boaz spoke to Ruth, so God speaks to us from His Word.

He accepts us (Ruth 3:8-10). Boaz might have refused to have anything to do with Ruth; but in his love for her, he accepted her. He even called her "my daughter" (see 2:8) and pronounced a blessing on her (see Eph. 1:3). Our heavenly Father and our Redeemer is seeking for a closer relationship with us, and we should not be afraid to draw near and share His love (John 14:21-24; James 4:7-8). If we could only realize in even a small way the great love our Kinsman Redeemer has for us, we would forsake everything else and enjoy His fellowship.

He assures us (Ruth 3:11-13). In the midnight darkness, Ruth couldn't see the face of Boaz, but she could hear his voice; and that voice spoke loving assurance to her: "Fear not!" *Our assurance is not in our feelings or our circumstances but in His Word.*

How firm a foundation, ye saints of the Lord,
Is laid for your faith in His excellent Word.

During the Boxer Rebellion, when the workers with the China Inland Mission were experiencing great suffering, the founder James Hudson Taylor, then in his late seventies, said to some colleagues, "I cannot read; I cannot think; I cannot even pray; but I can trust." "So then faith comes by hearing, and hearing by the word of God" (Rom. 10:17, NKJV).

"Fear not" is the word of assurance that the Lord gave to many of His servants: to Abraham (Gen. 15:1), Isaac (26:24), Jacob (46:3), Moses and the nation of Israel (Ex. 14:13), Joshua (Josh. 8:1; 10:8), King Jehoshaphat (2 Chron. 20:17), the Jewish remnant returning to their land (Isa. 41:10, 13-14; 43:1, 5; 44:2), the Prophet Ezekiel (Ezek. 3:9), the Prophet Daniel (Dan. 10:12, 19), Joseph (Matt. 1:20), Zacharias (Luke 1:13), Mary (1:30), the shepherds (2:10), Paul (Acts 27:24), and the Apostle John (Rev. 1:17). You and I can say with these spiritual giants, "The Lord is my helper; I will not fear" (Heb. 13:6, NKJV).

Not only did Boaz calm Ruth's fears, but he also made a promise to her concerning the future: "I will do for you all that you request" (Ruth 3:11, NKJV). Whatever God starts, He finishes; and what He does, He does well (Phil. 1:6; Mark 7:37). It was not Ruth's obligation to do for herself what only Boaz could do.

What seemed to Naomi to be a simple procedure has now turned out to be a bit more complicated, because there was a man in Bethlehem who was a nearer kinsman. Boaz didn't withhold this problem from Ruth, for he didn't want her to return home with false hopes in her heart. Joy and peace that are based on ignorance of the true facts are but delusions that lead to disappointments. The great concern of Boaz was the redemption of Ruth, even if another kinsman redeemer had to do it.

When you see this as a picture of our redemption in Jesus Christ, it impresses you strongly that *God obeyed His own law when He accomplished our salvation in Christ.* His law said, "The soul who sins shall die" (Ezek. 18:4, NKJV), and God didn't seek for some way to evade this. "He who did not spare His own Son, but delivered Him up for us all" (Rom. 8:32). Of course, there was no other "kinsman" who could redeem a lost world. "Neither is there salvation in any other: for there is none other name under heaven given among men, whereby we must be saved" (Acts 4:12, KJV).

4. Ruth received gifts from Boaz. (Ruth 3:15-17)

During her days as a gleaner, Ruth had received generous treatment from Boaz.

His workers had allowed her to follow the harvesters; they protected her from harm; they deliberately dropped sheaves for her to pick up. Boaz had shared the noon meal with Ruth, even handing her the parched grain with his own hands (2:14). On that first day of gleaning, Ruth had gone home with a little more than half a bushel of grain; but now Boaz filled her cloak with two bushels of grain, which would be more than two weeks' supply.

Boaz not only calmed Ruth's fears and gave her assurance for the future, but he also met her present needs in a gracious and generous way. She had not asked him for anything, but he gave the grain to her because he loved her. He was about to marry her, and he didn't want his prospective bride gleaning in the fields like a poor laborer.

Naomi's question in 3:16 has puzzled translators and interpreters. Why would her own mother-in-law ask her who she was? *The Living Bible* paraphrases the question, "Well, what happened, dear?" and both the NIV and the NASB read, "How did it go, my daughter?" But the *Authorized Version* translates the Hebrew text as it stands: "Who are you, my daughter?" In other words, "Are you still Ruth the Moabitess, *or are you the prospective Mrs. Boaz?"*

Ruth remembered Boaz's words, as she had done before (2:19-21); and she shared with Naomi all that Boaz had promised. Then Ruth showed Naomi the generous gift Boaz had given them. A man who sends a generous gift to his prospective mother-in-law is certainly a good choice for a husband!

Naomi could no longer say that her hands were empty (1:21). Now they were full because of the grace of the kinsman redeemer. Ruth's faith and obedience had brought about a complete transformation in their lives, and now they were living by grace.

5. Ruth waited for Boaz to work. (Ruth 3:18)

It is "through faith and patience" that we inherit the promises (Heb. 6:12; 10:36). Since Naomi and Ruth believed that Boaz would accomplish what he said he would do, they waited patiently until they received the good news that Ruth would be a bride. "Commit your way to the Lord, trust also in Him, and He will do it" (Ps. 37:5).

I confess that *waiting* is one of the most difficult things for me to do, whether it's waiting for a table at a restaurant or waiting for a delayed flight to take off. I'm an activist by nature, and I like to see things happen on time. Perhaps that's why the Lord has often arranged for me to wait. During those times, three phrases from Scripture have encouraged me: "Sit still" (Ruth 3:18, KJV), "Stand still" (Ex. 14:13, KJV), and "Be still" (Ps. 46:10, KJV).

"Sit still" was Naomi's counsel to Ruth, and wise counsel it was. Ruth would have accomplished nothing by following Boaz around Bethlehem, trying to help him keep his promises. "Their strength is to sit still" (Isa. 30:7, KJV). Our human nature gets nervous and wants to help God out; and when we try, we only make matters worse.

"Stand still" was the command of Moses to the people of Israel when the Egyptian army was pursuing them. There was no need to panic, for God had the situation well in hand. Then the Lord commanded the people to "go forward" (Ex. 14:15), and He led them safely through the sea. There is a time to stand and a time to march, and we must be alert to know which one God wants us to do.

"Be still, and know that I am God" (Ps. 46:10, KJV) is a wonderful antidote for a restless spirit. The Hebrew word translated "be still" means "take your hands off, relax." It's so easy for us to get impatient with the Lord and start meddling in matters that we ought to leave alone. He is God, and His hands can accomplish the impossible. Our hands may get in the way and make matters worse.

Boaz was busy working for Ruth, and Naomi was confident that he wouldn't rest until he had settled the matter. "Being confident of this very thing, that He which hath begun a good work in you will perform [complete] it until the day of Jesus Christ" (Phil. 1:6, KJV). It encourages my heart to know that Jesus Christ is working unceasingly for His people as He intercedes in heaven (Heb. 8:34), and that He is working in us, seeking to conform us to His perfect will (13:20-21; Phil. 2:12-13).

Have you put yourself at the feet of the Lord of the Harvest, and are you trusting Him to work?

One evidence of your trust will be your willingness to sit still and let Him have His way.

CHAPTER FOUR
LOVE FINDS A WAY
Ruth 4

(In which Boaz and Ruth get married, and Naomi finds her empty heart full of joy and her empty hands full of a baby boy)

The Book of Ruth opens with three funerals but closes with a wedding. There is a good deal of weeping recorded in the first chapter, but the last chapter records an overflowing of joy in the little town of Bethlehem. "Weeping may endure for a night, but joy cometh in the morning" (Ps. 30:5, KJV). Not all of life's stories have this kind of happy ending; but this little book reminds us that, for the Christian, *God still writes the last chapter.* We don't have to be afraid of the future.

This chapter focuses on three persons: a bridegroom, a bride, and a baby.

1. The bridegroom (Ruth 4:1-10)

The law of the kinsman redeemer is given in Leviticus 25:23–34, and the law governing levirate marriage is found in Deuteronomy 25:5-10. The purpose of these laws was to preserve the name and protect the property of families in Israel. God owned the land and didn't want it exploited by rich people who would take advantage of poor people and widows. When obeyed, these laws made sure that a dead man's family name did not die with him and that his property was not sold outside the tribe or clan. The tragedy is that the Jewish rulers didn't always obey this law, and the prophets had to rebuke them for stealing land from the helpless (1 Kings 21; Isa. 5:8–10; Hab. 2:9-12). The nation's abuse of the land was one cause of their Captivity (2 Chron. 36:21).

The meaning of redemption. The word *redeem* means "to set free by paying a price." In the case of Ruth and Naomi, Elimelech's property had either been sold or was under some kind of mortgage, and the rights to the land had passed to Ruth's husband, Mahlon, when Elimelech died. This explains why Ruth was also involved in the transaction. She was too poor, however, to redeem the land.

When it comes to *spiritual* redemption, all people are in bondage to sin and Satan (Eph. 2:1-3; John 8:33-34) and are unable to set themselves free. Jesus Christ gave

His life as a ransom for sinners (Mark 10:45; Rev. 5:9-10), and faith in Him sets the captive free.

Each time I visit a bookstore, I try to observe what subjects are getting prominent notice; and in recent years, it's been the theme of *deliverance.* I see shelves of books about addiction and codependence and how to find freedom. In a world that's enjoying more political freedom than ever before, millions of people are in bondage to food, sex, drugs, alcohol, gambling, work, and dozens of other "masters." While we thank God for the help counselors and therapists can give, it is Jesus Christ who alone can give freedom to those who are enslaved. "Therefore if the Son makes you free, you shall be free indeed" (John 8:36, NKJV).

The marks of the redeemer. Not everybody could perform the duties of a kinsman redeemer. To begin with, *he had to be a near kinsman* (Lev. 25:25). This was the major obstacle Boaz had to overcome because another man in Bethlehem was a nearer relative to Ruth than he was (3:12-13). When you see this as a type of Jesus Christ, it reminds you that He had to become *related* to us before He could redeem us. He became flesh and blood so He could die for us on the cross (Heb. 2:14-15). When He was born into this world in human flesh, He became our "near kinsman"; and He will remain our "kinsman" for all eternity. What matchless love!

In order to qualify, the kinsman redeemer also *had to be able to pay the redemption price.* Ruth and Naomi were too poor to redeem themselves, but Boaz had all the resources necessary to set them free. When it comes to the redemption of sinners, nobody but Jesus Christ is rich enough to pay the price. Indeed, the payment of money can never set sinners free; it is the shedding of the precious blood of Christ that has accomplished redemption (1 Peter 1:18-19; see Ps. 49:5–9). We have redemption through Christ's blood (Eph. 1:7), because He gave Himself for us (Titus 2:14) and purchased eternal redemption for us (Heb. 9:12).

There was a third qualification: The kinsman redeemer *had to be willing to redeem.* As we shall see in this chapter, since the nearer kinsman was not willing to redeem Ruth, Boaz was free to purchase both the property and a wife. The nearer kinsman had the money but not the motivation: He was afraid he would jeopardize his own family's inheritance.

The method of redemption. In ancient times, the city gate was the official court where judicial business was transacted in the presence of the elders (Deut. 21:18-21; 2 Sam. 15:2; Job 29:7ff). When Boaz arrived at the gate, he gathered ten men to witness the transaction. Just then, the nearer kinsman walked by—another evidence of God's providence—and Boaz hailed him. Now everything was ready for the great transaction that would ultimately involve the coming of the Son of God into the world.

The key theme of this chapter is *redemption.* The words "redeem," "buy," and "purchase" are used at least fifteen times. *There can be no redemption without the paying of a price.* From our point of view, salvation is free to "whosoever shall call on the name of the Lord" (Acts 2:21, KJV); but from God's point of view, redemption is a very costly thing.

The other kinsman was willing to buy the land until he learned that Ruth was a part of the transaction, and then he backed out. His explanation was that, in marrying Ruth, he would jeopardize his own inheritance. If he had a son by Ruth, and that son were his only surviving heir,

Mahlon's property *and part of his own estate* would go to Elimelech's family. The fact that Ruth was a Moabitess may also have been a problem to him. (Both Mahlon and Chilion had married Moabite women and died!)

Boaz was undoubtedly relieved when his relative stepped aside and opened the way for Ruth to become his wife. It's worth noting that the nearer kinsman tried to protect his name and inheritance; *but we don't even know what his name was or what happened to his family!* Boaz took the risk of love and obedience, and his name is written down in Scripture and held in honor. "He who does the will of God abides forever" (1 John 2:17, NKJV). This also explains why Orpah's name is missing in Ruth 4:9-10.

The custom of taking off the shoe probably relates to the divine commandment to walk on the land and take possession (Gen. 13:17; Deut. 11:24; Josh. 1:3). In years to come, the ten witnesses would be able to testify that the transaction had been completed because they saw the kinsman hand his shoe to Boaz. It symbolized the kinsman's forfeiture of his right to possess the land. Boaz now had the land—and Ruth!

I have mentioned before that Boaz is a picture of Jesus Christ, our Kinsman Redeemer; and this scene is no exception to that. Like Boaz, Jesus wasn't concerned about jeopardizing His own inheritance; instead, He made us a part of His inheritance (Eph. 1:11, 18). Like Boaz, Jesus made His plans privately, but He paid the price publicly; and like Boaz, Jesus did what He did because of His love for His bride.

However, there are also some contrasts between Boaz and the Lord Jesus Christ. Boaz purchased Ruth by giving out of his wealth, while Jesus purchased His bride by giving Himself on the cross. Boaz didn't have to suffer and die to get a bride. Boaz had a rival in the other kinsman, but there was no rival to challenge Jesus Christ. Boaz took Ruth that he might raise up the name of the dead (Ruth 4:10), but we Christians glorify the name of the living Christ. There were witnesses on earth to testify that Ruth belonged to Boaz (vv. 9-10), but God's people have witnesses from heaven, the Spirit, and the Word (1 John 5:9-13).

Five times in Ruth 4:1-2 you find people *sitting down.* When Jesus Christ finished purchasing His bride, He sat down in heaven (Heb. 1:3; Mark 16:19) because the transaction was completed. "It is finished!"

2. The bride (Ruth 4:11-12)

It's a wonderful thing when the covenant community sincerely rejoices with the bride and groom because what they are doing is in the will of God. In my pastoral ministry, I've participated in a few weddings that were anything but joyful. We felt like grieving instead of celebrating. The popular entertainer George Jessel defined marriage as "a mistake every man should make," but the last place you want to make a mistake is at the marriage altar. Contrary to what some people believe, marriage is not "a private affair." This sacred union includes God and God's people, and every bride and groom should want the blessing of God and God's people on their marriage.

The people prayed that Ruth would be fruitful in bearing children, for in Israel children were considered a blessing and not a burden (Ps. 127:3-5). Alas, that's not the attitude in society today. In the United States each year, a million and a half babies are legally destroyed in the womb, and the pieces of their bodies removed as though they were cancerous tumors. A

Christian nurse said to me one day, "In one part of our hospital, we're working day and night to keep little babies alive. In another part, we're murdering them. What is God going to say?"

It was important that the Jewish wives bear children, not only to perpetuate the nation, but also because it would be through Israel that God would send the Messiah to earth. The Jews abhorred both abortion and the exposing of children to die—practices that were common in other nations. Jacob's two wives, Leah and Rachel, bore to him eight sons who "built" the nation by founding the leading tribes of Israel (Gen. 29:31-30:24; 35:18). The use of the word *Ephrathah* in Ruth 4:11 is significant, for the Hebrew word means "fruitful." The people wanted Ruth to be fruitful and famous and bring honor to their little town. It was the place where Rachel was buried (Gen. 35:19), but more importantly, it would be known as the place where Jesus Christ was born.

The neighbors also wanted the house of Boaz to be like that of Perez (Ruth 4:12; see Matt. 1:3). The family of Perez had settled in Bethlehem (1 Chron. 2:5, 50-54), and Boaz was a descendant of Perez (v. 18). Tamar, the mother of Perez, was not a godly woman; but her name is found in our Lord's genealogy (Matt. 1:3).

What wonderful changes came into Ruth's life because she trusted Boaz and let him work on her behalf! She went from loneliness to love, from toil to rest, from poverty to wealth, from worry to assurance, and from despair to hope. She was no longer "Ruth the Moabitess," for the past was gone, and she was making a new beginning. She was now "Ruth the wife of Boaz," a name she was proud to bear.

One of the many images of the church in the Bible is "the bride of Christ." In Ephesians 5:22-33, the emphasis is on Christ's love for the church as seen in His ministries: He died for the church (past), He cleanses and nourishes the church through the Word (present), and He will one day present the church in glory (future). Christ is preparing a beautiful home for His bride and one day will celebrate His wedding (Rev. 19:1-10; 21-22).

3. The baby (Ruth 4:13-22)

God had been gracious to Ruth back in Moab by giving her the faith to trust Him and be saved. His grace continued when she moved to Bethlehem, for He guided her to the field of Boaz where Boaz fell in love with her. God's grace continued at the town gate where the nearer kinsman rejected Ruth and Boaz purchased her. After the marriage, God poured out His grace on Ruth and Boaz by giving her conception (Gen. 29:31; 30:1-2; 33:5) and then by giving her the safe delivery of a son, whom they named Obed ("servant").

God would use this baby to be a source of blessing to many.

Obed was a blessing to Boaz and Ruth. This was no ordinary baby, for it was God's special gift to Boaz and Ruth; and what a blessing little Obed was to their home! But *every* baby is a special gift from God and should be treated that way. Every baby deserves a loving home and caring parents who want to raise the child "in the training and admonition of the Lord" (Eph. 6:4, NKJV). What a great privilege it is to bring new life into the world and then to guide that life so it matures to become all that God has planned!

Obed was also a blessing to Naomi. His grandmother informally "adopted" him as her own son and became his foster mother. The women of Bethlehem shared Naomi's joy when they said, "Praise be to the Lord, who this day has not left you without a kinsman-redeemer" (Ruth 4:14,

NIV). The reference is to Obed, not Boaz.

Obed was a "restorer of life" to Naomi. Every grandparent can bear witness that grandchildren are better than the Fountain of Youth, for we "get young again" when the grandchildren come to visit. Though not all grandparents agree with it, they all know the saying: "They're called 'grandchildren' because they're grand when they come and grand when they leave." *There's no better way to get a new lease on life than to start investing yourself in the younger generation.* Every baby that is born into this world is a vote for the future, and grandparents need to focus on the future and not on the past. When you're holding a baby, you're holding the future in your arms.

Obed would be a blessing to Naomi in another way: He would one day care for the family that brought him into the world, including his grandmother Naomi. Boaz had redeemed the family inheritance; now Obed would continue the family line, protect the inheritance, and use it to sustain Naomi. He would live up to his name and be a "servant" to Naomi, his "foster mother."

The guarantee for this ministry would not be the law of the land but the love of Ruth for her mother-in-law. Obed would early learn to love Naomi even as Ruth loved her. Obed was an only son, but his affection for his mother and grandmother would be equal to that of seven sons.

Obed would bring blessing to Bethlehem. The child would bring fame to both the family name and the name of his native town. Elimelech's name almost disappeared from Israel, but Obed would make that name famous and bring glory to Bethlehem. This happened, of course, through the life and ministry of King David (v. 22) and of David's greater Son, Jesus Christ. Naomi would have the comfort of knowing that the family name would not perish but increase in fame.

Obed would bring blessing to Israel. Obed was the grandfather of King David, one of Israel's greatest rulers. When the name of David is mentioned, we usually think of either Goliath or Bathsheba. David did commit a great sin, but he was also a great man of faith whom God used to build the kingdom of Israel. He led the people in overcoming their enemies, expanding their inheritance and, most of all, worshiping their God. He wrote worship songs for the Levites to sing and devised musical instruments for them to play. He spent a lifetime gathering wealth for the building of the temple, and God gave him the plans for the temple so Solomon could do the job. Whether he had in his hand a sling or sword, a harp or hymnal, David was a great servant of God who brought untold blessings to Israel.

Obed would bring blessing to the whole world. The greatest thing God did for David was not to give him victory over his enemies or wealth for the building of the temple. The greatest privilege God gave him was that of being the ancestor of the Messiah. David wanted to build a house for God, but God told him He would build a house (family) for David (2 Sam. 7). David knew that the Messiah would come from the kingly tribe of Judah (Gen. 49:8-10), but nobody knew which family in Judah would be chosen. God chose David's family, and the Redeemer would be known as "the son of David" (Matt. 1:1).

Little did those Bethlehemites know that God had great plans for that little boy! Obed would have a son named Jesse; and Jesse would have eight sons, the youngest of which would be David the king (1 Sam. 16:6-13).[1] Remember that the next time you behold a baby or a child, that little one might be one for whom God has planned a great future. The medieval teacher who always tipped his hat to his pupils had the right idea, for among them perhaps was a future general or emperor.

The Moabites were not to enter the congregation of the Lord "even to the tenth generation" (Deut. 23:3). But the little Book of Ruth closes with a ten-generation genealogy that climaxes with the name of David!

Never underestimate the power of the grace of God.

INTERLUDE: **REFLECTIONS ON RUTH**

The main purpose of the Book of Ruth is historical. It explains the ancestry of David and builds a bridge between the time of the judges and the period when God gave Israel a king.

But the Bible is more than a history book. There are many practical lessons to be learned from these events—lessons that can encourage us in our spiritual walk. The Book of Ruth is no exception.

This little book certainly reveals the providence of God in the way He guided Ruth and Naomi. It encourages me to know that God still cares for us even when we're bitter toward Him, as Naomi was. God directed Ruth, a "new believer," and used her faith and obedience to transform defeat into victory. God is concerned about the details of our lives, and this fact should give us courage and joy as we seek to live each day to please Him.

The Book of Ruth beautifully illustrates God's work of salvation. The story opens with Ruth as an outsider, a stranger, but it ends with Ruth as a member of the covenant community because she has married Boaz, her kinsman redeemer. He paid the price for her to be redeemed.

But the book also illustrates the believer's deepening relationship with the Lord. In chapter 1, Ruth doesn't even know that Boaz exists. In chapter 2, Ruth is a poor laborer, gleaning in the field of Boaz and receiving his gifts. To her, Boaz is only a mighty man of wealth who shows kindness to her. The turning point is in chapter 3 where Ruth yields herself at the feet of Boaz and believes his promises. The result is recorded in chapter 4: Ruth is no longer a poor gleaner, for now she has Boaz, *and everything he owns belongs to her.*

Too many of God's people are content to live in chapter 2, picking up the leftovers and doing the best they can in their difficult situation. They want God's gifts, but they don't want a deeper communion with God. What a difference it would make if they would only surrender themselves to the Lord and focus on the Giver instead of the gifts! Ponder John 14:21-24.

The Book of Ruth reminds us that God is at work in our world, seeking a bride and reaping a harvest; and we must find our place in His program of winning the lost. The events in the Book of Ruth occurred during the period of the judges, a time not much different from our own day. If you focus only on the evils of our day, you'll become pessimistic and cynical; but, if you ask God what field He wants you to work in and faithfully serve Him, you'll experience His grace, love, and joy.

Judges is the book of "no king" (17:6; 18:1; 19:1; 21:25). First Samuel is the book of "man's king," when God gave Saul to Israel because they asked for him. Things will get so bad in our world that the nations will one day cry out for a king to feed them and protect them. That king will appear; and we call him the Antichrist.

But 1 Samuel isn't the end of the story, for 2 Samuel is the book of God's *king!* David did appear on the scene, and he did establish the kingdom in the name of the Lord. Likewise, when man's king has done his worst, God's King will appear, judge this evil world, put away ungodliness, and then establish His glorious kingdom.

Meanwhile, even though we must live in an evil time like the age of the judges when there was no king in Israel, we can still seek first the kingdom of God and be loyal subjects of the King of kings (Matt. 6:33). The name Elimelech means "my God is king," but Elimelech didn't live up to his name, for he doubted God and disobeyed Him. Even though there is no king in Israel and all around us everything seems to be falling apart, there can be a King in our lives, reigning in our hearts.

It was Ruth's commitment that made the difference in her life and in the lives of the people she loved.

Have you put yourself at the feet of the Lord of the harvest? Until you do, God can never be to you all that He wants to be.

Endnotes

Chapter 4

1. In 1 Chronicles 2:13-15, the writer states that Jesse had seven sons, but this is not an error or contradiction. The unnamed son must have died either unmarried or without posterity. Therefore, his name was dropped out of the official genealogy.

1 SAMUEL

A SUGGESTED OUTLINE OF 1 SAMUEL

Key Theme: The establishment of a king in Israel

Key Verse: 1 Samuel 12:22

I. THE FAILURE OF THE PRIESTHOOD—1–7

The birth of Samuel—1:1–2:11
The failure of Eli—2:12-36
The call of Samuel—3
The rescue of the Ark—4–6
The new spiritual beginning—7

II. THE FAILURE OF THE FIRST KING—8–15

Israel requests a king—8
Saul is made king—9–10
Saul's first victories—11
The nation renews the covenant—12
Saul loses the throne—13–15

III. THE TRAINING OF THE NEW KING—16–31

David is anointed—16:1-13
David serves Saul—16:14-23
David kills Goliath—17
Saul becomes jealous of David—18–19
The love of David and Jonathan—20
David driven into exile—21–27, 29–30
Saul's defeat and death—28; 31

CONTENTS

CHAPTER ONE
"THE LORD OF HOSTS IS WITH US"
1 Samuel 1–3

One of the awesome titles of our great God is "Lord of Hosts" or "Lord of the armies." This title is used nearly 300 times in Scripture and is found for the first time in 1 Samuel 1:3. "Lord of hosts" describes God as the sovereign Lord of the host of the stars (Isa. 40:26), the angelic host (Ps. 103:20-21) and the armies of Israel (Ex. 12:41; Ps. 46:7, 11). In the *Authorized Version,* "hosts" is transliterated "Sabaoth" in Romans 9:29 and James 5:4. In his hymn "A Mighty Fortress Is Our God," Martin Luther rightly applied this title to Jesus Christ:

> Did we in our own strength confide,
> Our striving would be losing,
> Were not the right Man on our side,
> The Man of God's own choosing.
> Dost ask who that may be?
> Christ Jesus, it is He;
> Lord Sabaoth His name,
> From age to age the same,
> And He must win the battle.

The story of the people of Israel recorded in the Bible is a living demonstration of the fact that the Lord *does* win the battle, that He is sovereign in all things. People and events recorded in Scripture are part of what theologians call "salvation history," God's gracious plan to send the Savior into the world to die for sinners. The Book of Ruth ends with the name of David (Ruth 4:22), and 1 Samuel tells the story of David's successful preparation for reigning on the throne of Israel. It was from David's family that Jesus Christ, the "Son of David," was born. The Books of Samuel, Kings, and Chronicles record many sins and failures on the part of God's people, but they also remind us that God is on the throne, and when He isn't allowed to rule, He overrules. He is the Lord of Hosts and His purposes will be accomplished.

1. God directs history.

"What are all histories but God manifesting Himself," said Oliver Cromwell over three centuries ago, but not everybody agrees with him. The British historian Edward Gibbon, who wrote *The Decline and Fall of the Roman Empire,* called history "little more than the register of crimes, follies, and misfortunes of mankind," and Lord Chesterfield, his contemporary, called history "a confused heap of facts." But Dr. A.T. Pierson, preacher and missionary statesman of the last century, said it best when he wrote, "History is His story." This is particularly true of the history recorded in the Bible, for there we have the inspired account of the hand of God at work in the affairs of mankind to bring the Savior into the world.

The Book of Judges is the book of "no king" and describes a nation in which anarchy was the norm. "In those days there was no king in Israel, but every man did that which was right in his own eyes" (Judg. 17:6; and see 18:1; 19:1; and 21:25). Israel wasn't a united people, as during the days of Joshua, but it was a loose confederation of tribes with God-appointed judges ruling in widely separated areas. There was no standing army nor were there permanent military leaders. Men from the different tribes volunteered to defend the land when they were summoned to battle.

But during those dark days of the Judges, a love story took place that's recorded in the Book of Ruth. Boaz married Ruth the Moabitess and from their union came Obed, the father of Jesse who became the father of David the king. *There was no king in Israel, but God was already at work preparing the way for His chosen servant (Ps. 78:56-72).* If Judges is the book of "no king," then 1 Samuel is the book of "man's king." The people of Israel asked for a king and God gave them Saul, from the tribe of Benjamin, who turned out to be a tragic failure. But the Lord had prepared David for the throne, and 2 Samuel is the book of "God's king."

You cannot read the records of the past without seeing the hand of "the Lord of Hosts" at work in the events of what we call history. The Lord is mentioned over sixty times in 1 Samuel 1–3, for He is the chief actor in this drama. Men and women are free to make their decisions, good or bad, but it is Jehovah, the Lord of history, who ultimately accomplishes His purposes in and through the nations (Acts 14:15-17; 17:24-26; Dan. 4:25, 32). Indeed, "history is His story," a truth that is a great encouragement to God's people who suffer for their faith. But this truth is also a warning to unbelievers who ignore or oppose the will of God, because the Lord of hosts will ultimately triumph.

Samuel was God's "bridge builder" at a critical time in Jewish history when the weak confederation of tribes desperately needed direction. He was the last of the judges (1 Sam. 7:15-17; Acts 13:20) and the first of a new line of prophets after Moses (3:24). He established a school of the prophets, and he anointed two kings—Saul who failed and David who succeeded. At a time when the ages were colliding and everything seemed to be shaking, Samuel gave spiritual leadership to the nation of Israel and helped to move them toward national unification and spiritual rededication.

In human history, it may appear to us that truth is "forever on the scaffold" and wrong is "forever on the throne," but that isn't heaven's point of view. As you study 1 Samuel, you will see clearly that God is always in control. While He is long-suffering and merciful and answers the prayers of His people, He is also holy and just and punishes sin. We live today in a time of radical worldwide change, and the church needs leaders like Samuel who will help God's people understand where they've been, who they are, and what they are called to do.

2. God answers prayer. (1 Sam. 1:1-28)

During the period of the judges, the Israelites were in dire straits because they lacked godly leadership. The priesthood was defiled, there was no sustained prophetic message from the Lord (3:1), and the Law of Moses was being ignored throughout the land. As He often did in Israel's history, God began to solve the problem by sending a baby. Babies are God's announcement that He knows the need, cares about His people, and is at work on their behalf. The arrival of a baby ushers in new life and a new beginning; babies are signposts to the future, and their conception and birth is a miracle that only God can do (Gen. 30:1-2). To make the event seem even greater, God sometimes selects barren women to be the mothers, as when He sent Isaac to Sarah, Jacob and Esau to Rebekah, and Joseph to Rachel.

A divided home (1 Sam. 1:1-8). Elkanah was a Levite, a Kohathite from the family of Zuph (1 Chron. 6:22-28, 34-35). The Levites were scattered throughout the land and went to Shiloh to minister at the tabernacle whenever they were needed. Elkanah lived in Ramah on the border of Ephraim and Benjamin (see Josh. 18:25). Elkanah's famous son Samuel would be born in Ramah (1 Sam. 1:19-20), live there (7:17), and be buried there when he died (25:1).[1]

In many ways, Elkanah seems to be a good and godly man, except that he had two wives. Apparently Hannah was his first wife, and when she proved barren, he married Peninnah so he could have a family. We don't know why Elkanah didn't wait on the Lord and trust Him to work out His plan, but even Abraham married Hagar (Gen. 16) and Jacob ended up with four wives! While bigamy and divorce were not prohibited by Jewish law (Deut. 21:15-17; 24:1-4), God's original plan was that one man be married to one woman for one lifetime (Mark 10:1-9).

Each year Elkanah took his family to Shiloh to worship (Ex. 23:14-19), and together they ate a meal as a part of their worship (Deut. 12:1-7). This annual visit to the tabernacle should have been a joyful event for Hannah, but each year Peninnah used it as an opportunity to irritate her rival and make fun of her barrenness. When Elkanah distributed the meat from the sacrifice, he had to give many portions to Peninnah and her children, while Hannah received only one portion. Elkanah gave her a generous share, but his generosity certainly didn't compensate for her infertility. [2]

The name "Hannah" means "a woman of grace," and she did manifest grace in the way she dealt with her barrenness and Peninnah's attitude and cruel words. Elkanah was able to have children by Peninnah, so Hannah knew that the problem lay with her and not with her husband. It seemed unfair that a woman with Peninnah's ugly disposition should have many children while gracious Hannah was childless. She also knew that only the Lord could do for her what he did for Sarah and Rachel, but why had God shut up her womb? Certainly this experience helped to make her into a woman of character and faith and motivated her to give her best to the Lord. She expressed her anguish only to the Lord and she didn't create problems for the family by disputing with Peninnah. In everything she said and did, Hannah sought to glorify the Lord. Indeed, she was a remarkable woman who gave birth to a remarkable son.

A devout prayer (1 Sam. 1:9-18). During one of the festive meals at Shiloh, Hannah left the family and went to the tabernacle to pray. She had determined in her heart that the Lord wanted her to pray for a son so that she might give him back to the Lord to serve Him all his life. It's an awesome fact that, humanly speaking, the future of the nation rested with this godly woman's prayers; and yet, how much in history has depended on the prayers of suffering and sacrificing people, especially mothers.

The original tabernacle was a tent surrounded by a linen fence, but from the description in the text we learn that God's sanctuary now included some sort of wooden structure with posts (1:9) and doors (3:2, 15) and in which people could sleep (vv. 1-3). This structure and the tabernacle together were called "the house of the Lord" (1:7), "the temple," "the tabernacle of the congregation," and God's "habitation" (2:32). It was here that aged Eli, the high priest, sat on his priestly throne to oversee the ministry, and it was there that Hannah went to pray. She wanted to ask the Lord for a son and to promise the Lord her son would serve Him all the days of his life.

What an example Hannah is in her praying! It was a prayer born out of sorrow and suffering, but in spite of her feelings, she laid bare her soul before the

Lord. It was a prayer that involved submission, for she presented herself to the Lord as His handmaid, to do whatever He wanted her to do (see Luke 1:48). It was a prayer that also involved sacrifice, because she vowed to give her son back to the Lord, to be a Nazirite (Num. 6) and serve the Lord all his life. In praying like this, was Hannah "bargaining" with the Lord? I don't think so. Bearing a son would have removed her disgrace and perhaps ended her rival's persecution, but giving up the son was another matter. Perhaps it would have been easier for her to go on living in barrenness than to have a child for three years and have to give him up forever. I wonder if God had given Hannah an inner conviction that her son would play an important part in the future of the nation.

Hannah's faith and devotion were so strong that they rose above the misunderstanding and criticism of the nation's highest spiritual leader. When you give your best to the Lord, it's not unusual to be criticized by people who ought to encourage you. Moses was criticized by his brother and sister (Num. 12), David by his wife (2 Sam. 6:12-23), and Mary of Bethany by an apostle (John 12:1-8), yet all three were commended by the Lord. In the first four chapters of 1 Samuel, Eli comes across as a poor example of a believer, let alone a high priest. He was probably self-indulgent (4:18) and definitely tolerant of the sins of his two sons (2:22-36), and yet he was quick to judge and condemn the devotions of a godly woman. "In prayer it is better to have a heart without words, than words without a heart," said John Bunyan, and that's the way Hannah prayed.

Those who lead God's people need spiritual sensitivity so they can "rejoice with those who rejoice, and weep with those who weep" (Rom. 12:15 NKJV). Eli accused her of pouring out too much wine, when all she was doing was pouring out her soul to God in prayer (1 Sam. 1:15). Five times Hannah called herself a "handmaid," which signified her submission to the Lord and His servants. We don't read that Eli apologized to her for judging her so severely, but at least he gave her his blessing, and she returned to the feast with peace in her heart and joy on her countenance. The burden was lifted from her heart and she knew that God had answered her prayer.

A distinguished son (1 Sam. 1:19-28). When the priests offered the burnt offering early the next morning, Elkanah and his family were there to worship God, and Hannah's soul must have been rejoicing, for she had given herself as a living sacrifice to the Lord (Rom. 12:1-2). When the family arrived home, God answered her prayers and gave her conception, and when her child was born, it was a son whom she named Samuel. The Hebrew word *sa-al* means "asked," and *sama* means "heard," and *el* is one of the names for God, so Samuel means "heard of God" or "asked of God." All his life, Samuel was both an answer to prayer and a great man of prayer.[3]

Certainly Hannah told Elkanah about her vow, because she knew that Jewish law permitted a husband to annul a wife's vow if he disagreed with it (Num. 30). Elkanah agreed with her decision and allowed her to remain at home with her son when the rest of the family went on its annual trip to Shiloh. We can't help but admire Elkanah for what he said and did, for this was his firstborn son by his beloved Hannah and father and son would be separated for the rest of their lives. A firstborn son had to be redeemed by a sacrifice (Ex. 13:11-13), but Elkanah was giving his son as a living sacrifice to the Lord. As a Levite, a Nazirite, a prophet, and a judge, Samuel would faithfully serve the Lord and Israel and help to usher in a new era in Jewish history.

Mothers usually weaned children at the age of three, and surely during those precious years, Hannah taught her son and prepared him for serving the Lord. He did not have a personal knowledge of the Lord until later when God spoke to him (1 Sam. 3:7-10). Hannah was a woman of prayer (1:27) and taught her son to be a man of prayer. When she and Elkanah took their son to Shiloh to give him to the Lord, they brought along the necessary sacrifices so they could worship the Lord. The *Authorized Version* reads "three bullocks" while other translations read "a three-year-old bull" (NIV, NASB). However, the fact that the parents took a skin of wine and an ephah of meal, enough to accompany three sacrifices, suggests that three bullocks is the correct number, for three-tenths of an ephah of grain was needed for each bull sacrificed (Num. 28:12).

When Elkanah and Hannah presented their son to the Lord, Hannah reminded Eli that she was the woman who had prayed for a son three years before.[4] Did the old man remember the occasion and did he recall how unfairly he had dealt with this sorrowing woman? If he did, there's no record of it; but he received the boy to become a servant of the Lord at the tabernacle and be trained in the law of the Lord.

Considering the low level of spiritual life in Eli and the wicked ways of his sons, it took a great deal of faith for Elkanah and Hannah to leave their innocent son in their care. But the Lord was with Samuel and would preserve him from the pollution around him. Just as God protected Joseph in Egypt, so He would protect Samuel in Shiloh, and so He can protect our children and grandchildren in this present evil world. Judgment was coming to Eli and his family, but God would have Samuel prepared to guide the nation and move them into the next stage of their development.

The story thus far makes it clear that the life and future of a nation depends on the character of the home, and the character of the home depends on the spiritual life of the parents. An African proverb says, "The ruin of a nation begins in the homes of its people," and even Confucius taught, "The strength of a nation is derived from the integrity of its homes." Eli and his sons had "religious" homes that were godless, but Elkanah and Hannah had a godly home that honored the Lord, and they gave Him their best. The future hope of the people of Israel rested with that young lad in the tabernacle learning to serve the Lord. Never underestimate the power of the home or the power of a little child dedicated to God.

3. God receives praise and worship. (1 Sam. 2:1-11)

After Hannah left her son with Eli, she could have gone off alone and had a good cry, but instead she burst into a song of praise to the Lord. The world doesn't understand the relationship between sacrifice and song, how God's people can sing their way into sacrifice and sacrifice their way into singing. "And when the burnt offering began, the song of the Lord began also" (2 Chron. 29:27, KJV). Before He went to the garden where He would be arrested, Jesus sang a hymn with His disciples (Matt. 26:30); and Paul and Silas sang hymns to the Lord after they had been humiliated and beaten (Acts 16:20-26). Frequently in the psalms you find David praising God in the midst of difficult circumstances. After being beaten by the religious leaders in Jerusalem, the apostles "departed from the presence of the council, rejoicing that they were counted worthy to suffer shame for His name" (Acts 5:41, NKJV).

Hannah's song near the beginning of 1 Samuel should be compared with David's song found near the end of 2 Samuel (22), as well as with Mary's song in Luke 1:46-55. All three songs tell of God's grace to undeserving people, God's victory over the enemy, and the wonderful way God turns things upside down in order to accomplish His purposes. What Mary expressed in her song is especially close to what Hannah sang in her hymn of praise.

The joy of the Lord (1 Sam. 2:1). Hannah was praying and rejoicing at the same time! She was thinking of God's blessing to the nation of Israel as well as to herself and her home. When prayer is selfish it isn't spiritual and it does not honor the Lord. Hannah knew in her heart that God was going to do great things for His people and that her son would play an important part in accomplishing God's will. Her worship came from her heart and was saturated with the joy of the Lord.

The word "horn" in verses 1 and 10 symbolizes strength or a strong person (see Pss. 75:4-5, 10; 89:17, 24; 92:10; 132:17). To have your "horn exalted" meant to receive new strength from God and be especially helped by Him at a time of crisis. An "enlarged mouth" means a mouth boasting of God's victory over His enemies. Defeated people have to keep their mouths shut, but those who share God's victory have something to talk about to the glory of God.

"I rejoice in thy salvation" suggests more than Hannah's being delivered from barrenness. Hannah sees this miracle as the beginning of new victory for Israel who time after time had been invaded, defeated, and abused by their enemies (Judg. 2:10-23). But the word "salvation" is *yeshua*—Joshua—one of the names of the promised Messiah. King David would be God's *yeshua* to deliver Israel from her enemies, and Jesus, the Son of David, would be God's *yeshua* to deliver all people from the bondage of sin and death.

The majesty of the Lord (1 Sam. 2:2-3). It's good for us to begin our praying with praising, because praise helps us focus on the glory of the Lord and not on the greatness of our needs. When we see the greatness of God, we start to see life in perspective. Hannah knew the character of God and exalted His glorious attributes. She began by affirming His *holiness* and *uniqueness.* The two go together because in both Hebrew and Greek the word "holy" means "wholly other, set apart, separated." Orthodox Jews confess daily, "Hear, O Israel: the Lord our God is one Lord" (Deut. 6:4, KJV). There is no other God, and whenever Israel turned to idols for help, they lost the blessing of the Lord.

The "Rock" is one of the repeated images of the Lord in the Scriptures. It's found in the "Song of Moses" (Deut. 32:4, 15, 18, 30-31, 37) and in David's song (2 Sam. 22:32). The rock speaks of the Lord's strength, stability, and steadfastness and magnifies the fact that He does not change. We can depend on Him, for His character is unchangeable and His promises never fail. "For I am the Lord, I change not" (Mal. 3:6 KJV).

The Lord is also "a God of knowledge" (1 Sam. 2:3), so people had better be careful what they say and how they say it. There's no place for pride and arrogance when you stand before a God who knows you through and through, everything you've thought, spoken, and done. God heard all of Peninnah's haughty words spoken against Hannah, and He also heard Hannah's prayer from her heart. God is omniscient and knows all things, and He is omnipresent and beholds all things.

Hannah rejoiced because this holy God is a *just judge* of the actions of His people. Unlike the people involved in human judicial proceedings, the Lord knows everything and is able to weigh us and our actions accurately. He weighed Belshazzar and found him "wanting" (Dan. 5:27). The Lord weighs our motives (Prov. 16:2) and our hearts (24:11-12), and His scales are accurate. Like Hannah, we may be misunderstood and maligned by people, but the Lord will always act justly.

The grace of the Lord (1 Sam. 2:4-8a). God is holy and just and is always true to His Word and His character. But He is also merciful and gracious and often does things that catch us by surprise. Hannah described some of His acts and affirmed that the Lord turned everything upside down! The "Song of Mary" (The Magnificat) in Luke 1:46-55 expresses some of these same truths.

The mighty warriors fail while the stumbling weaklings win the battle (1 Sam. 2:4; see Ecc. 9:11). The rich people with plenty of food are looking for something to eat and are willing to labor for it, while the poor, hungry people have more than they need (1 Sam. 2:5a). The barren woman gives birth to seven children, while the woman with many children is exhausted and feeble and can't even enjoy her family (v. 5b). The truth in this statement is reflected in the fact that Hannah bore five more children (v. 21).

Because He is sovereign, the Lord is in charge of life and death and everything in between (v. 6). He can rescue us from the grave or permit us to die. If He allows us to live, He can make us rich or poor, exalted or abased, for He knows what's best. This doesn't suggest that people should meekly comply with difficult circumstances and do nothing about them, but that we can't change these circumstances without the Lord's help (Deut. 8:18). In His grace, God can choose the poor and raise them up to sit among the princes (see Ps. 113:7-8 and Luke 1:52). He takes them from the dust and the garbage heap and puts them on glorious thrones! But isn't that what God did for Jesus (Phil. 2:1-10) and what Jesus did for us when He saved us? (Eph. 2:1-10) Indeed, because of the cross, the Lord has "turned the world upside down" (Acts 17:6), and the only people who have clear vision and true values are those who have trusted Jesus.

The protection of the Lord (1 Sam. 2:8b-10a). God has established the world so that it can't be moved, and what happens on our planet is under His watchful care.[5] We may think that God has abandoned the earth to Satan and his demonic powers, but this is still our Father's world (Ps. 24:1-2), and He has set His King on heaven's throne (Ps. 2:7-9). As God's people walk on this earth and walk in the light, the Lord will guard and guide their steps, but the wicked will walk in spiritual darkness because they depend on their own wisdom and strength. It may seem that the wicked "have it made," but one day the storm of God's wrath will burst upon them in fierce judgment. God is long-suffering with those who resist Him, but their day is coming.

The reign of the Lord (1 Sam. 2:10b). This is a remarkable statement that the Lord will give an anointed king to Israel and strengthen him to serve Him and the nation. Hannah certainly knew the Law of Moses because in them she found the promises of a future king. God told Abraham and Sarah that kings would come from them (Gen. 17:6, 16), and He repeated this promise to Jacob (35:11). In his last words to his sons, Jacob announced that Judah would be the royal tribe (49:10); and in Deuteronomy 17:14-20, Moses gave instructions concerning a future king. When Israel asked for a king, God was prepared to grant their request. In many respects, King David fulfilled this prophecy; but the ultimate fulfillment is in Jesus the Christ ("Anointed One") who will one day sit on David's throne and rule over His glorious kingdom (Luke 1:32-33, 69-75).

Hannah and Elkanah left their son in Shiloh and returned to Ramah with joyful hearts and great expectation to see what the Lord would do. What a wonderful thing it is when a husband and wife are dedicated to the Lord, worship Him together, pray together, and trust His Word. Hannah went to the place of worship with a broken heart, but the Lord gave her peace because she prayed and submitted to His will.

4. God judges sin. (1 Sam. 2:12-36)

Up to this point, the focus has been on Elkanah and his family (1:1–2:11), but now it will shift to Eli and his family (2:12–3:21). Throughout this section, you will see a deliberate contrast between Samuel and the two sons of Eli, Hophni and Phinehas. Eli's sons "abhorred the offering of the Lord" (2:17), but "Samuel ministered before the Lord" (v. 18). The two brothers committed evil deeds at the tabernacle and invited God's judgment, but Samuel served at the tabernacle and grew in God's favor (v. 26). The priestly line would end in Eli's family, but Samuel would be called of God to carry on a holy priesthood (2:34–3:1). From the human viewpoint, it looked as though Eli's evil sons were getting away with their disobedience, but God was preparing judgment for them while He was equipping His servant Samuel to continue His work.

God's judgment deserved (1 Sam. 2:12-21). Since Eli was an old man with failing vision (4:15), he left the work of the tabernacle to his two sons, and they took advantage of their father by doing what they pleased. Hophni and Phinehas did not personally know the Lord but were "sons of Belial," a Hebrew term that described worthless people who openly practiced lawlessness (Deut. 13:13; Judg. 19:22; 1 Sam. 25:25; Prov. 16:27). In 2 Corinthians 6:15, Paul uses Belial as a synonym for Satan. The law stated precisely what portions of the sacrifices belonged to the priests (Lev. 7:28-36; 10:12-15; Deut. 18:1-5), but the two brothers took the meat that they wanted and also took the fat parts that belonged to the Lord. They even took raw meat so they could roast it and not have to eat boiled meat. They "abhorred the offering of the Lord" (1 Sam. 2:17) and "trampled on" (scorned) the Lord's sacrifices (v. 29).

Hophni and Phinehas not only showed disrespect for the sacrifices on the altar, but they also had no regard for the women who served at the door of the tabernacle (v. 22; Ex. 38:8). Instead of encouraging them in their spiritual walk, the two brothers seduced them. These women were not official servants appointed by the law but were volunteers who assisted the priests and Levites. Perhaps they helped care for the little children who came with the adult worshipers, or they may have been there just to be close to the presence of the Lord. Ministerial immorality is in the news today, and it's a tragic thing, but it's really nothing new.

In contrast to the wickedness of Eli's sons is the faithfulness of Samuel (1 Sam. 2:18-21). He was somewhat of an apprentice priest, learning the work of the sanctuary, and even wore a linen robe with an ephod (vest) over it, just as the adult priests and Levites did. Each year when his parents came to Shiloh, his mother would bring a new set of garments for the growing lad. In Scripture, garments often speak of the spiritual life (Isa. 61:10; Zech. 3:1-5; Eph. 4:22-32; Col. 3:8-17; 1 Peter 5:5), and a change of clothing symbolizes a new beginning (Gen. 35:2; 41:14; 45:22; Ex. 19:10; Rev. 3:18). Each year's new garments spoke not only of a boy growing physically but also spiritually (1 Sam. 2:21), and this reminds us of our Lord who "increased in wisdom and stature, and in favor with God and men" (Luke 2:52, NKJV).

God was about to bring judgment to the house of Eli, but the Lord blessed Elkanah and Hannah and their house, for He gave her five more children (1 Sam. 2:21; see Ps. 113:9). This was the gracious gift of God and an answer to the prayer of Eli (1 Sam. 2:20) who was pleased with Samuel and grateful for his ministry. Hannah gave one child to the Lord and the Lord gave back five!

God's judgment disregarded (1 Sam. 2:22-26). Godly people told Eli about his sons' sins, and he spoke to them about their conduct, but it did no good. He wasn't much of a godly father or spiritual leader, and his sons disregarded his warnings. It's tragic when a father—and a spiritual leader at that—loses his influence over his own family and can only wait for God's hand of judgment to fall. Lot lost his influence with his family (Gen. 19:12-14), and after David sinned with Bathsheba, his influence over his sons was greatly weakened. Hophni and Phinehas had no respect for the Lord or for the office of their father the high priest, so all God could do was judge them and replace them with faithful servants.

God's judgment declared (1 Sam. 2:27-36). An anonymous "man of God" appeared at Shiloh to declare the terms of God's judgment on Eli and his family. The title "man of God" is used some seventy times in the Old Testament and usually refers to a prophet sent by the Lord. First, the prophet dealt with *the past* (vv. 27-28) and reminded Eli that his position as high priest was a gift of God's grace. The Lord had chosen Aaron to be the first high priest and given him the privilege of passing this honor on to his eldest son (Ex. 4:14-16; 28:1-4). It was a privilege for the high priest and his sons to offer sacrifices on the brazen altar, burn incense on the golden altar, wear the sacred garments, and eat of the holy offerings. Then the messenger focused on *the present* (1 Sam. 2:29) and accused Eli of putting his sons ahead of the Lord and sharing in their sins. (The "you" at the beginning of v. 29 is plural and includes Eli with his sons.) To tolerate sin and not deal with it severely is to participate in that sin. As high priest, Eli had the authority to discipline his sons, but he refused to do so. "Do not share in the sins of others" (1 Tim. 5:22 NIV). If Eli had been a man of God, concerned for the glory of God, he would have remonstrated with his sons and called them to repent; and if they refused, he would have replaced them.

The burden of the prophet's message was centered on *the future* (1 Sam. 2:30-36). God had given the priesthood to Aaron and his descendants forever, and nobody could take this honor (Ex. 29:9; 40:15; Num. 18:7; Deut. 18:5). However, God's servants can't live any way they please and expect the Lord to honor them; for "them who honor me I will honor" (1 Sam. 2:30). The privilege of the priesthood would remain with the tribe of Levi and the house of Aaron, but God would take it away from Eli's branch of the family. Eli's descendants would become weak and die off and there would be no more old men like Eli in the family. They would have to beg for their food and would plead for an opportunity to serve (v. 36). In David's day the descendants of Eleazar outnumbered those of Ithamar at least two to one (1 Chron. 24:1-5), so Eli's family did slowly die out. But even worse, very soon Eli's two pampered sons would die on the same day. Even the tabernacle would experience distress (1 Sam. 2:32, NIV), which turned out to include the capture of the Ark and ultimately the moving of the tabernacle from Shiloh to Nob (21:1-6; Jer. 7:14). However, at Nob many of the priests were slain by Doeg, which was a partial fulfillment of this prophecy.

Eli descended from Aaron through Ithamar, Aaron's fourth son, but God would abandon that line and turn to the sons of Eleazar, Aaron's third son and successor in the high priesthood.[6] Under David, both Zadok and Abiathar served as high priests (2 Sam. 8:17), but when Solomon became king, he removed Eli's great-great grandson Abiathar from the high priesthood because he had cooperated with David's son Adonijah in his attempt to seize the throne. Solomon appointed Zadok to serve as high priest, and he was of the house of Eleazar. (See 1 Kings 2:26-27, 35.) In the list of Jewish high priests in 1 Chronicles 6:3-15, the names from Eli to Abiathar are missing. By confirming Zadok as high priest, Solomon fulfilled the prophecy given by the man of God nearly a century and a half before.[7]

But the future wasn't all bleak, for the man of God announced that God would raise up a faithful priest who would please God's heart and do God's will (1 Sam. 2:35). The immediate reference is to Zadok, but ultimately it points to Jesus Christ who alone could have a "sure house" and be God's anointed priest "forever." Our Lord came from the tribe of Judah, so He had no connection with the house of Aaron, but was made a high priest after the order of Melchizedek (Heb. 7–8).

5. God rewards faithfulness. (1 Sam. 3:1-21)

Once again we see the contrast between the wickedness of Eli's family and the faithfulness of the boy Samuel (v. 1). He ministered before the Lord under the guidance of Eli at a time when God wasn't speaking to His people very often. The spiritual leaders were corrupt, and God's people weren't obeying His law anyway, so why should God say anything new to them? It was a tragic day in the nation of Israel when the living God no longer sent His people signs and prophetic messages (Ps. 74:9; Ezek. 7:26; Amos 8:11-12; Micah 3:6). The silence of God was the judgment of God.

But God was about to change the situation and speak His precious Word to a young boy who would listen and obey.

An attentive ear (1 Sam. 3:1-9). Samuel was probably twelve years old when the Lord spoke to him one night as he lay in the tabernacle "annex" where Eli was also sleeping. The "lamp of God" was the seven-branched golden candlestick that stood in the holy place before the veil, to the left of the golden altar of incense (Ex. 25:31-40; 27:20-21; 37:17-24). It was the only source of light in the holy place, and the priests were ordered to keep it burning always (27:20) and to trim the wicks when they offered the incense each morning and evening (30:7-8). The lamp was a symbol of the light of God's truth given to the world through His people Israel. Alas, the light of God's Word was burning dimly in those days, and God's high priest was barely able to see! The Ark was there, containing the law of God (25:10-22; 37:1-9; Heb. 9:1-5), but the law was not honored by God's people.

The Lord spoke to Samuel four times (1 Sam. 3:4, 6, 8, 10), and the first three times, Samuel thought it was Eli calling him. One of the marks of a faithful servant is an attentive ear and an immediate response. But Samuel had never heard God's voice, so he didn't know who was calling to him. Like Saul of Tarsus, Samuel's call and conversion occurred at the same time, except that Samuel's experience was at night while Saul saw a blazing light when he heard God's voice (Acts 9:1-9). Eli was discerning enough to realize that God was speaking to the boy, so he told him how to respond.

An obedient will (1 Sam. 3:10-14). Samuel obeyed Eli, went back to his sleeping place, and waited for the voice to come again. This time God spoke the boy's name twice, for the Shepherd calls His sheep by name and gets their attention (John 10:3, 14).[8] Not only that, the Lord came and stood near Samuel as He spoke to him. This experience wasn't a dream or a vision but a manifestation of the presence of the Lord. Samuel's response was, "Speak, for your servant is listening" (1 Sam. 3:10, NIV), and he left out the word, "Lord" (see v. 9). Why? Samuel didn't yet have a personal knowledge of the Lord (v. 7), so he couldn't know whose voice it was that had spoken to him. Perhaps he was being careful not to accept it as the voice of Jehovah when he had no way to be sure.

Because Samuel was obedient to God and to Eli, he heard the message from the Lord and learned what God planned to do. This was certainly a weighty message to give to a young boy, but in so doing, perhaps God was rebuking the spiritual lethargy of the adults, for to which of them could God give this message? When God can't find an obedient adult, He sometimes calls a child. "And I will make mere lads their princes" (Isa. 3:4, NASB).

Samuel didn't know the message the unknown prophet had delivered to Eli, but the message God gave him confirmed it. The Lord would judge the house of Eli because Eli's two sons "made themselves vile [contemptible]" and Eli did nothing to restrain them. Though Eli and his sons were priests, they could offer no sacrifice that would atone for their sins! Their sins were deliberate and defiant, and for such sins no sacrifice could be offered (Num. 15:30). Not only had they defiled themselves, but they had also defiled the priesthood. The Lord had been long-suffering toward the house of Eli, but they hadn't repented and turned from their sins; now it was too late.

A humble heart (1 Sam. 3:15-18). Samuel had heard the voice of God and received the message of God, but he still got up early and went back to his old tasks. He opened the doors of the sanctuary so the people could come to sacrifice,[9] and he said nothing to Eli about what God had told him. This shows remarkable maturity on the part of a young boy. Most youths would have been proud of their experience with the Lord, rushed around delivering the message, and would not have stooped to open doors. It was only when Eli commanded him that Samuel related the message of judgment that God had given to him.

Was Eli's response to the message active submission or passive resignation to something that couldn't be changed? I vote for resignation, the same attitude that Hezekiah displayed when Isaiah told him his foolish actions would one day bring ruin to the kingdom of Judah (Isa. 39). Eli was an old man who had not been a good father or a faithful priest, and he had already been warned that judgment was coming. His two sons would perish in one day and his family would lose the privilege of the priesthood, so what was there to live for? God had chosen Samuel to be judge, priest, and prophet, so the light of truth would keep burning in Israel. All the old man could do was to wait patiently for the sword to fall.

Eli had his faults as we all do, and we must appreciate his positive attitude toward young Samuel, his successor as the spiritual leader in Israel. It isn't every veteran servant who can graciously lay down his tools and let the young apprentice take over. Until the very end of his life, Eli at least had a concern for the Ark of God and the future of the nation; and the news of Israel's defeat and the capture of the Ark caused his death. If Eli had shown some of this concern when his sons were young like Samuel, things would have been different.

A godly walk (1 Sam. 3:19-21). For the second time we're told that Samuel grew (2:21; 3:19), but the affirmation is added, "the Lord was with him." This statement will also be made about youthful David (16:18; 18:12, 14). The Lord was against Eli and his sons, but His blessing was upon Samuel and his ministry. Unlike the other judges, Samuel's words and influence would reach the entire nation. The people recognized that God had called Samuel to be a prophet and declare the Word of God and the will of God. Once again, the Lord appeared from time to time at Shiloh and revealed Himself to His prophet. Israel was about to experience a new beginning that would lead to new challenges and dangers as well as new blessings and victories.

CHAPTER TWO
ISRAEL'S DEFEAT—GOD'S VICTORY
1 Samuel 4–6

The Ark of the Covenant is mentioned at least thirty-five times in these three chapters and represents Jehovah God, the central person in all of Israel's history. The Ark was the most important piece of furniture in the tabernacle and resided in the Holy of Holies. In the Ark were the two tablets of the law, and on it was the golden "mercy seat" where God's glorious presence dwelt. This was the throne of God from which He spoke to His people (Ex. 25:10-22). To the eye of faith, God is very evident and active in all the events recorded in these chapters. None of these events happened by accident; they were all part of God's plan to chasten His people, judge sinners, and eventually establish His anointed king

1. The faithful Word of God (1 Sam. 4:1-22)

No sooner does God begin to reveal His Word to His people than the enemy shows up to attack them. The Philistines are mentioned in Scripture as early as the days of Abraham (Gen. 21:32; see 10:14), and in the Books of Samuel they're mentioned over 150 times. They were originally a seagoing people from the Aegean region who invaded the territory along the Mediterranean coast (Phoenicia) and sought to control all of the land we know as Palestine. (The name "Palestine" is a form of the word "Philistine.") The Philistines were very distressed when Israel conquered the Promised Land and many times attempted to drive them out. It's likely that this particular battle was Israel's response to one of those Philistine invasions.

Israel was defeated (1 Sam. 4:1-10). Aphek was a northern Philistine city about three miles west of the Jewish city of Ebenezer ("stone of help").[1] Shiloh lay about twenty miles east of Ebenezer. In their initial confrontation, the Philistines defeated Israel and killed 4,000 men, and the elders of Israel were perplexed over this defeat. Wasn't Israel God's chosen nation, and didn't He give them the land as their possession? Then why was Israel defeated by their idol-worshiping neighbors? If the elders had recalled the terms of God's covenant, they would have realized that this shameful defeat was caused by Israel's disobedience to God's law (Lev. 26:39; Deut. 28:25).

The Lord had clearly told them how to fight their wars (Deut. 20), but instead of searching their hearts and confessing their sins, the people decided to imitate Moses and Joshua and take the Ark of the Covenant into the battle with them. (See Num. 10:33-36; Josh. 3–4 and 6.) But this approach was merely "using God" to accomplish their own purposes. Unlike Moses and Joshua, they didn't seek the will of the Lord, they weren't walking by faith, and they certainly weren't seeking to glorify God. Even worse, the two wicked priests Hophni and Phinehas would be carrying the holy Ark of God! How could God bless two sinful men whom He had already consigned to judgment? (1 Sam. 2:29, 34–4:4,17) But Israel's hope was that the presence of the Ark would save the Jews from the hand of their enemies.[2]

When Hophni and Phinehas appeared in the camp carrying the Ark of God, the soldiers and elders shouted enthusiastically, but their carnal self-confidence was just the prelude to another defeat. The Ark may have been with them in the camp, but the Lord was against them. Their joyful shout may have bolstered their spirits, but it was no guarantee of victory. All it did was motivate the Philistine army to determine to fight harder and win the battle, which they did, killing 30,000 Jewish soldiers. God will not be "used" just to make sinful people achieve their own selfish purposes. God's promise is, "Them who honor me I will honor" (2:30).

The Ark was taken (1 Sam. 4:11a). Five times in verses 11-22 you find the phrase "the Ark of God was [is] taken" (vv. 11, 17, 19, 21-22). Never in the history of Israel had the Ark of God ever fallen into enemy hands! So holy was the Ark that it was kept behind the veil in the tabernacle and seen only by the high priest on the annual Day of Atonement (Lev. 16). When the Jewish camp moved during the nation's years of wandering, the first thing the high priest did was cover the Ark with the veil (Num. 4:5-6), and only then would he attend to the other pieces of furniture.

The Ark of God was the throne of God (2 Sam. 6:2, NIV; also Pss. 80:1 and 99:1), but now God's throne was in enemy territory! The Jews had forgotten that the Ark was God's throne in Israel *only if Israel was submitted to Him and obedient to His covenant.* Anything else was nothing but ignorant superstition, like people trusting good-luck charms. It wasn't a sin to take the Ark into battle if the people were truly devoted to the Lord and wanted to honor Him. God put the Ark into pagan hands, but Eli's two sons had lived like pagans while ministering before the Ark, so what was the difference? God would use the Ark to teach both the Jews and the Philistines some important lessons.

The two priests were slain (1 Sam. 4;11b). This fulfilled the Word of God spoken to Eli by the anonymous prophet (2:27-36) and to Samuel when he was called by the Lord (3:11-18). God had been long-suffering with Hophni and Phinehas as they desecrated His sacrifices and defiled His people, but now their time was up and their sins had found them out.

The high priest died (1 Sam. 4:12-18). Eli knew that his sons had entered the Holy of Holies and taken the Ark to the battlefield, but he was unable to stop them, just as he had been unable to control them in past years. He wasn't worrying about his sons as he sat in his special seat by the tabernacle; he was trembling for the safety of the Ark of God. But didn't Eli realize that God was still on the heavenly throne even if His earthly throne had been cheapened and transformed into a good-luck charm? Wasn't the Lord able to protect His own furniture and His own glory?

The messenger ran first to the busiest part of Shiloh and delivered the sad news of Israel's defeat, and the people's loud lamenting caught Eli's attention. The messenger ran to Eli to gave him the bad news: Israel was defeated, there was a great slaughter, Hophni and Phinehas were both slain and—as if saving the worst news for the last—the Ark of God had been taken by the Philistines. Eli must have suffered a stroke or a heart attack, for he fell back, broke his neck, and died. He was "a heavy man,"[3] probably caused by eating too much meat from the sacrifices (2:29) and leading a sedentary life. The death of Eli and his two sons was the beginning of the fulfillment of God's prophecy that Eli's branch of the priesthood would be destroyed and a new line introduced.

The glory of God departed (1 Sam. 4:19-22). The wife of Phinehas had more spiritual insight than her father-in-law, her husband, and her brother-in-law. The two brothers used the Ark as a good luck charm, Eli was concerned with the safety of the Ark, but she was burdened for the glory of God. She named her son Ichabod—"the glory is gone"—and then she died.[4] The presence of God's glory in the camp was a special sign that the Israelites were the people of God (Ex. 40:34; Rom. 9:4), but now the glory had departed and God's special favor was gone. When King Solomon dedicated the temple, the glory of God returned (1 Kings 8:10), but before the destruction of Jerusalem, the Prophet Ezekiel saw the glory leave the temple and the city (Ezek. 8:4; 9:3; 10:4, 18; 11:22-23). Ezekiel also saw the future millennial temple and the return of the glory of God (Ezek. 43:1-5). The glory of God didn't return to this earth until the birth of Jesus Christ, the Savior of the world (Luke 2:8-11; John 1:14). Today, God's glory dwells in His people individually (1 Cor. 6:19-20) and in His church collectively (Eph. 2:19-22).

So significant was this tragic event that Asaph the psalmist included it in one of his psalms (Ps. 78:60-61). But he tells us that much more happened than the capture of the Ark by the Philistines, for the Lord abandoned the tabernacle at Shiloh and allowed the enemy to destroy it (Jer. 7:12-14; 26:6, 9). The Philistines eventually returned the Ark and it remained first in Beth-shemesh and then Kiriath-jearim (1 Sam. 6:13-21). The priests must have constructed some kind of tabernacle at Nob (1 Sam. 21:1ff), but in Solomon's day, it was at Gibeon (1 Chron. 21:29; 1 Kings 3:4). Eventually Solomon incorporated the tabernacle into the temple which he built (2 Chron. 5:5).

The wicked sons of Eli thought their scheme would save the glory of God, but it only took the glory of God away!

2. The vindicating power of God (1 Sam. 5:1-12)

The five key cities of the Philistines were

Ashdod, Gaza, Ashkelon, Gath, and Ekron, and each had a ruler or "lord" (6:16-17). The Philistines first put the Ark into the temple of their god Dagon in Ashdod as evidence that Dagon was stronger and greater than Jehovah. At the beginning of the battle, the Philistines were frightened when they heard that the God of Israel was in the camp, but now they were making fun of Him and exalting their own gods. In their mythology, Dagon was the principal god of the Philistines and the father of Baal, the storm god, whose worship brought so much trouble to Israel.

However, Dagon didn't have a chance, for Jehovah God was and is well able to take care of Himself! The next morning, the worshipers found Dagon prostrate before the Ark like one of the worshipers. Like every dead idol, Dagon had to be righted again (Ps. 115), but things were even worse the next morning. The stump of Dagon was prostrate before the Ark of the Covenant, but his head and hands had been cut off and placed at the threshold of the temple! But that wasn't the end, for the Lord not only humiliated the god of the Philistines, but he judged the people who worshiped that god. When the Philistines captured the Ark and arrogantly treated the Lord as though He were just another god, they invited the judgment of God.

When you put the evidence together, it seems that the Lord sent infected mice or rats (1 Sam. 6:4) among the people and spread a terrible plague. According to the covenant, the Lord should have sent this affliction on the unbelieving Jews (Deut. 28:58-60), but in His grace, He punished the enemy. Some students believe this was the bubonic plague and that the people experienced painful inflammatory swellings of the lymph glands, especially in the groin. Others think it was a plague of tumors, perhaps severe hemorrhoids (see 1 Sam. 5:9), although it's difficult to understand the part the rats played in this affliction. Whatever the punishment was, it pained and humiliated the Philistines who attributed their suffering to the presence of the Ark.

But the five lords of the Philistines were anxious to preserve the glory of their victory. If they could prove that the calamity was a coincidence, they could retain the Ark and continue to magnify Dagon's superiority over Jehovah. The easiest way to do this was to move the Ark to another city and see what happened, so they took it to Gath—and the same thing happened! Then they carried it to Ekron, where the people protested and told them to take it elsewhere! God killed a number of citizens ("deadly destruction") and also sent a painful plague to the people of Ekron just as He had done to the inhabitants of Ashdod and Gath. God had vindicated Himself and proved that it was His hand that had destroyed the statue of Dagon and that brought affliction to the Philistine people. Nobody could call the eruption of these plagues a mere coincidence. But the lords of the Philistines still had to figure out how to get rid of the Ark without humiliating themselves and perhaps bringing more judgment on their land.

3. The wise providence of God (1 Sam. 6:1-18)

The experiences described in 5:1-12 occurred during a period of seven months, at the end of which the five lords decided it was time to get rid of the Ark. They wouldn't admit it, but Jehovah had vindicated Himself before the Philistines and humiliated their false god. Still wanting to save face, the lords sought some way to send the Ark back to Israel without directly involving themselves or their people.

Man proposes (1 Sam. 6:1-9). The Philistine wise men came up with a scheme that would test the God of Israel one more time. If Jehovah, represented by the Ark, was indeed the true and living God, *let Him take the Ark back to where it belonged!* The lords set up a plan that would absolve them of responsibility and blame. They would take two cows that had calves and separate them from the calves. They would hitch the cows to a new cart, put the Ark on the cart, and turn the cows loose. If the cows didn't move at all, or if they went to their calves, it would be "proof" that the God of Israel wasn't in control and the Philistines had nothing to fear. If the cows meandered all over without any sense of direction, the lords could draw the same conclusion. The situation being what it was, the cows would probably head for their calves, because that was the natural thing to do. The cows needed to get rid of their milk and the calves needed the nourishment.

But that wasn't all. The wise men decided that the nation had to send "appeasement gifts" to Jehovah in the form of golden models of the mice and the tumors. If the cows didn't head for Israelite territory, the Philistines could always reclaim their gold. If the cows went over the border into Israel, the Lord would be appeased and wouldn't send Philistia any more plagues. This plan enabled the Lord to receive glory without the lords of the Philistines being embarrassed. When you consider that the cows were nursing their calves and lowing for them, and that the cows had never drawn a cart before, the odds were that they wouldn't go down the road that led from Ekron to Beth-Shemesh. The five lords and their wise men had it all figured out.

God disposes (1 Sam. 6:10-18). But they were wrong. The lords of the Philistines didn't know the true and living God, but the cows did, and they obeyed Him! "The ox knows its owner and the donkey its master's crib" (Isa. 1:3, NKJV). They crossed the border and came to the priestly city of Beth-Shemesh (Josh. 21:13-16) where the men were working in the fields harvesting the wheat. They joyfully welcomed the return of the Ark, and the Levites took it off the cart and put it on a great stone in the field.

Grateful that the throne of God had been restored to His people, the Levites offered the cows as burnt offerings to the Lord, and in their joy ignored the fact that only male animals could legally be offered (Lev. 1:3). Other men from the city brought additional sacrifices. They also put the golden gifts on the rock and offered them to the Lord. Since Shiloh had been destroyed and there was no sanctuary available for worship, they used the large rock as an altar, and the Lord accepted their offerings. What the Lord is looking for is a broken and contrite heart, not a slavish obedience to the letter of the law (Ps. 51:15-17). The enemy was near at hand (1 Sam. 6:16) and the Jewish men didn't dare leave the place to which God had directed the cows.

God had done what Dagon could never do: He guided the cows, kept their attention on the right road, overcame their desire to go to their calves, and brought them to the priestly city of Beth-Shemesh. His providence rules over all. Alas, the priests and Levites didn't do their job well, and what should have been a great cause for joy turned out to be a cause of sorrow because of man's foolishness. Eventually the Ark would be given a safe resting place until King David would move it to a specially prepared place in Jerusalem (2 Sam. 6:12ff).

4. The holy wrath of God (1 Sam. 6:19-20)

The men of Beth-Shemesh should have covered the Ark, because it wasn't supposed to be seen by anyone except the high priest, and this mistake was costly. Some of the people became curious and looked into the Ark and were slain. If the pagan Philistines were judged for the way they treated the Ark, how much more responsible were the Jews who knew the law and were living in a levitical city!

Students have debated the accuracy of the number of people who were killed, because 50,000 seems too high for a town like Beth-Shemesh. Some make the number only 70 and say that the 50,000 is a scribal error, and perhaps it is. The Hebrews used letters for numbers and it would be easy for a copyist to make a mistake. Others include in the 50,000 the 4,000 plus "the great slaughter" (4:17) on the battlefield, but the text specifically says it was the irreverent people who looked into the Ark who were slain. (See 1 Sam. 6:19; Lev. 16:13; Num. 1:50-51; 4:5, 16-20.) It isn't likely that 50,000 people lined up and passed by the Ark, for the people queued up would have scattered when the first viewers were killed. Perhaps they were slain later. Certainly the Levites would have protected the Ark from the curious, for they knew the penalties for breaking the law of God. That 70 men were judged isn't difficult to believe, but 50,000 seems extravagant. However, since we don't know the population of Beth-Shemesh and its environs, we can't pass judgment on the text. One day an archeologist may solve the problem for us.

While God doesn't live in our church buildings or in any of its furnishings (Acts 7:48-50), we do want to show respect for anything dedicated to the the glory of God. The awesome event described here certainly warns us against religious curiosity and lack of reverence for the Lord. "It is a fearful thing to fall into the hands of the living God" (Heb. 10:31, KJV). In today's Western society, with its informality and lack of respect for the sacred, it's easy even for believers to get so "chummy" with the Lord that they forget He is "high and lifted up."

5. The merciful grace of God (1 Sam. 6:21–7:2)

The Lord could have withdrawn Himself from His people, but instead, He graciously allowed the Ark to be taken about ten miles to Kiriath Jearim where it remained in the home of Abinadab. The men of the city consecrated Abinadab's son Eleazar to guard the Ark. This was undoubtedly a levitical family, for after what had happened to the men of Beth-Shemesh, the men weren't likely to take any more chances by breaking the law! The Ark remained in Kiriath Jearim for perhaps a century, for the battle of Aphek was fought about 1104 B.C., and David brought the Ark to Jerusalem in about 1003 B.C. (2 Sam. 6). The Ark had been in the home of Abinadab twenty years when Samuel called an assembly of the people to turn from their sins and seek the Lord (1 Sam. 7:3).

The Ark of the Covenant represented the presence of the Lord with His people and the rule of the Lord over His people. The Lord had every right to abandon His sinful people, but He graciously remained with them, though not in the special tabernacle He had commanded them to build. It was a difficult time for the Jews, for they were not a united people, nor were they a godly people. Israel thought that their problems would be solved if they had a king like the other nations, but they would discover that having their own way would lead them into greater problems. God still gives His best to those who leave the choice with Him.

What the Ark was to Israel, Jesus Christ is to God's people today; and when He is given His rightful place of preeminence in our lives, He will bless us and work on our behalf. "But in your hearts set apart Christ as Lord," is the way Peter explained it (1 Peter 3:15, NIV). When Jesus Christ is Lord, the future is your friend, and you can walk through each day confident of His presence and His help.

CHAPTER THREE
THE CALL FOR A KING
1 Samuel 7-11

The Ark of the Covenant was now out of enemy hands and resting in the house of Abinadab in Kiriath Jearim in the territory of Benjamin (1 Sam. 1-2; Josh. 18:28). Shiloh had been destroyed by the Philistines and was no longer the location of the sanctuary of the Lord, and many years would pass before the Ark would be moved to Jerusalem by King David (1 Chron. 15). But having the Ark in Jewish territory didn't automatically solve Israel's problems, for during those twenty years when the Ark was in Abinidab's house, a new generation had arisen and was crying out for radical changes in Israel's government. For centuries, the people of Israel had looked to Jehovah as their King, but now they asked the Lord to give them a king just like the other nations. It was a critical time in the history of Israel, and it took the prayers and guidance of Samuel to bring them safely through this dangerous time of transition.

1. Seeking the Lord (1 Sam. 7:3-17)

Samuel discerned that the people were restless and wanting change, and he knew that times of transition bring out either the best or the worst in people. God called Samuel to build a bridge between the turbulent age of the judges and the new era of the monarchy, and it wasn't an easy task. There was one thing Samuel knew for certain: king or no king, the nation could never succeed if the people didn't put the Lord first and trust only in Him. That's why he called for a meeting at Mizpah, a city in Benjamin (Josh. 18:26), where he challenged God's covenant people to return to the Lord.

They put away their false gods (1 Sam. 7:3-4). Idolatry had been Israel's besetting sin. Jacob's family carried false gods with them (Gen. 35:2), and when the Jews were slaves in Egypt, they adopted the gods and goddesses of the Egyptians, and after the Exodus, worshiped some of these idols during the wilderness journeys (Acts 7:42-43). Moses commanded Israel to destroy every evidence of Canaanite religion, but the people eventually lapsed back into idolatry and worshiped the gods of the defeated enemy. Samuel specifically mentioned the Baals and Ashtoreths (1 Sam. 7:3-4). Baal was the Canaanite storm god to whom the Jews often turned when the land was suffering drought, and Ashtoreth was the goddess of fertility whose worship included unspeakably sensual activities. At Mount Sinai, the Jews didn't see a representation of God, but they heard His voice; and they knew that worshiping any image of their God was to practice false worship.

Putting away their false gods was only the beginning of their return to the Lord; the Jews also had to prepare their hearts for the Lord and devote themselves to the Lord alone (v. 3). This was in keeping with the first commandment, "You shall have no other gods before me" (Ex. 20:3, NIV). An idol is a substitute for God—anything that we trust and serve in place of the Lord. The Jews gave themselves to idols of wood, stone, and metal, but believers today have more subtle and attractive gods: houses and lands, wealth, automobiles, boats, position and recognition, ambition, and even other people. Anything in our lives that takes the place of God and commands the sacrifice and devotion that belong only to Him, is an idol and must be cast out. Idols in the heart are far more dangerous than idols in the temple.

They confessed their sins (1 Sam. 7:5-6). Samuel planned to lead the people in a time of worship and intercession for deliverance from their enemies, but if they had iniquity in their hearts, the Lord would not hear them (Ps. 66:18). It wasn't enough just to destroy their idols; the people also had to confess their sins and surrender themselves to the Lord. Two considerations suggest that this meeting occurred during the time of the Feast of Tabernacles. First, the people poured out water before the Lord, which became a practice at the Feast of Tabernacles, commemorating the times the Lord provided water in the wilderness (John 7:37-39). Second, the people fasted, and this was required only on the annual Day of Atonement, which preceded the Feast of Tabernacles.[1]

The key activity that day was their confession, "We have sinned against the Lord." God's covenant promise to Israel was that He would forgive their sins if they sincerely confessed them to Him (Lev. 26:40-45), for no amount of sacrifices or rituals could wash away their sins. "The sacrifices of God are a broken spirit, a broken and a contrite heart—these, O God, you will not despise" (Ps. 51:17, NKJV). Later in Israel's history, this promise of forgiveness and blessing was reiterated by Solomon at the dedication of the temple (2 Chron. 7:14).

They prayed for God's help (1 Sam. 7:7-11, 13-14). When the Philistines learned about this large gathering of Jews, they became suspicious that Israel was planning to attack, so the five Philistine lords summoned their troops and prepared to invade. Israel had no standing army and no one ruler to organize one, so they felt helpless. But their greatest weapon was their faith in Jehovah God, a faith that was expressed in prayer. "Some trust in chariots, and some in horses, but we will remember the name of the Lord our God" (Ps. 20:7, KJV). As we have seen, Samuel was a man of prayer (99:6), and God answered him that day. As he sacrificed the evening burnt offering, the Lord thundered against the Philistine soldiers and so confused them that it was easy for Israel to attack and defeat them. When we remember that Baal was the Canaanite storm god, it makes the power of God's thunder even more significant.

All the days of Samuel, the Lord kept the Philistines at a distance from Israel. Because of this victory, the Jews recovered cities they had lost in battle and even gained the Amorites as allies. Whenever God's people depend on their own plans and resources, their efforts fail and bring disgrace to God's name; but when God's people trust the Lord and pray, He meets the need and receives the glory. A man or woman of prayer is more powerful than a whole army! No wonder King Jehoash called the Prophet Elisha "the chariots and horsemen of Israel" (2 Kings 13:14), a title Elisha had used for his mentor Elijah (2 Kings 2:12 and see 6:17). Do we have such men and women of prayer today?

They commemorated the victory (1

Sam. 7:12). The setting up of stones to commemorate significant events has been a part of the Hebrew culture since Jacob set up a memorial at Bethel (Gen. 28:20-22; 35:14). Joshua set up twelve stones in the midst of the Jordan (Josh. 4:9) and twelve more on the western bank at Gilgal to mark the place where the waters opened and Israel crossed into the Promised Land (vv. 4:1-8, 19-21). A great heap of stones in the Achor Valley reminded the Jews of Achan's disobedience (vv. 7:24-26), and another heap marked the burial place of the king of Ai (8:29). Another heap stood at a cave at Makkedah to mark where five kings had been defeated and slain (10:25-27). Before his death, Joshua set up a "witness stone" to remind the Israelites of their vow to serve the Lord alone and obey Him (24:26-28).

"Ebenezer" means "stone of help" because the monument was a reminder to the Jews that God had helped them that far and would continue to help them if they would trust Him and keep His covenant. The founder of the China Inland Mission, J. Hudson Taylor, had a plaque displayed in each of his residences that read "Ebenezer—Jehovah Jireh," Together, these Hebrew words say, "The Lord has helped us to this point, and He will see to it from now on." What an encouragement to our faith!

They respected Samuel (1 Sam. 7:15-17). It's likely that this meeting at Mizpah marked the beginning of Samuel's public ministry to the whole nation of Israel, so that from that time on he was a focal point for political unity and spiritual authority. The nation knew that Samuel was God's appointed leader (3:20–4:1), and when he died, the entire nation mourned him (28:3). He made his home in Ramah and established a circuit of ministry to teach the people the law, to hear cases, to give counsel, and to pass judgment. His two sons assisted him by serving at Beersheba (8:1-2). Israel was blessed to have a man like Samuel to guide them, but the times were changing and Israel's elders wanted the nation to change as well.

2. Rejecting the Lord (1 Sam. 8:1-22)

Probably twenty or twenty-five years elapsed between the events recorded in chapter 7 and those in chapter 8. Samuel was now an old man, about to pass from the scene, and a new generation had emerged in Israel with new leaders who had new ideas. Life goes on, circumstances change, and God's people must have wisdom to adapt to new challenges without abandoning old convictions. Like more than one great leader, Samuel in his old age faced some painful situations and had to make some difficult decisions. He left the scene convinced that he had been rejected by the people he had served so faithfully. Samuel obeyed the Lord, but he was a man with a broken heart.

God had chosen Moses to lead the nation of Israel and Joshua to succeed him (Deut. 31:1-15), but Joshua wasn't commanded to lay hands on any successor. He left behind elders whom he had trained to serve God, but when they died, the new generation turned away from the Lord and followed the idols of the land (Judg. 2:10-15). There was an automatic succession to the priesthood, and the Lord could call out prophets when needed, but who would lead the people and see to it that the law was obeyed? During the period of the judges, God raised up leaders here and there and gave them great victories, but nobody was in charge of the nation as a whole. "In those days there was no king in Israel; every man did that which was right in his own eyes" (Judg. 21:25; see 17:6; 18:1; 19:1). The "nation" of Israel was a loose confederation of sovereign tribes, and each tribe was expected to seek the Lord and do His will.

Asking for a king (1 Sam. 8:1-9). Knowing that Israel needed a stronger central government, the elders presented their request to Samuel and backed it up with several arguments. The first two must have cut Samuel to the quick: he was now old and had no successor, and his two sons were not godly men but took bribes (1 Sam. 8:3-5). How tragic that both Eli and Samuel had sons who failed to follow the Lord. Eli was too easy on his wayward sons (2:29), and perhaps Samuel was away from home too much as he made his ministry circuit to the cities. Samuel's sons were miles away in Beersheba where their father couldn't monitor their work, but if the elders knew about their sins, surely their father must have known also.

When the elders asked to have a king "like all the nations" (8:5, 20), they were forgetting that Israel's strength was to be *unlike* the other nations. The Israelites were God's covenant people and He was their King. The glory of God dwelt in their midst and the law of God was their wisdom. (See Ex. 19:3-6; 33:15-16; Lev. 18:30 and 20:26; Num. 23:9.) But the elders were concerned about national security and protection from the enemies around them. The Philistines were still a powerful nation, and the Ammonites were also a threat (1 Sam. 12:12). Israel had no standing army and no king to lead it. The elders forgot that it was the Lord who was Israel's King and who gave her army the ability to defeat the enemy.

Samuel was a man of spiritual insight and he knew that this demand for a king was evidence of spiritual decay among the leaders. They weren't rejecting *him*; they were rejecting God, and this grieved Samuel's heart as he prayed to the Lord for wisdom. This wasn't the first time the people had rejected their Lord. At Sinai, their request was "Make us gods!" (Ex. 32:1) and after their humiliating failure at Kadesh Barnea, they said, "Let us make a captain, and let us return into Egypt" (Num. 14:4).[2] Whenever leadership in a church decays spiritually, that church becomes more like the world and uses the world's methods and resources to try to do God's work. The Jewish leaders in Samuel's day had no faith that God could defeat their enemies and protect His people, so they chose to lean on the arm of flesh.

God is never surprised by what His people do, nor is He at a loss to know what He should do. "The Lord brings the counsel of the nations to nothing; He makes the plans of the peoples of no effect. The counsel of the Lord stands forever, the plans of His heart to all generations" (Ps. 33:10-11, NKJV). There is every evidence in the Pentateuch that Israel would one day have a king. God promised Abraham, Sarah, and Jacob that kings would be among their descendants (Gen. 17:6, 16; 35:11), and Jacob had named Judah as the kingly tribe (49:10). Moses prepared the nation for a king when he spoke to the new generation preparing to enter the Promised Land (Deut. 17:14-20).

It wasn't Israel's request for a king that was their greatest sin; it was their insisting that God give them a king immediately. The Lord had a king in mind for them, David the son of Jesse, but the time wasn't ripe for him to appear. So, the Lord gave them their request by appointing Saul to be king, and He used Saul to chasten the nation and prepare them for David, the man of His choice. The fact that Saul was from the tribe of Benjamin and not from Judah is evidence enough that he was never expected to establish a dynasty in Israel. "So in my anger I gave you a king, and in my wrath I took him away" (Hosea 13:11, NIV). The greatest judgment God can give us is to let us have our own way. "And He gave them their request, but sent leanness into their soul" (Ps. 106:15, NKJV). However, the Lord wanted His people to go into this new venture with their eyes open, so He commanded Samuel to tell them what it would cost them to have a king.

Paying for a king (1 Sam. 8:10-22). What's true of individuals is true of nations: you take what you want from life and you pay for it. Under the kingship of Jehovah God, the nation had security and sufficiency as long as they obeyed Him, and His demands were not unreasonable. To obey God's covenant meant to live a happy life as the Lord gave you all that you needed and more. But the key word in Samuel's speech is *take*, not give. The king and his court had to be supported, so he would take their sons and daughters, their property, their harvests, and their flocks and herds. Their choice young men would serve in the army as well as in the king's fields. Their daughters would cook and bake for the king. He would take their property and part of their harvest in order to feed the officials and servants in the royal household. While these things weren't too evident under Saul and David, they were certainly obvious under Solomon (1 Kings 4:7-28). The day came when the people cried out for relief from the heavy yoke Solomon had put on them just to maintain the glory of his kingdom (12:1-4; see Jer. 22:13-17).

In spite of these warnings, the people insisted that God give them a king. Pleasing the Lord wasn't the thing uppermost in their minds; what they wanted was guaranteed protection against their enemies. They wanted someone to judge them and fight their battles, someone they could see and follow. They found it too demanding to trust an invisible God and obey His wonderful commandments. In spite of all the Lord had done for Israel from the call of Abraham to the conquest of the Promised Land, they turned their back on Almighty God and chose to have a frail man to rule over them.

3. Obeying the Lord (1 Sam. 9:1–10:27)

The focus now shifts from Samuel to Saul, God's choice for Israel's king. He was from the tribe of Benjamin, which had almost been exterminated because of their rebellion against the law (Judg. 19–20). Jacob compared Benjamin to "a ravening wolf" (Gen. 49:27), and the tribe was involved in numerous battles. Benjamin's territory lay between Ephraim and Judah, so Saul's tribe was adjacent to the royal tribe of Judah. In spite of what Saul said to Samuel in 1 Samuel 9:21, he belonged to a powerful and wealthy family that owned real estate and animals and had servants.

Physically, Saul was tall, good-looking, and strong, the kind of king people would admire. Even Samuel, with all his spiritual perception, got carried away when he saw him (10:23-24). His weakness for admiring the physical qualities even showed up when Samuel went to anoint David (16:1-7). Saul was obedient to his father and concerned about his father's feelings (9:5), and he was persistent in wanting to obey his father's will. To invest all that time and energy looking for the lost animals suggests that he wasn't a quitter. There was a certain amount of modesty in Saul (v. 21; 10:14-16), but there was no indication of spiritual life.

Samuel meets Saul (1 Sam. 9:1-25). Saul's home was in Gibeah, which was about five miles from Ramah where Samuel lived, and yet Saul didn't even know what all Israel knew (3:20), that a man of God named Samuel lived in Ramah (9:6). How Saul could live so close to Israel's spiritual leader and not know about him is a bit of a mystery and suggests that Saul simply lived and farmed with his family at Gibeah and minded his own business. Apparently he didn't attend the annual feasts and wasn't greatly concerned about spiritual matters. Like many people today, he wasn't against religion, but he didn't make knowing the Lord a vital part of his life. It's a good thing the servant knew about Samuel and that Saul heeded his advice!

A rather insignificant event brought Saul and Samuel together—the loss of some of Kish's donkeys. The animals were valuable, of course, and later somebody found them and returned them to Kish (10:2), but who would have thought that Israel's first king would be called to the throne while searching for donkeys! David was identified with sheep (Ps. 78:70-72; 1 Sam. 17:15) and saw the people of Israel as sheep who needed protection and guidance (2 Sam. 24:17). The Lord works in unusual ways, but if Saul had not obeyed his father and listened to his servant, the story might have been different.

It was evening when the two men arrived at the gates of Ramah, because the young ladies were going out to draw water. Asking the girls if the seer was there, they were given a long detailed answer. Perhaps the Jewish maids were happy to chat with a tall, handsome stranger! Even the time of Saul's arrival at the city was providential, for Samuel appeared just as Saul and his servant entered the city. Samuel was going up to a "high place" outside the city where he would offer a sacrifice to the Lord. Since there was no central sanctuary in Israel at that time, the people brought their sacrifices to a shrine that was dedicated to the Lord and located on a hill near the city. The pagan nations worshiped their false gods at the high places and also indulged in filthy practices there, but the people of Israel were forbidden to join them (Ps. 78:58; Hosea 4:11-14; Jer. 3:2).

The day before, the Lord had told Samuel that Saul was coming to Ramah, so he was prepared to meet him and give him God's message. Samuel couldn't say he was happy about the changes going on in Israel, but he was obedient to the Lord. The word "captain" in 1 Samuel 9:16 (KJV) simply means "leader." When Saul appeared, the Lord spoke again to Samuel and confirmed that this was indeed the man of His choice and that Samuel should anoint him as king. "God's anointed" was one of the titles for the king (12:3; 24:6; 26:9, 11, 16; Ps. 2:2, 6). The Lord would use Saul as He did Samson (Judg. 13:5), to begin to weaken the Philistines and prepare them for David's final conquest of this enemy of the Jews (1 Chron. 18:1).

Samuel's response to Saul's request must have shocked the young man. Saul discovered that he was speaking to the man he was seeking, that he would feast with him that day, that Samuel had a special message for him, and that the missing donkeys had been found and returned to his father. Furthermore, all the desire of Israel was fixed on Saul, because all Israel wanted a king. Saul didn't understand what Samuel was saying, but everything would be explained to him the next day. Samuel ignored Saul's protest that he was a nobody who belonged to an insignificant tribe, and he escorted Saul and his servant to the banquet hall at the high place where the feast would be held. Saul was given the special portion of the fellowship offering that belonged to the priest (1 Sam. 9:24; Lev. 7:32-33), and the cook informed him that the portion had been set aside especially for him. Strange things were happening! After the feast, Saul returned with Samuel to his house, and there they had a long talk in which Samuel rehearsed for Saul the events that had led up to this meeting.

Samuel anoints Saul (1 Sam. 9:26–10:16). Early the next morning, Samuel accompanied Saul and his servant to the edge of the city, sent the servant on ahead, and then anointed Saul as the first king of Israel. From that moment on, Saul was leader over God's people ("inheritance"), but only Samuel and Saul knew it. How could young Saul be sure that God had really chosen him? Samuel gave Saul three signs, special occurrences he would encounter as he made his way home.

First, he would meet two men who would tell him that the lost animals had been found (10:2), news that Saul had already heard from Samuel. Apparently these men knew who Saul was and that he had been away from home seeking the lost property. But this was a good experience for the young king, for it assured him that *God could solve his problems.* One of Saul's greatest failures as a leader was his inability to take his hands off of situations and let God work. In modern language, Saul was a "control freak." Yet while Saul and his servant were dining with Samuel, God was at work saving the lost animals.

The second sign would take place at the oak of Tabor where he would meet three pilgrims heading for Bethel (vv. 3-4). In spite of the nation's unbelief, there were still devoted people in the land who honored the Lord and sought His face.[3] There must have been a sacred place at Bethel dedicated to the Lord (Judg. 20:18, 26), and perhaps the three kids, the wine, and the three loaves of bread were gifts for the Levites serving there. Since as yet there was no central sanctuary, the three kids may have been for sacrifices. These men would greet Saul and give him two of the three loaves, and he was to receive them. God was showing Saul that not only could He solve his problems, but *He could also supply his needs.* As the first king of Israel, he would have to raise up an army and provide the food and equipment the men needed, and he would have to depend on the Lord.

The third sign had to do with spiritual power (1 Sam. 10:5-6). Saul would meet a band of prophets returning from worship at the high place, and they would be prophesying. The Holy Spirit of God would come upon Saul at that time and he would join the company of prophets in their ecstatic worship. In this sign, God told Saul that *He could endue him with the power he needed for service.* "And who is sufficient for these things?" is the question in the heart of every servant of God (2 Cor. 2:16), and the only correct answer is "our sufficiency is of God" (3:5). However, later Saul would become very self-sufficient and rebellious, and the Lord would take the Spirit from him (1 Sam. 16:14; 28:15).

When Saul turned from Samuel to start his journey home, God gave him "another heart" (10:9, see v. 6). Don't read New Testament "regeneration" into this statement; it refers primarily to a different attitude and outlook. This young farmer would now think and act like a leader, the king of the nation, a warrior-statesman whose responsibility it was to listen to God and obey His will. The Holy Spirit would further enable him to serve God as long as he walked in obedience to His will (v. 6). Because Saul became proud and independent and rebelled against God, he lost the Spirit's power, he lost his kingdom, and he eventually lost his life.

Each of these events took place just as Samuel promised. but the only one actually described in the text is Saul's encounter with the company of prophets (vv. 10-13). In the Old Testament era, God gave His Holy Spirit to chosen people to enable them to perform special tasks, and God could take the Spirit away as well. Believers today, who are under the New Covenant, have the Holy Spirit abiding within forever (John 14:16-17) as God's seal that we are His children (Eph. 1:13-14). When David asked God not to take the Holy Spirit from him (Ps. 51:11), he was thinking especially of what the Lord did to Saul (1 Sam. 16:14; 28:15). Believers today may grieve the Spirit (Eph. 4:30) and quench the Spirit (1 Thes. 5:19), but they cannot drive Him away.

The Spirit enabled Saul (probably for the first time in his life) to have a personal experience with the Lord and to express it in praise and worship. Had Saul continued to nurture this walk with the Lord, his life would have been much different. His pride and desire for power became his besetting sin. When the news got out that Saul had prophesied with a company of prophets, some of his friends spoke about him with disdain (1 Sam. 10:11-13). There's no evidence that he was overly wicked, but Saul was a secular person, not a spiritual person, and he was the last man his friends ever expected to have that kind of experience. The question, "Is Saul also among the prophets?" was asked of anybody who suddenly stepped out of character and did the unexpected. Since prophets often inherited their ministry from their fathers (Amos 7:14), and were even called "fathers" (2 Kings 2:12; 6:2), the second question was asked: "Who is their father?" Even after Saul was presented to the people as their king, not everybody in Israel was impressed with him (1 Sam. 10:27).

Saul returned home and went back to work on the farm as though nothing remarkable had happened. He said nothing to his family about being anointed king, and apparently the news about his prophetic experiences hadn't reached as far as Gibeah. The experiences of the previous days should have taught him that God was with him (v. 7), and that He would take care of him and meet his needs, if only he would trust and obey. He also should have realized that he could trust Samuel to give him God's message, and that to disobey Samuel meant to disobey the Lord. One more task awaited Saul, and that was to meet Samuel at Gilgal at a time that would be shown him (v. 8). This would be a test to see if Saul was truly devoted to the Lord and willing to obey orders. Unfortunately, he failed.

Samuel presents Saul to the people (1 Sam. 10:17-27). Samuel called another convocation at Mizpah for the purpose of presenting the new king to the people. True to his prophetic calling, he first preached a sermon and reminded the people of their redemption from Egypt by God's grace and power as well as their obligation under the covenant to obey the Lord. But they had disobeyed the Lord in asking for a king! They had sinned, but the Lord would answer their request.

Only the Lord and Samuel knew that the king had already been selected and anointed, but Samuel wanted the tribes to realize that Jehovah was in charge of the selection process. He had the tribes present themselves, probably represented by their elders, and the tribe of Benjamin was selected. This may have been selection by lot (14:40-42), or one of the priests may have used the Urim and Thummim to determine the Lord's will (Ex. 28:30). The clan of Matri was selected next, and from that clan, the family of Kish and finally, the young man Saul.

But Saul couldn't be found! And Samuel had to inquire further of the Lord to discover that the king was hiding among the wagons and baggage, certainly not an auspicious way to begin his reign! Was he hiding out of modesty or fear? Probably the latter, because true humility accepts God's will while at the same time depending on God's strength and wisdom. As Andrew Murray said, "True humility isn't thinking meanly of one's self; it's simply not thinking of one's self at all." Had Saul been focusing on the glory of God, he would have been present in the assembly and humbly accepting God's call. Then he would have urged the people to pray for him and to follow him as he sought to do the Lord's will.

This first official act on the part of Saul suggests that there was trouble ahead. Saul was a reluctant ruler who followed his emotions instead of building his faith. He would serve as a sacrificing courageous soldier one day and become a self-centered autocrat the next day. Shunning national popularity is one thing, but shunning God-given responsibility is quite another. "If God called a man to kingship," said G. Campbell Morgan, "he has no right to hide away."[4] Samuel did what he could to salvage an embarrassing situation. He presented Saul as God's chosen king, so the nation had to accept him, and he accented Saul's admirable physical characteristics. The people were impressed, but Samuel certainly knew that God didn't need tall, muscular men in order to get His work done. In a few years, He would use teenage David to kill a giant! (See Ps. 147:10-11.)

The wisest thing Samuel did that day was to link the kingship with the divine covenant (1 Sam. 10:25). His first speech about the king had been negative (8:10-18), but this address and document were positive and pointed out the duties of both king and people. Samuel no doubt elaborated on Moses' words from Deuteronmy 17:14-20 and reminded the people that even the king had to submit to the Lord and His Word. There was one God, one nation, and one covenant, and the Lord was still in charge.

When the assembly was ended, everybody went back home, including the king, and there accompanied him a group of valiant men who became his officers and inner circle. They followed Saul because the Lord moved them to do so. People gave Saul gifts as tokens of their homage to the king, but one group of men despised and ridiculed him. As king, Saul could have dealt severely with them, but he held his peace. And yet later, he was willing to kill Jonathan, his son, just because the boy had eaten some honey! Saul's emotional instability had him weeping over David one day and trying to kill him the next.

4. Serving the Lord (1 Sam. 11:1-15)

One of the reasons Israel asked for a king was so the nation could unite behind one leader and have a better opportunity to face their enemies. The Lord condescended to reach down to their level of unbelief, and He gave them a king who looked like a natural warrior. How sad it is that God's people trusted a man of clay whom they could admire, and yet they would not trust the Lord who throughout the nation's history had proven Himself powerful on their behalf. In His grace, God gave Saul an opportunity to prove himself and consolidate his authority.

The challenge (1 Sam. 1-3). The

Ammonites were descendants of Abraham's nephew Lot (Gen. 19:30-38) and therefore related to the Jewish people. The dangers posed by Nahash ("snake") and his army had helped to motivate the Jews to ask for a king, and now Nahash was encamped around Jabesh Gilead, a city about fifty miles from Saul's home. Rather than engage in a long and costly siege, Nahash offered to negotiate with the people in the city and let them live. All he demanded was that they submit to the humiliating and crippling punishment of having their right eyes gouged out. Archers and swordsmen would be handicapped in battle, and everybody would be humiliated and marked as defeated prisoners of war. Without having to kill anybody, Nahash could subdue the city, take its wealth, and enslave the people.

Wisely, the elders of the city asked for a week's delay, hoping to find somebody who could rescue them, and Nahash agreed, thinking that weak Israel couldn't muster an army. It's interesting that nobody from Jabesh Gilead responded to the call to arms when the nation had to punish the wickedness of Gilead in Benjamin (Judg. 21:8-9), but now they were asking their fellow Jews to come and rescue them!

The conquest (1 Sam. 11:4-11). It's strange that the messengers from Jabesh Gilead didn't hasten to contact Samuel and Saul first of all. Samuel their prophet had prayed and God gave victory over the Philistines, and Saul their new king had the nucleus of an army. It would take time for the Jews to get accustomed to the new form of government. When the news came, Saul was plowing in the field with the oxen. The Jews were noted for their loud and passionate expressions of grief, and when Saul heard the people weeping, he asked the cause. No sooner did the king understand the situation than he experienced an endowment of the Spirit of God and his own spirit was filled with righteous indignation that such a thing should happen in Israel.

Instantly Saul moved into action and in a dramatic way sent the message to the men of Israel that they were needed for battle. (Compare the actions of the Levite in Judg. 19.) He also identified himself with Samuel when he issued the call to arms, for he and Samuel were working together. The Lord worked on Saul's behalf by putting fear in the hearts of the people so that 330,000 men gathered for battle. Saul mustered the army at Bezek, about twenty miles from Jabesh Gilead, and then sent a message to the city that help was coming the next day before midmorning. Shrewdly, the citizens told the Ammonites that they would surrender the next day, and this gave Nahash the kind of false confidence that threw the army off guard.

Saul may have known the story of Gideon and his defeat of the Midianites, because, like Gideon, he divided his army into three parts and attacked at night (Judg. 7:16, 19). The morning watch was from 2 to 6 A.M., so he caught the enemy by surprise and completely routed them. Saul succeeded because he was empowered by the Spirit of God who both used Saul's natural gifts and gave him the wisdom and strength he needed. Being at the head of an inexperienced army of 330,000 men wouldn't be an easy task, but God gave the victory. The will of God will never lead us where the grace of God can't keep us and use us.

When Saul was chosen king, he was given *authority* from God and from the nation, but when he won this great victory, he gained *stature* before the people. It takes both to be an effective leader. The difficulties began later when Saul's pride inflated his authority and began to destroy his character and his stature. David was humbled by his success, but Saul became more and more proud and abusive. We admire Saul for not using the victory as a means of getting rid of his enemies but for giving glory to the Lord (1 Sam. 11:13; Lev. 19:18; Rom. 12:17). Effective leaders use their authority to honor God and build up their people, but ineffective leaders use the people to build up their authority. Later on, Saul began to do that, and it led to his failure.

Samuel seized the opportunity and called the nation together to give thanks to the Lord and to affirm the king and the kingdom. They met at Gilgal, near the Jordan River, a place that had solemn associations for the Jews (Josh. 4:19-5:11; 7:16; 10:8-15; 13:4). At the Mizpah assembly, they had accepted God's king, but at Gilgal they confirmed Saul as king before the Lord (1 Sam. 12:1). Our modern word would be "coronation." The peace offerings were part of a covenant ceremony in which the people sacrificed to God and then had a meal of some of the portions of the animals they gave to God. It was clear to everybody that the king and the nation had entered into a renewed covenant relationship with the Lord and were responsible to obey Him.

Samuel had anointed Saul privately (10:1) and then presented him to the people (vv. 17-27), and now Samuel led the nation in an act of dedication to the Lord. It was a time of spiritual revival and national rejoicing. Saul had passed his first test, but it wouldn't be long before he would fail in a much simpler test and lose his kingdom. Saintly Andrew Bonar used to say, "We must be as watchful after the victory as before the battle." Saul won his first battle, but he would lose the victory.

CHAPTER FOUR
REVIEWING AND REBUKING
1 Samuel 12–13

Saul and the people rejoiced greatly over the deliverance of Jabesh Gilead from the Ammonites, and Saul was careful to give the glory to the Lord (11:13). Samuel saw the victory as a great opportunity to "renew the kingdom" (v. 14) and remind the people that Jehovah God was still their King. The fact that Saul had led the army in a great victory would tempt the Israelites to put their faith in their new king, and Samuel wanted them to know that their future success rested in trusting Jehovah alone. The king was only God's servant for the people, and both king and people had to obey God's covenant. In his farewell message, Samuel defended his own ministry (vv. 1-5), reviewed God's mercies to Israel (vv. 6-11), and admonished the people to fear the Lord and obey the covenant (vv. 12-25). Samuel mentions the Lord at least thirty times in this message, because his heart's desire was to see the people return to the Lord and honor His covenant.

1. A leader's integrity (1 Sam. 12:1-5)

In asking for a king, the people had rejected the kingship of Jehovah and the leadership of Samuel, the last of the judges (7:6, 15-17). It must have been painful for Samuel to conduct this last meeting as their leader and transfer the civil authority to Saul. No doubt he had hoped that one of his sons would succeed him, but they weren't even considered (8:1-3). The twelve tribes had been governed by judges for nearly 500 years, but times had changed and the people wanted a king. Before leaving office as judge, Samuel had to set the record straight and bear witness that his hands were clean and the people could find no fault in him.

To many of the people at that assembly, Samuel had "always been there." Some of them had known him when he was a child and youth at Shiloh, learning to serve as a priest, and others remembered when he had begun to proclaim the Word of the Lord (3:20). He had walked before them almost all of his life, and now he stood before them "old and grayheaded" and challenged them to accuse him of using his authority to benefit himself. "Here I am" (12:3) makes us think of Samuel's responses the night the Lord called him (3:4-6, 8, 16). In the East, it was expected that civil officials would use their offices to make money, but Samuel hadn't taken that route. He obeyed the Law of Moses and kept his hands clean (Ex. 20:17; 22:1-4, 9; 23:8; Lev. 19:13; Deut. 16:19; 24:14). With such a godly example before them, we wonder why his sons took bribes.

Like Jesus, Samuel stood before the people and asked, "Which of you convicts me of sin?" (John 8:46, NKJV). The people heard what Samuel said and bore witness that he had spoken the truth. Samuel was a man of integrity; Saul would turn out to be a man of hypocrisy and duplicity. When the assembly gave their vote of confidence to Samuel, the prophet called the Lord and the new king to bear witness to what they had said. If the people ever changed their mind, they would have to deal with God and His appointed king!

It's a wonderful thing to get to the closing years of life and be able to review your life and ministry and not be afraid or ashamed. May we all be able to say with our Lord, "I have glorified You on the earth. I have finished the work which You have given Me to do" (John 17:4, NKJV).

2. A nation's iniquity (1 Sam. 12:6-25)

Having affirmed Samuel's credibility, the people now had to accept his analysis of the situation. He reviewed Israel's history from Moses to his own day and emphasized what the Lord in His grace had done for them.

Thank the Lord (1 Sam. 6-11). It was God, not the people, who appointed Moses and Aaron (v. 6) and who enabled them to do the mighty works they did for the people of Israel. Samuel wasn't afraid to point out Israel's sins and then challenge them to devote themselves to the Lord and to His covenant. It's often been said that the one thing we learn from history is that we don't learn from history, and Samuel didn't want his people to make that mistake.

But this was more than a lecture on history; it was also a court trial. Samuel's words in verse 7 have a judicial flavor: "stand still" carries the idea of "Stand up, court is in session!" and "reason" means "to decide a case of litigation." Samuel was going to prove to the people that the Lord had been righteous and faithful in all His dealings with Israel, but that the Jews had been faithless and disobedient. The Lord had covenanted with no other nation on earth except Israel, and Israel's obedience to that covenant made possible their enjoyment of God's promised blessings. These blessings included living in the Promised Land, being protected from their enemies, and having fruitful fields, flocks and herds, and families. If they failed to obey, the Lord would discipline them and take away their blessings. (See Deut. 28–30 and Lev. 26.) Every Jew knew this, but not every Jew really understood it.

Israel in Egypt cried out to the Lord for

help, and He sent them Moses and Aaron (1 Sam. 12:8). God delivered His people and took them to Canaan and gave them victory over the inhabitants of the land. But once they were in the land, they compromised their faith and joined in worshiping the false gods of their neighbors; so God had to discipline them (vv. 9-11). Now we are in the Book of Judges with its seven cycles of disobedience, discipline, and deliverance (Judg. 2:10-23). Samuel's point is that God always provided a leader when one was needed, and the nation wouldn't have needed a judge if the people had been faithful to God. In 1 Samuel 12:11, Jerubbaal ("let Baal contend [for himself]") is Gideon, and Bedan is probably Barak.[1] Samuel included himself, for he was the last of the judges (7:15).

Fear the Lord (1 Sam. 12:12-19). How should Israel have responded to this kind of national history? They should have expressed gratitude to the Lord and trusted Him for His continued care. They should have confessed their sin of unbelief and trusted Him alone. But what did they do? No sooner did the Ammonites attack than the Jews asked for a king and exchanged the rule of the Lord their King for the leadership of a mere man! God gave them what they asked for, but Israel lost something in the transaction.

However, all was not lost. God is never taken by surprise and He would not desert His people for His name's sake. If the people would fear the Lord and follow Him, He would continue to care for them and use their king to direct and protect them. Then Samuel demonstrated the awesome power of the Lord by "praying up a storm" during the dry season of wheat harvest (mid-May to mid-June). This miracle reminds us of the signs Moses and Aaron did in Egypt. Samuel was proving to the people that God could do anything for them if they trusted Him and obeyed, but that a mere king was helpless apart from the Lord. When the Jews begged Samuel for deliverance, they sounded like Pharaoh confessing his sin and begging Moses for relief (Ex, 8:8; 9:27-28; 10:16-17), and their repentance was probably just as insincere.

Obey the Lord (1 Sam. 12:20-25). Samuel moved from "Fear" to "Fear not" as he encouraged the people to accept the situation their unbelief created and make the most of it. How many times in our own lives do we get what we asked for and then wish we didn't have it! The Lord would not reject or forsake His people because of His holy covenant and His great faithfulness. God's purpose was to use Israel to bring glory to His name, and He would fulfill that purpose. The Jewish people knew the terms of the covenant: if they obeyed, the Lord would bless them; if they disobeyed, He would chasten them. Either way, He would be faithful to His Word; the major issue was whether Israel would be faithful. They had made a mistake, but God would help them if they feared and obeyed Him.

Samuel made it clear that, no matter what they decided, he would obey the Lord. Part of his obedience would be faithfully praying for the people and teaching them the Word of God. The Word of God and prayer always go together (Acts 6:4; John 15:7; Eph. 6:17-18). Samuel's heart was broken, but as a faithful servant of the Lord, he interceded for the people and sought to lead them in the right way. For God's people not to pray is to sin against the Lord, yet if there's one thing lacking in our churches today, it is prayer, particularly prayer for those in authority (1 Tim. 2:1-4).

When we consider the great things God has done for us, how could we do other than fear Him, thank Him, and serve Him in truth all the days of our lives? God's covenant with His people Israel was still in force: if they obeyed, He would bless; if they disobeyed, He would chasten. "Yet if you persist in doing evil," warned Samuel, "both you and your king will be swept away" (1 Sam. 12:25). Samuel may have been referring especially to the warning given by Moses in Deut. 28:36, *written into the covenant centuries before Israel had a king*: "The Lord will drive you and the king you set over you to a nation unknown to you or your fathers" (NIV). Unfortunately, Israel did disobey the terms of the covenant and God had to send them in exile to Babylon.

From time to time, churches and other Christian ministries face new situations and decide they must make organizational changes. Each ministry needs a Samuel to remind them of the spiritual principles that never change: the character of God, the Word of God, the necessity of faith, and the importance of obedience.

Methods are many, principles are few;
Methods always change, principles never do.

As the old Youth for Christ slogan expressed it, "Geared to the times but anchored to the Rock." Some changes are inevitable and necessary, but they need not destroy the work of God.

3. A king's irresponsibility (1 Sam. 13:1-14)

The narrative in chapters 13–15 focuses on Saul's early reign, especially his relationship to God and to Samuel. We see Saul making foolish and unwise decisions and trying to cover his disobedience with lies. It was the beginning of that tragic decline that ended in a witch's house and Saul's suicide on the battlefield. At chapter 16, David will come on the scene and the book will describe Saul's deepening conflict with God, himself, and David. We can trace the downward steps in his tragic failure.

Pride (1 Sam. 13:1-4). Saul had reigned two years when he began to establish a standing army.[2] Over 300,000 men had volunteered to deliver the people of Jabesh Gilead (11:8), but Saul chose only 3,000 and divided them between himself and his son Jonathan. Saul's camp was at Michmash and Jonathan's was about fifteen miles away in Gibeah. The fact that Israel was mustering an army put the Philistines on the alert. They had garrisons in different parts of the country and monitored the situation carefully.

It is as a brave and victorious soldier that Jonathan is introduced to us. When he attacked and defeated the Philistine outpost at Geba, it was a declaration of war, and the Philistines were quick to respond. This was the beginning of Israel's war of liberation, although it wasn't finished until after David became king. But who blew the trumpet and seemed to take the credit for the victory? Saul, son of Kish! As commander-in-chief, he was calling for more men, because he knew that many battles lay ahead, but we wish he had given proper credit to his courageous son.

Why did Saul call his fellow Israelites "the Hebrews" instead of "men of Israel"? The name may have come from Abraham's ancestor Eber (Gen. 10:21), or perhaps from the word meaning "to cross over." The ancestors of Abraham were those who "crossed over the River Euphrates" (Josh. 24:2-3). Canaan was "the land of the Hebrews" (Gen. 40:15); the Egyptians would not eat with "the Hebrews" (43:32); an Egyptian "beat one of the Hebrews" (Ex. 2:11). In Scripture, the word is used primarily by foreigners speaking to or of the Jews, or by the Jews speaking to foreigners about themselves. You get the impression that the word "Hebrew" was often used as a term of contempt. Did Saul not have respect for his people? Whatever reason he had for using the word, his command was clear: gather together at Gilgal, the place that Samuel had appointed (1 Sam. 10:8ff).

Unbelief and impatience (1 Sam. 13:5-9). The Philistine forces gathered at Michmash, less than twenty miles west of Gilgal, and it was obvious that Saul and his army were greatly outnumbered.[3] Saul's men began to hide and even deserted the army by crossing the river, and those who remained were paralyzed with fright. As Samuel had commanded, Saul waited for seven days (10:8), and the longer he waited, the more concerned he became. His army was melting away, the enemy was mobilizing, and the situation was hopeless.

Why did Samuel tarry? Was he deliberately trying to make Saul fail, or was he just reminding the new king who was still in control? Samuel had nothing to gain if Saul failed on the battlefield, and Samuel knew that God was in control, even in the appointment of the new king. Furthermore, this meeting had been planned some two years before (v. 8), and no doubt Samuel had reminded Saul of it more than once. *This rendezvous was the Lord's way of testing Saul's faith and patience.* Without faith and patience, we can't receive what the Lord promises (Heb. 6:12), and unbelief and impatience are marks of spiritual immaturity (James 1:1-8). Until we learn to trust God and wait on His timing, we can't learn the other lessons He wants to teach us, nor can we receive the blessings He's planned for us. Saul may have been handsome, strong, and taller than the other men, but if he didn't have a heart that was right with God, he didn't have anything. It's one thing to be victorious when you're leading an army of over 300,000 men (1 Sam. 11:8), but quite another thing when you have only 600! (v. 15) But this is where faith comes in.

Saul didn't want to go into the battle without first offering a sacrifice to the Lord, which in itself may have been a subtle form of superstition, like carrying the Ark into the battle. Later Samuel would remind Saul that God seeks obedience and not sacrifice (15:22). Without waiting for God's appointed priest, Saul offered the sacrifice, and just then Samuel arrived in the camp. If Saul had waited just a few minutes more, everything would have been all right; but his impatience cost him dearly.

Deception (1 Sam. 13:10-12). As Saul decays in character, we shall see him deceiving himself and others more and more. His first deception at Gilgal occurred when he greeted Samuel cordially and expected Samuel to give him a blessing. Saul was playing the hypocrite and acting as though he had done nothing wrong. "If we say that we have fellowship with him, and walk in darkness, we lie, and do not the truth" (1 John 1:6, KJV). His second lie consisted in blaming Samuel and the soldiers and not himself. It was Samuel's fault for arriving late and the army's fault for deserting their king. His words, "I saw" indicate that Saul was walking by sight and not by faith. He lied a third time when he said that he had to force himself to offer the sacrifice. Could he not have "forced himself" to pray or to call together some of the officers to beseech the Lord for His help? The will is the servant of the mind and heart, but Saul's thinking and desiring were totally out of the will of God.

People who are good at making excuses are rarely good at anything else, and those who are quick to blame others shouldn't complain if others blame them. When God confronted our first parents with their sin, Adam blamed Eve, and Eve blamed the serpent, but neither Adam nor Eve said humbly, "I have sinned." Throughout his career, King Saul was adept at minimizing his own sins and emphasizing the faults of others, but this isn't the way a man of God leads God's people.

Folly (1 Sam. 13:13-14).[4] It was foolish of Saul to think that he could disobey God and get away with it, and that his disobedience could bring God's blessing on himself and his army. "Let us do evil that good may come" (Rom. 3:8) is the logic of hell, not the law of heaven. He was foolish to conclude that the sacrifice of a king at the wrong time was as good as the sacrifice of a priest at the right time. He was foolish to walk by sight and not by faith in God's promise, "for whatsoever is not of faith is sin" (Rom. 14:23, KJV). Saul had the same kind of superstitious faith that Eli's sons had when they carried the Ark on the battlefield. He knew nothing of "the obedience of faith" (Rom. 16:26).

Saul's pride, impatience, disobedience, and deception were all seen and judged by the Lord, and Samuel announced the sentence: the crown would eventually be taken from Saul and given to another, in this case, David. Saul would continue as king, but he would not establish a lasting dynasty, and none of his sons would succeed him and rule over Israel. But even if Saul had not sinned, how could his dynasty continue "forever" (1 Sam. 13:13) when Saul was from the wrong tribe and God had already chosen David to be king of Israel? One answer is that Saul's eldest son, Jonathan, could have served with David, which in fact is what David and Jonathan had planned (20:31, 42; 23:16-18). Of course, the Davidic dynasty would have established the Messianic line, but someone from Saul's family would have served in court with the Davidic king.

Saul's sin at Gilgal cost him the dynasty, and his sin involving the Amalekites cost him the kingdom. He eventually lost his crown and his life (see 15:16-34, especially 23, 27-29; 16:1). God wanted a king with a heart that was right toward God, a man with a shepherd's heart, and He found that kind of heart in David (13:14; Pss. 78:72; 89:20; Acts 13:22). "This man [Saul] in his governing of Israel was a warrior and nothing more," said G. Campbell Morgan; "he was never a shepherd." But David had a shepherd's heart, because the Lord was his Shepherd (Ps. 23:1). David was under authority, so he had the right to exercise authority.

4. An army's insecurity (1 Sam. 13:15-23)

Saul had failed miserably, but in chapter 14 we will read about Jonathan's great success as a commander. This passage describes the sad condition of the army of Israel, which reveals how poor Saul's leadership was and how remarkable Jonathan's victory was. Saul walked by sight and had little faith, but Jonathan walked by faith and did exploits for the Lord.

A dwindling army (1 Sam. 13:15-16). Saul had mustered over 300,000 men to rescue the people of Jabesh Gilead and then had cut it down to 3,000, but now his forces numbered only 600. The Philistine army was "as the sand which is on the seashore in multitude" (v. 5), a simile also used for the army Gideon faced (Judg. 7:12)—and Saul's army was twice as large as Gideon's! The difference wasn't so much the size of the army as the strength of the leader's faith. Gideon trusted God for victory and God honored him; Saul disobeyed God and God punished him. Saul had mustered that huge army by means of fear (1 Sam. 11:7), so when his men began to fear the enemy instead of the king, they began to desert the camp and go to places of safety. Jonathan knew that the Lord didn't need great numbers to accomplish His purposes (14:6), but He did honor great faith.

A threatened army (1 Sam. 13:17-18, 23). The Philistines repeatedly sent out "raiding parties" to protect the roads and passes that the Jews might use if they attacked, and at the same time the Philistines kept any residents from helping the Jewish army. There were three such groups: one went north toward Ophrah, a second west to Beth-horon, and the third east toward Zeboim. A fourth detachment went south toward Gibeah to prevent the Jewish army from moving up to Geba (v. 23). With all these Philistine soldiers moving about in the area, what hope was there for the Jews? No matter which way Israel turned, they would meet the enemy! And yet the Lord was going to use Jonathan and his armor-bearer to win a great victory, for with God, nothing is impossible.

A deprived army (1 Sam. 13:19-22). It was bad enough that Saul lacked men, but it was even worse that his men were not properly equipped. When the Philistines moved in and subjected the land of Israel to their rule, they deported all the iron-workers so that the Jews couldn't make weapons or even repair their farm implements. They even had to pay exorbitant prices to have their implements sharpened. The Benjamites were skilled at using slings (Judg. 20:15-16), but slings were not practical in close combat, and what about the vast number of Philistine chariots? The Jewish army was small in number and had small supplies of weapons, but they had a great God, if only they would trust Him. All of this sets the stage for Jonathan's thrilling victory described in chapter 14, and that is contrasted with his father's sad defeat in chapter 15.

In the way it functions or doesn't function, the church of Jesus Christ today may sometimes resemble Saul's army, but if we do, it's our own fault. Through His great work on the cross, our Lord has defeated every enemy, and His power is available to His people. We have the armor and the weapons we need (Eph. 6:10ff), and His Word tells us all we need to know about the strategy of the enemy and the resources we have in Christ. All He asks is that we trust Him and obey His orders, and He will help us win the battle.

"Be strong in the Lord, and in the power of his might" (Eph. 6:10, KJV) for "the battle is the Lord's" (1 Sam. 17:47).

CHAPTER FIVE
A FOOLISH VOW AND A LAME EXCUSE
1 Samuel 14–15

Our task isn't an enjoyable one as we watch the character of King Saul steadily deteriorate. He has already demonstrated his unbelief and impatience (chap. 13), and now he will reveal further his disobedience and dishonesty. Saul's history will climax with the king visiting a witch and then committing suicide on the battlefield. Sir Walter Scott was right when he wrote in his poem "Marmion,"

> O what a tangled web we weave
> When first we practice to deceive!

These chapters teach us three powerful lessons that we must heed and obey if we want the blessing of God on our lives and service.

1. Faith in God brings victory. (1 Sam. 14:1-23)

The focus in this chapter is on Jonathan, Saul's oldest son, who had won the first major battle against the Philistines, but his father had taken the credit (13:1-7). It's a remarkable blessing of the grace of God that a man like Saul should have a son so magnificent as Jonathan. He was a courageous warrior (2 Sam. 1:22), a born leader, and a man of faith who sought to do the will of God. As the account progresses, it becomes clear that Saul is jealous of Jonathan and his popularity, and this jealousy increases when Jonathan and David became devoted friends.

Jonathan initiates the attack (1 Sam. 14:1-15). The Philistines had sent a detachment of soldiers to establish a new outpost to guard the pass at Michmash (13:23), and Jonathan saw this as an opportunity to attack and see the Lord work. Saul was hesitating in unbelief (14:2) while his son was acting by faith. God had called Saul to begin Israel's liberation from the Philistines, but most of the time he only followed up on what others started. In spite of all that the Lord had done for him and all that Samuel had taught him, Saul was not a man of faith who trusted the Lord and sought to glorify Him. Saul had a priest of the Lord attending him, a man named Ahijah from the rejected line of Eli (v. 3), but the king never waited for the Lord's counsel (vv. 18-20). Saul is a tragic example of the popular man of the world who tries to appear religious and do God's work, but who lacks a living faith in God and a heart to honor Him. Unfortunately, church history records the lives of too many gifted people who "used God" to achieve their own purposes, but in the end abandoned Him and ended life in disgrace.

Why didn't Jonathan tell his father that he had a plan to rout the enemy? Because Saul in unbelief would have vetoed such a daring venture of faith, and Jonathan had no desire to disagree with him at such a crucial time. Jonathan may have been insubordinate to his father and commander-in-chief, but his plan was still the wisest approach to take. With their false sense of security, the Philistine troops at the new outpost wouldn't be afraid of a couple of Jews who managed to cross the pass and climb the cliffs. Maybe the guards would see them as two Jewish men who wanted to desert the Hebrew army and find refuge with the enemy. Jonathan wasn't about to let the enemy attack first.

You can't help but admire Jonathan's faith in the Lord. Perhaps as he climbed the rocks, he meditated on God's promises of victory stated in the covenant. "You will chase your enemies, and they shall fall by the sword before you. Five of you shall chase a hundred, and a hundred of you shall put ten thousand to flight; your enemies shall fall by the sword before you" (Lev. 26:7-8, NKJV; see Deut. 28:7). Action without promises is presumption, not faith, but when you have God's promises, you can go forward with confidence. Jonathan may also have been thinking of Gideon when he told his armor-bearer, "Perhaps the Lord will help us, for nothing can hinder the Lord. He can win a battle whether he has many warriors or only a few" (1 Sam. 14:6, NLT; see Judg. 6-7). "If God be for us, who can be against us?" (Rom. 8:31)

But Jonathan's plan of attack differed from Gideon's in at least two ways: It was not a surprise attack at night, and he and his armor-bearer deliberately let themselves be seen by the Philistine guards. It was the guards' response that would give Jonathan the guidance he needed.[1] Should Jonathan wait for the Philistines to come over or should he go over and meet them on their own ground? When the two men disclosed themselves to the enemy, the Philistines only laughed and mocked them. They treated them like frightened animals that had emerged from their burrows or like soldiers who were deserting the Hebrew cause and joining the Philistine army.

This kind of arrogant self-confidence was exactly what Jonathan wanted to see, because this gave him and his armor-bearer opportunity to get close to the guards before attacking. Who would fear one soldier and his armor-bearer? But these two men had Almighty God on their side! "One of you routs a thousand, because the Lord your God fights for you, just as he promised" (Josh. 23:10). The two courageous Jews quickly killed twenty men, and then the Lord honored their faith by sending an earthquake, "a very great trembling"! "But the Lord your God will deliver them over to you, throwing them into great confusion until they are destroyed" (Deut. 7:23). Terror and confusion gripped the enemy camp and prepared the way for a great victory of the army of Israel.

Saul watches the battle (1 Sam. 14:16-19). Saul and his 600 men were back at Gibeah where Saul lived, and the watchmen on the walls could see the Philistine forces retreating and couldn't explain why. Did part of the Israeli army plan a sneak attack without Saul's permission? Who was missing? Jonathan and his armor-bearer! This was the second time that Jonathan had acted on his own (13:3), and it probably irritated Saul that his own son should be so independent. As we study the life of Saul, we will see more and more evidence that he was what some people call a "control freak." He envied other people's success, he was suspicious of any strategy he didn't originate or at least approve, and he was ruthless when it came to removing people who challenged his leadership or exposed his folly.

Saul asked the priest to bring him the Ark of the Lord and probably also the ephod.[2] He was probably planning to take the Ark to the battlefield with the army, a foolish tactic that had brought judgment in Eli's day (chap. 4); and the priest could use the ephod to determine God's will in the matter. But the priest never had a chance to determine God's will, for when Saul heard the noise of the battle increasing, he interrupted the divine proceedings and made his own decision. Once again, Saul's impatience and self-confidence got the best of him and he acted without knowing God's will or receiving God's blessing (Deut. 20:4-5). He was desperately anxious to prove himself as good a soldier as Jonathan and he desperately wanted to avenge himself against his enemies (1 Sam. 14:24). It was to fulfill his own personal agenda, not to honor God, that he rushed into the battle spiritually unprepared.

Israel enters the battle (1 Sam. 14:20-23). As Saul and his army moved toward the battlefield, they were joined by Israelites who had deserted to the enemy camp (v. 21) and by men who had fled the battle and hidden away (v. 22). We wonder what kind of soldiers these quitters turned out to be. The fact that Saul accepted these men may indicate that he was trusting his army and not trusting the Lord. Six hundred soldiers don't make a large army, so he welcomed even the weakest man to return. Yet in a few hours, Saul would be willing to kill his own son for eating some honey and breaking his father's foolish vow! Saul's emotional unbalance and contradictory thinking will show up again and again and do great damage to the kingdom. One day he will rush ahead like the horse, and the next day he will hold back like the mule (Ps. 32:9).

It was not Saul and his army who won the battle, but the Lord who used Jonathan and his armor-bearer (1 Sam. 14:23, see vv. 6, 12, and 45). The Israelite army followed the Philistines for the next fifteen miles, from Michmash to Beth Aven, and the Lord enabled them to defeat the enemy. But Saul had joined the battle so late, and his men were so weak and famished, that he couldn't achieve the kind of victory that would have been decisive (v. 30). One of the marks of a true leader is knowing when to act, and Saul had wasted time watching the battle from a distance and failing to seek the mind of the Lord.

2. Foolish words bring trouble. (1 Sam. 14:24-52)

The spiritual conditions of our hearts are revealed not only by the actions we perform but also by the words we speak. "For out of the abundance of the heart the mouth speaks" (Matt. 12:34). When you read King Saul's words recorded in Scripture, they often reveal a heart controlled by pride, foolishness, and deceit. He would say foolish things just to impress people with his "spirituality," when in reality he was walking far from the Lord.

A foolish vow (1 Sam. 14:24-35). Saul's heart was not right with God and he foolishly forced his army to agree to a vow of fasting until evening (v. 24). He didn't impose this fast because it was the will of God but because he wanted his soldiers to think he was a man wholly dedicated to the Lord. But this command was only more evidence of Saul's confused and superstitious faith. He thought that their fasting plus the presence of the Ark would impress the Lord and He would give them victory. But Jonathan and his armor-bearer were already enjoying victory without either the Ark or the fast!

No sensible commander would deprive his troops of food and energy while they were fighting the enemy. If the Lord commands it, then He would give the strength needed, but God gave Saul no such commission. Moses had fasted for forty days and nights when he was on the mountain with the Lord (Ex. 34:28), for the Lord sustained him. But Saul's soldiers were "distressed" (1 Sam. 14:24), "faint" (v. 28), and "very faint" (v. 31) because of this unnecessary fast. When we obey God's commands, we walk by faith, but when we obey unnatural human regulations, we only tempt the Lord. The first is confidence but the second is presumption. All of us need to heed the admonition given in Eccl. 5:2—"Do not be rash with your mouth, and let not your heart utter anything hastily before God" (NKJV).

When Jonathan and his armor-bearer joined the Israelite army in their march, they knew nothing about the king's foolish command, and Jonathan ate some honey from a honeycomb that had dropped to the ground. Then one of the soldiers told him that his father had put a curse on any soldier who ate any food that day. Why hadn't somebody warned Jonathan sooner? Perhaps they hoped that his innocent "disobedience" would open the way for all of them to eat! We wonder if Saul wasn't deliberately putting his son's life in jeopardy. However, Jonathan wasn't too worried, and he even dared to admit that his father's leadership had brought trouble to the land (v. 29).

Saul's foolish vow not only weakened

the soldiers physically and hindered their ability to pursue the enemy, but it also created in the men an abnormal craving for food. When the sun set and ushered in a new day, the vow was no longer in force, and the men acted like animals as they fell on the spoils, killing the sheep and oxen and eating the meat with the blood. When Jews slaughtered their animals, they were required to drain out the blood before preparing the meat, for blood was never to be used as food (Lev. 3:17; 7:26; 17:10-14; 22:28; Deut. 12:23-24; see Gen. 9:4). A truly spiritual vow brings out the best in people, but Saul's carnal vow brought out the worst.

As he often did, the king assumed "spiritual leadership" and commanded the men to bring the animals to a great rock to be slain and the blood easily drained out. He then built an altar so that the animals could be offered as fellowship offerings (Lev. 3; 7:11-34), parts of which the people were allowed to eat in a fellowship feast. Saul was feebly trying to turn a gastronomical orgy into a worship service, but he didn't succeed too well. The men were famished and more interested in eating than in worshiping the Lord.

A foolish judgment (1 Sam. 14:36-52). Surely Saul realized that his delay at Gibeah and the imposing of the foolish vow had already cost the Israelites a great victory, so he tried to make amends. He decided to move the army that very night and be ready to surprise the Philistines early the next morning. The army gave no resistance, but Ahijah the priest wisely suggested that they pause long enough to seek the will of the Lord. We aren't told what method Ahijah used to ascertain God's will, but whatever it was, God didn't answer. Even though Saul was not a godly man, his oath made in the Lord's name was legitimate; and if the Lord had ignored it, He would have dishonored His own name. Furthermore, the Lord was using this event to rebuke Saul as well as to honor Jonathan. Saul would discover that his men loved Jonathan and were prepared to defend him.

Saul already knew that Jonathan had been missing from the ranks (v. 17) and therefore he assumed that his son knew nothing about the vow. But if he had learned about the vow and still violated it, that made him an even greater sinner. Either way, Jonathan would be guilty and could be slain. We get the impression that Saul was almost determined that he would demote or destroy his own son, and it's clear that Jonathan didn't agree with his father's policies and practices. Hence, Saul made another oath (v. 39), and because his heart wasn't right nor his motive holy, he was taking the Lord's name in vain (Ex. 20:7).

This time they cast lots and the lot pointed to Saul and Jonathan. The second lot fell upon Jonathan. God could have changed the results (Prov. 16:33), but He wanted to bring the whole thing out in the open and humiliate King Saul, whose pride had caused the problem to begin with. The people praised Jonathan, not Saul, as the man who had brought the great victory to Israel, and if the Lord had used Jonathan in such a wonderful way, why should he be executed? By the time this matter was settled, it was too late to follow the Philistine army, so Saul and his men retreated. The victory did send the Philistines back home for a time, but they repeatedly threatened Israel (1 Sam. 14: 52). This victory did enhance Saul's reputation and helped him consolidate his kingdom. In verses 47-48 and 52, the writer summarizes some of Saul's major victories and informs us that he drafted every good man he met.

The facts about the royal family are summarized in vv. 49-51, but when they are compared with other texts (1 Sam. 9:2; 2 Sam. 21:8;1 Chron. 8:29-33; 9:39), they reveal some problems. Saul's grandfather was Abiel and his father Kish (1 Sam. 9:1-2). Ner was his uncle and Abner ("son of Ner") was captain of the army (14:51). Only three sons are mentioned (Jonathan, Ishvi, and Malchishua), while later texts speak also of Abinadab and Esh-Baal (1 Chron. 8:33; 9:39). He had two daughters, Merab and Michel, and all of these children were by his wife Ahinoam. His concubine Rizpah bore him Armoni and Mephibosheth (2 Sam. 21:8).

Jonathan, Malchishua and Abinadab all died with their father at Gilboa (1 Sam. 31:1-2), and Abner made Ish-bosheth king (2 Sam. 2:8ff). Ish-bosheth is probably the Esh-Baal of 1 Chronicles 8:33 and 9:39, for it wasn't unusual for Jewish men to have more than one name. But what happened to Ishvi? Was this also another name for Esh-Baal (Ish-bosheth), for the two names are not found together in any text. If so, then Saul had four sons by Ahinoam—Jonathan, the eldest, and then Ishhvi/Esh-Baal/Ish-bosheth, Malachishua, and Abinadab. Since the eldest and two youngest sons were killed in battle, this left Ish-Bosheth/Ishvi/Esh-Baal, Saul's second-born, to claim the crown. Of course, it's possible that Ishvi had died earlier, and this would have left Esh-Baal/Ish-bosheth to reign, or if Esh-Baal died, then Ishvi/Ish-bosheth survived to rule briefly.

3. Disobedience and deception bring judgment (1 Sam. 15:1-35).

This is a pivotal chapter in the story of Saul. The Lord gave him another opportunity to prove himself, but he failed again, lied about it, and was judged. Saul had a habit of substituting saying for doing and of making excuses instead of confessing his sins. No matter what happened, it was always somebody else's fault. He was more concerned about looking good before the people than being good before God. Consider the stages in this event that cost Saul the kingdom and eventually his life.

Disobeying God (1 Sam. 15:1-11). The Amalekites descended from Esau, the unbelieving brother of Jacob (Gen. 36:12, 15-16; Heb. 12:14-17) and the enemy of the Jewish people. The army of Amalek attacked the Jews shortly after Israel left Egypt, and they were defeated because God heard Moses' prayers and helped Joshua's army. At that time, the Lord declared perpetual war against Amalek (Ex. 17:8-16) and Balaam prophesied Amalek's ultimate defeat (Num. 24:20). See also Deuteronmy 25:17-19.

Some people find it difficult to believe that the Lord would command an entire nation to be destroyed just because of what their ancestors had done centuries before. Some of these critics may depend more on sentiment than on spiritual truth, not realizing how long-suffering the Lord had been with these nations and how unspeakably wicked they were (see 1 Sam. 15:18, 33; Gen. 15:16). God's covenant with the Jewish nation includes the promise, "I will curse him who curses you" (12:3), and God always keeps His Word. Nations like the Amalekites who wanted to exterminate the Jews weren't just waging war on Israel; they were opposing Almighty God and His great plan of redemption for the whole world. People are either for the Lord or against Him, and if they are against Him, they must suffer the consequences. Knowing

God's covenant with Abraham, Saul allowed the Kenites to escape (1 Sam. 15:6) because they had befriended Israel. They were descendants of the Midianites, and Moses married a Midianite woman (Ex. 2:16, 21-22; see Judg. 4:11). History shows that nations that have persecuted Israel have been severely judged.

We admire Saul for being careful to protect the Kenites, but he wasn't careful to obey God's will. Everything that was vile and worthless he destroyed, but he permitted King Agag to live, and he allowed the Israelite soldiers to save "the best" of the flocks and herds. But if the Lord says something is condemned, how can we say it's "the best"? "Woe to those who call evil good and good evil" (Isa. 5:20, NKJV). Saul certainly had sufficient men to get the job done right, but he decided to do it his own way. The prophet Samuel knew about Saul's disobedience before the army returned from the battle and it grieved him. The Hebrew word means "to burn" and suggests a righteous indignation, a holy anger. For the remainder of his life, Samuel mourned over Saul (1 Sam. 16:1) and cried out to God (15:11).

Serving God acceptably involves doing the will of God in the right way, at the right time, and for the right motive. God had given Saul another chance and he had failed miserably. No wonder his mentor Samuel was angry and brokenhearted. Saul was God's choice for king and Samuel wanted him to succeed. In the end, Saul's failure to exterminate all the Amalekites resulted in his own death (2 Sam. 1:1-10).

In the matter of God's "repenting" (1 Sam. 15:11), there is no contradiction between this statement and verse 29. (See endnote 4.)

Saul lies to Samuel (1 Sam. 15:12-15). In the eyes of the soldiers and the Jewish people, Saul had won a great victory over a long-time enemy, but in God's eyes he was a failure. Yet the king was so impressed with himself that he went to Carmel and erected a stone monument in his honor and then went to Gilgal, where he had previously failed the Lord and Samuel (13:4ff). Was he trying to avoid meeting Samuel? Perhaps, but his efforts were futile. It was fifteen miles from Samuel's home in Ramah to Gilgal, perhaps a day's journey for the old prophet.

Saul's greeting was sheer hypocrisy. He had no blessing to give Samuel and he had not performed the will of the Lord. First he lied to himself in thinking he could get away with the deception, and then he lied to Samuel who already knew the truth. He even tried to lie to God by saying he would use the spared animals for sacrifices! (See 1 John 1:5-10.) Saul blamed the soldiers for sparing the spoils, but surely as their commander-in-chief, he could have controlled them. "They" spared the best, but "we" utterly destroyed the rest! With Saul, it was always somebody else's fault.

Saul argues with Samuel (1 Sam. 15:16-23). Does Samuel's emphatic "Stop!" suggest that Saul was turning away, or does it mean "Stop telling lies"? Perhaps both are true, for Saul had no great desire to discuss his affairs with Samuel. But Samuel had a message from the Lord, and Saul knew he had better listen. The day would come when Saul would give anything to hear a word from the Lord (28:4-6).

Saul had once been a modest young man (9:21), but now for the second time he had willfully disobeyed the Lord's will and even erected a monument in honor of the event. He was to annihilate a nation that for centuries had done evil, but he ended up doing evil himself. Confronted with this accusation, Saul began to argue with God's servant and deny that he had done wrong. For the second time he lied when he said, "I have obeyed" (15:13, 20); for the second time he blamed his army (vv. 15, 21); and for the second time he used the feeble excuse of dedicating the spared animals as sacrifices for the Lord (vv. 15, 21).

The prophet rejected all three lies and explained why God couldn't accept the animals as legitimate sacrifices: the Lord wants living obedience from the heart, not dead animals on the altar. God doesn't need any donations from us (Ps. 50:7-15), and the sacrifice He desires is a broken and contrite heart (51:16-17). Sacrifice without obedience is only hypocrisy and empty religious ritual (Isa. 1:11-17; Jer. 7:21-26; Ps. 40:6-8). "For I desire mercy, and not sacrifice, and the knowledge of God more than burnt offerings" (Hosea 6:6, KJV). The religious leaders in Jesus' day didn't understand this truth (Matt. 9:9-13; 12:1-8), although occasionally somebody in the crowd would see the light (Mark 12:28-34).

Samuel was a Levite and a prophet, so he certainly wasn't criticizing the Jewish sacrificial system. The Lord through Moses had established Jewish worship and it was right for the people to bring their sacrifices to the Lord. This was His appointed way of worship. But the worshipers had to come to the Lord with submissive hearts and genuine faith, or their sacrifices were in vain. When David was in the wilderness and away from the priests and the sanctuary of God, he knew that God would accept worship from his heart. "Let my prayer be set before you as incense, the lifting up of my hands as the evening sacrifice" (Ps. 141:2, NKJV). Christian worship today must be more than simply going through a liturgy; we must worship God "in spirit and in truth" (John 4:24), "singing with grace in your hearts to the Lord" (Col. 3:16, NKJV).

But the prophet went on to reveal that the sins of rebellion and stubbornness (arrogance) controlled Saul's heart, and in God's sight, they were as evil as witchcraft and idolatry. (Later, Saul would actually resort to witchcraft.) Both sins were evidences of a heart that had rejected the Word of the Lord. To know God's will and deliberately disobey it is to put ourselves above God and therefore become our own god. This is the vilest form of idolatry.

Saul is rejected by God (1 Sam. 15:24-29). King Saul now moves from "I have obeyed the voice of the Lord" (v. 20) to "I have sinned."[3] However, this was not a true expression of repentance and sorrow for sin, because when he repeated it later, he added, "Honor me now . . . before the elders of my people" (v. 30). He was obviously more concerned about his reputation with the people than his character before God, and that is not the attitude of a man truly broken because of sin. Saul also admitted that he spared Agag and the animals because he feared the people instead of fearing the Lord and His commandment. But this was just another indication that he was more interested in being popular with people than in pleasing God.

Samuel refused to join Saul at the altar because he knew the Lord wouldn't receive the king's worship because He had rejected him. In his previous disobedience, Saul forfeited the dynasty (13:14), but now he lost his throne. He was no longer the king of Israel because Samuel would anoint young David to be king. Saul had already been warned about this judgment and now it would be fulfilled. As Samuel turned away, Saul clutched at the tassels on the hem of his garment (Num. 15:38-39) and tore the prophet's robe (see 1 Kings 11:29-39.) Samuel used the occurrence as an object lesson and announced that God had torn the kingdom from Saul's hand. Samuel called the Lord "the Strength of Israel," a name that speaks of God's glory, eminence, and perfection. How could such a wonderful God be guilty of changing or of telling lies? The Lord had announced that Saul would lose the kingdom, and nothing could change His mind.[4]

Saul is rejected by Samuel (1 Sam. 15:30-35). The Word of God simply did not penetrate Saul's mind and heart, and he continued to worry about maintaining his reputation rather than getting right with the Lord. Why Samuel changed his mind and decided to worship with Saul is a bit of a mystery, but the prophet's actions after that left no doubt where Samuel stood with reference to the king. Samuel publicly butchered King Agag and in that way let it be known that the king had failed to fulfill his commission. Samuel returned to his home in Ramah and Saul to his home in Gibeah, and Samuel made no more trips to see the king, either publicly or privately. Saul did visit Samuel once in Ramah (19:23-24).

Our hearts go out to Samuel who certainly suffered much because of the people and the king they so desperately wanted. When the kingdom was introduced in Israel, Samuel was replaced by a leader who was inferior to him in every way. Samuel did his best to advise the king and strengthen the kingdom, but Saul insisted on having his own way. Each time Saul was assigned a task, he failed, and when he was confronted, he lied and blamed others. When Israel experienced victories, it was usually Jonathan who led the way. It was a difficult time for Samuel, but God was still on the throne and had His true king waiting to be anointed.

King Saul had lost his dynasty, his character, and his throne and crown. He had also lost a godly friend. When David appears on the scene, Saul will lose his self-control and his good sense, and eventually he will lose his last battle—and his life.

CHAPTER SIX
GOD CHOOSES A KING
1 Samuel 16–17

Anyone who has ever been deeply disappointed by a friend or family member can understand why aged Samuel mourned so long over King Saul. Israel had rejected Samuel's leadership over them because he was too old, and they didn't want his sons to succeed him because they accepted bribes and perverted justice (8:3). But King Saul was guilty of disobeying God's clear commandments and also of lying about what he had done, and because of these sins, he had forfeited his throne. He was still in office and yet was unfit to lead the nation, and Samuel had broken fellowship with him (15:34-35). In his grief, Samuel must have felt like a dismal failure as a father, a spiritual leader, and a mentor to the new king. The word translated "mourn" means "to mourn for the dead" and reveals the depths of Samuel's sorrow.

There is a time to mourn (Ecc. 3:4), but there is also a time to act (Josh. 7:10), and for Samuel, that time had arrived. In spite of how he felt about himself, Samuel's work wasn't over yet, for God wanted him to anoint the new king, David, the son of Jesse. If Saul was "the people's king," then David was God's king, and the events recorded in these two chapters indicate clearly that God's hand was unquestionably on David, the leader of His choice.

1. God chose David. (16:1-13)

Had an election been held in Israel to choose a replacement for King Saul, it's not likely that the people would have chosen David, but he was God's first choice. "He also chose David his servant, and took him from the sheepfolds; from following the ewes that had young he brought him, to shepherd Jacob his people, and Israel his inheritance" (Ps. 78:70-71, NKJV). Let's consider some facts about this unusual young man.

David's city—Bethlehem (1 Sam. 16:1-5). In spite of the fact that it was a small town in Judah, Bethlehem was a well-known place to the Jewish people. It was when Jacob and his family were on their way to Bethel that his favorite wife, Rachel, died near Bethlehem while giving birth to Benjamin (Gen. 35:16-20). It was in Bethlehem that Ruth, the widow from Moab, found her husband, Boaz, and gave birth to Obed, David's grandfather (Ruth 4:13-22; Matt. 1:3-6). David himself would make Bethlehem a famous place, and so would Jesus, the Son of David, who would be born there as the Scriptures promised (Micah 5:2; Matt. 2:6). Bethlehem means "house of bread," and it was there that the living bread from heaven came to dwell in human flesh.

As Israel's judge and prophet, Samuel had the right to travel where he pleased in serving the Lord and His people. But these were difficult and dangerous times because Saul was a suspicious man and his spies would report anything Samuel did. From Samuel's home in Ramah, the road to Bethlehem passed by Gibeah where Saul had his headquarters, and Saul would want to know where Samuel was going and why he was going there. To avoid problems, God commanded His servant to take a heifer and announce that he would sacrifice a fellowship offering in Bethlehem for a select group of people, including Jesse and his sons. Then God would show Samuel which one to anoint as king.

The elders in Bethlehem knew that Saul and Samuel were estranged, so the arrival of Samuel gave them great alarm. Was Samuel recruiting followers to resist Saul? Would Saul interpret his presence in their little town as a declaration of war? Samuel quickly allayed their fears and told them to sanctify themselves and come to the sacrifice and the feast that would follow. "Sanctifying" meant that each of the guests would take a bath and change clothes (Ex. 19:10-15), because nobody ceremonially unclean could partake of the sacrificial feast (Lev. 7:19-21). For Jesse and his sons to be invited to this feast was a high honor, and, of course, nobody but Samuel knew why they were included.

David's family (1 Sam. 16:6-10). Before the guests sat down to enjoy the fellowship feast, Samuel looked over seven of Jesse's sons, thinking that the whole family was there, but he was operating by sight and not by faith. We don't know what Samuel's two sons looked like, but we do know that their father admired men who were handsome and well-built. Samuel had already forgotten this mistake he made about Saul (9:2; 10:23-24). David was the eighth son and only six of his brothers are named in Scripture: Eliab, the firstborn; Abinadab, the second; Shimea, the third, also called Shammah; Nethanel, or Nathaniel, the fourth; Raddai, the fifth; and Ozem, the sixth (1 Chron. 2:13-15). David is called the seventh in this genealogy, but 1 Samuel 16:10-11 makes it clear that he was the eighth and youngest son. Apparently one brother died without issue and his name dropped out of the genealogy. David also had two sisters: Zeruiah was the mother of Abishai, Joab, and Asahel; and Abigail, who was the mother of Amasa (1 Chron. 2:16-17). All of these men played important roles in David's kingdom.

No doubt there was no family in Bethlehem that could boast having seven such brothers, men of strength and stature, *and yet none of them was God's chosen king!* Samuel may have looked at their faces and forms, but the Lord examined their hearts. God alone can search the human heart and know what a person's motives really are (1 Chron. 28:9; Jer. 17:10; Rom. 8:27; Heb. 4:12).

David's occupation—a shepherd (1 Sam. 16:11). So insignificant was David in the family that Jesse didn't even call him from the flock to the feast![1] Saul was hiding among the baggage when Samuel called for him, but David was busy caring for his father's sheep. In Old Testament times, kings and their officers were looked upon as "shepherds" of the people (see Jer. 23; Ezek. 34), and David was a man with the heart of a shepherd (see 2 Sam. 7:8; 1 Chron. 21:17; Ps. 78:70-72). God's church today is a flock, and each spiritual leader needs to have the heart of a shepherd and lovingly care for God's lambs and sheep (John 10:1-18; 21:15-19; 1 Peter 5).

You can drive cattle but you have to lead sheep or they will scatter. The shepherd must know his sheep individually, love them, and take care of them according to their needs. For the most part, sheep are defenseless and do not see well, so they depend on the shepherd to guide and protect them. Though David was a literal shepherd who was called to be a "national" shepherd, he saw himself as one of the Lord's sheep and wrote about it in Psalm 23. This psalm wasn't the product of a young man but of a seasoned saint who looked back at a long life and confessed that the Lord had been faithful to him all the days of his life (23:6). David was exactly the kind of leader Israel needed to repair all the damage that Saul had done to the nation.[2]

God calls people who are busy, not people looking for ways to avoid responsibility. Moses (Ex. 3), Gideon (Judg. 6), Elisha (1 Kings 19:19-21), Nehemiah (Neh. 1), Amos (Amos 7:14-15), Peter, Andrew, James, and John (Mark 1:16-20), and Matthew (Matt. 9:9-13) were all busy when the Lord called them. God's pattern for leadership is stated in Matthew 25:21—"Well done, good and faithful servant; you were faithful over a few things, I will make you ruler over many things. Enter into the joy of your Lord" (NKJV). David had been faithful as a servant over a few things and God promoted him to being a ruler over many things—from a flock to a whole nation! Unlike Saul, David could be trusted with exercising authority because he had been under authority and had proved himself faithful.

David's appearance (1 Sam. 16:12a; see 17:42). While the physical appearance wasn't the most important thing for a king (16:7), David was so striking in his appearance that the Lord calls our attention to it. Saul was different from most Semitic people of that day because he was tall, but David's distinctive was that he was fair rather than swarthy. The word translated "ruddy" is the same as Esau's nickname "Edom—red" (Gen. 25:24-34). Some have interpreted this to mean that David was a redhead, but it may only mean that, unlike the average Semite, he was fair of skin and hair. Like Joseph, he was handsome (39:6) and had a winsome personality (1 Sam. 16:18). He was the kind of person who attracted people and won and held their confidence.

David's anointing (1 Sam. 16:12a-13). After looking at Jesse's seven sons, Samuel at last found the man of God's choice, a man after God's own heart (13:14). It's interesting that David ("beloved") was number eight, because in Scripture eight is often the number of a new beginning. God did use David to bring a new beginning to Israel, both governmentally and spiritually.[3]

In Scripture, only prophets, priests, and kings were anointed, and the anointing had to be performed by a person authorized by the Lord. In biblical imagery, oil can symbolize the Holy Spirit and the endowment of His power upon His servants (Zech. 4). The Hebrew word "Messiah" and the Greek word "Christ" both mean "anointed." The Spirit of God came upon young David in great power, and ever after that, David was God's man, but at the same time, the Spirit of God departed from Saul (1 Sam. 16:14).[4] Without the power of the Spirit, the servant of God is helpless to do the will of God and glorify Christ. As we abide in Christ, we receive the power we need, for Jesus said, "Without Me you can do nothing" (John 15:5, NKJV).

How much did David's father and brothers understand about this anointing? In view of David's subsequent association with King Saul, perhaps they interpreted the event as a consecration for David's special service to the king. It's likely that Samuel privately told David that he had been chosen by the Lord to be the next king. If so, his behavior while serving Saul was remarkably mature for a young man who one day would wear the crown. No doubt it was the assurance of this future hope that helped to keep David faithful during the ensuing years of trial and persecution.[5] But his trials and testings during those wilderness years helped to build his faith and develop his godly character and prepare him for the ministry that God had planned for him.

When David and Jonathan became friends (1 Sam. 18:1) and covenanted to be faithful to each other (18:3; 20:16), it's certain that David revealed to Jonathan that he was God's anointed king. When David became king, he would make Jonathan second in command (23:16-18). It's not likely that Jonathan told his paranoid father about David or their covenant, but somehow Saul discovered that David was his successor (20:30-31) and tried all the more to kill him. He expected his men to inform him about David and his whereabouts and Saul let them know that David was chosen to be the next king (22:6-8).

2. God prepared David. (1 Sam. 16:14-23)

David knew that the Lord had been present at his conception and had arranged for his genetic structure (Ps. 139:13-16). He ordained that David would be strong and handsome, that he would possess musical talent, that he would be prudent and brave. Just as Paul was a vessel prepared by God for a specific work (Gal. 1:15; Acts 9:15), so David was God's prepared servant to accomplish His purposes for His people.

Saul's attendants knew that something was seriously wrong with their master, and they rightly attributed it to the attacks of an evil spirit. God had permitted this spirit to trouble Saul (1 Sam. 16:14, 23; 18:10; 19:9) as part of His discipline because of the king's rebellion. By nature, Saul was a suspicious and revengeful man, and this gave the evil spirit a beachhead for his operations (Eph. 4:25-27). The one man in the kingdom who was prepared to minister to Saul was David!

David was a poet and musician, skilled at playing the harp and composing songs. By the end of his life, he was known as "the sweet psalmist of Israel" (2 Sam. 23:1). It's unusual to find such artistic talent in a man who was also a rugged soldier and fearless general. He wrote psalms, he organized the music ministry for the temple (1 Chron. 25), and provided instruments for the musicians (23:5). From the spoils of his many battles, he provided the materials for the temple, and he longed to have the privilege of building a house for the Lord. No matter how you examine his life and abilities, you find David to be a unique individual—and he was that way because God made him that way!

It was David's musical ability that introduced him into the royal court and then he was promoted to military service. The opportunities of life matched his giftedness, and David was wise to obey the will of the Lord. Just as he refused to wear Saul's armor when facing Goliath, so he rejected that which wasn't prepared and planned for him by the Lord. "He leads me in the paths of righteousness for his name's sake" (Ps. 23:3; Eph. 2:10).

The key to David's success in life is stated in 1 Sam. 16:18—"the Lord was with him." (See 18:12, 14, 28.) This was also the secret of the success of Joseph (Gen. 39:2-3, 21, 23), Joshua (Josh. 6:27), and Samuel (1 Sam. 3:19), and it is the basis for success in the Christian life today. David knew his gifts (Rom. 12:3), he experienced the power of God in using these gifts in his daily life. He loved the Lord and worshiped Him, and he surrendered himself to do the work God had called him to do. As long as he followed the Lord, God blessed and used him for his glory.

In their original meeting, Saul loved David (1 Sam. 16:21), so he obviously didn't know that his new attendant was to be the next king of Israel. However, that love was gradually replaced by envy and then fear (18:8-9, 12, 15), until Saul was determined to kill David. Saul became David's enemy (v. 19), but David never treated Saul like an enemy. David behaved wisely and tried to help Saul get over his fits of depression, but they only became worse. Without God, Saul was a total failure.

3. God guided David. (1 Sam. 17:1-27) David didn't remain in Saul's camp permanently but went back and forth between the camp and home as he was needed (v. 15, NIV). Whenever he was called to help Saul, he left his flock with a dependable man (v. 20) and hurried to the camp where now he even had his own tent (v. 54). It wasn't until after David killed Goliath that Saul took him permanently to be one of his armor-bearers (18:1-2). David was a Spirit-led man and his every decision had to be in the will of God and for the glory of God. Others might come and go as they pleased, but David was guided by the providential hand of God. We can see the guidance of God in the events reported in chapter 17.

Goliath is described as standing nine feet, nine inches tall, wearing a coat of mail that weighed 125 pounds and carrying a spear that weighed 15 pounds. He was a formidable opponent indeed. He had presented himself to the army of Israel each morning and evening for forty days, and apparently David arrived on the final day (17:16). Jesse chose just the right day to send David to the battlefield to carry food supplies to his three brothers and their commanding officer (vv. 17-18). Unlike modern armies, soldiers in ancient armies had to provide their own rations and help provide for others.

David was up very early that day and heard the morning challenge that Goliath gave to Saul and his army. If the Israelites could provide a champion who was able to defeat Goliath, the Philistines would submit to the Jews and be their servants, but if not, the Israelites must consider themselves defeated and become the servants of the Philistines (vv. 8-9). Unfortunately, nobody in the Jewish army volunteered, including King Saul, who stood head and shoulders above his men. Since Israel had come to a crisis in this confrontation, Saul made a generous offer to the man who would silence Goliath: he would marry one of the king's daughters, receive great riches from the king, and take his father's house off the tax rolls. Saul hoped that somebody would be tempted by the offer and try to defeat Goliath.

David's response to Goliath's arrogant speech was that of total disgust. Who was this uncircumcised Philistine to blaspheme the name of the God of Israel? Keep in mind that David was too young to serve in the army, but he was acting as though anybody in the camp who had faith in Jehovah could challenge Goliath and defeat him! But all he saw were men fleeing from the field at the very sight of the giant, and even King Saul was terrified (vv. 11, 24).[6] God had brought David to the camp for such a time as this, and he was ready to accept the challenge.

4. God encouraged David. (1 Sam. 17:28-39)

Whenever you step out by faith to fight the enemy, there's always somebody around to discourage you, and often it begins in your own home. David's eldest brother, Eliab, became angry when he heard that David was inquiring about Saul's offer and he ridiculed him (vv. 28-30). "We're soldiers and all you are is a shepherd boy! You came to see the battle! Go home and take care of your little flock and leave the fighting to us!" Of course, the fact that there had been no battle didn't embarrass Eliab, and he also forgot that David had originally come in order to deliver food for him, Abinadab, and Shammah. These three men had seen David anointed by Samuel but they didn't understand what it meant.

"[A] man's foes shall be they of his own household," promised Jesus (Matt. 10:36; see Micah 7:6), and that promise was true in David's life. It was also true in the life of Joseph, whose brothers hated him, lied about him, and sold him for a slave. Moses was criticized by his own brother and sister (Num. 12), and our Lord's earthly family at one time misunderstood Him and opposed His ministry (Mark 3:31-35; John 7:1-10). But David didn't allow Eliab's harsh words to discourage him, for he knew that God could help him defeat the giant.

But King Saul wasn't any more help, either in what he said or what he advised. "You are not able to go against this Philistine to fight with him; for you are but a youth, and he is a man of war from his youth" (1 Sam. 17:33, NKJV). Saul was echoing the report of the ten unbelieving spies who saw the giants in Canaan and decided that it was impossible to enter the land (Num. 13:28-29). When we walk by sight, we calculate everything from the human perspective, and this always leads to discouragement; but when we walk by faith, God comes into the equation, and that changes the results.

David had experienced the power of God in his own life and he knew that the Lord could turn weakness into power. While caring for the sheep, David had killed a lion and a bear, and he knew that the Lord could deliver him out of the hand of Goliath. It's as though he sees Goliath as just another animal attacking God's flock! Saul knew nothing personally about this wonderful power of God, so he advised David to wear his armor. Saul didn't have the faith to believe that God could do something new, so he suggested the old-fashioned time-honored method of warfare. King Saul was a grown man and a large one at that, and David was only a teenager, so imagine what the armor looked like on David's body! But men and women of faith obey God no matter what the experts say.

David's encouragement came from God, and this is one of the secrets of his life. "But David encouraged himself in the Lord his God" (1 Sam. 30:6). In spite of criticism and in spite of discouraging counsel and bad advice, David trusted the Lord his God, and God rewarded his faith.

5. God enabled David. (1 Sam. 17:40-58)

"All God's giants have been weak men, who did great things for God because they reckoned on His being with them." James Hudson Taylor, the founder of the China Inland Mission, wrote those words, but even more, he lived them. "I am the very little servant of an illustrious Master," he told a congregation in Australia. David understood what this meant, for he was but a teenager when he faced the giant; yet he knew that the Lord would be with him.

It was the Lord's victory (1 Sam. 17:40-47). It's unfortunate that this dramatic account is considered primarily a children's story or the basis for an allegory about defeating the "giants" in our lives. While there are many applications of a Bible passage, there is only one basic interpretation, and the interpretation here is that David did what he did for the glory of God. David came to the contest in the name of the Lord, the God of the armies of Israel, and he wanted Goliath, the Philistine army, and all the earth to know that the true and living God was Israel's God (v. 46). Goliath had ridiculed Israel's God and blasphemed His name, but David was about to set the record straight. David saw this as a contest between the true God of Israel and the false gods of the Philistines.

God wants to use His people to magnify His name to all the nations of the earth. This purpose was involved in the call of Abraham (Gen. 12:1-3) and God's choice of the people of Israel (Deut. 28:9-10). One purpose for Israel's sojourn in Egypt and the judgments God sent against Pharaoh was the proclaiming of God's name and glory to all the earth (Ex. 9:16). The parting of the Red Sea to let Israel out, and the opening up of the Jordan River to let them into Canaan, bore witness to all the nations that Israel's God was the true God (Josh. 4:23-24). Even the building of the temple was a witness to the Gentile nations of Israel's God so that they might know Him and fear Him (1 Kings 8:42-43). What the Lord did through David would be recorded and told around the world and bring great honor to the name of the Lord.

The very weapon that David used—a sling—was a shepherd's weapon, almost the toy of a child, and yet God used it to defeat the giant and rout the Philistine army. When Goliath saw a lad coming with a sling in one hand and a staff in the other, he laughed at him. "Am I a dog that you come at me with a stick?" But David announced that his real power was the name of the Lord of Hosts, the name that Goliath and the Philistines had insulted. David wanted the whole assembly—Israel and the Philistines—to know that the Lord doesn't need swords and spears but can deliver His people in His own way through the humblest of means. No wonder David and Jonathan became such fast friends, for they both had faith in a mighty God and wanted to fight His battles to glorify Him (1 Sam. 13:6; Pss. 33:16-22; 44:6-8).

It was David's victory (1 Sam. 17:48-51a). The Lord uses means to accomplish His purposes, and David was the prepared servant for this occasion. As a shepherd alone in the fields, he had learned to trust God, and as a faithful guardian of the flock, he had mastered the use of the sling. David had confident faith in God because he had found Him dependable in the crises of life, and he knew that the Lord would not desert him now. The Spirit of God lived in David's body and would enable him to win the battle. God guided the stone and it sank into the giant's forehead and he fell on his face before the two armies.[7] David stood over the fallen giant, took out the giant's sword, and cut off his head, an act that not only guaranteed the victim's death but also humiliated him and his army and announced total victory. Years later, David would write, "It is God who arms me with strength, and makes my way perfect. . . . He teaches my hands to make war so that my arms can bend a bow of bronze" (Ps. 18:32, 34, NKJV).

It became Israel's victory (1 Sam. 17:51b-54). Even as a youth, David displayed one of the marks of a great leader: he took the risk and opened the way so that others could share in the victory. The Philistines didn't keep their part of the bargain and submit to Israel (v. 9); instead, they fled in fear, so the Jews chased them at least ten miles to the cities of Gath (Goliath's hometown, v. 4) and Ekron, slaying the enemy soldiers all the way.[8] It turned out to be a tremendous victory for Saul's army. When the Israelites returned to the Philistine camp, they claimed the spoils of the victory that the Lord and David had won. David apparently accompanied the men in chasing the enemy (v. 57) and began to get the reputation of being a brave soldier (18:7). He stripped the giant and took his armor and put it in his tent. Later Goliath's sword will show up with the Jewish priests in Nob (21:1-9), so David must have dedicated it to the Lord by giving it to the priests.

When did David take Goliath's head to Jerusalem? Probably later when he conquered the city and made it his capital (2 Sam. 5:1-10). The city was known as Jebus in that day and was inhabited by the Jebusites (Judg. 19:10), so this verse was written into the text later when the name had been changed. When David moved into the city as king, he no doubt brought with him many precious trophies from his battles. The head of Goliath, as grisly as it was, would remind David that the Lord could be trusted to give the victory if we seek only to glorify Him.

It was not Saul's victory (1 Sam. 17:55-58). When Jonathan attacked the Philistine outpost (14:1-23), Saul was a spectator, and his bad decisions almost cost them a victory; and once again, Saul merely watched as David defeated the enemy single-handed. This would be Saul's pattern of leadership to the tragic end of his life.

Saul knew who David was, but he asked Abner who the lad's father was, for in that day, that was how people were identified. Jesse had been mentioned earlier in Saul's circle (16:18) but perhaps Abner wasn't present and Saul may easily have forgotten. (Do we know the names of our acquaintances' fathers?) As Saul's minstrel, David went back and forth between home and the camp, and he was present only when Saul was oppressed by the evil spirit; so we can excuse Saul for not knowing who Jesse was. The fact that the victor's family was relieved of paying taxes, and he would marry Saul's daughter was part of the bargain (17:25), so Saul would have to inquire about the father. Finally, Saul may have wanted to know if there were any more men like David back home. He probably didn't know that three of David's brothers were in his army, but he could have used a few more men like David! (See 14:52.) The result of the day's victory was that David was added permanently to Saul's staff.

It has well been said that there are people who make things happen, people who watch things happen and people who don't know that anything is happening. David had insight into Israel's plight and knew what was happening. He realized that it wasn't a physical conflict between two armies, but a spiritual battle between truth and error, faith and superstition, the true and living God and dead idols. David's faith lifted the war to a much higher plane, just as Paul did in Ephesians 6:10ff. Our battle is against the devil and his army, and human weapons are useless in that conflict.

Faith in God makes us participants with the Lord in the battle for truth. "And this is the victory that has overcome the world—our faith" (1 John 5:4). 9

CHAPTER SEVEN
A JEALOUS KING
1 Samuel 18–19

Jewish men had to be at least twenty years old before they could go to war (Num. 1:3), but David was probably only eighteen when he was made a high-ranking officer in the Jewish army (18:5, NIV). From the beginning of his new assignment, David found himself in a life-threatening conflict with King Saul. David didn't *create* problems for Saul; he *revealed* the deep-seated problems that were already there. David was an honest man of faith, but Saul was a deceitful, scheming man of the world. With great humility David had accepted his appointment as Israel's next king, while Saul was almost paranoid as he tried to protect his throne. God had abandoned Saul but had given His Spirit's power to David, and David moved from victory to victory as he led Saul's troops. We can trace some of the major stages in Saul's growing opposition to David.

1. Saul wants David killed. (1 Sam. 18:1-12)

At one time, Saul loved David (16:21, "liked him very much," NIV), but the king's attitude changed into jealousy and then hatred. The Lord was with David (18:12, 14, 28), however, and Saul was not permitted to harm him. During the ten years or so that David was a fugitive, the Lord not only thwarted Saul's plans repeatedly, but He even used the king's hostility to mature David and make him into a man of courage and faith. While Saul was guarding his throne, David was being prepared for his throne.

Love (1 Sam. 18:1-4). Too many Bible readers still view David and Jonathan as two frolicsome teenagers who liked each other because they had many common interests, but this picture is shallow and inaccurate. Jonathan had to be at least twenty years old to be in his father's army, and the fact that Jonathan was already commanding one-third of that army and had won two great victories (13:1-4; 14:1ff) indicates that he was a seasoned soldier and not a callow adolescent. Some biblical chronologists calculate that there could have been an age difference of twenty-five to twenty-eight years between David and Jonathan.

Jonathan listened to his father and David converse, and after that interview, took David to his own heart with the kind of manly affection that comrades in arms understand.[1] Jonathan was Saul's eldest son, destined for the throne of Israel, and the Lord had already given it to David, so their friendship was certainly unique. When Jonathan gave his official garments and his armor to David, making him a friend and equal, Jonathan was acknowledging that David would one day take his place, so David must have told Jonathan about his anointing. The two friends covenanted that when David became king, Jonathan would be second in command (20:16-17, 42; 23:16-18), and David covenanted to protect Jonathan's family from being slain.

Saul wasn't pleased with his son's friendship with David. For one thing, Jonathan was Saul's best commander and was needed to make the king look good. Saul was also afraid that Jonathan would divulge court secrets to David, and when Saul discovered that David was already anointed to succeed him, this made matters worse. He saw David as an enemy, a threat to his own son's future, although Jonathan didn't view it that way. But when a leader nurtures himself on pride, jealousy and fear, he suspects everybody.

Popularity (1 Sam. 18:5-7). "The crucible for silver and the furnace for gold, but a man is tested by the praise he receives" (Prov. 27:21, NIV). Just as the crucible and furnace test the metal and prepare it for use, so praise tests and prepares people for what God has planned for them. How we respond to praise reveals what we're made of and whether or not we're ready to take on new responsibilities. If praise humbles us, then God can use us, but if praise puffs us up, we're not yet ready for a promotion.

In his attitudes, conduct, and service, David was a complete success, and Saul's servants and the Jewish people recognized this and praised him publicly. This popular acclaim started after David's stunning defeat of Goliath, when the army of Israel chased the Philistines for ten miles, defeated them, and took their spoils (1 Sam. 17:52ff). As Saul and his men returned to camp, the women met the victors and praised both Saul and David. In true Hebrew fashion, their praise was exaggerated, but in one sense it was true. David's victory over Goliath made it possible for the whole army of Israel to conquer the Philistines, so each soldier's achievement was really a triumph for David.

Envy and anger (1 Sam. 18:8-11). "It is a dangerous crisis when a proud heart meets with flattering lips," said John Flavel, seventeenth-century British Presbyterian clergyman and author. What the women sang didn't seem to affect David, but their song enraged Saul. Saul had already forfeited the kingdom (15:28), but he still asked, "What can he have more but the kingdom?" Saul's response to David's success was exactly opposite that of John the Baptist when he was told of the great success of Jesus: "He must increase, but I must decrease" (John 3:30).

Envy is a dangerous and insidious enemy, a cancer that slowly eats out our inner life and leads us to say and do terrible things. Proverbs 14:30 rightly calls it "the rottenness of the bones." Envy is the pain we feel within when somebody achieves or receives what we think belongs to us. Envy is the sin of successful people who can't stand to see others reach the heights they have reached and eventually replace them. By nature, we are proud and want to be recognized and applauded; and from childhood we have been taught to compete with others. Dr. Bob Cook often reminded us that everybody wears a sign that reads, "Please make me feel important." Much modern advertising thrives on envy as it cleverly contrasts the "haves" and the "have-nots" and urges the "have-nots" to buy the latest products and keep up with the "haves." Envious people max out their credit cards to buy things they don't need just to impress people who really don't care!

But envy easily leads to anger, and anger is often the first step toward murder (Matt. 5:21-26). This explains why Saul threw his spear at David while David was trying to soothe the king and help him overcome his depression. The Lord enabled David to escape, and when he returned to the king a second time, Saul only tried again to kill him. These two events probably occurred after the Goliath victory but before David was made an officer in the army, and yet David remained faithful to his king.

Fear (v. 12). The Lord protected His servant David from Saul's murderous hand, a fact that frightened Saul even more (vv. 15, 29). Surely Saul knew he was fighting a losing battle, for the Lord was on David's side but had departed from him. However, Saul kept up a brave front as he tried to impress his officers with his authority. Even if Saul missed his target, the people around him didn't miss the message he was sending: "Saul is king and he wants David to be killed."

2. Saul plots to have David killed. (1 Sam. 18:13-30)

"Faith is living without scheming," but Saul was better at scheming than at trusting God. If Saul disobeyed God, he always had a ready excuse to get himself out of trouble, and if people challenged his leadership, he could figure out ways to eliminate them. Possessed by anger and envy, and determined to hold on to his crown, Saul decided that young David had to be killed.

Saul sends David into battle (1 Sam. 18:13-16). Since David was an excellent soldier and a born leader, the logical thing was to give him assignments that would take him away from the camp where the enemy could kill him. Saul made David commander over 1,000 and sent him to fight the Philistines. If David was killed in battle, it was the enemy's fault; and if he lost a battle but lived, his popularity would wane. But the plan didn't work because David won all the battles! After all, the Lord was with him and the power of God was upon him. Instead of eliminating David or diminishing his popularity, Saul's scheme only made him a greater hero to the people, and this increased Saul's fear of David all the more.

Saul demands an impossible feat (1 Sam. 18:17-27). Saul had promised to give one of his daughters in marriage to the man who killed Goliath (17:25), but this promise had not yet been fulfilled. The fact that David had killed Goliath wasn't enough, for Saul now expected David to "fight the battles of the Lord" in order to gain his wife, Saul's eldest daughter, Merab. Saul wasn't beneath using his own daughter as a tool to get rid of David. The details aren't given, but it seems that David had to fight a certain number of battles before the marriage could take place. Of course, the king was hoping that David would be slain during one of those battles, and then Saul would lose his enemy but still have his daughter.

However, David humbly declined the offer, saying that his family wasn't worthy to be related to the king; so Saul gave Merab to another suitor.[2]

Then Saul happily discovered that his younger daughter Michal was in love with David! Saul spoke to David about it and said he would give him a second chance to claim his reward. Once again David demurred, but Saul persisted. This time he asked selected servants to lie to David and tell him that Saul liked him and wanted him to marry Michal, and that Saul's attendants agreed with the proposal. But David put them off by telling the truth: he was from a lowly family and he didn't have any money to pay the bride price (Gen. 34:12; Ex. 22:16).

When David's reply was reported to Saul, the devious king saw in it a great opportunity to attack his enemies and get rid of David at the same time. Saul told his servants to tell David that all that the king required for a bride price was 100 foreskins from the "uncircumcised Philistines." Saul was certain that at some point in this endeavor, David would meet his death. Once again, Saul was using one of his daughters to help destroy an innocent man, and in this instance, it was a man she truly loved.

Whether the phrase "the appointed days" (1 Sam. 18:26) refers to a new deadline or the original deadline determined by Saul for Merab is really unimportant, because David and his men[3] accomplished even more than Saul had asked. David once more survived the battles and he brought the king 200 foreskins. Another of Saul's schemes had failed and he had to give Michal to David as his wife.

Saul is even more afraid (1 Sam. 18:28-30). We have seen this pattern before (vv. 12, 15), but now Saul's twisted emotions so controlled him that he was obsessed with the desire to kill his son-in-law. David never considered Saul to be his enemy (Ps. 18 inscription), but Saul remained David's enemy until the day he died on the battlefield. David continued to fight the Lord's battles, and the Lord continued to give him great success and to magnify his name above the names of Saul's best officers. David certainly paid close attention to what God was doing in him and for him, and no doubt the remembrance of these events encouraged him during the difficult days of his exile. "If God be for us, who can be against us?" (Rom. 8:31)

3. Saul looks for opportunities to have David killed. (1 Sam. 19:1-17)

Saul's mind and heart were so possessed by hatred for David that he openly admitted to Jonathan and the court attendants that he intended to have his son-in-law killed. Saul was now through with behind-the-scenes plots and was out to destroy David in the quickest way possible, and he ordered Jonathan and the royal attendants to join him in his endeavor. The hope of Israel lay in the heart and ministry of David, and yet Saul wanted to kill him! David would conquer Israel's enemies and consolidate the kingdom. He would gather much of the wealth used to build the temple. He would write psalms for the Levites to sing in praising God, and he would even design the musical instruments they played. God's covenant with David would keep the light shining in Jerusalem during the dark days of the nation's decline, and the fulfillment of that covenant would bring Jesus Christ the Messiah into the world. No wonder Satan was so determined to kill David!

Jonathan's intervention (1 Sam. 19:1-10). Surely Saul knew that Jonathan would pass the word along to his beloved friend David, but perhaps that's what the king desired. If he couldn't kill David, perhaps he could so frighten him that he would leave the land and never be seen again. Jonathan did report the king's words to David and suggested that his friend hide in the field the next morning when Jonathan would speak with his father on behalf of David. It's remarkable that such a magnificent son could belong to such a wicked father! Had Jonathan been a selfish man, he could have helped to eliminate David and secure the crown for himself, but he submitted to the will of God and assisted David.

Jonathan presented his father with two arguments: (1) David was an innocent man who was not deserving of death,[4] and (2) David had served Saul faithfully by winning great victories against Israel's enemies. David was a valuable man to have around and he had never sinned against the king. Jonathan didn't mention that David was also very popular with the soldiers and the common people, because making such a statement would only have aroused the king's anger and envy. Saul was enjoying a sane moment and agreed with his son, and even took an oath not to kill David. Saul was a liar and his oaths were meaningless (14:24, 44), but this did open the way for David to return to court.

When the Philistines attacked Israel again, David went out with his men and soundly defeated them. This only aroused Saul's envy and anger and once again he tried to pin David to the wall (18:10-11). Satan is a liar and a murderer (John 8:44), and because Saul was controlled by the evil one, he broke his oath and he threw his spear. David knew that the time had come for him to leave Saul's presence and hide, but first he went home to see his wife Michal. David would now begin about ten years of exile during which God would make a leader out of him.

Michal's deception (1 Sam. 19:11-17). Saul surmised that David would go home, so he sent men that night to watch David's house and kill him when he came out the next morning. Knowing her father's thought processes, Michal urged David to get out that night and flee to a place of safety. She let him down through a window and arranged a dummy in the bed by using an idol and some goats' hair. What Michal was doing with an pagan idol (teraphim) is a mystery, especially one as large as a man. (Rachel hid two teraphim under a saddle—Gen. 31:33-35.) It's possible that the idol was only a bust and that she used it and the goats' hair[5] for the head and used pillows to simulate the body. Michal was still depending on idols while married to a man after God's own heart, and like her father, she was a schemer.

While Michal was scheming, David was praying and trusting the Lord, and Psalm 59 came out of this experience. As you read this psalm, you see Saul's spies running here and there and waiting for David to emerge from his house, and you hear David comparing them to snarling dogs lurking in the city streets. But David's faith was in the Lord, for only the Lord could be his defense and his refuge. This doesn't mean that David rejected any plans for escape, because the Lord uses human means to accomplish His divine ends; but it does mean that David's faith was not in himself or in Michal's schemes, but in the Lord of the armies of Israel.

In the morning, when the agents demanded that Michal surrender her husband, she told them he was sick, and when they reported this to Saul, he told the men to bring him David, bed and all! But when they picked up the bed, the truth was revealed, and Michal was reproved by her father for being so deceptive, but she was only following his example! Like her father, she lied and claimed that David had threatened to kill her if she didn't cooperate.

4. Saul himself goes to kill David. (1 Sam. 19:18-24)

David fled to Samuel in Ramah, a godly friend he knew he could depend on, and Samuel took him to the fellowship of the prophets where they could worship God and seek His face. The word *naioth* means "dwellings" and was probably a section in Ramah where the "school of the prophets" assembled. There Samuel and David could worship and pray and ask God for wisdom, and the prophets would pray with them. But Saul's spies were everywhere and they reported to Saul where he could find David. The king sent three different groups of soldiers to capture David, but when they arrived at the place where the prophets had assembled, they were immediately possessed by the Spirit and began to praise and worship God! The Hebrew word translated "prophesy" can mean "to sing songs and praise God" as well as "to foretell events." Saul's soldiers didn't become prophets; they only uttered words inspired by the Spirit of God. God protected David and Samuel, not by sending an army but by sending the Holy Spirit to turn warriors into worshipers. "The weapons we fight with are not the weapons of the world. On the contrary, they have divine power to demolish strongholds" (2 Cor. 10:4, NIV).

Three groups of soldiers had failed, so Saul decided to go to Ramah himself. David's presence in Ramah was no secret because the people at the great cistern knew where he and Samuel were and they told Saul. Perhaps the entire town knew that some kind of "spiritual revival" was taking place at the school of the prophets. Saul hastened to the place only to be met by the Spirit of God and made to praise the Lord. He took off his outer royal garments and became like any other man, and he lay on the floor before Samuel. This would be their last meeting until that fateful night when Samuel came from the realms of the dead to pass judgment on the king (1 Sam. 28:7ff).

But Saul had had a similar experience after Samuel had anointed him king (10:9-13), and from it came the proverbial saying, "Is Saul also among the prophets?" After Saul's experience at Ramah, the proverb was resurrected. These two events prove that a person can have a remarkable religious experience and yet have no change in character. In Saul's case, both experiences were actually sent by the Lord, but Saul didn't profit from them. Special religious manifestations aren't evidences that a person is even saved (Matt. 7:21-23). Judas preached sermons and even performed miracles (Matt. 10:1-8), yet he was not a believer (John 6:67-71; 13:10-11; 17:12), and he betrayed the Lord and ended up committing suicide. Saul, like Judas, had many opportunities to see the Lord's hand at work, and yet he never had a life-changing experience with the Lord.

While Saul was occupied at the school of the prophets, David slipped away from Ramah and went to meet Jonathan somewhere near Gibeah. David and Jonathan would make one final effort at reconciliation with Saul, and it would almost cost Jonathan his life. Saul was a "double-minded man, unstable in all his ways" (James 1:8, NKJV). He would try to rule the land and defeat the Philistines while at the same time chasing David and seeking to kill him. The longer David eluded him, the more fanatical Saul became, until finally he ended his own life on the battlefield, lacking the help of the one man who could have given him victory.

CHAPTER EIGHT
DAVID IN EXILE
1 Samuel 20–22

David has been criticized and called impulsive because he left Ramah and his friend Samuel and fled to Gibeah to confer with Jonathan. But David knew that Saul's ecstatic experience would soon end and would leave his heart unchanged. Saul had promised Jonathan that he wouldn't try to kill David (19:6), but he had already broken that promise four times (vv. 20-24), so the wisest course for David was to get away from Saul and go into hiding. For David to remain at Gibeah wasn't an exercise of faith; it was an act of presumption and he was only tempting God. The drama in these three chapters involves four persons: Jonathan, Saul, David, and Doeg.

1. Jonathan—a faithful friend (1 Sam. 20:1-23)

In all literature, David and Jonathan stand out as examples of devoted friends. Jonathan had the more difficult situation because he wanted to be loyal to his father while at the same time being a friend to the next king of Israel. Conflict of loyalties, especially in the family, is one of the most painful difficulties we face in the life of faith (Matt. 10:34-39), but Christ calls for supreme devotion to Him and His will for our lives.

Conferring (1 Sam. 20:1-10, 18-23). David met Jonathan somewhere near Gibeah and wasted no time confronting his beloved friend with the key question: "What have I done that is so evil that your father wants to kill me?" David hadn't disobeyed any royal commands, incited any rebellion against the throne, or broken God's law, yet Saul was bent on destroying him.[1] David knew that Saul was an envious man who wanted to keep the throne for himself and hand it on to his descendants, but David had faith that the Lord would remove Saul from the scene in His good time and in His own way (26:7-11). David dearly loved Jonathan and didn't want to hurt him by criticizing his father, but now it was a matter of life or death.

Jonathan's reply sounds rather naïve, especially in the light of Saul's statement in 19:1 and his behavior at Ramah. Saul had thrown his spear at David at least three times (10–11; 19:9-10), and he had sent three groups of soldiers to capture him, and Saul finally went to Ramah himself to do the job (vv. 20-24). How much evidence did Jonathan need that his father was a disturbed man out to destroy God's anointed king? Jonathan mistakenly thought that his own relationship to his father was closer than it really was and that Saul would confide in him, but subsequent events proved him wrong, for Saul would even try to kill Jonathan!

David refuted Jonathan's argument by stating that the logical thing for Saul to do was to keep his eldest son in the dark. Saul knew that David and Jonathan were devoted friends and that Jonathan would be pained if he knew Saul's real intentions. The matter was so serious that David couldn't put his faith in what Saul told Jonathan. "There is but a step between me and death" (20:3). This was true both metaphorically and literally, for three times David had dodged the king's spear.

Jonathan offered to help in any way his

friend suggested, and David proposed a simple test of Saul's true feelings. It was customary for each Jewish family to hold a feast at the new moon (Num. 10:10; 28:11-15; Ps. 81:3), and Saul would expect David to attend. If Saul's son-in-law and leading military hero didn't attend the feast, it would be an insult to the king as well as the family, so David's absence would help reveal Saul's genuine attitude toward David. If Saul became angry, then David's assessment was correct, but if Saul excused David and didn't press the matter, then Jonathan was correct. The only problem with this scheme was that it required Jonathan to lie by saying that David had gone to Bethlehem to attend his own family's feast. David would be hiding in the field and waiting for Jonathan to tell him whether or not it was safe to come home.[2]

How would Jonathan safely get the message to David? (1 Sam. 20:10) He couldn't trust one of the servants to carry the word, so, in spite of the danger, he would have to do it himself. He devised a simple plan involving shooting three arrows out in the field where David was hiding (v. 20). Jonathan would call to the lad who was helping him and in this way signal David and tell him what to do. Even if some of Saul's spies were present, they wouldn't understand what was going on.

Covenanting (1 Sam. 20:11-17). From verse 11 to verse 23, David is silent while Jonathan reviews the covenant they had made with each other (18:1-4). Jonathan even took an oath and promised to give David the correct message on the third day of the feast, so he would know whether the king was friendly or angry.[3] Jonathan went beyond the immediate crisis to deal with future events. He knew that David would one day become king, and he prayed that the Lord would bless his reign. In their covenant, they agreed that Jonathan would serve next to David as second in command (23:16-18), and now Jonathan asked that if anything happened to him, David would promise not to wipe out his household, and David agreed. The phrase "the kindness of the Lord" (20:14) shows up in 2 Samuel 9 where David's compassionate care of Jonathan's crippled son, Mephibosheth, is described.

Jonathan reaffirmed his oath and included the whole house of David (1 Sam. 20:16), and he asked David to repeat his covenant oath as well. There's no mention of the offering of a covenant sacrifice (Gen. 15) or the signing of a covenant document, because the love the two men had for the Lord and each other was sufficient to make the agreement binding. Jonathan had brought much joy and encouragement to David during those difficult years, but it wasn't God's will that David permanently join himself to Saul and his family, for they belonged to the wrong tribe and represented a rejected and condemned monarchy. David never had a co-regent because Jonathan was killed in battle (1 Sam. 31:1-2), and David rejected Saul's daughter Michal as his wife and she died childless (2 Sam. 6:16-23). Had she borne any children, it would have brought confusion into the royal line.

2. Saul—a spiteful king (1 Sam. 20:24-42)

On the first day of the feast, David hid himself by the stone of Ezel and waited for Jonathan's signal, for it was remotely possible that the king might be favorably inclined and welcome him back into the official circle.

David's absence (1 Sam. 20:24-29). Constantly afraid of personal attack, Saul sat with his back to the wall, his commander Abner next to him, and Jonathan across from his father. David's place next to Jonathan was empty, but the king said nothing about it, convinced that David was ceremonially unclean and therefore unable to eat a holy feast that day. The feast consisted primarily of meat from the new moon fellowship offerings, and anyone ceremonially unclean was prohibited from participating (Lev. 7:20-21). Perhaps David had touched something unclean, or he may have had intercourse with his wife (15:16-18). If so, all he had to do was separate himself from other people for that day, bathe his body, and change clothes, and he could come back into society the next day.

But when the men met for their meal the second day, again David was missing, which suggested to Saul that his son-in-law's absence was caused by something more serious than simple ritual defilement. An unclean person could remove the defilement in a day, but David had been missing for two days. Suspicious of anything out of the ordinary in his official staff, Saul asked Jonathan why David was absent, disdainfully calling him "the son of Jesse" rather than by his given name that was now so famous. Later, Saul would try to humiliate the high priest, Ahimelech, by calling him "the son of Ahitub" (1 Sam. 22:11-12).

At this point Jonathan dropped his lie into the conversation and nothing went right after that. Jonathan didn't say that David's father Jesse had summoned him home but that one of his brothers had *commanded* him to attend the family feast. Perhaps Jonathan hoped his father would assume that the invitation came from one of David's three brothers serving in Saul's army (17:13), which might make the matter easier for Saul to accept. Jonathan also used a verb that means "to get away, to make a quick visit" so that Saul wouldn't suspect David of going home for a long visit and rallying his own troops so he could seize the throne.

Saul's anger (1 Sam. 20:30-34). When hateful feelings are in the heart, it doesn't take much for angry words to come out of the mouth (Matt. 12:34-35). Saul had probably been brooding over how David had insulted him by refusing to attend the feast, and the longer he brooded, the more the fire raged within. But instead of attacking David, King Saul attacked his own son! Had the Lord not intervened back in Ramah, Saul would have killed David in the very presence of the Prophet Samuel (1 Sam. 19:22-24), and now he reviled his own son while eating a holy feast!

The king's tirade seems to disparage his own wife, but rightly understood, his words describe his son as the lowest of the low. According to Saul, Jonathan's treachery in befriending David indicated that he was not Saul's son at all but the son of some other man, for a son of Saul would never betray his father. Therefore, Jonathan was slandering his own mother and saying she was a common prostitute, a rebel against the Law of Moses, and a woman who practiced perversion. Because Jonathan helped David and didn't protect his father's throne, he had shamed his mother as much as if he had exposed her nakedness. She bore him to be the successor to his father, and now Jonathan had refused the crown in favor of the son of Jesse. The king was shouting, "You are no son of mine! You must be illegitimate!"

Saul's great concern was the preservation of the kingdom *that the Lord had already taken from him*. God had made it very clear that none of Saul's sons would ever inherit the throne and David was the king of God's choice, so Saul was fighting the will of God and asking Jonathan to do the same thing. Saul was aware that his son knew where David was hiding and commanded Jonathan to find David and bring him in to be slain. When Jonathan remonstrated with his father and refused to obey the royal command, Saul threw his spear at his own son! Jonathan left the table in great anger and spent the rest of the day fasting.

Jonathan's alarm (1 Ssam. 20:35-42). Jonathan waited until the next day and then went out into the field with one of his young attendants as though he were going to practice shooting arrows. As he promised David, he shot three arrows (v. 20), one of which was sent far beyond the boy, making it necessary for Jonathan to shout to the lad. But his words were meant for David's ears: "Hurry! Go quickly! Don't linger!" When the boy came back with the arrows, Jonathan gave him the bow and sent him back to the city, and then he ran out to meet David.

This was not their last meeting (23:16-18), but it was certainly a profoundly emotional farewell. They both wept, but David wept the most. He didn't know how many years of exile lay before him, and perhaps he might never see his beloved friend again. Eastern peoples aren't ashamed to weep, embrace, and kiss one another when they meet or when they part (Gen. 31:55; Acts 20:37). Jonathan's, "Go in peace" must have encouraged David. Both men reaffirmed their covenant, knowing that the Lord heard their words and saw their hearts.[4] David left and traveled three miles to the priestly city of Nob, and Jonathan returned to Gibeah and continued to be an officer in his father's army.

Ten years later, the Philistines would kill Saul, Jonathan, and his brothers on the battlefield (1 Sam. 31:1-6).

3. David—a hopeful exile (1 Sam. 21:1–22:5)

When David fled to Nob, it marked the beginning of an exile that lasted about ten years (21:1–29:11). Not all of David's wilderness experiences are recorded, but enough history has been given to show us that he was a man of faith and courage. While it's difficult to determine the background of every psalm, it's likely that David's fugitive years are reflected in Psalms 7, 11–13, 16–17, 22, 25, 31, 34–35, 52–54, 56–59, 63–64, 142–143. Psalm 18 is his song of praise when God gave him triumph over his enemies.[5] It's wonderful that David wrote so many encouraging psalms during this period of great suffering, and from them God's people today can find strength and courage in their own times of testing. Our Lord quoted Psalm 22:1 and 31:5 when on the cross.

David goes to Nob (1 Sam. 21:1-9). This was a priestly town three miles south of Gibeah where the tabernacle was located. (The Ark was still in the house of Abinadab in Kiriath Jearim; 7:1.) Because of his friendship with Samuel, David knew he would find refuge and help among the priests there; and he had a strong personal devotion to the sanctuary of the Lord (Ps. 27:4-6). The fact that David arrived alone frightened Ahimelech, the high priest, who was a great-grandson of Eli and was also known as Ahijah (1 Sam. 14:3). He knew David's reputation and position and wondered that he was traveling without a royal entourage.

If "the king" in 21:2 refers to the Lord Jehovah (see 20:42), then David isn't lying, for David certainly was doing the Lord's business and would be for the rest of his life. But if this statement was a deliberate lie, then David was scheming instead of trusting. His motive was probably to protect the high priest from Saul's future investigations, but the plan failed; for Saul killed Ahimelech and all the priests except

Abiathar, because they conspired with his enemy. However, it is possible that David had asked some of his men to rendezvous with him at the cave of Adullam (see 22:2). David's reference to the ritual purity of his men suggests this.

David needed food, so Ahimelech gave him the sacred loaves from the tabernacle, food that was reserved only for the priests (Lev. 24:5-9). If the people had been bringing their tithes to the tabernacle as the law commanded, there would have been more food available, but it was a time of spiritual decline in the land. Jesus used this incident to teach a lesson on true obedience and spiritual discernment (Matt. 12:1-8; Mark 2:23-28; Luke 6:1-5).[6] Ahimelech wanted to be sure that David's soldiers were ritually clean, and David assured him that neither the men nor their equipment had been defiled (Lev. 15:16-18). David also asked for Goliath's sword, which for some reason was kept in the tabernacle alongside the ephod (Ex. 28:4-13). David could now proceed on his journey with food to strengthen himself and a sword for protection.

Doeg's presence at the tabernacle is a mystery. He was an Edomite and therefore not born a child of the covenant, but he was "detained before the Lord" at the sanctuary (1 Sam. 21:7). Perhaps he had become a Jewish proselyte and was following the Hebrew faith in order to hold his job. As Saul's chief shepherd, Doeg could easily have become defiled so that he had to bring a sacrifice to the Lord. David knew that Doeg would report to Saul what he had seen at Nob and that this would mean trouble (22:9ff).

From Nob to Gath (1 Sam. 21:10-15). Fear of Saul now temporarily replaced faith in the Lord, and David fled twenty-three miles to the enemy city of Gath, the home of the Philistine giant Goliath (17:4). It wasn't a safe place to go, but after seeing Doeg at Nob, David may have decided that his presence anywhere in Israel would only jeopardize the lives of his friends, so he decided to leave the land. Furthermore, the last place Saul would look for him would be in Philistia. David's reputation as a great warrior had preceded him,[7] and the king and his counselors didn't view his presence as a blessing. David then pretended to be mad, and this made it easy for him to escape unharmed. Had David waited on the Lord and sought His will, he might not have gotten into trouble.

Psalms 34 and 56 both came out of this bizarre experience. Psalm 56 was his prayer for God's help when the situation became dangerous, and Psalm 34 was his hymn of praise after God had delivered him, although he mentions "fear" (vv. 4, 7) and deliverance from trouble (1 Sam. 21:6, 17, 19). The emphasis in Psalm 56 is on the slander and verbal attacks of the Philistine leaders as they tried to get their king to deal with David. There's no question that David was a frightened man while he was in Gath, but he sustained his faith by remembering God's promises (vv. 10-11) and God's call upon his life (v. 12). According to Psalm 34, David did a lot of praying while in Gath (vv. 4-6, 17-22), and the Lord heard him. David learned that the fear of the Lord conquers every other fear (vv. 9-16). The Lord was indeed merciful to David to enable him to escape back to his own land. No matter how we feel or how dismal the circumstances appear, the safest place in the world is in the will of God.

From Gath to the cave of Adullam (1 Sam. 22:1-2). This was a well-known place in Judah, ten miles from Gath and about fifteen miles from Bethlehem, David's hometown. David was at least in friendly territory, and the fighting men from Judah and Benjamin came to join his band (1 Chron. 12:16-18). It was here that David longed for a drink of water from the well at Bethlehem and three of his mighty men broke through enemy lines to bring it to him (2 Sam. 23:13-17). Knowing how much that drink of water cost those three men who risked their lives, David poured it out as a drink offering to the Lord. Great leaders don't take their followers for granted or treat lightly the sacrifices that they make beyond the call of duty.

All of David's family joined him at the cave, which meant that his brothers deserted Saul's army and became fugitives like David. They knew that David was God's anointed king, so they linked up with the future of the nation. Many others saw in David the only hope for a successful kingdom, so they came to him as well: those who were in distress because of Saul, those in debt, and those discontented because of the way Saul was ruining the nation (see 1 Sam. 14:29). David ended up with 400 high quality fighting men, and the number later increased to 600 (23:13; 25:13; 27:2; 30:9). Some of his mighty men and their leaders are listed in 2 Sam. 23:8-39 and 1 Chron. 11:10-41. Saul had an army of 3,000 chosen men (1 Sam. 26:2).

True leaders attract the best people who see in the leader those qualities of character that they most admire. The people around David would never have been noticed in history were it not for their association with him, just as our Lord's disciples would have died unknown had they not walked with Jesus. God usually doesn't call the great and the powerful to be His servants, but those who have a heart for Him and an eagerness to obey His will (1 Cor. 1:26-31). David's little band of rejects represented the future of the nation, and God's blessing was with them. History reveals that it is the devoted remnant, small as it might be, that holds the key to the future of God's work on this earth.

Psalms 57 and 142 are associated with David's stay in the cave of Adullam, and both of them emphasize David's faith that God was his refuge. As David prayed, the cave became a holy tabernacle where by faith he could find shelter under the wings of the cherubim in the Holy of Holies (57:1). What looked like a cave to others was to David a divine sanctuary, for the Lord was his portion and his refuge (142:5). To David, the fugitive life was like being in prison (v. 7), but he trusted the Lord to see him through. He knew that God would keep his promises and give him the throne and the kingdom.

From Adullam to Moab (1 Sam. 22:3-4a). David honored his father and mother and sought to protect them, so he asked the king of Moab to shelter them until his days of exile were over. The Moabites were the descendants of Lot from his incestuous relationship with his older daughter (Gen. 19:30-38). In the days of Moses, the Moabites were not a people favored by the Jews (Deut. 23:3-6), but David's great-grandmother Ruth came from Moab (Ruth 4:18-22), and this may have helped David to gain their support.

From Adullam to "the stronghold" (1 Sam. 22:4b). After David had secured the safety of his parents, he returned to Adullam and then moved his company to "the stronghold" or "fortress," which many students believe was at Masada by the Dead Sea, about thirty-five miles southwest of Adullam. The Hebrew word *mesuda* means "fortress" or "stronghold," and can refer to natural hiding places in the wilderness. David lived in different "desert strongholds" (23:14, NIV) as he tried to protect himself and his friends and outwit Saul and his spies. But the Prophet Gad warned David that the wilderness fortress wasn't safe and that he should return to the land of Judah, so he relocated in the forest of Hereth in the vicinity of the cave of Adullam. *Hereth* means "thicket."

The Prophet Gad will appear again in the narrative of David's life. It was he who gave David the Lord's message after David had numbered the people (2 Sam. 24:11-19; 1 Chron. 21:9-19) and assisted David in setting up the musical ministry for the sanctuary of the Lord (2 Chron. 29:25). He also wrote a book about David's reign (1 Chron. 29:29). Later, Abiathar the priest would escape Saul's slaughter of the priests at Nob and join David, so that the king would have available the ministries of both prophet and priest.

4. Doeg: a deceitful servant (1 Sam. 22:6-23)

Now we discover why the writer mentioned Doeg in verse 7, for now he steps forth as a key actor in the drama. Wherever there is a scheming leader, he will have scheming followers, for we reproduce after our own kind. These are people who will do anything to gain the leader's approval and receive his rewards, and Doeg was such a man. This was the perfect time for him to use his knowledge to please the king and raise his own stature before the other officers. The fact that he was accusing God's anointed king didn't bother him, or that he lied about what the high priest said and did. It is no wonder that David despised Doeg and expressed his loathing in the words of Psalm 52.

The king's anger (1 Sam. 22:6-10). King Saul, spear in hand (18:10; 19:9; 26:7-22), was holding court under a tree on a hill[8] near Gibeah when word came to him that his spies[9] had discovered David's latest hiding place. This was probably the wilderness stronghold near the Dead Sea (1 Sam. 22:4-5), which explains why God sent the message to Gad that the company should return to Judah. Saul used this event as an occasion to berate his officers, all of whom were from his own tribe of Benjamin.[10] Always suspicious of treachery in the official ranks, Saul reminded the men that he was king and therefore was the only one who could reward them for their faithful service. David attracted men who were willing to risk their lives for him, but Saul had to use bribery and fear to keep his forces together. Saul was sure that his officers were conspiring against him because they had refused to tell him that David and Jonathan had covenanted together concerning the kingdom. Jonathan was the leader of a conspiracy that included some of the very men Saul was addressing. These traitors were working for David because David had promised to reward them. Furthermore, Saul was sure that David was plotting to kill him!

Doeg told the truth when he said he saw David at Nob and that Ahimelech the high priest gave him food and the sword of Goliath. But there's no evidence that the high priest used the Urim and Thummim to determine the will of God for David (Ex. 28:30; Num. 27:21). The sword of Goliath was kept near the ephod, and Ahimelech may have seen the high priest with the ephod in his hand, but this wasn't evidence that Ahimelech had consulted God on behalf of David. However, the lie made Doeg look good and David look bad.

The illegal trial (1 Sam. 22:11-15). It was but a short distance from Gibeah to Nob, so Saul immediately sent for the high priest, all his family, and the priests of Nob. Saul refused to address the high priest by his given name, but like Doeg called him "the son of Ahitub." The name Ahimelech means "brother of the king" and Saul wanted nothing to do with that, while "Ahitub" means "good brother." The king was obviously doing all he could to disgrace the high priest, when he should have been confessing his sins and seeking God's forgiveness. Saul was actually conducting an illegal trial, presenting four charges: Ahimelech gave David bread, he provided him with a weapon, he inquired of God for him, and he therefore was part of David's "conspiracy" to kill Saul so that he could become king. Never was Saul's paranoia more evident or more dangerous.

When Ahimelech heard these accusations, he first defended David before giving an account of his own actions. He reminded the king that David had been a faithful servant, an argument Saul's own son Jonathan had previously used (19:4-5). The entire nation honored David as a courageous and faithful warrior. But even more, David was Saul's son-in-law, a member of the royal family, one who had always done the king's bidding. He was held in high esteem in the king's household and even served as captain of Saul's personal bodyguard (22:14, NIV). If he had wanted to kill Saul, David certainly had plenty of opportunities to do so even before he fled. Perhaps the priest's words reminded the king that it was Saul who tried to kill David, not David who tried to kill Saul.

Ahimelech denied using the ephod to determine God's will for David. In fact, he stated boldly that if he had done so, it would have been the first time, because he had never done so before.[11] To do so would have been to forsake Saul for David! He closed his defense by stating that he and his family knew nothing about any conspiracy and therefore could in no way take part in a conspiracy.

The unjust sentence (1 Sam. 22:16-19). There was no evidence that Ahimelech had ever committed a capital crime, but Saul announced that he and his household must die. Even if the high priest had been guilty, which he was not, it was illegal to punish the whole family for the father's crime (Deut. 24:16). Their crime was knowing that David had fled and not reporting it to Saul. The things that Samuel had warned about the monarchy *and even more* were now taking place (1 Sam. 8:10-18). Saul had a police state in which each citizen was to spy on the others and report to the king anybody who opposed his rule. Israel had asked for a king "like the other nations," and that's what they received!

The guards nearest the king ("footmen," KJV) refused to slay the priests. This reminds us of the time Saul commanded the people to kill Jonathan for violating the oath, and they refused to obey him (14:41-46). Saul knew that Doeg was ready to do the evil deed, so he gave him permission to execute Ahimelech and his household, eighty-five priests of the Lord. A liar and murderer at heart (John 8:44), Doeg went beyond Saul's orders and went to Nob where he wiped out the entire population as well as the farm animals.

While this unjust trial and illegal sentence disturbs us, we must keep in mind that it was part of God's plan. This slaughter of the priests was a partial fulfillment of the ominous prophecy that had been given to unfaithful Eli (1 Sam. 2:27-36; 4:10-18), for God promised to replace the house of Eli with the house of Zadok (1 Kings 2:26-27; 4:2).

The protected priest (1 Sam. 22:20-23). The only survivor of the massacre at Nob was Abiathar, a son of Ahimelech, who then became the high priest. He knew that his only hope was to join David, so he fled to Keilah where David was now camped (23:6). When David moved from Hereth to Keilah isn't revealed in the text, but having a priest with an ephod was a tremendous help to David and his company. The 400 men had Gad the prophet, Abiathar the priest, and David the king; and they were fighting the battles of the Lord.[12] David took the blame for the slaughter of the priests, but he also took the responsibility of caring for Abiathar and making sure he was safe.

David was now officially an outlaw, but the Lord was with him and he would one day become Israel's greatest king.

CHAPTER NINE
DAVID THE DELIVERER
1 Samuel 23–24

In the second chapter of his book *Up from Slavery,* Booker T. Washington wrote, "I have learned that success is to be measured not so much by the position that one has reached in life as by the obstacles which he has overcome while trying to succeed." Measured by this standard—and it's a valid one—David was a very successful man. For ten years he was considered an outlaw, yet he fought the Lord's battles and delivered Israel from her enemies. He lived with his faithful men in the forsaken places of the land and often had to flee for his life, yet he knew that the Lord would finally deliver him and give him the promised throne. David's coronation was not only important to the people of Israel; it was important to all the people of God of every age. For out of David's family the Redeemer would ultimately come, Jesus of Nazareth, the Son of David, the Son of God.

1. David delivers Keilah from the Philistines. (1 Sam. 23:1-6)

Keilah was a border town in Judah, about twelve miles from the Philistine city of Gath and some ten miles west of the forest of Hereth where David and his men were camping (22:5). Situated that close to the enemy, Keilah was extremely vulnerable, especially during the harvest season when the Philistine army was searching for food. Had King Saul been concerned about defending his people instead, he would have sent a detachment of soldiers to protect Keilah, but he was obsessed with finding David and killing him.

The spies of both David and Saul were active in the land, and David's spies reported that the Philistines were attacking Keilah. David paused to determine the will of God, a practice every leader needs to imitate, for it's easy for our own personal interests to get in the way of God's will. How did David discover God's will when Abiathar the priest hadn't yet arrived in the camp? (23:6) The prophet Gad was with David (22:5), and it's likely that he prayed to the Lord for direction. Once Abiathar arrived with the ephod, David had him inquire of the Lord when there were important decisions to make (v. 9; 25:32; 26:11, 23).[1]

Once David got the go-ahead signal from the Lord, he mobilized his men, but they weren't too enthusiastic about his plans. It was acceptable to fight the Philistines, Israel's long-time enemies, but they didn't want to fight their own Jewish brothers. What if Saul turned against David and his men? The band of 600 men would then be caught between two armies! Unwilling to impose his own ideas on his men, David sought the Lord's will a second time, and once again he was told to go rescue the people of Keilah. It wasn't David's unbelief that created the problem, because he had faith in the Lord, but the fear in the hearts of his men made them unprepared for battle.

God more than kept His promise because He not only helped David slaughter the invading Philistines but also take a great amount of spoil from them. David moved into Keilah, which was a walled city, and it was there that Abiathar went when he fled from Nob carrying the precious ephod (22:20-23; 23:6). But Saul's spies were at work and learned that David was now in Keilah, a walled city with gates. Saul told his troops they were going to Keilah to rescue the city, but his real purpose was to capture David, and he was certain that David could not escape. Saul was not only willing to slaughter the priests of Nob, but he would have destroyed his own people in the city of Keilah just to lay hands on David. People who are controlled by malice and hatred quickly lose their perspective and begin to abuse their authority.

2. David delivers himself and his men from Saul. (1 Sam. 23:7-29)

While serving on Saul's staff, David had dodged the king's spears, thwarted an attempted kidnapping, and escaped the intended violence of three companies of soldiers and of Saul himself. Now that he was a fugitive with a price on his head and had over six hundred people to care for, David had to be very careful what he did and where he went. There might be another Doeg hiding in the shadows.

From Keilah to the wilderness of Ziph (1 Sam. 23:7-18). David's spies quickly let him know that Saul was planning to come to Keilah, so with Abiathar's help, David sought the Lord's guidance. His great concern was whether the people of Keilah would turn him and his men over to Saul. Since David had rescued the city from the Philistines, you would have expected the citizens to be grateful and to protect David, but such was not the case.[2] The Lord warned David to get out of the city because the people were prepared to turn him over to the king. No doubt the people of Keilah were afraid that if they didn't cooperate with Saul, he would massacre them as he did the people in Nob. David recalled how pained he was because of the tragedy at Nob, and he didn't want another city wiped out because of him. He led his men out and they "kept moving from place to place" (v. 13, NIV) until they settled in the wilderness of Ziph (v. 14).

When Saul got the word that David had left Keilah, he called off the attack, but he still sought him day after day and neglected the important affairs of the kingdom. However, the Lord was on David's side and made sure that Saul was never successful in his quest. Ziph was a town fifteen miles southeast of Keilah in "the wilderness of Ziph" which was part of "the wilderness of Judah." This is a destitute area adjacent to the Dead Sea where David's faith and courage were greatly tested. When visitors to the Holy Land see this wilderness area, they often express amazement that David could ever survive living there.

David's beloved friend Jonathan risked his life to visit David in the wilderness and "helped him find strength in God" (v. 16, NIV). This was their last recorded meeting. Jonathan isn't mentioned again in 1 Samuel until 31:2 where we're told he died on the battlefield. Jonathan had no idea that he would be slain before David became king, because he talked with David about their future coregency and renewed with him the covenant they had made (18:8; 20:31). He assured David that God would surely make him king in His good time, and that David would always be delivered from Saul's schemes to capture him. Jonathan admitted that his father knew all these plans.

From Ziph to the wilderness of Maon (1 Sam. 23:19-28). The Ziphites weren't interested in following God's plan; their great concern was to protect themselves from the rage of King Saul. They knew where David was hiding so they conveyed this important information to Saul, carefully addressing him as "king." This was their way of assuring him that they were loyal to him and not to David. Saul was still manipulating people by making them feel sorry for him (v. 21; 22:8), and this combination of building personal pity and wielding ruthless power seemed to be working. But Saul's character was deteriorating very quickly, while the Lord was molding David into a courageous man of God.

Saul was a good enough warrior to know that he couldn't find David in the wilderness of Judah without some specific directions, so he asked the Ziphites to send him exact details. He wanted to know the hiding places in the rocks and caves that David frequented and the hidden paths that he took. Once he had the map, Saul could search out the area and quickly find his enemy. But David also had his spies working and knew what Saul was doing, and the Lord was watching over the future king. David moved out of the area of Ziph and three miles south into the wilderness of Maon.

But Saul wasn't about to give up, so he followed David into the wilderness of Maon, and the two armies met at "the rock," a well-known mountain in the area. Saul divided his army and sent half around one side of the mountain and half around the other side, a pincers movement that would have meant total defeat for David and his 600 soldiers. But the Lord was in control and brought the Philistines to attack somewhere in Judah, and Saul and his men had to abandon the attack. It was a close call for David, but God kept His promises. To commemorate this great escape, the Jews called the place "Sela Hammahlekoth," which means "the rock of parting." The Hebrew carries the idea of "a smooth rock" and therefore "a slippery rock," in other words, "the rock of slipping away." David quickly moved from Maon to Engedi, next to the Dead Sea, a place of safety with an ample water supply.

David wrote Psalm 54 on this occasion and in it prayed for salvation and vindication from the Lord. David knew that the flatterers in Saul's official circle, people like Doeg, were telling lies about him and making it look as though David wanted to kill the king. These fawning toadies were hoping to be rewarded by Saul, but they only went down in defeat because they gave allegiance to the wrong king. Leaders who enjoy flattery and praise, and who encourage and reward associates who seek only to gratify their leader's ego, can never build other leaders or accomplish the will of God to the glory of God. David developed officers who were "mighty men" (1 Chron. 21; 2 Sam. 24), but Saul attracted officers who were moral weaklings. "Therefore by their fruits you will know them" (Matt. 7:20).

3. David delivers Saul from death. (1 Sam. 24:1-22)

David had prayed in Psalm 54 that the Lord would vindicate him and give him opportunity to prove to Saul that he wasn't an outlaw who was trying to kill him and seize the throne. After all, Saul was not only David's king, but he was also his commander and his father-in-law, and regardless of Saul's evil attitude, David never considered Saul to be his enemy.[3] God answered David's prayer when Saul and his troops came to find him at Engedi.

David's temptation (1 Sam. 24: 1-4). David and his men were hiding in a large cave, of which there were many in that area, and Saul chose to use that very cave as a place where he could relieve himself. The Law of Moses was very strict when it came to matters of sanitation, especially in the army camp (Deut. 23:12-14). Each soldier was required to leave the camp to relieve himself, and he had to carry a small shovel or trowel among his weapons so he could dig a hole and cover his excrement. This meant that Saul was away from the camp and therefore quite vulnerable. He naturally wanted privacy and he felt that he was not in danger. The fact that he walked right into David's hiding place not only proved that his spies were incompetent but also that the Lord was still in control.

As David and his men pressed to the walls in the back of the cave, they quietly discussed the meaning of this remarkable occurrence. The men assured David that Saul's presence in the cave was the fulfillment of a promise God gave him that He would deliver Saul into David's hands.[4] But when did God say this? Were they referring to Samuel's words to Saul in 1 Samuel 15:26-29, or to God's message to Samuel in 16:1? Perhaps the idea came from Jonathan's words in 20:15, which some of the men might have heard personally. It's likely that the leaders of the 600 men discussed these matters among themselves, for their future was wrapped up in David's future, and obviously they came to some false conclusions. David never planned to kill Saul, for he was sure that the Lord would remove him from the scene in His own way and His own time (26:9-11).

To David's men, it seemed providential that Saul was at their mercy (24:4; Ex. 21:13), and both David and Saul agreed with them (1 Sam. 24:10, 18). But that wasn't the issue. The major question was, "How does the Lord want us to use this occasion?" David's men saw it as an opportunity for revenge, while David saw it as an opportunity to show mercy and prove that his heart was right. God was giving him an opportunity to answer his own prayer for vindication (Ps. 54:1). David stealthily crept up to the garment that Saul had laid aside, cut off a corner of the robe, and went back into the cave. Saul left the cave not realizing what had happened.

David's conviction (1 Sam. 24:5-7) David was too wise in the truth of God's word to interpret this event as a signal for him to kill Saul, for the law says, "You shall not murder" (Ex. 20:13, NIV). Slaying an enemy on the battlefield or an attacker in self-defense was one thing, but to assassinate an unsuspecting king was quite something else. David reminded his men that Saul was the anointed of the Lord, and that no Jew had the right to attack him. The Jews were not even to curse their rulers, let alone kill them, for cursing a ruler was in the same category as blaspheming the name of the Lord (22:28).

However, David's conscience bothered him because he had cut off the corner of Saul's robe. His action sent out three messages. First, it was an insolent act of disrespect that humiliated Saul, but it was also a symbolic gesture not unlike what Saul did to Samuel's robe after the Amalekite fiasco (1 Sam. 15:27-28). By cutting off a part of the royal robe, David was declaring that the kingdom had been transferred to him. Finally, the piece of cloth was proof that David did not intend to kill the king and that the flatterers in the court were all liars. David's men would have killed Saul in a moment, but their wise captain restrained them. Leaders must know how to interpret events and respond in the right way.

David's vindication (1 Sam. 24: 8-15). When Saul was far enough away from the cave that it was safe, David left the cave and called to him. By using the title "my lord the king" and bowing to the earth, David emphasized what he had said to his men and let Saul know that he was not a rebel. Even if you can't respect the man or woman in office, you must show respect to the office (Rom. 13:1-7; 1 Peter 2:13-17). David showed his respect by calling Saul "my master" (1 Sam. 24:6), "the Lord's anointed" (vv. 6, 10), "my lord" (vv. 8, 10), "the king" (vv. 8, 14) and "my father" (v. 14). David's bold public appearance also let Saul and his army know that their official spy system was most ineffective.

Using the piece of Saul's robe as evidence, David opened his defense by exposing the deception of the courtiers who slandered David to Saul. The logic was irrefutable: David had an opportunity to kill Saul and refused to do so. David even admitted that some of his men urged him to slay the king, but he rebuked them. David was not guilty of any evil against Saul or any transgression against the Lord, but Saul was guilty of trying to kill David. "The Lord will judge between us," said David, "and prove that your officers are liars, but I will not lift my hand against you." Saul had hoped that the hand of the Philistines (18:17) or the hands of David's soldiers (19:20-21) would kill David, but they failed. Ultimately, Saul died by his own hand on the battlefield (31:1-6).

David quoted a familiar proverb[5] to prove his point: "Wickedness proceeds from the wicked" (24:13, NKJV), which simply means that character is revealed by conduct. The fact that David did not slay the king indicated that David did not have the character of a rebel or a murderer. But at the same time, David was strongly suggesting that Saul's character was questionable because he wanted to kill his son-in-law! But what was the king really doing as he pursued David? Only chasing a dead dog and a flea that was jumping from one place to another! (Fleas and dogs go together.) The phrase "dead dog" was a humiliating term of reproach in those days (17:43; 2 Sam. 3:8; 9:8; 16:9), so David was humbling himself before the Lord and the king. David closed his defense by asserting a second time (1 Sam. 24:12, 15) that the Lord was the righteous judge and would plead the cause of His faithful servant (Pss. 35:1; 43:1; see 1 Peter 2:23).

David's affirmation (1 Sam. 24:16-22). King Saul once again revealed his confused mental state by lifting up his voice and calling to David, who had certainly spoken long enough for Saul to discern that it was indeed his son-in-law.[6] As for Saul's weeping, he had manifested temporary emotional reactions like that before, but they never brought about repentance or a change of heart.

Saul described three possible levels of life: the divine level, where we return good for evil; the human level, where we return good for good and evil for evil; and the demonic level, where we return evil for good. Saul admitted that David was a godly man who, by not slaying him, returned good for evil. But Saul was possessed by demonic forces and did evil to the one man who could have destroyed him. Now Saul openly confessed that he knew David would be the next king (23:17) and would consolidate the nation of Israel that Saul had torn apart. Even then, Saul's major concern was his own name and descendants, not the spiritual welfare of the people; he made David swear that he wouldn't wipe out his family when he became king. David had made a similar covenant with Jonathan (20:14-17, 42) and he was willing to make the same promise to Saul. How tragic that Saul's own sins destroyed his family, all but Jonathan's crippled son, Mephibosheth, whom David adopted (2 Sam. 9).

Because David knew God's calling and believed God's promise, he was able to be so bold before Saul and his army. It was indeed a holy boldness that came from a heart that was right with God. The day would come when David and his cause would be vindicated and the Lord would judge those who had opposed him. Saul went back home to Gibeah, but in spite of his tears and emotional speech, he took up his pursuit of David again (1 Sam. 26:2, 21).

David had won many battles, but one of his greatest victories occurred in that cave when he restrained himself and his men from killing Saul. "He who is slow to anger is better than the mighty, and he who rules his spirit than he who takes a city" (Prov. 16:32, NKJV). This is a good example for all of us to follow, but especially those to whom the Lord has entrusted leadership.

CHAPTER TEN
A WISE WOMAN AND A FOOLISH KING
1 Samuel 25–26

Personal relationships are a large part of our lives, the most important being our relationship to the Lord. If from childhood you and I had kept a list of all the significant people who came in and out of our lives, we'd be amazed at their number and the variety of roles they played. Leaving God out of the picture, the longshoreman philosopher Eric Hoffer said that other people were "the playwrights and stage managers of our lives: they cast us in a role and we play it whether we will or no." But you can't leave God out of the picture! After all, He's the one who writes the script for us, chooses the cast, and puts us into the scenes He's planned for us. If we follow His directions, life becomes the satisfying fulfillment of His will, but if we rebel, the plot turns into tragedy.

These two chapters record four events that reveal David's involvement with four different kinds of people.

1. David loses a friend. (1 Sam. 25:1)

The death of Samuel, Israel's prophet and judge, is mentioned twice in the book (28:3). Both references state that all Israel mourned his death and gathered to bury him. Of course, not every Israelite attended the funeral service, but the leaders of the tribes were present to pay their last respects to a great man. It was Samuel's faith and courage that helped the nation transition from political disunity to a somewhat united monarchy. Since Saul and Samuel had been alienated for over seven years, it's not likely that the king attended the funeral, but he would call on Samuel for help even after the prophet was dead (chap. 28).

The people of Israel didn't always obey Samuel when he was alive, but they were careful to honor him when he died. Such is human nature (Matt. 23:29-31). However, Samuel didn't prepare an elaborate tomb for himself at some important public place, but instead asked to be buried at his own house in Ramah, probably in the garden or in a courtyard. In his pride, King Saul had prepared a public monument to himself at Carmel (1 Sam. 15:12), but Samuel, who truly deserved recognition, humbly asked to be laid to rest at his own home.

David knew it would be dangerous for him to attend the funeral at Ramah, for Saul would have his spies there, so he retreated to the wilderness. David had shown his love and respect for Samuel while the prophet was alive, so there was no need for him to make a public appearance. Samuel had anointed David king of Israel and had often protected David and given him counsel. How wonderful it is when the saints of the older generation spend time with the younger leaders and help to prepare them to serve the Lord and His people, and how encouraging it is when the younger leaders listen and learn.

Samuel was the kind of spiritual mentor and counselor that every leader needs, because he put the concerns of God ahead of the politics of the hour. To Samuel, pleasing the Lord was far more important than being popular with the people. It broke his heart when Israel asked for a king, but he obeyed the Lord's orders and anointed Saul. It wasn't long before he was disappointed in Saul, but then the Lord led him to anoint David. Samuel died knowing that the kingdom would be in good hands.

David was in Masada ("the stronghold") when Samuel died (24:22), and he and his men left there for the "wilderness of Paran," more than a hundred miles south of Masada. Perhaps David felt that the loss of Samuel's influence and prayers meant greater danger for him and therefore he needed more distance between himself and Saul. Instead of "Paran," some texts read "Maon," a place of refuge near the Dead Sea where David had been before (23:24). The events in the story of Nabal occur in Maon near Carmel (25:2), and this suggests that Maon may have been David's hiding place. Perhaps David fled to Paran and then backtracked to Maon, but considering the nature of the terrain and the difficulty of travel, this idea seems untenable.

2. David discovers an enemy. (1 Sam. 25:2-13)

During David's previous stay in the wilderness of Maon (23:24ff), which is in the vicinity of Carmel,[1] his men had been a wall of protection for Nabal's flocks and those caring for them. Nabal was a very wealthy man, but he was not a generous man. When David returned to Nabal's neighborhood, it was shearing time, a festive event (2 Sam. 13:23) that occurred each spring and early fall. David hoped that Nabal would reward him and his men for their service, for certainly they deserved something for protecting Nabal's sheep and goats from the thieves that usually showed up at shearing time.

David's expectation was logical. Any man with 3,000 sheep and 1,000 goats could easily spare a few animals to feed 600 men who had risked their own lives to guard part of his wealth. Common courtesy would certainly dictate that Nabal invite David and his men to share his food at a festive season when hospitality was the order of the day. It wouldn't be easy to feed 600 men in the wilderness, so David sent ten of his young men to explain the situation and to ask to be invited to the feast. Nabal refused to listen.

The character of Nabal is described as "churlish and evil" (1 Sam. 25:3), which the NIV translates "surly and mean" and the NLT "mean and dishonest in all his dealings." (Did he become rich by being dishonest?) He was from the tribe of

Judah and the family of Caleb, one of the two spies who urged Israel to enter the Promised Land (Num. 13-14; Josh. 14:6-7).[2] But the name "Caleb" also means "a dog," so perhaps the writer was conveying this meaning as well. The man was like a stubborn vicious animal that nobody could safely approach (1 Sam. 25:17). One of his own servants *and his own wife* both called him "a son of Belial—a worthless fellow" (vv. 17, 25). The Hebrew word *beliya'al* means "worthlessness" and in the Old Testament refers to evil people who deliberately broke the law and despised what was good. (See Deut. 13:13; Judg. 19:22; 20:13; 1 Sam. 2:12.) In the New Testament, the word refers also to Satan (2 Cor. 6:15).

When the young men graciously presented their case, Nabal "railed on them," which the NIV translates "hurled insults at them." The Hebrew word describes the shrieking of a bird of prey as it swoops down to tear its victim. It's used to describe Saul's hungry men as they fell on the plunder and butchered the animals (1 Sam. 14:32; 15:19). His words are found in 25:10-11 and certainly reveal the heart of a man who is selfish, arrogant, and rebellious. Abigail recognized David as king (vv. 28 and 30) and called David "my lord," but Nabal compared David to a rebellious servant who abandoned his master! (v. 10) It's obvious that Nabal's sympathies lay with Saul and not with David, another evidence that he had no heart for spiritual matters as his wife did. When you note all the personal pronouns in verse 11, you immediately recognize his pride and self-importance. He didn't even give God credit for making him wealthy! (Deut. 8:17-18; Luke 12:15-21)

The young men reported Nabal's reply to David who immediately became angry and swore revenge on him. David could forgive Saul, who wanted to kill him, but he couldn't forgive Nabal who only refused to feed him and his men. Nabal was ungrateful and selfish, but those are not capital crimes; Saul was envious and consumed with the desire to kill an innocent man. David's anger got the best of him; he didn't stop to consult the Lord, and he rushed out to satisfy his passion for revenge. Had David succeeded, he would have committed a terrible sin and done great damage to his character and his career, but the Lord mercifully stopped him.

God's servants need to be on guard at all times lest the enemy suddenly attack and conquer them. "Be sober, be vigilant, because your adversary the devil walks about like a roaring lion, seeking whom he may devour" (1 Peter 5:8, NKJV). David was a godly man and a gifted leader, but the best of men are but men at their best.

3. David takes a wife. (1 Sam. 25:14-44)

When the Lord isn't allowed to rule in our lives, then He steps in and overrules. He saw that David was about to act rashly and foolishly, so He arranged for a wise and courageous woman to stop him.

Abigail's wise plan (1 Sam. 2514-19). When this anonymous young man reported his master's actions to Abigail, he was serving the Lord whether he knew it or not. He knew he couldn't talk to Nabal about anything (v. 17), so he immediately went to his mistress, a wise and prudent woman. In those days, the parents arranged marriages for their children, so we aren't surprised to see a wise woman married to a foolish man. (Alas, it often happens today without the help of parents!) No doubt Abigail's parents considered it fortunate that their daughter could marry such a wealthy man, and she obeyed their wishes, but her life with

Nabal must have been tedious. All her husband was interested in was money, food and drink, and having his own way.

The servant reported how David and his men had protected the shepherds and their flocks, and how Nabal had refused to repay them. Did the young man know that David and his men were on their way to confront Nabal, or did he simply surmise it? Perhaps it was the Lord who gave him a special intuition that trouble was coming. Nabal and his servants were defenseless against David's 400 men. But if David had succeeded in this venture, it would have given Saul the evidence he needed that David was a dangerous renegade who had to be dealt with drastically.

Abigail put together enough food for David's men but said nothing to her husband. She was the mistress of the house and could dispose of the family provisions as she saw fit, even to the extent of sharing it with others. Nabal would have opposed her even though she was doing it for his own good. She wasn't stealing from her husband; she was paying a debt that he refused to pay. In order to save a little money, Nabal was foolishly jeopardizing the lives of everybody in his household, especially his own.

Abigail's humble apology (1 Sam. 25:20-35). Only a sovereign Lord could have arranged the timing of David's attack and Abigail's approach so that the two bands met. Abigail bowed before David and acknowledged him as her lord and king; in fact, she used the word "lord" fourteen times in her speech. Nabal would not have approved of her words or her actions because he was a follower of Saul and considered David a rebel (v. 10). Abigail was a woman of faith who believed that David was God's king, and she saw King Saul as only "a man" (v. 29). She quickly confessed that her husband was a "worthless fellow" (v. 25, see v. 17) who lived up to his name—fool, and she explained that she had known nothing about David's request for food. She accepted the blame for "this iniquity" (vv. 24, 28).[3]

In the rest of her speech, Abigail focused on David and the Lord and not on David and Nabal, and her emphasis was on David's future. By now David was calming down and starting to realize that he was in the presence of a remarkable woman. She pointed out that the Lord had stopped David from avenging himself, and David admitted this was true (vv. 32-34). Abigail admitted that her husband deserved to be judged, but she wanted the Lord to do it, not the king. In fact, she promised that the Lord would judge *all* the enemies of the king.

Abigail reminded David that the Lord had given him "a sure house" ("lasting dynasty," NIV), so he didn't have to fear the future. David was safe, bound in "the bundle of life" by the Lord; but his enemies would be hurled out like the stone David used when he defeated Goliath (see Jer. 10:18). No matter what Saul planned to do to David, the Lord would keep His promises and make David ruler over Israel. Then David would be glad he hadn't shed blood in order to avenge himself or get to the throne. The Lord would treat David well and he had nothing to fear.

Abigail had only one request for herself: that David would remember her when he came into his kingdom (1 Sam. 25:31). Was this a veiled suggestion of marriage, should Nabal die? Or was Abigail merely looking ahead and seeing herself as a widow who could profit from friendship with the king? Perhaps she was cautioning David to remember her and her advice when he became king so he wouldn't be tempted to take things into his own hands and forget the will of the Lord. As it turned out, David didn't wait too long after Nabal's decease but took her as his wife!

David blessed the Lord for providentially stopping him from killing innocent people, and he also blessed Abigail for her wise advice. David was a smart man to listen to reproof wisely given (Prov. 15:5, 10, 31-33); it's not likely that Saul would have listened to a woman's counsel. David wrote in Psalm 141:5, "Let the righteous strike me; it shall be a kindness. And let him reprove me; it shall be as excellent oil; let my head not refuse it" (NKJV). How we receive reproof and counsel is a test of our relationship to the Lord and our willingness to live by His Word. David admitted that he was wrong, the Lord forgave him, and the Lord worked out the problem for him.

Abigail's unexpected marriage (1 Sam. 25:36-44). Nabal is feasting when judgment is just around the corner! He didn't stop to thank God for the blessings He had sent to him, or even to consider that these blessings came because of his wife's faith and in spite of his own meanness. Nabal's idea of happiness wasn't to praise God or feed the hungry, but to eat to the full and get drunk. Nabal made no profession of faith in the Lord but was like the people Paul described: "whose end is destruction, whose god is their belly, and whose glory is in their shame—who set their mind on earthly things" (Phil. 3:19, NKJV).

Wisely, Abigail waited to tell her husband what she had done. The news so stunned Nabal that he experienced a stroke and lay helpless for ten days, and then the Lord took his life. What caused the stroke? Was it pride and anger on learning that his wife had dared to help David without his permission? Or was it shock in realizing the danger he had been in and how close he and his household had come to being slain? What if Saul heard that Abigail had befriended David? The king might consider Nabal an enemy and punish him accordingly. Whether one or all of these considerations caused Nabal's paralysis, it was the Lord who ultimately took his life. Sad to say, he died as he had lived—a fool.

When David heard the news of Nabal's death, he praised the Lord for avenging him and preventing him from doing it himself. David's concern was the glory of God and the advancement of His kingdom. Abigail certainly must have been pleased to be set free from the yoke of such a wicked man, a man she probably married against her will. David had been so impressed with her character and wisdom that he thought she would make a good queen, so he sent messengers to ask for her hand in marriage. It was an opportunity no woman would refuse, and she submitted to her king and even offered to wash his feet! In marrying Abigail, David not only acquired a good wife, but he also got possession of all of Nabal's wealth and property, which was situated near Hebron where David later established his royal residence (2 Sam. 2:1-4; 5:5). He had already taken Ahinoam as his wife, since she is always named before Abigail (27:3; 30:5; 2 Sam. 2:2). She was the mother of David's firstborn son, Amnon, and Abigail bore him Kileab, also named Daniel (1 Chron. 3:2).

But what about David's first wife, Michal, Saul's daughter, who had helped to save David's life? After David fled from home, Saul gave her to another man, probably using the alliance as a means to strengthen his own position and to break David's connection with the throne. There was no legal divorce, so Saul forced Michal into an adulterous relationship. When David was reigning over the tribe of Judah in Hebron, he demanded that Michal be returned to him (2 Sam. 3:13-16). However, Michal didn't remain a loving wife and probably resented David's taking her father's throne. She died childless (6:16-23).

4. David spares the king. (1 Sam. 26:1-15)

Some students of the Old Testament have tried to prove that the account in this chapter is merely an adaptation of the one in chapter 24, but the evidence stands against this interpretation. There are differences in locations (a cave in En Gedi; Saul's camp near Hachilah), times (day; night), activities (Saul came to the cave; David went to the camp), David's responses (cutting off part of Saul's robe; taking Saul's spear and water jug), and David's words (spoke only to Saul; spoke to Abner and Saul). This second experience with Saul was certainly more daring on David's part since he was actually in Saul's camp. David's recent experience with Nabal and Abigail had reassured him of his future reign and had taught him a profitable lesson about revenge.

Treachery (1 Sam. 26:1-4). Like Nabal, the Ziphites were related to Caleb (1 Chron. 2:42), but being members of the tribe of Judah, they should have been loyal to David. Hoping to gain the king's approval, for a second time they betrayed David to Saul (1 Sam. 23:19ff; see Ps. 54). Saul had learned to appreciate David's skill as a tactician, so he took his 3,000 soldiers to search for David in the wilderness. But David was already far ahead of him, for his spies had located Saul's camp, and David was safe in the desert. The Lord kept David safe and delivered him whenever Saul was near. "He delivered me from my strong enemy, from those who hated me, for they were too strong for me" (Ps. 18:17, NKJV).

Audacity (1 Sam. 26: 5-12). The Lord must have instructed David to go to Saul's camp that night, because He sent a deep sleep upon Saul and his men. Saul and Abner, who was Saul's captain (14:10) and cousin (v. 50), were sleeping at the heart of the camp, surrounded by the wagons and baggage ("the trench" KJV). Because of the supernatural sleep sent by the Lord, David and his nephew Abishai were able to penetrate to where Saul and Abner lay.[4] This is the first mention of Abishai in Scripture. As usual, Saul's spear was at hand, the symbol of his office and his authority (26:7, 11; 22:6; 18:10; 19:9; 20:33).

Abishai was sure that it was God's will that he kill Saul and put an end to his selfish rule and his relentless persecution of Israel's true king, but David stopped him. David had settled this matter in the cave (24:1-6) and there was no need to consider it again. He had also seen what the Lord did to Nabal. David was sure that Saul's life would end at the right time and in the right way, either by natural death or by a judgment from God, and then the throne would be his. When Abishai looked at Saul, he saw an enemy, but David looked at him and saw "the Lord's anointed." Instead of taking Saul's life, David took his spear and water jug, just so he could prove to Saul a second time that he didn't have designs on the king's life. David didn't let Abishai take the spear lest he be tempted to use it.

It would have been easy to argue that David had been wrong in the cave and that God was giving him a second chance to kill Saul, but David's decision was based on principle and not circumstances. David knew that it was wrong to lay hands on God's anointed, even though the king wasn't serving as God wanted him to serve. David might not have been able to respect the man, but he did respect the office and the God who gave that office to Saul.

Mockery (1 Sam. 26:13-16). David and his nephew made their way to the hill opposite Saul's camp where they were safe and from which they could be heard, and David called back to the soldiers in the camp and especially to Abner, the king's bodyguard. He was careful not to humiliate Saul in the presence of his men, although Saul couldn't easily escape the embarrassment of the situation. David didn't identify himself to Abner but only referred to himself as "one of the people" (v. 15). The absence of the spear and water jug was evidence enough that someone indeed had been close to the king and could have killed him. Abner was guilty and could have been disciplined for not doing his duty.

Dishonesty (vv. 17-25). Saul recognized David's voice and responded by calling him "my son, David," but David didn't call him "my father" as he had before (24:11). His address was only "my lord, O king." Saul's daughter Michal was no longer David's wife (25:44), so David was no longer son-in-law to the king. Furthermore, Saul certainly hadn't treated David like a son.

Once again, David tried to reason with Saul and show him how wrong he was in his thinking and acting. David wanted to know what his crime was that Saul had to pursue him and seek to kill him. If David had broken one of God's laws, then he was willing to bring a sacrifice and have his sin forgiven by the Lord. But if Saul was treating David like a criminal because of the lies his officers had told him, then *they* were the offenders, not David, and they would pay for their sins. Saul and his officers had driven David out of his own land, the very inheritance that the Lord had given his family, and if David moved to other lands, how could he worship Jehovah away from the priesthood and the sanctuary?[5]

But if David wasn't guilty of any crime or sin, why should Saul invest so much time and energy in pursuing him? The king of Israel was chasing a partridge just for the privilege of shedding its blood! (Partridges don't like to fly. They run from one cover to another.)

Once again, Saul lapsed into one of his sentimental moods (see 24:17) and confessed that he was a fool and a sinner. He promised that he wouldn't harm David, but David didn't believe him. His only reply was, "Behold the king's spear! Let one of the young men come over and fetch it" (26:22). When David cut Saul's robe in the cave, he reminded him that his kingdom would be severed from him, but in taking the spear, he humiliated the king and robbed him of the symbol of his authority.

For the second time, David had spared Saul's life, and David knew that the Lord would reward him for what he had done (Ps. 7:8). But David didn't expect Saul to value his life as he had valued Saul's life, because he knew Saul couldn't be trusted. Rather, he asked that the Lord reward him with protection and safety just as he had protected the king. See Psalm 18:20-27.

The last recorded words of Saul to David are in 1 Samuel 26:25, a statement that affirms the greatness of David's deeds and the certainty of his kingship. The two men parted, Saul heading for ultimate disgrace and death, and David to ultimate glory and victory. However, David's unbelief would take him to the land of the Philistines and the city of Ziklag, where he would live for about a year and a half. Soon David's years of wandering and testing would end and he would be ready to sit on the throne of Israel and rule God's people. One day David would look back on those difficult years and see in his painful experiences only the goodness and mercy of the Lord (Ps. 23:6).

CHAPTER ELEVEN
LIVING WITH THE ENEMY
1 Samuel 27:1-28;2; 29–30

In his more mature years, David heard God say to him, "I will instruct you and teach you in the way you should go; I will guide you with My eye. Do not be like the horse or like the mule" (Ps. 32:8-9, NKJV). The horse is impulsive and rushes heedlessly into the battle, while the mule is stubborn and holds back; and all of us have had both experiences. God doesn't want to deal with us as men deal with animals; He wants to be close to us and guide us with His eye, the way a parent guides a child. When we behold the face of the Lord, we can see His smile or frown and we can discern from His eyes which way He wants us to go. These chapters record the experiences of David when he was living without that kind of intimate, loving guidance.

1. Departing from the land (1 Sam. 27:1-2)

David had been a fugitive for about seven years when he decided to flee to Gath, but the idea of leaving Israel had probably already been in his mind (26:19). David had every reason to stay in the land and continue to trust God for protection and provision. After all, he was the anointed king of Israel and knew that eventually God would give him the throne. Abigail assured him of this (25:27-31), and even Saul admitted that David would ultimately triumph (26:25). Saul didn't keep one of his promises to leave David alone, and the constant flattery of the liars in his inner circle encouraged the king to keep on pursuing David. Living the life of a wilderness exile with his life daily in the balance was starting to depress David, and now he had two wives and 600 men to care for.

"How long, O Lord? Will you forget me forever? How long will you hide your face from me? How long shall I take counsel in my soul, having sorrow in my heart daily? How long will my enemy be exalted over me?" (Ps. 13:1-2, NKJV) In about three years, David's exile would end and he would be ruling the people of Judah in Hebron, but he had no way of knowing this. It takes both faith and patience to receive what God has promised (Heb. 6:12), and David seemed to be wavering in both of these essentials. He needed the faith and courage expressed in Psalm 27:1-3, but before we criticize him too severely, let's recall the time when we've done the same thing.

This scene reminds us of a similar situation in the life of our Lord as He faced the cross (John 12:20-33). "Now is my soul troubled, and what shall I say? 'Father, save me from this hour'? But for this purpose I came to this hour. Father, glorify your name" (12:27-28, NKJV). Jesus had the Father's glory uppermost in His heart, while David was concerned primarily for his own safety and comfort. Yet God was using the difficulties in David's life to make him a man of God and to prepare him for the throne, but now he decided to go his own way and solve his own problems.

God's children must be careful not to yield to despondency. Moses was discouraged over his heavy workload and wanted to die (Num. 11:15), and Elijah ran from the place of duty because of fear and discouragement (1 Kings 19). When we start to look at God through our circumstances instead of looking at our circumstances through God's eyes, we will lose faith, patience, and courage, and the enemy will triumph. "Trust in the Lord with all your heart, and lean not on your own understanding" (Prov. 3:5, NKJV).

"My times are in your hand; deliver me from the hand of my enemies, and from those who persecute me" (Ps. 31:15).

2. Deceiving the enemy (1 Sam. 27:3–29:11)

At the beginning of his exile, David had fled to Gath for safety, only to discover that his life was still in danger, and then he had to act like a madman in order to escape (21:10-15). But at that time, David was alone, while now he had two wives and was the commander of 600 valiant soldiers. David was still a deceiver, and "faith is living without scheming." He deceived Achish concerning three matters: the request for a city, the raids his men conducted, and the desire to fight the king's battles.

His request for a city (1 Sam. 27:3-7). Undoubtedly the news had reached the Philistines that Saul was trying to kill David, and so any enemy of Saul would be warmly welcomed in Gath. Achish could make use of David's tactical skill and the battle-honed skills of his courageous men. But the total number of people David brought with him could well have been between 2,000–3,000 (30:1-3), and that was quite a crowd to drop into the city of Gath.

Actually, David didn't want to stay in Gath because there the king and his officers could investigate what he was doing, so he requested that the king give him and his people a city of their own. He was very diplomatic in the way he phrased his request, humbling himself before the king ("I am not worthy to live in the royal city.") and assuring Achish that his services were always available. Happy to get the extra people out of Gath, where they were probably straining the food and water supply, and ready to strengthen his own army, Achish quickly accepted the idea. He gave David Ziklag, a town about twenty-five miles southwest of Gath, on the border of Simeon but under Philistine control. The tribe of Simeon had its inheritance within the tribe of Judah, which explains why Ziklag was associated with both tribes (Josh. 15:31; 19:5). However, since Achish gave the town to David, it belonged to the kings of Judah ever after. There could not have been a better base of operations for David and his men, and they made good use of it.

His reports of the raids (1 Sam. 27:8-12). Achish thought that David and his band were attacking cities and towns in Judah, when in reality they were raiding the towns and camps of the allies of Achish! David was wiping out the people that Joshua and his successors failed to exterminate when they entered the land, following the orders given by Moses in Deuteronomy 20:16-18. At the same time, he was eliminating the danger of any survivors taking the word to Gath that David was a liar. David took Achish gifts from the spoils of battle and gave him false reports of their activities, and Achish believed him. When word got back to the people of Judah that David was attacking their enemies, this made him even more popular with the leaders.

His responsibility in the battle (1 Sam. 28:1-2; 29:1-11). This is the battle in which Saul and his sons were killed (31:1-6), and it was the providential hand of the Lord that kept David and his men from having to participate. Achish assured David that he and his men were expected to fight alongside the Philistine troops, but David's reply was evasive: "Then you will see for yourself what your servant can do" (28:2, NIV). The king interpreted this to mean, "Until now, you have received only verbal reports of the prowess of me and my men, but this battle will give us opportunity to display our skills before your very eyes." But is that what David meant? Certainly he wouldn't fight against his own people, and he probably had an alternate plan in mind. But the king was so impressed that he commissioned David to be his bodyguard for life![1]

The troops assembled and paraded, the five lords of the Philistines (6:16-17) leading their companies and David and his men bringing up the rear and guarding the king. When the princes (military commanders) of the Philistines saw their king with David and his 600, they protested, "What are these Hebrews doing here?" This question must have shocked Achish because he had the utmost confidence in David. He hastened to assure his commanders that he had watched David for over a year, in fact, from the first day David left Saul (21:10-15), and he trusted him.

The leaders couldn't argue with their king, but they could suggest a safety measure. They remembered that in a previous battle, some Hebrew soldiers in the Philistine army had deserted their posts and fought for Israel (14:21), and David and his men might do the same thing. True, Saul was David's enemy, but they might be reconciled and fight together. After all, the people used to sing, "Saul slew his thousands, and David his ten thousands" (28:5; 18:7; 21:11), which suggests that they were once fighting together. The safest thing to do was to send David back to Ziklag, far from the battle, and let him carry on his own military attacks elsewhere.

The king gave the message to David, who continued his deception by appearing to be deeply hurt by the order. Had he not proved himself to his king? He wanted to go out and "fight against the enemies of [his] lord, the king," another ambiguous statement that the king would interpret in his favor. But who was David's "lord and king"—King Saul (24:8; 26:17), Achish, or Jehovah? And who were David's enemies—the Jews or the Philistines? But Achish assumed that he was David's king, so he ordered him to quietly leave Gath and go back to Ziklag and not to upset the commanders in any way. They had a demanding battle ahead of them and Achish wanted them to be at their best. David obeyed and returned to Ziklag.[2]

Though the Lord was gracious to deliver David and his men from participating in this battle, He isn't obligated to step in and extricate His people from situations caused by their own sinful decisions. We reap what we sow, and in later years, David suffered from being deceived by members of his staff and even of his own family.

3. Delivering the captives (1 Sam. 30:1-20)

David and his band were kept from fighting with the Philistines, but they still had a battle to fight, this time with the Amalekites, the sworn enemies of the Lord and of the Jews (Ex. 17:8-16; Deut. 25:17). Because Saul had won an incomplete victory over the Amalekites (1 Sam. 15:1-11), they were still free to attack God's people.

Distress (1 Sam. 30:1-6a). Perhaps the

Lord permitted this raid on Ziklag to encourage David to get out of enemy territory and go back to Judah where he belonged. The Amalekite leaders knew that David was at Gath and that all attention was focused on the confrontation between Israel and the Philistines. This was a perfect time to retaliate against David for his raids and to pick up some booty as well. Since most of the men were with David, the residents of Ziklag could put up no resistance and the invaders simply kidnapped the people and took whatever wealth they could find. They burned the city, an act of vengeance on their part but perhaps a message from the Lord that it was time for David to think about returning to Judah.

We can but imagine the horror and grief of David and his 600 men who had never lost a battle. Their city was burned, their wealth had been confiscated, and their wives and children had been kidnapped. It was the mercy of the Lord that the Amalekites spared the lives of the women and children, for in their raids David and his men had certainly killed their share of enemy women and children (27:11). The verb "carried them away" (30:2) is literally "drove them off" and paints the picture of animals being driven off by the herdsmen. The men wore themselves out in weeping and David was "greatly distressed," a verb that means he was pressed into a tight corner, the way a potter would press clay into a mold.

Encouragement (1 Sam. 30:6b-15). Different people react in different ways to the same circumstances, because what life does to us depends on what life finds in us. Some of the people wanted to stone David, which was certainly a foolish response. They needed their leader now more than ever, and how would his death solve their problem? We don't blame the men for being grieved, but we question their allowing their hearts to run ahead of their heads. David knew that the encouragement he needed could only come from the Lord. He ordered Abiathar the priest to bring the ephod and together they sought the will of the Lord. Saul had consulted the Lord but had received no answer (28:3-6), but the Lord graciously replied to David's request. David was hardly in a place of complete obedience, but God answered him just the same (Ps. 103:3-10).

Assured by the Lord that his pursuit of the enemy would meet with success, David and his men took off on their beasts and traveled sixteen miles to the brook Besor where 200 men had to stop because they were exhausted. (The Hebrew word translated "faint" means "dead tired.") That might have discouraged David, but he and his 400 men continued to travel. But where should they go? The Lord hadn't told them where the Amalekites were camped, but David trusted the Lord to guide him. It was then that they found an Egyptian slave whom his Amalekite master had abandoned because he was ill. The man could have perished in the wilderness, but the Lord had kept him alive for the sake of His servant David. The slave's master must have been an important man because his servant knew the plans of the Amalekite raiding party and could lead David to their camp. The master hoped that the man would die, but the Lord kept him alive so David could rescue the families that had been kidnapped.

Victory (1 Sam. 30:16-20). In their exuberant false confidence, the Amalekites were celebrating their great victory when David and his men attacked and caught the camp by surprise. They killed all the Amalekites, except 400 young men who escaped, rescued all the people who had been kidnapped, and recovered all the belongings that had been taken from Ziklag. It was a total victory for David, but it was also a profitable victory, because David took the wealth and booty of the Amalekites and claimed it for himself.

As you review what the Lord did for David in that dark hour in his life, you can better understand how He helps His people when problems and crises come into their lives. First, the Lord encouraged David so that he didn't despair but trusted the Lord to help him. Whenever a crisis comes, we need the courage to face it, and we must not try to blame others or pretend that nothing is wrong. The Lord also gave David wisdom to know what to do and the strength to do it. He and his men were weary, but the Lord enabled David and 400 of his men to persevere in their quest for the Amalekite invaders. The Lord also provided David with the facts he needed so he could find where the enemy was camping in that vast wilderness. When we step out by faith and trust the Lord, He will guide us when we need it. Finally, God gave David and his men the strength they needed to defeat the enemy and recover the prisoners and their wealth.

"Commit your way to the Lord, trust also in Him, and He shall bring it to pass" (Ps. 37:5).

4. Dividing the spoils (1 Sam. 30:21-31)

When David said to his troops, "This is David's spoil" (v. 20), he wasn't claiming the wealth of the Amalekites for himself in a selfish way but only stating that he would see to its distribution. Each of his fighting men received their part and so did the 200 soldiers who were too weary to continue the pursuit. This generosity of David bothered some of the "evil men and troublemakers" in David's band (v. 21), but David paid them no heed. He politely laid it down as a rule in his army that all the spoils would be divided among all the men, including those who didn't actually fight the enemy. After all, it was the Lord who gave them the victory, so nobody had the right to claim the spoils for himself as if the Lord owed it to him. God was gracious and generous to deliver the enemy into their hands, and they should be gracious and generous to share the wealth with others.

David also sent presents from the spoils to the elders of the towns in southern Judah, the places where he and his men had hidden during his wanderings (23:23). The people of these towns had helped David escape Saul, and David felt they deserved some kind of payment for their kindness. After all, if Saul had heard what they did, their very lives might have been in jeopardy. But David was doing more than thank these leaders. He was also paving the way for the time when he would return to their land as Israel's king

Even though the town had been burned by the enemy, David returned to Ziklag to await news of the battle between Israel and the Philistines. He was sure he wouldn't have to wait there very long, and he was right, for the news came on the third day (2 Sam. 1:1-2). After he heard the report of the death of Saul and his sons, he sought the Lord's guidance and the Lord sent him to Hebron (2:1-4). David reigned over Judah for seven and a half years, and Hebron was his capital city (v. 11).

The Lord had kept His promises, and David's wilderness wanderings were now ended.

CHAPTER TWELVE
THE KING IS DEAD!
1 Samuel 28:3–25; 31; 1 Chronicles 10

First Samuel opens with the birth of a gifted baby, Samuel, and closes with the death of a guilty man, King Saul. The early chapters cluster around the tabernacle where God spoke to young Samuel, and the closing chapters focus on a forsaken man to whom God refused to speak. Samuel prayed and God defeated the Philistines; Saul sought for God's help but He didn't answer, and the Philistines defeated Israel. First Samuel is the book of man's king and is a record of Saul's decline, defeat, and death. Second Samuel is the record of God's king, David, and it shows how God made a mighty monarch out of a shepherd boy. King Saul's final days are recorded in these two chapters.

1. A night of deception and distress (1 Sam. 28:3-25)

Of all the "night scenes" in the Bible—and there are many of them—this one is perhaps the strangest and most dramatic. The spirit of a dead man returned to announce the doom of a despairing king who can find no way of escape. Samuel and Saul met for the last time, and it was not a happy meeting.

Saul didn't receive God's help (1 Sam. 28:3-6). We have already learned that Samuel was dead (25:1), but the fact is repeated here for perhaps two reasons. First, Israel was in trouble and Samuel wasn't there to rescue them as he had done before (7:7-14), and second, Saul was in trouble and Samuel wasn't there to give him God's counsel. When Samuel was alive, he had told Saul and the people what they needed to do to defeat the Philistines (7:3). However, their faith in God had gradually eroded under the leadership of King Saul, who was now deliberately seeking help from the evil one. It was Israel's darkest hour, but if God had deserted them, it was only because Saul had first deserted God.

The Philistine army was already mobilizing, and Saul and his army weren't prepared to meet them. When he saw them assembled, he became very frightened and trembled. The Philistines first gathered at Aphek while Israel assembled at Jezreel (29:1). Then the Philistines moved to Jezreel (v. 11) and finally to Shunem (28:4), where they prepared to attack the Israelite army stationed at Mount Gilboa (v. 4; 31:1).

Saul attempted to get in touch with the Lord through dreams, but there was no answer. He had no prophet with him, as David did (22:5), and David also had a priest with an ephod (23:6). The "Urim" mentioned in 28:6 must refer to a new ephod that somebody had made for Saul, because the ephod from the tabernacle was with David. No matter what means Saul tried, he received no answer from God.[1] But during most of his life, he didn't want God's will because he wanted to do things his own way. Is it any wonder that at the end of Saul's career, God deserted him?

"Then they will call on me, but I will not answer; they will seek me diligently, but they will not find me. Because they hated knowledge and did not choose the fear of the Lord, they would have none of my counsel and despised all my reproof, therefore they shall eat the fruit of their own way, and be filled to the full with their own fancies" (Prov. 1:28-31, NKJV).

Saul disobeyed God's Word (1 Sam. 28:7-14). The information in verse 3 about

Saul putting away the people involved in spiritistic practices prepares us for the shock of Saul seeking for a spirit medium to assist him. The Law of Moses condemns all forms of spiritism (Ex. 22:18; Lev. 19:31; 20:6; Deut. 18:9-13), so Saul was right in having these people expelled, but he was wrong to seek their help. In doing so, he was both a deliberate sinner and a hypocrite. The fact that some of his servants knew where a spirit medium lived suggests that Saul's clean-up campaign wasn't too thorough and that not all of his officers agreed with him. Some of them knew a medium Saul had overlooked.

The night before the battle (1 Sam. 28:19), Saul disguised himself by taking off every sign of royalty and dressing in common clothes. He had a ten-mile journey from Mt. Gilboa to Endor and would pass very near the Philistine lines, so it wouldn't do to be recognized as the King of Israel. Furthermore, he didn't want the medium to know who he was. Saul began his reign at the dawning of the day when he was anointed king by Samuel the prophet (9:26), but he ended his reign by going out at night to visit a spirit medium. He broke the very law he attempted to enforce.

The woman was no fool. She wanted to be sure this wasn't a trap to catch her and condemn her, for spiritism was a capital crime in Israel. Saul took an oath using the name of the Lord whose law he was breaking, that she would not be prosecuted, so she agreed to cooperate. Saul not only violated the law himself, but he encouraged her to violate it! He asked her to get in contact with Samuel, the man Saul didn't want to contact when the prophet was alive.

He discovered God's plan (vv. 15-19). Taking the plain meaning of the text, it seems clear that Samuel did appear to the woman *but she was shocked when it happened.* Samuel didn't come up from the realm of the dead because she was a good medium but because the Lord willed it to happen. This was not a demon imitating Samuel, or the medium using clever tricks, otherwise the woman wouldn't have been shocked. Her surprised loud cry was evidence that Samuel's sudden appearing was something she didn't expect to happen. She saw the prophet but Saul didn't (vv. 13-14), but Samuel spoke directly to Saul and not through the medium. Samuel was a prophet of God and needed no "mouthpiece" to convey the Lord's message. In fact, verse 21 suggests that the woman was not close to Saul during the time Samuel delivered his message to the king.

Saul had only one question for Samuel: "What shall I do?" The Philistines were ready to attack, Saul was a weak and worried man, and everything he did to ascertain the Lord's will didn't work. "God is departed from me." Seven times in his brief message Samuel used the word "Lord" as he reminded Saul that God had departed from him because he refused to obey God's will. God tore the kingdom from Saul because he hadn't obeyed in the matter of slaying the Amalekites (15:28), and for the first time, Samuel announced that David was the "neighbor" who would inherit the kingdom (28:17). But the direst news of all was that the next day Saul and his sons would be slain in battle and join Samuel in the realm of the dead.[2]

Saul despaired over his plight (1 Sam. 28:20-25). The king was sitting on a couch next to the wall, and when he heard Samuel's words, he fell helpless, full length on the floor. He had wanted a message from the Lord, but when it came, it wasn't the message he wanted to hear. He was trembling with fear at hearing the announcement of his death, and he was weak from fasting. Why would a general fast before a strategic battle? Was Saul trying to buy help from the Lord as he had done once before? (14:28) Some authorities believe that mediums required people to fast before they came to a séance, so perhaps Saul had that in mind. In either case, his actions were foolish, because fasting can't earn the blessing of the Lord if the heart isn't right with God.

The medium shifted into a motherly role and begged the king to eat something. He had a dangerous journey ahead of him back to his camp, and the next day he had to direct his troops in the battle against the Philistines. As he had foolishly done before, Saul tried to "play the man" and appear the hero, substituting bravado for sanity, but the pleas of the medium and Saul's men prevailed. The woman must have been fairly well to do to have a fattened calf readily available, because this was the diet of the wealthy and a rare delicacy for the common people. Indeed, it was a meal fit for a king, but it was also his "last supper" before leaving this life. Saul ate and then left the medium's house. The final statement in the chapter reminds us of Judas—"He then having received the sop went immediately out: and it was night" (John 13:30, KJV).

We can't help but feel sorry for Saul, and yet at the same time, we must admit that he brought his plight on himself. Had he obeyed the Lord he wouldn't have lost the kingdom, and had he stopped pursuing David and invested his time developing his army, he would have been better equipped to meet the Philistines at Jezreel. In spite of all the blessings God gave to Saul, and all the opportunities to grow spiritually, Saul was unprepared to lead, unprepared to fight, and unprepared to die.

2. A day of disgrace and defeat (1 Sam. 31:1-10; 1 Chron. 10)

Saul's military record is summarized in 1 Samuel 14:47-48. It's a commendable record that presents Saul as a conquering general and a national hero. He began his career as a great success; after all, the people did sing, "Saul has slain his thousands." It was after his failure to destroy the Amalekites that Saul began to go downhill. When David came on the scene, Saul's envy of the young man's success so obsessed him that the king became paranoid and dangerous. Saul had many good qualities, but none of them was humble, obedient faith in God. Because of his pride and disobedience, Saul lost everything.

Saul lost his army (1 Sam. 31:1; 1 Chron. 10:1). Saul's soldiers were no match for the Philistine army with its large divisions and its many chariots. Some of the men deserted and many others died on the battlefield. The Philistines preferred to fight on level ground because they depended on their chariots, while Israel tried to lure them into the hill country around Mount Gilboa. Israel was outnumbered and outclassed, but even if they had boasted superior forces, they still would have been defeated. Saul's hour of judgment had come. Without Samuel's prayers and David's anointed leadership, the army of Israel was destined for defeat.

Saul lost his life (1 Sam. 31:2-7; 1 Chron. 10:1-6). One of the first rules of ancient warfare was, "Kill the enemy king!" (See 1 Kings 22:31.) Saul was on the field with three of his four sons; for some reason, Ish-Bosheth (also known as Esh-Baal) was missing (2 Sam. 2:8; 1 Chron. 8:33; 9:39). The three sons died first, and then Saul was fatally struck by an arrow and asked his armor-bearer to kill him. The Philistines were notorious for abusing and humiliating victims, especially officers and kings. Saul feared that he would be tortured to death, so when the young man failed to respond to his plea, he fell on his sword and died.[3] The young man immediately took his own life, and eventually all of Saul's bodyguards and officers around him met their death. It was total victory for the Philistines.

Saul's reign was a tragic one and his death seemed inevitable, but how sad that three of his sons should die with him on the battlefield. Jonathan had dreamed of being coregent with David (1 Sam. 23:16-18), but that dream was never fulfilled. How often the sins of one bring pain and even death to others. "There is a sin leading to death" (1 John 5:16, NKJV). The sins of both Saul and Eli (4:1-18) cost them their lives and the lives of their sons. God is no respecter of persons.

Saul lost his honor (1 Sam. 31:8-10; 1 Chron. 10:8-10). Humiliating the prisoners and the dying and stripping the dead were the chief activities of a victorious army, for the spoils of battle were a big part of their wages for risking their lives. The Philistines took great joy in abusing Saul's body. They stripped off his armor and cut off his head, and after parading both from place to place in their land (1 Chron. 10:9), they displayed them in their temples. The armor was put in the temple of their goddess Ashtareth, and the head in the temple of Dagon. Finally, they publicly displayed the mutilated corpses of Saul and his sons on the outside of the city wall of Bethshan, a Philistine controlled city in the Jezreel Valley. For a Jew not to receive proper burial was both humiliating and sacrilegious, and for the body to be mutilated and then exposed was even more scandalous. The Philistines were letting their people and their idols know that they had won a great victory over their chief enemy, the people of Israel. Dagon had triumphed over Jehovah!

Saul lost his crown (2 Sam. 1:1-10). The account of Saul's death given to David by the Amalekite was primarily a lie. The man "happened" to be at the battle but was obviously there to steal loot, and he had taken the two insignias of royalty from Saul's dead body. He had not put Saul out of his misery because Saul had committed suicide and was dead when the man arrived. After removing the royal crown and bracelet, the Amalekite, (who may have been a mercenary in one of the armies) should have safely removed the body from the field and protected it until it could have proper burial. He thought that his heroic acts would win David's approval, but they only brought him death.

Because of Saul's sins, he first lost his dynasty (13:11-14) and then his kingdom (15:24-31), and finally he lost his crown. The warning of our Lord in Revelation 3:11 is applicable at this point: "Behold, I come quickly! Hold fast what you have, that no one may take your crown" (NKJV). "Look to yourselves, that we do not lose those things we worked for, but that we may receive a full reward" (2 John 8, NKJV).

3. An hour of daring and devotion (1 Sam. 31:11-13; 1 Chron. 10:11-13)

While the Philistines were making merry over defeating Israel and humiliating Saul and his sons, the men of Jabesh Gilead heard about the tragedy and came to the rescue. King Saul's first great victory had been the delivering of Jabesh Gilead from the Ammonites (1 Sam. 11:1-11), so the people of the city felt an obligation to vindicate Saul's memory. All of their valiant men traveled fifteen to twenty miles at night to the city of Bethshan and took possession of the four mutilated and decaying bodies. In order to make this trip, they had to cross the Jordan River and go through enemy territory. Saul hadn't been a spiritual leader, but he was a courageous leader and the first king of Israel. Even if we can't respect the man, we must show respect for the office.

The men risked their lives a second time and carried the bodies to Jabesh Gilead. There they burned the bodies to remove the mutilated and decayed flesh, and they left the bones for burial. They didn't cremate the bodies, because cremation wasn't a Jewish practice. In times of emergency, the Jews would burn corpses that were so mutilated and decayed they couldn't be properly washed and anointed for burial; and then they would give honorable burial to the bones. After the people of Jabesh Gilead buried the bones, they fasted for seven days. It was their tribute to Saul and his sons.

Saul had often held court under a tree in Ramah (22:6), and now he was buried with three of his sons under a tree near Jabesh Gilead. Later, David disinterred the bones of Saul and Jonathan and had them buried in their family's tomb in Benjamin (2 Sam. 21:13-14).

CHAPTER THIRTEEN
FOUR SUCCESSES AND TWO FAILURES
Review of 1 Samuel

When the American statesman Benjamin Franklin signed the Declaration of Independence on July 4, 1776, he remarked, "We must indeed all hang together, or most assuredly, we shall all hang separately." The road from signing a document to achieving national unity was a long one and a costly one, but eventually the United States of America emerged on the political scene and has been there ever since. Its two mottoes summarize the miracle that was accomplished: "E pluribus unum—Out of many, one" and "In God we trust." The first tells us what happened and the second tells us how it happened.

The nation of Israel had a similar challenge. After the death of Joshua, Israel gradually became a divided nation. Instead of trusting the Lord, the Jews began to worship the gods of their pagan neighbors, and the spiritual bonds that held the tribes together began to weaken and break. Before long, people were doing what was right in their own eyes and caring little about the covenant they had made with the Lord. Then the people called for a king, for someone who could bring unity to the nation and victory to the army. God answered their request and gave them Saul, but not to solve their problems—he only made some of them worse—but to prove to the people that their greatest need was to trust in Him and obey His Word. It wasn't until David appeared on the scene that national events began to take a different turn and light appeared at the end of the tunnel.

David was anointed by Samuel, and Samuel was the son of Elkanah and Hannah; so the story begins with Hannah, a humble woman whose submission and faith in God are an example for all of us to follow.

1. Hannah, a godly woman

The name Hannah means "grace," and she certainly lived up to her name. God gave her the grace she needed to suffer the insults hurled at her by Peninnah, Elkanah's second wife, and to endure the embarrassment and pain of childlessness. She received the grace she needed to speak kindly and gently when she was misunderstood and criticized (Col. 4:6). God gave her grace to conceive a son and dedicate him to the Lord—and then to sing about it! So beautiful and meaningful was Hannah's song that Mary borrowed from it when she praised the Lord for His grace to her (Luke 1:46-55).

Hannah was a woman with "faith and patience" (Heb. 6:12) who committed herself to God, asked for a son, and waited for God to answer in His own way and time. She was patient at home as she endured the verbal attacks of Peninnah, and she was patient with Eli when he falsely accused her of being drunk. She was fortunate to have a devout husband who loved her and encouraged her to obey the Lord. There were times when life was very difficult for Hannah, but she persevered in her faith, hope, and love and eventually won the victory.

Hannah realized what too many of us forget, that God works in and through "common people" to accomplish His purposes on earth. He didn't ask Hannah to lead an army, as He did Deborah (Judg. 4–5), or intercede with a king, as He did Esther. He simply asked her to fulfill her heart's desire and give birth to a son. "Delight yourself also in the Lord, and He shall give you the desires of your heart" (Ps. 37:4). All that Hannah wanted was to be a woman of God who obeyed the will of God. In doing this, she helped to save the nation of Israel.

There's so much treachery, bloodshed, and confusion recorded in 1 Samuel that it's refreshing to meet at the very beginning of the book a woman who represents the very best that God has to give. The leaders of Israel had failed, so God sought out a woman He could use to help bring truth, peace, and order to His people. She served God simply by being a woman and doing what only a woman could do—give birth to a baby and dedicate that child to the Lord.

"He settles the barren woman in her home as a happy mother of children. Praise the Lord" (Ps. 113:9, NIV).

2. Eli, a compromising priest

Eli was an indulgent father who occasionally reproved his sons for their sins but took no steps to discipline the men, let alone replace them. The work at the tabernacle went on in a routine sort of way, but there was no spiritual power evident nor was there any fresh word from the Lord. The picture we get of Eli is that of a fat, old man, sitting on his special chair as he directed the affairs of the tabernacle, all the while closing his eyes to what he saw and his ears to what he heard. He was the leader of Israel's religion and desperately needed to have a fresh experience with the Lord.

But we can commend Eli for putting his blessing on Hannah's prayer request (1 Sam. 1:17) and for welcoming little Samuel when she brought him to be dedicated to the Lord. Samuel's sons weren't the best companions for an innocent little boy, but the Lord and Eli saw to it that Samuel wasn't defiled. Eli taught Samuel the truths of God Word and instructed him concerning the work and ways of the tabernacle. Samuel was born a priest, but God would call him to minister as a prophet and judge.

Something else is commendable in Eli: when the Lord sent His message to young Samuel, Eli counseled the boy, listened to the message, and submitted to the Lord's will. "It is the Lord. Let Him do what seems good to Him" (3:18, NKJV). Whether this statement was a confession of helpless resignation or a mark of worshipful submission isn't easy to determine, but let's give Eli the benefit of the doubt. As he saw God at work in young Samuel's life, Eli must have encouraged him and prayed for him. There's no record that he was envious of the lad because God's messages were coming through him. Blessed are those older saints who help the new generation know God and live for Him! However Eli may have failed with his own sons, he helped to point Samuel in the right direction and the whole nation benefited from it.

Eli's last day of ministry was a tough one: his two sons died, the Ark was captured by the enemy, and his daughter-in-law died giving birth to a son. "Ichabod—the glory has departed!" But God was still on the throne and young Samuel was getting ready to step into the gap and bring spiritual direction to the nation. Eli hadn't been a great spiritual leader, but he was one small link in the chain that led to the anointing of David and eventually the birth of the Redeemer.

3. Samuel, a faithful servant

Samuel was born at a time when the nation and its religion were a stagnant pool, but he soon found himself trying to navigate on a stormy sea. Change was in the air, and priests were trained to protect tradition, not to promote alteration. The Jewish leaders wanted a king, someone who could unify the people and protect them from the surrounding nations. Samuel saw this move as an abandonment of the Kingship of Jehovah, but the Lord told him to go along with the people and anoint Saul as king. Samuel did his best to educate the people for life under a monarchy, but his words seemed to make little difference.

The people had voted Samuel out of his judgeship, but he was still God's priest and prophet, and he helped Saul get a good start. Samuel led the nation in renewing their covenant with the Lord, Saul rescued the people of Jabesh Gilead, and Samuel gave a moving farewell speech in which he promised to pray for the nation. But it soon became evident that Saul had very little spiritual discernment and that he was using the kingship to promote himself, not to assist the people. He lied about his willful disobedience, lost the kingdom, and sent Samuel home to Ramah with a broken heart.

Real change agents don't sit around complaining and remembering the good old days. When God told Samuel to go to Bethlehem and anoint a new king, he risked his life and obeyed, and David became a part of the scene. Scripture doesn't tell us how much mentoring Samuel gave David, but the prophet recognized God's hand on the lad and surely taught him about the Lord and His people. Samuel was God's living link between Israel's past and future, and he played his part well. He befriended David when he was in danger, prayed for him, and trusted God to care for him.

Samuel is an example to all older believers who are prone to glorify the past, resist change in the present, and lose hope in the future. Without abandoning the past, Samuel accepted change, did all he could to make things work, and when they didn't work, trusted God for a brighter future. God didn't abandon the kingdom; He just chose a better man to be in charge, and Samuel helped to mentor that man. Every leader needs a Samuel, a person in touch with God, appreciative of the past but willing to follow God into a new era, a man of faith and encouragement who sees the hand of God at work where others see only confusion.

Nobody could buy Samuel's conscience or accuse him of putting money ahead of ministry. The only blot on his record is the covetousness of his sons who used their ministry to line their own pockets. Nothing is said in Scripture about Samuel's wife, so perhaps she died young and this deprived the boys of her godly instruction and example. Samuel was often away from home, covering his ministry circuit, and this may have left the boys too much to themselves. It's useless to second-guess history. But after seeing what Samuel did for David, we can perhaps forgive what he didn't do for his own sons.

4. Saul, an unstable king

Saul's chief problem seemed to be his lack of a spiritual foundation on which to build a godly life. He may have stood head and shoulders above everybody else, but he was a midget when he stood next to David or even his son Jonathan. This lack of spiritual experience resulted in a second deficiency—a lack of confidence in himself and in the Lord. This had to be covered up by a leadership style that fed his ego and kept everybody around him in fear. At the start of his reign, when he was supposed to be encouraging the people, he was hiding in the baggage! Yet during his reign, he kept his spear constantly with him, not just to protect himself but also to remind everybody who was boss. He believed any lie about David that would give him reason to rally the troops and forget the needs of the nation.

When David arrived on the scene, he didn't create problems—he revealed them. An insecure man like Saul can't tolerate competition and competence, and this made David an enemy. The people loved David and honored him, and this only made Saul's paranoia grow faster. Saul became a double-minded man who was "unstable in all his ways" (James 1:8). On the one hand, he pursued David and tried to kill him, while on the other hand he wept when he saw David or heard his voice, and tried to appear apologetic and repentant. His was the shallow heart of our Lord's Parable of the Sower. There was no depth, the tears were temporary, and no lasting fruit ever appeared.

Paradoxical as it seems, it was *success* that helped to bring about Saul's ruin. Charles de Gaulle, president of France, said, "Success contains within it the germs of failure, and the reverse is also true." Those germs of failure are planted by the hands of pride, and pride was one of Saul's besetting sins. He was suddenly forced out of the predictable work of a farmer and herdsman into the unpredictable work of a king, and he didn't have the equipment to work with. The Lord would have helped him, as he did Moses, Joshua, and Gideon, but Saul chose to go his own way. When success comes before we're ready for it, it can destroy us and rob us of the things that make for true success. Saul didn't know the difference.

When Saul failed, he learned to substitute excuses for confessions, but his lies only entangled him worse. His life and royal service were part of a tragic masquerade that was applauded by his flatterers and abominated by the Lord. Saul didn't listen to Moses, Samuel, Jonathan, or David, and once he had rejected God's Word, the only voice left was that of the devil.

"I know of no more unhappy character than Saul when God had departed from him," said Charles Haddon Spurgeon. "But, somehow, there was not the anguish in the soul of Saul that there would have been if he had ever really known the Lord. I do not think that he ever did really, in his inmost soul, know the Lord. After Samuel anointed him, he was 'turned into another man,' but he never became a new man. . . ."[1] Campbell Morgan said, "The man in his government of Israel was a warrior and nothing more; he was never a shepherd."[2] He held a spear, not a shepherd's crook.

When God calls people to serve, He knows their capacity for doing the work He wants them to do, and He will never abandon them—if they trust and obey. That's where Saul failed. When God is left out of the equation, the answer is always zero.

Centuries later, another Saul appeared on the scene—Saul of Tarsus, who quickly became known as Paul, "the small one."[3] He said he was "less than the least of all saints" (Eph. 3:8), which is quite a contrast to the Old Testament Saul with his great stature and manly physique. King Saul died a suicide on the battlefield, but his namesake died a martyr outside the city of Rome. Before his death, he wrote to his beloved Timothy, "I have fought a good fight, I have finished my course, I have kept the faith" (2 Tim. 4:7).

Ten seconds after he died, King Saul wished he could have said those words.

5. Jonathan, a generous friend

British preacher and composer George Matheson was right when he called Jonathan "a rainbow in a storm."[4] You don't find Jonathan speaking a pessimistic word or questioning God's ability to accomplish what had to be done. He and his armor-bearer challenged the Philistine outpost and won. He openly defied his father's bizarre instructions and taught his fellow soldiers a lesson in sane military manners. Jonathan risked his life to help David escape and then went to him in his exile so he could encourage him. The natural heir to the throne, Jonathan stripped himself of his royal garments and his armor and gave them to David.

Jonathan didn't mind being second man. He loved David and love always puts other people first. Jonathan made a covenant with David to become coregent when David ascended the throne, a promise, alas, that David couldn't fulfill. Jonathan loved his father and his nation to the very end and died on the battlefield while trying to defend king and country. It's tragic that so noble a prince should die because of the poor leadership displayed by his father, but God didn't want Saul's line and David's line together in the throne room.

Jonathan leaves behind a beautiful example of what true friendship should be: honest, loving, sacrificing, seeking the welfare of others, and always bringing hope and encouragement when the situation is difficult. Jonathan never achieved a crown on earth, but he certainly received one in heaven. "Be faithful until death, and I will give you the crown of life" (Rev. 2:10).

6. David, a courageous shepherd

The eighth son and the "baby" of the family, David should have lived and died in anonymity, but he was a man after God's own heart, and God put His hand upon him. It's too bad that when his name is mentioned, people instantly remember his sin with Bathsheba and the murder of her husband, because, as terrible as those sins were, David was a great man and served God in a great way. We ought also to remember the way he built and protected the kingdom of Israel, or the many psalms he wrote, or the sacrifices he made on the battlefield to gather wealth for the building of the temple. God forgave David and David paid dearly for his sins, but God never cast David aside or refused his dedicated service. "So then each of us shall give account of himself to God" (Rom. 14:12, NKJV).

David was a man athirst for God. He envied the priests because they were privileged to dwell in God's house and live close to His presence. But He saw God in the mountains and rivers as much as in the sanctuary, and he heard God's voice in the thunder. For David, the world was alive with God, and the highest honor one could have—higher than being king—was to be God's servant and accomplish His purposes on earth.

God first trained David in solitude as he cared for the flock, and when the time was right, He thrust him on the stage and trained him even more in suffering. Some of his brothers criticized him, his king tried to kill him, and the king's courtiers lied about him, but David lived his life open before the Lord and never turned back. No, he wasn't perfect, nor did he claim to be, but his heart was fixed, and his consuming desire was to glorify God and finish his work.

Though on occasion he wavered because of doubts, David believed God's promises and never turned back in unbelief. Doubt is a temporary relapse of the heart, but unbelief is a permanent rebellion of the will, and David was never guilty of that. Even during his sojourns in enemy territory, he sought ways to accomplish something that would further God's kingdom.

David was a unique blending of soldier and shepherd, musician and military tactician, commander and commoner. In spite of his sins and failures—and we all have them—he was Israel's greatest king, and always will be until King Jesus reigns on David's throne as Prince of Peace. The next time we're tempted to emphasize the negative things in David's life, let's remember that Jesus wasn't ashamed to be called "the Son of David."

Four successes: Hannah, a housewife; Samuel, a prophet and priest; Jonathan, a prince and friend; and David, a shepherd.

Two failures: Eli, a priest, and Saul, a king.

And the Lord still says to us, "Let Jesus be king of your life. Be successful!"

Endnotes

Chapter 1

1. Ramah means "height" and Ramathaim means "the two heights." A number of cities had "ramah" in their names (Josh 13:26; 19:29; 21:38; Judg. 4:5; 1 Sam. 30:27), but it's likely that Elkanah and his family lived in Ramathaim ("double heights") on the border of Benjamin and Ephraim. Elkanah was a Levite by birth but an Ephraimite by residence.
2. The NIV and NASB both read "a double portion" and the NLT says "a special portion," but some students translate 1:5 "only one portion." It seems, however, that Elkanah was trying to show special love to his wife at a difficult time, so the gift must have been special.
3. Psalm 99:6 and Jeremiah 15:1 identify Samuel as a man of prayer, and he's named in Hebrews 11:32 as a man of faith. For instances of special prayer on his part, see 1 Samuel 7:8-9; 8:6; 12:18-19, 23; 15:11.
4. In her brief speech recorded in 1:25-28, Hannah frequently used different forms of the Hebrew word *sa-al*, which means "asked" and is a basis for the name "Samuel." The word "lent" in v. 28 (KJV) means "given." Hannah's surrender of Samuel to the Lord was final.
5. Of course, the earth isn't resting on the tops of pillars. This is poetic language based on the architecture of that day. See also Job 38:4; Psalm 75:3; 82:5; 104:5; Isaiah 24:18.
6. There is no record in Scripture how the high priesthood moved from Eleazar's line to Ithamar's and hence eventually to Eli.
7. The priests who serve in the temple during the Kingdom Age will be from the family of Zadok (Ezek. 40:45-46; 43:19; 44:10-16).
8. The repetition of names when God speaks is also found when the Lord spoke to Abraham

(Gen. 22:11), Moses (Ex. 3:4), Martha (Luke 10:41), and Paul (Acts 9:4; 26:14).

9. Samuel would have a ministry of "opening doors" for others. He opened the doors of kingship to Saul, who failed to use it for God's glory, and also to David, who used his position to serve God and the people. Samuel established a school of the prophets and opened doors of ministry to the men God sent to him. He opened the doors to a new beginning for the nation of Israel that was at low ebb both spiritually and politically.

CHAPTER 2

1. Obviously 1 Samuel was written after the events described, so the name "Ebenezer" is used here by anticipation. See 1 Samuel 7:12. However, it may have been another site with the same name.
2. The word "hand" is a key word in this story. The "hand of the enemy" is found in 4:3; 7:3, 8. The Philistines spoke about "the hand of these mighty gods" (4:8), and "the hand of the Lord" is mentioned in 5:6-7, 9, 11; 6:3, 5, 9; and 7:13.
3. The Hebrew word *kabod* shows up frequently in this account. It means "heavy" but also can mean "honor, glory, respectful" (people of "weight"). Eli was "heavy" but he wasn't "weighty" when it came to character and godliness, what Paul called the "weight of glory" (1 Cor. 4:17).
4. Rachel named her second son "Ben-oni," which means "son of my sorrow," but Jacob changed it to Benjamin" which means "son of my right hand" (Gen. 35:16-18).

CHAPTER 3

1. The pouring out of the water could also be seen as a drink offering, symbolizing total devotion to the Lord, for liquids poured out can't be recovered again. See Psalm 62:8; Lamentations 2:19; Philippians 2:17; 2 Timothy 4:6. The only official fast on the Jewish calendar was on the Day of Atonement, but that didn't prevent the people from fasting at other times. The situation was critical, and the nation needed to "come clean" with the Lord.
2. The nation of Israel rejected God the Father when they asked for a king, God the Son when they said, "We have no king but Caesar" (John 19:15), and God the Holy Spirit when they stoned Stephen (Acts 7:51-60).
3. Going "back to Bethel" signifies a return to the Lord. Abraham did it (12:8; 13:1-4) and so did Jacob (Gen. 28:18-19; 35:1ff).
4. *The Westminster Pulpit* (London: Pickering and Inglis, n.d), vol. 9, 14.

CHAPTER 4

1. The Hebrew letters for *r* and *d* and *k* and *n* are very similar and someone copying a Hebrew manuscript could easily make a mistake. The original manuscripts of the Scriptures are inspired and inerrant, but minor spelling and numerical errors could creep into the copies.
2. The Hebrew text of 1 Samuel 13:1 reads, "Saul was a son of a year in his reigning, and he reigned two years over Israel," a perplexing statement indeed. The NIV reads "Saul was thirty years old when he became king, and he reigned over Israel forty-two years," but these numbers are not in the original text. The NASB says he was forty years old when he started his reign and was king for thirty-two years, but, again, these numbers are pure conjecture. The KJV settles for "Saul reigned one year; and when he had reigned two years over Israel Saul chose him three thousand men" (13:1-2). Paul said that Saul reigned forty years (Acts 13:21). Since Saul's son Jonathan was old enough to be a commander in the army, Saul could well have been forty or older when he became king. If he reigned thirty years, he would have been seventy when he died. Some chronologists have conjectured that Saul was born in 1080 and became king in 1050 at age thirty. If Saul died at age seventy, that would have been in 1010. See *The Expositor's Bible Commentary*, vol. 3, 373, for Ronald F. Youngblood's suggested chronology. Obviously, not all Old Testament students agree, and this is understandable because the factual data are not complete. No doctrinal matter is affected by this problem.
3. Like the Latin, the Hebrew language uses letters to represent numbers, so it was easy for copyists to make errors. Some students believe that "30,000 chariots" is a scribal error and that the number should be 3,000. The *l* at the end of Israel could have been copied twice, and this would have turned

"three" into "thirty." In ancient warfare, the number of cavalry soldiers always exceeded the number of charioteers, and the Philistines mustered 6,000 cavalrymen. But regardless of the exact numbers, the Jewish army was definitely outnumbered by the enemy.

4. Saul called himself a fool in 1 Sam. 26:21, and David admitted he had done foolishly when he numbered the people (2 Sam. 24:10; 1 Chron. 21:8). However, David was sincere in his confession and truly repented of his sin. In 2 Chronicles 16:9, the seer Hanani told King Asa he had done a foolish thing in robbing God's temple in order to hire heathen soldiers to fight his battles. All disobedience to God is folly and leads ultimately to failure and pain.

CHAPTER 5

1. Jonathan's "test" wasn't an act of unbelief as was Gideon's fleece (Judg. 6:36-40). Jonathan already had the faith he needed to defeat the enemy, but he wanted to know how the Lord wanted him to attack. It's wrong for God's children to "put out the fleece" and set up conditions that God has to meet before they will obey Him. Sometimes the Lord stoops to our level of weakness and meets our conditions, but the practice doesn't build one's faith.
2. The phrase "bring the Ark" in verse 18 is unusual, because the Ark wasn't used for determining the will of God. "Bring the ephod" is what we expect to read, as in 1 Samuel 23:9 and 30:7. The ephod was that part of the high priest's official garments in which the Urim and Thummim were kept (Ex. 28:6-30). They were used to determine the will of God.
3. Twice Pharaoh said "I have sinned" (Ex. 9:27; 10:16), but his words were empty. As soon as the situation improved in Egypt, he went right back to opposing Moses and God. Balaam said, "I have sinned" (Num. 22:34) but continued to be an enemy of Israel. Judas admitted his sin but never really repented (Matt. 27:4). David said, "I have sinned" and really meant it (2 Sam. 12:13; 24:10, 17; Ps. 51:4), and so did the prodigal son (Luke 15:18, 21).
4. When the Bible speaks about the Lord "changing His mind" or "repenting," it is using human language to describe divine truth. God knows the future, including our responses to His commands, and God is never at a loss to know what to do. He does change His actions in response to what people do, but this has nothing to do with His changeless nature or attributes. Jonah announced that Nineveh would be destroyed, but the city repented and the Lord withdrew the judgment. From the human point of view, God seemed to change His mind, but not from the divine point of view. God is always true to His nature and consistent with His attributes and plans. Nothing catches Him by surprise.

CHAPTER 6

1. The Hebrew word translated "youngest" in verse 11 also means "smallest." Saul was famous for his height (9:2; 10:23), but David was not conspicuous in the crowd. From the beginning of his ministry, David was seen as a man with a humble spirit.
2. Early in his life, David acknowledged that Jehovah God was King (Ps. 59:13). Blessed is that leader who recognizes that he is second in command!
3. Noah was "the eighth person" (2 Peter 2:5) and eight persons were saved in the Ark to give a new beginning to civilization (1 Peter 3:20). Jewish boys were circumcised on the eighth day, which gave them a new status in the nation as "sons of the covenant," and the firstborn were dedicated to God on the eighth day (Ex. 22:29-30).
4. In the Old Testament, the Spirit of God came upon people whom the Lord called to accomplish certain purposes for God, but He might also leave them as He did Saul. This fact helps to explain David's prayer in Psalm 51:11. Believers today who share in the New Covenant are assured that they have the Spirit forever (John 14:16). True believers are sealed by the Spirit at conversion, and the seal speaks of permanent possession and protection (Eph. 1:13-14 and 4:30).
5. Some chronologists calculate that David was born about 1085 and was anointed in 1070 at the age of fifteen or sixteen. Five years later (1065) he fled from Saul and was in exile for the next ten years. In 1055, he was crowned king over Judah when he was thirty years old (2 Sam. 2).
6. Fear seems to have been a constant prob-

lem with Saul. See 13:11; 15:24; 17:11; 18:12; 28:5. Faith and fear don't lodge in the same heart (Matt. 8:26).

7. Was the giant wearing his helmet or was he so confident that he left it behind? But even a helmet couldn't keep a heaven-impelled stone from penetrating Goliath's skull. It's likely that Goliath was in a combat posture, bent slightly forward and approaching David, and this plus the weight of his armor caused him to fall face forward.
8. The phrase "Israel and Judah" in verse 52, found also in 15:4, suggests that Saul didn't have a unified nation or a united army. Apparently the royal tribe of Judah operated as a separate entity. After the death of Saul and his sons, it was the tribe of Judah that welcomed David as their king (2 Sam. 2:1-4).
9. Some Old Testament scholars think that David wrote Psalm 8 in honor of God's victory over Goliath. Both 1 Samuel 17 and Ps. 8 emphasize the name of God, the fowl of the air, and beasts of the field, and God's willingness to care for and use frail man.

Chapter 7

1. To make anything more out of their friendship than the mature affection of two manly believers is to twist the Scriptures. Had there been anything unlawful in their relationship, the Lord certainly would never have blessed David and protected him, and David could never have written Psalm 18:19-27 ten years later.
2. Merab and her husband had five sons, all of whom were sacrificed by the Gibeonites in order to end a famine in the land (2 Sam. 21:1-9).
3. The phrase "David's men" is found frequently in the Samuel narrative (18:27; 23:3-5; 24:3; 25:12-13). It seems that some of his soldiers stayed with him and became his "crack troops" during the days of his exile. They considered it a high honor to be known as "David's men," and indeed it was.
4. The shedding of innocent blood was a very serious crime in Israel. The six cities of refuge were set apart so that innocent people involved in manslaughter might not be treated as murderers (Deut. 19:1-10), and the ritual of the red heifer atoned for innocent blood shed by unknown murderers (Deut. 21:1-9). God hates the sin of shedding innocent blood (Prov. 6:16-17) and the prophets cried out against it (Isa. 59:7; Jer. 7:6; 22:17; 26:15). This was one of the sins that brought about the downfall in Jerusalem and the kingdom of Judah (2 Kings 21:16).
5. The goats' hair reminds us of Jacob's deceiving his father, Gen. 27:15-16. Surely Michal knew the story.

Chapter 8

1. David often mentioned in his psalms that his life was constantly in danger because people wanted to kill him: Psalms 34:4; 38:12; 40:14; 54:3; 63:9; 70:2. Psalm 18 summarizes David's ten years in exile and how the Lord sustained and helped him.
2. It seems that David had a special hiding place that only Jonathan knew about, the place by the stone Ezel where David hid when all his trouble with Saul began (19:2; 20:19, NIV). The Hebrew word *ezel* means "the departure," a significant thing when you realize that it was there that David and Jonathan departed from each other and David departed from the service of Saul.
3. Jonathan's promise that he will tell David the truth almost sounds like he is minimizing his father's hatred for David (vv. 12-13). Even the NIV translation doesn't change this impression: "If he is favorably disposed toward you. But if my father is inclined to harm you. . . ." Perhaps we should expect a son to be more sanguine about his father's temper than the victim of the abuse, but Jonathan soon found out that Saul would kill him, too, if he could.
4. Jonathan's words "The Lord be between me and thee" must not be equated with the agreement between Laban and Jacob (Gen. 31:43-53), the so-called "Mizpah benediction," which is not a benediction at all. David and Jonathan trusted God and each other and knew that God would care for them and fulfill His purposes. Laban and Jacob didn't trust each other and reminded each other that the Lord would watch them and make sure neither one would cross the boundary to attack the other.
5. Biblical scholars don't agree on the authenticity of all the historical inscriptions to the psalms, but the psalms that have no inscriptions present an even greater mystery. In this book, I assume that the inscriptions are accurate.

6. The fact that Jesus mentioned Abiathar and not Ahimelech may come from the fact that Abiathar was the only priest who survived the slaughter that Saul commanded.
7. The Philistines called David "king" because they knew how popular he was with the people of Israel. He was the "king" of the battlefield.
8. The word "Ramah" in the KJV (v. 6) means "height," and therefore the NIV translates the text "on the hill at Gibeah." It's obvious that Saul and his officers couldn't be in Gibeah and Ramah at the same time, even though the cities were less than five miles apart.
9. Saul had enlisted everybody to help him locate David and used bribery and intimidation to get results (23:7, 19, 25, 27; 24:1; 26:1).
10. The *New Living Translation* uses the verb "shouted" in verses 7, 11 and 16.
11. The KJV translation of verse 15 suggests that this wasn't the first time the high priest had consulted the Lord for David, and the NIV backs this up. But there is no indication that David had ever gone to Nob to ask the high priest to determine God's will for him, including the occasion described by Doeg. David was merely a civil servant in Saul's employ and had no right to ask the high priest to inquire for him. Later, when Abiathar escaped and joined David's band, he did use the ephod to seek the Lord's will.
12. Unfortunately, Abiathar sided with Adonijah in his quest for the throne, and Solomon replaced him with Azariah from the priestly family of Zadok. This was the final step in eliminating Eli's family from the levitical priesthood.

CHAPTER 9

1. David himself was called a prophet (2 Sam. 23:2; Acts 4:25), but this gift seems to have been used primarily in the writing of the Psalms, especially those that speak about the Messiah.
2. David had a double claim on the people of Keilah: he was their brother, a member of the tribe of Judah, and he was their deliverer.
3. In the superscription to Psalm 18, David separated Saul from his enemies.
4. Saul was sure that the Lord had delivered David into his hands (23:7), and David's men were sure the Lord had delivered Saul into David's hands! It all depends on your point of view!
5. David used a familiar proverb that is now a part of Scripture, but that doesn't mean that folksy proverbs carry the same authority as the inspired Word of God. There is practical wisdom in some proverbs, but they have a tendency to contradict one another. "Look before you leap" is balanced by "He who hesitates is lost," and "Absence makes the heart grow fonder" by "Out of sight, out of mind."
6. The writer may have seen in this question a reflection of Isaac's words to Jacob, who was impersonating Esau, "Are you really my son Esau?" (Gen. 27:24, NKJV). Yet it was Saul who was the liar, not David.

CHAPTER 10

1. This is not Mount Carmel, located far north on the border of Asher and Manasseh, near the Mediterranean Sea.
2. Caleb's family tree is found in 1 Chronicles 2:18-54, and it's interesting to note that Caleb's grandmother was named Ephratah (2:50), the ancient name of Bethlehem (Gen. 35:16). Another of Caleb's descendants was actually named Bethlehem (2:51, 54; 4:4). Since David and Nabal both belonged to the tribe of Judah, and since David was born in Bethlehem, perhaps the two men were distant relatives! If so, then David had a double claim on Nabal's hospitality. Note that David referred to himself as Nabal's "son" (v. 8), which suggests that he expected fatherly care from Nabal.
3. "This iniquity" may have included more than Nabal's selfishness and uncharitable attitude. David had taken an oath to slay Nabal and all his men, and it's possible that Abigail somehow heard about it. We get the impression that this wise woman knew what was going on in David's camp. If David didn't keep his oath, foolish as it was, he would sin against the Lord, but Abigail said that she would assume the guilt in his place. Rebekah offered to bear Jacob's curse if her plan failed (Gen. 27:11-13). But if God had wanted David to keep his oath, He would not have intervened as He did.
4. Abishai, Asahel, and Joab were sons of David's sister Zeruiah (1 Chron. 2:16) and nephews of David. Saul's captain Abner killed Asahel, and Joab and Abishai chased him and killed him, much to David's sor-

row (2 Sam. 2–3). Abishai became one of David's best military leaders and saved David's life when he was attacked by a giant (2 Sam. 21:15-17).

5. In that day, many people believed that the god you worshiped was limited to the territory of the people who worshiped him, and when you moved to another country, you adopted the gods of that country. Those who worshiped Jehovah had to do it in the land of Israel. David certainly didn't believe this lie but exalted Jehovah as the Lord of all the earth. See Psalms 8, 138–139.

CHAPTER 11

1. The phrase "keeper of my head" (KJV) means "bodyguard." Had Achish forgotten that David had cut off Goliath's head and kept it? (17:54) Achish's leaders were worried about what David would do with their soldiers' heads (29:4). There's another interesting paradox here. David was Saul's bodyguard (22:14) and Saul didn't trust him, but David was deceiving Achish and the king made him his bodyguard!
2. David left the king as the new day dawned (29:10-11), but Saul was meeting with a witch at night (28:8) and heading for defeat and death.

CHAPTER 12

1. There is no contradiction between 1 Samuel 28:6 ("When Saul inquired of the Lord") and 1 Chronicles 10:14, that Saul "inquired not of the Lord." Two different Hebrew words are used. In 1 Sam. 28, the word is *sha'al* and means "to ask, to request"; and the word in 1 Chron. 10 is *daresh,* which means "to seek with care." Saul did ask for help but it was not from the heart, nor did he constantly seek God's help as David and Samuel did. He was in trouble, so he called on the Lord.
2. The Hebrews used "sheol" to describe both the grave itself and the realm of the dead. The Greek equivalent is "hades." The bodies of both the saved and the lost go into the grave, but their souls have different destinies. Luke 16:19-31 indicates that sheol/hades was divided into two areas, a place of rest and blessing for the righteous and one of suffering for the wicked. When our Lord ascended to heaven, He emptied the paradise portion and took those souls to heaven. Today, when believers die, they go immediately into the presence of the Lord (2 Cor. 5:1-8). At the judgment of the great white throne, hades will be emptied of the spirits of the lost, and the grave will give up the bodies (Rev. 20:11-18). The unsaved will be found guilty and cast into hell, the lake of fire. Hades is the "jail" but hell is the penitentiary from which none escapes.
3. Saul was one of seven men in Scripture who took their own lives: Abimelech (Judg. 9:54); Samson (Judg. 16:26-30); Saul (1 Sam. 31:4); Saul's armor-bearer (1 Sam. 31:5); Ahithophel (2 Sam. 17:23); Zimri (1 Kings 16:18); and Judas (Matt. 27:6).

CHAPTER 13

1. *Metropolitan Tabernacle Pulpit,* vol. 48, 521.
2. *The Westminster Pulpit,* vol. 9, p. 17.
3. The name Paul comes from the Latin *paulus,* which means "little, small."
4. George Matheson, *Representative Men of the Old Testament: Ishmael to Daniel* (Hodder and Stoughton, 1900), 173.

2 SAMUEL and 1 CHRONICLES

A SUGGESTED OUTLINE OF 2 SAMUEL

Key Theme: The restoration of the nation of Israel by God's power
Key Verse: 2 Samuel 22:29-31

David unites the people. 1–7
A new king. 1:1–5:5
A new capital city. 5:6–6:23
A new dynasty. 7:1-29

I. DAVID EXPANDS THE BORDERS. 8:1–10:19
He defeats Israel's enemies. 8:1-14; 10:1-19
He organizes the kingdom. 8:15-18
He honors Mephibosheth. 9:1-13

II. DAVID DISOBEYS THE LORD. 11:1–20:26
David's sins. 11:1–12:31
Amnon's sins. 13:1-22
Absalom's sins. 13:23–19:8
David's return to Jerusalem. 19:9–20:26

III. DAVID CLOSES HIS REIGN. 21:1–24:25
Showing respect for Saul. 21:1-14
Defeating the Philistines. 21:15-22
Praising the Lord. 22:1–23:7
Honoring his mighty men. 23:8-38
Buying a site for the temple. 24:1-15

A SUGGESTED OUTLINE OF 1 CHRONICLES

Ancestry: genealogy of the twelve tribes. 1–9
Unity: the nation brought together. 10–16
Dynasty: God's covenant with David. 17
Victory: the borders expanded. 18–21
Efficiency: the nation organized. 22–29

I. THE TEMPLE MINISTRY. 22–26; 28:1–29:20
II. THE ARMY. 27
III. THE HEIR TO THE THRONE. 28–29

CONTENTS

CHAPTER ONE
DAVID, KING OF JUDAH
2 Samuel 1:1–2:7
(See 1 Chronicles 10:1-12)

For ten years David was an exile with a price on his head, fleeing from Saul and waiting for the time when God would put him on the throne of Israel. During those difficult years, David grew in faith and godly character, and God equipped him for the work He had chosen for him to do. When the day of victory did arrive, David was careful not to force himself on the people, many of whom were still loyal to the house of Saul. He took a cautious approach, and we can't help but admire David for his wisdom and patience as he won the affection and allegiance of the people and sought to unify the shattered nation. "So he shepherded them according to the integrity of his heart, and guided them by the skillfulness of his hands" (Ps. 78:72 NKJV).

1. Vindication (2 Sam. 1:1-16)

The Lord prevented David and his men from assisting the Philistines in their battle against Saul and Israel, so David returned to Ziklag. There he discovered that the Amalekites had invaded and taken all the people and goods and had left the town in ruins. God in His providence led David to the Amalekite camp. David routed the enemy, delivered the women and children, and reclaimed all the goods as well as the loot the Amalekites had collected in their raids. He then returned to Ziklag and awaited a report from the battlefield (1 Sam. 29–30).

A deceitful messenger (2 Sam. 1:1-10). On the day that David was slaughtering the Amalekites, the Philistines were overpowering Saul and his army at Mount Gilboa, where they killed Saul and three of his sons (1 Sam. 31; 1 Chron. 10:1-12). The next day, while David was returning to Ziklag, the Philistines were humiliating Saul by desecrating his body and the bodies of his sons, and the Amalekite messenger was starting off to bring the news to David. It took him at least three days to get to Ziklag, which was about eighty miles from the scene of the battle. So it was on David's third day in Ziklag that he received the tragic news that Israel had been defeated and that Saul and three of his sons were dead.[1]

Scripture gives us three accounts of the death of Saul and his sons: 1 Samuel 31:1-

13, the report of the messenger in 2 Samuel 1:1-10, and the record in 1 Chronicles 10:1-14. According to 1 Chronicles 10:4-5, Saul killed himself by falling on his sword, but the messenger said he had killed Saul to save him from experiencing further agony and humiliation. 1 Chronicles 10:14 informs us that it was God who killed Saul for his rebellion, especially the sin of seeking guidance from a medium. Only with great difficulty can the reports in 1 Samuel 31 and 1 Chronicles 10 be reconciled with the report of the messenger; therefore, it's likely the man was lying.

There's no question that the man had been on the battlefield. While he was searching for spoils, he found the corpses of Saul and his sons before the Philistines had identified them, and he took Saul's insignias of kingship, his golden armband, and the gold chaplet he wore on his helmet. However, the Amalekite didn't kill Saul as he claimed, because Saul and his sons were already dead. But by claiming that he did, he lost his own life.[2]

One of the key words in this chapter is *fallen*, found in verses 4, 10, 12, 19, and 27. When Saul began his royal career, he was described as standing head and shoulders "taller than any of the people" (1 Sam. 9:2; see 1 Sam. 10:23 and 16:7), but he ended his career a fallen king. He fell on his face in fear in the house of the spirit medium (1 Sam. 28:20), and he fell on the battlefield before the enemy (1 Sam. 31:4). David humbled himself before the Lord, and the Lord lifted him up; but Saul's pride and rebellion brought him to a shameful end. "Therefore let him who thinks he stands take heed lest he fall" (1 Cor. 10:12 NKJV).[3] Saul was anointed king at the dawning of a new day (1 Sam. 9:26-27), but he chose to walk in the darkness (1 Sam. 28:8) and disobey the will of God.

A grieving camp (2 Sam. 1:11-12). The Amalekite messenger must have been shocked and then afraid when he saw David and his men tearing their garments and mourning the death of Saul. He thought that everybody in Ziklag would rejoice to hear the news of Saul's death, knowing that this meant the end of their dangerous fugitive way of life. He probably expected to be rewarded for bringing such good news, but he obviously didn't know the heart of David. In David's eyes, Saul was never his enemy (2 Sam. 22:1); and on the two occasions when David might have slain Saul, he made it clear that he would never lay hands on the Lord's anointed (1 Sam. 24:1-7; 26:1-11).

The messenger claimed that he was an Amalekite, the son of a resident alien (2 Sam. 1:13). But if he had been living in the land of Israel, he surely would have known that the king of Israel was the anointed of the Lord. If a loyal Jew had found the four corpses, he would have sought to hide them and protect them from the enemy; but the Amalekites were the enemies of Israel, the very people Saul was supposed to wipe out (1 Sam. 15). It's likely that the messenger was a genuine Amalekite but not a resident alien in Israel. He was more likely a "camp follower" who made his living scavenging after the Philistine army. By claiming to be the son of a resident alien, the man was asking for certain privileges specified in the Law of Moses, privileges he certainly didn't deserve (Ex. 22:21; 23:9; Lev. 19:33; 24:22; Deut. 24:17).

A righteous judgment (2 Sam. 1:13-16). At evening, when the time of mourning had ended, David further interrogated the messenger and concluded that the man deserved to die. If the story he told was true, then the man had murdered God's anointed king and deserved to die. If the story was not true, the fact that the Amalekite fabricated a tale about killing the king revealed the depravity of his heart. "Out of your own mouth I will judge you" (Luke 19:22 NKJV). The Jews had been commanded to annihilate the Amalekites (Ex. 17:8-16; Deut. 25:17-19), so when David ordered the messenger to be slain, he was simply obeying the Lord, something Saul had failed to do (1 Sam. 15).

In slaying the messenger, David vindicated Saul and his sons and demonstrated publicly that he had not been Saul's enemy and did not rejoice at Saul's death. This was a dangerous thing to do, for David and his men were living in Philistine territory, and the Philistine king still thought David was his friend and ally. For David to take his stand with the dead king of Israel could be considered an act of treason. But the Lord had vindicated David and David had vindicated Saul, and David wasn't afraid. The conduct of David and his camp, when reported to the Jewish people, would help to convince them that David indeed was chosen by God to be their king.

2. Lamentation (2 Sam. 1:17-27)

David's grief over the death of Saul and Jonathan was sincere, and to help the people remember them, he wrote a touching elegy in their honor. He ordered this lament to be taught and sung in his ancestral tribe of Judah, and no doubt people in other tribes learned and appreciated it. The people of the East unashamedly display their emotions, and their poets frequently write songs to help them commemorate both joyful and painful experiences. Moses taught Israel a song to warn them about apostasy (Deut. 32), and the prophets often wrote funeral dirges to announce impending judgment (Isa. 14:12ff; Ezek. 27:lff; 28:11-19).

This lament came to be known as "The Song of the Bow" (v. 18)[4] and was recorded in the Book of Jasher (Josh. 10:12-13), a collection of poems and songs that commemorated great events in the history of Israel. "How are the mighty fallen" is the major theme of the elegy (vv. 19, 25, 27), and the emphasis is on the greatness of Saul and Jonathan even in defeat and death. David celebrated their skill and bravery and their willingness to give their lives for their country. Like Hebrews 11, nothing is recorded in the song that speaks of any sins or mistakes in the lives of Saul and Jonathan.

He addresses the people of Israel (2 Sam. 1:19-20). David calls the dead king and his army "Your glory, O Israel" and "the mighty."[5] They didn't display much glory or might in the battle of Gilboa, but Saul was still God's chosen leader and his soldiers were the army of the Lord of Hosts. We're prone to forget that Saul and his army had risked their lives to fight and win many significant battles (1 Sam. 14:47-48) and that the Jewish women did sing "Saul has slain his thousands" (1 Sam. 18:7). David urged the people not to spread the bad news of Israel's defeat, for the Philistines would take care of that. Gath was the capital city of the Philistines where the leaders would rejoice at their victory, and Ashkelon was the chief religious center, where the people would give thanks to their idols for helping their army defeat Israel.

He addresses the mountains of Gilboa (2 Sam. 1:21). This is where the battle was fought and Saul was defeated (2 Sam. 1:6; 1 Sam. 28:4; 31:1). David prayed that God would forsake the place and not send rain or dew to the fields or give the farmers fruitful harvests, even though this meant there could be no grain offerings for the

Lord. He asked that God's creation join him in mourning over the defeat of Israel and the fall of their king. When David referred to the shield, was he speaking literally or metaphorically, or both? Saul carried a shield, and Israel's king was compared to a shield (Ps. 84:9; 89:18). Warriors did anoint their leather shields to preserve them, but the king was also God's anointed leader. Saul and his three sons had lost their shields and their lives, and their shields were defiled by blood.

He praises Saul and Jonathan (2 Sam. 1:22-23). This is the heart of the song, depicting Saul and Jonathan as victorious warriors. Jonathan's arrows hit their mark and Saul's sword "did not return unsatisfied."[6] They were as swift as eagles (Deut. 28:49) and as strong as lions (2 Sam. 17:10). But to David, these men weren't just great soldiers; they were also gracious people who were beloved in life and in death loyal to each other and to the people. From his meeting with Samuel in the medium's house, Saul knew that he and his sons would die that day in battle (1 Sam. 28:19), yet he entered the contest determined to do his best. Jonathan knew that his father had disobeyed God and sinned against David, yet he stayed at his side in the fight. Even though the army of Israel was defeated, David wanted the people to remember the greatness of their king and his sons.

He addresses the daughters of Jerusalem (2 Sam. 1:24). In spite of his faults and failures, during his reign Saul had brought stability to the nation. The tribes had abandoned selfish independence and competition and were striving to work together to better their lot, including their economic position. Saul's victories over enemy nations, greater safety in the towns and farmlands, and tribal cooperation all combined to make Israel wealthier. David seems to be describing the wealthy women and their luxuries, perhaps the wives of some of Saul's officers David had seen while he was serving in Saul's court. "Clothed . . . in scarlet and finery" is a familiar phrase that means "basking in wealth."

He speaks to his beloved friend Jonathan (2 Sam. 1:25-26). It's common in funeral dirges to name and address the deceased. "Jonathan my brother" carries a double meaning, for they were brothers-in-law (David was married to Michal, Jonathan's sister) and also brothers in heart and spirit. David and Jonathan were beloved friends who had covenanted together to share the throne, David as king and Jonathan as second in command (1 Sam. 23:16-18). To read homosexual overtones into David's expressions of his love for Jonathan is to misinterpret his words. Solomon described the love of husband and wife as "strong as death" (Song 8:6 NKJV), and the friendship of David and Jonathan was that strong. First Samuel 18:1 NIV says, "Jonathan became one in spirit with David, and he loved him as himself." David closed his lament by repeating the poignant refrain "How are the mighty fallen" and comparing Saul and Jonathan to weapons of war that had been lost and could never be used again.

In composing and teaching this elegy, David may have had several purposes in mind. For one thing, he gave honor to Saul and Jonathan and taught the people to respect the monarchy. Since Saul was Israel's first king, the people might conclude that all their kings would follow his bad example and possibly ruin the nation, so David sought to strengthen the concept of monarchy. The song also made it clear to everybody that David held no grudges against his father-in-law and sovereign. Finally, David set an example for all of us to follow in paying loving tribute to those who have died in battle to protect their country.

3. Coronation (2 Sam. 2:1-4a)

David was Israel's lawful king and couldn't remain in Ziklag since it was in enemy territory. It's likely that Achish, the Philistine king, thought that David was still under his authority, but David knew that he must return to his own land and begin to reign over his own people. David was in the habit of seeking the Lord's will when he had to make decisions, either by having Abiathar the priest consult the ephod (1 Sam. 23:9-12) or by asking Gad the prophet to pray to God for a word of wisdom (1 Sam. 22:5).

David was from Judah,[7] so it was logical that he go to live among his own people, but in which city should he reside? God gave him permission to return to Judah and told him to live in Hebron, which was located about twenty-five miles from Ziklag. By moving there, David was back with his own people but still under the shadow of the Philistines. Hebron was important in Jewish history, for near the city was the tomb of Abraham and Sarah, Isaac and Rebecca, and Jacob and Leah. The city was in the inheritance of Caleb, a man of stature in Jewish history (Josh. 14:14). Abigail, one of David's wives, had been married to a Calebite, and David had inherited her property near the wilderness of Maon (1 Sam. 25:2). Hebron was probably the most important city in the southern part of Judah, so David moved there with his men, and they lived in the towns surrounding Hebron. For the first time in ten years, David and his men were no longer fugitives. His men had suffered with him, and now they would reign with him (see 2 Tim. 2:12).

When David settled in Hebron, his return to Judah was the signal for his people to recognize him as their leader, so the elders of Judah anointed David a second time and made him king (see 1 Sam. 16:13).[8] Had Saul's captain Abner also accepted God's will and submitted to David, a costly civil war would have been averted, but loyalty to the old regime (Abner was Saul's nephew) and a desire to protect his own interests motivated Abner to fight David instead of follow him.

While David was living in Ziklag, volunteers had come to him from the tribes of Benjamin, Gad, and Manasseh (1 Chron. 12:1-22), so he not only had a large and experienced army but also a representation from some of the other tribes. Before long, David would win the allegiance of all the nation of Israel.

In his accession to the throne of Israel, David illustrates the career of Jesus Christ, the Son of David. Like David the shepherd, Jesus came first as a humble servant and was anointed king privately. Like David the exile, Jesus is King today but doesn't yet reign on the throne of David. Like Saul in David's day, Satan is still free to obstruct God's work and oppose God's people. One day, Jesus will return in glory, Satan will be imprisoned, and Jesus will reign in His glorious kingdom (Rev. 19:11–20:6). God's people today faithfully pray "Thy kingdom come" (Matt. 6:10 KJV) and eagerly await the return of their King.

David was thirty years old when the elders of Judah made him their king, and he reigned in Hebron for seven and a half years (2 Sam. 2:11). How blessed were the people of Judah to have such a gifted and godly leader!

4. Appreciation (2 Sam. 2:4b-7)

David was a man with a shepherd's

heart who cared about his people (see 2 Sam. 24:17), and one of his first concerns was the fate of Saul and the three sons who died with him. When he asked the leaders of Judah about the burial of the royal family, they told him how the men of Jabesh Gilead had risked their lives to recover the four bodies, burn away the decayed and mutilated flesh, and then bury the bones back at Jabesh (1 Sam. 31:8-13). They remembered how Saul had rescued their city many years before (1 Sam. 11).

Jabesh Gilead was located across the Jordan in the tribe of Gad, and the men who recovered the bodies had to travel northwest and cross the Jordan River to reach Beth Shan, a round trip of perhaps twenty-five miles. It was a courageous endeavor, and David thanked them for their devotion to Saul and to the kingdom of Israel. They had displayed "kindness," and the Lord would show them "kindness and faithfulness." Twenty-five years later, David would disinter the remains of Saul and the sons who died with him and rebury them in their native tribe of Benjamin (2 Sam. 21:12-14)

But David used this occasion as an opportunity to invite the brave men of Jabesh Gilead to cast their lot with him. They had been valiant for Saul, and now they could be valiant for David. Some warriors from Gad had already joined David's army while he was in Ziklag (1 Chron. 12:8-15), affirming their confidence that he was God's anointed king. Unfortunately, the people of Jabesh Gilead didn't choose to submit to David but instead followed Abner and Saul's weak son Ish-Bosheth.

The people of Jabesh Gilead allowed their affection for Saul to blind them to God's plan for the nation. They had a good motive, but they made a bad choice. How often in the history of the church have God's people allowed human affection and appreciation to overrule the will of God! Jesus Christ is King and He deserves our submission, loyalty, and obedience. To put human leaders ahead of God's anointed King is to create division and weakness in the ranks of the Lord's followers and invite multiplied problems for the Lord's people. As Augustine of Hippo said, "Jesus Christ will be Lord of all or He will not be Lord at all."

CHAPTER TWO
DAVID WATCHES AND WAITS
2 Samuel 2:8–4:12

"In order to govern," said Napoleon on his deathbed, "the question is not to follow out a more or less valid theory but to build with whatever materials are at hand. The inevitable must be accepted and turned to advantage." If this statement is true, then David was a very effective leader during the seven and a half years he ruled in Hebron. While Joab led the army of Judah, David watched and waited, knowing that the Lord would one day open the way for him to reign as king over all Israel. God called David not only to be the king of His people, but also their shepherd and spiritual leader. David had to wait on God's timing while patiently enduring the consequences of the selfish ambitions and reckless actions of leaders who were motivated by pride and hatred. David learned to build with the materials at hand and to trust God to use disappointments to the advantage of his people.

1. Abner the kingmaker (2 Sam. 2:8-32)

The key actor in this drama was Abner, Saul's cousin and the commander of his army (1 Sam. 14:50). It was Abner who brought David to Saul after David killed Goliath (17:55-58) and who with Saul pursued David for ten years (26:5ff). Abner was rebuked and humiliated by David when he failed to protect the king (26:13-16) and Abner had no special love for David. The people of Israel honored David above Saul and eventually the nation would learn that David was God's choice as king of Israel. But David already had a commander, Joab, so when David became king, what would happen to Abner? Most of what Abner did during those seven and a half years wasn't for the glory of God or the strengthening of Israel, but for his own self-interest. He was taking care of number one.

Abner rejects David's kingship (vv. 8-11). The people of Judah obeyed God's will and anointed David as their king, but Abner disobeyed the Lord and made Saul's one remaining son, Ish-Bosheth, the king of "all Israel." Abner knew that David was God's choice, a gifted leader and a brave soldier, but he deliberately rebelled against the Lord and appointed Ish-Bosheth. Israel had asked for a king "like all the nations" (1 Sam. 8:5), and when a king died, the other nations appointed a king's eldest son to succeed him. Three of Saul's sons had died in battle, and Ish-Bosheth was all that remained of the royal family.

Scripture doesn't say much about Ish-Bosheth, but it's clear that he was a weak puppet ruler manipulated by Abner (3:11; 4:1). He was certainly old enough to fight in the army with his father and brothers, but Saul left him home to protect the dynasty. (He was probably also a weak soldier.) Saul and Abner both knew that God had taken the dynasty away from Saul (1 Sam. 13:11-14). Knowing that he and his sons would die in the battle, Saul probably arranged to make his fourth son king. Ish-Bosheth may have been crowned by the general, but he was never anointed by the Lord. He is called Esh-Baal in 1 Chronicles 8:33, which means "man of the Lord." The word "baal" means "lord" and was also the name of a Canaanite deity, so that may be why his name was changed.[1]

Abner took Ish-Bosheth to Mahanaim, on the east side of the Jordan. This was a Levitical city of refuge where he would be safe (Josh. 21:38), and there Abner established a capital for "all Israel." But it's likely that it took at least five years for Abner to pursuade the tribes (minus Judah) to follow their new king. Ish-Bosheth was crowned at the beginning of David's reign of seven years and six months and was assassinated after reigning only two years over "all Israel." This would have been the last two years of David's reign in Hebron. Ish-Bosheth didn't have a long reign over "all Israel," but everybody knew that Abner was in charge anyway.

There's a modern touch to this scenario, for our political and religious worlds are populated by these same three kinds of people. We have weak people like Ish-Bosheth, who get where they are because they have "connections." We have strong, selfish people like Abner, who know how to manipulate others for their own personal profit. We also have people of God like David who are called, anointed, and equipped but must wait for God's time before they can serve. During more than fifty years of ministry, I have seen churches and other ministries bypass God's chosen men and women and put unqualified people into places of leadership just because they were well-known or had "connections."

Abner got what he wanted, but within a few years, he lost it all.

Abner challenges David's army (vv. 12-17). When Abner made Ish-Bosheth king, he was actually declaring war on David, and he knew it. But by now Abner had all the tribes except Judah behind him and he felt he could easily defeat David in battle and take over the entire kingdom. Confident of victory, Abner called for a contest between the two armies, to be held at the great cistern about twenty-three miles north of Gibeon. This was not unlike the challenge Goliath issued when he called for one of Saul's soldiers to fight him (1 Sam. 17:8-10). But Abner was rebelling against God while David was God's chosen leader!

This is the first time we meet Joab, David's nephew and the commander of his army.[2] The two armies met at the reservoir, and twelve soldiers from the army of Benjamin faced twelve men from Judah—and all twenty-four men were killed! That day the battlefield received a new name—"the field of sharp edges" or "the field of daggers." Joab and Abner wasted no time getting their troops in battle formation, and "The battle that day was very fierce." Abner was defeated that day, a portent of things to come.

Abner kills David's nephew (vv. 18-23). Joab, Abishai, and Asahel were David's nephews, the sons of his sister Zeruiah (see 1 Chron. 2:13-16).[3] Whether on his own initiative or at his brother's orders, Asahel went after Abner, for he knew that slaying the enemy general could mean confusing and scattering the whole enemy army. If Joab commanded the fleet-footed young man to go after Abner, perhaps he was thinking of his own future, for Abner might threaten to take his position as head of the army.

The record makes it clear that Abner had no desire to harm or kill the lad, but Asahel was persistent. First Abner told him to turn aside and take what he wanted from one of the dead enemy soldiers. Then he warned Asahel that if he killed him, this would create a "blood feud" that could cause trouble for years to come. Abner knew Joab and had no desire to begin a possible lifelong family conflict. It was bad enough that Joab and Abner were rival generals. When Asahel refused to give up the chase, the clever Abner killed him by using one of the oldest tricks of the battlefield: he stopped suddenly and allowed Asahel to propel himself right into the end of spear. The butt end of a spear was often sharpened so the spear could be thrust into the ground and be ready for action (1 Sam. 26:7). Asahel fell to the ground and died.[4] Asahel died in the course of battle, even though it appears that Abner had no plans or even desire to kill him.

Abner calls for a truce (vv. 25-32). Asahel's two brothers, Joab and Abishai, must have been following close behind because they took up the pursuit of Abner, no doubt determined to avenge the blood of their brother. But Abner's troops rescued him, and he and the Benjamites retreated to the hill of Ammah. Abner knew he was beaten (vv. 30-31), so he called for a truce. He may have suspected that the death of Asahel would encourage Joab and Abishai to stop fighting and take care of burial. Judah and Benjamin were brothers, both sons of Jacob, and why should brother fight brother? But it was Abner who had initiated the battle, so he had only himself to blame. A scheming man, he had a plan in mind that would give him both armies without having to shed blood.

Joab knew the heart of David, that he wanted unity and peace, not division and war, so he blew the trumpet and stopped his troops from pursuing the enemy. He said to Abner, "God only knows what would have happened if you hadn't spoken, for we would have chased you all night if necessary" (v. 27 NLT). Abner and his men walked all night to return to Mahanaim, and Joab and his army returned to Hebron, stopping at Bethlehem along the way to give Asahel a proper burial. During that all-night march, Joab and Abishai hatched a plot to avenge the death of their brother.

2. Abner the negotiator (2 Sam. 3:1-21)

The phrase "a long war" (vv. 1, 6) suggests a state of hostility for two years, occasional clashes rather than one long battle after another. David was biding his time, knowing that God would keep His promises and give him the throne of Israel. David's government in Hebron was going from strength to strength (Ps. 84:7), while the alliance of tribes under Ish-Bosheth and Abner was getting weaker. However, the astute Abner was using his position in the house of Saul to strengthen his own authority, for he was getting ready to make David an offer the king couldn't resist (v. 6).

As for David, his family was also increasing (see also 1 Chron. 3:1-4), and the king now had a growing harem like any other eastern monarch. Of course, David's son Solomon would go far beyond what his father had done or what any Jewish king would do (1 Kings 11:3).[5] David had moved to Hebron with two wives, and now he had six sons by six different wives. Polygamy started with Lamech, a descendant of Cain (Gen. 4:19), and was tolerated in Israel; but it was forbidden to Israel's kings (Deut. 17:17).

Amnon, David's firstborn, would rape his half-sister Tamar (chap. 13) and be murdered by Tamar's full brother Absalom, who would be killed while trying to take the kingdom from his father (chap. 14-18). The fact that Absalom was related to royalty on his mother's side might have encouraged his crusade for the kingdom. No doubt David's marriage to Maacah was politically motivated so that David would have an ally near Ish-Bosheth. Chileab is called Daniel in 1 Chronicles 4:1. During David's final illness, Adonijah would try to capture the throne and would be executed by Solomon (1 Kings 1–2). We know nothing about Shephatiah and his mother Abitai, and Ithream and his mother Eglah. After relocating his capital in Jerusalem, David took even more wives and concubines and had eleven more sons born to him (5:13-16).

Abner defects to David (vv. 6-11). Abner was a pragmatic politician as well as a shrewd general, and his basic principle was, "Always join the winning side." When he perceived that the throne of Ish-Bosheth had no future, he decided to switch loyalties and thereby guarantee his own security and possibly save lives. David had a reputation for kindness, and he had shown remarkable patience with the house of Saul.

We aren't told that Abner actually had intercourse with Saul's concubine Rizpah, and he firmly denied it; but if he did, he committed a very serious offense. A deceased king's harem belonged to his successor, in this case, Ish-Bosheth (see 12:8 and 16:15-23), and any man who even asked for one of those women was asking for the kingdom and guilty of treason. This is what led to the death of Adonijah (1 Kings 2:13-25). It's possible that Abner did take Rizpah just to precipitate a quarrel with Ish-Bosheth and to declare his change of allegiance. If so, he succeeded. Of course, the king wasn't strong enough to oppose Abner, who now announced that he was on David's side. The phrase "throne of David" is used in verse 10 for the first time in Scripture, and as time passes, it will take on Messianic significance (Isa. 9:6-7).

Abner negotiates for David (vv. 12-21). This episode is a good example of ancient "shuttle diplomacy."

- Abner sent messengers to David offering to bring all Israel under his rule (v. 12).
- David sent messengers to Abner accepting his offer, provided Abner first sent Michal to him. She was David's wife and Ish-Bosheth's sister (v. 13).
- Abner told Ish-Bosheth to honor David's request, and David also sent Ish-Bosheth a message asking that Michal be sent to Hebron (v. 14).
- Abner conferred with the elders of Israel (vv. 17-18).
- Abner conferred with the leaders of Benjamin (v. 19).
- Abner and twenty representatives from the tribes came to Hebron, bringing Michal with them (vv. 15-16, 20).
- Abner and David agreed on how to transfer the kingdom, and they shared a feast and made a covenant (v. 21).

In the early stages of these negotiations it would have been dangerous and unwise for David and Abner to meet personally, so they depended on their officials to make the necessary contacts. David had no reason not to cooperate with Abner since he had never personally been at war with him or King Saul. Outright war was the only alternative to this kind of diplomacy, and David was a man of peace. David had married into Saul's family, so he had to show some respect both to Abner and Ish-Bosheth, and he was determined to unite the tribes as quickly as possible and with the least amount of bloodshed. He had waited over seven years, and it was time to act.

Why did David make the return of Michal a condition for further negotiation? First of all, she was still his wife, even though Saul had given her to another man. Ten years before, when they were wed, Michal loved David very much (1 Sam. 18:20), and we have reason to believe that David loved her. It was good diplomacy to invite his "queen" to join with him, and the fact that she came from the house of Saul helped to strengthen the bonds of unity. By claiming the daughter of Saul, David was also claiming all the kingdom; and when Abner brought Michal to Hebron, it was a public announcement that he had broken with the house of Saul and was now allied with David.

3. Abner the victim (2 Sam. 3:22-39)

It looked as though everything was in good order for a peaceful transition, but there were hidden land mines in the diplomatic field and they were ready to explode. Ish-Bosheth was still on the throne and David would have to deal with him and the loyal supporters of the house of Saul. Abner had killed Asahel, and Joab was biding his time until he could avenge his brother's death.

Joab reproaches David (vv. 22-25). David had sent Joab and some of his men on a raid to secure wealth to help support the kingdom. On his return, when Joab heard that David had received Abner and given him a feast, his anger erupted and he rebuked the king.[6] The key idea in this paragraph is that Saul's general and the man who killed young Asahel had come and gone "in peace" (vv. 21-23), and Joab couldn't understand it. His own heart was still pained at the death of his brother, and Joab couldn't understand his sovereign's policies. Of course, Joab was protecting his own job just as Abner was protecting his, but unlike David, Joab didn't have any faith in what Abner said or did. Joab was certain that Abner's visit had nothing to do with turning the kingdom over to David. The wily general was only spying out the situation and getting ready for an attack.

The text records no reply from David. Joab had never been easy to deal with (3:39), and the fact that he was a relative made the situation even more difficult. The dynamics of David's family—the multiplied wives, the many children and various relatives in places of authority —created endless problems for the king, and they weren't easy to solve. David's silence wasn't that of agreement, because he didn't agree with his general; it was the silence of restraint and the evidence of a deep desire to put the nation back together again. David wasn't promoting "peace at any price," because he was a man of integrity; but he wasn't prepared to let his impetuous general conduct a personal vendetta in the name of the king. The sentiments of Psalm 120 could certainly apply to David's situation at this time.

Joab deceives Abner and kills him (vv. 26-27). Joab accused Abner of being a liar (v. 25) but practiced deception himself! We're often guilty of the sins we say others commit, and "it takes a thief to catch a thief." Joab must have sent the messengers in the name of the king or Abner would have been more cautious. Abner hadn't seen Joab at the king's house, so he probably assumed that David's general was still away on his raiding expedition. Joab and his brother Abishai (v. 30) were waiting for Abner, took him to a secluded part of the city gate, and stabbed him under the fifth rib, the same place he had stabbed Asahel (2:23).

Everything about the death of Abner was wrong. The two brothers knew what their king wanted, yet they deliberately put their own interests ahead of that of the kingdom. Asahel had been pursuing Abner on the battlefield, so he was another casuality of war; but the death of Abner was murder. Hebron was a city of refuge, a sanctuary where an accused murderer could get a fair trial, but the two brothers never gave the elders in Hebron a chance to hear the case. Abner killed Asahel in self-defense; but when Joab and Abishai killed Abner, it was pure revenge, and Abner never had an opportunity to defend himself. Asahel's death occurred in broad daylight where everybody could witness what happened, but Abner was deceived and led into the shadows. Abishai had accompanied David into Saul's camp and had seen him refuse to kill his father-in-law (1 Sam. 26:6ff), so he knew that David would never countenance the murder of Saul's general. We wonder if Abner died thinking that David had been involved in the plot to kill him.

David honors Abner (vv. 28-39). When David heard the news of Abner's death, he immediately disclaimed any part in what his two nephews had done. In fact, he went so far as to call down a curse on the house of Joab, naming some of the plagues that Moses had warned about in the Covenant (Deut. 28:25-29, 58-62). David issued a royal edict that commanded Joab and his army to mourn over Abner and to attend his funeral. The phrase "all the people" is used seven times in vv. 31-37 (KJV) and refers to the men in Joab's army (2:28; 12:29). David commanded them all to tear their garments, put on sackcloth, and weep over the death of a great man, and David himself followed the bier to the place of interment. Because Joab and Abishai were among the official mourners, it's likely that many of the people didn't know that they were the murderers. David didn't call them to trial, and it's likely that his statements in verses 29 and 39 were spoken privately to his inner council. He tried to shield them as much as possible, although they certainly didn't deserve it.

As he did for Saul and Jonathan, David wrote an official elegy to honor the dead general (vv. 33-34, 38). He made it clear that Abner hadn't died because of some foolish act on his part, and he had never been a prisoner at any time in his military career. He had fallen before wicked men who had deceived him. David further honored Abner by burying him in the royal city of Hebron and not taking him back to Benjamin. Later, David said to his confidential servants that Abner was "a prince and a great man." David also appointed Abner's son Jaasiel as chief officer over the tribe of Benjamin.

David's lament for himself in verse 39 was heard by his select "inner circle" and expressed the problems David had with his own family. The word "weak" doesn't suggest that David was not strong enough to be king, but rather that he was "restrained and gentle" in contrast to the "hard" approach of his nephews. David had experienced God's gentleness (22:36), and he tried to deal with others as God had dealt with him. He no doubt went too far in this approach when it came to his own family (18:5, 14), but David was a man after God's own heart (Ps. 103:8-14). All David could do was leave the judgment with the Lord, for He never makes a mistake.

4. Ish-Bosheth the loser (2 Sam. 4:1-12)

If David thought he was weak because of the behavior of his nephews, he should have considered the situation of Ish-Bosheth following the death of Abner. David was at least a great warrior and a gifted leader, while Ish-Bosheth was a mere puppet in the hands of his general, and now the general was dead. The people of the tribes in his kingdom knew that Abner's death meant the end of the reign of their king, and they no doubt expected a swift invasion by David and his army. The common people knew nothing of David's intentions or of his recent meeting with Abner. It was a day of distress for Ish-Bosheth and his people.

The account of Baanah and Rechab reminds us of the Amalekite in 2 Samuel 1, the man who claimed he killed Saul. These two men were minor officers in Abner's army who thought they could earn rewards and promotion from David if they killed Ish-Bosheth, and like the Amalekite, they were wrong. The only living heir to Saul's throne was a crippled twelve-year-old boy named Mephibosheth, so if Baanah and Rechab killed the king, the way would be open for David to gain the throne and unite the nation. (We will meet Mephibosheth again in 9:1-13; 16:1-4; 19:24-30; and 21:7-8.)

Their excuse for entering the king's house was to secure grain for their men, and while the king was asleep and unprotected, they killed him. If the murder of Abner was a heinous crime, this murder was even worse; for the man's only "crime" was that he was the son of Saul! He had broken no law and injured no person, and he wasn't given opportunity to defend himself. His murderers didn't even show respect to his dead body, for they beheaded him so they could take the evidence to David and receive their reward. Even worse, the two murderers told David that the Lord had avenged him!

David's answer made it clear that at no time in his career had he ever broken God's commandment by murdering somebody in order to accomplish his purposes. The Lord had watched over him and protected him during ten years of exile and now more than seven years as king in Hebron. As when Saul and Abner died, David made it very clear that he was not involved in any way. It would have been very easy for David's enemies to start slanderous rumors that the king had engineered both deaths in order to clear the way for ascending the throne of Israel.

At the king's command, his guards killed the two confessed murderers, cut off their hands and feet, and hung their corpses up as evidence of the king's justice. To mutilate a corpse in this way and then expose it publicly was the ultimate in humiliation (Deut. 21:22-23). David had the head of Ish-Bosheth buried in Hebron in the sepulchre of Abner, for they were relatives.

The four "kings" that Paul wrote about in Romans 5 were certainly active in these scenes from David's life. Sin was reigning (5:21) as men lied to each other, hated each other, and sought to destroy each other. Death also reigned (5:14, 17) as Asahel, Abner, and Ish-Bosheth were slain, along with nearly four hundred soldiers who died at the battle of the pool of Gibeon. But God's grace also reigned (5:21), for He protected David and overruled men's sins to accomplish His divine purposes. "Where sin abounded, grace did much more abound" (5:20 KJV). But David "reigned in life" (5:17) and let God control him as he faced one emergency after another. He was a man empowered by God, and God brought him through each crisis and helped him to succeed.

In the midst of today's troubles and trials, God's people can "reign in life by Jesus Christ" if we will surrender to Him, wait on Him, and trust His promises.

CHAPTER THREE
DAVID, KING OF ISRAEL
2 Samuel 5–6
(See also 1 Chronicles 3:4-8; 11:1-9;13:5–16:3)

What a remarkable and varied life David lived! As a shepherd, he killed a lion and a bear, and these victories prepared him to kill the giant Goliath. David served as an attendant to King Saul and became a beloved friend of Saul's son Jonathan. For perhaps ten years, David was an exile in the wilderness of Judea, hiding from Saul and learning to trust the Lord more and more. He had patiently waited for the Lord to give him the promised throne, and now that time had come. It is through faith and patience that God's people inherit what He has promised (Heb. 6:12), and David had trusted God in the most difficult circumstances. David inherited a divided people, but with God's help he united them and built Israel into a strong and powerful kingdom. These chapters describe the steps David took to unite and strengthen the nation.

1. David accepted the crown. (5:1-5)

The assassination of Ish-Bosheth left the eleven tribes without a king or even an heir to Saul's throne. Abner was dead, but he had paved the way for David to be made king of all twelve tribes (3:17-21). The next step was for the leaders of all the tribes to convene at Hebron and crown David king.

The qualifications for Israel's king were written in the Law of Moses in Deuteronomy 17:14-20. The first and most important requirement was that he was to be chosen by the Lord from the people of Israel, a king "whom the Lord your God chooses" (17:15, 20 NKJV). The people knew that Samuel had anointed David king some twenty years before and that it was God's will that David ascend the throne (2 Sam. 5:2). The nation needed a shepherd, and David was that shepherd (Ps. 78:70-72). Saul had been "the people's king" but he wasn't the Lord's first choice, for God had given him as a judgment against Israel because they wanted to be like the other nations (1 Sam. 8; Hos. 13:11). The Lord loved His people and knew they needed a shepherd, so He equipped David to be their king. Unlike Saul, who was a Benjamite, David was from the royal tribe of Judah (Gen. 49:10) and was born and raised in Bethlehem. Because of this, he was able to establish the dynasty that brought the Messiah Jesus Christ into the world, and He, too, was born in Bethlehem.

The people who gathered at Hebron reminded David that he belonged to the whole nation and not just to the tribe of Judah (2 Sam. 5:1). At the beginning of David's career, the people recognized that God's hand was upon him, for God gave him success in his military exploits. Present at Hebron were representatives from all the tribes, and they enthusiastically gave their allegiance to the new king (1 Chron. 12:23-40). The total number of officers and men is 340,800, all of them loyal to David. The people remained with David for three days and celebrated God's goodness to His people.[1]

The foundation of the Jewish nation was God's covenant with His people as expressed in the Law of Moses, especially Deuteronomy 27–30 and Leviticus 26. If the king and the people obeyed God's will, He would bless and care for them; but if they disobeyed and worshiped false gods, He would discipline them. Each new king was required to affirm the supremacy and authority of God's law, promise to obey it, and even make a copy of it for his own personal use (Deut. 17:18-20). David entered into a covenant with the Lord and the people, agreeing to uphold and obey God's law and to rule in the fear of the Lord (see 1 Sam. 10:17-25; 2 Kings 11:17).

When David was a teenager, Samuel had anointed him privately (1 Sam. 16:13), and the elders of the tribe of Judah had anointed him when he became their king at thirty years of age (2 Sam. 2:4). But now the elders of the whole nation anointed David and proclaimed him as their king. David was not an amateur, but a seasoned warrior and a gifted leader who obviously had the blessing of the Lord on his life and ministry. After experiencing years of turbulence and division, the nation at last had a king who was God's choice and the people's choice. God takes time to prepare His leaders, and much to be pitied is the person who "succeeds" before he or she is ready for it.

2. David established a new capital city. (5:6-10; 1 Chron. 11:4-9)

Abner and Ish-Bosheth had established their capital at Mahanaim (2:8), over the

Jordan River on the boundary of Gad and Manasseh, while David's capital was at Hebron in the tribe of Judah. But neither city was suitable for a new ruler who was seeking to unify the nation and make a new beginning. David wisely chose as his capital the Jebusite city of Jerusalem on the border of Benjamin (Saul's tribe) and Judah (David's tribe). Jerusalem had never belonged to any of the tribes, so nobody could accuse David of playing favorites in setting up his new capital.

Political considerations were important, but so was security, and the topography of Jerusalem made it an ideal capital city. Built on a rocky hill and surrounded on three sides by valleys and hills, the city was vulnerable only on the north side. The Valley of Hinnom lay on the south, the Kidron Valley on the east, and the Tyropean Valley on the west. "Beautiful for situation, the joy of the whole earth, is mount Zion, on the sides of the north, the city of the great King" (Ps. 48:2 KJV). "Out of Zion, the perfection of beauty, God hath shined" (Ps. 50:2 KJV). The Jewish people have always loved the city of Jerusalem, and today it is revered by Jews, Christians, and Muslims. To be born in Jerusalem was a high honor indeed (Ps. 87:4-6).

The Lord must have guided David in a special way when he chose Jerusalem to be his capital, because Jerusalem would play a strategic role in the working out of His great plan of salvation. God had promised the Jews that He would appoint a place where they could come to worship Him (Deut. 12:1-7), and He must have revealed to David that Jerusalem was that place. Later, David would purchase property on Zion which would become the site for the temple that his son Solomon would build (2 Sam. 24). The church sees the earthly Jerusalem as a city of legalistic bondage, but the heavenly Jerusalem as a symbol of the covenant of grace in Christ Jesus (Gal. 4:21-31) and the eternal home of Christ's people (Heb. 12:18-24; Rev. 21–22). God has set His King on the throne (Ps. 2:6), and one day He will speak in His wrath and judge those who oppose Him and His truth.

The Jebusites who lived in Jerusalem thought that their citadel was impregnable and that even the blind and the lame could defend it, a boast that made David angry. He knew that the Lord had promised Moses that Israel would conquer all the nations living in Canaan, including the Jebusites (Ex. 23:23-24; Deut. 7:1-2; 20:17), so by faith he planned his attack. He promised that the man who entered the city and subdued it would be the commander of his army, and he even told him how to do it: go up through the water shaft. David's nephew Joab accepted the challenge, captured the city, and became captain of David's troops. Excavations on Mount Zion have revealed a water shaft that would have been difficult but not impossible to climb. David occupied the mount and called the southern part "the City of David." In years following, David and his successors strengthened the fortress by building walls.

The word "millo" (v. 9) means "fullness" and refers to a stone embankment that was built on the southeastern side of the mount to support additional buildings and a wall. Archaeologists have uncovered what they call "a stepped-stone structure," about 1,500 feet long and 900 feet wide, that was a supporting terrace for other structures, and they assume this was the "millo." Both Solomon and King Hezekiah strengthened this part of Mount Zion (1 Kings 9:15, 24; 11:27; 2 Chron. 32:5). God's blessing was on David and gave him prosperity in everything he undertook for his people.

It was probably at this time that David brought the head of Goliath to Jerusalem as a reminder of God's faithfulness to His people (1 Sam. 17:54).

3. David formed political alliances. (5:11-16; 1 Chron. 3:5-9; 14:1-7)

Israel was a small nation that was distinguished from her neighbors by her special covenant relationship with the true and living God (Num. 23:7-10), and the Jews were warned not to form alliances with their neighbors that would compromise their testimony. Unless his successor bore the same name, Hiram was probably just beginning his reign as king of Tyre, for he befriended both David and Solomon during their reigns (1 Kings 5).

It's likely that David's palace was built for him after his successful wars against the Philistines (5:17-25), and this may have been Hiram's way of recognizing David's accession to the throne. No doubt the Phoenician king also appreciated the fact that David had defeated his warlike neighbors, the Philistines. From a practical point of view, it was necessary for the Phoenicians to be on good terms with the Jews because Israel could easily block the trade route to Tyre, and the Phoenicians depended on Jewish farmers for their food. (See Acts 12:20.) David interpreted Hiram's kindness as another evidence that the Lord had indeed established him on the throne of Israel.

The mention of David's palace and his alliance with Hiram offered the writer opportunity to mention David's family, the "house" that the Lord was building for him (Ps. 127). Deuteronomy 17:17 prohibited Israel's king from taking many wives, but David seems to have ignored this law, as did Solomon after him (1 Kings 4:26; 11:1-4). At least one of David's wives was a princess (3:3), which suggests that the marriage was for the sake of political alliance, and no doubt there were other similar marriages. This was one way to cement good relationships with other nations.

There are four lists of David's children in Scripture—those born while he reigned in Hebron (2 Sam 3:2-5) and those born after he moved to Jerusalem (5:13-16; 1 Chron. 3:1-9; 14:4-7). His first wife was Saul's daughter Michal (1 Sam. 18:27), who was childless (2 Sam. 6:23). In Hebron, Ahinoam of Jezreel gave birth to Amnon, David's firstborn (2 Sam. 3:2); Abigail the widow of Nabal gave birth to Chileab, or Daniel (2 Sam. 3:3); princess Maacah bore Absalom (3:3) and his sister Tamar (2 Sam. 13:1); Haggith gave birth to Adonijah (3:4); Abital bore Shephatiah (3:4); and Eglah bore Ithream (3:5). In Jerusalem, Bathsheba bore David four children (1 Chron. 3:5): Shimea (or Shammah), Shobab, Nathan, and Solomon. His other wives, who are not named (1 Chron. 3:6-9), bore David Ibhar, Elishua, Eliphelet (or Elpelet), Nogah, Nepheg, Japhia, Elishama, Eliada (or Beeliada, 1 Chron. 14:7), Eliphelet.[2]

David also had children by his concubines, so he had a large family to manage. It's no wonder that some of them got involved in various court intrigues and brought sorrow to the king. The law clearly stated that the king was not to multiply wives, but both David and Solomon ignored this law, and both paid dearly for their disobedience. It's likely that some of the wives, like Maacah, represented alliances that David made with neighboring kings to help guarantee the security of Israel.

4. David defeated the Philistines. (5:17-25; 1 Chron. 14:8-17)

As long as David was minding his own business in Hebron, the Philistines thought he was still one of their vassals;

but when he became king of the whole nation of Israel, the Philistines knew he was their enemy and they attacked him. It's probable that these attacks occurred before David relocated in Jerusalem, because he and his men went down to "the stronghold" (5:17), the wilderness area where he had lived in the days when Saul was out to kill him (1 Sam. 22:4; 23:13-14).[3] David got word of the approaching Philistine army, quickly maneuvered his soldiers, and met the invaders in the Valley of Rephaim, just a short distance from Jerusalem.

As he had done before, David sought the mind of the Lord in planning his attack, probably by using the Urim and Thummim, or he may have had the prophet Gad seek the Lord's will. Assured by the Lord that He would give Israel victory, David met the Philistines two miles southwest of Jerusalem, and he forced them to retreat. They left the field so quickly that they left their idols behind, and David and his men burned them. The Philistines were sure the presence of their gods would assure them victory, but they were wrong. David gave God all the glory and called the place Baal-perazim, which means "the Lord who breaks out."

Some commentators believe that the Gadite warriors joined David's army at this time (1 Chron. 12:8-15), and this was probably the occasion when three of David's "mighty men" broke through the Philistine lines and obtained for David water from the Bethlehem well (2 Sam. 23:13-17; 1 Chron. 11:15-19). It took a great deal of faith and courage for them to do this, and what they did was in response to a *desire in David's heart* and not an order from his lips. They obtained the water because they loved their king and wanted to please him. What an example for us to follow!

The Philistines returned to fight David a second time, and David sought the Lord's will a second time. Unlike Joshua after the victory at Jericho (Josh. 6–7), David didn't assume that the same strategy would work again. God gave him a new battle plan, he obeyed it, and the Lord gave him the victory. What was the sound in the tops of the trees? Only the wind? Angels (Ps. 104:4)? God coming to lead His people to victory? The strategy worked and David pursued the enemy all the way from Gibeon to Gezer, a distance of fifteen to twenty miles. By this victory Israel regained the territory that Saul lost in his last battle. In subsequent campaigns, David also took back the cities the Philistines had taken from Saul (2 Sam. 8:1; 1 Chron. 18:1). David had repeated battles with the Philistines, and the Lord gave him one victory after another (2 Sam. 21:15-22).

The people had long recognized that David was a brave and skillful warrior, and these two victories added greater glory to God and honor to His servant. By defeating the Philistines, David gave notice to Israel's enemies that they had better be careful what they did to him and his people.

5. David relocated the holy Ark. (2 Sam. 6:1-23; 1 Chron. 13:1-13; 15:1–16:3)[4]

The Ark of the Covenant was to be kept in the Holy of Holies of the tabernacle, for it symbolized the glorious throne of God (Pss. 80:1; 99:1 NIV); but for over seventy-five years, the Ark had been absent from the divine sanctuary at Shiloh. The Philistines captured the Ark when Eli was judge (1 Sam. 4) and then returned it to the Jews because the Lord sent judgment on the Philistines. First the Ark was sent to Beth Shemesh and then was taken to Kiriath Jearim and guarded in the house of Abinadab (1 Sam 5:1–7:1). During the reign of David, there were two high priests, Zadok and Ahimelech (2 Sam. 8:17), and it's possible that one served at the sanctuary, which was in Shiloh and then moved to Gibeon (2 Chron. 1:1-6), while the other ministered at court in Jerusalem. David pitched a tent for the Ark in the City of David, but the furnishings in the tabernacle weren't moved to Jerusalem until after Solomon completed the temple (1 Kings 8:1-4; 2 Chron. 5:1-5).

The first attempt (vv. 1-11). Why did David want the Ark in Jerusalem? For one thing, he wanted to honor the Lord and give Him His rightful place as King of the nation. But David also had a secret desire in his heart to build a sanctuary for the Lord (see chap. 7; Ps. 132:1-5), and the first step would be to place the Ark in the capital city. David knew that the Lord desired a central sanctuary (Deut. 12:5, 11, 21; 14:23-24; 16:2, 6, 11; 26:2), and he hoped the Lord would let him build it. David's dream didn't come true, but he did buy the land on which the temple was built (2 Sam. 24:18ff), and he provided the temple plans and the wealth and materials needed for its construction (1 Chron. 28–29).

Surely there was a political reason as well for moving the Ark to Jerusalem, for it symbolized "one nation under God." David involved all the key leaders in the land in planning the event and issued a general invitation to the priests and Levites to come to Jerusalem from all their cities. "So David assembled all the Israelites, from the Shihor River in Egypt to Lebo Hamath [or "the entrance to Hamath"], to bring the Ark of God from Kiriath Jearim" (1 Chron. 13:5). Hamath marked the northernmost boundary assigned by God to Israel (Num. 34:8). It was David's hope that past divisions and tribal differences would be forgotten as the people focused on the Lord. The presence of the Ark meant the presence of the Lord, and the presence of the Lord meant security and victory.

But one thing was missing: there is no record that David sought the mind of the Lord in this matter. Relocating the Ark to Jerusalem seemed a wise idea and everybody was enthusiastic about doing it, but the king didn't follow his usual pattern of asking the Lord for His directions. After all, what pleases the king and the people may not please God, and what doesn't please God will not have His blessing. David's first attempt failed miserably because the Levites didn't carry the Ark on their shoulders. God had given specific directions through Moses how the tabernacle was to be erected, dismantled, and transported (Num. 4), and the major pieces of furniture were to be carried on the shoulders of the Levites who descended from Kohath (vv. 4:9-20). When they used a new cart drawn by oxen, they were following the pattern of the pagan Philistines (1 Sam. 6), not the pattern given to Moses on Mount Sinai.

The lesson here is obvious: God's work must be done in God's way if it is to have God's blessing. The fact that all the leaders of Israel agreed to use the cart didn't make it right. When it looked like the Ark would fall from the cart, Uzzah presumptuously took hold of it to steady it, and he was killed. But God had warned about this in the Law of Moses, and every Israelite surely knew of it (Num. 1:51; 4:15, 20). There's no evidence that Abinadab was a Levite or that his sons Uzzah and Ahio were even qualified to be near the Ark, let alone touch it. David quickly had the Ark taken into the house of Obed-Edom, who was a Levite (1 Chron. 15:18, 21, 24; 16:5; 26:4-8, 15), and there it remained for three months.

At the beginning of new eras in biblical history, God sometimes manifested His power in judgment to remind the people that one thing had not changed: God's people must obey God's Word. After the tabernacle was erected and the priestly ministry inaugurated, Aaron's sons Nadab and Abihu were struck dead for willfully trying to enter the sanctuary (Lev. 10). When Israel entered the land of Canaan and began to conquer the land, God had Achan executed for disobeying the law and taking loot from Jericho (Josh. 6–7). During the early days of the New Testament church, Ananias and Sapphira were killed for lying to God and His people (Acts 5). Here, at the start of David's reign in Jerusalem, God reminded His people that they were not to imitate the other nations when they served Him, for all they needed to know was in His Word.

The church today needs to heed this reminder and return to the Word of God for an understanding of the will of God. No amount of unity or enthusiasm can compensate for disobedience. When God's work is done in man's way, and we imitate the world instead of obeying the Word, we can never expect the blessing of God. The crowds may approve what we do, but what about the approval of God? The way of the world is ultimately the way of death.

The second attempt (vv. 12-19). When David heard that the presence of the Ark was bringing blessing to the household of Obed-Edom, he wanted that blessing for himself and his people. The Ark belonged in the tent he had erected for it in Jerusalem. Since 1 and 2 Chronicles were written from the priestly viewpoint, the account of the second attempt is much fuller than the record in Samuel (1 Chron. 15:1–16:3). David was now determined to do God's work in God's way, so he sent the Levites on the ten-mile trip to the house of Obed-Edom, and they brought the Ark to Jerusalem on their shoulders.To make sure the Lord wouldn't "break through" with another judgment, the Levites paused after their first six steps and the priests offered a bull and a fattened calf. When no judgment fell, they knew God was pleased with what they were doing (1 Chron. 17:26).[5] When the procession reached the tent in Jerusalem, the priests offered fourteen more sacrifices (1 Chron. 15:26).

David danced enthusiastically in worship before the Lord and dressed for the occasion in a priestly linen ephod (v. 14). Later, his wife accused him of shamelessly exposing himself (v. 20), but 1 Chron. 15:27 informs us that he was also wearing a royal robe under the ephod. Though he was not from the tribe of Levi, David was acting as both king and priest—a picture of Jesus, the Son of David, who holds both offices "after the order of Melchizedek" (Heb. 6:20–8:13; Ps. 110). In the days of Abraham, Melchizedek was the king and priest of Salem (Gen. 14:17-24), and now David was worshiping as king and priest of Jerusalem. The procession was accompanied by Levites playing musical instruments and singing songs of praise to the Lord.

David's dance was personal and sincere, and he did it before the Lord as he celebrated the coming of His presence into the capital city. It's probable that some of the psalms (24, 47, 95, 99, 68, 105, 106, 132; see 1 Chron. 16:7-36) reflected his thoughts and feelings on that occasion. In ancient times, dancing played a part in both pagan and Hebrew worship (Ps. 149:3) as well as in the celebrations of special occasions, such as weddings, family gatherings (Luke 15:25), and military victories (Judg. 11:34). Usually it was the women who danced and sang before the Lord (Ex. 15:20-21; 1 Sam. 18:6; Ps. 68:24-26), and on occasions when both men and women danced, they were segregated. Religious dances are mentioned or hinted at in the Book of Psalms (26:6-7; 30:11; 42:4; 150:4).

There is no New Testament evidence that dancing as a "worship art form" was used either in the Jewish synagogue or the liturgy of the early church. The Greeks introduced dancing into worship in the post-Apostolic church, but the practice led to serious moral problems and was finally banned. It was difficult for congregations to distinguish between "Christian dances" and dances honoring a pagan god or goddess, so the church abandoned the practice and later church fathers condemned it.

When the Ark was safely installed in the tent, David blessed the people (another priestly act) and gave each person some bread and flesh (or wine) and a cake of raisins. Once again we're reminded of the priest-king Melchizedek, who came from Salem and gave Abraham bread and wine (Gen. 14:18-19). But when David went home to bless his own family, he discovered that his wife was ashamed of him and even despised him for dancing so enthusiastically in public (vv. 16, 20-23). It's interesting that the text says that she saw "King David" and not "her husband" (v. 16) and that she is called "the daughter of Saul" and not "David's wife" (v. 20). When she spoke to him, Michal used the third person ("How glorious was the king") and not the more personal second person, and her speech was very sarcastic. How sad that David's day of happy celebration ended with this kind of insensitive and heartless reception from his own wife, but often God's servants go quickly from the glory of the mountain to the shadows of the valley.

There's no evidence that David was guilty of any of the things his wife accused him of doing. He was properly attired and certainly didn't expose himself to the people, and his dance was before the Lord, who knew what was in his heart. David recognized in Michal the pride and spiritual blindness of her father, Saul, whose one desire was to gain and keep his popularity with the people. David preferred to live and serve so as to please the Lord. He reminded Michal that the Lord had chosen him to replace her father as king and that he would do what the Lord prompted him to do. In other words, David didn't need the spiritual counsel of the carnal daughter of a deposed and disgraced king. Perhaps Michal didn't like what David said about her father's neglect of the Ark (1 Chron. 13:3). David loved Michal and wanted her back when he became king (3:12-16), but love can easily be bruised when we least expect it.

Michal said that David had disgraced himself before the people, but David countered her false accusation with a declaration that she would be disgraced even more, and from that day on he ignored his marriage duties toward her. For a wife to bear no children was a disgrace in that day, especially if her husband rejected her. But Michal's barrenness was a blessing from the Lord. It prevented Saul's family from continuing in Israel and therefore threatening the throne of David. David and Jonathan had covenanted to reign together (1 Sam. 23:16-18), but God rejected that plan by allowing Jonathan to be slain in battle. The Lord wanted the line and throne of David to be kept apart from any other dynasty, because David's line would culminate in the birth of the Messiah, Jesus Christ. That will be the theme of the next chapter in David's story.

CHAPTER FOUR
DAVID'S DYNASTY, KINDNESS, AND CONQUESTS
2 Samuel 7–10
(See also 1 Chronicles 17–19)

In these four chapters we see King David involved in four important activities: accepting God's will (chap. 7), fighting God's battles (chap. 8), sharing God's kindness (chap. 9), and defending God's honor (chap. 10). However, these activities were nothing new to David, for even before he was crowned king of all Israel he had served the Lord and the people in these ways. Wearing a crown and sitting on a throne didn't change David, for in his character and conduct he had lived like a king all his young life. How tragic that from chapter 11 on, we see David disobeying the Lord and suffering the painful consequences of his sins. Andrew Bonar was correct when he said, "We must be as watchful after the victory as before the battle."

1. Accepting God's will (2 Sam. 7:1-29; 1 Chron. 17:1-27)

In the ancient world, what did kings do when they had no wars to fight? Nebuchadnezzar surveyed his city and boasted, "Is not this great Babylon, that I have built?" (Dan. 4:30). Solomon collected wealth and wives, entertained foreign guests, and wrote books, while Hezekiah seems to have supervised scholars who copied and preserved the Scriptures (Prov. 25:1). But it appears from 2 Samuel 7:1-3 that in David's leisure hours, the king thought about the Lord and conferred with his chaplain Nathan about improving the spiritual condition of the kingdom of Israel. David wasn't simply a ruler; he was a shepherd with a heart concern for his people. In rest, he thought of work he could do, and in success he thought of God and His goodness to him.

In this chapter, the Lord revealed to Nathan and David what is usually called the Davidic Covenant.[1] This declaration not only had great meaning for David in his day, but it has significance today for Israel, the church, and the world at large.

What the covenant meant to David (vv. 1-9). That David wanted to build a house for the Lord doesn't surprise us, because David was a man after God's own heart and longed to honor the Lord in every possible way. During his years of exile, David had vowed to the Lord that he would build Him a temple (Ps. 132:1-5), and his bringing the Ark to Jerusalem was surely the first step toward fulfilling that vow. Now it troubled David that he was living in a comfortable stone house with cedar paneling while God's throne was in a tent, and he shared his burden with Nathan.

This is the first appearance of Nathan in Scripture. Gad had been David's prophet during his exile (1 Sam. 22:5), and after David's coronation, Gad didn't pass from the scene (2 Sam. 24:1-18). In fact, he and Nathan worked together keeping the official records (1 Chron. 29:25, 29) and organizing the worship (2 Chron. 29:25), but Nathan seems to have been the prophetic voice of God to David during his reign. It was Nathan who confronted David about his sin (chap. 12) and also who saw to it that Solomon was crowned king (1 Kings 1:11ff). David had four sons by Bathsheba and named one of them Nathan (1 Chron. 3:1-5).[2] When Nathan told David to do what was in his heart, he wasn't affirming that David's desires were actually God's will. Rather, he was encouraging the king to pursue his desires and see what the Lord wanted him to do. God answered by giving Nathan a special message for the king, and Nathan faithfully delivered it.

In the first part of the message, God reminded David that at no time had He ever asked any tribe or tribal leader to build Him a house. God had commanded Moses to make a tabernacle for His dwelling, and He had been satisfied to travel with His pilgrim people and dwell with them wherever they camped. Now that Israel was in the land and had peace, they needed a caring leader, not a temple, and that's why God called David to shepherd the people of Israel. God had been with David to protect his life and prosper his service and had made David's name great. In spite of his desires and his oath, David would not build the temple. The best thing he could do for the Lord was to continue shepherding the people and setting a godly example.

This announcement must have disappointed David, but he accepted it graciously and gave the Lord thanks for all His goodness to him. When Solomon dedicated the temple, he explained that God accepted David's desire for the deed: "Whereas it was in your heart to build a house for My name, you did well that it was in your heart" (1 Kings 8:18 NKJV; see 2 Cor. 8:12). God's servants must learn to accept the disappointments of life, for as A. T. Pierson used to say, "Disappointments are His appointments."

What the covenant means to Israel (vv. 10-15). The foundation for God's purposes and dealings with the people of Israel is His covenant with Abraham (Gen. 12:1-3; 15:1-15). God chose Abraham by His grace and promised him a land, a great name, multiplied descendants, and His blessing and protection. He also promised that the whole world would be blessed through Abraham's seed, and this refers to Jesus Christ (Gal. 3:1-16). God called Israel to be the human channel through which His Son and His Word would come to the world. God's covenant with David builds on this covenant with Abraham, for it speaks about the nation, the land, and the Messiah.

The Lord began with the subject of Israel's land (v. 10) and promised "rest" to His people. The word "rest" is an important word in the prophetic vocabulary and refers to a number of blessings in the plan of God for His people. The concept of "rest" began with God's rest when He completed creation (Gen. 2:1-3), and this was a basis for Israel's observance of the Sabbath (Ex. 20:8-11). After God delivered Israel from Egypt, He promised them "rest" in their own land (Ex. 33:14; Deut. 25:19; Josh. 1:13, 15). David was so busy fighting wars that he couldn't build the temple (1 Kings 5:17),[3] but when God gave rest to Israel, Solomon built the temple using the plans and materials that God gave his father David (1 Kings 5:1-4; 8:56; Ps. 89:19-23).

The concept of "rest" goes beyond any of these matters because it speaks also of the spiritual rest that believers have in Christ (Matt. 11:28-30; Heb. 2:10-18; 4:14-16). The concept also looks ahead to Israel's future kingdom and the rest that God's people will then enjoy when Jesus Christ sits upon David's throne (Isa. 11:1-12; 65:17-25; Jer. 31:1-14; 50:34).

Then the Lord turned from promises concerning the land and the nation to promises concerning David's throne and family (vv. 11-16). Every king is concerned about the future of his kingdom, and the Lord promised David something above and beyond anything he could have imagined. David wanted to build God a house (the temple), but God promised to build David a house—a dynasty forever! The word "house" is used fifteen times in this chapter and refers to David's palace (vv. 1-2), the temple (vv. 5-7, 13), and David's dynasty, culminating in Messiah, Jesus Christ (vv. 11, 13, 16, 18-29).

God's first announcement of the coming of the Savior was given in Genesis 3:15, informing us that the Savior would be a human being and not an angel. Genesis 12:3 tells us that He would be a Jew who would bless the whole world, and Genesis 49:10 that He would come through the tribe of Judah. In this covenant, God announced to David that Messiah would come through his family, and Micah 5:2 prophesied that He would be born in Bethlehem, the City of David (see Matt. 2:6). No wonder the king was so elated when he learned that Messiah would be known as "the Son of David" (Matt. 1:1)!

In this section, the Lord speaks about Solomon as well as about the Savior, who is "greater than Solomon" (Matt. 12:42). Solomon would build the temple David longed to build, but his reign would end; however, the reign of Messiah would go on forever. David would have a house forever (vv. 25, 29), a kingdom forever (v. 16), and a throne forever (vv. 13, 16), and would glorify God's name forever (v. 26).

All of this is fulfilled in Jesus Christ, the Son of David (Ps. 89:34-37; Luke 1:32-33, 69; Acts 2:29-36; 13:22-23; 2 Tim. 2:8) and will be manifested when He returns, establishes the promised kingdom, and sits on David's throne. The spiritual blessings God offered to David are today offered in Jesus Christ to all who will trust Him (Isa. 55:1-3; Acts 13:32-39). They will be fulfilled literally by Jesus Chirst in the future kingdom promised to Israel (Isa. 9:1-7; 11:1-16; 16:5; Jer. 33:15-26; Ezek. 34:23-24; 37:24-25; Hos. 3:5; Zech. 12:7-8).[4] The throne of David ended in 586 B.C. with Zedekiah, the last king of Judah, but the line of David continued and brought Jesus Christ the Son of God into the world (Matt. 1:12-25; Luke 1:26-38, 54-55, 68-79).

Humanly speaking, the nation of Israel would have perished quickly had not God been faithful to His covenant with David, who was "the light [lamp] of Israel" (21:17). No matter to what depths the kings and people descended, the Lord preserved a lamp for David and for Israel (1 Kings 11:36; 15:4; 2 Kings 8:19; 2 Chron. 21:7; Ps. 132:17). Whether they recognized it or not, the Jewish people were heavily indebted to David for their temple, the instruments and songs used in the temple, the organization of the temple ministry, and the protection the nation had from the enemy nations. We today are indebted to David for keeping the light shining so that the Savior could come into the world. In spite of the nation's sins, God chastened His people, but He did not break His covenant or take His mercy away (v. 15; 22:51; 1 Kings 3:6; 2 Chron. 6:42; Ps. 89:28, 33, 49).

What the covenant means to believers today (vv. 18-29). We have already noted that there is a church today because God used David's family to bring the Savior into the world, and there is a future for Israel because God gave David a throne forever. The way that David responded to this great Word from God is a good example for us to follow today. He humbled himself before the Lord and at least ten times called himself the servant of God. Servants usually stand at attention and wait for orders, but David sat before the Lord. The covenant God gave David was unconditional; all David had to do was accept it and let God work. Like a little child speaking to a loving parent, the king called himself "David" (v. 20), and he poured out his heart to the Lord.

First he focused on *the present* as he gave praise for the mercies God bestowed on him (vv. 18-21). It was God's grace that had brought David this far—from the sheepfolds to the throne—and now God had spoken about his descendants far into the future. In verses 18-20 and 28-29, David addressed God as "Lord God," which in Hebrew is "Jehovah Adonai, the Sovereign Lord." (In vv. 22 and 25, it's "Jehovah Elohim," the God of power.) Only a God of sovereign grace would give such a covenant, and only a God with sovereign power could fulfill it. "Do you deal with everyone this way, O Sovereign Lord?" (v. 19 NLT). In one sense, the answer is no, because God chose the house of David to bring His Son into the world; but in another sense, the answer is yes, because any sinner can trust Jesus Christ and be saved and enter into the family of God. David saw the promises of this covenant as a "great thing" (v. 21) because of the dependability of God's Word and God's love.

In verses 22-24, David looked at *the past* and God's amazing grace toward Israel. The Lord chose Israel instead of the other nations on the earth, and He revealed Himself to Israel by giving the law at Mount Sinai and speaking the Word through His prophets. The Jews were to remember the uniqueness of the Lord and not bow before the idols of the other nations. (See Deut. 4:34; 7:6-8; 9:4-5; Neh. 9:10.) God is the Lord of all nations but He did great things for Israel, His chosen people. David recognized the wonderful truth that God had chosen Israel to be His people forever!

The third part of David's prayer and praise (vv. 25-29) looked to *the future* as revealed in the covenant just delivered to the king. God gave the Word, David believed it, and David asked God to fulfill that Word for His people. He wanted Israel to continue as a nation and the Lord to be magnified through Israel. He asked that his house be built just as the Lord had promised (v. 27), even though it was disappointing to David that he wasn't permitted to build a house for the Lord. "Thy kingdom come" is the thrust of verse 27, and "Thy will be done" the thrust of verse 28. It was enough for David simply to hear the promises and believe them; he also prayed to the Lord to fulfill them.

In his humility, faith, and submission to God's will, David is a good example for us to follow.

2. Fighting God's battles. (2 Sam. 8:1-18; 1Chron. 18)

This chapter summarizes the victories of the army of Israel over their enemies, events that most likely occurred between chapters 6 and 7 of 2 Samuel (see 7:1). The Lord helped David, Joab, and Abishai to overcome Israel's enemies on the west (v. 1), east (v. 2), north (vv. 3-12), and south (vv. 13-14). For a parallel account, see 1 Chronicles 18-19. King Saul had fought many of these same enemies (1 Sam. 14:47).

We must look at David's military activities in the light of God's covenants with Israel through Abraham (Gen. 12, 15), Moses (Deut. 27–30) and David (2 Sam. 7). The Lord had promised Israel the land from the River of Egypt to the Euphrates River (Gen. 15:17-21; Deut. 1:6-8; 11:24; 1 Kings 4:20-21), and the Lord used David to help fulfill the promise. Israel had lost territory to her enemies during the reign of King Saul, and David recaptured it, but he also expanded Israel's borders and acquired land that hadn't been conquered in Joshua's day (Josh. 13:1-7). David established vassal treaties with most of these nations and set up garrisons in their lands to maintain Israel's authority (v. 6). A man of faith, David believed God's promises and acted upon them for the blessing of his people.

But David's victories also meant peace and safety for the people of Israel so they could live normal lives and not be constantly threatened by their neighbors. Israel had a great work to perform on earth in bearing witness to the true and living God and bringing the written Scriptures and the Messiah into the world. Furthermore, David's victories enriched the treasury of the Lord so that the material was available for Solomon to build the temple (vv. 11-13; 1 Chron. 22). The church today doesn't use military weapons to fight God's battles (John 18:36-38; 2 Cor. 10:3-6; Eph. 6:14-18), but we could use the faith and courage of David and his soldiers and reclaim lost territory for the Lord.

West: the Philistines (v. 1) were the traditional enemies of the Jews and seized every opportunity to attack them. In 2 Samuel 21:15-22, at least four different Philistine campaigns are mentioned (see also 1 Chron. 20:4-8), and the text describes the slaying of several giants as well as the defeating of the Philistines. Israel captured several cities, including Gath, the home of Goliath. As a youth, David had killed Goliath, but during the first campaign he was unable to slay the giant Ishbi-benob, and David's nephew Abishai had to rescue him (21:15-17). David's men advised him to stop waging war personally, and he heeded their advice. Blessed is that leader who admits his weaknesses and admits when he needs to make changes! The name "Metheg-ammah" means "the bridle of the mother city" and probably refers to a key Philistine city that Israel captured, the location of which is a mystery to us. To "take the bridle" of anything means to gain control and force submission.

East: the Moabites (v. 2) had been friendly to David because they thought he was Saul's enemy (1 Sam. 14:47), and David was related to the Moabites through his great-grandmother Ruth (Ruth 4:18-22). While living in exile, David had even put his parents in the custody of the king of Moab (1 Sam. 22:3-4). The Moabites were actually related to the Jews because Abraham's nephew Lot was the father of their ancestor Moab (Gen. 19:30-38). Because the Moabites had hired Balaam the prophet to curse Israel and then led Moab in seducing the men of Israel (Num. 22–25), the Lord declared war on Moab, and David was only continuing that crusade. Most conquerors would have slaughtered the entire army, but David spared every third soldier and settled for tribute from the nation.

North: the Arameans and Syrians (vv. 3-13). Zobah was located north of Damascus and was part of a confederacy of nations called "the Syrians" in some translations, but more accurately they are "the Arameans." However, their neighbors the Syrians tried to come to their rescue and were defeated themselves, so that the whole area north to the Euphrates came under David's authority. This gave Israel important military installations and also control of the valuable caravan routes that passed through that territory. Israel could levy duty as the traders passed through and thereby increase its income. By defeating the Arameans and the Syrians, David also made friends with their enemies and received tribute from them (vv. 6-10).

South: the Edomites (vv. 12-14). First Chronicles 18:12-13 names the Edomites as the enemy (see 1 Kings 11:14b-18), but it's possible that the Syrians and Arameans at this time were in control of Edom and were also involved in the battle. It appears that while Israel was attacking the Syrians and Arameans in the north, the Moabites attacked them from the south, but the Lord gave Israel a great victory. Though David and Joab were the conquering leaders in this battle, it was the Lord who received the glory when David commemorated the victory in Psalm 60. "Over Edom I will cast My shoe" (60:8 NKJV) is a metaphorical expression that may have a dual meaning: (1) God claims Edom as His territory, and (2) God treats Edom like a slave who cleans the master's shoes. It expresses the humiliation God brought to the proud Edomites whom David conquered.

David also defeated the Amalekites (v. 12), a commission that his predecessor Saul had failed to fulfill (1 Sam. 15). From the days of Moses, the Lord had declared war on Amalek (Ex. 17:8-12; Num. 14:45; Deut. 25:17-19), and David was only continuing the crusade. Just as the Lord promised (7:9), David was victorious over his enemies. David's reputation increased dramatically because of these victories (v. 13), and David was careful to give God the glory (8:11-12).

Administration in Jerusalem (vv. 15-18).[5] Winning battles is one thing and managing the affairs of the growing nation is quite another, and here David proved himself capable. He ruled with justice and righteousness and served all the people (v. 15). David described such a leader in 23:1-7 and compared him to the sunrise and the sunlight after rain. Certainly David brought the dawning of a new day to Israel after the darkness of Saul's reign, and God used David to bring calm after the storm. God loves righteousness and justice (Ps. 33:5) and manifests both as He rules over His universe (Pss. 36:6; 99:4; Isa. 5:16; Jer. 9:24; Amos 5:24). David indeed was a man after God's own heart.

A good ruler must appoint wise and skilled subordinates, and this David did. David's nephew Joab had treacherously killed Abner (3:27-39), but David made him head of the army. We know little about Jehoshaphat or his position in David's government. The "recorder" ("secretary" NIV) was probably the officer who kept the records and advised the king as would a secretary of state. He may have been the chairman of the king's council. The scenario in Isaiah 36 indicates that the secretary/recorder was a person of high rank (see vv. 3, 22).

Zadok and Ahimelech were both serving as priests, for the Ark was in Jerusalem and the tabernacle was at Gibeon (1 Chron. 16:39ff). Ahimelech the priest was slain by Doeg at Saul's command (1 Sam. 22:6ff) and his son Abiathar survived the slaughter of the priests at Nob and joined David's band at Keilah (22:20; 23:6). He accompanied David during his exile years and must have fathered a son whom he named Ahimelech after the boy's martyred grandfather. When he came of age, the boy served with his father and Zadok. You find Zadok and Abiathar working together when the Ark was brought to Jerusalem (2 Sam. 15:24, 35) and when Absalom revolted against David (2 Sam. 17:15; 19:11-12).

Seriah the scribe ("secretary" NIV) was also known as Sheva (20:25), Shavsha (1 Chron. 18:16), and Shisha (1 Kings 4:3). The reference in Kings informs us that two of his sons inherited his position. The most remarkable appointment is that of Benaiah, the officer over David's bodyguard and a mighty warrior (23:20-23), who was a priest (1 Chron. 27:5). In the Old Testament, it wasn't unusual for a priest to become a prophet (Jeremiah, Ezekiel), but for a priest to become an army officer was unusual. The Cherethites and Pelethites were exceptional mercenaries from other nations who made up David's personal bodyguard. Benaiah became an invaluable aide to Solomon (1 Kings 1:38, 44).

While not all of David's sons proved to be worthy men, he had them serving as officers in his government. It was not only good for them, but it was one way for him to get information concerning what was going on in the nation. The title "chief rulers" ("royal advisers" NIV) is a translation of the Hebrew word for "priests." Since David belonged to the tribe of Judah, neither he nor his sons could enter the holy precincts of the tabernacle and minister as priests, so the word probably means "confidential advisers." These were men who had access to the king and assisted him in directing the affairs of the kingdom.

3. Sharing God's kindness (2 Sam. 9:1-13)

"The kindness of God" is the one of two themes in this chapter (vv. 1, 3, 7), and it means the mercy and favor of the Lord to undeserving people. Paul saw the kindness of God in the coming of Jesus Christ and His work on the cross (Titus 3:1-7 [3:4]; Eph. 2:1-9 [2:7]), and we see in David's dealings with Mephibosheth a picture of God's kindness to lost sinners. David had promised both Saul and Jonathan that he would not exterminate their descendants when he became king (1 Sam. 20:12-17, 42; 24:21), and in the case of Jonathan's son Mephibosheth, David not only kept his promise but went above and beyond the call of duty.

The second major theme is the kingship of David. The name "David" is used by itself six times in the chapter: six times he's called "the king," and once the two are united in "King David" (v. 5). Nobody in all Israel except David could have shown this kindness to Mephibosheth because David was the king. He had inherited all that had belonged to King Saul (12:8) and could dispose of it as he saw fit. Surely we have here a picture of the Son of David, Jesus Christ, who through His death, resurrection, and ascension has been glorified on the throne of heaven and can now dispense His spiritual riches to needy sinners. The name "David" means "beloved," and Jesus is God's beloved Son (Matt. 3:17; 17:5), sent to earth to save lost sinners.

Finding Mephibosheth (vv. 1-4). It's important to note that David's motivation for seeking Mephibosheth was not the sad plight of the crippled man but David's desire to honor Jonathan, the father. He did what he did "for Jonathan's sake" (1 Sam. 20:11-17). Mephibosheth was five years old when his father died in battle (4:4), so he was now about twenty-one years old and had a young son of his own (v. 12). David couldn't show any love or kindness to Jonathan, so he looked for one of Jonathan's relatives to whom he could express his affection. So it is with God's children: they are called and saved, not because they deserve anything from God, but for the sake of God's Son, Jesus Christ (Eph. 1:6; 4:32). God in His grace gives us what we don't deserve, and in His mercy doesn't give us what we do deserve.

David found out where Mephibosheth was living by asking Ziba, who served as an "estate manager" for Saul. Ziba answered David's questions about Mephibosheth, but he turned out to be very deceitful and lied to the king about Mephibosheth when David fled from

Absalom (16:1-4) and when David returned to Jerusalem (19:17, 24-30). The combination of David's impulsiveness and Ziba's deceit cost Mephibosheth half his property.

Calling Mephibosheth (vv. 5-8). What were the lame prince's thoughts when the summons came to appear before the king? If he believed what his grandfather had said about David, he would have feared for his life; but if he had listened to what his father told him about David, he would have rejoiced. Someone had to help the young man to the palace, where he fell before David—something difficult for a person with crippled legs—and acknowledged his own unworthiness. The king spoke his name and immediately assured him that there was nothing to fear. David then unofficially "adopted" Mephibosheth by restoring to him the land that his father, Jonathan, would have inherited from Saul, and then by inviting him to live at the palace and eat at the king's table. David had eaten at Saul's table and it had nearly cost him his life, but Mephibosheth would eat at David's table and his life would be protected.

The fact that David made the first move to rescue Mephibosheth reminds us that it was God who reached out to us and not we who sought Him. We were estranged from God and enemies of God, yet He loved us and sent His Son to die for us. "But God demonstrates His own love toward us, in that while we were still sinners, Christ died for us" (Rom. 5:8 NKJV). For David to rescue and restore Mephibosheth cost him only the land of Saul, which he had never paid for to begin with; but for God to restore us and bring us into His family, Jesus had to sacrifice His life. Our inheritance is much more than a piece of real estate on earth: it's an eternal home in heaven!

Enriching Mephibosheth (vv. 9-13). David took him into his own family, provided for him, protected him, and let him eat at his own table. It wouldn't be easy to care for a grown man who was lame in both feet, but David promised to do so. Whereas previously Mephibosheth had Ziba and his fifteen sons and twenty servants working for him (v. 10), now all the resources and authority of the king of Israel were at his disposal! Ziba and his sons and servants would still work the land for Mephibosheth and give him the profits, but those profits would be insignificant compared with the king's wealth. David's words "eat at my table" are found four times in the passage (vv. 7, 10, 11, 13) and indicate that Jonathan's son would be treated like David's son.

Mephibosheth looked upon himself as a "dead dog" (v. 8), and we were "dead" in our trespasses and sins when Jesus called us and gave us new life (Eph. 2:1-6). We have a higher position than that which David gave Mephibosheth, for we sit *on the throne* with Jesus Christ and reign in life through Him (Rom. 5:17). God gives us the riches of His mercy and grace (Eph. 2:4-7) and "unsearchable riches" in Christ (Eph. 3:8). God supplies all our needs, not out of an earthly king's treasury, but according to "his riches in glory" (Phil. 4:19). Mephibosheth lived the rest of his life in the earthly Jerusalem (v. 13), but God's children today are already citizens of the heavenly Jerusalem, where they will dwell forever with the Lord (Heb. 12:22-24).

This touching event in the life of David not only illustrates the believer's spiritual experience in Christ, but it also reveals to us that David was indeed a man after God's own heart (1 Sam. 13:14; Acts 13:22). He was a shepherd who had a special concern for the lame sheep in the flock.[6]

One last fact should be noted: when some of Saul's descendants were chosen to be slain, David protected Mephibosheth from death (21:1-11, especially v. 7). There was another descendant named Mephibosheth (v. 8), but David knew the difference between the two! The spiritual application to believers today is obvious: "There is therefore now no condemnation to those who are in Christ Jesus" (Rom. 8:1 NKJV). "For God did not appoint us to wrath, but to obtain salvation through our Lord Jesus Christ" (1 Thes. 5:9 NKJV). "He who believes in Him is not condemned; but he who does not believe is condemned already, because he has not believed in the name of the only begotten Son of God" (John 3:18 NKJV).

Mephibosheth is a difficult name to remember and pronounce, but he reminds us of some wonderful truths about "the kindness of God" shown to us through Jesus Christ our Savior and Lord.

4. Vindicating God's honor. (2 Sam. 10:1-19; 1 Chr. 19:1-19)

Once again, David wanted to show kindness, but this time his attempt led to war instead of peace. His overtures to his neighbor were misunderstood, and David had to defend his own honor as well as the honor of the Lord and His people.

A public offense (vv. 1-5). King Saul's first military victory was over Nahash and the Ammonite army when they attacked Jabesh Gilead (1 Sam. 11). Like the Ammonites, the Moabites were descendants of Lot (Gen. 19:30ff) and therefore relatives of the Jews. How did David become friendly with the Ammonites when his predecessor was at war with them? It probably occurred when David was in exile and appeared to be at war with Saul. During those "outlaw years," David tried to build a network of friendships outside Israel that he hoped would help him when he became king. The phrase "show kindness" can carry the meaning of "make a covenant,"[7] so it may have been David's desire not only to comfort Hanun but also to make a treaty with him.

David sent a delegation of court officials to Hanun, but immaturity and ignorance triumphed over wisdom and common sense. The inexperienced new king listened to his suspicious advisers and treated David's men as though they were spies. (Years later, Solomon's son Rehoboam would make a similar mistake and follow unwise counsel. See 1 Kings 12.) The Ammonites shaved the ambassadors' faces, leaving but one side of each beard intact, and then cut the men's official garments off at the waist. Jewish men were supposed to keep their beards intact (Lev. 19:27; 21:5; Deut. 14:1-2), and to tamper with a man's beard was a great insult. All Jews were to be dressed modestly, so exposing the men's bodies was even more embarrassing. It was treating them as though they were prisoners of war (Isa. 20:3-4), and it also meant removing some of the tassels on their garments that identified them as Jews (Deut. 22:12; Num. 15:37-41).

The first battle (vv. 6-14). The members of the delegation could easily secure other garments, but it would take time for their beards to grow; so they stayed in Jericho until they looked presentable. However, new beards couldn't erase old wounds. When King Hunan allowed his officials to mistreat the delegation, he not only insulted the men personally, but he also insulted King David who sent them and the nation they represented. In short, it was a declaration of war.

But King Hunan wasn't prepared for war, especially against a seasoned general like Joab and a famous king like David; so he paid a thousand talents of silver (1 Chron. 19:6) to hire troops from the north, including Syrians and Arameans, nations that David eventually defeated (8:12).[8] These 33,000 soldiers joined with the Ammonite army in attacking the Jewish army. Actually, Joab faced two armies who were using a pincer movement to defeat Israel, with the Syrians and Arameans coming from the north and the Ammonites coming from the south. Joab wisely divided his forces and put his brother Abishai in charge of the southern front, and with the Lord's gracious help, Joab so defeated the northern troops that his victory frightened the southern troops to flee to Rabbath, the fortified capital city of Ammon.

The second battle (vv. 15-19). David came personally to lead the battle against the Syrians,[9] and he and the army of Israel defeated them, and the Syrians became vassal states in David's growing empire. Joab wisely waited to set up a siege against the Ammonite capital of Rabbah at that time, so he waited to renew the attack in the spring of the year (11:1). He took the city and David came to finish the siege and claim the honors (12:26-31). It was while Joab and his men were besieging Rabbah that David remained in Jerusalem and committed adultery with Bathsheba.

David indeed was a man of war and fought the battles of the Lord, and the Lord was with him to give him victory. He extended the Israelite empire to the River of Egypt on the south, to the Euphrates River on the north, and on the east he conquered Edom, Moab, and Ammon, and on the north defeated the Arameans and the Syrians, including Hamath. Because of God's gifts and help, David undoubtedly became Israel's greatest king and greatest military genius. He was blessed with courageous men like Joab and Abishai, plus his "mighty men" (2 Sam. 23; 1 Chron. 11:10-47).

CHAPTER FIVE
DAVID'S DISOBEDIENCE, DECEPTION, AND DISCIPLINE[1]
2 Samuel 11–12

Unlike the average campaign biography or press release, the Bible always tells the truth about people. It should encourage us to know that even the best men and women in the biblical record had their faults and failures, just as we do, and yet the Lord in His sovereign grace was able to use them to accomplish His purposes. Noah was a man of faith and obedience, and yet he got drunk. Twice Abraham lied about his wife, and Jacob lied to both his father, Isaac, and to his brother Esau. Moses lost his temper when he struck the rock, and Peter lost his courage and denied Christ three times.

Here we see David, the man after God's own heart, who committed adultery and then murdered a man in a last-ditch effort to cover his own sin. For at least nine months, David refused to confess his sins, but then God spoke to Him and he sought the face of the Lord and made a new beginning. But he paid dearly for his sins for, as Charles Spurgeon said, "God does not allow his children to sin successfully." Alas, David suffered the consequences of his sins for the rest of his life, and so shall we if we rebel against Him, for the Lord chastens those He loves and seeks to make them obedient. The good things that we receive in life, we pay for in advance, for God prepares us for what He has prepared for us. But the evil things we do are paid for on the installment plan; and bitter is the sorrow brought by the consequences of forgiven sin.

These two chapters describe seven stages in David's experience. As we study, let's remember Paul's admonition, "Therefore let him who thinks he stands take heed lest he fall" (1 Cor. 10:12 NKJV).

1. The conceiving (2 Sam. 11:1-3)

David's temptation and sin illustrate the truth of James 1:14-15—"But each one is tempted when he is drawn away by his own desires and enticed. Then, when desire has conceived, it gives birth to sin; and sin, when it is full-grown, brings forth death" (NKJV). It isn't difficult to see how it all developed.

Idleness (vv. 1-2a). The account of David's sins is given against the background of Joab's siege of Rabbah, the key city of the Ammonites (11:1, 16-17; 1 Chron. 20:1-3). The Ammonite army had fled to the walled city of Rabbah (10:14), and Joab and the Israel troops were giving the people time to run out of food and water, and then they would attack. David sent Joab and the troops to lay siege to Rabbah, but he himself remained in Jerusalem. It was probably April or May and the winter rains had stopped and the weather was getting warmer. Chronologists calculate that David was about fifty years old at this time. It's true that David had been advised by his leaders not to engage actively in warfare (2 Sam. 21:15-17), but he could have been with his troops to help develop the strategy and give moral leadership.

Whatever the cause, good or bad, that kept David in Jerusalem, this much is true: "Satan finds some mischief still for idle hands to do."[2] Idleness isn't just the absence of activity, for all of us need regular rest; idleness is also activity to no purpose. When David was finished with his afternoon nap, he should have immediately moved into some kingdom duty that would have occupied his mind and body, or, if he wanted to take a walk, he should have invited someone to walk with him. "If you are idle, be not solitary," wrote Samuel Johnson; "if you are solitary, be not idle." Had David followed that counsel, he would have saved himself and his family a great deal of heartache.

When David laid aside his armor, he took the first step toward moral defeat, and the same principle applies to believers today (Eph. 6:10-18). Without the helmet of salvation, we don't think like saved people; and without the breastplate of righteousness, we have nothing to protect the heart. Lacking the girdle of truth, we easily believe lies ("We can get away with this!"), and without the sword of the Word and the shield of faith, we are helpless before the Enemy. Without prayer we have no power. As for the shoes of peace, David walked in the midst of battles for the rest of his life. He was safer on the battlefield than on the battlement of his house!

Imagination (v. 2b). A man can't be blamed if a beautiful woman comes into his line of vision, but if the man deliberately lingers for a second look in order to feed his lust, he's asking for trouble. "You heard that it was said, You shall not commit adultery," said Jesus. "But as for myself, I am saying to you, Everyone who is looking at a woman in order to indulge his sexual passion for her, has already committed adultery with her in his heart" (Matt. 5:27-28, *Wuest's Expanded Translation).* When David paused and took that longer second look, his imagination went to work and started to conceive sin. That would have been a good time to turn away decisively and leave the roof of his palace for a much safer place. When Joseph faced a similar temptation, he fled from the scene (Gen. 39:11-13). "Watch and pray, lest you enter into temptation. The spirit indeed is willing, but the flesh is weak" (Matt. 26:41 NKJV).

"Lead us not into temptation" was the prayer David should have prayed. By lingering and looking, David tempted himself. By sending the messengers, he tempted Bathsheba; and by yielding to the flesh, He tempted the Lord.

Information (v. 3). When God forbids something and calls it sin, we shouldn't try to get more information about it. "I want you to be wise in what is good, and simple concerning evil" (Rom. 16:19). David knew what the law said about adultery, so why did he send to inquire about the woman?[3] Because in his heart, he had already taken possession of her, and now he was anxious to have a rendezvous with her. He learned that Bathsheba was a married woman, and that fact alone should have stopped him from going on with his evil plan. When he found out she was the wife of one of his courageous soldiers who was even then on the battlefield (23:9), he should have gone to the tent of meeting, fallen on his face and cried out to God for mercy. From the brief genealogy given, David should have realized that Bathsheba was the granddaughter of Ahithophel, his favorite counselor (23:34; 16:23). No wonder Ahithophel sided with Absalom when he revolted against his father and seized the kingdom!

David knew the law and should have remembered it and applied it to his own heart. "You shall not covet your neighbor's wife" (Ex. 20:17); "You shall not commit adultery" (Ex. 20:14). David also knew that the palace servants saw and heard everything that went on and reported it to others, so there wasn't much chance he could escape detection. The fact that he was showing interest in his neighbor's wife was probably already public knowledge. But even if nobody but the messenger knew it, the Lord God knew it and didn't approve of what David was doing. God gave David time to come to his senses and seek forgiveness, but he only hardened his heart and continued to pretend that all was well.

2. The committing (2 Sam. 11:4)

One of the puzzles in this event is the willingness of Bathsheba to go with the messengers and submit to David's desires. The Hebrew word translated "took" (laqah) can mean simply "to get, receive, or acquire" or it can be translated "lay hold of, seize, or take away." However, there seems to be no evidence of force or violence in the text and the reader assumes that Bathsheba co-operated with the messengers. But why?

Did Bathsheba even know why David wanted her? If so, didn't she stop to consider that, having just finished her monthly period (v. 2), she was ripe for conception? Maybe she *wanted* to have a baby by the king! First Kings 1 reveals that Bathsheba was more a tiger than a housecat. "Did the young wife construct the situation?" asks Professor E. M. Blaiklock. "There is more than suspicion that she spread the net into which David so promptly fell."[4] Perhaps she thought David had news from the front about her husband, but it wasn't the king's job to deliver military announcements. Did she miss her husband's love and take her purification bath in public as a deliberate invitation to any man who happened to be watching? If she refused David's requests, would he punish her husband? (That happened anyway!)

No Jewish citizen had to obey a king who himself was disobeying God's law, for the king covenanted with God and the people to submit to the divine law. Did she think that submitting to David would put into her hands a weapon that might help her in the future, especially if her husband were killed in battle? We can ask these questions and many more, but we can't easily answer them. The biblical text doesn't tell us and educated guesses aren't much help.

The sin that David's lust had conceived was now about to be born, a sin that would bring with it sorrow and death. According to Proverbs 6, David was about to be robbed (v. 26), burned (vv. 27-28), disgraced and destroyed (vv. 30-33), just for a few minutes of forbidden pleasure. Hollywood movies, television, and modern fiction use stories about adultery as a means of entertainment, which only shows how bad things have become. Famous people admit they've been unfaithful to their spouses, but it doesn't seem to hurt either their popularity or their incomes. "No-fault divorces" simplify the procedure, but they don't prevent the painful emotional consequences of infidelity. Ministers and other counselors know that it isn't easy for victims to heal and rebuild their lives and homes, yet the media go on teaching people how to break their marriage vows and apparently get away with it.

David and Bathsheba sinned against God, for it is God who established marriage and wrote the rules that govern it. So serious was adultery in the nation of Israel that both the adulterer and the adulteress were taken out and stoned to death (Lev. 20:10; Deut. 22:22-24; John 8:1-6). God takes seriously the marriage vows brides and grooms make, even if they don't (Mal. 2:14; Heb. 13:4).

3. The covering (2 Sam. 11:5-27)

"And the woman conceived, and sent and told David, and said, I am with child" (v. 5 KJV). These are the only recorded words of Bathsheba in the entire episode, but they were the words David didn't want to hear. You can paraphrase her brief message, "The next step is yours." Being the tactician that he was, David immediately devised a plan to cover up his sin. He called Uriah home from the battlefield, hoping that this brave soldier would go home and spend time with his wife. In fact, David ordered him to go home (v. 8), but the soldier disobeyed and stayed with the king's servants that night. David even sent food from his own table so Uriah and his wife could enjoy a feast, but Uriah never took it home. We wonder if Uriah had heard something that made him suspicious. Palace servants are notorious gossips.

David had to think up another scheme, and his next expedient was to have a second interview with Uriah the next day, during which the king chided him for not going home. A true soldier, Uriah gently rebuked the king for suggesting that one of his own soldiers put personal pleasure ahead of duty, especially when their fellow soldiers were out on the battlefield. Even the Ark of God was in a tent, so why should Uriah enjoy his home and wife? First Samuel 21:5 suggests that David's soldiers abstained from intercourse while fulfilling their military duties (a regulation based on Lev. 15:16-18); so Uriah must have been surprised when his commander suggested such a thing.

David's third expedient was to invite

Uriah to have a meal with him before he returned to the battle. During the meal, David passed the cup so frequently that Uriah became drunk. But Uriah drunk proved to be a better man than David sober, for he once again refused to go home. Uriah was a soldier at heart, and even when alcohol tore down his defenses, he remained faithful to his calling. There was but one expedient left: Uriah had to die. If David couldn't entice Uriah to go home, he would have to get him out of the way so he could marry Uriah's widow, and the sooner they married, the better the scheme would work. David was breaking the Ten Commandments one by one. He coveted his neighbor's wife and committed adultery with her, and now he would bear false witness against his neighbor and order him to be killed. David thought he was deceiving everybody, but he was deceiving only himself. He thought he could escape guilt when all the while he was adding to his guilt, and he could not escape God's judgment. "He who covers his sins will not prosper" (Prov. 28:13 NKJV).

Joab had Rabbah under siege and ordered his men not to go too near the wall lest they be shot at and killed. Occasionally some Ammonite soldiers would come out the city gate and try to entice the Jewish soldiers to come closer and attack them, but Joab's orders were obeyed. Shrewd Joab may have read between the lines of David's letter and deduced that the only thing Uriah had that David could want would be Uriah's beautiful wife, so he cooperated with the plan. After all, knowing David's scheme would be another weapon Joab could use for his own protection someday. Besides, Joab had already killed Asahel, Abner (2 Sam. 2:17-24; 3:27ff), and would one day murder Amasa (20:6-10), so he understood these things. Joab knew he couldn't send Uriah up to the walls alone or it would look suspicious, so several of "the king's servants" (v. 24) died with him just so David could cover his sins. "The king's servants" may refer to David's bodyguard, the best of the Israelite troops (8:18).

Bathsheba's expressions of grief for her dead warrior husband were undoubtedly sincere, but they were mitigated by the knowledge that she would soon be living in the palace. People probably raised their eyebrows when she married so quickly after the funeral, and married the king at that, but when some six months later she delivered a baby boy, eyebrows went up again. Second Samuel 3:1-5 suggests Bathsheba is the seventh wife of David, but when you add Michal, who was childless, Bathsheba becomes the eighth. In Scripture, the number eight is often the sign of a new beginning, and with the birth of Solomon to David and Bathsheba, this hope was fulfilled.

However, David had unfinished business to take care of because the Lord was displeased with all he had done.

4. The confessing (2 Sam. 12:1-14)

Nathan had the privilege of delivering the message about God's covenant with David and his descendants (2 Sam. 7), but now the prophet had to perform spiritual surgery and confront the king about his sins. David had been covering his sins for at least six months, and Bathsheba's baby was about to be born. It wasn't an easy task the Lord had given Nathan, but it's obvious that he prepared carefully for his encounter with the guilty king.

The trial (vv. 1-6). In telling a story about the crime of another, Nathan prepared David for dealing with his own sins, and it's possible that David thought Nathan was presenting him with an actual case from the local court. Nathan was catching David off guard and could study the king's response and better know what to do next. Since David had been a shepherd himself, he would pay close attention to a story about the theft of an innocent lamb; and as king, he was obligated to see that poor families were given justice.

God directed Nathan to choose his words carefully so that they would remind David of what he had said and done. The prophet said that the ewe lamb "did eat of his [the poor man's] own meat, and drank of his own cup, and lay in his bosom" (v. 3 KJV). This should have reminded David of Uriah's speech in 11:11: "Shall I then go to my house to eat and drink, and to lie with my wife?" (NKJV). But it wasn't until Nathan told about the rich man stealing and killing the lamb that David showed any response, and then he was angry at another man's sins! (See 1 Sam. 25:13, 22, 33 for another example of David's anger.) David didn't seem to realize that he was the rich man, Uriah was the poor man, and Bathsheba was the ewe lamb he had stolen. The "traveler" whom the rich man fed represents the temptation and lust that visited David on the roof and then controlled him. If we open the door, sin comes in as a guest but soon becomes the master. (See Gen. 4:6-7.)

David passed judgment on the rich man without realizing he was passing judgment on himself. Of all blindness, the worst kind is that which makes us blind to ourselves. "Many men seem perfect strangers to their own character," said Joseph Butler, and David was among them.[5] How easy it is to be convicted about other people's sins (Matt. 7:1-3)! Stealing and killing a domestic animal wasn't a capital offense in Israel, but David was so angry he exaggerated both the crime and the punishment. Until now, he had been minimizing the consequences and doing nothing, when actually what he did to Uriah *was* worthy of death. Both David and Bathsheba should have been stoned to death (Lev. 20:10; Deut. 22:22-24; John 8:1-6). Knowing the law, David realized that four sheep had to be given to repay the owner whose ewe lamb had been stolen (Ex. 22:1).

The verdict (vv. 7-9). The prophet realized that though David was very angry, he was also unguarded and ready for the sword of the Spirit to pierce his heart (Heb. 4:12; Eph. 6:17). With one quick thrust, Nathan said, "You are the man!" (v. 7 NKJV) and proceeded to hold up the mirror that revealed how dirty the king really was. Nathan explained to David why he stole Uriah's little ewe lamb. First, the king forgot the goodness of the Lord who had given him everything he had *and would have given him more* (v. 7-8). Second, David had despised God's commandment and acted as though he had the privilege of sinning (v. 9). By coveting, committing adultery, bearing false witness, and killing, David had broken four of the Ten Commandments, *and he thought he could get away with it!* It was bad enough that David arranged to have Uriah killed, but he used the sword of the enemy to do it!

The sentence (vv. 10-12). David's adultery with Bathsheba was a sin of passion, a sin of the moment that overtook him, but his sin of having Uriah killed was a premeditated crime that was deliberate and disgraceful. This may be why 1 Kings 15:5 emphasizes "the matter of Uriah the Hittite" and says nothing about Bathsheba. But the Lord judged both sins and David paid dearly for his lust and deceit. God repaid David "in kind" (Deut. 19:21; Ex. 21:23-25; Lev. 24:20), a spiritual principle that David expressed in his "victory psalm" after Saul died (Ps. 18:25-27).

The sword did not depart from the king's household, and his wives were taken and violated just as he had taken Bathsheba. Indeed, David did pay fourfold, for Bathsheba's baby died, and his sons Amnon, Absalom, and Adonijah were slain (13:29; 18:14-15; 1 Kings 2:25). David's beautiful daughter Tamar was raped by her half brother (chap. 13), and David's concubines were humiliated publicly by Absalom when he captured the kingdom (16:22). For the rest of David's lifetime, he experienced one tragedy after another, either in his family or in the kingdom. What a price he paid for those few minutes of passion with his neighbor's wife!

The punishments God assigned to David were already stated in the covenant God had with Israel and which the king was expected to obey (Lev. 26; Deut. 27–30). If the nation rebelled against God, He would slay their sons in battle (Lev. 26:17; Deut. 28:25-26), take away their children (Lev. 26:22; Deut. 28:18), give their wives to others (Deut. 28:30), and even take Israel out of its land into foreign exile (Deut. 28:63-68). Because of Absalom's rebellion, David was forced to flee Jerusalem and live in the wilderness. But the covenant also included a section on repentance and pardon (Deut. 30; Lev. 26:40ff), and David took it seriously.

The pardon (vv. 13-14). The condemned prisoner knew that the verdict was true and the sentence was just, so without any argument, he confessed: "I have sinned against the Lord" (v. 13).[6] Nathan assured David that the Lord had put away his sin. "If we confess our sins, He is faithful and just to forgive us our sins, and to cleanse us from all unrighteousness" (1 John 1:9 NKJV). "If You, Lord, should mark iniquities, O Lord, who could stand? But there is forgiveness with You, that You may be feared" (Ps. 130:3-4 NKJV).

No wonder David later wrote that the Lord "forgives all your iniquities . . . [and] redeems your life from destruction. . . . As far as the east is from the west, so far has He removed our transgressions from us" (Ps. 103:3-4, 12 NKJV).

But there was a "however" in Nathan's reply, for though God in His grace had forgiven David's sins, God in His government had to permit David to experience the consequences of those sins, beginning with the death of Bathsheba's baby. All during David's months of silence, he had suffered intensely, as you can detect when you read his two prayers of confession (Pss. 32 and 51). Psalm 32 pictures a sick old man instead of a virile warrior, and Psalm 51 describes a believer who had lost almost everything—his purity, joy, witness, wisdom, and peace—a man who was afraid God would take the Holy Spirit from him as He had done to Saul. David went through intense emotional and physical pain, but he left behind two prayers that are precious to all believers who have sinned.

Because of Christ's finished work on the cross, God is able to save lost sinners and forgive disobedient saints, and the sooner the lost and the disobedient turn to the Lord and repent, the better off they will be. David wrote, "I said, 'I will confess my transgressions to the Lord,' and You forgave the iniquity of my sin. For this cause everyone who is godly shall pray to You in a time when You may be found" (Ps. 32:5-6 NKJV). "Seek the Lord while He may be found, call upon Him while He is near" (Isa. 55:6 NKJV).

5. The chastening (2 Sam. 12:15-23)

Chastening is not punishment meted out by an angry judge who wants to uphold the law; rather, it's difficulty permitted by a loving Father who wants His children to submit to His will and develop godly character. Chastening is an expression of God's love (Prov. 3:11-12), and the Greek word used in Hebrews 12:5-13 means "child training, instruction, discipline." Greek boys were taken to the gymnasium early in life and taught to run, wrestle, box, swim, and throw, exercises that were assigned so the boys would develop "a sound mind in a sound body." In the Christian life, chastening isn't always God's response to our disobedience; sometimes He's preparing us for challenges yet to come, like a coach preparing athletes for the Olympics. If there were no painful consequences to sin or subsequent chastening from the hand of God, what kind of a daring and irresponsible world would we be living in?

Bathsheba delivered the son that Nathan had predicted would die, but David still fasted and prayed and asked God for healing for the child. The Lord didn't interrupt David's prayers and tell him to stop interceding; after all the sins David had committed, it didn't hurt him to spend the day in prayer. During those months of silence and separation from God, David had a lot to catch up on! The baby lived only a week and the parents weren't able to circumcise and name their son on the eighth day. Their son Solomon ended up with two names (vv. 24-25), but this son didn't even have one.

Why would a loving and just God not answer a grieving and repentant father's prayers and heal the child?[7] After all, it wasn't the baby's fault that his father and mother had sinned against the Lord. For that matter, why did God allow Uriah and some fellow soldiers to die at Rabbah just so David could marry Bathsheba? Keep asking similar questions and you will end up with the ultimate question, "Why does a loving God permit evil in the world?" Eventually David looked back and saw this painful experience as God's "goodness and mercy" (Ps. 23:6) both to him and to the baby. "Shall not the Judge of all the earth do right?" asked Abraham (Gen. 18:25 NKJV). When he heard the bad news of God's judgment on his family, even backslidden Eli confessed, "It is the Lord. Let Him do what seems good to Him" (1 Sam. 3:18 NKJV). There are no easy answers to settle our minds, but there are plenty of dependable promises to heal our hearts, and faith is nurtured on promises, not explanations.

This much is sure: David's week of fasting and prayer for the baby showed his faith in the Lord and his love for Bathsheba and her little son. Very few Eastern monarchs would have shed a tear or expressed a sentence of sorrow if a baby died who had been born to one of the harem "wives." In spite of his many sins, David was still a tender shepherd and a man after God's own heart; he had not been "hardened by the deceitfulness of sin" (Heb. 3:13). He washed himself, changed his apparel, worshiped the Lord, and returned to life with its disappointments and duties. In Scripture, washing oneself and changing clothes symbolizes making a new beginning (Gen. 35:1-2; 41:14; 45:22; Ex. 19:10; Lev. 14:8-9; Jer. 52:33; Rev. 3:18). No matter how long or how much the Lord chastens us, "He will not always strive with us, nor will He keep his anger forever" (Ps. 103:9 NKJV). Because of God's grace and mercy, we can always make a new beginning.

David's words in verse 13 have brought great comfort to people who have experienced the death of a little one, but not every Old Testament student agrees that the king's words are a revelation from God. Perhaps he was just saying, "My son can't come back from the grave or the world of departed spirits, but one day I shall go there to him." But what kind of comfort does it bring us to know that everybody eventually dies? "He shall not return to me" states that David believed that his dead son would neither be reincarnated nor would he be resurrected before the Lord's time. It also affirms that David expected to see and recognize his son in the future life. Where was David eventually going? "I will dwell in the house of the Lord forever" (Ps. 23:6 NKJV; see also 11:7; 16:11; 17:15).[8]

6. The comforting (2 Sam. 12:24-25)

No matter how devastated the chastening hand of our loving Father makes us feel, there is comfort available from the Lord (see Isa. 40:1-2, 9-11, 28-31). Before her son died, God called Bathsheba "Uriah's wife" (v. 15), possibly because that's who she was when the boy was conceived; but in verse 24, she is David's wife, which suggests that, like David, she is also making a new beginning. What an evidence of God's grace that "the wife of Uriah" is mentioned in the genealogy of Messiah (Matt. 1:6), along with Tamar (v. 3; Gen. 38) and Rahab and Ruth (v. 5; Josh. 2 and 6:22-25; Ruth 1, 4; Deut. 23:3).

At least nine months are compressed into verses 24 and 25, nine months of God's grace and tender mercy. It was God who caused the conception to occur and who saw to it that the baby would have the "genetic structure" that he would need to accomplish God's will (Ps. 139:13-16). In a very special way, "the Lord loved him" and even gave Solomon ("peaceable") a special name, "Jedidiah—loved by the Lord." Since "David" means "beloved," father and son were bound together by similar names. God had told David that this son would be born and that he would build the temple (7:12-13; 1 Chron. 22:6-10), and He kept His promise. Every time David and Bathsheba looked at Solomon, his very presence reminded them that God had forgiven their past and guaranteed their plans for the future.

7. The conquering (2 Sam. 12:26-31; 1 Chron. 20:1-3)

But there was still kingdom work for David to do, including helping Joab finish the siege of Rabbah (10:14; 11:1; 12:26-31). Little by little, the Israelite army had taken over the city, first the area where the royal palace stood (v. 26), and then the section that controlled the water supply (v. 27). Joab was now ready for that final assault that would bring the siege to an end, but he wanted the king to be there to lead the army. Whatever his faults, Joab at least wanted to bring honor to his king. David went to Rabbah and led the troops in the final foray that brought the city to its knees.

No king could wear a crown very long that weighed from fifty to seventy-five pounds, so David's "coronation" was a brief but official act of state, claiming Ammon as his territory. (The imperial state crown used by the kings and queens of England weighs less than three pounds, and monarchs have found wearing it a bit of a burden!) The crown was very valuable, so David took it along with the abundant spoil he found in the city. Most of this wealth probably went into the Lord's treasury and was used in the building of the temple.

David put some of his prisoners of war to work with saws, picks, and axes, and others to making bricks. God in His grace gave David this victory even though he had been a rebellious man. He and his army then returned to Jerusalem where he would experience further chastening, this time from adult members of his own family. He had forced the Ammonites to drop their swords, but now the sword would be drawn in his own family.

CHAPTER SIX
DAVID'S UNRULY SONS
2 Samuel 13–14

We have seen in the first ten chapters of 2 Samuel how God empowered David to defeat Israel's enemies and establish and expand the kingdom. Then David committed the sins of adultery, murder, and deception (chap. 11-12), and the rest of the book describes David wrestling with problems caused by his own children. His days are dark and disappointing, but he still depends on the Lord, and the Lord enables him to overcome and prepare the nations for the reign of his son Solomon. What life does to us depends on what life finds in us, and in David was a muscular faith in the living God.

Absalom is the chief actor in this part of the drama, for it was Absalom who helped to turn the drama into a tragedy.[1] The three heirs to David's throne were Amnon, David's firstborn, Absalom, his third son,[2] and Adonijah, who was born fourth (1 Chron. 3:1-2). God had warned David that the sword would not depart from his own household (12:10), and Absalom (which means "peaceful") was the first to take up that sword. David's judgment against the rich man in Nathan's story was, "He shall restore the lamb fourfold" (12:6), and that judgment fell upon David's own head. Bathsheba's baby died; Absalom killed Amnon for raping Tamar; Joab killed Absalom during the battle of Mount Ephraim; and Adonijah was slain for trying to usurp the throne from Solomon (1 Kings 2:12-25).

David was reigning over Israel, but sin and death were reigning within his own family (Rom. 5:14, 17, 21). God had forgiven David's sins (12:13), but David was discovering that the consequences of *forgiven* sin are very painful. God had blessed David with many sons (1 Chron. 28:5), but now the Lord would turn some of those blessings into curses (Mal. 2:1-2). "Your own wickedness will correct you, and your backslidings will rebuke you" (Jer. 2:19 NKJV). The events in chapters 13 and 14 unfold like a tragic symphony in five movements: from love to lust (13:1-14), from lust to hatred (13:15-22), from hatred to murder (13:23-36), from murder to exile (13:37-39), and from exile to reconciliation (14:1-23).

1. From love to lust (2 Sam. 13:1-14)

Absalom is mentioned first because chapters 13-19 focus on the "Absalom story," and Tamar was Absalom's full sister. Both Tamar and Absalom were noted for their physical beauty (13:1; 14:25). Their mother was Maacah, a princess from the royal house of Talmai in Geshur, a small Aramean kingdom near what we know as the Sea of Galilee. David had no doubt taken Maacah as his wife in order to establish a peace treaty with her father. The fact that Absalom had royal blood in his veins from both his father and his mother may have spurred him on in his egotistical quest for the kingdom.

Amnon was the oldest of David's sons and the apparent heir to the throne, so perhaps he felt he had privileges that the other sons didn't have. It was evil for him to nurture an abnormal love for his half sister and he should have stopped feeding that appetite the moment it started (Matt. 5:27-30). The sin was not only unnatural, but it violated the standard of sexual purity established by God's law (Lev. 18:9-11; 20:17; Deut. 27:22). However, he became so infatuated with Tamar that he really thought he loved her and became ill thinking about it. The virgin princesses were kept secluded in their own quarters, apart even from their male relatives, and Amnon's imagination worked overtime as he thought about her.

Jonadab was Amnon's cousin, the son of David's brother Shammah, here called Shimeah (1 Sam. 16:9), and he was a very crafty man, probably a minor official in the palace. He will show up again in 14:32 after Amnon has been killed by Absalom's servants. Anybody in our lives who makes it easy for us to sin is certainly not much of a friend; in fact, by following Jonadab's advice, Amnon ended up becoming a rapist, committing incest, and getting killed.

Amnon must have begun to recover from his "love sickness" because he had to pretend to be ill when David came to visit him. Perhaps Amnon was thinking, "If my father committed adultery and murder and got away with it, surely I can get away with rape." Such is the destructive power of a bad example. "If the godly compromise with the wicked, it is like polluting a fountain or muddying a spring" (Prov. 25:26 NLT). David's family was now polluted and the consequences would be calamitous. David was known for his wisdom and keen insight (14:17, 20), but after the "Bathsheba affair," he seems to have lost ground. By ordering Tamar to obey her half brother's wishes, he sent her into pain and humiliation; and when two years later David allowed Amnon to attend Absalom's feast, he sent his firstborn to his death. David the deceiver was himself deceived!

Tamar baked the special cakes for Amnon, who asked everyone to leave so he could enjoy the meal with his sister, and then he forcibly violated her. What he thought was love was really only lust, a passion that so controlled him that he became like an animal. Of course she resisted him as long as she could. Her refusal to cooperate was based on the law of God and the responsibility of the nation of Israel to be different from their pagan neighbors (v. 12). David's sin had given occasion to the enemy to blaspheme God (12:14). Her use of the words "folly" and "fool" (vv. 12-13 KJV) remind us of Genesis 34 and Judges 19–20, two other despicable rape scenes in Scripture. (See Gen. 34:7; Judg. 19:23-24; 20:6, 10.) Tamar tried to stall for time by suggesting that he ask the king for permission to marry her (v. 13), even though she knew that such a marriage was prohibited by the Law of Moses (Lev. 18:9-11; 20:17; Deut. 27:22).[3]

2. From lust to hatred (2 Sam. 13:15-22)

Amnon thought he loved Tamar. First he was distressed over her (vv. 1-2), and then he became ill longing for her (v. 2) even to the point of looking haggard (v. 4). But after he committed the shameful act, he hated Tamar vehemently and wanted to get rid of her! True love would never violate another person's body just to satisfy selfish appetites, nor would true love try to persuade someone to disobey the law of God. In his sensual cravings, Amnon confused lust with love and didn't realize that there is a fine line between selfish love (lust) and hatred. Before he sinned, he wanted Tamar all to himself; but after he sinned, he couldn't get rid of her fast enough.

Sexual sins usually produce that kind of emotional damage. When you treat other people like things to be used, you end up throwing them aside like broken toys or old clothes. The word "woman" is not in the Hebrew text of verse 17, so Amnon was saying, "Throw this thing out!" This explains why Tamar accused Amnon of being even more cruel by casting her aside than by raping her. Having lost her virginity, Tamar was not a good prospect for marriage, and she could no longer reside in the apartments with the virgins. Where would she go? Who would take her in? Who would even want her? How could she prove that Amnon was the aggressor and that she hadn't seduced him?

She went to the apartment of her brother Absalom, because in a polygamous society, it was the responsibility of a full brother to protect the honor of a full sister.[4] When Absalom saw her tears, her torn garment, and the ashes on her head, he realized that she was in great pain and humiliation, and he deduced that Amnon had violated her. His question "Has that Amnon[5], your brother, been with you?" (v. 20 NIV) reveals this, for the phrase "been with you" was a euphemism for "gone to bed with you." Palace gossips don't miss much, so it's probable that Absalom heard of Amnon's "illness" and Tamar's intended visit to his apartment. But if Absalom was so concerned about his sister, why didn't he warn her to stay away from Amnon? The king had ordered Tamar to visit her half brother, and Absalom's words couldn't change the king's command. About all Absalom could do was caution her not to be left alone with him.

Tamar may have said that she was going to the king to tell him what happened, but her brother suggested that she wait. Why? Because Absalom's cunning brain was already at work on a scheme that would accomplish three purposes: avenge Tamar, get rid of Amnon, and put himself next in line for the throne! His statement "He is your brother" (v. 20) means, "If it were any other man, I would avenge you immediately; but since it's your brother, I'll have to be patient and wait for an opportunity." Absalom was trying to avoid a public scandal that would grieve the family and hurt his own plans to seize the throne.

King David did hear about the tragedy and became very angry, but what could he say? The memory of his own sins shut his mouth, and how could he punish his firstborn son and the heir to his throne? According to the law, if a man raped a virgin not engaged to be married, he had to pay her father a fine and marry her, and he could never divorce her (Deut. 22:28-29). However, the law also prohibited the marriage of half brothers and half sisters, so marriage was out of the question (Lev. 18:9). David had committed two capital crimes—adultery and murder—and God had not applied the law to him.

So, neither David nor Absalom said anything to Amnon about his wicked deed. In fact, Absalom never spoke to him at all ("neither good nor bad") but simply waited for the right time to kill Amnon and avenge his sister. However, Amnon's friend Jonadab knew that Absalom wanted to kill Amnon, for he said, ". . . by the intent of Absalom this has been determined since the day that he violated his sister Tamar" (13:32 NASB). If Jonadab figured out what was going on, perhaps others suspected something also. Amnon's lust had turned to hatred, but now it was Absalom who was nurturing hatred in his heart, and that hatred would give birth to murder (Matt. 5:21-22). Then, with

Amnon out of the way, Absalom could become king.[6]

3. From hatred to murder (2 Sam. 13:23-36)

The French author Emile Gaboriau wrote, "Revenge is a luscious fruit which you must leave to ripen." For two years Absalom waited to avenge the rape of his sister, but when the time came, he was ready to act. Thanks to the generosity of their father, the princes not only held government offices but they also owned lands, flocks, and herds. Absalom had his land and flocks at Baal Hazor, about fourteen miles north of Jerusalem. It was customary in Israel to arrange great feasts at sheep-shearing time and invite members of the family as well as friends to share the festive occasion.

Absalom asked his father to come to the feast and bring his officials with him, but David declined, explaining that so many guests would be an unnecessary financial burden to his son. Absalom was hoping for that kind of response because he didn't want David and his guards present when Amnon was murdered. Then he asked if David would permit his successor Amnon to attend the feast, a request that made David feel apprehensive. But David knew that the crown prince often took his place at public functions that demanded royal presence, so why couldn't he represent the throne at Absalom's feast? Furthermore, two years had passed since Amnon violated Tamar and Absalom hadn't done anything against him. To guarantee some kind of safety for Amnon, David went the extra mile and permitted all the adult king's sons to attend the feast, assuming that Absalom wouldn't dare attack Amnon with so many of his family members present.

But during those two years, Absalom had perfected his plan and made arrangements for escape. His father David had arranged for the murder of Uriah the Hittite and had survived, so why shouldn't his son Absalom survive? Like his father, Absalom used other hands to do the deed, and at a time when the victim least expected it. David had made Uriah drunk but had failed to achieve his purpose, while Absalom made his brother drunk and accomplished what he had set out to do. Absalom followed his father's evil example and committed premeditated murder.

When Absalom gave the command and his servants killed Amnon, the princes at the feast fled for their lives, no doubt convinced that Absalom was planning to wipe out the royal family and take the throne. The young men mounted their mules, which were considered a "royal animal" (18:9; 1 Kings 1:33, 38, 44), and they hastened back to Jerusalem as fast as the animals could move. But Absalom also fled (vv. 34, 37) and probably his servants with him.

In verses 30-36, which are a parenthesis, we move from Baal Hazor to Jerusalem and see the escaping princes from David's point of view. Before the guards on the wall could clearly observe the men riding furiously toward Jerusalem and recognize them as the king's sons, a messenger arrived from Absalom's house announcing that all the king's sons had been slain! (Bad news travels fast and often is exaggerated.) David tore his garments and fell to the ground in grief (see 12:16), no doubt blaming himself for allowing his sons to attend Absalom's feast. David's nephew Jonadab, who knew more than he admitted,[7] gave the true account that only Amnon had been killed; but even this was a terrible blow to David, for Amnon was his firstborn and heir to the throne. The fleeing princes arrived safely and everyone joined in expressing grief because Amnon was dead and Absalom was the murderer.

The problem with revenge is that it doesn't really solve any problems and eventually turns around and hurts the perpetrator. "In taking revenge," wrote Francis Bacon, "a man is but even with his enemy, but in passing it over, he is superior."[8] No one was treated more unjustly and inhumanely than Jesus Christ at His trial and crucifixion, yet He refused to retaliate; and He is our example (1 Peter 2:18-25). The old slogan "Don't get mad—get even" may satisfy some people, but it can never be pleasing to the Lord. The Christian way is the way of forgiveness and faith, trusting the Lord to work everything out for our good and His glory (1 Peter 4:12-19).

4. From murder to exile (2 Samuel 13:37-39)

Twice we're told that Absalom fled (vv. 34, 37), and he probably did it during the confusion that ensued when the king's sons fled. Only Absalom and his guilty servants knew what was going to happen at the feast, so everybody else was caught unawares. They were all witnesses of the "murder most foul" and could easily testify that Absalom was guilty.

Absalom fled eighty miles northeast to the home of his maternal grandparents in Geshur, where his grandfather Talmai was king (3:3). No doubt this safe haven had been arranged beforehand, and it's likely that Talmai would have enjoyed seeing his grandson crowned king of Israel. Back in Jerusalem, David mourned over his firstborn son Amnon, but in Geshur, the exiled son was no doubt plotting how he could take the kingdom away from his father. Normal grief heals in its time, and after three years, David was comforted concerning the death of the crown prince.

The statement "And the soul of king David longed to go forth unto Absalom" (v. 39 KJV) has been given at least two interpretations. It means either that David wanted very much to see his son again, which is understandable, or that David planned to go after Absalom and deal with him, but his anger gradually quieted down. I prefer the second interpretation. If David had really wanted Absalom back home, he could have accomplished it very easily, since Joab was for it (14:22) and David's in-laws in Geshur would have cooperated. However, when Absalom did come home, David kept him at a distance for two years (14:28)! If the king was anxious to see his son again, he went about it in a peculiar way. It appears that a struggle was going on in David's heart: he knew that his son deserved punishment, but David was known for being lenient with his sons (1 Kings 1:6). David initially planned to deal severely with Absalom but decided against it as his attitude changed. As explained in chapter 14, David compromised by finally bringing Absalom home, but he punished him by delaying full reconciliation. It was five years before father and son saw each other face-to-face (13:38; 14:28).

5. From exile to reconciliation (2 Sam. 14:1-33)

Joab knew his king very well and recognized the signs of David's yearning for his exiled son. As head of the army, Joab was concerned that Israel have a crown prince ready to reign just in case something happened to David, who was now close to sixty. But Absalom couldn't come home unless David gave permission, and the king wouldn't give permission until he was convinced it was the right thing to do. It was the king's duty to uphold the law, and Absalom was guilty of plotting the murder of his half brother Amnon.[9]

David loved his son and undoubtedly was convicted about the way he had pampered him, but how could he get out of this dilemma? Joab provided the solution to the problem.

Joab reasons with the king (vv. 1-20). Just as Nathan had confronted David the sinner by telling him a story (12:1-7), so Joab confronted David the father and king by putting a fabricated account of a family problem into the mouth of a woman who was both wise and a very good actress. She came to the king dressed in mourning and told him about her family troubles. Her two sons had an argument in the field and the one killed the other. (This sounds like Cain and Abel, Gen. 4:8-16.) The other relatives wanted to slay the guilty son and avenge his brother's blood (Num. 35:6ff; Deut. 19:1-14), but she opposed them. Killing her only son would put an end to her family and "quench her coal" (v. 7). According to the law, the surviving son was guilty and should be slain (Ex. 21:12; Lev. 24:17), but she wanted the king to pardon her surviving son.

Nathan's story about the ewe lamb touched the heart of David the shepherd, and this story about a warring family moved the heart of David the father. His first response was to assure her he would "take up the case" (v. 8), but that wasn't good enough for her. Sometimes the wheels of government turn slowly, and her case was a matter of life and death. When she said she would assume the guilt of whatever decision he made, David promised to protect her if anybody approached her about the matter (vv. 9-10). But the woman still wasn't satisfied, so she asked the king to take an oath to assure her that her son would not be slain, and David agreed (v. 11). Taking an oath in the Lord's name was binding and could not be ignored.

The woman now had David in a corner (vv. 12-17). If he had agreed to protect a guilty son whom he did not know, how much more was he obligated to protect his own son whom he loved! She had come to him with a matter involving the future of one small family, but the matter concerning Absalom concerned the future of an entire nation. The king didn't want to see her only son and heir destroyed, but he was willing for the crown prince to be left in exile. He forgave the murderer of her son, so could he not forgive the man who plotted the murder of Amnon? How much longer will the king wait before he sends for his son? After all, life is brief, and when life ends, it's like water spilled into the earth and can't be recovered. Slaying the murderer can't bring back the victim, so why not give him another chance?

God is no respecter of persons, and His law is true, but even God devises ways to show mercy and forgive offenders (v. 14). He punishes sin, to be sure, but He also seeks for ways to reconcile sinners with Himself. (She may have had in mind Ex. 32:30-35 and 34:6-9.) Had He not forgiven David's sins? The woman confessed that she was afraid that her family would slay her son and rob her of the inheritance God had given them.

It was a stirring speech and David took it to heart. But being a wise man, he realized that the full import of the woman's plea went far beyond the boundaries of her family and property. David had insight enough to know that she was speaking about the king,

Absalom, and the future of the nation of Israel, God's inheritance. At this point he also must have understood that the entire story was pure fiction and that somebody else was behind all that the so-called widow had spoken. Then the truth came out that indeed it was Joab who had plotted the whole thing, but his motive was a noble one: "Your servant Joab did this to change the present situation" (v. 20 NIV).

Joab gives thanks to the king (vv. 21-27). No doubt it was Joab who brought the woman to have this audience with the king, and he probably remained in the room and heard all that the woman and the king said to each other. David had sworn to protect the woman and her son, so the king could do nothing but allow Absalom to come home; and he ordered Joab to go to Geshur and bring the exile back to Jerusalem. Joab's words in verse 22 suggest strongly that he had discussed the subject with David on more than one occasion, and he was overjoyed that the matter was now settled. Geshur was about eighty miles from Jerusalem, and Joab would waste no time making the journey; so Absalom could have been back home a week or ten days later.

However, there were restrictions placed on the crown prince. He had to remain on his own land, which almost amounted to house arrest, and he wasn't allowed to go to the palace and see his father. Perhaps David was testing his son to see if he could be trusted, or David may have thought that these restrictions would assure the people that the king wasn't pampering his difficult son. However, these limitations didn't hinder the expansion of Absalom's popularity, for the people loved and praised him. The fact that he had plotted the murder of his half brother and had proved his guilt by running away meant very little to the people, for people must have their idols, and what better idol than a young handsome prince? Lack of character was unimportant; what really mattered was status, wealth, and good looks.[10] In contemporary language, Absalom was a he-man, someone with "machismo," and the people envied and admired him. Times have not changed.

Whatever Absalom may have had, one thing he didn't have was a large number of sons to carry on his "famous" name. The three sons mentioned in verse 27 must have died very young, because 18:18 informs us that Absalom had no sons living at that time. We aren't surprised that he named his daughter after his sister Tamar. Always the egotist, Absalom erected a pillar to remind everybody of his greatness.

Joab brings Absalom to the king (vv. 28-33). A deceptive "wise woman" could see the king's face, but the king's own son was banished from his presence. Absalom put up with this arrangement for two years, trusting that Joab would bring about reconciliation between himself and his father, but Joab did nothing. Absalom knew that being banished from the king's presence meant he wasn't expected to be heir to the throne, and more than anything else, Absalom wanted to be king of Israel. A shrewd man like Joab must have realized that Absalom had designs on the throne and that the prince's growing popularity could provide him the support he needed to take over the kingdom. Knowing how volatile the situation was, the discerning general stayed away from Absalom lest he give the impression he was being controlled by the egotistical prince.

After two years of waiting, during which he had summoned Joab twice and been ignored, Absalom decided that drastic action was necessary. He commanded his servants to set fire to his neighbor's barley crop, and his neighbor happened to be Joab.[11] This got the general's attention, for the law required that an arsonist repay the owner of a field whose crop he had destroyed (Ex. 22:6). People knew about the fire, so Joab could visit Absalom without fear of being misunderstood.

Absalom presented Joab with two alternatives: either take him to the king and let him receive his son and forgive him, or take him to court and prove that he was guilty of a capital crime and deserved to die. Absalom would rather be slain than go on living in shameful house arrest. Joab was on the horns of a dilemma, for it was he who had masterminded Absalom's return to Jerusalem. Joab knew that the people would never permit their favorite royal personage to be tried and convicted of a crime, but how could Joab guarantee that the king would be reconciled to his son? Joab gave Absalom's message to David and David invited his son to come to see him, and the king received him with a kiss of reconciliation. Father and son were together after five years of separation (13:38; 14:28).

There is no record that Absalom was repentant and sought his father's forgiveness, or that he visited the temple and offered the required sacrifices. Father and son were together again, but it was a fragile truce and not a real peace. Absalom still had his hidden agenda and was determined to seize David's throne. Now that the prince was free, he could be visible in the city and enjoy the adulation of the crowds, while at the same time quietly organizing his sympathizers for the coming rebellion. David was about to lose his throne and crown, his concubines, his trusted adviser Ahithophel, and ultimately his son Absalom. It would be the darkest hour in David's life.

CHAPTER SEVEN
DAVID'S ESCAPE TO THE WILDERNESS
2 Samuel 15:1–16:14

It's one thing to experience God's power when you're facing giants or fighting armies, and quite something else when you're watching people tear your world apart. God was chastening David, but David knew that God's power could help him in the hour of pain as well as in the hour of conquest. He wrote in one of his exile psalms, "Many are they who say of me, 'There is no help for him in God.' But You, O Lord, are a shield for me, my glory and the One who lifts up my head" (Ps. 3:2-3 NKJV). David recognized that God's loving hand of discipline was upon him, and he admitted that he deserved every blow. But he also believed that God's gracious hand of power was still at work in his life, that the Lord hadn't forsaken him as He forsook Saul. The Lord was still working out His perfect will, and never did David rise to greater heights of faith and submission than when he was forced to leave Jerusalem and hide in the wilderness.

The passage introduces us to three kings.

1. Absalom—Israel's counterfeit king (2 Sam. 15:1-12)

If ever a man was equipped to be a demagogue[1] and lead people astray, that man was Absalom. He was a handsome man whose charm was difficult to resist (14:25-26), and he had royal blood in his veins from both his father and his mother. The fact that he had no character wasn't important to most of the people who, like sheep, would follow anybody who told them what they wanted to hear and gave them what they wanted to have. Newspaper editor H. L. Mencken's definition of a demagogue is rather extreme, but he gets the point across: "One who preaches doctrines he knows to be untrue to men he knows to be idiots." Novelist James Fenimore Cooper expressed it accurately: "One who advances his own interests by affecting a deep devotion to the interests of the people."

Absalom was not only a consummate liar, but he was a patient man who was able to discern just the right hour to act. He waited two years before having Amnon murdered (13:23), and now he waited four years before openly rebelling against his father and seizing the throne (v. 7).[2] When you read the "exile psalms" of David, you get the impression that at this time King David was ill and didn't have his hands on the affairs of the kingdom, thus giving Absalom opportunity to move in and take over.[3] With great skill, the egotistical prince used every device at his disposal to mesmerize the people and win their support. David had won the hearts of the people through sacrifice and service, but Absalom did it the easy way—and the modern way—by manufacturing an image of himself that the people couldn't resist. David was a hero; Absalom was only a celebrity. Alas, many of the people had gotten accustomed to their king and now took him for granted.

Absalom's campaign must have begun shortly after his reconciliation with his father, for now he was free to go wherever he pleased. His first move was to begin riding in a chariot pulled by horses and accompanied by fifty men who were his bodyguard and who announced his presence. The prophet Samuel had predicted this kind of behavior by Israel's kings (1 Sam. 8:11) and Moses had warned against the acquisition of horses (Deut. 17:16). David wrote in Psalm 20:7 (NKJV), "Some trust in chariots, and some in horses; but we will remember the name of the Lord our God."

Since David wasn't available to the people, Absalom met them personally on the road to the city gate when they came early each morning to have their grievances examined and their cases tried. The city gate was the "city hall" of the ancient cities (Ruth 4:1ff; Gen. 23:10; Deut. 22:15; 25:7), and he knew there would be many disgruntled people there wondering why the court system wasn't functioning efficiently. (See 2 Sam. 19:1-8.) Absalom would greet these visitors like old friends and find out where they came from and what their problems were. He agreed with all of them their complaints were right and should be settled in their favor by the king's court. It was gross flattery of the most despicable kind, but the people loved it. Absalom boasted that he would handle kingdom matters better if only he were a judge (v. 4), which was a subtle way of criticizing his father. When people started to bow to him because he was the crown prince, he reached out his hand and stopped them, pulled them to himself and kissed them (v. 5). This reminds us of the hypocritical kisses of Judas when he greeted Jesus in the garden (Matt. 26:47-50; Mark 14:45).

It took only four years for Absalom's magnetism to draw together a large number of devoted followers throughout the whole land. The people Absalom met returned home and told their friends and neighbors that they had spoken personally to the crown prince, and over the four-year period, this kind of endorsement won Absalom many friends. His rapid success at influencing the minds and hearts of a nation warns us that one day a leader will arise who will control the minds of people around the world (Rev. 13:3; 2 Thes. 2). Even the people of Israel will be deceived and sign a covenant with this ruler, and then he will turn on them and seek to destroy them (Dan. 9:26-27). Jesus told the Jewish leaders of His day, "I have come in My Father's name, and you do not receive me; if another comes in his own name, him you will receive" (John 5:43 NKJV).

Absalom had been deceiving his siblings and the Jewish nation for years, and when the right time came, he took a bold step and lied to his father (vv. 7-9). The prince was no longer under house arrest, so there was no need to get permission to leave Jerusalem, but in so doing he achieved several purposes. First, he could tell anybody who asked that he had his father's permission to go to Hebron to fulfill the vow he had made while exiled in Geshur. Second, it allayed any fears that might arise because of Absalom's former feast at which Amnon was killed. Third, it gave credence to his invitation to two hundred key people in David's administration who willingly attended the feast. When the guests saw these two hundred important people in Hebron, they must have been impressed. The fact that this was a feast connected with the fulfilling of a vow gave it the aura of a religious assembly (Deut. 23:21-23), for sacrifices were offered to the Lord. What could go wrong at a feast dedicated to the Lord? Absalom was now using the name of the Lord to hide his sins.[4]

Absalom's masterstroke was to win the support of Ahithophel, David's smartest counselor; and when the guests saw him at the feast, they felt confident that all was well. But Ahithophel did more than attend the celebration; he also joined Absalom in revolting against King David. It was probably Ahithophel who masterminded the entire operation. After all, David had violated Ahithophel's granddaughter Bathsheba and ordered her husband killed. (See 23:34; 1 Chron. 3:5.) This was Ahithophel's great opportunity to avenge himself on David. However, in supporting Absalom, Ahithophel was rejecting Bathsheba's son Solomon, whom God would choose to be the next ruler of Israel. At the same time, Ahithophel was taking steps toward his own death for, like Judas, he rejected the true king and went out and committed suicide. (See 17:23; Pss. 41:9; 55:12-14; Matt. 26:21-25; John 13:18; Acts 1:16.) Ahithophel had deceived David his king and sinned against the Lord, who had chosen David.

Why did Absalom decide to start his insurrection in Hebron? For one thing, it was the former capital of Judah, and perhaps there were people there who resented David's moving the capital to Jerusalem. Absalom was born in Hebron and could claim special kinship with the residents. Hebron was a sacred city to the Jews because it was assigned to the priests and had a connection with Caleb (Josh. 21:8-16). Located about twenty miles southwest of Jerusalem, Hebron was a walled city and the ideal city from which to invade Jerusalem and seize the throne. With two hundred of David's officials "imprisoned" behind Hebron's walls, it would be simple for Absalom to take over the kingdom.

2. David—Israel's true king (2 Sam. 15:13-23)

Absalom and Ahithophel had their trumpeters and messengers ready to act, and at the signal, the word quickly spread throughout the land: "Absalom is king! He reigns from Hebron!" The anonymous messenger who informed David actually helped to save the king's life. However lethargic David may have been before now, he immediately moved into action, because David always did his best during a crisis.

David takes charge (vv. 13-16). His first official order was for his family, officials and special bodyguard to leave Jerusalem immediately. If Absalom had the whole nation following him, it would be easy for armies from Judah and the northern tribes to surround Jerusalem and leave no way of escape. David knew that the same Absalom who killed Amnon would also kill his brothers and possibly even his father, so it was imperative that everybody flee. Furthermore, if Absalom had to attack Jerusalem, he would slaughter the inhabitants, and there was no reason for hundreds of innocent people to die. It was just like David to risk his own life and abandon his own throne in order to protect others. The servants pledged their loyalty to the king (v. 16) and so did his bodyguard (vv. 18-22). The ten concubines David left behind to manage the household would be violated by Absalom (16:20-23), an act that declared he had taken over his father's kingdom.

David mobilizes the forces (vv. 17-22). David and the people with him escaped to the northeast, moving from Jerusalem opposite the direction of Hebron. When they came to the last house in the suburbs of Jerusalem, they rested and David reviewed his troops. These included David's personal bodyguard (the Cherethites and the Pelethites, 8:18; 23:22-23) as well as six hundred Philistines who had followed David from Gath and were under the command of Ittai (1 Sam. 27:3). Ittai assured David that they were completely loyal to the king. This Gentile's testimony of fidelity to David (v. 21) is one of the great confessions of faith and faithfulness found in Scripture and ranks with that of Ruth (1:16) and the Roman centurion (Matt. 8:5-13).[5]

David weeps (v. 23). The key word in this section is "passed over" or "crossed over," used nine times. David and his people crossed the Kidron (v. 23), which in winter flowed powerfully on the east side of Jerusalem and had to be crossed to reach the Mount of Olives. The scene reminds us of our Lord's experience when He went to the garden (John 18:1). At that very hour, Judas, one of His own disciples, was betraying Him and arranging for His arrest. The people wept as they quickly moved along and their king wept with them, though perhaps for a different reason (vv. 23, 30). His own son had betrayed him, along with his friend and confidential adviser, and the foolish people for whom the king had done so much were ignorant of what was going on. David might have prayed as Jesus did on the cross, "Father, forgive them, for they know not what they do" (Luke 23:34).

Was David feeling the weight of guilt as once again Absalom, his beloved son, defied God's will and broke his father's heart? He and his son had been reconciled, but the young man had shown no contrition for his sins nor had he asked forgiveness from his father or from the Lord. "The sword shall not depart from your household" had been the ominous sentence from the mouth of God's prophet, and it was being fulfilled. Bathsheba's baby had died and Amnon had been murdered. David didn't want Absalom to die (18:5), but the young man would be slain by Joab, the third "installment" in David's painful payment (12:6). Adonijah would also die in an aborted attempt to become king (1 Kings 1), and then the debt would be paid.

For the second time in his life, David is forced to flee into the wilderness to save his life. As a young man, he fled the jealous rage of King Saul, and now he was seeking refuge from the hypocritical deceptions of his son Absalom and his former counselor, Ahithophel. By leaving Jerusalem, David had spared the city a bloodbath, but now he and his family were in danger, and what was the future of the kingdom and God's covenant with David?

3. Jehovah—Israel's sovereign King (2 Sam. 15:24–16:14)

When you read David's exile psalms, you can't help but see his trust in God and his conviction that no matter how disordered and disturbed everything was, the Lord was still on His throne. No matter how David felt, he knew that the Lord would always keep His covenant and fulfill His promises. Psalm 4 might well have been the song David sang to God that first evening away from home, and Psalm 3 what he prayed the next morning. In Psalms 41 and 55, he poured out his heart to the Lord, and the Lord heard him and answered in His time. Psalms 61, 62, and 63 allow us to look into David's troubled heart as he asks God for guidance and strength. Note that each of these three psalms ends with a strong affirmation of faith in the Lord. We today can have courage and assurance in our own times of difficulty as we see how the Lord responded to David and his great needs.

The Lord acknowledges David's faith (15:24-29). Zadok and Abiathar shared the high priestly duties and had helped to bring the Ark to Jerusalem (1 Chron. 15:11ff), so they thought it wise to take the Ark to David. Absalom had usurped his father's throne, but the priests would not allow him to have the throne of God. They joined David's camp and brought many of the Levites with them, and Abiathar offered sacrifices (v. 24 NIV) and no doubt called upon God to guide and protect the king.

But David told them to take the Ark back to Jerusalem! He didn't want the throne of God treated like a good-luck charm as in the days of Eli when the glory departed from Israel (1 Sam. 4). Absalom and his men were trying to turn David's glory into shame (Ps. 4:2), but God's favor was upon the king and He would restore him to his throne. David had seen God's power and glory in His sanctuary (Ps. 63:2 and he would see it by faith there in the wilderness. But even if God rejected David, the king was prepared to accept Jehovah's sovereign will (v. 26).[6] Eli had made a similar statement (1 Sam. 3:18), but it was resignation, not dedication. In David's case, the king was totally yielding to the Lord and saying, "Not my will but your will be done."

Faith without works is dead, so David assigned the two priests to be his eyes and ears in Jerusalem and to send him all the information that would help him plan his strategy. Zadok's son Ahimaaz and Jonathan the son of Abiathar would be the messengers and bring the information to him. David was a gifted tactician, and when you read 1 Samuel 19–28, you discover that he had an effective spy system that kept him informed of Saul's every move. David would have agreed with the counsel attributed to Oliver Cromwell, "Put your trust in God, my boys, and keep your powder dry." Whatever Absalom might do to the king's officials, he wasn't likely to lay hands on the Lord's priests and Levites, and they could go about their work almost unnoticed. When the two priests and their sons returned to Jerusalem with the Ark, Absalom's followers must have interpreted their action as four votes for the new king.

The Lord sees David's tears (15:30). "The Bible was written in tears, and to tears it will yield its best treasures," said A. W. Tozer.[7] David was a strong and courageous man, but he wasn't afraid to weep openly. (Real men *do* weep, including Jesus and Paul.) We read about David's tears in Psalm 6, which might well have been an exile psalm (vv. 6-8), as well as in Psalms 30:5, 39:12, and 56:8. "Depart from me, all you workers of iniquity; for the Lord has heard the voice of my weeping" (Ps. 6:8 NKJV). "The sacrifices of God are a broken spirit, a broken and a contrite heart—these, O God, You will not despise" (Ps. 51:17 NKJV).

David certainly had much to weep over, for his sins had brought sorrow and death to his family. Amnon had been murdered and Tamar violated, and now Absalom—the king's own son—was in the process of usurping the throne of Israel and heading for certain death. David's friend and counselor Ahithophel had turned against him, and the people for whom David had often risked his life were abandoning him to follow an egotistical rebel who was never chosen by God. If ever a man had a right to weep, it was David. Like disobedient children being spanked, it's easy for people to weep when they're being chastened for their sins, and then forget about the pain when the spanking is over. But David's tears went much deeper. He was not only concerned for the welfare of his rebellious son but also for the safety of the nation and the future of Israel's God-given ministry to the world. God's covenant with David (2 Sam. 7) assured him that his throne would last forever, and this is fulfilled in Christ; but the promise also implied that Israel would not be destroyed or the lamp of David permanently extinguished (1 Kings 11:36; 15:4; 2 Kings 8:19; 21:7; Ps. 132:17). God would be faithful to keep His covenant, and David knew that his throne was safe in the hands of the Lord.

The Lord answers David's prayer (15:31-37). Another messenger arrived in David's camp and informed the king that Ahithophel had deserted him for Absalom (see v. 12). "Even my own familiar friend in whom I trusted, who ate my bread, has lifted up his heel against me" (Ps. 41:9 NKJV). "For it is not an enemy who reproaches me; then I could bear it. . . . But it was you, a man my equal, my companion and my acquaintance" (Ps. 55:11-14). What do you do when one of your closest confidants betrays you? You do what David did—you pray and you worship. "O Lord, I pray thee, turn the counsel of Ahithophel into foolishness. And it came to pass, that when David was come to the top of the mount . . . he worshipped" (v. 31 KJV).

And then David saw Hushai, who was the answer to his prayer! Hushai is called "David's friend" (v. 37; 1 Chron. 27:33), which implies he was a friend at court and a special counselor to the king. He was an Arkite, which means he came from a group of people who descended from Canaan and thus were Gentiles (Gen. 10:17; 1 Chron. 1:15). The town of Arka was located in Syria, about two hundred miles north of Damascus and five miles east of the sea. David's conquests had reached that far north, and some of the people had begun to worship the true God of Israel and to serve the king.

As he had done with Zadok and Abiathar and their two sons, so David did with Hushai: he sent him back to Jerusalem to "serve" Absalom. All five men were taking risks for the sake of the Lord and the kingdom, but they considered it an honor to serve their king and help restore him to the throne. All of the people to whom David gave special assignments could say, "We are your servants, ready to do whatever my lord the king commands" (v. 15 NKJV). This would be a fine statement for believers to adopt today as an expression of their devotion to Christ.

Hushai came to Jerusalem just as Absalom arrived, and the people's excitement at greeting the new king probably enabled Hushai to enter the city without being noticed, or perhaps he strengthened his position by joining the crowd. Of course, later Hushai would greet the king and go to work doing all he could to obstruct his plans and keep David informed. If there's one thing better than *getting* an answer to prayer it's *being* an answer to prayer, and Hushai was the answer to David's prayer. Humanly speaking, were it not for Hushai's counsel to Absalom, David might have been slain in the wilderness.

The Lord meets David's needs (16:1-4). When David met Hushai, it was an answer to prayer, but when he met Ziba, the encounter met an immediate need but created a problem that wasn't settled until David returned to the throne. Ziba had been one of Saul's land managers as well as a custodian of Jonathan's crippled son, Mephibosheth (chap. 9). Knowing that Ziba was an opportunist with evil motives, David was suspicious about Ziba's presence, his gifts, and the absence of Mephibosheth, who had been cared for by David. Ziba had brought a string of donkeys (NIV) for David and his family to use, as well as generous amounts of bread, wine, and fruit. The gifts were needed and appreciated, but David was concerned about the motive behind them.

Ziba lied to the king and did his best to discredit his young master, Mephibosheth. David was weary and deeply wounded within, and it wasn't the best time for him to be making character decisions. He accepted Ziba's story—which was later discredited (19:26-27)—and made a rash judgment that gave Ziba the property that rightfully belonged to Mephibosheth. "He who answers a matter before he hears it, it is folly and shame to him" (Prov. 18:13). God's leaders must constantly be on guard lest they make unwise decisions on the basis of incomplete information.

God honors David's submission (16:5-14). Through Ziba's lies, Satan attacked David as a serpent who deceives (2 Cor. 11:3; Gen. 3:1-7), and then through Shimei's words and stones, Satan came as a lion who devours (1 Peter 5:8). Ziba told lies and Shimei threw stones, and both were making it hard for David. The king was now near Bahurim[8] in the tribe of Benjamin, where the pro-Saul forces were still strong. Shimei was on the hillside opposite David and above him, and it was easy for him to throw stones and clumps of dirt at David and his people. David was exhausted and discouraged, and yet he never rose to greater heights than when he allowed Shimei to go on attacking him. Abishai was only too willing to cross over and kill the man who was attacking the king, but David wouldn't allow it. Abishai had also wanted to kill Saul in the camp of Israel (1 Sam. 26:6-8), and he assisted his brother Joab in murdering Abner (2 Sam. 3:30), so David knew that his words were not to be treated lightly.

"Get out, get out, you man of blood, you scoundrel!" shouted Shimei, but David didn't retaliate. Shimei was blaming David for the death of Saul and his sons, for after all, David was officially in the Philistine army when they died. The fact that David was miles away from the battlefield when their deaths occurred didn't seem to matter to Shimei. This loyal Benjamite probably blamed David for the death of Saul's son Ish-Bosheth, who inherited Saul's throne, and also Abner, Saul's loyal commander; and, of course, Uriah the Hittite as well. "You have come to ruin because you are a man of blood!" (v. 8). Shimei was breaking the law while giving vent to his hatred of David, for Exodus 22:28 says, "You shall not revile God, nor curse a ruler of your people" (NKJV).

David's attitude was one of submission because he accepted Shimei's abuse as from the hand of God. David had already announced that he would accept anything the Lord sent to him (15:26), and now he proved it. When David considered that he was an adulterer and a murderer who deserved to die, yet God let him live, why should he complain about some stones and dirt? And if Absalom, David's own son, was out to kill him, why should a total stranger be punished for slandering the king and throwing things at him? David had faith that God would one day balance the books and take care of people like Absalom and Shimei. Perhaps David was thinking of Deuteronomy 32:35: "It is mine to avenge; I will repay" (NIV; see Rom. 14:17-21). When David regained the throne, he pardoned Shimei (19:16-23), and later Solomon restricted him to Jerusalem where he could be watched. When Shimei arrogantly overstepped his bounds, he was arrested and executed (1 Kings 2:36-46).

David and the people went beyond Behurim some twenty miles to the ford of the Jordan River, possibly near Gilgal or Jericho, and there they rested. Very early the next morning they crossed the river and proceeded to Mahanaim (17:22, 24), where Jacob had prepared to meet his brother Esau and had wrestled with God (Gen. 32). Perhaps David remembered that event and gained courage as he thought of the army of angels that God sent to protect Jacob.

What did all this suffering accomplish for David? *It made him more like Jesus Christ!* He was rejected by his own people and betrayed by his own familiar friend. He gave up everything for the sake of the people and would have surrendered his own life to save his rebellious son who deserved to die. Like Jesus, David crossed the Kidron and went up Mount Olivet. He was falsely accused and shamefully treated, and yet he submitted to the sovereign will of God. "[W]ho, when He was reviled, did not revile in return; when He suffered, He did not threaten, but committed Himself to Him who judges righteously" (1 Peter 2:23 NKJV).

David had lost his throne, but Jehovah God was still on the throne and would keep His promises with His servant. Faithful to His covenant, the Lord remembered David and all the hardships that he endured (Ps. 132:1), and He remembers us today.

CHAPTER EIGHT
DAVID'S BITTERSWEET VICTORY
2 Samuel 16:15–18:33

When General Douglas MacArthur spoke before the United States Congress on April 19, 1951, he made the famous statement, "In war there is no substitute for victory." But more than one military expert has maintained that armed forces can only win battles and that in the long run, nobody really wins a war. Why? Because the price is too high. For every word in Hitler's book *Mein Kampf,* 125 people died in World War II. In view of modern atomic weapons, nobody would "win" World War III.

David's army and Absalom's army were about to engage in battle in a civil war that neither father nor son could "win," but both sides could lose. If David won, it meant death for his son Absalom and his friend Ahithophel; if Absalom won, it could mean death for David and other members of his family. In modern terms, it was a "catch-22" situation; in ancient terms, it would be a "pyrrhic victory."[1]

Absalom was trusting his charm, his popularity, his army, and the wisdom of Ahithophel, but David was trusting the Lord. "Hear my cry, O God; attend to my prayer. From the end of the earth I will cry to You, when my heart is overwhelmed; lead me to the rock that is higher than I" (Ps. 61:1-2 NKJV).

What did David experience during those difficult days?

1. David's throne was usurped. (2 Sam. 16:15-23)

This paragraph picks up the narrative that was interrupted at 15:37 so we could learn about David's escape and his encounters with Ziba and Shimei. Thanks to David's speedy departure, Absalom's rebellion was a bloodless coup and he took Jerusalem unopposed, which was just what David wanted (15:14). Unlike Absalom, David was a man with a shepherd's heart who thought first about the welfare of his people (24:17; Ps. 78:70-72).

Hushai won Absalom's confidence (vv. 16-19). As soon as possible, Hushai entered the king's audience chamber and officially presented himself to the new king. He didn't want Absalom to think he was a spy, although that's exactly what he was. He was God's man in Jerusalem to frustrate the counsel of Ahithophel. Absalom was no doubt surprised to see his father's counselor in Jerusalem, but his sarcastic greeting didn't upset Hushai, who spoke respectfully to him. Hushai's words to Absalom must be read very carefully or they will be misunderstood.

Hushai gave the usual respectful greeting "God save the king," *but he didn't say "King Absalom."* In his heart, he was referring to King David, but the new king didn't understand what Hushai was saying. In his pride, Absalom thought Hushai was calling him the king. Again, note that Hushai doesn't mention Absalom's name or say that he will serve the new king. In verse 18, Hushai is speaking about David, for the Lord had never chosen Absalom to be Israel's king; and Hushai didn't promise to serve Absalom but to serve "in the presence" of David's son. In other words, Hushai would be in the presence of Absalom, *but he would be serving the Lord and David.* A proud man, Absalom interpreted Hushai's words to apply to himself, and he accepted Hushai as another counselor. This decision was of the Lord and prepared the way for Absalom's defeat.

Absalom followed Ahithophel's counsel (vv. 20-23). Absalom had two important tasks to perform before he could rule the kingdom of Israel. The first was that he had to seize his father's throne and let it be known that he was officially the king. Unlike his father David, who sought the mind of the Lord through the Urim and Thummim or from a prophet, Absalom looked to human experience and wisdom—and from a human point of view, Ahithophel was among the very best. However, Ahithophel didn't seek the mind of the Lord nor did he want the will of the Lord. His primary goal was to avenge himself against David for the sin he had committed against his granddaughter Bathsheba and her husband, Uriah the Hittite.

It was customary for a new king to inherit the previous king's wives and harem, so when Absalom followed Ahithophel's counsel, he was declaring that he was now king of Israel (see 3:7, 12:8 and 1 Kings 2:22). By taking his father's concubines, Absalom was making himself totally abhorrent to his father and breaking down every possible bridge for reconciliation. The new king was telling his followers that there was no turning back and the revolution would continue. But unwittingly, he was doing even more: he was fulfilling Nathan's prophecy that David's wives would be violated in public (12:11-12). David had been on the roof of his house when he lusted after Bathsheba (11:2-4), and that's where David's wives would be violated.

2. David's prayer was answered. (2 Sam. 17:1-28)

Having achieved his first purpose and taken over the royal authority, Absalom now had to deal with the second matter and make sure that David and his followers didn't return and take back the kingdom. The solution was simple but drastic: he had to find his father and kill him. For guidance, Absalom turned to his two counselors for help.

Hushai's counsel prevailed (vv. 1-14).[2] Humanly speaking, if Absalom had followed Ahithophel's plan, David would have been slain and Absalom's problems solved. But David had prayed that God would turn Ahithophel's counsel into foolishness (15:31), and God used Hushai to do just that. Note that Ahithophel put himself front and center by using phrases like "Let me now choose . . . I will arise . . . I will come . . ." and so on. He wanted to be the general of the army because he wanted personally to supervise the murder of his enemy King David. His plan was a good one: use a small army that could move swiftly, attack suddenly at night, and have David's death as the one great goal. Ahithophel would then bring back David's followers and they would swear loyalty to the new king. It would be a quick victory and very little blood would be shed.

Hushai wasn't in the room when Ahithophel outlined his plan, so Absalom called him in and told him what his favorite counselor had said. Directed by the Lord, Hushai took an entirely different approach and focused on the ego of the young king. Hushai's reply isn't a series of "I will" statements about himself but rather a series of statements about the new king that couldn't help but ignite Absalom's imagination and inflate his ego. Hushai laid an effective verbal trap, and Absalom fell into it.

First, Hushai explained why Ahithophel's counsel wasn't wise "at this time," although it had been wise at other times (vv. 7-10). As for focusing only on the murder of David, Absalom knew that his father was a great tactician and a mighty warrior, surrounded by experienced soldiers who feared nothing. All of them were angry because they'd been driven from their homes. They were like a bear robbed of her cubs. (Hushai is a master of metaphor!) Furthermore, David was too smart to stay with the troops; he would hide in a safe place where he couldn't be trapped. His men would be on guard and would set ambushes and kill anybody who came near. David's army was too experienced in war to be unprepared for a sudden attack. A sudden attack by a small army would not work. If the invading army were repulsed, word would spread that Absalom's forces had been defeated, and then all his men would flee. Absalom would then begin and end his reign with a military disaster.

Then Hushai presented a plan that overcame all these difficulties. First, the new king himself must lead the army, and it must be the biggest army he could assemble "from Dan to Beersheba." This suggestion appealed to Absalom's inflated ego, and in his imagination he could see himself leading the army to a great victory. Of course, he wasn't a seasoned military man, but what difference did that make? What a way to begin his reign! Absalom didn't stop to consider that it would take time to gather his forces "from Dan to Beersheba," time that David could use to cross the Jordan River and "get lost." Hushai, of course, was interested in buying time for David so he could "get lost."

With such a large army at his command, Absalom didn't have to depend on a difficult surprise attack but could "fall on" David's men over a wide area, like the morning dew that falls on the ground. Wherever David's men fled, they would see Absalom's forces and there would be no escape. Instead of sparing David's forces, Absalom's army would wipe them out so they couldn't cause trouble in the future. Realizing that Absalom might be worried about the time element, Hushai answered his objections in verse 13. If during the delay in rounding up his troops Absalom heard that David had taken his men into a walled city, the task would be even easier. The whole nation would obey their new king and work together taking the city apart, stone by stone! What a demonstration of power!

Ahithophel's matter-of-fact speech was forgotten as Hushai's grand plan, punctuated with vivid mental pictures, gripped the hearts and minds of Absalom and his leaders. God had answered David's prayer and confused the counsel of Ahithophel. Absalom would ride at the front of his army, intent on victory, but he would meet with humiliating defeat. "The Lord brings the counsel of the nations to nothing; He makes the plans of the peoples of no effect. The counsel of the Lord stands forever, the plans of His heart to all generations" (Ps. 33:10-11 NKJV).

David's spy system worked (vv. 15-22). David and his people were camped at the fords of the Jordan, about twenty miles from Jerusalem, and the two runners were waiting at En Rogel in the Kidron Valley, less than a mile from Jerusalem. Hushai gave the message to the two priests and told them to tell David to cross over the Jordan as quickly as possible. He was not to delay. If Absalom changed his mind and adopted Ahithophel's plan, then all might be lost. Zadok and Abiathar told an anonymous maidservant; she took the message to Jonathan and Ahimiaaz, who immediately ran a mile south to the house of a collaborator in Bahurim. However, a young man saw them leave and recognized the priests' sons. Wanting to impress the new king, he told Absalom what was happening, and Absalom's guards started out after the two young men.

At this point, the account reads like the story of the two spies recorded in Joshua 2. Rahab hid the two spies under stalks of flax on the roof of her house. The wife in Bahurim hid the two runners in a cistern, covered the opening with a cloth, and sprinkled grain on the cloth. The cloth looked like it was there to provide a place to dry grain in the sun. Not obligated to assist Absalom in his evil plans, the woman sent the guards off in the wrong direction, and the young men were saved. They arrived at David's camp, gave the king the facts, and urged him to cross the Jordan immediately, which he did. The guards returned to Jerusalem empty-handed, but Absalom didn't see their failure as a serious problem. How wrong he was!

Ahithophel took his own life (v. 23). Why? Was it because Absalom hurt his feelings by rejecting his counsel? No, it was because he knew that Hushai's counsel would bring about Absalom's defeat, and Ahithophel was serving the wrong king. As a traitor against King David, Ahithophel would either be slain or banished forever from the kingdom. Rather than humiliate himself and his family in his death, he put his affairs in order and hanged himself. His suicide reminds us of what Judas did (Matt. 27:5) and points to what David had written in two of his wilderness psalms (Pss. 41:9; 55:12-15; see John 13:18). In Acts 1:15-22, Peter referred to two other psalms that concerned Judas (Pss. 69:25 and 109:8).

Ahithophel had been a faithful servant of the king and the kingdom until he determined in his heart to get vengeance on David for what he did to Bathsheba and Uriah. This desire for revenge so obsessed him that he ceased to be a servant of the Lord and began to serve his own sinful desires. He knew of Absalom's ambitions but kept them hidden from David, and he cooperated with the crown prince in the palace coup. But with all of his wisdom, Ahithophel was supporting the wrong king, and the Lord had to judge him. Both Ahithophel and Absalom ended up hanging from a tree. How tragic it is when a man or woman leads an exemplary and useful life and then fails dishonorably at the end. There are old fools as well as young fools, and Ahithophel was one of them. All of us need to pray that the Lord will help us to end well.

Friends cared for David (vv. 24-29). David and his party forded the river and came to Mahanaim, the former capital of the ten tribes when Saul's son Ish-Bosheth was king (2:8). It was at Mahanaim ("two camps, two hosts") that Jacob saw the army of angels God had sent to protect him (Gen. 32), but David had no such vision. However, God often uses human "angels" to help His servants, and this time it was Shobi, Machir, and Barzillai. They brought provisions for the king and his people and saw to it that they were adequately cared for. God prepared a table for David as his enemies were approaching (Ps. 23:5).

Absalom's army was commanded by Amasa, who was David's nephew and Joab's cousin (v. 25). Of course, Absalom was commander in chief (17:11). How sad that son was fighting against father, uncle against nephew, cousin against cousin, and citizen against citizen. War is bad enough, but a civil war makes an even worse war. Absalom and his men crossed the Jordan, intending to meet David's army somewhere near the forest of Ephraim, about three miles northwest of Mahanaim. The forest of Ephraim was probably named by some Ephraimites who crossed the river and settled on the western side in the region of Gilead.

3. David's son was slain. (2 Sam. 18:1-18)

Knowing that the enemy was soon to arrive, David numbered his troops, divided them into three companies, and placed Joab, Abishai, and Ittai as their commanders. Whatever approach

Absalom and Amasa used, David's men would be able to maneuver and help each other. David offered to accompany the army, but the people told him to stay in a place of safety in the walled city. (See 21:15-17, which occurred long before Absalom's rebellion.) "There are ten thousand of us but only one of you!" they argued. They knew that Absalom's soldiers would go after the king and not worry about the soldiers. If David stayed in the city, he could send out reinforcements if they were needed. David accepted their decisions; he didn't want to fight his son anyway.

But neither did he want the army to fight his son! Absalom had stood at the gate in Jerusalem and attacked his father (15:1-6); now David stood at a city gate and instructed the soldiers to go easy on Absalom. Absalom certainly hadn't been gentle with his father! He had murdered Amnon, driven David out of Jerusalem, seized his throne, violated David's concubines, and now he was out to kill David. That doesn't sound like the kind of man you would want to protect, but if David had one fault, it was pampering his sons (1 Kings 1:5-6; see 1 Sam. 3:13). But before we criticize David, we must remember that he was a man after God's own heart. Let's be thankful that our Father in heaven hasn't dealt with us according to our sins (Ps. 103:1-14). In His grace, He gives us what we don't deserve, and in His mercy He doesn't give us what we do deserve. Jesus didn't deserve to die, for He was sinless; yet He took the punishment that belonged to us. What a Savior!

The battle spread out across the area, and many soldiers died because of the density of the forest. We don't know how many men perished on each side, but it's likely that most of the ten thousand dead belonged to Absalom's army. Both the sword and the forest devoured their victims. (This metaphor has been used before in 1:22 and 2:26.) But God didn't need a sword to stop the rebel Absalom; He simply used the branch of a tree! How much his heavy head of hair contributed to this accident isn't recorded, but it's ironic that the thing he was so proud of (14:25-26) turned out to assist in his death. Indeed, pride does lead to judgment. Another example is Samson (Judg. 16). "He catches the wise in their own craftiness, and the counsel of the cunning comes quickly upon them" (Job 5:13 NKJV).

The soldiers who encountered Absalom hanging from the tree didn't dare touch him, but Joab had his own agenda. It was Joab who had orchestrated the reconciliation of David and Absalom, and now Joab ignored David's orders and killed the young man.[3] Absalom rejected Ahithophel's plan to "kill the king only," but Joab accepted it! There's a hint in verse 11 that Joab had quietly spread the word that he would reward any soldier who killed the rebellious son. The soldier who could have won the reward refused to kill Absalom for two reasons: he didn't want to disobey the king, and he wasn't sure Joab would defend him if the king found out about it. After all, David killed the man who said he killed Saul (1:1-16) as well as the two men who killed Saul's son Ish-Bosheth (4:1ff). The soldier knew that Joab didn't want to be caught issuing an order to kill the king's son when the king commanded otherwise. The death of Absalom marked the end of the war and the rebellion, so Joab withdrew his troops.

Both Absalom and Ahithophel died on trees, and to an Israelite, hanging a body on a tree was evidence that the deceased was cursed by God (Deut. 21:22-23; Gal. 3:13). When you consider the crimes these two men committed, is it any wonder they were cursed? Yet God in His grace forgave David of the same crimes and allowed him to live. At one time, Absalom was the most popular man in the kingdom, but he ended up being buried in a pit, his body covered with stones. Apparently his three sons had died (14:27), so there was no one left in his family to perpetuate his name; so he erected a pillar to keep his name alive (v. 18). Even the original pillar is gone, and the so-called Tomb of Absalom seen today in the Kidron Valley is from the days of the Herods. "The memory of the righteous is blessed, but the name of the wicked will rot" (Prov. 10:7 NKJV).

4. David's heart was broken. (2 Sam. 18:19-33)

The war was over and the rebellion ended. All that remained was for Joab to notify the king and return him safely to Jerusalem. But it was a bittersweet victory for David. When the enemy is your own son, there can be no triumph and no celebration.

Ahimaaz was a well-known runner (v. 27), and he volunteered to take the news to the king at Mahanaim, some three miles away. As enthusiastic as the young man was, he didn't realize what he was asking; for David was known to take out his anger and sorrow on the messengers (1:4-16; 4:8-12)! Although the word "tidings" that Ahimaaz used could apply to any kind of news, it usually referred to "good news," and there was no good news that day. Joab knew his king very well and knew that the report of Absalom's death must be conveyed with compassion and skill. To keep Ahimaaz safe, Joab selected a person known only as "the Cushite," who was possibly one of his own servants. Better that a foreign servant be slain than the son of a Jewish priest. However, after the Cushite left, Ahimaaz continued to annoy Joab and ask for permission to run. There was nothing good or bad to add to the news, so why run? Weary of hearing the young man's pleas, Joab gave him permission to go.

Ahimaaz reminds us of those bothersome people who want to be important but have nothing much to say. He took the long, easy route to Mahanaim through the valley, while the Cushite took the short, direct route over difficult terrain. Ahimaaz was a young man without a real message or the ability to convey that message in the right way. As the Cushite ran, he meditated on how to tell King David that his son was dead. What's the sense in running if you don't know how to share the news?

The scene shifts to Mahanaim where David is seated between the outer and inner gates of the city, waiting for the watchman in the tower to give him word that a messenger is on his way from the battlefield.[4] Even though he was unprepared to speak to the king, Ahimaaz put forth every effort and passed the Cushite on the road. David said, "He is a good man. He comes with good news" (v. 27 NIV). It's obvious that the character of the messenger has nothing to do with the contents of the message, but David was grasping for any straw of hope available.

Before he arrived at the gate, Ahimaaz was so anxious to give the news that he called out, "All is well."[5] Then he came to the king, bowed before him and told him that Joab had won the battle. When David asked about Absalom, the young messenger was not prepared or equipped to share the bad news, so he made an excuse that was undoubtedly a lie. In his feeble attempt to go down in history as the man who brought the news from the forest of Ephraim to Mahanaim, Ahimaaz ended up having nothing to say that David wanted to hear. What he said was correct, but he didn't say enough. He ended up standing to one side and watching the Cushite deliver the right message in the right way.

During my pastoral ministry, I've occasionally had to be the bearer of bad news. I can recall praying, pondering, and putting myself in the place of the waiting people, all the while trying to assemble words that would bring the least amount of hurt. It wasn't easy. Someone has defined "tact" as "the knack of making a point without making an enemy," and the Cushite had tact.

The text says that David "trembled violently" when he comprehended that Absalom had been slain. No doubt he had prayed that the worst would not happen, but it happened just the same. In one sense, David pronounced his own sentence when he said to Nathan, "And he shall restore the lamb fourfold" (12:5), for this was the final payment of David's great debt. The baby had died, Tamar was raped, Amnon was slain and now Absalom was dead. David tasted once again the pain of forgiven sin.

David's tears reveal the broken heart of a loving father. Speaking about David's sorrow, Charles Spurgeon said, "[I]t would be wise to sympathize as far as we can, than to sit in judgment upon a case which has never been our own."[6] David wept when he heard about the death of Jonathan and Saul (1:11-12), the murder of Abner (3:32), and the murder of Amnon (13:33-36), so why shouldn't he weep over the death of his beloved son Absalom? Once again, we see the heart of God revealed in the heart of David, for Christ died for us when we were sinners and living as the enemies of God (Rom. 5:7-10). David would have died for Absalom, but Jesus *did die for us!*

David's problem wasn't that he grieved over his son, for grief is a very human response and tears are a part of the healing. His problem was that he grieved excessively and wouldn't permit himself to be comforted. His response was abnormal. He neglected himself and his responsibilities and had to be soundly rebuked by Joab before he would take steps to return to Jerusalem and save the kingdom. His troubles weren't over, but the Lord would empower him to be the ruler He wanted him to be.

The Lord can heal a broken heart, if we give all the pieces to Him and obey Him by faith.

CHAPTER NINE
DAVID'S RETURN AND RENEWED PROBLEMS
2 Samuel 19:1-40

The repeated theme in this chapter is "bringing back the king" (vv. 10, 11, 12, 15, 41). David was across the Jordan in Mahanaim, but he belonged in Jerusalem. All the tribes, including David's own tribe of Judah, had participated in Absalom's rebellion to some extent; now it was time for them to bring their king back to Jerusalem. Years of intrigue and intertribal conflict left Israel a deeply divided nation, and there was a desperate need for a strong display of unity and loyalty. This chapter describes five steps David took to bring about the healing of the nation.

1. David focuses his perspective. (19:1-8)

The saintly Scottish pastor Andrew Bonar (1810–1892) used to say, "Let us be as watchful after the victory as before the battle." It's possible to win the battle but lose the victory, which is what happened to David after Joab defeated Absalom and his army. What should have been a day of celebration for David's army at Mahanaim became a confused time of embarrassment and shame as the people[1] stole back into the city as if they had been humiliated by defeat. They had risked their lives for king and country, and were now treated like criminals!

It was very unlike David to be insensitive to the sacrifices his men made as they served him (see 23:13-17; 1 Sam. 30:21-30), but that day he was so obsessed with the death of Absalom that he could think of nothing else. By isolating himself from his men, the king turned a military victory into an emotional defeat. David was not only a great warrior but also a deeply emotional poet and musician, a man who could go from the depths of despair into the heights of glory while writing one psalm. David had experienced a difficult time after the death of Amnon (13:37-39), and the death of his favorite son Absalom left him inconsolable. David's attitude puzzled his followers, who saw Absalom as a liar, a murderer, a traitor, and a rebel.

Certainly we expect a father to grieve over the tragic death of a son and overlook the son's mistakes and sins. But leaders must still lead, even if their hearts are broken; that's one of the prices that leaders must pay. On October 10, 1950, Sir Winston Churchill was introduced at the University of Copenhagen as "the architect of victory" in World War II. Churchill replied: "I was only the servant of my country and had I, at any moment, failed to express her unflinching resolve to fight and conquer, I should at once have been rightly cast aside." David the father forgot that he was also David the king and that he still had his crown because his brave soldiers put the good of the nation ahead of their own personal interests.

Joab's short but cutting speech jolted the king back to reality, and David took his place at the gate—where his men came to him and where he acknowledged their brave service. It's likely that David didn't yet know that it was Joab who engineered Absalom's death and burial, otherwise his response might have been different. It didn't take long for David to find out what Joab and his men did and this helped to precipitate David's naming Amasa as general of the army (v. 13; and see 1 Kings 2:5).

The one thing that's missing in the entire Absalom episode is David's seeking the mind of the Lord as he made decisions. The younger David called for the Urim and Thummim or asked for the counsel of a prophet, but apart from his prayer in 15:31, we don't find David requesting guidance. Of course, the wilderness psalms record his concerns and prayers, so we know he wasn't depending on himself and his leaders alone. But we wish David had sought God's direction as he dealt with Absalom and the problems he created. When it came to dealing with his sons, David needed all the help he could get, but perhaps he wouldn't admit it. It's never too late for God to work.

2. David strives for unity. (2 Sam. 19:9-15)

When David finally arrived in Jerusalem, it was a signal to the nation that the rebellion was ended and their true king was back on the throne. But en route to Jerusalem, David made some royal decisions that sent out other important messages to the people. His first message was that he wanted his kingdom to be a united people. The old prejudices and animosities must be buried and the nation must be united behind its king. Within the tribes the people were divided between the followers of Absalom and the followers of David (vv. 9-10), and the old division between "the ten tribes (Israel) and Judah" still persisted (vv. 40-43).

David began with Judah (vv. 11-12). The leaders from all twelve tribes should have united in sending a formal invitation to David to return and reign, but party squabbles and tribal friction kept things in ferment. David knew that the trouble would only increase if he waited too long to regain his city and his throne, so he marched right ahead. After all, he was God's anointed king (v. 22) and didn't need to call for a referendum before taking up his fallen scepter.

Judah was the royal tribe (Gen. 49:10); David was from the tribe of Judah; his capital city was in Judah, and the elders of Judah had first made him king (2:1-4), so he logically turned first to the elders of Judah for help. Using his two priests as intermediaries, David told the elders of Judah that the Israelites in the other tribes were talking about returning the king to Jerusalem, but he had heard nothing from his own tribe. Absalom had begun his rebellion in Hebron, which was in Judah, and the leaders of Judah must have cooperated with him, so it was time they displayed their allegiance to David, their rightful king. It's likely that all the tribal leaders who had foolishly followed Absalom were wondering what David would do to them once he regained his throne.

David appointed Amasa to be his general (vv. 13-14). The news of this appointment must have shocked the leaders of the nation and then brought them great relief, for it meant that David was pardoning all the officials who had followed Absalom. Amasa had been Absalom's general whose assignment it was to search for David and destroy him, but now David was making his nephew (and Joab's cousin) the leader of his great army.

But why replace Joab? For one thing, David learned that it was Joab who had slain Absalom in disobedience to the orders the king had given. Even though he deserved death, Absalom could have been taken alive and brought to David to be dealt with later; and Joab didn't have the authority to defy his sovereign and act as judge and executioner. If Joab did this to the king's son, what might he do to the king himself? This brings up a second reason David replaced Joab: Joab had been gradually increasing his authority ever since David had been told to stop waging war personally (21:15-17).

In the ancient East, the king was commander in chief of the army, and whoever took his place, for whatever reason, became a man of high esteem and authority. It was Joab who told David to come to Rabbah for the final conquest; otherwise, Joab would take the city and name it after himself! By the time of the battle of the forest of Ephraim, Joab had at least ten armor-bearers (18:15)! Joab had a record of eliminating anybody who threatened his authority. He and his brother Abishai killed Abner, who had been King Saul's general (3:27ff); and before the story ends, Joab will kill Amasa (20:4-13).

Joab and his brothers, though capable warriors, caused much grief to David from the early in his reign (3:39; 16:10; 19:22). Of course, Joab knew all about the murder of Uriah (11:14ff), and perhaps this piece of information carried more power than his sword. When he killed Absalom, Joab went too far, and David saw this as an opportunity to get rid of his power-hungry general. Amasa had led the rebel army, so by appointing him to Joab's position, David united the army and declared an amnesty to all the rebel soldiers, giving the nation a new beginning.

As the other tribes debated and delayed, the men of Judah united behind David with all their hearts, and they sent him an official invitation to return home. David went down to the Jordan near Gilgal, and the men of Judah met him there. The first place Israel camped after Joshua had led them across the Jordan, Gilgal was less than twenty miles from Jerusalem and a key city in Jewish history. There the males of the new generation entered into covenant with Jehovah and were circumcised (Josh. 3–5), and it was at Gilgal that Samuel renewed the covenant when Saul became king (1 Sam. 11:14-15). The text doesn't state it, but perhaps David also renewed the covenant at Gilgal and assured the people that Jehovah was still on the throne and His Word was still in force. Perhaps it was a time of rededication for the king, for throughout the rest of the book, we see David very much in charge.

3. David declares general amnesty. (2 Sam. 19:16-23)

Not only were the men of Judah at the Jordan to welcome David, but his enemy Shimei the Benjamite was there[2] with a thousand men from his tribe (see 16:5-14). Ziba, the land manager for Mephibosheth (9:1-10), was also in the crowd with his fifteen sons and twenty servants, and they crossed the river to meet him on the western shore and help escort him to the other side. Somebody provided a ferryboat that went back and forth across the Jordan to carry the king's household so they wouldn't have to ford the river. When David arrived on the western bank of the river, Shimei prostrated himself and begged for mercy.

There's no doubt that Shimei deserved to be killed for the way he treated David (Ex. 22:28), and Abishai was willing to do the job, but David stopped his nephew just as he had done before (16:9). The first time David stopped Abishai, his reason was that the Lord had told Shimei to curse the king, so David would take his abuse as from the hand of the Lord. But now his reason for sparing Shimei was because it was a day of rejoicing, not a day of revenge. But even more, by pardoning Shimei, King David was offering a general amnesty to all who had supported Absalom during the rebellion.

David kept his word and didn't have Shimei killed for his crime, but when David was about to die, he warned Solomon to keep an eye on Shimei (1 Kings 2:8-9). Solomon put him under house arrest and told him not to leave Jerusalem, but when Shimei disobeyed the king, he was taken and slain (1 Kings 2:36-46). Shimei had a weakness for resisting authority and treating God's appointed ministers with disdain (Jude 8), and that's why David cautioned Solomon. Shimei didn't appreciate David's mercy or Solomon's grace, and his independence and arrogance finally caught up with him.

4. David corrects an error. (2 Sam. 19:24-30)

Mephibosheth, the lame prince, had been "adopted" into David's household and permitted to eat at the king's table (9:1ff), a gift from David in honor of Jonathan, Mephibosheth's father and David's beloved friend. When David became king of all Israel, he inherited everything that had belonged to Saul, including his land, and some of the land he turned over to Mephibosheth to help support him and his family. David commanded Saul's servant Ziba to care for the land and to obey Mephibosheth, which he promised to do. But when David was escaping from Jerusalem, Ziba showed up without his master and brought help to David and his people. At that time, David made an impulsive decision and gave all the land to Ziba (16:1-4). Ziba also showed up to help David cross the river and return home (19:17).

Ziba wasn't on hand to help him, so it would have been difficult for the crippled prince to travel the twenty miles or so from Jerusalem to the Jordan, but he did it.[3] He knew that Ziba had slandered him by telling David that he hoped the rebellion would succeed and the crown be returned to the house of Saul. Mephibosheth wanted an opportunity to speak to David personally, deny Ziba's lies, and affirm his own allegiance to the king, all of which he did. The repeated address "my lord the king" came from his heart. He was loyal to the king.

As David listened to Mephibosheth's explanation, he realized that he had jumped to conclusions when he gave all the land to Ziba, but David didn't have time to conduct a hearing to settle the matter. Mephibosheth made it clear that he wasn't asking his king for anything. The king had given him life, so what more was there to desire? To paraphrase his speech, "I have more than I deserve, so why should I seek the throne? I was destined to die and you not only saved me but took me into your own family circle."

David's response isn't easy to understand. On the surface, he seemed to be saying, "There's no need to go into the matter again. You and Ziba divide the land." But was David the kind of man who went back on his word? How would that kind of decision be received by the thousand Benjamites who came to the Jordan to welcome David? After all, doing something kind to Mephibosheth would have strengthened David's ties with both the tribe of Benjamin (Saul's tribe) and also the ten tribes that had originally followed the house of Saul. Taking away half of Mephibosheth's inheritance hardly fit into the joyful and forgiving atmosphere of the day, and yet by dividing the estate, David was also forgiving Ziba of his lies and treachery to his master. By dividing the land between Ziba and Mephibosheth, David was taking the easy way out.

But Mephibosheth's reply must have stunned David: "Rather, let him take it all, inasmuch as my lord the king has come back in peace to his own house" (v. 30 NKJV). But thanks to David's impetuous judgment, Ziba already had it all! This situation reminds us of the "case of the dead baby" that Solomon had to solve (1 Kings 3:16-28). When he offered to divide the living baby, the child's true mother protested, and that's how Solomon discovered her identity. Unlike a living baby, land isn't harmed when it's divided; but perhaps David was testing Mephibosheth to see where his heart was. The text doesn't tell us, but perhaps Mephibosheth did receive all the land as in the original contract. Either way, the lame prince was cared for as Ziba worked the land.

5. David rewards the faithful. (2 Sam. 19:31-40)

Barzillai was one of three wealthy landowners who met David when he arrived at Mahanaim and together supplied his needs and the needs of his people (17:27-29). He returned to his home in Rogelim, twenty to twenty-five miles north. When he heard that David was returning to Jerusalem, he came down to see him off. Unlike Shimei, he had no sins to confess, nor was there a misunderstanding to straighten out as with Mephibosheth. Barzillai wanted no favor from the king. All he wanted was to have the joy of sending him off safely, knowing that the war was over. These two trips must have been difficult for an eighty-year-old man, but he wanted to give his best to his king.

David wanted to reward Barzillai by caring for him at his palace in Jerusalem. Not only did David want to express his thanks, but by having so important a man in Jerusalem, it would strengthen ties with the trans-Jordanic citizens at a time when unity was an important commodity. But Barzillai graciously refused David's offer on the grounds that he was too old. Older people don't like to pull up their roots and relocate, and they want to die at home and be buried with their loved ones. At his age, Barzillai couldn't enjoy the special pleasures of life at court, and he would only be a burden to the king, who had enough to think about.

However, Barzillai was willing to let his son Chimham take his place (1 Kings 2:7) and go to Jerusalem to live. What Barzillai didn't need for himself he was willing for others to enjoy. Said Matthew Henry, "They that are old must not begrudge young people those delights which they themselves are past the enjoyment of, nor oblige them to retire as they do." Barzillai crossed the river with David and Chimham and went a short distance with them, and then they said good-bye, David affectionately kissing his friend and benefactor.[4] In Jeremiah's time, there was a site known as Geruth Kimham ("habitation of Chimham") near Bethlehem (Jer. 41:17), which may have been where Barzillai's son settled down with his family.

But David's troubles weren't over yet, for the long-running feud between the ten tribes and Judah would surface again and almost cause another civil war. Shakespeare was right: "Uneasy lies the head that wears a crown."[5]

CHAPTER TEN
DAVID'S NEW STRUGGLES
2 Samuel 19:41–20:22
(See also 1 Chronicles 20:4-8)

The humorous poet Ogden Nash was sounding a serious note when he wrote, "People could survive their natural troubles all right if it weren't for the trouble they make for themselves." Ouch!

As we read the account of David's later life, we can see the truth of that statement. All parents have predictable problems with their children, but the sins of David's children seemed to set new records, especially those of Absalom. All leaders have problems with their followers, but in David's case, the sword flashed repeatedly in Israel with brother fighting against brother. How painful are the consequences of forgiven sin! These chapters describe four different conflicts that David had to deal with after Absalom's rebellion had been crushed.

1. Tribal conflict (19:41–20:4, 14-26)

A crisis will bring out the best in some people and the worst in others. The representatives of the tribes were gathered at Gilgal to escort their king back to Jerusalem, and instead of rejoicing at the victory God had given His people, the tribes were fighting among themselves. The "men of Israel" were the ten northern tribes, and they were angry at the southern tribe of Judah, which had also absorbed the tribe of Simeon. Israel was angry because Judah had not waited for them to arrive on the scene to help take David home. Judah had "kidnapped" the king and had ignored and insulted the other ten tribes. Judah replied that David was from their tribe, so they had the greater responsibility to care for him. Israel argued that they had ten shares in David but Judah had only two, as though the king were some kind of security on the stock market. Apparently nobody urged the tribes to call on Jehovah for His help and to remember that Gilgal was the place where Israel had made a new beginning in Joshua's day (Josh. 3–5).

The conflict between Judah and Israel had deep roots, just like the political conflicts that divide many nations today. When King Saul assembled his first army, it was divided between Israel and Judah (1 Sam. 11:8), and this division continued throughout his reign (15:4; 17:52; 18:16). After the death of Saul, the ten tribes of Israel followed Saul's son Ish-Bosheth, while Judah followed David (2 Sam. 2:10-11). Judah, of course, was obeying the will of God, for the Lord had named David as the nation's next king. This tribal rivalry existed even in David's day (11:11; 12:8). "Every kingdom divided against itself is brought to desolation," said Jesus, "and every city or house divided against itself shall not stand" (Matt. 12:25 KJV). When Rehoboam became king after the death of Solomon his father, the rift widened and the kingdom divided into Judah and Israel.

All it takes to light the fires of conflict is a speech from a would-be leader, and Sheba was that leader. Being a Benjamite, he favored the house of Saul, and he was probably an officer in the northern army. If the ten tribes seceded from the kingdom, perhaps he could become commander of their army. Sheba didn't declare war; all he did was dismiss the army and the citizens who came from the northern tribes and tell them not to follow David any longer. But in essence it was a declaration of war, for Sheba marched through the northern tribes trying to gather a following (v. 14). It appears that not many people responded, and Sheba and his followers ended up in the walled city of Abel.

Joab again took command of David's troops and followed Sheba to Abel, surrounded the city, and began to lay siege to it. For the third time in the "David story," a woman changes the course of events. Abigail was the first (1 Sam. 25), and the woman of Tekoa was the second (2 Sam. 14). The wise woman called to Joab from the wall and assured him that her city was not in league with any rebels and therefore didn't deserve to be attacked. Perhaps she was thinking about the law in Deut. 20:10-16 requiring that a city first be given an offer of peace before it was attacked. When Joab explained that it was only Sheba he was after, she persuaded the citizens to kill the rebel leader and save the city. However, Sheba wasn't a scapegoat; as a rebel against the king, he deserved to be slain. Sheba wanted to be head of the army, but instead, his head was thrown over the wall to the army.

The chapter closes with a second listing of David's officers (8:15-18), and two new officers are added: Adoram (or Adoniram) was in charge of the forced labor, and Ira the Jairite served as David's chaplain. The "forced labor" was done by prisoners of war, but Israelites were occasionally conscripted to assist with government building projects. During Solomon's reign and after, the officer in charge of these labor projects didn't have an easy time of it (1 Kings 4:6; 5:14; 12:18ff; 2 Chron. 10:18-19).

Now we must back up a bit to discover how Joab regained the command of David's army.

2. Personal conflict (20:4-13)

When David heard about Sheba's call to rebellion, he immediately sent word to Amasa, his new commander (19:13), to gather the troops within three days and come to Jerusalem. An experienced strategist, David knew that insurrection had to be nipped in the bud or it would gain momentum among the dissatisfied people in the land, and this could lead to another war. Thousands of David's subjects had been willing to follow Absalom, and it seemed that the ten northern tribes were ready to follow anybody.

But Amasa didn't show up with the army within the three allotted days, and David gave the command of the army to Abishai. Amasa had been commander of Absalom's army, so perhaps David was afraid he had turned traitor and joined up with Sheba. The most logical explanation for Amasa's delay was that the men didn't trust him and were unwilling to follow him and risk their lives. Taking Joab's officers and David's "mighty men" with him, Abishai quickly assembled the army of Judah and headed north to stop Sheba. Imagine their surprise when they met Amasa and his army at the great rock in Gibeon, about six miles northwest of Jerusalem. Amasa was on his way to report to David and get his orders.

Though he had no official position, Joab went along with his brother Abishai to help in any way that he could. The two men had fought together in the battle of the forest of Ephraim and defeated Absalom. Joab had no love for Amasa, who had betrayed David and led Absalom's army (17:25). Furthermore, it was Amasa who took Joab's place as commander of the troops, an appointment that must have humiliated Joab. (David made that change because it was Joab who killed Absalom.) Joab knew that he and his brother Abishai could deal successfully with Sheba's revolt but that Amasa was too weak and inexperienced to lead a victorious army.

As when they murdered Abner (3:27-39), Joab and Abishai must have quickly plotted together when they saw Amasa approaching. Joab had killed Abner[1] and Absalom, so his hands were already stained with blood. The trick with the sword gave Amasa the idea that this was just a casual meeting, but it was Joab's crafty way of catching Amasa off guard. (See Judg. 3:20-23.) Once more, the sword was at work in David's household, for Amasa was his cousin. There was no reason why Amasa should be killed. True, he had joined forces with Absalom, but David had declared a general amnesty that included Joab, who had killed Absalom. Joab could have easily taken the command away from Amasa, but the old campaigner was of such a disposition that he preferred to destroy those who stood in his way. He wanted none of Absalom's leaders to live and create more problems for David.

Joab left Amasa lying in a pool of blood on the highway, a sight that brought the marching army to a halt. Here was their commander dead before the battle had even begun! Joab and Abishai took off after Sheba, but the army wasn't following. It was what we call today "a gaper's block." One of Joab's men was wise enough to move the corpse to the side of the highway and cover it up. Then he rallied Amasa's troops to support Joab and David, and the soldiers responded. The politically correct thing to say would have been "David and Abishai," because David had given the command to Abishai; but Joab had taken back his old position and wouldn't let it go (v. 23). Once again, David had to give in to Joab's power tactics.

We trust that somebody buried the body, for it was considered a serious thing in Israel for a body not to have proper burial.

3. Ethnic conflict (2 Sam. 21:1-14)

The book closes with a record of two national calamities—a drought caused by King Saul's sin (21:1-14) and a plague caused by King David's sin (24:1-25). Between these two tragic events, the writer gives us a summary of four victories (21:15-22) and a list of David's mighty men (23:8-39), as well as two psalms written by David (22:1–23:7). Once again we see David the soldier, the singer, and the sinner.

Sin (vv. 1-4). Nowhere in Scripture are we told when or why Saul slaughtered the Gibeonites and thus broke the vow that Israel had made with them in Joshua's day (Josh. 9). Joshua tried to make the best of his mistake, because he put the Gibeonites to work as woodcutters and water carriers; but Israel's vow obligated them before God to protect the Gibeonites (Josh. 10). Saul killed several Gibeonites but intended to wipe them all out, so it was a case of "ethnic cleansing" and genocide.

Saul's religious life is a puzzle. Attempting to appear very godly, he would make foolish vows that nobody should keep (1 Sam. 14:24-35), while at the same time he didn't obey the clear commands of the Lord (1 Sam. 13, 15). He was commanded to slay the Amalekites and didn't, yet he tried to exterminate the Gibeonites! Another piece of the puzzle is that Jeiel, Saul's great-grandfather, was the progenitor of the Gibeonites (1 Chron. 8:29-33; 9:35-39), so Saul slaughtered his own relatives.

Gibeon became a Levitical city (Josh. 21:17), and the tabernacle was there at one time (1 Kings 3:4-5). The city was located in the tribe of Benjamin—Saul's tribe—and perhaps that is a clue to Saul's behavior. It was bad enough to have the pagan Gibeonites alive and well in the land of Israel, but did they have to reside in Benjamin? One of Saul's "leadership" tactics was to reward his men with houses and lands (1 Sam. 22:7), and perhaps to do this he confiscated property from the Gibeonites. Whatever his motive and method, Saul in his grave brought judgment on the people of Israel as the drought and famine continued for three years (21:1, 10).

The first year of drought might have been caused by some unexpected change in the weather, and during the second year people would say, "It's bound to improve." But when for the third year the land suffered drought and famine, David sought the face of the Lord. It was written in the Lord's covenant with Israel that He would send the rain to the land if His people would honor and obey Him (Deut. 28:1-14). David knew that the sin of murder would pollute the land (Num. 35:30-34), and that's exactly what was causing all the trouble. Perhaps through his prophet Nathan or his chaplain Ira, the Lord said to David, "It is because of Saul and his bloodthirsty house, because He killed the Gibeonites" (v. 1 NKJV). Saul had been dead for over thirty years, and the Lord had patiently waited for this sin to be dealt with.[2]

Retribution (vv. 5-9). When he learned the facts, David immediately offered to make restitution for the terrible sins of his predecessor, because he wanted the Gibeonites to be able to bless the people of Israel and thereby enjoy God's blessing (Gen. 12:1-3). But the Gibeonites didn't want money; they knew that no amount of money could ransom a murderer or recompense the survivors (Num. 35:31-33). The Gibeonites made it clear that they knew their place in Israel as servants and resident aliens, and they had no right to press their case.[3] But it would take the shedding of blood to atone for the Gibeonite blood that had been shed (Ex. 21:24; Lev. 24:19-21; Deut. 19:21). The nation was suffering because of Saul's sins, and if David killed just any man, that wouldn't solve the problem. The Gibeonites asked that seven of Saul's male descendants be sacrificed before the Lord and this would end the drought and famine.

David knew that the Jews were forbidden to offer human sacrifices (Lev. 18:21; 20:1-5; Deut. 12:29-32; 18:10), nor did he see the deaths of the seven men as sacrifices with atoning value. We today who have the New Testament and understand the Gospel of Jesus Christ view this entire episode with mingled disgust and dismay, but we must keep in mind that we're dealing with law, not grace, and Israel, not the church. The Law of Moses required that an unsolved murder be atoned for by sacrifice (Deut. 21:1-9), so how much more a known slaughter perpetrated by a king! However, we must keep in mind that the death of the seven men was not atonement but legal retribution.

Though David didn't commit the crime, he had to choose the seven men who would die, and that wasn't an easy thing to do. (Perhaps David thought about those who had died because of his sin—Bathsheba's baby, Uriah the Hittite, Amnon, Absalom and Amasa.) Because of his vow to Jonathan to protect his descendants (1 Sam. 20:12-17)[4], the king avoided naming Mephibosheth and chose two sons of Saul's concubine Rizpah as well as five sons of Saul's daughter Merab, who was married to Adriel (v. 8 NIV).[5] We aren't told how the seven men were executed, although "fell together" (v. 9) suggests they were pushed off a cliff. This happened during barley harvest in the middle of April, and the seven corpses were exposed for about six months, until the rains arrived and the drought ended in October. To hang up a corpse was to disgrace the person and put him under a curse (Deut. 21:22-23).

Compassion (vv. 10-14). The law required exposed bodies to be taken down by sundown and buried. To be sure that Saul's crime was sufficiently dealt with, David allowed the bodies to remain exposed until the rains came, signifying that the Lord was blessing His people again. During that time Rizpah protected the bodies of her sons and nephews, an act of love and courage. It was Rizpah who was involved when Abner abandoned the house of Saul and joined with David (3:6-12).

But David went a step further. He had the bones gathered up, along with the bones of Saul and his sons that the men of Jabesh-Gilead had interred (1 Sam. 31), and brought the whole family together in their family tomb (vv. 12-14). To have proper burial with one's ancestors was the desire of every Israelite, and David granted this blessing to Saul and his family. Whatever questions remain concerning this unusual event, this much is true: one man's sins can bring sorrow and death to his family, even after he is dead and buried. We must also give credit to David for dealing drastically with sin for the sake of the nation, and yet for showing kindness to the house of Saul.

4. National conflict (21:15-22; 1 Chron. 20:4-8)

These four conflicts took place much earlier in David's reign, probably after he made Jerusalem his capital and the Philistines opposed his rise to power. All four involve "descendants of the giants"[6] from Philistia, one of whom was a brother of Goliath (v. 19).

In the first conflict (vv. 15-17), David fought so much that he grew faint, because the Philistines would focus on him rather than the other soldiers. Ishbi-benob wanted to slay David and had a bronze spear that weighed seven and a half pounds. However David's nephew Abishai, who more than once irritated David, came to the king's rescue and killed the giant. It was then that the military leaders decided the king was too vulnerable and valuable to be sacrificed on the battlefield. The king was the "lamp of Israel" and had to be protected. (See 1 Kings 11:36; 15:4; 2 Kings 8:19; 2 Chron. 21:7.)

The second contest with the Philistines (v. 18; 1 Chron. 20:4) took place at Gob, a site we can't locate with any accuracy, where Israel won the battle because one of David's mighty men killed the giant. (See 1 Chron. 11:29.) The fact that the names of these giants were preserved shows that they were well-known warriors.

The third conflict with the Philistines (v. 19) was again at Gob, and this time the brother of Goliath (1 Chron. 20:5) is the giant that was slain. We know little about Elhanan except that he came from Bethlehem and was one of David's mighty men (23:24).

The fourth battle took place in Gath in enemy territory (vv. 20-22; 1 Chron. 20:6-8), and David's nephew Jonathan killed the giant who had, like Goliath, defied Israel and Israel's God. (See 1 Sam. 17:10.)

When as a youth David killed Goliath, he certainly gave the men of Israel a good example of what it means to trust God for victory. It's good to know how to kill giants yourself, but be sure to help others kill the giants in their lives.

CHAPTER ELEVEN
DAVID'S SONG OF VICTORY
2 Samuel 22
(See also Psalm 18)

First Samuel 2 records the song Hannah sang when she brought her son Samuel to serve the Lord at the tabernacle, and 2 Samuel 22 records the song of David after the Lord helped him defeat his enemies (v. 1; Ps. 18, title). How significant that two books full of burdens and bloodshed are bracketed by praise! No matter how dark the days or how painful the memories, we can always praise the Lord.

In this song, David offered thanks to the Lord for the many victories He had given him and for the gracious way He had worked to bring him to the throne of Israel. Note that Saul is not included among David's enemies, for no matter what Saul did to him, David never treated Saul like an enemy. It's likely that 2 Samuel 22 is the original version, but when the song was adapted for corporate worship David wrote a new opening: "I will love thee, O Lord, my strength" (Ps. 18:1 KJV). The Hebrew word used here for "love" means "a deep and fervent love," not just a passing emotion. He also deleted from verse 3 "my savior; thou savest me from violence." There are other differences, but they do not deter us from grasping the glorious message of this song of praise.

It's unlikely that this song was written just after the defeat of Saul and the beginning of David's reign in Hebron. From verse 51 we infer that David wrote this psalm after God made His dynastic covenant with him (2 Sam. 7) and gave him the victories recorded in 2 Samuel 8 and 10. We further infer from verses 20-27 that he wrote the psalm before his terrible sins in connection with Bathsheba and Uriah (2 Sam. 11-12), for he could never have written verses 20-27 after that sad episode.

The emphasis in this psalm is on what the Lord in His grace and mercy did for David.

1. The Lord delivered David. (2 Sam. 22:1-19)

"Deliver" is a key word in this song (vv. 1, 2, 18, 20, 44, 49), and it carries with it the meanings of "drawing out of danger, snatching, taking away, allowing to escape." For at least ten years before he became king, David was pursued by Saul and his army, and the record shows that Saul tried to kill David at least five times. (See 1 Sam. 18:10-11; 19:8-10, 18-24.) After he became king, David had to wage war against the Philistines, the Ammonites, the Syrians, the Moabites, and the Edomites, and God enabled him to triumph over all his enemies.

David began by praising the Lord for who He is—a rock, a fortress, and a deliverer (v. 20)—images that certainly came out of David's years in the wilderness when he and his men hid in caves and natural fortresses. "God is my rock" (v. 3) can be translated, "My rock-like God." The image of the Lord "the rock" goes back to Genesis 49:24 and is used often in "The Song of Moses" in Deuteronomy 32 (vv. 4, 15, 18, 30-31). Hannah used it in her song (1 Sam. 2:2), and it's found frequently in the psalms. A rock reminds us of strength and stability, that which is dependable and unchanging. No matter how David's enemies tried to destroy him, he was always guided and protected by the Lord. God was a shield around him and a deliverer in every time of danger.

The image of the rock gives way to the image of the flood (vv. 4-7), and this leads to the vivid picture of the storm (vv. 8-20. While he was exiled in the wilderness, David certainly saw many rainstorms (see Ps. 29) that transformed the dry riverbeds into raging torrents (Ps. 126:4). No matter what the season, David was constantly fighting the strong currents of Saul's opposition. Waves of death, floods of ungodly men, the cords of sheol (the land of the dead), and the hidden traps of death all made David's life difficult and dangerous. No wonder he told Jonathan, "There is but a step between me and death" (1 Sam. 20:3 NKJV).

What do you do when you're drowning in a flood of opposition? *You call on the Lord and trust Him for the help you need (v. 7).* David was a man of prayer who depended on the Lord for wisdom, strength, and deliverance, and the Lord never failed him. Why did God wait all those years before delivering David and putting him on the throne? For one thing, the Lord was building himself a leader, and this could be done only by means of trial, suffering, and battle. But the Lord also had his own timetable, for "when the fullness of the time had come" (Gal. 4:4 NKJV), out of David's family the Messiah would come to the world.

When the Lord answered David's cries and delivered him from Saul and the enemies of the people of God, it was like a great thunderstorm being released over the land (vv. 8-20). David describes

God's intervention as an earthquake (v. 8) followed by lightning, fire, and smoke (v. 9). The Lord was angry! (See Pss. 74:1 and 140:10.) Against the background of the black sky, the Lord swooped down on a cloud propelled by the cherubim.[1] The storm raged! In Scripture, a storm can picture an advancing army (Ezek. 38:9; Dan. 11:40; Hab. 3:14) or the judgment of God (Jer. 11:6; 23:19; 25:32). God's arrows were like the lightning, His voice like the thunder, and the winds like the angry breath of His nostrils. No wonder His enemies fled in terror! David didn't see himself as a great commander who led a victorious army, but as God's servant who trusted Jehovah to win the victory. He gave all the glory to the Lord. God not only "came down" (v. 10), but He "reached down" and plucked David out of the dangerous waters.

2. The Lord rewarded David. (2 Sam. 22:20-28)

For at least ten years, David had been in "tight" places, but now the Lord had brought him out "into a spacious place" (v. 20 NIV). God could give him a larger place because David had been enlarged in his own life through his experiences of trial and testing. "Thou hast enlarged me when I was in distress" (Ps. 4:1 KJV). David had often cried out, "The troubles of my heart are enlarged," but at the same time, God was enlarging His servant and preparing him for a bigger place (18:19, 36). "I called on the Lord in distress; the Lord answered me and set me in a broad place" (Ps. 118:5 NKJV). In the school of life, God promotes those who, in times of difficulty, learn the lessons of faith and patience (Heb. 6:12), and David had learned his lessons well.

David's righteousness (vv. 21-25). A superficial reading of these verses might lead us to believe that David was bragging about himself, but this isn't the case at all. David was praising the Lord for enabling him to live a blameless life in dangerous and uncomfortable situations. Just think of how difficult it would be to keep the law of the Lord in the Judean wilderness while fleeing for your life! In all that he did, David sought to please the Lord, obey His law, and trust His promises. These verses describe David as a man of integrity (see Ps. 78:72), a "man after God's own heart" (1 Sam. 13:14). David knew and claimed God's covenant promises and the Lord honored him. King Saul violated the terms of the covenant, and the Lord judged him.

This doesn't mean that David was spotless and always did the right thing. He had his days of despair when he fled to the enemy for help, but these were incidents in a life that was otherwise wholly devoted to the Lord. David honored only the Lord and never turned to idols. He did not dishonor the name of the Lord; he was careful to love and protect his parents (1 Sam. 22:1-4); and when he had opportunities to slay Saul, David refused to touch the Lord's anointed and commit murder. There is no evidence that during his "battle years" David was a thief, an adulterer, or a false witness against others. (Actually, it was Saul and his men who lied about David.) David was a generous man who didn't cultivate a covetous heart. We don't know how David honored the Sabbath when he was away from the covenant community, but there's no reason to believe that he broke the fourth commandment. Measured by the righteousness of the law, David was a man with clean hands and a pure heart (Ps. 24:3-6), and he received his reward from the Lord.

The Lord's faithfulness (vv. 26-28). The Lord never violates His own attributes.

God deals with people according to their attitudes and their actions. David was merciful to Saul and spared his life on at least two occasions, and the Lord was merciful to David. "Blessed are the merciful: for they shall obtain mercy" (Matt. 5:7 KJV). David was faithful to the Lord, and the Lord was faithful to Him. David was upright; he was single-hearted when it came to serving God. He was not sinless—no man or woman on earth is—but he was blameless in his motives and loyal to the Lord. In that sense, his heart was pure: "Blessed are the pure in heart: for they shall see God" (Matt. 5:8 KJV).

Unlike Saul, David was not perverse in heart but submitted to the will of God (v. 27). The NIV reads, "to the crooked you show yourself shrewd," reminding us that faith is living without scheming or making excuses, two practices at which Saul excelled. The Hebrew word translated "froward" (KJV) or "crooked" (NIV) comes from a root that means "to wrestle." David didn't fight God or God's will, but Saul did; and that's why David was exalted but Saul was abased (1 Peter 5:5-6; James 4:10).

Finally, David was humble and broken before the Lord, while Saul promoted himself and put himself first. "You rescue those who are humble, but your eyes are on the proud to humiliate them" (v. 28 NLT). Hannah touched on this important theme in her song to the Lord (1 Sam. 2:3, 7-8). When Saul began his reign, he stood head and shoulders above everybody else (1 Sam. 10:23-24), but at the end of his life, he fell on his face in a witch's house (28:20) and fell as a suicide on the battlefield (31:1-6). "Therefore let him who thinks he stands take heed lest he fall" (1 Cor. 10:12 NKJV). David fell on his face in submission, and the Lord lifted him up in honor. Saul lifted himself up and eventually fell on his face in humiliation.

God is always faithful to His character and His covenant. Knowing the character of God is essential to knowing and doing the will of God and pleasing His heart. David knew God's covenant so he understood what God expected of him. The character of God and the covenant of God are the foundations for the promises of God. If we ignore His character and covenant, we will never be successful in claiming His promises.

3. The Lord enabled David. (2 Sam. 22:29-43)

In this stanza of his song, David looked back and recalled how the Lord helped him during those difficult years of exile.

The Lord enlightened David (v. 29). The image of the burning lamp can refer to God's goodness in keeping people alive (Job 18:5-6; 21:17). David's life was constantly in danger, but the Lord kept him alive and provided all he needed. But a burning lamp also speaks of the reign of a king. David's men were afraid that one day he would be slain in battle and the "light of Israel" be put out (2 Sam. 21:17). Even after David died, the Lord was true to His covenant promise and kept David's lamp burning by maintaining David's dynasty (1 Kings 11:36; 15:4; 2 Kings 8:19; 2 Chron. 21:7; Ps. 132:17).

But God enlightened David in another way, for He revealed His will to him through the words of the prophets and the use of the Urim and Thummim. Saul made his own decisions, but David sought the mind of the Lord. During the dark days of his exile, David could say, "The Lord is my light and my salvation; whom shall I fear? The Lord is the strength of my life; of whom shall I be afraid?"[2] (Ps. 27:1 NKJV).

The Lord empowered David (vv. 30-35). The picture here is that of a courageous warrior letting nothing stand in the way of victory. God empowered David to face the enemy without fear, running through a troop and the barricades they put up, and even scaling a wall to take a city. God's way is perfect (v. 31) and He made David's way perfect (v. 33), because David trusted in Him. God shielded David in the battle because David relied wholly on the flawless Word of God.

David's body belonged to the Lord (see Rom. 12:1), and God used his arms, feet and hands (vv. 33-35) to overcome the enemy. David was a gifted warrior, but it was the anointing power of the Lord that enabled him to succeed on the battlefield. Like a fleet-footed deer, he could reach the heights; even his ankles didn't turn (v. 37 NIV). God made David's arms strong enough to bend a bow of bronze and shoot arrows with great power. In the strength of the Lord, David was invincible.

The Lord enlarged David (vv. 36-43). God enlarged David's path (v. 37) and put him into a larger place (v. 20), a wonderful truth we have already considered. The remarkable statement "thy gentleness hath made me great" (v. 36 KJV) reveals David's utter amazement that Almighty God would condescend to pay any attention to him. David always saw himself as an ordinary Jewish shepherd with no special position in Israel (1 Sam. 18:18, 23), but the Lord "stooped down" to make him great. He made David a great warrior and gave him a great name (2 Sam. 7:23), and David acknowledged this incredible mercy from God, but David's greatest desire was to make Jehovah's name great before the nations (7:18-29).

The gracious condescension of the Lord is a theme that is too often neglected by God's people. As with David, God the Father condescends to work in our lives to fit us for the work of His choosing (and see Isa. 57:15), and God the Son certainly humbled Himself for us when He came to earth as a servant and a sacrifice for sin (Phil. 2:5-11). The Holy Spirit condescended to come to earth and live in the people of God! David didn't look back on those difficult exile years and see the "hardness" of God but the gentleness of God. He saw only goodness and mercy following him (Ps. 23:6). The servant in the parable who called the master "a hard man" (Matt. 25:24) certainly didn't have the same outlook as King David!

We might cringe as we read David's description of his victories, but we must remember that he was fighting the battles of the Lord. If these nations had defeated and destroyed Israel, what would happen to God's great plan of salvation? We wouldn't have a Bible, and we wouldn't have a Savior! In rebelling against the Lord and worshiping idols, these pagan nations had sinned against a flood of light, so they were without excuse (Rom. 1:18ff; Josh. 2). The Lord had been patient with them for many years (Gen. 15:16), but they had spurned His grace. David pursued his enemies when they tried to get away (vv. 38, 41); he defeated them, crushed them, and ground them into the dirt! They became like mire in the streets.

4. The Lord established David. (2 Sam. 22:44-51)

It is one thing to fight wars and defeat the enemy, but it is quite something else to keep these nations under control. David not only had to unify and lead the twelve tribes of Israel, but he also had to deal with the nations that were subjected to Israel.

The Lord enthroned David (44-46). The Gentile nations didn't want a king on the throne of Israel, especially a brilliant strategist, brave warrior, and beloved leader like David. However, God not only established him on the throne, but also promised him a dynasty that would never end. The Lord promised David a throne, and He kept His promise. He also helped David to unite his own people and deal with those who were still loyal to Saul. The word "strangers" in verses 45-46 (KJV) means "foreigners" and refers to Gentile nations. The Lord's victories frightened these peoples and drove them into hiding places. Eventually they would come out of their feeble fortresses and submit to David.

The Lord exalted David (vv. 47-49). David's shout of praise, "The Lord lives" (v. 47), was his bold witness to these subjected peoples that their dead idols could not save them or protect them (see Ps. 115). Only Jehovah, the God of Israel, is the true and living God, and David's victories and enthronement proved that God was with him. David was always careful not to exalt himself, but to exalt the Lord. David closes his song with high and holy praise for the Lord God of Israel. He exalted the Lord, and the Lord exalted him (Matt. 6:33; 1 Sam. 2:30). If we magnify our own name or our own deeds, we will sin, but if the Lord magnifies us, we can bring glory to His name (Josh. 3:7).

The Lord elected David (vv. 50-51). God's sovereign choice of David to be king, and His dynastic covenant with him, form the foundation for all that God did for His servant. Israel was called to be a witness to the nations, and it was David's responsibility to build a kingdom that would honor the name of the Lord. It's too bad that because of his sin with Bathsheba he brought reproach to God's name (2 Sam. 12:14). Nevertheless, David was God's king and God's anointed, and the covenant between God and David still stands and will ultimately be fulfilled in the reign of Jesus Christ in His kingdom.

Paul quoted verse 50 in Romans 15:9 as part of the wrap-up of his admonition to the believers in the churches in Rome that they receive one another and stop judging one another. The Gentile believers in Rome were enjoying their freedom in Christ, while many of the Jewish believers were still in bondage to the Law of Moses. Paul points out that Christ came to minister to both Jews and Gentiles by fulfilling God's promises to the Jews and dying for both Jews and Gentiles. From the very beginning of the nation, when God called Abraham and Sarah, the Lord had it in mind to include the Gentiles in His gracious plan of salvation (Gen. 12:1-3; Luke 2:29-32; John 4:22; Eph. 2:11ff).

The sequence in Romans 15:8-12 is significant. Jesus confirmed the promises made to Israel (v. 8), and Israel brought the message of salvation to the Gentiles (v. 9). Both believing Jews and Gentiles as one spiritual body now praise the Lord together (v. 10); and all the nations hear the good news of the Gospel (v. 11). When Jesus returns, He will reign over both Jews and Gentiles in His glorious kingdom (v. 12). From the very beginning, it was God's plan that the nation of Israel be His vehicle for bringing salvation to a lost world. "Salvation is of the Lord" (Jonah 2:9 NKJV) and "Salvation is of the Jews" (John 4:22 NKJV). The Gentiles owe a great debt to the Jews (Rom. 15:27), and Gentile Christians ought to pay that debt. They can show their appreciation to Israel by praying for their salvation (Rom. 9:1-5; 10:1) and for the peace of Jerusalem (Ps. 122:6), lovingly witnessing to them as God gives opportunity (Rom. 1:16), and sharing in their material needs (Rom. 15:27).

As you review this psalm, you can see what it was that thrilled the heart of David. He saw God and mentioned Him at least nineteen times. He saw God in the affairs of life, both the happy occasions and the storms that came. He saw God's purpose in his life and in the nation of Israel and rejoiced to be a part of it. But most exciting of all, in spite of the troubles David had experienced, he still saw the gentle hand of God, molding his life and accomplishing His purposes (v. 35). The enlarged troubles (Ps. 25:17) "enlarged" David (Ps. 4:1) and prepared him to take enlarged steps (2 Sam. 22:37 KJV) in the enlarged place God had prepared for him (22:20). That can be our experience as well.

CHAPTER TWELVE
DAVID'S MEMORIES AND MISTAKES

2 Samuel 23–24
(See also 1 Chronicles 11:10-41; 21:1-26)

The death of King David is not recorded in 2 Samuel, but in 1 Kings 2:1-12. However, 2 Samuel 23–24 record his last psalm, the names of his greatest soldiers, and the sad account of his sin of numbering the people. Chapters 21–24 serve as an "appendix" to 2 Samuel and seem to focus on the divine and human sides of leadership. A leader's decisions may have serious consequences, as proved by the sins of Saul (chap. 21) and David (chap. 24). Leaders must depend on the Lord and give Him the glory, as David's two psalms declare; and no leader can do the job alone, as indicated by the list of David's mighty men. Second Samuel 23–24 give us three portraits of David that illustrate the greatness and the humanness of this leader's life.

1. David the inspired singer (2 Sam. 23:1-7)

At least seventy-three of the psalms in the Book of Psalms are assigned to David, but his last one is found only here in 2 Samuel 23. The phrase "the last words of David" means "his last inspired written words from the Lord." The psalm may have been written during the closing days of his life, shortly before he died. Since the theme of the psalm is godly leadership, he may have written it especially for Solomon, but it has much to say to all of God's people today.

The privileges of leadership (vv. 1-2). David never ceased to marvel that God would call him to become the king of Israel, to lead God's people, fight God's battles, and even help to write God's Word. It was through David's descendants that God brought the Messiah into the world. From the human point of view, David was a "nobody," a shepherd, the youngest of eight sons in an ordinary Jewish family; nevertheless, God selected him and made him to become Israel's greatest king. The Lord had given David skillful hands and a heart of integrity (Ps. 78:70-72) and equipped him to know and do His will. As the son of Jesse, David was a member of the royal tribe of Judah, something that was not true of his predecessor Saul. (See Gen. 49:10.)

David didn't promote himself to achieve greatness; it was the Lord who chose him and elevated him to the throne (Deut. 17:15). The Lord spent thirty years training David, first with the sheep in the pastures, then with Saul in the army camp, and finally with his own fighting men in the Judean wilderness. Great leaders are trained in private before they go to work in public. "Talents are best nurtured in solitude," wrote Goethe; "character is best formed in the stormy billows of the world." David had both. He had been faithful in private as a servant, so God was able to elevate him publicly to be a ruler (Matt. 25:21). The Lord followed the same procedure when He prepared Moses, Joshua, Nehemiah, the apostles, and even His own Son (Phil. 2:5-11; Heb. 5:8). Dr. D. Martyn Lloyd-Jones used to say, "It is a tragic thing when a young man succeeds before he's ready for it." David was ready for the throne.

God empowers those whom He calls, and He anointed David with His Spirit (1 Sam. 16:12-13). Dr. A. W. Tozer said, "Never follow any leader until you see the oil on his forehead," which explains why so many gifted men came to David and joined his band. It takes more than talent and training to be an effective leader and to be able to recruit and train other leaders. Jesus reminded His disciples, and reminds us, "Without Me, you can do nothing" (John 15:5 NKJV). Religious leaders who follow the principles of what the world calls "success" rarely accomplish anything permanent that glorifies God. "He who does the will of God abides forever" (1 John 2:17 NKJV). It's good to be educated by men, but it's even more important to be trained by the Lord. "Our Lord was thirty years preparing for three years' service," wrote Oswald Chambers. "The modern stamp is three hours of preparation for thirty years of service."

But the Spirit not only empowered David for battle, He also inspired him to write beautiful psalms that still minister to our hearts. When you think of the trials that David had to endure in order to give us these psalms, it makes you appreciate them even more. David made it clear that he was writing the Word of God, not just religious poetry. Peter called David "a prophet" (Acts 2:30) and at Pentecost quoted what David wrote about the Messiah's resurrection and ascension (Acts 2:24-36). When you read the Psalms, you are reading the Word of God and learning about the Son of God.

The responsibilities of leadership (vv. 3-7). God didn't train David just to put him on display, but because He had important work for him to do; and so it is with every true leader. David was to rule over God's own people, "the sheep of his pasture" (Ps. 100:3), which is an awesome responsibility. It demands character and integrity ("just" = righteous) and a submissive attitude toward the Lord ("the fear of God"). Without righteousness and the fear of God, a leader becomes a dictator and abuses God's people, driving them like cattle instead of leading them like sheep. David was a ruler who served and a servant who ruled, and he had the welfare of his people on his heart (24:17). It encourages me today to see that even secular business specialists are comparing effective leaders to shepherds who care.[1]

David used a beautiful metaphor to picture the work of the leader: rain and sunshine that together produce useful fruit instead of painful thorns (vv. 4-7). David exemplified this principle in his own life, for when he came to the throne it meant the dawning of a new day for the nation of Israel. In this, he reminds us of what happened when Jesus came to earth (see Ps. 72:5-7; Isa. 9:2; 58:8, 60:1, 19; Mal. 4:1-3; Matt. 4:13-16; Luke 2:29-32). With the coronation of David, the storms that Saul had caused in the land were now over and the light of God's countenance was shining on His people. Under David's leadership, there would be a harvest of blessing from the Lord.

With God's help, leaders must create such a creative atmosphere that their colaborers will be able to grow and produce fruit. Ministry involves both sunshine and rain, bright days and cloudy days, but a godly leader's ministry will produce gentle rain that brings life and not storms that destroy. What a delight it is to follow a spiritual leader who brings out the best in us and helps us produce fruit for the glory of God! Unspiritual leaders produce thorns that irritate people and make progress very difficult (vv. 6-7).

In his song, David went beyond the principles of leadership to celebrate the coming of Messiah (v. 5). David mentioned the covenant the Lord made with him (2 Sam. 7), a covenant that guaranteed him a dynasty forever and a throne forever, a covenant that was fulfilled in Jesus Christ (Luke 1:32-33, 68-79). The statements in verse 5 are best read as questions: "Is not my house right with God? Has he not made with me an everlasting covenant, arranged and secured in every part?" (NIV) The first question doesn't suggest that all of David's children were godly, for we know that they were not. It only declares that David's house (dynasty) was secure because of God's covenant promises. Nothing could change this covenant; it was everlastingly secured by the character of God.

In verse 5, David again used the image of fruit: "Will he not bring to fruition my salvation and grant me my every desire?" (NIV) David's desire was that God would fulfill His promise and send the Messiah, who would be born from David's descendants. The throne of Judah ended historically in 586 BC with the reign of Zedekiah, but that wasn't the end of David's family or the nation of Israel. The Lord providentially preserved Israel and David's seed so that Jesus Christ could be born in Bethlehem, the City of David. The nation was small and weak, but the Messiah came just the same! "A shoot will come up from the stump of Jesse; from his roots a Branch will bear fruit" (Isa. 11:1 NIV; see 4:2, 6:13, and 53:2). However, one day the evil people of the earth will be uprooted like thorns and burned (vv. 6-7; see Matt. 3:10, 12; 13:40-42).

2. David the gifted leader (2 Sam. 23:8-38; 1 Chron. 11:10-47)

Here are listed the names and some of the exploits of the leading men who followed David and stood with him during the difficult years of exile and during his reign.

The first "three mighty men" (vv. 8-12; 1 Chron. 11:10-14). Josheb-Basshebeth is named first; he was also known as Adino and Jashobeam (v. 8; 1 Chron. 11:11). He was chief of the captains in David's army and was famous for killing eight hundred enemy soldiers "at one time." First Chronicles 11:11 says he killed three hundred men. As we've already noted, the transmission of numbers from manuscript to manuscript by copyists sometimes led to these minor differences. Did the fear of the Lord drive all these men over a cliff, or did Jashobeam's courage inspire others to enter the battle and he got the credit for the victory? How he accomplished this feat isn't disclosed, but it's unlikely that he killed them one at a time with his spear.

Eleazar (vv. 9-10) was from the tribe of Benjamin (1 Chron. 8:4) and fought beside David against the Philistines, probably at Pas Dammim (1 Sam. 17:1; 1 Chron. 11:12-13). While many of the Israelite soldiers were retreating, he remained in his place and fought until the sword was "welded" to his hand. The Lord honored the faith and courage of David and Eleazar and gave Israel a great victory, after which the other soldiers returned to the field to strip the dead and claim the spoils. Like David, Eleazar wasn't selfish about sharing the spoils of battle because the victory had come from the Lord (1 Sam. 30:21-25).

The third "mighty man" was Shammah (vv. 11-12), who also was used of the Lord to bring victory at Pas Dammim (1 Chron. 11:13-14). But why risk your life to defend a field of lentils and barley? Because the land belonged to the Lord (Lev. 25:23) and was given to Israel to use for His glory (Lev. 18:24-30). Shammah didn't want the Philistines to control what belonged to Jehovah, for the Jews were stewards of God's land. To respect the land meant to honor the Lord and His covenant with Israel.

The second "three mighty men" (vv. 13-17; 1 Chron. 11:15-19). These three aren't named, but they were a part of the "thirty" listed in verses 24-29. This suggests that they were not the three men named previously. All people are created equal before God and the law, but all people are not equal in gifts and abilities; some people have greater gifts and opportunities than others. However, the fact that we can't achieve like "the first three" shouldn't keep us from doing less than our best and perhaps establishing a "second three." God doesn't measure us by what He helped others do but by what He wanted us to do with the abilities and opportunities He graciously gave us.

The fact that David was hiding in a cave near Bethlehem suggests that this event took place either during the time that David was fleeing from Saul or shortly after he was made king in Hebron and the Philistines attacked him (2 Sam. 5:17; 1 Chron. 14:8). It was harvest time, which meant there had been no rain and the cisterns were empty. No water was available in the cave, and David thirsted for the water from the well at Bethlehem that he used to drink from when he was a boy. The text suggests that David spoke to himself about the water and didn't issue any orders, but the three men wanted to please their leader more than anything else. They were close enough to hear his whispered words, loyal enough to take his wish as their command, and brave enough to obey at any cost. They traveled twelve miles, broke through enemy lines, and came back with the water. What an example for us to follow in our relationship with the Captain of our salvation!

No matter what the Lord put in David's hands, he used it to honor God and help God's people—a sling, a sword, a harp, a scepter, even a cup of water—and this occasion was no exception. When David looked into the cup, he didn't see water; he saw the blood of the three men who had risked their lives to satisfy his desire. To drink that water would demean all his men and cheapen the brave deed of the three heroes. It would communicate that their lives really weren't important to him. Instead, David turned the cave into a temple and poured the water out as a drink offering to the Lord, as he had seen the priests do at the tabernacle. The drink offering accompanied the giving of another sacrifice, such as the burnt offering, and was not offered independently. It was an act of dedication that symbolized a person's life poured out in the service of the Lord. The three men had given themselves as a sacrifice to the Lord to serve David (Rom. 12:1), so David added his offering to theirs to show them he was one with them in their devotion to Jehovah. To paraphrase his own words in 24:24, David would not treat as nothing that which had cost those three men everything. All leaders need to follow David's example and let their followers know how much they appreciate them and the sacrifices they make.

Jesus gave Himself as a sacrifice for us, and also as a drink offering (Ps. 22:14; Isa.

53:12). Paul used the image of the drink offering to describe his own dedication to the Lord (Phil. 2:17; 2 Tim. 4:6). Mother Teresa often said, "We can do no great things, only small things with great love." But doing small things because we love Christ turns them into great things. According to Jesus, whenever we show love and kindness to others and seek to meet their needs, we give Him a cup of cold water (Matt. 25:34-40).

Two special "mighty men" (vv. 18-23; 1 Chron. 11:20-25). Abishai (vv. 18-19) was David's nephew and the brother of Joab, the commander of David's army. He was also the brother of Asahel, who was slain treacherously by Abner; and Joab and Abishai killed Abner, much to David's regret (2 Sam. 2–3). Abishai was a courageous man who is commended here for killing three hundred enemy soldiers. However, sometimes he had more zeal than wisdom. While in Saul's camp with David one night, he wanted to kill King Saul, an offer that David rejected (1 Sam. 26); and he also offered to cut off Shimei's head because he cursed David (16:9-11; 19:21). He led the army in the siege of Rabbah (10:10-14) and saved David's life during a battle with a giant (21:15-17). Abishai was loyal to David during Absalom's rebellion and was in charge of a third of David's army (18:2, 12).[2] Abishai was also in charge of "the second three" and was held in high honor.

Benaiah (vv. 20-23; 1 Chron. 11:22-25) was a remarkable man who was born to serve as a priest (1 Chron. 27:5) but became a soldier and the commander of David's bodyguard (8:18; 20:23). In the Bible, there are priests who became prophets, such as Jeremiah, Ezekiel, and John the Baptist, but Benaiah is the only priest named who became a soldier. He performed valiantly on the battlefield and fought some interesting battles. F. W. Boreham has a wonderful sermon about Benaiah killing the lion in which he points out that Benaiah met the worst of enemies (a lion) in the worst of places (a pit) under the worst of conditions (on a snowy day) – and he won! Benaiah was loyal to the house of David and supported Solomon when he came to the throne (1 Kings 1:8-10). When Joab tried to make Adonijah king, it was Benaiah who executed him, thus fulfilling David's command to Solomon (1 Kings 2:5-6). Solomon made Benaiah the head of his army in Joab's place (1 Kings 2:35; 4:4; 1 Chron. 27:5-6). Benaiah's son Jehoiada didn't follow a military career but became a counselor to King Solomon, replacing Ahithophel (27:34).

The Thirty (vv. 24-39; 1 Chron. 11:26-47). Saul may have stood head and shoulders above everybody else, but it was David who had the kind of character and stature that attracted men who were looking for true leadership. One mark of real leaders is that they have devoted followers and not just self-seeking flatterers and parasites. (The official term is "sycophants," from a Greek word meaning "an informer." The American and English slang expression would be "bootlicker.") Saul's officers were men he couldn't trust and who had to be bribed into loyal service (see 1 Sam. 22:6ff), but David's men would have died for their leader, and some of them did.

Since ancient peoples often had two or more names that could have alternate spellings, it's not easy to correlate the list in 2 Samuel 23 with the one in 1 Chronicles 11. Some names on the Samuel list are missing from the Chronicles list, but the latter list contains sixteen extra names (11:41-47). Perhaps they were replacements or alternates.[3] Those not mentioned in the

Chronicles list are Shammah son of Agee (v. 11), Elika (v. 25), Eliam (v. 34), and Igal (v. 36). The differences between the two lists are minor and doubtless the composition of this group changed from time to time as men died and were replaced.

In this list, the men are divided into four groups: the three mighty men (vv. 8-12), the second three mighty men (vv. 13-17),[4] two special leaders (vv. 18-23), and "The Thirty" exceptional soldiers (vv. 24-39).[5] But does verse 36 record one man's name ("Igal the son of Nathan who was the son of Hagri") or the names of two men ("Igal the son of Nathan, and the son of Hagri")? Except for the three men who brought David the water, the names of all the other men are given, so it seems strange that one man's name would be omitted. It's likely that verse 36 registers the name of one man, which means there were thirty-two soldiers in "The Thirty"—the twenty-nine named on the list, plus the three unnamed men of verses 13-17. Perhaps the term "The Thirty" was simply a code name for David's elite soldiers, regardless of how many there were, just as "The Twelve" was a code name for the Lord's apostles. If you add to the thirty-two men the three mighty men of verses 8-12, plus Abishai and Benaiah, you have the total of thirty-seven given in verse 39.

Two names are familiar to us: Asahel, the nephew of David and brother of Joab and Abishai (v. 24), and Uriah the Hittite, the husband of Bathsheba (v. 39; 1 Chron. 11:41). Both of them were dead, but their names remained on the list of great warriors. How tragic that David took the life of one of his best soldiers just to cover up sin!

Two other facts are worth noting. First, David didn't do the job alone; he had the help of many devoted followers. We think of David as a mighty warrior, and he was, but how far would he have gotten without his loyal and gifted soldiers? Most of the men listed came from Judah. This is to be expected since Judah was David's tribe and he reigned there before the nation was united. But "The Thirty" also included three men from Benjamin, the tribe of Saul, and several soldiers from neighboring nations. All these men recognized that God's hand was upon David and they wanted to be a part of what God was doing. The diversity of the commanders in his army speaks well of his leadership.

Second, God noted each man, had most of their names recorded in His Word, and will one day reward each one for the ministry he performed. David's name is mentioned over a thousand times in the Bible, while most of these men are mentioned but once or twice. However, when they meet the Lord, "then each one's praise will come from God" (1 Cor. 4:5 NKJV).

Joab was commander of the entire army (20:23), but he's mentioned in this military roster only in connection with his brothers Abishai (v. 18) and Asahel (v. 24; 1 Chron. 11:20, 26). In the end, Joab was disloyal to David and tried to put Adonijah on the throne, and this cost him his life (1 Kings 2:28-34).

3. David the repentant sinner. (2 Sam. 24; 1 Chron. 21)

Second Samuel 24:1 states that God incited David to number the people, while 1 Chronicles 21:1 names Satan as the culprit. Both are true: God permitted Satan to tempt David in order to accomplish the purposes He had in mind. Satan certainly opposed God's people throughout all of Old Testament history, but this is one of four instances in the Old Testament where Satan is named specifically and seen openly at work. The other three are when he tempted Eve (Gen. 3), when he attacked Job (Job 1–2) and when he accused Joshua the high priest (Zech. 3).[6]

A proud king (vv. 1-9; 1 Chron. 21:1-6). There was nothing illegal about a national census, if it was done according to the rules laid down in Exodus 30:11-16 (and see Num. 3:40-51). The half shekel received at the census was used to pay the bills for the sanctuary of God (Ex. 38:25-28). As a good Jewish citizen, Jesus paid his temple tax (Matt. 17:24-27), even though He knew that much of the ministry at the temple in that day was corrupt and had been rejected by His Father (Matt. 23:37–24:1). The phrase "the people" used in 2 Samuel 24:2, 4, 9, 10 refers to the Jewish military forces and is used this way in the Authorized Version of 1 Samuel 4:3, 4, 17. But the census that David ordered wasn't to collect the annual temple tax; it was a military census to see how big his army was, as verse 9 makes clear. But there had been military censuses in Israel in the past and the Lord hadn't judged the nation (Num. 1 and 26). What was there about this census that was wrong?

Joab and his captains were against the project (v. 4) and Joab's speech in verse 3 suggests that David's command was motivated by pride. The king wanted to magnify his own achievements rather than glorify the Lord. David may have rationalized this desire by arguing that his son Solomon was a man of peace who had no military experience. David wanted to be certain that, after his death, Israel would have the forces needed to preserve the peace. Another factor may have been David's plan to organize the army, the government, and the priests and Levites so that Solomon could manage things more easily and be able to build the temple (1 Chron. 22–27).

Whatever the cause, the Lord was displeased (1 Chron. 21:7), but He permitted Joab and his captains to spend the next nine months and twenty days counting the Israelites twenty years old and upward who were fit for military service. Sometimes God's greatest judgment is simply to let us have our own way. The census takers left Jerusalem, traveled east across the Jordan, and started counting at Aroer in the vicinity of the Dead Sea. Then they moved north through Gad and Gilead to Israel's northernmost border, where David had conquered the territory and expanded his kingdom (2 Sam. 8). The men then went west to Tyre and Sidon and then south to Beersheba in Judah, Israel's farthest border city.

From Beersheba, they returned to Jerusalem, but they didn't count the Levites (who were exempted from military duty, Num. 1:49; 2:33) and the men of Benjamin. The tabernacle was located at Gibeon in Benjamin (1 Chron. 16:39-40; 21:29) and Joab may have thought it unwise to invade holy territory on such a sinful mission. Anyway, Saul had come from Benjamin and there may still have been pockets of resistance in the tribe. Benjamin was too close to home and Joab didn't want to take any chances. The incomplete total was 1,300,000 men.[7]

A convicted king (24:10-14; 1 Chron. 21:7-13). Realizing that he had been foolish in pursuing the project, David confessed his sin and sought the Lord's face. At least six times in Scripture we find David confessing "I have sinned" (2 Sam. 12:13; 24:10, 17; Ps. 41:4 and 51:4; 1 Chron. 21:8). When he confessed his sins of adultery and murder, David said, "I have sinned"; but when he confessed his sin of numbering the people, he said, "I have sinned *greatly*" (italics mine). Most of us would consider his sins relating to Bathsheba far worse than the sin of numbering the people, and far more foolish, but David saw the enormity of what he had done. David's sins with Bathsheba took the lives of four of David's sons (the baby, Amnon, Absalom, and Adonijah) plus the life of Uriah; but after the census, God sent a plague that took the lives of seventy thousand people. The Lord must have agreed with David that he had indeed sinned greatly.

David's sin with Bathsheba was a sin of the flesh, a yielding to lust after an afternoon of laziness (11:2; Gal. 5:19), but the census was a sin of the spirit (see 2 Cor. 7:1), a willful act of rebellion against God. It was motivated by pride, and pride is number one on the list of the sins that God hates (Prov. 6:16-17). "Pride is the ground in which all the other sins grow," wrote William Barclay, "and the parent from which all the other sins come." Both Scripture and civil law make a distinction between sudden sins of passion and willful sins of rebellion and treat the guilty parties differently (Deut. 19:1-13; Ex. 21:12-14). The census was willful rebellion, and David sinned against a flood of light. Furthermore, God gave David over nine months' time to repent, but he refused to yield. In the various scenes in David's history, Joab doesn't come across as a godly man, but even Joab was opposed to this project, and so were his officers. David should have heeded their counsel, but he was determined to have a census.

God in His grace forgives our sins when we confess them (1 John 1:9), but in His righteous government, He allows us to reap the consequences. In this case, the Lord even gave David the privilege of choosing the consequences. Why? Because David's disobedience was a sin of the will, a deliberate choice on David's part, so God allowed him to make another choice and name the punishment. Gad[8] gave the king three choices and told him to consider them, make a decision, and give his answer when the prophet returned.

Between the first and second visits, David must have sought the face of the Lord, for God lowered the famine period from seven years to three years, which explains the seeming discrepancy between 2 Samuel 24:13 and 1 Chronicles 21:12. In His mercy, God shortened the days of the suffering for His chosen people (Matt. 24:22). The three punishments are named in God's covenant with Israel (Deut. 28), so David shouldn't have been surprised: *famine*—28:23-24, 38-40; *military defeat*—28:25-26, 41-48; *pestilence*—28:21-22, 27-28, 35, 60-61.[9] In Jewish law, the unintentional sin of the high priest was equivalent to the sin of the entire congregation (Lev. 4:1-3, 13-14), so how much more would the penalties apply to a king who had sinned intentionally! Knowing the mercy of the Lord, David wisely chose pestilence for his punishment.

A repentant king (24:15-25; 1 Chron. 21:14-30). The plague started the next day at morning and continued for the appointed three days, with the judgment angel ending his work at Jerusalem, just as Joab and his men had done (v. 8). David's shepherd's heart was broken because of this judgment and he pleaded with the Lord to punish him instead. Why would God kill seventy thousand men and yet keep David alive? We must note that 24:1 says that God was angry *with Israel* and not with David, so He must have been punishing the people for some sin they had committed. It's been suggested that this plague took the lives of the Israelites who had followed Absalom in his rebellion and didn't want David as their king. This may be so, but the text doesn't tell us.

God permitted David to see the judgment angel hovering over Jerusalem near the threshing floor of Araunah (Ornan), a Jebusite. The Jebusites were the original inhabitants of Jerusalem, so Ornan had submitted to David's rule and become a reputable citizen of Jerusalem. We aren't told that David heard God's command to the angel to cease plaguing the people, but David knew that God was merciful and gracious, so he begged for mercy for "the sheep of his pasture" (Ps. 100:3). The elders of Israel were with David (1 Chron. 21:16) and with him fell to the ground in humble contrition and worship. It was David's sin that precipitated the crisis, but perhaps they realized that the nation had also sinned and deserved to feel God's rod of discipline.

Once again, the prophet Gad appeared on the scene, this time with a message of hope. David was to build an altar on Ornan's threshing floor and there offer sacrifices to the Lord, and the plague would cease. As king, David could have appropriated the property (1 Sam. 8:14) or even borrowed it, but he insisted on purchasing it. David knew the high cost of sinning and he refused to give the Lord something that had cost him nothing. For fifty shekels of silver he purchased the oxen for sacrifices and the wooden yokes for fuel, and for six hundred shekels of gold, he purchased the entire threshing floor (24:24; 1 Chron. 21:25). When the priest offered the sacrifices, God sent fire from heaven to consume them as a token of His acceptance (1 Chron. 21:26; Lev. 9:24).

Knowing that the king was well able to purchase his property, why was Ornan so anxious to give it to David absolutely free? Or was his offer just another instance of traditional Eastern courtesy in the art of bargaining? (See Gen. 23.) Perhaps Ornan remembered what happened to Saul's descendants because of what Saul did to the Gibeonites (21:1-14) and he didn't want the lives of his sons threatened (1 Chron. 21:20). The King James translation of verse 23 is a bit awkward and gives the idea that Ornan himself was a king, so the NIV or NASB should be consulted.

The land that David purchased was no ordinary piece of property, for it was the place where Abraham had put his son Isaac on the altar (Gen. 22) and where Solomon would build the temple (1 Chron. 22:1; 2 Chron. 3:1). After the plague had ceased, David consecrated the site to the Lord (Lev. 27:20-21) and used it as a place of sacrifice and worship. The altar and tabernacle were at Gibeon, but David was permitted to worship at Jerusalem. The land was sanctified and would one day be the site of God's temple. David announced, "This is the house of the Lord God, and this is the altar of the burnt offering for Israel" (1 Chron. 22:1), and from that time began to get everything ready for Solomon to build the temple.

If you were asked to name David's two greatest sins, you would probably reply, "His adultery with Bathsheba and his numbering of the people," and you would be right. *But out of* those *two great sins, God built a temple!* Bathsheba gave birth to Solomon and God chose him to succeed David on the throne. On the property David purchased and on which he erected an altar, Solomon built the temple and dedicated it to the glory of God. What God did for David is certainly not an excuse for sin (Rom. 6:1-2), because David paid dearly for committing those sins. However, knowing what God did for David does encourage us to seek His face and trust His grace when we have disobeyed Him. "But where sin abounded, grace abounded much more" (Rom. 5:20). What a merciful God we serve!

CHAPTER THIRTEEN
DAVID'S LEGACY
1 Chronicles 22–29

David "served his own generation by the will of God" (Acts 13:36 NKJV). When you serve your own generation faithfully, you also serve future generations. "He who does the will of God abides forever" (1 John 2:17 NKJV). The legacy of David enriched God's people Israel for centuries. Not only did David provide all that was needed for the building of the temple, he also wrote songs and designed musical instruments to be used in the worship services (23:5). Even more, it was through David's family that the Savior came into the world, "the Root and Offspring of David" (Rev. 22:16), so David still enriches the church today.

When we hear David's name, we may think first of Bathsheba and David's sins, but these chapters present David the builder, the man who risked his life to gather wealth for the building of a temple to the glory of God. He's a great example for believers of every age who want to make their lives count for Christ and leave behind their own legacy of spiritual blessing.

1. Spiritual motivation

Some Bible readers today might be tempted to scan these chapters, skip all the lists of names, and go on to read about the reign of Solomon in 2 Chronicles; but to do so would be a great mistake. Think of the encouragement and guidance these chapters must have given to the Jewish remnant that returned to Jerusalem after the Babylonian captivity. (See the books of Ezra, Nehemiah, Haggai, and Zechariah.) These courageous people had to rebuild the temple and organize its ministry, and reading these chapters would remind them that they were doing God's work. God gave each detail of the original temple and its ministry to David, who then gave it to Solomon. Those "lists of names" helped Zerubbabel and Joshua the high priest examine the credentials of those who wanted to serve in the temple (Ezra 2:59-64), and refuse those who were not qualified.

These chapters encouraged the Jews in their labors centuries ago, and they can encourage us today as we seek to build the church (Eph. 2:19-22). When you read 1 Corinthians 3:9-23 and compare it with 1 Chronicles 22, 28, and 29, you see parallels that ought to encourage us to build the church the way God's Word commands.[1] David knew that God's temple had to be built with gold, silver, and costly stones (22:14; 29:1-5), and Paul took these materials and applied them spiritually to the local church. They stand for the wisdom of God as found in the Word of God (Prov. 2:1-10; 3:13-15; 8:10-21). Wood, hay, and straw can be picked up on the surface, but if you want gold, silver, and jewels, *you have to dig for them.* We don't build the local church on clever human ideas or by imitating the world; we build by teaching and obeying the precious truths of the Word of God. (See 1 Cor. 3:18-20 for Paul's view of the wisdom of this world.)

Solomon didn't have to draw his own plans for the temple, because the Lord gave the plans to David (28:11-12). As we read the Word and pray, the Lord shows us His plans for each local church. "Work out your own salvation [Christian ministry] with fear and trembling" (Phil. 2:12-13 NKJV) was written to a congregation of believers in Philippi, and though it has personal application for all believers, the emphasis is primarily on the ministry of the congregation collectively. Some local church leaders run from one seminar to another, seeking to learn how to build the church, when they probably ought to stay home, call the church to prayer, and seek the mind of God in His Word. God has different plans for each church, and we're not supposed to blindly imitate each other.

The temple was built to display the glory of God, and our task in the local church is to glorify God (1 Cor. 10:31; 14:25). When Solomon dedicated the temple, God's glory moved in (1 Kings 8:6-11); but when Israel sinned, the glory moved out (Ezek. 10:4, 18-19; 11:22-23). We wonder how many local churches go through the motions of worship Sunday after Sunday, yet there's no evidence of the glory of God.

The temple was to be "a house of prayer for all nations" (Isa. 56:7), but the religious leaders in Jesus' day had made it into a den of thieves (Matt. 21:13; Lk. 19:46; Jer. 7:11). A den of thieves is the place where thieves run to hide after they've done their wicked deeds, which suggests that a service in a local church can be a good place to go to pretend to be spiritual (1 John 1:5-10). How many local churches are known for their effective ministry of prayer? They may be houses of music, education, and even social activities, but are they houses of prayer?

The temple was built and God honored it with His presence because the leaders and people gave their best to the Lord, sacrificed, and followed His directions. This is a good example for us to follow today. We are privileged to assist in the building of the church, and our motive must be only the glory of God.

2. Careful preparation (1 Chron. 22:1-19)

The Lord didn't permit David to build the temple, but He did honor the preparation David made for his son Solomon to do the job. "Well begun is half done" says the old proverb, and David was careful to have Solomon, the people, and the materials prepared for the great project. (See vv. 3, 5 and 14.)

The site, materials, and workers (vv. 1-4). We're not sure when the Lord began to give David the plans for the temple and its personnel, but the purchase of Ornan's property seemed to be the signal for action. When God sent fire from heaven to consume David's offerings (21:26), David knew that his sin was forgiven and that he was back in fellowship with the Lord. But David also perceived that his altar was now very special to the Lord and he continued to sacrifice there instead of going to the tabernacle at Gibeon. The Lord let him know that Mount Moriah was the place where He wanted the temple to be built. It's possible that David wrote Psalm 30 at this time, even though as yet there was no actual building to dedicate. By faith, he dedicated to the Lord the property he had purchased and the building that would one day stand on it.[2]

David enlisted both Jews and resident aliens (1 Kings 5:13-18) to help construct the temple. This division of David's government was under Adoram (2 Sam. 20:24), also called Adoniram (1 Kings 4:6).[3] The 30,000 Jewish workers cut timber in Lebanon for a month and then returned home for two months, while the 150,000 "alien" laborers cut and delivered massive stones from the hills, supervised by Jewish foremen (1 Kings 5:13-18, and see 9:15-19; 2 Chron. 2:17-18). The fact that Gentiles worked along with the Jews suggests that the temple was indeed a house for all nations. We must not think that these resident aliens were treated as slaves, because the Law of Moses clearly prohibited such practices (Ex. 22:21; 23:9; Lev. 19:33).

For years, David had been amassing the materials for the temple, the total value of which was beyond calculation. Much of it came from the spoils of the battles David had fought and won (18:9-11; 26:26-28). David the warrior had defeated Israel's enemies and taken their wealth so that Solomon his son would have the peace and provisions necessary to build the house of God.

Solomon the builder (vv. 5-16). Some biblical chronologists believe David was about sixty years old when he inaugurated the temple building program, but we don't know how old Solomon was. David said his son was "young and inexperienced" (22:5; 29:1 NIV), and after his accession to the throne, Solomon called himself "a little child" (1 Kings 3:7). This explains why David admonished and encouraged his son several times to obey the Lord and finish the work God had assigned to him (22:6-16; 28:9-10, 20-21). David also admonished the leaders to encourage and assist their new king in this great project. David wanted everything to be prepared before his own death so that Solomon would have everything he needed to build the house of God.

David encouraged Solomon by assuring him that the temple project was the will of God; therefore, the Lord would help him finish it (vv. 6-10). God had enabled his father to fight the Lord's battles and bring about peace for Israel, and now it was time to build God's house (2 Sam. 7:9). The Lord had told David that a son would be born to him to accomplish this task (7:12-16; 1 Chron. 17:11; see Deut. 12:8-14). The emphasis David made was that the temple was to be built, not for the glory of the name of David or even of Solomon, but the name of the Lord (vv. 7, 8, 10, 19). David wanted to be sure that Solomon would honor the Lord and not build a monument to honor himself.

David further encouraged his son by reminding him of the faithfulness of God (vv. 11-13). If he would trust the Lord and obey Him fully, the Lord would maintain the peace and security of Israel and enable him to complete the project (see 28:7-9, 20). The words "Be strong, and of good courage; dread not, nor be dismayed" remind us of how Moses encouraged Joshua his successor (Deut. 31:5-8, 23); the Lord repeated that encouragement after Moses died (Josh. 1:6, 9). Moses and Joshua were faithful men, and God saw them through all their trials and enabled them to complete their work. He would do the same for Solomon.

The third encouragement David gave his son was the great amount of wealth the king had accumulated for the project, along with the large number of workers who were conscripted (vv. 14-16). It seems incredible, but the king said he had amassed 3,750 tons of gold and 37,500 tons of silver, and that there was so much bronze and iron that it couldn't be weighed. At least Solomon wouldn't have to take up any collections!

The leaders of Israel (vv. 17-19). David ordered the leaders to cooperate with Solomon and help him complete the project. He reminded them that the peace and rest they enjoyed was only because God had used David to defeat Israel's foes and expand her borders. (Note the mention of "rest" in vv. 9 and 18 and in 23:25.) But the temple was for the Lord, so it was imperative that the leaders seek Him and have their hearts right before Him. David had his throne in Jerusalem and he wanted the Ark—the throne of God—to be there also. His only concern was that the name of the Lord be glorified.

3. Temple organization (1 Chron. 23:1–27:34)

David knew that the ministers of the temple also had to be organized and prepared if God was to be glorified. Too often local church building programs concentrate so much on the financial and the material that they ignore the spiritual, and then a backslidden and divided congregation meets to dedicate the new edifice! A gifted administrator, David organized the Levites (chap. 23), the priests (chap. 24), the temple singers (chap. 25), and the temple officers (chap. 26). David wanted to be sure that everything in God's house would be done "decently and in order" (1 Cor. 14:40 NKJV). In making these decisions, David and his two priests drew lots (24:5-6, 31; 25:8; 26:13-14, 16). This was the process Joshua used when he gave the tribes their inheritance in the Promised Land (Josh. 14:2; 23:4).

But organization wasn't an end in itself, for these people were being organized for service. The phrase "for the service of the house of the Lord" (or its equivalent) is used several times in these chapters to remind us that ministry is the major responsibility of God's servants in God's house. (See 23:24, 26, 28, 32; 25:1, 6, 8, 30; 28:13, 14, 20, 21; 29:5, 7; 2 Chron. 31: 16, 17.) It's one thing to fill an office, but quite something else to use that office to serve the Lord and His people.

The Levites (23:1-32; see also chap. 6). The author of Chronicles doesn't record the family struggle that occurred when Solomon became king (1 Kings 1–2), but verse 1 indicates an earlier appointment and 29:22 a second one. However, verse 1 may simply mean that David announced Solomon as his successor, as in 28:4-5, while 29:22 describes the actual coronation. (We get the impression that Solomon's coronation described in 1 Kings 1 was very hastily arranged.) Solomon's formal public accession to the throne is described in 29:21-25.

The Levites assisted the priests in the sanctuary ministry and were required by the law to be at least thirty years old (v. 3; Num. 4:3; see also Num. 8:24). Later that was lowered to twenty years (v. 24). The 38,000 Levites were divided into four groups, each with a specific ministry: 24,000 Levites who helped the priests in the sanctuary, 6,000 who were "officers and judges" (see 26:1-32), 4,000 who were gatekeepers ("porters" KJV; see 26:1-19), and 4,000 who were singers (see 25:1-31). There was one temple, one high priest, one divine law, and one Lord to serve, but there was a diversity of gifts and ministries, not unlike the church today. The fact that the Levites took care of the sanctuary while the priests served at the altar didn't mean that their work was less important to the ministry or to the Lord. Each servant was important to the Lord and each ministry was necessary.

David not only organized the sanctuary musicians, but he also provided them with proper musical instruments to use in praising the Lord (v. 5; 2 Chron. 29:25-27; Amos 6:5). Nothing that the priests and Levites did in the temple was left to chance or human invention, but was ordained by the Lord. Nadab and Abihu, the sons of Aaron, the first high priest (24:1-2), were killed by the Lord for devising their own form of worship (Lev. 10).

The Levitical duties are given in verses 24-32. The Israelites were at rest in their land and no longer a nomadic people, so the Levites didn't have to carry the various parts of the tabernacle from place to place (see Num. 4). The construction of the temple meant that the Levites would need new assignments. One of their tasks would be to keep the temple clean and in good repair and make sure that the temple precincts were ceremonially pure. They also saw to it that the supply of meal was available for the offerings. Whenever the daily, monthly, and annual sacrifices were offered, the Levite choir would provide praise to the Lord.

The priests (24:1-31). It was important that the priests truly be descendants of Aaron. In David's day, he had two high priests, Zadok, a descendant of Aaron through Eleazar, and Ahimelech, the son of Abiathar, who was from the line of Ithamar. Abiathar was David's friend and priest during his exile days (1 Sam. 20:20ff) and also during the rebellion of Absalom (2 Sam. 15:24-29). Unfortunately, Abiathar wasn't loyal to Solomon and sided with Adonijah in his quest for the throne, and Solomon had to banish him from Jerusalem (1 Kings 2:22-27). Abiathar came from the line of Eli, and that line was rejected and judged by God (1 Sam. 2:30-33; also see 2 Sam. 22:26-27). The twenty-four families (clans) of priests were assigned by lot to serve in the sanctuary at scheduled times and the rest of the time would be in the priestly cities instructing the people. This procedure was still being followed when Zacharias served in the temple (Luke 1:5-9). He was from the clan of Abijah (24:10).

The musicians (25:1-31). Apart from the ritual blowing of the trumpets (Num. 10), nowhere in the Law of Moses is there any mention of music in connection with Jewish worship, yet this chapter describes an elaborate organization of twenty-four courses of singers and musicians. David was a writer of psalms and a gifted musician (2 Sam. 23:1-2; 1 Sam. 16:18) and it's likely that the sanctuary musical worship came to fruition under his direction (v. 6), and the Lord approved these innovations (2 Chron. 29:25). Harps, lyres, and cymbals are mentioned here (v. 1), and trumpets are mentioned elsewhere (1 Chron. 13:8; 15:24, 28; 2 Chron. 5:13; 20:28). There were also choirs (1 Chron. 15:27).

Three gifted Levites were put in charge of the instrumental music and the singing in the worship services. Asaph wrote at least twelve psalms (50, 73–83) and played the cymbals (16:5). Heman was also called "the king's seer" (v. 5), which suggests that he had a special gift of discerning the Lord's will. The Lord promised to give Heman a large family (v. 5 NIV), and all his children were musicians. Jeduthun's name is related to "Judah" and means "praise," a good name for a choir director. Jeduthun is also associated with Psalms 39, 62 and 77.

The word "prophesy" is used three times in verses 1-3 to describe the ministry of Asaph, Heman, and Jeduthun. The word usually refers to the ministry of the prophets in declaring God's Word. As has often been said, "The prophets were *forth*-tellers as well as *fore*-tellers." They spoke to present needs and didn't just predict future events. Miriam led the women in praising the Lord, and she was called a prophetess (Ex. 15:20). The root of the Hebrew word *naba* means "to bubble, to boil up," referring to the fervor and excitement of the prophet declaring God's message. Others say it comes from an Arabic root that means "to announce." The point is that the men who led Israel's sanctuary worship were not necessarily prophets in the technical sense, but they and their singers declared the Word (God's message) with enthusiasm and joy.

Temple officers (26:1-32). These officials included gatekeepers (vv. 1-19), treasurers (vv. 20-28), and miscellaneous officials scattered outside Jerusalem (vv. 29-32). The gatekeepers were assigned to guard the temple gates, with four guards at the north and south gates and six at the east and west gates (vv. 17-18 NLT). Two guards watched over the storehouse, and there were also guards outside the temple area. There are details about the temple area that aren't recorded in Scripture, and this makes it difficult for us to be exact in our description.[4] It seems that the gatekeepers watched the people come and go and made sure that nobody was deliberately defiling the temple or behaving in a way that disgraced the sanctuary of the Lord.

The treasurers (vv. 20-28) guarded the two temple treasuries, one for general offerings and the other for "dedicated things" from the people, especially the spoils of war (vv. 20-28). (See 2 Kings 12:4-16.) Saul and David added to this treasury, but so did other leaders, such as Samuel the prophet and Abner and Joab, the two generals.

The third group of temple officers (vv. 29-32) were the "officers and judges" assigned to tasks away from the temple and even west of the Jordan. They kept the king in touch with the affairs of the tribes of Reuben and Gad and the half tribe of Manasseh. But these officers were also responsible to keep these tribes involved in "every matter pertaining to God" (v. 32 NIV), that is, the all-important religious events of the nation. Separated from the other tribes, the trans-Jordanic Israelites might easily grow careless about observing the annual feasts or even the weekly Sabbaths. This explains why these officers are listed among the temple workers. It's also likely that these officers were also responsible to collect taxes.

4. Military administration (1 Chron. 27:1-34)

For Solomon to be able to build the temple, Israel had to remain a strong nation, at peace with her neighbors, for young Solomon wasn't a military genius like his father David. It was necessary to organize the army, the tribal leaders, and the managers and counselors who served the king personally.

The captains (vv. 1-15). David's army consisted of 288,000 men—not an excessively large standing army—made up of twelve divisions of 24,000 each, so that each man served one month out of the year. However, if a military emergency arose, the entire army could be called up. Each monthly military division was in the charge of one of David's "mighty men," who are listed in 1 Chronicles 11. The twelve commanders are: Jashobeam (vv. 2-3; see 11:11); Dodai (v. 4; see 11:12); Benaiah, head of David's personal bodyguard (vv. 5-6; see 11:22-25); Asahel, David's nephew (v. 7; see 11:26); Shamhuth (v. 8; see 11:27); Ira (v. 9; see 11:28); Helez (v. 10; see 11:27); Sibbecai (v. 11; see 11:29); Abiezer (v. 12; see 11:28); Maharai (v. 13; see 11:30); another Benaiah (v. 14; see 11:31); and Heldai (v. 15; see 11:30).

The tribal leaders (vv. 16-24). Each of the tribes had a leader (Num. 1–2, 4) and the tribes were broken down into smaller units (tens, fifties, hundreds, thousands; Ex. 18:17-23), each unit with a leader. For some reason, Gad and Asher are not mentioned in this list, but to reach the number twelve, Levi is included along with both tribes of Joseph (Ephraim and Manasseh). The king could summon twelve men and through them eventually get the ear of all the people.

The mention of the tribes and their leaders brought to mind David's ill-fated census (21:1-17; 2 Sam. 24). This extra piece of information helps us understand why the numbers differ in the two accounts (24:9; 21:5), because Joab didn't finish the census and not all the numbers were recorded.

The king's managers (vv. 25-31). During Saul's reign, there was some kind of tax structure (1 Sam. 17:25), but this is not mentioned in the records of David's reign. Under Solomon, the taxes became intolerable (1 Kings 4:7, 26-28;12:1-24). David owned royal farms, orchards, vineyards, flocks, and herds, and from these he met the needs of the palace personnel. David had storehouses for his produce, and since his tastes weren't as expensive as Solomon's, what David received from the Lord went much further.

The king's counselors (vv. 32-34). Every leader needs an inner circle of counselors who will advise him, force him to examine his own decisions and motives, and help him seek the mind of the Lord. Jonathan, David's uncle, is given high recommendations. Jehiel appears to have been tutor to the sons in the royal family. Ahithophel had been David's trusted friend and wise adviser, but he sided with Absalom in the rebellion and committed suicide when Absalom rejected his counsel (2 Sam. 15:30-31; 16:15–17:23). Hushai was the man whose counsel was accepted by Absalom, which led to the downfall of the rebel army. Ahithophel's replacement was "Jehoiada son of Benaiah." This Benaiah is probably the son of David's trusted head of the royal bodyguard, Benaiah the priest. Abiathar the priest was one of David's must trusted helpers (1 Sam. 22:20-23), and though Joab and David were not intimates, David needed the head of his army in his inner circle if only to know what he was thinking. Joab didn't always have David's interests at heart.

5. Sincere consecration (1 Chron. 28:1–29:20)

No amount of human machinery and organization can take the place of heartfelt consecration to the Lord. David was going to leave the scene, an inexperienced son would follow him, and the construction of the temple was a task beyond any one man or group of men. Apart from the blessing of the Lord, the people could not hope to succeed. Leaders come and go, but the Lord remains; and it is the Lord whom we must please.

David challenges the leaders (28:1-8). David assembled at Jerusalem the leaders mentioned in the previous chapters and reviewed for them the story of his great desire to build a temple for the Lord. It's good for people to know the heart of their leader and how God has worked in his or her heart. He emphasized that it was the Lord who chose and anointed him and who chose Solomon to be his successor. He reminded the leaders of God's gracious covenant with the house of David and of their responsibility to obey the law of the Lord. If they kept the terms of the covenant and obeyed God, He would keep His promises and bless the nation. As long as they obeyed the terms of God's covenant, they would possess the land and enjoy its blessings.

David charges Solomon (28:9-10). Solomon had a great responsibility to set the example and obey the law of the Lord. A "perfect heart" means a heart wholly dedicated to the Lord, one that's not divided. It's unfortunate that in his later years Solomon became a double-minded man and began to worship idols, for this led to God's discipline and the division of the kingdom. For the second time, David admonished Solomon to "be strong" (22:13), and he would do it a third time before he finished his speech (v. 20). Dr. Lee Roberson has often said, "Everything rises and falls with leadership." If leadership is faithful to the Lord and trusting in Him, God will give success.

David conveys his gifts for the project (vv. 11-21). David's first gift to Solomon was a written plan for the temple and its furnishings (vv. 11-19). While the temple followed the pattern of the tabernacle in a general way, what Solomon built was larger and much more elaborate than what Moses built. David reminded Solomon that these plans were not suggestions from the Lord; they were a divine commission. The organization of the priests and Levites was also commanded by the Lord. Moses had to make everything according to the pattern God gave him on the mount (Ex. 25:9, 40; Heb. 8:5), and so did Solomon. The plans for the temple spelled out how much material should go into each piece of furniture and each part of the building (vv. 13-19), and nothing was to be changed.

David's second gift was another word of encouragement to strengthen Solomon's will and his faith (v. 20). Like Moses encouraging Joshua (Deut. 31:6-7), David told Solomon that the Lord would never forsake him and that he could find in God all the wisdom and strength he needed to complete the project.[5]

The third gift Solomon received from his father was a people prepared to work with him and complete the project (v. 21). We've seen how David organized the various levels of leaders, both civil and religious, so they could work harmoniously and follow their new king. Just as the Lord provided skillful people to construct the tabernacle (Ex. 35:25-35; 36:1-2), so He would provide the workers that Solomon needed to build the temple of Jehovah. This promise was fulfilled (2 Chron. 2:13-14). Furthermore, all the people would listen to their new king's commands and obey him.

David's fourth gift was his own store of wealth that he had accumulated for the building of the temple (29:1-5). According to 22:14, the spoils of battle devoted to the Lord amounted to 3,750 tons of gold and 37,500 tons of silver. David added from his own wealth 110 tons of gold and 260 tons of silver (v. 4). This means that David was responsible for providing 3,860 tons of gold and 37,760 tons of silver. But the king then urged his leaders to give generously to the "building fund" (vv. 6-9), and they contributed 190 tons of gold, plus another 185 pounds, 375 tons of silver, 675 tons of bronze, and 3,750 tons of iron, as well as precious stones. This sounds like Paul's "gold, silver, and precious stones" (1 Cor. 3:12). The remarkable thing about the leaders and their offering is that they gave willingly and "rejoiced with great joy" at the privilege! This time we're reminded of Paul's words in 2 Corinthians 8:1-5 and 9:7.

David calls on the Lord (29:10-21). This magnificent prayer begins with praise and adoration to the Lord (vv. 10-14). God had blessed David richly, so he blesses God thankfully! His words are a short course in theology. He blesses the God of Israel and acknowledges His greatness, power, glory, victory, and majesty. God owns everything! God is sovereign over all! His name is great and glorious! But who are David and his people that they should be able to give so lavishly to the Lord? After all, everything comes from Him, and when we give, we only return to the Lord that which He has graciously already given to us.

In contrast to the eternal God, David declares that he—the king!—is like any other human, an alien and a stranger on the earth. God is eternal, but human life is brief and nobody can prevent the inevitable hour of death. (Here David sounds like Moses in Ps. 90.) Since all things come from God, and life is brief, the wisest thing we can do is give back to God what He gives to us and make an investment in the eternal.

He assures the Lord that the offerings came from his heart and the hearts of his people, and that they gave joyfully and with sincerity. David prays that his people might always have hearts of generosity, gratitude, and joy, and that they might always be loyal to their God. In other words, may they worship God alone and not make wealth their God.

Like any godly father, David closed his prayer by interceding for his son Solomon, that he would always be obedient to what was written in the law, and that he might succeed in building the temple to the glory of God. ("Palace" in v. 19 KJV means "any large palatial structure.") He then called on the congregation to bless the Lord, and they obeyed and bowed low and even fell on their faces in submission and adoration. What a way to begin a building program!

6. Joyful celebration (1 Chron. 29:21-25)

The next day, David provided sacrifices for the Lord and a feast for his leaders. The burnt offerings were sacrificed to express the people's total dedication to the Lord. But David also offered fellowship offerings, and a part of each sacrifice was used for a fellowship meal. It was a joyful occasion that climaxed with the coronation of Solomon. It was very important that the representatives of all Israel agree that Solomon was God's appointed king; otherwise, he could never have led them in the building of the temple. David was anointed privately by Samuel (1 Sam. 16:13) and publicly at Hebron on two occasions (2 Sam. 2:4; 5:3), so he was anointed three times. At the same celebration, Zadok was anointed high priest, which suggests that Abiathar was set aside. Eventually Abiathar turned traitor and supported Adonijah and was sent into retirement (1 Kings 2:26-27, 35).

The book closes on a sober note as it records the death of King David. A Russian proverb says, "Even the greatest king must at last be put to bed with a shovel." True, but some bring glory to God even from the grave! From that day on, the Jewish kings were all measured against David (1 Kings 3:3; 15:5; 2 Kings 18:3; 22:2; 14:3; 15:3, 34; 16:2; 18:3; 20:3).

David's legacy is a long one and a rich one. He unified the nation, gave the people peace in their land, and extended the borders of the kingdom. God chose him to establish the dynasty that eventually brought Jesus the Savior into the world. He provided much of the wealth that was used to build the temple, and the king who constructed it. He also purchased the site on which the temple would be built. God gave David the plans for the temple, and David recruited the workers to build it.

David wrote songs for the Levites to sing as they worshiped God, and he also provided the musical instruments. He organized the temple ministry and taught the people that the worship of God was the number-one priority for them and the nation. Before he died, he encouraged Solomon, challenged the leaders, and gave to the new king a united people, enthusiastic about building the house of God. We today learn from David's life both what to do and what to avoid. We read and meditate on David's hymns, and sometimes we sing them.

Endnotes

Chapter 1

1. It's interesting that 1 Samuel records the scene of a messenger bringing bad news of defeat to Eli the priest (1 Sam. 4), and here a similar messenger brings what he

thought was good news to David the king. Eli keeled over and died, but here the messenger was slain. In 1 Samuel, the Ark was taken by the enemy, but later recovered by Israel; here the bodies of the royal family were taken and later recovered and buried.

2. Saul's death reminds us of Revelation 3:11: "Behold, I am coming quickly! Hold fast what you have, that no one may take your crown" (NKJV).
3. King Saul's namesake, Saul of Tarsus, began his ministry by falling (Acts 9:4; 22:7; 26:14), but at the end of his life, we see him standing boldly with his Lord (2 Tim. 4:16-17).
4. The KJV gives the impression that David wrote this song to encourage young men to learn how to use the bow, but the Hebrew text doesn't support this. The elegy was called "The Song of the Bow" possibly because of the reference to Jonathan's bow in verse 22. The name identified the tune that was used to sing the song. Certainly David wasn't encouraging the archers to practice more because Saul and Jonathan lost the battle, because his song extols their military prowess.
5. The Hebrew word translated "glory" can also be translated "gazelle." David saw Saul as a majestic deer that had been slain on the mountain.
6. "The sword devours" (i.e., eats, drinks) is a familiar metaphor in the Old Testament (Deut. 32:42; 2 Sam. 2:26; 11:25; Isa. 31:8; Jer. 12:12). Saul's sword devoured much blood and was satisfied.
7. It appears that the tribe of Judah, while cooperating with Saul and the other tribes, had been maintaining somewhat of a "separated" posture in those days (see 1 Sam. 11:8; 15:4; 17:52; 18:16; 30:26).
8. David was anointed three times: first privately by Samuel (1 Sam. 16:13), then publicly by the elders and people of Judah (2 Sam. 2:4), and finally publicly by the whole nation (5:3).

Chapter 2

1. The name "baal" also belonged to Saul's granduncle (1 Chron. 9:36), and Jonathan's lame son, Mephibosheth, was also called "Merib-Baal" (1 Chron. 8:34).
2. Joab was David's nephew, but David didn't seem to have much control over him (see 3:39 and 18:5, 14.) At the end of David's reign, Joab conspired to make David's son Adonijah the next king; when Solomon took the throne, he had Joab executed for treason (1 Kings 2).
3. According to 2 Samuel 17:25, Zeruiah was either David's half sister or stepsister. If Nahash was the mother of Abigail and Zeruiah, then she was Jesse's second wife. If Nahash was the father, then he sired Abigail and Zeruiah, died, and his unidentified wife married Jesse. Whoever she was, Zeruiah certainly was the mother of three remarkable men.
4. First Chronicles 27:7 tells us that Asahel's son Zebadiah succeeded his father as commander of his division.
5. There's an interesting pattern in 2 Samuel in which you find a list of names (children or officials) at the end of historical sections: 1:1–3:5; 3:6–5:16; 5:17–8:18; 9:1–20:26.
6. The situation reminds us of the Parable of the Prodigal Son (Luke 15:11-32). Abner, the "prodigal soldier," was coming home, and David gave him a banquet. Joab, the faithful "elder brother," might say to David, "I've been faithful to you and risked my life, and yet you never gave me a banquet!"

Chapter 3

1. How could this many people converge on Hebron and eat and drink for three days without upsetting the town and its economy? Where would all the food come from? First Chronicles 13:1 may give us the answer. While the chronicler gives us the totals of the military units loyal to David, perhaps only the officers of these military units attended the coronation, a total of about 3,750 men. Not every soldier was present, but every soldier was represented and through his officer gave his allegiance to the new king.
2. The name "Eliphelet" is found twice in the list and is also given as "Elpelet."
3. If the brave deed of the three mighty men occurred at this time, then David was in the Cave of Adullam (2 Sam. 23:13).
4. Some Old Testament scholars put this event later in David's career, after David's sin with Bathsheba and his numerous battles against his enemies (2 Sam. 8–12). See *A Harmony of the Books of Samuel, Kings and Chronicles* by William Day Crockett (Baker Book House, 1964).

5. It's not likely that these sacrifices were offered after every six steps as the procession moved toward Jerusalem. That would have made for a very long journey and would have required a great number of sacrifices. Once David was sure of God's approval, they marched on with confidence.

CHAPTER 4

1. The word "covenant" isn't used in 2 Samuel 7 but David used it in 23:5 when referring to the revelation given to him through Nathan.
2. Most scholars have concluded that Bathshua and Bathsheba were the same person. It was not unusual for a person in the ancient world to have more than one name or the name have more than one spelling.
3. First Chronicles 22:8 and 28:1-3 inform us that the fact that David shed much blood was another reason why God chose Solomon to build the temple.
4. In His covenant with Abraham, God promised him many descendants and later compared their number to the dust of the earth (Gen. 13:16) and the stars of the heaven (Gen. 15:1-6), suggesting an earthly people and a heavenly people. The Jews are God's earthly people and are promised an earthly kingdom, but all who trust Christ are of the seed of Abraham (Gal. 3:1-18) because all of us are saved by faith, not by obeying a law.
5. This is the third of four "official lists" found in 2 Samuel, and each one closes a major division of the book: 1:1–3:5 (David's sons in Hebron); 3:6–5:16 (David's sons in Jerusalem); 5:17–8:18 (David's officers in Jerusalem); and 9:1–20:26 (David's officers later in his reign).
6. One school of interpreters feels that David was only putting Mephibosheth under "house arrest" to make certain that he didn't create any problems in the kingdom. Subsequent events proved that it was Ziba the manager who needed to be watched! And how much damage could a crippled young man do to Israel's greatest king? David brought Mephibosheth to his palace table, not to protect himself but to show his love to him for his father's sake.
7. "Kindness" (mercy) is sometimes connected with the making of a covenant. (See Deut. 7:9, 12; Josh. 2:12; 1 Sam. 20:8, 14-17; Dan. 9:4.)
8. Keep in mind that 2 Samuel wasn't written in chronological order, and verses like 8:12 are summaries of wars that the writer describes later.
9. In a prior battle, David was nearly killed by a giant named Ishbi-benob, and his nephew Abishai rescued him. At that time, the military leaders told David not to go to go to war anymore (2 Sam. 21:15-17), and he complied. His appearance at the Syrian campaign (10:15-19) was to take charge of troop movements but not to engage in hand-to-hand combat.

CHAPTER 5

1. There is no account of David's great sins found in 1 Chronicles. The book was written from the viewpoint of the priesthood; the emphasis is on the greatness of the kings, not their sins. David and Solomon are described as "ideal rulers."
2. Isaac Watts, "Divine Songs for Children" (1715).
3. The word "sent" is repeated often in chapters 11 and 12. See 11:1, 3, 4, 5, 6 (twice), 8, 12, 14, 18, 22; 12:1, 25, 27. David's sins kept a lot of people on the move!
4. *Professor Blaiklock's Handbook of Bible People,* by E. M. Blaiklock (London: Scripture Union, 1979), p. 210.
5. Joseph Butler, *Fifteen Sermons* (Charlottesville, VA: Ibis Publishing, 1987), p. 114
6. Saul used the words "I have sinned" three times, but didn't mean them (1 Sam. 15:24, 30; 26:21). David said "I have sinned" at least five times (2 Sam. 12:13; 24:10, 17 [1 Chron. 21:8, 17]; Pss. 41:4; 51:4). David was the Prodigal Son of the Old Testament, who repented and "came home" to find forgiveness (Luke 15:18, 21). For others who used these words see Exodus 9:27; Numbers 22:34; Joshua 7:20; 2 Samuel 19:20; Matthew 27:4.
7. As with Jonah and the city of Nineveh, God's decree of judgment can be interrupted by the repentance of the people involved. (Nineveh didn't fall until over a century later.) The prediction that Bathsheba's baby would die was fulfilled that week because God chose to act at that time. God's character and purposes don't change, but He does change His timing and His methods to accomplish His purposes.
8. Since Scripture gives no definitive revelation on the subject of infant salvation, the-

ologians have wrestled with the problem and good and godly believers disagree. For a balanced and compassionate theological study, see *When a Baby Dies* by Ronald H. Nash (Zondervan, 1999).

CHAPTER 6

1. Even after his death, Absalom's name and memory reminded people of evil (2 Sam. 20:6; 1 Kings 2:7, 28; 15:2, 10; 2 Chron. 11:20-21).
2. It's likely that David's second son, Chileab (or Daniel), died young, for apart from the royal genealogy, he is not mentioned in the biblical account (1 Chron. 3:1).
3. Perhaps she was thinking of Abraham and Sarah (Gen. 20:12), but that was before the Law of Moses.
4. When Dinah was raped (Gen. 34), it was her full brothers Simeon and Levi who avenged her (see Gen. 29:32-35; 30:17-21.)
5. The Hebrew for "Amnon" is a diminutive form: "Has that little Amnon been with you?" Absalom didn't hide his utter dislike for his half brother.
6. Did anybody know that Solomon was God's choice for the next king? Perhaps not, for the Lord hadn't revealed it. According to some chronologists, Solomon's birth occurred before Amnon's sin against Tamar, but Bathsheba had given birth to three other sons before she gave birth to Solomon (2 Sam. 5:14; 1 Chron. 3:5; 14:4). God promised David that one of his sons would succeed him and build the temple (2 Sam. 7:12-15), but it isn't recorded that He announced the name of the son at that time. Amnon and Absalom had already been born, and the announcement sounds as if the designated son would be born in the future. First Chronicles 22:6-10 indicates that at some point the Lord had told David that Solomon would be his successor (see 28:6-10; 29:1). Whether they knew it or not, both Amnon and Absalom were fighting a losing battle.
7. It seems strange that Jonadab would make this announcement, because by doing so, he was almost confessing that he knew something about the plot. However, David and his servants knew that Jonadab was Amnon's confidant, and no doubt they concluded that he and Amnon had discussed Absalom's attitude and concluded that there was danger in the air. Jonadab was too shrewd a man to implicate himself before the king.
8. See "Of Revenge" in *The Essays of Francis Bacon.*
9. God solved this problem for lost sinners by sending His Son to die on the cross, and thus He upheld the law but at the same time provided salvation for all who trust Christ. See Romans 3:19-31.
10. How heavy was the hair that Absalom's barber cut from his head? It all depends on the weight of the "royal shekel" (v. 26). If it was 11.5 grams, then the haircut produced about five pounds of hair. Baldness was ridiculed in Israel (2 Kings 2:23).
11. The parallels between Absalom and Samson are interesting. Both were distinguished by their hair, for Samson was a Nazirite (Judg. 13:1-5), and both set fields on fire (Judg. 15:4-5). The loss of his hair caused Samson's defeat (Judg. 16:17ff), and it's probable that Absalom's thick hair helped to trap his head in the tree branches, where Joab found him and killed him (2 Sam. 18:9-17).

CHAPTER 7

1. The word "demagogue" comes from two Greek words: *demos* (people) and *agogos* (guiding). A true leader uses his authority to help people, but a demagogue uses people to gain authority. Demagogues pretend to be concerned about the needs of the people, but their only concern is to get into power and enjoy the fruits of their dishonesty.
2. Hebrew texts vary from "four" to "forty." If forty is the correct number, we don't know the starting point—forty years from what event? Some chronologists date Absalom's rebellion at between 1023 and 1027 BC. This would be approximately forty years from David's anointing by Samuel, but why select that event? It seems reasonable to accept "four" as the correct number and date it from Amnon's reconciliation with his father (14:33).
3. Most students identify Psalms 3, 4, 41, 55, 61–63, and 143 as "exile psalms," and some add Psalms 25, 28, 58, and 109. Both Psalms 41 and 55 indicate that David was not well, and see 61:6-7. If indeed David was ill, then he was unable to meet the people and hear their problems; and Absalom took advantage of this situation.

4. David once lied about attending a feast as a device to deceive King Saul (1 Sam. 20:6). Thus do our sins find us out.
5. David faced a similar test when he was serving as commander of the bodyguard of Achish, king of the Philistines (1 Sam. 29).
6. David's statement "Behold, here am I" reminds us of Abraham (Gen. 22:1, 11), Jacob (Gen. 31:11; 46:2), Moses (Ex. 3:4), Samuel (1 Sam. 3:4, 16), and Isaiah (Isa. 6:8). It is a statement of surrender.
7. *God Tells the Man Who Cares* (Christian Publications, 1970), p. 9.
8. It was at Bahurim that David's wife Michal said good-bye to her second husband as she was returned to David, and the man wept bitterly (3:13-16). Now it was David who was weeping.

CHAPTER 8

1. In 279 BC, the army of Pyrrhus, king of Epirus, defeated the Romans at Asculum at such great cost that he said, "One more such victory and we are lost."
2. For a detailed study of the speeches of Ahithophel and Hushai, and why God used Hushai's counsel, see chapters 1–4 of my book *Preaching and Teaching with Imagination* (Baker Books).
3. The word in 18:14 translated "darts" in the KJV and "javelins" in the NIV can mean rod, staff, or even scepter. They were probably javelins sharpened at one end. Joab thrust them into Absalom's body, and then the ten men around the tree finished the job.
4. The scene reminds us of Eli the priest waiting at the gate for news concerning the Ark of the Covenant (1 Sam. 4:12ff).
5. This is the familiar Hebrew word *shalom,* which among other things means "peace, health, well-being." David uses the word in his questions: "Is the young man Absalom *shalom*?" (vv. 29, 32).
6. *The Metropolitan Tabernacle Pulpit,* vol. 24, p. 505.

CHAPTER 9

1. "The people" in 2 Samuel is a phrase that identifies David's followers, especially his army. See 15:17, 23-24, 30; 16:14; 17:2-3, 16, 22; 18:1-4, 6, 16; 19:2-3, 8-9, 39. Another term for his army is "the servants of David" (2:13, 15, 17, 30-31; 3:22; 8:2, 6, 14; 10:2, 4; 11:9, 11, 13, 17; 12:18; 15:15; 16:6; 18:7, 9; 19:6; 20:6).
2. Shimei identified himself with "the house of Joseph" (v. 20), and this is the first time this phrase is used in the Old Testament. It refers to the ten tribes headed by Ephraim, Joseph's younger son. The ten northern tribes were often called "Ephraim" or "sons of Joseph."
3. The KJV translation "to Jerusalem" in verse 25 should read, "from Jerusalem."
4. The "Absalom episode" began with David kissing Absalom after his son's two years of house arrest (14:33), and ended with David kissing Barzillai.
5. *Henry IV, Part 2,* act 3, scene 1.

CHAPTER 10

1. Joab killed Abner because Abner had killed Joab's brother Asahel, and it was done near Gibeon, where Joab met Amasa (2:12ff). Perhaps the memory of his brother's murder aroused Joab, even though Amasa had nothing to do with it.
2. Why the Gibeonites didn't bring the matter before David much earlier is a mystery, for as resident aliens in the land, they had their civil rights. During the first part of his reign, David was securing and extending the kingdom, and in the last years he was dealing with the troubles caused by his own sins, so perhaps it took time to get the king's ear. By sending drought and famine, the Lord kept the terms of the covenant (Lev. 26:18-20; Deut. 28:23-24).
3. The Law of Moses gave resident aliens certain rights, and Israel was warned not to oppress the strangers in the land (Ex. 22:21; Lev. 19:34; Deut. 24:17). Apparently neither Joshua's vow nor the Law of Moses restrained Saul from trying to liquidate the Gibeonites.
4. But David also made a similar promise to Saul (1 Sam. 24:20-22), and here he was having Saul's descendants slain. However, the killing of five men wasn't the equivalent of wiping out all of a man's family.
5. We're told in 6:23 that Michal died without having any children, so the text should read Merab (see NIV). She was Saul's daughter by Ahinoam (1 Sam. 14:49) and was married to Adriel (1 Sam. 18:17-19).
6. The Hebrew text reads "descendants of Rapha." The word means "giant" (Deut. 2:11, 20; Josh. 12:4; 13:12; 17:15; 1 Chron. 20:4, 6, 8.)

CHAPTER 11

1. In Ezekiel 1, the prophet saw God's glorious throne on a magnificent crystal platform, with cherubim at each corner, like "wheels" carrying the throne from place to place. The image of God's throne like a chariot reminds us that He can come down from heaven to help His people and nothing can thwart Him.
2. Light as an image of God is frequently found in Scripture (Ps. 84:11; Isa. 60:19-20; Ezek. 1:4, 27; Dan. 2:22; Micah 7:8; Mal. 4:2; Luke 2:32; John 8:12; 1 Tim. 6:16; 1 John 1:5; Rev. 21:23.)

CHAPTER 12

1. In the Old Testament, God viewed the rulers of Israel as shepherds, which explains passages like Jeremiah 10:21, 12:10, 23:1-8, 25:36; Ezekiel 34:1-18; Zechariah 10:2, 11:15-17. The word "pastor" means "shepherd."
2. Second Samuel 8:13 gives David credit for the great victory against the Edomites, while 1 Chronicles 18:12 attributes the victory to Abishai. The inscription of Ps. 60 states that Joab was also a part of the event. It's likely that David was in charge and Joab and his brother Abishai commanded the field forces. It was customary in those days for the king to get the credit for such victories (see 2 Sam. 12:26-31).
3. For an excellent comparative chart of David's mighty men, see pages 478-479 of the Old Testament volume of *The Bible Knowledge Commentary*, edited by John Walvoord and Roy Zuck (Victor).
4. Some students think that the three who brought the water from the Bethlehem well were the men named in verses 8-12, but verse 13 seems to indicate they were a different trio, a part of "The Thirty."
5. The two terms "The Three" and "The Thirty" are found frequently in this chapter. For "The Three" see verses 9, 13, 16-19, 22, 23; for "The Thirty" see verses 13, 23-24. In 1 Chronicles 11, "The Three" are mentioned in verses 12, 15, 18-21, 24, 25; and "The Thirty" in verses 15, 25, and 42.
6. For a study of these four appearances of Satan and how they apply to believers today, see my book *The Strategy of Satan* (Tyndale House).
7. First Chronicles 21:5 records 1,100,000 men, but we need to remember that Joab didn't complete the census (1 Chron. 27:23-24) and different sums were recorded at different times during the nine months of the survey. Also, note that 2 Samuel 24:9 specifies "800,000 valiant men," that is, an experienced standing army, while there could have been another 300,000 men who were of age but not seasoned in battle. This gives us the 1,100,000 total of 1 Chronicles 21:5.
8. The prophet Gad first appears in Scripture after David fled from Saul (1 Sam. 22:5). He must have been an expert on Jewish liturgy because he assisted David in organizing the Levites for their part in the temple worship services. He also kept an official record of the events of David's reign (1 Chron. 29:29).
9. More than once God sent plagues to Israel to chasten His people (Num. 11:31-34; 14:36-38; 16:46-50; 21:4-9; 26:9-10). Of course, this was in agreement with His covenant, which the people had broken.

CHAPTER 13

1. It's too bad that many well-meaning preachers misinterpret 1 Corinthians 3:9-23 and preach about "building your life." You can make that application, but the basic interpretation has to do with building the local church. For an exposition of this passage, see my book *Be Wise* (Victor).
2. The psalm certainly fits David's experiences described in 1 Samuel 24 and 1 Chronicles 21. His pride led him to sin (vv. 6-7) and the nation was under the penalty of death. But God answered his plea for deliverance, and His anger lasted for a short time.
3. Adoram wasn't a popular man. After Solomon's death, Solomon's son Rehoboam took the throne. The people were tired of Solomon's taxes and vast building programs, and they stoned Adoram to death (2 Kings 11:18).
4. First Chronicles 26:18 in the KJV has been a popular verse with people who like to criticize the Scriptures: "At Parbar westward, four at the causeway, and two at Parbar." What does "Parbar" mean? Many Hebrew scholars say it means "colonnade" and refers to an area west of the temple proper. The NLT reads, "Six were assigned each day to the west gate, four to the gateway leading up to the Temple, and two to the courtyard." A footnote says that "courtyard" could also be translated "colonnade," but "the meaning of the Hebrew is uncertain."

5. Forgive a personal note at this point. Back in the fifties, when I was pastoring my first church, the Lord led us into a building program. I'm not a builder and I have a problem even reading a blueprint, and I was very worried. One day in my personal devotional time, during the course of my regular Bible reading, I came to 1 Chronicles 28:20, and the Lord gave it to me as His promise of success. It carried me through.

1 KINGS

A SUGGESTED OUTLINE OF 1 KINGS

Theme: Irresponsible leadership destroys nations
Key verses: 1 Kings 9:4-9

I. THE KINGDOM PROTECTED (1 KINGS 1:1–2:46)

The last days of David (1:1–2:12
The first acts of Solomon (2:13-46)

II. THE KINGDOM ENRICHED (1 KINGS 3:1–10:29)

God's gift of wisdom (3:1-28)
Organizing the government (4:1-34)
Building the temple (5:1–6:38; 7:13-51)
Dedicating the temple (8:1–9:9)
Building the royal houses (7:1-12)
Miscellaneous royal projects (9:10-24)
Solomon's glory (10:1-29)

III. THE KINGDOM DIVIDED (1 KINGS 11:1–14:31)

Solomon's folly (11:1-43)
Rehoboam's folly (12:1-24; 14:21-31)
Jeroboam's folly (12:25–14:20)

IV. THE KINGDOMS DESTROYED (1 KINGS 15:1–22:53)

Judah (15:1-24)
Israel (15:25–22:53)

The two books of Kings record about four hundred years of the history of Israel and Judah, while the two books of Chronicles see the history of the united kingdom and then the kingdom of Judah from the priestly point of view. Besides recording history, these books teach theology, especially the faithfulness of God in keeping His covenant, the sovereignty of God in directing the destinies of all nations, and the holiness of God in opposing idolatry. Especially important is the way all four books magnify the Davidic dynasty and thus prepare the way for the coming of the Messiah. The books of Kings identify eight kings of Judah, descendants of David, who pleased the Lord: Asa (1 Kings 15:9-15); Jehoshaphat (22:41-43); Joash, or Jehoash (2 Kings 12:1-3); Amaziah (14:1-4); Azariah, or Uzziah (15:1-4); Jotham (15:32-38); Hezekiah (18:1-3); and Josiah (22:1-2). The rulers of the Northern Kingdom were not a godly lot and were not part of David's dynasty.

CONTENTS

CHAPTER ONE
SUNSET AND SUNRISE
1 Kings 1:1–2:46
(1 Chronicles 29:22-30)

"A crisis isn't what makes a person; a crisis shows what a person's made of." In one form or another, you find this statement in the writings of insightful thinkers from antiquity to the present. Another version is, "What life does to you depends on what life finds in you." The same sun that hardens the clay melts the ice.

The kingdom of Israel was facing a crisis because King David was on his deathbed. In facing this crisis, different people responded in different ways.

1. Adonijah the opportunist (1 Kings 1:1-10)

A real leader looks at a crisis and asks, "What can I do that will best help the people?" An opportunist looks at a crisis and asks, "How can I use this situation to promote myself and get what I want?" Opportunists usually show up uninvited, focus attention on themselves and end up making the crisis worse. Adonijah was that kind of person.

The occasion (vv. 1-4). Adonijah was David's oldest living son and was probably thirty-five years old at this time. David's firstborn, Amnon, was killed by Absalom; his second son, Kileab (or Daniel), must have died young because there's no record of his life; and the third son, Absalom, was slain by Joab (1 Chron. 3:1-2). As David's eldest son, Adonijah felt that he deserved the throne. After all, his father was a sick man who would soon die, and it was important that there be a king on the throne of Israel. Like his older brother Absalom (2 Sam. 15:1-6), Adonijah seized his opportunity when David wasn't at his best and was bedfast. However, Adonijah underestimated the stamina and wisdom of the old warrior and ultimately paid for his pride with his life.

Abishag became a companion and nurse for David and was probably officially considered a concubine, so there was nothing immoral about their relationship. She will become a very important person in the drama after David's death (2:13-23). Adonijah made the mistake of thinking that his father was unable to function normally and therefore interfere with his plans, but he was wrong. Instead of being a sympathetic son, Adonijah decided to claim the throne for himself. If he won the support of his siblings, the government leaders, the priests, and the army, he could pull off a coup and become the next king

The traitors (vv. 5-7). Following the example of his infamous brother Absalom (2 Sam. 15:7-12), Adonijah began to promote himself and generate popular support. Like Absalom, he was a handsome man who had been pampered by his father (v. 6; 2 Sam. 13–14), and the unthinking people joined his crusade. Wisely, Adonijah got the support of both the army and the priesthood by enlisting Joab the general and Abiathar the high priest. Both of these men had served David for years and had stood with him during his most difficult trials, but now they were turning against him. Yet Adonijah knew that the Lord had chosen Solomon to be Israel's next king (2:15), and Abiathar and Joab certainly understood this as well. When the Lord gave David His covenant (2 Sam. 7), He indicated that a future son would succeed him and build the temple (1 Chron. 22:8-10), and that son was Solomon (1 Chron. 28:4-7). Adonijah, Abiathar, and Joab were rebelling against the revealed will of God, forgetting that "[t]he counsel of the Lord stands forever" (Ps. 33:11, NKJV).

The faithful (vv. 8-10). Again, like his brother Absalom, Adonijah hosted a great feast (2 Sam. 15:7-12) and invited all his brothers except Solomon (v. 26). He also ignored several other important leaders in the kingdom, including Zadok the high priest, Benaiah the leader of the king's personal guard, Nathan the prophet, and David's "mighty men" (2 Sam. 23).[1] This was a coronation feast and the guests were proclaiming Adonijah as king of Israel (v. 25). Perhaps some of them thought that the ailing King David had actually laid his hands on Adonijah and named him king. After all, Adonijah's brothers were at the feast, which suggested they made no claim to the throne. But surely the guests were aware of the absence of Solomon, Zadok, Benaiah, and Nathan. And did anyone ask when and where Nathan had anointed Adonijah, and if he had been anointed, why the event was so secret? The faithful servants of God and of David had been left out, an obvious clue that Adonijah had named himself as king without any authority from David or the Lord.

Often in Bible history it appears that "truth is fallen in the street, and equity [justice] cannot enter" (Isa. 59:14, NKJV), but the Lord always accomplishes His purposes. "The wicked is snared in the work of his own hands" (Ps. 9:16, NKJV). Adonijah's great feast was the signal David's loyal servants needed to inform David that it was time to name Solomon the next king of Israel.

2. Nathan the loyalist (1 Kings 1:11-53)

If ever King David had a loyal friend and adviser, it was the prophet Nathan. Nathan brought the good news about God's covenant with David and his descendants (2 Sam. 7:1-17), and Nathan also shepherded David through those dark days after the king's adultery with Bathsheba (2 Sam. 12). Nathan must have had musical gifts as well because he helped David organize the worship in the sanctuary (2 Chron. 29:25-26). When Solomon was born, Nathan told the parents that the Lord wanted the boy also named "Jedidiah—beloved of the Lord" (2 Sam. 12:24-25). When Nathan heard about Adonijah's feast and his claim to the throne, he immediately went to work.

Nathan informed Bathsheba (vv. 11-14). Though we haven't read anything about

Bathsheba since the birth of Solomon, we must not conclude that she had been unimportant in the affairs of the palace. Her conduct in this chapter alone is evidence that she was a courageous woman who wanted to do the will of God. To be sure, it was her son who was to be the next king, and had Adonijah succeeded in gaining the throne, both Bathsheba and her son would be killed (vv. 12, 21). But the fact that Nathan turned immediately to Bathsheba suggests that he knew what the future queen mother could do. Also, the way Adonijah approached her and Solomon received her (2:13-19) indicates that both men recognized her as a woman of influence. It's unfortunate that too many people think of Bathsheba only as "the adulteress" when it was her intervention that saved Israel from disaster at a critical hour.

Bathsheba informed David (vv. 15-21). The prophet had given Bathsheba the words to speak, a brief statement of only two questions that she expanded into a very moving speech. The key word in the dialogue of this entire scenario is "swear," used in verses 13, 17, 29, and 30. Nathan and Bathsheba knew that David had promised that Solomon would be the next king because Solomon was God's choice. David had publicly announced the appointment of Solomon when he announced the building of the temple (1 Chron. 22, 28). When God gave a special name to Solomon, this certainly suggested that he would be David's successor (2 Sam. 12:24-25).

Bathsheba bowed before the king (v. 16, and see 23, 31, 47, 53) and then reminded him of his oath that Solomon would be the next king of Israel. She then informed him that Adonijah was hosting a coronation banquet and that Abiathar and Joab were there with all the royal sons except Solomon. Obviously the banquet was not to honor Solomon! Adonijah had proclaimed himself king, but all Israel was waiting for David's official word concerning his successor. Her *coup de grace* was the obvious fact that if Adonijah became king, he would quickly get rid of both Bathsheba and her son. What David did was a matter of life or death. Abishag was witness to all that Bathsheba said (v. 15).

Nathan informed David (vv. 22-27). While Bathsheba was speaking to her husband, Nathan came into the palace and was announced, so Bathsheba left the room (v. 28) and Nathan entered the bedchamber. He asked the king two questions: Did David announce that Adonijah would sit on his throne, and had the king done this in secret without telling his servant the prophet (vv. 24, 27). Sandwiched between these two questions was his report that Adonijah was now celebrating his coronation, all the king's sons except Solomon were at the feast, and so were Abiathar and all the military commanders. Nathan didn't mention Joab, but Bathsheba had already done that. What Nathan revealed was that Joab had brought his officers with him, so the army was backing Adonijah. However, David's loyal servants—Nathan, Zadok, and Benaiah—had been ignored. That being the case, Nathan wondered if Adonijah really had the authority to proclaim himself king.

It's very likely that Nathan's recitation of these facts brought to David's memory the terrible days of Absalom's rebellion and he didn't want the nation to experience another civil war. Solomon was a man of peace (1 Chron. 22:9). Reared in the palace, he had no experience of war as did his father; and if there was a civil war, how could he build the temple?

David instructed his loyal servants (vv. 28-37). David responded immediately to the crisis and told Nathan to call Bathsheba back to his bedside. The two were alone (v. 32). David spoke to Bathsheba and reaffirmed the fact that her son Solomon was to be the next king of Israel. He had sworn this to her privately and would not back down on his oath. But then David went even further and *made Solomon his coregent that very day!* "I will surely carry out this day . . ." (v. 30). If David waited too long, Adonijah's rebellion could grow in strength; and after David died, who would have authority to act? By making Solomon his coregent immediately, David stayed in control and Solomon would do his bidding. Solomon was no longer merely prince or even heir apparent: he was now coregent with his father and the king of Israel.

David then asked them to call his loyal servants—Nathan the prophet, Zadok the priest, and Benaiah the head of his personal bodyguard—men he knew he could trust. He instructed them to proclaim Solomon king in a public demonstration at Gihon. This was an important place of springs on the eastern slope of Mount Zion less than a mile up the valley (north) from En Rogel where Adonijah was hosting his great feast (v. 9). It wouldn't take long for the news to get to Adonijah! Solomon was to ride David's royal mule, and it was to be announced that Solomon was sharing David's throne as king and would be David's successor. Zadok and Nathan were to anoint Solomon with the holy anointing oil from the tabernacle. The trumpet would be blown, declaring to the people that this was an official event. Solomon was now king and ruler over all Israel and Judah.[2] (See 4:20, 25.)

Benaiah was the son of a priest (1 Chron. 27:5), but he chose a military career and became one of David's mighty men (2 Sam. 23:20-23) and the leader of David's personal guard, the Cherethites and Pelethites (v. 38; 2 Sam. 8:18). After hearing David's instructions, Benaiah spoke up enthusiastically in agreement and thus gave both David and Solomon the support of the soldiers under his command. Later, Solomon would execute Joab for his treachery in following Adonijah and would give his position to Benaiah (2:35). Benaiah was as loyal to Solomon as he had been to David.

The Lord informed Israel (vv. 38-53).[3] Zadok, Nathan, and Benaiah, protected by David's personal troops, obeyed David's instructions to the letter and announced to all Israel that Solomon was king. The people were ecstatic as they played their musical instruments and shouted "God save King Solomon." This shout echoed down the valley and reached En Rogel where the people were shouting "God save King Adonijah" (v. 25).

As they finished their meal, Adonijah and his guests heard the shouting and the sound of the trumpet and wondered what was going on in Jerusalem. Had David died? Was it a declaration of war?

Their questions were answered by the arrival of Jonathan, the son of Abiathar the priest who had assisted David during Absalom's rebellion (2 Sam. 17:17-22). Adonijah thought that Jonathan was bringing good news, but it turned out to be the worst possible news for Adonijah, Abiathar, and Joab. Jonathan's report is that of an eyewitness who saw Solomon riding the king's mule and watched as Zadok and Nathan anointed the new king. But verses 47-48 describe what transpired in David's bedchamber (vv. 36-37), and we wonder where Jonathan obtained this information. Did he hear Benaiah tell his troops that they would now be loyal to Solomon as they had been to David? Did Nathan or Zadok quote David's words to the people?

Jonathan made it clear that Solomon was *at that very moment* the king of Israel. Adonijah, his fellow conspirators, and his guests knew what that meant: they were all under great suspicion. The guests, including the naïve princes, all rose up and fled back to the city for safety, and Adonijah fled to the tabernacle for asylum. This was the tent in

Jerusalem, which housed the Ark (1 Chron. 16:1, 37). The tabernacle with the other furnishings was at Gibeon (1 Chron. 16:39-40; 1 Kings 3:4). There was an altar there and Adonijah took hold of the horns of the altar, which is what people in danger did before the establishment of the six cities of refuge (2:28; Ex. 21:13-14). A place of asylum at least delayed judgment and gave the accused an opportunity for a hearing (Deut. 19).

Solomon showed mercy to his brother and allowed him to return to his home in Jerusalem. This amounted to house arrest because the king's guards could keep Adonijah under constant surveillance. But Solomon also warned his brother to be careful how he behaved, for as an insurgent, Adonijah was worthy of death.[4] If he stepped out of line, he would be executed. Adonijah bowed before Solomon, but his heart was submitted neither to the Lord nor his brother.

3. David the realist (1 Kings 2:1-11; 1 Chron. 29:26-30)

David "served his own generation by the will of God" (Acts 13:36, NKJV), but he was also concerned about Solomon and the next generation. David had his enemies, some of whom were in his own household and inner circle, and he wanted to be certain that the new king didn't inherit old problems. During his long reign of forty years, David had unified the nation, defeated their enemies, successfully organized kingdom affairs, and made more than adequate preparation for the building of the temple. He sang his last song (2 Sam. 23:1-7) and then gave his last charge to Solomon.[5]

"Put the Lord first" (vv. 1-4). The Old Testament records the last words of Jacob (Gen. 49), Moses (Deut. 33), Joshua (23:1–24:27), and David (1 Kings 2:1-11). "I go the way of all the earth" is a quotation from Joshua at the end of his life (Josh. 23:14), and "Be strong and show yourself a man" sounds like the Lord's words to Joshua at the start of his ministry (Josh. 1:6). Solomon was a young man who had lived a sheltered life, so he needed this admonition. In fact, from the very outset of his reign, he would have to make some tough decisions and issue some difficult orders. David had already commissioned Solomon regarding building the temple (1 Chron. 22:6-13), a task that would take seven years. One day Solomon would come to the end of his life, and David wanted him to be able to look back with satisfaction. Blessed is that person whose heart is right with God, whose conscience is clear and who can look back and say with the Master: "I have glorified You on the earth. I have finished the work which You have given Me to do" (John 17:4, NKJV).

David's words parallel those of Moses when he commissioned Joshua (Deut. 31). First Moses admonished Joshua to "be a man" and face his responsibilities with courage and faith (vv. 1-8), and then Moses gave the law to the priests and admonished the people (including Joshua) to know it and obey it. The king was expected to be familiar with the law and the covenant (Deut. 17:14-20), for in obeying God's Word he would find his wisdom, strength, and blessing.[6]

But David also reminded his son of the special covenant the Lord had made concerning the Davidic dynasty (v. 4; 2 Sam. 7:1-17). He warned Solomon that if he disobeyed God's law, he would bring chastening and sorrow to himself and the land, but if he obeyed God's commandments, God would bless him and the people. More importantly, God would see to it that there was always a descendant of David sitting on the throne. David knew that Israel had a ministry to perform in providing the vehicle for the promised Redeemer to come to earth, and the future of God's redemptive plan rested with Israel. How tragic that Solomon didn't fully follow God's law and was the means of promoting idolatry in the land and then causing the kingdom to be divided.

"Protect the kingdom!" (vv. 5-9). David knew that there were perils lurking in the shadows in the kingdom and he warned Solomon to act immediately and deal with two dangerous men. *Joab,* commander of David's army, was the first to be named. He had stood by David through many difficult trials, but from time to time he had asserted his own will and been guilty of murdering innocent men. Joab was David's nephew and the brother of Abishai and Asahel, and all of them were noted warriors. But Joab killed Abner because Abner had killed Asahel (2 Sam. 2:12-32). Joab also killed David's son Absalom even though he knew David wanted him taken alive (2 Sam. 18). He murdered Amasa, whom David had appointed leader of his forces (2 Sam. 20), and he supported Adonijah in his quest for the throne (1 Kings 1:7). Joab had been involved in David's scheme to kill Bathsheba's husband, Uriah (2 Sam. 11:14ff), and perhaps the crafty general was using his knowledge to intimidate the king. David didn't mention Uriah or Absalom to Solomon, and Solomon already knew that Joab was a traitor to the king.

The second dangerous man was *Shimei (vv. 8-9).* He was a Benjamite and a relative of Saul who wanted to see Saul's line restored to the throne. He cursed David when David was fleeing from Absalom (2 Sam. 16:5-13). To curse the king was a violation of the law (Ex. 22:28), but David accepted this unkindness as a discipline from the Lord. Later, when David returned to the throne, Shimei humbled himself before the king and David forgave him (2 Sam. 19:18-23). But David knew that there was always a pro-Saul element in the northern tribes, so he warned Solomon to keep Shimei under surveillance.

David not only remembered dangerous men like Joab and Shimei, but he also remembered helpful men like *Barzillai (v. 7),* who had provided him and his people with what they needed when they fled from Absalom (2 Sam. 17:27-29). David had wanted to reward Barzillai with a place at his table, but the old man preferred to die in his own home. He asked David to give the honor to his son Kimham (2 Sam. 19:31-38); but now David instructed Solomon to care for Barzillai's sons and not Kimham alone.

David did go "the way of all the earth," and "died in a good old age, full of days and riches and honor . . ." (1 Chron. 29:28, NKJV). Solomon was already king and his throne was secure, so there was no need for any official decisions or ceremonies.

4. Solomon the strategist (1 Kings 2:12-46)

The new king had his agenda all prepared: deal with Joab, deal with Shimei, reward the sons of Barzillai, and build the temple. But his first major crisis came from his half brother Adonijah.

Adonijah's request (vv. 13-25). Solomon had graciously accepted Adonijah's submission to the new regime (1:53), although Solomon certainly knew that the man was deceitful and ready to strike again. The fact that Adonijah went to the queen mother with his request suggests that he expected her to have great influence with her son. Adonijah's declaration in verse 15 shows how confused he was in his thinking, for if Solomon was God's choice for the throne, and Adonijah knew it, why did he attempt a coup and try to seize the crown? Like Absalom, he thought that a popular demonstration and the cheers of the people meant success. Perhaps Adonijah said "it was his [Solomon's] from the Lord" just to impress Bathsheba.

Students differ in their interpretation of Bathsheba's role in this scenario. Some say she was very naïve in even asking Solomon, but Bathsheba had already proved herself to be a courageous and influential woman. It's likely that she suspected another plot because she knew that possession of a king's wife or concubine was evidence of possession of the kingdom. This was why Absalom had publicly taken David's concubines (2 Sam. 16:20-23), for it was an announcement to the people that he was now king. It's difficult to believe that the king's mother was ignorant of this fact. I may be in error, but I feel that she took Adonijah at his word, *knowing that Solomon would use this as an opportunity to expose Adonijah's scheme.* By having Abishag as his wife, Adonijah was claiming to be coregent with Solomon!

Solomon immediately detected the reason behind the request and said, "Ask for him the kingdom also!" The king knew that Adonijah, Abiathar, and Joab were still united in gaining control of the kingdom. By asking for Abishag, Adonijah issued his own death warrant, and Benaiah went and took the traitor's life. David wasn't there to feel the pain of another son's death, but the execution of Adonijah was the final payment of the fourfold debt David had incurred (2 Sam. 12:5-6). The baby died, Absalom killed Amnon, Joab killed Absalom, and Benaiah executed Adonijah. David paid for his sins fourfold.

Abiathar's removal (vv. 26-27). But Solomon didn't stop there: he also defrocked Abiathar the priest, who had supported Adonijah, and sent him into retirement at the priestly city of Anathoth, about three miles from Jerusalem. This had been the home of Jeremiah the prophet. In deposing Abiathar, Solomon fulfilled the prophecy given to Eli that his family would not continue in the priesthood (1 Sam. 2:27-36; see Ezek. 44:15-16). Zadok was made high priest (v. 35), and his descendants filled the office until 171 B.C. Solomon recognized the fact that Abiathar had faithfully served his father David, so he didn't have him executed.

Joab's execution (vv. 28-35). Joab no doubt had an efficient spy system, and when he heard the news that Adonijah had been slain, he knew he was next on the list. He fled to the tabernacle David had erected in Jerusalem for the Ark of the Covenant (2 Sam. 6:17) and there claimed asylum by taking hold of the horns of the altar. However, only people who were guilty of manslaughter could do this and claim the right to a trial, and Joab was guilty of both murder and disloyalty to King David and King Solomon. Joab defied both Benaiah and Solomon by refusing to come out of the sacred enclosure, but Solomon was not to be treated in such an arrogant manner by a man who was obviously a traitor and a murderer. Though he was a soldier, Benaiah belonged to a priestly family, so it was legal for him to enter the sacred precincts, and he went and killed Joab at the altar and then buried him. Solomon then promoted Benaiah to be the commander of the army in the place of Joab (v. 35).

It's important to understand that Solomon wasn't simply acting in revenge in the place of his father David. Solomon explained that the death of Joab took away the stain of the innocent blood that Joab had shed when he killed Abner and Amasa. The shedding of innocent blood polluted the land (Num. 35:30-34) and the victim's blood cried out to God for vengeance (Gen. 4:10). The cities of refuge were provided for people who had accidentally killed somebody. They could flee to one of the six cities and be protected until the elders had investigated the case. But murderers like Joab were not to be given any mercy but were to be executed so that the innocent blood they had shed would pollute the land no more (Deut. 19:1-13; 21:1-9; Lev. 18:24-30). Saul's treatment of the Gibeonites had polluted the land and created trouble for David (2 Sam. 21:1-14), and Solomon didn't want that to happen during his reign.

Shimei's daring (vv. 36-46). Since Shimei was related to Saul (2 Sam. 16:5; 1 Sam. 10:21), he was a potential troublemaker who might arouse the tribe of Benjamin against the new king, and perhaps even stir up the ten northern tribes of Israel. David had brought unity and peace the nation and Solomon didn't want Shimei creating problems. He ordered him to move to Jerusalem, build himself a house, and stay in the city. If he left the city and crossed the Kidron Valley, he would die. Jerusalem wasn't that large a city at that time, so Solomon's men could keep their eyes on the Benjamite who had cursed David and thrown dirt and stones at him.

Shimei obeyed for three years and then disobeyed. When two of his slaves ran away and went twenty-five miles to Gath, Shimei decided to go personally and bring them back. Surely he could have hired somebody else to go get the slaves, but he went himself. Perhaps he thought he had fulfilled the terms of the agreement, or maybe he thought the guards weren't watching him. Most likely he was deliberately defying Solomon and pushing the limits just to see what he would do. He found out. Solomon knew that Shimei had left Jerusalem, and when he returned, the king confronted him with his crime. Solomon delivered a brief but powerful speech that condemned him for what he did to David and what he had just done to Solomon, and it ended with Benaiah executing Shimei the traitor.

Solomon was to be a "man of peace" (1 Chron. 22:6-10), and yet he began his reign by ordering three executions. But true peace must be based on righteousness, not on sentiment. "But the wisdom that is from above is first pure, then peaceable . . ." (James 3:17, NKJV). The land was polluted by the innocent blood that Joab had shed, and the land could be cleansed only by the execution of the murderer. David didn't execute Joab, even after Joab killed Absalom, because David knew that he himself had blood on his hands (Ps. 51:14). David was guilty of asking Joab to shed Uriah's innocent blood, but Solomon's hands were clean. Solomon was indeed a "man of peace," and he achieved that peace by bringing about righteousness in the land.

From the human viewpoint, it was sunset for David and sunrise for his son Solomon, but not from the divine viewpoint. "But the path of the just is like the shining sun, that shines ever brighter unto the perfect day" (Prov. 4:18, NKJV). As a leader, David was "as the light of the morning . . . even a morning without clouds" (2 Sam. 23:4, KJV), and for the sake of David, the Lord kept the lamp burning in Jerusalem (1 Kings 11:36; 2 Kings 8:19). Even today, when we read and sing his psalms and study his life, that light shines on us and helps to direct our way.

CHAPTER TWO
WISDOM FROM ABOVE
1 Kings 3–4
(2 Chronicles 1)

When Solomon ascended the throne, the people of Israel soon learned that he was not another David. He was a scholar, not a soldier, a man more interested in erecting buildings than fighting battles. David enjoyed the simple life of a shepherd, but Solomon chose to live in luxury. Both David and Solomon wrote songs, but Solomon is better known for his proverbs. We have many of David's songs in the Book of Psalms, but except for Psalms 72 and 127, and the Song of Solomon, we have none of Solomon's three thousand songs.

David was a shepherd who loved and served God's flock, while Solomon became a celebrity who used the people to help support his extravagant lifestyle. When David died, the people mourned; after Solomon died, the people begged his successor King Rehoboam to lighten the heavy yoke his father had put on their necks. David was a warrior who put his trust in God; Solomon was a politician who put his trust in authority, treaties, and achievement. "King Solomon was among the wisest fools who ever wore a crown," wrote Frederick Buechner.[1]

Solomon is mentioned nearly three hundred times in the Old Testament and a dozen times in the New Testament. He's listed in the genealogy of Jesus Christ (Matt. 1:6-7) and is cited as an example of splendor (Matt. 6:29; Luke 12:27) and wisdom (Matt. 12:42; Luke 11:31). He is identified as the builder of the temple (Acts 7:47). One of the colonnades in the temple was named after him (John 10:23; Acts 3:11; 5:12). His father, David, was recognized as the ideal leader, and his record became the standard by which every succeeding king of Judah was measured. However, nobody pointed to Solomon as a good example of a godly ruler.

Chapters 3 and 4 describe events that occurred during the first three years of Solomon's reign, before he began to build the temple (6:1), and they describe Solomon in several roles.

1. The peacemaker (1 Kings 3:1a)

Solomon's name comes from the Hebrew word *shalom* which means "peace," and during his reign, the kingdom was at peace with its neighbors. His father, David, had risked his life on the battlefield to defeat enemy nations and claim their lands for Israel, but Solomon took a different approach to international diplomacy. He made treaties with other rulers by marrying their daughters, which helps to explain why he had seven hundred wives who were princesses, as well as three hundred concubines (11:3). It appears that Solomon entered into treaty arrangements with every petty ruler who had a marriageable daughter! Yet Moses in the law warned the Jewish kings not to multiply wives (Deut. 17:14-20).

His first bride after he became king was the daughter of the pharaoh of Egypt, Israel's old enemy. This alliance indicates that Egypt had slipped much lower on the international scene and that Israel was now much higher, because Egyptian rulers didn't give their daughters in marriage to the rulers of other nations.[2] It's significant that Solomon didn't put his Egyptian wife[3] into the royal palace where David had lived, because it was near the Ark of the Covenant (2 Chron. 8:11), but housed her in another place until her own palace was completed. He spent seven years building the temple of God but thirteen years building his own palace (1 Kings 6:37–7:1).

Solomon's complex system of treaties cut at the very heart of Israel's unique position as the people of God among the nations of the world. They were God's holy people, a chosen people among whom the Lord himself dwelt (Ex. 33:16; Deut. 4:7-8, 32-34). God had made no covenants with the Gentile nations, nor had He given them His Word, His sanctuary, or His holy priesthood (Rom. 9:1-5). God said to the Jews, "I am the Lord your God, who has separated you from other people" (Lev. 20:24, 26, KJV). As long as Israel trusted the Lord and obeyed Him, the nation would "dwell safely alone" (Deut. 33:28). The prophet Balaam described Israel as "a people dwelling alone, not reckoning itself among the nations" (Num. 23:9, NKJV).

The Lord placed Israel among the Gentile nations to be a witness to them of the true and living God, a "light among the Gentiles" (Isa. 42:6). If Israel had continued to be faithful to the terms of God's covenant (Deut. 27–30), the Lord would have blessed them and used them as an "object lesson" to the pagan nations around them. Instead, Israel imitated the Gentiles, worshiped their idols, and abandoned their witness to the true God. For that reason, God had to chasten them and then send them into captivity in Babylon. God wanted Israel to be the "head" of the nations, but because of her compromise, she became the "tail" (Deut. 28:13, 44). Solomon may have thought he was making political progress by bringing Israel into the family of nations, but the consequence was really spiritual regress. Solomon also entered into lucrative trade agreements with other nations (10:1-15, 22), and the nation prospered; but the price he paid was too high.

The kingdom of Israel prospered only as she trusted God and obeyed the terms of His covenant. If they were true to the Lord, He promised to give them all they needed, to protect them from their enemies, and to bless their labors. But from the very beginning of the Jewish monarchy, Israel's leaders made it clear that they wanted to be "like the other nations" (1 Sam. 8), and Solomon led them closer to that goal. Ultimately, Solomon married many pagan wives and began to worship their false gods, and the Lord had to chasten him. See 1 Kings 11.

2. The builder (1 Kings 3:1b)

Solomon is remembered as the king during whose reign the temple was built (chaps. 5–7; 2 Chron. 2–4). His alliance with Hiram, king of Tyre, gave him access to fine timber and skilled workmen. But he also built his own palace (7:1-12), which seems to have consisted of living quarters plus "the house of the forest of Lebanon," where arms were stored and displayed (10:16-17, KJV), the Hall of pillars, and the Hall of Judgment. He also built a house in Jerusalem for his Egyptian princess wife (2 Chron. 8:11). Official state visitors were overwhelmed by the splendor of these structures (chap. 10).

Though he wasn't a warrior himself, Solomon was concerned about the security of the land. He expanded and strengthened the "Millo" (9:24; 11:27), a protective wall or embankment that David had begun to build (2 Sam. 5:9). The word *millo* means "filling." Solomon had a special interest in horses and chariots and built stables in special "chariot cities" (4:26; 9:17-19; 10:26-29). He became quite a "horse dealer" himself and imported horses and chariots and sold them to other nations (2 Chron. 1:14-17; 9:25-28), no doubt making a good profit on the sales. He also built "store cities" in strategic places (9:15-19; 2 Chron. 8:1-6). At that time, Israel controlled several important trade routes that needed to be protected, and military personnel were housed in these cities, along with supplies of food and arms.

Solomon violated the Law of Moses not only by marrying many wives but also by multiplying horses and depending on chariots (Deut. 17:14-17). Contrary to God's command, Solomon went back to Egypt for both! The king was required to copy out for himself the Book of Deuteronomy (Deut. 17:18-20), and we wonder how Solomon responded when he read the command about wives and horses. Or did he ever meditate on what his father wrote in Psalm 20:7 (and see also 33:16-19)? During Solomon's reign, the outward splendor and wealth of Israel only masked an inward decay that led eventually to division and then destruction.

3. The worshiper (1 Kings 3:2-15)

Solomon certainly made a good beginning, for he "loved the Lord, walking in the statutes of David his father" (v. 3, KJV); but a good beginning doesn't guarantee a good ending. Saul, the first king of Israel, started out with humility and victory, but he ended up being rejected by the Lord and committing suicide on the battlefield. Solomon himself would write in Ecclesiastes 7:8, "The end of a thing is better than its beginning" (NKJV) and "A good name is better than precious ointment, and the day of death than the day of one's birth" (7:1, NKJV). We receive our name soon after birth, and between birth and death, we either enhance that name or debase it. After death, we can't change a bad name into a good name or a good name into a bad name. "Great is the art of beginning," wrote the American poet Longfellow, "but greater the art is of ending."

Consecration (vv. 2-4). God purposed that the people of Israel have a central place of worship and not imitate the nations in Canaan by building "high places"[4] wherever they chose. When Israel entered the land, they were instructed to destroy these "high places" and the idols that were worshiped there (Num. 33:52; Deut. 7:5; 12:1ff; 33:29). However, until the temple was built and centralized worship was established in the land, the people of Israel worshiped the Lord in the "high places." In time, the phrase "high place" began to be used to mean "a place of worship" and the Jews worshiped Jehovah at these temporary shrines.

Gibeon was such a sacred place, for the tabernacle was located there. As a first step toward the construction of the tabernacle, David had moved the Ark of the Covenant to Jerusalem, but the rest of the tabernacle, including the altar of sacrifice, was still at Gibeon, located five miles north of Jerusalem. Solomon assembled the leaders of Israel and arranged for them to go to Gibeon with him and worship the Lord (2 Chron. 1:1-6). This event would not only be an act of consecration but it would manifest to the people the unity of the nation's leaders. Solomon offered a thousand burnt offerings to the Lord as he and his officers together praised the Lord and sought His face. The burnt offering pictured total dedication to the Lord.

Revelation (v. 5). The assembly lasted all day and the people remained at Gibeon for the night, including King Solomon who was given a remarkable dream from the Lord. David had both Nathan and Gad as his counselors, but there seems to have been no prophet in Solomon's circle of advisers. Twice the Lord spoke to the king through dreams (see 9:1-9). The Lord sometimes communicated His messages through dreams not only to His own servants but also to those of other nations, such as Abimelech (Gen. 20), the Egyptian servants of Pharaoh (Gen. 40), and Pharaoh himself (Gen. 41).

Solomon heard the Lord say, "Ask! What shall I give you?" (v. 5, NKJV). The Lord's command and question were a revelation of God's grace as well as a test of Solomon's heart. (The word "ask" is found eight times in this passage.) What people ask for usually reveals what they really desire, and what they desire depends on how they envision their life's calling. Had Solomon been a warrior, he might have asked for victory over his enemies; but he saw himself as a youthful leader who desperately needed wisdom so he could adequately serve God's chosen people. He had succeeded David,

Israel's greatest king, and Solomon knew that the people couldn't help but compare and contrast father and son. But even more, he had been called to build the temple of the Lord, an awesome task for such an inexperienced leader. Solomon knew he couldn't accomplish that great venture without wisdom from heaven.

Petition (vv. 6-9). Solomon's prayer was brief and to the point, and it was spoken with true humility, for three times he called himself "your servant." First, Solomon reviewed the past and thanked God for the faithfulness and steadfast love shown to his father (v. 6). Solomon acknowledged God's goodness in keeping his father through many trials and then giving him a son to inherit his throne. Solomon is referring here to the covenant God gave to David when he expressed his heart's desire to build a temple for God (2 Sam. 7). In that covenant, God promised David a son who would build the temple, and Solomon was that son. Solomon admitted that he wasn't the king because God recognized his abilities but because He kept His promises to his father David.

Then, Solomon moved into the present and acknowledged God's grace in making him king (v. 7). But he also confessed his youthfulness and inexperience and therefore his desperate need for God's help if he was to succeed as Israel's king. Solomon was probably twenty years old at this time and certainly much younger than his advisers and officers, some of whom had served his father. He called himself a "little child" (1 Chron. 22:5; 29:1ff), a mark of both honesty and humility. The phrase "to go out or come in" refers to giving leadership to the nation (Num. 27:15-17; Deut. 31:2-3; 1 Sam. 18:13, 16; 2 Kings 11:8).

In his prayer, the king not only confessed his own smallness but also the nation's greatness (v. 8). The people of Israel were the people of God! This meant that God had a great purpose for them to fulfill on earth and that their king carried a great responsibility in ruling them. God had multiplied the nation and fulfilled His promise to Abraham (Gen. 12:2; 13:16; 15:5), Isaac (Gen. 26:1-5), and Jacob (Gen. 28:10-14), and Solomon wanted the blessing to continue.

The king concluded his prayer by anticipating the future and asking the Lord for the wisdom needed to rule the nation (v. 9). Wisdom was an important element in Near Eastern life and every king had his circle of "wise men" who advised him. But Solomon didn't ask for a committee of wise counselors; he asked for wisdom for himself. In that day, the wise person was one who was skillful in the management of life.[5] It meant much more than the ability to make a living; it meant the ability to make a life and make the most out of what life might bring. True wisdom involves skill in human relationships as well as the ability to understand and cooperate with the basic laws God has built into creation. Wise people not only have knowledge of human nature and of the created world, but they know how to use that knowledge in the right way at the right time. Wisdom isn't a theoretical idea or an abstract commodity; it's very practical and personal. There are many people who are smart enough to make a good living but they aren't wise enough to make a good life, a life of fulfillment that honors the Lord.

Solomon asked God to give him "an understanding heart," because no matter how smart the mind may be, if the heart is wrong, all of life will be wrong. "Keep your heart with all diligence, for out of it spring the issues of life" (Prov. 4:23, NKJV). The word translated "understanding" means "hearing"; Solomon wanted a "hearing heart." True understanding comes from hearing what God has to say, and to the Old Testament Jew, "hearing" meant "obeying." When the Lord speaks to us, it's not that we might study and pass judgment on what He said, but that we might obey it. An understanding heart has insight and exercises discernment. It is able to distinguish the things that differ (Phil. 1:9-11). It knows what is real and what is artificial, what is temporal and what is eternal.[6] This kind of understanding is described in Isaiah 11:1-5, a prophecy concerning the Messiah. Believers today can claim the promise of James 1:5.

Approbation (vv. 10-13). God was pleased with Solomon's request for wisdom, for it showed that the king was concerned with serving God and His people by knowing and doing God's will. Solomon never read Matthew 6:33, but he practiced it—and the Lord gave to him the additional blessings that he didn't ask for! God always gives His best to those who leave the choice with Him. When you read the Book of Proverbs, you find that the love of wisdom and the practice of discernment can lead to these extra blessings (see Prov. 3:1-2, 10, 13-18). In the subsequent chapters, we will learn about Solomon's wealth and honor and how he attracted visitors from other nations who wanted to hear his wisdom.

Obligation (v. 14). The Lord was careful to remind Solomon that his obedience to God's covenant and his devotion to the Lord were the keys to his future blessings. Solomon was required to write out his own personal copy of Deuteronomy (Deut. 17:18-20), and this would include the covenant spelled out in Deuteronomy 28–30. Solomon also knew the terms of the covenant God made with his father David (2 Sam. 7:1-17) and that it required obedience on the part of David's son and successor (vv. 12-16). God promised to lengthen Solomon's life if he obeyed the Word (Prov. 3:2, 16), for he would be honoring God and his father David and could claim the promise of Exodus 20:12 (see Eph. 6:1-3). It's unfortunate that Solomon with all his wisdom forgot this part of the agreement and gradually drifted into sin and disobedience, and God had to chasten him.[7]

When Solomon returned to Jerusalem, he went to the tent that housed the Ark and there offered more sacrifices (v. 15). The Ark represented the presence of God among His people and the rule of God over His people (Pss. 80:1; 99:1). Solomon acknowledged the sovereign rule of God over his own life and the life of the nation. In other words, Solomon knew that he was second in command. It was when he started to forget that basic truth that he got himself into trouble.

4. The discerner (1 Kings 3:16-28)

God's chosen leaders can't always remain on the heights of spiritual glory but must take that glory and blessing with them into the place of duty and service. Jesus left the Mount of Transfiguration for the valley of conflict (Matt. 17:1-21), and Paul left the heights of heaven to carry on earth the pain of a thorn in the flesh (2 Cor. 12:1-10). Solomon had been worshiping at Gibeon and Jerusalem, but now he has returned to the responsibilities of the throne.

Like his father David, Solomon gave the common people access to the king (2 Sam. 14). God had given Solomon a special gift of wisdom and now he could put it to use. He had stood before the Ark, the throne of God, and now his people could stand before his throne and seek help. But for Solomon to receive two prostitutes at his throne was certainly an act of condescension. Like Jesus, he welcomed "publicans and sinners" (Luke 15:1-2), except that Jesus did more than solve their problems: He changed their hearts and forgave their sins. In every way, Jesus is "greater than Solomon"(Matt. 12:42).

Although prostitution seemed to be tolerated in Israel, the Law of Moses laid down some severe restrictions and punishments (Lev. 19:29; 21:7, 9, 14; Deut. 23:18). The Book of Proverbs warned young men about the wiles of the harlot ("the strange woman") and Paul instructed believers to avoid prostitutes (1 Cor. 6:15-16). These two women lived together with other prostitutes in a brothel, they became pregnant about the same time and both delivered babies. One can't help but feel sorry for the little ones who came into the world in such a place, without fathers to provide for them and protect them. But the kind of men who would visit prostitutes might not be the best fathers!

Since there were no witnesses to the birth of the two babies or the death of the one, the case couldn't be tried in the courts in the normal way. It would be one woman's word against the word of the other, even though it was obvious that one of the women was a liar. Using the divine wisdom God gave him, Solomon bypassed the word of the women and went right to their hearts, for the heart of every problem is the problem in the heart. By suggesting that they "divide the baby" between them, Solomon revealed the heart of the true mother and gave her baby to her. We aren't told what he did with the mother who had lied and stolen (kidnapped) the baby. We trust that the true mother abandoned her sinful ways and raised her son in the ways of the Lord.

For weeks, the account of this event was the main topic of conversation in all Israel, and Solomon's decision announced to everybody that the king was indeed a wise man.

5. The administrator (1 Kings 4:1-28; 2 Chron. 1:14-17)

David was a gifted administrator (2 Sam. 8:15-18; 20:23-26) and his son inherited some of that ability. Even though Solomon had great wisdom and authority, he couldn't handle the affairs of the kingdom alone. A good leader chooses capable associates and allows them to use their own gifts and thereby serve the Lord and the people.

Special officers (vv. 1-6). Azariah was the high priest (v. 2). He was the son of Ahimaaz and the grandson of Zadok, the priest who had served David so faithfully. It appears that Ahimaaz had died and therefore his son was given the office. See 2 Samuel 15:27, 36; 1 Chron. 6:8-9. The word *ben* in Hebrew can mean son or grandson. While David had only one scribe, Solomon had two (v. 3), and they were the sons of David's scribe, Shisha. He was also known as Seriah (2 Sam. 8:17), Sheva (2 Sam. 20:25) and Shavsha (1 Chron. 18:16). Solomon's kingdom was much larger and more complex than that over which his father ruled, so the keeping of records would have been more demanding.

Jehoshaphat had been recorder during David's reign (2 Sam. 8:16; 20:24), and Benaiah had been appointed head of the army by Solomon (2:35). He was born into a priestly family but chose a military life instead. Abiathar had been exiled because of his part in the plot involving Adonijah (2:27), and Zadok had died and been replaced by his grandson. Since both Zadok and Abiathar had served with David, they are found in the official roster. Azariah was in charge of the twelve officers who supervised the twelve districts that Solomon had marked out in Israel (vv. 7-19). Whether his father was Nathan the prophet (1:11), Nathan the son of David (2 Sam. 5:14), or another man named Nathan is not explained. Nathan was a popular name in Israel.

Zabud was a priest who served as special adviser to the king; Ahishar managed the complex affairs of the king's household; and Adoniram was in charge of the men who were drafted to labor in the public works of the kingdom (9:15-23; 2 Chron. 2:2, 17-18; 8:7-10). These would not be Israelites but foreigners in the land. However, in the building of the temple, Solomon did conscript Israelites to devote four months a year to public service (5:13-18). Adoniram was also known as Adoram and he was stoned to death by the people when Rehoboam became king (1 Kings 12:18-20). Samuel had warned the people that their king would do such things (1 Sam. 8:12-18).

Special commissioners (vv. 7-19, 27-28). Solomon marked out twelve "districts" of various sizes and put a commissioner over each district. The boundaries of the districts ignored the traditional boundaries of the tribes and even incorporated territory that David had taken in battle, and each district was to provide food for the king's household for one month. It's likely that the commissioners also collected taxes and supervised the recruiting of soldiers and laborers for the temple and Solomon's other building projects. By establishing new districts that crossed over old boundaries, Solomon may have hoped to minimize tribal loyalty and eliminate some of the tension between Judah and the northern tribes. Instead, the plan only aggravated the tension, particularly since Judah wasn't included in the redistricting program. Being the royal tribe that contained the royal city, Judah was administered separately.

Any king with seven hundred wives and three hundred concubines, plus numerous officers and frequent guests, would have a large household to feed. The Queen of Sheba came with "a very great train" that must have included several hundred people. According to verses 22-23, the meals for one day in the palace required 185 bushels of fine flour, 375 bushels of coarse meal, ten oxen fattened in the stall and twenty oxen from the pasture, one hundred sheep, and various kinds of game and fowl. Solomon also needed grain for his many horses, which may have been how the coarse meal (barley) was used. The conquered nations may have looked upon these monthly donations as part of their tribute to King Solomon, but the Jewish tribes considered the whole system to be a humiliating form of extortion. After Solomon's death, it was no wonder that the ten tribes rose up in revolt against "all the king's horses and all the king's men."

For some reason, five of the commissioners are identified by their fathers, for *ben* in Hebrew means "son of" (8-11, 13). The son of Abinadab (v. 11) may have been a son of David's own brother and therefore a cousin to Solomon (1 Sam. 16:8; 17:13). He also married one of Solomon's daughters, as also did Ahimaaz (v. 15). It's likely that Solomon instituted this supply system several years into his reign since he didn't have adult children when he was crowned. Baana was probably a brother to Jehoshaphat the recorder (vv. 12 and 3). These twelve men had great power in the land and were a part of the corrupt bureaucracy that Solomon wrote about in Ecclesiastes 5:8-12.

Special disctinctions (vv. 20-28). The nation of Israel became famous for its large population, its peace and security, its buildings, its wise king, and its satisfying lifestyle, "eating, and drinking, and making merry" (v. 20, KJV). Of course, the population grew because of God's promise to the patriarchs (Gen. 15:5; 17:8; 22:17; 26:4; 32:12) and His promises in the covenant (Deut. 28:1-14). The enlarged territory was also a part of God's promise (Gen. 15:18; Ex. 23:31; Deut. 1:7; Josh. 1:4). The tributary nations submitted to Solomon's rule and brought him gifts and tribute annually, and Solomon enjoyed great blessing because of God's covenant with David (2 Sam. 7). Contrary to God's law, Solomon multiplied horses in the land (Deut. 17:16) and built special cities for housing them (v. 26; 10:26-29; 2 Chron. 1:14-17; 9:25, 28).[8]

6. The scholar (1 Kings 4:29-34)

King David appreciated and enjoyed God's created world and wrote hymns of praise about the Creator and His creation, but Solomon looked upon nature more as an object of study. God gave Solomon wisdom and breadth of understanding beyond that of the great wise men of the east, and he was able to lecture accurately about the living things in God's creation. Ecclesiastes 2:5 informs us that Solomon planted great gardens, and no doubt it was in these that he observed the way plants and trees developed.

Ethan and Heman are mentioned in 1 Chronicles 15:19 as members of David's musical staff assigned to direct sanctuary worship. Ethan is probably the man also known as Jeduthun who wrote Psalms 39 and 89 (1 Chron. 16:41-42; 25:1, 6), and Psalm 88 is assigned to Heman. These men were also known for their wisdom. Other than 1 Chronicles 2:6, we have no further information about Calcol and Darda.

Most of Solomon's three thousand proverbs have been lost, for fewer than six hundred are recorded in the Book of Proverbs. Also lost are "the annals of Solomon" (11:41) as well as the books about Solomon written by Nathan, Ahijah, and Iddo (2 Chron. 9:29). We do find many references to nature in Proverbs, Ecclesiastes, and the Song of Solomon, so Solomon's scientific enquiries did yield spiritual truth and practical lessons for life. He became an international celebrity and important people from all over the known world came to see his treasures and hear his wisdom.

Peace and prosperity reigned while Solomon was king, but no matter how successful things appeared to citizens and visitors, all was not well in the kingdom. During the period between his ascension to the throne and his dedication of the temple, Solomon appears to have walked with the Lord and sought to please him. But Alexander Whyte expressed it vividly when he wrote that "the secret worm . . . was gnawing all the time in the royal staff upon which Solomon leaned."[9] Solomon didn't have the steadfast devotion to the Lord that characterized his father, and his many pagan wives were planting seeds in his heart that would bear bitter fruit.

CHAPTER THREE
FULFILLING DAVID'S DREAM

1 Kings 5:1–6:38; 7:13-51
(2 Chronicles 2–4)

"Surely I will not come into the tabernacle of my house, nor go up into my bed; I will not give sleep to mine eyes or slumber to mine eyelids, until I find out a place for the Lord, an habitation for the mighty God of Jacob" (Ps. 132:3-5, KJV). So wrote King David, for it was his passionate desire to build a temple for the glory of the Lord. "One thing have I desired of the Lord, that will I seek after; that I may dwell in the house of the Lord all the days of my life, to behold the beauty of the Lord, and to inquire in his temple" (Ps. 27:4, KJV).

The Lord knew David's heart but made it clear that He had other plans for His beloved servant (2 Sam. 7). David was so busy fighting wars and expanding and defending the borders of the kingdom of Israel that he didn't have time to supervise such a complex and demanding enterprise. Solomon, the man of peace, was God's choice to build the temple, and his father prepared him for the task and encouraged him (1 Chron. 22 and 28).

Since the days of Moses, the people of Israel had brought their sacrifices and offerings to the tabernacle, but now they were no longer a pilgrim people but a nation settled in their own land. The tabernacle was a fragile, portable building, and the time had come for Israel to build a temple to their great God. The nations around them had temples dedicated to their false gods, so it was only right that the people of Israel dedicate a magnificent temple to honor Jehovah of Hosts, the true and living God. In the second month (our April/May) of the year 966, the fourth year of his reign, Solomon began the work,[1] and these chapters record several stages of the project.

1. Securing the materials (1 Kings 5:1-12; 2 Chron. 2:1-16)

As he anticipated the building of the temple, David had set aside some of the spoils of battle especially for the Lord (1 Chron. 22:14). This amounted to 3,750 tons of gold, 37,500 tons of silver, and an unmeasured amount of bronze, iron, wood, and stone. All this wealth he presented publicly to Solomon (1 Chron. 29:1-5). David also added his own personal treasure and then invited the leaders of the nation to contribute as well (1 Chron. 29:1-10). The final totals were 4,050 tons of gold and over 38,000 tons of silver, not to speak of thousands of tons of bronze and iron, as well as precious stones. It was a great beginning for a great project.

David also gave Solomon the plans for the temple that had been given to him by the Lord (1 Chron. 28). David had also assembled some artisans and laborers to follow those plans and work in wood and stone to prepare material for the temple (1 Chron. 22:1-4). Hiram, king of Tyre, had provided workers and materials for the building of David's palace (2 Sam. 5:11), and David had enlisted their help in preparing wood for the temple (1 Chron. 22:4). Solomon took advantage of this royal friendship to enlist Hiram to provide the workers and timber needed for the temple.

Hiram had sent Solomon his greetings on the occasion of his coronation, and Solomon had sent back official thanks plus a request for his help in the construction of the temple. In his message, Solomon indicated that he knew that his father had discussed the building of the temple with Hiram, so Hiram wasn't hearing about it for the first time. David had even told Hiram about God's covenant (2 Sam. 7) and God's choice of Solomon to build the house of God. Solomon made it clear that he was constructing, not a monument to the glory of his father, but a temple to the honor of the name of the Lord (v. 5; see 8:16-20, 29, 33, 35, 41-44).

Solomon also requested a master artisan who could make the intricate and beautiful furnishings required for the temple (7:13-14; 2 Chron. 2:7), and King Hiram sent him Hiram (or Huram-Abi; 2 Chron. 2:13-14). He was the son of a mixed marriage, for his father was a Phoenician and his mother was from the tribe of Naphtali.[2] He was gifted as a metal worker and cast the two pillars at the entrance of the temple as well as the metal furnishings within the temple. As when Moses built the tabernacle, the Lord assembled the needed workers and empowered them to do their work (Ex. 31:1-11; 35:30-35).

Solomon's letter was really a commercial contract, for in it he offered to pay for the wood by providing food annually for Hiram's household (5:11), and also to pay the workers one large payment for their labor (2 Chron. 2:10). Until the work was completed, King Hiram's household received annually 125,000 bushels of wheat and 115,000 gallons of pure olive oil. The workers would receive one payment of 125,000 bushels of wheat, 125,000 bushels of barley, and 115,000 gallons of wine and of olive oil, all of which would be divided among them. In his reply, Hiram accepted the terms and outlined the procedure. His men would cut the trees in Lebanon, prepare the logs, and then take them down the coast to Joppa (modern Jaffa; 2 Chron. 2:16), either on ships or bound together as rafts. At Joppa Solomon's men would claim the timber and transport it overland to the building site, about thirty-five miles away, as the crow flies.[3]

As any pastor and church board can attest, building programs are not easy, and they either bring out the best or the worst in God's people. But like Moses who supervised the building of the tabernacle, Solomon had a great deal going for him. Both men knew that God had chosen them to direct the work and that He would enable them to finish successfully. Both leaders had an incredible amount of wealth and materials at their disposal before they started, and both received the construction plans from the Lord Himself. Both were blessed to have leaders who gave generously to support the project.

2. Conscripting workers (1 Kings 5:13-18; 9:15-23; 2 Chron. 2:2, 17-18; 8:7-10)

It would take a great deal of manpower to fell the trees, trim the logs, and transport them to the construction site for the builders to use. David's incomplete census had revealed that there were 1,300,000 able-bodied men in the land (2 Sam. 24:9) and Solomon conscripted only 30,000 to labor on the temple, about 2.3 percent of the total available labor force. Ten thousand of the men spent one month each quarter in Lebanon assisting Hiram's men in their work, and then they had two months at home. These men were Jewish citizens and were not treated like slaves (9:22; see Lev. 25:39-43). We aren't told if they shared in any of the wages Solomon promised Hiram's workers, but they probably didn't.

Solomon also took a census of the non-Israelite aliens in the land and drafted 150,000 of them to cut and transport stones for the temple (5:15-18; 9:15-23; 2 Chron. 2:17-18; 8:7-10). Of this group, 70,000 carried burdens and 80,000 cut limestone blocks from the hills. In charge of this group were 3,000 overseers and 300 supervisors who were aliens, and over the entire group were 250 Jewish officers. The stone blocks had to be cut carefully so they would fit together perfectly when assembled at the temple site (6:7), and that would demand careful planning and expert supervision.

Even though the conscription involved a very small portion of the male citizens, the Jewish people resented Solomon taking 30,000 of their men to work in Lebanon four months out of the year. This critical attitude helped to strengthen the people's revolt against Rehoboam and to precipitate the division of the nation after Solomon's death (12:1-21). Indeed, when it came to labor and taxes, Solomon did indeed put a heavy yoke on the people.

Both Jews and Gentiles assisted in the construction of the temple, and this fact is significant, for the temple was to be "a house of prayer for all nations" (Isa. 56:7; Matt. 21:13; Luke 19:46). After the captivity, the Persian government assisted the Jews in rebuilding their temple, and Herod's temple had a special area for the Gentiles. Sad to say, some of the Jewish religious leaders turned the court of the Gentiles into a market for selling sacrifices and changing foreign money into Jewish currency. The church today is a temple of God composed of believers in Jesus Christ, both Jews and Gentiles (Eph. 2:11-22). It is being "built up" to the glory of the Lord as "living stones"—both Jews and Gentiles—are added to the temple by the Holy Spirit (1 Peter 2:5).

Hiram's workmen in Lebanon were not worshipers of the Lord, and the aliens in the land of Israel were not Jewish proselytes, yet God used both of these groups of "outsiders" to help build His holy temple. The Lord would "have all men to be saved" (1 Tim. 2:4, KJV), but even if they aren't believers, He can use them to fulfill His purposes. He used Nebuchadnezzar and the Babylonian army to chasten Israel, and called Nebuchadnezzar "my servant" (Jer. 25:9), and He used Cyrus king of Persia to set Israel free and help them rebuild their temple (Ezra 1). This should encourage us in our praying and serving, for the Lord can use people we least appreciate to get His will done on earth. God can even work through unconverted government officials to open doors for His people or meet the needs they might have.

3. Building the temple (1 Kings 6:1-38; 2 Chron. 3:1-17)

What were David's two greatest sins? Most people would reply, "His adultery with Bathsheba and his taking a census of the people," and their answers would be correct. As a result of his sin of numbering the people, David purchased property on Mount Moriah where he built an altar and worshiped the Lord (2 Sam. 24). David married Bathsheba and God gave them a son whom they named Solomon (2 Sam. 12:24-25). Now we have Solomon building a temple on David's property on Mount Moriah! God took the consequences of David's two worst sins—a piece of property and a son—and built a temple! "But where sin abounded, grace abounded much more" (Rom. 5:20, NKJV). This isn't an encouragement for us to sin, because David paid dearly for both of those transgressions, but it is an encouragement to us go on serving God after we've repented and confessed our sins. Satan wants us to think that all is lost, but the God of all grace is still at work (1 Peter 5:10).

The outer structure (vv. 1-10, 36-38; 2 Chron. 3). The ancient world had a "short cubit" or "common cubit" of almost eighteen inches and a "long cubit" of almost twenty-one inches. The common cubit was used for the temple (2 Chron. 3:3), which means that the structure was ninety feet long, thirty feet wide, and forty-five feet high. A porch thirty feet wide and fifteen feet deep stood at the front of the temple, and a courtyard for the priests surrounded the sanctuary. It was separated from an outer courtyard by a wall composed of stone blocks and wood (v. 36; 2 Chron. 4:9). Jeremiah 36:10 calls the court of the priests "the upper courtyard," which suggests that it stood higher than the outer courtyard. The doors of the temple faced east, as did the gate of the tabernacle.

Unlike the tabernacle, the temple had three levels of rooms attached to outer walls of the temple on the south, west, and north walls. Each chamber was seven and a half feet high. The walls that supported these chambers were constructed like three stairsteps, and the chambers stood on wooden supports that rested on these stairs. The rooms on the upper level were ten and a half feet wide, on the second level nine feet wide, and on the lowest level seven and a half feet wide. These chambers were probably used for storage. At the middle of the south wall of the temple was a door leading to the lowest level of rooms and to a spiral stairway leading to the middle and top floors. On each level there must have been a narrow passage connecting the rooms. In the north and south walls, above the third level of rooms, were narrow windows that let in a small amount of light (v. 4). There were no windows in the tabernacle of Moses. However, the light necessary for ministry in the holy place came from ten lampstands, five along the north wall and five along the south wall. Of course, so large and heavy a structure required a strong foundation (v. 38).

A divine message (vv. 11-13). We don't know who brought this message (probably a prophet) or when it was delivered, but the Lord sent His Word to the king at a time when he was either discouraged with the building program or (more likely) starting to become proud of what he was accomplishing. The Lord reminded Solomon, as He must constantly remind us, that He's not impressed with our work if our walk isn't obedient to Him. What He wants is an obedient heart (Eph. 6:6). God would fulfill His promises to David and Solomon (2 Sam. 7), not because Solomon built the temple but because he obeyed the Word of the Lord. A similar warning was included in the covenant God gave Moses in Deuteronomy 28–30, so it was not a new revelation to Solomon. This was the second time God spoke to Solomon about obedience (see 3:5ff), and He would speak to him about it again after the dedication of the temple (9:3-9).

The inner structure (vv. 14-35). When the basic building was completed, the workers focused on the inside of the temple, which was the most important part, for it was there that the priests carried out the ministry of the Lord. The interior walls from ceiling to floor were paneled with cedar boards, overlaid with gold (v. 22), on which were carved open flowers and gourds, and the floor was covered with planks of pine (or fir), also overlaid with gold (vv. 15 and 30). A pair of beautifully carved folding doors led into the Holy Place from the court of the priests (vv. 31-35). Like the cherubim, these doors were made of olive wood covered with gold, and they even had hinges of gold (7:50). Golden chains hung across the outside of the doors (v. 21).

At the west end of the Holy Place, sixty feet from the doors, hung the beautiful veil that marked off the Holy of Holies, also called the Most Holy Place (2 Chron. 3:10). This created a room that was a cube, measuring thirty feet on every side (v. 20).[4] In the tabernacle of Moses, the Holy of Holies was also a cube, but it measured only fifteen feet per side. In fact, the dimensions of the temple were twice those of the tabernacle—ninety feet by thirty feet as opposed to forty-five feet by fifteen feet. The walls of the Holy of Holies were paneled with cedar wood and covered with gold, and the floor was made of gold-plated fir planks. Even the nails used in the Holy of Holies were plated with gold. It was in the Holy of Holies that the Ark of the

Covenant was kept.

The Ark of the Covenant represented the throne of God who was "enthroned between the cherubim" (Ps. 80:1, NIV). It was a wooden chest, forty-five inches long, twenty-seven inches wide, and twenty-seven inches high. Because the two tables of the law were in the Ark, it was also called "the Ark of the Testimony" (Ex. 25:22). Across the top of the Ark was a golden "mercy seat," and at each end was a cherub made of olive wood and covered with gold. The cherubim were fifteen feet high and their wings were fifteen feet across, so that as the Ark sat in the Holy of Holies, the four wings reached from wall to wall. (See vv. 23-28 and Ex. 25:10-22 and 37:1-9). Once a year, the high priest was permitted to enter the Holy of Holies, sprinkle the blood of the sacrifice on the mercy seat and thus cover the sins of the people for another year (Lev. 16).

Hiram cast two large pillars of bronze, each twenty-seven feet high and eighteen feet in circumference.[5] They were free-standing, about four inches thick, and hollow (Jer. 52:21). A decorative capital four feet high rested on top of each pillar (2 Kings 25:17). It was comprised of an inverted bowl, lotus petals, and a network or interwoven chain of pomegranates. The two pillars were named "Jachin" ("he establishes") and "Boaz" ("in him is strength") and they stood outside the entrance to the Holy Place, Jachin to the north and Boaz to the south. The "he" in these definitions surely refers to God, and the pillars bore witness to the Jewish people that it was God who established their nation and Israel's faith in Jehovah was the source of their strength. Some see in this a reference to David's dynasty, established by God (2 Sam. 7) and continued by Him.

4. Furnishing the temple (1 Kings 7:13-51; 2 Chron. 4)

The furnishings of the temple were important to the priests, for without the divinely ordained furniture, they couldn't do their ministry or please the Lord.

The brazen altar (2 Chron. 4:1). As you approached the temple from the east, you came to the entrance to the inner courtyard of the priests. It was to this entrance that the people brought their sacrifices and offerings to be presented to the Lord. On the right, toward the north, stood the altar of brass, thirty feet square and fifteen feet high (2 Chron. 4:1), where the fire was kept burning and the priests offered the sacrifices (see 8:64; 9:25; see Ex. 27:1-8; 38:1-7). The height of the altar suggests that there must have been steps leading up to a ledge on which the priests could stand and minister (see Ezek. 43:13-17). Some students believe that the altar itself wasn't fifteen feet high but was shorter than that and stood on a stone base that raised it higher. The tabernacle altar was only four and a half feet high.

The laver or molten sea (vv. 23-26; 2 Chron. 4:2-5, 10). To the left of the entrance, on the south side of the court (v. 39), stood the huge "molten sea" that replaced the smaller laver that had stood in the tabernacle court (vv. 23-26; see Ex. 30:17-21; 38:8). It was round and made of brass a handbreadth thick with the image of lilies around the rim, and it could hold over 17,000 gallons of water.[6] This large basin measured fifteen feet across and was seven and a half feet high. It stood on the backs of twelve cast statues of oxen, in groups of three, with each group facing a different direction. Perhaps these twelve oxen represented the twelve tribes of Israel. (See 2 Kings 16:17.)

There must have been a system for removing small amounts of water so the priests could wash their hands and feet, but this system isn't explained in the text. Perhaps there were spigots at the base of the basin. If the priests didn't keep their hands and feet clean as they ministered in the temple, they were in danger of death (Ex. 30:20). In Scripture, water for drinking is a picture of the Spirit of God (John 7:37-39), while water for washing is a picture of the Word of God (Ps. 119:9; John 15:3; Eph. 5:25-27). As the priests labored for the Lord in the temple, they became defiled and needed to be cleansed; and as we serve the Lord, we too can become defiled and need the "washing of water by the word." Jesus pictured this truth in John 13 when He washed the disciples' feet.

The ten stands and lavers (vv. 27-39; 2 Chron. 4:6). These were beautifully decorated metal wagons, six feet square and four and a half feet high, with handles at each corner. Each stand could hold a basin that held 230 gallons of water. The stands were kept in the court of the priests right next to the sanctuary, five on the north side and five on the south side. Since the stands were on wheels, they could easily be moved from place to place. They were used for the washing and preparing of the sacrifices (2 Chron. 4:6) and perhaps for the general cleanliness of the temple. The dirty water could then be wheeled away and disposed of in a proper place and the basins filled with clean water from the molten sea.

It's worth noting that these very practical and useful stands were also very beautiful, which teaches us that God sees beauty in holiness and the holiness of beauty (Ex. 28:2; Pss. 29:2; 96:6, 9; 110:3).

The golden incense altar (6:20, 22; 7:48). The altar was made of cedar covered with gold, but we have no dimensions given in the text. It stood before the veil that separated the Holy Place from the Holy of Holies, and on it the priests burned incense each morning and evening when they cared for the lamps (Ex. 30:1-10; 37:25-29). In Scripture, the burning of incense is a picture of our prayers rising up to the Lord (Ps. 141:1-2; Rev. 5:8; Luke 1:8-10). The Lord gave Moses the recipe for the mixture of spices that was used in the tabernacle and temple worship (Ex. 30:34-38), and this mixture was not to be counterfeited or used for any other purpose. The golden altar was used for no other purpose, and on the annual Day of Atonement, the high priest applied blood to this altar to cleanse and purify it (Ex. 30:10). Without "clean hands and a pure heart" (Ps. 24:3-5), we can't approach the Lord and expect Him to hear and answer prayer (Ps. 66:18; Heb. 10:19-25).

The golden lampstands and tables (vv. 48-49; 2 Chron. 4:7-8, 19-20). In the tabernacle that Moses constructed, there was only one table for the loaves of bread, but the temple had ten golden tables, five in a line on each side of the Holy Place. The tabernacle had one golden lampstand with seven lamps on it, but the temple had ten golden lampstands in the Holy Place, five along the north wall and five along the south wall. They provided the light needed for the ministry in the Holy Place.

The miscellaneous utensils (vv. 40-50; 2 Chron. 4:7-8, 11-22). The priests required many different utensils in order to carry on their work, including wick trimmers, bowls for sprinkling water and sacrificial blood, dishes, ladles, large pots for cooking the meat from the peace offerings, and shovels for removing the ashes. The temple was an imposing structure that contained expensive furnishings made of gold and polished bronze, but the daily ministry would have been impossible without these small utensils.

It's difficult to calculate the cost of this

building in modern currency. It isn't enough just to know the price of the precious metal today, but we also need to know its purchasing power. Then we must calculate what Solomon paid for manpower and materials and try to express it in contemporary equivalents. When you consider that there was gold overlay on the inside walls and floors, the furniture, the doors, and the cherubim, you have no hesitation concluding that this was a very costly building. And yet all this beauty was destroyed and this wealth was confiscated when the Babylonian army captured Jerusalem and destroyed the temple (see Jer. 52). Nebuchadnezzar robbed the temple and deported the captives in stages, and eventually his men burned the city and the temple so they could get their hands on all the gold that was there.

How painful it is to realize that Solomon, the man who constructed the temple, was the man who married a multitude of foreign wives and encouraged idolatry in Israel, the very sin that turned the nation away from God and brought upon them the fiery judgment of the Lord.

CHAPTER FOUR
GOD'S HOUSE AND SOLOMON'S HEART
1 Kings 8:1–9:9, 25-28 (2 Chronicles 5–7)

"Fellow citizens, we cannot escape history." Abraham Lincoln spoke those words to the American Congress on December 1, 1862, but King Solomon could have spoken them to the Jewish leaders when he dedicated the temple during the Feast of Tabernacles in the twenty-fourth year of his reign.[1] No matter where the Jews are in this world, or what the century is, they have their roots in Abraham, Moses, and David. King David is mentioned twelve times in this section[2] and Moses is mentioned three times. During his prayer, Solomon referred to God's covenant with his father (2 Sam. 7) and also to the covenant God gave to Moses recorded in Deuteronomy 28–30. The main thrust of his prayer is that God would hear the prayers directed toward the temple and forgive those who sinned, and this request is based on the promise given in Deuteronomy 30:1-10. Israel's kings were commanded to make their own copy of the Book of Deuteronomy (Deut. 17:18-20), and Solomon's many references to Deuteronomy indicate that he knew the book very well.

What kind of a "house" did Solomon dedicate that day?

1. A house of God (1 Kings 8:1-11; 2 Chron. 5:1-14)

Solomon assembled at Jerusalem the leaders of the tribes of Israel and whoever of the citizens could attend, from the north to south (v. 65), that they might assist him in dedicating the house of God. The word "house" is used twenty-six times in this passage (thirty-seven times in 2 Chron. 5–7), for this structure was indeed the "house of God." (vv. 10, 11, 17, etc.). But what made this costly building the house of the Lord? Not simply that God commanded it to be built and chose Solomon to build it, or that He gave the plans to David and provided the wealth to construct it. Those matters were important, but the thing that made this temple the house of the Lord was the presence of the Lord God Jehovah in the sanctuary.

The Ark was brought in (vv. 1-9; 2 Chron. 5:1-9). In the Holy of Holies, Jehovah was "enthroned between the cherubim" (Ps. 80:1 NIV). The pagan nations had their temples, altars, priests, and sacrifices, but their temples were empty and their sacrifices useless. The true and living God dwelt in the temple on Mount Moriah! That's why Solomon's first act of dedication was to have the Ark of the Covenant brought from the tent David had pitched for it (2 Sam. 6:17) and placed into the inner sanctuary of the temple.[3] The tabernacle equipment and furnishings were also brought to the temple and stored there (2 Chron. 5:5). The Ark of the Covenant was the only piece of the original furniture that was kept in active service, for nothing could replace the throne of God or the law of God that was kept in the Ark. That this dedication service took place during the Feast of Tabernacles was significant, for the Ark had led Israel all during their wilderness journey.

The priests placed the Ark before the large cherubim that Hiram had made, whose wings spanned the width of the Holy of Holies (6:23-30). The cherubim on the original golden mercy seat looked at each other, while the new cherubim looked out toward the Holy Place where the priests ministered. The angels of God not only "look into" the mysteries of God's grace (1 Peter 1:12), but they also behold the ministry of God's people and learn about God's grace (1 Cor. 4:9; 11:10; Eph. 3:10; 1 Tim. 5:21). At one time, a pot of manna and the staff of Aaron stood before the Ark (Ex. 16:33; Num. 17:10; Heb. 9:4), both of which were reminders of rebellion in Israel (Ex. 16:1-3; Num. 16). But the nation was now making a new beginning and those items weren't needed. The important thing was that Israel obey the law of God that was kept in the Ark. The Jews were no longer a pilgrim people, but the staves were left in the Ark as a reminder of God's faithfulness to them during those forty years of discipline.

The glory came down (vv. 10-11; 2 Chron. 5:11-14). The Ark was but a symbol of the throne and presence of God; it was the actual presence of the Lord in His house that was important. Once Solomon and the people had honored God and placed His throne in the Holy of Holies, the glory of God came and filled the house of the Lord. The glory cloud had guided Israel through the wilderness (Num. 9:15-23), but now the glory came to dwell within the beautiful temple Solomon had built. As the glory filled the house, the priests praised God with voice and instruments, for the Lord inhabits the praises of His people (Ps. 22:3).

The presence of God's glory was the distinguishing mark of the nation of Israel (Ex. 33:12-23; Rom. 9:4). The sins of the people caused God's glory to depart from the tabernacle (1 Sam. 4:19-22), but now the glory had returned. But the nation would sin again and be taken to Babylon, and there Ezekiel the prophet would have a vision of the glory of God leaving the temple (Ezek. 8:1-4; 9:3; 10:4, 18-19; 11:22-23). However, God would also allow Ezekiel to see the glory return to the kingdom temple (43:1-5). The glory came to earth in the person of Jesus Christ (John 1:14; Matt. 17:1-7), but sinners crucified "the Lord of glory" (1 Cor. 2:8). When Jesus returned to heaven, the cloud of glory accompanied Him (Acts 1:9) and the temple was left "desolate" (Matt. 23:38–24:2).

Since the coming of the Spirit at Pentecost (Acts 2), God's glory has resided in each of God's children individually (1 Cor. 6:19-20) as well as in the church local (1 Cor. 3:16) and the church universal (Eph. 2:19-22). Until Jesus comes to take us to the eternal glory, our privilege and responsibility is to bring glory to Him as we serve here on earth. Each local assembly, worshiping the Lord in spirit and truth, should manifest the glory of the Lord (1 Cor. 14:23-25).

2. A house of testimony (1 Kings 8:12-21; 2 Chron. 6:1-11)

God not only graciously dwells with His people, but He also gives them His Word and faithfully keeps His promises. That's the major theme of this section, for in it Solomon glorified Jehovah by reviewing the history of the building of the temple.

The mystery of God (vv. 12-13; 2 Chron. 6:1-2). The king was standing on his special platform (2 Chron. 6:13), facing the sanctuary, the priests were at the altar (5:12) and the people were gathered in the assembly, and all of them had just seen a marvelous manifestation of the glory of God. Yet Solomon opened his address by saying, "The Lord said He would dwell in the dark cloud" (v. 12, NKJV). Why speak of darkness when they had just beheld God's radiant glory? Solomon was referring to the words of the Lord to Moses at Mount Sinai: "Behold, I come to you in the thick cloud, that the people may hear when I speak with you, and believe you forever" (Ex. 19:9, NKJV). There was indeed a thick cloud of darkness on the mountain (Ex. 19:16; 20:21; Deut. 4:11; 5:22) and Moses went into that darkness with great fear (Heb. 12:18-21). Solomon was connecting the events of that day to Israel's past experience at Sinai, for the people of God must not be cut off from their roots in history.

God is light (1 John 1:5) and dwells in light (1 Tim. 6:16), but He cannot fully reveal Himself to man because "there shall no man see me, and live" (Ex. 33:20, KJV). The emphasis at Sinai was on *hearing* God, not *seeing* God, lest the Jewish people would be tempted to make images of their God and worship them. Like the church today, Israel was to be a people of the Word, hearing it and obeying. King David envisioned the Lord with darkness under His feet and darkness as His canopy (Ps. 18:9, 11; see 97:2). There is mystery about God that humbles us, because we don't always understand Him and His ways, but this mystery also encourages us to trust Him and rest upon His Word. Solomon didn't want the people to think that God was now their "neighbor" and therefore they could speak to Him or about Him any way they pleased. "But the Lord is in His holy temple. Let all the earth be silent before Him" (Hab. 2:20, NASB).

Like a servant reporting to his master, Solomon announced that he had built the house to be God's dwelling place (v. 13). This reminds us that Moses finished work of building and erecting the tabernacle (Ex. 40:33), that our Savior finished all that the Father instructed Him to do (John 17:4), and that both John the Baptist and Paul finished their courses successfully (Acts 13:25; 2 Tim. 4:7). All of us will give an account of our life and service when we see the Lord (Rom. 14:10-13), and it behooves us to be faithful to the calling He has given us, so that we end well.

The goodness and faithfulness of God (vv. 15-21). Over more than fifty years of ministry, it's been my privilege to assist many local churches in dedicating new sanctuaries; and in my messages, I've tried to emphasize the work of God in the history of His people. As A. T. Pierson used to say, "History is His story." It's easy for new church members and new generations that come along to take for granted or forget the history of their church. The weekly Sabbath, the annual feasts (Lev. 23), and the presence of the temple would bear witness to the Jewish people, young and old, that Jehovah was their God. The word "remember" is used at least fourteen times in the Book of Deuteronomy because God didn't want His people to forget the lessons of the past.

God in His goodness and grace made a covenant with David concerning his family and his throne (2 Sam. 7), and He included in that covenant the promise of a son who would build the temple. What God spoke with His mouth, He accomplished with His hand (v. 15), and what He promised to David, He performed through Solomon (v. 20). But God did these things for the honor of His name, not for the glory of either David or Solomon (vv. 16-20). God's name is referred to at least fourteen times in Solomon's address and prayer. The king was careful to give God all the glory. Whenever the people would come to worship, they would remember that the goodness and faithfulness of the Lord made the temple possible.

3. A house of prayer (1 Kings 8:22-53; 2 Chron. 6:12-42)

According to 2 Chronicles 6:13, Solomon knelt on the special platform near the altar as he prayed this prayer, his hands lifted to heaven. Our traditional posture for prayer ("hands folded and eyes closed") was unknown to the Jews. Their posture was to look up by faith toward God in heaven (or toward the temple) and lift their open hands to show their poverty and their expectancy as they awaited the answer (v. 38, 54; Ex. 9:29, 33; Pss. 63:4; 88:9; 143:6). This practice was carried over into the early church (1 Tim. 2:8). The word "heaven" is found at least a dozen times in verses 22-54.

Solomon opened his prayer with praise and thanksgiving to the Lord, the covenant-making and covenant-keeping God. "There is no God like thee" (v. 23; compare Ex. 15:11 and Deut. 4:39). He then referred to God's covenant with his father, David, the covenant that appointed Solomon as David's heir and the builder of the temple (2 Sam. 7). But Solomon also claimed the covenant promise of the Davidic dynasty and prayed that David's royal line would continue just as God had promised. Of course, the ultimate fulfillment of that promise is in Jesus Christ (Luke 1:26-33, 67-75; Acts 2:29-30; Rom. 1:3).

As Solomon prayed, he was overwhelmed by the contrast between the greatness of God and the insignificance of the work he had done in building the temple. How could Almighty God, the God of the heavens, dwell in a building made by men's hands? Solomon had expressed this same truth to King Hiram before he began to build (2 Chron. 2:6), and the prophet Isaiah echoed it (Isa. 66:1). Stephen referred to these words from Solomon and Isaiah when he defended himself before the Jewish council (Acts 7:47-50), and Paul emphasized this truth when preaching to the Gentiles (Acts 17:24). Solomon realized that God's willingness to dwell with His people was wholly an act of grace.

The burden of his prayer is in verses 28-30: that the Lord would keep His eyes on the temple and His ears open to the prayers of the people and answer them when they prayed toward the temple. He asked the Lord to forgive the sins of the people when they prayed (vv. 30, 34, 36, 39, 50) and in so doing maintain "the cause of his people Israel" (v. 59). Solomon knew the terms of the covenant found in Deuteronomy 28–29, and the calamities he mentioned in his prayer are the very disciplines the Lord promised to send if Israel disobeyed His law. But Solomon also knew that Deuteronomy 30 promised forgiveness and restoration if God's people would repent and turn to the Lord. Jonah looked toward the temple and prayed, and God forgave him (Jonah 2:4), and Daniel prayed for the people as he looked toward Jerusalem (Dan. 6:10). "My house shall be called a house of prayer for all nations" (Isa. 56:7, NKJV; Matt. 21:13; Mark 11:17; Luke 19:46).

Solomon presented to the Lord seven specific requests.

(1) Justice in the land (vv. 31-32; 2 Chron. 6:22-23). Solomon had begun his reign by judging between two women (3:16-28), but it would be impossible for him to handle every case of personal conflict in the land and still perform all the duties of the king. Judges were appointed in Israel to hear local cases (Ex. 18:13-27; 21:5-6; 22:7-12; Deut. 17:2-13; 25:1), and the priests were also available to apply the law and render decisions (1 Chron. 23:4; 26:29). If a man was accused of sinning against his neighbor, the accused could take an oath at the temple altar and the Lord would declare whether or not the man was innocent. How this verdict was declared isn't explained, but perhaps the priest used the Urim and Thummim (Ex. 28:30; Lev. 8:8). Justice in the land is essential if citizens are to enjoy "life, liberty, and the pursuit of happiness." How tragic that, in later years, it was the godless kings of Israel and Judah who allowed injustice into the land.

The judges' responsibility was to "condemn the wicked . . . and justify the righteous," but when it comes to our salvation, God justifies the ungodly (Rom. 4:5) on the basis of the sacrifice Christ made on the cross (Rom. 5:6). God has condemned all people as unrighteous (Rom. 3:23) so that He might show grace to all mankind and save those who will put their trust in His Son.

(2) Military defeat (vv. 33-34; 2 Chron. 6:24-25). This defeat is caused because the people have sinned in some way (Josh. 7) and the Lord is displeased with them. If Israel obeyed the terms of the covenant, there would be peace in the land and God would give Israel victory over any enemies who attacked them. But if Israel sinned, God would allow their enemies to triumph over them (Lev. 26:6-8, 14-17, 25, 33, 36-39; Deut. 28:1, 7, 15, 25-26, 49-52). If this defeat brought the people to repentance, then God would forgive them and see to it that the prisoners were released and returned home.

(3) Drought in the land (vv. 35-36; 2 Chron. 6:26-27). Israel had title to the land because of God's covenant with Abraham, but they could possess it and enjoy its blessings only if they obeyed God's law. One of the severest disciplines listed in the covenant was drought in the land (Lev. 26:19; Deut. 28:22-24, 48). The Lord promised His people that He would send the rain in its season (Deut. 11:10-14) only if they honored Him. Since the Israelites were a pastoral and agricultural people, rain was absolutely necessary for their survival. Whenever the people obeyed the Lord, they enjoyed bumper crops and their flocks and herds were healthy and multiplied. The purpose of drought was to bring the people to a place of repentance, and God promised to forgive their sins and send the rain. See 1 Kings 18.

(4) Other natural calamities (vv. 37-40; 2 Chron. 6:28-31).[4] God warned in the covenant that Israel's disobedience would bring divine discipline to them. He would send famine (Lev. 26:26, 29; Deut. 28:17, 48), blight (Lev. 26:20; Deut. 28:18, 22, 30, 39-40), invasions of insects (Deut. 28:38, 42), and various sicknesses and plagues (Lev. 26:16, 25; Deut. 28:21-22, 27, 35, 59-61). However, if they obeyed Him, He would shelter His people and their land from these calamities. But once again, Solomon asked the Lord to forgive His people when they confessed their sins, and to restore their land (see 2 Chron. 7:13-14).

In his prayer, Solomon frequently mentioned the land (vv. 34, 36-37, 40-41, 46-48) because this was part of Israel's inheritance from the Lord. When the people began to sin, God punished them first *in the land* (see the Book of Judges), and when they persisted in their rebellion, He allowed enemy nations to take them *out of the land*. In 722 B.C., the Assyrians conquered Israel and assimilated the people, and in 606–586 the Babylonians defeated Judah, burned Jerusalem and the temple, and took many of the people captive to Babylon. When God punished His people out of their land, He finally cured them of their idolatry.

(5) Foreigners who came to pray (vv. 41-43; 2 Chron. 6:32-33). These were not the "resident aliens" in Israel who settled in the land and had certain privileges and responsibilities under the law (Lev. 16:29; 17:10, 12; 18:26; 19:34; 20:2; 25:6, 45). The "foreigners" were people who would come to Israel because they had heard of the greatness of the Lord and His temple. (Gentile workers had helped to build the temple.) It was the responsibility of Israel to be a "light" to the pagan Gentile nations and to demonstrate to them the glory of the true and living God. Solomon had this in mind when he asked the Lord to hear and answer the prayers of people outside the covenant, so that "all peoples of the earth may know Your name and fear You" (v. 43 NKJV; see v. 60). If these people began to pray to the Lord Jehovah, perhaps they would come to trust and worship Him.

From the very beginning of the nation, when God called Abraham and Sarah to leave Ur and go to Canaan, God declared that He wanted Israel to be a blessing to the whole world (Gen. 12:1-3). God's judgments against Pharaoh and Egypt were a witness to the nations (Ex. 9:16), as was His opening of the Red Sea at the Exodus (Josh. 2:8-13). When God dried up the Jordan so Israel could enter the Promised Land, He revealed His power and glory to the other nations (Josh. 4:23-24). His blessing on Israel in the land of Canaan was a witness to the pagan nations (Deut. 28:7-14), and so was David's victory over Goliath (1 Sam. 17:46). God blesses us that we might be a blessing, not that we might horde the blessing and boast. The Jews prayed, "God be merciful to us and bless us, and cause His face to shine upon us, that Your way may be known on earth, Your salvation among all nations" (Ps. 67:1-2, NKJV). The church today needs to pray that prayer and keep that purpose in mind.

(6) Armies in battle (vv. 44-45; 2 Chron. 6:34-35). When God sent His people into battle, it was a "holy war" that could be won only by His strength and wisdom. Using the silver trumpets, the priests sounded the call to arms (2 Chron. 13:12-16; Num. 10:1-10). They assisted the armies to ascertain God's will (1 Sam. 23:1-2), and they encouraged the men to fight for the glory of the Lord and trust Him alone (Deut. 20:1-4). Even in the midst of battle, the soldiers could look toward the temple and ask the Lord for His help. When he described the Christian soldier's equipment, Paul included prayer as one of the essentials for victory (Eph. 6:18-19). The French writer Voltaire said, "It is said that God is always on the side of the heaviest battalions," but the truth is that God is on the side of those who pray in His will.

(7) Defeat and captivity (vv. 46-53; 2 Chron. 6:36-39). The pronoun "they" in verse 46 refers to the people of Israel, and Israel's history shows that the nation was prone to sin. All of us are sinners (Prov. 20:9; Rom. 3:23), but God's special blessings on Israel and His covenant with them made their disobedience that much more serious. By disobeying God's law and imitating the sins of their idolatrous neighbors, the Jews were sinning against a flood of light. In the covenant, God warned that repeated rebellion would lead to captivity (Lev. 26:27-45; Deut. 28:49-68). The other disciplines took away from the Jews the blessings of the land, but captivity took them away from the land itself. The Jewish people did experience defeat and captivity. Assyria conquered the northern kingdom of Israel in 722 and Babylon conquered the southern kingdom of Judah in 606–586 and took the Jews captive to Babylon. This terrible event was predicted by Isaiah (6:11-12; 11:11-12; 39:6) and Micah (4:10), and Jeremiah revealed that the Babylonian captivity would last for seventy years (Jer. 25:1-14; 29:11-14). When the prophet Daniel understood what Jeremiah wrote, he began to pray that God would keep His promises (Deut. 30:1-10) and set the nation free (Dan. 9:1ff). No doubt many other believing Jews ("the remnant") also interceded, and God stirred Cyrus, king of Persia, to allow the Jews to return to their land and rebuild their temple (Ezra 1; 2 Chron. 36:22-23).

Solomon gave the Lord several reasons why the Lord should forgive His people when they repented and returned to Him.

After all, they were His people whom He had purchased and delivered from Egyptian bondage (v. 51). Israel was His special people, separated from the other nations to glorify God and accomplish His mission on earth. Again, Solomon revealed his knowledge of the Book of Deuteronomy (4:20; 7:6; 9:26-29; 32:9).

He closed his prayer by asking the Lord to keep His eyes upon the temple and the people who worshiped there, and to keep His ears open to the requests of the people who prayed at the temple or toward the temple (2 Chron. 6:40-42). His benediction in verse 41 is found in Psalm 132:8-10.[5] Israel was no longer a pilgrim people, but they still needed the Lord to guide and help them. (See also the words of Moses in Num. 10:35-36.) Thanks to David's victories on the battlefield, God had kept His promise and given Israel rest; but as Andrew Bonar said, "Let us be as watchful after the victory as before the battle." Solomon closed the prayer with a plea that the Lord not reject him, the anointed king, David's son and heir. "Remember the mercies of your servant David" (2 Chron. 6:42, NKJV), referring to God's promises to David in the covenant (2 Sam. 7; Ps. 89:19-29).

These "sure mercies of David" (Isa. 55:3, NKJV) involve the coming of Jesus Christ, the Son of David, to be the Savior of the world (Acts 13:32-40).

4. A house of praise (1 Kings 8:54-61; 2 Chron. 7:1-3)

The king had been kneeling on the special platform near the altar, his hands lifted to God, but now he stood to give the people a blessing from the Lord. Usually it was the priests who blessed the people (Num. 6:22-27), but on a special occasion such as this, the king could give the blessing as David did (2 Sam. 6:18, 20). Solomon blessed the whole assembly and through them the entire nation, and he gave thanks to God for His great mercies.

As Solomon reviewed the history of the Jewish nation, his conclusion was that the promises of God had never failed, not even once. God's people had often failed the Lord, but He had never failed them. He promised Moses that He would give the nation rest, and He did (Ex. 33:14). By His power, He enabled Joshua to overcome the nations in Canaan and claim the land for Israel's inheritance. Moses told the people that when they had entered into the promised rest, God would give them a central sanctuary where they could offer their sacrifices and worship God (Deut. 12:1-14); and now that temple had been provided. In his farewell speech to the leaders, Joshua emphasized the same truth (Josh. 23:14-15, and see 21:45). But Joshua also reminded them that the warnings would be fulfilled as well as the promises, and he cautioned them to obey the Lord in all things.

Solomon especially emphasized one promise that God gave to the patriarchs and repeated often in Jewish history, that the Lord would not leave His people or forsake them. God was with Abraham during his life, and He promised to be with Isaac (Gen. 26:3, 24) and Jacob (Gen. 28:15; 31:3; 46:1-4). He renewed this promise to Moses (Ex. 3:12; 33:14), and Moses repeated it to Joshua (Deut. 31:6-8, 17). The Lord Himself also gave the promise to Joshua (Josh. 1:5, 9; 3:7; see 6:27). He also gave it to Gideon (Judg. 6:15-16), and the prophet Samuel repeated it to the nation (1 Sam. 12:22). David encouraged Solomon with this promise when he appointed him to build the temple (1 Chron. 28:20).

After the days of Solomon, the Prophet Isaiah repeated this promise and gave comfort to the Jewish people who would experience the Babylonian captivity (Isa. 41:10, 17; 42:16; 44:21; 49:14-16). The Lord used it to encourage Jeremiah (Jer. 1:8, 19; 20:11), and Jesus gave it to His disciples before He ascended to the Father (Matt. 28:19-20). The church today can claim the promise just as did believers long ago (Heb. 13:5). See also Psalms 27:9; 37:25, 28; 38:21.

Solomon also asked God to help him and his people to have hearts that were inclined to the Lord and eager to obey His commandments (v. 58). He knew the Book of Deuteronomy and must have had 5:29 in mind—"Oh, that they had such a heart in them that they would fear Me and always keep all My commandments, that it might be well with them and with their children forever!" (NKJV). Solomon admonished the people to have sincere hearts and to follow the Lord wholeheartedly (v. 61).

Finally, Solomon asked the Lord to remember the prayer that he had spoken with his lips and from his heart (vv. 59-60). Our spoken words are but breath and sound, and they vanish almost immediately. It encourages us to know that no believing prayer spoken to the Lord is ever forgotten, for God remembers our prayers and answers them in His time and in His own way. (See Rev. 5:8 and 8:3.) Solomon's prayer was not selfish. He wanted the people of Israel to be faithful to the Lord so that all the nations of the earth might come to know and trust the God of Israel. How encouraging to know that the prayer of one man could touch and influence a whole world! God still wants His house to be called "a house of prayer for all nations."

The Lord answered Solomon's request by sending fire from heaven to consume the sacrifices on the altar, and once again the glory of God filled the house (2 Chron. 7:1-3). God sent fire from heaven when Aaron the priest blessed the people (Lev. 9:23-24), and also when Elijah the prophet called upon God (1 Kings 18:38). Now he sent fire when Solomon the king offered his prayer and his sacrifices to the Lord. But the people all responded by bowing to the ground and praising the Lord. Imagine the sound of thousands of people shouting, "Truly He is good, truly His lovingkindness is everlasting" (2 Chron. 7:3, NASB). God had accepted the prayer of the king and the worship of the people!

5. A house of fellowship (1 Kings 8:62-66; 2 Chron. 7:4-10)

The assembly that gathered for the dedication of the temple came from the southernmost boundary of the kingdom ("the river of Egypt" = the Wadi of Egypt) to the northernmost boundary ("the entrance to Hamath") and formed a "great congregation" (v. 65, NKJV; and see 4:21). Many of them brought sacrifices to the Lord and Solomon himself provided 22,000 cattle and 120,000 sheep and goats. The new altar was too small for the offering of so many animals, so to expedite matters, the king sanctified the courtyard and it was used for sacrifices.

It was customary to feast and rejoice during the week set aside for the Feast of Tabernacles. The feast celebrated God's gracious care of His people during their years in the wilderness, and the people of Israel could look back and give thanks. But now they could look around and give thanks for the new temple, the promises of God, and the presence of the glory of the Lord. Just like the other sacrifices, the peace offering (or fellowship offering, Lev. 3 and 7:11-34) was presented to the Lord, but part of the meat was given to the priests and part was retained by the worshiper. He and his family could enjoy a feast and even invite friends to share it with them. The Jews raised their animals for milk, wool, and young and didn't often eat meat, so the fellowship feast after the sacrifice was a real treat. The dedication lasted a week, the feast lasted another week, and the event closed with a day of solemn assembly (2 Chron. 7:8-9). The sacrifices must have been offered day after day, for the meat of the fellowship offering could be eaten only two days and all leftovers had to be burned the third day (Lev. 19:5-8).

While some churches go overboard on eating—"the Upper Room has become the supper room"—there is nothing wrong with God's people eating together. Jesus often used meal settings to teach the Word, and the early church occasionally held what was called "a love feast" (*agape*), a potluck meal that may have been the only decent meal some of the members had all week, especially the slaves (1 Cor. 11:20-22, 33-34; Jude 12). The members of the various Jerusalem assemblies often ate together (Acts 2:42-47; 4:35; 6:1), and hospitality was a virtue often encouraged in the epistles (Rom. 12:13; 16:23; 1 Tim. 3:2; 5:10; Titus 1:8; 1 Peter 4:9; 3 John 8). "Therefore, whether you eat or drink, or whatever you do, do all to the glory of God" (1 Cor. 10:31, NKJV).

However, the peace offering symbolizes Jesus Christ who is our peace (Eph. 2:14) and who has given us the gift of His peace (John 14:27). Because of His sacrifice on the cross, we have "peace with God" (Rom. 5:1), and by surrendering to Him, we can have "the peace of God" in our hearts (Phil. 4:6-9). God's people "feed" on Jesus Christ as we read the Word and make it a part of our lives, and as we obey what it commands. Jesus Christ is the center of our fellowship, just as at the dedication of the temple the peace offerings were the center of the fellowship.

God doesn't live in the church buildings we erect, but when we assemble in these buildings dedicated to Him, we ought to emphasize worship, fellowship, joy, and witness. Such meetings are occasions for both joy and solemnity. "Serve the Lord with fear, and rejoice with trembling" (Ps. 2:11, NKJV). When the Holy Spirit is in control, both rejoicing and reverence will characterize the gathering.

6. A house of responsibility (1 Kings 9:1-9; 2 Chron. 7:11-22)

The presence of God's glory in the temple and the coming of fire from heaven to consume the sacrifices assured Solomon that his prayer had been heard and was accepted by the Lord. But there would not always be that same splendor of glory in the temple, nor would fire from heaven consume every sacrifice; so the Lord spoke His Word to Solomon, for "the Word of the Lord endures forever" (1 Peter 1:25).

Promise (vv. 1-3; 2 Chron. 7:11-16). As He had done at Gibeon (3:4-5), the Lord appeared to Solomon and spoke the Word that he needed to hear. He assured the king that He had heard his prayer and would answer it. His eyes would be on the house Solomon had built and dedicated, and His ears would be alert to hear the prayers of His people. The people and their king had dedicated the house to the Lord, but now He would sanctify the house and make it His own. God's name was on the house, God's eyes were watching, and His ears listening. It was indeed the house of the Lord.

The text in 2 Chronicles 7:11-16 mentions some of the specific requests that Solomon had made in his prayer, and the Lord promised to answer every request. He was willing to forgive His people when they sinned if only they would humble themselves, pray, seek His face, and turn from their sins. God has never made a covenant with any other nation but Israel, but since Christian believers today are God's people and called by His name, they can claim this promise.

Obedience (vv. 4-5; 2 Chron. 7:17-18). The Lord made the matter very personal and spoke specifically to Solomon, referring to the covenant God had made with his father, David (2 Sam. 7). The Lord reaffirmed the terms of the covenant and assured Solomon that David would always have a king on the throne so long as his descendants obeyed the law and walked in the fear of the Lord. Solomon couldn't expect God's blessing just because David was his father and he had obeyed David and built the temple. Solomon had to be a man like his father, a man after God's own heart (1 Sam. 13:14), a man of integrity (Ps. 78:72). It's interesting that the Lord said nothing about David's adultery, deception, and plot to murder Uriah. These had been serious transgressions for which David had paid dearly, but David had confessed them and the Lord had forgiven him.

Warning (vv. 6-9; 2 Chron. 7:19-22). God had given the Jewish people His Word, and He expected them to obey it, and the king had to practice the law and set the example for others. It's tragic that after the death of Solomon the nation divided and both kingdoms gradually declined until they were destroyed. The Lord in these words was only rehearsing the terms of the covenant found in Leviticus 26 and Deuternomy 28-30, a covenant that the Jewish people knew well. The kingdom of Judah did turn to idols, disobey the Lord, and invite His chastening. The Babylonian army devastated the land, destroyed Jerusalem, and robbed and burned the temple Solomon had dedicated. Instead of being a blessing to all the nations of the earth, the ruined city and temple would shock visitors from other nations and move them to ridicule.

Before we pass judgment on David's royal line, let's consider how many local churches, schools, denominational agencies, and other Christian ministries have abandoned the true faith and ceased to bring glory to the Lord. We could honestly write "Ichabod—the glory has departed" on many an edifice in which Christ was once honored and from which the gospel of Jesus Christ was sent out to a lost world.

From Solomon's death in 931 until the reign of Zedekiah (597–586), the Davidic dynasty would continue for God would keep His promise to David. But the only Jew alive today who qualifies to sit on David's throne *and can prove it from the genealogies,* is Jesus of Nazareth, Son of David, Son of God. One day He will reign from David's throne and "the earth will be filled with the knowledge of the glory of the Lord, as the waters cover the sea" (Hab. 2:14, NKJV).

CHAPTER FIVE
THE KINGDOM, POWER, AND GLORY
1 Kings 7:1-12; 9:10–10:29 (2 Chronicles 8:1–9:28)

Most people remember King Solomon as the man who built the temple of God in Jerusalem, but during his reign, he was occupied with many different activities. These chapters record a series of vignettes depicting some of the things Solomon did to advance his kingdom and enhance his life. But these activities also reveal Solomon's character and expose some of the areas of weakness that later produced a bitter harvest. Gradually, Solomon became more interested in prices than in values, and in reputation rather than character, and in the splendor of the kingdom rather than the good of the people and the glory of the Lord.

1. Solomon builds a palace. (1 Kings 7:1-12)

The work on the temple structure was completed in seven years,[1] but it took several more years for Hiram and his crew to decorate the interior and construct the furnishings. While they were busy at the temple, Solomon designed and built a palace for himself that was a combination of personal residence, city hall, armory, and official reception center. "I enlarged my works," he wrote, "I built houses for myself" (Ecc. 2:4, NASB).

When you read this description of the project, you get the impression that it involved several isolated structures, but 1 Kings 9:10 refers to "the two houses [buildings]," the temple and the "palace." The palace was twice as large as the temple and probably had two if not three stories. It was 150 feet long, 75 feet wide, and 45 feet high. (The temple was 90 x 30 x 45.) The total structure included two porches or colonnades, Solomon's own residence, a residence for his Egyptian wife[2] (and perhaps part of his harem), a throne room ("hall of justice"), and a spacious reception hall, all tied together by a large courtyard set off by walls like those at the temple.

We don't have a detailed description to guide us, but it appears that when you approached the building, you came to a smaller porch that served as the main entrance (v. 7). This led to a larger porch or colonnade with cedar pillars, which probably served as a waiting room. From here you moved into "the hall of pillars," a large assembly hall with sixty cedar pillars (vv. 2-3), forty-five of which held up the cedar-beamed ceiling that formed the floor of the second story. Fifteen pillars were placed opposite each other against the side walls, to the right and left of the entrance, and fifteen down the center of the room, all bearing the cedar beams. The other fifteen pillars were placed strategically where needed, especially at the entrance (see v. 6, NIV).

Because of the abundance of these cedar pillars from Lebanon, the structure was known as "the Palace of the Forest of Lebanon." The assembly hall was no doubt used for official government occasions. In this hall, Solomon displayed three hundred large shields and two hundred smaller shields, all made of wood covered with gold (10:16-17). The larger ones used seven and a half pounds of gold each, a total of 1,500 pounds, and the smaller shields three-and a half pounds apiece, making 1,025 pounds, a total of 2,525 pounds of gold for all five hundred shields. Since gold is too soft to provide protection, these shields were not used in battle but were there to impress visitors. They were taken from the building only when displayed on special ceremonial occasions.

From the hall you moved into the throne room, the "Hall of Justice," where Solomon met with his officers, settled disputes referred to him, and gave judgment concerning governmental affairs. It was there he had his magnificent throne described in 10:18-20. Solomon's living quarters, and, we assume, the queen's quarters, were behind this throne room (7:7-8 NIV). Of course there were other entrances to various parts of the building, all of them protected by the king's special bodyguard, and Solomon had a private concourse that led from his residence to the temple. Next to the temple of the Lord, Solomon's "palace" must have been an imposing structure.

2. Solomon disappoints a friend. (1 Kings 9:10-14; 2 Chron. 8:1-2)

Hiram, king of Tyre, had been David's good friend, and David had told him about his plans to build a temple for the Lord (5:1-3), plans the Lord didn't permit David to carry out. After David's death, Solomon became Hiram's friend (Prov. 27:10) and contracted with Hiram to help build the temple (5:1-12). Hiram would send timber and workers if Solomon would pay the workers and provide Hiram with food in return for the timber. Solomon also conscripted Jewish men to cut stone (5:13-18) and the aliens in the land to help bear burdens (9:15, 20-23; 2 Chron. 8:7-10).

But 1 Kings 9:11 and 14 inform us that Hiram also supplied Solomon with 120 talents of gold (about four and a half tons)! King Solomon had at least 3,750 tons of gold available before he began to build the temple (1 Chron. 22:14-16), and the fact that he had to get gold from Hiram surprises us. The gold, silver, and other materials for the temple that are inventoried in 1 Chronicles 22, 28–29 were all dedicated to the Lord, so they couldn't be used for any other building. This means Solomon needed the gold for the "palace" complex, perhaps for the gold shields, so he borrowed it from Hiram, giving him the twenty cities as collateral. These cities were conveniently located on the border of Phoenicia and Galilee.[3]

Apart from the fact that Solomon shouldn't have been so extravagant in building his "palace," he didn't have the right to give twenty cities away just to pay his debts. All the land belonged to the Lord and could not be deeded away permanently (Lev. 25:23). One purpose for the Year of Jubilee (Lev. 25:8ff) was to make sure the land that had been sold was returned to the original owners and so that no clan or tribe could be deprived of their inheritance. But Solomon was starting to behave like his Egyptian father-in-law who had wiped out the population of an entire Canaanite city and given the city to his daughter as a wedding gift (v. 16).

But Hiram didn't like the cities that Solomon gave him! After looking them over, he called them "Cabul" which sounds like a Hebrew word that means "good for nothing." He didn't think the collateral was worth the investment he had made. However, the story seems to have had a happy ending. Solomon must have paid back the loan because Hiram returned the cities to him and Solomon rebuilt them for the Israelites (2 Chron. 8:1-2). Did Solomon pay off the loan with the 120 talents of gold that the Queen of Sheba gave him (10:10)?

Solomon exhibits in this incident some character traits that disturb us, including the extravagant cost of the "palace" that necessitated a loan, and then giving a friend poor collateral that wasn't even his to give away. Humanly speaking, were it not for Hiram, the temple would not have been built, and this was no way for Solomon to treat a generous friend.

3. Solomon strengthens his kingdom. (1 Kings 9:15-24; 2 Chron. 8:1-11)

When the Lord appeared to Solomon in Gibeon, He promised to give him riches and honor to such an extent that there would be no king like him all the days of his life (3:13). He kept that promise and made Solomon's name famous and his accomplishments admired by people in other nations. Solomon's father, David, had conquered enemy territory and added it to the kingdom, but he hadn't attempted to build an international network that would make Israel powerful among the nations. David was a mighty general who feared no enemy, but Solomon was a shrewd diplomat and politician who missed no opportunity to increase his wealth and power. This section lists for us the achievements of Solomon both at home and abroad.

We don't usually think of Solomon as being a military man, but this one exploit is recorded in Scripture (2 Chron. 8:3). Hamath was a city north of Damascus at the farthest northern border of the kingdom of Israel (Num. 34:8; Josh. 13:5). People from this area attended the dedication of the temple (8:65; 2 Chron. 7:8). The city was situated on a very important trade route from which Solomon could collect custom and duty and also guard against invaders. Along with Hamath, Solomon fortified Hazor, Megiddo, and Gezer and made them "store cities," that is, places where chariots, horses, arms, and food were stored for the use of the Jewish troops. Solomon knew that if he didn't protect the outlying areas of the kingdom, he might find himself at war with his neighbors, his treaties notwithstanding.

Solomon also strengthened and extended "the Millo," the terraced area next to the walls of Jerusalem that buttressed the wall and gave more protection to the city. The word *millo* means "to fill." This was an "earth-fill fortification" that was begun by David (2 Sam. 5:9) and continued by Solomon (9:24; 11:27). The king and his family, the people of the city, and the wealth in the temple and the palace all had to be protected.

To accomplish all this work, the king conscripted the aliens in Israel, the descendants of the Canaanites who had once ruled the land (v. 20; Gen. 15:18-21; Josh. 3:10). In building the temple, he had also enlisted the temporary help of the Jewish men (5:13-14; 9:15, 22-23), but no Jewish worker was treated like a slave. The Jews were made officers and leaders in these building projects.

4. Solomon worships the Lord. (1 Kings 9:25; 2 Chron. 8:12-16)

Annually, the adult Jewish males in Israel were required to appear at Jerusalem to celebrate Passover, Pentecost, and Tabernacles, (Ex. 23:14-19; Deut. 16:1-17). To Christian believers today, these three feasts signify the death of Christ, the Lamb of God, for our sins (John 1:29; 1 Cor. 5:7); the resurrection of Christ and the coming of the Holy Spirit (1 Cor. 15:23; Acts 2); and the future regathering of God's people in the kingdom (Rev. 20:1-6). To the Jewish people, Passover looked back to their deliverance from Egyptian bondage while Tabernacles commemorated God's care during their years in the wilderness. Firstfruits (Pentecost) celebrated the goodness of God in sending the harvest.

Solomon lived in Jerusalem, but he set an example by going to the temple and offering sacrifices. Of course, it was the priests who offered both the sacrifices and the incense. The burnt offering signified total dedication to the Lord; the fellowship or peace offerings spoke of peace with God and communion with Him and one another; and the burning incense was a picture of prayer offered to the Lord (Ex. 30:1-10; Ps. 141:2; Rev. 8:3). There are no instances in Scripture of the common people bringing incense to be offered on the golden altar, since this was a task the priests performed twice daily for the whole nation. However, Psalm 72, "A Psalm for Solomon," mentions continual prayer to be made for the king (v. 15), and there is no reason why Solomon could not have provided some of the spices needed for the special incense (10:2, 10; Ex. 30:34-38).

The account in 2 Chronicles 8 indicates that Solomon also provided the sacrifices that were needed during these feasts as well as on the special Sabbaths and the new moon festivals. He obeyed the Law of Moses in this regard, and he also followed the plan instituted by his father, David, for the ministry of the priests and Levites in the temple (1 Chron. 23–26). Asaph was chief over the musicians (1 Chron. 16:4-5), and there were 4,000 singers divided into twenty-four courses. Each singer ministered at the temple two weeks every year. There was also a special choir of 288 singers (1 Chron. 25:7). Solomon was careful to see to it that David's songs and instruments were used and that his plan for organizing the priests and Levites was honored.

5. Solomon expands his influence. (1 Kings 8:26–10:13; 2 Chron. 8:17-9:12)

Solomon was a great entrepreneur. He made trade agreements with many nations, built a navy, and hired Hiram's expert seamen to manage it for him. Being an inland people for the most part, the Jews were not given to maritime pursuits, so Solomon depended on the Phoenicians, a coastal people, to handle this aspect of his enterprises. Importing products from the east enriched Solomon's coffers and helped to make the kingdom more international in its outlook. This outreach surely gave opportunities for the Jews to bear witness of their God to the pagan Gentiles, but there's no record that there was such a ministry. Solomon had to maintain a huge budget and he needed as much money as he could get. On one trip they brought back 420 talents of gold, about sixteen tons of gold. The ships also brought luxury items like ivory, apes, and peacocks. It appears that Solomon also had a zoo (Ecc. 2:4-9). The words of the English poet Oliver Goldsmith come to mind:

> Ill fares the land, to hast'ning ills a prey,
> Where wealth accumulates, and men decay . . .[4]

The visit of the Queen of Sheba (10:1-13) was undoubtedly motivated both by Solomon's mercantile endeavors as well as her own desires to meet Solomon, see the glories of his kingdom, and test his highly esteemed wisdom. Sheba was a wealthy and highly civilized nation located in southwest Arabia, and the queen brought with her expensive gifts that also served as samples of what her country had to offer (Isa. 60:6; Jer. 6:20; Ezek. 38:13). She "told him all her heart" and he told her what she wanted to know. What she heard and what she saw left her breathless. She had heard the reports but she didn't really believe them until she saw it all for herself. We're reminded of the experience of Thomas (John 20:24-29).

The record of her visit gives us an opportunity to get a glimpse of life in the palace. The queen not only marveled at Solomon's palace, but she was impressed by the meals (4:7, 22-23), the livery and conduct of the servants, the seating of the officers and guests, and the incredible wealth that was displayed on and around the tables. She walked with Solomon on his private concourse to the temple where she watched him worship. (See 10:5 and 2 Chron. 9:4, NIV margin.) The wisdom of Solomon's words and the wealth of Solomon's kingdom were just too much for her, and she was no pauper herself! She brought Solomon expensive gifts, including an abundance of spices and 120 talents of gold (four and a half tons). Solomon reciprocated by giving her whatever she asked for out of his royal bounty.

The queen couldn't contain herself. She announced publicly that Solomon and his servants had to be the happiest people on earth, yet it was Solomon who later wrote the Book of Ecclesiastes and declared, "Vanity of vanities, all is vanity!" We wonder if Solomon's officers and servants didn't gradually grow accustomed to all the pomp and circumstance of court life, especially the gaudy display of wealth. Even Solomon wrote, "Better is a little with the fear of the Lord, than great treasure with trouble. Better is a dinner of herbs [vegetables] where love is, than a fatted calf with hatred" (Prov. 15:16-17, NKJV). Hearing Solomon's words of wisdom may have excited the dinner guests, but the officers and servants had heard it before. One of the dangers of living in that kind of situation is that we begin to take things for granted, and before long, we don't value them at all. This can apply to spiritual treasures as well as material wealth.

When the queen said, "Blessed be the Lord, your God," she wasn't affirming her personal faith in Jehovah. People in those days believed in "territorial deities." Each nation had its own god or gods (1 Kings 20:28) and when you left your land, you left your gods behind (1 Sam. 26:19). Once she returned home, the queen would worship the gods of her own land, even though she had seen the glories of the God of Israel and heard His wisdom. Jesus didn't commend the Queen of Sheba for her faith but for the fact that she made every effort to travel about 1,500 miles to hear the wisdom of Solomon, when the Son of God, one "greater than Solomon," was in the midst of the Jewish people (Matt. 12:39-42). The tragedy of lost opportunity!

It's interesting to contrast this account of the meeting of Solomon and the Queen of Sheba with the account of Solomon's first act of justice as king when he met two prostitutes (3:16ff). They were commoners but she was a queen, and they had very little but she was very wealthy. Yet the king's door was open to all three of these women and he sought to help them. Of course, the Queen of Sheba negotiated a trade pact with Solomon, but there's no evidence that she trusted the true and living God.

The commercial network that Solomon established certainly helped the economy of the nation and brought many influential visitors to Jerusalem, but did it help the king and his people draw near to God? Israel wasn't supposed to be isolated from the community of nations, because she was to be a light to the Gentiles, but she was supposed to be separated from the sins of those nations that didn't know the true and living God. Along with the influx of foreign merchandise came the influx of foreign ideas, including ideas about religion and worship; and eventually Solomon himself, influenced by his foreign wives, succumbed to idolatry (11:1ff).

6. Solomon lives in splendor. (1 Kings 10:14-29; 2 Chron. 9:13-28)

When God promised to give Solomon wisdom, He also promised him riches and honor (3:13). It isn't a sin to possess wealth or to inherit wealth. Abraham was a very wealthy man who gave all his wealth to his son Isaac (Gen. 24:34-36). Earning money honestly isn't a sin, but loving money and living just to acquire riches is a sin (1 Tim. 6:7-10).

Solomon himself wrote, "Whoever loves money never has money enough; whoever loves wealth is never satisfied with his income. This too is meaningless" (Ecc. 5:10, NIV). Someone has wisely said, "It's good to have the things that money can buy, provided you don't lose the things money can't buy."

Solomon's annual income was 666 talents of gold, or about twenty-five tons.[5] It came from several sources: (1) taxes, (2) tolls, customs, and duty fees, (3) trade, (4) tribute from vassal rulers, and (5) gifts. His use of conscripted labor was also a form of income. It took a great deal of money to support his splendid manner of life, and after Solomon's death, the people of Israel protested the yoke they were wearing and asked for the burden to be lightened (12:1-15).

Why did Solomon need five hundred shields that required 2,525 pounds of gold to make? Why did he need an ivory throne overlaid with gold? Why must he and his guests drink only from golden vessels? To what purpose were the thousands of horses and chariots he assembled? Why did he need seven hundred wives and three hundred concubines? *In pursuing each of these goals, Solomon disobeyed the very Word of the Lord!* The Lord warned in Deuteronomy 17:14-20 that Israel's king was not to multiply horses and go to Egypt to get them, nor was he to multiply wives or gold. Solomon not only acquired thousands of horses, but he became a horse dealer himself! Deuteronomy 17:20 warns the king that he must remain humble before the Lord "and not consider himself better than his brothers." It's not difficult to believe that Solomon's heart was lifted up with pride, and pride always leads to destruction and a fall (Prov. 16:18).

To the world of that day, and especially to the Jewish people, Solomon became a model of wealth and splendor, and no doubt many envied him. But Jesus said that one of the Father's lilies was more beautifully arrayed than Solomon in all his glory (Matt. 6:28-30). True beauty comes from within, from "the hidden person of the heart" (1 Peter 3:4, NKJV). The more we must add to our possessions before people will admire us, the less true wealth and beauty we really have.

David had prophets and priests who advised him and even warned and rebuked him, but nobody seems to have admonished Solomon to pay more attention to making a life instead of amassing a fortune. A Roman proverb says, "Riches are like salt water—the more you drink, the more you thirst." Henry David Thoreau said that a man is rich in proportion to the number of things he can afford to do without; and Jesus asked, "For what profit is it to a man if he gains the whole world, and loses his own soul?" (Matt. 16:26, NKJV).

CHAPTER SIX
THE FOOLISH WISE MAN
1 Kings 11:1-43 (2 Chronicles 9:29-31)

"Scripture never blinks the defects of its heroes," wrote the gifted British expositor Alexander Maclaren. "Its portraits do not smooth out wrinkles, but, with absolute fidelity, give all faults."[1] This inspired biblical honesty is seen in the record of the life of King Solomon. God gave Solomon unusual wisdom, incredible wealth, and great opportunities, but in his older years, he turned from the Lord, made foolish decisions, and didn't end well. "A man's own folly ruins his life" (Prov. 19:3, NIV). Solomon wrote those words and probably believed them, but he didn't heed them.

It isn't difficult to trace the steps in Solomon's downward path.

1. Solomon disobeyed God's Word. (1 Kings 11:1-8)

Going back to Egypt may have been Solomon's first step in turning away from the Lord. He secured a bride from Egypt (v. 1; 3:1; 9:24) and he purchased horses and chariots there (4:26-28; 10:26-29). Both of these actions revealed Solomon's unbelief. He married the Egyptian princess in order to establish a peace treaty with her father, and he wanted horses and chariots because he didn't really believe that Jehovah could protect the land. What his father David had written was not in Solomon's creed: "Some trust in chariots, and some in horses; but we will remember the name of the Lord our God" (Ps. 20:7, NKJV). His marriages and his procuring of horses and chariots were in direct disobedience to the Lord's clear commands (Deut. 17:16; 7:1-6; Ex., 23:31-34; 34:15-16; Josh. 23:12-13). Solomon's bad example in choosing wives from pagan nations created problems for Ezra and Nehemiah over four centuries later (Ezra 9:2; 10:2-3; Neh. 13:23-27).

In terms of "biblical geography," Egypt represents the bondage of the world.[2] The wilderness pictures the unbelief of God's people today as, like Israel, they wander and fail to lay hold of their inheritance in Christ.[3] The Promised Land represents the rest God gives to those who trust Christ, submit to Him, and go forth to conquer by faith. All believers have been delivered from the world system that is contrary to God (Gal. 1:4), and all believers are exhorted to claim their inheritance in Christ now and not to wander aimlessly through life. No Christian believer has to trust the world for anything, because we have received in Christ every blessing that we need (Eph. 1:3; 2 Peter 1:1-4). We are in the world physically but not of the world spiritually (John 17:14:19), and all our needs come to us from the Father in heaven (Matt. 6:11; Phil. 4:19).

The danger of marrying pagan unbelievers is spelled out in v. 2, NKJV, which is a quotation from Deuteronomy 7:4: "they will turn away your heart after their gods." That's exactly what happened to Solomon (vv. 3, 4, 9). The Ammonites and Moabites were descendants of Abraham's nephew Lot (Gen. 19:30ff). The Ammonites worshiped the hideous god Molech and sacrificed their infants on his altars (Lev. 18:21; 20:1-5; and see Jer. 7:29-34; Ezek. 16:20-22). Chemosh was the chief god of the Moabites, and Ashtereth (Astarte) was the goddess of the people of Tyre and Sidon. As the goddess of fertility, her worship included "legalized prostitution" involving both male and female temple prostitutes, and that worship was unspeakably filthy. (See Deut. 23:1-8; 1 Kings 14:24; 15:12; 22:46.) The Babylonians also worshiped this goddess and called her Ishtar.

Solomon had exhorted the people to have hearts that were "perfect with the Lord" (8:61, KJV), that is, undivided and totally yielded to Him alone; yet his own heart wasn't perfect with God (v. 4). Solomon didn't totally abandon Jehovah but made Him one of the many gods that he worshiped (9:25). This was a direct violation of the first two commandments given at Sinai (Ex. 20:1-6). The Lord Jehovah is the only God, the true and living God, and He will not be put on the same level as the false idols of the nations. "For I am God, and there is no other; I am God, and there is none like Me" (Isa. 46:9, NKJV).

Solomon's compromise wasn't a sudden thing, for he gradually descended into his idolatry (Ps. 1:1). First he permitted his wives to worship their own gods; then he tolerated their idolatry and even built shrines for them. Eventually he began to participate in pagan practices with his wives. His sensual love for his many wives was more compelling than his spiritual love for the Lord, the God of Israel. He was a man with a divided and disobedient heart, and people who are double-minded and unstable are dangerous (James 1:8). How could Israel be a light to the Gentile nations when their king was openly worshiping and supporting the idols of those nations? He used to offer sacrifices and burn incense only to the Lord Jehovah, but when he got older, he started to include the false gods his wives worshiped (8:25; 11:8).

When you read the Book of Ecclesiastes, you discover that when Solomon's heart began to turn from the Lord, he went through a period of cynicism and despair. He even questioned whether his life was worth living. Without a close walk with the Lord, his heart was empty, so he pursued pleasure, became involved in commercial ventures with many foreign nations, and engaged in vast building programs. However, he still found no enjoyment in life. At least thirty-eight times in Ecclesiastes, Solomon wrote, "Vanity of vanities."

His love for spiritual values was replaced by a love for physical pleasures and material wealth, and gradually his heart turned from the Lord. First he was friendly with the world (James 4:4), then spotted by the world (James 1:27), and then he came to love the world (1 John 2:15-17) and be conformed to the world (Rom. 12:2). Unfortunately, the result of this decline can lead to being condemned with the world and losing everything (1 Cor. 11:32). That's what happened to Lot (Gen. 13:10-13; 14:11-12; 19:1ff), and it can happen to believers today.

2. Solomon ignored God's warning. (1 Kings 11:9-13)

The Lord wasn't impressed with Solomon's royal splendor, for the Lord looks on the heart (1 Sam. 16:7) and searches the heart (1 Chron. 28:9; Jer. 17:10; Rev. 2:23). It was Solomon who wrote, "Keep your heart with all diligence, for out of it spring the issues of life" (Prov. 4:23, NKJV), yet in his old age, his own heart was far from the Lord. Since the discovery of the circulation of the blood by William Harvey in the 17th century, everybody knows that the center of human physical life is the heart. But what's true physically is also true morally and spiritually. We're to love God with all our heart (Deut. 6:5) and receive His Word into our hearts (Prov. 7:1-3). God wants us to do His will from our hearts (Eph. 6:6). If our heart is wrong toward God, our entire life will be wrong, no matter how successful we may appear to others.

When Solomon was born, he was greatly loved by the Lord and given the special name "Jedidiah" which means "beloved of the Lord (2 Sam. 12:24-25). But now we read that God was angry with Solomon because the king's heart had turned from the Lord. Solomon was turning his back on a wealth of blessing God had given to him and sinning against a flood of light. To begin with, the Lord had given Solomon a father who, though he wasn't perfect (and who is?), was devoted to the Lord with a single heart. David had prayed for Solomon and encouraged him to do the will of God and build the temple. Twice the Lord had appeared to Solomon (3:5; 9:2) and reminded him of the terms of the covenant He had made with his father (2 Sam. 7). Solomon certainly knew the terms of the covenant in Deuteronomy 28–30, for he referred to them in his prayer when he dedicated the temple.

We don't know how God delivered this warning to Solomon; perhaps it was through a prophet. But God warned Solomon that, after his death, the kingdom would be divided and his son would reign over only the tribes of Judah and Benjamin. The other ten tribes would become the northern kingdom of Israel. The verb "tear" in verse 11 is picked up in the "action sermon" of Ahijah the prophet when he tore Jeroboam's new robe into twelve parts (vv. 29ff). This division of the kingdom wouldn't be the peaceful work of a diplomat but the painful work of an angry Lord.

Were it not for God's covenant with David and His love for Jerusalem, the city where His temple stood, He would have taken the entire kingdom away from Solomon's descendants. God promised David a dynasty that would not end, and therefore He kept one of David's descendants on the throne in Jerusalem until the city was taken by the Babylonians and destroyed. Of course, the ultimate fulfillment of that covenant promise is in Jesus Christ (Luke 1:32-33, 69; Acts 2:29-36; Ps. 89:34-37). God's name was upon the temple (1 Kings 8:43), so He preserved Jerusalem; and God's covenant was with David, so He preserved David's dynasty. Such is the grace of God.

There is no evidence that Solomon took this warning to heart. Had he remembered his own dedication prayer, he could have looked toward the temple and confessed his sins to the Lord.

3. Solomon resisted God's discipline. (1 Kings 11:14-25)

Solomon's many marriages had been his guarantees of peace with the neighboring rulers, and Solomon's reign had been a peaceful one. But now his system would start to fall apart, for the Lord raised up "adversaries" against Solomon (vv. 14, 23, 25) and used them to discipline the rebellious king. That God would discipline David's disobedient heirs was a part of the covenant (2 Sam. 7:14-15) and was reaffirmed to Solomon when God spoke to him at Gibeon (3:14). It was repeated while Solomon was building the temple (6:11-13) and after the temple was dedicated (9:3-9). See also 1 Chronicles 22:10 and Psalm 89:30-37. The king certainly could not have been ignorant of the dangers of disobeying the Lord. Three of Solomon's opponents are mentioned specifically.

Hadad the Edomite (vv. 14-22). Solomon had women from Edom in his harem (v. 1), but this didn't stop Hadad from making trouble for Israel. David and Joab had won a great victory over Edom and wiped out the male population (2 Sam. 8:13-14; 1 Chron. 18:11-13; see Ps. 60 title), but Hadad, one of the princes, had fled with some of his father's leaders and found asylum with Pharaoh in Egypt. This must have been a new Pharaoh who didn't find it necessary to recognize Solomon's marriage treaty with the Egyptian princess. Even more, he not only gave Hadad food and a place to live, but he also gave him his own sister-in-law as his wife, and Hadad had a son by her. This meant that Egypt and Edom were now in league against Israel.

The death of King David and his general Joab meant that it was safe for Hadad and his band to return to Edom. There Hadad planned to strengthen the nation and direct a series of attacks against the Israelites. Hadad knew he couldn't take over Solomon's kingdom, but the Lord used him to harass Solomon and his troops in a series of border attacks. This constant irritation from the south should have reminded Solomon that God was disciplining him and calling him back to a life of obedience.

Rezon of Damascus (vv. 23-25). When David defeated the Syrians at Zobah (2 Sam. 8:5-8), a young man named Rezon fled to Damascus with his band of soldiers and set himself up as king. David apparently recognized him as king, and Rezon must have been a capable man because the power of Syria increased under his leadership. But Rezon allied himself with Hadad, leader of Edom, and began to harass Solomon from the north. Rezon established a dynasty of strong rulers in the area (known as Aram), all of whom gave trouble to the kings of Judah (15:18-20; 20:1ff; 2 Kings 8-13 and 15-16 *passim.*) Rezin was king of Aram (Syria) during the time of Isaiah the prophet (Isa. 7:1-8; 8:6; 9:11).

4. Solomon opposed God's servant. (1 Kings 11:26-43; 2 Chron. 9:29-31)

Hadad attacked Solomon from the south and Rezon from the north, but Jeroboam was one of Solomon's own leaders who threatened the king from within the official ranks. He was an Ephraimite who displayed excellent management qualities and caught the eye of the king. Since Jeroboam was from the tribe of Ephraim, Solomon put him in charge of the Jewish labor force from the house of Joseph, namely the tribes of Ephraim and Manasseh. By now, the nation had grown weary of Solomon's building projects and especially of the way he conscripted Jews to do the work (5:13-18), and young Jeroboam had his introduction to the undercurrents of opposition against the king. This knowledge, plus the fact that Solomon had put him over northern tribes, would assist him when the time came to establish the ten northern tribes in their own kingdom.

One day in the course of his own work, Jeroboam was stopped by Ahijah the prophet from Shiloh who had a message for him from God. During Solomon's reign, prophets didn't play a prominent role, but prophets will be very important from now until the end of the kingdom of Judah. Whenever the kings or the priests defied the Word of God, the Lord often sent a prophet to warn them. Prophets were "forth-tellers" more than "foretellers." They came with a message from God for that present day, and if they revealed anything about the future, it was to help them call people back to obedience to God's will.[4]

Ahijah dramatized his message by tearing Jeroboam's new garment into twelve parts and giving him ten of them. This was God's way of saying that Jeroboam would become king of the ten northern tribes of Israel.[5] Ahijah explained why two tribes were still reserved for the house of David and also why Solomon's son was being given only those two tribes. Solomon had sinned greatly by introducing idolatry into the land, a sin that would eventually destroy the nation and lead them into captivity.

It was for David's sake that God protected Judah and Jerusalem. Solomon hadn't kept the terms of the covenant God made with his father (2 Sam. 7), but God would be faithful to His Word (2 Sam. 7:11-13). The lamp would burn for David until the end of the Jewish monarchy with the fall of Zedekiah (2 Kings 25; see 1 Kings 11:36; 15:4; 2 Kings 8:19; 21:7; Ps. 132:17).

Ahijah closed his message by warning Jeroboam that what happened to him was wholly of God's grace. He had better take his calling seriously and obey the Word of the Lord, or God would discipline him just as He had to discipline Solomon. God would give Jeroboam an enduring dynasty if he obeyed the law of God. However, that dynasty would not replace the dynasty of David in Judah, for from David's dynasty the Messiah would come and fulfill the covenant promises. God humbled David's successors by giving them only two tribes, but He wouldn't humble them forever. There would be a healing of the division of the nation when Messiah came (Jer. 30:9; Ezek. 34:23; 37:15-28; Hos. 3:5; Amos 9:11-12), and then the king would reign over the whole nation.[6]

Since Ahijah and Jeroboam were alone in the field when the message was delivered (v. 29), we don't know how the word of Jeroboam's special call reached Solomon's ears. Jeroboam may have told some of his close associates who were distressed by the way the king was treating the people, or perhaps God gave Ahijah permission to send the message to Solomon. This message was God's last word of discipline and rebuke for the wayward king, for what more could He do to awaken the king than to take most of the kingdom away from his successor? Solomon should have fallen on his face in repentance and contrition and sought the face of the Lord, but instead he tried to kill his rival. Jeroboam fled to Egypt for safety. The new Pharaoh was Shishak, a man who had no obligations to the house of David.

Solomon had forsaken the Lord (v. 33; see 9:9), and this would be the recurring sin of many kings of Israel and Judah (18:18; 19:10, 14; 2 Kings 17:16; 21:22; 22:17). The sin of idolatry cut at the very heart of Israel's faith, Jehovah was the only true and living God, the God of Abraham, Isaac, and Jacob.

Solomon reigned from 971 to 931. Did he return to the Lord before he died? Bible students don't agree in their interpretations and answers. Certainly his admonition in Ecclesiastes 12:13-14 points in the direction of repentance and restoration, and we trust this was so. The accomplishments of his very full life were recorded not only in 1 Kings and 2 Chronicles, but also in some books that we don't possess, including the Acts of Solomon (possibly an official register), a book by Nathan the prophet, as well as records by Ahijah and Iddo. Solomon is the first Jewish king whose death was recorded in the "official words" of verses 41-43 and 2 Chron. 9:29-31. See also 2 Chronicles 9:29; 12:15; 26:22; and 32:32.

Like King Saul, Solomon was handed great opportunities but didn't make the most of them. He knew a great deal about animals, plants, bringing wealth to the nation, and constructing buildings, but he was defective in sharing the knowledge of the Lord[7] with the Gentiles who came to his throne room. Like his father, David, Solomon had a gift for enjoying women, but when Solomon sinned, he didn't have David's sincere heart and broken spirit of repentance. The grandeur of the kingdom and not the glory of the Lord was what motivated Solomon's life.

He left behind the temple of God, his royal palace, a nation in bondage, an economy in trouble, as well as the books of Proverbs, Ecclesiastes, and the Song of Solomon. The nation was united during his reign, but there was a hairline split in the nation that eventually revealed itself in open rebellion and division. Solomon's hunger for wealth and achievement put a heavy financial burden on the nation, and after his death, the people revolted.

But the people did worse than that: they followed Solomon's bad example and began to worship the gods of their neighbors. It was this sin more than any other that brought about the downfall of the Jewish nation. "Solomon imported the wives," wrote William Sanford LaSor, "the wives imported the gods; Solomon tolerated it, encouraged it, built places of worship for these idolaters. What can you expect the people to do but follow along?"

May our allegiance always be sincere and loyal to Jesus Christ, the one "greater than Solomon," who died for us, who lives for us, and one day will come for us!

CHAPTER SEVEN
HE WOULD NOT LISTEN

1 Kings 12:1-24; 14:21-31 (2 Chronicles 10:1–12:16)

"Then I hated all my labor in which I toiled under the sun," Solomon wrote in Ecclesiastes, "because I must leave it to the man who will come after me. And who knows whether he will be a wise man or a fool?" (Ecc. 2:18-19, NKJV).

His successor was his son Rehoboam, who occasionally made a shrewd decision but for the most part was a foolish ruler. At the beginning of Rehoboam's reign, a selfish decision on his part divided the nation, and during his fourth year, Rehoboam decided to turn from the Lord and worship idols, and that brought the judgment of the Lord. His reign could hardly be called successful.

According to 1 Kings 14:21, Rehoboam was forty-one years old when he began to reign.[1] Since Solomon reigned for forty years (11:42), this means that Rehoboam was born before Solomon became king. But the same text informs us that Rehoboam's mother was an Ammonite woman named Naamah,[2] which means that the Egyptian princess Solomon married was not his first wife (3:1). His father David had married a princess from Geshur, a nation in Syria, and she became the mother of Absalom (2 Sam. 3:3). This was undoubtedly a political move on David's part, so perhaps Solomon's marriage to an Ammonite woman didn't upset David in his latter years. The Hebrew text of 14:21 reads "Naamah *the* Ammonite" (italics mine), suggesting that she was distinguished above the other Ammonite women in the court. This would include Solomon's Ammonite wives and concubines, which Rehoboam inherited when he became king.

What life does to us depends on what life finds in us. During Rehoboam's reign of seventeen years, the way he responded to situations revealed what kind of a person he really was. At least four characteristics stand out in his short reign.

1. An arrogant king (1 Kings 12:1-17; 2 Chron. 10:1-19)

Alexander Maclaren called this account "a miserable story of imbecility and arrogance," and he was right. The story reveals that, whatever gifts Rehoboam may have possessed, he didn't have the gift of relating to people and understanding their needs. David was a king who loved his people and risked his life for their welfare. Solomon was a king who didn't serve the people but used the people to satisfy his own desires. Reheboam was a king who ignored the lessons of the past and turned his ears away from the voices of the suffering people. He was unfit to rule.

The assembly at Shechem (vv. 1-3; 2 Chron. 10:1-3). Solomon must have made it clear that Rehoboam was to be the next king, but it was still necessary for the people to affirm the choice and enter into covenant with God and the king. This had been done when Saul became king (1 Sam. 10:17) and also when David and Solomon were each crowned (2 Sam. 2:4; 5:1ff; 1 Kings 1:28ff). Rehoboam and his officers appointed Shechem as the meeting place, and Jeroboam and the men of the Northern Kingdom attended.[3] Jeroboam had returned from his asylum in Egypt and was the acknowledged leader of the northern ten tribes. Rehoboam knew this man was his enemy, but he didn't dare openly oppose him lest he alienate the people. Surely Rehoboam also knew the prophecy given by Ahijah that Jeroboam would become ruler of the Northern Kingdom, but perhaps he didn't think it would really occur. No doubt he thought that the Davidic dynasty and the Solomonic prosperity would carry the day. He forgot 2 Sam. 7:12-14.

If Rehoboam selected Shechem for this important meeting, it was one of the smartest things he ever did. Shechem was located about forty miles north of Jerusalem, a good central city for such an important meeting. It was situated in the tribe of Manasseh, and this would please the people in the northern ten tribes. Joseph's tomb was at Shechem (Josh. 24:32), the tabernacle had been in Shiloh in Ephraim, and Samuel the prophet was from the hill country of Ephraim (1 Sam. 1:1). Abraham, the father of the Jewish nation, had been in Shechem (Gen. 12:6) and so had Jacob (Gen. 33:18). Joshua had confirmed the covenant with Israel at Shechem (Josh. 24), so Shechem was a place of great historical and spiritual significance to the Jewish people.

Ephraim, and Manasseh, the descendants of Joseph, considered themselves the leading tribes in Israel and openly expressed their resentment of the leadership of Judah (Ps. 78:60, 67). David had welcomed volunteers from Ephraim and Manasseh into his warrior band (1 Chron. 12:30-31); but for years, Ephraim and Manasseh had sown seeds of division and dissension in the land (see Judg. 8:1; 12:1). Perhaps Rehoboam thought that being crowned at Shechem would be a step toward peace and unity between the north and the south, but it turned out to be just the opposite.

The appeal of the ten tribes (vv. 4-5; 2 Chron. 10:4-5). Led by Jeroboam, the leaders of the northern tribes protested the heavy yoke that Rehoboam's father had laid on them, including high taxes and forced labor. When Solomon reorganized the land into twelve districts (4:7-19), it appears that Judah wasn't included, and this policy may have been followed when he conscripted laborers (5:13-18). We can easily understand how the other tribes would respond to such blatant favoritism. Why should these hardworking people sacrifice just so the king could live in a magnificent house, be pampered by servants, and eat daily at a festive table? The people were wearing a galling yoke and they were tired of it.

Back in the days of the judges, when Israel had asked for a king, Samuel warned them that having a king would be a very costly luxury (1 Sam. 8:10-22). The very things Samuel warned about were done by Solomon and would be continued by Rehoboam unless he altered his policies. It must have irritated Rehoboam that Jeroboam was the spokesman for the ten northern tribes, for surely he knew about the prophecy of Ahijah and that his father Solomon had tried to kill Jeroboam (11:29-40). Furthermore, Jeroboam was a favorite in Egypt and Rehoboam didn't know what plans he and Pharaoh had made together. The kingdom was not in good shape and only Rehoboam could make things better. Visitors to Israel were awestruck by what they saw, but they couldn't detect the moral and spiritual decay that was creeping through the foundations of the kingdom, beginning in the throne room.

The people were willing to serve Rehoboam if only he would serve them and make life a bit easier for them. All of God's truly great leaders had been servants to the people—Moses, Joshua, Samuel, and especially David—but Solomon had chosen to be a celebrity and not a servant, and Rehoboam was following his bad example. When the Son of God came to earth, He came as a servant (Luke 22:24-27; Phil. 2:1-13), and He taught His disciples to lead by serving. Jesus washed His disciples' feet as an example of humble service (John 13:1-17), and He wants us to follow His example, not the examples of the "great leaders" in the secular world (Matt. 20:25-28).

The advice of the counselors (vv. 6-11; 2 Chron. 10:6-11). Let's give Rehoboam credit for asking for a delay to give him time to think and seek counsel. However, time solves no problems; it's what leaders *do with time* that really counts. There's no evidence that the king sought the Lord in prayer or that he consulted with the high priest or with a prophet. We get the impression that his mind was already made up but that he was willing to go through the motions in order to please the people. One of the marks of David's leadership was that he was willing to humble himself and seek the mind of God, and then pray for God's blessing on his decisions. Leaders who try to impress people with their skills, but take no time to seek God, only prove that they don't know the most important thing in spiritual leadership: they are second in command. (See Josh. 5:13-15.)

In making important decisions, we should seek sound spiritual counsel (Prov. 11:14; 15:22; 24:6), but let's be sure the counselors we talk to are mature saints who are able to guide us aright. The British writer Frank W. Boreham said, "We make our decisions, and then our decisions turn around and make us." Sometimes we forget our decisions, but our decision can never forget us, because we reap what we sow. If the path we choose turns out to be a detour, then let's admit it, confess our sin, and ask the Lord to lead us back to the right road.

The elders gave Rehoboam the best advice: be a servant of the people and the people will serve you. However, Rehoboam had already made up his mind, so he immediately rejected that answer and turned to his contemporaries whom he knew would give him the answer that he wanted. He had no intention of weighing the facts, seeking God's will, and making the wisest choice. In more than fifty years of ministry, I've seen so-called Christian leaders take the Rehoboam approach, do terrible damage to the work of the Lord, and then walk away from the mess, leaving behind poison and debris that will take years to remove.

The ancient world honored age and maturity, but our modern society worships youth. In our churches and parachurch ministries, there's a desperate need for generational balance, with the older and younger generations communicating with each other and learning from each other, just like a family (Titus 2:1-8; 1 Tim. 5:1-2). A friend told me he wanted to start a church only for people fifty and older, and I suggested he put an undertaker on the staff. God meant for His church to include male and female, old and young, and those in between, and that all of them should learn from one another. There are old fools as well as young fools, and age is no guarantee of wisdom or even useful experience. The young people in my life help me catch up with the present, and I help them to catch up on the past, and so we all stay balanced and love one another.

The young counselors were interested primarily in being important and magnifying themselves and the authority of the new king. They thought the best way to do that was to make a show of force. Youth, in general, seek to have authority and freedom, until they make the painful discovery that they may not be ready to use these precious gifts wisely. After admonishing both the elder saints and the younger ones, Peter wrote, "Yes, all of you be submissive to one another, and be clothed with humility, for 'God resists the proud, but gives grace to the humble'" (1 Peter 5:5, NKJV).

The announcement of the king (vv. 12-17; 2 Chron. 10:12-17). A man forty-one years old who had grown up in the palace, who had been given three days to consider a matter, and who even had access to those who could determine the will of God, should never have made this kind of a decision. His father had even written a book of practical proverbs about wisdom, one of which said, "A soft answer turns away wrath, but a harsh word stirs up anger" (Prov. 15:1, NKJV). However, Rehoboam's leadership was motivated by pride, not humility, and pride knows nothing of gentleness and kindness. "There is one who speaks like the piercings of a sword, but the tongue of the wise promotes health" (Prov. 12:18, NKJV). Apparently Rehoboam hadn't taken time to read and copy Deuteronomy 17:18-20.

The king answered the people roughly, which is the same Hebrew word that is translated "grievous" in verse 4. The way he spoke was rough and the words he used were harsh. Instead of lightening the yoke, Rehoboam announced that he would make it heavier and more cutting. His little finger was bigger than his father's waist, and if his father used whips, he would use scourges. ("Scorpions" was the name for a whip with metal pieces in it, similar to the Roman scourge.) Both in his words and his manner, the new king made it clear to the people that he was important and powerful and they were unimportant and weak, a dangerous message indeed.

Rehoboam represented the third generation of the Davidic dynasty, and so often it's the third generation that starts to tear down what the previous generations have built up. The people of Israel served the Lord during Joshua's days and during the days of the elders he had trained, but when the third generation came along, they turned to idols, and the nation fell apart (Judg. 2:7-10). I've seen this same phenomenon in businesses and local churches. The founders worked hard and sacrificed much to start the business or the church, and the second generation was faithful to the examples and beliefs of the founders. But when the third generation arrived, they inherited everything without working for it or paying for it, and they tore down what others had worked so hard to build up. Of course, if the second generation doesn't teach the third generation the ways of the Lord, or if they won't receive the teaching, it's no wonder the new generation goes astray (Deut. 11:18-21; 32:46; Eph. 6:4).

The consequences of Rehoboam's speech were predictable: "all Israel" (meaning the ten northern tribes)[4] announced their decision to leave the other two tribes and establish their own kingdom. They shouted the words of Sheba, a troublemaker in David's day (2 Sam. 20:1), left the assembly, and made Jeroboam their king. The only exceptions were the citizens of the ten tribes who had settled in Judah for one reason or another. They remained faithful to the throne of David.

Solomon's first official decision brought him the reputation for great wisdom (3:16-28), but his son's first official decision told the nation that he was foolish and unwise. For centuries, the Jews considered the division of the nation the greatest tragedy in their history and measured every other calamity by it (Isa. 7:17).

2. An angry king (1 Kings 12:18-24; 2 Chron. 10:18-19; 11:1-4)

While Rehoboam was still in Shechem, he attempted some belated diplomacy and sent one of his trusted officers to the assembled ten tribes to try to bring peace or at least keep the discussion going. His choice of mediators was unwise because Adoram was in charge of the forced labor, and forced labor was one of the irritating areas in the dispute.[5] Perhaps Adoram was authorized to negotiate easier labor arrangements or even lower taxes, but if he was, he failed miserably. The people stoned him and the frightened king took off for Jerusalem as soon as he heard the news. Rehoboam had followed the wrong counsel, used the wrong approach, and chosen the wrong mediator. What else wrong could he do?

He could declare war!

After all, he was the king, and by declaring war he could assert his authority and demonstrate his military strength, and perhaps Jeroboam his rival might be one of the casualties. Didn't Solomon, his father, want to have Jeroboam killed (11:40), and wasn't his father the wisest man in the world? Didn't the ten northern tribes rebel against the king and even kill an innocent man whose only task was to encourage peace? The beloved King David declared war on the Ammonites for only *embarrassing* his envoys (2 Sam. 10), while Rehoboam's envoy was *murdered*. The ten northern tribes were dividing what the Lord had put together and they deserved to be chastised. They had even called an assembly and appointed Jeroboam as their king! To defy the covenants of God and desert the Davidic line was wicked. It seemed that every consideration pointed logically to one conclusion—war.

Every consideration except one: was this war the will of God? After Rehoboam had assembled an army of 180,000 men,[6] he discovered that he had wasted his time. The Lord sent the prophet Shemaiah[7] to tell the king to call off the fight and send the men home. Though what happened was the consequence of Rehoboam's foolishness and Jeroboam's aggressiveness, it was God who had ruled and overruled to bring about the division, thus fulfilling Ahijah's prophecy. Each man had acted freely and so had their counselors, yet the Lord's will was done. (See Acts 2:23.) Our sovereign God is so great that He lets people make their own decisions and yet accomplishes His purposes.

The plan of God was only one factor; a second factor was that it was wrong for Judah and Benjamin to fight against their brothers (v. 24). It seems strange, yet family and national conflict appears repeatedly in the history of Israel. Abraham and Lot disagreed (Gen. 13), and Abraham reminded his nephew that they shouldn't fight because they were brothers (13:8). Jacob and Esau had a lifelong battle that their descendants continued for centuries (Gen. 27:41-46; Ps. 137:7; Obad. 10-13). Joseph's brothers hated him (Gen. 37), and Aaron and Miriam criticized their brother Moses (Num. 12). Saul was David's enemy and on many occasions tried to kill him. "Behold, how good and how pleasant it is for brethren to dwell together in unity" (Ps. 133:1, NKJV).[8]

Frequently in Old Testament history we find a prophet confronting a king with "Thus says the Lord." Whenever a king, a priest, or even another prophet stepped out of line, a prophet would step forward and rebuke him; and if the prophet's message was ignored, God's hand of judgment would fall. (See 1 Kings 13:21-22; 14:6-11; 16:1-4; 20:28ff; 2 Kings 1:16; 22:14-15.) Israel was to be a people of God's Word, and God's Word must be held higher than even the word of the king.

To Rehoboam's credit, he called off the attack, although in the years that followed, there were repeated border skirmishes and other irritating conflicts between Rehoboam and Jeroboam (14:20; and see 15:6, 16, 32; 2 Chron. 11:1). However, it's possible that Rehoboam was grateful that his plans never succeeded. Like his father, he wasn't a military man and he couldn't be sure of winning. It was God's plan there be two kingdoms, and that settled the matter. At least he submitted to the Word of God.

At this point in the record, the writer interrupted the Rehoboam story to tell us about Jeroboam. The Rehoboam account is amplified in 2 Chronicles 11:5-22 and then picked up and concluded in 1 Kings 14:21-36 (2 Chron. 12:1-16).

3. An astute king (2 Chron. 11:5-22)

Rehoboam heard and obeyed God's message from Shemaiah, and the Lord began to give him wisdom and bless his life and his work. Had he stayed on that course, he would have led Judah into godliness and true greatness, but he turned from the Lord and lost the blessings he and his people could have enjoyed.[9]

God blessed his building projects (vv. 5-12). His father, Solomon, had strengthened the borders of the kingdom by putting up fortress cities for his soldiers, horses, and chariots (1 Kings 9:15-19; 2 Chron. 8:1-6), and Rehoboam followed his good example. The cities he selected formed a wall of protection for Jerusalem on the east and west and across the south. The king knew that Jeroboam was a favorite in Egypt, so perhaps he had Pharaoh in mind when he set up this line of defense. It's interesting that he didn't put defense cities across the northern border. After Shemaiah's warning, perhaps the king hesitated to provoke the northern tribes or to give the suggestion that Judah was preparing for war. He may have hoped that an "open door policy" would ease the tension and make it easier for the people in the ten tribes to come to Jerusalem.

God blessed his people (vv. 13-17). King Jeroboam ordained his own priests and turned the ten northern tribes into a center for worshiping idols, but for three years Rehoboam kept the people of Judah true to the Law of Moses. As a result, the priests and Levites in Israel who were devoted to the Lord came into Judah and enriched the nation greatly. Some priests and Levites merely "sided with Rehoboam" (v. 13) and remained in Israel, but others gave up their property in Israel and moved permanently to Judah (v. 14). A third group stayed in Israel but traveled to Jerusalem three times a year for the annual feasts (v. 16). (To some extent, we have these same three groups in the churches today.) The addition of these godly priests and Levites and their families to the population of Judah strengthened the kingdom and brought the blessing of the Lord. "Blessed is the nation whose God is the Lord; and the people whom he hath chosen as his own inheritance" (Ps. 33:12, KJV).

God blessed his family (vv. 18-23). Like both David and Solomon, Rehoboam disobeyed the Word and took many wives (Deut. 17:17). Only two of his wives are named in the record: Mahalath, a granddaughter of David through both her father and mother, and Maacah, the daughter of Absalom. Since David's son Absalom had only one daughter, Tamar (2

Sam. 14:27), Maacah could have been his granddaughter. Maacah's father's name is given as Abishalom in 1 Kings 15:2, and in 2 Chronicles 13:2, Maacha is called the daughter of Uriel of Gibeah. If this Uriel was indeed the husband of Tamar, the only daughter of Absalom, then Maacah was the granddaughter of Absalom and the great-granddaughter of King David. At least two of Rehoboam's eighteen wives were from solid Davidic stock.

It was important that kings and queens have large families so that there would be an heir to the throne and replacements if anything should happen to the crown prince. King Rehoboam was blessed with many children—twenty-eight sons and sixty daughters. The king did a very wise thing when he appointed his grown sons to royal offices and distributed them throughout Judah and Benjamin. This accomplished several things that made for peace and efficiency in the palace. To begin with, the princes weren't engaged in their own pursuits and getting involved in palace intrigues, as some of David's sons had done to the sorrow of their father. Rehoboam had grown up in the lap of luxury, but he was smart enough to put his sons to work.

The second benefit was that Rehoboam could assess their character and skills and decide which son would succeed him. God called David to be king and later told him that Solomon would be his successor. There's no evidence that God named Solomon's successor, so Solomon must have appointed Rehoboam to take the throne. After watching his sons, Rehoboam selected Abijah, son of Maacah,[10] to be his heir, even though Jeush, his son by Mahalath, was the firstborn (vv. 18-19). First, Rehoboam made Abijah "ruler among his brethren" (v. 22, KJV; "chief prince," NIV), which suggests that Abijah was his father's right-hand man, perhaps even coregent. Rehoboam recognized in this son the ability that was needed for a successful reign. Unfortunately, Abijah didn't live up to his name, "Jehovah is father."

The "many wives" that Rehoboam secured for his sons may have been "treaty wives" to guarantee peace between Judah and her neighbors. This was the plan his father, Solomon, followed.

4. An apostate king. (1 Kings 14:21-31; 2 Chron. 12:1-16)

Rehoboam walked with the Lord for three years after becoming king (2 Chron. 11:17), but in the fourth year of his reign, when his throne was secure, he and all Judah turned away from Jehovah to worship idols (2 Chron. 12:1-2). "And he did evil, because he did not prepare his heart to seek the Lord" (2 Chron. 12:14, NKJV). The phrase "forsaken [abandoned] the commandment of the Lord" occurs frequently in the record of the reigns of the kings of Judah and Israel (1 Kings 18:18; 19:10, 14; 2 Kings 17:16; 21:22; 22:17; 2 Chron. 12:1, 5; 13:10-11; 15:2; 21:10; 24:18, 20, 24; 26:6; 29:6; 34:25). David had warned Solomon about this sin (1 Chron. 28:9, 20) and so had the Lord Himself (1 Kings 3:14; 9:4-9; 11:9-13), but Solomon in his latter years worshiped both the Lord and the abominable idols of the heathen. Solomon was influenced by his pagan wives to worship idols; perhaps Rehoboam was influenced by his Ammonite mother. Whatever the influence, the king knew that he was breaking the covenant and sinning against the Lord.

God's holy jealousy (vv. 21-24). When the Bible speaks of the Lord being "a jealous God" (14:22), it refers to His jealous love over His people, a love that will not tolerate rivals. Israel was "married" to the Lord at Mount Sinai when they entered into the covenant, and the worship of idols was a terrible breach of that covenant, like a wife committing adultery.[11] Surely Rehoboam knew what God said to the nation at Mount Sinai: "For I, the Lord your God, am a jealous God" (Ex. 20:5, NKJV). This same truth is included in The Song of Moses as well: "They have provoked Me to jealousy by what is not God; they have moved Me to anger by their foolish idols" (Deut. 32:21 NKJV; see also Ps. 78:58; Jer. 44:3). Paul used the marriage picture when he warned the church to avoid pagan idolatry (1 Cor. 10:22), and James called worldly believers "adulterers and adulteresses" (James 4:4, KJV).

The king allowed and encouraged the building of idolatrous shrines in the land ("high places"), the erecting of sacred stones ("images") and phallic images and Asherah poles ("groves"). He also permitted the shrine prostitutes, male ("sodomites") and female, to serve the people at these shrines, a detestable practice expressly forbidden by the Law of Moses (Deut. 23:17-18). Idolatry and immorality go together (Rom. 1:21-27), and it wasn't long before the pagan sins condemned by the law became commonly accepted practices in Judah (Lev. 18, 20; Deut. 18:9-12). The Jewish people were no longer a light to the Gentiles; instead, the darkness of the Gentiles had invaded the land and was putting out the light.

Before we pass judgment on the king and people of Judah, perhaps we had better examine our own lives and churches. Surveys indicate that, when it comes to sexual morality, the "born-again" people in the churches don't live much differently than the unsaved people outside the church. The materialistic and humanistic idols of the unsaved world have made their way into the church and are both tolerated and promoted. The Lord punished Rehoboam for his sins. How long will it be before the Lord punishes His church?

God's loving discipline (vv. 25-31; 2 Chron. 12:1-16). For a year, the Lord was patient with Rehoboam and the people of Judah; but by the fifth year of Rehoboam's reign, the long-suffering of the Lord had come to an end. God directed Shishak, king of Egypt, to invade Judah with a huge army and, in spite of Rehoboam's new defenses, he defeated town after town.[12] (One Egyptian inscription states that Shishak took 156 cities in Israel and Judah.) When the Egyptians got as far as Jerusalem, the prophet Shemaiah once again appeared on the scene with a message from God, short and to the point: "This is what the Lord says, 'You have abandoned me; therefore, I now abandon you to Shishak'" (12:5).

Whenever God's people experience discipline because of their sins, they can make a new beginning by hearing the Word of God and humbling themselves before the God of the Word. This was the promise God gave His people when Solomon dedicated the temple (2 Chron. 7:13-14). Rehoboam and his officers humbled themselves before the Lord and He stopped Shishak from attacking Jerusalem. However, Judah was now subject to Shishak and had to pay him tribute. God's people discovered that their "freedom to sin" brought them into painful and costly bondage to Egypt, for the consequences of sin are always costly.

To satisfy Shishak's demands, Rehoboam gave him gold from the temple and from the king's palace. This included the five hundred gold shields that Solomon had made for the palace (1 Kings 10:16–17). Rehoboam was too poor to make duplicate shields, so he replaced them with shields made of bronze, and the royal ceremonies went on as if nothing had happened. How often the precious treasures of former generations are lost because of sin and then replaced by cheap substitutes. Life goes on and nobody seems to know the difference. That's what happened to the church at Laodicea (Rev. 3:17-19).

After the invasion of Shishak in 925 B.C., Rehoboam reigned for twelve more years and died in 913 B.C. Had he continued to walk with the Lord and to lead his people to be faithful to God's covenant, the Lord would have done great things for him. As it was, his sins and the sins of the people who followed him left the nation weaker, poorer, and in bondage. As Charles Spurgeon said, "God does not allow His people to sin successfully."

Rehoboam went the way of all flesh and died at the age of fifty-eight. We trust that the humbling that he and his leaders experienced lasted for the rest of their lives and that they walked with the Lord.

CHAPTER EIGHT
A NEW KING, AN OLD SIN
1 Kings 12:25–14:20

King Jeroboam I[1] was a doer, not a philosopher; he was a man who first caught Solomon's attention because he was busy, efficient, dependable, and productive (11:26-28). He was the ideal popular leader who knew how to fight the people's battles and champion their causes. Ask him about his personal faith in the Lord and his answers might be a bit foggy. He had lived in Egypt long enough to develop a tolerance toward idolatry as well as an understanding of how religion can be used to control the people. In this skill, Jeroboam was one with Nebuchadnezzar (Dan. 3), Herod Agrippa I (Acts 12:19-25), and the Antichrist (Rev. 13, 17), and today's latest demagogue. But Jeroboam made three serious mistakes during his twenty-two-year reign.

1. He didn't believe God's promises. (12:25-33)

Success in life depends on doing God's will and trusting God's promises, but Jeroboam failed in both. When Ahijah gave Jeroboam God's message that guaranteed him the throne of the kingdom of Israel (11:28-39), the prophet made it clear that political division did not permit religious departure. God would have given Jeroboam the entire kingdom except that He had made an everlasting covenant with David to keep one of his descendants on the throne (2 Sam. 7:1-17). This protected the Messianic line so that the Savior could come into the world. The Lord tore the ten tribes away from Rehoboam because Rehoboam had followed Solomon's bad example and turned the people to idols. This should have been a warning to Jeroboam to be faithful to the Lord and stay away from false gods. The Lord also promised to build Jeroboam a "sure house" (a continued dynasty) if he obeyed the Lord and walked in His ways (v. 38, KJV). What a promise, yet Jeroboam couldn't believe it.

Fear (vv. 25-28). One of the first evidences of unbelief is fear. We get our eyes off the Lord and start looking at the circumstances. "Why are you fearful, O you of little faith?" Jesus asked His disciples (Matt. 8:23-27, NKJV), reminding them that faith and fear can't coexist in the same heart for very long. Jeroboam's fear was that the Southern Kingdom would attack him and his own people desert him and go back to Jerusalem to worship. The law not only appointed the temple in Jerusalem as the only place of sacrifice (Deut. 12), but it also commanded all Jewish men to go to Jerusalem three times a year to observe the appointed feasts (Ex. 23:14-17). What if the people decided to remain in Judah and not return to Israel? Even if they returned north after worshiping, how long could they live with divided loyalties? Perhaps Jeroboam recalled the plight of Saul's successor, Ish-Bosheth, who tried to rule over the ten northern tribes but failed and was slain (2 Sam. 4). If there was ever a popular movement in Israel toward uniting the two kingdoms, Jeroboam would be a dead man.

Security (v. 25). Like both Solomon (9:15-19; 11:27) and Rehoboam (2 Chron. 11:5-12), King Jeroboam fortified his capital city (Shechem) and strengthened other key cities against any invaders. Penuel (Peniel) was east of the Jordan and was famous as the place where Jacob wrestled with the angel of the Lord (Gen. 32). It appears that Jeroboam later moved his capital from Shechem to Tirzah (14:17), or perhaps he had a second palace there. Instead of trusting the Lord to be his shield and defender, Jeroboam trusted his own defenses and strategy.

Substitutes (vv. 26-33). The easiest solution to Jeroboam's problem of holding the loyalty of his people was to establish a worship center for them in the territory of Israel. But what authority did he have to devise a rival religion when the Jews had received their form of worship from the very hand of God? He certainly couldn't build a temple to compete with Solomon's temple in Jerusalem, or write a law that matched what Moses received from Jehovah, or set up a sacrificial system that would guarantee the forgiveness of sins. He was no Moses and he certainly couldn't claim to be God!

What Jeroboam did was to take advantage of the tendency of the Jewish people to turn to idols, and the desire of most people for a religion that is convenient, not too costly, and close enough to the authorized faith to be comfortable for the conscience. Jeroboam didn't tell the people to forget Jehovah but to worship Him in the form of a golden calf. In both Egypt and the land of Canaan, the king had seen statues of calves and bulls that were supposed to be "holding up" the invisible forms of the gods. In the pagan religions that Jeroboam was copying, calves and bulls symbolized fertility. Jeroboam turned his back on the most important message given at Mount Sinai: Israel's Lord Jehovah is a God who would be *heard* but not *seen* or *touched.* Hearing His Word is what generates faith (Rom. 10:17), and faith enables us to obey. But most people don't want to live by faith; they want to walk by sight and gratify their senses.

Jeroboam's words in verse 28 suggest that Aaron's golden calf (Ex. 32:1-8, especially v. 4) was also in his mind.[2] But the king went one better: he made *two* calves and put one at Bethel, on the farthest southern border of the kingdom, just a short distance from Jerusalem, and the other at Dan, on the farthest northern border (see Hos. 8:5-6; 13:2-3). Worshiping the Lord couldn't be more convenient! "It is too much for you to go up to Jerusalem," the king told the people (v. 28), and they were more than willing to believe him. The king built shrines at Bethel and Dan and allowed the people to make their own high places closer to home. By royal fiat, he instituted a "do-it-yourself religion" and, as in the Book of Judges, everybody did what was right in his own eyes (Judg. 17:6; 18:1; 19:1; 21:25). If the Canaanites and Egyptians could worship calves, so could the Hebrews! He forgot about Exodus 20:1-3 and 22–23—but the Lord didn't forget!

A religion needs ministers, so Jeroboam appointed all kinds of people to serve as "priests" at the altars in Dan and Bethel (13:33-34; 2 Chron. 11:13-17). The only requirement was that each candidate bring with him a young bull and seven rams (2 Chron. 13:9).[3] God had made it clear when He gave Moses the law that only the sons of Aaron could serve as priests at the altar (Ex. 28:1-5; 29:1-9; 40:12-16) and that if anybody from another tribe tried to serve, he would be put to death (Num. 3:5-10). Even the Levites, who were from the tribe of Levi, were not allowed to serve at the altar on penalty of death (Num. 3:5-10, 38; 4:17-20; 18:1-7). Unauthorized priests at unauthorized temples could never have access to God or present sacrifices acceptable to God. It was a man-made religion that pleased the people, protected the king, and unified the nation—except for the faithful Levites who abandoned the Northern Kingdom and moved to Judah to worship God according to the teaching of the Scriptures (2 Chron. 11:13-17).

The law of Moses required the Jews to celebrate seven divinely appointed feasts each year (Lev. 23), so Jeroboam instituted a feast for the people of the Northern Kingdom. The Feast of Tabernacles was scheduled for the seventh month for one full week. This was a joyous festival when the people recalled their wilderness years by living in booths and celebrating the goodness of the Lord in giving the harvest. Jeroboam's feast was set for the eighth month so that the people had to choose which one they would attend, and this separated the loyal Jews from the counterfeit worshipers in Israel. But why travel all the way to Jerusalem when Bethel and Dan were much easier to reach?

Along with setting up his own religious calendar, temples, altars, and priesthood, Jeroboam made himself a priest (vv. 32-33)! He offered incense and blood sacrifices just as the authorized priests did at the temple, except that the Lord never acknowledged his sacrifices. The sacrifice on the fifteenth day of the eighth month was in connection with the feast that he had ordained, and this sacrifice may have been in imitation of the annual Day of Atonement. He had all the ingredients needed for a "religion" but lacked the most necessary one—the Lord God Jehovah!

Apostasy. We live today in an age when "manufactured religion" is popular, approved, and accepted. The blind leaders of the blind assert that we live in a "pluralistic society" and that nobody has the right to claim that only revelation is true and only one way of salvation is correct. Self-appointed "prophets" and ministers put together their own theology and pass it off as the truth. They aren't the least bit interested in what Scripture has to say; instead, they substitute their "feigned [plastic] words" (2 Peter 2:3, KJV) for God's unchanging and inspired Word, and many gullible people will fall for their lies and be condemned (2 Peter 2:1-2). Jeroboam's "religion" incorporated elements from the Law of Moses and from the pagan nations that the Jews had conquered. His system was what is today called "eclectic" (selective) or "syncretic" (combining many parts), but God called it heresy and apostasy. When the prophet Isaiah confronted the new religions in his day, he cried out, "To the law and to the testimony! If they do not speak according to this word, it is because there is no light in them" (Isa. 8:20, NKJV).

Because Jeroboam didn't believe God's promise given by the prophet Ahijah, he began to walk in unbelief and to lead the people into false religion. The religion he invented was comfortable, convenient, and not costly, but it wasn't authorized by the Lord. It was contrary to the revealed will of God in Scripture and it had as its purpose the unification of his kingdom, not the salvation of the people and the glory of God. It was man-made religion and God totally rejected it. Centuries later, Jesus told the woman of Samaria (the former kingdom of Israel), "You worship what you do not know; we worship that which we know, for salvation is from the Jews" (John 4:22, NASB). When He made that statement, He instantly wiped out every other religion and affirmed that the only way of salvation is from the Jews. Jesus was a Jew and the Christian faith was born out of the Jewish religion. Our modern "pluralistic society" notwithstanding, the Apostle Peter was right: "And there is salvation in no one else; for there is no other name under heaven that has been given among men, by which we must be saved"(Acts 4:12, NASB).

2. He didn't heed God's warnings. (1 Kings 13:1-34)

This long chapter is not about young and old prophets; it's about King Jeroboam and his sins. The young prophet's ministry is very important in this account, for all that he said and experienced, including his death, were a part of God's warning to King Jeroboam. According to verse 33, the king didn't turn back to God: "After this event Jeroboam did not return from his evil ways" (NASB). In this chapter, a prophet died, but in the next chapter, the crown prince died! Obviously, God was trying to get Jeroboam's attention.

The message (vv. 1-2). The anonymous prophet came from Judah because there were still faithful servants of God there whom the Lord could use. He met Jeroboam at the shrine in Bethel, which eventually became "the king's sanctuary" (Amos 7:10-12). When you devise your own religion, as Jeroboam did, you can do whatever you please, and Jeroboam chose to be a priest as well as a king. Jeremiah and Ezekiel were priests who were called to be prophets, but the Mosaic Law didn't permit kings to serve as priests (2 Chron. 26:16-23). Jesus Christ is the only King who is also Priest (Heb. 7–8), and all who believe in Christ are "kings and priests" (Rev. 1:6, KJV) and "a royal priesthood" (1 Peter 2:9). Jeroboam's "priesthood" was spurious and rejected by the Lord. That may be why the anonymous prophet from Judah delivered his message while the king was at the altar.

The prophet spoke to the altar, not to the king, as though God no longer wanted to address Jeroboam, a man so filled with himself and his plans that he had no time to listen to God. The message declared that the future lay with the house of David, not with the house of Jeroboam. Because of Jeroboam's evil ways, the kingdom of Israel would become so polluted with idolatry and its accompanying sins that the kingdom would be wiped out within two centuries. In 722, the Assyrians captured Israel and the ten northern tribes moved off the scene.[4] David's dynasty continued until the reign of Zedekiah (597–586). He was Judah's last king before the Babylonian conquest of Jerusalem in 586.

The prophet's message looked ahead three hundred years to the reign of godly King Josiah (640–609) who rooted out the idolatry in the land, including the king's shrine at Bethel (2 Kings 23:15-16). Josiah desecrated the altar by burning human bones on it, and then he tore down the altar and let the ashes spill out. The prophecy was fulfilled just as the prophet announced. So sure was this promise that the prophet even named the king! (See also Isa. 44:28; 45:1, 13.)

The miracles (vv. 4-6). The king paid no attention to the message from God; all he wanted to do was punish the messenger. He was infuriated to hear that a king from Judah would one day desecrate and destroy his successful religious system. When Jeroboam stretched out his hand and pointed to the prophet, the Lord touched his arm and it suffered a stroke. What a humiliating experience for such a powerful king and priest! At that moment, the pagan altar split and the ashes came pouring out. Often the Lord authenticated His Word by giving miraculous signs (Heb. 2:1-4) but only to give emphasis to the message. In spite of Jeroboam's stubborn pride and willful disobedience, the Lord graciously healed his arm. (See Ex. 8:8; Acts 8:24.) It's too bad that the king was more concerned about physical healing for his body than moral and spiritual healing for his soul.

The king witnessed three miracles in just a few minutes, yet there's no evidence that he was convicted of his sins. Of themselves, miracles don't bring conviction or produce saving faith, but they do call attention to the Word. When Jesus raised Lazarus from the dead, some of the witnesses believed in Jesus while others went straight to the Jewish religious leaders and stirred up trouble (John 11:45-54). Miracles aren't necessary for evangelism (John 10:40-42), and those who claimed to believe on Christ only because of His miracles were really "unsaved believers" (John 2:23-25).

The maneuver (vv. 7-10). Jeroboam was a clever man and tried to trap the prophet by inviting him to the palace for a meal. Satan comes as the lion to devour us (1 Peter 5:8), and when that fails, he comes as a serpent to deceive us (2 Cor. 11:3; Gen. 3:1ff). The king's "Lay hold of him!" became "Come home with me!" But the prophet refused, for he knew his commission from the Lord compelled him to leave Bethel and not tarry. Had the prophet eaten a meal with the king, that one simple act would have wiped out the effectiveness of his witness and ministry. In the east, sharing a meal is a sign of friendship and endorsement. The prophet certainly didn't want to be a friend to such an evil man or give others the impression that he endorsed his wicked works. "Like a trampled spring and a polluted well is a righteous man who gives way before the wicked" (Prov. 25:26, NASB). A compromising servant of God muddies the waters and confuses the saints. The prophet refused the king's friendship, food, and gifts. Like Daniel, he said, "Let your gifts be for yourself, and give your rewards to another" (Dan. 5:17, NKJV).

The mistake (vv. 11-34). The faithful man from Judah couldn't be deceived by a wicked king but he could be fooled by an old retired prophet![5] This narrative presents some things to puzzle over, but we must not forget the main message: if the Lord punished a deceived prophet for his disobedience, how much more would he punish a wicked king who was sinning with his eyes wide open? If a true prophet disobeyed and was disciplined, what will happen to the false prophets? The prophet from Judah didn't compromise in his message, but he did compromise in his conduct, and he paid for his disobedience with his life. The Lord was saying to King Jeroboam, "If the righteous one is scarcely saved, where will the ungodly and the sinner appear?" (1 Peter 4:18, NKJV; see also Prov. 11:31).

There are some characteristics of the old prophet that bother me. First of all, what was he doing living in Bethel when by traveling just a few miles he could be in Judah? We get the impression that the prophet wasn't exactly a spiritual giant, otherwise the Lord would have called him to rebuke the king. The fact that he lied to a fellow prophet raises some questions about his character. It's also disturbing that he wept over the younger man's death *when he helped to cause it*, and then buried the man he helped to kill. Was he trying to atone for his own sins against the prophet?

The younger prophet did his work well and got out of town. Had he kept going and not lingered under the tree he would have escaped the tempting offer of the old prophet. God's servants often face great temptations after times of great success and excitement. (See 1 Kings 18 and 19.) The old man's sons witnessed the confrontation with Jeroboam at the altar and told their father what the prophet from Judah had said about the king and about his commission from the Lord (vv. 8-10). When the old prophet caught up with the messenger of the Lord, he deliberately tempted him to disobey the Lord's commission, *and the younger man fell into the trap!* The older prophet should not have tempted a fellow servant to disobey, but the younger man shouldn't have hastened to accept the older man's words. If God gave the man from Judah the message and the instructions for delivering it, then God could also give him the changes in the plan.

When an emotionally disturbed man told Charles Spurgeon that God had told him to preach for Spurgeon the next Sunday at the Metropolitan Tabernacle, Spurgeon replied, "When the Lord tells me, I'll let you know." Other believers can use the Word to encourage us, warn us, and correct us, but *beware of letting other believers tell you God's will for your life.* The Father loves each of His children personally and wants to convey His will to each personally (Ps. 33:11). Yes, there's safety in a multitude of counselors, provided they're walking with the Lord, but there's no certainty that you have the will of God just because a committee approved it.

Since he knew what the prophet from Judah was supposed to do, why did the old man deliberately lie to the young man and encourage him to disobey the Lord? Was the old man worried that the visiting prophet might stir things up in comfortable Bethel and create problems for him and other satisfied compromisers? Perhaps the young prophet was feeling proud of what he had done—preaching a powerful message and performing three miracles—and the Lord used the old man to test him and bring him back to essentials. By telling the lie, the old prophet tempted the young man, but by going back to Bethel, the young prophet tempted himself (he was out of God's will) and tempted the Lord. Why didn't the young visitor seek the face of the Lord and find out His will? The text tells us only the events, not the motives in the hearts of the participants, so we can't answer any of these questions with finality.

One of the strangest events of all is that the Lord sent His Word to the old prophet who was out of His will! But God spoke to Balaam, who was not necessarily a separated and dedicated man, as well as to Elijah (1 Kings 18) and Jonah (Jonah 3–4). After the meal, the younger prophet started back home and the lion met him and killed him. But even this event had miracle aspects to it, because the lion didn't maul the body or attack the mule, and the mule didn't run away. The animals must have remained there a long time because witnesses told the tale in Bethel and people came out to see the sight, including the old prophet who carried the body away and buried it. Surely the news arrived at the palace, and perhaps the king rejoiced that his enemy was dead. But the prophet's words were not dead! And the very death of the prophet was another warning to Jeroboam that he had better start to obey the Word of God.

The old prophet must have recovered his courage, for he publicly declared that the prophecy given at the Bethel altar would be fulfilled (vv. 31-32), and it was (2 Kings 23:15-18). Three hundred years later, King Josiah saw the old prophet's tomb and took courage that the Lord does fulfill His Word. But did any of these unusual events convict the heart of King Jeroboam and bring him to a place of repentance? "But even after this, Jeroboam did not turn from his evil ways" (v. 33, NLT). However, God's next warning would come closer to home.

3. He didn't receive God's help. (1 Kings 14:1-20)

We don't read in Scripture that Jeroboam sought the Lord's will, prayed for spiritual discernment, or asked the Lord to make him a godly man. He prayed for healing for his arm, and now he asked the prophet Ahijah to heal his son, the crown prince and heir to the throne. It's obvious that physical blessings were more important to him than spiritual blessings. Like many nominal believers and careless church members today, the only time Jeroboam wanted help from God's servant was when he was in trouble.

The pretending wife (vv. 1-3). Abijah wasn't a little child at this time. He was old enough to be approved by the Lord (v. 13) and appreciated by the people, for they mourned over him when he died (v. 18). No doubt the godly remnant in Israel pinned their hopes on the young prince, but God judged the royal family and the apostate citizens by calling the boy away from the cesspool of iniquity that was called Israel. "The righteous man perishes, and no man takes it to heart; and devout men are taken away, while no one understands. For the righteous man is taken away from evil" (Isa. 57:1, NASB).

The king wanted help from the prophet, but he was too proud to admit it or to face Ahijah personally. The prophet still lived in Shiloh (11:29) because he was too old and infirm to relocate in Judah, and he wanted to be faithful to the very end and warn Jeroboam of the consequences of his sins. Did the king think a disguise would fool the godly prophet, blind as he was? Ahijah could see more in his blindness than Jeroboam and his wife could see with their gift of sight.[6] The gifts the queen carried were those of a common laborer, not gifts fit for a king to give.

The discerning prophet (vv. 4-6). It was about twenty miles from Tirzah to Shiloh, but the prophet knew she was coming before she even arrived in the city. The aged prophet knew who was coming, why she was coming and what he was supposed to tell her. "The secret of the Lord is with those who fear Him" (Ps. 25:14, NKJV). "Surely the Lord does nothing, unless He reveals His secret to His servants the prophets" (Amos 3:7, NKJV). Jeroboam sent his wife to Ahijah, but Ahijah said that he was sent to her! He gave her the message she was to give to her husband, and it wasn't a very happy one.

The revealing message (vv. 7-16). First, the prophet reminded Jeroboam of *God's grace in the past (vv. 7-8a)*. The Lord had chosen Jeroboam and raised him from being a district leader to ruling over the Northern Kingdom.[7] God had torn ten tribes away from the house of David and had given them to Jeroboam. But then Ahijah revealed *Jeroboam's sins in the present (vv. 8b-9)*. Unlike David, who had a heart wholly dedicated to the Lord, Jeroboam did more evil than Saul, David, and Solomon put together. He turned from the true God of Israel and made false gods, and then allowed the people of the ten tribes to worship them. He organized a counterfeit religion, provoked the Lord to anger, and refused to listen to the prophets who were sent to warn him.

This led to Ahijah's **revelation of Jeroboam's future (vv. 10-16).** To begin with, unlike King David, Jeroboam would not establish a dynasty, even though God had promised to bless him with a "sure house" if he obeyed the Lord (11:38, KJV). All of Jeroboam's male descendants would be cut off; the Lord would make a "clean sweep" of Jeroboam's family and take away every potential heir, just the way servants remove dung from a house. (God didn't think much of the king's children!) But even worse, none of them except Abijah, the ailing crown prince, would have a decent, dignified burial. Between the scavenger dogs in the city and the carrion birds in the fields, the children's corpses would be devoured and never buried, a terrible humiliation for any Jew.

Then Ahijah got to the matter at hand, the future of the sick heir to the throne. Abijah would die, have a dignified burial, and be mourned by the people. The one son of wicked Jeroboam who could have ruled justly would be taken from them, not because he was wicked but because he was good and God wanted to spare him the suffering that lay ahead of the kingdom (Isa. 57:1). As he looked ahead (v. 14), Ahijah then saw Nadab, Jeroboam's son and heir, reign for two years and then be assassinated by Baasha, a man from the tribe of Issachar (15:25-31). Baasha would not only kill Nadab, but he would exterminate the family of Jeroboam, in fulfillment of Ahijah's prophecy (15:29).

Then the blind prophet looked even further ahead (vv. 15-16) and saw the entire kingdom of Israel defeated by the enemy (Assyria), rooted out of the land, and scattered among the nations. This happened in 722 B.C. The kingdom of Israel had a new religious system, but they were still under the Lord's covenant (Lev. 26; Deut. 28–30). That covenant warned that their disobedience to God's law would bring military defeat and national dispersion to the nation (Deut. 28:25-26, 49-52; Lev. 26:17, 25, 33-39; and see Deut. 7:5 and 12:3-4). What would be the cause of this terrible judgment? "[T]he sins of Jeroboam, who did sin, and who made Israel to sin" (v. 16, KJV). Just as David was God's standard for measuring the good kings, Jeroboam was God's example of the worst of the bad kings. See 1 Kings 15:34; 16:2-3, 7, 19, 26, 31; 22:52; 2 Kings 3:3; 9:9; 10:29, 31; 13:2, 6, 11; 14:24; 15:9, 18, 24, 28; 17:21-22.

The distressing fulfillment (vv. 17-20). Jeroboam apparently had a palace in Tirzah as well as the palace in Shechem, and it must have been at the edge of the city. Ahijah had told Jeroboam's wife that the child would die as soon as she entered the city (v. 12), but v. 17 indicates that he died when she stepped on the threshold of the door. All Israel did mourn the loss of this son and they gave him a funeral suited to a crown prince. The king's hand had been healed and his altar destroyed (13:1-16), and now his son had died. His army would be defeated by the king of Judah, also named Abijah (2 Chron. 13).

How many times did God have to warn him before he would repent?

Nobody could sin like Jeroboam, son of Nebat. During his twenty-two years as king of Israel, he led his family and the nation into ruin. One day Jeroboam died and was succeeded by his son Nadab who was assassinated. The day would come when not a single male descendant of King Jeroboam would be alive, nor would you be able to identify the ten tribes of Israel.

"Indeed I tremble for my country when I reflect that God is just; that His justice cannot sleep forever. . . ."[8] Thomas Jefferson wrote those words in 1781, but they are just as applicable to us today.

CHAPTER NINE
KINGS ON PARADE
1 Kings 15:1–16:28 (2 Chronicles 13–16)

Were it not for the overruling hand of a sovereign God, the Jewish nation could never have accomplished what God called them to do: bearing witness of the one true and living God, writing the Scriptures, and bringing the Savior into the world. There were now two kingdoms instead of one, and leaders and common people in both kingdoms had departed from the Lord to serve idols. The priests still carried on the temple ministry in Judah, but during the 345 years from Rehoboam to Zedekiah, only eight of Judah's nineteen kings were classified as "good." As for Israel's twenty kings, for the most part they were all self-seeking men who were classified as "evil." Some were better than others, but none was compared with David.

Keep in mind that the books of Kings and Chronicles don't record history from exactly the same perspective. The focus in 1 and 2 Kings is on the kings of Israel, but in 1 and 2 Chronicles, the emphasis is on David's dynasty in Judah. The Northern Kingdom of Israel, later called Samaria, is mentioned in Chronicles only when it had dealings with Judah. Another thing to remember is that the two kingdoms used different systems in keeping official records. In Judah, the king's reign was counted from the beginning of the next calendar year after he began his reign, while in Israel, the count began with the year the king actually ascended the throne. Also, some kings had their sons as coregents during the closing years of their reign. These factors complicate calculating how long some kings reigned, and this helps us understand why biblical chronologists don't always agree.

1. A dynasty continues (1 Kings 15:1-24; 2 Chron. 13–16)

The Northern Kingdom of Israel had nine dynasties in about 250 years while the Southern Kingdom faithfully maintained the Davidic dynasty for 350 years, and that was the dynasty from which the Lord Jesus Christ, the Son of David, would come (Matt. 1:1). With all of its faults, the kingdom of Judah was identified with the true and living God, practiced authorized worship in the temple, and had kings who came from David's family. Two of these kings are named in these chapters—Abijah and Asa.

Abijah (vv. 1-8; 2 Chron. 13). This son of Rehoboam was handpicked by his father because of his proven ability (2 Chron. 11:22), but he wasn't a godly man (15:3). He reigned only three years (913–910). He was from David's line through both parents, for David's infamous son Absalom was Abijah's paternal grandfather. Abijah may have had David's blood flowing in his veins, but he didn't have David's perfect heart beating in his breast. Abijah's father, Rehoboam, had kept up a running war with Jeroboam, and Abijah carried on the tradition.

However, Abijah knew his history and had faith in what God said to Moses and David. He had the courage to preach a sermon to Jeroboam and his army of 800,000 men, twice as large as Judah's army, reminding them of the true foundation for the Jewish faith (2 Chron. 13:4ff). For his platform, he used Mount Zemaraim, a prominent place located on the border between Benjamin and Israel (Josh. 18:22). He opened his sermon by reminding Jeroboam that the line of David was the true royal dynasty as stated in God's unchanging covenant with David (vv. 4-5; 2 Sam. 7) The phrase "covenant of salt" means "a perpetual covenant" (Num. 18:19).

Anticipating the argument that the Lord had also made Jeroboam king, Abijah explained why the nation divided (2 Chron. 13:6-7). Jeroboam had rebelled against both Solomon and Rehoboam and had to flee to Egypt to be safe. Then Rehoboam, in his immaturity, listened to unwise counsel and made a foolish decision that led to Jeroboam becoming king.[1] But God's original plan was that the line of David would reign over a united kingdom. In 1 and 2 Chronicles, the emphasis is on the legitimacy of the Davidic dynasty (1 Chron. 17:14; 28:5; 29:11, 23; 2 Chron. 9:8).

Having settled the matter that the sons of David should sit on the throne, Abijah reminded Jeroboam that only the sons of Aaron could serve in the temple (2 Chron. 13:8-12). The only divinely authorized temple of the Lord was in Jerusalem, and there the priests, the sons of Aaron, conducted the form of worship commanded by the Lord through Moses. Judah worshiped the one true and living God, while Israel worshiped two golden calves. Israel's priests were hirelings, not divinely appointed servants of the Lord. In Judah, the people honored the Lord God Jehovah. "God himself is with us!" Therefore, if Israel attacked Judah, Israel was fighting against the Lord!

Abijah's sentries weren't doing a very good job, for while Abijah was speaking, some of Jeroboam's soldiers moved behind him and set up an ambush. If Judah did attack, they'd find their smaller army fighting on two fronts, surely a dangerous situation. It's important to have good theology, but it's also important to have good strategy and alert guards on duty. But Abijah was up to the challenge and he cried out to God for deliverance. At the same time, the priests blew their trumpets (Num. 10:8-10) and the army of Judah gave a great shout, just as the people had done at Jericho (Josh. 6), and the Lord sent immediate victory.[2] Over half of Jeroboam's army was slain by the army of Judah, and Abijah's soldiers moved north to capture the city of Bethel, ten miles from Jerusalem. From Bethel they moved five miles north and took Jeshanah and four miles northeast to take Ephrain (Ephron). Abijah not only defeated the army of Israel and recovered some lost territory, but he gave Jeroboam a blow from which he never recovered. Then the Lord struck Jeroboam and he died (2 Chron. 13:20; 1 Kings 14:19-20).

It was for the glory of His own name that the Lord acted as He did. In 1 Kings, Abijah isn't marked out as a godly ruler, but we commend him for his understanding of God's truth and his faith in God's power. Abijah was no Joshua, but the God of Joshua was still the God of His people and proved Himself faithful. Abijah become more and more powerful, fathered many children, and helped to continue the dynasty of David. God uses imperfect people to do His will, if only they will trust Him.

Asa (vv. 9-24; 2 Chron. 14–16). Abijah's son Asa ruled for forty-one years (910–869). He began his reign with a heart like that of David (1 Kings 15:11; 2 Chron. 14:2), but though a good king for most of his life, during the last five years of his reign, he rebelled against the Lord. The word "mother" in 15:10 (KJV) should be "grandmother" for it refers to the same person mentioned in v. 2. The Jewish people didn't identify relatives with the same precision we do today. There were three major divisions to Asa's life and reign.

(1) Peace and victory (1 Kings 15:9-11; 2 Chron. 14:1–15:7). Thanks to his father's victory over Jeroboam (2 Chron. 13), Asa had peace during the first ten years of his reign (2 Chron. 14:1). During that time, he led a national reformation, cleansed the land of idolatry, and urged the people to seek the Lord (vv. 2-5). He also fortified the land by building defense cities and assembling an army of 580,000 men (vv. 6-8). The emphasis, however, wasn't on military achievements but on seeking the Lord (v. 7). It was God who gave them peace because they sought His face. They used that time of peace to prepare for any war that might occur, for faith without works is dead. It's a good thing Asa was prepared, because the Egyptian army attacked Judah, led by Zerah, who was a Cushite. The two armies met at Mareshah, about twenty-five miles southwest of Jerusalem.

Like his father, Asa knew how to call on the Lord in the day of trouble (14:11; 13:14-18). The king wasn't ignorant of his plight, because he identified Judah as "those who have no power." Zerah's army was almost twice as large as Asa's, and Asa's men had no chariots. Whether by many soldiers or by few, the Lord could work in mighty power. He may have had the words of Jonathan in mind when he prayed that way (1 Sam. 14:6). He might also have been thinking of what Solomon asked in his prayer of dedication (2 Chron. 6:34-35). Sudden deliverance in the midst of battle is a repeated theme in 2 Chronicles (13:14-18; 14:11-12; 18:31; 20:1ff; 32:20-22).

Asa's motive wasn't simply to defeat a dangerous enemy but to bring glory to Jehovah. Like David approaching Goliath, he attacked the enemy army "in the name of the Lord of hosts, the God of the armies of Israel" (1 Sam. 17:45, KJV). In response to Asa's prayer of faith, the Lord soundly defeated the Egyptian army and enabled Asa and his men to pursue them south to Gerar. There the men of Judah and Benjamin plundered the cities around Gerar and brought back an immense amount of spoils. This defeat of the Egyptian army was so thorough and so humiliating that the Egyptians didn't attack the people of Judah again until nearly three hundred years later when King Josiah met the forces of Pharaoh Neco at Carchemish (2 Chron. 35:20-24).

The Lord sent the prophet Azariah to meet Asa and the victorious army and give them a message of encouragement and warning (see also 1 Kings 12:21-24; 2 Chron. 16:7). More than one general has won a battle but afterwards lost the war because of pride or carelessness, and the Lord didn't want Asa to fall into that trap. Azariah's message was the same as that of King Asa: seek the Lord, obey Him, trust Him, and be strong in the Lord (2 Chron. 15:1-7; see also 14:4 and Deut. 4:29). Azariah reviewed the the dark days of the judges, when the nation didn't have a king, a godly priest, or anyone to enforce the law (Judg. 2:11-21). Because the people had turned to idols, their land was overrun by the enemy and it wasn't safe to travel (Judg. 5:6; 19:20). This was a fulfillment of God's covenant warning (Deut. 28:25-26, 30, 49-52). But whenever the people cried out to God and forsook their idols, He mercifully forgave them and defeated the enemy. Azariah admonished the king and the people to get to work, build the nation, and serve the Lord faithfully.

(2) Reformation and renewal (1 Kings 15:12-15; 2 Chron. 15:8-19). This is the second phase of Asa's reformation, and certainly he dealt more severely with sin in the land than in the first phase. He expelled the shrine male prostitutes, for this practice was prohibited by God's law (Deut. 23:17), as was sodomy itself (Lev. 18:22; 20:13; see also Rom. 1:27 and 1 Cor. 6:9). He also removed his own grandmother from being the queen mother because she had an idolatrous shrine in a grove. That took some courage! We aren't told where this dedicated wealth had been kept, but Asa brought it to the temple treasury because it had been dedicated to the Lord. This was probably booty taken from the enemies he and his father had defeated with the Lord's help.

Once again, he removed the idols from the land, and he also repaired the altar of sacrifice that stood in the court of the priests before the temple. How or why the altar was damaged, the text doesn't say; but without the altar, the priests had no place to offer sacrifices. Solomon dedicated the temple in about 959, and Asa's fifteenth year was 896 (2 Chron. 15:10), so the altar had been in constant use for over sixty years. Perhaps it was just worn out, but a neglected altar isn't a very good testimony to the state of religion in the land. The Hebrew word can also mean "to renew," so perhaps the altar was rededicated to the Lord.

It's one thing to remove idols and repair the altar, but the greatest need was to rededicate the people. In the fifteenth year of his reign, Asa called for a great assembly to gather at Jerusalem to worship the Lord and renew the covenant.[3] Not only did the people of Judah and Benjamin attend, but devout people came to Jerusalem from Ephraim, Manasseh, and Simeon. The thing that drew them was the obvious fact that the Lord was with Asa. Since they assembled in the third month, they were probably celebrating the Feast of Pentecost (Lev. 23:15-22). The king brought the spoils of battle to be dedicated to the Lord, including valuable metals (1 Kings 15:15) and animals for sacrifice (2 Chron. 15:11).

At significant times throughout Jewish history you find the leaders and the people renewing their commitment to the Lord, a good example for the church to follow today. After the nation crossed the Jordan and entered the land, they renewed their covenant with the Lord (Josh. 8:30ff). Joshua called for a similar meeting near the close of his life (Josh. 24). When Saul was named king, Samuel called for an assembly and a time of renewal (1 Sam. 11:14–12:25). King Joash and King Josiah both renewed the covenant between themselves and the people and God (2 Kings 11:4ff; 23:1ff). Spiritual revival or renewal doesn't mean asking God for something new but for the renewal of our devotion to that which He has already given to us. Asa didn't reorganize the priesthood or remodel the temple, nor did he import new worship ideas from the pagan nations around him. He simply led the people in rededication to the covenant that God had already given them. They sought the Lord with all their hearts and He heard them.[4] God was pleased with this new step of commitment and He gave Judah and Benjamin peace for another twenty years.

(3) Relapse and discipline (1 Kings 15:16-24; 2 Chron. 16:1-14). Apparently King Asa had become careless in his walk with the Lord, because the Lord sent Baasha, king of Israel, to war against him.[5] Baasha fortified Ramah, which was located about six miles north of Jerusalem. From this outpost he would be able to monitor his own people who might go to Jerusalem and also launch his own attack on Judah.

After all that the Lord had done for Asa, you would think he would have called the people together to confess sin, seek the Lord, and learn His will about this serious situation. But instead, in his unbelief, he resorted to politics. He took the dedicated treasures from the temple and gave them to Ben-hadad, king of Syria, and entered into a pact with a pagan nation. (David had defeated Syria! See 2 Sam. 8:3-12 and 1 Chron. 18:3-4.) With Syria attacking Israel from the north, Baasha would have to abandon Ramah and move north to defend his country. King Asa not only followed the bad example of his father Abijah in making an unholy alliance, but he insisted that Ben-hadad lie and break his treaty with Israel! Scripture doesn't tell us when Abijah made a pact with Ben-hadad, but perhaps he married one of the Syrian princesses and in that way secured peace, following the example of Solomon (2 Chron. 13:21).

Ben-hadad took the silver and gold, broke his promise with Israel, and helped Judah. He captured the cities of Ijon, Dan, and Abelmaim in the north, and then marched through the tribe of Naphtali and took all the important storage cities. In this way, he gained control over the major trade routes and crippled Baasha's power and income. Having achieved his purpose, Asa conscripted the people to go to Ramah and carry off the stones and timber, and with that material the king built two fortified cities: Mizpeh about two and a half miles north of Ramah, and Geba about the same distance to the east. Judah had extended its border as far as Bethel (2 Chron. 13:17), and these new military sites would make their position even more secure.

Everyone was happy with the results of the treaty except the Lord. He sent the prophet Hanani to rebuke the king and give him the Word of the Lord. It was the task of the prophet to rebuke kings and other leaders, including priests, when they had disobeyed the law of the Lord. The prophet's message was clear: if Asa had relied on the Lord, the army of Judah would have defeated both Israel and Syria. Instead, Judah merely gained a few towns, the Lord's treasury was robbed and the king was now in a sinful alliance with the Syrians. Hanani reminded Asa that the Lord hadn't failed him when Zerah and the huge Egyptian army attacked Judah. The king had done a foolish thing in hiring the Syrians. Judah would pay for his mistake for years to come, and Syria did become a constant problem to the kingdom of Judah.

The fundamental problem was not Judah's lack of defenses but the king's lack of faith. Unlike David, whose heart was sincere before the Lord (see 1 Kings 15:5, 11), Asa's heart was divided—one day trusting the Lord and the next day trusting in the arm of flesh. A perfect heart isn't a sinless heart but a heart wholly yielded to the Lord and fully trusting Him. King Asa revealed the wickedness of his heart by becoming angry, rejecting the prophet's message, and putting him in prison. Apparently some of the people opposed Asa's foreign policy and his mistreatment of God's servant, so the king brutally oppressed them.

God gave Asa time to repent, but he refused to do so. In the thirty-ninth year of Asa's reign, the Lord afflicted him with a disease in his feet, which must have brought him considerable pain and inconvenience. Once again, he turned his back on the Lord and refused to confess his sins and seek Jehovah, but he turned for help to his physicians. Two years later, he died, and the throne was given to his son Jehoshaphat, who had probably served as coregent during the last years of his father's life.[6] Asa was a man who made a good beginning and lived a life of faith, but when it came to his final years, rebelled against the Lord. The people made a very great bonfire in his honor, but in God's sight, the last years of Asa went up in smoke (1 Cor. 3:13-15).[7]

2. A dynasty concludes. (1 Kings 15:25–16:22)

At this point, the historian turns to the account of the kings of Israel and will remain there until the end of the book. The story of the kings of Judah is found primarily in 2 Chronicles. David's dynasty is mentioned in 1 and 2 Kings only where there is some interaction between Judah and Israel. The dynasty that began with Jeroboam is now about to end.

Nadab is assassinated (15:25-31). Jeroboam reigned over Israel for 22 years (14:20) and became the prime example in Scripture of an evil king (see 15:34; 16:2, 19, 26, etc.). Nadab inherited his father's throne as well as his father's sinful ways. He had reigned only two years when a conspiracy developed that led to King Nadab being assassinated by Baasha, a man from Issachar. Nadab was with the army of Israel, directing the siege of Gibbethon, a Philistine city south of Ekron. This border city had been a source of friction between Israel and the Philistines. It actually belonged to the tribe of Dan (Josh. 19:43-45) and was a Levitical city (Josh. 21:23), and Nadab wanted to reclaim it for Israel.

Baasha not only killed the king but he seized his throne and proceeded to fulfill the prophecy of Ahijah that Jeroboam's family would be completely wiped out because of the sins Jeroboam committed (14:10-16). Had Jeroboam obeyed God's Word, he would have enjoyed the blessing and help of the Lord (11:38-39), but because he sinned and caused the nation to sin, the Lord had to judge him and his descendants. That was the end of the dynasty of Jeroboam I.

Baasha disobeys God (15:32–16:7). Baasha set up his palace at Tirzah and reigned over Israel for twenty-four years. Instead of avoiding the sins that brought about the extinction of Jeroboam's family—and he was the man who killed them—Baasha copied the lifestyle of his predecessor! It has well been said that the one thing we learn from history is that we don't learn from history. Baasha had destroyed Jeroboam's dynasty, but he couldn't destroy the Word of God. The Lord sent the prophet Jehu to give the king the solemn message that after he died, his family would be exterminated, and another dynasty would be destroyed because of the father's sin. Baasha's descendants would be slain and their corpses become food for the dogs and the vultures. For a Jew's body not to be buried was a terrible form of humiliation.[8]

Elah is assassinated (16:8-14). Baasha had a normal death, but his son and successor did not. Elah appears to be a dissolute man who would rather get drunk with his friends than serve the Lord and the people. Arza was probably the prime minister. Both men forgot the words of Solomon, who knew a thing or two about kingship: "Woe to you, O land, when your king is a child, and your princes feast in the morning! Blessed are you, O land, when your king is the son of nobles, and your princes feast at the proper time—for strength and not for drunkenness" (Ecc. 10:16-17, NKJV).

The assassin this time is Zimri, the captain of half of the charioteers in the army of Israel. As a noted captain, he had access to the king, and what better time to kill him than when he was drunk? Like Elah's father, Zimri seized the throne, and once he was in power, he killed every member of Baasha's family. Baasha had fulfilled the prophecy of Abijah and Zimri fulfilled the prophecy of Jehu. But it must be pointed out that a person who fulfills divine prophecy is not innocent of sin. Both Baasha and Zimri were murderers and guilty of regicide, and the Lord held them responsible and accountable. The dynasty of Jeroboam was no more and the dynasty of Baasha was no more. In Judah, the dynasty of David continued.

CHAPTER TEN
LET THE FIRE FALL!
1 Kings 17–18

Elijah the Tishbite[1] suddenly appears on the scene and then leaves as quickly as he came, only to reappear three years later to challenge the priests of Baal. His name means "The Lord (Jehovah) is my God," an apt name for a man who called the people back to the worship of Jehovah (18:21, 39). Wicked King Ahab had permitted his wife Jezebel to bring the worship of Baal into Israel (16:31-33) and she was determined to wipe out the worship of Jehovah (18:4). Baal was the Phoenician fertility god who sent rain and bountiful crops, and the rites connected with his worship were unspeakably immoral. Like Solomon who catered to the idolatrous practices of his heathen wives (11:1-8), Ahab yielded to Jezebel's desires and even built her a private temple where she could worship Baal (16:32-33). Her plan was to exterminate the worshipers of Jehovah and have all the people of Israel serving Baal.

The prophet Elijah is an important figure in the New Testament. John the Baptist came in the spirit and power of Elijah (Luke 1:17), and some of the people even thought he was the promised Elijah (John 1:21; Mal. 4:5-6; Matt. 17:10-13). Elijah was with Moses and Jesus on the Mount of Transfiguration (Matt. 17:3), and some students believe that Moses and Elijah are the two witnesses described in Rev. 11:1-14. Elijah wasn't a polished preacher like Isaiah and Jeremiah, but was more of a rough-hewn reformer who challenged the people to abandon their idols and return to the Lord. He was a courageous man who confronted Ahab personally and rebuked his sin, and he also challenged the priests of Baal to a public contest. He was not only a worker of miracles, but he also experienced miracles in his own life. These two chapters record seven different miracles that Elijah either performed or experienced.

1. A nationwide drought (1 Kings 17:1)

The Jewish people depended on the seasonal rains for the success of their crops. If the Lord didn't send the early rain in October and November and the latter rain in March and April, there would soon be a famine in the land. But the blessing of the semiannual rains depended on the people obeying the covenant of the Lord (Deut. 11). God warned the people that their disobedience would turn the heavens into bronze and the earth into iron (Deut. 28:23-24; see Lev. 26:3-4, 18-19). The land belonged to the Lord, and if the people defiled the land with their sinful idols, the Lord wouldn't bless them.

It's likely that Elijah appeared before King Ahab in October, about the time the early rains should have begun. There had been no rain for six months, from April to October, and the prophet announced that there would be no rain for the next three years![2] The people were following Baal, not Jehovah, and the Lord could not send the promised rain and still be faithful to His covenant. God always keeps His covenant, whether to bless the people for their obedience or to discipline them for their sins.

God had held back the rain because of the fervent prayers of Elijah, and He would send the rain again in response to His servant's intercession (James 5:17-18). For the next three years, the word of Elijah would control the weather in Israel! The three and a half years of drought would prepare the people for the dramatic contest on Mount Carmel between the priests of Baal and the prophet of the Lord. Like a faithful servant, attentive to his master's commands, Elijah stood before the Lord and served him. (Later, his successor, Elisha, would use this same terminology. See 2 Kings 3:14 and 5:16.) An extended drought, announced and controlled by a prophet of Jehovah, would make it clear to everybody that Baal the storm god was not a true god at all.

2. Food from unclean birds (1 Kings 17:2-7)

After Elijah left the king's presence, Jezebel must have instigated her campaign to wipe out the prophets of the Lord (18:4). As the drought continued and famine hit the land, Ahab began his search for Elijah, the man he thought caused all the trouble (18:17). In one sense, Elijah did cause the drought, but it was the sins of Ahab and Jezebel that led the nation into disobeying God's covenant and inviting His chastening. The Lord had a special hiding place for His servant by a brook east of the Jordan, and He also had some unusual "servants" prepared to feed him. The Lord usually leads His faithful people a step at a time as they tune their hearts to His Word. God didn't give Elijah a three-year schedule to follow. Instead, He directed his servant at each critical juncture in his journey, and Elijah obeyed by faith.

"Go, hide yourself!" was God's command, and three years later the command would be, "Go, show yourself!" By leaving his public ministry, Elijah created a second "drought" in the land—an absence of the Word of the Lord. God's Word was to the Jewish people like the rain from heaven (Deut. 32:2; Isa. 55:10): it was essential to their spiritual lives, it was refreshing, and only the Lord could give it. The silence of God's servant was a judgment from God (Ps. 74:9), for not to hear God's living Word is to forfeit life itself (Ps. 28:1).

At the brook Cherith ("Kerith Ravine," NIV), Elijah had safety and sustenance. Until it dried up, the brook provided water, and each morning and evening the ravens brought him bread and meat. The raven was considered "unclean" and "detestable" on the Mosaic list of forbidden foods (Lev. 11:13-15; Deut. 14:14), yet God used these birds to help sustain the life of his servant. The ravens didn't bring Elijah the carrion that they were accustomed to eat, because such food would be unclean for a dedicated Jew. The Lord provided the food and the birds provided the transportation! Just as God dropped the manna into the camp of Israel during their wilderness journey, so He sent the necessary food to Elijah as he waited for the signal to relocate. God feeds the beasts and the ravens (Ps. 147:9; Luke 12:24), and He can use the ravens to carry food to His servant.

As the drought grew worse, the brook dried up, leaving the prophet without water; but he never made a move until the Word of the Lord came to tell him what to do. It has well been said that the will of God will never lead us where the grace of God cannot keep us and care for us, and Elijah knew this from experience. (See Isa. 33:15-16.)

3. Food from empty vessels. (1 Kings 17:8-16)

Elijah lived at Cherith probably a year, and then God told him to leave. God's instructions may have shocked the prophet, for the Lord commanded him to travel northeast about a hundred miles to the Phoenician city of Zarephath. God was sending Elijah into Gentile territory, and since Zarephath was not too far from Jezebel's home city of Sidon, he would be living in enemy territory! Even more, he was instructed to live with a widow whom God had selected to care for him, and widows were usually among the neediest people in the land. Since Phoenicia depended on Israel for much of its food supply (1 Kings 5:9; Acts 12:20), food wouldn't be too plentiful there. But when God sends us, we must obey and leave the rest to Him, for we don't live on man's explanations—we live on God's promises.

"Because of our proneness to look at the bucket and forget the fountain," wrote Watchman Nee, "God has frequently to change His means of supply to keep our eyes fixed on the source." After the nation of Israel entered the Promised Land, the manna ceased to fall into the camp and God changed His way of feeding the people (Josh. 5:10-12). During the early days of the church in Jerusalem, the believers had all that they needed (Acts 4:34-35), but a few years later, the saints in Jerusalem had to receive help from the Gentile believers in Antioch (Acts 11:27-30). Elijah was about to learn what God could do with empty vessels!

The fact that the woman had been instructed by the Lord (v. 9) isn't proof that she was a believer in the God of Israel, for the Lord gave orders to a pagan king like Cyrus (2 Chron. 36:22) and even called him his "shepherd" (Isa. 44:28). The widow spoke of Jehovah as "the Lord *your* God" (v. 12, italics mine), for she could easily discern that the stranger speaking to her was a Jew; but even this isn't evidence she was a believer. It's probable that Elijah remained with her for two years (18:1), and during that time, the widow and her son surely turned from the worship of idols and put their faith in the true and living God.

The woman's assets were few: a little oil in a flask, a handful of barley in a large grain jar ("barrel", KJV), and a few sticks to provide fuel for a fire. But Elijah's assets were great, for God Almighty had promised to take care of him, his hostess, and her son. Elijah gave her God's promise that neither the jar of grain nor the flask of oil would be used up before the end of the drought and famine. God would one day send the rain, but until then, He would continue to provide bread for them—and He did.

In our modern society, with its credit cards and convenient shopping, we need to remember that each meal we eat is a miracle from the hand of God. We may live far from the farmers who grow our food, but we can't live without them. "Give us this day our daily bread" is more than a line in a prayer that we may too casually recite. It's the expression of a great truth, that the Lord cares for us and uses many hands to feed us.

Back of the loaf is the snowy flour,
And back of the flour is the mill,
And back of the mill is the wheat, sun, and shower,
The farmer—and the Father's will.

4. Life for a dead boy (1 Kings 17:17-24)

This is the first recorded instance in Scripture of the resurrection of a dead person. The evidence seems clear that the widow's son actually died and didn't just faint or go into a temporary swoon. He stopped breathing (v. 17) and his spirit left the body (vv. 21-22). According to James 2:26, when the spirit leaves a body, the person is dead. The great distress of both the mother and the prophet would suggest that the boy was dead, and both of them used the word "slay" with reference to the event (vv. 18 and 20, KJV).

The mother's response was to feel guilty because of her past sins. She believed that her son's death was God's way of punishing her for her misdeeds. It isn't unusual for people to feel guilty in connection with bereavement, but why would she point her finger at her guest? She recognized Elijah as a man of God, and perhaps she thought his presence in the home would protect her and her son from trouble. Or maybe she felt that God had informed her guest about her past life, something she should have confessed to him. Her words remind us of the question of the disciples in John 9:2, "Master, who did sin, this man, or his parents, that he was born blind?"

Elijah's response was to carry the lad to his upstairs room, perhaps on the roof, and to cry out to the Lord for the life of the child. He couldn't believe that the Lord would miraculously provide food for the three of them and then allow the son to die. It just didn't make sense. Elijah didn't stretch himself out on the boy's dead body in hopes he could transfer his life to the lad, for he knew that only God can impart life to the dead. Certainly his posture indicated total identification with the boy and his need, and this is an important factor when we intercede for others. It was after Elijah stretched himself on the child for the third time that the Lord raised him from the dead, a reminder that our own Savior arose from the dead on the third day. Because He lives, we can share His life by putting our faith in Him. (See 2 Kings 4:34 and Acts 20:10.)

The result of this miracle was the woman's public confession of her faith in the God of Israel. She now knew for sure that Elijah was a true servant of God and not just another religious teacher looking for some support. She also knew that the Word he had taught her was indeed the Word of the true and living God. During the time he lived with the widow and her son, Elijah had shown them that God sustains life (the meal and oil didn't run out) and that God imparts life (the boy was raised from the dead).

Elijah hadn't been in public ministry for a long time, yet his private ministry to the woman and her son was just as important both to the Lord and to them. The servant who won't "hide himself" and minister to a few people isn't really ready to stand on Mount Carmel and call down fire and rain from heaven. People who have proved themselves faithful with a few things in small places can be trusted by the Lord with many things before many people in the bigger places (Matt. 25:21). Elijah had proved the power of God in Baal's own home territory, so he was now ready to challenge and defeat Baal in the kingdom of Israel.

During these three years as an exile and a hunted man (18:10), Elijah has learned a great deal about the Lord, about himself and about the needs of people. He has learned to live a day at a time, trusting God for his daily bread. For three years, people have been asking, "Where is the prophet Elijah? Is he able to do anything to ease the burdens we carry because of this drought? But the Lord is more concerned about the worker than the work, and He has been preparing Elijah for the greatest challenge of faith in his entire ministry.

Before we leave the account of Elijah's sojourn with the widow of Zarephath, we must consider how our Lord used this story in the sermon He preached in the synagogue in Nazereth (Luke 4:16-30). During the first part of the sermon, the listeners approved of what Jesus said and complimented Him on His "gracious words." But then He reminded them of the sovereign grace of God that reached other nations besides the covenant people of Israel. The great Jewish prophet Elijah actually ministered to a Gentile widow and her son and had even lived with them, and yet he could have ministered to any of the many widows in the nation of Israel. His second illustration was from the ministry of Elisha, Elijah's successor, who actually healed a Gentile general of leprosy (2 Kings 5:1-15). Certainly there were plenty of Jewish lepers he might have cured!

Our Lord's emphasis was on the grace of God. He wanted the proud Jewish congregation in the synagogue to realize that the God of Israel was also the God of the Gentiles (see Rom. 3:29) and that both Jews and Gentiles were saved by putting their faith in Him. Of course, the Jews wouldn't accept the idea that they were sinners like the Gentiles and had to be saved, so they rejected both the messenger and the message and took Jesus out of the synagogue to cast Him down from the hill. Elijah's ministry to the widow and her son was proof that God is no respecter of persons and that "all have sinned and fall short of the glory of God" (Rom. 3:23). Whether a person is a religious Jew or a pagan Gentile, the only way of salvation is through faith in Jesus Christ.

5. Fire from heaven (1 Kings 18:1-40)

For three years, Elijah had hidden himself at the brook Cherith and then with the widow in Zarephath, but now he was commanded to "show himself" to wicked King Ahab. But along with God's command was God's promise that He would send rain and end the drought that He had sent to punish the idolatrous nation for over three years.

Obadiah meets Elijah (vv. 1-16). Students don't agree on the character of Obadiah, the governor of the palace. A man of great authority, he was administrator of the royal palace as well as steward and supervisor of whatever estates the king possessed. But was he a courageous servant of God (his name means "servant of Jehovah") or a timid compromiser who was afraid to let his witness be known? The text informs us that Obadiah "feared the Lord greatly" and proved it during Jezebel's "purge" by risking his life to rescue and support one hundred prophets of the Lord.[3] That doesn't sound like a man who was compromising his testimony! Why should he tell the king and queen what he was doing for the Lord? The Lord had put Obadiah in the palace to use his God-given authority to support the faithful prophets at a time when openly serving the Lord was a dangerous thing.

The king and Obadiah were searching the country for grass and other foliage that could be used to feed the horses and mules used in the army. Ahab wasn't especially concerned about the people of the land, but he wanted his army to be strong just in case of an invasion. It's remarkable that the king was willing to leave the safety and comfort of the palace to scour the land for food for the animals. It seems that when Ahab was away from Jezebel, he was a much better man.

The Lord led Elijah to the road that Obadiah was using and the two men met. Obadiah had such reverence for Elijah and his ministry that he fell on his face on the earth and called him, "My lord, Elijah." But Elijah's aim was to confront wicked King Ahab, and he wasn't about to go looking for him; so he commissioned Obadiah to tell the king where he was. We can understand Obadiah's concern lest the king come back and not find the prophet. During the three years Ahab had been searching for Elijah, no doubt he had followed up many false leads, and Ahab wasn't interested in wasting time and energy at such a critical point in the nation's history. Furthermore, Ahab might punish Obadiah or even suspect him of being a follower of Elijah's God. But when Elijah assured the officer that he would remain there and wait for the king, Obadiah went off to give Ahab the message.

Not all of God's servants are supposed to be in the public eye like Elijah and the other prophets. God has His servants in many places, doing the work He's called them to do. Nicodemus and Joseph of Arimathea didn't make a big fuss about their faith in Christ, yet God used them to give proper burial to the body of Jesus (John 19:38-42). Esther kept quiet about her Jewish heritage until it was absolutely necessary to use it to save the life of the nation. Over the centuries, there have been numerous believers who have kept a low profile and yet made great contributions to the cause of Christ and the advancement of His kingdom.

Elijah meets King Ahab (vv. 17-19). Everything that Elijah did was according to the Word of the Lord (v. 36), including confronting the king and inviting him and the priests of Baal to a meeting on Mount Carmel. Ahab called Elijah "the troublemaker in Israel," but it was really Ahab whose sins had caused the problems in the land. Surely Ahab knew the terms of the covenant and understood that the blessings of the Lord depended on the obedience of the king and his people. Both Jesus and Paul would be called "troublemakers" (Luke 23:5; Acts 16:20; 17:6), so Elijah was in good company.

Mount Carmel was located near the border of Israel and Phoenicia, so it was a good place for the Phoenician god Baal to meet Jehovah, the God of Israel. Elijah told Ahab to bring not only the 450 prophets of Baal but also the 400 prophets of the Asherah (Astarte), the idols that represented Baal's "wife." It seems that only the prophets of Baal showed up for the contest (vv. 22, 26, 40).

The prophets of Baal meet the God of Israel (vv. 20-40). Representatives were present from all ten tribes of the Northern Kingdom, and it was this group that Elijah addressed as the meeting began. His purpose was not only to expose the false god Baal but also to bring the compromising people back to the Lord. Because of the evil influence of Ahab and

Jezebel, the people were "limping" between two opinions and trying to serve both Jehovah and Baal. Like Moses (Ex. 32:26) and Joshua (Josh. 24:15) before him, Elijah called for a definite decision on their part, but the people were speechless. Was this because of their guilt (Rom. 3:19) or because they first wanted to see what would happen next? They were weak people, without true conviction.

Elijah weighted the test in favor of the prophets of Baal. They could build their altar first, select their sacrifice and offer it first, and they could take all the time they needed to pray to Baal. When Elijah said he was the only prophet of the Lord, he wasn't forgetting the prophets that Obadiah had hidden and protected. Rather, he was stating that he was the only one openly serving the Lord, and therefore he was outnumbered by the 450 prophets of Baal. But one with God is a majority, so the prophet had no fears. Surely the prayers of 450 zealous prophets would be heard by Baal and he would answer by sending fire from heaven! (See Lev. 9:24 and 1 Chron. 21:26.)

By noon, Elijah was taunting the prophets of Baal because nothing had happened. "He who sits in the heavens shall laugh; the Lord shall hold them in derision" (Ps. 2:4, NKJV). The prophets of Baal were dancing frantically around their altar and cutting themselves with swords and spears, but still nothing happened. Elijah suggested that perhaps Baal couldn't hear them because he was deep in thought, or busy in some task,[4] or even traveling. His words only made them become more fanatical, but nothing happened. At three o'clock, the time of the evening sacrifice at the temple in Jerusalem, Elijah stepped forward and took charge.

Who originally built the altar that Elijah used? Probably a member of the believing remnant in Israel who privately worshiped the Lord. But the altar had been destroyed, probably by the prophets of Baal (19:10), so Elijah rebuilt it and sanctified it. By using twelve stones, he reaffirmed the spiritual unity of God's people in spite of their political division. Elijah had given the prophets of Baal some advantages, so now he gave himself some handicaps. He had a trench dug around the altar and filled it with water. He put the sacrifice on the wood on the altar and had everything drenched with water.

At the time of the evening sacrifice, he lifted his voice in prayer to the God of the covenant, the God of Abraham, Isaac, and Jacob. His request was that God be glorified as the God of Israel, the true and living God, and make it known that Elijah was His servant. But even more, by sending fire from heaven, the Lord would be telling His people that He had forgiven them and would turn their hearts back to the worship of the true God. Elijah may have been thinking of God's promise to Solomon in 2 Chronicles 7:12-15. Suddenly, the fire fell from heaven and totally devoured the sacrifice, the altar, and the water in the trench around the altar.[5] There was nothing left that anybody could turn into a relic or a shrine. The altar to Baal still stood as a monument to a lost cause. The prophets of Baal were stunned, and the people of Israel fell on their faces and acknowledged, "The Lord, He is God!"

But Elijah wasn't yet finished, for he commanded the people to take the false prophets of Baal and slay them. This was in obedience to the Lord's command in Deuteronomy 13:13-18 and 17:2-5. The test had been a fair one, and the prophets of Baal had been exposed as idolaters who deserved to be killed. The law required that idolaters be stoned to death, but Elijah had the prophets killed with the sword (19:1). This action, of course, angered Jezebel, from whose table these men had been fed (v. 19), and she determined to capture Elijah and kill him.

6. The rains return. (1 Kings 18:41-45)
Elijah had announced three years before that it was his word that stopped the rain and only his word could start it again (17:1). He was referring to the power of his prayers, the words that he spoke to the Lord (James 5:17-18). It had been a long and disappointing day for King Ahab, and Elijah sent him to his retainers to get something to eat.[6] Elijah went to the top of Carmel to pray and ask the Lord to send the much-needed rains. "Every day we live," wrote missionary Amy Carmichael, "we have to choose whether we should follow in the way of Ahab or of Elijah." Matthew 6:33 comes to mind.

Elijah's unusual posture was almost a fetal position and indicated the prophet's humility, his great concern for the people, and his burden for the glory of the Lord. Unlike the answer to the prayer at the altar, the answer to this prayer didn't come at once. Seven times Elijah sent his servant to look toward the Mediterranean Sea and report any indications of a storm gathering, and six of those times the servant reported nothing. The prophet didn't give up but prayed a seventh time, and the servant saw a tiny cloud coming from the sea. This is a good example for us to follow as we "watch and pray" and continue to intercede until the Lord sends the answer.

The little cloud wasn't a storm, but it was the harbinger of the rains that were to come. Elijah commanded the king to mount his chariot and return to his palace in Jezreel as soon as possible. We aren't told how he broke the news to Jezebel that Baal had been publicly humiliated and declared to be a false god, and that the prophets of Baal that she supported had been slain. But neither the drought nor the famine had brought Ahab and Jezebel to repentance, and it wasn't likely that the fire from heaven or the coming of the rain would change their hearts (Rev. 9:20-21; 16:8-11). All the evidence notwithstanding, Jezebel was determined to kill Elijah (19:1-2).

7. Strength for the journey (1 Kings 18:46)
Soon the heavens were black with clouds and great torrents of rain began to fall on the land. The Lord not only proved that he was the true and living God, but He also put His approval on the ministry of His servant Elijah. Elijah had neither chariots nor retainers to drive them, but he did have the power of the Lord; and he ran ahead of Ahab and reached Jezreel ahead of the king, a distance of about seventeen miles. This was quite a feat for an older man and in itself was another sign to the people that God's powerful hand was upon His servant.

God had chastened His people with drought and famine but had cared for His special servant Elijah. God had sent fire from heaven to prove that He was the true and living God. Now He had answered the prayer of His prophet and had sent the rains to water the land. You would think that Elijah would be at his very best spiritually and able to face anything, but the next chapter records just the opposite. As great a man as Elijah was, he still failed the Lord and himself.

CHAPTER ELEVEN
THE CAVE MAN
1 Kings 19

It encourages me when I read James 5:17, "Elijah was as human as we are" (NLT). I have a tendency to idealize the men and women in Scripture, but the Bible is the "word of truth" (2 Tim. 2:15) and describes the warts and wrinkles of even the greatest. When James wrote those words, he undoubtedly had 1 Kings 18 and 19 in mind, for in these chapters we see Elijah at his highest and at his lowest. When the psalmist wrote that "every man at his best state is altogether vanity" (Ps. 39:5, KJV), he included all of us except Jesus. An old adage reminds us, "The best of men are but men at their best," and Elijah's history proves how true this is.

However, the outstanding leaders in Scripture, with all their humanness, knew how to find their way out of what John Bunyan called "the slough [swamp] of despond" and get back on track with the Lord. We can learn from their defeats as well as their successes. Furthermore, by studying passages like 1 Kings 19, we're reminded to give glory to the Master and not to His servants (1 Cor. 1:27-29). We're also reminded to prepare for what may happen after the victories God gives us. How quickly we can move from the mountaintop of triumph to the valley of testing! We need to humble ourselves before the Lord and get ready for the trials that usually follow the victories.

If Elijah could have described to a counselor how he felt and what he thought, the counselor would have diagnosed his condition as a textbook case of burnout. Elijah was physically exhausted and had lost his appetite. He was depressed about himself and his work and was being controlled more and more by self-pity. "I only am left!" Instead of turning to others for help, he isolated himself and—worst of all—he wanted to die. (Elijah never did die. He was taken to heaven in a chariot. See 2 Kings 2.) The prophet concluded that he had failed in his mission and decided it was time to quit. But the Lord didn't see it that way. He always looks beyond our changing moods and impetuous prayers, and He pities us the way parents pity their discouraged children (Ps. 103:13-14). The chapter shows us how tenderly and patiently God deals with us when we're in the depths of despair and feel like giving up.

The chapter begins with Elijah running away and trying to save himself. Then the prophet argues with the Lord and tries to defend himself. Finally, he obeys the Lord and yields himself and is restored to service. In all of this, Elijah was responding to four different messages.

1. The enemy's message of danger (1 Kings 19:1-4)

When the torrential rain began to fall, Jezebel was in Jezreel and may have thought that Baal the storm god had triumphed on Mount Carmel. However, when Ahab arrived home, he told her a much different story. Ahab was a weak man, but he should have stood with Elijah and honored the Lord who had so dramatically demonstrated His power. But Ahab had to live with Queen Jezebel and without her support, he knew he was nothing. If ever there was a strong-willed ruler with a gift for doing evil, it was Jezebel. Neither Ahab nor Jezebel accepted the clear evidence given on Mount Carmel that Jehovah was the only true and living God. Instead of repenting and calling the nation back to serving the Lord, Jezebel declared war on Jehovah and His faithful servant Elijah, and Ahab allowed her to do it.

Why did Jezebel send a letter to Elijah when she could have sent soldiers and had him killed? He was in Jezreel and the deed could have been easily accomplished on such a wild and stormy night. Jezebel wasn't only an evil woman; she was also a shrewd strategist who knew how to make the most of Baal's defeat on Mount Carmel. Ahab was a quitter, but not his wife! Elijah was now a very popular man. Like Moses, he had brought fire from heaven, and like Moses, he had slain the idolaters (Lev. 9:24; Num. 25). If Jezebel transformed the prophet into a martyr, he might influence people more by his death than by his life. No, the people were waiting for Elijah to tell them what to do, so why not *remove him from the scene of his victory?* If Elijah disappeared, the people would wonder what had happened, and they would be prone to drift back into worshiping Baal and letting Ahab and Jezebel have their way. Furthermore, whether from Baal or Jehovah, the rains had returned and there was work to do!

Jezebel may have suspected that Elijah was a candidate for a physical and emotional breakdown after his demanding day on Mount Carmel, and she was right. He was as human as we are, and as the ancient church fathers used to say to their disciples, "Beware of human reactions after holy exertions." Her letter achieved its purpose and Elijah fled from Jezreel. In a moment of fear,[1] when he forgot all that God had done for him the previous three years, Elijah took his servant, left Israel, and headed for Beersheba, the southernmost city in Judah. Charles Spurgeon said that Elijah "retreated before a beaten enemy." God had answered his prayer (18:36-37) and God's hand had been upon him in the storm (18:46), but now he was walking by sight and not by faith. (See Ps. 16:7-8.)

For three years, Elijah had not made a move without hearing and obeying the Lord's instructions (17:2-3, 8-9; 18:1), but now he was running ahead of the Lord in order to save his own life. When God's servants get out of God's will, they're liable to do all sorts of foolish things *and fail in their strongest points.* When Abraham fled to Egypt, he failed in his faith, which was his greatest strength (Gen. 12:10ff). David's greatest strength was his integrity, and that's where he failed when he started lying and scheming during the Bathsheba episode (2 Sam. 11–12). Moses was the meekest of men (Num. 12:3), yet he lost his temper and forfeited the privilege of entering the Promised Land (Num. 20:1-13). Peter was a courageous man, yet his courage failed and he denied Christ (Mark 14:66-72). Like Peter, Elijah was a bold man, but his courage failed when he heard Jezebel's message.

But why flee to Judah, especially when Jehoram, king of Judah, was married to Ahab's daughter Athaliah (2 Kings 8:16-19; 2 Chron. 21:4-7). This is the infamous Athaliah who later ruled the land and tried to exterminate all of David's heirs to the throne (2 Kings 11). The safest place for any child of God is the place dictated by the will of God, but Elijah didn't stop to seek God's will. He traveled 90 to 100 miles to Beersheba and left his servant there. Did he say, "Stay here until I return?" or did he just set the man free for his own safety. If the enemy came after Elijah, his servant would be safer someplace else. Furthermore, if the servant didn't know where Elijah was, he couldn't inform against him.

Beersheba had a special meaning to the Jews because of its associations with

Abraham (Gen. 21:22, 33), Isaac (26:33), and Jacob (46:1). The "juniper tree"[2] is actually a flowering shrub ("the flowering broom tree") that flourishes in the wilderness and provides shade for flocks and herds and travelers. The branches are thin and supple like those of the willow and are used to bind bundles. (The Hebrew word for this shrub means "to bind.") The roots of the plant are used for fuel and make excellent charcoal (Ps. 120:4). As Elijah sat under its shade, he did a wise thing—he prayed, but he didn't pray a very wise prayer. "I've had enough!" he told the Lord, "so take my life."[3] Then he gave his reason: "I'm no better than my fathers." But God never asked him to be better than anybody else, but only to hear His Word and obey it.

The combination of emotional burnout, weariness, hunger, and a deep sense of failure, plus lack of faith in the Lord, had brought Elijah into deep depression. But there was also an element of pride involved, and some self-pity, for Elijah was sure that his courageous ministry on Mount Carmel would bring the nation to its knees. Perhaps he was also hoping that Ahab and Jezebel would repent and turn from Baal to Jehovah. His expectations weren't fulfilled, so he considered himself a failure. But the Lord rarely allows His servants to see all the good they have done, because we walk by faith and not by sight, and Elijah would learn that there were 7,000 people in Israel who had not bowed to Baal and worshiped him. No doubt his own ministry had influenced many of them.

2. The angel's message of grace (1 Kings 19:5-8)

When the heart is heavy and the mind and body are weary, sometimes the best remedy is sleep—just take a nap! Referring to Mark 6:31, Vance Havner used to say that if we didn't come apart and rest, we'd come apart—and Elijah was about to come apart. Nothing seems right when you're exhausted.

But while the prophet was asleep, the Lord sent an angel to care for his needs. In both Hebrew and Greek, the word translated "angel" also means "messenger," so some have concluded that this helpful visitor was another traveler whom the Lord brought to Elijah's side just at the right time. However, in verse 7, the visitor is called "the angel of the Lord," an Old Testament title for the second person of the Godhead, Jesus Christ, the Son of God. In passages like Genesis 16:10, Exodus 3:1-4 and Judges 2:1-4, the angel of the Lord speaks and acts as God would speak and act. In fact the angel of the Lord in Exodus 3:2 is called "God" and "the Lord" in the rest of the chapter. We assume that this helpful visitor was our Lord Jesus Christ.

Elijah and the Apostle Peter were both awakened by angels (Acts 12:7), Elijah to get some nourishment and Peter to walk out a free man. The angel had prepared a simple but adequate meal of fresh bread and refreshing water, and the prophet partook of both and lay down again to sleep. (Jesus prepared a breakfast of bread and fish for Peter and six other of His disciples; John 21:9, 13.) We aren't told how long the Lord permitted Elijah to sleep before He awakened him the second time and told him to eat. The Lord knew that Elijah planned to visit Mount Sinai, one of the most sacred places in all Jewish history, and Sinai was located about 250 miles from Beersheba, and he needed strength for the journey. But no matter what our destination may be, the journey is too great for us and we need God's strength to reach the goal. How gracious God was to spread a "table in the wilderness" for His discouraged servant (Ps. 78:19, and see Ps. 23:5). Elijah obeyed the messenger of God and was able to travel for forty days and nights on the nourishment from those two meals.

When you review God's ministries to Elijah as recorded in 1 Kings 18 and 19, you see a parallel to the promise in Isaiah 40:31. For three years, the prophet had been hidden by God, during which time he "waited on the Lord." When the Lord sent him to Mount Carmel, He enabled Elijah to "mount up with wings as eagles" and triumph over the prophets of Baal. After Elijah prayed and it began to rain, the Lord strengthened him to "run and not be weary" (18:46), and now He sustained him for forty days so he could "walk and not faint" (19:8). Elijah wasn't wholly living in the will of God, but he was smart enough to know that he had to wait on the Lord if he expected to have strength for the ministry and for the journey that lay before him.

God's angels are His special ambassadors, sent to minister to His people (Heb. 1:14; Ps. 91:11). An angel rescued Daniel from being devoured by lions (Dan. 6:22), and angels attended Jesus during His temptation in the wilderness (Mark 1:12-13). An angel strengthened Jesus in the Garden of Gethsemane (Luke 22:43) and encouraged Paul on board ship in the storm (Acts 27:23). The angels in heaven rejoice when a sinner is converted (Luke 15:7, 10). When we arrive in heaven and God privileges us to review our earthly walk, we will no doubt discover that strangers who helped us in different ways were actually the angels of God, sent by the Lord to assist and protect us.

3. The Creator's message of power (1 Kings 19:9-14)

It was about 200 miles from Beersheba to Sinai, a journey of perhaps ten days to two weeks. It had been three weeks at the most since Elijah fled from Jezreel, but the trip expanded to consume forty days (19:8)! If Elijah was in such a hurry to put miles between himself and Jezebel's executioners, why did he take such a long time to do it? Perhaps the Lord directed his steps (Ps. 37:23) —and his stops—so that he would spend one day for every year the Israelites had been in the wilderness after they were delivered from Egypt. It was Israel's unbelief and fear at Kadesh Barnea that led to their judgment (Num. 13–14), and it was Elijah's unbelief and fear that led to his journeying in the desert. (Our Lord also spent forty days in the wilderness when He was tempted; Matt. 4:2.) Since he was heading for Sinai, Elijah may have planned the trip so he could spend forty days in the wilderness to imitate Moses who spent forty days on the mount with the Lord (Ex. 34:28). Elijah had to deal with Baal worship and Moses had to deal with the worship of the golden calf (Ex. 32).[4]

Elijah made the cave his home and waited upon the Lord. In contemporary religious language, he was "making a retreat" in order to solve some problems and get closer to the Lord. He was so depressed that he was willing to give up his calling and even his life. When the Lord finally came and spoke to Elijah, it wasn't to rebuke him or instruct him but to ask him a question: "What are you doing here?" The prophet's reply didn't really answer the question, which explains why God asked it a second time (v. 13). Elijah only told the Lord (who already knew) that he had experienced many trials in his ministry, but he had been faithful to the Lord. But if he was a faithful servant, what was he doing hiding in a cave located hundreds of miles from his appointed place of ministry?

In this reply, Elijah reveals both pride and self-pity, and in using the pronoun "they," he exaggerates the size of the opposition. He makes it look as though every last Jew in the Northern Kingdom had turned against him and the Lord, when actually it was Jezebel who wanted to kill him. The "I only am left" refrain[5] makes it look as though he was indispensable to God's work, when actually no servant of God is indispensable. God then commanded him to stand on the mount at the entrance of the cave, but it doesn't appear that Elijah obeyed him until he heard the still, small voice (v. 13). Another possibility is that he did go out of the cave but fled back into it when God began to demonstrate His great power.

"The Lord passed by" reminds us of the experience of Moses on the mount (Ex. 33:21-22). All Elijah needed to get renewed for service was a fresh vision of the power and glory of God. First, the Lord caused a great wind to pass by, a wind so strong that it broke the rocks and tore the mountain, but no divine message came to the prophet. Then the Lord caused a great earthquake that shook the mount, but nothing from God came out of the earthquake. The Lord then brought a fire, but it, too, gave Elijah no message from the Lord. Certainly the prophet must have thought of the giving of the law as he witnessed this dramatic display of power (Ex. 19:16-18).

What was God trying to accomplish in Elijah's life by means of these awesome and frightening object lessons? For one thing, He was reminding His servant that everything in nature was obedient to Him (Ps. 148)—the wind, the foundations of the earth, the fire—and He didn't lack for a variety of tools to get His work done. If Elijah wanted to resign from his divine calling, the Lord had someone else to take his place. As it turned out, Elijah didn't resign but was given the privilege of calling his successor, Elisha, and spending time with him before being taken to heaven.

The wind, the earthquake, and the fire are all means that the Lord has used to manifest Himself to mankind. Theologians call these demonstrations "theophanies," from two Greek words (*theos* = God; *phaino* = to manifest, to appear) that together mean "the manifestation of God." The pagan nations saw these great sights and worshiped the powers of nature, but when the Jews saw them, they worshiped the God who created nature. (See Judg. 5:4-5, Ps. 18:16-18 and Hab. 3.) But these same demonstrations of the awesome presence and power of God will be seen in the last days before Jesus returns to earth to establish His kingdom. The Old Testament prophets called this period "the day of the Lord." (See Joel 2:28-3:16, Isa. 13:9-10, Matt. 24:29, and Rev. 6-16.) Perhaps the Lord was saying to Elijah, "You feel like you've failed to judge the sin in Israel, but one day I will judge it and my judgment is final and complete."

After this dramatic display of power, there was "a still, small voice," which has also been translated "a gentle whisper, a tone of a gentle blowing." When the prophet heard that voice, he stepped out of the cave and met the Lord. The mighty power and the great noise of the previous exhibitions didn't stir Elijah, but when he heard the still, small voice, he recognized the voice of God. For the second time (see Jonah 3:1), he heard the same question, "What are you doing here, Elijah?" and once again, Elijah repeated the same self-centered evasive answer.

God was saying to Elijah, "You called fire from heaven, you had the prophets of Baal slain, and you prayed down a terrific rainstorm, but now you feel like a failure.

But you must realize that I don't usually work in a manner that's loud, impressive, and dramatic. My still, small voice brings the Word to the listening ear and heart. Yes, there's a time and place for the wind, the earthquake and the fire, but most of the time, I speak to people in tones of gentle love and quiet persuasion." The Lord wasn't condemning the courageous ministry of His servant; He was only reminding Elijah that He uses many different tools to accomplish His work. God's Word comes down like the gentle shower that refreshes, cleanses, and produces life (Deut. 32:2; Isa. 55:10).

In this day of mammoth meetings, loud music, and high-pressure promotion, it's difficult for some people to understand that God rarely works by means of the dramatic and the colossal. When He wanted to start the Jewish nation, He sent a baby—Isaac; and when He wanted to deliver that nation from bondage, He sent another baby—Moses. He sent a teenager named David to kill the Philistine giant, and the boy used a sling and a stone to do it. When God wanted to save a world, He sent His Son as a weak and helpless baby; and today, God seeks to reach that world through the ministry of "earthen vessels" (2 Cor. 4:7, KJV). Dr. J. Oswald Sanders states that "the whispers from Calvary are infinitely more potent than the thunder of Sinai in bringing men to repentance."[6]

4. The Lord's message of hope (1 Kings 19:15-21)

Elijah had nothing new to say to the Lord, but the Lord had a new message of hope for His frustrated servant. The Lord had many reasons for rejecting His servant and leaving him to die in the cave, but He didn't take that approach. "He has not dealt with us according to our sins, nor punished us according to our iniquities. . . . For He knows our frame; He remembers that we are dust" (Ps. 103:10, 14, NKJV).

First, the Lord told Elijah to return to the place of duty. When we're out of the Lord's will, we have to retrace our steps and make a new beginning (Gen. 13:3; 35:1-3). The honest answer to the question "What are you doing here, Elijah?" was "Nothing! I'm having a personal pity party!" But Elijah was called to serve, and there were tasks to perform. When Joshua was brokenhearted because of Israel's defeat at Ai, he spent a day on his face before God; but God's answer was, "Get up! Why do you lie thus on your face?" (Josh. 7:10, NKJV). When Samuel mourned over the failure of Saul, God rebuked him. "How long will you mourn for Saul, seeing I have rejected him from reigning over Israel? Fill your horn with oil, and go … " (1 Sam. 16:1, NKJV); and Samuel went and anointed David to be the next king. *No matter how much or how often His servants fail Him, God is never at a loss to know what to do.* Our job is to obey His Word and get up and do it!

Elijah's first responsibility was to anoint Hazael to be king of Syria. This was a Gentile nation, but it was still the Lord who chose the leaders. "[The] Most High rules in the kingdom of men, and gives it to whomever He chooses" (Dan. 4:25, NKJV). Then he was to anoint Jehu to be king of Israel, for even though the nation had divided, Israel was still under the divine covenant and was responsible to the Lord. His third task was to anoint Elisha to be his own successor. Elijah had complained because the past generation had failed and the present generation hadn't done any better (v. 4). Now God called him to help equip the future generation by anointing two kings and a prophet.[7] This is the Old Testament version of 2 Timothy 2:2.

The people the Lord named weren't especially significant in the social structure of that day. Hazael was a servant to King Bed-hadad, Jehu was a captain of the army, and Elisha was a farmer. But by the time Elisha and Jehu completed their work, Baal worship was almost wiped out in Israel (2 Kings 10:18-31). No one generation can do everything, but each generation must see to it that people in the next generation are called and trained and that the tools are made available for them to continue the work of the Lord. God was calling Elijah to stop weeping over the past and running away from the present. It was time for him to start preparing others for the future. When God is in command, there is always hope.

But the Lord did more than send His servant out to recruit new workers. He also gave him the assurance that his work and their work would not be in vain. God would use the swords of Hazael and Jehu, and the words and works of Elisha, to accomplish His purposes in the land. Even more, He assured Elijah that his own ministry hadn't been a failure, for there were still 7,000 people in the land who were faithful to Jehovah. Indeed, the prophet was not alone, *yet God sent him to touch the lives of three individuals.* The Lord didn't command Elijah to gather all 7,000 faithful people together in a mass meeting and preach a sermon. There's certainly a place for sermons and large meetings, but we must never underestimate the importance of working with individuals. Jesus spoke to huge crowds, but He always had time for individuals and their needs.

The phrase "I have left" in verse 18 (KJV) means "I have reserved for myself." This is "the remnant according to the election of grace" that Paul wrote about in Romans 11:1-6. No matter how wicked the world scene may appear, God always has a remnant that is faithful to Him. Sometimes that remnant is small, but God is always great and accomplishes His purposes.

Without delay, Elijah retraced his steps and returned to the place of duty. It was 150 miles from Sinai to Abel Meholah (v. 16) where he would find Elisha plowing a field. Elisha's name means "God has salvation." The fact that Elisha was using twelve yoke of oxen—twenty-four expensive animals—indicates that his family was probably better off financially than most Israelites.[8] Elijah didn't say a word to the young man but merely cast his mantle (outer garment) over him to indicate that the Lord had called him to serve the prophet and then be his successor. Elisha and his family were part of that "remnant of grace" that God had set apart for Himself. No matter how bleak the days may seem, God has His people and knows when to call them.

Elisha's conduct seems to contradict what Jesus said in Luke 9:57-62, but this is not so. Elisha was wholehearted in his obedience to follow after Elijah, while the men in the Gospel record had hesitations and reservations, and Jesus knew it. Elisha proved his commitment by killing two of the oxen and using the wooden farm implements as fuel to cook them for a farewell feast. In contemporary terms, he was "burning his bridges behind him." He had no intention of taking his hand off the plow and then going back to it. Elijah's reply means, "What have *I* done? I didn't call you, the Lord did. Am I stopping you? Do as the Lord wants you to do." The *New Living Translation* reads, "Go on back! But consider what I have done to you." How Elisha's family and friends viewed this sudden change of vocation isn't shared with us, but there's no indication they were opposed to

Elisha's decision.

As you review the chapter, you can see the mistakes that Elijah made and how the Lord overruled them and accomplished His will. Elijah walked by sight and not by faith, yet the Lord sustained him. He looked at himself and his failures instead of at God's greatness and power. He was more concerned about doing more than his ancestors had done in the past instead of calling and preparing new servants for the future. He isolated himself from God's people and thereby lost the strength and encouragement of their fellowship and prayers. But let's not be too hard on Elijah, for he did have a sensitive ear to the still, small voice of the Lord, and he did obey what God told him to do. The Lord rebuked him gently and brought him out of his cave and back into active service. Let's keep these things in mind and recall them the next time we're under our juniper tree or in our cave!

Finally, let's be among those who look to the future and seek to enlist others to serve the Lord. To glamorize or criticize the past accomplishes little; what's important is that we do our job in the present and equip others to continue it after we're gone. God buried His workers, but His work goes right on.

CHAPTER TWELVE
AHAB, THE SLAVE OF SIN
1 Kings 20:1–22:53

In his novel *Moby Dick,* Herman Melville gave the name Ahab to the deranged captain of the whaling vessel *Pequod.* (Melville also included a "prophet" named Elijah.) The Ahab in the Bible is a weak man who destroyed himself and his family because he allowed his evil wife, Jezebel, to turn him into a monster. The name Jezebel is familiar to people today and has even made it into the dictionary: "Jezebel—an evil, shameless woman." To call a woman "a Jezebel" is to put her on the lowest level of society (see Rev. 2:20-23). The prophet Elijah described the man accurately when he told Ahab, "I have found you, because you have sold yourself to do evil in the sight of the Lord" (1 Kings 21:20, NKJV).

These chapters describe four events in Ahab's life: three battles with the Syrians (Aram) and a land-grab scam that involved an illegal trial and several murders. Because he wasn't rightly related to the Lord and His Word, Ahab was enslaved to sin, but "the wages of sin is death" (Rom. 6:23), and Ahab received his wages with dividends. We will look at the four events and see Ahab's varied responses.

1. Believing God's promise (1 Kings 20:1-30)

This is the first of two occasions when wicked King Ahab showed a glimmer of spiritual understanding. Israel was just coming out three years of famine when Ben-hadad, King of Syria, decided to attack and take advantage of their plight. King David had defeated these northern nations (called Syria in the older translations, Aram in the newer ones), but these nations had gradually regained their independence. Another factor in Ben-hadad's attack was the growing strength of Assyria in the north. Ben-hadad wanted to control the trade routes through Israel because he had lost the northern routes to Assyria, and he also wanted to be sure that Israel would provide men and weapons in case of an

Assyrian invasion.

The siege (20:1-12). The thirty-two "kings" who allied with Ben-hadad were the rulers of northern city-states whose safety and prosperity depended a good deal on the strength of Syria. We aren't told how long the siege of Samaria lasted, but Syria ultimately brought Ahab to the place of submission. First, Ben-hadad demanded Ahab's wealth and family, and Ahab agreed. Ben-hadad planned to hold the family hostage just to make sure Ahab didn't back out of his agreement. Instead of Ahab calling for Elijah or another prophet and seeking the help of the Lord, he quickly capitulated. (Contrast this decision with Saul's decision in 1 Samuel 11.) Ben-hadad wasn't satisfied with this arrangement and wanted more, but his covetousness led to his defeat. In addition to taking the king's wealth and the royal family, Ben-hadad wanted to send officers to search all the royal buildings and take whatever they wanted! Agreeing with this request was much too humiliating for proud Ahab, so he and his advisers refused to accept it.

When he received Ahab's message, Ben-hadad was probably drunk and feeling very brave, because he made an unwise decision. He could have gotten most of what he wanted without sacrificing a single soldier, but now he made an oath to grind Samaria to powder, and he had to live up to his boast. To his credit, Ahab replied with a familiar proverb that could have applied to him as much as to Ben-hadad. It's the equivalent of, "Don't count your chickens before they hatch."

The promise (20:13-21). In opposing Ben-hadad, Ahab had nothing to stand on, but God in His grace sent him a message of hope: the Lord would give Ahab the victory. The Lord wasn't doing this because Ahab deserved it but because He wanted to honor His own name before the wavering king of Israel and his people. As He did on Mount Carmel, so Jehovah would do on the battlefield: He would demonstrate that He alone is God (18:36-37). We commend Ahab for receiving the promise and asking for further instructions. Perhaps Jezebel wasn't home that day to influence him the wrong way.

Following the example of Solomon (1 Kings 4:7ff), Ahab's father, Omri, had divided the kingdom of Israel into a number of political districts, each in the charge of a "provincial leader" who was also an army officer. The Lord selected these leaders to lead the attack against Syria, and Ahab was to lead the small army of 7,000 men. They went out at noon, knowing that Ben-hadad and his officers would be eating and drinking and be in no condition to fight a battle. Even when Ben-hadad's scouts reported that a company of men was approaching the Syrian camp, the Syrian king wasn't afraid but told the guard to take them alive. The military strategy for capturing prisoners would be different from that for destroying an invading army, so Ahab's men caught the Syrian guards by surprise and proceeded to wipe out the Syrian army. Instead of measuring the dust of Samaria as he threatened (v. 10), Ben-hadad jumped on his horse and escaped with his life. But because Ahab believed God's Word and acted upon it, God gave him a great victory.

The challenge (20:22-30). Another anonymous prophet spoke to Ahab and cautioned him to strengthen his forces and be prepared for another invasion. While Ahab was listening to God's message, Ben-hadad was listening to his officers explain Syria's great defeat. They were healing their king's wounded pride while at the same time protecting their own lives. They explained that their great army wasn't at fault; the defeat was the fault of the terrain. The gods of the Syrians were "gods of the plains," while Israel's God was a "god of the hills." Change the location and Syria will have the victory.

We now have a different scenario, because not only was the enemy challenging God's people, *he was challenging God Himself!* This was the Mount Carmel contest all over again, and the Lord wouldn't let it go unchallenged. Jehovah is the Lord of all the earth! He sent another man of God to assure Ahab of victory, but only because He wanted Ahab, the army of Israel, and the men of Syria to know that Jehovah alone is God. The Lord gave Israel victory on the battlefield, and when the enemy fled into the city of Aphek, God sent an earthquake and killed 27,000 Syrian soldiers.[1] By the grace of God, Ahab won a second great victory!

2. Disobeying God's command (1 Kings 20:31-43)

When God sent King Saul to fight the Amalekites, He made it clear that He wanted the Israelites to completely destroy them (1 Sam. 15). Saul disobeyed the Lord and as a result lost his kingdom. The Lord must have given a similar command to King Ahab (v. 42), but he, too, disobeyed. Ahab won the battle but lost the victory. What the enemy couldn't accomplish with their weapons, they accomplished with their deception. If Satan can't succeed as the lion who devours (1 Peter 5:8), he will come as a serpent who deceives (2 Cor. 11:3). Even Joshua fell into a similar trap (Josh. 9).

Ben-hadad's officers were clever men who knew it was worth the risk to appeal to Ahab's pride. God had given the victory, but Ahab would take the credit and claim the spoils. In their dress and their attitude, the officers pretended to show humble submission to Ahab as he waited in his chariot (v. 33). Ahab certainly enjoyed the "honor" he was receiving after the great victory, but not once did he give the glory to the Lord. To hear that Ben-hadad was his servant made his heart glad, and he was more than willing to spare the man's life. Later, Hazael would kill Ben-hadad and become the king (2 Kings 8).

Ben-hadad immediately entered into a treaty with Ahab and gave back to Israel the cities his father had taken (1 Kings 15:20). He also gave Ahab permission to sell Israel's produce and wares in the market at Damascus, which amounted to a trade agreement. That the king of Israel should make such a treaty with the enemy is remarkable, but Ahab had no convictions (except those of his wife) and always took the easy way out of any situation. Furthermore, he needed the support of Aram in case the Assyrians should decide to move south. This treaty lasted three years (22:1).

The Lord couldn't allow Ahab to disobey and get away with it, so He instructed one of the sons of the prophets to confront the king about his sin. The "sons of the prophets" were young men who had special prophetic gifts and met in groups to study with elder prophets like Samuel (1 Sam. 7:17; 28:3), Elijah, and Elisha (2 Kings 2:3-7, 16; 4:38, 40). Knowing that he would have to catch Ahab by surprise to get his attention, the man wisely set up an "action sermon" that would arouse the king's interest.[2] The young man told a fellow student about God's orders and asked him to strike him with a weapon, but the man refused. We can understand a friend not wanting to injure a friend, but like Ahab, the young prophet was disobeying God, and it cost him his life. This certainly put the fear of God into the other students, because the next one the young man approached was only too willing to comply. Disguised as a wounded soldier, he was ready to deliver his message.[3]

In those days, a person could approach the king to help decide matters that needed legal clarification; and when Ahab saw this "injured soldier" sitting by the side of the road, his curiosity was aroused. Now we have a replay of Nathan's approach to David after David committed adultery with Bathsheba (2 Sam. 12), for just as David determined his own sentence, so Ahab announced his own guilt! Hearing that the "soldier" had lost an important prisoner of war and would have to forfeit his life or pay an enormous fine (75 pounds of silver), the king replied, "So shall your judgment be; you yourself have decided it" (v. 40, NASB). The king could have granted the man a pardon and saved his life, but he preferred to let him die. *But in so doing, Ahab was declaring his own guilt and passing sentence on himself!*

How did Ahab recognize that the young man was one of the sons of the prophets? It's not likely that Ahab was that close to Elijah's followers to know them personally. When the bandage was removed, did it reveal some identifying mark? Had Ahab seen the man on Mount Carmel? We have no way of knowing, but the sight must have shocked the king. The man that Ahab judged now became Ahab's judge and announced that one day the Syrians would slay Ahab. But instead of repenting and seeking the Lord's forgiveness, Ahab went home and pouted like a child (v. 43; see 21:4).

3. Breaking God's laws (1 Kings 21:1-16)

Ben-hadad was the man Ahab should have killed, but he set him free; and Naboth was the man Ahab should have protected, but Ahab killed him! When you sell yourself to do evil, you call evil good and good evil, light darkness and darkness light (Isa. 5:20). The infamous episode of Naboth's vineyard reveals the lawlessness of King Ahab and his evil wife, Jezebel. Consider the sins they committed and consequently the commandments of God that they disdained and disobeyed.

Idolatry. The first two commandments in the Decalogue declare that the Lord is the only true God and that true worshipers do not worship and serve other gods, whether things in God's creation or things they make themselves (Ex. 20:1-6). "The essence of idolatry is the entertainment of thoughts about God that are unworthy of Him," wrote A. W. Tozer.[4] Jezebel brought Baal worship into Israel and Ahab permitted it to spread throughout the land. When you turn away from truth, it's evidence that you're believing lies, then you start loving lies, and before long, you're controlled by lies.

Covetousness (vv. 1-4). Ahab and Jezebel had a summer palace at Jezreel, but the king couldn't enjoy it fully without a vegetable garden. Powerful people acquire one thing after another, but in all their acquiring, there's never any real satisfaction. "A man is rich in proportion to the number of things he can afford to let alone," wrote Henry David Thoreau in chapter two of *Walden.* Then he added later in the book, "Superfluous wealth can buy superfluities only. Money is not required to buy one necessity of the soul."

The king wanted Naboth's vineyard because he coveted a garden convenient to the palace.

"Thou shalt not covet" is the last of the Ten Commandments (Ex. 20:17) but perhaps it's the most difficult one to obey. Even more, a covetous heart often leads us to disobey all the other commandments of God. The first nine Commandments focus on forbidden outward conduct—making and worshiping idols, stealing, murdering, and so on—but this commandment deals primarily with the hidden desires of the heart. It was the Tenth Commandment that helped Saul of Tarsus, the Pharisee, realize what a sinner he really was (Rom. 7:7-25); and it was this commandment that the wealthy young ruler refused to acknowledge when he looked into the mirror of the law (Matt. 19:14-30).

Ahab masked his covetousness by first offering to buy the vineyard or trade it for another piece of property. It was a reasonable offer, but Naboth was more concerned about obeying God's Word than pleasing the king or even making money. Naboth knew that the land belonged to the Lord and that He loaned it to the people of Israel to enjoy as long as they obeyed His covenant. All property had to be kept in the family (Lev. 25:23-28), which meant that Naboth was forbidden to sell his land to the king. Displaying his usual childishness, Ahab went home, went to bed, and pouted.

False witness (vv. 5-10). "Thou shalt not bear false witness against thy neighbor" is the ninth commandment and emphasizes the importance of speaking the truth, whether in court or over the back fence. Truth is the cement that holds society together, and when truth is gone, everything starts to fall apart (Isa. 59:14). Jezebel was a resolute woman who never allowed the truth to stand in the way of what she wanted, so she fabricated an official lie, on official stationery, sealed with the official seal. But no amount of royal adornment could change the fact that Ahab and Jezebel were breaking God's law.

What right did Jezebel have to write Naboth's death warrant? Her husband was king! Since she came from Phoenicia, she had the Gentile view of kingship, which included being important, getting what you want, and using your authority to take care of yourself. Samuel warned about this kind of monarch (1 Sam. 8:14), and Jesus cautioned His disciples not to follow that philosophy of governing but to serve the people in love (Matt. 20:20-28). A true leader uses his authority to build the people, while a dictator uses the people to build his authority, and people are expendable. Jezebel even threw in some religion and told the local authorities to proclaim a fast. If you can sugarcoat your scheme with something religious, the people will quickly accept it. But no matter how legal and spiritual that royal edict may have looked, in the sight of God it was only a lie—and God judges liars. Everything that God hates, Ahab and Jezebel did (Prov. 6:16-19).

Murder (vv. 11-13). The procedure Jezebel outlined was in agreement with the law (Deut. 17:6-7; 19:15; Num. 35:30), but the accusation was false, the witnesses were liars, and the judges had been bought off by royal intimidation. In every town there were "men of Belial—worthless fellows" who would do anything for money or just to become important. Nobody but Ahab and possibly Jezebel heard Naboth's refusal to sell, and there was nothing in his words that could be interpreted as blasphemy. To curse God was a capital crime (Lev. 24:13-16), and cursing the king was dangerous because he was God's appointed ruler (Ex. 22:28; Acts 23:5).[5]

Stealing (vv. 14-16). The weak rulers in Naboth's city followed Jezebel's orders, conducted their illegal trial, took Naboth and his sons (2 Kings 9:26) outside the city, and stoned them. Nobody in the family was alive who could inherit the land, so Ahab felt he was free to take it. The officers notified Jezebel, not Ahab, of the execution, so it's obvious who had the power in the royal family. But the land didn't belong to Ahab, and the law says, "Thou shalt not steal" (Ex. 20:15, KJV). The vineyard hadn't even belonged to Naboth—it belonged to the Lord. Ahab was stealing property from God!

If ever two people were guilty of blaspheming God and breaking His laws, it was Ahab and Jezebel, and judgment was about to fall.

4. Hearing God's sentence (1 Kings 21:16-29)

"Surely the Lord does nothing, unless He reveals His secret to His servants the prophets" (Amos 3:7, NKJV). We have heard nothing from or about Elijah since he called Elisha to be his successor, but now God brings His servant into center stage to confront the king. As He always does when he gives an assignment, He told Elijah just what to say to the evil king. Ahab had shed innocent blood and his guilty blood would be licked up by the dogs. What a way for the king of Israel to end his reign!

Previously, Ahab called Elijah "the troubler of Israel" (18:17), but now he makes it more personal and calls the prophet "my enemy." Actually, by fighting against the Lord, Ahab was his own enemy and brought upon himself the sentence that Elijah pronounced. Ahab would die dishonorably and the dogs would lick his blood. Jezebel would die and be eaten by the dogs. All of their posterity would eventually be eradicated from the land. They had enjoyed their years of sinful pleasure and selfish pursuits, but it would all end in judgment.

Instead of going home to pout, Ahab actually repented! What his wife thought about his actions isn't recorded, but the Lord who sees the heart accepted his humiliation and told it to His servant. The Lord didn't cancel the announced judgments but postponed them until the reign of Ahab's son Joram. See 2 Kings 9:14-37. Ahab was slain on the battlefield and the dogs licked his blood at the pool of Samaria (22:37-38). Because of the postponement of the judgment, the dogs licked his son Joram's blood on Naboth's property, just as Elijah predicted (2 Kings 9:14-37). Later events proved that Ahab's repentance was short-lived, but the Lord at least gave him another opportunity to turn from sin and obey the Word. How much more evidence did Ahab need? But the influence of his wife couldn't easily be broken, for when Ahab married her, he sold himself into sin.

5. Receiving God's judgment (1 Kings 22:1-53; 2 Chron. 18)

At this point we are introduced to godly Jehoshaphat, king of Judah. A summary of his reign is found in 22:41-50 and even more fully in 2 Chronicles 17–20. He followed in the way of David and sought to please the Lord (17:1-6). He sent teaching priests throughout the land to explain God's law to the people (17:7-9) and assigned the other priests to serve as faithful judges to whom the people could bring their disputes. God gave Judah peace, and Jehoshaphat took advantage of this opportunity to fortify the land (17:10-19).

He was a good king and a godly leader, but he got involved in three costly compromises. The first was the "bride compromise" when he married his son to a daughter of Ahab and Jezebel (2 Chron. 18:1; 21:4-7; 1 Kings 22:44; 2 Kings 8:16-19). This led to the "battle compromise," when

Jehoshaphat got entangled in affairs of his son's father-in-law when Syria attacked Israel (18:2–19:3). Ahab's evil influence affected the reign of Jehoshaphat's grandson Ahaziah (2 Chron. 22:1-9), and the "battle compromise" almost cost Jehoshaphat his life (1 Kings 22:32-33). The third compromise was the "boat compromise," when Jehoshaphat foolishly joined forces with Ahab's son Ahaziah (1 Kings 22:48-49; 2 Chron. 20:31-37) and tried to get rich by importing foreign goods. The Lord wrecked his fleet and rebuked him for his sinful alliance.

One of Jehoshaphat's great achievements was the defeat of the Moabites, Ammonites, and Edomites, a great force that attacked Judah (2 Chron. 20:10). The king humbled himself before the Lord, called for a nationwide fast, and encouraged the people to seek the face of the Lord. At a mass meeting in Jerusalem, Jehoshaphat prayed for God's guidance and help, reminding the Lord of His covenant with Abraham (v. 7) and God's acceptance of Solomon's prayer when he dedicated the temple (vv. 8-9; 6:12–7:22). If the people would look toward the temple and pray, God promised He would hear and answer. The Lord could see the great army approaching, and the king asked Him to judge them. (The name "Jehoshaphat" means "whom God judges," that is, "God pleads his cause.")

The prayer was followed by a declaration of the Word from Jehaziel (20:14-17), assuring the king and his people that the Lord would indeed intervene and give Judah victory. "The battle is not yours, but God's" (v. 15). The king and the people believed the Lord's promise and praised Him even before the battle started. The next day, Jehoshaphat sent the army out with the singers at the very front! God caused the three enemy armies to fight among themselves and destroy themselves, leaving the spoils of war for the army of Judah. The army had praised God before the battle and at the very time of the battle, and now they praised him at the temple after the battle. Faith, prayer, and praise are great weapons!

In chapter 22, the writer of 1 Kings focused primarily on the "battle compromise."

Ahab compromises God's king (vv. 1-6). When after three years, Ben-hadad hadn't kept his agreement to give Israel back the cities his father took (21:34), Ahab decided it was time to fight Syria and take them back. Jehoshaphat's son was married to Ahab's daughter, so Jehoshaphat had to be friendly toward Ahab and help him fight his battles. He was disobeying the Lord when he took this step (2 Chron. 19:1-3), but one compromise often leads to another. As the descendant of David, Jehoshaphat should have kept his distance from Ahab and never allowed the Davidic line to mingle with that of Ahab. All the court chaplains,[6] paid to agree with the king, assured Ahab that he would win the battle, but Jehoshaphat was wise enough to ask Ahab for some Word from the Lord.

Yes, there was a prophet of the Lord in Israel, and he was where true prophets are often found—in prison. Ahab sent for his enemy Micaiah, and while the two kings were waiting, the prophets put on quite a demonstration. Zedekiah, who seemed to be their leader, made some iron horns to illustrate how Israel would push back and gore the Syrians and win the battle. All the other prophets agreed and shouted their approval. But it takes more than enthusiasm to win a war, especially when God has decreed otherwise.

Ahab ignores God's warning (vv. 7-28). Micaiah was under a great deal of pressure to agree with the false prophets and assure Ahab he would defeat Syria. Not only was Micaiah outnumbered four hundred to one, but the officer who brought him to the two kings warned him to agree with the majority. Often in Scripture, it's the *minority* that's in the will of God, and Micaiah was determined to be faithful, not popular. The sight of the two kings on their thrones, dressed in their royal robes, must have been impressive, but it didn't sway Micaiah. His words in verse 13 were spoken in sarcasm and Ahab knew it, but Ahab's reply wasn't honest. He was just trying to impress Jehoshaphat and make him think he really did want to know and do God's will.

The Lord had given Micaiah two visions, both of which announced judgment to King Ahab. In the first, he saw Israel wandering hopelessly, like sheep without a shepherd, obviously a description of a nation without a leader (Num. 27:15-22). Jesus used this image to depict the Jewish people without spiritual direction (Matt. 9:36). Ahab got the message: he would be killed in the battle.

The second vision explained how this would be accomplished: a lying spirit would give Ahab false confidence so he would enter the battle. That the God of truth should allow a lying spirit to accomplish His work is a puzzle to some people, but it's no different from God permitting Satan to attack Job (Job 1–2) or to motivate Judas to betray Jesus (John 13:21-30). God deals with people on the basis of their character. "With the pure You will show Yourself pure; and with the devious [crooked, NIV] You will show Yourself shrewd" (Ps. 18:26, NKJV). Ahab was fighting against God, and like any good boxer or wrestler, the Lord anticipated his moves and countered with the right response. Ahab was a consummate liar and the Lord dealt with him according to his character.

God didn't lie to Ahab; quite the contrary, through the lips of Micaiah He told the truth and gave Ahab fair warning of what lay ahead. The fact that God warned Ahab *before the battle* clears the Lord of the charge of being guilty of his death. The reaction of Zedekiah proves that the four hundred false prophets didn't believe Micaiah either. A much greater mystery is why a godly man like King Jehoshaphat went into the battle at all and risked his life. Ahab ordered the true prophet to be taken back to prison and given bread and water, as if punishing the prophet would change his message. The test of a true prophet was the actual fulfillment of his words (Deut. 18:17-22; Num. 16:29), and Micaiah knew this. That's why his parting message to Ahab was, "If you ever return in peace, the Lord has not spoken by me" (v. 28, NKJV).

Ahab meets his death (vv. 29-40, 51-53). How could King Jehoshaphat not discern what Ahab was doing to him? If Ahab had put a target on Jehoshaphat's back, he would not have made it easier for the enemy to kill him! If Jehoshaphat had died, then his son would have taken the throne, and Ahab's daughter would have been the Jezebel of Judah! If Ahab then united the two thrones and blended the Davidic line with his own line, what would have happened to the Davidic covenant and the Messianic line? But God is sovereign in all things and protected Jehoshaphat, while at the same time allowing a random arrow to hit an opening in Ahab's armor and kill him. Ahab was disguised and yet was killed, while Jehoshaphat was in his royal robes and never touched. Ahab had set the king of Syria free when he should have destroyed him, and now the Syrians killed Ahab.

Micaiah's prophecy was fulfilled and so were the prophecies of Elijah (20:42; 21:19-21).

Ahab's son Ahaziah took the throne and continued the evil ways of his father and mother (vv. 51-53). He reigned only two years, and his brother Joram (or Jehoram) succeeded him. The prophecy about the dogs licking blood on Naboth's property was actually fulfilled in the death of Joram (21:29; 2 Kings 9:25-26).

CHAPTER THIRTEEN
REFLECTIONS ON RESPONSIBILITY
Reviewing 1 Kings

Newspaper columnist Abigail Van Buren wrote, "If you want your children to keep their feet on the ground, put some responsibility on their shoulders." Responsibility isn't a curse; it's a blessing. Adam and Eve had work to do in paradise before sin came into the world, and the perfect Son of God worked as a carpenter before He began His public ministry. Booker T. Washington said, "Few things help an individual more than to place responsibility upon him, and to let him know that you trust him."

After killing his brother Abel and lying about it, Cain asked, "Am I my brother's keeper?" He was dodging both responsibility and accountability, a practice that's becoming very popular today. A bumper sticker announces, "The Devil made me do it" and people smile when they read it. When our first parents sinned, they ran and hid from God, and when they were confronted with their sin, they blamed others. Finally, they had to take the responsibility for what they had done, and with responsibility came hope and promise. Irresponsible people may run away, make excuses, cover up, or blame others, but if they do, they will never know the meaning of healthy character, integrity, a clear conscience, and the joy of walking with God.

First Kings begins with the death of King David and ends with the death of King Ahab, and between those two events many other people either succeeded or failed, lived or died, because of decisions that were either responsible or irresponsible. The world of David and Ahab was nothing like our world today, but human nature hasn't changed and the basic principles of life are quite stable. We ought to be able to reflect on what we've learned from 1 Kings and draw some practical conclusions for life today.

1. David: One person can make a difference.

The more you ponder the life of David, warts and all, the more you see his greatness. He was born with leadership ability, courage, and practical common sense, and the Holy Spirit gave him sensitivity to God's will and a special power that set him apart as God's man. His predecessor, King Saul, almost destroyed the nation, but David accepted the difficult responsibility of putting it back together again and building it into a mighty kingdom. David defeated Israel's enemies; collected great treasures for building the temple; organized the army, the government, and the ministry at the sanctuary; wrote songs for the Levites to sing; and even invented musical instruments for them to play. What a man!

God's covenant with David assured Israel of a king forever and was ultimately fulfilled in the coming of Jesus Christ into the world. It was because of His promise to David that the Lord kept one of his descendants on the throne during the years of Judah's decline. Throughout the history of the monarchy, God measured every king against David, and though some of them were exceptional, none of them quite reached his level.

One person can make a difference, if that person is willing to accept responsibility and walk with God. Anybody can run with the herd, but when God finds individuals who are willing to stand alone if necessary, He goes to work and builds leaders. The words of Dr. Lee Roberson have echoed in my mind for many years: "Everything rises or falls with leadership."

2. Solomon: Success often leads to failure.

It's good to have the things that money can buy, provided you don't lose the things that money can't buy. Solomon was a brilliant man who could discuss everything from how to grow herbs to how to build fortresses, yet he made a mess out of his life and paved the way for the division of the kingdom. During the golden age of Solomon, the nations marveled at his wisdom and envied his wealth (and perhaps his many wives), but Solomon himself turned out to be a hollow man who forsook the Lord who had so richly blessed him. He was perhaps the wisest fool in Bible history.

When you read between the lines, you find that his living in luxury, surrounded by glamour and pleasure, introduced into Israel the viruses that eventually ate the spiritual heart out of the nation. Yes, we need education, but we also need to ask God for the wisdom to use it as we should. We also need money for food, clothing, and shelter—"For your heavenly Father knows that you need all these things," said Jesus (Matt. 6:32)—but to acquire money just for money's sake is to surrender to covetousness and become so concerned about prices that we ignore values.

Solomon was irresponsible in many areas of life, and his son Rehoboam inherited some of that mindset and ended up dividing the nation. God made a leader out of David by sending him out to care for sheep; challenging him with a lion, a bear, and a giant; forcing him to run for his life for ten years; and making him wait for the promised throne. Solomon grew up pampered and protected; he could have used a few years' service in the wilderness. By accumulating wives, horses, and wealth, he brought peace to the nation, but it was a peace purchased at the price of obedience to the law of God.

There's no virtue in ignorance and poverty, but there's no magic in knowledge and wealth. The government leaders tell us, "If people were just smarter and richer, we'd solve society's problems." People do become smarter and richer, and they create a whole new set of problems. Billy Sunday once said, "When I was a kid, we'd go down to the railroad yard and steal things from the freight cars. Now a fellow goes to university and learns how to steal the whole railroad!" People are so smart they can sit at a computer keyboard and rob a bank thousands of miles away. Human nature doesn't change.

3. National strength and national character begin in the home.

If David had displayed in his home the kind of discipline and strength he showed on the battlefield, Jewish history might have been different. Part of the problem lay with his having too many wives, plus the fact that it isn't always easy for the children of celebrities to grow up normally. But whatever the causes, some of

David's children turned out really bad, and what they were and what they did affected the nation.

According to Genesis 3, Satan came as a liar and his first target was human marriage. He's been attacking it ever since. According to Genesis 4, he came as a murderer and his second target was the human family. He encouraged Cain to be envious and angry so that Cain would kill Abel. It's been said that in the modern home, the stereo and the TV set are better adjusted than the members of the family. People complain because children can't pray in school, but few parents encourage them to pray at home.

Home is a school for character, where we learn to love, listen, obey, and assist. In short, it's where we learn to be responsible.

4. Rehoboam: Generations must work together.

Whether it's in the home, in the chambers of government, or in the sanctuary of the local church, generations must work together and learn from each other. Solomon's son Rehoboam foolishly turned a deaf ear to the experience of the mature and chose to win only the applause of his peers, and as a result he lost most of his kingdom. By putting labels on different generations and letting them do their own thing—"Well, that's just the way they are!"—we've weakened social solidarity, divided the family, cut whole generations off from the heritage of the past, and convinced young people that they really can make it alone.

God has decreed that parents shall be older than their children. He has also commanded parents to love their children, teach them how to listen and obey, protect them from evil, and be good examples before them. But parents can also learn from their children. It's a two-way street. I cultivate the friendship of young people, because I need them and they need me. I help them catch up on the past and they help me catch up on the present. I'm not always right and they're not always wrong. The older generation hands the next generation a valuable heritage from the past, but if we don't understand the world they're living in and the way they feel about it, we can't help them use that heritage for their good and the good of society.

Paul saw the local church as a family in God (Titus 2:1-8), with one generation ministering to another. Younger people treat the older folks as they would their parents or grandparents, and older saints treat the younger ones as they would their own children. When a family gets together, they don't always agree on everything, but they try to help each other during the various stages of life. That's the way it should be in the home, the church, and the nation.

5. Jeroboam: wasted opportunity

God offered Jeroboam a priceless opportunity to build the kingdom of Israel for the glory of God, but he wasted it. Instead of looking back to David and imitating his leadership, and looking up to the Lord for help, Jeroboam let his ego take over and did things his own way. He invented his own religion to make it easy for the people to disobey the Lord. He abandoned the divine authority of God's Word and appointed priests who were unspiritual and unqualified. God sent him signs and messages, but he refused to submit. "The sins of Jeroboam" are mentioned over twenty times in Scripture.

The division of the Jewish nation was a tragedy, but if both Rehoboam and Jeroboam had listened to the Lord, they could have rescued both kingdoms from ruin. Once opportunity is lost, it won't be repeated. Each opportunity is a test of the vision and values of the people in charge. The Lord gave Jeroboam a sure promise (11:29-40), but the king wouldn't take it seriously and trust God to fulfill it. Opportunity doesn't shout, it whispers, and our ears must be attentive. Opportunity knocks, it doesn't kick down the door, and we had better be alert to open the door. The American poet John Greenleaf Whittier wrote

> For of all sad words of tongue or pen,
> The saddest are these: "It might have been!"

To ignore God-given opportunity is to waste the past, jeopardize the future, and frustrate the present.

6. Baal: The insidious cancer of idolatry

Jeroboam put up his golden calves and Jezebel brought in Baal worship, and before long, the people of the Northern Kingdom had turned from Jehovah to the worship of dumb idols. An idol is not only an insult to God but it's an insult to man, for men and women were created in the image of God to reflect the glory of the true and living God. To create a god in your own image and worship it is a dangerous thing, for we become like the gods we worship (Ps. 115:8).

If you want to be religious and still enjoy the pleasures of sin, then the worship of idols is the road to take. But its freedom leads to bondage and its pleasures eventually lead to pain and death. Whether the idol we worship is money, prestige, authority, sex, entertainment, or our own self-righteous satisfaction, it can never equal what we receive when we worship the true and living God through His Son, Jesus Christ.

7. Elijah: Reformation and renewal

A nation, a church, a family, or an individual is never so far gone that the Lord can't gave a new beginning. Elijah was Ahab's enemy because Ahab was following his own agenda and not the Lord's. Elijah was God's servant and risked his life to bring the nation back to the God of Abraham, Isaac, and Jacob. True reformation should lead to spiritual renewal. It isn't enough to tear down the pagan altars and remove the priests of Baal. We must rebuild the Lord's altar and ask God for new fire from heaven to consume the sacrifices.

Reformation means getting rid of the accretions of the new things to get back to the foundations of the old things. When Israel abandoned her covenant with Jehovah, she ceased to be the people of God and became like the other nations. The beautiful temple that once housed the glory of God became a pile of ruins that bore witness to the sins of an ungrateful and unbelieving people. God's chosen people forgot their glorious past and deliberately manufactured a future that brought shame and ruin.

The key issue in any nation's faith has always been the struggle between the true prophets and the false prophets, both of whom claim to speak in the name of the Lord. The false prophets tell us what we want to hear while the true prophets tell us what we need to hear. The false prophets don't make a deep and thorough diagnosis of the nation's sicknesses; they barely scratch the surface. True prophets cut deep and expose the hidden cancers; like John the Baptist, they apply the ax to the root of the trees (Matt. 3:10) and don't waste their time plucking off dead leaves from the dying branches.

"Where is the Lord God of Elijah?" asked Elisha as he began his prophetic ministry (2 Kings 2:14, NKJV). We know the answer: "The Lord is in his holy temple" (Hab. 2:20). But the real question isn't "Where is the Lord God of Elijah?" but "Where are the Elijahs?" God is still seeking for men and women whose hearts are right with Him, people He can use to recover the past, renew the present, and rescue the future.

8. Ahab and Jezebel: the abuse of power

Some years ago I began to read a biography of Adolph Hitler, but the longer I read it, the more depressed I became, until finally I stopped reading the book. I never did finish it. I respond the same way to Ahab and Jezebel. He was spineless and she was heartless and together they were the embodiment of wickedness. If they were living today, Hollywood would make a feature movie about them and they'd be featured in a miniseries on television. Cameras in hand, the press would follow their every move and report every activity in detail. It would make no difference that Ahab and Jezebel were godless unbelievers who lacked character and high ideals. The public feeds its sick imagination on that kind of garbage and keeps asking for more. Thanks to fallen human nature, there's always more.

Page through a review of the twentieth century and marvel at how the nations of the world ever survived such a concerted abuse of power. Much of it was brutal, leading to the annihilation of millions of innocent people. Some of it was done with finesse, the abusers wearing their white gloves, but it still led to destruction. Abusers who didn't use knives, guns, and ovens, used words, and this includes professed Christians in the church. The world looked on and said, "Behold, how they hate one another!" I've been in ministry for over fifty years, and in the past ten years, I've heard more church horror stories than I did in the previous forty years.

Whether it's administrative power, financial power, physical and mental power, or the ultimate power of life and death, the power we have comes from God and must be used according to His will. King and queens, emperors and prime ministers, dictators and generals, parents and teachers, the FBI and the KGB—all of them are accountable to the Lord and will one day answer to Him.

King Jesus is the greatest example of the right use of authority. He is a Servant who leads and a Leader who serves, and He does it because He loves us.

9. God is sovereign!

Since the days of Job, people have been trying to make sense out of what goes on in this world, and nobody has yet discovered the key. We have a hard enough time predicting the weather let alone fully understanding the dynamics of history or even the personal situations in our own lives. A famous movie star said, "Life is like a B-picture script. It is that corny. If I had my life story offered to me to film, I'd turn it down."[1] American playwright Eugene O'Neill had a character in *Strange Interlude* say, "Our lives are merely strange, dark interludes in the electric display of God the Father." That's not very encouraging.

Knowing that our God is sovereign in all things gives us the courage and faith we need to live and serve in this fallen world. "The Lord brings the counsel of the nations to nothing; He makes the plans of the peoples of no effect. The counsel of the Lord stands forever, the plans of His heart to all generations" (Ps. 33:10-11, NKJV). He has given us the right to make choices and decisions, and He will not force His will upon us; but if He isn't allowed to rule, He will overrule. In spite of our resistance and rebellion, His will shall be done "on earth as it is in heaven." He runs the universe by His wise decrees and doesn't call a committee meeting to find the consensus of His creatures. "Man's will is free," writes A. W. Tozer, "because God is sovereign. A God less than sovereign could not bestow moral freedom upon His creatures. He would be afraid to do so."[2]

Yet, how longsuffering God is with both the saved and the lost! He allowed Jezebel to kill some of the prophets of the Lord, and He allowed Elijah to run away from the place of duty. The greatest judgment God can send is to allow people to have their own way and then suffer the consequences. "How long, O Lord, how long?" has been the painful prayer of believers on earth (Ps. 13:1-2) and in heaven (Rev. 6:10), but our times are in His hands and He knows the end from the beginning. When the news of the day upsets me, I pause and worship the eternal sovereign God who is never surprised or caught unprepared. This keeps me from fretting and getting discouraged and it helps to keep my life in balance.

The Book of 1 Kings has revealed to us the sinfulness of the human heart, the faithfulness of a loving God, and the seriousness of being a part of God's believing remnant. Before Jesus returns to set up His kingdom, many things are going to get worse and we may become discouraged and be tempted to quit. Then we'll remember that responsibility means our response to His ability. God is still on the throne, so we'll join the heavenly multitude and sing the song of the overcomers: "Alleluia, for the Lord God omnipotent reigneth" (Rev. 19:6, KJV).

Endnotes

Chapter One

1. We aren't able to identify with certainty Shimei and Rei (v. 8), unless they were David's brothers Shimea and Raddai who held offices in the kingdom (1 Chron. 2:13-14, NIV). There was also a Shimei, son of Ela, who served in Solomon's court (1 Kings 4:18). The Shimei in 1 Kings 1:8 certainly wasn't the same Shimei who cursed David during Absalom's rebellion (2 Sam. 16:5-12; 19:18-23).
2. David ruled over a united kingdom, so the phrase "over Israel and over Judah" seems strange to us. But this record was written many years after these events occurred and after the kingdom had been divided.
3. 1 Chronicles 29:23-25 records another coronation service for Solomon. Whether this is the same one described in 1 Kings 1 or a later celebration that was larger and more carefully planned, we can't be sure. It seems unlikely that the ailing David got up from his deathbed, made the speeches recorded in 1 Chronicles 28:1–29:20, witnessed Solomon's second anointing, and then returned to his room to die. 1 Chronicles 29:22 states that Solomon was "acknowledged as king" and anointed "a second time," so the event in 1 Kings 1 has to be his first. It's possible that the author of Chronicles dropped this information in at this point as a summary of the last events in the life of David (29:21-30). In times of crisis, it wasn't unusual for the new king to have a hasty coronation and then a larger and more formal one later. There are some chronological problems here, but in view of the volatile situation, it isn't impossible that God gave David strength to participate in the great public events described in 1 Chronicles 28–29. Solomon's second anointing was necessary to establish once and for all that he was indeed the king. David was anointed three times (1 Sam. 16:13; 2 Sam. 2:4 and 5:3).
4. Since Adonijah was the leader of the rebellion, he was the most responsible. Solomon not only pardoned Adonijah but he also pardoned the other sons of David who were at the feast (1:9). Solomon realized that they had been duped by Adonijah and attended the feast in innocence. Once there, they discovered the reason for the celebration, but it would have been dangerous to leave, knowing that all the army officers were there. Jonathan's news report gave them

the opportunity they needed to escape.

5. Chronologists don't find it easy to calculate Solomon's age at his accession to the throne, nor do we know how long David lived after Solomon became coregent. David was thirty years old when he began to reign in Hebron (2 Sam. 5:1-5), and he reigned seven years there and thirty-three years in Jerusalem, making him seventy years old when he died. If he was fifty when he committed adultery with Bathsheba, and if Solomon was the son born next after the death of their baby (2 Sam. 12:24-25), then Solomon could have been eighteen or nineteen years old when he became king. However, 1 Chronicles 3:5 suggests strongly that Solomon was their fourth son, which could make him as young as fifteen when he became king. David described Solomon as "young and tender [inexperienced, NIV]" (1 Chron. 22:5, KJV), but perhaps this was the language of an aged father as he looked at his successor. Raised in the security of the palace, Solomon wasn't the well-rounded man that his father was; but does any leader think his son is ready to take over?
6. For examples of kings obeying God's law, see 2 Kings 14:6; 18:4, 6.

CHAPTER TWO

1. Frederick Buechner, *Peculiar Treasures* (New York: Harper and Row, 1979), p. 161.
2. Solomon's wife's dowry from Pharaoh was the Philistine city of Gezer (1 Kings 9:16). Egypt had conquered Philistia and still held authority over it. This was not Solomon's first wife, because his firstborn son and successor, Rehoboam, had an Ammonite mother named Naamah (14:21). Solomon must have married before he became king because Rehoboam was forty-one years old when he took the throne, and Solomon reigned forty years.
3. The Jews were not to marry the women who belonged to the pagan nations in the land of Canaan (Ex. 34:16; Deut. 7:1ff), a law that Solomon eventually violated. There seemed to be no regulation concerning a Jew taking an Egyptian wife. Jewish tradition says that his wife did adopt the Jewish faith.
4. They were called "high places" *(bamah)* because they were usually located in the hills, away from the cities, in the midst of nature and "closer" to heaven. The word *bamah* means "elevation." Worship at these pagan shrines usually involved unspeakable orgies. Some Jews worshiped Baal at the high places during the period of the Judges (Judg. 6:25; 13:16). During the days of Samuel and Saul, sacrifices weren't always offered at the tabernacle altar (1 Sam. 7:10; 9:11-25; 13:9; 14:35; 16:5). David built an altar on Mount Moriah (1 Chron. 21:26), no doubt anticipating the day when the temple would stand there. Worship at the high places was a constant temptation and sin during the days of the Jewish monarchy, and no sooner did one king destroy these pagan shrines than his successor would rebuild them.
5. See my book on Proverbs, *Be Skillful* (Victor, 1995).
6. Two different Hebrew words are translated "understanding" in this passage. In verse 9, the word *shama* means "to hear, listen, obey." The Hebrew daily confession of faith is called "the Shema," and begins "Hear, O Israel . . . " (Deut. 6:4-5). The word used in verses 11-12 is *bin* and means "to distinguish, to discern, to separate." Together, the words mean "to hear with the intention to obey, and to exercise discernment so as to understand."
7. The Bible records four times when God spoke to Solomon: at Gibeon (3:10-15), during the building of the temple (6:11-13), after the completion of his building projects (9:3-9), and when Solomon disobeyed the Lord and worshiped idols (11:9-13). Note that in the first three instances, the emphasis was on obedience.
8. Solomon didn't need 40,000 horses when he had only 1,400 chariots (1 Kings 10:26; 2 Chron. 1:14), so the figure 4,000 in 2 Chronicles 9:25 is no doubt the correct one. If each chariot had two horses, that would leave 1,200 horses for the fortress cities Solomon had armed and also for other state services.
9. *Bible Characters from the Old and New Testaments* (Kregel: 1990), p. 284.

CHAPTER THREE

1. After the Babylonian captivity, the Jewish remnant began to rebuild the temple at the same time of the year (Ezra 3:8).
2. 2 Chronicles 2:14 identifies his mother with Dan, not Naphtali, but when you remem-

ber how Solomon established new districts and borders, this is no problem. The tribes of Dan and Naphtali were united in the eighth district of Naphtali, supervised by Ahimaaz (4:15).

3. Hiram also provided Solomon with wood for his palace complex. Apparently Solomon ran up a bill he couldn't pay immediately because Hiram also loaned him some gold. As collateral, Solomon gave Hiram twenty cities on the border of Galilee and Phoenicia, but Hiram wasn't pleased with them (1 Kings 9:10-14). Later, Solomon was able to pay his debt and reclaim the cities (2 Chron. 8:1). Of course, all these payments of food and gold came out of the pockets of the Jewish people, so it's no wonder they protested and asked for relief after Solomon died (1 Kings 12:1-15).
4. The height of the temple was forty-five feet, which meant there was an "attic space" fifteen feet high above the Holy of Holies. We aren't told if or how this space was used.
5. 2 Chronicles 3:15 gives the height of the pillars as thirty-five cubits, which some take to mean the *combined* height.
6. 1 Kings 7:26 says the basin held 2,000 baths, or about 11,000 gallons of water, while 2 Chronicles 4:5 says 3,000 baths or over 17,000 gallons. The larger amount may have been its full capacity while the smaller amount was what was normally kept in the molten sea. Water was a precious commodity in the east and it would take a lot of labor to fill up the huge basin.

CHAPTER FOUR

1. The sequence of events as recorded in 1 Kings appears to be as follows. First, the temple structure was built in seven years (6:1-38). Then, the royal palaces were built in thirteen years (7:1-12), making a total of twenty years for all this construction (9:10). During that time, Hiram was constructing the furnishings of the temple and supervising the work within the building (7:13-51). When all this work was completed, Solomon dedicated the temple (8:1-66), following which God appeared to Solomon the second time (9:1-9). The Lord's words to Solomon in 9:3 [2 Chron. 7:12] are not as meaningful if the dedication had taken place thirteen years before.
2. The text mentions the city of David (v. 1), God's choice of David (v. 16), and especially God's covenant with David (vv. 15-18, 20, 24-26). The Lord kept His promise and gave David a son who built the temple that David wanted to build (v. 20). When the people left the dedication service and the feast that followed, they rejoiced at the good things the Lord had "done for David" (v. 66).
3. David's first attempt to bring the Ark to Jerusalem failed miserably, but his second attempt was successful. Solomon followed his father's example by offering many sacrifices as the priests carried the Ark from the city of David to the temple. However, unlike his father, Solomon didn't dance in the holy procession.
4. Amos 4 describes how God did send many of these judgments to the kingdom of Israel.
5. It's generally accepted by students that Psalm 132 was composed for use when the Ark was brought to the temple and the temple was dedicated. The petitioner asked God to bless the king (Solomon) for the sake of David (vv. 1, 10), that is, because of the covenant God made with David in 2 Samuel 7. David wanted to build the temple (vv. 2-9), but God chose his son to do it. The Lord also promised to keep David's descendants on the throne (vv. 11-12, 17) and defeat Israel's enemies (v. 18).

CHAPTER FIVE

1. The timber and the stones had to be brought from a distance and the stones carefully cut to fit into the structure without any further dressing. All of this took time. Doing the delicate gold work within the temple, plus making the many pieces of furniture and utensils, would also require time. This explains why it took twenty years to finish both structures.
2. Nothing is said about Solomon's wife Naamah, the Ammonitess, who gave birth to Rehoboam, Solomon's firstborn son and successor (14:21).
3. Control of the cities would give Hiram whatever resources were available, including taxing the citizens or conscripting them for service. It was not a nice way for Solomon to treat his own people.
4. "The Deserted Village" by Oliver Goldsmith, lines 51 and 52.
5. It's futile to connect the number 666 with

Revelation 13:18. When you add Hiram's loan of 120 talents of gold (9:14) with the 420 talents brought in by the navy (9:28) and the 120 talents given by the queen of Sheba (10:10), you have a total of 660 talents of gold. It is said that the number six in Scripture is the number of man, always short of the number seven, the perfect number that belongs only to God. If this is true, then Solomon's 666 talents represents man's ultimate wealth, not the true eternal wealth that comes only from God. We brought nothing into this world, and we shall take nothing out (1 Tim. 6:7; Job 1:21; Ps. 49:17).

CHAPTER SIX

1. *Expositions of Holy Scripture,* by Alexander Maclaren, on 1 Kings 11:4-13.
2. I like F. W. Robertson's definition of "the world." You find it in volume 4 of his collected sermons, p. 165. "The world is that collection of men in every age who live only according to the maxims of their time." In amassing wealth and multiplying wives, and in his desire to live in splendor, Solomon was imitating the eastern potentates and not following the Word of God or the example of his father, David.
3. In spite of what songwriters say, crossing the Jordan and entering the land of Canaan is not a picture of going to heaven. We certainly won't have to fight our way into heaven! It's a picture of turning our back on the past and entering by faith into our present inheritance in Christ, the blessings He wants us to enjoy, and the work He wants us to do. All of this is explained in the Book of Hebrews.
4. For instances of prophets courageously confronting kings, see 13:1-10; 14:1-18; 16:1-4; 20:22ff; 22:1ff; 2 Kings 1.
5. Samuel had ripped Saul's garment and used the event to preach a message (1 Sam. 15:27), and David had cut a piece from Saul's garment (1 Sam. 24:4-6). The image is an obvious one.
6. Students of Old Testament history have noted that early in the nation's history, there was rivalry between the ten northern tribes and the two southern tribes, so it wasn't easy to divide the nation. See Judges 5:14-16; 2 Samuel 19:41-43; 20:2; 1 Kings 1:35; 4:20, 25. This rivalry will be healed when Messiah reigns (Isa. 11:13).
7. William Sanford LaSor, *Great Personalities of the Old Testament* (Revell, 1959), p. 125.

CHAPTER SEVEN

1. Some question that a man forty-one years old could be called "young and indecisive" (2 Chron. 13:7), but age and maturity are two different things. During the latter part of Solomon's reign, Rehoboam took eighteen wives and sixty concubines, and his family consisted of twenty-eight sons and sixty daughters (2 Chron. 11:18-21).
2. With two exceptions, when information is given about a king of Judah, the name of his mother is included. It was important that David's line be identified accurately. The exceptions are Jehoram (2 Kings 8:17) and Ahaz (2 Kings 16:2).
3. Some students think that Jeroboam was holding a meeting for the Northern Kingdom and Rehoboam saw this as an opportunity to get a hearing and build some bridges into the Northern Kingdom. If so, Rehoboam certainly turned a good opportunity into a terrible calamity.
4. The phrase "all Israel" can mean both kingdoms (9:30; 12:1) or only the northern ten tribes (10:16; 11:13). The reader must consider the context and be discerning.
5. Did this man have several names or were there three different men with similar names, each of whom served a different king? Adoram was over the forced labor when David was king (2 Sam. 20:24) and Adoniram when Solomon reigned (4:6). The man Rehoboam sent was named both Adoram and Hadoram (2 Chron. 10:18). It's difficult to believe that one man could serve so many years, but perhaps he did. Some students believe that three men are involved: Adoram served David, Adoniram served Solomon, and the first Adoram's son or grandson (Adoram/Hadoram) served Rehoboam. But would Rehoboam send an untried and relatively unknown officer on such an important diplomatic mission? It's more likely that Adoram is another form of Adoniram, the man who served Solomon, because it was Solomon's yoke that the people were opposing, not David's.
6. In David's last census, Joab reported 500,000 able-bodied men in Judah available to bear arms (2 Sam. 24:9), while there were 800,000 men available in the northern

tribes. Those numbers were over forty years old, but perhaps the population hadn't changed that much.

7. In 1 Kings 12:22, Shemiah is called "a man of God," a title often used for prophets, especially in 1 and 2 Kings (1 Kings 12:22; 13:1, 26; 17:18, 24; 20:28; 2 Kings 1:9, 11; 4:7, 9, 16, 22, 25, 27, 40, 42; 5:14). Moses bore this title (Deut. 33:1; Josh. 14:6) and Paul applied it to Timothy in 1 Timothy 6:11, and to all dedicated believers in 3:17.
8. The Jewish people should be recognized and applauded for being the only nation in history that has left an accurate portrait of their leaders and a factual report of their history. The Bible is a Jewish book, yet it doesn't always show Israel in a good light. Of course, the Scriptures are inspired by God, but it still took a good deal of honesty and humility to write the record and admit that it is true.
9. In both Kings and Chronicles, the message of obedience and blessing comes through loud and clear. However, we must not conclude that everybody who obeys God will escape suffering and trial, for more than one good king had personal troubles, and some were assassinated. No king was perfect, but God's covenant with Israel assured them that He would bless the nation if they obeyed His will.
10. Abijah was also known as Abijam (1 Kings 14:31; 15:1, 7-8, KJV). This change in spelling may reflect a desire to eliminate from the name of an ungodly man (1 Kings 15:3) the syllable "Jah," which refers to Jehovah.
11. This theme is expanded and illustrated in the Book of Hosea. The Prophet Hosea's wife became a prostitute and he had to buy her back out of the slave market.
12. This is not the Pharaoh who made a treaty with Solomon and gave him a daughter to be his wife. The new Pharaoh was not friendly toward Judah.

CHAPTER EIGHT

1. Don't confuse Jeroboam I with Jeroboam II, Israel's fourteenth king, who reigned from 782–753. His history is found in 2 Kings 14:23-29.
2. It's unlikely that Aaron was trying to introduce a new god to Israel but rather was presenting Jehovah in the form of the golden calf (Ex. 32). The calf was supposed to be a "help" to the Jews in their worship of the Lord. Aaron certainly knew that Jehovah was the only true God, but he also knew that the weak people couldn't live by faith in an invisible Jehovah, especially when their leader Moses had been absent for forty days. This fact doesn't exonerate Aaron, but it does help us better understand the mind-set of the people. It was easier to worship the invisible Lord by means of the visible calf, and it wasn't long before the idolatry gave birth to indecency and immorality (Ex. 32:6, 19; 1 Cor. 10:1-8). No matter what excuse Aaron gave, he had sinned in giving the people what they wanted and not what they needed. Jeroboam also gave the people what they wanted, and false teachers are doing the same thing today (2 Peter 2; Jude 1ff).
3. According to Exodus 29 Aaron and his sons needed for their consecration one bull for a sin offering, a ram for a burnt offering, and another ram for a fellowship offering. It took seven days for the consecration service to be completed. Obviously, Jeroboam wasn't following God's directions.
4. People talk about "the ten lost tribes of Israel," but this is not a biblical concept. God knows where children of Abraham are and He will call them together when it's time. Some nations have claimed to be the descendants of the so-called ten lost tribes, but these claims are unfounded. Jesus spoke of the "twelve tribes of Israel" (Matt. 19:28; Luke 22:30), and Paul spoke of "our twelve tribes" as living entities in his day (Acts 26:7), and James wrote his epistle to "the twelve tribes scattered abroad" (James 1:1, KJV). In his vision of future events, John the apostle saw twelve tribes sealed by God (Rev. 7:4) and twelve gates named for the twelve tribes (21:12).
5. Nowhere in Scripture do we read of any servant of the Lord "retiring" and doing nothing for the Lord as he waited to die. Instead of relocating in Judah, or staying in Israel to oppose the false religion, the old man accepted the *status quo* and became comfortable. Moses and the other prophets served to the very end, and there's no evidence that the apostles abandoned their calling when they became old. Dr. William Culbertson, for many years dean and then president of Moody Bible Institute in

Chicago, often ended his public prayers with, "And, Lord, help us to end well."

6. Saul disguised himself and both Samuel and the witch saw through it (1 Sam. 28). Wicked King Ahab disguised himself in battle, hoping King Jehoshaphat would be killed, but a random arrow hit him just the same (1 Kings 22:30ff). Godly King Josiah foolishly interfered with Pharaoh Neco, disguised himself, and was killed in battle (2 Chron. 35:20-25). God can see through disguises.
7. The prophet Nathan took a similar approach in confronting King David (2 Sam. 12:7-8a).
8. Thomas Jefferson, *Notes on Virginia,* in *The Life and Selected Writings of Thomas Jefferson,* edited by Adrienne Koch and William Peden (N.Y.: Modern Library), p. 258.

CHAPTER NINE

1. This interpretation of Rehoboam's foolish decision is that of his son and not that of the Lord. It did not come from an inspired prophet. We would expect a son to defend his father.
2. Joshua's victory at Jericho seems to be the backdrop for this event. The Lord is called "captain" (v. 12; Josh. 5:13-15, KJV), the priests blew the trumpets, and the people shouted (Josh. 6:1-21). The victory was completely from the Lord.
3. The calling of assemblies is a significant thing in the history of the Jews, both before and after the division of the kingdom. (See 1 Chron. 13:2-5; 28:8; 29:1; 2 Chron. 5:6; 20:3ff; 30:1ff.)
4. The fact that submitting to the covenant was a matter of life or death (2 Chron. 15:13) doesn't imply that Judah had become brutal or that the sword brought about the revival. Those who refused to seek God and renew the covenant were declaring that they were practicing idolatry, and according to Deuteronomy 13:6-9, idolaters were not to be spared. The people who refused to submit knew what the covenant said, so in declaring their allegiance to a foreign god, they were taking their own lives in their hands.
5. There's a chronological problem here since Baasha ascended the throne during Asa's third year and reigned for twenty-four years (1 Kings 15:33). This means he died in Asa's twenty-seventh or twenty-eighth year and therefore could not have attacked Judah in Asa's thirty-sixth year. Dr. Gleason Archer suggests that the word translated "reign" in 2 Chronicles 16:1 (KJV, NIV) should be understood as "kingdom," that is, "in the thirty-sixth year of the kingdom of Judah." Therefore, the writer was dating this event from the division of the kingdom in 931–930, and not from Asa's accession to the throne in 910. The Hebrew word translated "reign" is translated "kingdom" or "realm" in 2 Chronicles 1:1, 11:17 and 20:30. Some students see these numbers as a copyist's error, for in the Hebrew, the difference between the letters used for 36 and 16 is very slight. See Archer's *Encyclopedia of Bible Difficulties* (Zondervan), pp. 225-226.
6. The inability of the physicians to help Asa must not be interpreted as a divine rejection of the medical profession. God can heal either with or without means (Isa. 38:21), and Paul had Luke "the beloved physician" on his missionary staff (Col. 4:14). Even Jesus said that sick people need a physician (Luke 5:27-32). To use 2 Chronicles 16:12 as an argument for "faith healing" and against going to the doctor is to misinterpret and apply a very plain statement. Asa's sickness was a judgment from the Lord, and his going to the physicians was a rebellion against the Lord. He refused to repent, so God refused to let him be healed.
7. Asa's body was placed in his prepared tomb. The burning had nothing to do with cremation, a practice that the Jews considered reprehensible.
8. The phrase "because he killed him" in verse 7 indicates that though Baasha fulfilled God's will when he killed Nadab and then wiped out the house of Jeroboam, he was still responsible for his motives and his actions. Baasha didn't enter into his grisly work as a holy servant of God but as an evil assassin who wanted the throne.

CHAPTER TEN

1. "Tishbite" probably refers to the town of Tishbe in Gilead, located west of Mahanaim.
2. The six-month period from April to October is the factor that explains the seeming discrepancy between 1 Kings 18:1 (three years) and Luke 4:25 and James 5:17 (three years and six months). When the expected early rains didn't appear in October, Elijah explained the cause. The

drought was already six months old by the time Elijah visited Ahab.

3. On the schools of the prophets, see 1 Samuel 10:5 and 2 Kings 2:3-7 and 6:1-2.
4. The Hebrew word in verse 27 that is translated "pursuing" in the KJV and "busy" in the NIV can also mean "relieving himself." Idolaters make their gods in their own image.
5. Satan is a counterfeiter of the miracles of God (2 Thes. 2:9-10) and could have sent fire from heaven (Job 1:9-12; Rev. 13:13), but the Lord restrained him.
6. Some have suggested that Ahab ate some of the sacrificial meat, but that doesn't seem possible. Elijah's sacrifice was completely consumed and the sacrifice to Baal was never exposed to any fire.

Chapter Eleven

1. The Hebrew text reads "and when he saw," as do the KJV and the NIV margin. The Septuagint reads "he was afraid," and the NIV and the NASB both adopted this text. What did he see that made him afraid? The dangerous situation? The dangerous messenger? We aren't told and it's useless to speculate.
2. "Sitting under the juniper tree" is a common English phrase that describes a person who is angry at God, sick of life, embarrassed by failure, and ready to call it quits.
3. The scene reminds us of Jonah at Nineveh as he argued with the Lord (Jonah 4). Moses also wanted to die because of the impossible workload he tried to carry (Num. 11:14-15).
4. The Hebrew text of verse 9 reads "the cave" as if a well-known cave was meant. Some students believe that Elijah occupied the same part of Sinai that Moses did when he saw the glory of God (Ex. 33:12-23).
5. See Psalm 12:1, Micah 7:2, and Isa. 57:1.
6. *Robust in Faith* (Moody Press), p. 135.
7. Elijah called Elisha (19:19-21), and Elisha anointed Hazael (2 Kings 8:7-15). By the authority of his master, Elisha's servant anointed Jehu (2 Kings 9:1-10). From God's point of view, it was Elijah who did all of this.
8. Once again, we see the Lord calling people who were busy. This was true of Moses, Gideon, David, Nehemiah, Amos, and the apostles.

Chapter Twelve

1. As we have noted before, deciphering the transcription of numbers in the Hebrew language has sometimes caused problems for students, since letters are used for numbers and some letters look very similar. Could that many people be killed just by walls falling on them? But the collapsing of the walls would leave the city defenseless and make it possible for Ahab's troops to kill anybody seeking refuge in the city. The seven days of waiting, the falling of the walls, and the deception afterward all makes us think of the fall of Jericho (Josh. 6). However, Ahab was certainly no Joshua!
2. God sometimes told the prophets to use "action sermons" to get His message across to people who were spiritually blind and deaf. For example, Isaiah dressed like a prisoner of war for three years (Isa. 20); Jeremiah wore a wooden yoke and then an iron one (Jer. 27–28); and Ezekiel "played war," ate prisoners' rations, and cooked over a dung fire (Ezek. 4).
3. Disguises seem to play a significant role in 1 Kings. See 14:2 and 22:30.
4. *The Knowledge of the Holy* (Harper, 1961), p. 11. See Psalm 50:21.
5. When in his refusal Naboth said "The Lord forbid" (v. 3), he wasn't taking an oath or blaspheming God's name. But deceivers like Ahab and Jezebel know how to turn nothing into something. Exaggeration is a subtle form of lying.
6. The prophets of Baal had been slain (18:40) but could have been replaced. However, knowing Jehoshaphat's devotion to the Lord, Ahab wasn't likely to parade four hundred prophets of Baal before him. These men were probably attached to the shrines at Dan and Bethel where Jeroboam had put the golden calves. (See Amos 7:10-13.) It was still idolatry, but of a more refined type. These false prophets used the name of the Lord and claimed to speak by His authority (22:11-12). This is the same kind of false prophet that Jeremiah had to put up with years later.

Chapter Thirteen

1. Kirk Douglas in *Look,* Oct. 4, 1955.
2. *The Knowledge of the Holy* (Harper, 1961), p. 118.

2 KINGS

A SUGGESTED OUTLINE OF 2 KINGS

Theme: God's judgment of Israel and Judah

I. THE MINISTRY OF ELISHA (2 KINGS 1–13)
II. THE FALL OF SAMARIA (2 KINGS 14–17)
III. THE CAPTIVITY OF JUDAH (2 KINGS 18–25)

CONTENTS

CHAPTER ONE
THE PARTING OF THE WAYS
2 Kings 1–2

Elisha ("my God saves") had been Elijah's servant and apprentice for probably ten years, but now time had come for the Lord to call His courageous servant home. We get the impression that they were men with different dispositions, Elijah being the "son of thunder" and Elisha the gracious healer. This doesn't mean that Elijah was never tender or that Elisha was never stern, for the biblical record shows otherwise. But in general, Elijah came like John the Baptist, putting the ax to the root of the trees, while Elisha followed with a quiet ministry like that of Jesus (see Matt. 3:1-12 and 11:16-19). In the closing events of this spiritual partnership, we see revealed four important truths about the God of Israel.

1. God judges sin. (2 Kings 1:1-18)
After the death of wicked King Ahab, the nation of Moab took advantage of Ahaziah, his son and successor, and broke the bonds of vassalage that had chained them to Israel (v. 1; see 3:4-5). Years before, David had defeated Moab (2 Sam. 8:2) and Ahaziah's successor, Jehoram (Joram), would join with Jehoshaphat, king of Judah, to fight against the Moabites (3:6ff). But the Lord is in charge of the nations of the earth (Acts 17:24-28; Dan. 5:19, 21; 7:27), and His decrees determine history. Ahaziah was an evil man (1 Kings 22:10, 51-53), but when the Lord isn't allowed to rule, He overrules (Ps. 33:10-11).

Idolatry (vv. 2-4). A decade or so before Ahaziah's accident, Elijah had won his great victory over Baal (1 Kings 18), but Ahab and Jezebel hadn't been convinced or converted and neither had their family (1 Kings 22:51-53). When Ahaziah was severely injured by falling through a lattice, he turned for guidance to Baal and not to the Lord God of Israel. "Baal" simply means "lord," and "Baal-Zebul" means "Baal is prince." But the devout remnant in Israel, who worshiped Jehovah, made changes in that name and ridiculed the false god of their neighbors. "Baal-Zebel" means "lord of the dung," and "Baal-Zebub means "lord of the flies," one of the names Jesus' enemies used to insult Him. (Matt. 10:25).

Why did the king decide to send messengers forty miles away to Ekron to consult the priests of Baal? True, Elijah had slain the 450 prophets of Baal (1 Kings 18:19, 22, 40), but that was ten years ago. Surely other priests of Baal were available in the land. The king's parents had fed hundreds of these priests at their table (1 Kings 18:19), and it wouldn't have been difficult for King Ahaziah to import priests of Baal to serve as court chaplains. Perhaps he sent to Ekron for help because he didn't want the people in Samaria to know how serious his condition was. The temple of Baal at Ekron was very famous, for Baal was the chief god of that city, and one would expect a king to send there for help. Note that Ahaziah asked the priests of Baal for a prognosis and not for healing.

God keeps His servants informed about matters that other people know nothing about (John 15:15, Amos 3:7). This "angel of the Lord" could well have been our Lord Jesus Christ in one of His preincarnate appearances (Gen. 16:7;18; 21:17; 22:11; 48:16). When God's servants are walking with their Lord, they can be confident of His directions when they need them. This had certainly been Elijah's experience (see v. 15 and 1 Kings 17:3, 9; 18:1; 21:18). Elijah intercepted the royal envoys and gave them a message that would both rebuke and sober the king. Why did he want to consult the dead god of Ekron when the living God of Israel was available to tell him what would happen? He would surely die! This ominous declaration was made three times during this event—twice by Elijah (vv. 4 and 16) and once by the messengers (v. 6). Instead of being spokesmen for Baal, the messengers became heralds of God's Word to the king!

Pride (vv. 5-12). It seems incredible that the king's messengers didn't know who Elijah was and didn't learn his identity until they returned to the palace! Elijah was Ahab's enemy (1 Kings 21:20) and Ahaziah was Ahab's son, so certainly Ahaziah had said something to his courtiers about the prophet. The description the messengers gave of Elijah reminds us of John the Baptist who ministered "in the spirit and the power of Elijah" (Luke 1:17; Matt. 3:4). The phrase "a hairy man" (KJV) suggests his garment rather than his appearance. The NIV reads "with a garment of hair." Like John the Baptist, Elijah wore the simple camel's hair garment of the poor and not the rich robe of a king (Matt. 11:7-10).

The announcement that he would die should have moved Ahaziah to repent of his sins and seek the Lord, but instead, he tried to lay hands on the prophet. (This reminds us of King Herod's seizure of John the Baptist; Matt. 14:1-12.) Ahaziah knew that Elijah was a formidable foe, so he sent a captain with fifty soldiers to bring him to the palace; but he underestimated the prophet's power. Did Ahaziah think that he could kill the prophet and thereby nullify the prophecy? (The Lord's words in v. 15 suggest that murder was in the king's mind.) Or perhaps the king hoped to influence Elijah to change the prophecy. But Elijah took his orders from the King of kings and not from earthly kings, especially a king who was an idolater and the son of murderers. Years before, Elijah ran away in fear when he received Jezebel's threat (1 Kings 19), but this time, he remained where he was and faced the soldiers unafraid.

The captain certainly didn't use the title "man of God" as a compliment to Elijah or as a confession of his own faith, for "man of God" was a common synonym for "prophet." Elijah's reply meant, "Since you called me a man of God, let me prove it to you. My God will deal with you according to your own words." The fire that came from heaven killed all fifty-one men. This judgment was repeated when the second company of fifty arrived. Note that the second captain ordered Elijah to "come down quickly." Don't keep your king waiting! The memory of the contest on Mount Carmel should have warned the king and his soldiers that Elijah could bring fire from heaven (1 Kings 18).[1]

We must not interpret these two displays of God's wrath as evidence of irritation on the part of Elijah or injustice on the part of God. After all, weren't the soldiers only doing their duty and obeying their commander? These two episodes of fiery judgment were dramatic messages from the Lord that the king and the nation had better repent or they would all taste the judgment of God. The people had forgotten the lessons of Mount Carmel, and these two judgments reminded them that the God of Israel was "a consuming fire" (Deut. 4:24 and 9:3; Heb. 12:29). King Ahaziah was a proud man who sacrificed two captains and one hundred men in a futile attempt to prevent his own death. These were not innocent men, the victims of their ruler's whims, but guilty men who were willing to do what the king commanded. Had they adopted the attitude of the third captain, they too would have lived.

Disobedience (vv. 13-18). Insisting that Elijah obey him, the king sent a third company of soldiers, but this time the captain showed wisdom and humility. Unlike the king and the two previous captains, he submitted himself to the Lord and His servant. The third captain's plea for himself and his men was evidence that he acknowledged Elijah's authority and that he would do God's servant no harm. The Lord's words in verse 15 suggest that the danger lay in the hands of the captains and not in the hands of the king. Perhaps the king had ordered them to kill Elijah en route to the palace or after he had left the palace. If the king had to die, he would at least take Elijah with him!

The king was in bed when Elijah confronted him and for the second time told him he would die. How many times must the Lord repeat His message to a wicked sinner? The king would leave this world with "you will surely die" ringing in his ears, yet he refused to obey the Word of God. Again, we're reminded of Herod's response to John the Baptist, for Herod listened to John's words but still wouldn't repent (Mark 6:20). After about two years on the throne, Ahaziah did die, just as Elijah had predicted, and his younger brother Jehoram (or Joram) became king. Note that the current king of Judah was also named Jehoram (v. 17). To avoid confusion, we shall refer to Ahaziah's brother, the king of Israel, as Joram, and Jehoshaphat's son, the king of Judah, as Jehoram.

Before leaving this passage, we need to remind ourselves that a proud and unrepentant world will one day experience the fire of the wrath of God. It will happen "when the Lord Jesus is revealed from heaven with His mighty angels, in flaming fire taking vengeance on those who do not know God, and on those who do not obey the gospel of our Lord Jesus Christ. These shall be punished with everlasting destruction from the presence of the Lord and from the glory of His power" (2 Thes. 1:7-9, NKJV). God "commands all men everywhere to repent" (Acts 17:30, NKJV), which means that those who do not repent are rebels against the Lord. The gospel isn't only a message to believe; it's also a mandate to obey.

2. God wants us to remember. (2 Kings 2:1-6)

King Ahaziah died but Elijah didn't die! He was taken up into heaven in a whirlwind, accompanied by fiery horses drawing a chariot of fire. Like Enoch of old, he walked with God and then suddenly went to be with God (Gen. 5:21-24; Heb. 11:5). Both men illustrate the catching away of the saints when Jesus returns (1 Thes. 4:13-18). But before Elijah left Elisha to carry on the work, he walked with his successor from Gilgal to beyond the Jordan, and what a walk that must have been! The Lord had at least three purposes in mind when He led these two servants to walk together.

Taking advantage of the present. Elisha knew that his master was going to leave him (vv. 1, 3, 5), and he wanted to be with him to the very end, listen to his counsel and learn from him. It appears that Elijah wanted Elisha to tarry behind and let him go on alone, but this was merely a test of Elisha's devotion. When Elijah threw his mantle on Elisha and made him his successor, the younger man promised, "I will follow you" (1 Kings 19:20), and he kept that promise.

During the years that the two men had worked together, surely they came to love and appreciate one another in a deeper way. "It is not good that the man should be alone" (Gen. 2:18) applies to ministry as well as marriage. Moses and Aaron labored together, and David and Jonathan encouraged each other. Paul journeyed first with Barnabas and then with Silas, and Dr. Luke seemed to be a regular companion to the apostle. Even our Lord sent out His disciples two-by-two (Mark 6:7; see Ecc. 4:9-12). We are not only fellow workers with the Lord, but also with the Lord's people, and there must be no competition as we serve the same Lord together (John 4:34-38; 1 Cor. 3:1-9).

We never know when a friend and fellow worker will be taken from us. God told Elisha that Elijah was leaving him, but we don't know when it is our time or a friend's time to go to heaven. What great opportunities we miss by wasting time on trifles when we could be learning from each other about the Lord and His Word! It rejoices my heart when I see younger Christians and Christian workers appreciating the "senior saints," the veterans of Christian service, and learning from them. One day, these "giants" will be called home and we'll no longer be able to learn from them.

These two men represented different generations and opposite personalities, yet they were able to walk together. What a rebuke this is to those in the church who label the generations and separate them from each other. I heard one youthful pastor say that he didn't want anybody in his church over the age of forty, and I wondered where he would get the wise counsel that usually comes with maturity. I thank God for the "Elijahs" in my life who were patient with me and took time to instruct me. Now I'm trying to share that same blessing with others.

Preparing for the future. At Bethel, Jericho, and Gilgal, the two men visited the "sons of the prophets" (vv. 5, 7, 15; 4:1, 38-40; 6:1, 7; 9:1; see 1 Kings 20:35), companies of dedicated men who were called of God to study the Scriptures and teach the people. Samuel led one of these "schools" at Ramah (1 Sam. 7:17; 28:3; see 10:5, 10; 19:20-23). These groups would be similar to the mentoring groups in our churches, or even like our Bible schools and colleges. The work of the Lord is always one generation short of extinction and we must be faithful to obey 2 Timothy 2:2—"And the things that you have heard from me among many witnesses, commit these to faithful men who will be able to teach others also" (NKJV).

These young prophets knew that their master was about to leave them, so these final meetings must have been very emotional. We have "farewell messages" in Scripture from Moses (the Book of Deuteronomy), Joshua (Josh. 23–24), David (1 Chron. 28–29), Jesus (John 13–16), and Paul (Acts 20:17-38 and 2 Tim.), but the Lord didn't record for us what Elijah said to his beloved students. Certainly he told them to obey Elisha just as they had obeyed him, to remain true to the Word of God and to do everything God told them to do as they battled against idolatry in the land. It was their responsibility to call the people back to obeying God's covenant (Deut. 27–30) so that He might be pleased to bless and heal their land.

During the years that I was privileged to instruct seminary students, I occasionally heard some of them say, "Why should we attend school? Charles Spurgeon never went to seminary, and neither did Campbell Morgan or D. L. Moody!" I would usually reply, "If any of you are Spurgeons, Morgans, or Moodys, we'll no doubt discover it and give you permission to stop your education. But let me remind you that both Spurgeon and Moody founded schools for training preachers, and Campbell Morgan was once president of a training college and also taught at a number of schools. Meanwhile, back to our studies."

God has different ways of training His servants, but He still expects the older generation to pass along to the younger generation the treasures of truth that were given to them by those who went before, "the faith . . . once for all delivered to the saints" (Jude 3, NKJV).

Reviewing the past. Gilgal, Bethel, Jericho, and the Jordan River were important places in Hebrew history, each of them carrying a significant message. Before he left the land and went to heaven, Elijah wanted to visit these sites one last time and take Elisha with him. Our eternal God doesn't reside in special places, but we who are creatures of time and history need these visible reminders to help us remember and better understand what God has done for His people. The past is not an anchor to hold us back but a rudder to guide us, and the Lord can use these "tangible memories" to strengthen our faith. The British poet W. H. Auden wrote, "Man is a history-making creature who can neither repeat his past nor leave it behind." It's important for us to remember what God did in the past and to pass this treasure along to our children and grandchildren (Pss. 48:9-14; 71:17-18; 78:1-8; 145:4). That's one of the major themes of Moses' farewell address to the new generation about to enter the Promised Land (Deut. 4:9-10; 6:4-9; 11:19-21; 29:29). "Remember" is found fourteen times in Deuteronomy and "forget" at least nine times.

Gilgal (v. 1) was the first place the Israelites camped after they crossed the Jordan River and entered the Promised Land (Josh. 4:19-20). It was there that the new generation of Jewish men submitted to circumcision and officially became "sons of the covenant" (Josh. 5:2-9). Gilgal was the place of new beginnings and Elijah wanted his successor to remember that. Each new generation is an opportunity for God to raise up new leaders, and each time His people repent and return to Him, He can restore them and renew them. At that time, Gilgal was the center of idolatrous worship (Hos. 4:15; 9:15; 12:11; Amos 4:4 and 5:5), but Elijah didn't abandon it.

From Gilgal the two men walked to Bethel (vv. 2-3), about fifteen miles west of Gilgal. Abraham worshiped there (Gen. 12:8; 13:3) and so did Jacob. It was at Bethel that Jacob saw the angels ascending and descending the ladder (or staircase) that reached to heaven. There he heard God promise to be with him and care for him (Gen. 28:11-19). Bethel means "house of God," and there Jacob worshiped the Lord and vowed to obey Him. Years later, Jacob returned to Bethel and, like Abraham (Gen. 13:3), made a new beginning in his walk with the Lord (Gen. 35). King Jeroboam had put a golden calf at Bethel and made it the site of idolatrous worship (1 Kings 12:26-32; Amos 3:14; 4:4-6), but Elijah looked beyond the city's present desecration to the time when it was a place of blessing and renewal.

At Bethel, the students spoke to Elisha about his master's departure. Perhaps they thought they knew something that nobody else knew, an attitude not uncommon among some students. The same scene was repeated when Elijah and Elisha arrived at Jericho (v. 5). In both cities, Elisha politely assured the students that he was aware of what was about to happen, but that their discussing it only added to the pain of his separation from his master.

Their approach to what God was doing was purely cerebral, but to Elisha, the loss of his beloved master brought pain to his heart. The mark of a true student of the Scriptures is a burning heart, not a big head (Luke 24:32; 1 Cor. 8:1).

The two men then went fifteen miles west to Jericho, the site of Joshua's first victory in the Promised Land (Josh. 5:13–6:27). It was also the place where Achan disobeyed and took of the spoils that belonged to the Lord alone, a sin that led to Israel's defeat at Ai (Josh. 7). Certainly the wonderful victory at Jericho showed Israel how to conquer the land: get your orders from the Lord; obey them by faith, no matter how foolish they may seem; give all the glory to Him alone. The two times Joshua failed to follow this formula, he experienced defeat (Josh. 7, 9). Joshua had put under a curse anybody who rebuilt Jericho (Josh. 6:26), but during the reign of evil King Ahab, the city was rebuilt (1 Kings 16:34). Jericho would remind Elisha of the victory of faith, the tragedy of sin and the majesty of the Lord who deserves all the glory.

Elijah and Elisha walked five miles east and came to the Jordan River, and surely the record in Joshua 1–4 came into their minds and into their conversation. The Lord opened the Red Sea to let His people out of Egypt (Ex. 12–15), and then He opened the Jordan River to let them into their inheritance. What good is freedom if you don't claim your inheritance? As the nation followed the Ark of the Covenant, the Lord opened the swollen waters of the river, and the people passed over on dry land! To commemorate this miracle, Joshua built a monument in the midst of the river and another one on the shore. Nothing is too hard for the Lord, for with God, all things are possible! *And Elijah duplicated that great miracle!*

This is a good place to point out the similarities between Moses and Elijah. Both opened bodies of water, Moses the Red Sea (Ex. 14:16, 21, 26) and Elijah the Jordan River. Both called down fire from heaven (Ex. 9:24; Lev. 9:24; Num. 11:1 and 16:35), Both men saw the Lord provide food, Moses the manna (Ex. 16) and quails (Num. 11), and Elijah the oil and flour for the widow, plus his own meals (1 Kings 17:1-16). In the land of Egypt, Moses prayed and God altered the weather, and Elijah prayed and God stopped the rain and then three years later started the rain again. Moses gave the law to the people of Israel and Elijah called them to repent and return to the true and living God. Both were associated with mountains (Sinai and Carmel), and both made journeys through the wilderness. Both men had unique endings to their lives: God buried Moses in a grave nobody can find, and God carried Elijah to heaven by a whirlwind. Both Moses and Elijah were privileged to be present with Jesus on the Mount of Transfiguration (Matt. 17:4; Mark 9:5; Luke 9:33).

Elijah is a good model for believers to imitate when it comes to the inevitability of one day leaving this earth, either through death or the rapture of the church. He didn't sit around and do nothing, but instead visited three of the prophetic schools and no doubt ministered to the students. He didn't say to his successor "I'm going to leave you" and thus dwell on the negative, but said "I'm going to Bethel—to Jericho—to the Jordan" and kept busy until the very moment the Lord called him. Even more, he didn't ask his successor to give him anything, because we can't take anything in our hands from earth to heaven (1 Tim. 6:7), but instead he offered to give Elisha a gift before the end came.[2] One of the best gifts we can leave is a prepared servant of God to take our place!

3. God rewards service. (2 Kings 2:7-12) As Elijah and Elisha stood by the Jordan River, they were watched by fifty of the sons of the prophets, men who stood afar off. They knew that Elijah was going to leave that day (vv. 3 and 5), but they didn't know how he would depart or when God would call him. It's likely that only Elisha actually saw Elijah go up into heaven (v. 10), and after the prophet disappeared, the fifty students thought he hadn't really left them (vv. 16-18). They saw Elijah open the waters of the Jordan and close them again, and they saw Elisha repeat the miracle, but they didn't see what Elisha saw when the whirlwind took Elijah to heaven. The fifty men were spectators that saw only part of what happened, but Elisha was a participant in the miracle and the heir to Elijah's ministry.

Elijah didn't give his successor three wishes; he simply asked him to name the one gift he wanted more than anything else. Every leader needs to be right in his priorities, and Elisha had a ready answer: he wanted a double portion of the spirit of his master. This was not a request for twice as much of the Holy Spirit, or for a ministry twice as great as that of Elijah, but for a greater degree of the inner spirit that motivated the great prophet. The request was based on Deuteronomy 21:17, the law of inheritance for the firstborn. Though there were many "sons of the prophets," Elisha saw himself as Elijah's "firstborn son" who deserved the double inheritance that Moses commanded. Like a firstborn son serving a father, Elisha had walked with Elijah and attended to his needs (3:11; 1 Kings 19:21), but the only inheritance he desired was a double measure of his master's inner spirit of courage, faithfulness, faith in God, and obedience to God's will. In saying this, Elisha was accepting the prophetic ministry that Elijah had begun and declaring that he would carry it on to completion, with God's help.

Elijah was honest with his friend and told him that such a gift was not his to grant, for only the Lord could do it. However, if the Lord allowed Elisha to see his translation from earth to heaven, that would be proof that his request had been granted. Then it happened! As the two friends walked along talking, a fiery chariot drawn by fiery horses came between them, and a whirlwind lifted Elijah out of sight—*and Elisha saw it happen!* This meant his request had been granted and the Lord had equipped him to continue the ministry of Elijah. Elijah was certainly the "prophet of fire," for Scripture records at least three instances of his bringing fire from heaven (1 Kings 18:38; 2 Kings 1:10 and 12), so it was right that God send fiery horses and a chariot of fire to accompany His servant to glory.

Elisha's response was one of grief, like a son mourning over the loss of a beloved father. But he paid great tribute to Elijah when he called him "the chariot of Israel and its horseman" (v. 12). This one man was the equivalent of a whole army! In His covenant with Israel, the Lord promised that, if the nation obeyed Him, He would enable a hundred Israelites to chase ten thousand enemy soldiers (Lev. 26:6-8), and Moses promised that God would cause one man to chase a thousand and two men to chase ten thousand (Deut. 32:30). One with God is a majority.

4. God honors faith. (2 Kings 2:13-25) Elijah was gone and Elisha couldn't turn to him for help, but the God of Israel was still on the throne. From now on, Elisha's faith would put him in touch with the power of God and enable him to accomplish God's work in Israel. Three miracles are recorded here, each with spiritual messages that we need to understand today.

Crossing the river (vv. 13-18). Why did Elijah leave the Promised Land and go to the other side of the Jordan? Was he abandoning his own country and people? Certainly God's whirlwind could have lifted him just as easily from Bethel or Jericho. Technically, Elijah was still in Israelite territory when he crossed the river, since Reuben and Gad and the half tribe of Manasseh had their inheritance east of the Jordan. But there was more involved. By taking Elisha west of the Jordan, Elijah forced him to trust God to get him across the river and back into the land! Elijah's successor was now like Joshua: he had to believe that God could and would open the river for him. The students who were watching must have wondered what their new leader would do.

In taking up Elijah's mantle, Elisha was making it clear that he accepted the responsibilities involved as he succeeded the great prophet and continued his work. By using the mantle to open the waters of the Jordan, he was declaring that his faith was not in the departed prophet but in the ever-present living God. Certainly we ought to honor the memories and accomplishments of departed leaders. "Remember those who led you, who spoke the word of God to you; and considering the result of their conduct, imitate their faith" (Heb. 13:7, NASB). But too many dead founders and leaders still control their former ministries from their graves, and their successors find it difficult to make the changes needed for survival. Elisha didn't make that mistake, for he called on the God of Elijah to assist him, and the Lord honored his faith. Elisha wasn't a clone of Elijah, but the two men had this in common: they both had faith in the true and living God. That's why Hebrews 13:7 commands us to remember past spiritual leaders and "imitate their faith."

Elisha's miraculous crossing of the Jordan River not only demonstrated the power of God and the faith of His servant, but it also announced to the sons of the prophets that Elisha was their new leader. When God opened the Jordan so Israel could cross, He used that miracle to magnify Joshua's name and declare that His hand was upon the new leader (Josh. 3:7-8; 4:14). A. W. Tozer used to say that "it takes more than a ballot to make a leader," and he was right. Regardless of how they were trained or chosen, true spiritual leaders assure their followers of their divine calling by demonstrating the power of God in their lives. "Therefore by their fruits you will know them" (Matt. 7:20, NKJV).

The fifty sons of the prophets who saw Elisha cross the river on dry ground had no problem submitting to him and accepting his leadership because God's power was evident in his ministry.

But the fifty students didn't believe that their former leader had actually gone to heaven; they asked for on-site verification. God had openly demonstrated that Elisha was their new leader, so why search for Elijah? And why would the Lord catch His servant up in the whirlwind only to abandon him in some forsaken part of the country? Is that the kind of God they served? Furthermore, it was impossible for the students to search out every part of the land, so why even begin? The entire enterprise was ridiculous and Elisha permitted the search only because he was annoyed by their repeated requests. New leaders must not be vexed by the interest their followers have in their former leader. When the search parties returned to Elisha at Jericho, he at least had the privilege of telling them, "I told you so!"

Healing the bad water (vv. 19-22). Not only did Elisha enjoy the loyalty of the sons of the prophets, but the leaders of Jericho also respected him and sought his help. It should be no surprise to us that the water at Jericho was distasteful and the soil unproductive, for the city was under a curse (Josh. 6:26). The Old Testament Jew thought of salt in terms of God's covenant (Num. 18:19) and personal purity in worship (Lev. 2:13). The phrase "to eat salt" meant "to share hospitality," so that salt implied friendship and loyalty between people and between God and man. The salt didn't purify the water or heal the soil; that was the work of God. This miracle reminds us of the miracle at Marah ("bitter"), when Moses threw in a piece of wood and healed the water (Ex. 15:22-26). At Marah, God revealed Himself to His people as "Jehovah-Rapha—the Lord who heals."

If you visit Jericho today, tour guides will point out "Elisha's fountain" and invite you to take a drink.

Once more, we have a miracle that speaks of a new beginning. Elisha even emptied the salt from a new bowl. The miracle was an "action sermon" that reminded the people that the blessings of God were for a nation that was loyal to His covenant. To disobey His law meant to forfeit His blessings (Deut. 28:15ff).

Judging the mockers (vv. 23-25). This event took place at Bethel, one of the centers for idol worship in the land (1 Kings 12:28-33; Amos 7:13). The Hebrew word translated "little children" in the KJV really means "youths" or "young men." It refers to people from twelve to thirty years old who were able to discern right from wrong and make their own decisions. This was not a group of playful children making a clever joke but a gang of smart-aleck youths maliciously ridiculing God and God's servant.

"Go up" refers to the recent ascension of Elijah to heaven. Fifty men saw Elijah vanish from the earth in an instant, and certainly they reported what had happened and the event was discussed widely. The youths were saying, "If you are a man of God, why don't you get out of here and go to heaven the way Elijah did? We're glad he's gone and we wish you would follow him!" For a young person to call any grown man "bald head" would be a gross affront, and to repeat the nickname would make the offense even worse. Gray hair was a "crown of glory" (Prov. 16:31) among the Jews, but baldness was a rare thing among them and by some people was considered a disgrace (Isa. 3:24).

What we have here is a gang of irreverent and disrespectful ruffians mocking God's servant and repeating words they probably heard at home or in the marketplace. Because he knew the Word of God, Elisha understood that what they were doing was a violation of God's covenant, so he called down a curse upon them. (One of the covenant warnings was that God would send wild beasts to attack the people. See Lev. 26:21-22.) These young men were not showing respect to the Lord God of Israel, to Elijah or to Elisha, so they had to be judged. The two bears mauled the youths but didn't kill them, and for the rest of their days, their scars reminded everybody that they couldn't trifle with the Lord and get away with it.

You frequently find the Lord sending special judgments at the beginning of a new period in Bible history, as though God were issuing a warning to His people that the new beginning doesn't mean that the old rules have been changed. After the tabernacle ministry began, God killed Nadab and Abihu for offering "strange fire" before the Lord (Lev. 10). After Israel's first victory in the Promised Land, God ordered Achan to be slain because he took treasures from the spoils of war that were wholly dedicated to God (Josh. 7). At the outset of David's reign in Jerusalem, he had the Ark of the Covenant brought to the city, and Uzzah was killed for touching it (2 Sam. 6:1-7). When Ananias and Sapphira lied to the leaders in the early church, God took their lives (Acts 5). Now, at the beginning of Elisha's ministry, the mauling of the youths gave fair warning that the Lord God of Elijah was still reigning and still took His covenant seriously.

The attitude displayed by these youths, as it spread through the land, is what eventually led to the fall of both Samaria and Judah. "And the Lord God of their fathers sent warnings to them by His messengers. . . . But they mocked the messengers of God, despised His words, and scoffed at His prophets, until the wrath of the Lord arose against His people, till there was no remedy" (2 Chron. 36:15-16, NKJV).

Elisha had been with Elijah at Gilgal, Bethel and Jericho, and had crossed the Jordan with him, but now he went to Mount Carmel, the scene of Elijah's greatest triumph. As far as we know, Elisha wasn't there when Elijah called down fire from heaven. Perhaps as Elisha visited the place where the altar had stood, he meditated on what the Lord had done and he was renewed in his spirit. No doubt he gave thanks to God that he was part of such a wonderful heritage. But you can't live in the past, so he left that sacred place and headed for Samaria, capital city of the Northern Kingdom and home of King Joram, son of Ahab. There he would be involved in a war involving Israel, Judah, and Moab against Edom, and Elisha would provide the weapon that would win the battle for the three kings.

CHAPTER TWO
AMAZING GRACE!
2 Kings 3–4

From the outset of his ministry, Elisha proved himself to be a worker of miracles like his master and predecessor, Elijah, for he opened the Jordan River and crossed on dry land, and then he purified the water at Jericho. Except for calling down judgment on a group of arrogant young men (2:23-25), Elisha's miracles were primarily revelations of God's grace and mercy. Elijah reminds us of John the Baptist with his ax, winnowing fork, and baptism of fire (Matt. 3:1-12; Luke 1:17); but Elisha reminds us of our Savior who had compassion on the multitudes and "went about doing good" (Acts 10:38). The six miracles recorded in these two chapters certainly magnify the grace of God.

1. Grace defeats the enemy. (2 Kings 3:1-27)

When Ahaziah died, his brother Joram became king of Israel (1:17). He was also called Jehoram, but since that was also the name of Jehoshaphat's son and the coregent of Judah, we'll distinguish the two rulers by calling the king of Israel Joram. Being a son of Ahab and Jezebel, the new king was hardly a godly man, but at least he removed an image dedicated to Baal (1 Kings 16:32-33) and he showed some respect for Elisha. However, neither Baal worship nor the golden calves were removed from the land during his reign, and the image of Baal that Joram removed found its way back and Jehu had to destroy it (10:27).

A costly rebellion (vv. 4-8; see 1:1). The land of Moab was especially suited for raising sheep, but an annual tribute to Israel of 100,000 lambs and the wool of 100,000 rams was certainly demanding. Ahab's death and Ahaziah's brief reign of less than two years gave Mesha opportunity to rebel. When Joram, a younger man, took the throne of Israel, it seemed like an opportune time for Moab to break the yoke once and for all. But Joram didn't want to lose all that free income, nor did he want his people to think he was a weak ruler, so he took a military census and prepared for war.

Jehoram, now coregent of Judah, was married to Joram's sister Athaliah, so it seemed only right for Joram to ask King Jehoshaphat to go with him to punish Moab. A year before, the Moabites and Ammonites had declared war on Judah and Jehoshaphat, had soundly defeated them with the Lord's help (2 Chron. 20). Joram wanted allies like that at his side! The two kings decided not to attack from the north because the northern border of Moab was heavily fortified and the Ammonites might interfere, but to make an attack from around the southern extremity of the Dead Sea. Joram's army would march south through Judah and pick up Jehoshaphat's men, and then both armies would march through Edom and join with the Edomite army at the more vulnerable southern border of Moab.

A needy army (vv. 9-14). The plan was a good one. Joram's army left Samaria and after a three-day march joined Jehoshaphat's army in Judah, probably at Jerusalem. Then both armies proceeded south to Edom, a journey of about four days. So, after this seven-day march, the armies arrived at the valley at the southern end of the Dead Sea, between the mountains of Judah and Moab. Everything was going well except that they were out of water. The soldiers were thirsty and so were the baggage animals and the cattle brought along for food.

Conveniently forgetting that his father's god Baal was the rain god, King Joram responded to the situation by blaming the Lord for their plight (v. 10). Jehoshaphat, on the other hand, suggested that they consult the Lord and see what He wanted them to do. He had given the same advice to Ahab years before when they had joined forces to fight the Syrians (1 Kings 22). Joram didn't know any prophets of the Lord and didn't even know that Elisha was in the area. One of his own officers had to tell him that the prophet had joined the troops, certainly by the leading of the Lord. At that hour, Elisha was the most valuable man in the combined armies of the three nations. Elisha had compared Elijah to the army of Israel (2:12), but now Elisha was more powerful than three armies!

We aren't told where Elisha was, but the three kings humbled themselves and went there to ask for his help. When Jehoshaphat joined with Ahab to fight the Syrians, the Lord's prophet rebuked him for compromising (2 Chron. 19:1-4); but now, the presence of a descendant of King David was the key to victory. Elisha made it clear that he wasn't helping Joram, son of Ahab, but Jehoshaphat, son of David. Once again, it is God's covenant with David that introduces the grace of God and brings about God's rescue of His people. Joram's reply still smacked of unbelief: "We're all in this together and are in danger of being defeated!" But when it came to confronting kings, Elisha was as fearless as his mentor, Elijah.

A divine intervention (vv. 15-27). The music of the harpist brought quietness to the prophet's mind and heart and helped to facilitate his communion with the Lord. Then Elisha revealed God's plan. The kings were to command their soldiers to dig ditches or pits in the dry valley. God would send rain in the distant mountains, but the Moabite army wouldn't know it because there would be no sound of wind or storm. The rain would create a flood that would move down from the mountains and cover the arid plain. Some of the water would collect in the pits or trenches and be available for the men and beasts to drink. But God would also use those pools to deceive and defeat the Moabite army. Elisha didn't explain how.

Then Elisha added that God would enable the three armies to defeat the Moabites, but it must be a complete victory. They were to tear down, stone by stone, all the fortified cities in Moab and throw the stones in the fields. They must also cut down the trees and stop up the wells.[1] In other words, the three armies should so destroy Moab's resources that they would not be able to regroup and start fighting back.

The priests back in Jerusalem were offering the early morning sacrifice when the rain that fell in the mountains came flooding into the valley. It filled the trenches and formed pools on the earth, and the soldiers, cattle, and baggage animals were all able to drink to the full. *But the Moabite army assembled at the border knew nothing about the rain!* God arranged that the reflection of the sun on the pools gave the illusion of blood, and the Moabites were deceived into thinking that the three armies had slaughtered each other. (This had happened to the armies of Moab, Ammon and Edom when they attacked King Jehoshaphat, 2 Chron. 20:22-30.) Confident of their safety and the opportunity for wealth, the Moabites attacked the camp of the three kings and were soundly defeated and chased away.

The three armies obeyed God's command and moved into Moab bent on destroying their cities and doing as much damage to their natural resources as possible. The king of Moab and his army retreated to Kir Hareseth, the capital at that time, and the invading armies laid siege to it but couldn't break through. The king of Moab tried to get through the lines to Edom, perhaps to persuade his former allies to help him, but the plan didn't work. His final step was to turn to his god Chemosh and offer him the life of the crown prince. He did this publicly, on the wall of the city, and the result was that the armies called off the siege and returned to their own lands.

A strange ending (v. 27) Joram succeeded in punishing Moab for breaking their agreement, but what was it that ended the war? The phrase "great indignation against Israel" (KJV and NKJV) has been translated "the fury against Israel" (NIV), "there came great wrath against Israel" (NASB), "the anger against Israel was great" (NLT), and "Great indignation came upon Israel" (*Berkeley*). The *New English Bible* reads, "The Israelites were filled with such consternation at this sight, that they struck camp and returned to their own land." The marginal reading is, "There was such great anger against the Israelites."

We can't believe that the false god Chemosh did anything to stop the invaders or that Jehovah would allow a brutal pagan sacrifice to take glory from His name. "I am the Lord: that is my name: and my glory will I not give to another, neither my praise to graven images" (Isa. 42:8). This leaves us with three possibilities. Perhaps the sacrifice gave fresh courage and zeal to the Moabites so that their army attacked with new enthusiasm and drove the invaders back. Or, perhaps the Israelites were so disgusted at the sacrifice that they packed up and left, and the other two kings followed with their armies. Human sacrifices were forbidden by the Mosaic Law (Lev. 20:1-5) and Jehoshaphat may have felt guilty that his siege had caused the death of the crown prince. But the three armies had slain many people as they moved through Moab, and it's not likely that they regretted the death of the king's successor. Furthermore, the emphasis is on Israel and not Judah, and King Joram of Israel wouldn't be upset at the offering of a human sacrifice. He came from a family of murderers!

If the Lord sent His wrath against Israel, why did He do so? Did He judge King Joram and his army alone (Israel = the Northern Kingdom) or Israel and Judah together? Throughout the text, "Israel" refers to the Northern Kingdom and not the united tribes, so Joram and the army of Israel must have been the target. Twice Joram had questioned whether Jehovah could or would do anything (vv. 10, 13), and Elisha made it clear that he wasn't paying any attention to the apostate king (vv. 13-14). Yet Joram was sharing in a great victory because of the faith of the king of Judah! Perhaps the Lord demonstrated His wrath against the army of Israel alone to teach Joram a lesson, just as He sent drought and fire from heaven to teach his father, Ahab, a lesson. When Israel had to leave the field, the other two kings left with them, and this ended the siege. The capital city was not destroyed and the Moabite king and his forces were neither captured nor killed, so it was an incomplete victory. However, for the sake of the house of David, God in His grace gave victory to the three kings.

2. Grace pays the debt. (2 Kings 4:1-7)[2] From the great international conflict, Elisha returned to the concerns of the schools of the prophets, for a true spiritual leader has a concern for individuals. He followed the example of his mentor, Elijah, who had ministered to families (1 Kings 17:8-24). The fact that the woman was a widow and the mother of two sons shows that the sons of the prophets weren't a celibate monastic group. Elisha knew this particular man and that he had a reputation for godliness. His death would have ended whatever income he earned, and for a widow to raise two sons unaided would have been a difficult thing at that time. Even dedicated people training for ministry have their trials and difficulties.

According to Hebrew law, a creditor could take the debtor and his children as servants, but he was not to treat them like slaves (Ex. 21:1-11; Lev. 25:29-31; Deut. 15:1-11). It would be heartbreaking for this woman to lose her husband to death and her two sons to servitude, but God is the "judge of the widows" (Deut. 10:18; Pss. 68:5; 146:9) and He sent Elisha to help her.[3]

God often begins with what we already have. Moses had a rod in his hand, and God used that to accomplish great things (Ex. 4:2). Peter and his partners had fishing nets in their hands (Luke 5), and the lad had a few loaves and fishes (John 6). All that the poor widow had was a little oil in a vessel, but "little is much when God is in it." Most of her neighbors would have unused empty vessels sitting around, so she wasn't robbing anybody by borrowing them, and once she had sold the oil, she could return the vessels. Elisha instructed her to shut the door so that nobody would see that a miracle was occurring in her house, and no doubt she warned her sons to keep quiet. The amount of oil she received was limited by the number of vessels she had, and that was controlled by her faith. (See also 13:10-19.) "According to your faith let it be to you" (Matt. 9:29, NKJV). When she sold the oil, she had enough money to pay off the debt and maintain herself and her two sons.

The Lord doesn't always perform miracles of this kind to help us pay our debts, but He does meet our needs if we trust and obey. If we give everything to Him, He can make a little go a long way. This miracle also reminds us of the greatest miracle of all, the gracious forgiveness of our debts to the Lord through faith in Jesus Christ (Luke 7:36-50; Eph. 1:7; Col. 2:13). It didn't cost Elisha anything for God to provide the needed money to pay the debt, but it cost Jesus Christ His life to be able forgive us our sins.

3. Grace imparts the life. (2 Kings 4:8-37)

Shunem was about twenty miles northwest of Abel-meholah, Elisha's hometown, and twenty-five miles or so beyond Shunem was Mount Carmel (see v. 25). The average traveler on foot could cover fifteen to twenty miles per day, so Shunem was the perfect halfway point for Elisha whenever he went to Mount Carmel to pray, meditate, and seek the Lord in a new way. Since Mount Carmel was a very special place because of Elijah's ministry, perhaps there was also a school of the prophets there.

A great woman (vv. 8-10). The unnamed woman was great in social standing and in wealth. But she was also great in perception, for she noticed that Elijah often passed that way on his ministry trips. She also discerned that he was a man of God, and she wanted to serve the Lord by serving His prophet. We get the impression that her husband lacked his wife's spiritual insight, but at least he didn't oppose her hospitality to the itinerant preacher. He permitted her to have a permanent "prophet's chamber" built on the roof of the house and to outfit it with a lamp, a table and chair,[4] and a bed. It was large enough to walk around in (v. 35) and apparently offered room enough for Gehazi, Elisha's servant (v. 13). The woman also saw to it that the two men were fed.

In this day of motels and hotels, hospitality to God's people, and especially God's servants, is becoming a neglected ministry and a lost blessing. Yet, one of the qualifications for an elder is "given to hospitality" (1 Tim. 3:2; Titus 1:8), and Hebrews 13:2 exhorts all believers to practice this virtue (see Gen. 18). We should open our hearts and homes to others and not complain about it (1 Peter 4:9).

A great gift (vv. 11-17). The prophet and his servant were resting in the room when Elisha expressed a desire to do something special for the woman because of her kindness to them, and he asked Gehazi to call her so he could discuss the matter with her. Elisha addressed his words to Gehazi, possibly because the woman held Elisha in such high regard that she didn't feel worthy to speak with him. But her reply was humble and brief: "I am content among my own people." She didn't want Elisha to intercede with the great God because she had no desire to be treated like a great person. She ministered to them because she wanted to serve the Lord.

After she left the prophet's chamber, Gehazi suggested that she might want a son. Her husband was older than she, so perhaps conception was impossible; but if God could do it for Abraham and Sarah, He could do it for them. It was likely that her husband would precede her in death, and without a family, she would be left alone. Gehazi called her a second time, and this time Elijah spoke to her personally. He gave her a promise that sounded very much like God's words to Abraham and Sarah (v. 16; Gen. 17:21; 18:14). How many blessings husbands with nominal faith have received because of the dedication of their godly wives! The promise was fulfilled and the woman gave birth to a son. Grace brought life where once there had been no life.

A great sorrow (vv. 18-28). The boy was still a child when these events occurred, for his mother was able to hold him on her lap and carry his limp body up to Elijah's chamber on the roof (vv. 20-21). The cause of the lad's illness isn't specified, but perhaps the heat of the harvest season affected him. The mother called to the father in the field and asked him to provide her with a servant and a donkey, but she didn't inform him that the boy had died. The fact that she was leaving suggested that the boy was safe, probably taking a nap. No doubt she feared her husband would order instant burial, for nobody wants a corpse in the house during the hot harvest season. Her husband wondered why she wanted to see Elisha when it wasn't a special holy day, but her only reply was, "Peace—*shalom.*" She would also say this to Gehazi (v. 26).

Gehazi's attitude toward the woman's coming reveals a dark streak in his character that shows up even more in the next chapter (v. 27; see Matt. 15:23; 19:13-15). Perhaps the woman and her servant intruded on their afternoon siesta. But Elisha discerned that something was wrong that the Lord hadn't revealed to him. Even Jesus occasionally asked for information (Mark 5:9; 9:21; John 11:34). Of course the woman was bitter and heartbroken, and it sounds like she was blaming Elisha for the tragedy. She hadn't asked for a son, and if Elisha and Gehazi hadn't interfered, her joy wouldn't have been snatched from her.

A great miracle (vv. 29-37). The woman and the servant must have ridden very fast to get to Mount Carmel in time for Elisha and Gehazi to return home with her the same day; and the animal must have been exhausted from such a strenuous trip in the harvest sun. Why did Elisha send Gehazi ahead? He was probably the younger of the two men and could run faster and get to the house much more quickly. It was important that somebody get back to guard the corpse so that the father wouldn't discover it and have it buried. Gehazi laid his staff on the boy's body, but nothing happened. (Was this because of what was hidden in his heart?) The woman rode the donkey and Elisha followed after her, but we aren't told that he received special power as Elijah did when he ran before Ahab's chariot (1 Kings 18:46).

Once again the door was shut on a miracle (4:4; and see Luke 8:51). First, the prophet prayed, and then, following the example of Elijah (1 Kings 17:17-24), he stretched himself out over the corpse. He got up and walked in the room, no doubt praying and seeking God's power, and then he lay on the boy a second time. This time the boy came back to life, sneezed seven times and opened his eyes. The text doesn't explain the significance of the sneezes, unless it was God's way of expelling something toxic from his lungs. You would think that Elisha would have been overjoyed to take the boy downstairs to his mother, but instead, he called Gehazi, who in turn called the mother.[5] See Hebrews 11:35.

But the story doesn't end there (see 8:1-6). Later, when Elisha announced the coming of a seven-year famine, he also advised the woman to relocate, so she went to dwell with the Philistines. When she returned to claim her property, Gehazi was speaking with the king and telling him about the resurrection of the boy, and his mother showed up in the palace! The king authorized the officials to return her property to her along with whatever income she had lost because of her absence. The death of the boy turned out to be a blessing in disguise.

Only God's grace can impart life, whether to a barren womb or to a dead boy, and only God's grace can impart spiritual life to the dead sinner (John 5:24; 17:1-3; Eph. 2:1-10). It was God who gave the boy life, but He used Elisha as the means to do it. So it is with raising sinners from the dead: God needs witnesses, prayer warriors, and concerned saints to bring that life to them. Said Charles Spurgeon, "The Holy Ghost works by those who feel they would lay down their own lives for the good of others, and would impart to them not only their goods and their instructions, but themselves also, if by any means they might save some. O for more Elishas, for then we should see more sinners raised from their death in sin."[6]

4. Grace removes the curse. (2 Kings 4:38-41)

Elisha visited the sons of the prophets at Gilgal during the time of the famine (8:1), and he commanded Gehazi his servant to make a stew for the men. Vegetables were scarce so some of the men went looking in the fields for herbs they could add to the stew. The student who came with a cloak filled with gourds wasn't knowledgeable about such matters but just brought whatever looked edible. In fact, nobody knew what these gourds were!

What were the evidences that there was poison in the pot? The bitter taste of the stew was perhaps the first clue, and the men probably suffered stomach pains and nausea. There had been death in the water at Jericho (2:19-22), and now there was death in the pot at Gilgal. It had been introduced innocently by a well-meaning student, but it had to be removed. But it was a time of famine and food was scarce. Elisha dropped some flour into the pot, and the Lord removed the poison from the stew.

As far as we know, there were no poisonous plants growing in the Garden of Eden. They showed up with the thorns and thistles after Adam sinned (Gen. 3:17-19). Today, there is a great deal of "death in the pot," for we live under the curse of the law of sin and death, and sin and death are reigning in this world (Rom. 5:14-21). But when Jesus died on the cross, He bore the curse of the law for us (Gal. 3:13), and for those who have trusted Christ, grace is reigning (Rom. 5:21) and they are "reigning in life" (Rom. 5:17). The sting of death has been removed (1 Cor. 15:50-57)!

5. Grace satisfies the hungry. (2 Kings 4:42-44)

In the northern kingdom of Israel, there was no official temple dedicated to Jehovah, and many of the faithful priests and Levites had left apostate Israel and moved to Judah (1 Kings 12:26-33; 2 Chron. 11:13-17). Since there was no sanctuary to which the people could bring their tithes and offerings (Lev. 2:14; 6:14-23; 23:9-17; Deut. 18:3-5), they brought them to the nearest school of the prophets where they would be shared by people true to the Mosaic Law. The firstfruit offerings of grain could be roasted heads of grain, fine flour baked into cakes, or even loaves of bread. All of this would be most welcome to the sons of the prophets, and certainly the Lord honored the people who refused to bow down to the golden calves at Dan and Bethel.

There were one hundred hungry men in the group, and though the gifts the man brought were honored by the Lord, they couldn't feed all of the men adequately. The situation parallels that of Christ and the disciples (Matt. 14:13-21; 15:29-33, and parallels in the Gospels). Gehazi's question "How can I set this before a hundred men?" (v. 43, NIV) sounds like Andrew's question about the five loaves and two fish, "[H]ow far will they go among so many?" (John 6:9, NIV).

But Elisha knew that the Lord had this difficult situation well under His control. He commanded his servant to set out the bread and grain, and when Gehazi obeyed, there was not only plenty of food for everybody, but there was food left over. The Word of the Lord had announced and accomplished the impossible.

When our Lord fed the five thousand, He used the miracle as a backdrop for preaching a strong salvation message about the Bread of Life (John 6:25ff). Elisha didn't preach a sermon, but the miracle assures us that God knows our needs and meets them as we trust Him. Today we have freezers and supermarkets to supply us with food, and there are food banks to help those who are poor. But in Elisha's time, people prepared and consumed their food a day at a time. That's why Jesus taught us to pray, "Give us this day our daily bread" (Matt. 6:11). During his years in the wilderness as an exile, David depended on God's provision, and he was able to say, "I have been young, and now am old; yet I have not seen the righteous forsaken, nor his descendants begging bread" (Ps. 37:25, NKJV). Out of the riches of His grace, the Lord meets our every need.

CHAPTER THREE
THREE MEN—THREE MIRACLES
2 Kings 5:1–6:7

Elisha was a miracle-working prophet who ministered to all sorts of people who brought him all kinds of needs. In this section, we see Elisha healing a distinguished general, judging his own servant, and helping a lowly student get back to work. It may seem a long way from the lofty head of the army to a lost axhead, but both were important to God and to God's servant. Like our Lord when He ministered here on earth, Elisha had time for individuals and he wasn't influenced by their social standing or their financial worth. "Casting all your care upon Him, for He cares for you" (1 Peter 5:7, NKJV).

But as important as the miracles are in this section, the theme of *ministry* is even more important. The Lord not only gave new life to Naaman, He also gave him a new purpose in life, a new ministry. He would return to Syria (Aram) as much more than a general, for now he was an ambassador of the true and living God of Israel. Naaman gained a new purpose in life, but, alas, Gehazi lost his ministry because of his covetousness and deception. When Elisha recovered the lost axhead, the student got back his "cutting edge," and his ministry was restored to him.

1. Naaman—ministry received. (2 Kings 5:1-19)

The Prophet Elijah is named twenty-nine times in the New Testament while Elisha is named only once. "And many lepers were in Israel in the time of Elisha the prophet, and none of them was cleansed except Naaman the Syrian" (Luke 4:27, NKJV). Naaman was a Gentile and the commander of the army of an enemy nation, so it's no wonder the congregation in Nazareth became angry with the Lord, interrupted His sermon and carried Him out of the synagogue. After all, why would the God of Israel heal a man who was a Gentile and outside the covenant? He was an enemy who kidnapped little Jewish girls, and a leper who should have been isolated and left to die. These people knew nothing about the sovereign grace of God. Like Naaman, they became angry, but unlike Naaman, they didn't humble themselves and trust the Lord. Naaman's experience with Elisha illustrates to us the gracious work of God in saving lost sinners.

Naaman needed the Lord (vv. 1-3). The king of Syria was Ben Hadad II, and as commander of the army, Naaman was the number two man in the nation. But with all his prestige, authority, and wealth, Naaman was a doomed man because under his uniform was the body of a leper. It appears from verse 11 that the infection was limited to one place, but leprosy has a tendency to spread and if left unchecked, it ultimately kills. Only the power of the God of Israel could heal him.

Although Naaman didn't realize it, the Lord had already worked on his behalf by giving him victory over the Assyrians. Jehovah is the covenant God of Israel, but He is also Lord of all the nations and can use any person, saved or unsaved, to accomplish His will (see Isa. 44:28; 45:13; Ezek. 30:24-25). The Lord also did a gracious thing when He permitted Naaman to bring the captive Jewish girl into his house to be his wife's maid. The girl was a slave, but because she trusted the God of Israel, she was free. Even more, she was a humble witness to her mistress. Her words were so convincing that the woman told her husband and he in turn informed the king. Never underestimate the power of a simple witness, for God can take words from the lips of a child and carry them to the ears of a king.

Although there is no direct scriptural statement that leprosy is a picture of sin, when you read Leviticus 13, you can clearly see parallels. Like leprosy, sin is deeper than the skin (v. 3), it spreads (v. 7), it defiles (v. 45), it isolates (v. 46), and it is fit only for the fire (vv. 52, 57).

Seeking the Lord (vv. 4-10). Naaman couldn't leave Syria without the king's permission, and he also needed an official letter of introduction to Joram, king of Israel. After all, Syria and Israel were enemies, and the arrival of the commander of the Syrian army could be greatly misunderstood. Both Naaman and Ben Hadad wrongly assumed that the prophet would do whatever the king commanded him to do and that both the king and the prophet would expect to receive expensive gifts in return. For that reason, Naaman took along 750 pounds of silver and 150 pounds of gold, plus costly garments. The servant girl had said nothing about kings or gifts; she only pointed to Elisha the prophet and told her mistress what the Lord could do. Unsaved people know nothing about the things of the Lord and only complicate that which is so simple (1 Cor. 2:14). We aren't saved by bringing gifts to God, but by receiving by faith His gift of eternal life (Eph. 2:8-9; John 3:16, 36; Rom. 6:23).

This was King Joram's opportunity to honor the Lord and begin to build peace between Syria and Israel, but he failed to take advantage of it. Although 3:11 suggests that Joram and Elisha weren't close friends, the king did know who Elisha was and what he could do. He also surely knew that Israel's task was to bear witness to the godless nations around them (Isa. 42:6; 49:6). But Joram's concerns were personal and political, not spiritual, and he interpreted the letter as a declaration of war.[1] Alarmed by the thought, he impulsively tore his clothes, something that kings rarely did; but his mind was blinded by unbelief and fear and he didn't understand what the Lord was doing.

The prophet was in his home in the city of Samaria, but he knew what the king had said and done in his palace, for God hides from His servants nothing they need to know (Amos 3:7). His message to Joram must have irritated the king, but at the same time Elisha was rescuing Joram from personal embarrassment and possible international complications. Yes, there was a king on the throne, but there was also a prophet in Israel! The king was helpless to do anything, but the prophet was a channel of God's power.

Elisha knew that Naaman had to be humbled before he could be healed. Accustomed to the protocol of the palace, this esteemed leader expected to be recognized publicly and his lavish gifts accepted with exaggerated appreciation, because that's the way kings did things. But Elisha didn't even come out of his house to welcome the man! Instead, he sent a messenger (Gehazi?) instructing him to ride thirty-two miles to the Jordan River and immerse himself in it seven times. Then he would be cleansed of his leprosy.

Naaman had been seeking help and now his search was ended.

Resisting the Lord (vv. 11-12). If Naaman began his journey at Damascus, then he had traveled over one hundred miles to get to Samaria, so another thirty miles or so shouldn't have upset him. But it did, for the great general became angry. The basic cause of his anger was pride. He had already decided in his own mind just how the prophet would heal him, but God didn't work that way. Before sinners can receive God's grace, they must submit to God's will, for "God resists the proud, but gives grace to the humble" (1 Peter 5:5, NKJV; see Rom. 10:1-3). Dr. Donald Grey Barnhouse used to say, "Everybody has the privilege of going to heaven God's way or going to hell their own way."

The Lord had already been working on Naaman's pride and there was more to come. King Joram wasn't able to heal him, the prophet didn't come to court or even come out to greet him, and he had to dip in the dirty Jordan River, not once, but seven times. And he a great general and second in command over the nation of Syria! "Ah, that is just the trouble," said evangelist D. L. Moody when preaching on this passage. "He had marked out a way of his own for the prophet to heal him, and was mad because he didn't follow his plans." Is it any different today? People want to be saved from their sins by participating in a religious ritual, joining a church, giving money to the church, reforming their lives, doing good works, and a host of other substitutes for putting faith in Jesus Christ. "Not by works of righteousness which we have done, but according to his mercy he saved us" (Titus 3:5).

Naaman had another problem: he preferred the rivers back in Damascus to the muddy Jordan River.[2] He thought his healing would come from the water, so it was logical that the better the water, the better the healing. He would rather have his own way and travel over a hundred miles than obey God's way and go thirty-two miles! He was so close to salvation and yet so far away!

Trusting the Lord (vv. 13-15a). Once again, the Lord used servants to accomplish His purposes (vv. 2-3). If Naaman wouldn't listen to the command of the prophet, perhaps he would heed the counsel of his own servants. "Come now, and let us reason together, says the Lord" (Isa. 1:18). Elisha didn't ask him to do something difficult or impossible, because that would only have increased his pride. He asked him to obey a simple command and perform a humbling act, and it was unreasonable not to submit. When Naaman told his story back in Syria and got to this point, his friend would say, "You did what?" Faith that doesn't lead to obedience isn't faith at all.

When he came up from the water the seventh time, his leprosy was gone and his flesh was like that of a little child. In New Testament language, he was born again (John 3:3-8). "Assuredly, I say to you, unless you are converted and become as little children, you will by no means enter the kingdom of heaven" (Matt. 18:3, NKJV). By his obedience he demonstrated his faith in God's promise, and the Lord cleansed him of his leprosy. To quote D. L. Moody again, "He lost his temper; then he lost his pride; then he lost his leprosy; that is generally the order in which proud rebellious sinners are converted." Naaman gave a clear public testimony that the Lord God of Israel was the only true and living God and was the God of all the earth. He renounced the false gods and idols of Syria and identified himself with Jehovah. What an indictment this testimony was against the idol-worshiping king and people of Israel!

Serving the Lord (vv. 15b-19). Like every new believer, Naaman still had a lot to learn. He had been saved and healed by trusting in God's grace, and now he had to grow in grace and faith and learn how to live to please the God who saved him. Instead of hurrying home to share the good news, Naaman returned to the house of Elisha to thank the Lord and His servant. (See Luke 17:11-19.) That meant traveling another thirty miles, but he must have rejoiced during the entire trip. It was natural for him to want to reward Elisha, but had the prophet accepted the gift, he would have taken the credit to himself and robbed God of glory. God saves us "to the praise of the glory of His grace" (Eph. 1:6, 12, 14). He also would have given Naaman, a new convert, the impression that his gifts had something to do with his salvation. Abraham had refused the gifts from the king of Sodom (Gen. 14:17-24), Daniel would refuse the king's offer (Dan. 5:17), and Peter and John would reject Simon's money (Acts 8:18-24).

Naaman was starting to grow in his understanding of the Lord, but he still had a long way to go. Elisha refused his gifts, but Naaman asked if he could take some native soil with him to Syria to use in his worship of Jehovah. In those days, people had the idea that the gods of a nation resided in that land, and if you left the land, you left the god behind. But Naaman had just testified that Jehovah was God in all the earth (v. 15)! However, taking that soil was a courageous act, because his master and his friends would surely ask Naaman what it meant, and he would have to tell them of his faith in the God of Israel.

In his second request, Naaman showed unusual insight, for he realized that the king would expect him to continue his official acts as the commander of the army. This included accompanying the king into the temple of Rimmon, the Syrian equivalent of Baal. Naaman was willing to perform this ritual outwardly, but he wanted Elisha to know that his heart would not be in it. Naaman anticipated that his healing and his changed life would have an impact on the royal court and eventually lead to the king's conversion. Instead of criticizing believers who serve in public offices, we need to pray for them, because they face very difficult decisions.[3]

It's interesting that Elisha didn't lecture him or admonish him but just said, "Go in peace." This was the usual covenant blessing the Jews invoked when people were starting on a journey. The prophet would pray for him and trust God to use him in his new ministry in Syria. Naaman's leprosy was gone, he still had the treasures, he carried soil from Israel, and he knew the true and living God. What a witness he could be in that dark land—and Naaman's servant girl would join him!

2. Gehazi—ministry revoked. (2 Kings 5:20-27)

While Naaman was seeking to live the truth and please the Lord, Elisha's servant was wallowing in deception and unholy desires. "Thou shalt not covet" is the last of the Ten Commandments (Ex. 20:17), but when you break this one commandment, you tempt yourself to break the other nine. Covetous people will make idols out of material wealth, bear false witness, steal, dishonor God's name, abuse their parents, and even murder. Gehazi had been decaying in his spiritual life, and this was the climax. He had pushed away the woman whose son died (4:27), and he had no power to raise the boy to life (4:31). Now his covetousness took control, it led to lying, and it finally resulted in Gehazi becoming a leper. The disease on the outside typified the decay on the inside.

He lied to himself (v. 20). When he refused the gifts, Elisha hadn't been "easy" on Naaman but had taught the young believer a difficult lesson. Gehazi was measuring his master's conduct the way the world would measure it, not the way God measured it. Like our Lord's disciples when Mary anointed Jesus, he asked, "Why this waste?" (Mark 14:3-9), only in Gehazi's situation, it was a wasted opportunity to get wealth. He actually believed he would be a better and a happier man if he took some gifts from Naaman and that he had the right to do it. "Take heed and beware of covetousness, for one's life does not consist in the abundance of the things he possesses" (Luke 12:15, NKJV).

Surely Gehazi knew that Naaman's salvation and healing were wholly by the grace of God and that taking gifts might give the Syrian general the impression that he could do something to save himself. When he returned to Syria, Naaman would have to account for the missing treasures, and this could only weaken his testimony. Abraham refused gifts from the king of Sodom so he wouldn't compromise his testimony before the people of Sodom who needed to know the Lord (Gen. 14). Peter and John refused Simon's offer lest they give the Samaritans the idea that God's gifts could be purchased with money (Acts 8:20ff). The Apostle Paul even refused financial support from the church at Corinth lest the people think he was just another traveling philosopher, out to collect money.[4]

Gehazi took the Lord's name in vain

when he said "As the Lord lives" (v. 20, see v. 16), for he had sin in his heart and was planning to sin even more. We get the impression that Gehazi had no fear of God in his heart and privately used God's name carelessly. Had he revered the name of God—the third commandment, Exodus 20:7—he would not have been controlled by greed.

He lied to Naaman (vv. 21-24). Naaman's caravan wasn't too far away and Gehazi was able to run and catch up with it (see 4:26, 29). Naaman did a noble thing when he stopped his chariot and stepped down to meet Elisha's servant. (See Acts 8:31.) Perhaps Elisha had another message for him, or perhaps there was a need to be met. For a Syrian general to show such deference to a Jewish servant was certainly an indication that God had wrought a change in his heart. Naaman greeted him with "Shalom—is all well?" and Gehazi replied "Shalom—all is well." But all wasn't well! When a man's heart is filled with greed and his lips are filled with lies, he is far from enjoying *shalom,* which means "peace, well-being, fulfillment, prosperity, safety."

In carrying out his evil plan, Gehazi not only used God's name in vain, but he also used God's work as a "cloak of covetousness" (1 Thes. 2:1-6). Using Elisha's name, he lied to Naaman when he asked for gifts for two sons of the prophets from Bethel and Gilgal. These schools were located in the area of Mount Ephraim. We must not criticize Naaman for believing Gehazi's lies, for after all, he was a young believer and lacked the discernment that comes with a maturing spiritual experience. "My master has sent me" was a deliberate falsehood, although unknown to Gehazi, his master knew what he had done. Naaman not only gave Gehazi more than he requested and wrapped it neatly, but he also assigned two of his servants to carry the gifts for him. When the three men arrived at the hill on which Samaria was built (or perhaps a hill between them and Samaria), Gehazi took the bundle and sent the men back, lest somebody recognize them and start asking questions. Gehazi was near his master's house and he had to be careful not to let him know what he had done.

He lied to Elisha (vv. 25-27). Acting very innocent, Gehazi went and stood before his master, awaiting orders; but he found himself on trial! Gehazi had forgotten that "all things are naked and open to the eyes of Him to whom we must give account" (Heb. 4:13, NKJV). God knew what Gehazi had done and He communicated it to His servant. The scene reminds us of how Joshua interrogated Achan (Josh. 7) and Peter interrogated Ananias and Sapphira (Acts 5), all of whom had coveted wealth and lied about it.

Elisha not only saw what his servant had done, but he saw into his servant's heart and knew why he did it. Gehazi longed to be a wealthy man with land, flocks and herds, expensive clothing, and servants to obey his orders. He wasn't content to labor by the side of Elisha the prophet; he wanted to have security and comfort. There's certainly nothing wrong with being wealthy, if that's God's will for your life, for Abraham and Isaac were wealthy and so was David. But it is wrong to get that wealth through deceit and to make that wealth your god. Gehazi used the ministry God gave him as a means of deceiving Naaman, and that is contrary to God's will (1 Thes. 2:1-6; 2 Cor. 2:17; 4:2).

God judged Gehazi by giving him leprosy and promising that at least one of his descendants in each generation would be a leper. The covetousness that ate away at his heart became leprosy eating away at his body. Gehazi had hoped to leave great wealth to his descendants, but instead, he left great shame and sorrow for years to come. In Israel, lepers were considered unclean and weren't allowed to be in the community and live normal lives. Gehazi could no longer be Elisha's servant; he had lost his ministry. "Not greedy for money" is one of the qualifications for God's servants (1 Tim. 3:3). One of the marks of the last days is that people will love money more than they love God or other people (2 Tim. 3:1-5).

3. The student—ministry restored. (2 Kings 6:1-7)

Elisha wasn't only a traveling preacher and a miracle-working prophet, but he was also the overseer of several schools of the prophets where young men called to ministry were trained and encouraged. We know there were schools in Gilgal, Bethel, and Jericho (2:1-5) and also in Samuel's hometown of Ramah (1 Sam. 19:22-24), but there may have been others. Both Elijah and Elisha were concerned that the next generation know the Lord and understand His Word, and this is the church's commission today (2 Tim. 2:2). D. L. Moody and Charles Spurgeon were not privileged to have formal training for ministry, but both of them started schools that are still training God's servants today. It's good to serve our own generation, but let's not forget the generations to come.

This account picks up the story from 4:44. God had blessed the school at Jericho and it was necessary to enlarge their quarters. The students studied together when the prophet visited them, for they met with him and sat before him to hear him teach (v. 1). They also ate together (4:38-44), but they lived in their own family dwellings (4:1-7). It's a good sign when God is raising up a new generation of servants and when the veteran ministers of God take time to teach them.

But new growth brings new obligations, and the facilities at Jordan had to be enlarged. Schools today would do fundraising and hire architects and contractors, but in Elisha's day, the students did the work. Not only that, but the leader of the school went with them and encouraged the work. Elisha had a shepherd's heart and was willing to go with his flock and share their burdens.

The Jewish people didn't have hardware stores stocked with tools such as we have today. Iron tools were precious and scarce, which explains why the student had to borrow an ax so he could help prepare the timber. (When I was in seminary, I didn't own any tools.) Not only were tools scarce, but they weren't constructed with the strength and durability of our tools today. In fact, Moses gave a special law relating to damage that might result when an axhead flew off the handle (Deut. 19:4-5), so it must have happened frequently. If the law of borrowed animals also applied to borrowed tools (Ex. 22:14-15), then that poor student would have to reimburse the lender for the lost axhead, and that would probably upset the budget for weeks to come. Without the axhead, the student couldn't work and that would add to somebody else's burdens. All in all, the sunken axhead caused a great deal of trouble.

The student was quick enough to see where it fell and honest enough to report the accident to Elisha. The Jordan isn't the cleanest river in the Holy Land (5:12) and it would be very difficult for anybody to see the axhead lying at the bottom. The prophet didn't "fish out" the axhead with a pole. He threw a stick into the water at the place where the axhead sank, and the

Lord raised the iron axhead so that it floated on the surface of the river and could be picked up. It was a quiet miracle from a powerful God through a compassionate servant.

There are some spiritual applications that we can learn from this incident, and perhaps the first is that *whatever we have has been "borrowed."* Paul asked, "And what do you have that you did not receive?" (1 Cor. 4:7, NKJV), and John the Baptist said, "A man can receive nothing unless it has been given to him from heaven" (John 3:27, NKJV). Whatever gifts, abilities, possessions, and opportunities we have are from God, and we will have to give an account of them when we see the Lord.

This student lost his valuable tool *while he was serving the Lord.* Faithful service is important, but it can also be threatening, for we might lose something valuable even as we do our work. Moses lost his patience and meekness while providing water for the people (Num. 20:1-13), and David lost his self-control while being kind to his neighbor (1 Sam. 25:13). God's servants must walk carefully before the Lord and take inventory of their "tools" lest they lose something they desperately need.

The good news is that *the Lord can recover what we have lost and put us back to work.* If we lose our "cutting edge," He can restore us and make us efficient in His service. The important thing is to know that you have lost it, and when and where you have lost it, and honestly confess it to Him. Then get back to work again!

While we're on the subject of axes, Ecc. 10:10 offers some good counsel: "If the axe is dull and he does not sharpen its edge, then he must exert more strength. Wisdom has the advantage of giving success" (NASB). The modern equivalent is, "Don't work harder—work smarter." Wisdom tells a worker to sharpen the tool before the work begins. But our text from Kings reminds us further to make sure that the sharp axhead is firmly set into the handle. Don't work without a cutting edge and don't lose your cutting edge.

CHAPTER FOUR
THE BATTLE IS THE LORD'S
2 Kings 6:8–7:20

From our point of view, it would have been more logical for the Lord to appoint Elijah, the "son of thunder," to confront the enemy armies that invaded Israel; but instead, He appointed Elisha, the quiet farm boy. Elisha was like the "still, small voice" that followed the tumult of the wind, the earthquake, and the fire (1 Kings 19:11-12), just as Jesus followed John the Baptist who had an ax in his hand. By declaring the righteousness of God and calling for repentance, Elijah and John the Baptist both prepared the way for their successors to minister, for without conviction there can be no true conversion.

As always in Scripture, the key actor in the drama is the Lord, not the prophet. By what he said and did, as well as by what he didn't do, Elisha revealed the character of the God of Israel to King Joram and his people. Jehovah is not like the idols of the nations (Ps. 115), for He alone is the true and living God.

1. The God who sees. (2 Kings 6:8-14)
Whenever the Syrians planned a border raid, the Lord gave Elisha the information and he warned the king. Baal could never have done this for King Joram, for idols have "Eyes . . . but they do not see" (Ps.

115:5, NKJV). The Lord sees not only the actions of people but also their thoughts (Ps. 94:11; 139:1-4) and their hearts (Prov. 15:3, 11; Jer. 17:10; Acts 1:24). Most of the people in the northern kingdom of Israel were unfaithful to the Lord, and yet in His mercy He cared for them. "Behold, He who keeps Israel shall neither slumber nor sleep" (Ps. 121:4, NKJV).

The king of Syria was sure there was a traitor in his camp, for the mind of the unbeliever interprets everything from a worldly viewpoint. Idolaters become like the gods they worship (Ps. 115:8) so Ben Hadad was as blind as his god Rimmon (5:18). However, one of Ben Hadad's officers knew what was going on and informed the king that the prophet Elisha was in charge of "military intelligence" and knew what the king said and did even in his own bedroom.

The logical solution then was to eliminate Elisha. Once again you see the ignorance of the king, for if Elisha knew every scheme the king planned for the border raids, surely he would know this scheme as well—and he did! Ben Hadad's spies found Elisha in Dothan, located about twelve miles north of the capital city of Samaria. Elisha's home was in Abel-meholah, but in his itinerant ministry, he moved from city to city. Humanly speaking, he would have been safer in the walled city of Samaria, but he had no fear, for he knew God was caring for him. The arrival that night of a company of foot soldiers, cavalry, and charioteers didn't upset the prophet in the least. This was not the full army but rather an enlarged "band" such as engaged in border raids (v. 23; 5:2; 13:20; 24:2).

When God's servants are in His will and doing His work, they are immortal until their work is done. The disciples tried to discourage Jesus from going back to Judah, but He assured them He was on a "divine timetable" and was therefore perfectly safe (John 11:7-10). It was only when His "hour had come" (John 13:1; 17:1) that His enemies had the power to arrest Him and crucify Him. If the Father's eye is on the sparrow (Matt. 10:29), then surely He is watching over His precious children.

2. The God who protects. (2 Kings 6:15-17)

This servant was not Gehazi, for he had been removed and replaced. The young man was an early riser, which speaks well of him, but he was still deficient in his faith. Seeing the city surrounded by enemy troops, he did the normal thing and turned to his master for help.

A woman told evangelist D. L. Moody that she had found a wonderful promise that gave her peace when she was troubled, and she quoted Psalm 56:3, "What time I am afraid, I will trust in thee." Moody said he had a better promise for her, and he quoted Isaiah 12:2, "Behold, God is my salvation; I will trust, and not be afraid." We wonder what promises from the Lord came to Elisha's mind and heart, for it's faith in God's Word that brings peace in the midst of the storm. Perhaps he recalled David's words in Ps. 27:3, "Though an army may encamp against me, my heart shall not fear; though war may rise against me, in this I will be confident" (NKJV). Or the words of Moses from Deuteronomy 20:3-4 may have come to mind, "Do not let your heart faint, do not be afraid . . . for the Lord your God is He who goes with you, to fight for you against your enemies, to save you" (NKJV).

Elisha didn't trouble himself about the army; his first concern was for his frightened servant. If he was going to walk with Elisha and serve God, the young man would face many difficult and dangerous situations, and he had to learn to trust the Lord. We probably would have prayed that the Lord would give peace to the lad's heart or calmness to his mind, but Elisha prayed for God to open his eyes. The servant was living by sight and not by faith and couldn't see the vast angelic army of the Lord surrounding the city. Faith enables us to see God's invisible army (Heb. 11:27) and trust Him to give us the victory. Jacob had a similar experience before he met Esau (Gen. 32), and Jesus knew that, if His Father so desired, the angelic army could deliver Him (Matt. 26:53). "As the mountains surround Jerusalem, so the Lord surrounds His people" (Ps. 125:2 (NKJV). "The angel of the Lord encamps all around those who fear Him, and delivers them" (Ps. 34:7, NKJV). The angels are servants to God's people (Heb. 1:14), and until we get to heaven, we will never fully know how much they have helped us.

3. The God who shows mercy (2 Kings 6:18-23)

Elisha didn't ask the Lord to command the angelic army to destroy Ben Hadad's feeble troops. As with nations today, defeat only promotes retaliation, and Ben Hadad would have sent another company of soldiers. God gave Elisha a much better plan. He had just prayed that the Lord would open his servant's eyes, but now he prayed that God would cloud the eyes of the Syrian soldiers. The soldiers weren't made totally blind, otherwise they couldn't have followed Elijah; but their sight was clouded in such a way that they were able to see but not comprehend. They were under the delusion that they were being led to the house of Elisha, but Elisha was leading them to the city of Samaria!

When Elisha went out to meet the Syrian troops, did he lie to them (v. 19)? No, because he was no longer in the city of Dothan and was actually going to Samaria. The prophet was actually saving their lives, for if King Joram had been in charge, he would have killed them (v. 21). Elisha did bring the troops to the man they wanted. When the army arrived at Samaria, the guards must have been shocked to see the prophet leading the troops, but they obediently opened the gates and then God opened their eyes. Imagine their surprise when they found themselves at the heart of the capital city and at the mercy of the Israelites.

King Joram would have slain all of the Syrian soldiers and claimed a great victory for himself, but Elisha intervened. The king graciously called Elisha "my father" (v. 21), a term used by servants for their master (5:13), but later, he wanted to take off Elisha's head (vv. 32)! Like his wicked father, Ahab, he could murder the innocent one day and then "walk softly" before the Lord the next day (1 Kings 21). Double-minded people are unstable (James 1:8).

Elisha's reply took the matter entirely out of the king's hands. Had Joram defeated this army in battle? No! If he had, he could kill his prisoners; but if he hadn't, then whoever captured the prisoners would decide what to do. These were not prisoners of war; they were Elisha's guests, so the king's responsibility was to feed them. Joram knew that having a meal with them was the same as making a covenant with them (Gen. 26:26-31), but he obeyed. In fact, he went beyond the prophet's request for bread and water and prepared a great feast for the soldiers.

Solomon wrote, "If your enemy is hungry, give him food to eat; if he is thirsty, give him water to drink. In doing this, you will heap burning coals on his head, and the Lord will reward you" (Prov.

25:21-22, NIV). In Romans 12:20-21, Paul quoted these words and applied them to believers today, and see also the words of Jesus in Matthew 5:43-48 and Luke 6:27-36. King Joram wanted to kill the Syrians, but Elisha "killed them with kindness." By eating together, they made a covenant of peace and the Syrian bands would no longer raid the borders of Israel.

Would this approach avert conflicts today? We must remember that Israel is a covenant nation and that the Lord fought their battles. No other nation can claim these privileges. But if kindness replaced long-standing and deeply rooted ethnic and religious differences among peoples, as well as national pride and international greed, there would no doubt be fewer wars and bombings. The same principle applies to ending divorce and abuse in families, riots and lootings in neighborhoods, uproars on campuses, and division and conflict in our communities. "Blessed are the merciful: for they shall obtain mercy" (Matt. 5:7).

4. The God who keeps His covenant. (2 Kings 6:24-33)

The border raids stopped, but Ben Hadad II decided it was time again for war.[1] Rulers have to prove themselves to their people, and defeating and looting a neighbor is one of the best ways to reveal your strength and wisdom. This time he sent the full army and he seems to have caught Joram totally unprepared. Perhaps the peace along the borders lulled Joram into thinking that Syria was no longer a threat. Joram doesn't seem to have been very astute when it came to military matters.

The siege of Samaria lasted so long that the people in the city were starving. It seems that Elisha had counseled the king to wait (v. 33), promising that the Lord would do something, but the longer they waited, the worse the circumstances became. But it must be remembered that God warned that He would punish His people if they failed to live up to the terms of His covenant. Among His punishments were military defeat (Lev. 26:17, 25, 33, 36-39; Deut. 28:25-26, 49-52) and famine (Lev. 26:26, 29; Deut. 28:17, 48), and Israel was now experiencing both. Had King Joram called his people to repentance and prayer, the situation would have changed (2 Chron. 7:14). People were reduced to eating unclean food, such as a donkey's head and dove's droppings, and for these they paid exorbitant prices—two pounds of silver for the head and two ounces of silver for the dung.[2]

But even worse, people were eating their own children! This, too, was a predicted punishment for breaking God's covenant (Lev. 26:29; Deut. 28:53-57). King Joram met two such women as he walked on the wall and surveyed the city. One woman called to the king for help, and he thought she wanted food and drink. Joram's reply really put the blame on the Lord and not on the sins of the nation. God alone could fill the threshing floor and the winepress and provide food and drink. But the woman didn't want food and drink; she wanted justice. Her friend hadn't kept her part of the bargain but had hidden her son!

Joram was appalled that the nation had fallen so low, and he publicly tore his robe, not as a sign of sorrow and repentance but as evidence of his anger at God and Elijah (see 5:7). When he did, he exposed the fact that he was wearing a rough sackcloth garment beneath the royal robe, but what good is sackcloth if there's no humility and repentance in the heart? His next words make it clear that he took no responsibility for the siege and the famine and that he wanted to murder

Elisha. He even used the oath that he learned from his evil mother, Jezebel (v. 31; 1 Kings 19:2). Joram's father, Ahab, called Elijah "the one who troubled Israel" (1 Kings 18:17), and Joram blamed Elisha for the plight Samaria was in at that time. The king sent a messenger to arrest Elisha and take him out to be killed.

The prophet wasn't upset or worried, for the Lord always told Elisha everything he needed to know. As the prophet sat in his house with the elders of the land, leaders who had come to him for counsel and help, he knew that the arresting officer was on his way. He also knew that the king himself would follow him to make sure the execution was a success. Elisha had already made it clear that he didn't accept the authority of the king of Israel because Joram was not of the line of David (3:14). Joram was the son of Ahab the murderer, the king who with his wife, Jezebel, killed the Lord's prophets who were opposing Baal worship (1 Kings 18:4). They also killed their neighbor Naboth so they could confiscate his property (1 Kings 21).

Elisha commanded the elders to hold the door shut until both men were outside. Being kept waiting at the door didn't help the king's temper one bit, and he called to Elisha, "It is the Lord who has brought this trouble on us! Why should I wait any longer for the Lord?" (v. 33, NLT). He should have said, "I am the cause of this great tragedy and I repent of my sins! Pray for me!" There was provision in the covenant for confession and forgiveness (Deut. 30) if only King Joram and his people had taken advantage of it. The Lord always keeps His covenant, whether to bless if His people obey or to discipline if they disobey.

5. The God who fulfills His promises. (2 Kings 7:1-20)

Did Elisha and the elders allow the king to enter the room along with his attendant and messenger? They probably did, but Joram was a somewhat subdued man when the door was finally opened to him, not unlike his father, Ahab, when Elijah indicted him for the murder of Naboth (1 Kings 21:17ff). The only messages the Lord had sent to the rebellious King Joram were the army around the city and the starvation within the city, and the king still had not repented.

Good news from the Lord (vv. 1-2). How fortunate it was for the kingdom of Israel that they had Elisha the prophet living and ministering among them! Throughout Hebrew history, in times of crisis, the prophets had God's message for God's people, whether they obeyed it or not. King Joram could turn to the priests of Baal, but they had nothing to say. The Lord spoke through "his servants the prophets" (21:10)

Joram wanting something to happen now; he would wait no longer. But Elisha opened his message with "tomorrow about this time." What would happen? Food would once more be available and the inflationary prices would fall drastically. The fine flour for the people and the barley for the animals would cost about twice as much as in normal times. This was a great relief from the prices the people had paid for unclean food.

The officer who attended the king didn't believe the words of the prophet and scoffed at what Elisha said. "Will it become like Noah's flood," he asked, "with food instead of rain pouring out of heaven?" (See Gen. 7:11. The Hebrew word translated "windows" in the KJV means "floodgates.") To the humble heart that's open to God, the Word generates faith; but to the proud, self-centered heart, the Word makes the heart even harder. The same sun that melts the ice will harden the clay. The next morning, all the people in the city except this officer would awaken to life, but he would awaken to death.

Good news from the enemy camp (vv. 3-16). The scene shifts to outside the locked gates of Samaria where four lepers lived in isolation (Lev. 13:36). Nobody had told them about Elijah's promise of food. They were discussing their precarious situation when they came to an insightful conclusion: if they stayed at the gate, they would die of hunger, but if they went to the enemy camp, they might receive some pity and some food. Even if the Syrians killed them, it was better to die quickly from a sword's thrust than to die slowly from hunger. Lest they be observed from the city wall, they waited until twilight before going to the Syrian camp. Most of the camp would be resting and the lepers would have to deal only with some of the guards.

But nobody was there! The Lord had caused them to hear a sound which they interpreted as the coming of a vast army, and the Syrians had left their camp as it was and fled twenty-five miles to the Jordan River, scattering their possessions as they ran (v. 15). The Lord had defeated the Moabites by a miracle of sight (3:20-23) and now He defeated the Syrians by a miracle of sound. They thought the armies of the Egyptians and the Hittites were coming to destroy them.[3] The four lepers did what any hungry men would have done: they ate to the full and then looted the tents for wealth, which they hid.

However, as night came on, they stopped to have another conference and assess the situation. Why should an entire city be starving, and mothers eating their own children, while four dying men are selfishly enjoying the resources in the abandoned camp? Furthermore, when morning comes, the whole city will discover that the enemy has fled, and they'll wonder why the men didn't say something. When the truth comes out, the four men would be punished for keeping the good news to themselves.[4]

It was night when they found their way back to the city and approached the guard at the gate. Since these four men lived just outside the gate, the guard must have known them. The lepers gave him the good news and he shared it with the other guards, and one of the officers took the message to the king. Once again revealing his unbelief and pessimism (3:10, 13), Joram said that the whole thing was a trick, that the enemy was hiding and only trying to draw the people out of the city so they could move in. That was how Joshua had defeated the city of Ai (Josh. 8). It wasn't so much that he doubted the word of the lepers as that he rejected the word of Elisha. Had he believed the Word of the Lord, he would have accepted the good news from the lepers.

One of the officers had the good sense to reason with the king. Let some officers take a few horses and chariots and go investigate the terrain. If it all turns out to be a trick and they are killed, they would have died had they stayed in the city, so nothing is lost. The officer wanted five horses but the king let him have only two chariots with probably two horses per chariot. The men found the camp devoid of soldiers. Then they followed the escape route all the way to the Jordan River, a distance of twenty-five miles, and saw on the ground the clothing and equipment that the Syrians had discarded in their flight.

The spies raced back to the city and shared the good news that the Syrian army was gone and their camp was just waiting to be looted. It was indeed a day of good news as the people found food to eat and to sell back in the city, not to speak of valuable material goods that could be converted into cash. But the main lesson isn't that God rescued His people when they didn't deserve it, but that God fulfilled the promise He gave through His prophet Elisha. Note the emphasis on "the word of the Lord" in verses 16-18.

Jesus has promised to come again, but in these last days, people are questioning and even denying that promise. Fulfilling what Peter wrote in 2 Peter 3, the scoffers have now come and are asking, "Where is the promise of his coming?" The church is like those four lepers: we have the good news of salvation and we must not keep it to ourselves. If people don't believe the Word of the Lord, they won't be ready for His coming; but if we don't give them the message, they can't be ready for His coming. What will we say when we meet the Lord?

Bad news for the king's officer (vv. 17-20). It appears that this officer had gradually accepted the pessimistic unbelieving attitude of his king. To him, it was impossible for the prices to fall that low in one day and for fine flour and barley to be available so quickly. But God did it! The very people he thought would die of starvation came rushing out of the gate. They knocked him down, trod on his helpless body, and he died. The Word of the Lord lived on but the man who denied that Word was killed. "Heaven and earth will pass away," said Jesus, "but My words will by no means pass away" (Matt. 24:35, NKJV).

CHAPTER FIVE
REAPING THE HARVEST OF SIN

2 Kings 8:1–9:37
(2 Chronicles 21:1–22:9)

Eliphaz said some foolish things to his suffering friend Job, but he also stated some eternal principles, one of them being, "Even as I have seen, those who plow iniquity and sow trouble reap the same" (Job 4:8, NKJV). Solomon repeated this truth in Proverbs 22:8, "He who sows iniquity will reap sorrow" (NKJV), and the prophet Hosea put it graphically when he said, "They sow the wind, and reap the whirlwind" (Hos. 8:7, NKJV). Jeroboam, Omri, and Ahab had led the northern kingdom of Israel into idolatry, and Jehoram, who married a daughter of Ahab, had introduced Baal worship into the kingdom of Judah. Both kingdoms were rebellious against the Lord and polluted by idolatry, but now the day of judgment had arrived for Ahab's dynasty, the day that the Prophet Elijah had predicted (1 Kings 21:21, 29).

1. The greatness of God. (2 Kings 8:1-6)

Obviously this event had to take place before the healing of Naaman (2 Kings 5), since the king wasn't likely to welcome a leper into the palace, and Gehazi was a leper (5:27). The author of 2 Kings doesn't claim to follow a strict chronology, and we're not even sure which king Gehazi was entertaining with stories about his master. Perhaps this event occurred early in the reign of King Joram. This account reminds us of the greatness of the Lord. The events that follow reveal the sinfulness of people, but this section gives us a reminder that God is great and will accomplish His purposes in spite of the sinfulness of people, great and small.

God controls nature (8:1-2). We were introduced to the wealthy Shunamite woman and her family in 4:8-37. God often used famines to chasten His people when they were disobedient and needed to be reminded of their covenant obligations (Deut. 28:17, 48). This famine may have been the one mentioned in 4:38. The prophet warned the woman to escape the famine by going to the land of the Philistines and becoming a resident alien there. Knowing in advance that the famine was coming, she was able to secure a temporary home in Philistia ahead of the others who would flee Israel. Note that her husband isn't mentioned; but since he was older than she (4:14), it's likely he was dead.

This famine came because the Lord called for it, and He could command it because He is Lord of all. "Moreover He called for a famine in the land; He destroyed all the provision of bread" (Ps. 105:16, NKJV). In the beginning, God spoke and creation came into being (Gen. 1), and God speaks today and creation obeys His will (see Ps. 148). In these times of discipline and distress, if God's people would pray and confess their sins, God would have delivered them (2 Chron. 7:14). When people ignore God's Word, the Lord may speak through His creation and remind them who is in charge.

God controls life and death (8:3-5). The account of the miracles in the life of the Shunamite woman reveals the awesome power of God. She had no children and her husband was now old, but as with Abraham and Sarah (Gen. 17), the Lord gave them both new life and the woman conceived a son. But the son was struck with an illness and died, yet the Lord raised him from the dead. God keeps us among the living (Ps. 66:9), and "in his hand is the life of every creature and breath of all mankind" (Job 12:10, NIV). "For in him we live, and move, and have our being" (Acts 17:28). Famines remind us that God alone can make nature fruitful, and death reminds us that God alone gives life and has the power and authority to take it away. "No one has power over the spirit to retain the spirit, and no one has power in the day of death" (Ecc. 8:8, NKJV).

God providentially controls the events in life (8:5-6). At the very moment Gehazi was describing this wonderful resurrection miracle, the mother of the child walked into the throne room! She had returned home only to discover that strangers had taken over her estate and robbed her of seven years' produce. In those days, it was common for people to bring such problems directly to the king and he would decide how property should be divided. The fact that Gehazi stood there as witness to her ownership of the land made it easy for the king to pass judgment. Years before, when her son had died, little did the mother realize that one day that bitter experience would play an important part in the preservation of her property.

Our English word "providence" comes from two Latin words, *pro* and *video*, which together mean "to see ahead, to see before." God not only knows what lies ahead; but He plans what is to happen in the future and executes His plan perfectly. Perhaps a better word is "prearrangement." In no way does God's providence interfere with our power of choice or our responsibility for the choices we make and their consequences. (See 1 Chron. 29:11; Job 41:11; Ps. 95:3-5; 135:6; 139:13-18; Dan. 4:35; James 4:13-15.)

This happy episode in the king's

palace reveals to us the character of God and prepares us for the tumultuous events that follow. Hazael will murder Ben Hadad and become king of Syria. Jehu will sweep through the land and kill kings, princes, and pagan priests as he wipes out the house of Ahab and the worship of Baal. Evil Queen Jezebel and Queen Mother Athaliah will both meet their death and pay for their wicked deeds. What a time in history! Nevertheless, the Lord was on His throne, judging sin and fulfilling His Word. No matter what occurs in history, God is in control. He knows all things and can do all things. He is present everywhere, working out His will. He is a holy God who is longsuffering with sinners but eventually judges those who disobey Him. Our world may be shaking (Heb. 12:25-29), but our God can be trusted to do what is right.

2. The wickedness of the human heart. (2 Kings 8:7-15)

When the Lord met with the Prophet Elijah on Mount Horeb (1 Kings 19:8-18), He gave him a threefold commission: to anoint Hazael king of Syria, to anoint Jehu king of Israel, and to anoint Elisha to minister as his successor (1 Kings 19:15-16). Before his translation to heaven, Elijah had fulfilled only one of those commissions, the anointing of Elisha (1 Kings 19:19-21), so we assume that he told Elisha to take care of the other two assignments. Jehu would become God's appointed scourge to rid the land of Ahab's evil descendants as well as Ahab's false religion.

The mission of Elisha (vv. 7-13). It took faith and courage for Elisha to travel to Damascus. After all, he had often thwarted Syria's plans for raiding Israel's border towns (6:9-12) and he had humiliated the Syrian army by leading them into Samaria and sending them home with full stomachs but empty hands (6:14-23). Because of Elisha, the Syrian army fled from Samaria and the Jewish people were able to loot their camp (7:1ff). But Elisha had also healed Naaman the Syrian of his leprosy (5:1ff), and when Elisha brought the Syrian raiding party to Samaria, he showed them mercy and saved their lives.

The fact that Ben Hadad the Syrian king was very ill and wanted help from the Lord made Elisha's arrival more significant. This was a pagan Gentile king seeking the help of a prophet of Jehovah, but perhaps the conversion of Naaman had something to do with it. Even more, Ben Hadad sent Hazael, one of his high officials, to meet Elisha and give him expensive gifts. The gifts were probably more like "bribes" and the king was hoping that his generosity would cause Elisha to give him a good answer. But like his master, Elisha undoubtedly refused to accept the gifts (5:15-16). By calling the king of Syria "your son," Hazael was seeking to add more honor to Elisha (see 6:21). Then he asked the key question: would the king of Syria recover from his sickness?

Elisha's reply appears to be deliberately ambiguous, for the Hebrew text can be read "You will certainly recover" or "Your will certainly not recover" (see NIV margin). The prophet seems to be saying, "The sickness will not take his life, but he will die by another means." In other words, the sickness was not terminal but the king's life was about to be terminated. As a high officer of the king, Hazael wanted to give the king good news, so he didn't convey to him the second part of the message. Elisha was not lying to Hazael. Hazael's question "Will the king recover from his sickness?" was answered "Yes and no." No, the sickness would not kill the king, but, yes, something else will kill him. However, Elisha didn't reveal what that "something else" was or when it would happen.

Elisha stared at Hazael, as though reading his mind and heart, and then the prophet broke into weeping. The Lord had shown him some of the violence and bloodshed that Hazael would perpetrate, brutal acts that were normal practices in ancient warfare (15:16; Hos. 13:16; Amos 1:3-5). Hazael's reply indicated that he recognized his subordinate status in the government and wondered where he would get the authority to do those things.[1] In calling himself "the dog," he wasn't referring to a vicious nature—"Am I some kind of dog that I would do these things?"—but rather that he was a nobody, a humble servant of the king, a man without such great authority. Elisha's reply stunned him: Hazael would have all the authority he needed because he would become king of Syria. The text doesn't tell us, but this may have been the point at which Elisha anointed Hazael with the sacred oil. If so, then Hazael was the only king of Israel, the Northern Kingdom, to have the anointing of the Lord.

Even before Elisha announced Hazael's great promotion, the prophet may have seen in Hazael's heart his plan to murder the king. Or, did the prophet's words stir up the desire in Hazael's heart? Either way, Elisha wasn't to blame for what Hazael decided to do. Hazael accepted the fact that he would be the next king, but he didn't ask how this would come about. Elisha made it clear that the king would die, but not because of his illness. "If the king is going to die anyway," Hazael might reason, "then why wait? Why not take his life now and become king much sooner?" When the human heart is bent on evil, it can invent all kinds of excuses. "The heart is more deceitful than all else and is desperately sick; who can understand it?" (Jer. 17:9, NASB).

When the king asked for Elisha's message, Hazael gave him the first half and said, "You will surely recover." In this, he told the truth, for the king would not die from his illness. But to make sure that the second half of the message was fulfilled, Hazael smothered him with a heavy wet cloth and seized the throne for himself. He ruled Syria for forty-one years (841–801 B.C.).

3. The foolishness of compromise. (2 Kings 8:16-29; 2 Chron. 21)

The writer now shifts to the southern kingdom of Judah and tells us how King Jehoram brought apostasy and judgment to the land. For five years Jehoram served as coregent with his father Jehoshaphat, and when Jehoshaphat died, he took the throne. Jehoram was married to Athaliah, a daughter of Ahab, and Jehoshaphat had joined Ahab in fighting against the Syrians at Ramoth Gilead (1 Kings 22). In other words, the wall of separation was gradually crumbling between David's dynasty in Judah and the descendants of Ahab in Israel. The future of God's great plan of salvation depended on the continuation of the Davidic dynasty, so Jehoram was playing right into the enemy's hands. By compromising with the evil rulers of Israel, Jehoram displeased the Lord and weakened the nation.

A reign of terror (vv. 16-22). When he became king, Jehoram followed the example of Jezebel and murdered all his brothers and anybody who might threaten his authority (2 Chron. 21:1-7). His father had given each of the sons a fortified city to rule, and Jehoram didn't want them to unite against him. Instead of calling them together to pray and worship God at the temple and to seek His blessing, he followed the ways of Ahab and Jezebel and ruled by the sword. Jehoram wanted his brothers out of the way so they couldn't oppose his policy of promoting the worship of Baal. Jezebel had won again.

God could have destroyed the king and his kingdom, but for David's sake, He kept the dynasty alive (v. 19; see 1 Kings 11:36 and 15:4, and Pss. 89:29-37 and 132:17). But the Lord brought several defeats to Judah, including the revolts of Edom and Libnah (vv. 20-22; 2 Chron. 21:8-11). David had defeated and subdued Edom (2 Sam. 8:13-14; 1 Kings 11:15-17) but now they were free from Judah and put their own king on the throne. Jehoram's troops had invaded Edom but were surrounded by the army of Edom and barely broke through their lines to escape.

A word of warning (2 Chron. 21:12-15). We have noted before that the writer of 2 Kings didn't follow a strict chronology, and this is another instance. The translation of the Prophet Elijah to heaven is recorded in 2 Kings 2:11, but King Jehoram of Judah, son of Jehoshaphat, is mentioned in 1:17. This means that Elijah was alive and ministering during the early part of Jehoram's reign. We don't know how much time elapsed between the accession of Joram, king of Israel, and the events recorded in 2 Kings 2 that led up to the translation of Elijah. Writing this letter to the king of Judah may have been one of Elijah's last ministries.[2]

The prophet reminded Jehoram of three great kings of Judah: David, who founded the royal dynasty; Asa, a godly king who purged the land of evil (1 Kings 15:9-24; 2 Chron. 14–16); and Jehoram's father, Jehoshaphat.[3] Instead of following in the ways of these kings, Jehoram patterned himself after Ahab. As a consequence, the people followed his bad example and it wasn't difficult for him to make Baal worship popular in Judah, the one place where Jehovah should have been worshiped without compromise.

Not only was Jehoram an idolater, but he was also a murderer and killed his own brothers; so the Lord would now cause him to reap what he had sown. The enemy would invade and loot the kingdom of Judah and take Jehoram's treasures as well as his wives and sons. Then, the king would be afflicted with an incurable bowel disease that would give him great pain and ultimately take his life. Both of these predictions came true. The Philistines and the Arabs invaded Judah, robbed the palace of its treasures, and took Jehoram's wives and sons, except for young Ahaziah, also known as Jehoahaz. The king contracted a painful, lingering bowel disease and died after two years. But the people didn't mourn his death, nor did they stage the traditional "royal bonfire" in his honor. But perhaps the most humiliating thing was that his body wasn't placed in a royal sepulcher, although he was buried in the city of David.[4]

Was Jehoram's compromise worth it? Of course not! "There is a way which seems right to a man, but its end is the way of death" (Prov. 16:25, NASB).

Unfortunately, he was followed by his son Ahaziah, who was also a follower of the Ahab clan, for his mother, Athaliah, was a daughter of Ahab.[5] Ahaziah joined with his uncle King Joram to take Ramoth Gilead from Hazael, king of Syria, and there Joram was wounded. He went to his palace at Jezreel to recover, and King Ahaziah went down to visit and encourage his uncle. Why does the writer give us these seemingly trivial details? To let us know that the Lord was putting together the people who would be slain because of their sins. "His going to Joram was God's occasion for Ahaziah's downfall" (2 Chron. 22:7, NKJV). To have the king of Judah and the king of Israel together in one place would make it easy for Jehu to obey the commandment of the Lord.

4. The suddenness of opportunity. (2 Kings 9:1-13)

The scene now shifts to Ramoth Gilead where Israel and Judah had combined their forces to recover the city from the Syrians. One of the key commanders of the Israeli army was Jehu, the son of Jehoshaphat, but not the Jehoshaphat who was king of Judah and the father of Jehoram. Unknown to Jehu, the Prophet Elisha had dispatched one of the young sons of the prophets to anoint him king of Israel. This was the third assignment God gave Elijah (1 Kings 19:15-16). Instead of going to the battlefield himself, Elisha wisely gave the young man the authority to anoint Jehu privately. Elisha advised the student to flee the scene as fast as he could, for obviously there was going to be serious conflict.

Jehu was having a staff meeting in the courtyard when the young man approached and asked for a private audience with the commander. They went into a private room in the house and there the young man anointed Jehu to be the new king of Israel. It's interesting that the young prophet called the people of Israel "the people of the Lord" (9:6). Even though Israel and Judah were separate kingdoms and not obedient to the covenant, the people were still the chosen ones of the Lord and Abraham's descendants. God's covenants with Abraham (Gen. 12:1-3) and with David (2 Sam. 7) would still stand. The people had turned away from the Lord, but He had not forsaken them.

The young man didn't end his work with the anointing but went on to explain to Jehu the work God wanted him to do. His main task was to wipe out the family of Ahab in Israel and execute God's judgment upon them because of the innocent people they had killed. He specifically mentioned Jezebel's crimes and her judgment, referring to the words Elijah spoke when he confronted Ahab (1 Kings 21:21-24). That prophecy may have been forgotten by Ahab's descendants, but God remembered it, and the time had come to fulfill it. Just as God had wiped out the descendants of Jeroboam and Baasha (1 Kings 15:25–16:7), He would use Jehu to destroy the house of Ahab.

The officers in the courtyard must have wondered who the young man was and why his message to Jehu was so confidential. Did he come from the front? Would there be a change in the battle plan? When the young man ran out of the house and fled, the officers were sure he was out of his mind. More than one servant of God has been accused of madness, including Paul (Acts 26:24; 2 Cor. 5:13) and Jesus (Mark 3:20-21, 31-35; John 10:20). Actually, it's the lost world that is mad and God's people who are the sane ones.

Was it a mark of humility in Jehu that he didn't immediately announce that he was king? The officers had to pull the truth out of him, but once they knew, they accepted their commander's promotion and openly acknowledged it. As far as the biblical record is concerned, Jehu is the only king of Israel who was anointed by an appointed servant of the Lord. Jehu's opportunity came suddenly, but he accepted it by faith and immediately began to serve the Lord. A Chinese proverb says, "Opportunity has a forelock but not a pigtail. Once it is past, you cannot grasp it." As the tenth king of Israel, Jehu started a new dynasty and reigned for twenty-eight years (10:36).

5. The swiftness of God's judgment. (2 Kings 9:14-37; 2 Chron. 22:1-9)

Here is the situation as Jehu began his crusade. Ahaziah was reigning in Judah and following the counsel of his wicked mother, Athaliah, and the leaders in the house of Ahab in Israel. Baal was his god and he had no interest in the law of the Lord. Ahaziah had gone to Jezreel to visit King Joram, who was recovering from wounds received at Ramoth Gilead and did not know that God had given Israel a new king. Jehu wanted to catch his enemies by surprise, so he ordered his officers not to spread the word that he was king.

The death of Joram (vv. 16-26). It was about forty-five miles from Ramoth Gilead to Jezreel, but Jehu was a fast and daring charioteer and his men were accustomed to traveling at speeds that were alarming in those days. The word "peace" (shalom) is repeated eight times in this section (vv. 17-19, 22, 31), but the event was actually a declaration of war. Without slowing his pace, Jehu received Joram's two messengers and commanded them to ride with his company, and they obeyed. However, when his two messengers failed to return to Jezreel, Joram became suspicious and ordered his own chariot to be readied for an escape.

In a move that made Jehu's work much easier, Joram and Ahaziah each mounted his royal chariot and rode out to meet the man who had now been identified as Jehu. Perhaps the two kings were hoping that Jehu was bringing good news from the front. Joram's question "Have you come in peace?" might have meant "Has the battle at Ramoth ended in our favor?" or "Is your mission one of peace?" If it was the latter, it suggests that Jehu might have been somewhat of a "loose cannon" in Joram's army, and perhaps Joram suspected he had designs on the throne. Jehu's reply6 instantly told the king that danger was in the air, and he tried to get away. Joram warned his nephew Ahaziah, who did escape but was later caught, but one well-directed arrow ended the life of Joram. As a patient recuperating from wounds, Joram wouldn't be wearing his armor. Providentially, he died on the property of Naboth that Ahab and Jezebel had taken after killing Naboth and his sons. Thus the Lord fulfilled the prophecy He gave to Elijah (1 Kings 21:18-24).

Jehu not only executed the king of Israel, but he also killed all the royal princes (2 Chron. 22:8).

The death of Ahaziah (vv. 27-29; 2 Chron. 22:1-9). The reports of Ahaziah's death in 2 Kings 9:27-29 and 2 Chronicles 22:7-9 aren't easy to harmonize, but we suggest a scenario. Ahaziah was wounded as he fled from Jezreel (v. 27). He made it to Beth-haggan and then turned northwest at the Ascent of Gur and headed for Megiddo where he tried to hide from Jehu. But Jehu's men tracked him down and killed him at Megiddo. Ahaziah's servants carried his body from Megiddo to Jerusalem where he was buried with the kings, for he was a descendant of David. Had he not compromised with Joram, worshiped Baal, and followed his mother, Athaliah's, counsel, he would have been spared all this shame and defeat.

The death of Jezebel (vv. 30-37). It didn't take long for Jezebel and the palace residents to hear that Jehu was in Jezreel, that he was king, and that he had killed her son Joram. She put on her makeup, "attired her head," and watched at an upper window, waited for him to show up. When she saw him come through the gate, she called, "Is it well, Zimri, your master's murderer?" (v. 31, NASB). About fifty years before, Zimri had killed King Elah and made himself king and then had proceeded to exterminate the family of Baasha (1 Kings 16:8-20). Since Zimri ruled for only seven days and then died a suicide, Jezebel was obviously trying to warn Jehu that his authority was weak and his days were numbered. She might even have been suggesting that Jehu form an alliance with her and strengthen his throne.

But Jehu knew his mandate from the Lord. When he called for evidence of loyalty from the palace personnel, two or three servants responded, and they threw Jezebel out the window to the courtyard below. Jehu rode his horse over her body until he was sure she was dead. Since he was now king, Jehu went into the palace and called for something to eat. As he was dining, he remembered that, evil as she was, Jezebel was a princess, the daughter of Ethbaal, the Sidonian ruler (1 Kings 16:29-31); so he ordered the servants to bury her body. But it was too late. Smelling human blood, the wild dogs showed up and ate her body, leaving only her skull, feet and the palms of her hands. It was a gruesome scene, but it was what Elijah had predicted would happen (1 Kings 21:21-24). God's Word never fails but accomplishes His purposes on the earth (Isa. 55:10-11).

CHAPTER SIX
THE SWORD AND THE CROWN
2 Kings 10–11
(2 Chronicles 22:10–23:21)

Studying these two chapters gives you the feeling that you're reading the morning paper or watching the ten o'clock news on television. You meet two leaders—Jehu, former army commander and now ruler of the northern kingdom of Israel; and Jehoiada, high priest at the temple in Jerusalem in the Southern Kingdom. As you watch these two men, you recognize the fact that the same forces for good and for evil were at work in their world that are at work in our own world today.

You also recognize the difference between leaders who are motivated by selfish ambition and leaders who are motivated by spiritual dedication. Jehu was proud of his "zeal for the Lord" (10:16), but that "zeal" was a pious cloak that hid the egotism and anger that really motivated his service. God gave Jehu an important work to do, but the king went beyond the assigned boundaries and carried his mandate too far. The Lord commended Jehu for what he accomplished (10:30), but He also chastened him for his pride and compromise. Humanly speaking, were it not for the courageous service of the high priest, Jehoiada, and his wife Jehosheba, the Davidic dynasty would have come to an end. The future of God's promises to David, that involved His great plan of salvation, was all wrapped up in a little baby boy named Joash.

Let's identify the forces that were at work in that day, forces that are still at work in our world today,

1. Fear and double-talk (2 Kings 10:1-10)

Years before, Elijah had prophesied that the line of godless King Ahab would come to an end and that every last descendant of Ahab would be slain (1 Kings 21:20-29). The Lord gave this mission to Jehu when He anointed him king of Israel (2 Kings 9:6-10). Even though the nation was divided into two kingdoms, the Jews were still God's covenant people and their kings couldn't do whatever they pleased. Ahab and Jezebel had promoted Baal worship in Israel, and when Jehoram, king of Judah, married Athaliah, a daughter of Ahab, he encouraged Baal worship in Judah (8:16-18). By this evil marriage, Jehoram not only corrupted Judah with idol worship, but he corrupted the line of David and jeopardized the fulfillment of the messianic promises.

Jehu had already killed Joram, king of Israel, and Ahaziah, king of Judah (9:14-29), and he had also slain Jezebel, the evil wife of Ahab (9:30-37). Now Jehu was on a "search and destroy" mission to find and kill every one of Ahab's descendants. His first challenge was to get control of the capital city of Samaria where Ahab's male descendants were being protected and prepared for places of leadership in the government. Jehu knew that his forces couldn't easily take a walled city like Samaria, but being a clever strategist, he knew how to get his enemies to surrender. Once he had taken Samaria, the other key cities in the land would also surrender.

Samaria accepts Jehu's rule (vv. 1-5). Jehu was in Jezreel (9:30), about twenty-five miles north of Samaria, and from there, he communicated with the leaders in Samaria—the palace administrators, the military leaders, and the tutors and guardians of the princes. He knew that if he could intimidate these respected leaders, he could take over the city without a fight. His first challenge was that they choose one of Ahab's male descendants, put him on the throne and then defend his right to reign. This was probably a suggestion that the new king or a champion of his choice fight Jehu one-on-one and the winner take all. (See 1 Sam. 17:8ff and 2 Sam. 2:9.)

Jehu even pointed out their advantages: they were in a walled city and they had armor and weapons as well as chariots and horses. Jehu was using a technique that revolutionaries have used successfully for centuries: making a bold proposal and letting the leaders' imaginations create fear in their hearts. Adolf Hitler wrote, "Mental confusion, contradiction of feeling, indecisiveness, panic: these are our weapons." Three different groups of leaders had to unite on this decision, and these men knew that Jehu had killed two kings and disposed of Jezebel. Furthermore, he seemed invincible, for nobody had stood in his way. The message they sent to Jehu at Jezreel was one of complete unconditional surrender. They promised to do whatever he commanded and they agreed not to name a new king. In short, they accepted Jehu as their king.

Samaria obeys Jehu's orders (vv. 6-10). Now Jehu shows himself to be the master of political double-talk. He accepted their submission to his rule and then ordered them to "take the heads" of the seventy descendants of Ahab and bring them to Jezreel. This could mean "bring the leaders among the group to me and we'll discuss matters," or it could mean "behead all seventy and bring me their heads." It was the second interpretation that the leaders followed, so they immediately killed Ahab's descendants and sent messengers to Jezreel with the heads. When they arrived that evening, Jehu ordered the messengers to stack up the heads at the entrance of the city, certainly a grisly reminder to the people of Jezreel that it didn't pay to get in Jehu's way.

But the next morning, Jehu again showed himself a master politician by absolving himself of any guilt! He admitted that he had killed Joram, the former king of Israel, but since he had not left Jezreel, he couldn't have murdered the seventy young men. Then he reminded them of the divine promise that all of

Ahab's descendants would be eliminated, so the responsibility ultimately lay with the Lord and His prophet Elijah. In one brief speech, Jehu washed his hands of the mass murder and also allied himself with the Lord and the Prophet Elijah!

Jehu practiced what is today called "double-speak." Taxes are now "revenue enhancement" and potholes are "pavement deficiencies." People are no longer bald; they are only "follicularly deprived." Hospital technicians gave a fatal dose of nitrous oxide to a mother about to deliver and killed both the mother and the child. They called the tragedy "a therapeutic misadventure." Poor people are now "fiscal underachievers" and soldiers no longer kill the enemy, they "service the target." David was right when he wrote, "They speak falsehood to one another; with flattering lips and with a double heart they speak" (Ps. 12:2, NASB).

2. Selfish ambition (10:11-17)

Jehu's divine commission had now become a personal crusade, motivated by his own selfish ambition. Novelist Joseph Conrad wrote in the preface to Some Reminiscences, "All ambitions are lawful except those which climb upward on the miseries and credulities of mankind." Lawful ambition uses truth and builds on the past, while unlawful ambition uses lies and destroys the past. Dictators must annihilate their enemies in order to be safe, but in so doing, they destroy the past and the information and help they need for moving into the future. A German aphorism says, "Every eel hopes to become a whale," and Jehu was now driving in that lane.

He goes too far (vv. 11-14). To prove that he intended to obey God and purge the land of Ahab's family, Jehu proceeded to kill all of Ahab's descendants that he found in Jezreel. But he didn't stop there; he went beyond his divine commission and killed Ahab's close friends, his chief officers, and the priests who served in the palace. It was a wholesale slaughter based on "guilt by association." The Lord wanted to rid the land of Ahab's family so that none of them could usurp the throne, but for Jehu to kill Ahab's friends, officers, and priests was totally unnecessary. In fact, Jehu later had serious problems with the Syrians (10:22-23) and could have used some of the wisdom and experience of the court officers he killed. By wiping out these former leaders, Jehu destroyed a valuable source of political wisdom and skill.

He then left Jezreel and went to Samaria to claim his throne. On the way, he met a group of travelers who were going to Jerusalem to visit King Ahaziah, who was related to them. They didn't know that King Ahaziah, King Joram, and Queen Jezebel were all dead and that Jehu had killed them and was now in charge. Since Ahaziah had married into Ahab's family (8:18), it seemed logical to Jehu that anybody related to Ahaziah belonged to the enemy, so he had all forty-two men slain. But these men weren't related by blood to Ahab; they were descendants of David! Jehu was now attacking the Davidic dynasty! (See 2 Chron. 22:8.)

He enlists a friend (vv. 15-17). Jehu now encountered an ally, Jehonadab the Rechabite, and used him to give respectability to his own ambitions. The Rechabites were a people that belonged to the Kenites, the descendants of Moses' brother-in-law Hobab (Judg. 4:11). They identified with the tribe of Judah (Judg. 1:16) but stayed to themselves and followed the traditions laid down by their ancestors (Jer. 35). They were respected highly by the Jewish people, but, being nomads and tent-dwellers, the Rechabites were separated from the everyday city life and politics of the Jews.

Jehonadab was just the kind of man Jehu needed to make his crusade look credible. When Jehonadab took Jehu's hand and stepped into the royal chariot, he declared that he was heart and soul behind the new king. Certainly Jehonadab disapproved of Baal worship and rejoiced to hear that Ahab's family was being eradicated. However, when he met Jehu, Jehonadab didn't know the motives that were driving the king and the ruthless methods he was using.

Every ambitious leader needs a respectable second man to help "sell" his policies and practices to the public. It was bad enough that Jehu had begun to murder innocent people, but now he was "using" an innocent man to make his crimes look like the work of the Lord. However, this is the way many unscrupulous leaders operate. Jehu's statement "see my zeal for the Lord" (v. 16) reminds us of the words of Elijah when he was running from Jezebel and hiding in the cave (1 Kings 19:10, 14). The Hebrew word can be translated "jealous" or "zealous."

When Jehu and Jehonadab arrived at Samaria with the company of soldiers, Jehu presented himself as their king and the people submitted to him. Jehu had already intimidated the rulers of the city, so he met no opposition when he rode through the city gate. The city officers turned Ahab's remaining relatives over to him and Jehu killed them all.

3. Deception (2 Kings 10:18-28)

Jehu had finished the work of ridding the nation of Ahab's family, so there were no descendants who could challenge his right to the throne. But what about the Baal worship that had infected the land? That was Jehu's next responsibility and he decided to use deception as his major weapon.

As king of Israel, Jehu could have dealt with the Baal worshipers in one of three ways. He could have commanded them to leave the land, or he could have obeyed Deuteronomy 13 and killed them. He might even have tried to convert them, although it would have been easy to "convert" if the sword was hanging over your head. He also could have ordered the temple of Baal to be torn down. Jehu had the promised support of the leaders in Samaria (v. 5), so why did he choose to lie to the people and then kill them? God's servants are not allowed to "do evil that good may come" (Rom. 3:8, NASB; see 1 Thes. 2:3), yet that's the course that Jehu took. He had authority from Moses to kill the idolaters, and that he did; but why did he deceive them first?

He lied to them about himself, claiming that he was more devoted to Baal than Ahab had been. He also lied about the service in the temple of Baal. However, this may have been another instance of Jehu's "double-speak," for there *was* a "great sacrifice" to Baal—the lives of the priests and the worshipers in Baal's temple! Jehu was a military man whose life was so dedicated to strategy and conquest that, unlike David, he couldn't bring faith and the glory of God into his battles. Jehu seems to have had a lust for blood and a joy in outsmarting his enemies, and we never read that he sought the mind of the Lord in any of his endeavors.

First, he assembled the prophets, ministers, and priests of Baal and commanded them to announce a great sacrifice for Baal. Coming from the king through the religious leaders, the announcement would carry much more weight and be more believable. Jehu even sent messengers throughout the land to command the Baal worshipers to attend the great sacrifice in Samaria. The house of Baal in Samaria was built by Ahab for Jezebel (1 Kings 16:31-32), so Jehu would destroy "the house of Ahab" in two senses: his physical "house" or family and the house he built for Baal.

Once the people were in the temple, Jehu made sure that no true worshipers of Jehovah were among the worshipers of Baal. He commanded that the Baal worshipers wear the special garments that were used during their services, and he and Jehonadab admonished the priests not to allow any outsiders to participate (v. 23). Jehu gave the impression that he wanted "pure worship" for the great sacrifice. Once the Baal worshipers were ready inside the temple, Jehu instructed his eighty soldiers outside the temple to be ready to enter the temple as soon as the sacrifice was ended.

Does the "he" in verse 25 (KJV) refer to Jehu or to the high priest of Baal? The NIV and the NASB both opt for Jehu, but not knowing the layout of the temple or the order of the service, it's difficult to decide. How could the king be visible at the altar and, without raising suspicion, leave the altar and go outside to command the soldiers? It's likely that Jehu provided the animals for the sacrifices, so in that sense, *he* was "sacrificing to Baal" whether he was at the altar or not. The soldiers killed all the Baal worshipers in the temple and threw their bodies outside into the court. Then some of the men went into the inner shrine of the temple and removed the wooden images of the gods and the stone image of Baal and destroyed them. What once was the sacred house of Baal was turned into a public latrine.

Jehu's plan worked and enabled him in one day to wipe out Baal worship in the land. By lying to the people, he accumulated a larger crowd of Baal worshipers than if he had gone after them one by one, but it's unfortunate that his first public act as king in Samaria was an act of deception. Would anybody trust him after that?

4. Compromise (2 Kings 10:29-36)

Once things quieted down, Jehu had a long reign of twenty-eight years; but he followed the ways of Jeroboam and worshiped the golden calves at Dan and Bethel. The calves were supposed to be only symbols of Jehovah, but it was idolatry just the same. In spite of his zeal for the Lord, Jehu was an idolater at heart who used the Lord's name only to cover up his sins. By being a part of the "national religion," Jehu united the people and gained their respect. Jehu was a consummate politician to the very end.

The Lord commended Jehu for the work he had done and rewarded him by giving him the longest dynasty in the history of the Northern Kingdom—over one hundred years. He was succeeded by Jehoahaz, Joash, Jeroboam II and Zechariah, all of whom were bad kings. But the Prophet Hosea announced that the Lord was displeased with Jehu for murdering innocent people (Hos. 1:4; 2:21). Jehu established his dynasty by killing King Joram at Jezreel (2 Kings 9:15ff), and for this God would judge him. "Jezreel" means "God scatters" and He would scatter the Northern Kingdom by allowing the Assyrians to conquer them in 722 B.C. Jehu's great-great-grandson Zechariah reigned only six months and was assassinated by Shallum who reigned only one month. The dynasty began with a murder and ended with a murder.

Even during Jehu's lifetime, the Lord chastened him by allowing Israel's old enemy Syria (Aram) to take territory from the tribes east of the Jordan. Having the enemy living right across the Jordan River wasn't a comfortable situation for the nation. Jehu was an effective soldier but he wasn't much of a builder, and he's remembered only for the people he killed. He could have assembled a group of gifted men to assist him in promoting the true faith in the land, but he settled for following the crowd and worshiping the golden calves.

5. Retaliation (2 Kings 11:1; 2 Chron. 22:10)

We move now to the southern kingdom of Judah where the throne was empty because Jehu had killed King Ahaziah near Jezreel (9:27-28). The queen mother, Athaliah, a daughter of Ahab, saw her opportunity and seized the throne, reigning for six years. As the founder of Baal worship in Judah, she had no desire to see the Davidic dynasty succeed. She tried to kill all the royal princes, but one survived. David's family was rapidly being destroyed. When Jehoram became king of Judah, he killed all his brothers and some of the princes of Israel to prevent them from dethroning him (2 Chron. 21:4), and the Arabian invaders had killed Jehoram's older sons (22:1). Jehu had killed some of David's descendants (22:8), and now Athaliah had ordered the "royal seed" to be wiped out. Satan certainly did his utmost to keep the promised Messiah from being born in David's family in Bethlehem!

Athaliah was retaliating because of all that Jehu had done in eradicating Ahab's family and Baal worship in Israel. To return evil for good is demonic; to return good for evil is godlike; and to return evil for evil and good for good is human. Wherever there is conflict in this world, you will usually find this spirit of revenge and retaliation. As individuals used to fight duels to uphold their personal honor, so nations sometimes fight wars to protect their national honor. But by killing the royal seed, Athaliah was rebelling against the Lord Jehovah who had promised David that he would have a descendant sitting on his throne in Jerusalem.

Most of us don't go to that extreme in seeking to "pay back" our enemies, but revenge isn't an unknown thing among God's people. Moses in the law admonished his people not to practice revenge (Lev. 19:18), and Solomon gave the same counsel (Prov. 20:22; 24:29). Jesus taught against personal revenge (Matt. 5:38-48), as did the apostles Paul (Rom. 12:17-21) and Peter (1 Peter 3:8-9). Planning and executing revenge does far more harm to the perpetrator than to the victim. Many famous authors have written about "sweet revenge," but experience shows that revenge is very bitter. A Jewish proverb says, "The smallest revenge will poison the soul." If you are going to pay back an enemy, choose a good one, because paying back an enemy is a very expensive luxury.

6. Faith and courage (2 Kings 11:2-12; 2 Chron. 22:11–23:11).

When wicked Athaliah killed the heirs to David's throne, the faithful remnant in Judah must have wondered where God was and what He was doing. Why would He make a covenant promise to David and not keep it? How could He allow the queen mother to do such an evil deed and jeopardize the future of the messianic line? But God was still on the throne and had His servants prepared to act. In a world that seems to be controlled by deceit and selfish ambition, there are still people like Jehoiada and Jehosheba who have faith in God's Word and courageously do His will.

Protection (vv. 2-3; 22:11-12). Jehoiada was the high priest and Jehosheba, his wife, was a princess, a daughter of King

Jehoram and a sister to King Ahaziah, whom Jehu had slain. This made her an aunt to little Joash. That such a godly woman should come out of that family is a miracle of the grace of God. Knowing what Athaliah planned to do, the priest and the princess stole one-year-old Joash from the royal nursery and hid him with his nurse, first in a room where old bedding was stored and then in a room in the temple. As he grew older, he mingled and played with the other children in the temple area and wasn't recognized as an heir to the throne.[1]

Presentation (vv. 4-12; 23:1-11). Jehoiada and Jehosheba and the boy's nurse had the patience to wait for God's time, for faith and patience go together (Heb. 6:12). "Whoever believes will not act hastily" (Isa. 28:16, NKJV). In His gracious providence, the Lord watched over the child as well as the three people who knew who he was and where he was; for if Queen Athaliah had known what they were doing, she would have killed them along with the prince.

While waiting those six years, the high priest had thought and prayed and the Lord told him how to take Athaliah off the throne and put Joash on the throne. First, he called together the five officers who were in charge of the temple guard, presented the king to them and had them take an oath to obey his orders and tell no one what was going to transpire. After outlining his plan, he sent them throughout the kingdom of Judah to order the Levites living away from Jerusalem and the heads of the Jewish families (clans) to come to Jerusalem on a specific Sabbath day. They were to assemble at the temple as though they were there to worship the Lord.

Jehoiada's plan was simple but effective. The five officers each commanded one hundred men. Two companies would ordinarily be on duty daily and be replaced on the Sabbath Day, but on this particular Sabbath they would remain on duty and guard the king. A third company would guard the palace where Athaliah lived, and this would give her a false sense of security. A fourth company was assigned to the gate Sur (or "the foundation gate"—23:5), which may have led from the nearby palace to the temple area. The fifth company assembled at the gate behind the guardhouse, a normal place for the temple guards to gather. Anybody watching at the temple would have no reason to suspect that anything dramatic was about to occur. They would see the guards march in and take their usual places, and they might notice that the crowd of worshipers in the temple was larger than usual.

Even King David was involved in the plan! The high priest distributed to the men the weapons that David had confiscated in his many battles, and the guards protected David's own heir with those weapons. It was David who purchased the property on which the temple stood (2 Sam. 24:18ff), and it was David who provided the wealth that enabled Solomon to build the temple. Some of it came from his own personal treasury and the rest from the spoils of the battles he had fought for the Lord (1 Chron. 28–29). He wrote many of the songs the Levites sang in the temple services, and now he was providing the weapons to defend his own dynasty. David not only served his own generation (Acts 13:36) but every generation that followed. What an example for us to follow!

When everybody was in place, Jehoiada brought out the seven-year-old king and presented him to the people. Jehoiada put the crown on Joash's head and gave him a copy of the law of God that he was to obey (Deut. 17:14-12; 31:26). The high priest anointed him and the people joyfully welcomed him as their ruler. "God save the king" is literally "Let the king live!" (See 1 Sam. 10:24; 2 Sam. 16:16; 1 Kings 1:25, 39.) God had kept His covenant promise and put one of David's descendants on the throne of Judah!

7. Obedience (2 Kings 11:13-21; 2 Chron. 23:12-21)

God had protected the young king and had enabled Jehoiada and the officers to present him to the people, but the work wasn't over yet.

The execution of Athaliah (vv. 13-16; 23:12-15). The repeated shout "God save the king!" startled Athaliah and she hastened out of the palace to see what was happening. The first thing she discovered was that she was trapped. There were guards around the palace and between the palace and the temple courts, so there was no opportunity for her to escape or for her own soldiers to come to her rescue. She hurried to the temple court where she saw the young king standing by the pillar (1 Kings 7:21), protected by the captains. She also saw that the assembly was made up not only of priests, Levites and military personnel, but also "the people of the land," that is, the landholding citizens whose work, wealth, and influence were important to the nation.

How paradoxical that she should shout "Treason! Treason!" when *she* was the real traitor. Joash was a descendant of David and had every right to the throne, while Athaliah had seized the throne and had no claim to it. Jehoiada ordered the five military captains to escort her out of the temple area and told the guards to slay anybody who followed her. Once they were back on the palace grounds, near the Horse Gate, they killed her with the sword.

The dedication of the people (v. 17; 23:16). Jehoiada had already given the holy covenant to the king (v. 12), but it was necessary that both the people and the king affirm their allegiance to one another and to the Lord. Israel was a theocracy and God was their King. The king ruled as God's chosen representative, and the people obeyed the king as they would obey the Lord, for the law of Israel was the law of the Lord. Israel was a covenant nation, for at Mount Sinai their ancestors had sworn allegiance to the Lord and His Word (Ex. 18–19). *No other nation on earth has this same covenant relationship to the Lord* (Ps. 147:19-20).

The elimination of Baal worship (vv. 18-21; 23:17). As Jehu had done in Samaria, so Jehoiada did in Jerusalem: he and the people destroyed the temple of Baal and killed the chief priest of Baal before the altar of Baal.[2] No doubt they also executed the other people who were leaders in Baal worship. They also destroyed the temple of Baal and the altar and images that it contained. Because of Athaliah and her compromising husband Jehoram and their son Ahaziah, the kingdom of Judah had been infected with idolatry for at least fifteen years, and now the infection was exposed and removed.

The restoration of the Davidic dynasty (11:19-21; 23:20-21). What a joyful crowd it was that escorted the king from the temple to the palace, where they placed him on the throne! Satan's attempt to end the Davidic line had failed, and the messianic promise was still in force. The people had done the will of God and obeyed His Word, and for the first time in many years, righteousness and peace reigned in the land.

The organization of the temple ministry (11:18b; 2 Chron. 23:18-19). We learn from 2 Kings 12 that the temple of the Lord had been grossly neglected and abused during the time that Athaliah was the power behind the throne. Jehoiada immediately took steps to remedy this situation by following David's orders (1 Chron. 23–26) and putting the proper priests and Levites into places of ministry. It was important that they offer the daily sacrifices to the Lord and sing praises to Him. It was also essential that the doors of the temple be guarded so that no unclean person might enter and defile the other worshipers. *Revival is simply obeying God's Word and doing what He commanded our fathers to do.* We don't need the novelties of the present; we need the realities of the past.

When God began to restore true worship in Jerusalem and Judah, He started with one dedicated couple—Jehoiada the high priest and his wife, Jehosheba. They enlisted the nurse who cared for Joash, and God protected all four of them for six years. Then Jehoiada enlisted the five military captains, who in turn assembled their five hundred soldiers. The scattered priests, Levites, and people of the land came together as one to honor the Lord and obey His Word. Sin was purged, God's will was accomplished and the name of the Lord was glorified!

God could do it then, and He can do it today—but we must trust Him to have His way.

CHAPTER SEVEN
FOCUSING ON FAITH
2 Kings 12–13
(2 Chronicles 24)

It's a well-known principle that what a person believes ultimately determines how a person behaves. Eve believed the Devil's lie that she wouldn't die; she ate the forbidden fruit, and she eventually died. With his eyes wide open, Adam believed he should imitate his wife, so he took the fruit and ate it; and he plunged the human race into sin and death (Gen. 3; Rom. 5:12-21; 1 Tim. 2:14). When we believe the truth, God works for us, but when we believe a lie, the Devil works against us. When our Lord was tempted by Satan, He countered Satan's lies with God's truth and said, "It is written" (Matt. 4:1-11). The three kings presented in these chapters illustrate three different kinds of faith, none of which is the kind God's people should have today.

1. Joash—shallow faith (2 Kings 12:1-21)

In His parable about the sower (Matt. 13:1-9, 18-23), Jesus explained that, from a spiritual viewpoint, there are four kinds of hearts, and they respond to the seed of the Word in four different ways. When the hard-hearted hear the Word, the seed can't get in, so Satan snatches it away. Shallow-hearted people receive the Word but provide no room for it to take root, so the shoots grow up but don't last. A plant can't grow and bear fruit if it doesn't have roots. Those with crowded hearts receive the seed but the shoots are smothered by the weeds that should have been pulled up. The person with the heart that bears fruit is honest, repentant, understands the Word and embraces it by faith. When it came to his own personal faith, King Joash had a shallow heart. Let's note the stages in Joash's spiritual experience.

Obeying (vv. 1-3; 2 Chron. 24:1-3). Joash was only seven years old when he ascended the throne of Judah (11:4), and he had a long reign of forty years. It's obvious that a child of seven can't rule a nation, so the high priest Jehoiada was his tutor and mentor. Joash seemed to be a willing student, and during all the years that Jehoiada instructed him, the king obeyed the Lord. When the king was ready for marriage, it was Jehoiada who picked out his two wives. Both David and Solomon had gotten into trouble because of too many unwise marriages, so the high priest limited Joash to two wives. It was important that Joash rebuild the family of David, for the house of David had almost been destroyed by Jehoram (2 Chron. 21:4), Jehu (2 Kings 10:12-14), Arab invaders (2 Chron. 22:1), and Queen Athaliah (2 Kings 11:1).

The only thing Joash and Jehoiada didn't do was remove the high places in Judah, the local shrines where the people worshiped the Lord. They were supposed to go to the temple to worship (Deut. 12), but during the dark days of Athaliah's reign, the temple had been ignored and even allowed to decay. However, Jehoiada and King Joash would lead the people in repairing the temple so that they had a fine place for worshiping the Lord. The godly people in Judah must have rejoiced that an obedient descendant of David was on the throne. What they didn't know was that Joash's faith was shallow, and that he obeyed God only to please Jehoiada. Joash was an excellent follower but not a good leader. When Jehoiada died, Joash went his own way and disobeyed the Lord.

Struggling (vv. 4-16; 2 Chron. 24:4-14). It was clear to the people of Judah that godly Jehoiada was the power behind the throne, and this probably gave them a feeling of security. But as the king matured in age and experience, he must have been frustrated by this arrangement. It's a normal thing for young people to want the freedom to be themselves and make their own decisions, and this desire must have been intensified in Joash's life because of the authority he possessed. But with Jehoiada running things, Joash could say with King David, "And I am weak today, though anointed king" (2 Sam. 3:39, NKJV).

It isn't easy to mentor a young king and know just when to loosen and lengthen the restraining cords. Parents know this from raising their children to adulthood. Perhaps Jehoiada was taking charge too much and not gradually handing responsibility over to Joash. On the other hand, perhaps Jehoiada held the reins longer because he saw some weaknesses in the king's character and wanted to give him time to correct them. Maybe it was just a "generational problem." Whatever the cause, the king decided it was time to be set free from the rule of the Jewish priesthood and to begin to assert his authority. He chose the repairing of the temple as his focal point for freedom.

No doubt Joash and Jehoiada had discussed the need for repairing the temple, but for some reason, the high priest wasn't enthusiastic enough to get things started. Old age may have been a factor. We don't know how old Joash was when Jehoiada issued the order to have the temple offerings diverted into the building project (vv. 4-5). This would include money from the census (Ex. 30:11-16; Num. 2:32), money from personal vows (Lev. 22:18-23; 27:1ff), and money from the trespass offerings (v. 17; Lev. 5:14-6:7). But the plan didn't work, probably because the priests depended on these sources of income for the funds they needed to maintain the temple ministry and to meet their own needs. As far as the census was concerned, the priests and Levites may have hesitated because they remembered that David's census had brought judgment to the land (1 Chron. 22).

The text doesn't tell us how long Joash waited for Jehoiada to act, but when he was thirty years old and had reigned for twenty-three years, the king decided to act on his own. He called in Jehoiada and cautiously rebuked the priests for not doing the job. He also told the high priest that the throne would now direct the building program. The priests could keep the money that was rightfully theirs according to the Mosaic Law, because the new approach to financing the project would be freewill offerings from the people. Jehoiada informed the priests and Levites, who must have rejoiced that their income wouldn't be diverted and that they no longer had to get involved in repairing the temple. Having been involved in church building programs, I can sympathize with them!

The arrangement was simple, and it worked. Jehoiada prepared a large offering box, placed it in the temple by an entrance near the altar, and encouraged the people to bring their offerings for the repair of the temple. Of course, there were temple guards that kept their eye on the box. When the people found out that the project was now under royal supervision and in the hands of the laity, this encouraged them to give even more. They knew that every gift they brought and placed in the box would go directly into the building project and not be diverted into other ministries, so they gave generously. King Josiah followed a similar plan when he repaired the temple nearly two hundred years later (2 Kings 22:1-7).

However, Joash didn't ignore the priesthood in this project, for the counting and distributing of the money was handled jointly by representatives of the king and the high priest (v. 10). Without realizing it, Joash was following Paul's principle of involving the people and making sure everything was kept open and aboveboard (2 Cor. 8:16-24). The workers were so honest and faithful that nobody kept records of the income and expenditures, a fact that may have upset the royal auditors. The only project they didn't include was replacing the gold and silver utensils that had been stolen from the temple (2 Chron. 24:7), but enough money was left over to take care of that need (2 Chron. 24:14).

Believers today know that the Lord doesn't live in church buildings or in any other kind of building (John 4:23-24; Acts 7:48-50; 17:24), but this doesn't mean that it's wrong to dedicate structures to His service and glory. The early churches didn't have their own buildings but met in homes and in accessible public places such as the temple in Jerusalem. It wasn't until the fourth century that the law permitted them to construct and meet in their own buildings. Some of the saints today oppose church buildings and say they're a waste of God's money, while others almost worship their buildings and get their priorities confused. Campbell Morgan clarifies the issue with this warning:

> Whereas the house of God today is no longer material but spiritual, the material is still a very real symbol of the spiritual. When the Church of God in any place in any locality is careless about the material place of assembly, the place of its worship and its work, it is a sign and evidence that its life is at a low ebb.[1]

I recall preaching one Sunday evening to a congregation that met in a church building that was in such disrepair that it couldn't help but embarrass the members and the visitors they brought. It was doubtful that any of the members lived in houses in that condition (Hag. 1:1-6). I asked one of the church leaders why they didn't fix things up, and he replied somewhat sarcastically, "Oh, most of our budget has to go to foreign missions. And do you know what the missionaries do with the money we send them? They fix their buildings!" It wasn't a matter of either home or foreign but of balance. As Dr. Oswald J. Smith used to say, "The light that shines the farthest will shine the brightest at home." The executive director of a foreign mission ministry told me, "It took me ten years to learn that Acts 1:8 didn't use the word *or* but the word *and.* The Lord doesn't tear things down at home in order to build things up overseas." Blessed are the balanced!

Forsaking (vv. 17-18; 2 Chron. 24:15-22). Jehoiada died at the advanced age of one hundred and thirty. He was so beloved by the people that he was buried with the kings (2 Chron. 24:15-16). But when Jehoiada passed off the scene, King Joash showed his true colors and abandoned the faith. His apostasy wasn't the fault of Jehoiada, for the high priest had faithfully taught Joash the Scriptures. The problem was Joash's shallow faith and his desire to please the leaders of the land, "the officials of Judah" who visited Joash and asked him to be more lenient in matters of religion (24:17-18). He relented, and once again idolatry moved into Judah and Jerusalem.

Joash's apostasy was a sin of willful rebellion against God, for the king knew what the Law of Moses taught about idolatry. But it was also a sin of ingratitude for all that Jehoiada had done for him. *Jehoiada and his wife had saved the king's life!* The high priest had taught him the truth of God's Word and had stood at Joash's side as he learned how to govern the people. But the king had never taken the truth into his heart and allowed it to take root. The soil of his heart was shallow and he had obeyed God's law only because his mentor was watching. He even took wealth from the very temple he had repaired and gave it to a pagan king for ransom!

Joash is a warning to us today. It isn't enough simply to know God's truth; we must obey His truth "from the heart" (Eph. 6:6). Truth in the mind can lead to obedience, but truth in the heart and obedience from the heart will produce godly character. God's Word and God's will must be internalized—received into the heart (Ps. 119:9-11)—or we can never develop consistent Christian character. Until duty and discipline become delight, we are only reluctant servants who obey God because we have to, not because we want to. Jehoiada was a "religious prop" on which the king leaned. When the prop was removed, the king fell.

During more than fifty years of ministry, I have occasionally witnessed the "Joash tragedy." A godly wife dies and the widower soon drops out of church and starts to live a worldly life. Sons or daughters go off to college and gradually leave the faith because father and mother aren't there to counsel and warn them. I've known some high-profile Christian leaders who "used" their children in their ministries, but when the children were on their own, they turned their backs on their parents and the Lord. A good beginning is no guarantee of a good ending. King Josiah had every encouragement to become a godly man, but he didn't take advantage of his opportunities by taking God's truth into his heart. When the Lord sent prophets to warn him, he refused to listen. He even plotted with his leaders to have Zechariah, the son of Jehoiada, stoned to death because he rebuked the king for his sins.[2] Imagine murdering the son of the very people who saved your life!

Suffering (vv. 19-21; 2 Chron. 24:23-

27). When the king of Judah became an idolater and a murderer, the Lord began to discipline him. First He brought the prophets to warn Joash, but he wouldn't listen. Then He brought Judah's long-time enemy Syria against Judah,[3] and Joash was severely wounded in the battle. He finally robbed the temple and bribed Hazael not to attack Jerusalem. However, Joash didn't recover from his wounds, for two of his officials murdered him because he had ordered the death of Zechariah, son of Jehoiada.[4] Second Chronicles 24:26 informs us that the two assassins were sons of non-Jewish women, one from Moab and the other from Ammon. The Moabites and the Ammonites were the descendants of Abraham's nephew Lot who had an incestuous relationship with his two daughters (Gen. 19:30-38). The people buried Joash in Jerusalem but not in the sepulcher of the kings where Jehoiada the high priest was buried (2 Chron. 24:25, 16).

The boy king, who made such a good beginning, had a bad ending, and it was because he forsook the way of the Lord. We wonder if the Prophet Ezekiel was thinking about Joash when he wrote Ezekiel 18:24-32.

2. Jehoahaz—crisis faith. (2 Kings 13:1-9)

Now the focus moves from Judah to Israel and the reign of Jehu's son Jehoahaz. It's no surprise that he chose Jeroboam as his model, because his father had done the same thing (10:29). Jehoahaz would rather worship the golden calves than the living God, but when he found himself in trouble, he turned to the Lord for help.

The people of Israel shouldn't have been surprised when the Lord brought the Syrians against them, because the people knew the terms of the covenant God had made with them before they entered the land of Canaan. If they obeyed Him, He would give them victory over their enemies, but if they disobeyed, He would cause them to fall before their enemies (Lev. 26:17, 25, 33, 36-39; Deut. 28:25-26, 49-52). People still believe Satan's lie, "You will not surely die" (Gen. 3:4, NKJV). "Do whatever you enjoy," says the Enemy, "because there are no serious consequences to sin." But whether to chasten or to bless, God is always true to His Word.

The situation became so painfully desperate that Jehoahaz cried out to God for help, just the way Israel had done during the period of the judges (Judg. 2:10-23). God in His mercy heard and answered the king's prayer and promised to send a deliverer, but only after Jehoahaz was off the scene (v. 22). Hazael died and his son and successor Ben-Hadad was a weaker ruler, so it was possible for someone to break the iron grip Syria had on Israel. Historians aren't agreed as to who this deliverer was. Some point to the Assyrians who began to attack Syria in the days of Ben-Hadad and weaken his power. Others feel the deliverance came through one or both of Jehoahaz's successors, Jehoash (v. 25) and Jeroboam II (14:25-27). The statement "Israel dwelt in their tents" (v. 5) means "they lived in peace and didn't have to seek refuge in the walled cities."

Did the promised blessing of God change the king? Apparently not, for he didn't remove the idols from the land (v. 6; 1 Kings 16:33) nor did he encourage the people to return to the Lord. Crisis faith is rarely deep or lasting. Once people see hope of deliverance and their pain eases up, they forget the Lord and return to their old ways until the next crisis. The Syrians left Jehoahaz with a mock army that was more of an embarrassment than it was an encouragement. Yet God had promised that if His people trusted Him and obeyed His Word, their enemies would flee before them (Deut. 28:7; 32:30; Lev. 26:8).

But crisis faith is undependable. How many times I've heard hospital patients say, "Pastor, if God heals me and gets me out of here, I'll be the best Christian you ever met." God did heal them and allow them to go home, but I never met them again in church. Yes, there are such things as "foxhole conversions" and "deathbed conversions," and we don't want to discourage anyone from turning to God in the hour of crisis. The British historian William Camden wrote, "Betwixt the stirrup and the ground / Mercy I asked, mercy I found."

But how many times can we call on the Lord when we're in trouble and then ignore Him when we're safe? People who depend on crisis faith need to heed the warnings of Proverbs 1:24-33 and Isaiah 55:6-7, and they shouldn't assume that because God heard and helped them, they're automatically going to heaven.

3. Jehoash—ignorant faith. (2 Kings 13:10-25)

For some reason, the death of Jehoash is mentioned twice, once before the historian records his life (vv. 12-13) and again at the end of the story (14:15-16). His great defeat of Amaziah, king of Judah, is also mentioned before it's described (14:8-14; 2 Chron. 25). But the most important thing about Jehoash was that he had sense enough to visit the Prophet Elisha and seek some blessing from him. Consider five facts about Jehoash.

He followed the wrong examples (vv. 10-13). Like his father, he modeled himself after Jeroboam I, the first king of Israel. This meant he visited the golden calves and bowed down to idols. And, like his father, he turned to the Lord only when he was in trouble and time was running out. The Syrians were still in control and the Prophet Elisha was about to die.

He made a wise decision (v. 14). We haven't heard from or about Elisha since 9:1, when he sent one of the sons of the prophets to anoint Jehu to be king of Israel. This means over forty years of silence as far as the record is concerned, yet Elisha was at work in the land and the Lord was with him. Now he was an old man and about to die, and the king of Israel went to see him. Let's at least give Jehoash credit for visiting the prophet and seeking his help. Was it Elisha who told Jehoahaz that God would send a deliverer (vv. 4-5)? Was his son Jehoash that deliverer? Only Elisha knew God's plan and the king was wise enough to visit him.

It's too bad spiritual leaders aren't appreciated during their lifetime but are greatly lauded after they die. The Pharisees were better at building tombs for the dead than they were at showing thanks to the living (Matt. 23:29-32). Faithful servants of God never "retire" even though they may leave their lifelong vocation and step back from public ministry. Even from his deathbed, Elisha was serving the Lord and his people. As long as God gives us strength and sanity, we should serve Him the best we can in whatever ways He opens for us. How grateful I am for "senior servants" who have counseled and encouraged me, and the memories of their lives and ministries are still a blessing to me (Heb. 13:7-8, NIV).

The king showed respect for the prophet and even addressed him with the same words Elisha used for Elijah when Elijah was taken to heaven (2:12). Elisha was like a father to the nation and was more valuable than all their armies! Elisha knew that Jehoash was in trouble because of the Syrians and graciously used his failing strength to help the king. Yes, Jehoash was a compromising king who disobeyed God, but Jehovah is "the Lord, the Lord God, merciful and gracious, longsuffering, and abounding in goodness and truth" (Ex. 34:6, NKJV). He had promised deliverance for His people and He would keep His promise. However, Elisha gave Jehoash God's promise of victory but did it in a way that required the king to exercise intelligent faith.

He made a great mistake (vv. 15-19). King Jehoash was not a man of faith, but he could follow directions. However, he lacked the spiritual discernment and insight that people have who live in the Word and walk by faith. When the prophet put his hands on the king's hands, it obviously symbolized a conveying of power from God. When Elisha commanded him to shoot an arrow toward the area where the Syrians were in control, it clearly spoke of victory over the enemy (Deut. 32:42; Ps. 120:4). This much the king could have understood because Elisha gave him a clear promise of victory.

But when Elisha told him to take the remaining arrows and strike the ground with them, he didn't have the spiritual understanding he needed to make the most of it. Had he been a faithful worshiper of the living God, he would have seen the truth; but he was blind like the dead idols he worshiped (Ps. 115:3-8). Shooting one arrow guaranteed victory, but the number of times he smote the ground determined how many victories God would give him. Because Jehoash had ignorant faith, he limited himself to only three victories over the Syrians.

As sick as he was, the Prophet Elisha expressed righteous anger over the king's ignorance and unbelief. What an opportunity Jehoash missed for utterly destroying his enemies! "According to your faith let it be to you" (Matt. 9:29, NKJV). It isn't enough for us simply to *know* God's will and obey it, as important as that is, but we should also *understand* God's will and God's ways (Eph. 5:17; Ps. 103:7). The commandments and acts of God reveal to us the character of God if our spiritual eyes are open (Eph. 1:17-20). This is how we understand the ways of God and how better to serve Him, and this is how the Lord increases our faith.

He received a great encouragement (vv. 20-21). When Elisha died, the king may have wondered if his promises died with him. To encourage the king, the Lord graciously performed a miracle after Elisha died. The Jews didn't embalm corpses as did the Egyptians. They merely washed the body and wrapped it in clean cloths along with spices. One day, when the arrival of Moabite raiders interrupted a committal service of a man recently deceased, the mourners quickly put the body into Elisha's tomb and fled. But God used that occasion to give the man life! Surely this miracle was talked about among the people and the king may have heard the account from the lips of the men who saw it. This miracle told him that, though the prophet was dead, Jehovah was still the living God and the God of power. His promises would not fail.

The Prophet Elijah never died but was caught up into heaven (2:11-12), but the Prophet Elisha died and was buried. However, Elisha performed a miracle even after he was dead. God has different plans for each of His servants and it's not our business to compare one with the other or to question what He does (John 21:19-23).

He won the three victories (vv. 22-25). The Syrians were determined to destroy Israel and make it a part of their empire, but the Lord had other plans. His covenant with the patriarchs (Gen. 12:1-3) and His grace toward their descendants moved Him to look upon Israel's affliction and rescue them from their enemies. It was only when the people sinned so flagrantly that they blasphemed the name of the Lord and defiled His land that God permitted both Israel and Judah to be defeated and taken into bondage. In 722, Assyria conquered the northern kingdom of Israel, and in 586, Jerusalem fell to the Babylonians. The people of Judah returned to their land after the seventy years of captivity expired, but the people of Israel were assimilated into the Assyrian empire.

King Jehoash won three great victories against the Syrians, and this was sufficient to enable him to recover towns that Hazael and Ben-Hadad had taken from Israel, and then King Jeroboam II recovered the rest of the land. The Lord enabled Jehoash to increase his military power (v. 7) and overcome the Syrians led by Ben-Hadad III. God's promise came true and God's people were spared. During the reigns of Jehoash and Jeroboam II, the kingdom of Israel reached its zenith and there was prosperity in the land. However, with all its achievements and wealth, it was still a land filled with idolatry and much sin. During the reign of Jeroboam II, the Prophets Hosea and Amos ministered to the people of Israel. When you read their books, you see the true conditions of the land.

CHAPTER EIGHT
NINE KINGS—FIVE ASSASSINATIONS
2 Kings 14–15
(2 Chronicles 25–27)

"Political history is far too criminal and pathological to be a fit subject of study for the young," wrote poet W. H. Auden. Edward Gibbon, author of *The Decline and Fall of the Roman Empire,* defined history as "little more than the register of the crimes, follies, and misfortunes of mankind."[1]

The history recorded in these five chapters seems to agree with Auden and Gibbon, for it reeks of selfish intrigue, bloodshed, moral decay, and repeated rebellion against the law of the Lord. Ancient Israel wasn't much different from society today. Not one king of Israel encouraged his people to repent and seek the Lord; and in Judah, Amaziah and Uzziah both committed acts of arrogant ambition that brought judgment from God. When Jeroboam II became king of Israel in 782 B.C., little did the people realize that in sixty years, the kingdom would be no more. As we look at these nine rulers, we can gain some practical insights into the will and ways of God as well as the terrible wages of sin.

1. Amaziah, a presumptuous king (2 Kings 14:1-20; 2 Chron. 25)

Amaziah was the ninth king of Judah[2] and the son of Joash (Jehoash), the "boy king," who in his later years turned away from the Lord, killed God's prophet, and was himself assassinated (2 Chron. 24:15-26). Amaziah made an excellent beginning, but he later abandoned the Lord and was also assassinated (14:17-20).[3] He saw to it that the men were executed who had killed his father, and he obeyed Deuteronomy 24:16 by judging only the offenders and not their families.[4] Had he continued to obey God's Word, his life and reign would have been much different. Consider some of his sins.

Unbelief (14:7; 25:5-13). Amaziah decided to attack Edom and regain territory that had been lost (8:20-22). The venture was a good one, but the way he went about it was definitely wrong. He took a census and found he had 300,000 men, but instead of trusting the Lord to use these men, he hired 100,000 mercenaries from Israel to increase his forces. His faith was in numbers and not in the Lord (Ps. 20:7), but even worse, the soldiers he hired came from apostate Israel where the people worshiped the golden calves. God sent a prophet to rebuke the king and warn him that the Lord was not with the kingdom of Israel, so the hired soldiers would only bring defeat. "But if you go, be gone! Be strong in battle! Even so, God shall make you fall before the enemy; for God has power to help and to overthrow" (25:8, NKJV). The prophet was a bit sarcastic, but he made his point.

One of the recurring themes in Israel's history is their sin of forming alliances with the ungodly because they didn't have faith in the Lord. Solomon married heathen wives and by this entered into treaties with his neighbors, but his wives influenced him to worship idols (1 Kings 11). King Ahab married Jezebel, a Phoenician princess and a worshiper of Baal (1 Kings 16:30-33), and this brought Baal worship into the kingdom. King Jehoshaphat allied with Ahab to fight the Syrians and was almost killed. Jehoshaphat also entered into a business partnership with King Ahaziah, but the Lord broke it up by destroying Jehoshaphat's fleet. "Do not be unequally yoked together with unbelievers" (2 Cor. 6:14, NKJV) is an admonition that needs to be heard and heeded by the church today. It's not by imitating the world and uniting with the world, but by being different from the world that we manifest the power and grace of God and accomplish His will.

According to 2 Chron. 25:2, Amaziah was not wholehearted in his relationship to the Lord (see NIV), and this revealed itself in the way he argued with the prophet about the will of God (25:9). The king was unwilling to send the mercenaries home because it would have meant forfeiting the one hundred talents of silver he had paid to the king of Israel. This amounted to nearly four tons of silver. Amaziah was "counting the cost" and adjusting his priorities, hoping he could change God's mind. The prophet wisely replied that God could give him much more if he would only trust Him and obey His will (Matt. 6:33).

If we would seek the Lord's will *before* we rush into disobedience, we would avoid a great deal of trouble; but even after we change our minds and decide to obey the Lord, often there are still painful consequences to endure. The soldiers returned to Israel very angry because of the way they had been treated. Why were they angry? For one thing, they lost an opportunity to profit from the spoils of battle. Furthermore, who was the king of Judah to say that God thought more highly of Judah's soldiers than He did the army of Samaria? What an embarrassment for these brave mercenaries to be sent home empty-handed, having never fought the battle! How could they explain to the king and their friends back home that the army had been declared unclean and rejected? Their solution was to give vent to their anger by attacking some of the border cities in northern Judah. They killed three thousand people and took the spoils as their compensation (25:13).[5]

Because he finally obeyed the Lord, Amaziah's army defeated the Edomites. They killed ten thousand men in the Valley of Salt, where David had won a great victory (1 Chron. 18:12). Then they destroyed ten thousand prisoners of war by casting them down from the heights of the city of Sela (Petra) that was cut right out of the mountain (Obad. 1-4). So elated was Amaziah with his achievement that he renamed the city "Joktheel," which means "God destroys" (14:7).

Idolatry (25:14-16). The saintly Scottish minister Andrew Bonar said, "Let us be as watchful after the victory as before the battle," an admonition that King Amaziah desperately needed to hear and heed. The Lord Jehovah had given His servant an outstanding victory over a strong enemy in a difficult place, *and yet Amaziah took back to Judah the gods of the defeated enemy* (2 Chron. 25:14-16)! Surely the king of Judah didn't think that by taking these idols he would paralyze the Edomites and prevent future wars! Every Jew was taught that the Lord Jehovah was one God and the only true and living God, and therefore the gods of the nations were nothing (Deut. 6:4-5; Ps. 115). Worshiping idols was a direct violation of the Law of Moses (Ex. 20:1-6), and worshiping the gods of a defeated enemy was simply unreasonable. After all, what did those gods accomplish for the Edomites? Yet Amaziah began to worship the gods of Edom, offer them sacrifices, and consult them.

When the Lord sent His messenger to the king to warn him, Amaziah interrupted the prophet and threatened to kill him if he continued to speak. But the prophet had one last word: God would destroy the king for his sin. In fact, God would permit the king to destroy himself! The greatest judgment God can send to people is to let them have their own way.

Pride (14:8-14; 25:17-24). Amaziah defeated the Edomites because he obeyed the Lord, but then the Edomites defeated Amaziah when he took their gods home with him. Inflated by his great success and unconcerned about his great sin, Amaziah looked for other worlds to conquer and decided to challenge Joash (Jehoash), king of Israel. He not only ignored the warning of the prophet God sent, but he forgot the words of his ancestor Solomon, "Before destruction the heart of man is haughty, and before honor is humility" (Prov. 18:12, NKJV). Even King Jehoash warned him that his pride would ruin him (14:10), but Amaziah was bent on defeating Israel and becoming the ruler of a united kingdom.

Jehoash's reply (14:9; 25:18) reminds us of the parable Jotham spoke (Judg. 9:7-20), and both of them deal with pride and judgment. Amaziah's problem was pride: he saw himself as a strong cedar, when in reality he was only a weak thistle that could be crushed by a passing wild beast. The truly humble person sees things as God sees them and doesn't live on illusions. Pride blinds the mind, distorts the vision, and so inflates the ego that the person can't tell truth from fiction.

Rejecting a second warning from the Lord, Amaziah invaded Israel where his army was soundly defeated. He was taken captive fifteen miles from Jerusalem and went from the palace to the prison. The army of Israel invaded Judah and destroyed six hundred feet of the wall of Jerusalem, leaving the city vulnerable to future attacks. They also took treasures from the palace and from the temple of the Lord, and they even took some of the leaders as hostages. King Amaziah was in exile in Samaria for fifteen years (14:17) and then returned to Jerusalem briefly as coregent with his son (14:21; 26:1, 3). But his idolatry disturbed some of the leaders and they formed a conspiracy to assassinate him. He fled to Lachish where he was captured and killed (14:18-20; 25:27).

Amaziah is a tragic figure in Jewish history. He was presented with great opportunities and experienced great help from the Lord, but he was a double-minded man who didn't wholeheartedly serve the Lord. He had his own agenda and didn't take time to seek the mind of the Lord. "Pride goes before destruction, and a haughty spirit before a fall" (Prov. 16:18, NKJV).

2. Jeroboam, a prosperous king (14:23-29)

The record now turns from Judah to Israel and to Jeroboam II who had the longest reign of any of Israel's kings, forty-one years. He was not a good king when it came to spiritual matters, but he brought prosperity to the nation and delivered it from its enemies. Even back in those ancient days, the average citizen didn't care about the character of the nation's leaders so long as the people had food on their tables, money in their purses, and no fear of being invaded by their enemies.

Thanks to Assyria's victories over Syria, both Israel and Judah were finally relieved of the bondage of that persistent enemy and both had opportunity to use their wealth and manpower for building instead of battling. Israel was able to drive the Syrians out of the border outposts and Jeroboam also recovered the territory that had been lost to Syria. The kingdom of Israel reached the dimensions achieved in the days of Solomon (vv. 25 and 28; 1 Kings 8:65). The Lord permitted these victories, not because the people or their king deserved them, but because He had pity on His people who were suffering under the rule of Syria (14:26; see Ex. 2:23-25).

The prosperity of Israel was only a veneer that covered sins and crimes that were an abomination in the sight of the Lord. The Prophets Amos (1:1) and Hosea (1:1) ministered during Jeroboam's reign and warned that judgment was coming. Judgment did come in 722 B.C., when the Assyrians invaded Israel, deported many of the Jewish people, and imported Gentiles from other conquered nations to mix with the Israelites. This policy eventually produced a mixed race, part Jew and part Gentile, as well as a hybrid religion with its own temple and priesthood on Mount Gerizim (John 4:20-22). After the Babylonian captivity, the orthodox Jews who returned to Judah would have nothing to do with the Samaritans (Ezra 4:1-4; Neh. 2:19-20; see John 4:9).

What were the sins of this prosperous kingdom? For one thing, the rich were getting richer at the expense of the poor, who were exploited and abused. The wealthy landowners barely cared for their slaves, and the courts disobeyed the law and decided cases in favor of the rich and not in fairness to the poor. In the midst of this corruption, the leaders practiced their "religion," attended services, and brought their sacrifices (Amos 2:1-8; 4:1-5). While the wealthy men and their wives lived in luxury, the poor were downtrodden and robbed of their civil rights (Amos 6:1-7; Hos. 12:8). The "religious" crowd longed for "the day of the Lord" to come, thinking that this momentous event would bring even greater glory to Israel (Amos 5:18-27). The people didn't realize that "the day of the Lord" actually meant divine judgment on the nation, for God's judgment begins with His own people (1 Peter 4:17). Israel was given to idolatry, which led to moral decay and worldly corruption (Hos. 6:4; 7:8; 9:9; 11:7; 13:2).[6] Jeroboam II ruled from 793 to 753, and in 722 B.C. the Assyrians invaded Israel and brought to an end the nation of Israel.

British poet and playwright Oliver Goldsmith said it perfectly in his poem *The Deserted Village:*

> Ill fares the land, to hast'ning ills a prey,
> Where wealth accumulates, and men decay . . .

3. Uzziah (Azariah), an illustrious king (2 Kings 15:1-7; 2 Chron. 26)

His given name was Azariah, which means "Jehovah has helped," but when he became king of Judah at age sixteen, he took the "throne name" Uzziah, which means "Jehovah is strength." The people made him king when his father Azariah was taken to Samaria after his foolish war against Jehoash, king of Israel (2 Kings 14:13).

During his father's fifteen years of captivity in Samaria, Uzziah ruled Judah and sought to do the will of God. After his father's death, Uzziah continued on the throne until he foolishly attempted to become a priest and God judged him by making him a leper. At that time, his son Jotham became coregent with his father. The record declares that Uzziah was king of Judah fifty-two years (2 Chron. 26:3), including his coregencies with his father Azariah (fifteen years) and also with his son Jotham (possibly ten years).

From the very beginning of his reign, Uzziah showed himself to be a faithful worshiper of Jehovah, even though he didn't try to eliminate the "high places," the hill shrines where the Jewish people worshiped. They were supposed to go to the temple with their gifts and sacrifices for the Lord, but it was more convenient to visit a local shrine. Some of the high places were still devoted to pagan deities, such as Baal (2 Chron. 27:2), and it wasn't until the reigns of Hezekiah and Josiah that the high places were removed (2 Chron. 31:1; 2 Kings 23).

Uzziah's accomplishments (2 Kings 14:22; 2 Chron. 26:2, 6-15). He was very successful in his military exploits. He recovered from Edom the city of Elath, although later it was lost to Syria and Israel (2 Kings 16:5-6; 2 Chron. 28:17). Their possessing Elath gave Judah access to the sea, and this helped in their trade with other nations. Uzziah had Zechariah as his counselor and sought to know and please the Lord. "As long as he sought the Lord, God made him to prosper" (26:5).

God prospered his armies and helped them to conquer the Philistines, the Arabians, and the Ammonites. After defeating the Philistines, he destroyed the walls of their key cities. This victory gave him additional access to the sea. To keep control over this newly acquired territory, Uzziah built cities in Philistia and settled them with Jewish soldiers and officers. After conquering the Ammonites, Uzziah's fame increased even more. But these victories on foreign soil didn't deter him from strengthening things at home. He built towers on the walls of Jerusalem and repaired the damage that was done by the army of Israel (2 Kings 14:13). He had a well-trained army and provided them with the weapons and armor they needed,[7] and he also encouraged the building of "war machines" that shot arrows and threw stones (26:11-15).

But Uzziah wasn't just a gifted soldier

and a careful builder; he was also a farmer at heart. He sought to develop the land by building cisterns and putting the people to work with the flocks and herds as well as the fields and vineyards. He built towers in the fields where the guards could watch for invaders and protect the people. "Those who labor in the earth are the chosen people of God," wrote Thomas Jefferson in his *Notes on the State of Virginia.* Though a soldier, a builder, and a monarch, Uzziah was a man of the soil. He would have agreed with Booker T. Washington who said, "[T]here is as much dignity in tilling a field as in writing a poem."

Uzziah's arrogance (15:5; 26:16-21). Unfortunately, Uzziah imitated his father and allowed his accomplishments to swell his head. Amaziah wanted to be known as a great general, but Uzziah wanted to serve as both king and priest. In the Old Testament economy, the Lord separated the kings and priests, and while a priest could become a prophet (Ezekiel, Zechariah, John the Baptist), no prophet or king could become a priest. Only in Jesus Christ do we find the offices of prophet, priest, and king combined, and His priesthood is "after the order of Melchizedek" (Ps. 110:4; Gen. 14:18-20; Heb. 5–7). For Uzziah to covet the priesthood was ignorance, for he knew the Law of Moses; and for him to try to seize it by force was arrogance, for he knew what happened to others who had attempted to claim what wasn't rightfully theirs. (See Lev. 10; Num. 12, 16.)

"But when he became strong, his heart was so proud that he acted corruptly" (26:16, NASB). There's no question that Uzziah was an illustrious king whose name was known far and wide (26:15), but what the Lord did for him should have produced humility and not pride. Uzziah should have said with David, "Who am I, O Lord God? And what is my house that You have brought me thus far?" (2 Sam. 7:18, NKJV). Instead, he convinced himself that he deserved to be a priest as well as a king. He knew that the high priest burned the holy incense on the golden altar each morning and evening (Ex. 30:7-8), so he procured a censer and went into the temple precincts where only the priests were allowed to go (Num. 16:40; 18:7).

Azariah the high priest, along with eighty other priests, stood in his way and refused to allow him passage. It took a great deal of courage for them to oppose such a popular king, but their first allegiance was to the Lord. They could have compromised and perhaps won favors from the king, but they had but one desire, and that was to obey and glorify the Lord. The king became angry, refused to retreat, and raged at the priests for their interference. The Hebrew word translated "angry" in 26:19 implies "raging like a storm."

Had the king immediately left the temple and sincerely repented of his sins, the Lord would have forgiven him, but Uzziah stood his ground and insisted on his way. It was then that the Lord intervened and put the leprosy on his forehead where the priests could clearly see it. They knew that lepers belonged outside the camp, not inside the temple (Lev. 13:45-46), and they hurriedly forced the king out of the holy precincts. King Uzziah couldn't see the leprosy on his forehead, so perhaps it began to appear on other parts of his body so that he knew for certain that he was infected. The law demanded that those who intruded into the holy temple were to be put to death (Num. 18:7), but God graciously spared the king's life and gave him leprosy, a "living death."

Being a leper, the king couldn't appear

in public or even live in the palace. He was quarantined in an isolated house while his son Jotham ruled the land as coregent. When Uzziah died, he was buried in the royal cemetery, but apparently not in the tombs of the kings. He had a wonderful beginning but a tragic ending, and this is a warning to us that we be on guard and pray that the Lord will help us to end well. A good beginning is no guarantee of a successful ending, and the sin of unholy ambition has ruined more than one servant of the Lord. Uzziah the soldier was defeated by his pride; Uzziah the builder destroyed his own ministry and testimony; and Uzziah the farmer reaped the painful harvest of what he had sown. He is a warning to all who nurture unholy ambitions to intrude into that which God hasn't appointed for them. (See Ps. 131.)

4. Five notorious kings (2 Kings 15:8-31)

From Jeroboam I, the first king of Israel, to Hoshea, the last king of Israel, not one king is called "good." However, the kingdom of Judah didn't fare much better, for out of twenty kings who ruled after the kingdom divided, only eight of them could be called "good."[8] In this section of 2 Kings, we meet with five kings of Israel who were notorious for their godless character and evil deeds. Four of them were assassinated! Shallum reigned only one month, Zechariah six months, and Pekahiah for two years. Menahem, the cruelest of them all, reigned for ten years, and Pekah for twenty years. As the Northern Kingdom stumbled toward destruction, their rulers hastened the coming of the judgment of God. God often gives a nation just exactly the leaders it deserves.

Zechariah (vv. 8-12). Twenty-nine men in Scripture are named Zechariah; this one was the son of Jeroboam II, the last great king of the northern kingdom of Israel. Zechariah didn't have the political skills of his father and he chose to imitate the sins of his namesake, Jeroboam I. Zechariah was the great-great-grandson of Jehu and therefore the last of that dynasty. God promised Jehu that his descendants would occupy the throne of Israel for four generations (2 Kings 10:30), and that promise was fulfilled. Zechariah was a king, not because of his sanctity, ability, or popularity, but because he was providentially born into the royal family. Only two major facts are recorded about him: he did evil in the sight of the Lord, and he was assassinated publicly by Shallum, who then took the throne. Zechariah reigned only six months, and his death ended Jehu's dynasty.

Shallum (vv. 13-15). We know very little about this man. He organized a conspiracy and murdered Zechariah; he reigned as king of Israel for one short month; and he was the victim of a conspiracy that led to his own death. "Whoever digs a pit will fall into it, and he who rolls a stone will have it roll back on him" (Prov. 26:27, NKJV). Shallum was killed by Menahem, one of his own officers who was military commander at Tirzah, the early capital of Samaria (1 Kings 14:17; 15:21, 33). If Shallum had any descendants, they probably didn't admit it. What was there about Shallum to be proud of?

Menahem (vv. 6-22). Since he was a man feared by the people and had the army under his control, Menahem was able to rule for ten years and die a natural death. Because the people of Tiphsah (a city we can't identify) wouldn't accept his kingship, he broke his way into the city and killed his enemies. He was a brutal man who followed the Syrian custom of ripping up pregnant women (v. 16; see 8:12), something that Hosea the Prophet warned would happen (Hos. 13:16). When the Assyrians invaded the land, Menahem taxed all the wealthy citizens over a pound of silver and gave Pul (Tiglath-Pileser) thirty-seven tons of silver as tribute. The Assyrians left, but they came back twenty years later and took over the entire land. King David would have trusted God, fought the Assyrians, and defeated them; but Menahem's policy was to compromise and conciliate.

Pekahiah (vv. 23-26). Menahem's son inherited the throne but ruled for only two years. His father had been a military commander and had assassinated King Shallum, and Pekahiah was killed in his own palace by Pekah, a military commander, who then became king. The fact that Pekah was assisted by fifty men from Gilead suggests that he was in charge of the military forces east of the Jordan River.[9] It's likely that Pekahiah and Pekah disagreed about the right policy Israel should follow regarding Assyria. Pekahiah, like his father Menahem, sought to appease the Assyrians and give them what they wanted, while Pekah, a military man, took a hard line against Assyria and favored Syria.

Pekah (vv. 27-31). Thanks to the protection of his army, Pekah was able to reign twenty years. When a military man takes over, it's very difficult to get rid of him. In spite of Menahem's appeasement of the Assyrians, they invaded Israel again and in the course of four campaigns (738, 734, 733, and 732) not only took a number of key cities but also captured much territory from Hamath and Naphtali in the north to Gilead and Galilee. The Assyrians also took Philistia as far south as Gaza, and even captured Damascus in Syria. Many Jews and Philistines were deported to Assyria. Pekah was slain by Hoshea, son of Elah, who was pro-Assyrian in his political views. We will hear more about Hoshea in 2 Kings 17. He reigned for nine years and was probably deported to Assyria where he died (17:1; 18:10-11).[10]

5. Jotham, a virtuous king (2 Kings 15:32-38; 2 Chron. 27)

Jotham, son of Uzziah, began to reign when he was twenty-five years old and ruled for sixteen years (27:1). He was coregent with his father after Uzziah was smitten with leprosy for invading the temple precincts. Jotham would be considered a good king, although his son Ahaz was a bad king. In fact, from Jotham, the eleventh king of Judah, to Zedekiah, the twentieth and last king of Judah, only Jotham, Hezekiah, and Josiah could be called good kings. That's three kings out of ten. The Lord kept David's lamp burning in Jerusalem all those years, but there came a time when He had to bring in the nation of Babylon and punish His people for their sins.

Like his father, Uzziah, Jotham was both a builder and a warrior. He repaired the walls of Jerusalem and the Upper Gate of the temple. He also built cities in the Judean mountains and fortresses and towers in the wooded areas. His army confronted the armies of Israel and Syria, and he won a great victory over the Ammonites and put them under a very heavy annual tribute—nearly four tons of silver and 62,000 bushels each of wheat and barley (27:5). "So Jotham became mighty, because he prepared his ways before the Lord his God" (27:6, NKJV). We wonder how much more good he would have accomplished had he lived longer.

In Hebrew history we frequently find a

godly father begetting an ungodly son and an ungodly father raising a godly son. Good king Jehoshaphat begat bad king Jehoram, but godly King Joash gave the nation a godly son (Amaziah), grandson (Uzziah), and great-grandson (Jotham). However, Jotham's son Ahaz was not a good king or a godly man, yet he begat good King Hezekiah, who in turn was the father of Manasseh, perhaps the most wicked king of the lot—and he had a reign of fifty-five years! Ezekiel the Prophet in Babylon dealt with this interesting phenomenon in chapter 18 of his prophecy.

God is sovereign in His gifts to individuals and nations. The Lord was longsuffering toward His people during those difficult and evil days, and He was faithful to keep His promises to David. But time was running out. After Ahaz died, only Hezekiah and Josiah would honor the Word of God and seek to obey His will. Yet, in spite of the sins and failings of the people, the Lord maintained a godly remnant in the nation, and from that godly remnant the Messiah would eventually be born.

"Known to God from eternity are all His works" (Acts 15:18, NKJV).

CHAPTER NINE
A TALE OF TWO KINGDOMS
2 Kings 16–17
(2 Chronicles 28)

An English proverb says, "Consider well who you are, where you came from, what you do and where you are going." The first two considerations were easily answered in both Israel and Judah, for both nations would have said, "We are God's chosen people, descendants of our father Abraham." As for the third question, both kings would have had to admit, "We do what our wicked predecessors did." King Ahaz of Judah didn't follow the godly example of his ancestor David, and Hoshea, king of Israel, imitated the wicked kings that ruled before him. They were free to make these decisions, *but they were not free to change the consequences of their decisions,* which brings us to the fourth question, "Where are you going?" For both rulers, God's answer was clear: "You and your people are plunging rapidly toward judgment and ruin." Solomon's words were about to be proved in both kingdoms: "Righteousness exalts a nation, but sin is a reproach to any people" (Prov. 14:34, NKJV).

1. Judah, a compromising nation (2 Kings 16:1-20; 2 Chron. 28:1-27)

Ahaz was the son of Jotham, a good king, and the father of Hezekiah, a very good king, but he himself was not a godly man or even a good man. Instead of discovering and doing the will of God, Ahaz imitated the wicked kings of Israel and even the pagan practices of Assyria.[1] He even adopted the horrible worship practices of the pagans and sacrificed his son (2 Chron. 28:3 says "children," plural) to a pagan god, Baal or Molech, a practice that was clearly prohibited in the Law of Moses (Lev. 18:21; Deut. 18:10). Each Jewish son was to be redeemed by a sacrifice and therefore belonged to the Lord (Ex. 13; Num. 18:14-16). How could a son who belonged to God be sacrificed to an idol? But Ahaz was a compromiser both in his religious practices and his political leadership.

Political compromise (vv. 5-9; 2 Chron. 28:5-21). Pekah, the king of Israel, and

Rezin, king of Syria, wanted Ahaz to join with them in opposing Assyria, but Ahaz refused because he was pro-Assyrian. In fact, he trusted Assyria instead of trusting the Lord. In retaliation, Syria and Israel planned to remove Ahaz from the throne and put their own puppet king in his place, but the Lord protected David's throne, even though Ahaz didn't deserve it. (For the complete story, read Isa. 7–9.)

According to 2 Chronicles 28:5-8, it was the Lord who brought these two kings against Judah, to punish Ahaz for his sins. Pehak and Rezin did a great deal of damage to Judah but they weren't able to take Jerusalem. One of the sons of Ahaz was killed, along with two key officers of state. The invading armies killed thousands of soldiers and took thousands of prisoners of war to Samaria. It looked like Israel was going to swallow up Judah!

The Lord raised up a prophet in Israel[2] who warned the Samaritan army that by taking these people of Judah as prisoners, Israel was breaking God's law and inviting God's judgment. After all, the people of Judah and the people of Samaria were part of one family, the family of Abraham. The Prophet Obed (not the same man as in 15:8) pointed out three sins the army of Israel committed. First, they were in a rage against the people of Judah and captured and killed them indiscriminately. Second, they planned to make slaves out of their own brothers and sisters, and this was contrary to God's law (Lev. 25:39ff). In doing these things, they showed no fear of the Lord and therefore were asking for Him to judge them (2 Chron. 28:9-11). Yes, God was angry with Judah (28:9, 25), but there was danger He would become angry at Israel for the way they treated Judah (28:11-13). After Obed's message, some of the leaders in Israel stood and affirmed what he had said and urged the army not to sin against the Lord and their brothers and sisters.

A remarkable thing happened: the people accepted God's message, repented, and changed their treatment of the prisoners. The Israelites not only fed and clothed them, and gave special help to the injured and feeble, but the soldiers even returned the loot they had taken from Judah. This was an instance of being "good Samaritans" on a national level (Luke 10:25-37), and it reminds us of Elisha's kindness to the Syrian soldiers who came to capture him (2 Kings 6:15-23). When the prisoners (with the spoils of battle) arrived back in Judah, they were living witnesses of the grace and goodness of the Lord, but there's no record that Ahaz led the nation in a great praise service.

This remarkable event carried another message to Judah: the time would come when the Babylonians would invade the land and take thousands of captives away to Babylon. This experience with the kingdom of Israel was somewhat of a "dress rehearsal" for the people of Judah, but Babylon wouldn't treat them as the Israelites did. Most of the Jewish captives would die in Babylon, and after seventy years, only a feeble remnant would return to rebuild the temple and try to establish the nation again.

Does the Lord still chasten nations today as He did in ancient days? The Jewish people, of course, belonged to a covenant nation, even though it was now divided into two kingdoms; and they were responsible to obey the covenant of the Lord. But what about the Gentile nations that have no covenant relationship with God? The Prophet Amos makes it clear that God knows the sins of the Gentile nations and holds them accountable (Amos 1–2). God never gave His law to the Gentiles (Ps. 147:19-20), but the demands of that law are written in the hearts of all people (Rom. 2:12-16), so the disobedient Gentiles are guilty before the Lord. As you read the Old Testament, you find God judging Sodom and Gomorrah (Gen. 18–19), Egypt (Ex. 1–14), the Gentile nations in and around Canaan (Num. 31–32; Joshua 1–12), and even Babylon (Jer. 50–51). However, because the Jews knew the true and living God and had the witness of His law, they were even more accountable. How tragic that apostate Israel and not enlightened Judah showed concern about obeying the message of God. Judah had the temple, the law, and the priesthood, but they didn't have the Lord. "Blessed is the nation whose God is the Lord" (Ps. 33:12).

Religious compromise (16:10-18; 2 Chron. 28:22-25). Not only did Israel and Syria attack Judah but God also brought the Edomites and the Philistines against Jerusalem. Ahaz sent word to the king of Assyria to come and help him. His message was that of a flattering flunky, what we today would call a "bootlicker." He called himself Tiglath-pileser's "servant" and "son," a strange posture for a descendant of David to take before a pagan ruler. To encourage the Assyrian king even more, Ahaz took wealth from the temple, the palace, and the princes and sent him a gift. Actually, Ahaz made Judah a vassal nation under the control and protection of Assyria. Ahaz had no living faith in the Lord and put his trust in the army of Assyria instead, and this cost him dearly. Indeed, Assyria did defeat Syria, but then Tiglath-pileser summoned his "son" and "servant" to Damascus to give an account of himself and to receive orders. Gone were the days when the kings of Judah and their armies were feared by the nations!

King Uzziah had tried to meddle with the ministry in the temple and the Lord gave him leprosy, but Urijah the high priest did anything the king commanded, even if it meant disobeying the Law of Moses. We aren't sure whether copying the pagan altar was wholly the idea of Ahaz or whether the king of Assyria commanded it. Perhaps Tiglath-pileser wanted this altar in the Jewish temple to remind the king and people of Judah that they were now under the authority of Assyria. Ahaz was not devoted to the faithful worship of Jehovah, so it's likely that this altar was copied simply to satisfy his pride. He would have a royal altar like the one in Damascus! Consequently, the God-designed altar of the Lord was shoved to one side.

All of this is a picture of what often happens in Christian ministries today: somebody sees something out in the world that would "fit" into the Lord's work, and the church starts to imitate the world. Moses was commanded to make the tabernacle according to what God showed him on the mount (Ex. 25:40; 26:30; Heb. 8:5), and likewise the temple was constructed according to the plans God gave to David (1 Chron. 28:11, 12, 19). The Jews didn't appoint a building committee and vote on the design. But today, the church is becoming so like the world that it's getting difficult to tell them apart. A. W. Tozer wrote,

> Aside from a few of the grosser sins, the sins of the unregenerated world are now approved by a shocking number of professedly "born-again" Christians, and copied eagerly. Young Christians take as their models the rankest kind of worldlings and try to be as much like them as possible. Religious leaders have adopted

> the techniques of the advertisers: boasting, baiting, and shameless exaggeration are now carried on as a normal procedure in church work. The moral climate is not that of the New Testament but that of Hollywood and Broadway.[3]

Ahaz thought that the Lord would be pleased with sacrifices offered on this magnificent new altar, but he was wrong. The Lord doesn't want sacrifice; He wants obedience (1 Sam. 15:22-23); and Ahaz worshiped the gods of the heathen nations (2 Chron. 28:23). No fire from heaven ignited the sacrifices placed on that pagan altar (Lev. 9:24), because the Lord had rejected it. The religious novelties in churches today may excite and entertain the people, but they don't edify the church or exalt the Lord. The sanctuary becomes a theater, worship becomes entertainment, ministry becomes performance, and a congregation becomes an audience. The measure of all this is not the glory of God but the applause of the people.

But replacing God's altar with a pagan altar was just the beginning. King Ahaz also "remodeled" the laver and the ten movable stands that held the ten basins for preparing sacrifices (1 Chron. 28:17; 1 Kings 7:23-40). Apparently he needed the precious metal for his own purposes, so he took it from the Lord. But to please the king of Assyria, Ahaz had to remove his own royal entryway to the temple as well as the royal canopy (or dais for his throne) that he had placed in the temple. Tiglath-pileser was now in charge, not King Ahaz,

However, the king could never have made all these changes without the cooperation of Urijah, the high priest (16:10, 11, 15, 16). When King Uzziah tried to rebel against the Word of the Lord and enter the temple, the high priest Azariah with eighty other priests successfully withstood him (2 Chron. 26:16ff); but Urijah and his priests compromised, disobeyed the Law of Moses and gave in to their king. Once compromise begins, it continues to grow; and all that it takes for evil to triumph is for weak people like Urijah to let leaders have their way. Ahaz not only replaced the altar and removed metal from the furnishings, but he finally took all the vessels for himself, closed the doors of the temple, and set up altars in the streets of Jerusalem (2 Chron. 28:24-25). "Do you not know that a little leaven leavens the whole lump of dough?" (1 Cor. 5:6, NASB; see Gal. 5:9). Once we allow worldliness to get into the church fellowship, it will quietly grow, pollute the fellowship and eventually take over. It was not until the reign of his son Hezekiah that the temple Ahaz defiled was reopened and sanctified for ministry (2 Chron. 29:1-29).

When Ahaz died, he was buried in Jerusalem but not in the royal tombs (16:19-20; 28:26-27). In this, he joined Jehoram (2 Chron. 21:20), Joash (24:25), and Uzziah (26:23), and Manasseh would join them (33:20). The unbelief and unfaithfulness of Ahaz did great damage to the kingdom of Judah, some of which his son Hezekiah would be able to repair.

2. Israel, a captive nation (2 Kings 17:1-41; 18:9-12)

Hoshea was the last ruler of the northern kingdom of Israel, for in his day (722 B.C.), the Assyrians invaded the land, deported many of the citizens, and repopulated Israel with Gentile peoples from lands Assyria had conquered. The kingdom of Israel became Samaria, named after the capital city, and it was a nation whose citizens were not pure Jews but a comingling of many ethnic strains.

God had given His people so many blessings, and now those blessings would fall into the hands of Assyria and Babylon. The Jews had a living Lord, but they replaced Him with dead idols. Their wealthy land was confiscated by enemy nations, the people were taken captive, and eventually Jerusalem and the temple were destroyed (586 B.C.). God in His mercy preserved a faithful remnant so a light would remain shining and He could fulfill the promises He had made to His people.

Israel lost its leader (17:1-5). Hoshea had assassinated Pekah and seized the throne of Israel (15:29-31). Tiglath-pileser had died and Shalmaneser V was now king of Assyria, and Hoshea gave homage to him and brought him tribute. However, Hoshea secretly made a treaty with Egypt to enlist them to fight for Israel and help them break the Assyrian yoke.[4] Ever since Abraham fled to Egypt to escape a famine and only got himself and his wife into trouble (Gen. 12:10ff), various Jewish leaders have vainly looked to Egypt for help. (See Gen. 26:2; Num. 14:1-4; Deut. 17:16; Isa. 30:1-2; 31:1.) So it is with believers today who turn to the world for help instead of waiting on the Lord and trusting Him. When Shalmaneser discovered the plot, he took Hoshea prisoner and left the throne of Israel empty.[5]

In 725, Shalmaneser began to besiege Samaria, but then he died (or was killed) and his leading general, Sargon II, took over. The siege lasted three years, and in 722, the city capitulated. Assyria had already taken the tribes east of the Jordan (1 Chron. 5:24-26), so now they possessed everything but Judah, and that would fall to Babylon.

Israel lost its land (v. 6; 18:9-12). As we have seen, Assyria's policy was to relocate conquered peoples and replace them with prisoners from other nations.[6] It was clearly stated in God's covenant with His people that their disobedience would bring defeat in war (Deut. 28:25, 49-50, 52), oppression and slavery (Deut. 28:29, 33, 48, 68), and captivity (Deut. 28:36, 43, 63-68); and all of this happened to both Israel and Judah. The land belonged to the Lord (Lev. 25:2, 23, 38) and the people were His "tenants." Not only was the land His, but so were the people (Lev. 25:55). They would possess the land and enjoy its blessings as long as they kept the terms of the covenant, but repeated disobedience would bring discipline *within* the land and ultimately discipline *outside* the land. That's exactly what happened. Because of the people's sins during the period of the judges, seven different nations invaded the land, took the crops, and enslaved the people right in their own land. After the division of the nation, Israel was taken captive by Assyria and Judah by Babylon. God kept the terms of His covenant.

Israel disobeyed its law (vv. 7-17). These verses read like a legal court case against the northern kingdom of Israel. The law was a gift from God, an agreement that guaranteed His provision and protection if the people did His will. But they forgot how God had delivered them from Egypt and set them free. They ignored the Law of Moses that commanded them not to worship false gods but to destroy the heathen idols, temples, and shrines (Deut. 7, 13). Israel began with secret worship of idols (v. 9), but this eventually became public, and Jehovah was acknowledged as one god among many. The Lord sent prophets who admonished and warned the people, but the people paid little attention.

As their ancestors had done so many

times, the Jewish people stiffened their necks and hardened their hearts and refused to obey the Lord (Deut. 9:6, 13; 10:12-22; Neh. 9:16, 17, 29; Ps. 106). Since we become like the god we worship (Ps. 115:8), the people became "vanity" (emptiness, nothingness) because they worshiped vain idols (v. 15). In fact, they turned to idols and made a golden calf while Moses was communing with God on Mount Sinai (Ex. 32). After the division of the kingdom, King Jeroboam made *two* golden calves for the people to worship (1 Kings 12:25ff). As is often the case, it is the children who suffer for the sins of the parents, for the Jewish fathers began to offer their sons and daughters on the fiery altars of the heathen gods.

Israel angered its Lord (vv. 18-33). The anger of the Lord is His holy wrath; it must not be compared to a child's temper tantrum. The Lord was longsuffering toward His people and made ample provision to bring them back to Himself, but they refused. God's wrath is anger motivated by love, which is anguish. It's the anguish of a father who wants the best for his children, but they prefer to go their own way. These verses inform us that the division of the kingdom into Judah and Israel was an act of God as He sought to protect David's dynasty from the idolatry in Israel. However, King Jereboam's false, manmade religion infected Judah, and it was only by the grace of God that a faithful remnant remained.

The phrase "to fear the Lord" means "to worship the Lord according to the Law of Moses" (vv. 25, 28, 32, 34). The mixture of religions among the various peoples resulted in what we today would call "pluralism." At first, the Jews didn't worship God at all, and He disciplined them for their unfaithfulness (v. 25). The Jewish people worshiped Jehovah *plus the gods of the other nations*. God will not share worship with false gods, so it's no wonder He became angry. All the people in the land should have repented, turned from their false gods, and turned to the Lord; but instead, the Lord's people accepted the false gods of other nations.

The king of Assyria believed that each god was associated with the land from which the people came, and therefore the new residents didn't know how to worship the Lord of Israel. They could never learn from the Israelites left behind because they had been worshiping the golden calves since the days of King Jeroboam. The king of Assyria ordered one of the Jewish priests to be sent to Israel to teach the people how to worship "the god of the land." But this priest went to Bethel, the site of one of the shrines dedicated to the golden calf! How much he knew about the true Jewish faith and what he taught aren't revealed to us, but the situation doesn't appear to be encouraging.

Many people today would applaud this "world congress of religions," but the Lord abhors it. In a democracy, we learn to accept pluralism, but this doesn't mean we approve of it or believe that all religions are equal. In the United States, all religions are equal before the law and may be freely practiced, but Christians still believe that "there is no other name under heaven given among men by which we must be saved (Acts 4:12, NKJV). Jesus rejected the Samaritan religion because "salvation is of the Jews" (John 4:19-24). The Jewish people who were left in the land appointed their own priests and ignored the standards established by God through Moses (v. 32). The people set up their own religious ceremonies and integrated with this new system some of the beliefs of their new neighbors. There was something for everybody, and it didn't matter what you believed or how you worshiped, just as long as you were religious (vv. 29-33). Does this sound familiar?

Israel did not learn her lesson (vv. 34-41). It's often been said that the one thing we learn from history is that we don't learn from history. In spite of the way the Lord had warned them and chastened them, the people continued to worship the Lord along with the other gods, and they did it their own way. They ignored their history as the people of God delivered from Egyptian bondage. They forgot God's laws and covenants, especially God's commandments concerning idolatry (Ex. 20:1-6). Like many professed Christians today, the people of Israel worshiped the Lord where and how they pleased, but they also paid respect to the false gods of the other nations.

What finally happened to these ten disobedient tribes? We hear about "the ten lost tribes of Israel," but the Bible never uses that phrase. Many people in the ten tribes assimilated with the peoples brought into the land by the Assyrians, and this produced the Samaritan people. But there's no evidence in Scripture that the ten tribes of Israel are "lost." Long before the Assyrians captured the Northern Kingdom, dedicated people from the ten tribes moved to Judah and remained faithful to the Lord (1 Kings 12:16-20; 2 Chron. 11:5-16; 19:4-10). Godly King Hezekiah invited true believers to come to Judah and worship God according to the Scriptures, and many of them came (2 Chron. 30:1-14, 25-27). Josiah's reforms had a tremendous effect on the Jewish people (2 Chron. 34:1-7, 33; 35:17-19).

Though Jesus spoke about "the lost sheep of the house of Israel" (Matt. 10:5-6), the New Testament knows nothing about any "lost tribes of Israel." (See Matt. 4:12-16 and Luke 2:36-38.) Paul spoke about "our twelve tribes" (Acts 26:7) and James wrote his epistle "to the twelve tribes scattered abroad" (James 1:1). If we take Revelation 7:1-8 literally, then in the last days the Lord will find people from the tribes of Israel.

The main message from this tragic chapter is that false worship leads to corrupt practices, and corrupt practices result in divine condemnation and judgment. Disobedient and compromising leaders—both kings and priests—failed to teach the people the Word of God, and as each new generation came along, the nation drifted further from the Lord. There came a day when God's anger was displayed against His people, and that was the end of the political entity known as Israel, the Northern Kingdom.

CHAPTER TEN
THE MAKING OF A KING—PART I

2 Kings 18:1–20:11
(2 Chronicles 29:1–31:21; 32:24-26; Isaiah 38)

The name Hezekiah means "the Lord strengthens," and during his reign of twenty-nine years (715–687), King Hezekiah needed God's strength to accomplish all that he did. Like Asa (1 Kings 15:11), Jehoshaphat (22:43), and Josiah (2 Kings 22:2), his model was King David, which means that, while Hezekiah wasn't perfect, he did seek to obey the Lord and please Him. He was one of the few kings who actually removed the high places and put an end to idol worship in the hills. He restored temple worship and encouraged the people from both Judah and Israel to come to the temple in Jerusalem and worship the Lord. The Lord had commanded that there be one central place of worship, and that was at Jerusalem (Deut. 12).

The sequence of events in Hezekiah's life as recorded in Scripture is not strictly chronological. Most students agree that the events recorded in Isaiah 38 and 39—his illness and his welcome of the Babylonian ambassadors—actually antedated the Assyrian invasion (Isa. 36–37). We will take this approach as we study Hezekiah's life and ministry and seek to integrate the material in Kings, Chronicles, and Isaiah.

1. Hezekiah the reformer (2 Kings 18:4; 2 Chron. 29:3–31:21)

It's interesting that 2 Kings has but one verse describing Hezekiah's reforms (18:4), while 2 Chronicles devotes three chapters to this important part of his life. However, 2 Kings mentions how King Hezekiah destroyed the bronze serpent made by Moses (Num. 21:5-9), but this isn't mentioned in Chronicles. The serpent was a religious relic that had reached the status of an idol. "Nehushstan" probably means "a piece of bronze, a brass thing." How easy it is for human nature to want to honor religious relics that have no power! Hezekiah was a man of faith who trusted the living God and followed His law, and he didn't want the people worshiping a dead, useless image.

He cleansed the temple (29:3-19). Hezekiah didn't waste any time getting Judah back to the worship of the true and living God. His father, Ahaz, had defiled the temple and finally closed the doors and stopped the Levitical ministry (28:24). Hezekiah commanded the priests to sanctify themselves so they would be able to cleanse the temple and restore the worship that the Lord had commanded through Moses. The abandoning of the temple worship by the people of the Northern Kingdom had led to their captivity, and the defiling and neglecting of the temple by Ahaz had brought discipline to Judah, including invasions by Syria, Edom, and Philistia. The temple worship was at the heart of the Jewish nation, and if that was wrong, everything else would be wrong.

But Hezekiah wasn't interested in a mere housecleaning project, because he had it in his heart not only to rededicate the temple and the people but also to enter into a covenant with the Lord (v. 10). Fourteen leaders are named in verses 12-14, men who set the example and led the way for a new beginning for temple ministry. If the spiritual leaders aren't right with God, how can He bless His people? All three Levitical families were represented—Mahath and Joel from the Kohathites, Kish and Azariah from Marari, and Joah and Eden from the Gershonites (see Num. 3–4). The clan of Elizaphan belonged to the Kohathites (Num. 3:30) and had achieved an honorable reputation because of their faithful service. They were represented by Shimri and Juel. The other men listed were among the temple singers related to Asaph (from Gershon), Heman (from Kohath) or Jeduthun (from Merari), well-known musicians, singers, and worship leaders. King Hezekiah knew that there had to be music and praise or the temple worship would displease the Lord. These leaders and their helpers sanctified themselves before the Lord so that He could use them to sanctify His temple.

On the first day of the first month, they began to cleanse the temple, beginning in the Holy of Holies and the Holy Place. They carried out the accumulated trash and remnants of idolatrous worship, took it down to the Kidron Valley, and burned it. After sanctifying the building they cleansed the porch. This included removing the pagan altar that Ahaz had built, and placing the Lord's altar where it belonged (2 Kings 16:10ff). The Levites also cleansed the vessels and instruments used in the temple services and put them in their proper places. It took sixteen days to complete the work, which meant they missed Passover, which was on the fourteenth day of the first month. However, Hezekiah held a great Passover during the second month (ch. 30).

If we are to have revival in the Lord's work, we must begin with cleansing. Over the years, individuals and churches can gradually accumulate a great deal of "religious rubbish" while ignoring the essentials of spiritual worship. It's not by doing some unique new thing that we experience new blessing from the Lord, but by returning to the "old things" and doing them well. If we confess our sins (2 Chron. 7:14), light the lamps, burn the incense (a picture of prayer, Ps. 141:1-2), and offer ourselves as living sacrifices (v. 7; Rom. 12:1-2), the Lord will see and hear and will send His blessing.

He consecrated the temple (vv. 20-36). The king and the rulers of the city met together at the temple and offered sacrifices to the Lord. They brought sacrifices for the kingdom (Judah and Israel), the temple, and the kingdom of Judah in particular. The sin offerings were offered to atone for the sins of the people, and the priests included both Israel and Judah (v. 24—"all Israel"). The burnt offerings symbolized total dedication to the Lord. As the sacrifices were being offered to the Lord, the musicians and singers offered their praise to the Lord, following David's instructions, using David's songs, and playing David's instruments (vv. 25-27, 30; 1 Chron. 23:5-6).

But this wasn't a dedication service planned only for the king and his leaders, for the people in the congregation sanctified themselves and brought their offerings as well (vv. 28-36). They brought a large number of sacrifices, including three thousand sheep, which were probably given as fellowship offerings. Part of the fellowship offering was kept by the worshiper and eaten with his family as a fellowship meal. Hezekiah was following the example of Solomon when he dedicated the temple more than two hundred years before (1 Kings 8:62ff). It was a time of great rejoicing for the king and his people. Keep in mind that many devout people from the apostate northern kingdom of Israel (now Samaria) had fled to Judah so they could worship the Lord according to the Law of Moses, so this dedication service involved all the tribes.

He celebrated Passover (30:1-27). Three times each year, the Jewish men were required to go to Jerusalem to celebrate the feasts of Passover, Pentecost, and Tabernacles (Ex. 23:14-17; 34:22-24). To the Christian believer today, Passover speaks of the death of Christ, the Lamb of God who died for us (1 Cor. 5:7; John 1:29). On Pentecost, the Holy Spirit came upon the early church (Acts 2); and Tabernacles speaks of the future kingdom when Jesus shall reign and we shall reign with Him (Zech. 14). Passover commemorated the release of the Jewish people from Egyptian bondage, so it was a national celebration. For this reason, Hezekiah invited Jews from both Judah and Israel (Samaria) to come to Jerusalem for the feast. The Law of Moses made provision for celebrating the Passover in the second month (Num. 9:6-13), and Hezekiah took advantage of this provision. Neither the temple nor the priests and Levites had been ready the first month (vv. 1-3).

The emphasis in the invitation was on "all Israel" (vv. 5-6) and not just the people of Judah. Since the days of Solomon, there had not been a Passover involving the entire nation, and Hezekiah wanted to unite the people spiritually even though they were divided politically. The Northern Kingdom (Samaria) was under the rule of Assyria and the Jewish remnant living there worshiped the gods of the Gentile nations. They needed to return to the God of Abraham, Isaac, and Jacob (v. 6). The Jewish people had a common ancestry and a common worship, and it was time to put the Lord first, forget past differences and celebrate. The repeated words "turn again" and "return" reveal the desire of Hezekiah's heart (vv. 6, 9). If the people all turned in repentance to God, God would return to bless His people. Hezekiah built his appeal around the words of Solomon in 2 Chronicles 7:14.

Alas, the remnant in bondage to Assyria was just as stiff-necked as their ancestors were when God dealt with them in the wilderness. Here was an opportunity to make a new beginning and glorify the Lord by seeking His compassion, grace and mercy (v. 9), but most of the people outside Judah rejected the invitation. They mocked Hezekiah's words and laughed at his messengers, but so doing, they rejected the blessing the Lord had for them. However, there were some people who had the courage to disagree with their families and friends and go to Jerusalem for the feast, among them men from the northern tribes of Asher, Manasseh, and Zebulun. They came a long distance with humble hearts, seeking the blessing of the Lord. God gave the worshipers who gathered oneness of mind and heart so that it was the Lord who was the center of the event and not some political agenda.

The celebration is described in 30:13-27. The people removed the altars that King Ahaz had put up in Jerusalem (v. 14), for there could be no united worship unless they met at the one appointed altar in the temple court. What a paradox that the people were eager to worship the Lord, but the priests and Levites were ceremonially unclean and therefore unable to minister at the altar! But they remedied the situation and brought the burnt offerings that were to be offered daily (Ex. 29:38-43; Num. 28:1-8). During the reign of King Ahaz, the appointed temple services had been stopped, and the priests allowed themselves to become disqualified to serve at the altar; but between Hezekiah's accession to the throne and the celebration of the Passover, there had been time for them to prepare themselves.

But many common people in the large congregation were also unclean (Ex. 12:14-16; 13:6-10), perhaps because they had left their homes quickly or because they had been defiled during the journey to Jerusalem (Num. 9:9-10). But Hezekiah knew that God was concerned about the hearts of the worshipers and not the details of meeting ceremonial requirements, and he prayed that God would cleanse and accept them (1 Sam. 15:22-23; Isa. 1:10-17; Hoses 6:6; Micah 6:6-8; Mark 12:32-33). God answered his prayer, because it's the heart that God wants and not mere religious ritual. If there were any legalists in the congregation, they must have been very upset, but their attitude would only rob them of God's blessing. (See Luke 18:9-14 and Ps. 51:10-11 and 15-16.) If God's people today would prepare their hearts for worship with as much care as they prepare their "Sunday best," the Lord would send His blessings on His church.

There was so much joy and blessings that Hezekiah and the people decided to continue the celebration for another week, and the king generously provided the sacrifices needed for the offerings, and this provided food for the people.

The king's example motivated the leaders of Judah to bring extra sacrifices as well, so there was plenty of food for everybody. Spontaneous giving comes from spontaneous worship of the Lord and heartfelt gratitude to Him. When Solomon dedicated the temple, he also kept the people there another week (7:8-9).

He commenced and organized the temple ministry (31:1-21). When the second week of the feast ended, before the people left for home, the priests pronounced the benediction God commanded them to give in Numbers 6:22-27, and the worshipers left Jerusalem with the blessing of the Lord upon them. But as they carried the blessing home, they also obeyed the Lord and destroyed the idols in Judah, Benjamin, Ephraim, and Manasseh. It's one thing to have an exciting time praising God in a two-week special meeting, but it's quite something else to return home afterward and live like people who have met the Lord.

King Hezekiah knew that the blessings of the Passover feast wouldn't continue unless the people could participate in the regular ministry at the temple. It's wonderful to have a great feast at Christmas or on some special anniversary, but you can't live all year on one or two special meals. For that reason, Hezekiah followed David's instructions (1 Chron. 23–26) and organized the priests and Levites for ministry at the temple. He set a good example by providing from his own flocks and herds the sacrifices needed day by day and month by month. King Hezekiah sought the Lord and did everything for Him from his heart (v. 21).

After staffing and organizing the temple ministry, Hezekiah also admonished the people to bring their tithes and offerings to the temple for the support of the priests and Levites (v. 4; Num. 18:8-32; Deut. 12:1-19; 14:22-29). He allocated special chambers in the temple for storing the gifts and he appointed faithful men to oversee the distribution of the food. The priests and Levites depended on these gifts for their own support and that of their families (see Neh. 13:1-14). The king seemed especially concerned about the little children who had been weaned (vv. 16, 18). He wanted none of God's servants or their families to go hungry.

In the third month (May/June), the time of grain harvest, the people brought the grain and the priests and Levites heaped it up. During the seventh month (Sept./Oct.), when the orchard and vineyard harvests came in, these gifts of fruits and wine were added to the store. Like the gifts brought for the building of the tabernacle (Ex. 36:5-7) and the construction of the temple (1 Chron. 29:1-20), the tithes and offerings brought to the newly consecrated temple were far more than the king expected. A worshiping people will always be a generous people, especially when their leaders set the example, and Judah was no exception.

2. Hezekiah the negotiator (2 Kings 18:7-16)

Judah had been a vassal state under Assyria since the reign of King Ahaz, Hezekiah's father (16:7-18). When Sargon, ruler of Assyria, died in battle, and Sennacherib took the throne, it seemed to Hezekiah an opportune time to break that yoke. Sennacherib was involved in other empire concerns, so Hezekiah didn't send him the annual tribute. Judah had been victorious over the Philistines, so the kingdom was feeling strong. In 722 B.C., Assyria attacked Israel and captured the city of Samaria, and this meant that the Assyrian army was now right next door to Judah.

In 715 B.C., Sennacherib invaded Judah

and headed toward Jerusalem.[1] Hezekiah's faith was very weak, so he humbled himself before the king and paid the tribute money that he owed—eleven tons of silver and one ton of gold. Some of the wealth came from the king's own treasure, but it's disappointing to see that Hezekiah took the rest of it from the temple of the Lord. He followed the bad example of his father (16:8). King David didn't negotiate with his enemies or try to buy them off; he attacked and defeated them. Of course, Sennacherib withdrew from Judah, but he had every intention of returning.

3. Hezekiah the sufferer (2 Kings 20:1-11; 2 Chron. 32:24-26; Isa. 38:1-8)

According to the chronologers, this is the next important event in the life of Hezekiah. It took place fifteen years before his death in 687, so his sickness and healing, as well as the visit of the Babylonian ambassadors, occurred in the year 702 B.C.. The next year, the Assyrians returned and attacked Jerusalem.

Did the Lord send this sickness to discipline Hezekiah because he compromised with the Assyrians? The record in 2 Chronicles 32:24 tells us that the king had become proud and this was one way that the Lord humbled him. The fact that the Prophet Isaiah visited him with such a solemn message indicates how serious this experience really was, for the king was going to die. "Set your house in order" involved most of all appointing an heir to the throne. Hezekiah had become king at the age of twenty-five (2 Kings 18:1) and died in 687. His son Manasseh became king in 687 at the age of twenty-two, which means he was born in 709, so he would have been seven years old when Isaiah told his father he was going to die. Joash had ascended the throne at the age of seven (11:4ff), but he had Jehoiada the godly priest to advise him. Obviously, the throne of David was in jeopardy.

Hezekiah's response was to turn away from all around him and pray to the Lord.[2] If his statement in 20:3 and Isaiah 38:2 sounds like boasting, keep in mind that Hezekiah was only claiming the promise of 2 Chronicles 6:16-17. This promise was part of the Lord's gracious covenant with David and his descendants (2 Sam. 7:1-17), and Hezekiah was simply reminding the Lord that he had been faithful to obey His law. In other words, as a faithful son of David, he was "qualified" to live. God's message to the king through Isaiah emphasized the importance of King David and the continuation of his descendants on the throne in Jerusalem.

God answered Hezekiah's prayer by telling Isaiah how to bring about healing and also by giving Isaiah two great promises to share with Hezekiah. First, the king would recover and worship at the temple within three days; and second, if the Assyrians returned, the Lord would defend and deliver the city of Jerusalem. Remember, Hezekiah's illness occurred *before* the second invasion of Sennacherib's army. To assure the king of the truth of these promises, God gave him a miraculous sign: the shadow on the steps of Ahaz (a large sundial) went backward ten degrees. As the sun went down, the shadow would naturally get longer, but suddenly, the shadow became shorter. Did God reverse the movement of planet Earth or simply cause the shadow itself to go back on the steps? God doesn't explain His miracles and it's unwise for us to do it for Him.

God disciplines us because He loves us and wants to prevent us from disobeying Him and losing His blessing (Heb. 12:1-11). Chastening isn't the work of a stern judge as he punishes a criminal. It's the ministry of a loving father as he seeks to bring out the very best in his children, for the Father wants us to be "conformed to the image of His Son" (Rom. 8:29, NKJV)

4. Hezekiah the singer (Isa. 38:9-22)

The Prophet Isaiah recorded the psalm Hezekiah wrote after he had been healed and given fifteen more years of life (Isa. 38:9-20). It's likely that Hezekiah wrote other psalms as well (see v. 20, KJV and NASB) because we read about "the men of Hezekiah" in Proverbs 25:1. This title suggests that the king had a special "guild" of scholars who worked with the Scriptures and copied the manuscripts.[3] The psalm that Hezekiah wrote in commemoration of his sickness and deliverance certainly is filled with vivid imagery that teaches us a great deal about life and death. This is especially true in the NIV translation.

Hezekiah saw life as a journey that ended at the gates of death, or "Sheol," the Hebrew word for the realm of the dead (v. 10). He was in the prime of his life and yet was being robbed of the rest of his years. (He was probably thirty-seven or thirty-eight years old.) Perhaps he was thinking of Psalm 139:16 where David declares that God has written in His book the number of each person's days. Hezekiah lamented that he was leaving the land of the living and would see his friends no more.[4] Keep in mind that the full light had not yet been given concerning immortality, the intermediate world, and the Resurrection (2 Tim. 1:10).

But death is not only the end of a journey; it's also like taking down a tent (v. 12). Paul used the tent image in a similar way (2 Cor. 5:1-4) and so did Peter (2 Peter 1:13-14). But Hezekiah also pictures his impending death as a weaving being taken off the loom (v. 12). God "wove us" in our mother's womb (Ps. 139:13-16) before birth, and during our lives, He wanted to weave us into something beautiful and useful for His glory. Hezekiah was being cut off before the pattern was completed. Day and night, the king was in anxiety and suffering, like a helpless bird being attacked by a hungry lion (vv. 13-14). All he could do was mourn like a dove or cry out like a thrush or a swift.

In verse 15, the atmosphere changes and he gives thanks to God for His mercy in rescuing him from the pit (vv. 17-18). God not only saved his life, but He cleansed his record and put his sins behind His back (v. 17; see Isa. 43:25; Micah 7:19). The Lord had disciplined the king because of his pride (2 Chron. 32:24), but now the king promised to "walk humbly" for the rest of his life (v. 15). Hezekiah dedicated himself to praising the Lord and telling the next generation what the Lord had done for him. Perhaps that's when he organized "the men of Hezekiah" so that the biblical manuscripts would be carefully copied and protected.

However, Hezekiah's pride reared its ugly head again and the king once more had to be rebuked.

CHAPTER ELEVEN
THE MAKING OF A KING—PART II

2 Kings 18:17–19:37; 20:12-21 (2 Chronicles 32:27-33; Isaiah 36–37; 39)

We have seen King Hezekiah as an effective reformer who cleansed and consecrated the temple and restored the priestly ministry. But Hezekiah the negotiator capitulated to Assyria and paid tribute in order to avoid war. Then God sent a severe illness to Hezekiah to humble him and he cried out to God for mercy. Following that victory, Hezekiah stumbled again by welcoming the Babylonian envoys and showing them what they had no right to see. This was not a praiseworthy hour in Hezekiah's life.

1. Hezekiah the boaster (2 Kings 20:12-19; 2 Chron. 32:27-31; Isa. 39)

Scripture pictures our adversary the Devil as a serpent and a lion (Gen. 3:1ff; 2 Cor. 11:1-4; 1 Peter 5:8-9). Satan usually comes first as a serpent to deceive us, but if that doesn't work, he returns as a lion to devour us. This was Hezekiah's experience. First the Babylonian ambassadors came to Jerusalem to learn how wealthy and strong Judah was, and then the Assyrian army came to ravage the land, capture Jerusalem, and deport the Jewish people to Assyria. The ambassadors deceived Hezekiah because he didn't seek God's wisdom from Isaiah the prophet, but the king did seek the Lord when the Assyrians invaded the land, and the Lord gave him victory.

Hezekiah's pride (20:12-13; 32:27-30; 39:1-2). We have already learned that Hezekiah had a problem with pride (2 Chron. 32:25-26). His near-fatal sickness did humble him, but the visit of the Babylonian envoys made it clear that the old sin was still very much alive. The envoys came to Judah with two purposes in mind: (1) to find out how strong the kingdom was, and (2) to try to influence Hezekiah to unite with Babylon in opposing Assyria. Because he didn't fully grasp their true purpose, Hezekiah assumed that it was a great honor to be visited by officials from the king of Babylon. At that time in history, Assyria was the strongest empire and Babylon was an empire on the rise. Why should Hezekiah worry about Babylon? Because one day Assyria would move off the scene and Babylon would be the key nation in the Near East. From 606 to 586, Babylon would invade Judah, destroy Jerusalem and the temple, and take the nation into captivity. Babylon first came as the serpent, then she returned as the lion.

The envoys brought expensive gifts from the king of Babylon as well as personal letters expressing his pleasure that Hezekiah had recovered from his dangerous illness. Hezekiah should have realized that Merodach-Beladan had no personal interest in the health of the king of Judah but only wanted to obligate Hezekiah to become an ally of Babylon. It's likely that the envoys helped to inflate Hezekiah's ego by complimenting him on his military resources and personal wealth. (See 2 Chron. 32:27-30.) Foolishly, Hezekiah gave them the grand tour and showed them his treasures and weapons. It appears that Hezekiah was better at managing his scribes and writing his psalms than he was at overseeing the politics of the kingdom. All that Hezekiah possessed came from the hand of God and belonged to God, so why should Hezekiah boast about it? He may have made a good impression on the envoys but he grieved the Lord and endangered the kingdom and the city.

Pride is one of Satan's chief weapons in his battle against the Lord and His people. Satan himself committed the sin of pride when he rebelled against God and sought the worship and obedience that God alone deserves (Isa. 14:12-15). Pride makes us rob God of the glory that belongs to Him alone. Pride gives us a feeling of false security and this leads us into sin and defeat. Charles Spurgeon said to his London congregation, "Be not proud of race, face, place, or grace." Good advice! William Barclay wrote, "Pride is the ground in which all the other sins grow, and the parent from which all the other sins come."

Isaiah's prophecy (20:14-18; 29:3-8). Hezekiah should have conferred with Isaiah as soon as the diplomatic pouch arrived with news that the Babylonian envoys were coming to Jerusalem. When the prophet heard that a foreign entourage had come and gone, he went to the king and asked two important questions: "What did they say and where did they come from?" The king never did answer the first question, but he did admit that the men had come from Babylon. That envoys should come to Judah from "a far country" obviously pleased the king, and no doubt he was pleased to find an ally in the battle against Assyria.

As you read the Book of Isaiah, you soon discover that the prophet already knew something about the future of Babylon (see 13–14 and 20:1-10). At that time in history, most people would have pointed to Assyria as the threatening world power, for Babylon was just starting to get recognition on the world scene. Assyria had defeated the kingdom of Israel, but it would be Babylon that would conquer the kingdom of Judah, and Isaiah 39:5-7 is Isaiah's first clear prophecy of that event. A century after Hezekiah's death, Babylon would destroy Jerusalem and the temple, and some of Hezekiah's descendants would go into captivity and his wealth would be carried to Babylon.

The Lord's patience (20:19). Hezekiah's response wasn't a sigh of relief that his generation had escaped judgment, but rather was an expression of his acceptance of the will of God. Hezekiah's pride had been broken once again (2 Chron. 32:26), but for the sake of the nation and the throne of David, he was grateful there would be peace. The Lord had been longsuffering toward Hezekiah and the king didn't realize that another great trial was about to begin—Assyria's assault against Jerusalem. However, the king had learned some valuable lessons from his sickness and his mishandling of the affair of the Babylonian envoys. How gracious it is of the Lord to prepare us for what He has prepared for us!

2. Hezekiah the commander (18:17-37; 2 Chron. 32:1-19; Isa. 36)

"After these deeds of faithfulness, Sennacherib king of Assyria came and entered Judah" (2 Chron. 32:1, NKJV). The "deeds of faithfulness" were Hezekiah's labors to cleanse and consecrate the temple, the priests, and the Levites, and to restore true worship in Judah. One would think that God would reward his service by giving him peace, but instead, the Lord allowed the Assyrians to return to Judah and threaten Jerusalem. Hezekiah was faithful to the Lord, but it seems as though the Lord wasn't faithful to Hezekiah. After all, the king had done "that which was good and right and truth before the Lord his God" (2 Chron. 31:20) and had done it "with all his heart" (v. 21). Why, then, didn't the Lord protect Judah from another invasion?

"It is the standing puzzle of the Old Testament," said Alexander Maclaren, "how good men come to be troubled, and how bad men come to be prosperous."[1] We have little trouble understanding why the Assyrians destroyed the northern kingdom of Israel; after all, the nation was worshiping idols and rebelling against the law of God. But Judah had returned to the Lord under Hezekiah's leadership, and though the king had made some mistakes, his heart was sincere before God.

But God had His divine purposes to fulfill in Hezekiah's life and in the life of the nation. It was an easy thing for God to send an angel to destroy 185,000 Assyrian soldiers, but it was much more difficult to work with King Hezekiah and transform him into a man of faith. When we allow God to have His way, the trials of life work *for* us and not *against* us, and they bring great glory to the Lord. The king needed to learn that he was second in command (see Josh. 5:13-15) and that the Lord alone was sovereign.

The preparation (2 Chron. 32:1-8). Hezekiah knew that the Assyrians were coming, so he met with his leaders and took steps to strengthen Jerusalem. By working with his leaders he united them in sympathy and strategy, an important factor for leadership in war. The Assyrian records state that their army took forty-six fortified cities in Judah before settling in Lachish and planning the siege of Jerusalem. By blocking up the water supply outside the city, Hezekiah prevented the invaders from having ample supplies of fresh water. Hezekiah had already dug the tunnel between the Gihon spring and the city of Jerusalem (2 Kings 20:20) so that the people in the city would not die of thirst. Even today, this tunnel is a popular place for visitors to the Holy Land.

Hezekiah also had the wall of Jerusalem repaired and strengthened, and he put extra towers on it. He even constructed a second outside wall and then strengthened the "Millo," the terraces that butted up against the walls (see 11:8; 1 Kings 11:27). He organized the army, appointed officers, gave them weapons, and then encouraged them by making a speech. His address reflected the words of Moses to Israel and to Joshua (Deut. 31:1-8) and God's words to Joshua (Josh. 1:1-9; see also 2 Kings 6:16). Hezekiah was wise to use God's Word to encourage his soldiers and remind them of the past victories of God's people because they had trusted the Lord.

The confrontation (18:17-18; 36:1-3). Hezekiah's near-fatal illness occurred in 702 B.C. and so did the visit of the Babylonian envoys. This means that it was the very next year—701 B.C.—that the Assyrians invaded the land. Hezekiah had fourteen more years to live and he certainly didn't want to do it in captivity. However, the Prophet Isaiah had already told him that God would deliver Judah and defend Jerusalem for the sake of King David (20:6), so Hezekiah had a great promise to believe. God's people don't live on explanations; they live on promises.

The Assyrian army chose Lachish for their central camp, thirty miles southwest of Jerusalem, and brought "a great host" against Jerusalem. Three of the Assyrian officers told Hezekiah to send out three of his officers to arrange for the terms of surrender. These are titles and not personal names: Tartan = supreme commander, Rabsaris = chief officer, and Rabshakeh = field commander. Representing Hezekiah were Eliakim, the palace administrator, Shebna, the secretary, and Joah, the recorder (see Isa. 22:15-25; 36:3).

They met at the very place where Isaiah had confronted Ahaz, Hezekiah's father, and told him not to make a treaty with the Assyrians (Isa. 7; 2 Kings 16:5-9). Treaty or no treaty, Isaiah had predicted that the Assyrians would return, and his words had now come true.

The six officers didn't have a quiet conversation but stood far enough apart that the field commander had to raise his voice. Of course, the Assyrians wanted the people on the wall to hear what was going on, because they wanted to frighten them. The officers refused to speak in

Aramaic, the trade language of that day, but used the familiar Hebrew (18:26-27; 32:18; 36:11-12). It's significant that the Assyrian leaders learned the Hebrew language so they could better wage war. God's servants today need to follow this example so they can proclaim the message of peace.

The proclamation (18:19-36; 32:9-19; 36:4-21). It's important to identify three "speeches" if we want to understand the dynamics of this event. First, the field commander spoke to Hezekiah and the Jews and blasphemed their God (18:17-36). Then Hezekiah went to the temple and spoke to God about what the field commander had said (19:1-19). Finally, God spoke to Hezekiah (through Isaiah the Prophet) about the judgment the Assyrians would receive at His hand (19:20-34). God always has the last word.

The field commander was a subtle man who knew how to weave words together and get his message across. Of course, he wasn't too concerned about speaking the truth, for he knew that most people (including the Jews in Jerusalem) live on "seems" instead of "is" and think with their emotions instead of their minds. The basic theme of his address was *faith* (18:19-20; 32:10; 36:4-5), and he asked the people, "What are you really trusting? Can anybody deliver you?" Note the repetition of the words "deliver" and "my hand," and note also how he tried to belittle Hezekiah by calling Sennacherib "the great king" (18:19, 28; Isa. 36:4, 13). What the Rabshekah didn't realize was that Jehovah is the Great King and that He heard every word the Field Commander was saying. "For the Lord Most High is awesome; He is a great King over all the earth" (Ps. 47:2, NKJV). Jerusalem was "the city of the great King" (Ps. 48:2), and the Lord Himself has said, "I am a great King" (Mal. 1:14, NKJV).

The Field Commander began to name what Judah was trusting, all the while pointing out that each of them would fail. He began with *Egypt (18:21, 24; Isa. 36:6, 9)*, and no doubt there were officials in Judah who thought Pharaoh could help them. There had always been a strong Egyptian party in Judah after the kingdom divided, and the Prophet Isaiah had warned the leaders not to go to Egypt for help (Isa. 30:1-7; 31:1-3). But Egypt was nothing but a "splintered reed" that would pierce your hand if you leaned on it.[2]

In 18:22 and 30 (32:12; Isa. 36:7, 10), the commander tried to convince them that they couldn't trust *the Lord their God* to deliver them. How could they trust Jehovah when Hezekiah had removed the altars of the Lord from the city? Was the Lord pleased with what the king did? The Commander knew that there were people in Jerusalem who were unhappy because they could no longer worship at different altars and in the high places but had to go to the temple. But the Commander was so bold as to affirm that he and the Assyrian army had come to Jerusalem in obedience to the commandment of the Lord (18:25; 36:10; see 2 Chron. 35:21). After all, the Lord had used Assyria to chasten and destroy the kingdom of Israel, so why wouldn't He use Assyria to conquer Judah?

If the people of Judah were trusting in their *military resources*, said the commander, they were really in trouble, for they didn't have sufficient horses or enough cavalry men to put on them. If the king would "make a bargain" (enter into a treaty) with Sennacherib, the Assyrians would stop the siege and the people's lives would be spared.

In reply to the interruption by Eliakim, Shebna, and Joah (18:26), the field commander gave a special message to the people on the wall. If they didn't surrender, the day would come when they would be so hungry and thirsty that they would eat and drink their own excrement (18:27; 36:12). The report in 2 Chronicles 32:11 states that the field commander began his speech by warning the people of inevitable death by famine and thirst if they refused to surrender.

But the year before, the Prophet Isaiah had told Hezekiah that God would defend Jerusalem and destroy the Assyrians (20:6; Isa. 38:4-6), and it was this promise that the king gave to the people (18:29-30). Once again, we marvel at how much the commander knew about the affairs of Hezekiah. The commander was doing everything he could to tear down the people's confidence in their king. The Rabshakeh painted a glowing picture of what would happen if Judah surrendered. They would live at peace in their own land until they would be deported to Assyria, a land very much like Judah (18:31-32; 36:16-17). Whenever the enemy makes an offer, there is always that fatal "until" attached to it.

The commander's final argument was purely pragmatic and very illogical: none of the gods of the nations already conquered could defeat Sennacherib, so Jehovah would fail as well (18:33-35; 36:18-20). But Jehovah isn't like the dead powerless idols of the nations: He is the true and living God! In obedience to the king's command, the people on the wall said nothing to the field commander, and that's the best way to respond to ignorant people who blaspheme the Lord and know nothing of His truth and greatness.

The humiliation (18:37–19:13; 36:22–37:13) The three officials left the fuller's field and returned to the city to tell Hezekiah what the field commander had said. In humility before the Lord and in acknowledgement of their own helplessness, the three men tore their garments and looked to the Lord for His help. They told their king what the field commander had said, and the report must have broken Hezekiah's heart. How could anybody be so arrogant and so blaspheme the name of the Lord? The Rabshakeh had reproached the living God by daring to associate Him with the dead idols of the nations. Hezekiah also tore his clothes and humbled himself before the Lord.

The king knew that he needed a word from the Lord, so he sent his officers to Isaiah the Prophet and asked him to pray and seek God's help. (This is the first mention of Isaiah in 2 Kings.) The king's metaphor about birth is a picture of extreme danger. The child has come to the time of birth, but the mother hasn't strength enough to deliver it, so both mother and child are in danger of losing their lives. The king also knew that only a remnant of God's people from Israel and Judah were faithful to Him (19:4, 30), but for their sake and the sake of David, the Lord would be willing to work.

Isaiah told Hezekiah not to be afraid (Ps. 46:1-3) because the Lord had heard the blasphemy of the Rabshakeh and would deal with Sennacherib. The Assyrian king would hear a report and the Lord would give him such a fearful spirit that he would return home. The report was that Tirhakah, king of Egypt,[3] was coming to Judah, which meant Sennacherib would have to wage war on two fronts (19:9; 37:9). He didn't want to do that, so he temporarily abandoned the siege and went back to Lachish to prepare for war. However the field commander sent one last message to Hezekiah, this time a letter (19:8-13; 37:8-13) and simply repeated what he had already said.

3. Hezekiah the intercessor (2 Kings 19:14-19; 2 Chron. 32:20; Isa. 37:14-20)
When the outlook is bleak, try the uplook. That's what King Hezekiah did when he received the blasphemous letter from the king of Assyria. Often in my own ministry I have had to spread letters before the Lord and trust Him to work matters out, and He always has.

Hezekiah looked beyond his own throne and the throne of the "great king" Sennacherib and focused his attention on the throne of God "who was enthroned between the cherubim" (19:15; 37:14, NIV; see Pss. 80:1; 99:1). Since he was not a high priest, Hezekiah couldn't enter the Holy of Holies where the mercy seat sat upon the Ark of the Covenant, but he could "enter" by faith even as believers can today (Heb. 10:19-25). At each end of the mercy seat was a cherub, and the mercy seat was the throne of God on earth (Ex. 25:10-22). Not only is the Lord the King of Israel and the King of all nations, but He is the creator of the heavens and the earth. Hezekiah was lost in worship as he realized the greatness of the Lord, the only true God. This is a good example to follow when we pray about life's problems. When we focus on the Lord and see how great He is, it helps to put our problems in perspective,

The king had one great burden on his heart: that the God of Israel be glorified before the nations of the earth. Sennacherib had blasphemed the Lord and Hezekiah asked God to act on behalf of Judah so that His name would be honored. "Hallowed be thy name" is the first request in the Lord's Prayer (Matt. 6:9). Being a faithful Jew, the king knew that the gods of the defeated nations weren't gods at all (Isa. 2:20; 40:19-20; 41:7; 44:9-20). He asked the Lord to save the people of Judah, not for their sake but for the glory of His great name.[4]

Some people rush into the Lord's presence whenever they face a problem, but the Lord never hears their voices at any other time. This wasn't true of King Hezekiah. He was a man who at all times sought the blessing of the Lord on His people. He sought to know the Word of God and the will of God, and this gave him power in prayer. Blessed is that nation whose leaders know how to pray!

4. Hezekiah the victor (2 Kings 19:20-37; 2 Chron. 32:20-22; Isa. 37:21-38)
The Lord told Isaiah to get His message to the king, and the prophet obeyed. The answer to Hezekiah's prayer was threefold: (1) God would deliver Jerusalem, (2) God would defeat the Assyrian army and they would depart, and (3) God would care for the people and they would not starve. But God also had a message of rebuke to Sennacherib because of his pride and blasphemy. Hezekiah's faith was rewarded and his prayer was answered.

Rebuke (19:20-28; 37:22-29). God had used Assyria to chasten the northern kingdom of Israel, and the Lord had given Sennacherib victory over other nations, but the Assyrian king had never given God the glory. In fact, his field commander had reproached the name of the Lord (19:4, 16, 22, 24; 37:4, 17, 23, 24) and blasphemed the God of Israel. But "the virgin, the daughter of Zion"—the city of Jerusalem—would toss her head in disdain and laugh at the defeat of Assyria. The Lord used the image of a virgin because the Assyrians would not be able to take the city and violate it the way pagan soldiers did to women taken captive. But the Lord would treat the Assyrians like cattle and put hooks in their noses and lead them.

The Lord quoted back to the Rabshakeh and to Sennacherib the very words they had used in boasting about their victories. Chariots are made primarily for the flat lands, but they boasted that their chariots had ascended the high mountains of Lebanon. The dry lands and deserts didn't stop them, nor did the rivers. Other kings used barges to cross rivers, but they dried up the Nile and walked across on dry land. (Is this a reference to Israel at the Jordan, Joshua 4–5? There is no evidence that Assyria ever conquered Egypt.) They cut down cities and people the way a farmer mows the grass, and nothing stood in their way.

But it was the Lord who planned these conquests and enabled Assyria to succeed (37:26-27). The nation was His weapon to judge Israel and the other nations and to chasten Judah. (Isa. 10:5-19). How foolish for the ax to boast against the woodsman, and how foolish for Sennacherib to take credit for what the Lord had done! Instead of honoring the Lord, Sennacherib raged against the Lord (19:27; 37:28-29) and exalted himself against the God of heaven. Whatever reasons or excuses world leaders may give for what they do, the basic cause is rebellion against God and His law (Ps. 2:1-6; Acts 4:23-31). But the Lord would treat the Assyrians like cattle, put hooks in their noses, and lead them away! The Assyrians were known for doing this to their prisoners of war, but now they would be the victims.

Provision (19:29; 37:30). The Assyrians had taken possession of Judah, pillaged the land and taken the fortified cities, and now they were besieging Jerusalem. How long could the food hold out? And even if Jerusalem did survive, how long would it take to restore the land, plant the crops, and get a harvest? The field commander warned that the people of Jerusalem would die of famine and thirst if they didn't submit to Assyria (2 Chron. 32:11). But the Lord of the harvest was in control. September and October were the months devoted to sowing, and March and April were devoted to reaping the harvest. The orchards and vineyards produced their harvest from July to September. No doubt the Assyrians came in the harvest season and confiscated the food. With the Assyrians in the land and Jerusalem under siege, the people couldn't work their farms; but God promised that when the Assyrians left, food would grow of itself until the men could work the fields, orchards, and vineyards. God would not permit His people to starve.

Some students have seen a relationship between this prophecy and Psalm 126, one of the "Songs of the ascents [degrees]." (See chapter 10, endnote 3.) The psalm speaks of a dramatic and sudden deliverance for Jerusalem, which certainly wasn't the case at the end of the Babylonian captivity. Could this have been Jerusalem's deliverance from the Assyrian army, when God killed 185,000 soldiers? If so, the prayer in Psalm 126:4 would certainly be applicable. As the men went out in the fields to sow, they would be weeping for joy that the land was delivered, but they might also weep because the seed they were sowing could have been made into bread for their children. Seed was scarce, yet God cared for His people.

Deliverance (19:28, 30-37; 32:21-22; 37:31-38). God promised that He would deliver His "remnant" from their enemies and they would "take root" and become fruitful again. Not only would Sennacherib never enter the city, but he wouldn't even shoot an arrow at it, attack it, or build a siege mound next to it! In one night, God's angel killed 185,000 Assyrian soldiers and that put an end to the siege of Jerusalem. The Rabshakeh had boasted that one of the Assyrian junior officers was stronger than 2,000 Jewish charioteers (36:8-9), but when the Lord wanted to wipe out 185,000 enemy soldiers, all He had to do was send one of His angels!

It was a humiliating defeat for the Assyrians, but the event brought great glory to the Lord and honor to Hezekiah (2 Chron. 32:23; see Ps. 126:2-3). Sennacherib left the scene and went home, and there one of his sons killed him. His gods were unable to give him victory in Judah and they couldn't protect him from his own family in his own homeland. Why did God deliver His people? For the glory of His own name, of course, and for the sake of David whom He loved (19:34). Why does He bless His people today? For the sake of His own glory and because of His love for His own Son who died for us.

Death (2 Kings 20:20-21; 2 Chron. 32:27-33). "And Hezekiah prospered in all that he did," states 2 Chronicles 32:30 (NASB). Because of the blessing of the Lord, he had immense wealth, huge flocks and herds, and large storage buildings for grain and wine. "He trusted in the Lord, the God of Israel" (2 Kings 18:5, NASB). "And the Lord was with him; wherever he went he prospered" (2 Kings 18:7, NASB). He was a model of the "blessed man" in Psalm 1., the person who obeys the Word, meditates on it, and depends upon the power of God.

Hezekiah was not only in favor with God, but he was also beloved by his people. He was buried with the kings in Jerusalem, "and all Judah and the inhabitants of Jerusalem honored him at his death" (2 Chron. 32:33). Like all of us, Hezekiah had his lapses of faith and his failures, but was undoubtedly one of the greatest kings in Jewish history.

CHAPTER TWELVE
THE END IS NEAR
2 Kings 21:1–23:30
(2 Chronicles 33:1–35:27)

"We live in the twilight of a great civilization, amid the deepening decline of modern culture," writes eminent theologian Carl F. H. Henry. "Those strange beast-empires of the books of Daniel and Revelation seem already to be stalking and sprawling over the surface of the earth."[1]

Similar words could have been written about Judah during the days of the three kings studied in this chapter—Manasseh, Amon, and Josiah. The Jewish nation had given the world a witness to the one true and living God, but now many of the people worshiped foreign idols. Israel gave the world the prophets and the Scriptures, but most of the leaders of Judah no longer listened to God's Word. Josiah was Judah's last good king. The Lord had covenanted to protect David's throne so that the promised Redeemer might one day come, but now the government of Judah was decaying and the very existence of the kingdom was in jeopardy. The future of God's plan of redemption for a lost world rested with the faithful remnant that resisted the inroads of pagan culture and remained true to the Lord.

God's promise hadn't changed: "If my people, which are called by my name, shall humble themselves, and pray, and seek my face, and turn from their wicked ways; then will I hear from heaven, and will forgive their sin, and will heal their land" (2 Chron. 7:14). Each of these three kings had to learn something about humility. It was almost too late when

Manasseh humbled himself (2 Chron. 33:12, 19); Amon never did submit to the Lord (33:23); and Josiah truly humbled himself before the Lord and was used to bring a spiritual awakening to the land (34:19, 27). "True humility is a healthy thing," wrote A. W. Tozer. "The humble man accepts the truth about himself."[2]

1. Manasseh—humiliated by affliction (2 Kings 21:1-18; 2 Chron. 33:1-20)

That godly King Hezekiah should have such a wicked son is another one of those puzzles in biblical history. If Manasseh was born in 709, then he was seven years old when his father was healed and the miracle of the shadow occurred. He was eight years old when the 185,000 Assyrian soldiers were slain. Apparently these miracles made little impression on his heart. Many scholars think that Manasseh was coregent with his father for perhaps ten years (697–687), from ages twelve to twenty-two, and the son lived in close relationship with a godly father.[3] But the remarkable thing is that Manasseh became the most wicked king in Judah's history, so much so that he is blamed for the fall of the Southern Kingdom (2 Kings 24:3; Jer. 15:1-4).

Manasseh's wickedness (23:1-15; 33:1-10). He lived a most ungodly life and yet had the longest reign of any king in Jewish history. It was as though the Lord took His hand off the nation and allowed all the filth to pour out of people's hearts. In character and conduct, he was even worse than the Amorites whom Joshua defeated in Canaan, a nation with a reputation for brutality and wickedness (21:11; Gen. 15:16). All that his godly father, Hezekiah, had torn down, Manasseh rebuilt as he led the nation back into idolatry, including the worship of Baal. He also made a detestable idol which he placed in the temple of the Lord (21:3; 2 Chron. 33:7, 15), and he encouraged the people to worship "all the starry hosts" (21:3; 33:3, 5; see Deut. 4:19 and 17:1-7). There was to be but one altar in the temple court, but Manasseh added altars dedicated to various gods (see 16:10-16) and thus made Jehovah one "god" among many. Yet the Lord had put His name in only one place—the temple in Jerusalem (21:4, 7; Deut. 12:11; 1 Kings 8:20, 29; 9:3); and now a multitude of false gods shared that honor with Him. Manasseh followed the religion of Molech and caused his sons to pass through the altar fire (Lev. 18:21; 20:1-5), and he consulted spiritists and mediums (21:6; 33:6; Lev. 19:31; Deut. 18:11).

In His mercy, the Lord sent prophets to warn the king and the people, but they refused to listen. Some of these witnesses were no doubt killed by the king (21:16), along with other godly people who opposed the worship of false gods. God reminded His people that their enjoyment of the land depended on their obedience to the law of the Lord. This was the basic requirement of the covenant God made with His people (Lev. 26; Deut. 28–29). God had promised to keep them in the Promised Land (2 Sam. 7:10), but now He warned them that they would be taken off the land and scattered among the nations (Deut. 28:64-68; Lev. 26:33-35). This judgment had already fallen on the Northern Kingdom with the invasion of the Assyrian army, and it would happen to Judah when the Babylonians came (606–586). Alas, Judah didn't learn from Israel's chastening.

We don't know which prophets delivered the message in 21:10-15, but nobody could misunderstand what they said. If Manasseh and the people didn't repent and turn from their evil ways, God would send judgment so severe that just hearing about it would make their ears tingle (21:12; 1 Sam. 3:11; Jer. 19:3). This describes a frightening response to news so terrible that it's like hearing a loud noise that makes your ears ring. The Hebrew word *salal* means "to tingle, to quiver," and is related to the word for cymbals and bells. When they heard the news of the approaching Babylonian army, it would be like hearing a sudden clash of cymbals! Wake up! Wake up! But it would be too late.

But God used a second image to awaken them. Like a careful builder, He would measure the nation with His plumbline, but it would be a measuring for tearing down and not for building up. Everyone was familiar with bricklayers using plumblines to keep the walls straight as they built, but nobody measures a building in order to destroy it. (See Isa. 34:11 and Amos 7:7-9, 17.) God's judgments are just and He will give them what they deserve, just as He gave Israel (Samaria) what she deserved. The third picture comes from the kitchen: God would empty the kingdom of Judah of its people just as a person wipes all the water out of a dish after washing it. It's the image of depopulating a land by death or deportation and leaving it empty (Jer. 51:34).

The word "forsake" in 21:14 means "to give over to judgment." God promised never to abandon His people (1 Sam. 12:22; 2 Sam. 7:23-24), but He also warned that He would chasten them if they disobeyed Him. God didn't break His promises; it was the people who broke His covenant. God is always faithful to His covenant, whether to bless obedience or punish disobedience.

Manasseh's repentance (33:11-13, 19). The writer of 2 Kings wrote nothing about the remarkable change in Manasseh's life, but we find the record in 2 Chronicles.[4] Apparently he displeased the king of Assyria in some way and God allowed the Assyrian officers to come to Judah and capture the king. This was no respectable act of taking somebody into custody, because they put a hook in his nose and bound him with chains (33:11, NIV). He was treated like a steer being led to the slaughter, and he deserved it. The city of Babylon was a second capital for Assyria at that time, and there they imprisoned him.

The whole experience was one of great humiliation for this wicked king, but the Lord used it to chasten him, break his pride, and bring him to his knees. He prayed to the Lord for forgiveness and the Lord kept His promise and forgave him (2 Chron. 7:14). Even more, the Lord moved the Assyrians to set him free and allow him to return to Jerusalem to rule over the people. What a trophy of the grace of God! Manasseh humbled himself (33:12), but the Lord first humbled him (33:19). True repentance is a work of God in the heart and a willing response of the heart to the Lord.

Manasseh's reformation (33:14-18, 20). When he returned home, Manasseh proved the reality of his conversion by seeking to undo all the evil he had done. He fortified Jerusalem and other cities in Judah, he removed his idol from the temple (33:7, 15), and he removed from the temple all the altars he had put up to false gods. Having purged the temple, he then repaired the altar of the Lord that had been neglected, and he offered thank offerings to the Lord who had rescued him. He commanded the people of Judah to serve the Lord and he set the example. He allowed them to offer sacrifices in the high places, but not to pagan gods—only to the God of Israel. "Therefore bear fruit in keeping with repentance," John the

Baptist told the Pharisees and Sadducees (Matt. 3:8, NASB), and that's exactly what Manasseh did.

After a long life and reign, Manasseh died and was buried in the garden at his own house, not in the sepulchers of the kings (see 28:27).

2. Amon—hardened by disobedience (2 Kings 21:19-26; 2 Chron. 33:21-25)

After his repentance, Manasseh tried to undo all the damage he had done to Jerusalem and Judah, but there was one place where he could make no changes—in the heart of his son Amon. The young man had been too influenced by his father's sins to take notice of his new life of obedience, and there were no doubt people at court who encouraged Amon to maintain the old ways. Whereas Manasseh humbled himself before the Lord, his son Amon refused to do so (33:23), and the longer he sinned, the harder his heart became.

"The wages of sin is death" (Rom. 6:23). Why Amon's own officials should assassinate him isn't made clear, but the reason probably wasn't spiritual. While it's true that the Law of Moses declared that idolaters should be slain (Deut. 13), there was nobody in the land with the authority to deal with an idolatrous king. It's likely that the conspirators were more interested in politics. Amon was probably pro-Assyrian—after all, they had released his father from prison—while the officials were pro-Babylonian, not realizing that the rise of Babylon would ultimately mean the fall of Judah. Amon's son Josiah was definitely pro-Babylonian and even lost his life on the battlefield trying to stop the Egyptian army from assisting Assyria against Babylon. The fact that the people made Josiah the next king would suggest that they didn't want a pro-Assyria king.

3. Josiah—humbled by God's Word (2 Kings 22:1–23:30; 2 Chron. 34:1–35:25)

Out of the twenty rulers of Judah, including wicked Queen Athaliah, only eight of them could be called "good": Asa, Jehoshaphat, Joash, Amaziah, Uzziah, Jotham, Hezekiah and Josiah. There's no question that Josiah was a great king, for even the Prophet Jeremiah used him as an example for the other rulers to follow. "He pled the cause of the afflicted and needy," said Jeremiah of Josiah, while the kings that followed Josiah exploited the people so they could build their elaborate palaces (Jer. 22:11-17). Josiah ruled for thirty-one years (640–609) and walked in the ways of the Lord because David was his model. No doubt his mother was a godly woman and guided her son wisely. He was only eight years old when they made him king, so the court officials were his mentors; but at age sixteen, Josiah committed himself to the Lord and began to seek His blessing.

Cleansing the land (34:3-7). Hezekiah had cleaned up after Ahaz, and Manasseh had cleansed up the consequences of his own evil practices, and now twenty-year-old Josiah had to undo the damage done by his father Amon. What a tragedy that all the leaders of Judah didn't maintain the law of the Lord and keep the nation honoring Jehovah. The four kings who followed Josiah undid all the good he had done and sold the nation into the hands of the Babylonians. Everything rises and falls with leadership, and young King Josiah provided aggressive spiritual leadership for the people. He had been seeking the Lord for four years and now he was prepared to cleanse the land.

He purged the land of the high places and called the people back to worship at the temple in Jerusalem. He destroyed the idols and the altars dedicated to Baal and other false gods, and he defiled the places where the people worshiped these idols. After purging Jerusalem and Judah, he moved into northern Israel (Manasseh, Ephraim, Naphtali) and rid that area of idolatry. It's interesting that the king of Judah could go to these tribes in Israel (Samaria) and exercise such authority, but a great many people had come to Hezekiah's Passover feast from Ephraim, Manasseh, Issachar, and Zebulun and returned home determined to please the Lord (2 Chron. 30:18). From 2 Chronicles 34:7, we learn that the king personally went on these trips and led the way in removing idolatry from the land.[5]

Repairing the temple (22:3-7; 34:8-13). Josiah's eighteenth year as king was indeed a stellar one. He repaired the temple of the Lord where the Book of the Law was discovered; he made a covenant with the Lord; he carried on further reforms in the land, and he hosted a great celebration of Passover. He was twenty-six at the time. The man who expedited the king's plans for repairing the temple was Shaphan, the father of a remarkable family. His son Gemariah joined with others in urging King Jehoiakim not to burn Jeremiah's scroll, and his grandson Micaiah heard Baruch read Jeremiah's second scroll in the temple and reported it to the king's secretaries (Jer. 36:11ff). His son Elasah carried Jeremiah's letter to the Jewish exiles in Babylon (Jer. 29:1-23), and his son Ahikam was among the men who consulted Huldah the Prophetess about the Book of the Law (1 Kings 22:12-20). Ahikam also interceded with King Jehoiakim not to kill the Prophet Jeremiah (Jer. 26:16-24). After the fall of Judah and Jerusalem, Shaphan's grandson Gadaliah was named governor of Judah. The only disappointing son of the four was Jaazaniah who worshiped idols in the temple of the Lord (Ezek. 8:11-12).

The people had been contributing money for the upkeep of the temple (v. 4), so the king ordered Shaphan to tell Hilkiah the high priest to distribute the funds to the workers and start repairing the temple. It wasn't enough just to destroy the idol worship in the land; the temple had to be available for the worship of the true and living God. As with the temple reconstruction under Joash (2 Kings 12), the workers were faithful and there was no need to keep elaborate records. Leadership is stewardship, and leaders must see to it that the work is done with integrity and God's money is used wisely.

Discovering the Scriptures (22:8-20; 34:14-28). It seems remarkable that the Book of the Law should be lost *in the temple!* That would be like losing the Bible in a church building and not missing it for years. This scroll was probably all five books of Moses, but Shaphan "read in the book"; that is, he read the king-selected passages, perhaps from the Book of Deuteronomy.[6] Shaphan gave the king a report on the building program and then, almost as an afterthought, told him about the newly discovered book. It's to Josiah's credit that he desired to hear what the book said, and when he heard it read, he was smitten with fear and grief. How people respond to God's Word is a good indication of their spiritual appetite and the strength of their desire to please the Lord.

If indeed Shaphan read from the Book of Deuteronomy, then what Josiah heard read from chapters 4–13 would convict him about the wicked things the nation *had already done*. Chapters 14–18 would disturb him because of what the people *had not done*, and the covenant spelled out in chapters 27–30 would warn him of *what God would do* if the nation didn't repent. In the terms of His covenant, the Lord made it clear that the nation would be punished severely if they disobeyed His law. So deeply moved was the king that he tore his robes and ordered the high priest and several officers to inquire of the Lord concerning Judah's spiritual condition. Josiah was only twenty-six years old and had been seeking the Lord for only ten years, yet his response to the Word of God was that of a mature believer.

Hilkiah didn't consult Jeremiah about this matter, or even the Prophet Zephaniah, one of Josiah's kinsmen (Zeph. 1:1), who was ministering at that same time. Perhaps Jeremiah was not in the city but at his family home in Anathoth, and Zephaniah may also have been out of Jerusalem. But the king's committee found a capable servant in Huldah the Prophetess, whose husband Shallum was in charge of the royal wardrobe.[7] Along with Huldah, the prophetesses in Scripture include Miriam (Ex. 15:20), Deborah (Judg. 4:4), Naodiah (Neh. 6:14), the wife of Isaiah the Prophet (Isa. 8:3), Anna (Luke 2:36), and the four daughters of Philip the evangelist (Acts 21:8-9).

Huldah's message was in two parts. The first part (22:15-17; 34:23-25) was addressed to "the man who sent you," meaning Josiah as a common man before the law of God, just like all the other people in Judah and Israel. The second part (22:18-20; 34:26-28) was addressed to "the king of Judah," that is, Josiah as an individual with spiritual needs and concerns. As far as the nation was concerned, God would indeed send His wrath because of their repeated disobedience, but as far as Josiah was concerned, he would be spared this impending judgment because of his godly life and humility before the Lord (see 2 Chron. 33:12, 23). Even though Josiah died as the result of wounds received in battle, he went to his grave in peace because Nebuchadnezzar and his army hadn't yet invaded the land. God called Josiah away before the terrible judgments fell.

Covenanting with the Lord (23:1-3; 34:29-33). The delegation reported Huldah's message to the king, who immediately called the elders, priests, and prophets together, with the people of the land, and shared the message with them. Then he called them to enter with him into a covenant with the Lord. The "renewing of the covenant" was a familiar event in Jewish history. When the new generation was about to enter Canaan, Moses had them renew the covenant, as recorded in Deuteronomy. On two occasions, Joshua called for a renewal of the covenant (Josh. 8:34ff; 24), and so also did Samuel (1 Sam. 7:2ff; 12:1ff). After Nehemiah and the people completed the rebuilding of the wall of Jerusalem, Ezra led them to rededicate themselves to Jehovah (Neh. 8–10). We must never assume today that because our churches are growing and our ministry prospering that God's people are necessarily at their best. There are times when corporate renewal of our dedication to Christ is the right thing to do.

The king stood by a pillar of the temple (see 11:14) and read the words of the law to the assembly. He covenanted with them to walk before the Lord in obedience and devotion. He set the example, for if the leaders don't walk with God, how can God give His people His best blessings? This meeting wasn't a demonstration of "civil religion" where everybody obeyed because the king commanded it. What Josiah pled for was a yielding of their hearts and souls to the Lord in sincerity and truth.

Reforming the land (23:4-20; 34:33).

The king then began to implement the terms of the covenant and obey the law of the Lord. First, he removed from the temple everything that belonged to idolatrous worship, burned it in the Kidron Valley and had the ashes taken to Bethel and scattered to defile the shrine of the golden calf that Jeroboam I had set up. He also broke down that shrine and destroyed everything associated with it (23:15; Hos. 10:5; Zeph. 1:4). He brought Manasseh's infamous idol out of the temple (see 21:7; 33:7), burned and pulverized it, and sprinkled the ashes on the graves of those who worshiped it so as to defile them. Josiah destroyed the houses of the sodomites (male religious prostitutes; 1 Kings 14:24 and 15:12), in obedience to Deuteronomy 23:17-18.

He also removed the Levitical priests who ministered at the high places throughout Judah (23:8), from the northern border (Geba) to the southern border (Beersheba), desecrated those places, and brought the priests to Jerusalem. They were not permitted to serve at the temple altar, but they were allowed to share the food from the sacrifices. Then he went to Topheth, the place of human sacrifice in the Valley of Hinnom, and defiled it. (See Isa. 30:33, Jer. 7:31-32, and 19:6, 11-14.) He removed the horses dedicated to the sun god and burned the chariots in the fire. Imagine stabling horses in the temple precincts! He pulled down and destroyed the altars to the heavenly host that had been placed by Ahaz on the roof of the temple buildings (16:1-4, 10-16; 21:3, 21-22), removed by Hezekiah and replaced by Manasseh. (See Jer. 19:13 and 32:29.) He also did away with the altars Manasseh had put in the temple court. All these things were smashed and thrown in the garbage dump in the Kidron Valley.

On the southern slope of the Mount of Olives, Solomon had provided special altars for his heathen wives where they could worship their gods (1 Kings 11:5-7), and these altars and idols Josiah removed and destroyed. To make sure the area would never be used for idol worship again, he buried human bones there and defiled it (Num. 19:16). He even took his crusade into Samaria and destroyed the shrine at Bethel that had been established by King Jeroboam (1 Kings 12:28-33). He took the remains of the dead priests of Bethel, buried nearby, and burned them on the altar, scattering the ashes to pollute the area. Thus he fulfilled the prophecy made three centuries before (1 Kings 13:31-32). When Josiah saw the grave of the man of God who had prophesied those very actions, he commanded that it be left intact.

What Josiah did at Bethel, he did throughout the land of Samaria, destroying idols and the shrines dedicated to them, and slaying the idolatrous priests who served at their altars (Deut. 13:6-11; 18:20). Don't confuse the idolatrous priests of verse 20 with the disobedient priests of verse 8. The latter were allowed to live in Jerusalem but were not permitted to serve at that temple altar. Finally, Josiah removed the various kinds of spirit mediums from the land (23:24), people who were at one time encouraged by King Manasseh (21:6). But in spite of all the good that Josiah did, he couldn't stop the Lord from sending judgment to Judah. The sins of Manasseh had been so great that nothing could prevent the Lord from pouring out His wrath on His people.

Celebrating the Passover (23:21-23; 35:1-19). In many respects, King Josiah was following the example of King Hezekiah in cleansing the nation of idolatry, repairing the temple and restoring the worship, and celebrating a great nationwide Passover in Jerusalem. While all the appointed feasts in Leviticus 23 were meaningful and important, the feast of Passover was especially significant. For one thing, Passover reminded the Jewish people of their national origin at the Exodus when the Lord delivered them from Egyptian bondage. This was a manifestation of the grace and power of God. He took them to Himself as His own people and entered into a covenant relationship with them at Mount Sinai. They were God's chosen people, God's covenant people, a people to bring glory to His name.

Hezekiah had celebrated his great Passover during the second month of the year, but Josiah celebrated during the first month. Note in 2 Chronicles 35 that there is an emphasis on the Levites and their important ministry during the Passover (vv. 2, 5, 8-12, 14-15, 18). According to 2 Kings 23:22 and 2 Chronicles 35:18, this Passover was even greater than the one celebrated in Hezekiah's time because "all Judah and Israel . . . were present" (35:18; see 30:18). Hezekiah's Passover lasted two weeks, but at Josiah's Passover the people offered almost twice as many sacrifices. At least 37,600 small animals were offered, plus 3,800 bulls. The priests and Levites were cleansed and sanctified, ready to serve, and there were many Levites who sang praises to the Lord and played instruments.

Josiah obeyed what he had read in the law of the Lord.

What is the meaning of King Josiah's admonition to the Levites about carrying the Ark (35:3)? Bearing the sacred Ark had been the task of the Kohathites (Num. 4), but the nation was no longer a pilgrim people and the Ark had been placed in the Holy of Holies in the temple. Inasmuch as the Book of the Law had been misplaced, and it was kept in the Ark (Deut. 31:24-29), it has been conjectured that perhaps the Ark had been taken out of the temple and hidden during the evil days of Manasseh and the Ark and the book were separated. It's also been suggested that Manasseh replaced the Ark with the image he had made and which he worshiped (23:4-6; 33:7). The Hebrew word translated "put" in 35:3 can be translated "leave," so the sense of his command might be, "Don't bring the Ark—we don't need it at this time. We're no longer on the march." Some of the enthusiastic Levites might have wanted to add the presence of the Ark to the great celebration, even though the law didn't require it.

Josiah ruled at a time when Assyria was on the decline and Babylon hadn't yet reached its zenith, the times were more peaceful, and the people could travel in greater safety. The celebration was indeed a great rallying time for the Jewish people from both Judah and Samaria. God's people need occasions like this when together they can celebrate the Lord and His goodness and fellowship with one another.

Sacrificing his life (23:28-30; 35:20-27). Nineveh, the capital city of Assyria, was taken by the Babylonians and the Medes in 612 B.C., and Assyria was definitely on the decline. In 608, Pharaoh Neco led his army from Egypt to assist the Assyrians against the Babylonians.[8] Josiah was pro-Babylon and wasn't too happy about the Egyptian forces marching along the western border of Judah, so he personally led the army of Judah against him. The two armies met at Megiddo, about fifty miles north of Jerusalem, and there Josiah was fatally wounded. His officers took him back to Jerusalem where he died and was buried with the kings.

Josiah had no mandate from the Lord

to interfere in the dispute between Egypt and Babylon, yet Pharaoh Neco claimed that the Lord had commanded him to help Assyria. According to 2 Chronicles 35:22, this message was "from the mouth of God." Egypt and Assyria failed in their attempt to hold back Babylon, but Neco's defeat of Josiah did give Egypt control of Judah for a few years (2 Chron. 36:3-4). Josiah was greatly mourned in Judah and Jeremiah even wrote laments to honor him (35:25; see Jer. 22:10). These laments have been lost and must not be confused with the Book of Lamentations.

From the death of Josiah in 608 to the destruction of Jerusalem by Babylon in 586—a period of twenty-two years—four different kings sat on David's throne, three of them sons of Josiah but not imitators of his faith. Jehoahaz and Jehoiachin each reigned for only three months. It was a sad time for the people of God, but there was still a believing remnant that followed the Lord and helped seekers in each new generation to know the Lord.

CHAPTER THIRTEEN
THE END HAS COME
2 Kings 23:29–25:30
(2 Chronicles 36)

"Every great nation fell by suicide." The British political leader Richard Cobden made that observation, and his statement is aptly illustrated in the history of the kingdom of Judah. Sudden political or military blows from the outside didn't destroy Judah. The nation committed suicide as it decayed morally and spiritually from within. These chapters tell the tragic story of the last years of a great nation. We can see the steps in their decline and the decisions of their kings who led the people downward to destruction.

1. They lost their independence (2 Kings 23:29-33; 2 Chron. 35:20–36:4)

King Josiah was a godly man who sincerely wanted to serve the Lord, but he made a foolish blunder by attacking Pharaoh Neco. His meddling in Egypt's affairs was a personal political decision and not a command from the Lord. Josiah wanted to prevent Pharaoh Neco from assisting Assyria in their fight against Babylon, little realizing that it was Babylon and not Assyria that would be Judah's greatest enemy. Josiah was mortally wounded by an arrow at Megiddo and died in Jerusalem. With the death of Josiah, the kingdom of Judah lost her independence and became subject to Egypt. This lasted from 609 to about 606, and then Egypt retreated and Babylon took over.

According to 1 Chronicles 3:15-16, Josiah had four sons: Johanan; Eliakim, who was renamed Jehoiakim; Mattaniah, who was renamed Zedekiah; and Shallum, also known as Jehoahaz. We know nothing about Johanan and assume he died in childhood. When Josiah died, the people put Josiah's youngest son Jehoahaz on the throne and bypassed the other two brothers. His given name was Shallum (Jer. 22:11) and Jehoahaz was the name he was given when he took the throne. Jehoahaz and Zedekiah were full brothers (23:31; 24:18). It's obvious that the Jeremiah mentioned in 23:31 isn't the Prophet Jeremiah since he was unmarried (Jer. 16:1-2).

Jehoahaz reigned only three months. When Neco was returning to Egypt with his army, he deposed Jehoahaz, made Eliakim king, renaming him Jehoiakim, and placed a heavy tax on the land. It's likely that Jehoiakim was pro-Egypt in politics while Jehoahaz favored alliances with Babylon, as had his father, Josiah. Pharaoh met Jehoahaz at the Egyptian military headquarters at Riblah and from there took him to Egypt where Jehoahaz died. The Prophet Jeremiah had predicted this event. He told the people not to mourn the death of Josiah, but rather to mourn the exile of his son and successor Shallum, for he would never see Judah again (Jer. 22:10-12). But unlike his godly father, Josiah, Jehoahaz was an ungodly man and an evil king and deserved to be exiled.

Jehovah called Israel to be a "people dwelling alone, not reckoning itself among the nations" (Num. 23:9, NKJV). Their faith was to be in the Lord alone, not in the treaties or compromises worked out by clever diplomats. Israel was God's "special treasure . . . a kingdom of priests and a holy nation" (Ex. 19:5-6, NKJV; see Deut. 7:6-11). It was Solomon who moved Israel from its separated position into the arena of international politics. He married seven hundred wives (1 Kings 11:3), most of whom represented treaties with their fathers or brothers who were rulers and men of influence. These treaties brought wealth into the nation and kept warfare out, but in the end, both Solomon and Israel were drawn into the idolatry of the nations around them (1 Kings 11:1-13).

Had the Jewish people obeyed the Lord and kept His covenant, He would have put them at the head of the nations (Deut. 28:1-14), but their disobedience led to their defeat and dispersal among the nations of the earth. Unfortunately, the church has followed Israel's bad example and entangled itself with the world instead of keeping itself separated from the world (2 Tim. 2:4; James 1:27; 1 John 2:15-17). Believers are in the world but not of the world, and this enables us to go into the world and share Jesus Christ with lost sinners (John 17:13-19). Campbell Morgan said that the church did the most for the world when the church was the least like the world. Be distinct!

2. They lost their land (2 Kings 23:34–24:7; 2 Chron. 36:5-8)

Having deposed Jehoahaz, Pharaoh Neco selected Josiah's second son to be the next regent, changing his name from Eliakim to Jehoiakim. Both names mean "God has established," but the new name used the covenant name "Jehovah" in place of "El," the common name for God. By doing this, Neco was claiming to be the Lord's agent in ruling Judah. Of course, the new king had to swear allegiance to Neco in the name of Jehovah, and his new name would remind him of his obligations. In order to pay tribute to Neco, the new king taxed the people of the land. He reigned for eleven years and during that time, Judah got more and more in trouble with the surrounding nations.

Jehoiakim was a wicked man. When Urijah the Prophet denounced him and then fled to Egypt, Jehoiakim sent his men to find him and kill him (Jer. 26:20-24). Jeremiah the Prophet announced that Jehoiakim would not be mourned when he died but would have the burial of a donkey, not the burial of a king (Jer. 22:18-19). It was Jehoiakim who cut to pieces and burned to ashes the scroll of Jeremiah's prophecy (Jer. 36). Unlike his father, Josiah, he had no respect for the Lord or His Word (Jer. 22:1-23).

However, the new empire of Babylon was about to replace Egypt as Judah's great enemy and master. Nebuchadnezzar their king attacked Egypt, but the battle ended in a stalemate and Nebuchadnezzar returned to Babylon to reequip and strengthen his forces for a return engagement. From Babylon's "retreat," Jehoiakim falsely concluded that Egypt was strong enough to resist Babylon, so after three years as a vassal king, he rebelled against Nebuchadnezzar and refused to pay the annual tribute. Until he could arrive at Jerusalem in person, Nebuchadnezzar ordered the armies of some of his vassal nations to attack and raid Judah. These raids were but a prelude to the great invasion of Judah that would lead to the destruction of Jerusalem and the temple. Isaiah had told King Hezekiah that this would happen (2 Kings 20:12-20) and King Manasseh had heard the same warning but not heeded it (21:10-15). Jeremiah had seen the vision of the boiling pot that faced the north, symbolizing the coming invasion from Babylon (Jer. 1:11-16; see 4:5-9; 6:22-26).

The scenario of the death of King Jehoiakim must be put together from information given in 2 Kings, 2 Chronicles, and the Book of Jeremiah. In 597, Nebuchadnezzar came to Jerusalem to punish the rebellious king; but before he arrived, his officers had captured Jehoiakim and bound him to take him prisoner to Babylon (2 Chron. 36:5-6). We aren't told whether he died a natural death or was killed (2 Kings 24:6); the verse mentions only his death ("slept with his fathers") and not his burial. He died in December 598, before Nebuchadnezzar arrived on the scene in March 597 (2 Kings 24:10ff). The Prophet Jeremiah warned that Jehoiakim would have an ignominious death and no burial. When the king died, his body was probably thrown into some pit outside the walls of Jerusalem. He lived a disgraceful life and fittingly was buried in a disgraceful manner.

3. They lost their wealth and their leading people (2 Kings 24:8-17; 25:27-30; 36:9-10)

Nebuchadnezzar appointed Jehoiakim's son Jehoiachin (Jeconiah, Coniah) to be the new king, but he lasted only three months. He was eighteen years old at the time.[1] When the Babylonian king, officials, and army arrived at Jerusalem in March, 597, Jehoiachin led the royal family and the leaders of the nation in surrendering to the enemy. Jeremiah had prophesied this humiliating event (Jer. 22:24-30).

The Babylonians took the king's treasures as well as treasures from the temple of the Lord. Some of the temple vessels had already been removed to Babylon (2 Chron. 36:7), but now the Babylonians stripped off all the gold they could find. Then they deported to Babylon over ten thousand key people, including members of the royal family, government officials, and valuable craftsmen. This is when the Prophet Ezekiel was taken to Babylon (Ezek. 1:1-3). All of this was but a foretaste of the terrible events that would occur when Nebuchadnezzar would return in 588 and lay siege to Jerusalem for two years. (See Isa. 39:1-8, Jer. 7:1-15 and Ezek. 20:1-49.)

Jehoiachin was a prisoner in Babylon for thirty-seven years and then was released by Nebuchadnezzar's son and heir, Evil-Merodoch (2 Kings 25:27-30; Jer. 52:31-34). The false prophet Hananiah had predicted that Jehoiachin would be set free to return to Judah (Jer. 28), but the king remained an exile, though treated with kindness after his pardon. Whenever the king of Babylon displayed his special prisoners on royal occasions, he put Jehoiachin's throne above the thrones of the other captive kings. As Jeremiah had predicted, none of Jehoiachin's children sat on David's throne (Jer. 22:28-30), because Josiah's third son, Mattaniah (Zedekiah) was appointed king to replace Jehoiachin.[2]

4. They lost their city and temple (2 Kings 24:18-25:21; 2 Chron. 36:11-21)

Jehoiakim had reigned for only three months when he was exiled to Babylon, but his successor, Zedekiah, ruled for eleven years. He pretended to submit to Babylon while at the same time courting Egypt and listening to the pro-Egypt leaders in the government of Judah (Ezek. 17:11-18). Zedekiah took an oath in the name of the Lord that he would be faithful to the king of Babylon (2 Chron. 36:13; Ezek. 17:11-14). He maintained diplomatic contact with Babylon (Jer. 29:3) and even visited the court of Nebuchadnezzar (Jer. 51:59), but he also sent envoys to Egypt to seek the help of Pharaoh Hophra.

In 605, during the reign of Jehoiakim, the Babylonians had deported some of Judah's best young men to Babylon to be trained for official duty, among them Daniel and his three friends (Dan. 1:1-2). The second deportation was in 597 (2 Kings 24:10-16) when over ten thousand people were sent to Babylon. But Zedekiah still favored getting help from Egypt, and in 588, the political situation seemed just right for Zedekiah to revolt against Babylon (2 Kings 24:20; 2 Chron. 36:13). Nebuchadnezzar responded by marching his army to Jerusalem, but when the Egyptian army moved to help King Zedekiah, the Babylonians withdrew temporarily to face Egypt. Nebuchadnezzar knew it was unwise to fight a war on two fronts. God sent Jeremiah to warn Zedekiah that Nebuchadnezzar would return (Jer. 37), but Zedekiah's faith was in Egypt, not in the Lord (Ezek. 17:11-21). Zedekiah even called an "international conference" involving Edom, Moab, Ammon, Tyre, and Sidon (Jer. 27), hoping that these nations would work together to keep Babylon at bay. However, Nebuchadnezzar stopped Egypt and then returned to Jerusalem and the punishment of Zedekiah.

The siege of Jerusalem began on January 15, 588, and continued until July 18, 586, when the famine was so severe the people were cooking and eating their own children (Lam. 4:9-10). The invaders broke through the walls and took the city, looting and destroying the houses and finally burning the city and the temple on August 14, 586. The Prophet Jeremiah had counseled Zedekiah and his officers to surrender to Nebuchadnezzar and thus save the city and the temple (Jer. 21; 38:1-6, 14-28), but they refused to obey God's Word and had Jeremiah arrested as a traitor! The officers put him under court guard and even dropped him into an abandoned cistern where he would have died had he not been rescued (Jer. 38:1-13). The hypocritical and weak Zedekiah told Jeremiah to ask the Lord what he should do (Jer. 21), but the king refused to accept the prophet's answer. Zedekiah asked Jeremiah to pray for him (Jer. 37:1-3), but the king was a proud man who refused to humble himself and pray for himself (2 Chron. 36:12-13; 2 Chron. 7:14).

When the Babylonian soldiers finally entered the city, King Zedekiah fled with his family and officers, but they were intercepted in the plains of Jericho and taken into custody. Jeremiah's prophecy had come true (Jer. 34:1–7; see also chapters 39 and 52). Zedekiah faced Nebuchadnezzar at his headquarters at Riblah where he was found guilty of rebellion and sentenced to be exiled to Babylon. But first, to give the king one last tormenting memory, the Babylonians killed his sons before his eyes—and then gouged out his eyes! Ezekiel in Babylon also prophesied that the king would attempt to escape and be captured and taken to Babylon, but he would not see the city (Ezek. 12:1-13). How could Zedekiah see the king of Babylon (Jer. 34:3) but not see the city of Babylon? The answer was: after he had seen the king, Zedekiah was blinded by his enemies.

After removing everything valuable from the city and the temple, on August 14, 586, the Babylonians finished breaking down the walls of the city and set fire to Jerusalem and the temple. The Babylonian officers captured the religious leaders of the city as well as the king's staff, the people who had opposed Jeremiah and given the king poor counsel, and had them slain before Nebu-chadnezzar at Riblah. The priests had polluted God's house with idols and encouraged the people to break the covenant of God (2 Chron. 36:14; see Lam. 4:13 and Ezek. 8–9). The leaders of the nation had refused to listen to God's servants, so God sent judgment (2 Chron. 36:15-16). There was "no remedy" and the day of judgment had arrived. Only the poor people remained in the land (24:14; 25:12; Jer. 39:10; 40:7; 52:16) to take care of what was left of the vineyards and farms.

King Zedekiah lived in Babylon until his death and, in fulfillment of the Lord's promise through Jeremiah (Jer. 34:4-5), was given a state funeral. He certainly didn't deserve such an honor, but the Lord did it for the sake of David, the founder of the dynasty.

3. They lost their hope (2 Kings 25:22-36; Jer. 40–44)

The Babylonians treated the Prophet Jeremiah with exceptional kindness and gave him the option of going to Babylon or remaining in the land (Jer. 40:1-6). Like a true shepherd, he chose to remain with the people, even though for the most part they had rejected him and his ministry for forty years. His heart was broken when he saw the ruins of the city and the temple, but he knew that the Word of the Lord had been fulfilled (2 Chron. 36:21). The people had not allowed the land to enjoy the rest God commanded (Lev. 25:1-7; 26:32-35), so now it would have a seventy-year "Sabbath" (Jer. 25:11-12; 29:10-14; Dan. 9:1-3).

The Babylonians appointed Gedaliah governor of Judah. He was the grandson of godly Shaphan, who served under King Josiah, and the son of Ahikam, who faithfully supported Jeremiah (2 Kings 22:1-14; Jer. 26:24). Gedaliah assured the Jews who remained in the land that the Babylonians would treat them well if only they would cooperate, the same counsel Jeremiah had sent earlier to the Jewish exiles in Babylon (Jer. 29:1-9). Certainly the people knew the promise the Lord had given through Jeremiah, that the captivity would last seventy years and then the exiles would be allowed to return to Judah. God's purpose was to give them "a future and a hope" (Jer. 29:11), but they had to accept that promise by faith and live to please Him.

However, a group of insurgents led by Ishmael, who belonged to the royal family (2 Kings 25:25; Jer. 41:1), decided to usurp Gedaliah's authority. (See Jer. 40–41 for the details discussed below.) Several factors were involved in this vicious assassination plot. To begin with, Ishmael had designs on the throne and resented Gedaliah's appointment as governor and his submission to the Babylonians. (See James 4:1-6.) The army officers told Gedaliah that the king of the Ammonites had sent Ishmael to take over the land (Jer. 40:13-16),[3] but Gedaliah refused to believe them. Had Gedaliah listened to this sound advice and dealt sternly with Ishmael, things would have been different for the remnant in Judah, but he was too naïve to face facts. A third factor was the arrival in Judah of a large group of Jews who had fled to neighboring lands (Jer. 40:11-12). Their allegiance was questionable and perhaps they were too easily influenced by Ishmael. All the neighboring nations had suffered from Babylon's expansion and would have been happy to be set free.

Ishmael killed Gedaliah and took the people captive, but Johanan and the other officers rescued the captives. Ishmael and eight of his men fled to the Ammonites. Johanan became the new leader of the remnant and decided that they should all flee to Egypt rather than obey Jeremiah's message and stay in the land and serve the Babylonians. In a show of hypocritical piety, Johanan and the leaders asked Jeremiah to seek the mind of the Lord about the matter, and he agreed to do so. The Lord kept them waiting for ten days and during that time proved that He could keep them safe and well in their own land.

Jeremiah's message to the remnant (Jer. 42:7-22) was in three parts. First, he gave them God's promise that He would protect them and provide for them in their own land (vv. 7-12). Then he warned them that it was fatal to go to Egypt (vv. 13-18). The sword of the Lord could reach them in Egypt as well as in their own land. There could be no temporary residence in Egypt and then a return to Judah, for none of them would return. Finally, Jeremiah revealed the wickedness in their hearts that led them to lie to him and pretend to be seeking God's will (vv. 19-22). These leaders were like many people today who "seek the will of God" from various pastors and friends, always hoping that they will be told to do what they have already decided to do. The Jews rejected God's message and went to Egypt, taking the Prophet Jeremiah with them (Jer. 43:1-7).

However, the biblical record doesn't end on this bleak note but records the proclamation of Cyrus that the Jewish remnant could return to their own land and rebuild Jerusalem and the temple (2 Chron. 36:22-23). The Book of Ezra opens with this proclamation (Ezra 1:1-4) and tells the story of the remnant's return to the land. This decree was issued in 538 when Cyrus defeated Babylon and established the Persian empire. The Babylonians began their assault on Judah when their army invaded Judah in 606–05 and deported prisoners, among them Daniel and his friends. From 606 to 538 is approximately seventy years, the time period announced by Jeremiah (Jer. 25:11-12; 29:10). Some students prefer to start the count with the destruction of the temple in 586. Seventy years later would take us to 516–15, the year the second temple was dedicated and the captivity officially ended.

As they had so often done during their history, the Jewish leaders lived by scheming instead of by trusting the promises of God. Jeremiah had given the people hope by promising that God was with them and would see to it they were protected and returned to their land (Jer. 29:11). But the leaders abandoned all hope when they fled to Egypt, for there they died and were buried. How tragic that the faithful Prophet Jeremiah, who had suffered so much for the people and the Lord, should be buried in some forgotten place in Egypt.

As we come to the close of this record of the tragic decline and destruction of a great nation, we need to take some lessons to heart. *No nation rises any higher than its worship of God.* The nation of Israel was torn into two kingdoms because of the sins of Solomon who turned to idols in order to please his pagan wives.

Because they worshiped idols and forsook the true God, the northern kingdom of Israel was taken captive by Assyria. It didn't take long for Judah to succumb and eventually be captured by Babylon. We become like the god we worship (Ps. 115:8), and if we refuse to worship the true and living God, we become as helpless as the idols that enthrall us.

The people who led Israel and Judah astray were conformers, weak people who followed the crowd and pleased the people. God warned them of their folly by raising up men and women who were distinctively different and sought to please the Lord, but these faithful witnesses were ignored, abused, and martyred. The cynical playwright George Bernard Shaw defined martyrdom as "the only way in which a man can become famous without ability." He was wrong. People who have suffered and died for the faith had the God-given abilities to trust Him, to put truth and character ahead of lies and popularity, and to refuse to "go with the flow" and be conformed to the world with its shallowness and sin.

At this critical time in history, God is seeking dedicated, distinctive people—not cookie-cutter, carbon-copy Christians. Friendship with the world is enmity with God (James 4:4) and to love the world and trust it is to lose the love of the Father (1 John 2:15-17). We are to be "living sacrifices" for the Lord (Rom. 12:1-2), distinctive people whose lives and witness point to Christ and shine like lights in the darkness. "A city that is set on a hill cannot be hid" (Matt. 5:14). Faith is living without scheming. Start to explain away the clear teachings of the Bible about obedience to the Lord and separation from sin, and you will soon find yourself sliding gradually out of the light and into the shadows and then into the darkness, eventually ending in shame and defeat.

"He who does the will of God abides forever" (1 John 2:17, NKJV).

Endnotes

Chapter One

1. James and John had been with Elijah on the Mount of Transfiguration and wanted to imitate him by calling down fire from heaven on their "enemies." Jesus rebuked them (Luke 9:52-58). The Christian response to opposition is given in Matt. 5:38-48 and Rom. 12:14-21.
2. The inference here is that, after going to heaven, Elijah could do nothing further for Elisha. See Luke 16:19-26.

Chapter Two

1. Deut. 20:16-20 applied to Israel's attacks on cities in Canaan where the Jews would inherit the land. It was forbidden to cut down the fruit trees and thereby ruin their own inheritance. However, in foreign lands, their army could follow a "scorched earth" policy.
2. There's no indication that the events in this chapter are presented in chronological order.
3. Neh. 5:5 and 8, Isa. 1:17 and 23, and Amos 2:6 indicate that the Jewish people didn't always share God's love for the helpless widows. The early church had a special concern for widows that should be revived in the church today (1 Tim. 5:1-16; James 1:27).
4. The word is not "stool" as in KJV but "chair," and can be translated "chair of honor" or "throne."
5. Gehazi's part in this entire episode is most interesting (vv. 15, 25, 29, 36). It appears that Elisha preferred to have his servant be the go-between for him and the great woman.
6. *Metropolitan Tabernacle Pulpit*, vol. 25, p. 121.

Chapter Three

1. Joram seems to have had a pessimistic outlook on life and expressed it by jumping to conclusions. When they ran out of water, he didn't believe that Elisha could provide water for the three armies (3:10, 13). When

he read the letter, he applied it to himself and totally ignored Elisha.

2. The water in the Abana (Amana) and Parphar came from the snow in the mountains around Damascus, so it was fresh and clean. Naaman had to learn that God's ways are above our ways (Isa. 55:8-9).
3. God also gave leprosy temporarily to Miriam because she criticized her brother Moses (Num. 12) and permanently to King Uzziah because he tried to be a priest (2 Chron. 26:16-21). Three sins must be avoided: covetousness, malicious criticism, and rebelling against God's calling in our lives.
4. In 1 Cor. 9:1-14, Paul taught that the Christian laborer was worthy of his hire, and he included himself. But in vv. 15-27, he argued that he had the right to refuse their support for the sake of reaching more people with the Gospel. It was a personal conviction that he didn't impose on all the churches or all of God's servants. Paul knew that in Corinth especially, accepting money could put a barrier between him and the people he was trying to reach.

CHAPTER FOUR

1. "Ben Hadad" was the title or "throne name" of the Syrian rulers, just as Pharaoh was the title of the Egyptian king.
2. The NIV translates "doves' dung" as "a half a pint of seed pods."
3. Over a century ago, secular scholars used to smile at the mention of the Hittites and refer to them as "a mythological people mentioned only in the Bible." But excavations have revealed a powerful Hittite civilization that was frequently at enmity with Israel. Once again the archaeologists' spades have had to affirm the truth of Scriptural record.
4. It takes very little imagination to apply this scene to the church today. Jesus has won the victory over Satan and "this is a day of good news." Believers are enjoying all the blessing of the Christian life while a whole world is suffering and dying. How can we keep the good news to ourselves? If we do, we will answer for it when we face the Judge. How can we be silent in a day of good news?

CHAPTER FIVE

1. The Hebrew text simply says "do this great thing" (v. 13). The NIV reads "accomplish such a feat." The NLT reads, "How could a nobody like me ever accomplish such a great feat?" To a professional soldier, doing what Elisha described in v. 12 would be a "great thing." The issue wasn't what would be done by Hazael but how he would have the authority to do it.
2. This is the only mention of Elijah in 1 and 2 Chronicles. The Elijah in 1 Chron. 8:27 was a member of the tribe of Benjamin.
3. Along with David, the kings most often singled out for their godliness are Asa, Jehoshaphat, Joash, Hezekiah, and Josiah.
4. 2 Kings 8:24 says that Jehoram was buried "with his fathers," and this seems to contradict 2 Chron. 21:20. It's possible that Jehoram was originally buried in the tombs of the kings but that his body was later removed to another site. Popular opinion was so against honoring Jehoram that his corpse was removed from the royal tombs and placed elsewhere in Jerusalem.
5. Athaliah is always identified with Ahab but not with Jezebel. Although she learned much evil from Jezebel, we can't assume that Jezebel was her birth mother. "The daughter of Omri" (8:26, KJV) should read "the granddaughter of Omri." See 2 Chron. 22:2, NIV.
6. The word "harlotries" or "whoredoms" in v. 22 refers to Jezebel's idolatrous worship of Baal. In the Old Testament prophets, adultery and prostitution were familiar images of idol-worship. Israel was married to the Lord when she accepted His covenant at Sinai and was warned to worship one God and not worship idols (Isa. 54:5; Jer. 3:14 and 31:32; Hos. 2:2). In the nation of Israel, just as adulteresses were stoned, so those who worshiped idols were slain (Deut. 13).

CHAPTER SIX

1. Often in the account of salvation history, the future of God's plan rests with a baby or a child. Cain killed Abel, but God sent Seth as the next link in the chain. Abraham and Sarah waited twenty-five years for their son Isaac to be born, and baby Moses was supposed to be drowned but lived to grow up and deliver Israel from Egypt.

During one of Israel's darkest hours, the Lord sent Samuel to Hannah and Elkanah. Now, the future of the messianic promise and the Davidic covenant rests with one little boy.

2. Jehoiada wouldn't allow the guards to kill Athaliah on the holy ground of the temple of Jehovah, but they could kill the priest of Baal before the very altar of Baal. Baal worship was a man-made religion and therefore a false religion. See John 4:22-23.

CHAPTER SEVEN

1. *The Westminster Pulpit*, vol. 8, p. 315.
2. Some believe that this was the man Jesus spoke about in Matt. 23:35 and Luke 11:51, but the text reads "son of Berechiah" (see Zech. 1:1). "From Abel [Genesis] to Zechariah [2 Chronicles]" would cover the entire Old Testament, since the Hebrew Bible ends with 2 Chronicles. Zechariah was a popular name among the Jews—there are twenty-seven found in the Bible—and it's not unlikely that more than one was stoned to death for his faith.
3. See 8:7-15; 10:32-33; 13:3, 22.
4. Many Jewish kings were assassinated. See 1 Kings 15:27; 16:8-10; 2 Kings 9:22-29; 15:10, 13-15, 25-26, 29-31.

CHAPTER EIGHT

1. *The Decline and Fall of the Roman Empire*, ch. 3. A decade before, Voltaire had written, "Indeed, history is nothing more than a tableau of crimes and misfortunes."
2. In numbering the rulers of Judah, I'm including wicked Queen Athaliah, who reigned for six years after the death of Ahaziah, and was Judah's seventh ruler. When young King Joash took the throne, Athaliah was slain.
3. Of the nine kings whose reigns are described in these chapters, five were assassinated: Amaziah (14:19-22), Zechariah (15:10), Shallum (15:14), Pekahiah (15:25), and Pekah (15:30).
4. The phrase "as soon as the kingdom was confirmed" (14:5) suggests that, after his accession, Amaziah faced opposition and had to overcome it gradually. We commend him for waiting patiently to receive the authority he needed to bring judgment against the men who murdered his father.
5. The text suggests that the mercenaries first reported to their king in Samaria and then from there returned to the border country and attacked the cities. The king must have approved their plan or they wouldn't have returned to Judah to fight. Later, Amaziah tried to get revenge but failed miserably (25:17ff).
6. Note that the Prophet Jonah ministered in Israel at that time (14:25), and this fact helps us better understand his refusal to preach to the city of Nineveh. During Jeroboam's reign, the kingdom of Israel was proud, complacent, and very nationalistic. They were God's chosen people and they didn't want any other nation to interfere. Jonah would rather see the Assyrians destroyed by the Lord and refused at first to take God's message to them.
7. In those days, the soldiers often had to provide their own weapons and armor.
8. They are Asa, Jehoshaphat, Joash, Amaziah, Uzziah, Jotham, Hezekiah, and Josiah. Of course, at the top of the list is King David.
9. The phrase in v. 25 "with Argob and Arieh" has challenged students. The NIV and NLT translations suggests that these were two of Pekahiah's officers who were killed along with the king, while the KJV and NASB see them as two men who helped Pekah murder the king. The first interpretation seems to be the better of the two. Pekahiah was guarded by only two aides while Pekah had eighty men with him.
10. Pekah united with Rezin, king of Syria, in trying to force Ahaz, king of Judah, to join forces with them in opposing Assyria. It was out of this context that the famous messianic promise of Isa. 7:14 was born.

CHAPTER NINE

1. The dates for the reign of Ahaz are usually given as 732 to 716, sixteen years, but some scholars feel that these were the sixteen years of his sole reign as king. He was probably a vice-regent for nine years and a coregent with Jotham another four years.
2. This happens frequently in 2 Chronicles. See 11:2, 5; 15:1-8; 18:1ff; 25:7-9, 15-16; and 36:12. Prophetic ministry involves wisdom from God to understand the times and being able to apply the Word to the situation.
3. *Keys to the Deeper Life* (Christian Publications), p. 22.

4. No "Pharaoh So" is found in Egyptian history, but it's possible that "So" refers to the Egyptian capital city of Sais, which is "So" in Hebrew. Hoshea sent to So (Sais) to enlist the help of Pharaoh.
5. Perhaps Hoshea had to present himself in person to Shalmaneser, as Ahaz had done to Tiglath-pileser (16:10), and the king of Assyria wouldn't allow him to return to Samaria. The government of Israel was very weak and the officers knew that the end was near.
6. In Col. 1:13, Paul used this military image: "translated us into the kingdom of his dear Son" (KJV). The word "translated" comes from a Greek word that means "to move a defeated population to another land." Jesus on the cross defeated sin, Satan, and death and the Father has transferred all who believe in His Son out of the kingdom of darkness and into the kingdom of life and light.

CHAPTER TEN

1. Most students believe that Judah was invaded twice by the Assyrian army, in 715 and in 701. The second invasion is given far more space in the biblical record because of the great miracle the Lord performed. It's difficult to see 2 Kings 18:7-16 as a part of the 701 invasion, but it was a prelude to it.
2. King Ahab turned to the wall and pouted because he didn't get his own way (1 Kings 21:4), but that wasn't the attitude of Hezekiah. Perhaps in looking toward the wall of his room he also looked toward the temple, which is what the Jews were supposed to do when they prayed (2 Chron. 6:21, 26, 29, 32, 34, 38).
3. J. W. Thirtle in his book *Old Testament Problems* (London: Morgan and Scott, 1916) proposed the theory that the fifteen "Songs of the Degrees (Ascents)" in the Book of Psalms (120–134) were compiled by Hezekiah to commemorate the fifteen extra years God gave him. Ten of these psalms are anonymous, while the other five are assigned to David (four psalms) and Solomon (one psalm). Thirtle believed that Hezekiah wrote the ten anonymous psalms to commemorate the shadow going back ten degrees on the stairway of Ahaz. After all, these are the "songs of the degrees." Since David was his hero, King Hezekiah must have tried his hand at writing psalms, and it's possible the Spirit of God gave him those ten psalms for that special collection.
4. Actually, when believers die, they leave the land of the dead (this world) and go to the land of the living (heaven)!

CHAPTER ELEVEN

1. *Expositions of Holy Scripture* (Baker, 1974), vol. 3 [2 Kings 8–Nehemiah], p. 244.
2. As you study the field commander's speech, it's tempting to believe that the Assyrians had someone in Jerusalem. The Rabshakeh not only knew about the Egyptian party, but he also knew that Hezekiah had removed the pagan altars (18:22), and that Isaiah had warned the people not to depend on horses and soldiers (18:23; Isa. 30:15-17).
3. The KJV calls him "king of Ethiopia," which refers to the region of the upper Nile. He was commander of the army at that time and eventually became ruler of Egypt.
4. Many great events in Jewish history were for the purpose of exalting Jehovah's name before all the nations. These include the Exodus (Ex. 9:16); the conquest of Canaan (Deut. 28:9-10); the entrance into Canaan (Josh. 4:23-24); the killing of Goliath (1 Sam. 17:46); and the building of the temple (1 Kings 8:42-43).

CHAPTER TWELVE

1. *Twilight of a Great Civilization* (Crossway Books, 1988), p. 15.
2. *God Tells the Man Who Cares* (Christian Publications), p. 138.
3. If Manasseh was twelve years old in 697, then he was born in 709. He was coregent with his father from 697 to 687 and served alone for the next forty-five years. He was seven years old in 702 when his father had that severe illness, and he became coregent five years later (697). Since Manasseh was the heir to David's throne, his father surely taught him to obey the Word.
4. 1 and 2 Chronicles were probably written and circulated when the Jews were captives in Babylon, so the Holy Spirit led the writer to emphasize the messages the exiles needed to hear. If God could forgive and restore such a wicked man as Manasseh, could He not also forgive and restore His captive people? King Manasseh is a living

witness to the truth of God's promise in 2 Chron. 7:14.

5. The emphasis in 2 Chronicles is on "all Israel," the uniting of the two kingdoms as the people of God. Many godly people from the Northern Kingdom had relocated to Judah so they would be under the spiritual leadership of God's Levitical priests in the temple dedicated to the Lord. The mention of Simeon in 34:6 reminds us that this tribe was politically a part of Judah (1 Chron. 4:24-43).
6. Some scholars claim that this whole episode was a "pious fraud" and that Hilkiah "found" the book in order to call Josiah's attention to the Law of Moses and the covenant Israel made with the Lord. But why would they take such a devious approach with a king who openly displayed his love for the Lord? Under the long reign of Manasseh, the law of God was ignored and openly disobeyed, and it wouldn't have been difficult for the temple copy of the Scriptures to be hidden for protection and then forgotten. However, this one scroll wasn't the last and only copy of God's law in the land, for the high priest and other temple officials certainly had copies. This was the opportune time for Josiah to hear the law of God, and the Lord arranged for it to happen.
7. There's no evidence that this Shallum was the uncle of Jeremiah (Jer. 32:7).
8. The Authorized Version of 2 Kings 23:29 says that Egypt "went up against the king of Assyria," when the Egyptians were actually assisting Assyria against the Babylonians. The NASB reads "Pharaoh Neco . . . went up to the king of Assyria."

CHAPTER THIRTEEN

1. Second Chron. 36:9 reads "eight years old," but the fact that he had wives (2 Kings 24:15) makes this very questionable, and it's unlikely that Nebuchadnezzar would appoint a young child to lead a vassal nation. After only a three months' reign, Jehoiachin was put in prison in Babylon (24:15), something the enemy wasn't likely to do to a child. Like ancient Latin, the Hebrew language uses the letters of the alphabet for numbers. The difference between eight and eighteen is the presence of a "hook" symbol over the letters for eighteen, and if the person who copied the manuscript failed to add the "hook," the error would be recorded and repeated. These occasional scribal errors in no way affect the inspiration of Scripture and do not touch upon any major teaching in the Bible.
2. The phrase "his father's brother" in 2 Kings 24:17 refers to Jehoiachin's father, Jehoiakim, whose brother was Mattaniah (Zedekiah) and therefore Jehoiachin's uncle. Zedekiah was the last king of the kingdom of Judah. Jeremiah's prophecy said that no son of Jehoiachin (Coniah) would occupy David's throne, and none ever did. After the exile, when the remnant returned to Judah to rebuild the temple, one of the leaders was Zerubbabel (Ezra 3:8; Hag. 1:1 and 2:20-23) who descended from Jehoiachin (Jeconiah) through Shealtiel (Matt. 1:11-12). However, though he came from David's line, he never sat on David's throne. Jeconiah never established a royal dynasty.
3. Perhaps the Ammonites hoped to restore the coalition described in Jer. 27 and revolt against Babylon. This, of course, would have been out of the will of God, but Ishmael would have jumped at the chance to become Judah's new leader.

EZRA

A SUGGESTED OUTLINE OF THE BOOK OF EZRA

Key theme: Restoring the spiritual heart of the nation
Key verse: Ezra 7:10

I. THE NATION IS RESTORED—1–6
1. A remnant returns with Zerubbabel and Joshua—1–2
2. The temple is rebuilt—3–6
   (1) The work begins—3
   (2) The work opposed—4
   (3) The work resumed—5
   (4) The work completed—6

II. THE PEOPLE ARE REDEDICATED—7–10
1. A second group arrives with Ezra—7–8
2. Confession of sin—9
3. Cleansing of sin—10

CONTENTS

CHAPTER ONE
THE PROVIDENCE OF GOD
Ezra 1–3

"Thank God He gives us difficult things to do!" said Oswald Chambers in *My Utmost for His Highest*.[1]

The first time I read that statement, I shook my head in disagreement; but I was young and inexperienced then, and it seemed smarter to do the easy things that made me look successful. However, I've lived long enough to understand the wisdom of Chambers' statement. I've learned that when God tells us to do difficult things, it's because He wants us to grow. Unlike modern-day press agents and spin doctors, God doesn't manufacture synthetic heroes; He grows the real thing. "The hero was a big man," wrote Daniel Boorstin; "the celebrity is a big name."[2]

In God's Hall of Heroes are the names of nearly 50,000 Jews who in 538 B.C. left captivity in Babylon for responsibility in Jerusalem. God had called them back home to do a difficult job: to rebuild the temple and the city and restore the Jewish community in their own land. This noble venture involved a four months' journey plus a great deal of faith, courage, and sacrifice; and even after they arrived in the Holy City, life didn't get any easier. But as you read the inspired record, you can see the providential leading of the Lord from start to finish; and "if God be for us, who can be against us?" (Rom. 8:31)

You see God's providence at work in three key events.

1. The release of the captives (Ezra 1:1-4)

More than a century before, the Prophet Isaiah had warned the Jews that the people of Judah would be taken captive by Babylon and punished for their sins (Isa. 6:11-12;11:11-12; 39:5-7), and his prophecy was fulfilled. In 605, Nebuchadnezzar deported the royal family and took the temple vessels to Babylon. In 597, he sent into exile 7,000 "men of might" and a thousand craftsmen (2 Kings 24:10-16); and in 586, he destroyed Jerusalem and the temple and exiled the rest of the Jews in Babylon, except for "the poor of the land" (2 Kings 25:1-21).

In 538, Cyrus the Great, king of Persia, conqueror of Babylon, issued a decree that permitted the exiled Jews to return to their land and rebuild their temple. This, too, had been prophesied by Isaiah (Isa. 44:28). What Cyrus did twenty-five centuries ago reminds us today of some important spiritual truths.

God is faithful to His Word. For at least forty years, the Prophet Jeremiah had warned the leaders of Judah that the Babylonian exile was inevitable (see Jer. 20:4-6; 21:7-10); and he pled with them to repent of their sins and surrender to Babylon. Only then could they save the city and the temple from ruin. The leaders didn't listen—in fact, they called Jeremiah a traitor—and the Holy City and the temple were destroyed in 587–586.

But Jeremiah also announced that the Captivity would be for seventy years (Jer. 25:1-14; 29:10; see Dan. 9:1-2). Bible students don't agree on the dating of this period, whether it begins with the Babylonian invasion in 606 or the destruction of the city and temple in 587–586. From 606 to 537–536, when the remnant returned to Judah, is seventy years; but so also is the period from the fall of

Jerusalem (586) to the completion of the second temple in 516. Regardless of which calculation you accept, the prediction and its fulfillment are astonishing.[3] Whether He promises chastening or blessing, God is always faithful to His Word. "Not one thing has failed of all the good things which the Lord your God spoke concerning you" (Josh. 23:14, NKJV). "There has not failed one word of all His good promise" (1 Kings 8:56, NKJV). "Heaven and earth shall pass away," said Jesus, "but My words shall not pass away" (Matt. 24:35).

God is faithful to His covenant. In spite of their sins, these exiles were God's chosen people and children of the covenant He had made with Abraham, Isaac, and Jacob (Gen. 12:1-3). The nation had broken the covenant, but the Lord had remained faithful to His Word. He had called the Jewish nation to bring blessing to all the earth, and He would see to it that they fulfilled their mission. Through them, the world would receive the knowledge of the one true and living God, the written Word of God, and ultimately the Savior of the world. "Salvation is of the Jews" (John 4:22).

God is in control of the nations. It was the Lord who raised up Nebuchadnezzar—"My servant" (Jer. 25:9; 27:6; 43:10)—to chasten the people of Judah; and then He raised up Cyrus to defeat the Babylonians and establish the Persian Empire. "Who has stirred up one from the east, calling him in righteousness to His service? He hands nations over to him and subdues kings before him" (Isa. 41:2, NIV; see also v. 25). The Lord called Cyrus "My shepherd" (44:28) and "His anointed" (45:1), and Isaiah prophesied that Cyrus would liberate the exiles and enable them to rebuild their city and temple (v. 13).

God's people need to remember that the Lord God is sovereign over all nations and can do what He pleases with the most powerful rulers. Nebuchadnezzar had to learn this lesson the hard way (Dan. 4:28-32), but then he confessed: "His [God's] dominion is an everlasting dominion, and His kingdom is from generation to generation. All the inhabitants of the earth are reputed as nothing; He does according to His will in the army of heaven and among the inhabitants of the earth. No one can restrain His hand" (Dan. 4:34-35).

God can do as He pleases with the rulers of the earth; and He has demonstrated this in His dealings with Pharaoh (Ex. 9:16; Rom. 9:17), Ahasuerus (The Book of Esther), Sennacherib (2 Kings 19:28), Augustus Caesar (Luke 2:1), and Herod Agrippa I (Acts 12:20-24). King Jehoshaphat said it perfectly: "O Lord, God of our fathers, are You not the God who is in heaven? You rule over all the kingdoms of the nations. Power and might are in Your hand, and no one can withstand You" (2 Chron. 20:6).

People don't have to be Christian believers for God to use them. Whether a mayor, governor, senator, prime minister, ambassador, or president, God can exercise His sovereign power to accomplish His purposes for His people. This is one reason Paul exhorts believers to pray for those in authority, not that our political agenda might be fulfilled, but that God's will might be accomplished on this earth (1 Tim. 2:1-8). "God can make a straight stroke with a crooked stick," said Puritan preacher John Watson; and that's what he did with Cyrus!

The king's decree boldly acknowledged the Lord and called Him "the Lord God of heaven" (Ezra 1:2), a title that's used seventeen times in Ezra, Nehemiah, and Daniel. The decree addressed two kinds of people: (1) those who wanted to return to their land and (2) those who preferred to remain in Babylon. The latter group was urged to give offerings to help finance the expenses of the journey and the restoration of the temple.[4]

The Jews also accepted gifts from their Gentile neighbors (v. 6, NIV). When the Jews left Egypt, they plundered the Egyptians (Ex. 12:35-36) and collected the wages the men should have received during their years of slavery. Now the Jews were making their "exodus" from captivity, so they collected wealth from their pagan neighbors and dedicated it to the Lord[5]

2. The return of the remnant (Ezra 1:5–2:70)

God not only stirred the spirit of Cyrus to grant freedom to the captives (1:1), but He also stirred the hearts of the Jews to give them the desire to return to Judah (v. 5). "For it is God who works in you both to will and to do for His good pleasure" (Phil. 2:13). The same God who ordains the end (the rebuilding of the temple) also ordains the means to the end, in this case, a people willing to go to Judah and work.

The treasure (Ezra 1:5-11). Not only did the travelers carry their own personal belongings, but they carried 5,400 gold and silver temple vessels which had been taken from Jerusalem by Nebuchadnezzar (2 Kings 25:8-17; Jer. 52:17-23; Dan. 1:2; 5:1-3).These items were carefully inventoried by the treasurer and delivered to Sheshbazzar, the appointed ruler of Judah.

Who was Sheshbazzar? He's mentioned four times in Ezra (1:8, 11; 5:14, 16) but not once in any of the other post-exilic books. He's called "the prince of Judah" (1:8, KJV, NIV), a title that can mean "leader" or "captain" and often referred to the heads of the tribes of Israel (Num. 1:16, 44; 7:2; Josh. 9:15-21). The word "Judah" in Ezra 1:8 refers to the district of Judah in the Persian Empire, not to the tribe of Judah; so Sheshbazzar was the appointed leader of "the children of the province [of Judah]" (Ezra 2:1).

Many Bible students believe that Sheshbazzar was another name for Zerubbabel, the governor of Judah, who with Joshua the high priest directed the work of the remnant as they rebuilt the city and the temple. He's mentioned twenty times in the postexilic books, and according to 2 Chronicles 3:16-19 was a grandson of King Jehoiakim and therefore a descendant of David.

Ezra 5:16 states that Sheshbazzar laid the foundation of the temple, while Ezra 3:8-13 attributes this to Zerubbabel, and Zechariah 4:9 confirms it. It seems logical to conclude that Sheshbazzar and Zerubbabel were the same person. It wasn't unusual in that day for people to have more than one given name, especially if you were a Jew born in a foreign land.

When you add the numbers given in Ezra 1:9-10, they total 2,499; but the total given in verse 11 is 5,400. A contradiction? Not necessarily, for it was important that Zerubbabel and the leaders keep a careful inventory of the temple treasure, and it's not likely they would make that big a blunder. The statement in 1:10, "and other vessels a thousand" suggests that verses 9-10 list the larger and more valuable items, while many smaller objects weren't even listed in categories.

The leaders (2:1-2). From the parallel list in Nehemiah 7, we must add the name of Nahamani (Ezra 2:7), bringing the total to twelve men, one for each of the tribes. The Nehemiah in verse 2 is not the man who rebuilt the walls of Jerusalem, because he didn't come on the scene until 444. And the Mordecai listed isn't the

Mordecai of the Book of Esther. "Jeshua" is Joshua the high priest, who is mentioned twenty-three times in the postexilic writings. He was an important part of the leadership of the remnant and served at the side of Zerubbabel the governor.

Geographically, the Southern Kingdom (Judah) included only the tribes of Judah and Benjamin; but over the years, people from the other ten tribes had moved to Judah, so that all twelve tribes were represented in the Captivity. The Bible says nothing about "ten lost tribes"; it appears that all twelve are accounted for (James 1:1; Acts 26:7).

Everything in God's work rises and falls with leadership. When God wants to accomplish something, He calls dedicated men and women to challenge His people and lead the way. A decay in the quality of a nation's leaders is an indication that trouble is ahead. The British essayist Walter Savage Landor wrote, "When small men cast long shadows, it's a sign that the sun is setting."

The families and clans (Ezra 1:3-35). The long lists of names given in Scripture, including the genealogies, may not be interesting to the average reader, but they're very important to the history of God's people. Unless there's an inheritance involved, most people today are more concerned about the behavior of their descendants than the bloodline of their ancestors; but that wasn't true of the Old Testament Jews. It was necessary for them to be able to prove their ancestry for many reasons.

To begin with, unless you could prove your ancestry, you couldn't enter into the rights and privileges of the Jewish nation, of which there were many. The Israelites were a covenant people with an important God-given task to fulfill on earth, and they couldn't allow outsiders to corrupt them. Furthermore, the Jews returning to Judah couldn't reclaim their family property unless they could prove their lineage. Of course, it was especially important that the priests and Levites certify their ancestry; otherwise they couldn't serve in the temple or share in the benefits of that service, such as the tithes and offerings and the assigned portions of the sacrifices.

In verses 3-20, the names of eighteen Jewish families are listed, totaling 15,604 males. When they took a census, the Jews usually included men twenty years of age and older (Num. 1:1-4); but we aren't certain what procedure was followed here. In Ezra 1:21-35, the volunteers were listed according to twenty-one cities and villages, a total of 8,540 men. We don't know the names of all these 24,144 men, but they were important to the Lord and to the future of the nation and its ministry to the world.

The priests and Levites were especially important to the nation (vv. 36-42), for without them, there would be no reason to rebuild the temple. Four groups of priests totaled 4,289 men, and they would be assisted by 341 Levites, some of whom were singers and gatekeepers. The Levites also assisted the priests in teaching the people the law of the Lord (Deut. 33:8-10; Neh. 8:5-8).

The 392 "Nethinim" (Ezra 1:43-54) and "children of Solomon's servants" (vv. 55-58) were workers in the temple who were not priests or Levites. In Hebrew, "Nethinim" means "those given" and seems to refer to prisoners of war who were given to the priests to perform menial tasks in the temple. (See Josh. 9:23, 27 and Num. 31:30, 47.) "Solomon's servants" were probably a similar group of men, established during Solomon's reign. Eighty years later, Ezra would have to send for more Levites and Nethinim to help with the temple ministry (Ezra 8:15-20).

The disqualified (Ezra 1:59-63). There were 652 people who couldn't prove their Jewish ancestry. (The towns mentioned were in Babylon, not Judah.) Zerubbabel and Joshua didn't send these people back home but allowed them the rights of "strangers and foreigners" (Ex. 22:21, 24; 23:9; Lev. 19:33-34; Deut. 10:18; 14:29).

We aren't told how many priests were unable to provide adequate credentials, but we are told that they were excluded from serving in the temple. No doubt some men thought they could enter the priesthood and have a much easier time living in Jerusalem, but Zerubbabel rejected them. God had made it clear that any outsider who attempted to serve at the altar would be put to death (Num. 1:51; 3:10). These men were treated as "strangers" and allowed to make the journey, but Zerubbabel the governor[6] excluded them from the priestly privileges until they could be tested by "the Urim and Thummim."[7] This was the means provided for the high priest to determine God's will (Ex. 28:30; Num. 27:21).

The totals (Ezra 1:64-67). The total that Ezra gives (42,360) is 12,542 more than the total you get when you add up the individual figures given in the chapter. Nehemiah also gives 42,360 (Neh. 7:66). However, in giving this list, Ezra didn't say that these several groups represented all the men who left Babylon, nor do we know how many more joined after the list was completed. It's possible that he counted men only from Judah and Benjamin, so that pilgrims from the other ten tribes make up the difference.

We do know that an additional 7,337 servants, both men and women, went along, which speaks well of their Jewish masters and mistresses, for these servants (slaves?) might have been sold in Babylon and remained there. Apparently, they preferred to be with the Jews. This many servants (one-sixth of the total) also suggests that some of the Jews had become wealthy in Babylon.

The 200 singers (Ezra 1:65) were not a part of the temple ministry but were "secular singers" who performed for Jewish festive occasions such as weddings (see 2 Chron. 35:25). From the time of the Exodus (Ex. 15), the Jews composed songs to honor God and celebrate the blessings of life. Over a dozen different musical instruments are named in Scripture. The captivity in Babylon hadn't been a time for singing (Ps. 137:1-4); but now that the Jews were "heading home," they had a song to sing.

3. The rebuilding of the temple (Ezra 2:68–3:13)

Ezra wrote nothing about the long trip (900 miles) or what the Jews experienced during those four difficult months. It reminds us of Moses' description of Abraham and Sarah's journey to Canaan: "and they went forth to go into the land of Canaan; and into the land of Canaan they came" (Gen. 12:5). "It is a strange narrative of a journey," said Alexander Maclaren, "which omits the journey altogether . . . and notes but its beginning and its end. Are these not the main points in every life, its direction and its attainment?"[8]

Investing in the work (Ezra 2:68-70). This was undoubtedly a thank offering to the Lord for giving them a safe journey. The people gave their offerings willingly and according to their ability, which is the way God's people are supposed to give today (2 Cor. 8:8-15; 9:6-15). According to Nehemiah 7:70-72, both the tribal leaders and Zerubbabel the governor gave generously, and the common people followed their good example.

Setting up the altar (Ezra 3:1-3). The seventh month would be Tishri, our September–October, a month very sacred to the Jews (Lev. 23:23-44). It opened with the Feast of Trumpets; the Day of Atonement was on the tenth day; and from the fifteenth to the twenty-first days, they celebrated the Feast of Tabernacles. But the first thing Joshua the high priest did was restore the altar so he could offer sacrifices for the people. The people were afraid of the strong nations around them who resented the return of the Jews, and they wanted to be sure they were pleasing to the Lord. Again, we see a parallel with Abraham, who built an altar when he first came into the land of Canaan (Gen. 12:7). This is an Old Testament picture of Matthew 6:33.

Joshua also restored the various sacrifices commanded by the Law, which would include a burnt offering each morning and evening and extra offerings for special days. It wasn't necessary to wait until the temple was completed before offering sacrifices to God. As long as there was a sanctified altar and a qualified priest, sacrifices could be given to the Lord. After all, it's not the external furnishings but what's in the heart that concerns God the most (1 Sam. 15:22; Ps. 51:16-17; Hosea 6:6; Mark 12:28-34).

Laying the foundation (Ezra 3:7-13). The work didn't begin until the second month of the next year, which means they spent nearly seven months gathering materials and preparing to build. It was in the second month that Solomon started building the original temple (1 Kings 6:1), and he gathered his materials in much the same way (Ezra 3:7; 1 Kings 5:6-12). Joshua and Zerubbabel were in charge of the project, assisted by the Levites. "If the foundations are destroyed, what can the righteous do?" asked David (Ps. 11:3); and there's only one answer: lay the foundations again! That's what spiritual revival is all about, getting back to the foundations of the Christian life and making sure they're solid: repentance, confession, prayer, the Word of God, obedience, and faith.

Note the emphasis on unity. The people gathered together (Ezra 3:1); the workers stood together (v. 9); the Levites sang together (v. 11); and all the while, the people were working together to get the foundation laid. Their tasks were varied, but they all had one goal before them: to glorify the Lord by rebuilding His temple. This is what Paul had in mind when he wrote "make my joy complete by being like-minded, having the same love, being one in spirit and purpose" (Phil. 2:2).

Following the example of David, when he brought up the Ark to Jerusalem (1 Chron. 16), and Solomon, when he dedicated the temple (2 Chron. 7:1-3), the priests and Levites sang praise to the Lord, accompanied by trumpets and cymbals; and the people responded with a great shout that was heard afar off. (See Pss. 47:1; 106:1; 107:1; 118:1-4; 135:3; 136; and 145:1-11.) The people united their hearts and voices in praise to the Lord for His goodness to them.

But at this point, their "togetherness" was interrupted as the young men shouted for joy and the old men wept "with a loud voice." Why were they weeping on such a joyful occasion? Because they had seen the original temple before it was destroyed over fifty years before, and the new edifice was nothing in comparison. (Haggai would later preach a sermon about this. See Hag. 2:1-9.) These godly old men longed for "the good old days," but it was the sins of their generation that had caused the fall of the kingdom to begin with! Had their generation listened to the Prophet Jeremiah and obeyed God's Word, Jerusalem and the temple would still be standing.

It's unfortunate when the unity of God's people is shattered because generations look in opposite directions. The older men were looking back with longing while the younger men were looking around with joy. Both of them should have been looking up and praising the Lord for what He had accomplished. We certainly can't ignore the past, but the past must be a rudder to guide us and not an anchor to hold us back. God's people are a family, not a family album filled with old pictures; they're a garden, not a graveyard covered with monuments to past successes.

We have similar generational disagreements in the church today, especially when it comes to styles of worship. Older saints enjoy singing the traditional hymns with their doctrinal substance, but younger members of the church want worship that has a more contemporary approach. But it isn't a question of accepting the one and rejecting the other, unless you want to divide families and split the church. It's a matter of balance: the old must learn from the young and the young from the old, in a spirit of love and submission (1 Peter 5:1-11). When they were new, many of our traditional hymns were rejected for the same reasons some people reject contemporary praise choruses today. "But each class [the young and the old] should try to understand the other's feelings," said Alexander Maclaren. "The seniors think the juniors revolutionary and irreverent; the juniors think the seniors fossils. It is possible to unite the shout of joy and the weeping. Unless a spirit of reverent regard for the past presides over the progressive movements of this or any day, they will not lay a solid foundation for the temple of the future. We want the old and the young to work side by side, if the work is to last and the sanctuary is to be ample enough to embrace all shades of character and tendencies of thought."[9]

Every local church is but one generation short of extinction. If the older believers don't challenge and equip the younger Christians and set a godly example before them (Titus 2:1-8; 1 Tim. 5:1-2), the future of the congregation is in jeopardy. The church is a family; and as a family grows and matures, some things have to fall away and other things take their place. This happens in our homes and it must happen in the house of God. To some people, "change" is a synonym for "compromise," but where there's love, "change" becomes a synonym for "cooperation with one another and concern for one another."

"Behold, how good and how pleasant it is for brethren to dwell together in unity!" (Ps. 133:1)

CHAPTER TWO
THE FAITHFULNESS OF GOD
Ezra 4–6

"Therefore know that the Lord your God, He is God, the faithful God" (Deut. 7:9, NKJV). Moses said that to the new generation of Israelites before they entered Canaan, a truth they would need as they faced the enemy and claimed their inheritance. New generations and old generations both need to be reminded that God is faithful.

"He who calls you is faithful, who also will do it" (1 Thes. 5:24, NKJV). Paul wrote that to some young Christians in Thessalonica, people who were being persecuted for their faith. They needed to be reminded that God's commandments are God's enablements.

"God being who He is," said A.W. Tozer, "cannot cease to be what He is, and being what He is, He cannot act out of character with Himself. He is at once faithful and immutable, so all His words and acts must be and must remain faithful."[1]

J. Hudson Taylor, pioneer missionary to inland China, described the successful Christian life as "not a striving to have faith . . . but a looking off to the Faithful One . . . "[2] He knew the words of Paul: "If we are faithless, He remains faithful. He cannot deny Himself" (2 Tim. 2:13, NKJV).

The Jewish remnant that returned to Jerusalem to rebuild the temple was depending on God's faithfulness to see them through. If God wasn't faithful to His covenant and His promises, then there was no hope. But the God who called them would be faithful to help them finish His work (Phil. 1:6), as long as they trusted Him and obeyed His Word.

In these three chapters, we see how God was faithful to His people in every stage of their work for Him.

1. Stage one: the work opposed (Ezra 4:1-24)

From the beginning, the remnant faced opposition from the mixed population of the land who really didn't want the Jews inhabiting Jerusalem and rebuilding the temple. Opportunity and opposition usually go together; and the greater the opportunity, the greater the opposition. "For a great and effective door has opened to me," wrote Paul, "and there are many adversaries" (1 Cor. 16:9).

Cooperation leading to compromise (Ezra 4:1-3). The first attack of the enemy was very subtle: the people of Samaria, the former Northern Kingdom, offered to work with the Jews to help them build the temple. These people claimed to worship the same God the Jews worshiped, so it seemed logical that they should be allowed to share in the work. On the surface, the Samaritans seemed to be acting like good neighbors, but their offer was insidious and dangerous.

The Samaritan people, being a mixture of many races, weren't true Jews at all. When the Assyrians conquered the Northern Kingdom, they deliberately mingled the nations they had defeated; and this led to racial and religious confusion (2 Kings 17:24-41). The Samaritans didn't worship the true and living God, for they "feared the Lord, yet served their own gods" (2 Kings 17:33; see John 4:22). The Jewish leaders had already rejected the professed Jews who had been in exile in Babylon (Ezra 2:59-63), so they weren't about to accept the people of the land who obviously didn't belong to the covenant nation and couldn't prove their Jewish lineage.

Why was the Samaritan offer so dangerous? Because if these outsiders had begun to mingle with the Jewish remnant while helping to build the temple, it wouldn't have taken long for the two groups to start socializing and intermarrying; and that was contrary to the Law of Moses (Ex. 34:10-17; Deut. 7:1-11; 12:1-3). Israel was a nation set apart from the other nations (Num. 23:9), because God had given them a special task to perform in the world (Gen. 12:1-3). If in any way the people of Israel were corrupted, the success of their God-given ministry would be jeopardized.

God's people today must maintain a separated position and not get involved with anything that will compromise their testimony and hinder God's work (2 Cor. 6:14–7:1;2 Tim. 2:3-5).

However, separation must never become isolation (1 Cor. 5:9-10) because God has a work for believers to do in this world (Matt. 5:13-16; John 17:14-18). Jesus was "holy, harmless, undefiled, separate from sinners" (Heb. 7:26); and yet He was the friend of sinners and sought to win them (Luke 15:1-2; Matt. 9:10-11; 11:19). God's people separate from the world so they can be a witness to the world.

Accusation leading to fear (Ezra 4:4-5, 24). Satan had come as the serpent to deceive (2 Cor. 11:3) and had failed; and now he came as the lion to devour (1 Peter 5:8), and he succeeded. The enemy told lies about the Jews and encouraged the people of the land to do everything possible to discourage the workers and hinder the work. They even hired counselors to influence the local officials to stop the project, and they succeeded.

"Then ceased the work of the house of God which is at Jerusalem" (Ezra 4:24). This was during the reign of Cyrus (559–530) who had given the Jews the right to return to their land and rebuild their temple. From 536 to 530, the work had progressed; but in 530, it stopped and didn't resume until the year 520, when Darius was king. This defeat wasn't because the king had issued a decree against them, but because the Jewish remnant feared the people of the land. The Jews had begun to get more interested in their own houses than in the house of God (Hag. 1:1-11).

Other opposition to God's work (Ezra 4:6-23). At this point in the narrative (vv. 6-23), Ezra cited other instances of the work being attacked, including the events that occurred during the time of Darius, who reigned from 522 to 486 (vv. 5, 24); Xerxes (v. 6) who was the Ahasuerus of the Book of Esther and reigned from 486 to 465; and Artaxerxes I (vv. 7-23), ruler from 465 to 424. Ancient writers often summarized historical events in this manner before moving on to finish their account. Ezra's main interest, of course, was in the opposition that came while the temple was being rebuilt during the reigns of Cyrus and Darius. The long parenthesis in vv. 6-23 deals with the rebuilding of the city (v. 12) and not the rebuilding of the temple. It's additional evidence of the fact that whenever God's people try to serve the Lord, somebody will oppose them [3]

In the seventh year of Artaxerxes I (458–457), Ezra the scribe took a group of liberated Jewish exiles to Jerusalem to start rebuilding the city (7:1). Eastern rulers depended on their local officials to act as spies and report anything suspicious. Rehum, the officer in charge, conferred with the other officials and decided that the rebuilding of the city was a threat to the peace of the empire. So he dictated a letter to Shimshai the scribe and had it sent to the king.

Rehum gave four reasons why the king must order the Jews to stop rebuilding Jerusalem. First, history showed that Jerusalem was indeed a "rebellious and wicked city"; unfortunately, this was a fact that even the Jews couldn't deny. If Jerusalem were restored, Rehum argued, it would rebel against the king and declare its independence (4:12).[4] As long as Jerusalem was in ruins, it was defenseless against the king's forces.

Second, an independent Judah would mean loss of revenue and tribute to the empire (v. 13);[5] but, third, a successful rebellion would also bring dishonor to the king. What king wants to have one of his provinces successfully rebel against him? This might encourage other provinces to follow their example. Finally, if the Jews succeeded in rebuilding and rebelling, they would no doubt conquer the entire territory across the Euphrates (v. 16); and this would really hurt the king and his empire.

The king's officers searched the archives and found proof that the Jews had indeed been ruled by mighty kings (David, Solomon, Josiah, Hezekiah) and also by rebellious kings, so Rehum's accusations were correct. During the declining years of Judah, their kings had made and broken treaties with Egypt, Assyria, and Babylon and had refused to pay tribute to Assyria and to Babylon. Their own record indicted them.

The king ordered the Jews to stop rebuilding the city. In fact, it's likely that the Persians wrecked the work the Jews had already completed, and the report that Nehemiah received from his brother described what the Persians had done, not what the Babylonians had done (Neh. 1:1-3). It wasn't until the arrival of Nehemiah in 445 that the work was resumed and the walls were finished and the gates restored.

2. Stage two: the work resumed (Ezra 5:1–6:12)

From 530 to 520, the Jews concentrated on building their own houses and neglected the house of the Lord. The Lord chastened His people to encourage them to obey His commands (Hag. 1:6), but they refused to listen. What means did God use to get the work going again?

God used preachers of the Word (Ezra 5:1-2). It was by the Word of the Lord that the world was created (Ps. 33:6-9), and by that same Word the Lord governs His creation and His people (Ps. 33:10-11). Church history shows that when God wants to arouse His people to do His will, He calls people to proclaim the Word of the Lord. The preaching of Martin Luther brought about what we call "the Reformation," a movement that transformed not only Germany but the entire Christian world. The preaching of John Wesley produced a spiritual awakening in Great Britain that swept many into the kingdom of God. Historians tell us that the Wesleyan Revival helped to rescue England from the kind of blood bath that France experienced during the French Revolution.

Never underestimate the power of the faithful preaching of God's Word. Charles Spurgeon, the famed British Baptist preacher, said, "I cannot help feeling that the man who preaches the Word of God is standing, not on a mere platform, but on a throne."[6]

Haggai began his ministry of the Word on August 29, 520 (Hag. 1:1), and five of his messages are recorded in the book that bears his name. A month or two later, he was joined by a young man named Zechariah, a priest whom God had called to be a prophet (Zech. 1:1). These two men delivered God's Word to the leaders and the remnant, "and they [the Jews] prospered through the prophesying [preaching] of Haggai, the prophet, and Zechariah" (Ezra 6:14).

Any work of God that isn't built on the Word of God will never prosper. Moses' success as the leader of Israel came from his faith in and obedience to God's Word (Deut. 4:10). Joshua's success in conquering the enemy in Canaan was based on his devotion to the Word of God (Josh. 1:8). When we obey God's Word, we can expect "great reward" (Ps. 19:11). If we want to know the power of God, we must also know the Word of God (Matt. 22:29).

God used local officials (Ezra 5:3-17). As governor of the province of Judah, Tattenai (Tatnai) was concerned about what the Jews were doing in Jerusalem, and rightly so. It was his responsibility to protect the interests of King Darius and the welfare of the empire and to see to it that peace and security were maintained. So, when the project was resumed, Tattenai investigated and asked two questions: (1) "Who gave you the authority to do this?" and (2) "What are the names of the men working on the building?"

The Jews didn't look upon the Persian officer as a troublemaker, but graciously answered his questions. After all, they had nothing to hide, and the eye of the Lord was upon them. God saw to it that the work was allowed to go on while Tattenai contacted the king to find out what to do.

God's people must "walk in wisdom toward those who are outside" (Col. 4:5, NKJV) and "walk honestly toward them that are outside" (1 Thes. 4:12), otherwise we have no effective witness where a witness is greatly needed. "Everyone must submit himself to the governing authorities, for there is no authority except that which God has established" (Rom. 13:1, NIV; and see 1 Peter 2:11-17). When it comes to the believers' relationship to civil authorities, there's no place for arrogance, accusation, or carnal anger masquerading as zeal for the Lord. Even where we disagree with officials, we can do it graciously (Dan. 1; 3; 6; Acts 4:19-20; 5:29; 1 Peter 2:13-25).

One of the things that worried Tattenai was the structure of the temple, with its large stones and timbered walls. It looked more like a fortress than a sanctuary! And the work was progressing so rapidly that he wondered if the Jews were planning to revolt.

The Jews knew their history and told Tattenai how the temple was built (the "great king" being Solomon) and why the temple was destroyed. They related how Nebuchadnezzar exiled the Jews in Babylon and how decades later Cyrus gave them permission to return to their land and rebuild their temple. Cyrus also gave them the temple treasures so that the ministry could be established again according to the Law of Moses. The facts were all there; the king's secretaries could check the archives to see that the Jews were telling the truth.

Careful to "[make] the most of every opportunity" (Eph. 5:15-16), the Jewish workers framed their answers to glorify the Lord. They didn't try to cover up the sins of the nation (Ezra 5:12) and they openly acknowledged that they were "the servants of the God of heaven" (v. 11). Both in their words and their demeanor, they presented a clear witness to this important Persian official, and God used him to certify their right to build and guarantee supplies from the king!

God used Darius the king (6:1-12). The royal secretaries searched the archives and located the scroll Cyrus had left containing the edict that governed the return of the Jews to their land. It authorized the Jews to rebuild their temple and even gave the limits of its dimensions.[7] Cyrus permitted large stones to be used for the walls and promised to pay the costs from the royal treasury. He also ordered the local officials to provide beasts for the daily sacrifices. His motive here may have been mixed, because he wanted the priests to pray for him and his sons, but the people of God are supposed to pray for those who are in authority (1 Tim. 2:1-4).

"Let the work of this house of God alone!" (Ezra 6:7) literally means, "Keep your distance!" Neither the local Persian officials nor the people of the land were to interfere, but rather do everything they could to support the work. The king described the terrible judgments that would come to anybody who didn't obey his edict (vv. 11-12). So, what started out as an investigation ended up as a royal decree that protected the Jews and provided for them!

But suppose the Jewish remnant had been offensive and treated Tattenai and his associates with defiance and disdain? His letter to headquarters might not have been as positive as it was, and this could have changed everything. Peter admonishes us to speak "with gentleness and respect"(1 Peter 3:15, NIV) when unsaved people question us, because this glorifies God and opens new opportunities for witness. God's eye is upon His people as they serve Him, so we need not fear what men can do to us.

3. Stage three: the work completed (Ezra 6:13-22)

On the twelfth day of the last month of 515, the temple was completed, about seventy years from the destruction of the temple by the Babylonians in 586, and about five and a half years after Haggai and Zechariah called the people back to work (5:1). God had been faithful to care for His people. He provided encouragement through the preaching of the prophets and even used the authority and wealth of a pagan king to further the work.

The joy of dedicating (6:13-18). Though there was no Ark in the Holy of Holies, and no glory filled the house, the temple was still dedicated[8] to the Lord because it was His house, built for His glory. Instead of weeping over what they didn't have, the Jews rejoiced over what they did have, and this is always the attitude of faith.

When King Solomon dedicated the temple that he built, he offered so many sacrifices that they couldn't be counted (1 Kings 8:5), plus 142,000 peace offerings which were shared with the people (1 Kings 8:63). The Jewish remnant offered only 712 sacrifices, but the Lord accepted them. Most important, they offered twelve male goats as sin offerings, one for each tribe, because they wanted the Lord to forgive their sins and give them a new beginning.

Joshua the high priest also consecrated the priests and Levites for their ministry in the completed temple. David had organized the priests into twenty-four courses so they could minister more effectively (1 Chron. 24:1-19). It wasn't necessary for all of them to serve all the time, for each course was assigned its week of ministry at the temple (Luke 1:5, 8). The statement "as it is written in the law of Moses" (6:18) refers to the consecration of the priests, not their organization. (See Lev. 8–9.)

The joy of remembering (Ezra 6:19-22). Passover was just a few weeks later and the Jews gathered in their families to remember how God had delivered them from bondage in Egypt (Ex. 12). Each year, the Jewish men were required to make three trips to Jerusalem to celebrate Passover, Pentecost, and the Feast of Tabernacles. During their years in exile, how the hearts of the Jews must have yearned for the day when once again they were free to go to their Holy City and worship God.

The leaders invited all the Jews and Jewish proselytes to share in the Passover, even those who couldn't prove their lineage. As long as the males were circumcised (Ex. 12:43-49) and had separated themselves from the paganism of the people of the land, they were welcome. It speaks well of the Jewish remnant that they reached out in this way and didn't try to establish an exclusive "holier than thou" fellowship.

The temple had been dedicated, and now the people were dedicating themselves to the Lord. During the seven days of the Feast of Unleavened Bread, the Jews had to remove all yeast (leaven) from their dwellings, a picture of personal purification. To a Jew, yeast was a symbol of evil; so Passover was a time to put away all evil from their lives. What good is a dedicated temple if you don't have a dedicated people? Once again, Jewish worship would take place in the Holy City in a restored temple dedicated to the Lord. No wonder the people were rejoicing! And it was all because of the faithfulness of God. He had "turned the heart of the king"[9] to assist the people, and now the work was completed (Prov. 21:1).

No matter what our circumstances may be, we can trust God to be faithful. "Great is Thy faithfulness" isn't just a verse to quote (Lam. 3:23) or a song to sing. It's a glorious truth to believe and to act upon, no matter how difficult the situation in life might be.

"I will sing of the mercies of the Lord forever; with my mouth I will make known Your faithfulness to all generations" (Ps. 89:1, NKJV).

CHAPTER THREE
THE GOOD HAND OF GOD
Ezra 7–8

When talk show hosts and hostesses ask successful people the "secret" of their great achievements, the answers they get are varied and sometimes contradictory. Some successful people will give credit to their sobriety and personal discipline, while others will boast that they lived just the way they pleased whether anybody liked it or not. "I always maintain my integrity" is counterbalanced by "I pushed my way to the top no matter who got stepped on."

But if we had interviewed Ezra and asked him the secret of his successful life, he would have said humbly, "The good hand of the Lord was upon me,"[1] a phrase that's found six times in Ezra 7 and 8 (7:6, 9, 28; 8:18, 22, 31). Nothing but the blessing of God can explain how an obscure Jewish priest and scholar, born in Babylonian Captivity, could accomplish so much for God and Israel when so much was working against him.

That God's good hand was upon this man doesn't minimize the importance of his personal piety or his great ability as a scholar, nor does it ignore the great help King Artaxerxes gave him.[2] God uses all kinds of people to accomplish His will, but if God's hand isn't at work in us and through us, nothing will be accomplished. It's the principle Jesus taught His disciples, "Without Me you can do nothing" (John 15:5, NKJV). What did God do for the people of Israel during those difficult days after the Babylonian Captivity?

1. He raised up a godly leader. (Ezra 7:1-6, 10)

It was the year 458 and Artaxerxes I was King of Persia (465–424). Nearly sixty years had passed since the completion of the temple in Jerusalem, and the Jewish remnant was having a very difficult time. It was then that God raised up Ezra to lead a second group of refugees from Babylon to Judah to bring financial and spiritual support to the work and to help rebuild the city.

Every person is important to God and God's work; but, as Dr. Lee Roberson has often said, "Everything rises and falls with leadership." When God wanted to deliver Israel from Egypt, He raised up Moses and Aaron. When Israel was divided and defeated, He called Samuel to teach the Word and David to serve as king. Richard Nixon was right when he said that leaders are people who "make a difference,"[3] and Ezra was that kind of man.

When God wants to judge a nation, He sends them inferior leaders (Isa. 3:1-8); but when He wants to bless them, He sends them men like Ezra.

His noble ancestry (Ezra 7:1-5). There were some priests in the Jewish remnant who couldn't prove their ancestry (2:61-63), but Ezra wasn't among them. He had the best of credentials and could prove his lineage all the way back to Aaron, the first high priest. Some famous spiritual leaders are named in this genealogy, men like Hilkiah, Zadok, and Phineas.[4] Of course, being blessed with godly ancestors is no guarantee of success for their descendants, but it's a good beginning. God promises to bless the descendants of the godly (Deut. 4:40; Ps. 128). "I don't know who my grandfather was," said Abraham Lincoln; "I am much more concerned what his grandson will be." Ezra knew the names of his ancestors and what these men had done, and he made the most of his heritage. He didn't squander the rich spiritual legacy they had entrusted to him but used it to honor the Lord and serve His people. What a tragedy it is when the descendants of godly families turn away from the Lord and lead lives of disobedience and rebellion (Judg. 2:10-15).

His remarkable audacity (Ezra 7:6). You wouldn't expect a priest and scholar like Ezra to dare to approach a mighty king and ask for permission to take a group of Jewish exiles to Jerusalem. Most scholars are retiring by nature, happy with their books and thoughts, and unwilling to get involved in the everyday affairs of life. The American poet and professor Archibald MacLeish wrote, "The scholar digs his ivory cellar in the ruins of the past and lets the present sicken as it will." But not Ezra!

Ezra's careful study of the Word of God had increased his faith (Rom. 10:17) and helped him understand God's plans for the Jewish remnant, and he wanted to be a part of those plans. Certainly as he studied the Old Testament Scriptures, he prayed for God to help His people; and God answered that prayer by calling him to go to Jerusalem. He gave Ezra the boldness to approach the king and the king a desire to cooperate with Ezra's requests.

When the first group of Jews left for Jerusalem in 537, it was because God moved upon the heart of Cyrus (Ezra 1:1-4); but now it was a lowly priest whom God used to touch the heart of King Artaxerxes.

His exceptional ability (7:10). When you recall that Ezra was born in Babylon, you can better appreciate his achievement as a skilled student of the Jewish Scriptures. Undoubtedly, some of the priests had brought copies of the Old Testament scrolls with them to Babylon, and these became very precious to the exiled spiritual leaders of the nation. There was no Jewish temple in Babylon, so the priests and Levites weren't obligated to minister, but some of them, like Ezra, devoted themselves to the study and teaching of the Word of God.[5]

When it comes to our relationship to the Word of God, Ezra is a good example for us to follow. He was a man with a prepared heart, devoted to the study of the Scriptures. "For Ezra had set his heart to study the law of the Lord" (v. 10, NASB). He would have agreed with the psalmist who wrote, "Oh, how I love Your law! It is my meditation all the day" (Ps. 119:97, NKJV). Even the king recognized and affirmed Ezra's great knowledge of the Scriptures (Ezra 7:11-14).

But Ezra did more than study the Word of God; he also practiced it in his daily life. It's in the obeying of the Word that we experience the blessing, not in the reading or the hearing of it (James 1:22-25). "This one is blessed in *what he does*" (v. 25, NKJV, italics added), not in what he thinks he knows. If our knowledge of the truth doesn't result in obedience, then we end up with a big head instead of a burning heart (1 Cor. 8:1; Luke 24:32); and truth becomes a toy to play with, not a tool to build with. Instead of building our Christian character, we only deceive ourselves and try to deceive others (1 John 1:5-10).

Ezra not only studied and obeyed the Word of God, but he also taught it to others. The priests and Levites were commanded by God to be teachers in Israel (Lev. 10:8-11; Deut. 33:10; Mal. 2:7), because that was the only way the people could learn God's truth. The common people couldn't afford to own scrolls of the Law, so it was up to the priests and Levites to read and explain the Scriptures to the people. "So they read in the book in the law of God distinctly, and gave the sense, and caused them to understand the reading" (Neh. 8:8). What a model for all preachers and teachers of the Bible to follow!

Each generation needs to discover the precious treasure of the Word of God, but that can't happen unless previous generations are faithful to learn the Word, guard it, obey it, and teach it. "And the things you have heard me say in the presence of many witnesses entrust to reliable men who will also be qualified to teach others" (2 Tim. 2:2, NIV).[6]

The three qualities mentioned in Ezra 7:10 are paralleled in our Lord's words in Matthew 13:52—"Therefore every scribe who has become a disciple of the kingdom of heaven is like a head of a household, who brings forth out of his treasure things new and old" (NASB). Ezra was a scribe who studied the Word, a disciple who obeyed and practiced the Word, and a householder who shared the Word with others. He's a good example for us to follow.

[Ezra 7:7-9 gives a summary of the journey to Jerusalem, the details of which we will study later.]

2. He directed a pagan ruler. (Ezra 7:11-28)

Just as God had worked in the heart and mind of Cyrus (1:1-4) and Darius (6:1-12), so He moved upon Artaxerxes I to permit Ezra and his people to return to their land. After hearing Ezra's requests, Artaxerxes took several steps to assist the Jews in this important undertaking.

Authorization (7:11-12, 25-26). First, Artaxerxes appointed Ezra as the leader of the group and also as the king's agent in Judah, even to the extent of giving him the right to inflict capital punishment on offenders (v. 26). From the way the king described Ezra in his official letter, it's clear that he was impressed with this Jewish priest-scribe and the Law which was the center of his life and ministry. The references to the law of God being in Ezra's hand (vv. 14, 25) may refer to actual scrolls that Ezra brought with him for his audience with the king, or perhaps it simply means "which you possess" (see v. 25, NIV).

Liberation (vv. 13-14). In his official letter, Artaxerxes gave the Jews the privilege to leave Babylon and go to Jerusalem with Ezra and join the remnant in rebuilding the city walls (4:12). Refer back to Ezra 4:7-23 for the account of the trials the Jews had in spite of the king's encouragement, and keep in mind that it was the rebuilding of the city, not the temple, that was involved, along with the spiritual restoration of the people. (See the suggested outline of the Book of Ezra.)

In 537, the first wave of Jewish refugees, about 50,000 of them, returned to Jerusalem under Zerubbabel's leadership to rebuild the temple. Now, in 458, Ezra was authorized to lead the second group, 1,500 men plus women and children, to help restore the walls and gates and to bring spiritual renewal to the people.

In 444, Nehemiah would arrive and finish the job of building the walls and hanging the gates.

Compensation (7:15-26). The Lord had told the struggling people in Jerusalem, "The silver is Mine, and the gold is Mine" (Hag. 2:8, NKJV), and now He proved it by opening the royal treasury and providing money to buy sacrifices to be offered at the temple in Jerusalem. The king commanded his officers beyond the river to give the Jews money out of the local royal treasury and defined the limits (Ezra 7:22). A hundred talents of silver would be nearly four tons of silver!

Then Artaxerxes gave Ezra the sacred articles from the original temple that hadn't been carried back by Zerubbabel (v. 19). Finally, he allowed Ezra to receive gifts from the Jews who remained in Babylon and from anybody else in the realm who wanted to contribute (see 1:4). Not every Jew wanted to go back, and not all were able; but all could contribute something to the work.

Like Darius before him (6:10), Artaxerxes was anxious that the God of Israel bless him and his sons and give success to his kingdom (7:23); so his generosity had somewhat of a selfish motive behind it. But it's doubtful if any person, king or commoner, ever does anything from an absolutely pure motive. It was remarkable that a pagan ruler would be this generous toward a captive people from whom he could hope to gain nothing. After all, if the God of Israel hadn't been able to protect the Jews from Babylonian Captivity, what could He do to help the Persians?

What Artaxerxes did for the Jews was clearly because of the good hand of God that was at work on behalf of God's chosen people. Finally, Artaxerxes exempted the priests, Levites, and temple servants from paying taxes or being conscripted for special duty to the empire (v. 24). Even if he had selfish motives, Artaxerxes was concerned that the temple ministry be strong and steady. To make certain that everything went smoothly as the Jews rebuilt the city, the king gave Ezra extensive authority to enforce the law (v. 26).

Celebration (vv. 27-28). This is the first occurrence of first-person narrative in the book; it continues through 9:15. He praises the Lord for moving the king to cooperate with his plans, and he sees this event as proof of God's mercy or covenant love. Ezra took no credit for this accomplishment; it was all the result of the "good hand of God" upon him. Without wasting any time, he assembled the chief men of the tribes and gathered the people who felt moved to travel to Jerusalem.

3. He gathered a willing remnant. (Ezra 8:1-30)

Many of the Jews were comfortable in Mesopotamia and quite satisfied to live and die there. During the Captivity, they had followed Jeremiah's counsel to be good citizens and settle down to normal lives (Jer. 29:1-7). Over the decades, the old generation had died and a new generation had arisen that had never seen

Jerusalem or the temple and probably had little interest in the welfare of their fellow Jews sacrificially laboring there. No doubt some of the Jewish men were in government employ or in business and were unable to relocate without paying a great price. Even our Lord had a problem enlisting disciples who were too settled in their successful lifestyles (Luke 9:57-62), and that explains why there's still a shortage of laborers (10:2).

Recruiting (Ezra 8:1-20). Wisely, Ezra gathered eighteen men who were the heads of Jewish families, knowing that they could influence their relatives, and the result was a total of 1,515 men, plus women and children (v. 21), who agreed to go with Ezra to Jerusalem. It wasn't as large a company as the first contingent that had gone with Zerubbabel and Joshua nearly eighty years before, but that didn't discourage them. If you compare the names in this list with those in Ezra 2:3-15, you'll see that many of Ezra's companions were related to those first settlers. The pioneer spirit seems to run in families.

The group left Babylon on the first day of the fifth month (7:9) and after about a week of travel stopped at the River Ahava (probably a canal) for three days before proceeding (8:15, 31). During that time, Ezra took inventory of the people and discovered that there were no Levites going with them,[7] so he sent a special committee of eleven leading men to recruit some Levites for the journey. The committee returned with only 38 Levites, but 220 temple servants came along with them. It's too bad the numbers weren't reversed; but even then, the laborers were few.

Trusting (vv. 21-23). Ezra's whole approach to this trip was a spiritual one; for if the good hand of God wasn't with them, everything would fail. But to receive the blessing and help of God, they had to humble themselves and seek His face, so Ezra called for three days of fasting and prayer, asking God to protect them on their long journey.

Ezra could have asked for an armed escort, but he felt that a request for protection would dishonor the Lord in the eyes of the pagan king. He had already told Artaxerxes that God's good hand was upon him and the Jews, so how could he then ask for human help? Ezra was relying on God's covenant with Abraham (Gen. 12:1-3), that those who bless the Jews are blessed by God, and there's a fine line between faith and presumption. Fourteen years later, Nehemiah didn't hesitate to request an armed escort from the king (Neh. 2:9); and Paul was glad for the Roman soldiers who protected him during his journey from Jerusalem to Caesarea (Acts 23). Were they less devoted than Ezra? Of course not! Undoubtedly the Lord gave Ezra special faith for this journey because He knew that Ezra's desire was only to glorify God. When you consider the factors involved in this expedition, you can see what great faith Ezra possessed. Here were several thousand Jews, inexperienced in travel and warfare, carrying a fortune in gold and silver, led by a scholar, not a soldier, and planning to travel through dangerous territory that was infested with brigands, and yet their leader didn't want an army to protect them! If anybody deserves the "Great Faith Award," it's Ezra!

Committing (Ezra 8:24-30). To twelve leading priests, Ezra committed the responsibility for the treasure: twenty-five tons of silver, nearly eight tons of silver and gold vessels, plus various other vessels and the offering given by the people. The twelve men represented the twelve tribes of Israel and had an obligation to them, but even more, it was the

Lord's treasure and these priests would one day give an accounting to Him.

In one sense, this event is a parable of the Christian life. God's people are on a difficult and dangerous journey to the heavenly Jerusalem (Heb. 12:22), and the Lord has committed certain of His treasures to us. Our task is to protect what He's given us and be ready to give a good account of our stewardship when we get to the end of the journey. The only difference is that, in our journey, God expects us to invest and increase the treasure and not just guard it. (See Matt. 25:14-30; 1 Tim. 1:11, 18-19; 6:20; 2 Tim. 1:13-14; 2:2.)

4. He gave them a safe journey. (Ezra 8:31-36)

As these Jewish èmigrès trudged through the wilderness, I wonder if they sang Psalm 121 to each other?

> I will lift up my eyes to the hills—
> From whence comes my help?
> My help comes from the Lord,
> who made heaven and earth.
> He will not allow your foot to be moved;
> He who keeps you will not slumber.
> Behold, He who keeps Israel
> shall neither slumber nor sleep.
> (Ps. 121:1-4, NKJV)

Arriving (Ezra 8:31). They left Babylon on the first day of the first month (7:9), tarried three days at the Ahava canal (8:15), and then left that encampment on the twelfth day of the first month (8:31), arriving at Jerusalem on the first day of the fifth month (7:9). They covered at least 900 miles in four months' time, and the good hand of God protected them and their possessions all the way.

Our God is the Alpha and the Omega; what He starts, He finishes (Rev. 1:8, 11; 21:6; 22:13; Isa. 41:4; 44:6). If God is at the beginning of the journey and we trust Him, He'll remain with us throughout the journey and take us to our destination. Each step of the way, God will see to it that we fulfill His loving purposes; and He will never forsake us (Isa. 43:1-2; Heb. 13:5-6).

Resting (Ezra 8:32). When my wife and I arrive home from an extended ministry trip, we find that it takes a couple of days to get rested and ready for the next assignment. Perhaps Ezra and his company arrived just before the Sabbath and wisely decided to prolong their rest. Sometimes the most spiritual thing we can do is to do nothing. Jesus told His busy disciples, "Come aside by yourselves to a deserted place and rest a while" (Mark 6:31, NKJV). As Vance Havner used to say, "If you don't come apart, you will come apart—you'll go to pieces."

Reckoning (Ezra 8:33-34). The priests took the treasure to the temple where it was weighed and inventoried, and all the facts were written down so an official report could be sent to the king. "Let all things be done decently and in order" (1 Cor. 14:40). God's servants must be faithful in every area of ministry, but especially in the matter of money. When you read 2 Corinthians 8–9, you see how scrupulous Paul and his associates were in handling the "relief offering" that the Gentile churches were sending to Jerusalem. "For we are taking pains to do what is right, not only in the eyes of the Lord but also in the eyes of men" (2 Cor. 8:21).

Worshiping (Ezra 8:35). The Jewish residents and the new arrivals gathered at the altar to worship God and declare their unity as His people. The twelve burnt offerings and twelve sin offerings were for the twelve tribes of Israel represented by the Jewish remnant in Jerusalem. Unlike the initial worship over seventy-five years before, when the altar was first set up, there's no record of anybody lamenting for "the good old days" (3:11-13).

The new arrivals were worshiping in their land, at their temple altar, for the first time in their lives! How Ezra's heart must have been stirred as he stood at the altar and participated in the worship service! "I was glad when they said to me, 'Let us go into the house of the Lord.' Our feet have been standing within your gates, O Jerusalem!" (Ps. 122:1-2, NKJV)

Clearance (Ezra 8:36). Having taken care of the spiritual matters that related to the nation and the temple, Ezra then presented himself and his credentials to the local Persian officials. "Render therefore to Caesar the things that are Caesar's, and to God the things that are God's" (Luke 20:25). He gave them the king's letter, and the officers were quick to obey the king's orders and assist the Jews in their projects. Ezra left Babylon with God's law in his heart and the king's letter in his hand and the good hand of God upon him. No wonder his mission was a success.

CHAPTER FOUR
THE GRACE OF GOD
Ezra 9–10

Ezra must have experienced great joy and satisfaction when he found himself in the Holy City, worshiping at the restored temple and ministering to the spiritual needs of the people. He certainly would have had an easier life had he remained "Scholar in Residence" for the exiles in Babylon, but "an easier life" wasn't on Ezra's agenda. God had called him to serve the Jewish remnant and teach them the Law of God, and he was obedient to God's call.

But four months after his arrival (7:9; 10:9), he learned that all wasn't well in Jerusalem because over 100 civil and religious leaders of the nation were guilty of deliberately disobeying the Law that Ezra had come to teach. How Ezra faced this difficult problem and solved it is an example for any Christian today who takes seriously God's repeated command, "You shall be holy; for I am holy" (Lev. 11:44, NKJV).[1]

1. Contamination: A sinful people (Ezra 9:1-2)

A group of laypeople informed Ezra that some of the leaders of the tribes, as well as some priests and Levites, had taken foreign wives for themselves and for their sons, and some of these men had even divorced their Jewish wives in order to marry heathen women (Mal. 2:10-16).

It was perfectly in order for these concerned Jews to report to Ezra what was going on, for he was one of their key spiritual leaders and carried great authority from the king (Ezra 7:25-26). It's likely that these concerned citizens had opposed the mixed marriages but were ignored, so they appealed to their leading priest and scribe for his help. The household of Chloe had informed Paul about some of the flagrant sins in the church at Corinth (1 Cor. 1:11), and he didn't rebuke them for it because there's a difference between "religious gossip" and honest concern. Covering sin never brings blessing to a nation or an individual (Prov. 28:13; see Deut. 17:1-7).

Disobedience (Ezra 9:1). The actions of these Jewish men were in violation of the Law of God (Ex. 34:15-16; Deut. 7:1-6). As the Book of Ruth testifies, it was legal for a Jewish man to marry a foreign woman if she fully renounced her old life and accepted her husband's faith; but this law didn't apply to the women native to the land of Canaan. According to Deuteronomy 20:1-15 and 21:10-14, a Jewish soldier could marry a female prisoner of war from a distant city, but he was forbidden to marry a Canaanite woman. But, when people decide to deliberately disobey the Word of God, they can usually find excuses to defend their actions. "There's a shortage of unmarried Jewish women," they might argue, "and we need to keep our families' names alive and help to increase the population." In other words, the end justifies the means. Blame the single Jewish women who wouldn't leave Babylon!

Did anyone offer to return to Babylon to find eligible wives for these single men?

Defilement (Ezra 9:2). God gave that marriage law to Israel in order to protect the nation from defilement. Because of these mixed marriages, the "holy seed" ("race," NIV) was being defiled by foreign women from the very nations God had commanded Israel to destroy (Deut. 7:1-6). The Jews weren't called a "holy nation" (Ex. 19:5-6) because they were better than anybody else, but because God had chosen them in His love and set them apart to do His will (Deut. 7:7-11). It's through Israel that "all families of the earth [shall be] blessed" (Gen. 12:3; 28:14), for the Jews gave the world three wonderful gifts: the knowledge of the true and living God, the written Word of God, and the Savior, Jesus Christ.

If it was wicked for single Jewish men to marry foreign women, how much greater was the guilt of married men who divorced their Jewish wives in order to marry pagan women! The Prophet Malachi denounced the Jewish men who did this (Mal. 2:13-16) and reminded them that Jehovah was seeking "a godly seed" (Ezra 9:15, KJV; "offspring," NIV, NKJV). This could refer to the promised Messiah as well as the future generations of Jews (Isa. 6:12-13). How could the Jews keep their nation "holy" if the men married out of the will of God? If the leaders of Israel continued to set such a bad example in defiling themselves, they would also defile the nation; and it wouldn't take long for Israel to lose their separated position in the world. Like Solomon (1 Kings 11), the men would start adopting the false gods and evil practices of their heathen wives; and before long, the true faith would be destroyed (Ex. 34:10-16). How then could God bring the Savior into the world?[2]

2. Concern: a privileged people (Ezra 9:3-15)3

How privileged the remnant was to have a spiritual leader like Ezra! He had been given special authority by the king (7:25-26), so you can see how serious it was for him to know what these men had done. Depending on the offense, Ezra could banish people from the community, confiscate their wealth, or even order their execution! But Ezra was first of all a man of God who sought God's best for his people, and he identified with them and made their burdens his burdens. He was supremely a man of prayer.

He didn't preach a sermon, although they needed to be reminded of what the Law said, nor did he immediately seek out the sinners and call them to confession and repentance, as important as that was. The first thing he did was to go to the temple, sit on the ground and express his grief before the people and before the Lord. As though he were mourning the dead, he tore his tunic and his cloak (9:5; see Gen. 37:29, 34; Josh. 7:6), and in further expression of sorrow, he plucked out hair from his head and his beard.[4] The people saw this and it reached their hearts.

Ezra was "appalled" (Ezra 9:3, NIV). The Hebrew word means "to be shocked, horrified, astonished, desolate." How could these men who were sons of the covenant commit such heinous sins? They had been so wonderfully helped by God in being freed from bondage and allowed to return to their land, and now they had rebelled against the Lord who had blessed them so much! And some of the offenders were priests and Levites who certainly knew the Law!

One of the maladies of society today is that people are no longer shocked by sin and willing to do something about it. Political leaders can flagrantly break the law and not only get away with it but be admired by the public and be elected to office again. Polls indicate that many Americans don't consider "character" to be an important factor when it comes to choosing leaders. In spite of all the noise about "religious revival" and "megachurches," God's people don't seem to be functioning well as salt and light in society. The salt has lost its flavor and no longer stings and prevents corruption, and the light is hidden under a bushel (Matt. 5:13-16).

During the time that Ezra sat fasting[5] and mourning, a crowd gathered around him made up of people who "trembled at the words of the God of Israel" (Ezra 9:4; see 10:9). The Jews had trembled greatly at Sinai when God spoke the Word (Ex. 19:16; Heb. 12:21), but later generations simply took God's Word for granted and didn't worry if they disregarded it. Too many Christians today are willing to read the Bible, study it, outline it, and even defend it; but they don't fear God and seek to obey what the Bible says. "But on this one will I look: on him who is poor and of a contrite spirit, and who trembles at My word" (Isa. 66:2, NKJV). Until God's people show respect for God and His Word, the Spirit of God can't work in mighty power as He longs to do.

At three o'clock in the afternoon, when the priests offered the daily evening sacrifice (Num. 28:1-4) and the people were assembling for prayer (Acts 3:1; Ps. 55:17; Dan. 6:10), Ezra began to call out to God and intercede for his people. As he wept (Ezra 10:1) and prayed, perhaps he was thinking of God's promise in 2 Chronicles 7:14, "If My people who are called by My name will humble themselves, and pray and seek My face, and turn from their wicked ways, then I will hear from heaven, and will forgive their sin and heal their land" (NKJV).

"We have sinned" (Ezra 9:5-7). Like both Nehemiah (Neh. 1:4-10) and Daniel (Dan. 9), Ezra identified himself with the people and their sins and spoke to God about "our iniquities" and not "their iniquities." Israel was one covenant nation before God, and the sins of one person affected all the people. For example, when Achan disobeyed God at Jericho, God said to Joshua, "*Israel* has sinned" (Josh. 7:11, NKJV, italics mine). The same principle applies to the local church (1 Cor. 5:6-8). Unless sin is dealt with, the whole assembly becomes defiled.

Like the publican in our Lord's parable (Luke 18:9-14), Ezra was too ashamed to look up to heaven as he prayed. The inability to blush because of sin is a mark of hypocrisy and superficial spiritual experience (Jer. 6:13-15). "Are they ashamed of their loathsome conduct? No, they have no shame at all; they do not even know how to blush" (Jer. 8:12, NIV). Words and actions that would have made earlier generations blush in shame are today part of the normal "entertainment" diet of the average TV viewer. When a nation turns sin into entertainment and laughs at what ought to make us weep, we are in desperate need of revival.

Why was Ezra so ashamed? *Because his people hadn't learned their lesson from all the trials that the nation had experienced (Ezra 9:7).* The new generation had grown up in Babylon and become so accustomed to the evil around them that they had no true fear of God. They should have been like Paul in Athens, who grieved over the wickedness that he saw (Acts 17:16), but instead, they first accepted Babylon's sinful way of life, then approved of it, and then enjoyed it. This compromising attitude went with them to Jerusalem and eventually revealed itself in their disobedience.

When you read the messages of the Prophet Malachi, you see how backslidden the priests were as they "served God" in the restored temple, and worldly spiritual leaders will produce worldly worshipers. While the older generation of Jews may have learned obedience through the chastening God sent them, the younger generation didn't learn the lessons their elders tried to teach them. The spiritual history of Israel, summarized in Ezra 9:7, is living proof that privileges bring responsibilities, and that much is required from those to whom much is given (Luke 12:48).

"We are unworthy of Your blessings" (Ezra 9:8-9). Ezra used five different images to picture what God's grace had done for the people who had returned to the land. In His grace, God had preserved a *remnant,* like a piece of cloth torn from a robe and kept safe (see 1 Kings 11:26-40). Throughout Jewish history, even when the nation turned from God, He always preserved a remnant that remained faithful to Him (1 Kings 19:18; Isa. 1:9; Mal. 3:16-17; Luke 2:38); and from that remnant, He made a new beginning.

Ezra then spoke about the *"nail in his holy place."* The image here is that of a nail pounded into the sanctuary wall or a tent peg driven into the ground, and it depicts security and stability, the foothold the Jews now had in their land. God had brought the remnant back to their land and given them favor with the king and the local officials, and had they trusted Him and obeyed His Word, He would have blessed them abundantly. But they chose to go their own way; so He had to chasten them with poor crops, bad weather, and serious economic problems (Hag. 1).

Third, God gave *light to their eyes,* by taking them out of Babylonian Captivity and returning them to their own land. To have your "eyes lightened" speaks of new life, new joy, and the dawning of a new day (Pss. 13:3; 34:5). It's similar to the next image, "to give us a little reviving in our bondage." The presence of the remnant in the land was like a resurrection from the dead! Their departure from Babylon was like the resurrection of a corpse from the grave.

Ezra's final image is that of *"a wall in Judah and in Jerusalem"* (Ezra 9:10), and it speaks of the protection God had given His people. He had worked in the hearts of kings—Cyrus, Darius, Xerxes, and Artaxerxes I—to gain them release from bondage and security in their own land. These were proud powerful rulers, but the Lord in His sovereignty used them to fulfill His purposes.

No wonder Ezra was ashamed. After all God had done for His people, they responded by disobeying His Word. *"We are speechless"* (Ezra 9:10-12). A knowledge of God's Word is indispensable for effective praying (John 15:7), and Ezra knew the Old Testament Scriptures thoroughly. In these verses, he refers to a number of passages from Moses and the prophets, including

Leviticus 18:24-26; Deuteronomy 7:1-6 and 11:8-9; Isaiah 1:19; 2 Kings 23:8-16; Ezekiel 5:11 and 37:25. It's obvious that these Jewish men were sinning against a flood of light.

The religious practices of the Canaanites were unspeakably vile and the stench reached to heaven. God had patiently held back His wrath, but the time of their judgment came when Israel invaded the land (Gen. 15:16). Wiping out the Canaanite civilization was like a surgeon removing a cancerous tumor or an engineer stopping a flood of poisonous sewage. Note the words that Ezra used in his prayer: unclean, filthiness, uncleanness, abominations.

God's law made it clear that Israel was to have no association with these nations, and now over 100 Jewish men had taken the first step by marrying into their families (Ezra 9:12). This could, of course, lead to peaceful relations and perhaps even wealth, but what about the future? What would happen to the children of these mixed marriages when it came time to obey God and become a part of the covenant? These men were sacrificing the future and paying a great price to do it. It wasn't worth it. No wonder Ezra was speechless and asked, "What shall we say after this?"

"We are guilty" (vv. 13-15). Guilt always shuts a person's mouth before God (Rom. 3:19). Sinners can give Him no logical reason for their sins and no acceptable excuses. Ezra not only confessed their sins but admitted that God had treated them far better than they deserved. He knew that God could easily destroy the remnant and start again with another people (Ex. 32:10; Num. 14:11-12), but, like Moses, he asked God to be gracious and forgiving.

Nobody could stand in His presence; nobody could speak in His presence. They were a guilty people, some of them because they deliberately broke God's law, and others because they allowed the offenders to get away with their sins. But God is righteous, and a righteous God must punish sin.

Before we try to untangle the problems of life, we must take time to seek God's face in prayer. This is not a long prayer. It can be read aloud very deliberately in only a few minutes, but it has tremendous depth. Charles Spurgeon used to say that it was the strength of our prayers, not the length of our prayers, that was important; and he was right. When you pray from a burdened heart, with a mind that's saturated with God's Word, then God will hear and answer.

3. Cooperation: a willing people (Ezra 10:1-8)

Never underestimate the power of the prayers of one dedicated believer (James 5:16-18), for the intercession of only one concerned person can make a difference in what God will do to and for His people. As Ezra prayed and wept at the altar before the house of God, "a very great congregation of men and women and children" came together, and they fell under conviction of sin.

"They too wept bitterly" (Ezra 10:1, NIV). This response wasn't something that Ezra worked up; it was something that he prayed down. The priests had offered a lamb on the altar, but Ezra gave the Lord an even greater sacrifice. "The sacrifices of God are a broken spirit, a broken and a contrite heart—these, O God, You will not despise" (Ps. 51:17, NKJV).

As I watch the contemporary religious scene, I note that churches occasionally feature "Christian comedians" and "Christian clowns," but not much is said about people who know how to weep and pray. As much as anyone else, I appreciate a sense of humor and a good laugh, but there comes a time when God's people need to stop laughing and start weeping and confessing. "Lament and mourn and weep! Let your laughter be turned to mourning and your joy to gloom. Humble yourselves in the sight of the Lord, and He will lift you up" (James 4:9-10, NKJV). That's God's formula for revival.

Shecaniah was the spokesman for the people, a man whose own relatives had sinned by marrying foreign women (Ezra 10:26). In my pastoral ministry, I've seen churches split and their witness almost destroyed because people have sided with their disobedient relatives in matters of discipline instead of with the Lord and His Word. Perhaps Shecaniah remembered what Moses wrote about the evils of being partial in judgment (Deut. 13:6-11; 17:1-13). Paul taught this same principle for the local church (1 Tim. 5:21).

To most of the people gathered around Ezra, the situation probably appeared hopeless; but not to Shecaniah, who said, "Yet now there is hope in Israel concerning this thing" (Ezra 10:2). He confessed that he and the rest of the nation were guilty, and then suggested a plan of action.

The plan was simple but demanding. First, the nation would corporately covenant to obey God's law. Then, Ezra and a group of men who "trembled at the Word" would decide how the matter would be settled; and the people promised to obey whatever was decreed. But everything had to be done according to the Law of Moses.

Ezra accepted the plan. He immediately swore in the leading priests and Levites as the committee to investigate the matter and see to it that the law was obeyed. But instead of participating immediately in the investigation, he withdrew into one of the rooms of the temple to fast and pray for God's guidance. He left it to the special committee to make the decisions and tell the people what to do. Wise is the leader who involves other people in the process, especially when the issue is so sensitive.

The committee issued a proclamation to the people of Jerusalem and of the outlying villages to appear in Jerusalem within three days or be in danger of expulsion from the community. At that time, each marriage would be investigated and the committee would discover who had violated the Mosaic Law.

A humble praying leader, a willing people, and a faithful and courageous committee worked together to accomplish a difficult task. What an example for the church to follow today!

4. Cleansing: an obedient people (Ezra 10:9-44)

On December 19, 458, the men of the two main tribes, Judah and Benjamin, plus exiles from the other tribes, gathered in the street before the temple to start the solemn investigation. (This meeting may have been convened at the Water Gate where Ezra later expounded the Law to the people, Neh. 8:1ff.)

It was December, the middle of the rainy season (October to mid-April), and the crowd trembled, not only because of the weather, but also because they were sure the heavy rain was a prelude to the judgment of God. Ezra made it clear that the mixed marriages would have to be dissolved, and he called upon the faithful Jews to separate themselves from those who had disobeyed God's law.

Once again, Ezra was given counsel by others, and he accepted it. (Blessed is the leader who has open ears to the ideas of others!) It was suggested that Ezra empower the committee of priests and

Levites to work with the leaders of the tribes, as well as the elders and judges of the towns (who knew their people), and let them determine who was guilty. It was impractical to try to interrogate so many people in one place, especially when the weather was so inclement; and the work couldn't be done in a day. Except for four men who dissented (Ezra 10:15), the crowd agreed with this idea and promised to obey.

Ten days later (v. 16), on December 29, Ezra and the leaders sat down together and began to investigate the matter; three months later, on March 27, 457, their work was finished. It must have been a difficult job to do, but they persisted with the help of the Lord. They discovered over 100 offenders,[6] including 27 priests, Levites, temple singers, and gatekeepers, people you would have expected to be models of obedience.

When spiritual leaders begin to sin, it doesn't take long for other people to follow. While we don't want to minimize the enormity of the sin, it should be noted that the number of offenders was very low when compared to the size of the population. Eighty years before, nearly 50,000 Jews had returned with Zerubbabel and Joshua, and during the ensuing years, the people surely multiplied. The total number of offenders was probably less than 1 percent of the residents. However, it's better to deal with these matters when the numbers are low, because the longer you wait, the more the sin will spread. Even one offender is one too many (Ecc. 9:18).

The guilty priests promised to put away their heathen wives, and they offered sacrifices to seek God's forgiveness (Ezra 10:18-19). We assume that the other offenders listed followed their example. God in His grace accepted their repentance and confession and granted them forgiveness.

The Book of Ezra opens in chapter 2 with a list of the names of the Jewish heroes who willingly returned to the land to serve the Lord. The book ends with a list of the sinners who disobeyed God but publicly made it right with the Lord and the people. But "making it right" didn't automatically heal every wound or remove every pain, because the women involved had to leave the community and go back to the heathen homes from which they had come, taking with them whatever children had been born to the union. It's easy to pull the nails out of the board, but it's impossible to pull out the holes that they leave behind.

Over thirteen years later, the problem of mixed marriages appeared again while Nehemiah was governor of Jerusalem (Neh. 13:23-31). It's possible for leaders to enforce the law and reform a nation's conduct, but only God can change the human heart and produce the kind of character that wants to do what's right. That's the difference between "reformation" and "revival."

Endnotes

Chapter One

1. *My Utmost for His Highest*, July 7.
2. Boorstin, Daniel J. *The Image: A Guide to Pseudo-Events in America* (New York: Harper and Row, 1964), 61.
3. If we calculate from the fall of Jerusalem (587–586) to when the first group of exiles returned (538), we have about fifty years. Perhaps we should see this as another evidence of God's mercy, for He shortened the time of their exile.
4. It may seem strange that not all the Jews elected to go back home, but they had been in Babylon several decades and had settled down to as normal a life as they could have away from their homes and temple. In fact,

the Prophet Jeremiah had instructed them to be the best citizens possible (Jer. 29:1–7). Lacking a temple and priesthood, the Jews developed synagogue worship during their captivity; and with the synagogue appeared the body of teachers we know as the scribes and Pharisees. Life in captivity was neither dangerous nor unbearable; and for many of the Jews, the long journey back to Judah was an impossible challenge. The Book of Esther and the Book of Daniel prove that God had work in Babylon for some of the Jews to do.

5. Is it right for God's people to accept and use for God's work wealth that comes from unbelievers? In one sense, the Babylonians owed this money to the Jews whom they plundered so ruthlessly during their invasion of Judah. The Prophet Haggai (2:8) makes it clear that all wealth belongs to God and He can distribute it as He sees fit. However, we need to follow the example of Abraham and refuse wealth that would compromise our testimony or put us under obligation to unbelievers (Gen. 14:18–24). Deuteronomy 23:17–18 warns us that money earned from sinful activities is not welcomed by God.
6. "Tirshatha" in the KJV, a Persian word translated "governor" in the NIV and NASB. The same title was given to Nehemiah (Neh. 7:65, 70; 8:9; 10:1). It means "the feared one" and is the equivalent of "Your Excellency" or "Your Reverence" in English. Charles Spurgeon's wife used to call him "the Tirshatha."
7. We aren't told why Joshua the high priest didn't have the Urim and Thummim, as they were an important part of his glorious vestments. During the Babylonian Captivity, the Jews didn't seem to have the special miracles from God that had often accompanied them (Ps. 74:9), although the Prophets Ezekiel and Daniel had wonderful revelations from God. There is no biblical evidence that the use of the Urim and Thummim was restored after the captivity.
8. Maclaren, Alexander. *Expositions of Holy Scripture* (Grand Rapids: Baker Book House, 1974), vol. 1, 77.
9. Ibid., vol. 3, 290.

CHAPTER TWO

1. Tozer, A.W. *The Knowledge of the Holy* (New York: Harper and Brothers, 1961), 85.
2. Taylor, Dr. and Mrs. Howard. *Hudson Taylor's Spiritual Secret* (London: China Inland Mission, 1949), 111.
3. Ezra 4:8–6:18 is written in Aramaic rather than Hebrew, and so is Ezra 7:12–26. These letters and the decree were copied from official documents kept in government archives.
4. Ezra 4:12 is the first place in Scripture where you find the word "Jews." It refers, of course, to the people of Judah.
5. Historians estimate that Artaxerxes I collected between 20 and 35 million dollars annually from his subjects.
6. Spurgeon, Charles. *Metropolitan Tabernacle Pulpit* (Pasadena, Texas: Pilgrim Publications, 1986), vol. 7, 13.
7. When he laid the foundation of the temple, Zerubbabel followed the dimensions given in the Law of Moses, but the edict allowed him to make a bigger structure.
8. The Hebrew word for "dedication" is *hanukkah*, which is the name of the Jewish holiday in December during which they remember the rededication of the temple in 165 B.C. The temple had been taken by the Gentiles and defiled, but the courageous Jews, led by Judas Maccabeus, captured it, cleansed it, and dedicated it to the Lord.
9. That Darius, King of Persia, should be called "king of Assyria" in 6:22 shouldn't disturb us. In Nehemiah 13:6, Artaxerxes, king of Persia, is called "king of Babylon." Darius' kingdom included Assyria, so the title applied.

CHAPTER THREE

1. Of course, God is spirit and doesn't possess literal hands such as we do. The phrase is what theologians call "anthropomorphic," that is, attributing to God something that is true of humans ("anthrop" = human; "morphos" = form). God doesn't have eyes, but He "sees" what's going on in the world; He doesn't have ears, but He "hears" our cries. Because He's a Person, God has the ability to act and respond, and the Bible uses human terminology to explain this. When Isaiah wanted to show the greatness of God, he said that God measured the waters "in the hollow of His hand" (Isa. 40:12); and the psalmist reminds us that all God has to do to feed His creatures is open His hand (Ps. 104:28). "You

open Your hand and satisfy the desire of every living thing" (Ps. 145:16, NKJV).

2. He was called "Artaxerxes Longimanus," which is Latin for "Artaxerxes the long-handed." (The Greek equivalent is "Macrochier.") He may have been called "the long-handed" because his great authority reached out so far, or because he was generous to his subjects. But it was God's hand that moved the king's hand to sign the edict that enabled Ezra to take a remnant of Jews to their land to serve the Lord.
3. Nixon, Richard. *Leaders* (New York: Warner Books, 1982), 1.
4. Hilkiah was high priest during the reign of godly King Josiah and found the Book of the Law while the temple was being repaired (2 Kings 22). Zadok was faithful to King David during David's most trying times, especially when Absalom and Adonijah tried to capture the crown (2 Sam. 15 and 17; 1 Kings 1–2). Phinehas was the courageous priest in Moses' day who was honored for opposing Israel's compromise with the Midianites (Num. 25; Ps. 106:30).
5. Many students believe that Ezra was one of the founders of the synagogue, which in Babylon took the place of the temple as a place for assembly, worship, and teaching.
6. Moses wrote what God told him (Ex. 24:4, 12; Deut. 28:58; 29:21; 30:10; 31:9, 19, 24) and also kept a record of Israel's journeys (Num. 33:2). He left Joshua "the Book of the Law" (Josh. 1:8) to which Joshua added his record (23:6). Samuel wrote in the book (1 Sam. 10:25) and others added to it (1 Chron. 29:29). The Book of the Law apparently was "lost" in the temple, of all places, and recovered during Josiah's day (2 Chron. 34–35). The Jewish scribes were very careful to copy the Scriptures accurately and preserve them from textual corruption. Thanks to their faithfulness and the providence of God, we have the Scriptures today.
7. Zerubbabel didn't have an abundance of Levites in his company, only 733 out of almost 50,000 men, less than 2 percent. One would think that God's special servants would be anxious to go back to their land and serve, but they decided to stay.

Chapter Four

1. This injunction is also found in Leviticus 11:45; 19:2; 20:7, 26; 21:8; and 1 Peter 1:15–16. When God repeats a command eight times, His people had better pay attention!
2. Christians are exhorted to marry "in the Lord" (1 Cor. 7:39) and not join themselves with unbelievers (2 Cor. 6:14–18). The Old Covenant distinction between Jews and Gentiles no longer applies, for God had made all nations of one blood and there is "no difference" (Acts 10; 17:26; Rom. 3:21–23). The Messiah has come, the work of salvation has been completed, and believing Jews and Gentiles may marry in the Lord and serve God.
3. Three great prayers of confession are found in the Old Testament: Ezra 9; Nehemiah 9; and Daniel 9.
4. When Nehemiah discovered sin, he plucked out the hair of the offenders! (Neh. 13:25).
5. The word "heaviness" (KJV; "self-abasement," NIV) suggests that Ezra fasted during this trying time, not because he was trying to earn God's blessing, but because he was just too burdened to eat.
6. Depending on how you translate the text and determine the various relationships, there were either 110 or 111 offenders.

NEHEMIAH

A SUGGESTED OUTLINE OF THE BOOK OF NEHEMIAH

I. CONCERN—1
1. Information—1:1-3
2. Intercession—1:4-9
3. Intention—1:10-11

II. CONSTRUCTION—2-3
1. Authority—2:1-10
2. Investigation—2:11-16
3. Challenge—2:17-20
4. Assignments—3:1-32

III. CONFLICT—4-6
1. Ridicule—4:1-6
2. Plots—4:7-9
3. Discouragement—4:10
4. Fear—4:11-23
5. Selfishness—5:1-19
6. Compromise—6:1-4
7. Slander—6:5-9
8. Threats—6:10-16
9. Intrigue—6:17-19

IV. CONSECRATION—7-12
1. The people—7:1-12:26
   a. Checking the genealogy—7
   b. Teaching the Word—8
   c. Confessing sin—9
   d. Making a covenant—10:1-12:26
2. The walls—12:27-47

V. CLEANSING—13

CONTENTS

CHAPTER ONE
DOES ANYBODY REALLY CARE?
Nehemiah 1

"The worst sin toward our fellow creatures is not to hate them, but to be indifferent to them: that's the essence of inhumanity."

George Bernard Shaw put those words into the mouth of the Rev. Anthony Anderson in the second act of his play *The Devil's Disciple.* The statement certainly summarizes what Jesus taught in the Parable of the Good Samaritan (Luke 10:25-37); and it rebukes all those who fold their arms complacently, smile benignly, and say somewhat sarcastically, "Ask me if I care!"

Nehemiah was the kind of person who cared. He cared about the traditions of the past and the needs of the present. He cared about the hopes for the future. He cared about his heritage, his ancestral city, and the glory of his God. He revealed this caring attitude in four different ways.

1. He cared enough to ask. (Neh. 1:1-3) Nehemiah was a layman, cupbearer to the great "Artaxerxes Longimanus," who ruled Persia from 464 to 423 B.C. He is identified as the son of Hachaliah to distinguish him from other Jews of the same name (Neh. 3:16; Ezra 2:2). Nehemiah means "The Lord has comforted."

A cupbearer was much more than our modern "butler" (see Gen. 40). It was a position of great responsibility and privilege. At each meal, he tested the king's wine to make sure it wasn't poisoned. A man who stood that close to the king in public had to be handsome, cultured, knowledgeable in court procedures, and able to converse with the king and advise him if asked (see 41:1-13). Because he had access to the king, the cupbearer was a man of great influence, which he could use for good or for evil.

That Nehemiah, a Jew, held such an important position in the palace speaks well of his character and ability (Dan. 1:1–4). For nearly a century, the Jewish remnant had been back in their own land, and Nehemiah could have joined them; but he chose to remain in the palace. It turned out that God had a work for him to do there that he could not have accomplished elsewhere. God put Nehemiah in Susa just as He had put Esther there a generation before, and just as He had put Joseph in Egypt and Daniel in Babylon. When God wants to accomplish a work, He always prepares His workers and puts them in the right places at the right time.

The Hebrew month of Chislev runs from mid-November to mid-December on our calendar; and the twentieth year of Artaxerxes was the year 444 B.C. Shushan (or Susa) was the capital city of the Persian Empire and the site of the king's winter palace. No doubt it was just another routine day when Nehemiah met his brother Hanani (see Neh. 7:2), who had just returned from a visit to Jerusalem, but it turned out to be a turning point in Nehemiah's life.

Like large doors, great life-changing events can swing on very small hinges. It was just another day when Moses went out to care for his sheep, but on that day he heard the Lord's call and became a prophet (Ex. 3). It was an ordinary day when David was called home from shepherding his flock; but on that day, he was anointed king (1 Sam. 16). It was an ordinary day when Peter, Andrew, James, and John were mending their nets after a night of failure; but that was the day Jesus called them to become fishers of men (Luke 5:1–11). You never know what God has in store, even in a commonplace conversation with a friend or relative; so keep your heart open to God's providential leading. I attended a birthday party one evening when I was nineteen years old, and a statement made to me there by a friend helped direct my life into the plans God had for me; and I will be forever grateful.

Why would Nehemiah inquire about a struggling remnant of people who lived hundreds of miles away? After all, he was the king's cupbearer and he was successfully secure in his own life. Certainly it wasn't his fault that his ancestors had sinned against the Lord and brought judgment to the city of Jerusalem and the kingdom of Judah. A century and a half before, the Prophet Jeremiah had given this word from the Lord: "For who will have pity on you, O Jerusalem? Or who will bemoan you? Or who will turn aside to ask how you are doing?" (Jer. 15:5, NKJV) *Nehemiah was the man God had chosen to do those very things!*

Some people prefer *not* to know what's going on, because information might bring obligation. "What you don't know can't hurt you," says the old adage; but is it true? In a letter to a Mrs. Foote, Mark Twain wrote, "All you need in this life is ignorance and confidence; then success is sure." But what we don't know *could* hurt us a great deal! There are people in the cemetery who chose not to know the truth. The slogan for the 1987 AIDS publicity campaign was "Don't die of ignorance"; and that slogan can be applied to many areas of life besides health.

Nehemiah asked about Jerusalem and the Jews living there because he had a caring heart. When we truly care about people, we want the facts, no matter how painful they may be. "Practical politics consists in ignoring facts," American historian Henry Adams said; but Aldous Huxley said, "Facts do not cease to exist because they are ignored." Closing our eyes and ears to the truth could be the first step toward tragedy for ourselves as well as for others.

What did Nehemiah learn about Jerusalem and the Jews? Three words summarize the bad news: remnant, ruin, and reproach. Instead of a land inhabited by a great nation, only a remnant of people lived there; and they were in great affliction and struggling to survive. Instead of a magnificent city, Jerusalem was in shambles; and where there had once been great glory, there was now nothing but great reproach.

Of course, Nehemiah had known all his life that the city of his fathers was in ruins, because the Babylonians had destroyed Jerusalem's walls, gates, and temple in 586 B.C. (2 Kings 25:1-21). Fifty years later, a group of 50,000 Jews had returned to Jerusalem to rebuild the temple and the city. Since the Gentiles had hindered their work, however, the temple was not completed for twenty years (Ezra 1–6), and the gates and walls never were repaired. Perhaps Nehemiah had hoped that the work on the walls had begun again and that the city was now restored. Without walls and gates, the city was open to ridicule and attack. See Psalms 48, 79, 84, and 87 to see how much loyal Jews loved their city.

Are we like Nehemiah, anxious to know the truth even about the worst situations? Is our interest born of concern or idle curiosity? When we read missionary prayer letters, the news in religious periodicals, or even our church's ministry reports, do we want the facts, and do the facts burden us? Are we the kind of people who care enough to ask?

2. He cared enough to weep. (Neh. 1:4) What makes people laugh or weep is often an indication of character. People who laugh at others' mistakes or misfortunes, or who weep over trivial personal disappointments, are lacking either in culture or character, and possibly both. Sometimes weeping is a sign of weakness; but with Nehemiah, it was a sign of strength, as it was with Jeremiah (Jer. 9:1), Paul (Acts 20:19), and the Lord Jesus (Luke 19:41). In fact, Nehemiah was like the Lord Jesus in that he willingly shared the burden that was crushing others. "The reproaches of them that reproached Thee are fallen upon Me" (Ps. 69:9; Rom. 15:3).

When God puts a burden on your heart, don't try to escape it; for if you do, you may miss the blessing He has planned for you. The Book of Nehemiah begins with "great affliction" (Neh. 1:3), but before it closes, there is great joy (8:12, 17). "Weeping may endure for a night, but joy cometh in the morning" (Ps. 30:5). Our tears water the "seeds of providence" that God has planted on our path; and without our tears, those seeds could never grow and produce fruit.

It was customary for the Jews to sit down when they mourned (Ezra 9:1-4; 2:13). Unconsciously, Nehemiah was imitating the grieving Jewish captives who had been exiled in Babylon years before (Ps. 137:1). Like Daniel, Nehemiah probably had a private room where he prayed to God with his face toward Jerusalem (Dan. 6:10; 1 Kings 8:28-30). Fasting was required of the Jews only once a year, on the annual Day of Atonement (Lev. 16:29); but Nehemiah spent several days fasting, weeping, and praying. He knew that somebody had to do something to rescue Jerusalem, and he was willing to go.

3. He cared enough to pray. (Neh. 1:5-10) This prayer is the first of twelve instances of prayer recorded in this book. (See 2:4; 4:4, 9; 5:19; 6:9, 14; 9:5ff; 13:14, 22, 29, 31.) The Book of Nehemiah opens and closes with prayer. It is obvious that Nehemiah was a man of faith who depended wholly on the Lord to help him accomplish the work He had called him to do. The Scottish novelist George MacDonald said, "In whatever man does without God, he must fail miserably, or succeed more miserably." Nehemiah succeeded because he depended on God. Speaking about the church's ministry today, the late Alan Redpath said, "There is too much working before men and too little waiting before God."

This prayer begins with **ascription of praise to God (1:5).** "God of heaven" is the title Cyrus used for the Lord when he announced that the Jews could return to their land (2 Chron. 36:22-23; Ezra 1:1-2). The heathen gods were but idols on the earth, but the God of the Jews was Lord in heaven. Ezra often used this divine title (5:11-12; 6:9; 7:12, 21, 23), and it is found four times in Nehemiah (1:4-5; 2:4, 20) and three times in Daniel (2:18-19, 44). Nehemiah began his prayer as we should begin our prayers: "Our Father which art in heaven, Hallowed be Thy name" (Matt. 6:9).

To what kind of a God do we pray when we lift our prayers to "the God of heaven"? We pray to a "great and awesome God" (Neh. 1:5, NKJV; and see 4:14, 8:6, and 9:32), who is worthy of our praise and worship. If you are experiencing great affliction (v. 3) and are about to undertake a great work (4:19; 6:3), then you need the great power (1:10), great goodness (9:25, 35), and great mercy (v. 31) of a great God. Is the God you worship big enough to handle the challenges that you face?

He is also a God who keeps His Word (1:5). The Lord had made a covenant with His people Israel, promising to bless them richly if they obeyed His Word, but warning that He would chasten them if they disobeyed (Lev. 26; Deut. 27-30). The city of Jerusalem was in ruins, and the nation was feeble because the people had sinned against the Lord. (See Ezra's prayer of confession in Ezra 9 and the prayer of the nation in Neh. 9.)

The greater part of Nehemiah's prayer was devoted to **confession of sin (1:6-9).** The God who promised blessing and chastening also promised forgiveness if His people would repent and turn back to Him (Deut. 30; 1 Kings 8:31-53). It was this promise that Nehemiah was claiming as he prayed for himself and the nation. God's eyes are upon His people and His ears are open to their prayers (1 Kings 8:29; 2 Chron. 7:14). The word *remember* is a key word in this book (Neh. 1:8; 4:14; 5:19; 6:14; 13:14, 22, 29, 31).

Note that Nehemiah used the pronoun "we" and not "they," identifying himself with the sins of a generation he didn't even know. It would have been easy to look back and blame his ancestors for the reproach of Jerusalem, but Nehemiah looked within and blamed himself! "We have sinned! We have dealt very corruptly!"

A few years ago, when the "media scandals" brought great reproach to the church, I wrote in my book *The Integrity Crisis:*

> To begin with, the integrity crisis involves more than a few people who were accused of moral and financial improprieties. *The integrity crisis involves the whole church.* I am not saying that people didn't sin, nor am I preaching "collective guilt," whatever that is. I only want to emphasize that, in the body of Christ, we belong to one another, we affect one another, and we can't escape one another. The press did not create the crisis, the church did; and the church will have to solve it (Nashville: Oliver Nelson, 1988; p. 18).

When one Jewish soldier, Achan, sinned at Jericho, God said that "the children of Israel committed a trespass" and that "Israel" sinned and transgressed the covenant (Josh. 7:1, 11). Since the sin of one man was the sin of the whole nation, it brought shame and defeat to the whole nation. Once that sin had been dealt with, God could again bless His people with victory.

How do we know that God forgives our sins when we repent and confess to Him? *He has so promised in His Word.* Nehemiah's prayer is saturated with quotations from and allusions to the covenants of God found in Leviticus and Deuteronomy. He certainly knew the Old Testament Law! In Nehemiah 1:8-9, he reminded God of His words found in Deuteronomy 28:63-67 and 30:1-10, just as we remind the Lord of His promise in 1 John 1:9. Nehemiah asked God to forgive His people, regather them to their land, and restore them to His favor and blessing.

This humble prayer closed with **an expression of confidence (Neh. 1:10-11).** To begin with, he had confidence in the power of God. When the Bible speaks of the eyes, ears, and hands of the Lord, it is using only human language to describe divine activity. God is spirit, and therefore does not have a body such as humans have; but He is able to see His people's needs, hear their prayers, and work on their behalf with His mighty hand. Nehemiah knew that he was too weak to rebuild Jerusalem, but he had faith that God would work on his behalf.

He also had confidence in God's faithfulness. "Now these are Thy servants and Thy people" (v. 10). In bringing Babylon to destroy Jerusalem and take the people captive, God chastened the Jews sorely; but He did not forsake them! They were still His people and His servants. He had redeemed them from Egypt by His great power (Ex. 14:13-31) and had also set them free from bondage in Babylon. Would He not, in His faithfulness, help them rebuild the city?

Unlike Elijah, who thought he was the only faithful Jew left (1 Kings 19:10), Nehemiah had confidence that God would raise up other people to help him in his work. He was sure that many other Jews were also praying and that they would rally to the cause once they heard that God was at work. Great leaders are not only believing people who obey the Lord and courageously move ahead, but they also challenge others to go with them. You can't be a true leader unless you have followers, and Nehemiah was able to enlist others to help him do the work.

Finally, Nehemiah was confident that God would work in the heart of Artaxerxes and secure for the project the official support that it needed (Neh. 1:10). Nehemiah couldn't simply quit his job and move to Jerusalem. He was an appointee of the king, and he needed the king's permission for everything he did. Furthermore, he needed the king's provision and protection so he could travel to Jerusalem and remain away from his post until the work was completed. Without official authority to govern, an official guard for the journey, and the right to use materials from the king's forest, the entire project was destined to fail. Eastern monarchs were absolute despots, and it was not easy to approach them or convince them. But "the king's heart is in the hand of the Lord; He directs it like a watercourse wherever He pleases" (Prov. 21:2, NIV).

Too often, we plan our projects and then ask God to bless them; but Nehemiah didn't make that mistake. He sat down and wept (Neh. 1:4), knelt down and prayed, and then stood up and worked because he knew he had the blessing of the Lord on what he was doing.

4. He cared enough to volunteer. (Neh. 1:11)

It has well been said that prayer is not getting man's will done in heaven but getting God's will done on earth. However, for God's will to be done on earth, He needs people to be available for Him to use. God does "exceedingly abundantly above all that we ask or think, according to the power that works *in us* (Eph. 3:20, NKJV, italics mine). If God is going to answer prayer, He must start by working in the one doing the praying! He works in us and through us to help us see our prayers answered.

While Nehemiah was praying, his burden for Jerusalem became greater and his vision of what needed to be done became clearer. Real prayer keeps your heart and your head in balance so your burden doesn't make you impatient to run ahead of the Lord and ruin everything. As we pray, God tells us *what* to do, *when* to do it, and *how* to do it; and all are important to the accomplishing of the will of God. Some Christian workers are like Lord Ronald in one of Stephen Leacock's short stories who "flung himself upon his horse and rode madly off in all directions."

Nehemiah planned to volunteer to go to Jerusalem to supervise the rebuilding of the walls. He didn't pray for God to send somebody else, nor did he argue that he was ill-equipped for such a difficult task. He simply said, "Here am I—send me!" He knew that he would have to approach the king and request a leave of absence. Eastern kings' words meant life or death. What would happen to Nehemiah's plans if he approached Artaxerxes on the wrong day, when the king was ill or displeased with something or someone in the palace? No matter how you look at it, Nehemiah was facing a test of faith; but he knew that his God was a great God and would see him through.

The king's cupbearer would have to sacrifice the comfort and security of the palace for the rigors and dangers of life in a ruined city. Luxury would be replaced by ruins, and prestige by ridicule and slander. Instead of sharing the king's bounties, Nehemiah would personally pay for the upkeep of scores of people who would eat at his table. He would leave behind the ease of the palace and take up the toils of encouraging a beaten people and finishing an almost impossible task.

And with the help of God, *he did it!* In fifty-two days, the walls were rebuilt, the gates were restored, and the people were rejoicing! And it all started with a man who cared.

Abraham cared and rescued Lot from Sodom (Gen. 18-19). Moses cared and delivered the Israelites from Egypt. David cared and brought the nation and the kingdom back to the Lord. Esther cared and risked her life to save her nation from genocide. Paul cared and took the Gospel throughout the Roman Empire. Jesus cared and died on the cross for a lost world.

God is still looking for people who care, people like Nehemiah, who cared enough to ask for the facts, weep over the needs, pray for God's help, and then volunteer to get the job done.

"Here am I, Lord—send me!"

CHAPTER TWO
THE MOUNTAIN STARTS TO MOVE
Nehemiah 2

Unknown to him, Nehemiah was about to join the glorious ranks of the "champions of faith"; and in the centuries to follow, his name would be included with heroes like Abraham, Joseph, Moses, Joshua, Esther, Deborah, and David. One person can make a big difference in this world, if that person knows God and really trusts in Him. Because faith makes a difference, we can make a difference in our world to the glory of God.

"Faith is a living, daring confidence in God's grace," said Martin Luther. "It is so sure and certain that a man could stake his life on it a thousand times." The promise is that "all things are possible to him who believes" (Mark 9:23, NKJV). Jesus said living faith can move mountains! (Matt. 17:20)

This chapter describes three evidences of Nehemiah's faith. As we study these evidences of faith, we must examine our own hearts to see whether or not we are really walking and working by faith.

1. He had the faith to wait. (Neh. 2:1-3) Since the Jewish month of Nisan would be our mid-March to mid-April, it would indicate that four months have passed since Nehemiah received the bad news about the plight of Jerusalem. As every believer should, Nehemiah patiently waited on the Lord for directions; because it is "through faith and patience" that we inherit the promises (Heb. 6:12). "He that believeth shall not make haste" (Isa. 28:16). True faith in God brings a calmness to the heart that keeps us from rushing about and trying to do in our own strength what only God can do. We must know not only how to *weep and pray,* but also how to *wait and pray.*

Three statements in Scripture have a calming effect on me whenever I get nervous and want to rush ahead of the Lord: "Stand still, and see the salvation of the Lord" (Ex. 14:13); "Sit still . . . until you know how the matter will turn out" (Ruth 3:18, NKJV); "Be still, and know that I am God" (Ps. 46:10). When you wait on the Lord in prayer, you are not wasting your time; you are investing it. God is preparing both you and your circumstances so that His purposes will be accomplished. However, when the right time arrives for us to act by faith, we dare not delay.

Eastern monarchs were sheltered from anything that might bring them unhappiness (Es. 4:1-2); but on that particular day, Nehemiah could not hide his sorrow. "By sorrow of the heart the spirit is broken" (Prov. 15:13), and Psalm 102 certainly describes Nehemiah's feelings about Jerusalem. Perhaps each morning, Nehemiah prayed, "Lord, if today is the day I speak to the king about our plans, then open the way for me."

The king noticed that his cupbearer was carrying a burden. Had Artaxerxes been in a bad mood, he might have banished Nehemiah or even ordered him killed; but instead, the king inquired why his servant was so sad. "The king's heart is in the hand of the Lord, as the rivers of water He turneth it whithersoever He will" (Prov. 21:1). World leaders are only God's servants, whether they know it or not. "O Lord God of our fathers, are You not the God who is in heaven? You rule over all the kingdoms of the nations. Power and might are in Your hand, and no one can withstand You" (2 Chron. 20:6, NIV).

2. He had the faith to ask. (Neh. 2:4-8) The king asked him, "What is it you want?" What an opportunity for Nehemiah! All the power and wealth of the kingdom were wrapped up in that question!

As he was accustomed to do, Nehemiah sent one of his quick "telegraph prayers" to the Lord (4:4; 5:9; 6:9, 14; 13:14, 22, 29, 31). But keep in mind that these "emergency prayers" were backed up by four months of fasting and praying. If Nehemiah had not been diligent to pray in private, his "telegraph prayers" might have gone unanswered. "He had only an instant for that prayer," wrote George Morrison. "Silence would have been misinterpreted. Had he closed his eyes and lingered in devotion, the king immediately would have suspected treason."[1]

It encourages my prayer life when I contrast the earthly throne of Artaxerxes with the throne of grace in heaven. Nehemiah had to wait for an invitation before he could share his burden with the king, but we can come to the throne of grace at any time with any need (Heb. 4:14-16). Artaxerxes saw the sorrow on Nehemiah's face, but our Lord sees our hearts and not only knows our sorrows but also feels them with us. People approaching the throne of Persia had to be very careful what they said, lest they anger the king; but God's people can tell Him whatever burdens them. (The word *boldly* in Heb. 4:16 means "freedom of speech.") You are never sure of the mood of a human leader, but you can always be sure of God's loving welcome.

Jewish rabbis often answer a question with a question, and Nehemiah followed that example. Instead of telling the king what he planned to do, he aroused the king's sympathy and interest with a question regarding how he should feel about the sad plight of his ancestral city and the graves of his forefathers. It was good psychology, and God used Nehemiah's reply to get the king's sympathetic attention (Luke 21:14-15). A pagan monarch would probably not sorrow over the ruins of Jerusalem, but he would certainly show respect for the dead.

Nehemiah was a true patriot whose dreams for the future were motivated by the values of the past. He did not try to duplicate the past, for that was impossible; rather, he built on the past so that Israel would have a future. To Nehemiah, the past was a rudder to guide him and not an anchor to hold him back. When Samuel Johnson called patriotism "the last refuge of a scoundrel," he was referring to that temporary zeal that uses "love of country" as propaganda for selfish purposes. United States Ambassador to the United Nations Adlai Stevenson said that patriotism was not "a short and frenzied outburst of emotion, but the tranquil and steady dedication of a lifetime." That certainly describes Nehemiah's kind of patriotism.

Not only had Nehemiah *prayed* for this opportunity, but he had also *planned* for it and had his answer ready. During those four months of waiting, he had thought the matter through and knew exactly how he would approach the project. His reply to the king can be summarized in two requests: "Send me!" (Neh. 2:4-6) and "Give me!" (vv. 7-10)

Nehemiah could not leave his post without the approval of the king, nor could he work in Jerusalem without the authority of the king. Pressure from local officials had stopped the work once before (Ezra 4), and Nehemiah didn't want history to repeat itself. He asked Artaxerxes to appoint him governor of Judah and to give him the authority he needed to rebuild the city walls. He told the king when he expected to return, but we don't know what that date was. According to Nehemiah 5:14, Nehemiah spent twelve years as governor. He went back to Persia briefly to report to the king, but then returned to Jerusalem to correct the abuses that appeared during his absence (13:6-7).

But Nehemiah asked for even more. He needed letters of introduction that would guarantee safe travel and hospitality between Susa and Jerusalem. He also requested letters of authority that would provide the materials needed for the construction of buildings and walls. (Nehemiah had done his research well. He even knew the name of the keeper of the king's forest!) Artaxerxes gave him what he asked, but it was the good hand of God that made the king so cooperative (see 2:18; and Ezra 7:6, 9, 28).

When Jesus sent His disciples out to minister, He first gave them the authority they needed to do the job; and He promised to meet their every need (Matt. 10:1-15). As we go forth to serve the Lord, we have behind us all authority in heaven and on earth (28:18); so we don't have to be afraid. The important thing is that we go where He sends us and that we do the work He has called us to do.

Nehemiah is a good example of how believers should relate to unsaved officials as they seek to do the work of God. Nehemiah respected the king and sought to work within the lines of authority that existed in the empire. He didn't say, "I have a commission from the Lord to go to

Jerusalem, and I'm going whether you like it or not!" When it comes to matters of conscience, we must always obey God rather than men (Acts 5:29); but even then, we must show respect for authority (see Rom. 13 and 1 Peter 2:11-25). Daniel and his friends took the same approach as did Nehemiah, and God honored them as well (Dan. 1).

The king's response is evidence of the sovereignty of God in the affairs of nations. We expect God to be able to work through a dedicated believer like Nehemiah, but we forget that God can also work through unbelievers to accomplish His will. He used Pharaoh to display His power in Egypt (Ex. 9:16; Rom. 9:17) and Cyrus to deliver His people from Babylon (Isa. 44:28; 45:1; Ezra 1:1-2). Caesar issued the decree that brought Mary and Joseph to Bethlehem (Luke 2:1-7), and two different Roman centurions—Claudius Lysias and Julius—saved Paul's life (Acts 21:26-40; 23:25-30; 27:1, 42-44). While it may be helpful to have believing officials like Joseph, Daniel, and Nehemiah, we must remember that God is not required to use only believers.

Moses and Nehemiah made similar decisions of faith and similar sacrifices (Heb. 11:24-26). As the representative of the deliverer of the Jews, would he be welcomed by the Gentile officials? Nehemiah performed no signs or wonders, nor did he deliver any prophecies; but he faithfully did his work and prepared a city for the coming Messiah (Dan. 9:24-27).

3. He had the faith to challenge others. (Neh. 2:11-18a)

Traveling (Neh. 2:9-10). No description is given of the trip from Susa to Jerusalem, a journey of at least two months' time. As a testimony to the faithfulness of God, Ezra had refused military protection for his journey (Ezra 8:21-23); but since Nehemiah was a governor on official business, he had a military escort. Nehemiah had just as much faith as Ezra; but as the king's officer, he could not travel without his retinue. For one thing, he would not oppose the will of the king; and he could not force his faith upon others.

When the official caravan arrived, it was bound to attract attention, particularly among those who hated the Jews and wanted to keep them from fortifying their city. Three special enemies are named: Sanballat, from Beth Horan, about twelve miles from Jerusalem; Tobiah, an Ammonite; and Geshem, an Arabian (Neh. 2:19), also called "Gashmu" (6:6). Sanballat was Nehemiah's chief enemy, and the fact that he had some kind of official position in Samaria only made him that much more dangerous (4:1-3).

Being an Ammonite, Tobiah was an avowed enemy of the Jews (Deut. 23:3-4). He was related by marriage to some of Nehemiah's co-laborers and had many friends among the Jews (Neh. 6:17-19). In fact, he was "near of kin" ("allied") to Eliashib the priest (13:4-7). If Sanballat was in charge of the army, then Tobiah was director of the intelligence division of their operation. It was he who gathered "inside information" from his Jewish friends and passed it along to Sanballat and Geshem. Nehemiah would soon discover that his biggest problem was not the enemy on the outside but the compromisers on the inside, a problem the church still faces today.

Investigating (Neh. 2:11-16). After his long difficult journey, Nehemiah took time to rest; for leaders must take care of themselves if they are going to be able to serve the Lord (Mark 6:31). He also took time to get "the lay of the land" without arousing the concern of the enemy. A good leader doesn't rush into his work but patiently gathers the facts firsthand and then plans his strategy (Prov. 18:13). We must be "wise as serpents" because the enemy is always watching and waiting to attack.

Leaders are often awake when others are asleep, and working when others are resting. Nehemiah didn't want the enemy to know what he was doing, so he investigated the ruins by night. By keeping his counsel to himself, Nehemiah prevented Tobiah's friends from getting information they could pass along to Sanballat. A wise leader knows when to plan, when to speak, and when to work.

As he surveyed the situation, he moved from west to south to east, concentrating on the southern section of the city. It was just as his brother had reported: The walls were broken down and the gates were burned (Neh. 2:13; 1:3). Leaders must not live in a dream world. They must face facts honestly and accept the bad news as well as the good news. Nehemiah saw more at night than the residents saw in the daylight, for he saw the potential as well as the problems. That's what makes a leader!

Challenging (Neh. 2:17-20). Nehemiah's appeal was positive; he focused on the glory and greatness of the Lord. He had been in the city only a few days, but he spoke of "we" and "us" and not "you" and "them." As he did in his prayer (1:6-7), he identified with the people and their needs. The city was a reproach to the Lord (1:3; 4:4; 5:9), but the hand of the Lord was with them; and He would enable them to do the work. God had already proved His power by working in the heart of the king, and the king had promised to meet the needs. It was Nehemiah's personal burden for Jerusalem and his experience with the Lord that convinced the Jews that the time was right to build.

It is to the credit of the Jewish nobles that they accepted the challenge immediately and said, "Let us rise up and build!" They were not so accustomed to their situation that they took it for granted and decided that nothing could be changed. Nor did they remind Nehemiah that the Jews had once tried to repair the walls and were stopped (Ezra 4). "We tried that once and it didn't work. Why try again?"

Christian leaders today face these same two obstacles as they seek to lead God's people into new conquests for the Lord. How often we hear, "We're content the way things are; don't rock the boat by trying to change things." Or, "We tried that before and it didn't work!"

It is worth noting that God sent the Jews a *leader from the outside.* Nehemiah came into the community with a new perspective on the problems and a new vision for the work. Too often in a local church, new members have a hard time "breaking into the system" because the veterans are afraid of new ideas that might lead to change. Since most of their leadership comes up through the ranks, parachurch ministries must also beware of the "dosed corporation" attitude. New workers from outside the organization might open the windows and let in some fresh air.

The good hand of God was upon the leader, and the followers "strengthened their hands" for the work (Neh. 2:8, 18). It takes both the hands of leadership and the hands of partnership to accomplish the work of the Lord. Leaders can't do the job by themselves, and workers can't accomplish much without leadership. Vincent de Paul said, "If in order to succeed in an enterprise, I were obliged to choose between fifty deer commanded by a lion, and fifty lions commanded by a deer, I should consider myself more certain of success with the first group than with the second."

Someone has defined *leadership* as "the art of getting people to do what they ought to do because they want to do it." If that definition is true, then Nehemiah certainly was a leader! Most of the people united behind him and risked their lives to get the work done.

Nehemiah was not only able to challenge his own people, but he was also able to stand up against the enemy and deal effectively with their opposition. Just as soon as God's people step out by faith to do His will, the enemy shows up and tries to discourage them. Sanballat and Tobiah heard about the enterprise (v. 10) and enlisted Geshem to join them in opposing the Jews. In chapters 4-7, Nehemiah will describe the different weapons the enemy used and how the Lord enabled him to defeat them.

They started off with ridicule, a device somebody has called "the weapon of those who have no other." They laughed at the Jews and belittled both their resources and their plans. They even suggested that the Jews were rebelling against the king. That weapon had worked once before (see Ezra 4).

Whether in the area of science, exploration, invention, business, government, or Christian ministry, just about everyone who has ever accomplished anything has faced ridicule. Our Lord was ridiculed during His life and mocked while He was hanging on the cross. He was "despised and rejected of men" (Isa. 53:3). On the Day of Pentecost, some of the Jews in the crowd said that the Christians were drunk (Acts 2:13). The Greek philosophers called Paul a "babbler" (17:18, NIV), and Festus told Paul he was out of his mind (26:24).

Nehemiah could have dealt with their ridicule in several ways. He might have ignored it, and sometimes that's the wisest thing to do (Prov. 26:4). But at the beginning of an enterprise, it's important that leaders encourage their people and let them know that God has everything in control. Had Nehemiah ignored these three men who were important in the community, he might have weakened his own position among the Jews. After all, he was the official governor, and he was doing official business.

Or, Nehemiah might have debated with the three enemy leaders and tried to convince them that their position was false. But that approach would only have given "official promotion" to the three men along with opportunity for them to say more. Why should Nehemiah give the enemy opportunity to make speeches against the God whom he served?

Of course, Nehemiah would not ask them to join the project and work with the Jews, although Sanballat and his friends would have welcomed the invitation (Neh. 6:1-4). In his reply, Nehemiah made three things dear: Rebuilding the wall was God's work; the Jews were God's servants; and Sanballat, Tobiah, and Geshem had no part in the matter. Sometimes leaders have to negotiate, but there are times when leaders must draw a line and defend it. Unfortunately, not everybody in Jerusalem agreed with their leader; for some of them cooperated with Sanballat, Tobiah, and Geshem and added to Nehemiah's burdens.

The stage is now set and the drama is about to begin.

But before we join the workers on the wall, let's ask ourselves whether we are the kind of leaders and followers God wants us to be. Like Nehemiah, do we have a burden in our hearts for the work

God has called us to do? (2:12) Are we willing to sacrifice to see His will accomplished? Are we patient in gathering facts and in planning our work? Do we enlist the help of others or try to do everything ourselves? Do we motivate people on the basis of the spiritual—what God is doing—or simply on the basis of the personal? Are they following us or the Lord as He leads us?

As followers, do we listen to what our leaders say as they share their burdens? Do we cling to the past or desire to see God do something new? Do we put our hands and necks to the work? (v. 18; 3:5) Are we cooperating in any way with the enemy and thus weakening the work? Have we found the job God wants us to complete?

Anyone can go through life as a destroyer; God has called His people to be builders. What an example Nehemiah is to us! Trace his "so" statements and see how God used him: "So I prayed" (2:4); "So I came to Jerusalem" (v. 11); "So they strengthened their hands for this good work" (v. 18); "So built we the wall" (4:6); "So we labored in the work" (v. 21); "So the wall was finished" (6:15).

Were it not for the dedication and determination that came from his faith in a great God, Nehemiah never would have accepted the challenge or finished the work. He had never seen the verse, but what Paul wrote in 1 Corinthians 15:58 was what kept him going: "Therefore, my beloved brethren, be steadfast, immovable, always abounding in the work of the Lord, knowing that your labor is not in vain in the Lord" (NKJV).

No matter how difficult the task, or how strong the opposition, Be Determined! As Dr. V. Raymond Edman used to say, "It is always too soon to quit."

CHAPTER THREE
WALL TO WALL WORKERS
Nehemiah 3

Nehemiah faced a great challenge and had great faith in a great God, but he would have accomplished very little had there not been great dedication on the part of the people who helped him rebuild the wall. With the kind of humility that befits a godly leader, Nehemiah gave all the credit to the people when he wrote, "So built we the wall . . . for the people had a mind to work" (Neh. 4:6).

British humorist Jerome K. Jerome said, "I like work, it fascinates me. I can sit and look at it for hours." When it comes to the work of the Lord, there is no place for spectators or self-appointed advisors and critics; but there is always room for workers. As you study this chapter, you will discover principles that apply to all human labor, especially the work of building the church.

1. The purpose of the work

Nehemiah was concerned about only one thing, the glory of God. "Let us build up the wall of Jerusalem, that we be no more a reproach" (2:17; and see 1:3; 4:4; 5:9). The Gentiles delighted in mocking their Jewish neighbors by pointing out the dilapidated condition of Jerusalem. After all, the Jews claimed that their capital city was "beautiful for situation, the joy of the whole earth" (Ps. 48:2). They said that God loved "the gates of Zion more than all the dwellings of Jacob" (87:2). If God loved Jerusalem so much, why were the walls in ruin and the gates burned? Why was the "holy city" a reproach? Why didn't the Jews do something?

For the most part, the world today ignores the church. If it does pay any attention to the church, it is usually to condemn or mock. "If you are the people of God," unbelievers ask, "why are there so many scandals in the church? If God is so powerful, why is the church so weak?" Whether Christians like it or not, we are living in a day of reproach when "the glory has departed" (1 Sam. 4:21).

The purpose of all ministry is the glory of God and not the aggrandizement of religious leaders or organizations (1 Cor. 10:31; 2 Cor. 4:5). The words of Jesus in His high priestly prayer ought to be the motivating force in all Christian ministry: "I have glorified Thee on the earth; I have finished the work which Thou gavest Me to do" (John 17:4). God has a special task for each of His children (Eph. 2:10); and in the humble, faithful doing of that task, we glorify His name.

Of course, the rebuilding of the walls and the setting of the gates also meant protection and security for the people. Jerusalem was surrounded by enemies, and it seemed foolish for the residents to improve their property when nothing was safe from invasion and plunder. Over the years, the citizens had become accustomed to their plight. Like too many believers in the church today, they were content to live with the status quo. Then Nehemiah arrived on the scene and challenged them to rebuild the city to the glory of God.

2. The pattern of the work

Nehemiah was a leader who planned his work and worked his plan, and the way he did it is an example for us to follow.

Thirty-eight individual workers are named in this chapter, and forty-two different groups are identified. There were also many workers whom Nehemiah did not name whose labors were important; and each worker—named and anonymous— was assigned a place and a task.

"A great many people have got a false idea about the church," said evangelist D.L. Moody. "They have got an idea that the church is a place to rest in . . . to get into a nicely cushioned pew, and contribute to the charities, listen to the minister, and do their share to keep the church out of bankruptcy, is all they want. The idea of work for them—actual work in the church—never enters their minds."

In 1 Corinthians 12 and 14, Paul compared individual Christians to members of the human body: Each member is important, and each has a special function to perform. I recall the relief that came to my own heart when I realized that God didn't expect me to do everything in the church, but rather to use the gifts He gave me in the tasks that He assigned. When I started doing that, I discovered I was helping others discover and develop their own gifts; and all of us accomplished more for the Lord.

The people finished this difficult task because they obeyed the same leader, kept their eyes on the same goal, and worked together for the glory of God. Neither the enemy outside the city nor the difficulties inside the city distracted them from their God-given task. Like Paul, they said, "This one thing I do" (Phil. 3:13).

The word *built* is used six times in Nehemiah 3 and means "rebuilt." George Morrison reminds us "that for this restoration no *new* material was needed. In the debris of the ruined masonry lay all the material required . . . and it seems to me that is always so when the walls of Zion are rebuilt" *(Morning Sermons,* London: Hodder and Stoughton, 1931, p. 249). It is not by inventing clever new things that we take away the church's reproach, but by going back to the old truths that made the church great in ages past. They lie like stones in the dust, waiting for some burdened Nehemiah to recover them and use them.

The word *repair* is used thirty-five times; it means "to make strong and firm." Nehemiah wasn't interested in a "quick fix," a whitewashed wall that would soon crumble (Ezek. 13:1-16; 22:28). They were building to the glory of God, and therefore they did their best.

The gates of Jerusalem had been destroyed by fire (Neh. 1:3; Jer. 17:27; Lam. 1:4), so Nehemiah requisitioned timber from the king's forest and had new gates constructed (Neh. 2:8) and put into place (6:1; 7:1). The gates were important to the safety of the people and the control of who went in and out of the city (7:3; 13:15-22). If the Lord loves the gates of Zion (Ps. 87:2), then His people ought to love them too.

Locks and bars are mentioned five times (Neh. 3:3, 6, 13-15). *Locks* refer to the sockets into which the bars were fitted, thus making it difficult for anyone outside to open the gates. It isn't enough that we simply do the work of God; we must also make sure that what we do is protected from the enemy. "Watch out that you do not lose what you have worked for, but that you may be rewarded fully" (2 John 8, NIV).

3. The people in the work

As you get acquainted with the various people mentioned in Nehemiah 3, you will find yourself saying, "This is just like the church today!" Circumstances change but human nature remains pretty much the same.

God uses all kinds of people. The chapter mentions rulers and priests (vv. 1, 12-19), men and women (v. 12), professional craftsmen (vv. 8, 32), and even people from outside the city (vv. 2, 5, 7). There was a place for everyone, and a job for everyone to do.

Leaders must set the example (Neh. 3:1). If anybody in the city should have been busy in the work, it was the priests, for the glory of the Lord was involved in the project. That the high priest used his consecrated hands to do manual labor shows that he considered the work on the wall to be a ministry to the Lord. "Therefore, whether you eat or drink, or whatever you do, do all to the glory of God" (1 Cor. 10:31, NKJV). Eliashib enlisted the other priests to work at the sheep gate in the northeast corner of the city. Since the sacrifices came into the city that way, the priests would be especially interested in that part of the project.

Sad to say, Eliashib did not remain true to his calling; for later he allied with the enemy and created serious problems for Nehemiah (Neh. 13:4-9). Some people who enthusiastically begin their work may drop out or turn against it for one reason or another. Eliashib's grandson married a daughter of Sanballat (v. 28), and this alliance no doubt influenced the high priest.

Some people will not work (Neh. 3:5). Tekoa was a town about eleven miles from Jerusalem, and some of their people traveled to Jerusalem to assist in the work. What a contrast between these people and their nobles! The Tekoites built in two places on the wall (vv. 5 and 27), while their nobles refused to bend the neck and work in even one place. Were these "aristocrats" so important in their own eyes that they could not perform manual labor? Yet Paul was a tentmaker (Acts 18:3), and Jesus was a carpenter (Mark 6:3).

The Tekoites were not the only "outsiders" to go to Jerusalem to work on the wall; for men also came from Jericho (Neh. 3:2), Gibeon, and Mizpah (v. 7). Their loyalty to their nation and their Lord was greater than their local interests. They were certainly safer back in their own communities, but they risked their lives to do the work of the Lord (Acts 15:25-26).

Some people do more work than others (Neh. 3:11, 19, 21, 24, 27, 30). Most workers are glad to lay down their tools when their job is finished, but these people asked for additional assignments. It isn't enough for us to say that we have done as much as others; we must do *as much as we can* as long as the Lord enables us. Jesus asked, "What do you do more than others? (Matt. 5:47, NKJV)

Some do their work at home (Neh. 3:10, 23, 28-30). At least six different workers, plus an unknown number of priests, repaired the portions of the wall that were nearest to their own houses. If all of us would follow this example, our neighborhoods and cities would be in much better shape! Of course, there is a spiritual lesson here: Christian service begins at home. A Chinese proverb says, "Better to be kind at home than to burn incense in a far place"; and Paul wrote, "Let them learn first to shew piety at home" (1 Tim. 5:4).

Some people work harder than others (Neh 3:20). Baruch is the only worker of whom it is said that the work was done "earnestly" ("zealously," NIV). The Hebrew word means "to burn or glow" and suggests that Baruch burned a lot of energy! "Whatever your hand finds to do, do it with all your might" (Eccl. 9:10, NIV). Paul admonished the slaves to work hard for their masters because they were really working for Christ (Eph. 6:5-8). Lazy workers not only rob themselves and the Lord, but they also rob their fellow workers. "He also that is slothful in his work is brother to him that is a great waster" (Prov. 18:9).

4. The places of the work

Nehemiah began his list of the "work stations" with the Sheep Gate in the northeast corner of the city (Neh. 3:1). Then he moved counterclockwise around the walls to the Gate Hammiphkad ("the Muster Gate"), which was adjacent to the Sheep Gate and just above the East Gate (v. 29). In his record, he names ten gates and several towers and other landmarks. He describes the work on the north wall first (vv. 1-7), then the western wall (vv. 8-13), then the southern point of the city (v. 14), and finally the eastern wall (vv. 15-32).

His primary purpose was to document for posterity and the official records the names and accomplishments of the people who worked on the wall. Without straining the text, however, we can glean from this chapter some spiritual illustrations to encourage us in our own personal lives and ministries.

The Sheep Gate (Neh. 3:1, 32). This was the gate through which the animals were brought into the city, including the temple sacrifices. The gate was near the temple area, so it was logical that the priests make this their special project. This is the only gate of which it is recorded that it was "sanctified," that is, dedicated to God in a special way.

This gate reminds us of Jesus Christ, the Lamb of God who died for the sins of the world (John 1:29; 5:2). Nehemiah could have begun his record with any of the gates, but he chose to start and end the report with the Sheep Gate. Jesus is the "Alpha and Omega, the beginning and the ending" (Rev. 1:8). Apart from Him and His sacrifice, we would have nothing eternal and satisfying. Nothing is said about the gate's "locks and bars," for the way is never closed to the lost sinner who wants to come to the Savior.

The Fish Gate (Neh. 3:3). This was located to the west of the Sheep Gate, and between the two stood the Tower of Hammeah ("the hundred") and the Tower of Hananeel (v. 1). These two towers were a part of the city's defense system and were close to the citadel, where the soldiers guarded the temple and protected the northern approach to the city which was especially vulnerable. Merchants used this gate when they brought fish from the Mediterranean Sea, and there may have been a fish market near the gate. In any event, it was a key entrance to the city.

The Old Gate (Neh. 3:6) is probably the Corner Gate (2 Kings 14:13; Jer. 31:38), located at the northwest corner of the city. Some students identify this with the "Mishneh Gate"; the Hebrew word means "second quarter" or "new quarter" (Zeph. 1:10, NIV). In Nehemiah's day, the northwest section of the city was "the mishneh" or "new quarter"; and this gate led into it. What a paradox: the old gate leads into the new quarter! But it is from the old that we derive the new; and if we abandon the old, there can be nothing new (see Jer. 6:16 and Matt. 13:52).

The Valley Gate (Neh. 3:13) is where Nehemiah began his nocturnal investigation of the ruins of the city (2:13). It was located at the southwest corner of the city walls, about 500 yards from the Dung Gate; and both opened into the Valley of Hinnom. The workers here not only restored the gate, but they also repaired the section of the wall between the two gates. It is likely that this long section of the wall—over 1,700 feet—was not as severely damaged as the other sections.

Every Christian needs a "valley gate," for God opposes the proud but gives grace to the humble (1 Peter 5:5-6). It is only as we yield to Christ and serve others that we can truly enter into the fullness of the life He has for us (Phil. 2:1-11).

The Dung Gate (Neh. 3:14) was located at the southernmost tip of the city, near the Pool of Siloam. It was a main exit to the Valley of Hinnom, where the city disposed of its garbage. The word *gehenna* means "Valley of Hinnom" and identified this area that Jesus used as a picture of hell, "where their worm dieth not, and their fire is not quenched" (Mark 9:44). King Manasseh had sacrificed children to idols in that valley (2 Chron. 33:6), and King Josiah had desecrated the place by turning it into a rubbish heap (2 Kings 23:10).

The sanitary disposal of waste materials is essential to the health of a city. This gate did not have a beautiful name, but it did perform an important service! It reminds us that, like the city, each of us individually must get rid of whatever defiles us, or it may destroy us (2 Cor. 7:1; 1 John 1:9).

The Fountain Gate (Neh. 3:15) was on the east wall, just north of the Dung Gate, in a very strategic location near the Pool of Siloam, the old City of David, and the water tunnel built by King Hezekiah (2 Kings 20:20). The Gihon Spring that fed the water system was an important source of water in the city.

In the Bible, water for drinking is a picture of the Holy Spirit of God (John 7:37-39), while water for washing is a picture of the Word of God (Eph. 5:26; John 15:3). Spiritually speaking, we have moved from the Valley Gate (humility) to the Dung Gate (cleansing) to the Fountain Gate (fullness of the Spirit).

The Water Gate (Neh 3:26) led from the old City of David to the Gihon Spring, located adjacent to the Kidron Valley. Jerusalem was one of the few great cities of antiquity that was not built near a great river, and the city depended on reservoirs and springs for its water. The text does not say that this gate was repaired, but only that the workers repaired the walls adjacent to it. The "Nethinims" ("those who are given") were probably temple servants, descendants of the Gibeonites who were made drawers of water (Josh. 9:23). They would naturally want to live near the most important source of water for the city.

If the Fountain Gate reminds us of the Spirit of God, the Water Gate reminds us of the Word of God. In fact, it was at the Water Gate that Ezra and the priests conducted a great "Bible conference" and explained the Scriptures to the people (8:1ff). That this gate is not said to have been repaired, as were the others, suggests that the Word of God stands forever and will not fail (Ps. 119:89; Matt. 24:35). The Bible does not need to be repaired or improved.

"The Ophel" (Neh. 3:26-27) was a hill south of the temple area, between the Horse Gate and the Water Gate. It was especially fortified and had a tower. The temple servants lived in that area because it was close to the water supply.

The Horse Gate (Neh 3:28) stood north of the Water Gate, adjacent to the temple area. It was here that wicked Athaliah was executed (2 Chron. 23:15). God warned His people not to trust in horses and chariots (Deut. 17:14-20), but Solomon imported them from Egypt (1 Kings 10:26-29), and they became an important part of the nation's defense system (Isa. 2:7). The Horse Gate reminds us that there is warfare in the Christian life (2 Tim. 2:1-4) and that we must always be ready to do battle (Eph. 6:10-18). It is significant that the priests repaired this gate as well as the Sheep Gate. Both were near the temple area.

The East Gate (Neh. 3:29) led directly to the temple and is probably what we know today as the Golden Gate. Tradition says that Jesus entered the temple on Palm Sunday through this gate. In the sixteenth century, the gate was sealed up with blocks of stone by the Turkish sultan, Sulayman the Magnificent. Jewish and Christian tradition both connect the Golden Gate with the coming of the Messiah to Jerusalem, and Muslims associate it with the future judgment.

Ezekiel saw the glory of the Lord depart from the temple at the East Gate (Ezek. 10:16-22; 11:22-25), and the Lord will return to the city the same way (43:1-5). So, we have every reason to associate this gate with the coming of the Lord and to remind ourselves to "abide in Him; that, when He shall appear, we may have confidence, and not be ashamed before Him at His coming" (1 John 2:28).

The Gate Hammiphkad (Neh. 3:31) was located at the northeast corner of the city. The Hebrew word has a military connotation and refers to the mustering of the troops for numbering and inspection. The NIV and NASB both translate it "the Inspection Gate." This is where the army was reviewed and registered. The north side of Jerusalem was the most vulnerable to attack, so this was a logical place to locate the army. When our Lord returns, He will gather His people together and review their works in preparation for giving out rewards for faithful service (1 Cor. 3:10-15; 2 Cor. 5:9-10; Rom. 14:10-12).

In this report, Nehemiah does not mention the Gate of Ephraim (Neh. 8:16; 12:39) or the Gate of the Guard (12:39). The former may have been on the north wall, looking toward the area of Ephraim; and the latter may have been associated in some way with "The Inspection Gate." Some translate it "The Prison Gate." It may have been the "court of the guard" named in 3:25.

Nehemiah's record ends with the Sheep Gate (v. 32), the place where he began (v. 1). Because they have rejected their Messiah, the people of Israel today have no sacrifice, no temple, and no priesthood (Hosea 3:4). Thank the Lord, here and there, individual Jews are trusting Christ; but the nation as a whole is blinded in unbelief (Rom. 11:25ff). When they see their Messiah, they will believe and be saved (Zech. 12:10-13:1).

No one person could have accomplished the work of repairing the walls and restoring the gates. It took leadership on Nehemiah's part and cooperation on the part of the people. Each had a place to fill and a job to do. So it is with the church today: We must work together if we are to finish the work to the glory of God.

"Therefore, my beloved brethren, be steadfast, immovable, always abounding in the work of the Lord, knowing that your labor is not in vain in the Lord" (1 Cor. 15:58, NKJV).

CHAPTER FOUR
WORKERS AND WARRIORS
Nehemiah 4

The Bible tells us to love our neighbors, and also to love our enemies; probably because they are generally the same people."

Those words from Gilbert Keith Chesterton were certainly true in Nehemiah's situation. His arrival in Jerusalem was a threat to Sanballat and his associates (2:10), who wanted to keep the Jews weak and dependant. A strong Jerusalem would endanger the balance of power in the region, and it would also rob Sanballat and his friends of influence and wealth.

When things are going well, get ready for trouble, because the enemy doesn't want to see the work of the Lord make progress. As long as the people in Jerusalem were content with their sad lot, the enemy left them alone; but, when the Jews began to serve the Lord and bring glory to God's name, the enemy became active.

Opposition is not only an evidence that God is blessing, but it is also an opportunity for us to grow. The difficulties that came to the work brought out the best in Nehemiah and his people. Satan wanted to use these problems as weapons to destroy the work, but God used them as tools to build His people. "God had one Son without sin," said Charles Spurgeon, "but He never had a son without trial."

When Sir James Thornhill was painting the inside of the cupola of St. Paul's Cathedral in London, at one point he finished an area and stepped back to view it. Had he gone back one step more, he would have fallen from the scaffolding and perhaps killed himself. Seeing the situation, a friend seized one of the brushes and rubbed paint over a part of the picture. The artist rushed forward to protect his work, and at the same time, his life was saved. When the picture of our life or ministry is not all we think it ought to be, perhaps the Master Artist is rescuing us from something far worse and preparing us for something far better.

Chapters 4 to 6 describe at least nine different tactics that the enemy used to try to stop the work on the walls. First, they attacked the Jewish people with *ridicule (4:1-6)* and *plots of war (vv. 7-9).* This resulted in difficulties *within* the Jewish ranks: *discouragement (v. 10), fear (vv. 11-23),* and *selfishness (5:1-19).* When attacks on the people failed to stop the work, the enemy then started to attack their leader, Nehemiah. They tried *compromise (6:1-4), slander (vv. 5-9), threats (vv. 10-14)* and *intrigue (vv. 17-19);* but none of these devices worked either. Nehemiah was "steadfast and unmovable" and led his people to finish the work in fifty-two days!

Referring to Satan, Paul wrote, "For we are not ignorant of his devices" (2 Cor. 2:11). This chapter presents four of Satan's devices for opposing the Lord's work, and it also tells us how God's people can be steadfast and defeat the enemy. If you start building, you will soon be battling; so, be prepared!

1. Ridicule (Neh. 4:1-6)

British critic and author Thomas Carlyle called ridicule "the language of the devil." Some people who can stand bravely when they are shot at will collapse when they are laughed at.

Shakespeare called ridicule "paper bullets of the brain," but those bullets have slain many a warrior.

It is not unusual for the enemy to insult the servants of God. Goliath ridiculed David when the shepherd boy met the giant with only a sling in his hand (1 Sam. 17:41-47). Jesus was mocked by the soldiers during His trial (Luke 22:63-65) and by the rabble while He was hanging on the cross (23:35–37); and some of the heroes of the faith had to endure mocking (Heb. 11:36). *When the enemy laughs at what God's people are doing, it is usually a sign that God is going to bless His people in a wonderful way.* When the enemy rages on earth, God laughs in heaven (Ps. 2:4).

Sanballat and his friends had begun to ridicule the Jews even before the work on the wall had begun. "They laughed us to scorn," wrote Nehemiah, "and despised us" (Neh. 2:19). What special relationship Sanballat had with the army of Samaria is not explained to us. Perhaps he had the army assembled as a show of strength to frighten the Jews. By making his initial speech before the army, Sanballat intensified the power of his ridicule as he made some important people laugh at the Jews.

First, Sanballat ridiculed *the workers* by calling them "feeble Jews" (4:2). The word *feeble* means "withered, miserable." The people were like cut flowers that were fading away. They had no human resources that people could see, but the enemy could not see their great spiritual resources. The people of the world don't understand that God delights in using feeble instruments to get His work accomplished (1 Cor. 1:18-31). The world glories in its wealth and power, but God's people glory in their poverty and weakness. When we are weak, then we are strong (2 Cor. 12:1-10).

Then Sanballat ridiculed *the work itself* by asking three taunting questions. "Will they fortify themselves?" must have evoked gales of laughter from the Samaritan army. How could a remnant of feeble Jews hope to build a wall strong enough to protect the city from the army? "Will they sacrifice?" implies, "It will take more than prayer and worship to rebuild the city!" This question was blasphemy against Jehovah God, for Sanballat was denying that God would help His people. "Will they finish in a day?" suggests that the Jews didn't know how difficult the task was and would soon call it quits.

In his final question, Sanballat ridiculed *the materials* they were using. The stones were taken out of the rubbish heaps and probably were so old and damaged that they would never last when set into the wall. While it is true that limestone is softened by fire, it is also true that the walls were "broken down," while the gates were "consumed with fire" (Neh. 2:13). In spite of what Sanballat said, there was still plenty of good material for the builders to use.

Tobiah the Ammonite was one of the visiting dignitaries at the Samaritan army inspection; and when it was his turn to make a speech, he ridiculed *the finished product (4:3).* You wouldn't need an army to knock down the wall; a solitary fox could do it! Of course, much that Sanballat and Tobiah said was true *from a human point of view;* for the Jewish remnant was weak and poor, and the work was too great for them. But they had great faith in a great God, and that's what made the difference.

How did Nehemiah respond to this ridicule? *He prayed and asked God to fight the enemy for him.* This is the third time you find Nehemiah praying (1:4-11; 2:4), and it will not be the last time. Nehemiah didn't allow himself to get detoured from his work by taking time to reply to their words. The Lord had heard the sneering taunts of Sanballat and Tobiah, and He would deal with them in His own way and His own time.

Nehemiah's prayer resembles the "imprecatory psalms," such as Psalms 69; 79; and 139:19-22. We must remember that Nehemiah was praying as a servant of God concerned for the glory of God. He was not requesting personal vengeance but official vindication for God's people. The enemy had blasphemously provoked God before the builders, and this was a terrible sin. The opposition of Sanballat and Tobiah against the Jews was in reality opposition against God.

The things people say may *hurt* us, but they can never *harm* us, unless we let them get into our system and poison us. If we spend time pondering the enemy's words, we will give Satan a foothold from which he can launch another attack closer to home. The best thing to do is to pray and commit the whole thing to the Lord; and then *get back to your work!* Anything that keeps you from doing what God has called you to do will only help the enemy.

2. Intimidating plots (Neh. 4:7-9)

A common enemy and a common cause brought four different groups together to stop the work on the walls of Jerusalem. The city was now completely surrounded by enemies! To the north were Sanballat and the Samaritans; to the east, Tobiah and the Ammonites; to the south, Geshem and the Arabs; and to the west, the Ashdodites. Ashdod was perhaps the most important city in Philistia at that time, and the Philistines did not want to see a strong community in Jerusalem.

God's people sometimes have difficulty working together, but the people of the world have no problem uniting in opposition to the work of the Lord (Ps. 2:1-2; Acts 4:23-30; Luke 23:12). As the enemy saw the work progressing, they became angry and decided to plan a secret attack against Jerusalem. Satan hates the Jews and has used one nation after another to try to destroy them (see Ps. 85 and Rev. 12). God chose the Jews to be His vehicle for giving the world the knowledge of the true God, the Scriptures, and the Savior (Rom. 9:1-5). "Salvation is of the Jews" (John 4:22), and Satan wanted to prevent the Savior from coming into the world. If he could destroy the nation, he would frustrate God's plan.

Nehemiah suspected that his enemies would launch an attack, so he posted a guard and encouraged the people to pray.

The workers held both tools and weapons (Neh. 4:17) and were prepared to fight when the signal was given. "Watch and pray" combines faith and works and is a good example for us to follow in our work and our warfare (see Mark 13:33; 14:38; Eph. 6:18; Col. 4:2-4).

The Christian's battle is not against flesh and blood, but against Satan and his demonic forces that use flesh and blood to oppose the Lord's work. If we hope to win the war and finish the work, we must use the spiritual equipment God has provided (Eph. 6:10-18; 2 Cor. 10:1-6). If we focus on the *visible* enemy alone and forget the *invisible* enemy, we are sure to start trusting our own resources; and this will lead to defeat.

3. Discouragement (Neh. 4:10)

Pressures from without often create problems from within. It isn't easy to carry on your work when you are surrounded by danger and daily face the demands of a task that seems impossible. If the Jews became discouraged, they would defeat themselves; and Sanballat and his allies would never have to wage war.

Discouragement is a key weapon in Satan's arsenal. It was discouragement that kept Israel from entering the Promised Land at Kadesh-Barnea (Num. 13). "We be not able to go up against the people; for they are stronger than we" (v. 31). The ten unbelieving spies "discouraged the heart of the children of Israel" (32:9); and as a result, the nation wandered in the wilderness forty years until the new generation was ready to conquer the land.

"We are not able!" is the rallying cry of all who take their eyes off the Lord and start looking at themselves and their problems. These discouraged Jewish workers were actually agreeing with the enemy who said they were feeble! (Neh. 2:19; 4:1-3) Sanballat had openly declared that the work would stop, and it almost did.

Why did this discouragement arise from the royal tribe of Judah? (See Gen. 49:8-12.) They had David's blood in their veins, and you would think they would be men and women of great faith and courage. The answer is found in Nehemiah 6:17-19: Some people in the tribe of Judah were secretly cooperating with the enemy. The ties of marriage were stronger than the bonds of commitment to the Lord. According to 13:15-22, some of the leaders of Judah were not wholly devoted to the Lord, but were more interested in making money. The combination of marriage and money divided their loyalties, and they became the cause of discouragement.

In over forty years of ministry, I have learned that, in the Lord's work, *discouragers are often doubters and compromisers.* There is usually something wrong in their spiritual walk. They frequently lack faith in God's Word, for one thing; and they are primarily interested in their own plans and pursuits. A double-minded person is unbelieving and unstable (James 1:5-8) and hinders the work of the Lord.

Nehemiah didn't pay much attention to these complainers but went right on with the work. That's the best thing to do. If you take time away from your work to listen to everybody who wants your attention, you will never get anything done. Nehemiah got his encouragement from prayer and the promises of God, and the occasional complaints of some of the people didn't upset him.

4. Fear (Neh. 4:11-23)

The Jews who lived in the outlying villages (3:2, 5, 7, 13) kept bringing a report to the city that the enemy was planning another surprise attack. Whether these

Jews were merely spreading rumors or helping to promote a conspiracy we don't know; but they told the story repeatedly. ("Ten times" is a Hebrew phrase meaning "many times." See Gen. 31:41 and Num. 14:22.) Nehemiah didn't respond immediately and probably was praying for God's guidance. He himself was not afraid of the enemy; but when he saw that his people were starting to become afraid, he began to act.

In his First Inaugural Address, on March 4, 1933, President Franklin Delano Roosevelt said to a nation in the grip of an economic depression, "The only thing we have to fear is fear itself." He may have borrowed the thought from Henry David Thoreau, American naturalist, who wrote in his journal on September 7, 1851, "Nothing is so much to be feared as fear." Why? Because fear paralyzes you, and fear is contagious and paralyzes others. Fear and faith cannot live together in the same heart. "Why are ye fearful, O ye of little faith?" (Matt. 8:26) Frightened people discourage others and help bring defeat (Deut. 20:8).

Nehemiah's first step was to post guards at the most conspicuous and vulnerable places on the wall. The enemy could then see that the Jews were prepared to fight. He armed entire families, knowing that they would stand together and encourage one another. The Jews not only repaired the walls near their own houses (Neh. 3:28-30), but they stood with their families to protect their homes and their city.

After looking the situation over, Nehemiah then encouraged the people not to be afraid but to look to the Lord for help. If we fear the Lord, we need not fear the enemy. Nehemiah's heart was captivated by the "great and terrible" God of Israel (4:14; see 1:5), and he knew that God was strong enough to meet the challenge. He also reminded the people that they were fighting for their nation, their city, and their families. If the nation was destroyed, what would become of God's great promises to Israel and His plan of redemption?

When we face a situation that creates fear in our hearts, we must remind ourselves of the greatness of God. If we walk by sight and view God through the problems, we will fail, as did the Jews at Kadesh-Barnea (Num. 13:26-33). But if we look at the problem through the greatness of God, we will have confidence and succeed. That was the approach David took when he faced Goliath (1 Sam. 17:45-47).

When the enemy learned that Jerusalem was armed and ready, they backed off (Neh. 4:15). God had frustrated their plot. "The Lord brings the counsel of the nations to nothing; He makes the plans of the peoples of no effect. The counsel of the Lord stands forever, the plans of His heart to all generations" (Ps. 33:10-11, NKJV). It is good to remind ourselves that the will of God comes from the heart of God and that we need not be afraid.

Nehemiah knew that he couldn't interrupt the work every time he heard a new rumor, so he set up a defense plan that solved the problem: Half of the men worked on the wall while the other half stood guard. He saw to it that the people carrying materials also carried weapons and that the workers on the walls carried swords. In this way, the work would not be interrupted, and the workers would be ready in case of an alarm. The man with the trumpet stayed close to Nehemiah so the alarm could be given immediately. The people were prepared to fight (Neh. 4:14), but they realized that it was God who fought with them and He alone could give the victory.

When Charles Spurgeon started his church magazine in 1865, he borrowed the title from Nehemiah and called the publication *The Sword and Trowel.* He said it was "a record of combat with sin and labor for the Lord." It is not enough to build the wall; we must also be on guard lest the enemy take it from us. Building and battling are both a normal part of the Christian life if we are faithful disciples (Luke 14:28-33).

Again, Nehemiah spoke words of encouragement to the people (Neh. 4:19-20). He reminded them that they were involved in a great work. After all, they were serving a great God and rebuilding the walls of a great city. He also reminded them that they were not working alone, even though they couldn't see all of their fellow workers on the wall. God was with all of them and would come to their defense.

No matter what the workers were doing, or where they labored on the wall, they all kept an ear open for the sound of the trumpet. What an example for us to follow as we await the return of the Lord! "For the Lord Himself shall descend from heaven with a shout, with the voice of the archangel, and with the trump of God" (1 Thess. 4:16).

Nehemiah also instituted a "second shift" and required the workers from the other towns to stay in Jerusalem at night and help guard the city. It is often while we sleep that the enemy does his most insidious work (Matt. 13:25), and we must be on guard.

Nehemiah not only organized the workers and guards and encouraged them to trust the Lord, but he also set the right kind of example before them (Neh. 4:23). He was a leader who served and a servant who led. He stayed on the job and was alert at all times. He inspected the city's defenses every night and made sure that the guards were on duty.

The late Dr. Alan Redpath explained why the Jews succeeded in getting their work done and keeping the enemy at bay: The people had a mind to work (v. 6), a heart to pray (v. 9), an eye to watch (v. 9), and an ear to hear (v. 20); and this gave them the victory *(Victorious Christian Service,* Revell, 1958; pp. 76-79).

They also had a godly leader with the faith to stand.

"Therefore ... be steadfast, immovable, always abounding in the work of the Lord" (1 Cor. 15:58, NKJV).

CHAPTER FIVE
STOP! THIEF!
Nehemiah 5

When the enemy fails in his attacks from the *outside,* he then begins to attack from *within;* and one of his favorite weapons is *selfishness.* If he can get us thinking only about ourselves and what we want, then he will win the victory before we realize that he is even at work.

Selfishness means putting myself at the center of everything and insisting on getting what I want when I want it. It means exploiting others so I can be happy and taking advantage of them just so I can have my own way. It is not only wanting my own way but expecting everybody else to want my way too. Why are selfish people so miserable? I think Thomas Merton said it best: "To consider persons and events and situations only in the light of their effect upon myself is to live on the doorstep of hell."

This chapter reveals to us the depths of

sin in the human heart and how each of us must learn to love our neighbors as ourselves. This moving drama has three acts.

1. A great cry (Neh. 5:1-5)

In the midst of a "great work" (4:19) for a "great God" (1:5), a "great cry" (5:1) was heard among the Jews. They were not crying out against the Samaritans, the Ammonites, or the Arabs, but against their own people! Jew was exploiting Jew, and the economic situation had become so desperate that even the wives (who usually kept silent) were joining in the protest.

Four different groups of people were involved in this crisis. First, there were the people who owned no land but who needed food (v. 2). The population was increasing; there was a famine (v. 3); and the people were hungry. These people could not help themselves so they cried out to Nehemiah for help.

The second group was composed of landowners who had mortgaged their property in order to buy food (v. 3). Apparently inflation was on the rise, and prices were going higher. The combination of debt and inflation is enough to wipe out a person's equity very quickly.

The third group complained because the taxes were too high, and they were forced to borrow money to pay them (v. 4). In order to borrow the money, they had to give security; and this meant eventually losing their property. The Persian king received a fortune in annual tribute, very little of which ever benefited the local provinces. Unlike our situation today, the taxes did not support local services; they only supported the king.

The fourth group was made up of wealthy Jews who were exploiting their own brothers and sisters by loaning them money and taking their lands and their children for collateral (Lev. 25:39-40). Jewish boys and girls had to choose between starvation or servitude!

It was not unlawful for Jews to loan money to one another, but they were not to act like money lenders and charge interest (Deut. 23:19-20). They were to treat one another with love even in the matter of taking security (24:10-13; Ex. 22:25-27) or making a brother a servant (Lev. 25:35-46). Both the people and the land belonged to the Lord, and He would not have anybody using either one for personal gain.

One reason for the "Year of Jubilee" (Lev. 25) was to balance the economic system in Israel so that the rich could not get richer as the poor became poorer. All debts had to be forgiven in the fiftieth year, all land restored to its original owners, and all servants set free.

These wealthy businessmen were selfishly exploiting the poor in order to make themselves rich. They were using their power to rob some and to put others into bondage. Greed was one of the sins the prophets had denounced before the Babylonian Captivity (Isa. 56:9-12; Jer. 22:13-19; Amos 2:6-7; 5:11-12). God has a special concern for the poor and will not hold those guiltless who take advantage of them.

2. A great assembly (Neh. 5:6-13)

It is one thing to confront foreign enemies and quite something else to deal with your own people when they fight one another. Young Moses learned that it was easier to dispose of an Egyptian master than to reconcile two Jewish brothers (Ex. 2:11-15). Nehemiah showed true leadership in his responses to the problem.

Anger (Neh. 5:6). This was not the flaring up of a sinful temper but the expression of righteous indignation at the way the businessmen were oppressing their brothers and sisters. "In your anger do not sin" (Eph. 4:26, NIV; see Ps. 4:4). Nehemiah was not a politician who asked, "What is popular?" or a diplomat who asked, "What is safe?" but a true leader who asked, "What is right?" His was a holy anger against sin, and he knew he had the Law of God behind him. Moses expressed this kind of holy anger when he broke the stone tables of Law (Ex. 32), and so did Jesus when He saw the hardening of the Pharisees' hearts (Mark 3:5).

Why didn't Nehemiah know about this scandalous economic problem sooner? Probably because he was so immersed in the one thing he came to do—the rebuilding of the walls—that he had no time to get involved in the internal affairs of the community. His commission as governor was to repair the walls and restore the gates, not to reform the community. Furthermore, Nehemiah had not been in the city long enough to learn all that was going on.

It is important to note that the building of the wall did not *create* these problems; it *revealed* them. Often when a church enters into a building program, all sorts of problems start to surface that people didn't even know were there. A building program is a demanding thing that tests our faith, our patience, and our priorities; and while it brings out the best in some people, it can often bring out the worst in others.

Consultation (Neh 5:7). "I consulted with myself" means literally "My heart consulted within me." A friend of mine calls this "putting my heads together." Actually, Nehemiah put his heart and his head together as he pondered the problem and sought God's direction. He got control of his feelings and his thoughts so that he could give constructive leadership to the people. "He who is slow to anger is better than the mighty, and he who rules his spirit than he who takes a city" (Prov. 16:32, NKJV). If a leader can't control himself, he will never be successful in controlling others.

Nehemiah decided to call a great assembly (Neh. 5:7) and publicly confront the people whose selfishness had created this difficult and painful situation. Theirs was a grievous public sin, involving the whole nation; and it demanded public rebuke and repentance.

Rebuke (Neh. 5:7-11). Nehemiah's rebuke of the exploiters consisted of six different appeals. First, he appealed to *their love* by reminding them that they were robbing their own fellow Jews, not the Gentiles (v. 7). The word "brother" is used four times in this speech. "Behold, how good and how pleasant it is for brethren to dwell together in unity!" (Ps. 133:1) "Let's not have any quarreling between you and me," Abraham said to Lot, "for we are brothers" (Gen. 13:8, NIV).

His appeal was based solidly on *the Word of God,* for the Law of Moses forbade Jews to exact interest from one another. The Jewish nation went into Babylonian Captivity an agricultural people, but some of them came out a mercantile people, having learned how to use money to make money. There is certainly nothing wrong with lending money (Matt. 25:27), providing you don't violate God's Word and exploit those who are helpless.

It is remarkable how much the Bible has to say about the right and wrong use of money. It is also remarkable how many professed believers ignore these truths and use their resources without consulting the Lord. They think that because they tithe, or give offerings to the Lord, they can do what they please with the rest of their income. They forget that we are stewards of all that God gives us, not just of what we give Him; and that He will hold us accountable for our stewardship.

In his third appeal, Nehemiah reminded them of *God's redemptive purpose for Israel (Neh. 5:8).* In the past, God redeemed Israel from Egypt; and more recently, He had redeemed them from Captivity in Babylon. But this verse informs us that Nehemiah and others of the leading Jews had helped redeem some of their people, and now their fellow Jews were putting people into bondage just to make money. These selfish money lenders were tearing down everything that God and Nehemiah were trying to build up.

What is freedom? It is life governed by truth and motivated by love. But the Jewish brokers were motivated by greed and ignoring the truth of God's Word. Their selfishness put both themselves and their creditors into bondage.

Israel's witness to their Gentile neighbors (v. 9) was the fourth appeal Nehemiah presented to the guilty money lenders. God called Israel to be a "light to the Gentiles" (Isa. 42:6; 49:6), but their conduct was certainly anything but a witness to their pagan neighbors. How could some of the Jewish citizens build the city wall on the one hand but enslave their neighbors on the other hand? If we truly fear the Lord, then we will want to honor Him before those who don't believe in Him.

Paul used a similar approach when he censured the Corinthian Christians for taking one another to court. "Dare any of you, having a matter against another, go to law before the unrighteous, and not before the saints? . . . But brother goes to law against brother, and that before unbelievers!" (1 Cor. 6:1, 6, NKJV) Far better to lose money than lose the privilege of your witness to the lost. You can always earn more money, but how do you restore a damaged testimony?

"The fear of our God" is not the servile dread of a slave toward a master but the loving respect of a child toward a parent. To fear the Lord means to seek to glorify God in everything we do. It means listening to His Word, honoring it, and obeying it. "The remarkable thing about fearing God," wrote Oswald Chambers, "is that when you fear God, you fear nothing else, whereas if you do not fear God, you fear everything else." Because Nehemiah's life was motivated by the fear of the Lord (Neh. 5:15), he did not fear what the enemy might do (vv. 14, 19). The fear of the Lord moved Nehemiah to be a faithful servant of the Lord.

To walk in the fear of God, of course, means to walk by faith, trusting God to deal with your enemies and one day balance the accounts. It means claiming Matthew 6:33 and having the right priorities in life. "The fear of the Lord leads to life, and he who has it will abide in satisfaction; he will not be visited with evil" (Prov. 19:23, NKJV).

In Nehemiah 5:10-11, Nehemiah appealed to *his own personal practice.* He was lending money to the needy, but he was not charging interest or robbing them of their security (Ex. 22:25). Unlike some leaders, Nehemiah was not saying, "Do what I say, not what I do!" He was not a hypocrite; he practiced what he preached. In fact, this chapter will conclude with Nehemiah pointing out all that God had enabled him to do for his people (Neh. 5:14-19). He was a good example as a believer and as a leader.

"The hundredth part" in verse 11 was the interest charged for the money, probably applied monthly, making a total of 12 percent interest a year. This practice had been going on before Nehemiah arrived on the scene and now the people were in despair as they tried to balance the family budget.

A man of action, Nehemiah told the brokers to restore both the interest and the security they had taken from their fellow Jews, as well as the property they had claimed in foreclosure. This drastic step of faith and love would not immediately solve all the economic problems of the people, but it would at least keep the problems from getting worse. It would also give the suffering people opportunity to make a fresh new start.

Nehemiah's sixth appeal was to remind them of *the judgment of the Lord (vv. 12-13).* The brokers promised to obey, so Nehemiah had them take an oath in the presence of the priests and the other officers of the city. This meant that their promise was not only between them and their neighbors, but between them and the Lord; and this was a serious thing. "When you make a vow to God, do not delay in fulfilling it. He has no pleasure in fools; fulfill your vow. It is better not to vow than to make a vow and not fulfill it" (Eccl. 5:4-5, NIV).

The great assembly was concluded with three actions that emphasized the seriousness of the occasion. First, Nehemiah shook out the folds of his robe, symbolic of what God would do with the money lenders if they didn't fulfill their vow. Shaking your robe or the dust off your feet was a typically Jewish act of condemnation (Acts 13:51; 18:6; Matt. 10:14).

Then the congregation responded with a collective "Amen," which was much more than a Jewish ritual. It was their solemn assent to what had been said and done at the assembly (see Neh. 8:6 and Deut. 27:14ff). The word *amen* means "so be it"; in other words, "May the Lord do all that you said!" It was an act of worship that made the entire assembly a part of the decisions that were made.

Then the whole congregation together praised the Lord. Why? Because God had enabled Nehemiah to help them begin to solve their problems, and he had directed the money lenders to acknowledge their sins and make restitution. This great assembly was not an "economic summit"; it was a worship service where Nehemiah had lifted a financial problem to the highest possible level. God's people need to follow his example and deal with every problem in the light of the will of God as declared in the Word of God.

3. A great example (Neh. 5:14-19)

D.L. Moody said, "A holy life will produce the deepest impression. Lighthouses blow no horns; they only shine." In our day of public scandals in almost every area of life, especially the political, how refreshing it is to meet a man like Nehemiah who put serving the people ahead of getting gain for himself.

Nehemiah never read Philippians 2:1-13, but he certainly practiced it. During his first term of twelve years as governor, and then during his second term of office (Neh. 13:6-7), he used his privileges for helping the people; he did not use the people to build a kingdom for himself. In that day, most officials exercised their authority in order to promote themselves and protect their personal interests. They had very little concern for the needs of the people. As children of God, our example is Jesus Christ and not the leaders of this world (Luke 22:23-30). "A cross stands in the way of spiritual leadership," writes J. Oswald Sanders, "a cross upon which the leader must consent to be impaled" *(Spiritual Leadership,* Moody Press, 1976; p. 105).

In what ways are these men examples to us? To begin with, Nehemiah and his assistants did not use the official expense account for their household expenses, nor did they tax the people in order to have something to eat. They paid their expenses out of their own pockets and didn't ask to be reimbursed.

The Apostle Paul followed a similar policy with the church at Corinth. He could have accepted support from them, as he did from other churches; but he chose to work with his own hands and preach the Gospel to them "without cost" (1 Cor. 9). Paul did not say that *every* Christian worker should do this, for "the laborer is worthy of his hire" (Luke 10:7; 1 Cor. 9:14). But every Christian should follow Paul's example in having a balanced spiritual attitude toward wealth and ministry. We must be willing to sacrifice personal gain for the spiritual good of others (see Acts 20:33-35 and 1 Sam. 12:3).

It has been said that leaders are people who accept more of the blame and less of the credit, but they are also people who quietly sacrifice so that others might have more.

Nehemiah and his associates not only paid their own bills, but they were also careful not to exploit the people in any way (Neh. 5:15). The servants of previous governors had used their positions for personal gain, perhaps taking bribes from the people and promising to represent them before the governor. For people in places of authority, the temptation to increase wealth and power is always present; but Nehemiah and his friends walked in the fear of the Lord and served honestly.

They were examples in a third way: They all participated in the rebuilding of the wall (v. 16). They were not advisors who occasionally emerged from their ivory towers, but workers who stood with the people in the construction and defense of the city. Jesus said, "I am among you as one who serves" (Luke 22:27, NIV); and Nehemiah and his aides had that same attitude.

Nehemiah was an example in another way: He not only paid for his own food, but he shared what he had with others (Neh. 5:17-18). He regularly fed over 150 guests, both residents and visitors, and he gave them a marvelous meal! (See 1 Kings 4:22-23 for Solomon's daily fare.) It is estimated that this amount of food would meet the needs of over 500 guests, so Nehemiah must have kept "open house" constantly. Or perhaps he shared what was left with the people working on the wall. At any rate, he was generous to others and asked for no reward.

Nehemiah 5:19 indicates perhaps the greatest thing about Nehemiah's service: He did what he did only to please the Lord. This is the fourth of his prayers (1:5ff; 2:5; 4:4), a wonderful expression of worship and humility. He didn't want praise or reward from the people; he wanted only the reward God would give him for his sacrificial service (see 13:14). Some of the people may not have appreciated their leaders as they should, but that didn't upset Nehemiah. He knew that the final assessment would come from the Lord, and he was willing to wait (1 Cor. 4:1-5).

If you are in a position of spiritual leadership, this chapter has some important lessons for you. To begin with, *expect problems to arise among your people.* Wherever you have people, you have the potential for problems. Whenever God's work is prospering, the enemy sees to it that trouble begins. Don't be surprised when your people can't always get along with each other.

Second, *confront the problems courageously.* "There is no problem so great that you can't ignore it" might be a good philosophy for a character in a comic strip, but it won't work in the Lord's service.

Every problem that you ignore will only go underground, grow deeper roots, and bear bitter fruits. Pray for God's help and tackle the problem as soon as possible.

Third, *be sure that your own integrity is intact.* A guilty conscience will rob you of the spiritual authority you need to give proper leadership, but every sacrifice you have made will give you the extra strength you need to defeat the enemy.

Finally, *see in every problem an opportunity for the Lord to work.* Solving problems in ministry is not an intellectual exercise but a spiritual experience. If we depend on the wisdom of the world, we will get what the world can do; but if we depend on the wisdom of God, we will get what God can do. All that we say and do must be motivated by love, controlled by truth, and done to the glory of God.

The work had been interrupted by the calling of the assembly and the solving of the economic problems, and now it was time for everybody to get back to his or her place on the wall. But Nehemiah's enemies would also be busy. This time they would aim their ammunition especially at Nehemiah and try to defeat him with four devilish devices.

CHAPTER SIX
WE HAVE HEARD THE ENEMY, AND HE IS A LIAR
Nehemiah 6

Under Nehemiah's gifted leadership, the people completed the rebuilding of the walls. Now all that remained to do was the restoration of the gates and the strengthening of the community within the walls. Since Sanballat and his friends had failed miserably in their attempts to stop the people from working, they decided to concentrate their attacks on Nehemiah. If they could eliminate him, or even discredit him, they could mobilize their allies living in Jerusalem (Neh. 6:17-18) and take over the city.

The average person doesn't realize the tremendous pressures and testings that people experience day after day in places of leadership. Leaders are often blamed for things they didn't do and criticized for things they tried to do. They are misquoted and misunderstood and rarely given the opportunity to set the record straight. If they act quickly, they are reckless; if they bide their time, they are cowardly or unconcerned. Referring to the pressures of leadership, President Harry Truman wrote in *Mr. Citizen,* "If you can't stand the heat, get out of the kitchen!"

People in places of *spiritual* leadership not only have the pressures that all leaders face, but they must also battle an infernal enemy who is a master deceiver and a murderer. Satan comes either as a serpent who deceives or a lion who devours (2 Cor. 11:3; 1 Peter 5:8), and Christian leaders must be alert and spiritually equipped to oppose him. It behooves God's people to pray earnestly, not only for those in *civil* authority (1 Tim. 2:1-3), but also for those in places of *spiritual* authority. If Satan can defeat a Christian leader, he can cripple a whole ministry and discredit the cause of Christ.

The enemy's main purpose was to generate fear in the heart of Nehemiah and his workers (Neh. 6:9, 13-14, 19), knowing that fear destroys faith and paralyzes life. Adolph Hitler wrote, "Mental confusion, contradiction of feeling, indecisiveness, panic; these are our weapons."

Both Jesus (Luke 13:31-37) and Paul (Acts 21:10-14) had to face the specter of fear, and both overcame it by faith.

Nehemiah didn't listen to the enemy's lies. He and the people completed the wall and hung the gates in only fifty-two days, much to the chagrin of their adversaries (Neh. 6:15-16). Satan used four strategies in attacking Nehemiah, strategies that he still uses against spiritual leaders today.

1. Compromise: "We will help you work". (Neh. 6:1-4)

Up to this point in the building program, Sanballat, Tobiah, and Geshem (Gashmu, v. 6) *opposed* everything that the Jews did; but now they offered to *cooperate* and help the Jews build the wall. They offered to meet Nehemiah in a village halfway between Jerusalem and Samaria, a quiet place where they could make plans on how to work together. "We're willing to meet you halfway," was their approach. "Now, don't be an unfriendly neighbor!"

Of course, the enemy's strategy was, "If you can't whip 'em, join 'em—and then take over!" Once the enemy gets a foothold in a ministry, he starts to weaken the work from within; and ultimately, the work will fail. While cooperation in the Lord's work is a noble thing, leaders must take care that they cooperate with the right people at the right time for the right purpose; otherwise they may end up cooperating with the enemy. Satan is a master deceiver and has his servants ready to join hands with God's people so he can weaken their hands in the work (2 Cor. 11:13-15).

Loving compromise and cooperation can be good and useful things *if there are no moral or spiritual issues involved.* Happy compromise can invigorate a marriage or strengthen a ministry (Phil. 2:1-4), but this is compromise among people who love each other and have the same purposes in mind. When you invite the devil to join your team, expect him to change the rules and the goals; and expect to be defeated.

Nehemiah rejected their offer because of three convictions. First, he knew that they were lying and wanted to kill him (Neh. 6:2). Nehemiah had the kind of spiritual discernment that leaders must possess if they are going to detect the enemy's strategy and defeat it. Second, he was convinced of the greatness of the work God had given him to do (v. 3). If Nehemiah allowed himself to be distracted and detoured from the work God had called him to do, where would his people go for leadership? A leaderless project is an aimless project and eventually falls apart. Leaders must be good examples and stay on the job.

During over forty years of ministry, as I have watched Christian leaders come and go, I have tried to take Paul's admonition to heart: "Therefore let him who thinks he stands take heed lest he fall" (1 Cor. 10:12, NKJV). I have noticed that when leaders become well-known, they often face the temptation to neglect their God-given work, join the "evangelical jet set," and start speaking all over the country or the world. Before long, the work at home starts to suffer, and often the leader's marriage and family suffer with it; and the enemy gets a foothold. Unless some radical changes are made in priorities, the result is tragic for both God's people and God's work.

This is not to say that Christian leaders must never leave home to minister elsewhere, for they are a gift *to the whole church* and not just to one work (Eph. 4:11-12). But when "the wider ministry" is more exciting than the work at home, leaders must beware; for the enemy is at work. Dr. Oswald J. Smith used to say, "The light that shines the farthest will shine the brightest at home."

Behind these two convictions was a third conviction: The Jews had nothing in common with Sanballat and his crowd, so there could be no basis for cooperation. Nehemiah had made that clear at the very outset of the project when he said to Sanballat, Tobiah, and Geshem, "But as for you, you have no share in Jerusalem or any claim or historic right to it" (Neh. 2:20, NIV). God's people are different from the people of the world and must maintain their separated position (2 Cor. 6:14-7:1). If Nehemiah had cooperated with Sanballat and his allies, how could he have led the nation to separate itself from the foreigners in the land? (Neh. 9:2; 10:28; 13:3) He would have been inconsistent.

Nehemiah had both discernment and determination: He refused to be influenced by their repeated offers (6:4; see 4:12). If their offer was wrong the first time, it would be wrong the fourth time or the fiftieth time; and there was no reason for him to reconsider. Decisions based only on *opinions* might be reconsidered, but decisions based on *convictions* must stand unless those convictions are changed. Otherwise, decision becomes indecision; and the leader who ought to be a guidepost becomes a weather vane.

2. Slander: "We'll tell everybody about you". (Neh. 6:5-9)

The fifth time the enemy approached Nehemiah, it was with an open letter accusing him of sedition. They had hinted at Jewish insurrection before the project had even begun (2:19), perhaps borrowing the idea from the people who had stopped the building of the temple years before (Ezra 4). Even our Lord was accused by His enemies of promoting sedition (Luke 23:1-5). It would be considered a serious charge in Nehemiah's day, because Persian kings tolerated no resistance from their subjects. Any hint of rebellion was immediately and ruthlessly put down.

It's interesting to see how often the enemy used *letters* in their attacks against the work (Neh. 6:5, 17, 19). An "open letter" to a royal governor would be both intimidating and insulting. Letters to officials were rolled up and secured with seals so that only those with authority could open and read them. Sanballat *wanted* the public to know the contents of the letter because he hoped to undermine Nehemiah's reputation and authority. If some of the Jewish workers believed what was in the letter, Sanballat could organize them and create division within the ranks. It was a splendid opportunity for the enemy to divide and conquer.

Statements like "it's been reported" and "they say" have caused trouble in many local churches and other ministries. In every organization, there are gossipmongers, hovering like vultures, just waiting for tidbits of slander that they can chew, swallow, and then regurgitate. An anonymous wit has defined *gossip* as news you have to hurry and tell somebody else before you find out it isn't true!

"I would rather play with forked lightning, or take in my hands living wires with their fiery current," said A.B. Simpson, founder of the Christian and Missionary Alliance, "than speak a reckless word against any servant of Christ, or idly repeat the slanderous darts which thousands of Christians are hurling on others, to the hurt of their own souls and bodies."

Not only did his enemies falsely accuse Nehemiah of fomenting a rebellion, but they also said he was planning to make himself king and had prophets prepared to announce his coronation (v. 7). If this report got back to the Persian king, there would be immediate reprisal; and that would be the end of the Jerusalem project.

Christian leaders must know how to handle false accusations, vicious letters, unfounded press reports, and gossip. Otherwise, these devilish weapons will so upset them that they will lose their perspective and spend so much time defending themselves that they will neglect their work. Nehemiah didn't make that mistake. He simply denied the reports, prayed to God for strength, *and went back to work.* He knew that his character was such that no honest person would believe the false reports. If we take care of our character, we can trust God to take care of our reputation.

On more than one occasion, Bible teacher G. Campbell Morgan was the target of savage gossip that accused him of unfaithfulness to the Christian faith. His usual approach was to say, "It will blow over. Meanwhile, I go quietly on with my work." Nehemiah would have approved of his approach.

3. Threats: "We will protect your life". (Neh. 6:10-14)

Shemaiah, a hireling prophet (v. 12), devised a clever plan for trapping Nehemiah. He shut himself up in his house and gave the impression that, like Nehemiah, his life was in danger. When Nehemiah came to see him, Shemaiah suggested that they both take refuge in the temple, where the enemy couldn't reach them (Ex. 21:13-14; 1 Kings 1:50-53). His words were very threatening: "They are coming to kill you; indeed, at night they will come to kill you" (Neh. 6:10, NKJV).

Since he had access to the temple, it's possible that Shemaiah was of priestly descent; but even this didn't influence Nehemiah's decision. He quickly detected the hoax and let it be known that he was not about to run away in the face of danger. In the first place, he was not that kind of a leader.

"Should such a man as I flee?" he asked (v. 11). He had previously said, "I cannot come down!" (v. 3) and now he declared, "I will not go in!" (v. 11) Nehemiah was a true shepherd and not a hireling like Shemaiah (John 10:12-13). If he had run away and hidden in the temple, it would have ruined his reputation forever.

Nehemiah rejected Shemaiah's proposal because it was contrary to the Law of Moses. It was forbidden for a layman to go beyond the altar of burnt offering at the temple. "The outsider who comes near shall be put to death" (Num. 18:7, NKJV). When King Uzziah tried to invade the holy precincts, God smote him with leprosy (2 Chron. 26:16-21). Nehemiah knew that Shemaiah was a *false* prophet because the message he delivered was contradictory to the Word of God (Deut. 13:1-5 and 18:20-22). "What saith the Scripture?" (Rom. 4:3) must be the test of any message, even if that message comes from somebody who claims to be one of God's servants. "To the law and to the testimony: if they speak not according to this word, it is because there is no light in them" (Isa. 8:20).

Nehemiah 6:14 indicates that there was a conspiracy against Nehemiah among the prophets, including a prophetess named Noadiah. This created a great deal of pressure for Nehemiah, for the Jews had great respect for their prophets. Nehemiah was outnumbered, yet he stood his ground. He was a layman opposed by a body of "professionals," yet he refused to give in. He prayed about them and left the matter with the Lord. In verses 9 and 14, we have the fifth and sixth of Nehemiah's "telegraph prayers" that he sent to the Lord in times of crisis. Of course, behind these brief intermittent prayers was a life of prayer that gave them strength.

4. Intrigue: "We will not give up". (Neh. 6:15-19)

The completion of the walls "in troublous times" (Dan. 9:25) was an embarrassment to the enemy, *but they did not give up.*

Satan is not a quitter but stays on the field even after it looks as if he has lost the battle. *Many a careless Christian has won the war but afterward lost the victory.* Satan is always looking for "an opportune time" (Luke 4:13, NIV) to attack the victors and turn them into victims. We need to heed the counsel of that saintly Scottish minister Andrew A. Bonar, who said, "Let us be as watchful after the victory as before the battle."

If you can't see Satan working, it's probably because he has gone underground. Actually, we are safer when we can see him at work than when his agents are concealed. Open opposition is good for God's work and God's workers because it keeps us alert and trusting the Lord. "Watch and pray!" was certainly one of Nehemiah's chief admonitions to his people (Neh. 4:9).

It seems incredible that *any* Jew would secretly cooperate with the enemy, let alone Jews who were *nobles* from the royal tribe of *Judah!* If any tribe had a stake in the future of "the city of David," it was the tribe of Judah; for God promised that a Savior and King would come from their tribe (Gen. 49:10; 2 Sam. 7). When these nobles cooperated with Tobiah, they were resisting the Lord, disobeying the Word, and jeopardizing their own future.

Why would they do such a treacherous thing? For one thing, Tobiah wrote them letters and influenced their thinking. Instead of seeking the truth, the nobles believed the enemy's lies and became traitors to their own people. Because they believed he was right, some of the men of Judah even took an oath of loyalty to Tobiah! In his letters, Tobiah no doubt flattered them and made promises to them; and they foolishly believed him. The nobles secretly shared the letters with others, and thus the conspiracy grew.

Don't believe everything you read or hear about Christian leaders. Consider the source and firmly refuse to accept as truth anything that can't be documented. Especially be wary of what the news media say about evangelical leaders; most media people are not too sympathetic with the Gospel. Looking for exciting stories, some reporters will magnify the insignificant into the sensational, while others will lift statements completely out of context. Sad to say, even the religious press is sometimes guilty of this kind of misrepresentation, including some militant publications that have forgotten how to "speak the truth in love" (Eph. 4:15). There are times when you wonder if perhaps we have reached the sad place that Jeremiah wrote about: "Beware of your friends; do not trust your brothers. For every brother is a deceiver, and every friend a slanderer" (Jer. 9:4, NIV).

How could these Jews turn their backs on their own heritage, their own brothers and sisters, and their own God? *The bonds of human connection were stronger than the bonds of spiritual affection.* Because Tobiah was tied to the tribe of Judah through marriage, the nobles of Judah gave the loyalty to him that they should have given to God (Neh. 6:18). The men of Judah forgot that they were "married" to Jehovah God and owed Him their love and loyalty.

But before we criticize these Jewish nobles, let's examine our own lives. Are we totally yielded to the Lord and fully obedient to Him? Do we ever permit human relationships to influence our decisions so much that we deliberately disobey the Word of God? In twenty-five years of pastoral ministry, I have seen more than one professed Christian leave a church fellowship because of something that was done to a relative in the church.

Commodore Josiah Tatnall is an almost forgotten name in American naval history. During the anti-European uprisings in China in 1859, Tatnall came to the aid of a British squadron in the Pei-Ho River and was criticized for it. In his dispatch to the U.S. Secretary of Navy, his defense was simply, "Blood is thicker than water."

That familiar statement was recorded by John Ray in his *English Proverbs* published in 1670; so it's been around for a long time. The meaning is obvious: Humanly speaking, you have greater obligation to a relative than you do to a stranger. But Jesus said, "He who loves father or mother more than Me is not worthy of Me. And he who loves son or daughter more than Me is not worthy of Me" (Matt. 10:37, NKJV). The "blood bond" that unites us to Christ is the strongest bond of all, and our loyalty to Him must come first.

The nobles of Judah weren't satisfied just to get their information and directions from Tobiah, but they felt it necessary to tell Tobiah everything Nehemiah said! No doubt they were hoping to win Tobiah's favor and thus earn a greater reward when Tobiah and his friends took over Jerusalem. In every sense, they were traitors to the nation and to the Lord. Meshullam was one of the workers on the wall (Neh. 3:4, 30), and yet his family was undermining the very work he was doing.

But these traitors went even further: They repeatedly told Nehemiah what a fine man Tobiah really was! "They that forsake the law praise the wicked; but such as keep the law contend with them" (Prov. 28:4). Had the nobles of Judah been studying and meditating on the Word of God, they would have had discernment and not been walking "in the counsel of the ungodly" (Ps. 1:1). They were blinded by lies and flattery and completely out of touch with reality. There was no light in them (Isa. 8:20).

But is the situation much different in churches today? It alarms me the way professed Christians, who claim to be "Bible taught," give their endorsement and support to people who are nothing but religious hucksters. You would think that the recent media scandals would wake people up, but such is not the case. "A horrible and shocking thing has happened in the land: The prophets prophesy lies, the priests rule by their own authority, and my people love it this way," wrote Jeremiah; and then he asked, "But what will you do in the end?" Jer. 5:30-31, NIV) Indeed, we are facing a day of reckoning. Then what?

Tobiah kept sending letters to his informers, and they in turn kept telling people to change their allegiance before Jerusalem was taken by the Gentiles. Nehemiah ignored the letters and threats and kept on working until the job was completed. After all, his work was "wrought of our God" (Neh. 6:16); and when God begins a work, He completes it (Phil. 1:6).

The story began with "So I prayed" (Neh. 2:4). Then we read, "So I came to Jerusalem" (v. 11). "So they strengthened their hands for this good work" is the next link in the chain (v. 18), followed by, "So built we the wall" (4:6) and, "So we labored" (v. 21).

Now we reach the end of this part of the story: "So the wall was finished" (6:15). But this marks a new beginning, for now Nehemiah must protect what he has accomplished. How he does this is the theme of the rest of the book.

CHAPTER SEVEN
"V" IS FOR VIGILANCE
Nehemiah 7

The walls were completed, the gates were restored, and the enemy was chagrined; but Nehemiah's work was not finished by any means. Now he had to practice the truth Paul emphasized in Ephesians 6:13, "And having done all, to stand." Nehemiah had been steadfast in building the walls and in resisting the enemy, and now he had to be steadfast in consolidating and conserving the gains. "Look to yourselves," warned the Apostle John, "that we lose not those things which we have wrought, but that we receive a full reward" (2 John 8).

A city is much more than walls, gates, and houses; a city is people. In the first half of this book, the people existed for the walls; but now the walls must exist for the people. It was time to organize the community so that the citizens could enjoy the quality of life God wanted them to have. God had great things in store for Jerusalem, for one day His Son would walk the city streets, teach in the temple, and die outside the city walls.

This chapter records three important steps that must be taken by any leader in order to protect the people and the work that has been done.

1. Enlisting leadership (Neh. 7:1-3)

Napoleon described a leader as "a dealer in hope," and Nehemiah certainly fits that description. Before the work began, he inspired the people by assuring them that God would prosper their efforts (2:18-20). When the people were afraid, he prayed that God would strengthen them (6:9). When the enemy threatened, Nehemiah stood his ground and called their bluff; and the work was completed in fifty-two days to the glory of God.

Assistants (Neh 7:2). Like all good leaders, Nehemiah knew he couldn't do the job alone. One of his first official acts was to appoint two assistants, his brother Hanani (see 1:2) and Hananiah, who was in charge of the citadel ("palace"; see 2:8). The citadel was a fortress in the temple area, guarding the north wall of the city, which was especially vulnerable to attack. Hanani and Hananiah would work with Rephaiah (3:9) and Shallum (v. 12), rulers of districts in the city.

Why was Nehemiah convinced that these men would be good leaders? They had two wonderful qualities: They were faithful to God and they feared God (7:2). Dr. Bob Jones, Sr., often said, "The greatest ability is dependability." If we truly fear the Lord, we will be faithful to do the work He has called us to do. When leaders fear people instead of fearing God, they end up getting trapped (Prov. 29:25); and that leads to failure.

Years ago, the German psychiatrist and philosopher Dr. Karl Jaspers said, "The power of leadership appears to be declining everywhere. More and more of the men we see coming to the top seem to be merely drifting." My former "boss" in Youth for Christ International, Dr. Ted Engstrom, wrote in his book *The Making of A Christian Leader* (Zondervan, 1976), "We see the tragedy of weak men in important places—little men in big jobs" (p. 12). British essayist Walter Savage Landor wrote, "When little men cast long shadows, it is a sign that the sun is setting." An ominous statement, indeed!

Not everybody is called to be a Nehemiah, but some of us can be Hananis, Hananiahs, Rephaiahs, or Shallums, and work with God-given leaders to help get the job done right. God is looking for faithful, God-fearing men and women who will have the courage and conviction to serve Him, come what may.

Gatekeepers (Neh. 7:1, 3). What good are strong new gates if nobody is guarding them and controlling who enters and leaves the city? What good are walls if the gates are open to every foe who wants to enter the city? I understand that the Great Wall of China was penetrated by the enemy at least four times, and each time the guards were bribed. Gates and walls are only as good as the people who guard them.

The gatekeepers ("porters" in v. 1) were given specific instructions as to when to open and close the gates (v. 3). To open the gates early in the morning would only invite the enemy to come in while the city was asleep and unprepared. To close and lock the gates without the guards on duty might give enemy agents opportunity to slip in unnoticed.

Guards. Nehemiah also had appointed two kinds of guards ("watches" v. 3): Those to patrol the walls at specific stations and those to keep watch near their own houses. Since many of the people had worked on areas of the wall near their homes (3:10, 23, 28-30), Nehemiah now challenged them to guard the areas they had built. With guards at the gates, watchmen on the walls, and a solid "neighborhood watch," the city was safe from outside attack.

All of this has a message for us today. *If God's people don't protect what they have accomplished for the Lord, the enemy will come in and take it over.* Paul's admonition must be heeded: "And having done all, to stand" (Eph. 6:13). What a tragedy that schools that once were true to the faith are today denying the faith, and churches that once preached the Gospel now have in their pulpits ministers who preach "another gospel." *Every Christian ministry is one short generation away from destruction, and God's people must be on guard.*

We need guards at the gates, faithful men and women who will not allow false Christians to get in and take over the ministry (2 Cor. 11:13-15). We need watchers on the walls to warn us when the enemy is approaching. Christian parents need to guard their homes lest the enemy gets in and captures their children. It is while God's servants are asleep and overconfident that the enemy comes in and plants his counterfeits (Matt. 13:25), so we must be awake and alert.

In this day when "pluralism" is interpreted by most people to mean "agree with everybody about everything and don't make waves," Christians need to remember that they are *different* and must test everything by the Word of God. There are many religions, but there is still "none other name under heaven given among men, whereby we must be saved" (Acts 4:12). Anything that changes that message or weakens our motivation to get that message out is of the devil and must be opposed. We need guards at the gates and watchers on the wall, or the enemy will take over.

2. Establishing citizenship (Neh. 7:4-69)

This section parallels Ezra 2:1-64. If you compare the two lists, you will see that some of Nehemiah's names and numbers differ from those recorded nearly a century before when the exiles returned from Babylon. This does not suggest that there are either errors or contradictions in the Bible. Errors in spelling names or copying numbers could easily creep in over a century, and none of these differences affects any matter of doctrine or duty.

Furthermore, the scribes who kept the public records certainly updated them after the community was established in Jerusalem. Ezra 2 lists the names of those who set out with Ezra, but it's possible that others joined the group after Zerubbabel's list was completed. For instance, Ezra 2:2 lists only *eleven* leaders, while Nehemiah 7:7 gives *twelve* names, adding Nahamani. "Nehum" in Nehemiah 7:7 is probably "Rehum" in Ezra 2:2. Variations such as this one are to be expected in ancient documents.

Reading this long list of difficult names might be boring to the modern student, but these people were God's "bridge" from the defeats of the past to the hopes of the future. These Jews were the "living link" that connected the historic past with the prophetic future and made it possible for Jesus Christ to come into the world. Ezra 2 and Nehemiah 7 are to the Old Testament what Hebrews 11 is to the New Testament: a listing of the people whose faith and courage made things happen.

Our modern cities are ethnic "melting pots"; but in Jerusalem at that time, the important thing was to be a Jew *and be able to prove your ancestry.* Genealogies were "lifelines" that linked the Jews not only to the heritage of the past but also to their hope for the future. Not to be able to prove your ancestry meant second-class citizenship and separation from all that God had given to Israel (Rom. 9:4-5). Nehemiah wanted to populate the holy city with citizens who knew they were Jews and were proud of it.

There are ten different groups listed here, starting with the *leaders who returned with Zerubbabel (Neh. 7:7).* These twelve men may have represented the twelve tribes of Israel, even though ten of the tribes had been assimilated by the Assyrians when the Northern Kingdom was captured in 722 B.C. The "Nehemiah" mentioned here is not the author of this book, since these men lived nearly a century before. It appears that these were the elders of the people who helped Zerubbabel, the governor, establish the nation.

Next are listed the various *families* or *clans* (vv. 8-25) and the number of people in each family who returned to the land. Verses 27-38 list the people according to their *villages.* It is interesting that the largest group in the entire list came from Senaah (v. 38), a town whose location is a mystery to us. It must have been a large community if nearly 4,000 people came from there. The Hebrew word means "hated," and some students think it refers to a category of citizen and not to a place. These may have been the "lower classes" in the Jewish society. Whoever they were, they worked on the walls (3:3) and helped restore the city.

It is worth noting that these returned exiles had maintained their identification with their native towns and villages. They knew where they came from and were not ashamed of it! Many people in our modern mobile population care little about family roots or even civic loyalty. Home is wherever one's work is, no matter where your original roots were planted. Also, in spite of their local loyalties, these Jews put the good of Jerusalem first (Ps. 137:1-6). True patriotism sees no conflict between loving one's home city and loving one's nation, for both are gifts from God.

The temple personnel are listed next: *priests (Neh. 7:39-42), Levites (v. 43), temple singers (v. 44), gatekeepers (v. 45),* and *various temple servants (vv. 46-60).* In the original return to the land, it was necessary for Ezra to send for Levites to serve in the restored temple (Ezra 8:15-20). Were the Levites so comfortable in Babylon that they were unwilling to serve in Jerusalem?

The temple servants ("Nethinim") had been organized by David to assist in the temple (Neh. 7:20) and may have been either prisoners of war or descendants of the Gibeonites (Josh. 9:22-27), who relieved the Levites of heavy routine tasks, like cutting wood and drawing water. "Solomon's servants" (Neh. 7:57) were also foreigners who labored for the king. That these non-Jews were willing to leave the secure life in Babylon for the difficulties of life in Jerusalem may indicate that they had come to trust the God of Israel. On the other hand, perhaps they were compelled to return by their masters.

The *singers* will play an important role in the life of the city. There are at least eighteen references to singers in the Book of Nehemiah and eight references to giving thanks to the Lord. There was not much singing during the exile, when the nation was out of fellowship with God (Ps. 137); but now they needed the musicians to maintain worship at the temple.

One group of people, including some priests, *could not prove their genealogies (Neh. 7:61-65).* For the priests, this would mean being cut off from the temple ministry and the income it provided from the tithes and offerings of the people. But the Law of Moses made it clear that only those whose family line was clearly in the family of Aaron could minister at the altar. Finally, there was a miscellaneous assembly of over 7,000 *servants (v. 67).* Since the total number of the congregation was over 42,000 (v. 66), about one-sixth of the population was in servitude. Jewish masters must have been very kind to their servants for so many of them to want to travel with them to Judea.

The animals were mentioned (vv. 68-69) because they were vitally important to the Jewish agricultural economy and to the work of rebuilding the nation.

The total of the figures in this list is 29,818; but Nehemiah's total is 42,360. When you add the 7,337 servants and the 245 singers to the 29,818 total, you get a total of 37,400, a difference of almost 5,000 from Nehemiah's figure. Some of these extra unnumbered people may have been priests who could not prove their genealogy (vv. 63-65), as well as others who didn't fit into any special category. If we knew all the facts about how Ezra 2 and Nehemiah 7 were compiled and copied, we would understand these seeming discrepancies.

The important thing is not to count the people but to realize that *these people counted.* In leaving Babylon, they did much more than put their names on a list. They laid their lives on the altar and risked everything to obey the Lord and restore the Jewish nation. They were "pioneers of faith" who trusted God to enable them to do the impossible.

Before we leave this section, it might be good for you to ask yourself, "If I had to prove my genealogy in order to get into God's city, could I do it?" You are heading for one of two destinies—heaven or hell—and only those who belong to God's family can enter heaven. You enter God's family by receiving Jesus Christ as your own Savior, and this alone guarantees your entrance into heaven (John 1:11-12; 3:16; 14:6).

3. Encouraging worship (Neh. 7:70-73) Citizenship and leadership together can make a state, but it takes worship to make that state into a godly nation. John Stuart Mill wrote, "The worth of a state, in the long run, is the worth of the individuals composing it." But the worth of the individual depends on his or her relationship to God, and this involves worship. If individual godliness declines, the morality of the nation declines.

The parallel passage is Ezra 2:68-70, which tells us that some of the Jewish leaders gave generously to the temple ministry. But Nehemiah informs us that the governor ("Tirshatha") and some of the common people also gave offerings to the Lord. It was only right that the leaders set the example. A thousand drams (Neh. 7:70) would be 19 pounds of gold, and 20,000 drams (vv. 71-72) would be about 375 pounds. It seems obvious that some of the Jewish leaders left Babylon very wealthy men, with precious metals and servants; but within a few years, the economy failed and the nation was in the grips of a crippling depression (Hag. 1).

But all of this money would have been useless were it not for the God-appointed ministers at the temple: the priests, Levites, singers, and helpers (Neh. 7:73). Moses had assigned special towns for the priests and Levites to live in (Num. 35:1-8; Josh. 21), but later Nehemiah had to move some of them into Jerusalem (Neh. 11:1-2).

It was now the seventh month (Oct.-Nov.), when Israel was expected to celebrate the Feast of Trumpets, the Day of Atonement, and the Feast of Tabernacles (Lev. 23:23-44). There could have been no better time for Nehemiah to call the people together to honor the Word of God, confess their sins, and dedicate themselves and their work to the Lord. What began with *concern (Neh. 1)* led to *construction (chaps. 2-3)* and *conflict (chaps. 4-7);* and now it was time for *consecration (chaps. 8-12).*

As we serve the Lord, we must always do our best; but without His help and blessing, even our best work will never last. "Unless the Lord builds the house, they labor in vain who build it; unless the Lord guards the city, the watchman stays awake in vain" (Ps. 127:1, NKJV). Nehemiah knew that there was a desperate need for the people to come back to the Lord and turn away from their secret sins that were grieving Him. Even though Nehemiah was the official representative of a pagan king, he did everything he could to glorify the God of Israel.

One of the key lessons we can learn from this long chapter is that *people are important to God.* When God wanted to take the next step in His great plan of redemption, He called a group of Jews to leave the place of exile and return to their own land. He gave them encouragement from the prophets and leadership from people who feared God and wanted to honor Him. The Lord didn't send a band of angels to do the job; He used common people who were willing to risk their futures on the promises of God.

Today, God is still calling people to leave their personal "Babylon" and follow Him by faith. The church is living in a day of reproach (Neh. 2:17), and there are "ruins" all around us that need to be rebuilt. "If the foundations be destroyed, what can the righteous do?" David asked (Ps. 11:3). The answer is plain: *The righteous can rebuild what has been torn down and start over again!* If you think that an enemy victory is final, then you have lost your faith in God's promises. There is always a new beginning for those who are willing to pay the price.

This chapter also reminds us that *God keeps accounts of His servants.* He knows where we came from, what family we belong to, how much we gave, and how much we did for Him. When we stand before the Lord, we will have to give an accounting of our lives before we can receive our rewards (Rom. 14:7-12); and we want to be able to give a good account.

A third lesson we must learn is that *the Lord is able to keep His work going.* The first group of Jewish exiles left Babylon for Judea in 538 B.C. and, in spite of many difficulties and delays, rebuilt the temple and restored the worship. Eighty years later, Ezra and another group returned; and fourteen years after that, Nehemiah arrived and rebuilt the walls and gates. During the days of Zerubbabel, God raised up the Prophets Haggai and Zechariah to give God's message to His people. No matter how discouraging the situation might be, God is able to accomplish His purposes if we will trust Him and do His will. John Wesley was right when he said that God buries His workers but continues His work. We must not be discouraged!

Finally, and most important, we must all be sure that *we know we are in the family of God.* No matter how much they argued or protested, the priests without legitimate genealogies could not enter the temple precincts and minister at the altar. God is not impressed with our first birth; what He wants is that we experience a second birth and become His children. If you are not certain of your spiritual genealogy, read John 3:1-18 and 1 John 5:9-13 and make sure that your name is written down in heaven (Luke 10:20).

CHAPTER EIGHT
THE PEOPLE AND THE BOOK
Nehemiah 8

French author Victor Hugo said over a century ago, "England has two books, the Bible and Shakespeare. England made Shakespeare but the Bible made England." Supporting that view, historians tell us that Elizabethan England was indeed a country of one book, and that book was the Bible.

When they arrived in America, the Pilgrim Fathers brought with them that same reverence for the Word of God. "The Bible came with them," said American statesman Daniel Webster, "and it is not to be doubted that to the free and universal reading of the Bible is to be ascribed in that age that men were indebted for right views of civil liberties." President Woodrow Wilson said, "America was born to exemplify that devotion to the elements of righteousness which are derived from the revelations of Holy Scripture."

Whether the Bible is "making" any nation today may be debated, but one thing is sure: The Scriptures helped to "make" the nation of Israel. They are a "people of the Book" as no other nation has been, and the church today would do well to follow ancient Israel's example. When God's people get away from loving, reading, and obeying the Word of God, they lose the blessing of God. If we want to be like fruitful trees, we must delight in God's Word (Ps. 1:2-3).

This explains why Nehemiah called for a "Bible conference" and invited Ezra the scribe to be the teacher. The walls were now finished and the gates were hung. The *material* needs of the city had been met; now it was time to focus on the *spiritual* needs of the people in the city. Chapters 8-13 of the book record that spiritual ministry: instructing the people (chap. 8), confessing sin (chap. 9), dedicating the walls (chaps 10-12), and cleansing the fellowship (chap. 13).

It is important to note that *Ezra and Nehemiah put the Word of God first in the life of the city.* What happened in Jerusalem from that point on was a by-product of the people's response to the Scriptures. "The primary task of the church and of the Christian minister is the preaching of the Word of God," said Dr. D. Martyn Lloyd-Jones. "The decadent periods and eras in the history of the church have always been those periods when preaching had declined" *(Preaching and Preachers,* pp. 19, 24). The Spirit of God uses the Word of God to cleanse and revive the hearts of the people of God.

If God is to work in and through His people, then they must respond positively to His Word; and this chapter describes three basic responses: understanding the Word (8:1–8), rejoicing in the Word (vv. 9-12), and obeying the Word (vv. 13-18). The whole person—mind (understanding), heart (rejoicing), and will (obeying)—must be captive to God's truth.

1. We must understand the Word of God (Neh. 8:1-8)

The Bible is not a "magic book" that changes people or circumstances because somebody reads it or recites it. *God's Word must be understood before it can enter the heart and release its life-changing power.* Note that six times in this chapter you can find "understanding" mentioned (vv. 2-3, 7-8, 12-13). Only those people old enough to understand the Scripture were permitted to be in the assembly (v. 3). In our Lord's "Parable of the Sower" (Matt. 13:1-9, 18-23), the emphasis is on understanding the Word of God. Jesus compared understanding and receiving the Word to the planting of seed in the soil, where it takes root and bears fruit.

Ezra was the ideal man to conduct this outdoor Bible school. He was a priest and scribe who "had prepared his heart to seek the law of the Lord, and to do it, and to teach in Israel" (Ezra 7:10). He had come to Jerusalem about fourteen years before Nehemiah had arrived and had already sought to bring the people back to the ways of the Lord (Ezra 7-10).

That the leaders chose the Water Gate for the site of the assembly is interesting. In the Bible, water for washing is a picture of the Word of God (John 15:3; Eph. 5:26), while water for drinking is a picture of the Spirit of God (John 7:37-39). When we apply the water of the Word to our lives, then the Spirit can work and bring the help we need. It is refreshing to the soul when you receive the Word and allow the Spirit to teach you.

Notice the various ministries that Ezra performed for the people during that special conference.

He brought the Book (Neh. 8:1-4). This was on the first day of the seventh month, which was the Jewish equivalent of our New Year's Day. The seventh month was a special time in the Jewish calendar because the Jews celebrated the Feast of Trumpets on the first day, the Day of Atonement on the tenth day, and the Feast of Tabernacles from the fifteenth day to the twenty-first day (Lev. 23:23-44). It was the perfect time for the nation to get right with the Lord and make a fresh new beginning.

The Book that Ezra brought was "the Book of the Law." This was probably the entire scroll of the Torah, the five Books of

Moses, the very foundation of the Jewish religion and civil law. It isn't likely that Ezra read and explained all five Books of Moses in that short a time. Perhaps he concentrated on explaining Deuteronomy and referred to the other books as he had need.

Ezra stood on a wooden platform ("pulpit") above the people so they could see and hear him better. He faced the public square where the people stood, and the wall and gate behind him may have served as a sounding board to help project his voice to the vast assembly. In verse 4, he named thirteen men who stood with him, perhaps leaders representing the tribes. Thirteen more men are named in verse 7 along with the Levites; perhaps they were teaching priests.

He opened the Book (Neh. 8:5-6). When Ezra lifted the scroll and unrolled it to the passage he would read, the people who were seated in the square honored the Word of God by standing up. They knew they would not be hearing a mere man speak his own ideas; they would be hearing the very Word of God (1 Thess. 2:13). The people remained standing while the Law was read and explained (Neh. 8:7). Ezra started his reading and teaching early in the morning and continued through midday (v. 3), which means the congregation stood and listened for five or six hours; and this continued for a week (v. 18). No doubt from time to time, he gave the people opportunities to rest; but the people were there to hear God speak and were willing to stand and listen.

After he opened the Word, "Ezra blessed the Lord, the great God" (v. 6). In many churches, there is a blessing *after* the reading of the Scripture; but there is certainly nothing wrong with praising the Lord for His Word *before* we read and hear it. The people affirmed his words by saying "Amen, Amen" (see 5:13), which means "So be it!" It was a united congregation (8:1) that honored the Scriptures and was willing to devote half of their day to hearing it read and taught. They didn't worship the Book; they worshiped the Lord who spoke to them from the Book.

Our churches today have a desperate need in their public services to show more respect for the Word of God. We are commanded to "give attention to the public reading of Scripture" (1 Tim. 4:13, NASB); and yet in many churches, the only Scripture publicly read is the text of the sermon. "Independent churches" criticize "liturgical churches" for being bound to tradition, but the so-called "liturgical churches" at least devote themselves to a systematic public reading of the Word of God. (The word "liturgy" simply means "a form of public worship." *Every* church has a liturgy, either a good one or a bad one.) We wonder how the Holy Spirit feels when He sees Bibles put on the church floor, or used as portable filing cabinets for miscellaneous papers, or even left behind in church where they are stacked up and finally given to the local city mission. We will *defend* the Bible as the Word of God, but we don't always *treat* it like the Word of God.

We are also in too big a hurry to have the meeting end. In some parts of the world, especially in Eastern Europe before the collapse of the Communist bloc, believers would stand for hours in crowded churches to hear Bible teaching. In the average Western evangelical church, the shorter the sermon, the better we like it.

He read and explained the Book (Neh. 8:7-8). The common people didn't own copies of the Scriptures, so they were thrilled to hear the Word of God. The word *distinctly* in verse 8 means that the Law was explained to the people in a language they could understand. The Word was translated and expounded in such a way that the people were able to apply it to their own lives. The Hebrew language would have undergone some changes since the days when Moses wrote the Pentateuch, and the everyday conversational Hebrew of the people would be different in some ways from ancient Hebrew. We need new translations of the Bible, not because the Bible changes, but because our language changes.

Suppose you had to use John Wycliffe's Version of the Bible, the oldest version in English. How much of this passage would you understand *if you did not already know it from another version?*

> alle ye that traueilen & teen chargid come to me & I schal fulfille you. take ye my yok on you & lerne ye of me for I am mylde and meke in herte: and ye schulen finde rest to youre soulis/ for my yok is softe & my charge liyt.

Wycliffe's translation goes back about 600 years (1382); but between Moses' writing of the Law and Ezra's reading of the Law, a thousand years had elapsed!

The Levites assisted Ezra in teaching the Law (v. 7), for this was one of their God-given ministries (Deut. 33:10; Mal. 2:7). They probably mingled with the people and, when there was a break in the reading, answered questions and told them how to apply the Law to their own lives. Here we have a balance between the public proclamation of the Word in the large assembly and the personal application in the smaller groups. Both are important.

2. We must rejoice in the Word. (Neh. 8:9-12)

As Ezra read and explained the Word, the assembly's first response was one of conviction and grief. They mourned over their sins, "for by the law is the knowledge of sin" (Rom. 3:20). The law can't save us; it can only convince us that we need to be saved and then point us to Jesus Christ the Savior (Gal. 3:24). The Jews had just observed the annual Day of Atonement, and the Lord had dealt with their sins (Lev. 16); so they should have been rejoicing in His forgiveness. On the Jewish calendar, the Feast of Tabernacles (Succoth) follows the Day of Atonement, giving God's people an entire week of happy celebration (23:26-44). The sequence is important: first conviction, then cleansing, and then celebration.

The Word of God brings conviction and leads to repentance, but it also brings us joy; for the same Word that wounds also heals. "Your words were found, and I ate them, and Your word was to me the joy and rejoicing of my heart; for I am called by Your name" (Jer. 15:16, NKJV). "The statutes of the Lord are right, rejoicing the heart" (Ps. 19:8). "Your testimonies I have taken as a heritage forever, for they are the rejoicing of my heart" (119:111, NKJV).

Assisted by the Levites, Nehemiah convinced the people to stop mourning and start celebrating. *It is as wrong to mourn when God has forgiven us as it is to rejoice when sin has conquered us.* The sinner has no reason for rejoicing and the forgiven child of God has no reason for mourning (Matt. 9:9–17). Yes, as God's children we carry burdens and know what it is to weep (Neh. 2:1-2); but we also experience power that transforms sorrow into joy.

The secret of Christian joy is to believe what God says in His Word and act upon it. Faith that isn't based on the Word is not faith at all; it is presumption or superstition. Joy that isn't the result of faith is not joy at all; it is only a "good feeling" that will soon disappear. Faith based on the Word will produce joy that will weather the storms of life.

It isn't enough for us to *read* the Word or *receive* the Word as others expound it; we must also *rejoice* in the Word. "I rejoice at Your word as one who finds great treasure" (Ps. 119:162, NKJV). In Bible days, people sometimes hid their wealth in jars buried in the ground (Matt. 13:44; Jer. 41:8). If a farmer plowing his field suddenly discovered a jar filled with gold, he would certainly rejoice. There are great treasures buried in God's Word, and you and I must diligently "dig" for them as we read, meditate, and pray; and when we find these treasures, we should rejoice and give thanks.

If we read and study the Word of God only from a sense of duty, then its treasures may never be revealed to us. It is the believer who rejoices in the Word, who delights to read and study it day by day, who will find God's hidden treasures. "Blessed is the man who fears the Lord, who finds great delight in his commands" (Ps. 112:1, NIV). "But his delight is in the law of the Lord, and in His law he meditates day and night" (1:2, NKJV).

Do you delight in God's Word? Would you rather have God's Word than food (119:103; Luke 10:38-42), or sleep (Ps. 119:55, 62, 147-148), or wealth? (vv. 14, 72, 137, 162) If you delight in His Word, God will delight in you and share His best blessings with you.

3. We must obey the Word. (Neh. 8:13-18)

Obligation and *appreciation* are certainly strong motives for seeing the Lord, but *celebration* is even stronger. When we obey the Lord and serve Him because we rejoice in Him, then our service will be a delight and not a drudgery. The old Bible commentator Matthew Henry wrote, "Holy joy will be oil to the wheels of our obedience." To the believer without joy, the will of God is punishment; but to the believer happy in the Lord, the will of God is nourishment (John 4:34). The Jews still had work to do in their city, and they needed the joy of the Lord to give them the strength to do it.

"When I think upon my God," wrote composer Franz Josef Haydn, "my heart is so full that the notes dance and leap from my pen and since God has given me a cheerful heart, it will be pardoned me that I serve Him with a cheerful spirit."

The Day of Atonement was celebrated on the tenth day of the month and the Feast of Tabernacles from the fifteenth to the twenty-first days. This meant that the leaders had just a few days available for getting the word out to the Jews in the surrounding villages that everybody was going to celebrate the Feast of Tabernacles. It is not enough to hear the Word of God; we must obey what it tells us to do (James 1:22-25). The people not only had joy in hearing the Word, but they also had "*great* gladness" in obeying it (Neh. 8:17, italics mine).

During the seven days of the feast, the Jews lived in booths made of branches and usually built on the flat roofs of their houses. It was a time for *looking back* and remembering the nation's forty years of wandering in the wilderness, when the people were homeless and lived in temporary shelters. But the feast was also a time for *looking around* at the harvest blessings from the hand of God. The Lord had given them a good land, and they were never to forget the Giver as they enjoyed the gifts (Deut. 8). The Feast of Tabernacles was also an occasion for *looking ahead* to the glorious kingdom God promised His people Israel (Zech. 14:4, 9, 16-20). It was a week-long festival of joyful praise and thanksgiving, focusing on the goodness of the Lord.

But the celebrating of the feast was not for enjoyment alone; it was also for enrichment and encouragement. "The joy of the Lord is your strength" (Neh. 8:10). The world's joy is temporary and artificial; and when the joy is gone, people are left with even greater weakness and emptiness. But the joy that comes from the Lord is real and lasting and enriches our lives. God doesn't give us joy *instead* of sorrow, or joy *in spite of* sorrow, but joy *in the midst of* sorrow. It is not *substitution* but *transformation.*

Jesus illustrated this truth by the birth of a baby (John 16:20-22). The same baby that gives the mother pain also gives the mother joy! Her pain is not *replaced* by joy but *transformed into* joy. The difficult circumstances of life are "pregnant" with joy, and by faith we must give that joy time to be born.

The Feast of Tabernacles was a time for sending food and gifts to others, especially to those who were needy. The Jews had found joy in *hearing* the Word of God, but now they found joy in *sharing* the blessings of God. The mind grows by taking in, but the heart grows by giving out; and it is important to maintain a balanced life.

Nehemiah 8:17 does not teach that the nation had ignored the Feast of Tabernacles since the days of Joshua, because that was not so. The feast was celebrated during King Solomon's day (2 Chron. 8:13) and also when the Babylonian exiles had returned to the land (Ezra 3:1-4). It was not the *fact* of the celebration that was so special but *the way* they celebrated, for it appears that everybody participated enthusiastically. Because every family made a booth, some of the people had to move from the houses into the streets and squares of the city. Apparently in previous years, not all the Jews had made booths and lived in them for the week of the feast. They had given only "token" acknowledgment of the feast. Furthermore, the joyful attitude of the people was beyond anything the nation had ever seen. It was truly a week of joyful celebration that brought glory to the Lord.

Ezra continued the "Bible conference" during the entire week of the feast, day by day reading and explaining the Word of God. The combination of joyful fellowship, feasting, and hearing the Word must have strengthened the people greatly. Then the week concluded with a solemn assembly (Num. 29:35), after which the people returned to their regular daily schedules.

Did the blessings of the celebration last? Yes, for a time; but then the people became careless again, and the leaders had to bring them back to the Word of God. But the failure of the people is not an argument against special times of Bible study or celebration. Someone asked evangelist Billy Sunday if revivals lasted, and he replied, "No, neither does a bath; but it's good to have one occasionally!"

From time to time in the history of the church, God's Spirit has burdened people to pray, search the Scriptures, and confess their sins; and from these sincere spiritual exercises, He has seen fit to bring fresh life to His people. It happened in Nehemiah's day, and it can happen again today.

Can God begin with you?

"If My people, who are called by My name, will humble themselves and pray and seek My face and turn from their wicked ways, then will I hear from heaven and will forgive their sin and will heal their land" (2 Chron. 7:14, NIV).

CHAPTER NINE
AMAZING GRACE!
Nehemiah 9

Jehovah God is the main subject of this chapter—who He is, what He does for His people, and what His people must do for Him. This prayer reviews the history of Israel and reveals both the majesty of God and the depravity of man. Israel responded to God's "great kindness" (Neh. 9:17), "great mercy" (v. 31), and "great goodness" (vv. 25, 35) with "great provocations" (vv. 18, 26) that resulted in "great distress" (v. 37).

It is interesting that three of Israel's great "national prayers" are recorded in Ezra 9, Nehemiah 9, and Daniel 9. Behind these prayers is the promise of 2 Chronicles 7:14 as well as the example of Moses when he interceded for the people (Ex. 32-33).

Dr. Arthur T. Pierson said, "History is His story"; and this chapter bears that out. "That men do not learn very much from the lessons of history is the most important of all the lessons that history has to teach," wrote Aldous Huxley; and philosopher George Santayana wrote, "Those who do not remember the past are condemned to relive it." The church today can learn much from the experiences of Israel, if we are willing to humble ourselves and receive the truth.

As you read this prayer, notice that it reveals the greatness of God (Neh. 9:1-6), the goodness of God (vv. 7-30), and the grace of God (vv. 31-38).

1. The greatness of God (Neh. 9:1-6)

The Feast of Tabernacles had ended, but the people lingered to hear more of the Word of God. Feasting had turned to fasting as the Word brought conviction and people started confessing their sins. In most churches today, a six-hour service—three hours of preaching and three hours of praying— would probably result in some requests for resignations; but to the Jewish people in that day, it was the beginning of a new life for them and their city.

When I was a young believer, churches often had two-week evangelistic campaigns; and it was not unusual for city-wide meetings to go for a month or six weeks in the summer. Gradually a change took place as "special meetings" were shortened to one week, then to a weekend; and now they are almost obsolete. In my itinerant ministry, more than once I have been reminded to watch the clock so the service could end on time. We live in the age of the digest and fast food, and this mentality has invaded our churches. We piously sing, "Take Time to Be Holy," but we aren't willing to pay the price to do it.

God's greatness is seen in the fact that *He receives our worship (vv. 1-5).* True worship involves many elements: hearing the Scriptures, praising God, praying, confessing sin, and separating ourselves from that which displeases God. Each of these elements is recorded in this paragraph.

Worship involves the Word of God, for the Word of God reveals the God of the Word. "The essence of idolatry," wrote A.W. Tozer in *The Knowledge of the Holy,* "is the entertainment of thoughts about God that are unworthy of Him" (p. 11). The better we know the Scriptures and respond to them, the better we will know God and become like Him. Israel was chosen by God to receive His Law (v. 13) and to know His will. Any worship service that ignores the Scriptures will not receive the blessing of God.

In the Scriptures, God speaks to us; and in prayer and praise, we speak to Him. "Stand up and bless the Lord your God!" (v. 5) is a command every true believer wants to obey. God's name is exalted above every name (Phil. 2:9-11), and we should honor it as we praise Him. It should be "exalted above all blessing and praise" (Neh. 9:5).

The people also took time to confess their sins (vv. 2-3) and seek the Lord's forgiveness. The annual Day of Atonement was past, but the worshipers knew that they needed constant cleansing and renewal from the Lord. We must not major on self-examination to the extent that we start ignoring the Lord, but we must be honest in our dealings with Him (1 John 1:5-10). Whenever you see sin or failure in your life, immediately look by faith to Christ and seek His forgiveness; *and keep on looking to Him.* The more you look at yourself, the more discouraged you will become. Focus on His perfections, not your own imperfections.

Finally, the people separated themselves from the world as they drew near to the Lord (Neh. 9:2; Ezra 6:21). Separation without devotion to the Lord becomes isolation, but devotion without separation is hypocrisy (see 2 Cor. 6:14-7:1). The nation of Israel was chosen by God to be a special people, separated from the pagan nations around them. "You are to be holy to Me because I, the Lord, am holy, and I have set you apart from the nations to be My own" (Lev. 20:26, NIV). The Apostle Peter applied those words to Christian believers in the church today (1 Peter 1:15; 2:9-10).

God's greatness is also seen in the fact that *He is God alone (Neh. 9:6a).* The nation of Israel was surrounded by idolatry and the degrading lifestyle that was associated with pagan worship. In his reading and explaining of the Law, Ezra had certainly emphasized the Ten Commandments (Ex. 20:1-17; Deut. 5:6-21), including the first two commandments that declare the uniqueness of God and the wickedness of idolatry. Even today, faithful Jews still recite "The Shema" (6:4-6) as their declaration of faith in the one and only true God.

One of Israel's ministries to the world was to bear witness to Jehovah, the true and living God. Their Gentile neighbors were surprised that the Jews had no idols (Ps. 115). When Israel turned to idols, as they often did, God disciplined them. In His eyes, their idolatry was like adultery (Jer. 3:1-5); for He had been "wedded" to them at Mt. Sinai when He gave them His covenant.

A third evidence of God's greatness is the fact that *He created the universe (Neh. 9:6b).* "In the beginning God created the heaven and the earth" (Gen. 1:1) is a statement that can be applied only to Jehovah, the God of Abraham, Isaac, and Jacob. Whenever God wanted to encourage His people, He would point to creation around them and remind them that He had made it all (Isa. 40). He used the same approach to remind them of the foolishness of worshiping idols (Isa. 41). To know that our Father in heaven is the Creator of all things is a great source of strength and peace. Idolatry means worshiping and serving the creature and the creation rather than the Creator (Rom. 1:25). "Thus does the world forget You, its Creator," wrote Augustine, "and falls in love with what You have created instead of with You."

God's greatness is seen in the fact of *His providential care for His creation (Neh. 9:6c).* He did not simply make everything and then abandon it to its own course. He is involved in the affairs of His creation: He sees when a sparrow falls (Matt. 10:29), and He hears when a raven cries out for food (Ps. 147:9). He has the stars all counted and named (v. 4), and He has even numbered the hairs on your head (Luke 12:7). "You open Your hand and satisfy the desire of every living thing" (Ps. 145:16, NKJV).

Finally, God's greatness is seen in the fact that *the hosts of heaven worship Him (Neh. 9:6d)*. You and I can't duplicate the mighty works of the angels, but we can imitate their devotion to the Lord as they worship before His throne. A*nd we have more cause to praise Him than they do!* We have been saved by the grace of God and shall one day be like the Lord Jesus Christ. We are not just servants; we are *children* of God (1 John 3:1-3) and will dwell with Him forever!

In our worship, it's wise to begin with the greatness of God. If we focus too much on what He gives or what we want Him to do, we may find our hearts becoming selfish. Sincere worship honors God in spite of circumstances or feelings or desires.

2. The goodness of God (Neh. 9:7-30)

This prayer rehearses the history of Israel, revealing God's goodness to His people and their repeated failure to appreciate His gifts and obey His will. The word "give" is used in one way or another at least sixteen times in this chapter (KJV), for our God is indeed the "giving God," who delights in meeting the needs of His people (1 Tim. 6:17). God gave Israel a land (Neh. 9:8, 15, 35), a law (v. 13), the ministry of the Spirit (v. 20), food and water (vv. 15, 20), deliverers (v. 27), and victory over their enemies (vv. 22, 24). What more could they want?

Centuries before, Moses had warned the people not to forget God, either His gracious hand of blessing or His loving hand of chastening (Deut. 8). Alas, the nation didn't thank God in times of blessing, but they were quick to turn to God for help in times of suffering (see Pss. 105-106). Let's not be too quick to judge them, because some of God's people today treat God the same way.

In my years of pastoral ministry, I have met people who had little interest in God or the church until a loved one was in the hospital or there was a death in the family. Then the pastor and all the church family had to drop everything and give them help! But just as soon as the crisis was over, these people were back to their old life again, ignoring the things of the Lord and living for the things of the world.

You can trace this tragic pattern in every stage of Israel's history.

Forming the nation (Neh. 9:7-18). It was an act of pure grace when God chose Abram and revealed Himself to him, for Abram was an idolater in a pagan city (Josh. 24:2-3). Eventually, God changed his name from Abram ("exalted father") to Abraham ("father of a multitude"), because He had promised to make him a great nation (Gen. 12:1-3; 17:1-8). Though Abraham had occasional lapses of faith, for a century he trusted the Lord and walked in obedience to His will. His obedient faith was made especially evident when he gave his son Isaac on the altar (Gen. 22; Heb. 11:17-19).

God's covenant (Gen. 12:1-3) was the basis for all that God did with and for Abraham and his descendants. It was God's purpose that *all the world* be blessed through Israel, and He did this in the sending of His Son, Jesus Christ (Gal. 3:8). God gave the land to Abraham and his descendants, even though during his lifetime Abraham owned nothing in the land but a cave for burying his dead (Gen. 23).

In the land of Egypt, the nation multiplied greatly, saw God's power over the pagan gods, and experienced deliverance from bondage by the mighty hand of God

(Ex. 1-15). God opened the sea to let Israel through and then closed it again to destroy the Egyptian army. It was complete deliverance; Israel was to have no further relationship with Egypt.

God led His people by day and by night, giving them food to eat and water to drink. He also gave them His holy Law, so that in their civil, personal, and religious life, they knew the will of God. The Sabbath was given as a special sign between God and His people (Ex. 31:13-17), but there is no evidence in Scripture that the Sabbath law was given to any of the Gentile nations.

In Nehemiah 9:16-18, Nehemiah tells us how the nation responded to all that God had done for them: They refused to bow to His authority ("hardened their necks"), listen to His Word ("hearkened not"), or obey His will. At Kadesh-Barnea, they tried to take matters in their own hands and appoint a new leader to take them back to Egypt (v. 17; Num. 14:1-5). When Moses was on the mountain with God, the people made and worshiped an idol (Neh. 9:18; Ex. 32). Moses interceded for the people, and God pardoned them.

How could these people turn their backs on God after all He had done for them? *They did not truly love Him.* Their obedience was only an outward form; it didn't come from their hearts. In their hearts, they were still living in Egypt and wanting to return there. They did not have a living faith in God but were willing to receive His help and enjoy His gifts. Read Psalm 78 for an "x-ray" of Israel's spiritual history.

Leading the nation (Neh. 9:19-22). During the forty years of Israel's discipline in the wilderness, the old generation died and a new generation was born; but God never forsook His people. He led them by the cloud and fire, taught them the Word, provided them with the necessities of life, and gave them victory over their enemies. God keeps His promises and fulfills His purposes. If we obey Him, we share in the blessing; if we disobey Him, we miss the blessing; but God's purposes will be fulfilled and His name glorified.

Like too many of God's people today, the Jews were shortsighted: They forgot the glorious purposes that God had in mind for the nation. Had they meditated on God's promises and purposes (Gen. 12:1-3; Ex. 19:1-8), they would not have wanted to go back to Egypt or mingle with the godless nations around them. Israel was a people who lived beneath their privileges and failed to accept fully God's will for their lives.

Chastening the nation (Neh. 9:23-30). God promised to multiply His people, and He kept His promise (Gen. 22:17). He also promised to give them a good land, and He kept that promise (13:14-18; 17:7-8). Under the leadership of Joshua, the army of Israel invaded Canaan, conquered the land, and claimed all its wealth. It was God who gave them victory and enabled them to possess cities, houses, lands, and wealth in the land of Canaan.

It was a "fat land" ("fertile," NIV), and Israel became a "fat people" (nourished, satisfied); and this led to their downfall. "But Jeshurun [Israel] grew fat and kicked; you grew fat, you grew thick, you are covered with fat; then he forsook God who made him" (Deut. 32:15, NKJV). Moses' warnings went unheeded (Deut. 8). Israel delighted themselves in God's great goodness but *they did not delight themselves in the Lord.* Like the prodigal son (Luke 15:11-24), they wanted the Father's wealth but not the Father's will.

"For every one hundred men who can stand adversity, there is only one who can stand prosperity," said Thomas Carlyle. Novelist John Steinbeck wrote, "If you want to destroy a nation, give it too much—make it greedy, miserable, and sick." It's possible for a local church to get proud of its "riches" and become poor in God's eyes (Rev. 3:14-22). The church that we may think is poor is probably rich in God's eyes (2:8-9).

"Give me neither poverty nor riches," prayed Agur the wise man. "Feed me with the food You prescribe for me; lest I be full and deny You, and say 'Who is the Lord?' Or lest I be poor and steal, and profane the name of my God" (Prov. 30:8-9, NKJV). Through the power of Christ, Paul had learned by experience "how to be abased" and "how to abound" (Phil. 4:12); and that is the lesson all of God's people need to learn.

Once in the land, Israel enjoyed rest during the days of Joshua and the elders who had served with him; but when those godly leaders were gone, the new generation turned away from the Lord (Judg. 2:6-15). God disciplined them, so they cried out for help; and God raised up deliverers to rescue them. Then they would walk in God's ways for a time, lapse back into sin; and the cycle would be repeated. The Book of Judges records the sad story of how God disciplined His people *in their own land* by allowing their pagan neighbors to rule over them.

Against the dark background of Israel's unfaithfulness shines the bright light of the faithfulness of God. When Israel obeyed Him, He was faithful to bless; when they disobeyed Him, He was faithful to chasten; when they asked for mercy, He was faithful to forgive. God is willing to give His people many privileges, but He will not give them the privilege of sinning and having their own way. God's purposes are more important than our pleasures, and He will accomplish His purposes even if He has to chasten us to do it.

Israel's sins finally became so disgusting to God that He decided to discipline them *away from their own land.* He used the Assyrians to destroy the Northern Kingdom, and then He brought the Babylonians to take the Southern Kingdom (Judah) captive and to destroy Jerusalem and the temple. It was as though God said to His people, "You enjoy living *like* the heathen so much, I'll let you live *with* the heathen." The nation's seventy years of captivity in Babylon taught them to appreciate the blessings they had taken for granted, and they never again returned to pagan idolatry.

God's chastening is as much an evidence of His love as is His bountiful supply of our needs (Heb. 12:1-11). We should be grateful that God loves us too much to allow us to become "spoiled children." *The Father is never as close to us as when He is chastening us.* "Blessed is the man You discipline, O Lord, the man You teach from Your law; You grant him relief from days of trouble, till a pit is dug for the wicked" (Ps. 94:12-13, NIV). "Before I was afflicted, I went astray; but now have I kept Thy Word" (119:67).

3. The grace of God (Neh. 9:31-38)

God was good to His people when His people were not good to Him. He sent them prophets to teach them and to warn them, but the nation refused to listen (2 Chron. 36:14-21). He was merciful to forgive them when they cried out for help, and He was long-suffering with them as they repeatedly rebelled against His Word. He could have destroyed the nation and started over again (see Ex. 32:10 and Num. 14:11-12), but He graciously spared them. In His mercy, God didn't give them what they deserved; and in His grace, He gave them what they didn't deserve.

As the Levites prayed, they acknowledged the sins of the nation and God's justice in sending punishment. "In all that has happened to us, you have been just; you have acted faithfully, while we did wrong" (Neh. 9:33, NIV). Note that the Levites used the pronoun "we" and not "they." As they prayed, they identified with the nation and acknowledged their own guilt. Nehemiah had prayed the same way at the beginning of the book (1:6-7). It is easy to be convicted about other people's sins, but God forgives only when we repent and confess our own sins.

In the past, although the nation had enjoyed abundant blessings, they still sinned against the God who had blessed them. Now those blessings had been taken away from them. They were back in the land, but they could not enjoy the land; for everything they worked for was given to somebody else! The Persian king was in control of everything, including their own bodies.

When God had been their king, the Jews had enjoyed great blessing; but when they rebelled against His will, they found themselves enslaved to kings who had no compassion on them. Samuel had warned them (I Sam. 8), and Moses had prophesied that the nation would forfeit its wealth to its conquerors (Deut. 28:15ff). Whatever we fail to give God, we cannot keep for ourselves. He will take it one way or another. Christians who refuse to honor God joyfully by faithful giving often end up having to spend that money reluctantly on obligations that are painful and unexpected, like doctor bills or home repairs (see Mal. 3:7-12).

The Levites had acknowledged God's greatness and goodness; and now, on the basis of His grace, they asked Him for a new beginning for the nation. They couldn't change the servitude they were in, but they could surrender themselves to a greater Master and seek His help. No matter who exercises dominion over us, if we are yielded to the Lord, we are free in Him (1 Cor. 7:22; Eph. 6:5-9). If God had been merciful to Israel in the past, forgiving their sins when they cried out to Him, would He not be merciful to them now?

But they did more than ask God for mercy; they also made a solemn covenant with God to obey His law and do His will. The nation had made a covenant with God at Mt. Sinai and then broken it (Ex. 24:3-8). They had renewed the covenant when they entered Canaan (Josh. 8:30-35) and after they had conquered the land (24:14-28), but then they rebelled against the Lord (Judg. 2:6-15).

Samuel had led the people in renewing their covenant vows (1 Sam. 11:14-12:25), but King Saul led the people back into sin and defeat. As soon as his throne was secure, David sought to bring the people back to the Lord (2 Sam. 6); and Solomon's prayer at the dedication of the temple was also a step in that direction. Sad to say, however, Solomon sinned against the Lord and almost destroyed his own kingdom.

Throughout the history of Israel, there was always a remnant of faithful people who trusted God, obeyed His will, and prayed for God to fulfill His promises (1 Kings 19:18; Isa. 1:9; Luke 2:38). This believing remnant was God's "lifeline" to maintain the ministry of Israel in the world. They kept the light of faith and hope burning in the land; and because of them, God was able to fulfill His promise and bring the Savior into the world. The Jews in Jerusalem in Nehemiah's day were a part of that remnant, and God heard their prayers.

Our God is a glorious God (Neh. 9:5).

He is powerful (v. 6), faithful (v. 8), and concerned about the needs of His people (v. 9). He is a pardoning God (vv. 17-19, 31), who is long-suffering when we sin (vv. 21, 30) but who chastens if we rebel (vv. 26ff). He is a generous God (vv. 24-25, 35), who gives us far more than we deserve. He is a God who keeps His promises even if we are unfaithful.

Surely this God deserves our loving obedience!

Perhaps the time has come for a new beginning.

CHAPTER TEN
AFTER WE SAY "AMEN"
Nehemiah 10

The story may be apocryphal, but it illustrates the point that this chapter makes.

In a certain church, there was a man who always ended his prayers with, "And, Lord, clean the cobwebs out of my life! Clean the cobwebs out of my life!"

One of the members of the church became weary of hearing this same insincere request week after week, because he saw no change in the petitioner's life. So, the next time he heard the man pray, "Lord, clean the cobwebs out of my life!" he interrupted with, "And while you're at it, Lord, *kill the spider*!"

It's one thing to offer the Lord a passionate prayer of confession, such as we have in chapter 9, and quite something else to live an obedient life after we say "Amen." But the people in the assembly were serious about their praying and were determined, by God's grace, to make a new beginning and live to please the Lord.

"The victorious Christian life," said Alexander Whyte, "is a series of new beginnings." The Lord is able to keep us from stumbling (Jude 24); but if we do stumble, He is able to lift us up and get us going again. "The steps of a good man are ordered by the Lord, and He delights in his way. Though he fall, he shall not be utterly cast down; for the Lord upholds him with His hand" (Ps. 37:23-24, NKJV). The nation had sinned, but now it was taking new steps of dedication and obedience.

But was their dedication real? There are at least three evidences given in this chapter that these people really meant what they prayed. These same evidences will be seen in our lives if our promises to the Lord are sincere.

1. Submission to the Word of God (Neh. 10:1-27, 29)

With Nehemiah's name heading the list, eighty-four persons put their seal on the covenant that they made with the Lord. This list included priests (vv. 2-8; see 12:1-7), Levites (10:9–13), and the leaders of the people (vv. 14-27). Many other citizens subscribed to the covenant who didn't "sign their names" individually (v. 28), including wives and children who didn't have the legal right to put a personal seal on an official document. All the people who had heard the Word of God read and explained were now committing themselves to obey what they had heard.

Putting a seal on this document was a serious matter because it meant taking a solemn oath before the Lord (v. 29; see 5:13). Perhaps they had heard Ezra read this passage from Deuteronomy: "All of you stand today before the Lord your God: your leaders and your tribes and your elders and your officers, all the men of Israel, your little ones and your wives . . . that you may enter into covenant with the Lord your God, and into His oath, which the Lord your God makes with us today, that He may establish you today as a people for Himself, and that He may be God to you, just as He has spoken to you, and just as He has sworn to your fathers, to Abraham, Isaac, and Jacob" (Deut. 29:10-13, NKJV).

The law governing vows and oaths is found in Numbers 30 and is introduced with these words: "When a man makes a vow to the Lord or takes an oath to obligate himself by a pledge, he must not break his word but must do everything he said" (v. 2, NIV). Since an oath involved the name and possible judgment of God, it was not to be taken lightly. Jesus warned against using empty oaths (Matt. 5:33-37; 23:16-22), and Solomon gave a similar warning (Eccl. 5:1-7).

Should believers today bind themselves with oaths as they seek to walk with the Lord and serve Him? Probably not. Our relationship to the Lord is that of children to a Father, and our Father wants our obedience to be based on love. I don't know of any examples in the New Testament of believers taking oaths of obedience to the Lord. Our obedience should be a joyful response to all that He has done for us in Christ (Col. 3:1ff). We don't succeed as Christians because we make promises to God, but because we believe the promises of God and act upon them. Oaths are often based on fear ("I had better do it or God will judge me!"), and fear is not the highest motivation for godly living, although it does play a part (2 Cor. 7:1).

2. Separation as the people of God (Neh. 10:28, 30-31)

The Jewish remnant was surrounded by idolatrous Gentiles, who wanted the Jews to become a part of their social, religious, and business society. But the Law of Moses prohibited God's people from living like the Gentiles, although it didn't stop the Jews from being good neighbors or even good customers (see 13:15-22). It was the ministry of the priests to teach the people "the difference between the holy and the common and show them how to distinguish between the unclean and the clean" (Ezek. 44:23, NIV).

Separation is simply total devotion to God, no matter what the cost. When a man and woman get married, they separate themselves from all other possible mates and give themselves completely to each other. It is total commitment motivated by love, and it is a balanced decision: We separate *from* others *to* the one who is to be our life's mate.

The Jews separated *from* the peoples around them and to the Lord and His Word (Neh. 10:28; 9:2). They also united with their brothers and sisters in promising to obey the Law of God (v. 29). Separation that ignores God and other believers is *isolation* and will eventually lead to sin. Only the Holy Spirit can give us the kind of balance we need to live a godly life in this ungodly world. The legalist wants to live by rules, but that style of life only keeps you immature and dependant on your spiritual leaders. The only way to grow in a balanced life is to give yourself totally to God and follow Him by faith.

Two special areas of concern were mentioned: marriage and the Sabbath. The danger in mixed marriages was the loss of faith on the part of the Jewish mate (Ex. 34:10-17). How could a Jew, married to a Gentile, observe the dietary laws or celebrate the annual festivals? He or she would be continually ceremonially unclean. Between the husband and wife there would be constant conflict, then occasional compromise, and finally complete conformity; and the Jewish mate would have abandoned his or her spiritual heritage.

Why would Jews want to marry pagan Gentiles in the first place? Apart from affection, which should have been controlled at the outset, perhaps they would marry for social status (Neh. 13:28) or to get ahead in business. Like some believers today who marry unbelievers, these Jews may have argued that marriage would give them opportunity to convert their mate to the true faith, although it is usually the other way around. God had a great purpose for Israel to fulfill, and the Jews' compromise with sin polluted the nation (Mal. 2:10–16). God wanted a "pure seed" so that through Israel He could send His Son into the world to be the Savior, and mixed marriages only brought confusion.

"As long as we love each other, it will work out!" is the argument many pastors hear from Christians who want to marry unsaved people. But the question is not, "Will this marriage work out?" but, "Will this marriage enjoy God's best blessing and fulfill God's will?" It's difficult to see how God can bless and use people who deliberately disobey His Word (2 Cor. 6:14-7:1; 1 Cor. 7:39).

The observance of the Sabbath was a distinctively Jewish practice (Neh. 9:14; Ex. 20:8-11; 30:12-18); the Gentiles around Jerusalem would treat the seventh day of the week like any other day and want to socialize and do business. While the Jewish Sabbath was not to be a day of bondage and misery, it was a day devoted to rest and contemplation of things spiritual. It was a weekly reminder to the nation that they were Jews and had a special calling in the world. Some of the Jewish merchants would be especially interested in getting business from the Gentiles, and to close up business on a day when people were shopping seemed a waste.

Moses didn't spell out specific rules for observing the Sabbath, but there was a precedent for not engaging in unnecessary work. They were not to light any fires on the Sabbath (Ex. 35:1-3), and one man was stoned because he gathered wood on the Sabbath (Num. 15:32-36). The prophets sternly rebuked the Jews for violating the Sabbath (Jer. 17:19-27; Amos 8:4-6; Isa. 56:1-2; 58:13-14), because their disobedience was a symptom of a deeper spiritual problem: rebellion against the Lord.

The solemn affirmation of faith reported in this chapter also included observing the Sabbatical Year (Lev. 25:1-7, 20–22; Deut. 15:1-11). Every seventh year, the Jews were to let the land lie idle so that it might restore itself, an excellent principle of ecology. Of course, the people would need a great deal of faith to trust God for food for two years; but God promised to care for them. After seven Sabbatical Years, they were to celebrate the fiftieth year as a "Year of Jubilee" (Lev. 25:8ff); and this meant trusting God for food for *three* years.

The evidence is that the nation had not faithfully celebrated these special Sabbatical observances. This was one reason why God sent them into Captivity (2 Chron. 36:21), that He might give the land seventy years of rest (Jer. 29:10). This would compensate for some 500 years of disobedience on the part of the nation (7 x 70), one year for each neglected Sabbatical Year or Year of Jubilee.

For the Jewish remnant to promise to commemorate the Sabbatical Year was a great step of faith, for many of the people were poor and the nation faced repeated agricultural and economic depression.

Not to have extra produce for a whole year would certainly affect their business with the Gentiles around them. The people's willingness to obey this law is a beautiful illustration of Matthew 6:33.

3. Their support for the house of God (Neh. 10:32-39)

The phrase "house of our God" is used nine times in this section and refers to the restored temple. The people were promising God that they would obey His laws and provide what was needed for the ministry at the temple. "We will not forsake the house of our God" (v. 39).

British expositor G. Campbell Morgan said: "Whereas the house of God today is no longer material but spiritual, the material is still a very real symbol of the spiritual. When the Church of God in any place in any locality is careless about the material place of assembly, the place of its worship and its work, it is a sign and evidence that its life is at a low ebb" (*The Westminster Pulpit*, vol. 8, p. 315).

Morgan is right. To be sure, God doesn't live in the houses in which we assemble to worship Him (Isa. 60:1-2; Acts 7:48-50), but the way we care for those buildings indicates what we think of our God (see Hag. 1). The restored Jewish temple didn't have the magnificence of the temple Solomon built (Ezra 3:8-13; Hag. 2:1-9), but it was God's house just the same and deserved the support of God's people.

Their promised support was specific and involved four different areas of ministry.

The temple tax (Neh. 10:32-33). The annual census of the people twenty years of age and older was accompanied by the collecting of a half-shekel tax to be used to support the ministry of the house of God (Ex. 30:11-16). The tax was a reminder to the people that God had redeemed them and paid a price to set them free, and that they should behave like people who belonged to God. The original tax was used to make silver sockets and hooks for the tabernacle (38:25-28), but in subsequent years it helped pay the expenses of the ministry.

Times were hard, so the leaders decided to adjust the tax and give a third of a shekel instead of a half. (By the time our Lord was ministering on earth, the tax was back to half a shekel; Matt. 17:24-27.) This temporary change didn't alter the meaning of the tradition or lessen the devotion of the people. God's people must use their common sense as they seek to obey the Lord. We must not put on ourselves burdens that God never expected us to carry (Acts 15:10), but neither should we look for the easiest and least demanding way to serve the Lord.

Nehemiah 10:33 describes how the money would be spent: to provide what was needed for the regular and special ministries at the temple, all of which were part of the "work of the house of our God." If the nation was to be in a right relationship with the Lord, the priests had to carry on their ministry faithfully.

We today don't have to provide animals, grain, and other materials in order for the church to worship the Lord; but we do have to help maintain the work of the ministry. This means paying salaries (Luke 10:7), sharing with the needy (1 Cor. 16:1-3), and being good stewards of all that God gives us (2 Cor. 8-9), so that the Gospel may be sent to the whole world. "For where your treasure is, there will your heart be also" (Matt. 6:21). If we are walking with the Lord, we will want to do our part in supporting the ministry of the church where God has put us.

The wood offering (Neh. 10:34). Since

the fire on the brazen altar was to be kept burning constantly (Lev. 6:12-13), it required a steady supply of wood; and wood was a precious commodity. The leaders drew lots and assigned the various clans the times when they were to bring wood for the altar. That such a humble thing as wood was important to God's service and could be sanctified for His glory is an encouragement to me. Not everybody in Israel could be a priest or Levite, or donate lambs or oxen for sacrifices, but everybody could bring some wood and help keep the fire burning.

There are no special directions in the Law concerning this offering, but tradition says that certain days of the year were set aside for the people to bring wood to the sanctuary. When God doesn't give us specific instructions, and we know there is a need to be met, we must figure out how to do the job. Since the priests needed wood for the altar, and the people could provide it, an equitable system was worked out.

The firstfruits (Neh. 10:35-37a). The Jews were taught to give God the first and the best, and this is a good example for us to follow today. "Honor the Lord with your wealth, with the firstfruits of all your crops" (Prov. 3:9, NIV). Because God saved the firstborn Jews from death in the land of Egypt, the firstborn of man and beast belonged to the Lord (Ex. 14:1-16; Lev. 27:26-27). The firstborn son had to be redeemed by a sacrifice (Ex. 34:19-20; Luke 2:22-24) because that child belonged to God.

Nowhere does Scripture tell us how much of the firstfruits the people were to bring to the temple (Ex. 23:19; 34:26), but the offering was to be brought before the people did anything else with their harvests. These were stored for the use of the temple servants (Neh. 12:44). No doubt the offering was to be measured by the blessing God had given to His people, as well as their devotion to Him.

The tithes (Neh. 10:37b-39). The word *tithe* means "a tenth." The Jews were to bring a tenth of their produce to the Lord each year for the support of the Levites (Lev. 27:30–34). The Levites then gave a "tithe of the tithe" to the priests (Num. 18:25-32). The Jews were also to tithe the 90 percent that was left and take it to the temple for the annual feasts (Deut. 26:1-11). To these two tithes was added a third tithe, received every third year for the poor (vv. 12-15; 14:28–29). When the spiritual life in Israel was at low ebb, there was little brought to the temple to support the ministry; and many of the Levites had to find other means of support. In times of spiritual quickening, the people would bring their offerings, and there would be plenty (2 Chron. 31:1-12; Mal. 3:8-11).

While there is no express command in the New Testament that God's people should tithe today, proportionate giving is certainly commended (1 Cor. 16:1-3). We are stewards of God's wealth and must make wise use of what He shares with us (4:1-2). If people under Old Testament Law could bring three tithes, how much more ought we to give today who live under the New Covenant of God's abundant grace? (See 2 Cor. 8-9 and note the repetition of the word "grace.") Tithing can be a great blessing, but those who tithe must avoid at least three dangers: (1) giving with the wrong motive, out of a sense of duty, fear, or greed ("If I tithe, God must prosper me!"); (2) thinking that they can do what they please with the 90 percent that remains; (3) giving only the tithe and failing to give love offerings to the Lord.

In light of all that God has done for us,

how can we rob Him of the offerings that rightly belong to Him? God didn't forsake His people when they were in need (Neh. 9:31), and they promised not to forsake the house of God (10:39). Years before, the Prophet Haggai had rebuked the people because they were so busy taking care of their own houses they had neglected the house of God (Hag. 1:4); and this warning needs to be heralded today. *Where there is true spiritual revival, it will reveal itself in the way we support God 's work, beginning in our own local church.* It isn't enough to pray or even commit ourselves to "faith promises" or pledges. We must so love the Lord that generous giving will be a normal and joyful part of our lives.

Sir Winston Churchill said, "We make a living by what we get, but we make a life by what we give." Jesus said, "Where your treasure is, there will your heart be also" (Matt. 6:21).

"We will not forsake the house of our God!" (Neh. 10:39)

CHAPTER ELEVEN
THE SHOUT HEARD 'ROUND THE WORLD
Nehemiah 11–12

Theologians remind us that God made the first garden (Gen. 1-2), but rebellious man built the first city (4:16-17), and the two have been in conflict ever since. In the ancient world, cities were places of wealth and power. In modern times, in spite of their magnificence, too often our cities are bankrupt institutions famous for pollution, poverty, and crime. How to finance and manage the great cities is a vexing problem to government leaders around the world. "We will neglect our cities to our peril," John F. Kennedy said, "for in neglecting them we neglect the nation."

Nehemiah followed the same philosophy. He knew that the nation of Israel could never be strong as long as Jerusalem was weak. But Jerusalem could not be strong unless the people were willing to sacrifice. Nehemiah calls on the people to present three sacrifices to the Lord for the sake of their city, sacrifices that God still calls His people to give for the sake of the church He is building in this world.

1. We must give ourselves to God. (Neh. 11:1-12:26)

Now that the walls and gates of Jerusalem were restored, it was important that the Jews inhabit their capital city and make the population grow. For one thing, people were needed to protect the city; for they never knew when the enemy might decide to attack. It may have been safer for the people to live in the small outlying villages that were no threat to the Gentile society, but somebody had to take the risk and move into the big city.

Also, if the people really loved God and their holy city, they would want to live there, if only as a witness to the skeptical Gentiles around them. After all, why rebuild the city if you don't plan to live there? But most of all, God had brought the remnant back home because He had a special job for them to do; and to abandon the restored city was to obstruct the working out of God's will through Israel.

In other words, God needed people—live bodies—in the holy city. The Jews were asked to heed a call not unlike the one Paul wrote in Romans 12:1: "I beseech you therefore, brethren, by the mercies of God, that you present your bodies a living sacrifice, holy, acceptable to God, which is your reasonable service" (NKJV).

Never underestimate the importance of simply being physically present in the place where God wants you. You may not be asked to perform some dramatic ministry, but simply being there is a ministry. The men, women, and children who helped to populate the city of Jerusalem were serving God, their nation, and future generations by their step of faith.

Some of these citizens volunteered willingly while others had to be "drafted" (Neh. 11:1-2). The people had promised to tithe their produce (10:37-38), so Nehemiah decided to tithe the people; and 10 percent were chosen by lot to move from the villages into Jerusalem. Since there were few residents in the city and since the housing situation was bad (7:4), it isn't surprising that many of the Jews were unwilling to move. We wonder what would happen in the average local church if 10 percent of the congregation were asked to relocate in order to strengthen and extend the work of the Lord!

We have grown accustomed to Nehemiah's practice of listing the names of the people involved in his projects. In chapter 3, he told us who the people were who worked on the wall and what part of the wall they repaired. Chapter 7 lists the names of the people who returned with Zerubbabel, and chapter 8 records the names of the leaders involved in the "Bible conference" at the Water Gate. Chapter 10 contains the names of eighty-four men who set their seals to the dedication covenant. In listing these names, Nehemiah was giving evidence of his sincere appreciation for each individual who assisted in the work. It also reminds us that our Father sees and records what His children do as they serve Him. Even if others don't recognize or appreciate your ministry, you can be sure that God knows all about it and will reward you accordingly.

The people of Judah and Benjamin who lived in Jerusalem are listed first (11:4-9). These two tribes composed the kingdom of Judah after the nation divided (1 Kings 11-12). "Valiant men" (Neh. 11:6) or "mighty men" (v. 14) can mean "brave fighting men" or "wealthy men of substance," such as Boaz (Ruth 2:1).

The priests, Levites, and temple workers are named next (Neh. 11:10-24). God had set aside special cities for them (Josh. 21), so they could have legitimately lived outside Jerusalem; but they chose to be with the people as they served God in the temple. Like Jeremiah, they chose to remain with God's people, even though it might have been safer and more comfortable elsewhere (Jer. 40:1-6).

A variety of people were needed for the temple ministry that was so important to the Jewish nation. The priests officiated at the altar, and the Levites assisted them. Some supervised the maintenance of the building (Neh. 11:16) while others ministered with prayer and praise (vv. 17, 22); and both were important. There were nearly 300 men appointed to guard the temple (v. 19). Since the tithes and offerings were stored in the temple, it was important that the building be protected. It took many people, with many skills, to maintain the ministry in Jerusalem.

When I was pastor of Calvary Baptist Church in Covington, Kentucky, one Sunday I started listing the people, seen and unseen, who helped make my pulpit ministry possible. While I was preaching, there were three technicians running the controls in the radio room, half a dozen men patrolling the parking lots, ushers at the doors and walking through the buildings to see that all was well, maintenance personnel keeping the equipment going, and an efficient pastoral staff backing me up. The musicians had led the congregation in praise and helped prepare them for hearing the Word.

During the previous week, scores of Sunday School workers had contacted hundreds of people, church members had invited many visitors to the services, the office crew had kept the organizational machinery running smoothly, church officers had encouraged and counseled, people had prayed—and all of this so that the pastor might be able to glorify Christ by proclaiming the Word of God! Believe me, it was a humbling experience; and it made me want to do my best for the Lord and for those wonderful people.

God uses many people with different gifts and skills to get His work done in this world. The important thing is that we give our bodies to the Lord so that He can use us as His tools to accomplish His work. Each person is important and each task is significant. Note that Nehemiah lists other temple ministers in 12:1-26.

In verse 23, Nehemiah states that the king of Persia helped support the ministry at the temple. Since the king wanted the Jewish people to pray for him and his family, he shared in the temple expenses (Ezra 6:8-10; 7:20-24). In our modern democracies, where there is a separation of church and state, this kind of support would be questioned. But the province of Judah was one small part of a great empire, ruled by an all-powerful king; and the king did for the Jews what he did for all the other provinces. Christians today are commanded to pray for civil leaders (1 Tim. 2:1-2; see Jer. 29:7), and this should be done daily and on each Lord's Day when the church assembles to worship.

Pethahiah (Neh. 12:24) was the "king's agent" who represented the Jews at court. People involved in government are God's ministers (Rom. 13:1-7), whether they realize it or not; and if they are faithful, they are seeing the Lord just as much as the priests and Levites in the temple.

In Nehemiah 12:25-36, Nehemiah names the villages where the Jews were living, some of which were quite a distance from Jerusalem. When the exiles returned to the land from Babylon, they would naturally want to settle in their native towns and villages. They would still be under the authority of Nehemiah and expected to be loyal to the king of Persia. This loyalty to their native cities was what helped make it difficult for Nehemiah to get people to reside in Jerusalem. While it is good to cultivate local loyalties, we must remember that there are larger obligations that must also be considered. The work of the Lord is bigger than any one person's ministry or the ministry of any one assembly.

2. We must give our praise to God. (Neh. 12:27-42)

The Jews were accustomed to having workers and watchers on the walls of Jerusalem, but now Nehemiah and Ezra assigned people to be worshipers on the walls. They conducted a dedication service with such enthusiasm that their shouts and songs were heard "even afar off" (v. 43).

The people had been dedicated (chaps. 8-10); now it was time to dedicate the work that the people had done. This is the correct order, for what good are dedicated walls and gates without dedicated people? Note that the emphasis was on *joyful praise* on the part of all the people. Singing is mentioned eight times in this chapter, thanksgiving six times, rejoicing seven times, and musical instruments three times.

The order for the dedication service was unique. The leaders and singers were divided into two groups, with Ezra leading one group and Nehemiah (following the choir) directing the second group. The processions started probably from the Valley Gate on the west wall, marching in opposite directions. Ezra's company (12:31-37) went south on the walls to the Dung Gate, then to the Fountain Gate and the Water Gate on the east wall of the city. Nehemiah's company went north (vv. 38-39) past the Old Gate, the Ephraim Gate, the Fish Gate, the Sheep Gate, and the Muster Gate ("gate of the guard"). Both groups met at the temple area where the service climaxed with sacrifices offered to the Lord.

Why did Ezra and Nehemiah organize this kind of a dedication service? Why not just meet at the temple area, let the Levites sing and offer sacrifices to the Lord, and send everybody home?

To begin with, it was the walls and gates that were being dedicated; and it was only right that the people see and touch them. I recall sharing in a service of dedication for a church educational building; but the service was held in the church sanctuary, not in the educational building. At some point in that service, we should have left the sanctuary and marched through the new building singing praises to God. As I ministered the Word, I felt as though I were performing a wedding for an absentee bride and groom!

But there is another reason for this unique service: The people were bearing witness to the watching world that God had done the work, and He alone should be glorified. The enemy had said that the walls would be so weak that a fox could knock them down (4:3), but here were the people *marching on the walls!* What a testimony to the unbelieving Gentiles of the power of God and the reality of faith. It was another opportunity to prove to them that "this work was wrought by our God" (6:16).

By marching on the walls, the people had an opportunity to see the results of their labors and realize anew that the work had not been done by one person. True, Nehemiah had been their leader, and they needed him; but "the people had a mind to work" (4:6). Various people and families had labored on different parts of the wall (chap. 3), but nobody "owned" the part he or she had worked on. The wall belonged to God.

You can expect serious problems after a church building program if individuals or groups in the church start claiming "territorial rights." I heard about one Sunday School class that actually sued the church when they were asked to vacate their classroom and locate elsewhere in the building. No matter how much work or money we have put into a building program, this does not earn us the right to claim and control some area of the building. *It all belongs to God and must be used for His glory.* As the Jews marched around the walls, they were symbolically saying just that. "Yes, we all had part in the work and a place to serve, but now we are giving it all to the Lord that He alone might be glorified!"

Let me suggest another reason for this march around the walls: It was a symbolic act by which they "stepped out by faith" to claim God's blessing. In that day, to walk on a piece of property meant to claim it as your own. God said to Abraham, "Arise, walk through the land … for I will give it unto thee" (Gen. 13:17); and He said to Joshua, "Every place that the sole of your foot shall tread upon, that have I given unto you" (Josh. 1:3). This joyful march around the walls was their way of saying, "We claim from our God all that He has for us, just as our forebears claimed this land by faith!"

Too often, a church dedication service marks the end and not the beginning of ministry as the congregation breathes a sigh of relief and settles down to business as usual. Vance Havner once described his impressions of a dedication service at which he had spoken: "The church people thought the new building was a milestone, but it looked to me like it was a millstone!" If we lose our forward vision and stop launching out by faith, then what God has accomplished will indeed become a millstone that will burden and break us.

But the most important thing about this dedication service was not the march around the walls. It was the expression of joyful praise that came from the choirs and the people. "By Him [Christ] therefore let us offer the sacrifice of praise to God continually, that is, the fruit of our lips, giving thanks to His name" (Heb. 13:15). "I will praise the name of God with a song, and will magnify Him with thanksgiving. This also shall please the Lord better than an ox or bullock that hath horns and hoofs" (Ps. 69:30-31).

The people offered their praise thankfully (Neh. 12:24, 27, 31, 38, 46), joyfully (vv. 27, 43-44), and loudly (vv. 42-43), accompanied by various instruments (vv. 27, 35-36). It was not a time for muted, meditative worship. It was a time for "pulling out all the stops" and praising the Lord enthusiastically.

This special service of dedication would have been a failure were it not for a man who had been dead for over 500 years. That man was King David. It was David who had organized the priests and Levites (v. 24; 1 Chron. 24:7-19) and written many of the songs for the temple choirs (Neh. 12:46). He had also devised musical instruments for use in worship (v. 36; 2 Chron. 29:26-27). David had served his generation faithfully (Acts 13:36), but in doing so, he had also served every generation that followed! In fact, it was David who captured the Jebusite city of Jerusalem and made it his capital, the City of David (2 Sam. 5:6-10). It was also David who had provided the blueprints and much of the wealth for the building of the temple (1 Chron. 28:11-19). "He who does the will of God abides forever" (1 John 2:17, NKJV).

It was not only the "professional musicians" who expressed praise to God, for the women and children also joined in the singing (Neh. 12:43). They had heard the Word at the Water Gate (8:2), so it was only right that they now express their worship; for learning the Word and worshiping the Lord must go together (Col. 3:12). We must never permit the accomplished ministry of worship leaders to take the place of our own spontaneous celebration of the Lord's goodness. Otherwise, we will become spectators instead of participants; and spectators miss most of the blessing.

So great was the people's praise that "the joy of Jerusalem was heard even afar off" (Neh. 12:43). This was now the third time in Israel's history that their shouting was "heard afar off." The soldiers shouted when the Ark of the Covenant came into their camp (1 Sam. 4:5), but that eventually led to shameful defeat. When the temple foundation was laid nearly a century before, the workers shouted for joy; but their joy was mingled with sorrow (Ezra 3:8-13). The shout from Jerusalem during this dedication service was unalloyed joy, to the glory of the Lord; and because of this record in the Word of God, *that shout has been heard around the world!*

3. We must give our gifts to God. (Neh. 12:44-47)

The people had covenanted with God to support the temple ministry (10:32-39), and they kept their promises. Some of the Levites were appointed to supervise the collecting of the produce and the storing of it in the temple. Keep in mind that these tithes and offerings represented the support of the temple workers so that they could serve the Lord.

The people brought their tithes and offerings, not only because it was the commandment of God, but also because they were "pleased with the ministering priests and Levites" (12:44, NIV). The ministers at the temple were exemplary both in their personal purity and in their obedience to God's Word (vv. 30, 45). They conducted the worship, not according to their own ideas, but in obedience to the directions given by David and Solomon. When believers have a godly ministry that exalts the Lord and obeys the Word, they are only too glad to bring their tithes and offerings to support it. A worldly ministry that seeks only to fulfill its own ambitions does not deserve the support of God's people.

The result of this joyful service of dedication was a plentiful supply of produce to sustain the work of the ministry. The people gave "not grudgingly or of necessity" but joyfully and gratefully (2 Cor. 9:7). Missionary leader J. Hudson Taylor used to say, "When God's work is done in God's way for God's glory, it will not lack God's support."

Our material gifts are really spiritual sacrifices to the Lord, if they are given in the right spirit. The Apostle Paul called the gifts from the Philippian church "an odor of a sweet smell, a sacrifice acceptable, well pleasing to God" (Phil. 4:18). Jesus accepted Mary's gift of precious ointment as an act of worship, and Hebrews 13:16 reminds us that doing good and sharing are sacrifices that please the Lord.

But before we can bring our material gifts to the Lord, we must first give ourselves to Him. Paul commended the churches of Macedonia because they "first gave themselves to the Lord" (2 Cor. 8:5, NKJV), before they shared in the missionary offering he was receiving for the needy believers in Jerusalem. Our gifts cannot be a substitute for ourselves.

It was a high and holy day in Jerusalem, a happy day because the work had been completed and God had been glorified in a wonderful way. Did the blessing last? No, it didn't; and we will find out why in the next study.

CHAPTER TWELVE
STANDING BY OUR PROMISES
Nehemiah 13

General William Booth, founder of The Salvation Army, once said to a group of new officers, "I want you young men always to bear in mind that it is the nature of a fire to go out; you must keep it stirred and fed and the ashes removed."

Nehemiah discovered that the fires of devotion had gone out in Jerusalem. His first term as governor lasted for twelve years (5:14), after which he returned to the palace to report to the king (13:6). He was gone perhaps a year; but when he returned to Jerusalem, he discovered that the situation had deteriorated dramatically, for the people were not living up to the vows they had made (chap. 10).

Nehemiah immediately began to act decisively to change the situation.

Without spiritual leadership, God's people are prone to stray like sheep. One successful pastor told me, "If we didn't keep our eyes on this work twenty-four hours a day, seven days a week, it would be invaded and soon fall apart." Moses was away from the people of Israel only a short time, and they became idolaters (Ex. 32). Paul would establish a church and leave it in the hands of the elders, only to have trouble begin soon after his departure. Then he would have to write them a letter or pay them a visit to straighten things out. (No wonder Paul exhorted the Ephesian church leaders as he did in Acts 20:28-32!) After Nehemiah was gone from Jerusalem only a short time, he came home to find the people defiled by compromise.

If you compare this chapter with chapter 10, you will see that the people failed to keep several of the promises that they had made to the Lord.

1. The separation promise (Neh. 13:1-9, 23-31)

The mixed multitude (Neh. 13:1-3). According to 10:28-29, the Jews had willingly separated themselves from the people of the land and united with their Jewish brothers and sisters to obey the Law and walk in the way of the Lord. But apparently their separation was incomplete, or some of the people formed new alliances; for they discovered that there were Ammonites and Moabites in their congregation, and this was contrary to the Law of Moses (Deut. 23:3-4).

Ammon and Moab were born from the incestuous union of Lot and two of his daughters (Gen. 19:30-38), and their descendants were the avowed enemies of the Jews. Somehow this "mixed multitude" had infiltrated the people of Israel in spite of previous purgings (9:2; 10:28). It was the "mixed multitude" that gave Moses so much trouble (Ex. 12:38; Num. 11:4-6), and it gives the church trouble today. The "mixed multitude" is composed of unsaved people who want to belong to the fellowship of God's people without trusting the Lord or submitting to His will. They want the blessings but not the obligations, and their appetite is still for the things of the world.

Balaam was a hireling prophet who tried to curse Israel but each time saw the curse turned into a blessing (Num. 22-24). Finally, however, he hit upon a scheme to defeat Israel: He encouraged the Moabites to be "neighborly" and invite the Jews to share in their religious feasts, which involved immorality and idolatry (Num. 25). Balaam knew that human nature would respond to the opportunity for sin and the Jews would disobey God. As a result of their sin, Israel was disciplined by God, and 24,000 people died.

The "mixed multitude" in the church today urges us to follow the philosophy of Balaam and do what the world wants us to do. I was told about a dedicated youth pastor whose ministry was bringing many teens to Christ and building them up in the faith. He didn't entice them with entertainment; he simply taught the Word, kept the young people busy witnessing, and met with them regularly for prayer. The church was being greatly helped by this group of dedicated teenagers.

But the enemy went to work. The youth pastor was called before the elders and asked, "What is your program for ministering to the carnal young people in the church?" He said that he had no special program for carnal teenagers, but that they were welcome to join in the Bible studies, prayer meetings, and witnessing trips. *The elders dismissed the youth pastor because he was not catering to the carnal teens in the church!*

When I was ministering over "Back to the Bible Broadcast," the manager of a Christian radio station phoned me to complain about my messages about Lot and worldliness among professing Christians. He felt I was being too hard on the carnal Christians. "If you keep that up," he said, "we're going to drop your program!"

The old Youth for Christ slogan is still true: In ministry, we must be "geared to the times and anchored to the Rock." If we understand the times (1 Chron. 12:32), we can relate to people more easily and apply the Word with greater skill; *but we must not imitate the world in order to try to witness to the world.* Years ago, Oswald Chambers wrote, "Today the world has taken so many things out of the church, and the church has taken so many things out of the world, that it is difficult to know where you are" (*The Servant As His Lord*, p. 17). "Today the world has so infiltrated the church," said Vance Havner, "that we are more beset by traitors within than by foes without. Satan is not fighting churches—he is joining them."

An enemy intruder (Neh 13:4-9). Not only were some of the Jews married to Ammonites or Moabites, but also *an Ammonite was living in the Jewish temple!* Tobiah the Ammonite (4:3) had been given a room in the temple by Eliashib the high priest (13:28). Eliashib is the first one named in the list of workers (3:1), and yet he had become a traitor. Why? Because one of his relatives was married to Sanballat's daughter (13:28), and Sanballat and Tobiah were friends. They were all a part of the secret faction in Jerusalem that was fraternizing with the enemy (6:17-19).

Just because a family has been active in the church a long time and has helped to build the work, it is no sign that each generation will be spiritual, or that any generation will *remain* spiritual. Children and grandchildren can drift from the faith and try to bluff their way on the testimony of their ancestors, and fathers and mothers can depart from the faith just to please their children. Eliashib's relative was privileged to be born into the priestly family, yet he threw away his future ministry by marrying the wrong woman (Lev. 21:14; Deut. 23:3); and Eliashib apparently approved of it.

All this happened while Nehemiah was away at the palace, which suggests that those he appointed to lead in his absence had failed in their oversight. *It doesn't take long for the enemy to capture leadership, and too often the people will blindly follow their leaders in the path of compromise and disobedience.*

It was bad enough that an Ammonite was living in the temple, and that a Jewish high priest had let him in; but this intruder was using a room dedicated to God for the storing of the offerings used by the Levites. He defiled the temple by his presence and robbed the servants of God at the same time. Nehemiah lost no time throwing out both the man and his furniture, rededicating the room to the Lord, and using it again for its intended purpose. Like our Lord, Nehemiah had to cleanse the temple; and it appears that he had to do it alone.

But this is not an easy thing to do. A new pastor may discover officers or leaders in the church who are not spiritual people but who are entrenched in their offices. What does he do? He knows that these leaders have relatives in the church who, like Eliashib, will cooperate with their family rather than contend for the faith. Should the pastor try to "clean house" and possibly split the church? Or should he bide his time, lovingly preach the Word, and pray for God to work? With either approach, the pastor will need courage and faith, because eventually the blessing of the Lord on the Word will arouse the opposition of the "mixed multitude."

Mixed marriages (Neh. 13:23-31). "We would not give our daughters as wives to the peoples of the land, nor take their daughters for our sons!" was the promise the Jews had made to the Lord (see 10:30, NKJV); but they did not keep it. In his survey of Jerusalem, Nehemiah saw women from Ashdod (see 4:7), Ammon, and Moab married to Jewish men; and he heard their children speaking foreign languages. (A child is more likely to learn how to speak from his mother, with whom he spends more time, than from his father who is away from home each day working.) If these children did not know the language of Israel, how could they read the Law or participate in the holy services? If a generation was lost to the faith, what was the future of the nation?

God's people and the people of the world can be identified by their speech. "They are from the world and therefore speak from the viewpoint of the world, and the world listens to them. We are from God, and whoever knows God listens to us; but whoever is not from God does not listen to us. This is how we recognize the Spirit of truth and the spirit of falsehood" (1 John 4:5-6, NIV).

While ministering at a summer Bible conference, I had dinner one evening in the home of the daughter of a well-known Christian musician and her husband. Both of them were able to talk about her father, now deceased, or about music and musicians; but when the conversation turned to the Word and the Lord, they were silent. I wondered if either of them really knew the Lord, or, if they did, if they were on speaking terms with Him. They had no problem talking about the things of the world, but they did not know "the language of Zion."

Nehemiah dealt with the problem by first expressing his horror that such a thing should be done in Israel (Neh. 13:25). In a similar situation, Ezra had plucked his own hair and beard (Ezra 9:3); but Nehemiah plucked the hair of some of the offenders! Ezra had dissolved the mixed marriages (Ezra 10), but Nehemiah only rebuked the offenders and made the people promise that they would not do it again.

Nehemiah also delivered a sermon, reminding the people that Solomon, one of Israel's greatest kings, was ruined by marrying foreign women (Neh. 13:26; 1 Kings 11:4-8). In Solomon's case, his mixed marriages were a threat to the throne and the kingdom; and in Nehemiah's day, mixed marriages even threatened the priesthood. The Law of Moses was clear, but both the priests and the common people had deliberately disobeyed it. Nehemiah then purified the priests and made certain that only those who were qualified served (Neh. 13:30). However, the problem with the priests was not completely settled, for the Prophet Malachi had to deal with disobedient priests in his day (Mal. 1-2).

How important it is that we take a stand for separation from sin "and having done all, to stand" (Eph. 6:13).

2. The support promise (Neh. 13:10-14)

"We will not forsake the house of our God," was the final statement the Jews made in their covenant with the Lord (10:39). This meant paying the temple tax, providing wood for the altar, and bringing the required tithes and offerings to the priests and Levites (vv. 32-39). Without the faithful support of the people, the ministry at the temple would languish; and the Levites would then scatter to the villages, where they could work the land and survive (13:10).

When Nehemiah returned to the city, he discovered that the people had failed to keep their promise. (This helps to explain why one of the storage rooms was available for Tobiah.) The priests and Levites were without support and were deserting their work in order to survive. The people ignored the warnings of Moses, "Take heed to yourself that you do not forsake the Levite as long as you live in your land" (Deut. 12:19, NKJV) and "You shall not forsake the Levite who is within your gates, for he has no part nor inheritance with you" (14:27, NKJV; and 18:1-8).

Nehemiah "contended" with them, which means he rebuked the leaders for breaking their promise and disobeying the Law. Before his survey of the city was completed, he also rebuked the nobles of Judah (Neh. 13:17) and the men married to foreign women (v. 25). While the Hebrew word can refer to arguing or even physical combat, it also carries the judicial meaning of "to plead a case." Since Nehemiah presented God's case and defended it from the Law, the offenders had to admit that he was right.

The temple officers in charge of the gifts had forsaken their posts because there was nothing coming in or going out, so Nehemiah "set them in their place" (v. 11; "stationed them at their posts," NIV). He then saw to it that the people brought to God the offerings that rightfully belonged to Him (Mal. 3:7-12). He appointed four men to supervise the treasury and distribute the tithes and offerings. Note that these men represented the priests, Levites, scribes, and laymen; but they all had one thing in common: They were faithful to the Lord. "Moreover it is required in stewards, that a man be found faithful" (1 Cor. 4:2).

When God's people start to decline spiritually, one of the first places it shows up is in their giving. "For where your treasure is, there will your heart be also" (Matt. 6:21). The believer who is happy in the Lord and walking in His will has a generous heart and wants to share with others. Giving is both the "thermostat" and the "thermometer" of the Christian life: It measures our spiritual "temperature" and also helps set it at the right level.

The prayer in Nehemiah 13:14 is the first one recorded since 6:14 and is the seventh of Nehemiah's "telegraph" prayers found in the book. You find three more such prayers in 13:22, 29, and 31. He was in the habit of talking to God as he served Him, a good example for us to follow. He reminded God of his faithfulness and prayed that what he had done would not be blotted out. Nehemiah was not pleading for blessings on the basis of personal merit, because he knew that God's blessings come only because of God's mercy (v. 22). This prayer is similar to the one recorded in 5:19 where Nehemiah merely asked God to remember him and what he had done. He wanted his reward from God, not from men.

Someone asked the American Episcopal bishop Phillips Brooks what he would do to resurrect a dead church, and he replied, "I would take up a missionary offering." *Giving to others is one secret of staying alive and fresh in the Christian life.* If all we do is receive, then we become reservoirs; and the water can become stale and polluted. But if we both receive and give, we become like channels; and in blessing others, we bless ourselves. American psychiatrist Dr. Karl Menninger said,

"Money-giving is a good criterion of a person's mental health. Generous people are rarely mentally ill people." Someone wrote in *Modern Maturity* magazine, "The world is full of two kinds of people, the givers and the takers. The takers eat well—but the givers sleep well."

3. The Sabbath promise (Neh. 13:15-22)

When they signed the covenant, the Jews promised not to do business with the Gentiles on the Sabbath Day (10:31); but Nehemiah found the people not only doing business on the Sabbath, but also doing their daily work and carrying unnecessary burdens. The Jewish merchants didn't want to lose the opportunity to make money from the Gentiles, and the Gentiles were quick to make a profit from their Jewish neighbors.

The child of God must choose spiritual wealth rather than material wealth and claim the promise of Matthew 6:33, "But seek first His kingdom, and His righteousness; and all these things shall be added to you" (NASB). Whoever wrote Psalm 119 made it clear that he chose God's Word rather than money (vv. 14, 72, 127, 162). King Saul made the wrong choice (1 Sam. 15), and so did Achan (Josh. 7) and Demas (2 Tim. 4:10).

In one of the churches I pastored, a lovely young couple began to attend with their little boy. Then I noticed that only the mother and son were attending, so I stopped at the home to see what had happened to the father. I learned that he had taken a second job on weekends so he could save enough money to get a better house. The wife confided that they really didn't need the extra money or a new house, but it was her husband's idea, and she couldn't stop him. The tragedy is, the extra money didn't go to a new house; it went to doctors and hospitals. The little boy contracted an unusual disease that required special medicine and care, and the father's extra income helped pay the bill.

I'm not suggesting that every family with a sick child is unfaithful in their stewardship, or that God makes children suffer for the sins of their parents. But I am suggesting that nobody can rob God and profit from it. If our priorities become confused and we start putting money ahead of God, then we must expect to be the losers.

Nehemiah took three steps toward changing the situation. First, he rebuked the Jews who were working and selling on the Sabbath and made them stop (Neh. 13:15). Then, he rebuked the nobles for allowing business on the Sabbath Day, reminding them that the nation's violation of the Sabbath was one cause for their captivity (vv. 16-18; Jer. 17:21-27). Did they want to have more wrath come on the people?

His third step was a very practical one: He ordered the city gates shut on the Sabbath Day. The guards had been willing to open the gates to the Gentile merchants, possibly because they were bribed; so Nehemiah put some of his own servants on duty. He also ordered the Levites to set a good example on the Sabbath and minister to the people.

The Lord's Day, the first day of the week, is not a "Christian Sabbath," because the Sabbath is the seventh day of the week and belonged especially to the Jews. Therefore, the Old Testament laws governing the Jewish Sabbath don't apply to the Lord's Day. But Sunday is a special day to God's people because it commemorates the resurrection of Jesus Christ from the dead as well as the coming of the Holy Spirit at Pentecost. We ought to use the Lord's Day to the glory of the Lord.

More and more, especially in our cities, Sunday has become a day for shopping, sports, and chores around the house. The shopping center parking lot is as full on Sunday afternoons as it is on Saturdays. I once interviewed the manager of a shopping mall and asked him how he felt about being open on Sundays.

"The employees and I would rather stay home," he replied, "but it's a big day for business, especially from people on their way home from church."

In our family, my wife and I tried to follow the simple principle of not doing on Sundays whatever could be done on any other day of the week, things like mowing the lawn, washing the car, shopping, and so on. The home didn't become a prison, but neither did it turn into a circus; and the children didn't seem to suffer for it.

The French agnostic, Voltaire, is supposed to have said, "If you want to kill Christianity, you must abolish Sunday." I'm not sure I agree with him, but I do know that many Christians have killed their joy, witness, and spiritual power by turning Sunday into an ordinary day and not putting Christ first in their week.

Nehemiah closes with two prayers (Neh. 13:29, 31) that God would remember him for his faithful service. His conscience was clear, for he knew he had done everything for the good of the people and the glory of God. There would probably be little appreciation from the people, in spite of his sacrifices; but he knew that God would reward him accordingly.

May those who come behind us find us faithful!

CHAPTER THIRTEEN
LOOKING FOR LEADERS
Nehemiah the Leader

During the French Revolution, a man was seen running down the street after a mob, moving quickly into danger.

"Stop! Stop!" somebody cried out. "Don't follow that mob!"

As the man continued to run, he called back, "I have to follow them! I'm their leader!"

Nehemiah was certainly not that kind of leader. He wasn't afraid of danger, but he was wise in his plans and careful in his decisions. The church today could use leaders like Nehemiah. We have a lot of rubbish to remove and rebuilding to accomplish before the world will believe that our God is real and our message is worth believing.

What are the characteristics of this man that we ought to emulate? Let me list twelve qualities that made Nehemiah a successful leader. As you read, try to think of passages in the Book of Nehemiah that illustrate these qualities.

1. He knew he was called of God.
When everything else fails, the call of God will give you the strength and resolution you need to get the job done. At first Moses resisted the call of God, but then he came to realize that God's calling was the greatest assurance of success (Phil. 1:6; 1 Thess. 5:24). Knowing that God had called him was the secret of Jeremiah's perseverance when everything around him was falling apart and his own people were against him. The worker who doesn't have a divine calling to the work is like

a house without a foundation or a ship without an anchor, unprepared for the storms of life.

Nehemiah started with a burden for Jerusalem, but the burden was not the call. He wept over the sad condition of the city (Neh. 1:4), but his tears were not the call. It was as he prayed to God and sought divine help that he received a call to leave his relatively easy job and go to Jerusalem to rebuild the walls. Because he knew God had called him, Nehemiah could approach the king and get help; and he could also enlist the help of the Jews in Jerusalem.

Before you quickly move into a place of ministry, be sure God has called you and equipped you for the job. You may not think you can do it, and others may have their doubts; but if God calls you, have no fear: He will see you through.

2. He depended on prayer.

The Book of Nehemiah starts and ends with prayer. And in between, Nehemiah often sends up quick prayers to heaven and asks for God's help. Nehemiah was the royal governor of the province, with all the authority and wealth of the king behind him; but he depended solely on God to help him finish the work.

The Christian worker who can get along comfortably without prayer isn't getting much done for God and certainly isn't threatening the enemy too much. "To be a Christian without prayer," said Martin Luther, "is no more possible than to be alive without breathing."

Nehemiah faced a gigantic task, a task too big for him but not too great for God. "Do not pray for tasks equal to your powers," said Phillips Brooks. "Pray for powers equal to your tasks." One mark of true spiritual leaders is their honest acknowledgment of their own inadequacy and their humble trust in the power of God.

We have Nehemiah's brief, spontaneous prayers recorded in the book, but behind those prayers was a life of prayer as seen in chapter 1. He certainly had a disciplined prayer life; for our "telegraph" prayers accomplish little if our hearts are not in tune with God. Most Christians never realize the hours that leaders must spend in prayer in order to get the job done. "Pray for great things," said evangelist R.A. Torrey, "expect great things, work for great things, but above all, pray." Nehemiah certainly followed that advice.

3. He had vision and saw the greatness of the work.

Leadership involves vision, revision, and supervision; but the greatest of these is vision. Leaders must see what others don't see and then challenge others to follow until they do see. "I am doing a great work, so that I cannot come down!" was Nehemiah's testimony (6:3), and he never lost that vision.

It's an old story but it bears repeating. A visitor was watching some men work on a building and began to question them. "What are you doing?" he asked one, who replied, "I'm making ten dollars a day." When he asked a second man the same question, the worker replied, "I'm laying stones in this building." But the third man answered, "Why, I'm building a cathedral!" He was the man with vision.

No matter what God has called you to do, it's a great work because it's part of the building of His church; and that's the greatest work in the world. I have often told people, "There are no small churches and there are no big preachers." In God's kingdom, every job is a big job and every servant is nothing apart from faith in the Lord.

If you lose the greatness of a vision, you

will begin to cut corners in your work, stop making sacrifices, and start looking for something else to challenge you. Nehemiah realized that what he was doing was far bigger than simply repairing gates and rebuilding walls. He was seeing the Lord God of heaven and getting the holy city ready for the coming of the Messiah!

4. He submitted to authority.

The call of God is not an invitation to become independent and ignore authority. Nehemiah respected the king and submitted his plans to him for his approval before he went to Jerusalem. He acknowledged what Paul wrote in Romans 13, that the powers that be are ordained of God for our good, and we should submit to them.

Even more, Nehemiah submitted to the authority of the Word of God. He invited Ezra to teach the Law to the people so that they too would obey the will of God. It is a basic rule of life that *those who exercise authority must themselves be under authority.* Nehemiah was a man who was dependable because he was accountable. In recent years, we have seen the sad consequences of religious leaders refusing to submit to authority and be accountable. When you read the Book of Nehemiah, you meet a man whose work prospered because he submitted to God, the Word, and the king.

5. He was organized in his work.

Instead of rushing impetuously into the task, Nehemiah secretly surveyed the situation and became acquainted with the facts. He talked with the Jewish leaders privately and told them his plan. There were no press conferences or "pep rallies." He was simply a man willing to wait for God's direction and then act as soon as the way was clear.

After making his plan, he enlisted his workers and sought to give them the same vision for the task that God had given to him. He had a job for everyone to do and a place for everyone to work. He gave recognition to his workers and encouraged them when the going was tough. He gave them a feeling of security even though the situation was dangerous.

Nehemiah's priorities were right: After the wall was finished, he held a "revival service" for the people and then publicly dedicated the walls. He planned his work and worked his plan, and God blessed him.

6. He was able to discern the tactics of the enemy.

Every Christian ministry needs an "intelligence department" that keeps its eye on the enemy and recognizes when he is at work. Nehemiah was not fooled by the enemy's offers or frightened by their threats. He could say with Paul, "We are not ignorant of his [Satan's] devices" (2 Cor. 2:11).

In our study, we have noted the various devices the enemy uses to try to stop the work; and every good leader will want to understand them. Leaders must spot the enemy before anybody else does and be ready to meet him quickly and efficiently. Leaders must recognize when Satan comes as a roaring lion or as a serpent, devouring or deceiving.

7. He worked hard.

That seems like a trite statement, but it isn't; for one of the secrets of Nehemiah's success was his willingness to sacrifice and work hard. Had he stayed back in the palace, serving the Persian king, he would have enjoyed an easy life. But once he was in Jerusalem, he went to work, he kept working, and he worked hard.

This is what Charles Spurgeon said to the ministerial students at his Pastors'

College in London: "Do not be afraid of hard work for Christ; a terrible reckoning awaits those who have an easy time in the ministry, but a great reward is in reserve for those who endure all things for the elect's sake. You will not regret your poverty when Christ cometh and calleth His own servants to Him. It will be a sweet thing to have died at your post, not turning aside for wealth, or running from Dan to Beersheba to obtain a better salary, but stopping where your Lord bade you hold the fort" *(An All Round Ministry,* p. 197).

"The laborer is worthy of his hire" (Luke 10:7), so let's be sure we are laborers and not loiterers. There is no place in the Lord's service for lazy people who give advice while they watch other people work.

8. He lived an exemplary life.
Whether it was working on the wall or feeding hundreds of guests, Nehemiah's life was blameless. His full time was devoted to the work, and he didn't permit himself to be distracted. He refused financial support that was legitimately his and instead spent his own money to help others. He identified with the people and stood right with them as together they built the walls.

The enemy would have rejoiced to discover something in Nehemiah's life that would have embarrassed him and hindered the work, but nothing could be found. Not that Nehemiah was sinless, for only Jesus Christ can claim that distinction; but his life was blameless. Paul exhorts us to become blameless and harmless, "children of God without fault in the midst of a crooked and perverse generation, among whom you shine as lights in the world" (Phil. 2:15, NKJV). The first qualification for the pastor (elder, bishop) is that he be "blameless" (1 Tim. 3:2; Titus 1:6).

There is no subsitute for integrity and the good conscience that goes with it. You can face any enemy, listen to any accusation, or confront any misunderstanding if you have integrity and a good conscience. You have nothing to hide and nothing to fear. It is when people start to lead a double life that they get into trouble, for nobody can serve two masters. Hypocrisy leads to further deception, until the deceivers get caught in their own traps. Sir Walter Scott was right when he wrote:

> O what a tangled web we weave
> When first we practice to deceive!

9. He sought to glorify God alone.
If Nehemiah had been interested only in promoting himself, he would have stayed in the palace; for there he was honored as the king's cupbearer and had an easy life. Or when he arrived in Jerusalem as the official governor, he would have used his authority to make life easier for himself. He could have "thrown his weight around" and avoided a great deal of sacrifice and toil.

But he did neither of those things. Instead, he came as a servant, identified with the people, and entered right into their trials and burdens and dangers. In this, he was certainly like our Lord Jesus Christ (Phil. 2:1-11).

Nehemiah was burdened because the city of Jerusalem no longer glorified God. It was a reproach. He was concerned because the people living in Jerusalem were an object of scorn to their Gentile neighbors. He determined to remove the reproach and give the Jews in Jerusalem cause to glorify God.

In the building of the walls and the repairing of the gates, God was glorified. In the way Nehemiah and his people confronted and defeated the enemy, God was glorified. In their dependence on the Lord, God was glorified. In the great service of dedication, the Lord was magnified. From beginning to end, the entire enterprise brought glory to the Lord.

I fear that the church today suffers from having too many celebrities and not enough servants. The praise too often goes to the workers and not to the Lord. Particularly at some religious conventions, there is so much praise given to men that the Lord is left out of the picture completely. *There is nothing good that God will not do for the worker who humbly serves and lets Him have the glory.*

10. He had courage.

There is no place for timidity in leadership. Once you know what God wants you to do, you must have the courage to step out and do it. You must be willing to take some risks and occasionally make some mistakes. You must be able to take criticism, be misunderstood, and even be slandered, without giving up. As Harry Truman said, "If you can't stand the heat, get out of the kitchen."

Nehemiah had the courage to live in a dangerous city and confront a subtle enemy. He had the courage to deal with the traitors among his own people and to call the people back to faithfulness to the Lord. He even threw Tobiah out of the temple! While you and I as Christian workers don't have the authority to pluck out beards or forcibly eject unwanted tenants, we need the same kind of courage Nehemiah had when he did those things.

Someone has said that success is never final and failure is never fatal: It's courage that counts. The ancient Greeks thought that courage was the "master virtue," because without courage you could never use your other virtues. No wonder the Spanish novelist Cervantes wrote, "He who loses wealth loses much; he who loses a friend loses more; but he who loses courage loses all."

11. He enlisted others to work.

True leaders don't try to do everything themselves. They not only enlist others, but they also create the kind of climate that enables others to become leaders as well. Real leaders aren't afraid to surround themselves with people who can do some things better than they can. Leaders don't feel intimidated by the excellence of others; in fact, they encourage it. Their job is to challenge others to do their best and help get the job done.

In my study of Christian biographies, I've noticed that God has occasionally raised up men and women who were like magnets in the way they attracted potential leaders to them. D.L. Moody was such a man, and so was Paul Rader. Amy Carmichael had this gift, and so did the late Dr. Bob Cook. Leaders develop other leaders, because they know how to discern spiritual gifts and the potential in a life.

12. He was determined.

Lech Walesa, the courageous Polish labor leader who became President of his country, said this about leadership: "To be a leader means to have determination. It means to be resolute inside and outside, with ourselves and with others." If anybody lived up to that description, it was Nehemiah.

Be determined! That's one of the key messages of the Book of Nehemiah. President of Wheaton (Ill.) College, Dr. V. Raymond Edman, used to remind his students, "It's always too soon to quit." Like Jesus Christ, Nehemiah set his face like a flint and kept on going (Luke 9:51; Isa. 50:7). Anyone who puts his hand to the plow and looks back is not fit to serve the Lord (Luke 9:62).

I read about a couple of boys who went around their neighborhood looking for jobs shoveling snow. They saw a man shoveling his driveway and asked if they could do the job.

"Can't you see I'm already half finished?" he said.

"That's why we asked," the boys explained. "You see, we get most of our work from people who got started but weren't able to finish."

Nehemiah was determined because the work he was doing was a great work and he was serving a great God. He was determined because the city was in great reproach, and he wanted it to bring great glory to God. He was determined because he was part of a great plan that God had for the world as He worked through the Jewish nation.

The church today needs leaders, men and women and young people who will determine under God to accomplish the will of God, come what may. The church needs leaders who will say with Nehemiah, "I am doing a great work, so that I cannot come down!"

More than anything else, I want to be able to say at the end of my ministry and my life, "I have glorified You on the earth. I have finished the work which You have given me to do" (John 17:4, NKJV).

So, the next time you feel like quitting, remember Nehemiah and stay on the job until the work is finished to the glory of God.

Be determined!

Endnotes

Chapter 2

1. Morrison, George. *Morning Sermons* (London: Hodder and Stoughton, 1935), p. 243

ESTHER

A SUGGESTED OUTLINE OF THE BOOK OF ESTHER

Theme: God's providence in protecting His people

Theme verses: 4:13-14

I. ESTHER'S CORONATION—CHAPS. 1–2

1. The dethroning of Vashti—1
2. The crowning of Esther—2

II. HAMAN'S CONDEMNATION —CHAPS. 3–7

1. Haman's intrigue—3
2. Mordecai's insight—4
3. Esther's intercession—5–7

III. ISRAEL'S CELEBRATION—CHAPS. 8–10

1. A new decree—8
2. A sure defense—9
3. A great distinction—10

CONTENTS

CHAPTER ONE
THE QUEEN SAYS "NO!"
Esther 1

(In which a family disagreement grows into a national crisis)

Let's begin by getting acquainted with the king. His Persian name was Khshayarshan, which in Hebrew becomes Ahasuerus and in the Greek language, Xerxes. His father was Darius I, and his grandfather was Cyrus the Great; so he came from an illustrious family. Ahasuerus ruled over the Persian Empire from 486 to 465 B.C. The empire was divided into twenty "satrapies," which in turn were subdivided into "provinces"; and the king was in absolute control.

Like most monarchs of that day, Ahasuerus was a proud man; and in this chapter, we see three evidences of his pride.

1. His boastfulness (Es. 1:1-9)

Eastern rulers enjoyed hosting lavish banquets because each occasion gave them opportunity to impress their guests with their royal power and wealth. Three banquets are mentioned in this chapter: one for the key military and political officers of the empire (vv. 1-4); one for the men of Shushan (Susa in Greek), site of the king's winter palace (vv. 5-8); and one for the women of Shushan (v. 9), presided over by Queen Vashti.

The king probably didn't assemble all his provincial leaders at one time; that would have kept them away from their duties for six months and weakened the empire. It's more likely that, over a period of six months, Ahasuerus brought the officers to Shushan on a rotating schedule. Then, having consulted with them, the king would bring them all together for the seven-day feast so they could confer collectively. In Esther 1:11, the writer indicates that the princes were also at this week-long festivity.

Along with these three banquets, at least six other feasts are recorded in this book: Esther's coronation banquet (2:18); Haman's celebration feast with the king (3:15); Esther's two banquets for Haman and the king (chaps. 5 and 7); the Jews' banquets when they heard the new decree (8:17); and the Feast of Purim (9:17-19). It's wonderful how God can accomplish His eternal purposes through such a familiar activity as people eating and drinking! (See 1 Cor. 10:31.)

What was the purpose behind the banquet for the nobles and officials of the empire? Scripture doesn't tell us, but secular history does. The Greek historian Herodotus (485-425 B.C.) may refer to these banquets in his *History*, where he states that Ahasuerus was conferring with his leaders about a possible invasion of Greece. Ahasuerus' father, Darius I, had invaded Greece and been shamefully defeated at Marathon in 490. While preparing to return to Greece and get revenge, Darius had died (486 B.C.); and now his son felt compelled to avenge his father and expand his empire at the same time. Herodotus claims that Ahasuerus planned to invade all of Europe and "reduce the whole earth into one empire."

According to Herodotus, the king's words were these: "My intent is to throw a bridge over the Hellespont and march an army through Europe against Greece, that thereby I may obtain vengeance from the Athenians for the wrongs committed by them against the Persians and against my father."[1]

The king's uncle, Artabanus, strongly opposed the plan, but the king persisted and succeeded in convincing the princes and officers to follow him.

It was important that Ahasuerus impress his nobles and military leaders with his wealth and power. When they saw the marble pillars, the gorgeous drapes hung from silver rings, the gold and silver couches on beautiful marble mosaic pavements, and the golden table service, what else could they do but submit to the king? Like the salesperson who takes you out to an exclusive restaurant for an expensive dinner, the king broke down their resistance. A proud man himself, he knew how to appeal to the pride in others.

Unfortunately, this ostentatious display of wealth couldn't guarantee the Persians a military victory. In 480 B.C., the Persian navy was destroyed at Salamis, while the king sat on a throne watching the battle; and in 479 B.C., the Persian army was defeated at Plataea. Thus ended Ahasuerus' dream of a world empire. If ever a man should have learned the truth of Proverbs 16:18, it was Ahasuerus: "Pride goes before destruction, and a haughty spirit before a fall" (NKJV).

People in authority need to remember that all authority comes from God (Rom. 13:1) and that He alone is in complete control. Pharaoh had to learn that lesson in Egypt (Ex. 7:3-5); Nebuchadnezzar had to learn it in Babylon (Dan. 3-4); Belshazzar learned it at his blasphemous banquet (Dan. 5); Sennacherib learned it at the gates of Jerusalem (Isa. 36-37); and Herod Agrippa I learned it as he died, being eaten by worms (Acts 12:20-23). Every man or woman in a place of authority is second in command, for Jesus Christ is Lord of all.

2. His drunkenness (Es. 1:10-12)

Scripture ignores these military matters because the writer's purpose was to explain how Esther became queen. It was at the conclusion of the seven-day banquet that Ahasuerus, "in high spirits from wine" (Es. 1:10, NIV), ordered his queen to display her beauty to the assembled guests; but she refused to obey. Her response, of course, was a triple offense on her part. Here was a woman challenging the authority of a man, a wife disobeying the orders of her husband, and a subject defying the command of the king. As a result, "the king became furious and burned with anger" (v. 12, NIV).

As you study the Book of Esther, you will discover that this mighty monarch could control everything but himself. His advisers easily influenced him; he made impetuous decisions that he later regretted; and when he didn't get his own way, he became angry. Susceptible to flattery, he was master of a mighty empire but not master of himself. "He who is slow to anger is better than the mighty, and he who rules his spirit, than he who captures a city" (Prov. 16:32). Ahasuerus built a great citadel at Shushan, but he couldn't build his own character. "Whoever has no rule over his own spirit is like a city broken down, without walls" (25:28, NKJV). The king could control neither his temper nor his thirst.

This is a good place to stop and consider alcohol and anger—two powerful forces that have brought more destruction to our society than even the statistics reveal.

While we appreciate the king's wisdom in not forcing his guests to drink (Es. 1:8), we can hardly compliment him on the bad example he set by his own drinking habits. The Bible doesn't *command* total abstinence, but it does emphasize it. The nation of Israel didn't drink strong drink during their wilderness pilgrimage (Deut. 29:5-6), and the priests were instructed not to drink wine or strong drink while serving in the tabernacle (Lev. 10:8-11). The Nazirites were forbidden not only to drink wine but even to eat the skin or seeds of the grape (Lev. 6:1-3). Though our Lord Jesus drank wine while here on earth, He is today a "total abstainer." People who claim Jesus as their example in social drinking, and even point out that He turned water into wine, should take Luke 22:18 into consideration: "For I say unto you, I will not drink of the fruit of the vine, until the kingdom of God shall come" (KJV). I wonder whether these people "follow His example" in any other areas of life, such as praying, serving, and sacrificing. (Probably not.)

Most of the advertisements that promote the sale of alcoholic beverages depict fashionable people in gracious settings, giving the subtle impression that "social drinking" and success are synonymous. But pastors, social workers, physicians, and dedicated members of Alcoholics Anonymous would paint a different picture. They've seen firsthand the wrecked marriages, ruined bodies and minds, abused families, and shattered careers that often accompany what people call "social drinking."

Longtime baseball coach and manager Connie Mack said that alcohol had no more place in the human body than sand had in the gas tank of an automobile. Alcohol is a narcotic, not a food; it destroys, not nourishes. The Bible warns against drunkenness (Prov. 20:1; 21:17; 23:20-21, 29-35; Isa. 5:11; Luke 21:34; Rom. 13:13-14; 1 Cor. 5:11; Eph. 5:18; 1 Peter 4:3-5); and even the Koran says, "There is a devil in every berry of the grape."

The best way to avoid drunkenness is not to drink at all. A Japanese proverb warns, "First the man takes a drink, then the drink takes a drink, and then the drink takes the man." And King Lemuel's mother taught him, "It is not for kings, O Lemuel, it is not for kings to drink wine; nor for princes strong drink" (Prov. 31:4, KJV).

As for the anger that King Ahasuerus expressed toward his lovely queen, it was ignorant, childish, and completely uncalled for. Had the king been sober, he would never have asked his wife to display her beauties before his drunken leaders. His pride got the best of him; for if he couldn't command his own wife, how could he ever command the Persian armies? Since Vashti had embarrassed the king before his own leaders, the king had to do something to save both his ego and his reputation.

Vashti was right, and Ahasuerus was wrong; and his anger was only further proof that he was wrong. Anger has a way of blinding our eyes and deadening our hearts to that which is good and noble. The Italian poet Pietro Aletino (1492-1557) wrote to a friend, "Angry men are blind and foolish, for reason at such a time takes flight and, in her absence, wrath plunders all the riches of the intellect, while the judgment remains the prisoner of its own pride." If anybody was a prisoner of pride, it was the exalted king of the Persian Empire!

To be sure, there's a holy anger against sin that ought to burn in the heart of every godly person (Rom. 12:9). Even our Lord manifested anger at sin (Mark 3:5), but we must be careful that our anger at sin doesn't become sinful anger (Eph. 4:26). Sometimes what we call "righteous indignation" is only unrighteous temper masquerading in religious garments. Jesus equated anger with murder (Matt. 5:21-26), and Paul warns us that anger can hinder our praying (1 Tim. 2:8).

Pride feeds anger, and as it grows, anger reinforces pride. "A quick-tempered man acts foolishly," warned the writer of Proverbs 14:17, a text perfectly illustrated by King Ahasuerus. Instead of being angry at Vashti, the king should have been angry at himself for acting so foolishly.

Before leaving this part of our story, I want to point out that the Gospel of Jesus Christ has helped to liberate and elevate women in society wherever it has been preached and obeyed throughout the world. "There is neither Jew nor Greek, there is neither bond nor free, there is neither male nor female: for ye are all one in Christ Jesus" (Gal. 3:28, KJV). We still have a long way to go in our recognition of the importance of women in the church, but thanks partly to the influence of the Gospel, society has made progress in setting women free from cruel bondage and giving them wonderful opportunities for life and service.[2]

3. His vindictiveness (Es. 1:13-22)

When the ego is pricked, it releases a powerful poison that makes people do all sorts of things they'd never do if they were humble and submitted to the Lord. Francis Bacon wrote in his *Essays*, "A man that studies revenge keeps his own wounds green, which otherwise would heal and do well." Had Ahasuerus sobered up and thought the matter through, he would never have deposed his wife. After all, she showed more character than he did.

The Persian king had seven counselors who advised him in matters of state and had the right to approach his throne. They also knew well how to flatter the king to secure their positions and get from him what they wanted. The phrase "understood the times" (v. 13) suggests that they were astrologers who consulted the stars and used other forms of divination. Eastern monarchs in that day depended on such men to give them instructions in matters personal, governmental, and military. (See Dan. 1:20; 2:2, 10, 17; 4:7; 5:7, 11, 17.)

Concerned about the repercussions of Vashti's disobedience, the king asked his seven counselors what he should do. The first thing they did was exaggerate the importance of the event: Vashti had done wrong not only to the king but also to the entire empire! Therefore, when the guests returned home, they would tell everybody that the queen was disobedient to her husband, and the consequences would be disastrous. The women in the empire would hold the men in contempt, and a general rebellion of wives against husbands and women against men would follow. (Commentators point out that the word "women" in Es. 1:17 means "women in general," while "ladies" in v. 18 refers to the women of the aristocratic class.) These counselors were playing it smart; for by exaggerating the problem, they also inflated their own importance and made the king more dependant on them.

But was the situation really that serious? When Vashti refused to obey, I wonder how many princes and nobles at the banquet said among themselves, "Well, the king's marriage is just like our marriages! His wife has a mind of her own, and it's a good thing she does!" It's doubtful that the king would have lost authority or stature throughout the empire had he shrugged his shoulders, smiled, and admitted that he'd done a foolish thing. "A fool shows his annoyance at once, but a prudent man overlooks an insult" (Prov. 12:16, NIV).

The seven wise men advised the king

to depose Vashti and replace her with another queen. They promised that such an act would put fear in the hearts of all the women in the empire and generate more respect for their husbands. But would it? Are hearts changed because kings issue decrees or congresses and parliaments pass laws? How would the punishment of Vashti make the Persian women love their husbands more? Are love and respect qualities that can be generated in hearts by human fiat?

How could seven supposedly wise men be so calloused in their treatment of Vashti and so foolish in their evaluation of the women of the empire? How could they be so brutal as to use the authority of the law to destroy one woman and threaten the peace of every home in the empire? They were encouraging every husband to act like King Ahasuerus and manage the home on the basis of executive fiat (Es. 1:22). What a contrast to Paul's counsel to husbands and wives in Ephesians 5:18-33!

Still motivated by anger and revenge, and seeking to heal his wounded pride, the king agreed to their advice and had Vashti deposed (Es. 1:19-21). He sent his couriers throughout the empire to declare the royal edict—an edict that was unnecessary, unenforceable, and unchangeable. King Ahasuerus was given to issuing edicts, and he didn't always stop to think about what he was doing (3:9-12). It was another evidence of his pride.

The king didn't immediately replace Vashti. Instead, he went off to invade Greece, where he met with humiliating defeat; and when he returned home, he sought solace in satisfying his sensual appetite by searching for a new queen and filling his harem with candidates. The women in his empire were not only to be subservient to the men, but they were also to be "sex objects" to give them pleasure. The more you know about Ahasuerus and his philosophy of life, the more you detest him.

The Bible doesn't tell us what happened to Vashti. Many biblical scholars believe she was Amestris, the mother of Artaxerxes who ruled from 464 to 425 B.C. It's likely that Esther was either out of favor or dead; for Amestris exercised great influence as the queen mother during her son's reign.

Artaxerxes was born in 483, the year of the great banquet described in Esther 1. It's possible that Vashti was pregnant with her son at that time and therefore unwilling to appear before the men. It was her son Artaxerxes who ruled during the times of Ezra (7:1, 7, 11-12, 21; 8:1) and Nehemiah (2:1; 5:14; 13:6).

In any case the stage was now set for the entrance of the two key persons in the drama: Haman, the man who hated the Jews, and Esther, the woman who delivered her people.

CHAPTER TWO
THE NEW QUEEN
Esther 2

(In which Esther becomes the king's wife, and Mordecai gets no reward for saving the king's life)

"God is preparing His heroes," said A.B. Simpson, founder of the Christian and Missionary Alliance, "and when the opportunity comes, He can fit them into their places in a moment, and the world will wonder where they came from."

Dr. Simpson might have added that

God also prepares His *heroines,* for certainly Esther was divinely prepared for her role as the new queen. *God is never surprised by circumstances or at a loss for prepared servants.* He had Joseph ready in Egypt (Ps. 105:17), Ezekiel and Daniel in Babylon, and Nehemiah in Susa; and He had Esther ready for her ministry to the Jews in the Persian Empire.

As you read this chapter, you will see at least three evidences of the hand of God at work in the affairs of the people.

1. The agreement of the king (Es. 2:1-4)

Nearly four years have passed since Vashti was deposed. During that time, Ahasuerus directed his ill-fated Greek campaign and came home in humiliation instead of honor. As he considered his rash actions toward his wife, his affection for Vashti rekindled; and though he had a harem full of concubines, he missed his queen. There is a difference between love and sex. The passing excitement of the moment is not the same as the lasting enrichment of a lifetime relationship.

The king's advisers were concerned that Vashti not be restored to royal favor; for if she regained her throne, their own lives would be in danger. After all, it was they who had told the king to remove her! But more was involved than the lives of the king's counselors, for the survival of the Jewish nation was also at stake. Queen Vashti would certainly not intercede on behalf of the Jews. She probably would have cooperated with Haman.

Knowing the king's strong sensual appetite, the counselors suggested that he assemble a new harem composed of the most beautiful young virgins in the empire. This was not a "beauty contest" where the winners were rewarded by having a chance for the throne. These young women were conscripted against their will and made a part of the royal harem. Every night, the king had a new partner; and the next morning, she joined the rest of the concubines. The one that pleased the king the most would become his new queen. It sounds like something out of *The Arabian Nights,* except that, in those tales, Emperor Shahriar married a new wife each day and had her slain the next morning. That way he could be sure she wouldn't be unfaithful to him!

I wonder how many beautiful girls hid when the king's officers showed up to abduct them? Heartbroken mothers and fathers no doubt lied to the officers and denied that they had any virgin daughters. Perhaps some of the girls married any available man rather than spend a hopeless life shut up in the king's harem. Once they had been with the king, they belonged to him and could not marry. If the king ignored them, they were destined for a life of loneliness, shut up in a royal harem. Honor? Perhaps. Happiness? No!

"The king's heart is in the hand of the Lord, like the rivers of water; He turns it wherever He wishes" (Prov. 21:1, NKJV). This doesn't mean that God forced Ahasuerus to accept the plan, or that God approved of the king's harems or of his sensual abuse of women. It simply means that, without being the author of their sin, God so directed the people in this situation that decisions were made that accomplished God's purposes.

The decisions made today in the high places of government and finance seem remote from the everyday lives of God's people, but they affect us and God's work in many ways. It's good to know that God is on His throne and that no decision is made that can thwart His purposes. "He does as He pleases with the powers of heaven and the peoples of the earth. No one can hold back His hand or say to Him: 'What have You done?' " (Dan. 4:35, NIV)

"There is no attribute of God more comforting to His children than the doctrine of divine sovereignty," said Charles Haddon Spurgeon. While we confess that many things involved in this doctrine are shrouded in mystery, it's unthinkable that Almighty God should not be Master of His own universe. Even in the affairs of a pagan empire, God is in control.

2. The choice of Esther (Es. 2:5-18)

We are now introduced to Mordecai and his cousin Esther, who, along with Haman, are the principal players in this drama. Once again, we see the hand of God at work in the life of this lovely Jewess. Consider the factors involved.

The influence of Mordecai (Es. 2:5-7). Mordecai is named fifty-eight times in this book, and seven times he is identified as "a Jew" (2:5; 5:13; 6:10; 8:7; 9:29, 31; 10:3). His ancestor, Kish, was among the Jews taken to Babylon from Jerusalem in the second deportation in 597 B.C. (2 Kings 24). Cyrus, King of Persia, entered Babylon in 539 and the next year gave the Jews permission to return to their land. About 50,000 responded (Ezra 1-2). In subsequent years, other Jews returned to Israel; but Mordecai chose to remain in the Persian capital.

While the Babylonians made life difficult for the Jews, the Persians were more lenient to aliens; and many Jews prospered in the land of their captors. Mordecai eventually held an official position in the government and sat at the king's gate (Es. 2:21). It's likely that he was given this position after Esther's coronation, because he had to walk back and forth in front of the house of the women in order to find out how his adopted daughter was doing (v. 11). If he were an officer of the king, he would have had access to inside information.

Esther was Mordecai's cousin and adopted daughter (v. 15). Her Persian name *Esther* means "star," and her Hebrew name *Hadassah* means "myrtle." (It's interesting that the myrtle tree bears a flower that looks like a star.) A beautiful woman, she was one of those taken into the king's harem. An English proverb says, "Beauty may have fair leaves, yet bitter fruit." We wonder how many young ladies in the empire regretted that they had been born beautiful!

One of the key elements in this story is the fact that the people in Shushan didn't know that Mordecai and Esther were Jews. The palace personnel found out about Mordecai when he told them (3:4), and the king learned about Esther at the second banquet she hosted for him and Haman (chap. 7).

This fact presents us with some problems. For one thing, if Mordecai and Esther were passing themselves off as Persians, they certainly weren't keeping a kosher home and obeying the laws of Moses. Had they been following even the dietary laws, let alone the rules for separation and worship, their true nationality would have quickly been discovered. Had Esther practiced her Jewish faith during her year of preparation (2:12), or during the four years she had been queen (2:16 with 3:7), the disguise would have come off.

Anyone has the right to conceal his or her true nationality, and this is not a sin. As long as nobody asked them, Mordecai and Esther had every right to conceal their racial origin. If people thought that the two cousins were Gentiles, well, that was their own conclusion. Nobody lied to them. "All truths are not to be spoken at all times," wrote Matthew Henry, "though an untruth is not to be spoken at any time." Nevertheless, that Esther and Mordecai did not acknowledge the God of Israel in the midst of that pagan society is unfortunate.

So much for their subterfuge. What about their nonkosher lifestyle? Even though the Law of Moses was temporary, and it would be ended with the death of Christ on the cross, that law was still in effect; and the Jews were expected to obey it. Daniel and his friends were careful to obey the law while they lived in Babylon, and the Lord blessed them for their faithfulness (Dan. 1). Why would He overlook the unfaithfulness of Mordecai and Esther *and still use them to accomplish His purposes?*

But even more serious than their lifestyle is the problem of a Jewess in a harem and ultimately marrying a Gentile. The Law of Moses prohibited all kinds of illicit sex as well as mixed marriages (Ex. 20:14; 34:16; Lev. 18; Deut. 7:1-4), and both Ezra and Nehemiah had to deal with the problem of Jews marrying Gentiles (Ezra 9-10; Neh. 10:30; 13:23-27). Yet, God allowed a pure Jewish girl to become the wife of a lustful Gentile pagan king, a worshiper of Zoroaster!

Some Bible students see this whole enterprise as an empire-wide "beauty contest" and Esther as a contestant who probably shouldn't have entered. They also assert that Mordecai encouraged her because he wanted to have a Jew in a place of influence in the empire in case there was trouble. Perhaps that interpretation is true. However, other students feel that the women were not volunteers but were selected and assembled by the king's special officers. The girls were not kidnapped, but everybody knew that the will of an Eastern monarch could not successfully be opposed. In this case I don't think we should condemn Esther for what happened to her since these circumstances were, for the most part, out of her control; and God did not overrule them for the good of her people.

When you consider the backslidden state of the Jewish nation at that time, the disobedience of the Jewish remnant in the Persian Empire, and the unspiritual lifestyle of Mordecai and Esther, is it any wonder that the name of God is absent from this book? Would you want to identify your holy name with such an unholy people?

The encouragement of Hegai (Es. 2:8-9). Just as Joseph found favor in Egypt (Gen. 39:21) and Daniel in Babylon (Dan. 1:9), so Esther found favor in Shushan. God is so great that He can work even in the heart and mind of the keeper of a harem! Hegai was a Gentile. His job was to provide pleasure for the king, and he didn't know the true God of Israel. Nevertheless, he played an important role in the plan that God was working out for His people. Even today, God is working in places where you and I might think He is absent.

Hegai had a year-long "beauty treatment" to prepare each woman for the king. It included a prescribed diet, the application of special perfumes and cosmetics, and probably a course on court etiquette. They were being trained to do one thing—satisfy the desires of the king. The one who pleased him the most would become his wife. Because of the providence of God, Hegai gave Esther "special treatment" and the best place in the house for her and her maids.

The nationality of Esther (Es. 2:10-11). Had Esther not been born into the Jewish race, she could never have saved the nation from slaughter. It would appear that the two cousins' silence about their nationality was directed by God because He had a special work for them to accomplish. There was plenty of anti-Semitism in the Gentile world, and Mordecai's motive was probably their own personal safety, but God had something greater in mind. Mordecai and Esther wanted to live in peace, but God used them to keep the Jewish people alive.

The approval of the king (Es. 2:12-18). Each night, a new maiden was brought to the king; and in the morning, she was sent to the house of the concubines, never again to be with the king unless he remembered her and called for her. Such unbridled sensuality eventually would have so bored Ahasuerus that he was probably unable to distinguish one maiden from another. This was not love. It was faceless, anonymous lust that craved more and more; and the more the king indulged, the less he was satisfied.

Esther had won the favor of everybody who saw her; and when the king saw her, he responded to her with greater enthusiasm than he had to any of the other women. At last he had found someone to replace Vashti! The phrase "the king loved Esther" (KJV) must not be interpreted to mean that Ahasuerus had suddenly fallen in love with Esther with pure and devoted affection. The NIV rendering is best: "Now the king was attracted to Esther more than to any of the other women" (v. 17). This response was from the Lord who wanted Esther in the royal palace where she could intercede for her people. "Known to God from eternity are all His works" (Acts 15:18, NKJV).

It's worth noting that Esther put herself into the hands of Hegai and did what she was told to do. Hegai knew what the king liked, and, being partial to Esther, he attired her accordingly. Because she possessed such great beauty "in form and features" (Es. 2:7, NIV), Esther didn't require the "extras" that the other women needed. (See 1 Peter 3:1-6.)

The king personally crowned Esther and named her the new queen of the empire. Then he summoned his officials and hosted a great banquet. (This is the fourth banquet in the book. The Persian kings used every opportunity to celebrate!) But the king's generosity even touched the common people, for he proclaimed a national holiday throughout his realm and distributed gifts to the people. This holiday may have been similar to the Hebrew "Year of Jubilee." It's likely that taxes were canceled, servants set free, and workers given a vacation from their jobs. Ahasuerus wanted everybody to feel good about his new queen.

3. The intervention of Mordecai (Es. 2:19-23)

The second "gathering of the virgins" mentioned in verse 19 probably means that the king's officers continued to gather beautiful girls for his harem, for Ahasuerus wasn't likely to become a monogamist and spend the rest of his life with Esther alone. Those who hold that this entire occasion was a "beauty contest" see this second gathering as a farewell to the "candidates" who never got to see the king. They were thanked and sent home. I prefer the first interpretation. Queen or no queen, a man like Ahasuerus wasn't about to release a group of beautiful virgins from his palace!

But most importantly, in verse 19 we now see Mordecai in a position of honor and authority, sitting at the king's gate (4:2; 5:13). In the East, the gate was the ancient equivalent of our modern law courts, the place where important official business was transacted (Ruth 4:1; Dan. 2:48-49). It's possible that Queen Esther used her influence to get her cousin this job.

Once again, we marvel at the providence of God in the life of a man who was not honoring the God of Israel. Neither Mordecai nor Esther had revealed their true nationality. Perhaps we should classify them with Nicodemus and Joseph of Arimathea who were "secret disciples" and yet were used of God to protect and bury the body of Jesus (John 19:38-42). Like these two men, Mordecai and Esther were "hidden" in the Persian capital because God had a very special work for them to do. Mordecai was able to use his position for the good of both the king and the Jews.

In Eastern courts, palace intrigue was a normal thing. Only a few officers had free access to the king (Es. 1:10, 14), and they often used their privileges to get bribes from people who needed the king's help. (This is why Daniel's fellow officers didn't like him; he was too honest. See Dan. 6.)

It's possible that this assassination attempt was connected with the crowning of the new queen and that Vashti's supporters in the palace resented what Ahasuerus had done. Or perhaps these two men hated Esther because she was an outsider. Although it wasn't consistently obeyed, tradition said that Persian kings should select their wives from women within the seven noble families of the land. These conspirators may have been traditionalists who didn't want a "commoner" on the throne.

Ahasuerus enjoyed almost unlimited authority, wealth, and pleasure. He was insulated from the everyday problems of life (Es. 4:1-4); but this didn't guarantee his personal safety. It was still possible for people to plot against the king and threaten his life. In fact, fourteen years later, Ahasuerus was assassinated!

God in His providence enabled Mordecai to hear about the plot and notify Queen Esther. When Esther told the king, she gave Mordecai the credit for uncovering the conspiracy; and this meant that his name was written into the official chronicle. This fact will play an important part in the drama four years later (6:1ff).

The phrase "hanged on a tree" (Es. 2:23, KJV) probably means "impaled on a stake," one of the usual forms of capital punishment used by the Persians, who were not known for their leniency to prisoners. The usual form of capital punishment among the Jews was stoning; but if they really wanted to humiliate the victim, they would hang the corpse on a tree until sundown (Deut. 21:22-23).

Mordecai received neither recognition nor reward for saving the king's life. No matter; God saw to it that the facts were permanently recorded, and He would make good use of them at the right time. Our good works are like seeds that are planted by faith, and their fruits don't always appear immediately. "Evil pursues sinners, but to the righteous, good shall be repaid" (Prov. 13:21, NKJV). Joseph befriended a fellow prisoner, and the man completely forgot his kindness for two years (Gen. 40:23; 41:1). But God's timing is always perfect, and He sees to it that no good deed is ever wasted.

The plot that Mordecai successfully exposed, however, was nothing compared to the plot he would uncover four years later, planned and perpetrated by Haman, the enemy of the Jews.

CHAPTER THREE
AN OLD ENEMY WITH A NEW NAME
Esther 3

(In which an evil man challenges the throne of Almighty God)

For four years, things have been peaceful in Shushan. Esther has reigned as queen, and Mordecai has tended to the king's business at the gate. Then everything changed, and all the Jews in the empire found themselves in danger of being killed—just to satisfy the hatred of a man named Haman.

The Book of Esther is one of five Old Testament books that the Jews call "The Writings" or "The Five Megilloth." (The word *megilloth* means "scrolls" in Hebrew.) The other books are Ruth, Ecclesiastes, The Song of Solomon, and Lamentations. Each year on the Feast of Purim, the Book of Esther is read publicly in the synagogue; and whenever the reader mentions Haman's name, the people stamp their feet and exclaim, "May his name be blotted out!" To Jews everywhere, Haman personifies everybody who has tried to exterminate the people of Israel. This chapter explains to us why Haman was such a dangerous man.

1. His ancestry (Es. 3:la)

Haman was an "Agagite," which could mean he came from a district in the empire known as Agag. But it could also mean that he was descended from Agag, king of the Amalekites (1 Sam. 15:8). If the latter is the case, then we can easily understand why Haman hated the Jews: God had declared war on the Amalekites and wanted their name and memory blotted off the face of the earth.

The story goes back to the time of Israel's Exodus from Egypt (Ex. 17:8-15), when the Amalekites attacked God's weary people in the rear ranks of the marching nation (Deut. 25:18). After Moses commanded Joshua to fight against Amalek, he interceded on the mountain, and Joshua won a great victory. God told Moses to write in a book that He had declared war on the Amalekites and would one day utterly destroy them because of what they had done to His people. Moses reminded the Israelites of the Amalekites' treacherous attack before they entered the Promised Land (Deut. 25:17-19).

It was Saul, the first king of Israel, whom God commanded to destroy the Amalekites (1 Sam. 15); and he failed in his commission and lost his own crown. (It was an Amalekite who claimed he put Saul to death on the battlefield. See 2 Sam. 1:1-10.) Because Saul didn't fully obey the Lord, some Amalekites lived; and one of their descendants, Haman, determined to annihilate his people's ancient enemy, the Jews. It's worth noting that King Saul, a Benjamite, failed to destroy the Amalekites; but Mordecai, also a Benjamite (Es. 2:5), took up the battle and defeated Haman. It's also worth noting that the founder of the Amalekites was a descendant of Esau (Gen. 36:12), and Esau was the enemy of his brother Jacob. This was another stage in the age-old conflict between the flesh and the Spirit, Satan and the Lord, the way of faith and the way of the world.

Everything about Haman is hateful; you can't find one thing about this man worth praising. In fact, everything about Haman, *God hated!* "These six things the Lord hates, yes, seven are an abomination to Him: A proud look, a lying tongue, hands that shed innocent blood, a heart that devises wicked plans, feet that are swift in running to evil, a false witness who speaks lies, and one who sows discord among brethren" (Prov. 6:16-19, NKJV). Keep these seven evil characteristics in mind as you read the Book of Esther, for you will see them depicted in this depraved man.

2. His authority (Es. 3:lb)

At some time between the seventh and twelfth years of the reign of Ahasuerus (v. 7; 2:16), the king decided to make Haman chief officer in the empire. Think of it: Mordecai had saved the king's life and didn't receive a word of thanks, let alone a reward; but wicked Haman did nothing and was promoted! There are many seeming injustices in this life; yet God knows what He's doing and will never forsake the righteous or leave their deeds unrewarded. (See Ps. 37.)

Haman probably fawned and flattered his way into this powerful new position because that's the kind of man he was. He was a proud man, and his purpose was to achieve authority and recognition. As we have seen, Ahasuerus was a weak and gullible man, susceptible to flattery and anxious to please people; so Haman's task wasn't a difficult one.

Some Bible students have seen in Haman an illustration of the "man of sin" who will one day appear and ruthlessly rule over humanity (2 Thes. 2; Rev. 13). Haman was given great authority from the king, and Satan will give great power to this wicked world ruler we call the Antichrist (Rev. 13:2, 4). As Haman hated the Jews and tried to destroy them, so the Antichrist will usher in a wave of worldwide anti-Semitism (12:13-17). At first, he will pretend to be friendly to Israel and will even make a covenant to protect them, but then he will break the covenant and oppose the very people he agreed to help (Dan. 9:24-27). As Haman was ultimately defeated and judged, so the Antichrist will be conquered by Jesus Christ and confined to the lake of fire (Rev. 19:11-20).

God permitted Haman to be appointed to this high office because He had purposes to fulfill through him. (See Rom. 9:17.) God takes His promises seriously and will not break His covenant with His people. My friend J. Vernon McGee used to say, "The Jew has attended the funeral of every one of the nations that tried to exterminate him"; and Haman was not to be an exception.

What people do with authority is a test of character. Do they use their authority to promote themselves or to help others? Do they glorify themselves or glorify God? Daniel was given a high position similar to Haman's, but he used his authority to honor God and help others (Dan. 6). Of course, the difference between Daniel and Haman is that Daniel was a humble man of God while Haman was a proud man of the world.

3. His vanity (Es. 3:2-6)

Not content with merely having a high office and using it, Haman wanted all the public recognition and honor that he could secure. Although the ancient people of the Near East were accustomed to giving public displays of homage, the king had to issue a special edict concerning Haman, or the people would not have bowed down to him. Haman was a small man in a big office; and the other nobles, more worthy than he, would not willingly recognize him. This fact is another hint that Haman got the office not by earning it but by stealing it. If he were a worthy officer, the other leaders would have gladly recognized him.

Pride blinds people to what they really are and makes them insist on having what they really don't deserve. The British essayist Walter Savage Landor (1775-1864) wrote, "When little men cast long shadows, it is a sign that the sun is setting." Haman was a little man, indeed, but his vanity compelled him to make himself look and sound bigger than he really was.

"Fools take to themselves the respect that is given to their office," wrote Aesop in his fable "The Jackass in Office"; and it applies perfectly to Haman. He was recognized, not because of his character or his ability, but because of the office he filled and because of the edict of the king. "Try not to become a man of success," said Albert Einstein, "but try to become a man of value." Men and women of value earn the recognition they deserve.

Haman's promotion may have brought out the worst in Haman, but it brought out the best in Mordecai; for Mordecai refused to pay homage to Haman. It must be remembered, however, that the Jews didn't violate the Second Commandment (Ex. 20:4-6) when they bowed down before people in authority any more than Christians do today when they show respect to leaders. For instance, Abraham bowed down to the sons of Heth when he negotiated with them for Sarah's grave (Gen. 23:7). Also Joseph's brothers bowed down before Joseph, thinking he was an Egyptian official (42:6). David even bowed down to Saul (1 Sam. 24:8), and Jacob and his family bowed before Esau (Gen. 33:3, 6-7). The Jews even bowed to one another. (See 2 Sam. 14:4 and 18:28.)

There were crowds of people at the gate, and some of them would be pleading for Haman to intercede for them. Consequently, Haman didn't notice that Mordecai was standing up while everybody else was bowing down. The other officials at the gate questioned Mordecai about his behavior, and it was then that Mordecai openly announced that he was a Jew (Es. 3:3-4). For several days, the royal officials discussed the matter with Mordecai, probably trying to change his mind; and then they reported his behavior to Haman. From that time on, Haman watched Mordecai and nursed his anger, not only toward the man at the gate, but also toward all the Jews in the empire.

Why did Mordecai refuse to bow down to Haman? What was there about being a Jew that prohibited him from doing what everybody else was doing? Even if Mordecai couldn't respect the man, he could at least respect the office and therefore the king who gave Haman the office.

I think the answer is that Haman was an Amalekite, and the Amalekites were the avowed enemies of the Jews. The Lord swore and put in writing that He had declared war on the Amalekites and would fight them from generation to generation (Ex. 17:16). How could Mordecai show homage to the enemy of the Jews and the enemy of the Lord? He didn't want to be guilty of what Joab said about King David, "You love your enemies and hate your friends" (2 Sam. 19:6, NKJV).

Mordecai's controversy with Haman was not a personal quarrel with a proud and difficult man. It was Mordecai's declaration that he was on God's side in the *national* struggle between the Jews and the Amalekites. Mordecai didn't want to make the same mistake his ancestor King Saul had made in being too lenient with God's enemies (1 Sam. 15). Because Saul compromised with the Amalekites, he lost his crown; but because Mordecai opposed them, he eventually gained a crown (Es. 8:15).

Keep in mind that the extermination of the Jews would mean the end of the messianic promise for the world. The reason God promised to protect His people was that they might become the channel through whom He might give the Word of God and the Son of God to the world. Israel was to bring the blessing of salvation to all nations (Gen. 12:1-3; Gal. 3:7-18). Mordecai wasn't nurturing a personal grudge against Haman so much as enlisting in the perpetual battle God has with those who work for the devil and try to hinder His will in this world (Gen. 3:15). Mordecai is not the only person in the Bible who for conscience' sake practiced "civil disobedience." The Hebrew midwives disobeyed Pharaoh's orders and refused to kill the Jewish babies (Ex. 1:15-22). Daniel and his three friends refused to eat the king's food (Dan. 1), and the three friends also refused to bow down to Nebuchadnezzar's image (Dan. 3). The apostles refused to stop witnessing in Jerusalem and affirmed, "We must obey God rather than men" (Acts 5:29). That statement can be a wonderful declaration of faith or a cowardly evasion of responsibility, depending on the heart of the person saying it.

But please note that, in each of these instances, *the people had a direct word from God that gave them assurance they were doing His will.* And further note that, in every instance, the believers were kind and respectful. They didn't start riots or burn down buildings "for conscience' sake." Because civil authority is ordained of God (Rom. 13), it's a serious thing for Christians to disobey the law; and if we're going to do it, we must know the difference between personal prejudices and biblical convictions.

Something else is involved: By confessing that he was a Jew, Mordecai was asking for trouble for both himself and the other Jews in the empire. *Obedience to conscience and the will of God in defiance of civil law is not a casual thing to be taken lightly.* Some of the "conscience protesters" we've seen on television, however, have seemed more like clowns going to a party than soldiers going to a battle. They could never stand with people like Martin Luther who challenged prelates and potentates with: "My conscience is captive to the Word of God. Here I stand, I cannot do otherwise!"

Mordecai may have had shortcomings with reference to his religious practices, but we must admire him for his courageous stand. Certainly God had put him and Esther into their official positions so that they might save their people from annihilation. Their neglect of the Jewish law is incidental when you consider their courage in risking their lives.

Like a cancerous tumor, Haman's hatred for Mordecai soon developed into hatred for the whole Jewish race. Haman could have reported Mordecai's crime to the king, and the king would have imprisoned Mordecai or perhaps had him executed; but that would not have satisfied Haman's lust for revenge. No, his hatred had to be nourished by something bigger, like the destruction of a whole nation. As with Judas in the Upper Room, so with Haman in the palace: he became a murderer. Mark Twain called anti-Semitism "the swollen envy of pygmy minds." And he was right.

4. His subtlety (Es. 3:7-15a)

Follow the steps that wicked Haman took as he executed his plan to destroy the Jewish people.

He selected the day (Es. 3:7). Haman and some of the court astrologers cast lots to determine the day for the Jews' destruction. This was done privately before Haman approached the king with his plan. Haman wanted to be sure that his gods were with him and that his plan would succeed.

The Eastern peoples in that day took few important steps without consulting the stars and the omens. A century before, when King Nebuchadnezzar and his generals couldn't agree on a campaign strategy, they paused to consult their gods. "For the king of Babylon stands at the parting of the road, at the fork of the two roads, to use divination: he shakes the arrows, he consults the images, he looks at the liver" (Ezek. 21:21, NKJV).[1] The Babylonian word *puru* means "lot," and from it the Jews get the name of their feast, Purim (Es. 9:26).

It's interesting that Haman began this procedure in the month of Nisan, the very month in which the Jews celebrated their deliverance from Egypt. As the astrologers cast lots over the calendar, month by month and day by day, they arrived at the most propitious date: the thirteenth day of the twelfth month (v. 13). This decision was certainly of the Lord, because it gave the Jews a whole year to get ready, and because it would also give Mordecai and Esther time to act. "The lot is cast into the lap; but the whole disposing thereof is of the Lord" (Prov. 16:33, KJV).

Was Haman disappointed with this choice? He may have wanted to act immediately, catch the Jews off guard, and satisfy his hatred much sooner. On the other hand, he would have nearly a year in which to nurse his grudge and anticipate revenge, and that would be enjoyable. He could watch the Jews panic, knowing that he was in control. Even if the Jews took advantage of this delay and moved out of the empire, he would still get rid of them and be able to claim whatever goods and property they would have left behind. The plan seemed a good one.

He requested the king's permission (Es. 3:8-11). Like Satan, the great enemy of the Jews, Haman was both a murderer and a liar (John 8:44). To begin with, he didn't even give the king the name of the people who were supposed to be subverting the kingdom. His vague description of the situation made the danger seem even worse. The fact that these dangerous people were scattered throughout the whole empire made it even more necessary that the king do something about them.

Haman was correct when he described the Jews as a people whose "laws are different from those of all other people" (Es. 3:8). Their laws were different because they were God's chosen people who alone received God's holy law from His own hand. Moses asked, "And what great nation is there that has such statues and righteous judgments as are in all this law which I set before you this day?" (Deut. 4:8, NKJV) and the answer is: "None!"

The fact that one man, Mordecai, disobeyed one law was exaggerated by Haman into the false accusation that *all* the Jews disobeyed *all* the laws of the land. The Prophet Jeremiah had instructed the Jews of the Exile to behave as good citizens and cooperate with their captors (Jer. 29:4–7), and the evidence seems to be that they obeyed. If the Jews in the Persian Empire had been repeatedly guilty of sedition or treason, Ahasuerus would have known about it by now. And even if some Jews in a few towns did disobey the king's laws, why should the whole nation of Israel be destroyed for the crimes of a few?

Haman's *coup de grace* came at the end of his speech when he offered to pay the king 10,000 talents of silver for the privilege of ridding the empire of these dangerous people. According to the Greek historian Herodotus (Book III, Section 95), the annual income of the entire Persian Empire was 15,000 talents of silver. In effect, Haman was offering the king an amount equivalent to two thirds of that huge amount. Haman must have been a fabulously wealthy man. Of course, he hoped to recoup some of this amount from the spoils taken from the Jews.

In Esther 3:11, the king's response ("The silver is given to thee," KJV) gives the impression that Ahasuerus rejected the money and offered to pay the expenses himself. In typical Oriental fashion, the king politely rejected the offer ("Keep the money," NIV), fully expecting Haman to insist that he accept it. (See Abraham's bargaining with the sons of Heth, Gen. 23.) Haman knew that the Greek wars had impoverished the king's treasuries, and he would never have offered so much money to so mighty a ruler if he didn't really intend to pay it. (See Es. 4:7.)

Without asking any questions, the king gave Haman his royal signet ring (see 8:2, 8), which granted him the authority to act in the king's name. He could write any document he pleased and put the king's seal on it, and the document had to be accepted as law and obeyed. It was a foolish thing for Ahasuerus to do; but true to character, he acted first and regretted it afterward. "He who answers a matter before he hears it, it is folly and shame to him" (Prov. 18:13, NKJV).

He immediately spread the word (Es. 3:12–14). Unknown to the Jews who were getting ready to celebrate Passover, Haman was busy with the king's secretaries, writing out the new law and translating it into the various languages of the peoples within the empire. In verse 13, the words of the law are similar to the instructions Samuel gave to King Saul when he sent him to destroy the Amalekites (1 Sam. 15:1–3). The one important difference was that Saul was not permitted to take any of the spoil, while Haman and his helpers hoped to plunder the Jews and accumulate great wealth. The official document was given to the royal couriers, who quickly carried it to every part of the empire.

If, in an ancient kingdom, a message of bad news could be so quickly prepared, translated, and distributed, why does it take the church so long to disseminate the good news of salvation through faith in Jesus Christ? To be sure, we have more people in our modern world than Ahasuerus had in his empire, but we also have better means of communication and transportation. *The problem must be with the couriers.* The message is ready to go, but we don't have enough people to carry it and enough money to send them.

The work was done quickly because Haman didn't want Ahasuerus to change his mind. Once the law was written and sealed, the doom of the Jews was also sealed; for the laws of the Medes and Persians could not be altered (Es. 1:19; 8:8; Dan. 6:8). Haman's subtle plan had worked.

5. His apathy (Es. 3:15b)

Haman could send out the death warrants for thousands of innocent people and then sit down to a banquet with the king! What a calloused heart he had! He was like the people the Prophet Amos described: "that drink wine in bowls, and anoint themselves with the chief ointments; but they are not grieved for the affliction of Joseph" (Amos 6:6). However, in the end, it was his own death warrant that Haman had sealed; for within less than three months, Haman would be a dead man (Es. 8:9).

Helen Keller said, "Science may have found a cure for most evils, but it has found no remedy for the worst of them all—the apathy of human beings" (*My Religion,* p. 162). Jesus vividly illustrated that apathy in the Parable of the Good Samaritan (Luke 10:25-37). He pointed out that two religious men, a priest and a Levite, ignored the needs of the dying man, while the Samaritan, a hated outsider, sacrificed to take care of him. Jesus also made it clear that loving the Lord ought to make us love our neighbor, and our neighbor is anyone who needs us.

Therefore, before we condemn wicked Haman, let's examine our own hearts. Billions of lost sinners in today's world are under a sentence of *eternal* death, and most Christians do very little about it. We can sit at our church banquets and Sunday dinners without even thinking about helping to get the message out that "the Father has sent the Son to be the Savior of the world" (1 John 4:14).

In June 1865, missionary to China, J. Hudson Taylor, had gone to stay with friends at Brighton, a popular British resort city by the sea. He was weary and ill and seeking the will of God for the future of his ministry. On Sunday, June 25, "unable to bear the sight of rejoicing multitudes in the house of God," he went for a walk on the sands and wrestled with God in agony of soul. God met him in a fresh way, and he trusted God to provide twenty-four workers to labor with him in China. Two days later, he went to the London & County Bank and opened an account in the name of the China Inland Mission! It was the beginning of a miracle ministry that continues today.[2]

The phrase in the account that tugs at my heart is "unable to bear the sight of rejoicing multitudes in the house of God." Certainly it's good to rejoice in the Lord and to do it in His house, but rejoicing must never be a substitute for responsibility. As a popular Gospel song expresses it: "God's tables are full but His fields are empty." We all want to enjoy the feast, but we don't want to share the message. We don't have to be hardened unbelievers like Haman to be apathetic and unconcerned about the plight of the world's billions of lost souls.

In contrast to the happiness of the king and his prime minister were the heaviness and bewilderment of the people in Shushan, Gentiles and Jews alike. What had caused this sudden change in policy? Why were the Jews suddenly targeted as enemies of the empire? Was there any way of escape?

The situation was not hopeless, however, for God had two people prepared and in place—Mordecai and Queen Esther—and He was ready to act.

CHAPTER FOUR
A DAY OF DECISION
Esther 4

(In which the queen goes into her counting house and counts the cost)

There were perhaps 15 million Jews scattered throughout the Persian Empire. Because of Haman's enmity and the king's stupidity, all of them were now appointed to die, unless they pulled up stakes and left the kingdom. But if they did that, where would they go? Even their own land of Israel wasn't safe because it was under the rule of Ahasuerus. Since the Persians ruled "from India to Ethiopia" (1:1), there were very few accessible places to which the Jews might flee.

In the Empire, the responses to Haman's decree were varied. Haman and the king completely ignored the plight of the Jews and sat down to a royal feast. Meanwhile, the people of the capital city were perplexed and didn't know what to do (3:15). Secluded in the royal harem, Queen Esther knew nothing about the danger that she and her people faced. While the Jews in the various provinces began to fast and mourn (4:3), only one man, Mordecai, was able to do anything about the peril; and he immediately began to act.

1. He expressed his concern. (Es. 4:1-3) Mordecai's appearance and actions (v. 1) were those of a person showing great grief (2 Sam. 1:11-12; 13:19) or deep repentance (Jonah 3; Neh. 9:1-2). Mordecai was neither afraid nor ashamed to let people know where he stood. He had already told the officers at the gate that he was a Jew; now he was telling the whole city that he was not only a Jew but also that he opposed the murderous edict. Although it can't be documented from his writings, a statement usually attributed to the British politician Edmund Burke certainly applies here: "All that is required for evil to triumph is for good men to do nothing."

"Deliver those who are drawn toward death, and hold back those stumbling to the slaughter. If you say, 'Surely we did not know this,' does not He who weighs the hearts consider it? He who keeps your soul, does He not know it? And will He not render to each man according to his deeds?" These solemn words from Proverbs 24:11-12 (NKJV) make it clear that we can't be neutral when human lives are at stake.

Mordecai ended his mournful pilgrimage at the king's gate, which was the commercial and legal hub of the city, a combination of marketplace and courtroom. That was as far as he could go because Oriental kings lived in an artificial paradise that sheltered them from the realities of life. "No sackcloth must come within their gates," said Scottish preacher George H. Morrison. "They must have a good time at any cost. They must live their easy and comfortable lives, as if there were no voices calling them" *(The Afterglow of God,* p. 72). How opposite from our Priest-King in heaven who welcomes us to bring our burdens and sorrows to Him!

What could Mordecai hope to accomplish at the gate with his sackcloth and his wailing? Well, perhaps somebody from the palace would take notice of him and get a message to Queen Esther. The queen's ladies-in-waiting knew Mordecai (Es. 2:11), although they didn't know the relationship between him and the queen; and Mordecai had already transmitted information to the queen through some of her retainers (2:22). Since Mordecai couldn't enter the house of the women, this was his only hope.

Esther received the report that Mordecai was dressed in sackcloth and ashes, mourning at the king's gate. Since she wasn't told the reason for her cousin's strange conduct, she did the logical thing and sent him fine clothes to put on lest his sackcloth arouse the concern of the king's officers and guards. What if the king should come out to the gate for an audience with the people? Mordecai would then be in trouble.

The queen's motives were fine, but her method was faulty. Before sending the new clothes to Mordecai, she should have found out what the problem really was. If Ahasuerus did appear at the gate, Mordecai's courtly garments might save him temporarily from the wrath of the king; but they couldn't rescue the Jews from the penalty of death that Haman had issued for them. Mordecai's mourning, however, finally got the attention of the queen; and that's what he wanted.

2. He explained their peril. (Es. 4:4-9) Mordecai's refusal of the new clothes gave him opportunity to get his vital message to the queen, for she sent one of her eunuchs to the gate to ask Mordecai what was wrong. I doubt that Hathach realized what an important part he was playing in God's plan to defeat Haman and save the Jews. So often in the work of the Lord, He uses obscure people to accomplish important tasks. What was the name of the lad who gave Jesus his loaves and fishes? Who were the men who rescued Paul by lifting him over that Damascus wall in a basket? What was the name of the little servant girl who told Naaman to go see the prophet? We don't know, but God used these people to accomplish His purposes. As great doors can swing upon small hinges, so great events can turn upon the deeds of "small" and sometimes anonymous people.

Mordecai not only knew all the facts about the decree, but he also had a copy of it for Esther to read for herself. This proves that he held a high position in the government, a position God had given him for the very purpose of saving the Jewish nation. But Mordecai did much more than inform the queen. He urged her to reveal her true nationality and go to the royal throne and intercede for her people.

When Mordecai told Hathach to tell the queen to ask for mercy "for her people," he divulged to him the fact that Esther was a Jewess. Did it shock Hathach, or was he perhaps a Jew himself, and that's why Mordecai entrusted him with this secret? Like Daniel and his three friends in Babylon, Jewish exiles in the Persian Empire were often pressed into royal service.

Now, the big question was: how would Queen Esther respond to this crisis?

3. He exhorted the queen. (Es. 4:10-14) Keep in mind that Mordecai couldn't speak directly to Esther but had to send his messages to her via Hathach. Esther had no way of sensing *personally* how Mordecai felt, nor could Mordecai fully understand how Esther was expressing herself. What a difference it makes when we can see the faces and hear the voices of the people we communicate with! Hathach certainly had a great responsibility placed on him as the living link between two distressed people who held in their hands the salvation of the Jewish nation.

In verses 10-11, Esther's reply was not an evasion but an explanation. She reminded Mordecai of what he already knew, that nobody, not even the queen, could rush into the throne room and ask for an immediate audience with the king. If she were to do so, she would take her life in her hands. Not only was the king of Persia sheltered from seeing sorrow and hearing bad news, but he was also protected from interruptions that might interfere with his schedule.

Again, I don't think this was an excuse on Esther's part, but rather a plea that Mordecai give her some guidance. He knew palace protocol, he was a man, and he was in touch with what was going on. She was isolated in the harem and incapable of devising the kind of strategy needed to solve the problem. Besides all this, she hadn't seen the king for a month; and it was possible that she had somehow fallen out of favor. Ahasuerus was unpredictable, and Esther didn't want to make matters worse.

I get the impression that Mordecai misinterpreted Esther's message. It sounded to him like she was trying to hide her nationality and avoid the responsibility of presenting herself to the king. Had he seen and heard her in person, he probably would have judged her differently.

In his reply, Mordecai reminded Esther of three solemn facts. First, he told her that her being a palace resident was no guarantee that she would be delivered from death. The royal edict said "all the Jews" (3:13), and Haman would see to it that every last Jew was discovered and slain, even those in the palace. For that matter, there were probably palace personnel who were still loyal to Vashti and would be happy to see Queen Esther removed.

Second, Mordecai reminded her that her silence wouldn't prevent deliverance from coming from some other source. The reference here is to the providence of God even though the name of God isn't mentioned. Knowing the Abrahamic Covenant (Gen. 12:1-3), Mordecai had faith that the people of Israel would be protected from annihilation. However, he warned her that even if deliverance did come, some of the Jews might still be slain, and Esther might be among them.

Why would God send "relief and deliverance" (NIV) to the Jewish people but allow Esther and her relatives to be slain? Perhaps Mordecai saw this as a punishment for her unwillingness to intercede for the people. To know to do good and not do it is sin (James 4:17). Therefore, instead of protecting herself by her silence, Esther would be putting herself into greater jeopardy. Haman and his agents would have little trouble finding her in the palace and taking her life.

Mordecai emphasized a third fact: Her being in the palace was not an accident, for she had "come to royal position for such a time as this" (Es. 4:14, NIV). He didn't say that God had put her there, but that's what his statement amounted to. If Esther would just take the time to review her life, she couldn't help but see that there had been divine leading all the way. Now, if God brought her to the throne, then He had a purpose in mind, and that purpose was now evident: She was there to intercede for her people. The statement of Joseph to his brothers comes to mind: "But as for you, you meant evil against me; but God meant it for good, in order to bring it about as it is this day, to save many people alive" (Gen. 50:20, NKJV).

As you ponder Mordecai's words, you will learn some basic truths about the providence of God that are important for Christians today. The first is that *God has divine purposes to accomplish in this world.* God's purposes involve the Jewish nation as well as the Gentile nations of the world. They also involve the church. God deals with individuals as well as with nations. His purposes touch the lives of kings and queens and common people, godly people and wicked people. There is nothing in this world that is outside the influence of the purposes of God.

Mordecai made it clear that *God accomplishes His purposes through people.* For reasons we don't fully understand, God permits wicked people to do evil things in this world; but He can work in and through unbelievers and His own people to accomplish His purposes. While He was not the author of his sins, God permitted the king's drunkenness and his foolishness in deposing Vashti. He used the king's loneliness to place Esther on the throne; and, in chapter 6, he will use the king's sleeplessness to reward Mordecai and start to overthrow the power of Haman. In great things and little things, God is sovereign.

The third truth that Mordecai emphasized was that *God will accomplish His purposes even if His servants refuse to obey His will.* If Esther rejected the will of God for her life, God could still save His people; but Esther would be the loser. When ministers and missionaries appeal to the church for volunteers for Christian service, they sometimes give the impression that God's work is at the mercy of God's workers; but this isn't true.

If you and I refuse to obey God, He can either *abandon us* and get somebody else to do the job, and we will lose the reward and blessing; or He can *discipline us* until we surrender to His will. Two examples come to mind. Since John Mark left the mission field and returned home (Acts 13:13; 15:36-41), God raised up Timothy to take his place (16:1-3). When Jonah ran from God, the Lord kept after him until he obeyed, even though he didn't obey from his heart. When God isn't permitted to rule, He overrules; and He always accomplishes His purposes.

The fourth lesson from Mordecai's speech is that *God isn't in a hurry but will fulfill His plans in due time.* God waited until the third year of the king's reign before taking Vashti off the throne. Then he waited another four years (Es. 2:16) before putting Esther on the throne. It was not until the king's twelfth year (3:7) that God allowed Haman to hatch his evil plot, and He decreed that the "crisis day" for the Jews would be almost a year away.

If you were reading the Book of Esther for the first time, you might become impatient with God and conclude that He was doing nothing. In chapters 1 and 2, a drunken king and his flattering advisers seem to be in charge. From chapter 3 to chapter 6, it looks as though wicked Haman is in control. Even after Haman is off the scene, it's the king's unalterable decree that keeps everybody busy. But *where is God?*

God is never in a hurry. He knows the end from the beginning, and His decrees are always right and always on time. Dr. A.W. Tozer compared God's sovereign purposes to an ocean liner, leaving New York City, bound for Liverpool, England. The people on board the ship are free to do as they please, but they aren't free to change the course of the ship.

"The mighty liner of God's sovereign design keeps its steady course over the sea of history," wrote Dr. Tozer. "God moves undisturbed and unhindered toward the fulfillment of those eternal purposes which He purposed in Christ Jesus before the world began" *(The Knowledge of the Holy,* p. 118*).*

The sovereignty of God doesn't suggest fatalism or blind determinism, both of which would make life a prison. Only a sovereign God is great enough to decree freedom of choice for men and women, and only a sovereign God could fulfill His wise and loving purposes in this world and even make evil cooperate in producing good (Gen. 50:20). The question is not, "Is God in control of this world?" but, "Is God in control of my life?" Are we cooperating with Him so that we are a part of the answer and not a part of the problem?

To quote Dr. Tozer again: "In the moral conflict now raging around us whoever is on God's side is on the winning side and cannot lose; whoever is on the other side is on the losing side and cannot win" (p. 119).

4. He expedited the plan. (Es. 4:15-17)

When we first met Esther and Mordecai, they were hiding their identity as Jews. Now Mordecai is enlisting other Jews in the struggle against Haman, and Esther is commanding her Gentile ladies-in-waiting to participate in the fast!

Even though the name of God is not mentioned in the text, this act of humiliation was obviously directed to the Lord and was certainly accompanied by prayer. Fasting and prayer are frequently found together in Scripture, for fasting is a preparation for concentrated and humble prayer. (See Ezra 8:2123; Ps. 35:13; Dan. 9:3; Acts 13:3.) Of itself, fasting is no guarantee that God will bless, for fasting must be accompanied by sincere humility and brokenness before the Lord (Isa. 58:1-10; Joel 2:12-13; Matt. 6:16-18). If fasting is only a formal religious ritual, it accomplishes no spiritual purpose.

Since Jews throughout the empire were already "fasting, weeping, and wailing" (Es. 4:3), it wasn't difficult for Mordecai to unite the Jews in Shushan to pray for Esther as she prepared to intercede before the king. This was a matter of life and death both for her and her people, and God used the crisis that Haman had created to bring a spiritual revival to His people scattered among the Gentiles. It's often the case that God's people have to experience trouble before they will humble themselves and cry out to God.

How should we interpret Esther's words, "And if I perish, I perish"? Do these words suggest unbelieving resignation ("Well, you forced me into it, so I'll do what you say, even if it kills me!") or trusting submission to the will of God ("I'll do God's will, whatever the cost!")? I vote for the second interpretation. To me, Esther echoes the same surrender and confidence that Paul expressed to the Ephesian elders: "But none of these things move me, neither count I my life dear unto myself, so that I might finish my course with joy, and the ministry, which I have received of the Lord Jesus, to testify the gospel of the grace of God" (Acts 20:24, KJV).

From the human point of view, everything was against Esther and the success of her mission. The law was against her, because nobody was allowed to interrupt the king. The government was against her, for the decree said that she was to be slain. Her sex was against her, because the king's attitude toward women was worse than chauvinistic. The officers were against her, because they did only those things that ingratiated themselves with Haman. In one sense, even the fast could be against her; for going three days without food and drink would not necessarily improve her appearance or physical strength. But "if God be for us, who can be against us?" (Rom. 8:31, KJV)

The answer of faith is—"Nobody!"

CHAPTER FIVE
A DAY IN THE LIFE OF THE PRIME MINISTER
Esther 5

(In which an evil man gathers enough rope to hang himself)

In recent years, the news media have had a heyday reporting the questionable (and usually illegal) behavior of well known people, including professional athletes, politicians, preachers, presidents of financial institutions, and even royalty. From "Watergate" to "Iran Gate" to "Pearly Gate," the investigative reporters have been kept busy digging up news to satisfy the public's insatiable appetite for scandal.

If all this journalistic activity accomplished nothing else, it certainly underscored the significance of the biblical warning, "Be sure your sin will find you out" (Num. 32:23, NKJV). People may succeed for a time in covering up disgraceful activities, but eventually the truth surfaces, and everybody knows what's going on. And the culprit discovers that *the wrong we do to others, we do to ourselves.*

The words of Psalm 7:14-16 make me think of Haman: "He who is pregnant with evil and conceives trouble gives birth to disillusionment. He who digs a hole and scoops it out falls into the pit he has made. The trouble he causes recoils on himself; his violence comes down on his own head" (NIV).

There is a law of retribution in this world declaring that the person who maliciously seeks to destroy others ends up destroying himself. The French existentialist Albert Camus wrote in his novel *The Fall:* "There's no need to hang about waiting for the last judgment—it takes place every day."

> Though the mills of God grind
> slowly,
> yet they grind exceeding small;
> Though with patience He stands
> waiting,
> with exactness grinds He all.
> (Friedrich von Logau)

Haman didn't realize it, but four forces had already begun to work together to destroy him.

1. Divine sovereignty (Es. 5:1-5)

Esther was concerned whether the king would acknowledge her presence and grant her an audience. If he didn't, it could mean her immediate execution; and she knew how unpredictable were his moods. The Jews had been fasting and praying for three days, asking God to intervene and save them from annihilation; and now Esther had to act.

What Esther did ranks among the great deeds of faith in Scripture and could have been recorded in Hebrews 11. It wasn't enough for the Jews to pray and have faith that God would work. Somebody had to act, for "faith without works is dead" (James 2:20, KJV). But Esther wasn't operating on the basis of "blind faith." She knew that God had covenanted with the Jews to deal with their enemies (Gen. 12:1-3). She also knew that the God of Israel was a forgiving God who would hear His people when they humbled themselves and prayed (2 Chron. 7:14). Furthermore, God had allowed a remnant of Jews to return to their land and rebuild the temple. Surely it wasn't God's will that they perish and their work stop. Unlike Esther, when we come to the throne of grace, we don't have to wonder what our Father thinks about us, because He always loves His people and welcomes them into His presence. *One of the greatest needs in the church today is for intercessors who will pray faithfully for a lost world and for a church that desperately needs revival.* "And He saw that there was no man, and wondered that there was no intercessor" (Isa. 59:16, KJV). When the needs are so great and the privilege of prayer is so wonderful, well might the Lord wonder that His people neglect the throne of grace. As John Newton wrote:

> Thou art coming to a King,
> Large petitions with thee bring;
> For His grace and power are such
> None can ever ask too much.

Let's note that Esther *prepared herself to meet the king.* (You'll recall that Ruth prepared herself to meet Boaz. See chap. 3.) If you knew you were going to meet the President of the United States at the White House, or royalty at Buckingham Palace, you would prepare for the meeting. Like Peter sinking into the sea, there are times when we have to rush into God's presence and cry out for help. But the power of those "emergency prayers" depends on our day-by-day fellowship with God, and that fellowship demands preparation. Preparing to pray is as important as the praying itself.

The king officially recognized his queen and invited her to share her petition. "There are many devices in a man's heart; nevertheless the counsel of the Lord, that shall stand" (Prov. 19:21, KJV). "The king's heart is in the hand of the Lord, as the rivers of water: He turneth it whithersoever He will" (Prov. 21:1, KJV; see Ezra 6:22). The sovereign God was in control.

Why didn't Esther immediately inform the king about Haman's evil plot? For at least four reasons. For one thing, it wasn't *the right time.* The king was unprepared to receive the shocking news that his number one officer was a scoundrel. In the midst of kingdom business, Ahasuerus might have considered her accusation an act of treason if not just a piece of palace gossip.

But neither was it *the right place* for her to intercede. There were no doubt retainers serving the king in the throne room, and it would have been a breach of palace etiquette for the queen to make her plea publicly. The sight of a weeping, pleading woman before the throne might have annoyed the king and made matters worse. Better she should speak to the king in the privacy of her own apartment than in the throne room.

The third reason was that Esther wanted Haman, *and only Haman,* present when she told the king about his prime minister's evil plot. With womanly intuition, Esther was confident that Haman, caught off guard, would in some way admit his guilt and do something foolish that would anger the king. It turned out that she was right on both counts.

But there was a fourth reason—one that Esther herself was unaware of at that time. One more event had to intervene before she could share her burden with the king, and it would take place that very night. The king would discover that he had never rewarded Mordecai for saving his life five years before, and he would rectify that mistake immediately. He would honor Mordecai, but at the same time humiliate Haman; and this experience would help prepare the king to hear Esther's petition.

Esther's banquet was already prepared. Thus, Haman and the king had to hurry to attend. In answer to prayer, God so worked in the king's heart that he not only cooperated willingly with his queen but he also made Haman cooperate. Such is the wonder of the providence of God.

2. False confidence (Es. 5:6-9a)

What an honor for Haman to attend a special banquet with the king and queen *alone* and in the queen's private apartment at that! It's unlikely that any official in the empire had ever been so honored. As Haman ate and drank with Ahasuerus and Esther, his confidence grew. He was indeed an important man in the kingdom, and his future was secure.

When the king asked Esther to state her petition, it gave the prime minister even more confidence; for here were the king and queen discussing a personal matter in his presence! Haman was not only the king's confidant, but now he was sharing in the intimate concerns of the queen as well. Since the queen had invited him to the banquet, she must certainly value his counsel.

At the banquet, we see three more evidences of the sovereignty of God. First, the Lord restrained Esther from telling Ahasuerus the truth about Haman. While there may have been fear in her heart, I don't think that's what held her back. The

Lord was working in her life and directing what she said, even though she wasn't aware of it. God was delaying the great exposure until after the king had honored Mordecai.

We also see the sovereign hand of God at work in the way the king accepted the delay and agreed to come to the second banquet. Monarchs like Ahasuerus aren't accustomed to being told to wait. "To man belong the plans of the heart, but from the Lord comes the reply of the tongue" (Prov. 16:1, NIV). "Many are the plans in a man's heart, but it is the Lord's purpose that prevails" (19:21, NIV). Whatever plans Ahasuerus had made for the next evening were canceled to make time for the queen's second feast.

A third evidence of God's sovereignty is that none of Esther's attendants who knew that she was a Jewess tried to convey this important information to Haman. Had Haman known the queen's nationality, he would have immediately devised some plan to prevent her from interfering. Palace intrigue is a dangerous game, and any of the attendants could have profited by telling Haman what they knew.

The fact that Esther invited Haman to the second banquet only increased this evil man's confidence (Es. 5:12), and that's exactly the response the queen wanted. As long as her enemy was overconfident, she knew it would lead to a fall. "He who trusts in himself is a fool, but he who walks in wisdom is kept safe" (Prov. 28:26, NIV). Like the rich fool in our Lord's parable (Luke 12:16-21), Haman was confident that he was set for life, when in reality he was just a few hours away from death.

Two other men come to mind whose false confidence led to their death: King Belshazzar and Judas Iscariot. King Belshazzar held a great feast during which he blasphemed the God of Israel; and by sending handwriting on the wall, God announced his doom. That very night Babylon was conquered and Belshazzar was slain (Dan. 5).

Judas, an apostle of the Lord, was not a true believer (John 6:70-71) but a traitor and a thief (12:6). In the Upper Room, he sat in the place of honor at the table, and none of the other disciples knew what was in his heart. But Jesus knew what Judas was and what Judas would do, and He hid this knowledge from the disciples. In fact, Jesus even washed Judas' feet! Confident that he had everything under control, Judas betrayed Jesus to the enemy and ended up committing suicide (Matt. 27:1-10).

The only safe place to put your confidence is in the Lord.

3. Pride (Es. 5:10-12)

The famous actor John Barrymore said, "One of my chief regrets during my years in the theater is that I couldn't sit in the audience and watch me."

It was with that kind of an attitude that Haman left the palace and returned home with a joyful heart. Fresh from an intimate dinner with the king and queen, and anticipating a second banquet the next evening, Haman launched himself on an ego trip that disgusts me each time I read it. Note the number of masculine personal pronouns here: *his* friends, *his wife, his* riches, *his* sons. (He had ten; 9:7-10.) The king had promoted him above everybody else. I'm reminded of that rich farmer in Luke 12:16-21 whose favorite word was I.

Didn't Haman know that "pride goes before destruction, and a haughty spirit before a fall"? (Prov. 16:18, NKJV) Or that "a man's pride will bring him low"? (29:23, NKJV) Anybody who boasts about position, wealth, family, or anything else ought to heed the words of John the Baptist: "A man can receive nothing, except it be given him from heaven" (John 3:27, KJV). "For who makes you differ from another?" asked Paul. "And what do you have that you did not receive? Now if you did indeed receive it, why do you glory as if you had not received it?" (1 Cor. 4:7, NKJV)

Many theologians are of the conviction that pride is the very essence of sin. (Perhaps that's why pride is number one on God's "hate list." See Prov. 6:16-19.) It was pride that turned Lucifer into Satan: "I will be like the Most High" (Isa. 14:14, NKJV). Satan used pride to tempt Eve: "You will be like God" (Gen. 3:5, NIV). British Bible scholar William Barclay wrote, "Pride is the ground in which all the other sins grow, and the parent from which all the other sins come."

What does a sinful person have to be proud of? We certainly can't be proud of our ancestry. The Puritan preacher William Jenkyn said, "Our father was Adam, our grandfather dust, and our great-grandfather-nothing." So much for the family tree! The only thing the Bible says is great about humanity is its sin: "And God saw that the wickedness of man was great in the earth" (Gen. 6:5, KJV). So much for our achievements!

Someone has said that pride is the only known disease that makes everybody sick except the person who has it. Unless cured, pride is a sickness unto death.

4. Malice (Es. 5:9b, 13-14)

When Haman left the queen's palace, he was walking on air; but the sight of Mordecai immediately brought him down to earth again. On previous occasions, Mordecai had refused to bow down to Haman (3:4-5), but now the courageous Jew even refused to stand up and acknowledge the presence of the illustrious prime minister. I once attended a press briefing at the White House; and when President Reagan entered the room, we all stood to our feet. When a presiding judge enters a courtroom, everyone rises and remains standing until the judge is seated. Whether we like the President or the judge personally is not the issue. We all show respect to the offices that they hold.

Haman was "filled with rage against Mordecai" (5:9, NIV). His hatred of the Jews in general and Mordecai in particular had so poisoned his system that he couldn't even enjoy talking about his greatness! "But all this gives me no satisfaction," he admitted, "as long as I see that Jew Mordecai sitting at the king's gate" (v. 13, NIV).

Malice is that deep-seated hatred that brings delight if our enemy suffers and pain if our enemy succeeds. Malice can never forgive; it must always take revenge. Malice has a good memory for hurts and a bad memory for kindnesses. In 1 Corinthians 5:8, Paul compared malice to yeast, because, like yeast, malice begins very small but gradually grows and finally permeates the whole of life. Malice in the Christian's heart grieves the Holy Spirit and must be put out of our lives (Eph. 4:30-32; Col. 3:8).

The insidious thing about malice is that it has to act; eventually it must express itself. But when you shoot at your enemy, beware! For the ammunition usually ricochets off the target and comes back to wound the shooter! If a person wants to self-destruct, the fastest way to do it is to be like Haman and cultivate a malicious spirit.

Haman had infected his wife and friends with his sinful hatred of the Jews, and they suggested that he ask the king for permission to hang Mordecai. A man with

Haman's authority could always trump up some charge, and the king wasn't about to take time to investigate. *Of course, this was before Ahasuerus discovered that Mordecai had saved his life!* Now we can better understand Esther's delay in offering her petition to the king. After the events in chapter 6, it would be impossible for Haman to get permission to execute Mordecai.

Not one to waste time, Haman ordered that the gallows be made. We're not sure whether the gallows itself was seventy-five feet high or whether it was put in a prominent place that lifted it to that height, such as the city wall or the roof of a building. But Haman's plan was obvious: He wanted to use Mordecai's execution to frighten the Jews and convince them that the king meant business when he approved the edict. The execution of a prominent Jew such as Mordecai would paralyze the wills of the Jewish people in the empire, and Haman would have them at his mercy.

There's another thing about this gallows that we're not sure of: Was it like the Western gallows, a device for hanging a person by the neck until dead? Or was it a stake on which a human body was impaled? The Persians were known for their cruel punishments, one of which was impaling live prisoners on sharp posts and leaving them there to suffer an agonizing death.

Whatever this gallows was, it turned out to be the instrument of Haman's own execution. God was standing in the shadows, keeping watch over His own.

"For the ways of man are before the eyes of the Lord, and He ponders all his paths. His own iniquities entrap the wicked man, and he is caught in the cords of his sin. He shall die for lack of instruction, and in the greatness of his folly he shall go astray" (Prov. 5:21-23, NKJV).

CHAPTER SIX
WARNING SIGNALS
Esther 6

(In which God sounds an alarm, but Haman won't listen)

You've probably seen the popular poster that reads: "Today is the first day of the rest of your life."

If anybody had said that to Haman as he left home early in the morning and hurried to the palace, they would have been wrong. They should have said, "Haman, today is the last day of your life!"

"As I live, saith the Lord God, I have no pleasure in the death of the wicked; but that the wicked turn from his way and live" (Ezek. 33:11, KJV).

"The Lord . . . is long-suffering toward us, not willing that any should perish but that all should come to repentance" (2 Peter 3:9, NKJV).

"O Jerusalem, Jerusalem, the one who kills the prophets and stones those who are sent to her! How often I wanted to gather your children together, as a hen gathers her chicks under her wings, but you were not willing!" (Matt. 23:37, NKJV)

On the basis of these three verses, we're safe in concluding that God's desire for sinners is not that they die but that they turn from their sins and be saved. There is joy in heaven when a sinner repents (Luke 15:7, 10), but the Lord won't force people to turn from their sins and trust His Son. "I wanted to . . . but you were not willing."

As much as we detest Haman and his foul deeds, we must keep in mind that God loves sinners and wants to save them. God is long-suffering and brings various influences to bear upon people's hearts as He seeks to turn them from their evil ways. We will see some of these influences at work in the events of this chapter.

1. A night of discovery (Es. 6:1-5)

Once again, we see the sovereign hand of God invisibly at work in the life of King Ahasuerus. God was working out His purposes whether the king knew it or not, and you can see in this paragraph at least five evidences of God's providence.

The king's insomnia (Es. 6:la). "Uneasy lies the head that wears a crown," wrote Shakespeare. Solomon agreed: "The sleep of a laboring man is sweet, whether he eat little or much; but the abundance of the rich will not suffer him to sleep" (Ecc. 5:12, KJV). Was it the cares of state that kept the king awake? Was he worried about his finances? Did he eat and drink immoderately at the queen's feast? Or, was he puzzled about the queen's mysterious request?

Some or all of these worries may have played a part in the king's wakefulness, but behind them was the sovereign hand of the living God who watches over His people and never slumbers or sleeps (Ps. 121:3-4). God wanted the king to stay awake because He had something to tell him.

While visiting the zoo, I became fascinated with the "nocturnal exhibit." Here were animals that most of us never see because they sleep in the daytime and do their active living at night. "While you are resting," said one of the posters, "Nature is busily at work helping to keep the balance of life stable." I thought to myself, "While I'm asleep, my Heavenly Father is busily at work making sure the new day will be just what He wants it to be." God's compassions never fail but are "new every morning" (Lam. 3:22-23) because God never sleeps and never stops working all things together for our good (Rom. 8:28).

The king's choice of entertainment (Es. 6:lb). Ahasuerus wasn't at a loss for sources of entertainment! He could have called a concubine from the harem, or he might have brought in the court musicians to play for him. He and his guards could have played a game together, or he might have asked for a troubadour to entertain him with a ballad. His decision to have a book read to him was certainly of God.

Can God direct us even in such minor matters as our recreations? He certainly can. When I was a young Christian, my attendance at a friend's birthday party turned out to be one of the most important events in my life. Because of that evening, I made a decision about my educational plans. That decision eventually led to my changing schools and meeting the girl who became my wife. Never underestimate the extraordinary things God can do through an ordinary event like a birthday party.

The servant's choice of books (Es. 6:lc). God directed Ahasuerus to ask for the kingdom chronicles to be read to him. (That would put anybody to sleep!) But God also directed that the servant take from the shelf the very book that recorded Mordecai's service to the king five years before. Certainly there were other volumes available, but that's the one the servant selected.

Can God direct in the books that people pick up and read? Yes, He can. Late in February 1916, a British student bought a book at a used-book stall in a railway station. He had looked at that book and rejected it at least a dozen times before, but that day he purchased it. It was *Phantastes* by George MacDonald, and the reading of that book eventually led to that young man's conversion. Who was he? C.S. Lewis, perhaps the greatest and most popular apologist for the Christian faith of the middle-twentieth century. He wrote to a friend that he had picked up the book "by hazard," but I believe God had directed his choice.

God can even direct *what we read* in a book. A young man in North Africa sought peace, first in sensual pleasures and then in philosophy, but only became more miserable. One day he heard a neighbor child playing a game and saying, "Take it and read! Take it and read!" The young man immediately picked up the Scriptures and "happened" to open to Romans 13:13-14; and those verses brought him to faith in Christ. We know that young man today as Augustine, Bishop of Hippo, and author of numerous Christian classics.

The king's servant picked out the very book that told about Mordecai's good deed and read that section to Ahasuerus. How marvelous is the providence of God!

The king's delay in rewarding Mordecai (Es. 6:2-3). This is a key matter; for had Mordecai been honored five years before, the events of this critical day could not have occurred. Rewards and punishments were basic to the Persian system of maintaining loyalty, and it was unusual for meritorious service not to be rewarded. Then why was Mordecai's good deed written down but forgotten? Did some junior clerk in the bureaucracy have a grudge against Mordecai? Did an office memo go astray? We don't know; but this we do know, that God was in charge and already had the day selected for Mordecai to be honored.

Is God in charge of schedules? He certainly is! After befriending Pharaoh's butler, Joseph thought it would lead to his being released from prison, but Joseph had to wait two more years until the time God had chosen for him to become second ruler in Egypt (Gen. 40:23-41:1). God had a specific day selected for the Jews to leave Egypt (Ex. 12:40-42; see Gen. 15:13-16), and even the birth of Jesus Christ in Bethlehem occurred "when the fullness of the time was come" (Gal. 4:4, KJV). In the midst of a confused and troubled world, the dedicated believer is able to say, "My times are in Thy hand" (Ps. 31:15, KJV) and find peace in God's will.

It has often been said that "God's delays are not God's denials." We sometimes get impatient and wonder why the wicked are prospering while the righteous are suffering, but God is never in a hurry. He is long-suffering toward the wicked because He wants them to repent, and He is patient with His people because He wants them to receive the right reward at the right time for the right purpose. If Mordecai was ever puzzled because the king promoted Haman but ignored him, he would soon find out that God had not made a mistake.

The timely arrival of Haman (Es. 6:4). It's possible that Haman had been up all night, enjoying the supervision of the construction of the gallows on which he planned to hang (or impale) Mordecai. It was very early in the morning, but Haman wanted to see the king as soon as possible and get permission for the execution (Prov. 6:18). From Haman's point of view, the earlier the hanging, the better. Mordecai's body would be on exhibition all day, and this would delight Haman and also put fear into the hearts of the Jews in the city. After executing Mordecai, Haman could be certain that everybody would obey the king's command and bow down to him.

Suppose Haman had arrived two hours later? The king would have consulted with other advisers, and Haman would have been left out of the celebration for Mordecai. God wanted Haman to spend the day honoring Mordecai and not gloating over Mordecai's corpse on the gallows. God was actually warning Haman that he'd better change course or he would end up being destroyed.

When you review these evidences of the providence of God, you can't help but want to praise and thank Him for the great God that He is. "The Lord brings the counsel of the nations to nothing; He makes the plans of the peoples of no effect. The counsel of the Lord stands forever, the plans of His heart to all generations" (Ps. 33:10-11, NKJV). "There is no wisdom, no insight, no plan that can succeed against the Lord" (Prov. 21:30, NIV). "If God be for us, who can be against us?" (Rom. 8:31, KJV)

2. A morning of decision (Es. 6:6-10)

It's one thing to enter the king's throne room, but now Haman was invited into the king's bedchamber. This new honor only increased Haman's pride and false confidence; he thought that he was in control of events and that Mordecai's doom was sealed. And when the king asked for Haman's advice on a personal matter, it inflated Haman's ego even more.

In verse 6, the king's question was vague and didn't identify "the man whom the king delights to honor" (NKJV). In his pride, Haman concluded that the king was speaking about him. After all, what other man in the empire deserved such honor from the king? After the way Mordecai had insulted him, Haman would now get double revenge: First Mordecai would see Haman honored by the king, and then Mordecai would be hanged on the gallows. Haman would then climax the day by feasting "merrily" (5:14) with the king and queen.

Little did proud Haman realize that, before the day would end, the situation would be completely reversed: Haman would be forced to honor Mordecai before all the people of the city; Esther's feast would turn out to be an exposé of the traitor; and Haman, not Mordecai, would end up on the gallows. "The righteous is delivered from trouble, and it comes to the wicked instead" (Prov. 11:8, NKJV).

"Before destruction the heart of a man is haughty, and before honor is humility" (18:12, NKJV). The first half of that verse applies to Haman and the last half to Mordecai. What a difference a little comma makes! Proverbs 29:23 gives the same message: "A man's pride shall bring him low, but the humble in spirit will retain honor" (NKJV). On which side of the comma do you live?

Thinking that the king was describing the honors he himself would receive, Haman asked for the very best: The man to be honored should be dressed in the king's own apparel; he should ride on the king's horse with the royal crest on its head; and one of the noble princes should lead the horse through the city and command the people to honor him. Such an event would almost be like a coronation!

The more I ponder the character of Haman, the more convinced I am that he wanted the throne for himself. As second man in the empire, if anything happened to Ahasuerus, Haman was certainly in the best position to capture the throne for himself. A proud man with selfish ambitions isn't content to take second place if there's any possible way to secure first place. If what is described in Esther 6:8-9 had actually been done for Haman, it would have given the people of Shushan the impression that Ahasuerus had chosen Haman to be his successor.

Note that King Ahasuerus called Mordecai "the Jew" (v. 10). You get the impression that the king completely forgot that he had permitted Haman to issue an edict to destroy the Jews. One day the king is an enemy of the Jews, and a few weeks later he honors one of the leading Jewish citizens! But Ahasuerus had a debt to pay, for Mordecai had saved his life. And perhaps in honoring Mordecai publicly, the king might help calm the troubled citizens of the city (3:15).

It was a morning of decision. The king had decided to reward Mordecai, and Haman had decided what the reward should be. What were the results?

3. A day of disgrace (Es. 6:11-14)

We wonder what Haman's response was when the king told him to do all those things for Mordecai. Was he shocked? Did he show his astonishment openly? Probably not, because you didn't express yourself that freely before an Eastern monarch. With the practiced duplicity that got him where he was, Haman bowed to the king's commandment and obeyed.

First, he had to go out to the king's gate, get Mordecai, and bring him into the palace. Then he had to dress Mordecai in the king's robes. After putting Mordecai on the king's horse, Haman had to lead the horse throughout the city and proclaim, "This is what is done for the man the king delights to honor!" (v. 9, NIV) After he had visited all the city streets, Haman had to lead the horse back to the palace, remove the royal garments from Mordecai,1 and send him back to his place at the city gate. What irony! For almost a whole day Haman was the servant of Mordecai, commanding the people to bow down and honor him! The thing Mordecai wouldn't do for Haman—bow down—Haman had to tell others to do for Mordecai!

How did this pageantry and prominence affect Mordecai? When it was over, he simply returned to his place at the gate and continued to serve the king. Applause doesn't change truly humble people, for their values are far deeper. God can trust His blessings with the humble because they seek to honor only the Lord.

Haman's reaction was quite different, for he was humiliated. He went home as soon as possible, his head covered as though he were grieving for the dead. This had been the way Mordecai had responded to the king's edict concerning the Jews (4:1-2). Again, the tables were turned.

Even if they did bow down to him, Haman had no desire to see the public, because he had been humiliated before them and he knew that they were laughing at him behind his back. Such is the difference between reputation and character. Haman was a famous man, a man of reputation, only because the king had made him so; but he was not a man of character. His reputation depended on his office, his wealth, and his authority, all of which could easily be taken from him.

What a contrast between Haman's family gathering in 6:13 and the one recorded in 5:10-12! Whereas before, Haman had boasted of his greatness, now he had to confess how he had been humiliated. If there had been any other official on the horse but Mordecai the Jew, Haman might have been able to handle the situation; but having to give honor to a Jew demoralized Haman completely.

At this point, his wife and counselors made an interesting statement: "If Mordecai, before whom you have begun to fall, is of Jewish descent, you will not prevail against him but will surely fall before him" (6:13, NKJV). *His humiliation in the streets and these words in his house should have alarmed Haman and moved him to change his course of action.* God was warning Haman, but the proud prime minister wouldn't heed the warning. Had he sincerely repented and asked for mercy, it's likely that he could have saved his own life and the lives of his ten sons.

The Persians were a very superstitious people, and the advisers saw in the events of the day a "bad omen" for Haman's future. Perhaps they were also familiar with God's covenant with Abraham (Gen. 12:1-3), or maybe they just knew Jewish history. At any rate, they saw Haman falling from his place of prominence; and this dire prediction should have brought him to the place of humility and repentance.

While Haman was discussing his misfortunes with his wife and advisers, the king's eunuchs arrived at the door to escort Haman to the queen's banquet. He had planned to go "merrily" to the feast, with Mordecai safely out of the way (5:14); but now everything had changed.

What would happen next? And what was the mysterious petition that Queen Esther would reveal at the banquet?

Off Haman went with the eunuchs to his last meal.

When God sounds the alarm, it pays to stop, look, and listen—and obey.

CHAPTER SEVEN
THE MASK COMES OFF
Esther 7

(In which Haman comes
to the end of his rope)

When they arrived at Esther's palace apartment, neither the king nor Haman knew that Esther was a Jewess. Haman was probably still distressed because of the events of the day, but he composed himself and hoped to enjoy the banquet. This is the seventh banquet recorded in the Book of Esther.

Had he known the nationality of the queen, Haman either would have run for his life or fallen on his face and begged the king for mercy. God had warned Haman through circumstances, through his advisers, and through his wife; but the prime minister would not heed the warnings. "The Lord detests all the proud of heart. Be sure of this: They will not go unpunished" (Prov. 16:5, NIV).

God's long-suffering led Haman into thinking he was safe. "Because sentence against an evil work is not executed speedily, therefore the heart of the sons of men is fully set in them to do evil" (Ecc. 8:11, NKJV). God's long-suffering today is an opportunity for people to repent (2 Peter 3:9), but our sinful world thinks it means God won't judge sinners at all. "For when they say, 'Peace and safety!' then sudden destruction comes upon them, as labor pains upon a pregnant woman. And they shall not escape" (1 Thes. 5:3, NKJV).

1. The queen's request (Es. 7:1-4)

Ever since the previous evening's banquet, Ahasuerus had been waiting to hear the queen's petition; so when the wine was served, he broached the subject. Of course, the statement "even to half of the kingdom" was a royal promise that wasn't to be taken literally (see 5:3; Dan. 5:16; Mark 6:23). It simply meant that the king would be generous. Therefore, tell him what you want.

During the previous twenty-four hours, Esther had probably rehearsed this speech many times; and now God gave her the strength to deliver it. Remember, she was taking her life in her hands, for if the king rejected her plea, that was the end.

She made it clear from the beginning that she depended on the favor of the king and wasn't trying to tell him what to do. She also said that her desire wasn't to please herself but to please the king. This was good psychology, especially when dealing with a chauvinistic monarch like Ahasuerus.

It was also wise on her part not to say, "There's a man in your kingdom who plans to destroy all of the Jews!" *She focused her petition on the fact that the queen's life was in danger and the king had to do something about it.* We have reason to believe Ahasuerus still loved his queen and didn't want any harm to come to her. As he sat there in her presence and beheld her beauty, her words moved him. What monster would want to kill the queen?

Not only was the queen's life in danger, but her people were also in danger of being slain. My guess is that this statement perplexed the king. Who were her people? Wasn't she a Persian? Has she been keeping a secret from me?

It was then that Esther reminded the king of the decree he had approved to wipe out the Jewish nation. In fact, her words are almost verbatim from the decree (Es. 3:13). Ahasuerus was smart enough to put two and two together and understand that Queen Esther was a Jewess, and he had unwittingly consented to her murder!

Esther continued by pointing out that the king had been paid to issue this decree (vv. 9-11). If he had sold the Jews as slaves, such a payment might have been just. But to sell them into death and total destruction was something for which nobody had enough money. "If it were only a matter of going into bondage," said Esther, "I would have kept quiet. Why bother the king with that? But wholesale murder is something I can't ignore."

Queen Esther bravely interceded for her people. How will the king respond? "Commit to the Lord whatever you do, and your plans will succeed. The Lord works out everything for His own ends—even the wicked for a day of disaster" (Prov. 16:3-4, NIV).

2. The king's rage (Es. 7:5-8)

At this point, try to imagine what was going through the mind of King Ahasuerus. Without openly accusing him, Esther has implicated the king in a horrible crime, and he was bound to feel guilty. The king knew that he had impetuously approved the decree. But he didn't realize that the decree was part of a conspiracy. He had signed the death warrant for his own wife! The king had to find a way to save his wife and save face at the same time.

In an absolute monarchy, the king is looked upon as a god and can do no wrong. This is why ancient monarchs always had a stable of scapegoats available—people who could take the blame for the ignorance or inefficiency of the throne. (Modern politicians often do the same thing.) Therefore, the king's question in verse 5 implied much more than, "Who is guilty?" The king was also looking for somebody to punish.

Ahasuerus had already received one surprise when he learned the nationality of his queen; and now he would be hit with another: His favorite officer was the adversary and enemy who had plotted the whole thing. Esther didn't reveal that Haman, like the king, had just learned from her own lips that she was a Jewess. Perhaps Ahasuerus concluded that Haman's crime was wanting to slay the queen and that he had decided to accomplish it by killing all the Jews. For that matter, maybe Haman was part of the Bigthan-Teresh conspiracy that Mordecai had exposed, a conspiracy to murder the king! (See 2:21-23.) *And like Esther, Mordecai was a Jew!*

Now we can better understand why God directed Esther to delay her pleas: He wanted to give Ahasuerus opportunity to learn what Mordecai had done, that Mordecai was a Jew and that he deserved to be honored. *If a Jew had saved the king's life, why should the king exterminate the Jews?*

"The king got up in a rage, left his wine and went out into the palace garden" (7:7, NIV). We've already noted that Ahasuerus was a man with a short temper (1:12); but on this occasion, his anger must have been volcanic. His masculine pride was hurt because he had misjudged the character of Haman. He had made a fool of himself by promoting Haman and by giving him so much influence. The king had also erred in approving the decree without first weighing all the facts (Prov. 18:13). As a result, he had endangered the lives of two very special Jews—Mordecai, who had saved his life, and Esther, his beloved wife.

No doubt the king walked to and fro in the garden, doing his best to control the anger that welled up within him. "The wrath of a king is as messengers of death" (Prov. 16:14, KJV). "The king's wrath is as the roaring of a lion" (19:12, KJV). No wonder Haman was afraid! He had been near enough to the king to recognize and interpret his every mood. He knew the king was about to become judge and jury and pass a sentence from which there was no escape.

But for Haman, there was one remote possibility: the mercy of the queen. Perhaps he could arouse her pity and get her to intercede for him. Esther knew Haman was a tool of the devil determined to destroy the Jewish people. Had he known originally that Esther was a Jewess, Haman might have cleverly worded the decree so that her life would be preserved; but he would still have had authority to annihilate all of her people. It was Haman's hatred for the queen's cousin Mordecai that started the whole conspiracy (Es. 3:5-6), and Esther wasn't about to abandon the one man who had meant so much to her.

In the Soncino Jewish commentary on Esther, Dr. S. Goldman makes this telling statement about 7:8: "The arrogant bully became, as usually in the face of disaster, a whining coward" *(The Five Megilloth, p.* 228). When the authority of the king had been behind him, Haman could courageously strut about, demand respect, and give orders. But now that the anger of the king was *against* him, Haman's true character was revealed. He was not a giant; he was only a midget full of pride and hot air! And all the king's horses and all the king's men couldn't put Haman's life back together again.

What a paradox! Haman had been furious because a Jewish *man* wouldn't bow down to him, and now Haman was prostrate before a Jewish *woman,* begging for his life! When the king entered the room and saw the scene, he accused Haman of trying to molest the queen. In his anger, the king would have exaggerated anything Haman did; and besides that, molesting the queen was a capital crime. Forget about the conspiracy; everybody could see for themselves that Haman was guilty of attacking the queen. For that crime alone, he deserved to die.

After escorting Mordecai around the city, Haman had covered *his head* in humiliation (6:12); but now the king's guards covered Haman's *face* in preparation for his execution. Had Haman covered his head in true humility and repentance, things would have been different, but he refused to listen to the warnings of the Lord. He was so controlled by pride and malice that he was blind to the dangers that lay ahead.

3. Haman's reward (Es. 7:9-10)

"The righteous is delivered from trouble, and it comes to the wicked instead" (Prov. 11:8, NKJV). The conspicuous gallows that Haman had constructed for Mordecai was convenient for the execution of Haman. Therefore, the king used it. Apparently Haman had let it be known in the palace that he planned to kill Mordecai, for the king's servant knew the purpose of the gallows. In his pride, Haman had boasted too much; and his words came back not only to haunt him but also to help slay him.

The day before, Haman had led Mordecai through the streets dressed in royal splendor; but now Haman was led through the streets with a covering over his face and a gallows at the end of the journey. Certainly Haman's wife Zeresh and their ten sons witnessed the execution, as did many of the Jews in the city. It must have given courage to the Jews to know that their enemy Haman was no longer on the scene.

"Do not be deceived: God cannot be mocked," warned Paul. "A man reaps what he sows" (Gal. 6:7, NIV). Haman sowed anger against Mordecai, and he reaped anger from the king. Haman wanted to kill Mordecai and the Jews, and the king killed Haman. "Even as I have seen, they that plow iniquity, and sow wickedness, reap the same" (Job 4:8, KJV). "He who sows wickedness reaps trouble" (Prov. 22:8, NIV).

This unchanging principle of sowing and reaping is illustrated throughout the Bible, *and it applies to both believers and unbelievers.* Jacob killed an animal and lied to his father, pretending to be Esau (Gen. 27:1-29); and years later Jacob's sons killed an animal and lied to him, pretending that Joseph was dead (37:31-35). Pharaoh gave orders to drown the Jewish baby boys (Ex. 1), and one day his army was drowned in the Red Sea (Ex. 14-15).

David secretly took his neighbor's wife and committed adultery (2 Sam. 11), and David's own son Absalom took his father's concubines and openly committed adultery with them (16:20-23). Furthermore, David's daughter Tamar was raped by her half brother Amnon (2 Sam. 13). David killed Bathsheba's husband (11:14-25), and three of David's own sons were slain: Absalom (2 Sam. 18), Amnon (13:23-36), and Adonijah (1 Kings 2:13-25). Saul of Tarsus encouraged the stoning of Stephen (Acts 8:1); and when he became Paul the missionary, he was stoned at Lystra (14:19-20).

But let's keep in mind that this law of sowing and reaping also applies to doing what is good and right. If we sow to the flesh, we reap corruption; but if we sow to the Spirit, we reap life everlasting (Gal. 6:8). No good deed done for the glory of Jesus Christ will ever be forgotten before God. No loving word spoken in Jesus' name will ever be wasted. If we don't see the harvest in this life, we'll see it when we stand before the Lord. Even a cup of cold water given in the name of Christ will have its just reward (Matt. 10:42; 25:31-46).

Haman was hanged, or impaled, on his own gallows, and his body taken down and buried. *All of Haman's wealth and glory couldn't rescue him from death nor could he take any of it with him.* "Those who trust in their wealth and boast in the multitude of their riches, none of them can by any means redeem his brother, nor give to God a ransom for him—for the redemption of their souls is costly. . . . Do not be afraid when one becomes rich, when the glory of his house is increased; for when he dies he shall carry nothing away; his glory shall not descend after him" (Ps. 49:6-8, 16-17, NKJV). In 1 Peter 1:18-19, Peter tells us how costly our redemption is: the shedding of the blood of Jesus Christ, the Son of God.

Not only is there a personal lesson here, but there is also a lesson about the nation of Israel: *Every enemy that has ever tried to destroy Israel has been destroyed.* "I will bless those who bless you, and I will curse him who curses you" is God's promise to Israel (Gen. 12:3, NKJV), and He has always kept it. God takes His promises seriously even if the nations of the world ignore them or challenge them.

This doesn't mean that God necessarily approves everything Israel has done or will do, but it does mean that God doesn't approve of those who try to destroy His chosen people. Whether it's Pharaoh in Egypt, Nebuchadnezzar in Babylon, Haman in Persia, or Hitler in Germany, the enemy of the Jews is the enemy of Almighty God and will not succeed.

"Then was the king's wrath pacified" (Es. 7:10, KJV). The Hebrew word translated "pacified" is used in Genesis 8:1 to describe the receding waters of the Flood. The king's anger had welled up within him and reached its peak when he executed Haman. Now it subsided, and the king was himself again. But though the adversary was out of the way, the problem was not completely solved; for the king's decree was still in effect *and could not be changed.* It was now the third month (Es. 8:9), and there were nine months to go before the fateful day when the Jews could legally be slain (3:13).

How would Esther and Mordecai solve this problem?

That is the topic of the next chapter.

CHAPTER EIGHT
FROM VICTIMS TO VICTORS
Esther 8

(In which the good news of a new law brings hope and joy)

Haman was dead, but his murderous edict was still very much alive. Long after wicked people are gone, the consequences of their evil words and deeds live on. Even today, innocent people are suffering because of guilty people who lie in their graves.

Unless something intervened, within nine months the Persians would attack the Jews and wipe them off the face of the earth. There were about 15 million Jews among the estimated 100 million people in the empire. Therefore, the odds were definitely against God's people. Of course, God's people have always been a minority; and "one with God is a majority." The Lord had brought Esther and Mordecai to the kingdom "for such a time as this," and they were prepared to act.

1. The promotion of Mordecai (Es. 8:1-2, 15)

According to the ancient historians, whenever a traitor was executed, the throne appropriated his property. Had Ahasuerus confiscated Haman's property for himself, he would have acquired a great deal of wealth; but he chose to give Haman's estate to Esther. More than an act of generosity, this gift was probably the king's way of atoning for his foolish decisions that had brought so much pain to Esther and her people. It's possible that Esther later shared some of this great wealth with the Jews so they could prepare themselves for the coming crisis.

Ahasuerus knew that both Esther and Mordecai were Jews, but now he was to learn that they were also cousins. Ahasuerus and Mordecai were relatives by marriage! When Haman was deposed, the king took back his royal ring (3:10), the insignia of the authority of the throne (8:8, 10; 3:12), and he gave the ring to Mordecai, making him prime minister. With a Jewish queen and a Jewish prime minister in the palace, the Jews in the empire were in a better political position than ever before.

Esther gave the management of Haman's vast estate into the hands of Mordecai, who had first opposed Haman and refused to bow down. Were it not for Mordecai's courage and encouragement of Esther, Haman would still be in control. "Wait on the Lord, and keep His way, and He shall exalt you to inherit the land; when the wicked are cut off, you shall see it. I have seen the wicked in great power, and spreading himself like a native green tree. Yet he passed away, and behold, he was no more" (Ps. 37:34-36, NKJV).

The king made sure that Mordecai had a uniform worthy of his office, and it's described in Esther 8:15. No longer did Mordecai wear old, borrowed robes (6:7-11) but new robes prepared especially for him. The official royal colors were blue and white (see 1:6). The golden "crown" was probably a large turban which, along with the robe of white and purple, identified Mordecai as an important man of great authority.

Everything that Haman had acquired from the king by his scheming, Mordecai received as gifts, because Mordecai was a deserving man. At the beginning of this story, Esther and Mordecai were hardly exemplary in the way they practiced their religious faith; but now we get the impression that things have changed. Both of them have affirmed their Jewish nationality and both were the means of calling all the Jews in the empire to prayer and fasting. In one sense, they spearheaded a Jewish "revival" and made being Jewish a more honorable thing in the empire.

God doesn't always give this kind of a "happy ending" to everybody's story. Today, not all faithful Christians are promoted and given special honors. Some of them get fired because of their stand for Christ! God hasn't promised that we'll be promoted and made rich, but He has assured us that He's in control of all circumstances and that He will write the last chapter of the story. If God doesn't promote us here on earth, He certainly will when we get to glory.

2. Esther's petition (Es. 8:3-6)

Wealth, prestige, and personal security could never satisfy Esther so long as her people were still in danger. To her, the most important thing in life was not her comfort but their deliverance; and she couldn't rest until the matter was settled. How unlike some believers today who ignore the needs of a lost world while they search for new ways to spend money and have fun! They think that attending church and bringing their offerings fulfills their Christian responsibilities and gives them the freedom to do whatever they please with the rest of their time and money. We need more people like Esther whose burden for condemned people was greater than any other thing in her life.

Years ago, in a Youth for Christ late-night prayer meeting, I heard attorney Jacob Stam pray, "Lord, the only thing most of us know about sacrifice is how to spell the word." I never forgot that statement, and I confess that it sometimes still haunts me. I recall another YFC staff meeting at which the late Bill Carle sang "So Send I You," and the Spirit of God brought all of us to our knees in prayer with a new dedication to help reach the world for Christ.

Esther couldn't do everything, but she could do something; and what she could do, she did. She approached the throne of the king and asked him to reverse the edict that Haman had devised. *It was her interceding at the throne that saved the people of Israel from slaughter.* She was asking nothing for herself, except that the king save her people and deliver her from the heavy burden on her heart.

As I've studied the Scriptures, I've been impressed with the many people who have prayed for the Jews. When Israel sinned, Moses met God on the mountain and interceded for them (Ex. 32). He was even willing for God to blot him out of the Book of Life if that's what it took to rescue the nation. Centuries later, the Apostle Paul said he was willing to be "accursed from Christ" if it would help save unbelieving Israel (Rom. 9:1-3, KJV).

On Mount Carmel, Elijah prayed for disobedient Israel (1 Kings 18); and in the palace, Nehemiah prayed for the Jews in Jerusalem (Neh. 1). Like Nehemiah, Ezra wept and prayed and asked God to help His sinful people (Ezra 9); and Daniel humbled himself and fasted and prayed that he might understand what God's plan was for Israel (Dan. 9). "I have set watchmen on your walls, O Jerusalem, who shall never hold their peace day or night. You who make mention of the Lord, do not keep silent, and give Him no rest till He establishes and till He makes Jerusalem a praise in the earth" (Isa. 62:67, NKJV).

"Pray for the peace of Jerusalem; they shall prosper who love thee" (Ps. 122:6, KJV). There can be no peace in this world until there is peace in Jerusalem, and there can be no peace in Jerusalem unless God's people obey this command and pray, "Thy kingdom come."

"It was a master stroke of the Devil when he got the church and the ministry so generally to lay aside the mighty weapon of prayer," wrote evangelist R.A. Torrey in *How to Obtain Fullness of Power in Christian Life and Service.* "The Devil is perfectly willing that the church should multiply its organizations and its deftly-contrived machinery for the conquest of the world for Christ, if it will only give up praying" *(Sword of the Lord* reprint, p. 59).

Esther's example encourages us to come to God's throne and intercede on behalf of others, especially the nations of the world where lost souls need to be delivered from death. One concerned person devoted to prayer can make a great difference in this world, for prayer is the key that releases the power of God. "Yet you do not have because you do not ask" (James 4:2, NKJV).

3. The king's proclamation (Es. 8:7-17)

The problem Esther and Mordecai faced was that the king, simply by executive fiat, couldn't cancel the first edict since the laws of the Medes and Persians were unalterable. In modern democratic nations, legislatures can reverse decisions and revoke laws, and the supreme court of the land can even declare laws unconstitutional; but not so in the ancient despotic Persian Empire. The voice of the king was the law of the land, and the king could do no wrong.

The king couldn't legally revoke his edict, but he could issue a new decree that would favor the Jews. The new decree would let everybody in the empire know that the king wanted his people to have a different attitude toward the Jews and look favorably upon them. The citizens didn't have to hire a lawyer to explain the new edict to them. You can be sure they got the message: Don't attack the Jews on March 7.

Since Mordecai was now prime minister, it was his job to draft the new decree. What he did was give the Jews permission to defend themselves against anybody who tried to kill them and take their property. There were many people in the empire like Haman, who hated the Jews, wanted to destroy them, and get their hands on their wealth. The new decree allowed the Jews to assemble and defend themselves, but they were not allowed to be the aggressors.

Scholars don't agree on the translation of verse 11. The *Authorized Version* gives the impression that the edict allowed the Jews to destroy the wives and children of their attackers and plunder their spoil, and the NASB seems to agree with this interpretation. The NIV connects "women and children" with the Jews being attacked and doesn't suggest that the Jews killed the women and children of their attackers. I prefer the NIV translation.

If you read 3:11-13, you will see the similarity of the wording of the two decrees. Mordecai used the "official language" of the government, because legal statements must be expressed in legal language. This language may seem strange to outsiders, but without it we would have confusion and misinterpretation. You can't write the law the way you write a poem or a recipe.

According to 8:9, the new edict was written on the twenty-third day of the third month, which on our calendar would be June 25, 474 B.C. (Remember, the Jewish calendar begins with the month of April.) The first decree was issued on April 17 (3:12). Thus, about seventy days had passed since Haman had declared war on the Jews. "D Day" for the Jews was March 7 (3:13). Therefore, the people had about eight months to get ready.

We must pause and consider whether it was really ethical for Mordecai to give the Jews the authority to kill and loot. People who deny the divine inspiration of the Bible like to point to the various "massacres" in Scripture as evidence that the God of the Bible is "a bully." Imagine worshiping a god that commanded the slaughter of whole populations!

First, let's consider the edict that Ahasuerus issued, for that's where all the trouble started. If it was wicked for Mordecai to tell the Jews to defend themselves, then it was even more wicked for Haman and Ahasuerus to tell the Persians to attack the Jews in the first place! Self-defense isn't a crime, but genocide definitely is. Do these critics approve of the *king's* edict? I certainly hope not! Well, if they don't approve of the king's decree, which permitted murder, then how can they disapprove of Mordecai's decree, which allowed the Jews the right to defend themselves? Better that Haman's decree had never been issued; but since it was published, better that Mordecai disarmed it by issuing his decree.

Now, let's look at the record in chapter 9, where you discover three important facts: The Jews killed only those who attacked them; they killed only the men (9:6, 12, 15); and they didn't lay hands on the loot, although they had the right to do so (vv. 10, 15-16). The fact that the Jews killed 800 men in the city of Shushan alone (vv. 6, 15) proves that there were many Persians just waiting for the opportunity to attack God's people. (It's estimated that there were probably half a million people in the capital city.)

The total number of the slain was 75,000 (v. 16) out of a population of perhaps 100 million people. But the fact that more than 75,000 people were prepared to slaughter *defenseless* Jews shows how many of the king's people hated God's people. And the fact that these people were even willing to attack *when they knew the Jews would protect themselves* is proof that anti-Semitism was very strong throughout the empire. The critics say it was wrong for the Jews to kill 75,000 would-be murderers. Would it have been better if the 75,000 Persians had killed ten times as many Jews?

Mordecai's decree was in complete harmony with God's covenant with Abraham: "I will bless those who bless you, and I will curse him who curses you" (Gen. 12:3, NKJV). Isaac also would have agreed with Mordecai; for when Isaac blessed Jacob, he said, "Cursed be everyone who curses you, and blessed be those who bless you" (27:29, NKJV). In addition, God promised Moses, "I will be an enemy to your enemies and an adversary to your adversaries" (Ex. 23:22, NKJV). And don't forget that quotation from Dr. J. Vernon McGee: "The Jew has attended the funeral of every one of the nations that tried to exterminate him."

It's one thing to write a liberating new edict and quite another thing to get the message out to the people. Mordecai put the secretaries to work translating and copying the decree, and then he sent the couriers to carry the good news to the people in the various provinces of the empire. The couriers "hastened" because they were "pressed on by the king's commandment" (Es. 8:14, KJV). The NIV translates it "spurred on by the king's command."

If only the church today were like those secretaries and couriers! How we need to tell the peoples of the world in their own languages the good news of salvation through faith in Jesus Christ! The King has commanded us, and we must go, but for some reason we linger. If a group of pagan scribes and messengers, without modern means of transportation and communication, could take Mordecai's decree to an entire empire, how much more should Christian workers be able to take Christ's Gospel to a lost world!

Ever since the fall of Adam, "the law of sin and of death" has been in force in this world (Rom. 8:2; 5:12-21); *and God will not rescind that law.* The wages of sin is still death (Rom. 6:23). Through the death and resurrection of Jesus Christ, God put another law into effect, "the law of the Spirit of life in Christ Jesus" (8:2). God obeyed the law of sin and death when He gave His Son, Jesus, to bear our sins and die on the cross. But then God raised Him from the dead and put a new decree into effect that makes it possible for sinners to be saved. Now He wants us to put that good news into every tongue and take that good news to every nation.

This chapter begins with Queen Esther in tears (Es. 8:3), but it ends with the Jews rejoicing and feasting (vv. 15-17). Happiness of one kind or another is mentioned in this paragraph at least seven times. (This is the eighth feast mentioned in the Book of Esther.) The Jews had been mourning and fasting, but now they were ecstatic with joy.

The thing that made the difference was not the *writing* of the decree or even its *distribution* in the various provinces. The thing that made the difference was the fact that *the Jews believed the decree.* It was their faith in Mordecai's word that changed their lives. They had hope, joy, and peace because they had faith in what the prime minister said. "Now may the God of hope fill you with all joy and peace in believing, that you may abound in hope by the power of the Holy Spirit" (Rom. 15:13, NKJV).

The statement that "many of the people of the land became Jews" (Es. 8:17, KJV) is variously interpreted. The obvious meaning is that many Gentiles in the empire forsook their pagan religions and became Jewish proselytes. But since the Jews were far from Jerusalem and the ministry of the priests, these "converts" couldn't be initiated fully into the Jewish faith. They became what were known later as "Godfearers" or "worshipers of God" (Acts 10:2; 16:14; 18:7).

I think the phrase means that many of the Gentiles in the empire sided with the Jews and acted as though they were Jews. They weren't ashamed to be identified with the Jews even though the Jews had enemies.

After President Reagan was shot, when he was being prepared for surgery, he jokingly said to the medical team, "I hope all of you are Republicans." One of the doctors replied, "Mr. President, today all of us are Republicans." That was the attitude of many of the people in the Persian Empire when Mordecai's edict was published: "Today, all of us are Jews."

The Book of Esther opens with the Jews keeping a very low profile, so much so that Esther and Mordecai wouldn't even confess their nationality. But now the Jews are proud of their race and so happy with what God had done that they were attracting others to their faith! Even the pagan Gentiles could see that God was caring for His people in a remarkable way.

Evangelist Billy Sunday said, "If you have no joy in your religion, there's a leak in your Christianity somewhere." If Christian believers today manifested more of the joy of the Lord, perhaps those outside the faith would be attracted to the church and be willing to consider the message of the Gospel.

It's worth trying.

CHAPTER NINE
GOD KEEPS HIS PROMISES
Esther 9 and 10

(In which the tables are turned, and then the tables are spread)

"Seek the peace of the city where I have caused you to be carried away captive." That was God's counsel to the Jews through the Prophet Jeremiah (Jer. 29:7, NKJV); and for the most part, they obeyed it. It wasn't the Jews who had declared war on the Gentiles, but the Gentiles who had declared war on the Jews!

"D Day" arrived for the Jews, the day appointed by Haman's decree for the slaughter of God's chosen people in the empire. But Mordecai's decree had changed that "D" from "destruction" to "deliverance." The Jews had permission to resist their enemies and had been given nine months to prepare for the encounter. The people in the empire who hated the Jews were hoping for victory, but "the tables were turned and the Jews got the upper hand over those who hated them" (Es. 9:1, NIV).

1. Vindication: the fear of the Jews (Es. 9:1-16)

The Jewish men were organized and armed, ready to meet any enemy who would attack them and their families and try to take their possessions. But the Lord had given them a greater weapon than their swords, because "the fear of the Jews fell upon them" (8:17, KJV; 9:2). This was a fear that God had sent into the hearts of the Gentiles to keep them from fighting His people.

This reminds us of the experience of Jacob as he traveled from Shechem to Bethel. "And they journeyed: and the terror of God was upon the cities that were round about them, and they did not pursue after the sons of Jacob" (Gen. 35:5, KJV). It was this same fear that went before Israel as they entered the Promised Land. "This day I will begin to put the dread and fear of you upon the nations under the whole heaven, who shall hear the report of you, and shall tremble and be in anguish because of you" (Deut. 2:25, NKJV, and see 11:25). Rahab told the two Jewish spies that the fear of Israel had paralyzed the nations in Canaan (Josh. 2:8-11; 5:1; 9:24), and that fear helped give Israel the victory.

One of the problems with our world today is that "there is no fear of God before their eyes" (Rom. 3:18, KJV). Like Pharaoh, people are saying, "Who is the Lord, that I should obey His voice?" (Ex. 5:2, KJV) *But have they seen anything in the people of God that would make them want to fear the Lord?* Is there such devotion to God among God's people that an outsider attending one of our meetings would fall down on his face, worship God, and "report that God is truly among you"? (1 Cor. 14:25, NKJV)

The fear of God protects those who fear God and believe His promises. Because the Jews believed Mordecai's decree, they had new courage and were not afraid of the enemy; and their courage put fear into the hearts of the enemy. (See Phil. 1:28.) Before King Jehoshaphat went out to battle, God's message to him was: "Believe in the Lord your God, and you shall be established; believe His prophets, and you shall prosper" (2 Chron. 20:20). That is still wise counsel.

But there was another aspect to this fear that helped give the Jews their victory, and that was the people's fear of Mordecai (Es. 9:3). The princes, deputies, governors, and officers of the king throughout the empire were in such awe of Mordecai that they even helped the Jews defend themselves against the Persians. God had given Mordecai his high position and his great reputation, and Mordecai used his authority to do the will of God.

Christians today who live in a democratic pluralistic society can't get into political office in order to use that office to promote their own religious faith and destroy those who disagree with them. Mordecai was prime minister in a government where his word was law. Christians today, however, can so live their faith that the power of God is seen in their lives, and the enemy will think twice before attacking. And yet, instead of the godless world being afraid of the church, the church is afraid of the world *and so imitates the world that it's difficult to tell the difference between the two.*

The church today is no longer "fair as the moon, clear as the sun, and terrible as an army with banners" (Song 6:10, KJV). Rather, we are "wretched, and miserable, and poor, and blind, and naked" (Rev. 3:17, KJV), which is the description of prisoners of war. Instead of being the conquerors, we're the prisoners! No wonder the world has no fear of the Lord.

"For though we live in the world, we do not wage war as the world does. The weapons we fight with are not the weapons of the world" (2 Cor. 10:3-4, NIV). Whenever the church has tried to use the weapons of this world to fight its battles, the consequences have been embarrassing if not disastrous. Wearing the whole armor of God (Eph. 6:l0ff), however, and depending on prayer and the Word of God (Acts 6:4), the Christian soldier can march forward with courage and faith.

The Persians who attacked the Jews were actually cooperating with Haman, an Amalekite; and this made them the enemies of God (Es. 9:5). In slaying those who attacked them, the Jews were only doing to the enemy what King Saul had refused to do (1 Sam. 15).

In Esther 9:5-15, we're given the report from Shushan; and, in verses 16-17, additional news is given about what happened in the other parts of the empire. During two days of conflict, the Jews killed 800 of their enemies in Susa alone (vv. 6, 15). It's remarkable that so many Persians would have dared to attack the Jews right in the king's own city where both Esther and Mordecai lived. Perhaps these people had been loyal to Haman and dependant on his bounty. Now they were angry because their hero had fallen and his wealth was gone.

Since the Jews were not the aggressors, it means that the ten sons of Haman had taken up arms and attacked the Jews; and all ten of them were slain. The bodies of the ten sons were hanged on Haman's gallows as a warning to the enemy. (In the text of the Hebrew Scriptures, the ten names are arranged on the page to look like a gallows. On the Feast of Purim, the synagogue reader reads these ten names all in one breath because the sons of Haman all died together.) The sight of ten corpses on Haman's gallows would certainly deter the Persians from attacking the Jews and would result in the saving of lives.

Some commentators have seen Esther's request in verses 12-13 as evidence of a vindictive spirit on her part, but this was not the case. Haman's strongest support was in the capital city where people had bowed down to him and benefited from his favors. Since it would be easy for them to get together and plan their strategy, Esther wanted to be sure that none of them would survive to cause further trouble. Perhaps she had received private intelligence that Haman's supporters had planned to attack again the next day, prompting her to ask Ahasuerus for permission to extend the Jews' right to defend themselves.

The Jews in the other parts of the empire killed 75,000 in one day, which shows how many people hated the Jews and wanted to destroy them. It averages out to about 600 per province. Since the Jews were greatly outnumbered in the empire, their victory was certainly a tribute to their faith and courage.

Three times in the record it's stated that the Jews didn't take any of the spoil (vv. 10, 15-16). It was in taking spoil from the enemy that King Saul lost his kingdom (1 Sam. 15:12-23), and the Jews didn't repeat his mistake. They were not out after wealth. They wanted only to protect themselves and vindicate their right to live safely in the empire. And remember, the Jews killed only those who first attacked them; the Jews were not the aggressors.

2. Celebration: the feast of the Jews (Es. 9:17-32)

It's sad when a nation (or a church) forgets its heroes and the providential events that have kept it alive. How easy it is for a new generation to come along and take for granted the blessings that previous generations struggled and sacrificed to attain! The Jews didn't make that mistake but established the Feast of Purim to remind their children year after year that God had saved Israel from destruction.

While Purim is not a Christian festival, Christians certainly ought to rejoice with their Jewish friends because every spiritual blessing we have has come through the Jews. The Jews gave to the world the knowledge of the true and living God, the Scriptures, and the Savior. The first Christians were Jewish believers, and so were the first missionaries. Jesus was a Jew who died on Passover, a Jewish feast day, and rose again from the dead on another Jewish holy day, the Feast of Firstfruits. The Holy Spirit came from heaven upon a group of Jewish believers on a Jewish holiday, Pentecost. "Salvation is from the Jews" (John 4:22). If there had been no Jews, there would be no church.

There's nothing wrong with *meaningful* tradition. The church is always one generation short of extinction; and if we don't pass on to our children and grandchildren what God has done for us and our fathers, the church will die of apathy and ignorance. "Come, my children, listen to me; I will teach you the fear of the Lord" (Ps. 34:11, NIV). It's when tradition gradually becomes *traditionalism* that we get into trouble. Theologian Jaroslav Pelikan said, "Tradition is the living faith of the dead; traditionalism is the dead faith of the living."

The Jews in the provinces finished their fighting on the thirteenth day of Adar (March) and spent the next day celebrating. But since the Jews in Shushan were still defending themselves on the fourteenth day, they didn't get to celebrate until the fifteenth. In the beginning, the Jews were united in their victory but divided in their celebration. It all depended on whether you lived in the city or the country. Mordecai, however, later issued a letter that instructed all the Jews to celebrate on both the fourteenth and fifteenth days of the month (Es. 9:20-22).

Today, the Jews begin their celebration with a fast on the thirteenth day of the month (v. 31), commemorating the date on which Haman's evil decree was issued (3:12). They go to the synagogue and hear the Book of Esther publicly read; and whenever the name of Haman is mentioned, they cry out, "May he be accursed!" or "May his name perish!" Children bring a special Purim rattle called a "gregar" and use it to make noise every time they hear Haman's name read.

On the morning of the fourteenth day of the month, the Jews again go to the synagogue, where the Esther story is read again and the congregation engages in prayer. The story about Moses and the Amalekites (Ex. 17:8-16) is also read. Then the celebrants go home to a festive holiday meal with gifts and special foods, and the celebrating continues on the next day. They also send gifts and food to the poor and needy so that everybody can rejoice together.

The name "Purim" is the plural of the Babylonian word *pur* which means "lot." It originates from Haman's casting of lots to determine the day when the Jews would be destroyed (Es. 9:24; 3:7). Even though there was no divine sanction given to this new feast, the Jews determined that it would be celebrated from generation to generation (9:26-28). Note the emphasis on teaching the children the meaning of Purim so that the message of the feast would not be lost in future generations.

There is a godly patriotism that goes beyond mere nationalism and civic pride and gives glory to God for what He has done. To see the hand of God in history and praise God for His goodness and mercy, and to ask God to forgive us for our sins, is perhaps the best way for the Christian patriot to celebrate a national holiday. But dedication must follow celebration. The

American political leader Adlai Stevenson said, "Patriotism is not short, frenzied outbursts of emotion, but the tranquil and steady dedication of a lifetime."

Not only did Mordecai the prime minister send a letter of instruction to the Jews in the empire, but Esther the queen also joined Mordecai in sending a second letter (vv. 29-32). Perhaps some of the Jews in the provinces didn't want to change from their original day of celebration (v. 19), and it was necessary for both the queen and prime minister to issue this second letter to keep peace in the nation. Too often God's people defeat the enemy and then celebrate the victory by fighting among themselves!

This second letter is described as "words of peace and truth" (v. 30), which suggests that there was a division among the Jewish people that needed to be healed. Not only did Esther and Mordecai send letters, but they also had the matter written into the book (diary?) that Mordecai used as his personal record (vv. 20, 32). It's possible that this book became a part of the official records of the empire.

The story of the victory of the Jews over their enemies was celebrated in an annual feast, recorded in two official letters, written in a journal, and ultimately included in the Old Testament Scriptures! What a rebuke to our modern "throw-away society" that has forgotten history and, like the Athenians of old, spends its time "in nothing else, but either to tell, or to hear some new thing" (Acts 17:21, KJV). Philosopher George Santayana was right when he said, "Those who do not remember the past are condemned to relive it."

3. Exaltation: the fame of Mordecai (Es. 10:1-3)

This brief chapter tells us that Mordecai, unlike his predecessor Haman, used his office to serve the king and help the Jews. Sometimes when people are elevated to high office, they forget their roots and ignore the needs of the common people. Mordecai wasn't that kind of man. Even though his political deeds are recorded in the official annals of the empire, what he did for his people has been recorded by the Lord and will be rewarded.

Why did the author mention the new tax program of King Ahasuerus? What does this have to do with Mordecai and the Jews? Some Bible students think that it was Mordecai who engineered this new system of tribute as *a substitute for war and plunder as a source of kingdom wealth. Now* that there was peace in the kingdom, the Jews were free to work, earn money, and prosper; and the prosperity of the Jews increased the prosperity of the empire in general. Mordecai reminded the king that the throne deserved a share in that prosperity. After all, it was the king who had chosen Esther, a Jewess, and promoted Mordecai, a Jew; and all three of them had worked together to save the Jews from destruction. Didn't the people of the empire, Jews and Gentiles alike, have an obligation to their monarch?

But the important message in this chapter is that God continued to use Mordecai to help the Jewish people. The Jews were aliens in a foreign land and subject to all kinds of harassment and abuse. Mordecai saw to it that they were treated with fairness. The last words of the book are variously translated. The *Authorized Version* says "and speaking peace to all his seed," suggesting that he encouraged the Jews and kept them at peace with one another. The NIV reads "and spoke up for the welfare of all the Jews." This implies that there were still forces at work in the empire opposing and threatening the Jews, but Mordecai represented them at court and protected them. "He did his best for his people, and was a friend at court for all of them" (TLB).

The exciting drama of Esther is over, but the blessings go right on. God preserved the Jewish nation so that we today can have a Bible and a Savior. Now it's our job to tell the whole world about this Savior and seek to win as many as we can to the Lord. We are the King's couriers, and we dare not fail.

Esther reaches across the centuries to join hands with believers today, and to say to the church: Be Committed!

Endnotes

Chapter One

1. See Herodotus, *The History, Book VII,* section 8.
2. One of the best presentations on this subject is *Daughters of the Church,* by Ruth A. Tucker and Walter Liefeld (Zondervan, 1987). See also A *Dictionary of Women in Church History,* by Mary L. Hammack (Moody Press, 1984).

Chapter Three

1. "Shaking the arrows" was something like our modern "drawing straws," with the arrows marked with the possible choices of action. "Consulting images" had to do with seeking help from the images of the gods they carried with them. "Looking at the liver" involved offering an animal sacrifice and getting directions from the shape and marks on the liver.
2. See *Hudson Taylor and the China Inland Mission: The Growth of a Work of God,* pp. 31-32.

Chapter Six

1. It's likely that Mordecai got to keep the garments since they had been worn by someone other than the king.